TECHNOLOGY

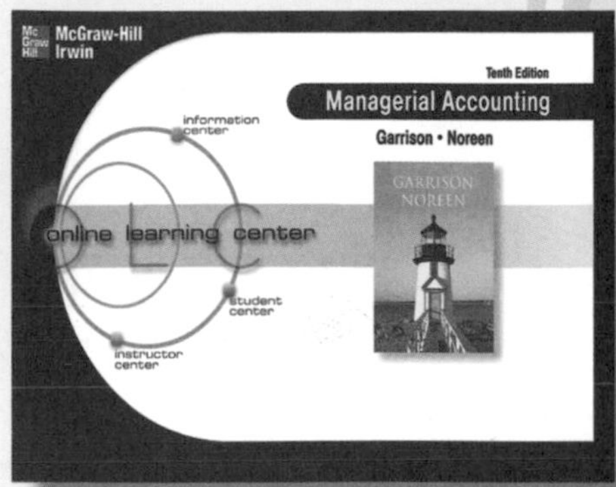

Online Learning Center

More and more students are studying online, and more and more instructors rely on the Internet to present and manage course material. That's why the **Managerial Accounting** team has provided the most complete and up-to-date collection of Web resources—whether it be alternate problems and solutions, an online tutorial, or links to professional resources. Whether you're an instructor building a lesson plan or a student preparing for an exam, the **Managerial Accounting OLC** is the perfect one-stop resource. Check it out at **www.mhhe.com/garrison10e**.

Knowledge **Gateway**

Knowledge Gateway

Developed with the help of our partner, Eduprise, the McGraw-Hill Knowledge Gateway is an all-purpose service and resource center for instructors teaching online. While training programs from WebCT and Blackboard will help teach you their software, only McGraw-Hill has services to help you actually *manage and teach* your online course, as well as run and maintain the software. Knowledge Gateway offers an online library full of articles and insights that focus on how online learning differs from a traditional class environment.

Course Management

The **Managerial Accounting OLC** is even better used in conjunction with a course management system, such as Blackboard or WebCT. Our Instructor Advantage service is ready to help you integrate your McGraw-Hill text and supplements into any 3rd-party course management platform; contact your McGraw-Hill representative for details.

If you're new to course management, we'd like to recommend PageOut, McGraw-Hill's course management system. With PageOut, you can construct a personalized course website in a matter of minutes—you don't even need to know a word of HTML. Better still, PageOut is FREE for all McGraw-Hill adopters. To learn how to use it in your accounting course, call one of our PageOut specialists at 1-800-541-7145.

Online Information Center
- Overview
- Table of Contents
- Author Biographies
- Preface
- Print and Electronic Supplements
- Link to PageOut
- Topic Tackler Demo
- NetTutor Demo

Online Instructor Center
- Instructor's Manual
- PowerPoint® files
- Solutions Manual
- Downloadable Images From the Text
- Excel Template Exercises and and Solutions
- Links to Professional Resources

Online Student Center
- Sample Study Guide and Working Papers
- Learning Objectives
- Chapter Overviews
- Glossary of Key Terms
- PowerPoint® files
- Internet Exercises
- Online Quizzes
- Links to URLs referenced in the text
- Online Factory Tours

Online Tutorial
- Excel Template Exercises
- Link to ALEKS Math Skills Assessor
- Practice Midterm and Final Exams
- Link to NetTutor Live Online Tutoring
- Downloadable Images From the Text

Other updates will be added throughout the term.

Managerial Accounting

Tenth Edition

Ray H. Garrison, D.B.A., CPA
Professor Emeritus
Brigham Young University

Eric W. Noreen, Ph.D., CMA
Professor Emcritus
University of Washington

Boston Burr Ridge, IL Dubuque, IA Madison, WI New York San Francisco St. Louis
Bangkok Bogotá Caracas Kuala Lumpur Lisbon London Madrid Mexico City
Milan Montreal New Delhi Santiago Seoul Singapore Sydney Taipei Toronto

McGraw-Hill Higher Education
A Division of The ***McGraw-Hill*** *Companies*

MANAGERIAL ACCOUNTING

Published by McGraw-Hill/Irwin, a business unit of The McGraw-Hill Companies, Inc. 1221 Avenue of the Americas, New York, NY, 10020.
Some ancillaries, including electronic and print components, may not be available to customers outside the United States.

This book is printed on acid-free paper.

domestic 2 3 4 5 6 7 8 9 0 VNH/VNH 0 9 8 7 6 5 4 3 2
international 2 3 4 5 6 7 8 9 0 VNH/VNH 0 9 8 7 6 5 4 3 2

ISBN 0-07-252812-5 (student edition)
ISBN 0-07-242338-2 (instructor's edition)

Publisher: *Brent Gordon*
Executive editor: *Stewart Mattson*
Senior developmental editor: *Tracey Douglas and Kristin Leahy*
Marketing manager: *Ryan Blankenship*
Senior project manager: *Pat Frederickson*
Lead production supervisor: *Heather D. Burbridge*
Senior designer: *Pam Verros*
Senior producer, Media technology: *Ed Przyzycki*
Senior supplement producer: *Carol Loreth*
Photo research coordinator: *Judy Kausal*
Photo researcher: *Sarah Evertson*
Cover design: *Adam Rooke*
Interior design: *Michael Warrell*
Cover photograph: © *Jonathan Kannair/Index Stock/PictureQuest*
Typeface: *10.5/12 Times Roman*
Compositor: *GAC Indianapolis*
Printer: *Von Hoffmann Press, Inc.*

Library of Congress Cataloging-in-Publication Data

Garrison, Ray H.
Managerial accounting / Ray H. Garrison, Eric W. Noreen.--10th ed.
p. cm.
Includes index.
ISBN 0-07-252812-5 (student ed. : alk. paper)--ISBN 0-07-242338-2 (instructor's ed. : alk. paper)
1. Managerial accounting. I. Noreen, Eric W. II. Title.
HF5657.4 G37 2003
658.15'11--dc21

2001055815

INTERNATIONAL EDITION ISBN 0-07-115100-1

www.mhhe.com

Dedication

To our families and
to our many colleagues who use this book.

About the Authors

Ray H. Garrison is emeritus Professor of Accounting at Brigham Young University, Provo, Utah. He received his B.S. and M.S. degrees from Brigham Young University and his D.B.A. degree from Indiana University.

As a certified public accountant, Professor Garrison has been involved in management consulting work with both national and regional accounting firms. He has published articles in *The Accounting Review, Management Accounting,* and other professional journals. Innovation in the classroom has earned Professor Garrison the Karl G. Maeser Distinguished Teaching Award from Brigham Young University.

Eric W. Noreen is a globe-trotting academic who has held appointments at institutions in the United States, Europe, and Asia. He is Professor Emeritus of Accounting at the University of Washington and was Visiting Price Waterhouse Professor of Management Information & Control at INSEAD, an international graduate school of business located in France.

He received his B.A. degree from the University of Washington and MBA and Ph. D. degrees from Stanford University. A certified management accountant, he was awarded a Certificate of Distinguished Performance by the Institute of Certified Management Accountants.

Professor Noreen has served as Associate Editor of *The Accounting Review* and the *Journal of Accounting* and *Economics*. He has published numerous articles in academic journals including: the *Journal of Accounting Research;* the *Accounting Review;* the *Journal of Accounting* and *Economics; Accounting Horizons; Accounting, Organizations and Society; Contemporary Accounting Research; the Journal of Management Accounting Research;* and the *Review of Accounting Studies*. He is a frequent presenter at workshops and conferences throughout the world.

Professor Noreen has taught management accounting at the undergraduate, master's, and doctoral levels and has won a number of awards from students for his teaching.

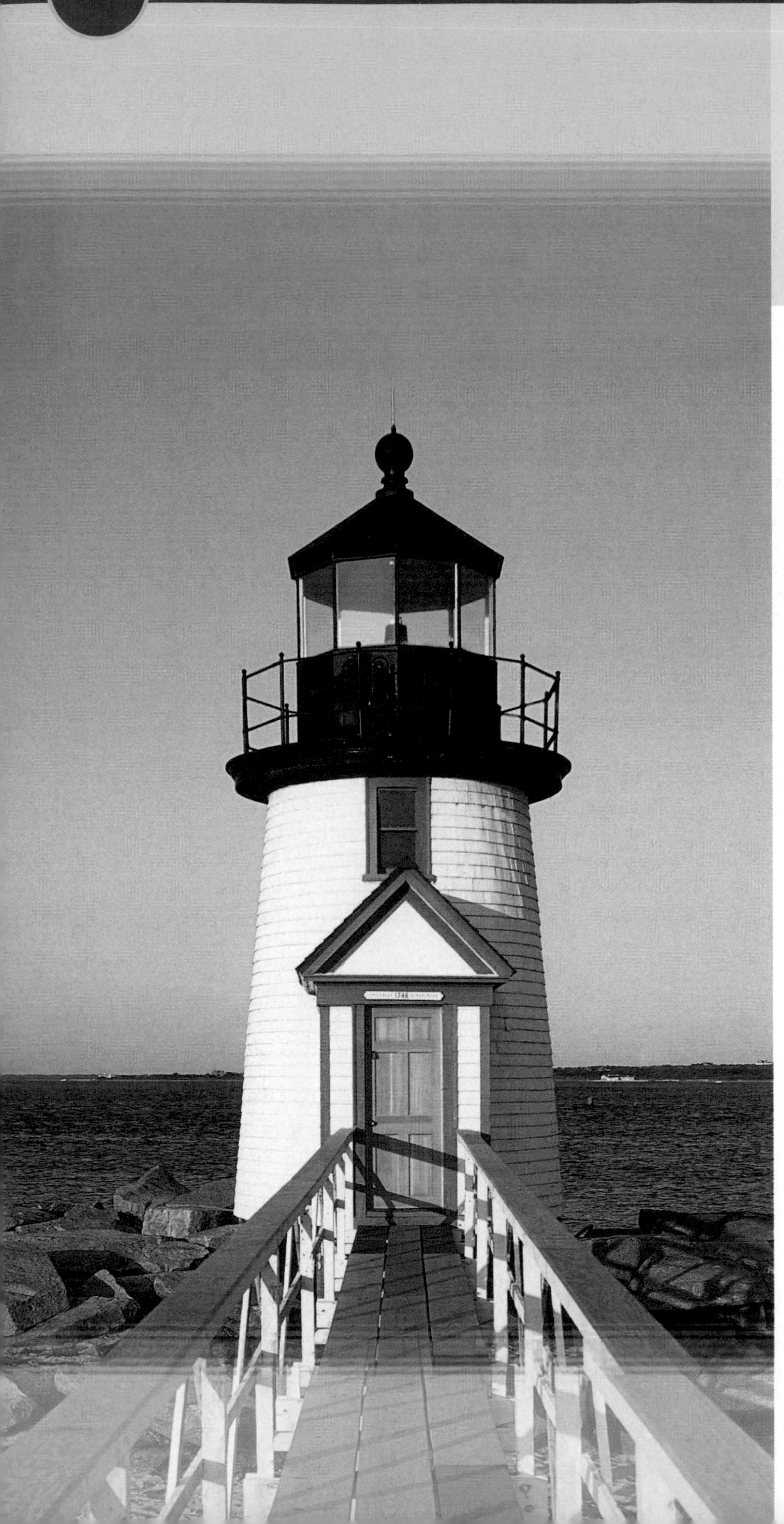

Your guide through

For centuries, the lighthouse has acted as a beacon of guidance for mariners at sea. More than an aid to navigation, the lighthouse symbolizes safety, permanence, reliability, and the comforts of the familiar.

For this reason, we have chosen to decorate the tenth edition of our "flagship" accounting publication, **Managerial Accounting** by Garrison and Noreen, with an image that we feel encapsulates the greatest strengths of this market-leading text.

Garrison is your guide through the challenging waters of managerial accounting. It identifies the three functions managers must perform within their organizations—plan operations, control activities, and make decisions—and explains what accounting information is necessary for these functions, how to collect it, and how to interpret it. To achieve this, **Managerial Accounting 10/E** focuses, now as in the past, on three qualities:

Garrison / Noreen:

the challenging waters of managerial accounting.

Relevance. Every effort is made to help students relate the concepts in this book to the decisions made by working managers. With insightful chapter openers, the popular Managerial Accounting in Action segments within the chapters, and stimulating end-of-chapter exercises, a student reading Garrison should never have to ask, "Why am I learning this?"

Balance. Garrison mixes its coverage to include a variety of business types, including not-for-profit, retail, service, and wholesale organizations as well as manufacturing. In the tenth edition, service company examples are highlighted with icons in the margins of the text.

Clarity. Generations of students have praised Garrison for the friendliness and readability of its writing, but that's just the beginning. Technical discussions have been simplified, material has been reordered, and the entire book has been carefully retuned to make teaching—and learning—from Garrison as easy as it can be. In addition, the supplements package is written by Garrison and Noreen, insuring that students and professors will work with clear, well-written supplements that employ consistent terminology.

The authors' steady focus on these three core elements has led to tremendous results. **Managerial Accounting** has been used by over 1.5 million students and is one of the few texts to win both the McGuffey and the Texty Awards from the Text and Academic Authors Association, which recognizes works for their excellence in areas of content, presentation, appeal, and teachability.

As seafarers looked to the lighthouse for direction along an unfamiliar shore, so too can Garrison act as a crucial compass for students seeking to master this challenging course area. It is a responsibility that has consistently brought out the best in the Garrison team and will continue to do so for many years to come.

What makes Garrison such a powerful learning tool?

Managerial Accounting is full of pedagogy designed to make studying productive and hassle-free. On the following pages, you will see the kind of engaging, helpful pedagogical features that make Garrison a favorite among both teachers and students.

Service

Owing to the growing number of service-based companies in business today, the tenth edition uses a helpful icon to distinguish service-related examples in the text.

Activity-Based Costing

The chapter on activity-based costing has been completely rewritten, allowing for greater accessibility. The more complex material has been moved to an appendix, where it may be included at the instructor's discretion.

Author-Written Supplements

Unlike other managerial accounting texts, Garrison and Noreen write all of the text's major supplements, ensuring a perfect fit between text and supplement. For more information on **Managerial Accounting's** supplements package, see pages xx and xxi.

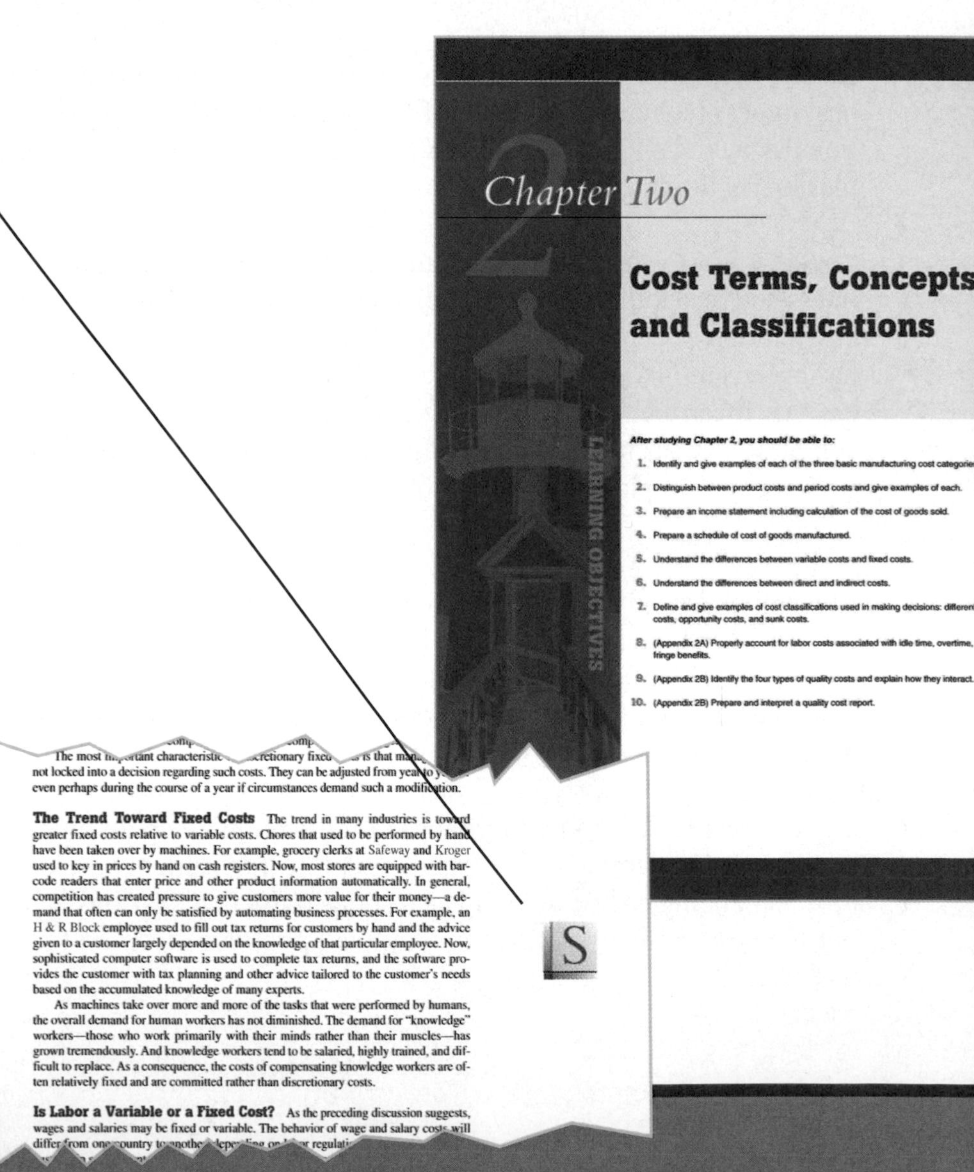

Chapter Two

Cost Terms, Concepts, and Classifications

LEARNING OBJECTIVES

After studying Chapter 2, you should be able to:

1. Identify and give examples of each of the three basic manufacturing cost categories.
2. Distinguish between product costs and period costs and give examples of each.
3. Prepare an income statement including calculation of the cost of goods sold.
4. Prepare a schedule of cost of goods manufactured.
5. Understand the differences between variable costs and fixed costs.
6. Understand the differences between direct and indirect costs.
7. Define and give examples of cost classifications used in making decisions: differential costs, opportunity costs, and sunk costs.
8. (Appendix 2A) Properly account for labor costs associated with idle time, overtime, and fringe benefits.
9. (Appendix 2B) Identify the four types of quality costs and explain how they interact.
10. (Appendix 2B) Prepare and interpret a quality cost report.

The most [illegible] characteristic [illegible] discretionary fixed [illegible] is that ma[illegible] not locked into a decision regarding such costs. They can be adjusted from year to y[illegible] even perhaps during the course of a year if circumstances demand such a modification.

The Trend Toward Fixed Costs The trend in many industries is toward greater fixed costs relative to variable costs. Chores that used to be performed by hand have been taken over by machines. For example, grocery clerks at Safeway and Kroger used to key in prices by hand on cash registers. Now, most stores are equipped with barcode readers that enter price and other product information automatically. In general, competition has created pressure to give customers more value for their money—a demand that often can only be satisfied by automating business processes. For example, an H & R Block employee used to fill out tax returns for customers by hand and the advice given to a customer largely depended on the knowledge of that particular employee. Now, sophisticated computer software is used to complete tax returns, and the software provides the customer with tax planning and other advice tailored to the customer's needs based on the accumulated knowledge of many experts.

As machines take over more and more of the tasks that were performed by humans, the overall demand for human workers has not diminished. The demand for "knowledge" workers—those who work primarily with their minds rather than their muscles—has grown tremendously. And knowledge workers tend to be salaried, highly trained, and difficult to replace. As a consequence, the costs of compensating knowledge workers are often relatively fixed and are committed rather than discretionary costs.

Is Labor a Variable or a Fixed Cost? As the preceding discussion suggests, wages and salaries may be fixed or variable. The behavior of wage and salary costs will differ from one country to another, depending on labor regulati[illegible]

Dissecting the Value Chain

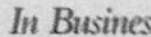

United Colors of Benetton, an Italian apparel company headquartered in Ponzano, is unusual in that it is involved in all activities in the "value chain" from clothing design through manufacturing, distribution, and ultimate sale to customers in Benetton retail outlets. Most companies are involved in only one or two of these activities. Looking at this company allows us to see how costs are distributed across the entire value chain. A recent income statement from the company contained the following data:

	Billions of Italian Lire	Percent of Net Sales
Net sales	2,768	100.0%
Cost of sales	1,721	62.2
Selling and general and administrative expenses:		
Payroll and related cost	166	6.0
Distribution and transport	57	2.1
Sales commissions	115	4.2
Advertising and promotion	120	4.3
Depreciation and amortization	42	1.5
Other expenses	275	9.9
Total selling and general and administrative expenses	775	28.0%

Even though this company spends large sums on advertising and runs its own shops, the cost of sales is still quite high in relation to the net sales—62% of net sales. And despite the company's lavish advertising campaigns, advertising and promotion costs amounted to only a lit- … bout 1,600 Italian lire at the time of

e all the costs that are involved in ured goods, these costs consist of ead. Product costs are viewed as d or manufactured, and they re- ale. So initially, product costs are Vhen the goods are sold, the costs l cost of goods sold) and matched assigned to inventories, they are

essarily treated as expenses in the bove, they are treated as expenses is means that a product cost such ring one period but not treated as l product is sold.

roduct costs. These costs are ex- they are incurred, using the usual financial accounting. Period costs manufactured goods. Sales com- costs. Neither commissions nor l or manufactured goods. Rather,

"In Business"

These helpful boxed features offer a glimpse into how real companies use the managerial accounting concepts discussed within the chapter. Every chapter contains from two to nine of these current examples.

Opening Vignette

BUSINESS FOCUS

Costs Add Up

Understanding costs and how they behave is critical in business. Labor Ready is a company based in Tacoma, Washington, that was started in 1989 with an investment of $50,000. The company fills temporary manual labor jobs throughout the United States, Canada, and the UK—issuing over 6 million paychecks each year to more than half a million laborers. For example, the food vendors at the new Seattle Mariners' Safeco Field hire Labor Ready workers to serve soft drinks and food at baseball games. Employers are charged about $11 per hour for this service. Since Labor Ready pays its workers only about $6.50 per hour and offers no fringe benefits and has no national competitors, this business would appear to be a gold mine generating about $4.50 per hour in profit. However, the company must maintain 687 hiring offices, each employing a permanent staff of four to five persons. Those costs, together with payroll taxes, workmen's compensation insurance, and other administrative costs, result in a margin of only about 5%, or a little over 50¢ per hour. Costs add up—make sure you learn what costs are commonly encountered in practice.

Source: Catie Golding, "Short-Term Work, Long-Term Profits," *Washington CEO*, January 2000, pp. 10–12.

"Managerial Accounting in Action"

These highly praised vignettes depict cross-functional teams working together in real-life settings, working with the products and services that students recognize from their own lives. Students are shown step-by-step how accounting concepts are implemented in organizations and how these concepts are applied to solve everyday business problems. First, "The Issue" is introduced through a dialogue. The student then walks through the implementation process. Finally "The Wrap-Up" summarizes the big picture.

Ch… …ystems Desig… …r Costing

in the performance and safety of the ride. Before we begin our discussion, recall from the previous chapter that companies generally classify manufacturing costs into three broad categories: (1) direct materials, (2) direct labor, and (3) manufacturing overhead. As we study the operation of a job-order costing system, we will see how each of these three types of costs is recorded and accumulated.

Managerial Accounting in Action

The Issue

YOST PRECISION MACHINING

Yost Precision Machining is a small company in Michigan that specializes in fabricating precision metal parts that are used in a variety of applications ranging from deep-sea exploration vehicles to the inertial triggers in automobile air bags. The company's top managers gather every morning at 8:00 A.M. in the company's conference room for the daily planning meeting. Attending the meeting this morning are: Jean Yost, the company's president; David Cheung, the marketing manager; Debbie Turner, the production manager; and Marcus White, the company controller. The president opened the meeting:

Jean: The production schedule indicates we'll be starting job 2B47 today. Isn't that the special order for experimental couplings, David?

David: That's right, Jean. That's the order from Loops Unlimited for two couplings for their new roller coaster ride for Magic Mountain.

Debbie: Why only two couplings? Don't they need a coupling for every car?

David: That's right. But this is a completely new roller coaster. The cars will go faster and will be subjected to more twists, turns, drops, and loops than on any other existing roller coaster. To hold up under these stresses, Loops Unlimited's engineers had to completely redesign the cars and couplings. They want to thoroughly test the design before proceeding to large-scale production. So they want us to make just two of these new couplings for testing purposes. If the design works, then we'll have the inside track on the order to supply couplings for the whole ride.

What makes Garrison such a powerful learning tool?

End-of-Chapter Material

Managerial Accounting has earned a reputation for the best end-of-chapter review and discussion material of any text on the market. Our problem and case material continues to conform to AECC and AACSB recommendations and makes a great starting point for class discussions and group projects. Other helpful features include:

Internet assignments teach students how to find information online and apply it to managerial accounting situations.

Writing assignments encourage your students to practice critical thinking.

82 Chapter 2 Cost Terms, Concepts, and Classifications

Required:
1. Prepare a schedule of cost of goods manufactured.
2. Prepare an income statement.
3. Assume that the company produced the equivalent of 10,000 uni What was the average cost per unit for direct materials? What was factory depreciation?
4. Assume that the company expects to produce 15,000 units of pro What average cost per unit and what total cost would you expect rect materials at this level of activity? For factory depreciation? (sume that direct materials is a variable cost and that depreciation that depreciation is computed on a straight-line basis.)
5. As the manager responsible for production costs, explain to the p average costs per unit between (3) and (4) above.

Ex

PROBLEM 2–20 Schedule of Cost of Goods Manufactured; Inco [LO1, LO2, LO3, LO4]
Skyler Company was organized on November 1 of the previous year. up losses, management had expected to earn a profit during June, the ment was disappointed, however, when the income statement for Jun income statement follows:

SKYLER COMPANY
Income Statement
For the Month Ended June 30

Sales.	
Less operating expenses:	
Selling and administrative salaries	$ 35,000
Rent on facilities	40,000
Purchases of raw materials.	190,000
Insurance	8,000
Depreciation, sales equipment	10,000
Utilities costs.	50,000
Indirect labor	108,000
Direct labor	90,000
Depreciation, factory equipment.	12,000
Maintenance, factory.	7,000
Advertising	80,000
Net operating loss.	

After seeing the $30,000 loss for June, Skyler's president state itable within six months, but after eight months we're still spilling re to throw in the towel and accept one of those offers we've had for th worse, I just heard that Linda won't be back from her surgery for at le

Linda is the company's controller; in her absence, the statement a assistant who has had little experience in manufacturing operations. A the company follows:

a. Only 80% of the rent on facilities applies to factory operations; the remainder applies to selling and administrative activities.
b. Inventory balances at the beginning and end of the month were as follows:

	June 1	June 30
Raw materials	$17,000	$42,000
Work in process	70,000	85,000
Finished goods	20,000	60,000

c. Some 75% of the insurance and 90% of the utilities cost apply to factory operations; the remaining amounts apply to selling and administrative activities.

The president has asked you to check over the above income statement and make a recommendation as to whether the company should continue operations.

Chapter 2 Cost Terms, C

Required:
1. Henry Ford made a now-famous statement that the Model T "cou as it was black." Explain what he meant by this statement.
2. How would Henry Ford or any other manufacturer with a na further efficiencies based on the traditional production model de
3. Are there any limits to lowering the cost of black Model Ts, volume, commodity product? Explain.
4. Once understood, the economies of mass production were applie ican economy. Universities, hospitals, and airlines are prime exa cepts of mass production, standardization, and specialization h costs of a university education. Of a stay in the hospital.

GROUP EXERCISE 2–30 If Big Is Good, Bigger Must Be Bette
Steel production involves a large amount of fixed costs. Since comp terms of price, American steel manufacturers (and many of their mar try counterparts) try to gain a competitive advantage by using econ in technology to increase productivity and drive unit costs lower. Th the result of their size.

Required:
1. How are fixed costs and variable costs normally defined?
2. Give examples of fixed costs and variable costs for a steel comp sure of production activity?
3. Give examples of fixed and variable costs for a hospital, unive What is the relevant measure of production or service activity fo
4. Using the examples of fixed and variable costs for steel comp the relationship between production output at a steel company a fixed costs, fixed cost per unit, total variable costs, variable c average unit cost.
5. With an *X* axis (horizontal axis) of tons produced and a *Y* axis graph total fixed costs, total variable costs, and total costs again
6. With an *X* axis of tons produced and a *Y* axis of unit costs, grap cost per unit, and total (or average) cost per unit against tons pr
7. Explain how costs (total and per unit) behave with changes i been set.

INTERNET EXERCISE 2–31 Internet Exercise
As you know, the World Wide Web is a medium that is constantly evo change without notice. To enable periodic update of site addresses, th the textbook website (www.mhhe.com/garrison10e). After accessi Center and select this chapter. Select and complete the Internet Exer

__Spreadsheets__ have become an increasingly common budgeting tool for managerial accountants; therefore, to assist students in understanding how budgets look in a spreadsheet, all figures pertaining to budgeting will appear as Microsoft Excel® screen captures.

Exhibit 5A–1 The Least-Squares Regression Worksheet for Brentline Hospital

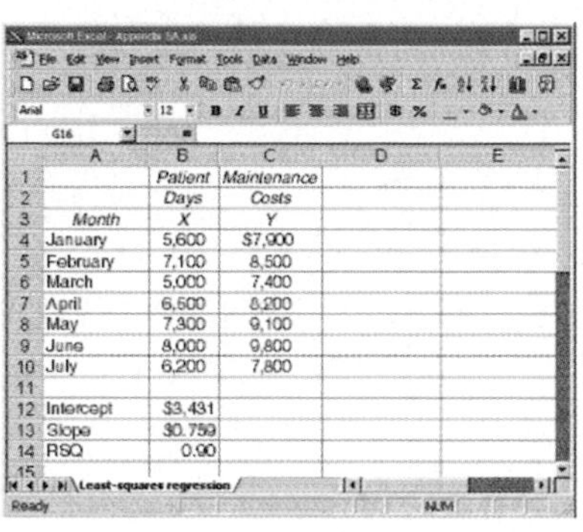

	A	B	C	D	E
1		Patient	Maintenance		
2		Days	Costs		
3	Month	X	Y		
4	January	5,600	$7,900		
5	February	7,100	8,500		
6	March	5,000	7,400		
7	April	6,500	8,200		
8	May	7,300	9,100		
9	June	8,000	9,800		
10	July	6,200	7,800		
11					
12	Intercept	$3,431			
13	Slope	$0.759			
14	RSQ	0.90			
15					

cally. Spreadsheet software, such as Microsoft® Excel, can also be used to do least-squares regression—although it requires a little more work than specialized statistical packages do.

To illustrate how Excel can be used to calculate the intercept *a*, the slope *b*, and the R^2, we will use the Brentline Hospital data for maintenance costs on page 204. The worksheet in Exhibit 5A–1 contains the data and the calculations.

As you can see, the *X* values (the independent variable) have been entered in cells B4 through B10. The *Y* values (the dependent variable) have been entered in cells C4 through C10. The slope, intercept, and R^2 are computed using the Excel functions INTERCEPT, SLOPE, and RSQ. In each case, you must specify the range of cells for the *Y* values and for the *X* values. In the above worksheet, cell B12 contains the formula =INTERCEPT(C4:C10,B4:B10); cell B13 contains the formula =SLOPE(C4:C10,B4:B10); and cell B14 contains the formula =RSQ(C4:C10,B4:B10).

According to the calculations carried out by Excel, the fixed maintenance cost (the intercept) is $3,431 per month and the variable cost (the slope) is $0.759 per patient-day. Therefore, the cost formula for maintenance cost is:

$$Y = a + bX$$

$$Y = \$3{,}431 + \$0.759X$$

Note that the R^2 (i.e., RSQ) is 0.90, which—as previously discussed—is quite good and indicates that 90% of the variation in maintenance costs is explained by the variation in patient-days.

b. Identify potential problems that could arise in each individual's position, either due to the type of position (i.e., line or staff) or to the location of the individual's position within the organization.

(CMA, adapted)

PROBLEM 1–7 Ethics in Business [LO4]
Consumers and attorneys general in more than 40 states accused a prominent nationwide chain of auto repair shops of misleading customers and selling them unnecessary parts and services, from brake jobs to front-end alignments. Lynn Sharpe Paine reported the situation as follows in "Managing for Organizational Integrity," *Harvard Business Review*, March-April, 1994:

> In the face of declining revenues, shrinking market share, and an increasingly competitive market . . . management attempted to spur performance of its auto centers. . . . The automotive service advisers were given product-specific sales quotas—sell so many springs, shock absorbers, alignments, or brake jobs per shift—and paid a commission based on sales. . . . [F]ailure to meet quotas could lead to a transfer or a reduction in work hours. Some employees spoke of the "pressure, pressure, pressure" to bring in sales.
>
> This pressure-cooker atmosphere created conditions under which employees felt that the only way to satisfy top management was by selling products and services to customers that they didn't really need.

Suppose all automotive repair businesses routinely followed the practice of attempting to sell customers unnecessary parts and services.

Required:

1. How would this behavior affect customers? How might customers attempt to protect themselves against this behavior?
2. How would this behavior probably affect profits and employment in the automotive service industry?

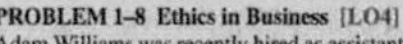

PROBLEM 1–8 Ethics in Business [LO4]
Adam Williams was recently hired as assistant controller of GroChem, Inc., which processes chemicals for use in fertilizers. Williams was selected for this position because of his past experience in chemical processing. During his first month on the job, Williams made a point of getting to know the people responsible for the plant operations and learning how things are done at GroChem.

During a conversation with the plant supervisor, Williams asked about the company procedures for handling toxic waste materials. The plant supervisor replied that he was not involved with the disposal of wastes and suggested that Williams might be wise to ignore this issue. This response strengthened Williams's determination to probe this area further to be sure that the company was not vulnerable to litigation.

Upon further investigation, Williams discovered evidence that GroChem was using a nearby residential landfill to dump toxic wastes. It appeared that some members of GroChem's manage-

__Ethics assignments__ serve as a reminder that good conduct is just as important as profits in business. Group projects can be assigned either as homework or as in-class discussion projects.

What's new about the Tenth Edition?

1

Chapter 1

The discussion of JIT, TQM, and Process Reengineering has been condensed.

The chapter has been reorganized by bringing forward the section that discusses organizational structure and the work of the management accountant.

The role of the CFO is discussed.

Links between e-commerce and subsequent chapters are discussed.

2

Chapter 2

The illustration of inventory flows in Exhibit 2–3 has been improved.

The alternative approach to computation of cost of goods sold has been eliminated.

New material dealing with ethical issues in the determination of product and period costs has been added.

Cost of quality material has been moved from an appendix at the back of the book to an appendix to Chapter 2.

3

Chapter 3

The section on use of information technology has been updated to cover new web-based technologies.

4

Chapter 4

Changes have been made in the format of the production report to improve its readability.

Rounding has been eliminated as an issue in all examples and end-of-chapter materials by ensuring that all computations carried out to the nearest whole cent yield exact answers.

5

Chapter 5

Scattergraph plots now precede the high-low method.

We now refer to the method for estimating fixed and variable costs based on the visual fit to the scattergraph plot as the **quick-and-dirty** method. The emphasis in the scattergraph section of the text is now on diagnosis of cost behavior patterns rather than as a way to estimate fixed and variable costs.

The term **regression line** is now reserved for the line that is computed by least-squares regression.

Hand calculation of the least-squares regression estimates has been eliminated. In the appendix we show how Excel or another spreadsheet application can be used to estimate slope, intercept, and the R^2 of the regression.

Chapter 6

The CVP graph is introduced before break-even analysis to provide a more intuitive basis for the mathematics.

Chapter 7

New "In Business" boxes have been added.

Chapter 8

The "Manufacturing Costs and Activity-Based Costing" section has been extensively rewritten.

The "Steps for Implementing Activity-Based Costing" have been more clearly highlighted.

"Step 4: Calculate Activity Rates" has been extensively rewritten.

The "Targeting Process Improvements" section has been moved later in the chapter, after the "Comparison of Traditional and ABC Product Costs" section.

A new section on "The Limitations of Activity-Based Costing" has been added.

Technically complex material has been moved to a new appendix entitled "ABC Action Analysis." This appendix covers "Activity Rates—Action Analysis Report," "Assignment of Overhead Costs to Products—Action Analysis Report," "Ease of Adjustment Codes," and "The Action Analysis View of the ABC Data."

Chapter 9

The Appendix covering Economic Order Quantity and the Reorder Point has been eliminated.

The mechanics of how to construct the various schedules in the master budget are more thoroughly explained in the text.

Chapter 10

A new exhibit, Exhibit 10–1, provides an overview of the variance reporting process.

Chapter 11

New "In Business" boxes have been added.

Chapter 12

Material on mandated segment reports has been added.

Chapter 13

A new, easy-to-understand example has been added illustrating the identification of relevant and irrelevant costs.

Material dealing with the reconciliation of the total and differential approaches has been added.

The section dealing with equipment replacement decisions has been eliminated. This subject is covered in the capital budgeting chapter.

The section on joint costs has been completely rewritten and features a new, appealing example.

Chapter 14

The material on income taxes that was in Chapter 15 has been simplified by eliminating MACRS depreciation and has been condensed and moved to Appendix 14D.

The section on automated equipment has been generalized and rewritten as a section on evaluating projects with uncertain future cash flows.

The section on interpolation in internal rate of return calculations has been eliminated.

Problem materials now ask for the internal rate of return to the nearest whole percent.

The present value tables have been expanded to include all rates of return between 5% and 25%.

Many new "In Business" examples have been added.

Chapter 15 (formerly Chapter 16)

New "In Business" boxes have been added.

Chapter 16 (formerly Chapter 17)

New "In Business" boxes have been added.

Chapter 17 (formerly Chapter 18)

New "In Business" boxes have been added.

Pricing Appendix

New "In Business" boxes have been added.

Can technology really help students and professors in the learning process?

Today, nearly 200,000 college instructors use the Internet in their respective courses. Some are just getting started, while others are ready to embrace the very latest advances in educational content delivery and course management.

That's why we at McGraw-Hill/Irwin offer you a complete range of digital solutions. Your students can use **Managerial Accounting's** complete Online Learning Center, NetTutor, and PowerWeb on their own, or we can help you create your own course website using McGraw-Hill's PageOut.

In addition to Web-based assets, **Managerial Accounting** boasts **Topic Tackler,** a CD-ROM that offers special chapter-by-chapter assistance for the most demanding managerial accounting topics. With McGraw-Hill's Presentation Manager CD-ROM, instructors have access to nearly every crucial supplement, from the instructor's resource manual to the test bank, in both print and electronic media.

McGraw-Hill is a leader in bringing helpful technology into the classroom. And with **Managerial Accounting,** your class gets all the benefits of the digital age.

NetTutor™

How can I easily integrate Web resources into my course?

ONLINE LEARNING CENTER (OLC)

More and more students are studying online. That's why we offer an Online Learning Center (OLC) that follows **Managerial Accounting** chapter by chapter. It doesn't require any building or maintenance on your part. It's ready to go the moment you and your students type in the URL.

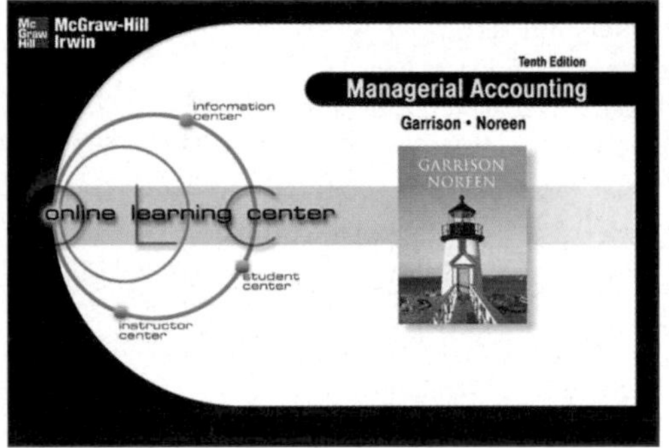

www.mhhe.com/garrison10e

As your students study, they can refer to the OLC website for such benefits as:

- Internet-based activities
- Self-grading quizzes
- Links to text references
- Links to professional resources on the Web and job opportunity information
- Learning objectives
- Chapter overviews
- Internet factory tours

A secured Instructor Resource Center stores your essential course materials to save you prep time before class. The instructor's manual, solutions, PowerPoint®, and sample syllabi are now just a couple of clicks away. You will also find useful packaging information and transition notes.

The OLC website also serves as a doorway to other technology solutions like PageOut which is free to **Managerial Accounting** adopters.

Many of my students work or have other obligations outside of class. How can they get book-specific help at their convenience?

NET TUTOR™

Net Tutor™

NetTutor is a breakthrough program that allows one-on-one assistance completely online. Qualified accounting tutors equipped with **Managerial Accounting** work online with your students on specific problems or concepts from their text.

NetTutor allows tutors and students to communicate with each other in a variety of ways:

The Live Tutor Center via NetTutor's WWWhiteboard enables a tutor to hold an interactive, online tutorial session with a student or several students. The WWWhiteboard acts as a virtual chalkboard where students can view tutor-created spreadsheets, t-accounts, and written explanations during hours that work with your students' schedules.

The Q&A Center allows students to submit questions at any time and retrieve answers within 24 hours.

The Archive Center allows students to browse for answers to previously asked questions. They can also search for questions pertinent to a particular topic. If they encounter an answer they do not understand, they can ask a follow-up question.

Students are issued five hours of free NetTutor time when they purchase a new copy of **Managerial Accounting**. Additional time may be purchased in five-hour increments. Tutors are available during the week to help students clear those afternoon and evening study hurdles.

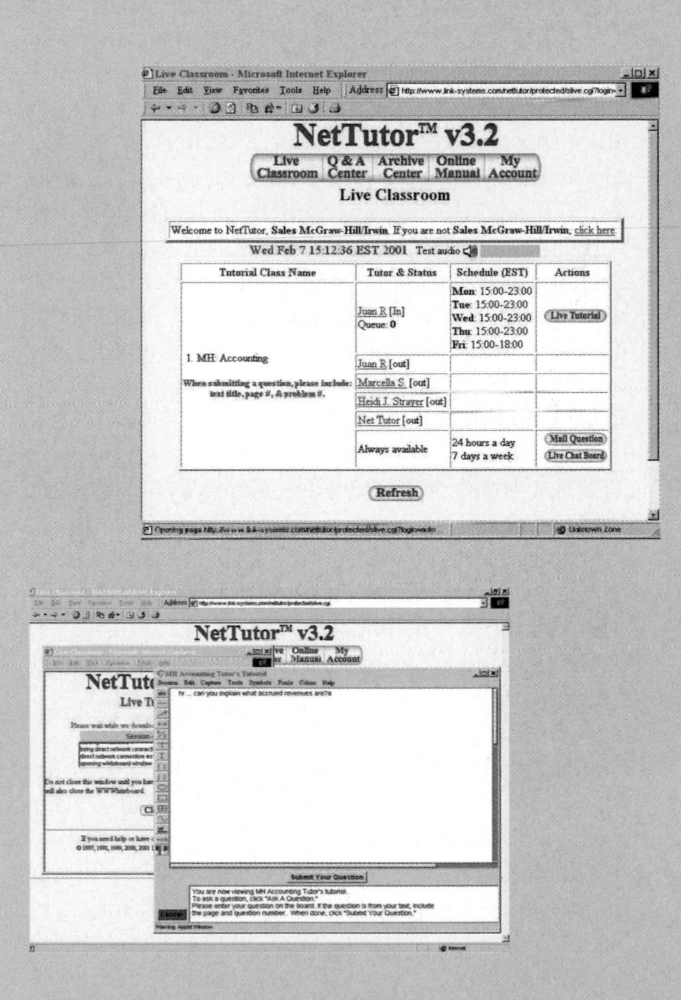

What help can I rely on from McGraw-Hill for setting up my online course?

KNOWLEDGE GATEWAY

Knowledge Gateway

Developed with the help of our partner, Eduprise, the McGraw-Hill Knowledge Gateway is an all-purpose service and resource center for instructors teaching online. While training programs from WebCT and Blackboard will help teach you their software, only McGraw-Hill has services to help you actually *manage and teach* your online course, as well as run and maintain the software. Knowledge Gateway offers an online library full of articles and insights that focus on how online learning differs from a traditional class environment.

The first level of Knowledge Gateway is available to all professors browsing the McGraw-Hill Higher Education website and consists of an introduction to OLC content, access to the first level of the Resource Library, technical support, and information on Instructional Design services available through Eduprise.

The second level is password-protected and provides access to the expanded Resource Library, technical and pedagogical support for WebCT, Blackboard, and TopClass, the online instructional design helpdesk, and an online discussion forum for users. The Knowledge Gateway provides a considerable advantage for teaching online—and it's only available through McGraw-Hill.

To see how these platforms can assist your online course, visit **www.mhhe.com/solutions**.

PAGEOUT & SERVICE

PageOut is McGraw-Hill/Irwin's custom website service. Now you can put your course online without knowing a word of HTML, selecting from a variety of prebuilt website templates. And if none of our ideas suit you, we'll be happy to work with your ideas.

If you want a custom site but don't have time to build it yourself, we offer a team of product specialists ready to help. Just call 1-800-634-3963, press 0 to get the receptionist, and ask to speak with a PageOut specialist. You will be asked to send in your course materials and then participate in a brief telephone consultation. Once we have your information, we build your website for you, from scratch.

INSTRUCTOR ADVANTAGE AND INSTRUCTOR ADVANTAGE PLUS

Instructor Advantage is a special level of service McGraw-Hill offers in conjunction with WebCT and Blackboard. A team of platform specialists is always available, either by toll-free phone or e-mail, to ensure everything runs smoothly through the life of your adoption. Instructor Advantage is available free to all McGraw-Hill customers.

Instructor Advantage Plus is available to qualifying McGraw-Hill adopters (see your representative for details). IA Plus guarantees you a full day of on-site training by a Blackboard or WebCT specialist, for yourself and up to nine colleagues. Thereafter, you will enjoy the benefits of unlimited telephone and e-mail support throughout the life of your adoption. IA Plus users also have the opportunity to access the McGraw-Hill Knowledge Gateway (see left).

How can I easily create an online course?

For the instructor needing to educate students online, we offer **Managerial Accounting** content for complete online courses. To make this possible, we have joined forces with the most popular delivery platforms currently available. These platforms are designed for instructors who want complete control over course content and how it is presented to students. You can customize the **Managerial Accounting** Online Learning Center content and author your own course materials. It's entirely up to you.

Products like **WebCT, Blackboard, eCollege,** and **TopClass** (a product of WBT) all expand the reach of your course. Online discussion and message boards will now complement your office hours. Thanks to a sophisticated tracking system, you will know which students need more attention—even if they don't ask for help. That's because online testing scores are recorded and automatically placed in your grade book, and if a student is struggling with coursework, a special alert message lets you know.

Remember, **Managerial Accounting's** content is flexible enough to use with any platform currently available. If your department or school is already using a platform, we can help. For information on McGraw-Hill/Irwin's course management supplements, including Instructor Advantage and Knowledge Gateway, see "Knowledge Gateway" on the previous page.

PAGEOUT

McGraw-Hill's Course Management System

PageOut is the easiest way to create a website for your accounting course.

There's no need for HTML coding, graphic design, or a thick how-to book. Just fill in a series of boxes with simple English and click on one of our professional designs. In no time, your course is online with a website that contains your syllabus!

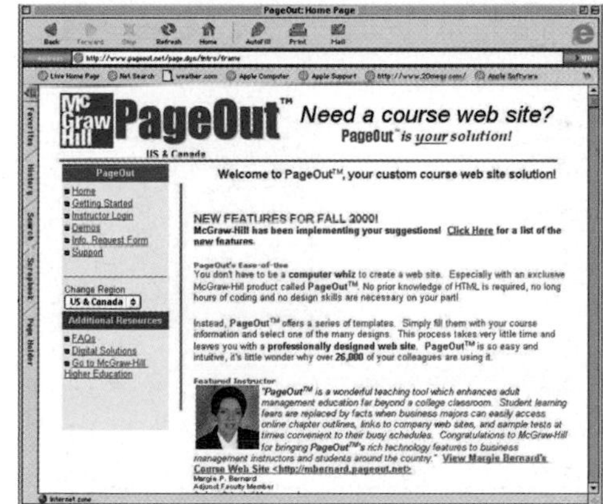

If you need assistance in preparing your website, we can help. Our team of product specialists is ready to take your course materials and build a custom website to your specifications. You simply need to call a McGraw-Hill/Irwin PageOut specialist to start the process. (For information on how to do this, see "Superior Service" on the next page.) Best of all, PageOut is free when you adopt **Managerial Accounting**! To learn more, please visit **http:///www.pageout.net**.

How can my students use their study time more effectively?

The online resource GradeSummit

tells your students everything they need to know in order to study effectively. And it provides you, the instructor, with valuable insight into which of your students are struggling and which course topics give them the most trouble.

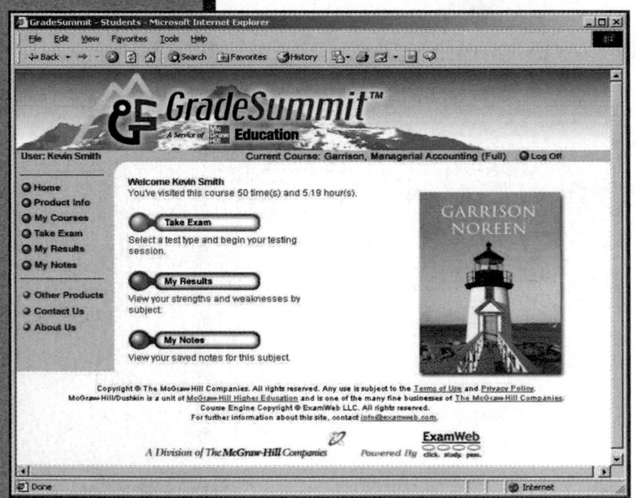

For the student, GradeSummit provides a series of practice tests written to coincide with **Managerial Accounting's** coverage. The tests can be taken in various formats according to student preference: *practice mode,* for instance, displays the correct answer immediately, while *exam mode* simulates a real classroom exam and displays results at the end. There's even a smart testing engine, *SummitExpress*, that automatically scales the difficulty level of the questions according to the student's responses.

Once a student has taken a particular test, GradeSummit returns a detailed results page showing exactly where the student did well and where he or she needs to improve. Students can compare their results with those of their other classmates, or even with those of every other student using the text nationwide. With that information, students can plan their studying to focus exclusively on their weak areas, without wasting effort on material they've already mastered. And they can come back to take a retest on those subjects later, comparing their new score with their previous efforts.

As an instructor, you'll know which students are falling behind simply by consulting GradeSummit's test logs, where results for every student in your course are available for review. Because GradeSummit's results are so detailed, you'll know exactly what topics are causing difficulties—an invaluable aid when it comes to planning lectures and homework.

Can the Internet help me keep my course up to date?

Keeping your course current can be a job in itself, and now McGraw-Hill does that job for you. PowerWeb extends the learning experience beyond the core textbook by offering all of the latest news and developments pertinent to your course, brought to you via the Internet without all the clutter and dead links of a typical online search.

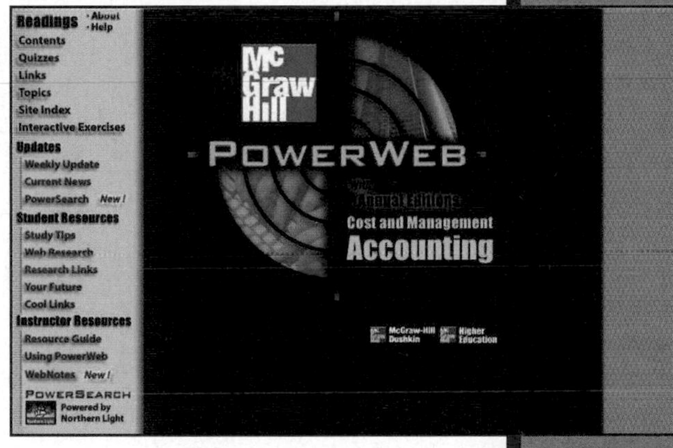

PowerWeb is a robust website that offers these *course-specific* features:

- Current articles related to managerial accounting.
- Daily and weekly updates with assessment tools.
- Informative and timely world news culled by a managerial accountant in academia.
- Refereed web links.
- Online handbook to researching, evaluating, and citing online sources.

In addition, PowerWeb provides a trove of helpful learning aids, including self-grading quizzes and interactive glossaries and exercises. Students may also access study tips, conduct online research, and learn about different career paths.

Visit the PowerWeb site at **http://www.dushkin.com/powerweb** and see firsthand what PowerWeb can mean to your course.

Supplements

INSTRUCTOR SUPPLEMENTS

Instructor CD-ROM

ISBN 0072531711

Allowing instructors to create a customized multimedia presentation, this all-in-one resource incorporates the Test Bank, PowerPoint® Slides, Instructor's Resource Guide, Solutions Manual, Teaching Transparency Masters, links to PageOut, and the Spreadsheet Application Template Software (SPATS).

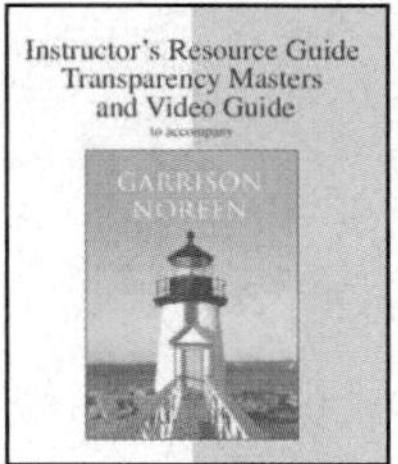

Instructor's Resource Guide and Video Manual

ISBN 007253155X

This supplement contains the teaching transparency masters and the video guide, extensive chapter-by-chapter lecture notes to help with classroom presentation, and useful suggestions for presenting key concepts and ideas.

Instructor's Edition

ISBN 007255522X

This special edition contains five types of annotations in the margins to help you plan your lessons: Instructor's Notes, Reinforcing Problems, In the Real World, Suggested Readings, and Check Figures.

Check Figures

These provide key answers for selected problems and cases. They are available on the text's website.

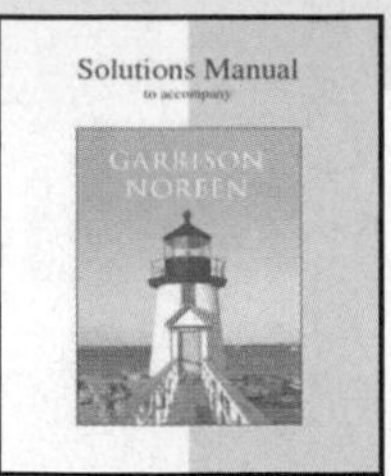

Solutions Manual and Disk

ISBN 0072539240

This supplement contains completely worked-out solutions to all assignment material and a general discussion of the use of group exercises. In addition, the manual contains suggested course outlines and a listing of exercises, problems, and cases scaled according to difficulty. This print supplement is packaged with a CD-ROM containing the Solutions Manual in Microsoft Word® format.

Solutions Transparencies

ISBN 0072531576

These transparencies feature completely worked-out solutions to all assignment material. The font used in the solutions is large enough for the back row of any lecture hall. Masters of these transparencies are available in the Solutions Manual.

Teaching Transparencies

ISBN 0072531630

Contains a comprehensive set of over 260 teaching transparencies covering every chapter that can be used for classroom lectures and discussion.

Ready Shows (PowerPoint® Slides)

ISBN 0072538821

Prepared by Jon Booker, Charles Caldwell, and Richard Rand, all of Tennessee Technological University, and Susan Galbreath of Lipscomb University, these slides offer a great visual complement for your lectures. A complete set of slides covers each chapter.

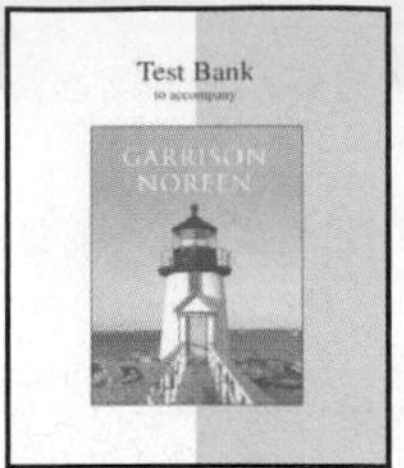

Test Bank

ISBN 0072531606

Nearly 2,000 questions are organized by chapter and include true/false, multiple-choice, and essay questions and computational problems.

Diploma Computerized Testbank

ISBN 007253172X

This test bank is now delivered in the Diploma Shell, new from Brownstone. Use it to make different versions of the same test, change the answer order, edit and add questions, and conduct online testing. Technical support for this software is available.

Excel Templates

Prepared by Jack Terry of ComSource Associates, Inc., these Excel templates offer solutions to the Student SPATS version. They are only available on the Instructor CD and the text's website.

Dallas County Community College Telecourse

These short, action-oriented videos, developed by Dallas County Community College, provide the impetus for lively classroom discussion. The focus is on the preparation, analysis, and use of accounting information for business decision making. (To acquire the complete telecourse, Accounting in Action, call Dallas TeleLearning at 972-669-6666, fax them at 972-669-6668, or visit their website at **http://telelearning.dcccd.edu.**)

STUDENT SUPPLEMENTS

Topic Tackler CD-ROM

ISBN 0072531746

Free with the text, the Topic Tackler CD-ROM helps students master difficult concepts in managerial accounting through a creative, interactive learning process. Designed for study outside the classroom, this multimedia CD delves into chapter concepts with graphical slides and diagrams, web links, video clips, and animations, all centered around engaging exercises designed to put students in control of their learning of managerial accounting topics.

Workbook/Study Guide

ISBN 0072531789

This study aid provides suggestions for studying chapter material, summarizes essential points in each chapter, and tests students' knowledge using self-test questions and exercises.

Ready Notes

ISBN 0072538368

This booklet provides Ready Slide exhibits in a workbook format for efficient note taking.

Student Lecture Aid

ISBN 0072531797

Much like the Ready Notes, this booklet offers a hard-copy version of all the Teaching Transparencies. Students can annotate the material during the lecture and take notes in the space provided.

Working Papers

ISBN 0072531762

This study aid contains forms that help students organize their solutions to homework problems.

Excel Templates

Prepared by Jack Terry of ComSource Associates, Inc., this spreadsheet-based software uses Excel to solve selected problems and cases in the text. These selected problems and cases are identified in the margin of the text with an appropriate icon. The Excel Templates are only available on the text's website.

Telecourse Guide

ISBN 0072531754

This study guide ties the Dallas County Community College Telecourse directly to this text.

Ramblewood Manufacturing, Inc. CD-ROM

ISBN for instructor version 0072536357
ISBN for student version 0072536667

This computerized practice set was prepared by Leland Mansuetti and Keith Weidkamp, both of Sierra College, and has been completely updated. This software simulates the operations of a company that manufactures customized fencing. It can be used to illustrate job-order costing systems with JIT inventory in a realistic setting. The entire simulation requires 10 to 14 hours to complete. A new feature prevents files from being transferred from one disk to another without detection. It is available on CD-ROM and runs on Microsoft Windows®.

Communication for Accountants: Effective Strategies for Students and Professionals

ISBN 0070383901

Authored by Maurice Hirsch of Southern Illinois University-Carbondale and Susan Gabriel and Rob Anderson, both of St. Louis University, this brief and inexpensive handbook addresses the need for accountants to communicate effectively through both writing and speaking.

Reviewers

Suggestions have been received from many of our colleagues throughout the world who have used the prior edition of **Managerial Accounting.** This is vital feedback that we rely on in each edition. Each of those who have offered comments and suggestions has our thanks.

The efforts of many people are needed to develop and improve a text. Among these people are the reviewers and consultants who point out areas of concern, cite areas of strength, and make recommendations for change. In this regard, the following professors provided feedback that was enormously helpful in preparing the tenth edition of **Managerial Accounting**:

Philip Blanchard, *University of Arizona*

Daniel Brickner, *Eastern Michigan University*

Betty Jo Browning, *Bradley University*

Steve Buchheit, *University of Houston*

Steven Christian, *Jackson Community College*

Barbara Croteau, *Santa Rosa Junior College*

Mary Curtis, *University of North Texas*

Alan Czyzewski, *Indiana State University*

Charles Davis, *Baylor University*

Deborah Davis, *Hampton University*

Patricia Doherty, *Boston University*

Peter Dorff, *Kent State University*

James Emig, *Villanova University*

Harriet Farney, *University of Hartford*

Jack Fay, *Pittsburg State University*

Jessica Frazier, *Eastern Kentucky University*

Jackson Gillespie, *University of Delaware*

Joe Goetz, *Louisiana State University*

Art Goldman, *University of Kentucky*

Michael Haselkorn, *Bentley College*

Cheryl Heath, *Montana State University – Billings*

Norma Holter, *Towson University*

David Jacobson, *Salem State College*

Holly Johnston, *Boston University*

Celina Jozsi, *University of South Florida*

Leroy Kauffman, *Western Carolina University*

Jong Kim, *California State University – Sacramento*

Shirly Kleiner, *Johnson County Community College*

Kathy Lancaster, *California Polytechnic State University – San Luis Obispo*

Chor Lau, *California State University – Los Angeles*

Larry Logan, *University of Massachusetts – Dartmouth*

Lisa Martin, *Western Michigan University*

Dan Matthews, *Midwestern State University*

Mark McCartney, *Saginaw Valley State University*

Cheryl McConnell, *Rockhurst College*

Harrison McCraw, *State University of Western Georgia*

David Medved, *Davenport University*

Douglas Morrison, *Clark College*

Joanne Nikides, *Palm Beach Community College – Lake Worth*

Michael O'Neill, *Seattle Central Community College*

Hugh Pforsich, *University of Idaho*

Leonardo Rodriguez, *Florida International University*

Eldon Schafer, *University of Arizona*

Anne Sergeant, *Iowa State University*

Ken Sinclair, *Lehigh University*

Soliman Soliman, *Tulane University*

Gina Stanley, *Concord College*

Gerald Thalmann, *North Central College*

Steven White, *Western Kentucky University*

Patricia Williams, *Friends University*

Consultants

Wagdy Abdallah, *Seton Hall University*

Sheila Ammons, *Austin Community College*

Mohamed Bayou, *University of Michigan—Dearborn*

Marvin Bouillon, *Iowa State University*

Suzanne Breitenbach, *Keller Graduate School of Business*

Thomas Buttros, *Indiana University at Kokomo*

Larry Carney, *Fontbonne College*

Ginger Clark, *University of Cincinnati*

Robert Close, *Consumnes River College*

Gail Cook, *University of Wisconsin—Parkside*

Rosalind Cranor, *Virginia Polytech Institute*

Jeremy Cripps, *Heidelberg College*

Larry Deppe, *Weber State University*

Peter Dorff, *Kent State University*

Alan Doyle, *Pima College*

Robert Dunn, *Auburn University*

Sheila Handy, *Lafayette College*

Thomas Hoar, *Houston Community College*

Bonnie Holloway, *Lake-Sumter Community College*

Susan Hughes, *Butler University*

Phillip Jones, *University of Richmond*

Carol Keller, *Coastal Carolina University*

J. Howard Keller, *IUPUI – Indianapolis*

Janice Klimek, *Missouri Western State College*

Terry Lindenberg, *Rock Valley College*

Lawrence Logan, *University of Massachusetts—Dartmouth*

Rex Mahlman, *Northwestern Oklahoma State University*

Carol Mannino, *Milwaukee School of Engineering*

Gary McCombs, *Eastern Michigan University*

Duncan McDougall, *Plymouth State College*

Noel McKeon, *Florida Community College*

David Morris, *North Georgia College and State University*

Doug Moses, *Naval Postgraduate School*

Kevin Nathan, *Oakland University*

Marina Nathan, *Houston Community College*

Kathy Otero, *University of Texas at El Paso*

Michael Pearson, *Kent State University*

Vaughan Radcliffe, *Case Western Reserve University*

David Remmele, *University of Wisconsin—Whitewater*

John Roberts, *St. John's River Community College*

Don Schwartz, *National University*

Mayda Shorney, *St. Gregory's University*

Donald Simons, *Frostburg State University*

Toni Smith, *University of New Hampshire*

Parvez Sopariwala, *Grand Valley State University*

Mel Stinnett, *Oklahoma Christian University*

Ephraim Sudit, *Rutgers University—Newark*

Kimberly Temme, *Maryville University*

Nicole Turner, *Florida Community College—Jacksonville*

Michael F. van Breda, *Southern Methodist University*

Kiran Verma, *University of Massachusetts—Boston*

Lee Warren, *Boston College*

Ronald Wood, *Pittsburg State University*

Martha Woodman, *University of Vermont*

We are grateful for the outstanding support from McGraw-Hill/Irwin. In particular, we would like to thank Brent Gordon, Publisher; Stewart Mattson, Executive Editor; Tracey Douglas and Kristin Leahy, Senior Developmental Editors; Ryan Blankenship, Marketing Manager; Pat Frederickson, Senior Project Manager; Heather Burbridge, Lead Production Supervisor; Pam Verros, Senior Designer; Carol Loreth, Senior Supplement Producer; and Judy Kausal, Photo Research Coordinator.

Finally, we would like to thank Beth Woods, Barbara Schnathorst, and Richey Kemmling for working so hard to ensure an error-free tenth edition.

We are grateful to the Institute of Certified Management Accountants for permission to use questions and/or unofficial answers from past Certificate in Management Accounting (CMA) examinations. Likewise, we thank the American Institute of Certified Public Accountants, the Society of Management Accountants of Canada, and the Chartered Institute of Management Accountants (United Kingdom) for permission to use (or to adapt) selected problems from their examinations. These problems bear the notations CMA, CPA, SMA, and CIMA respectively.

Ray H. Garrison • Eric Noreen

Brief Contents

Contents

Appendix A
Pricing Products and Services 804

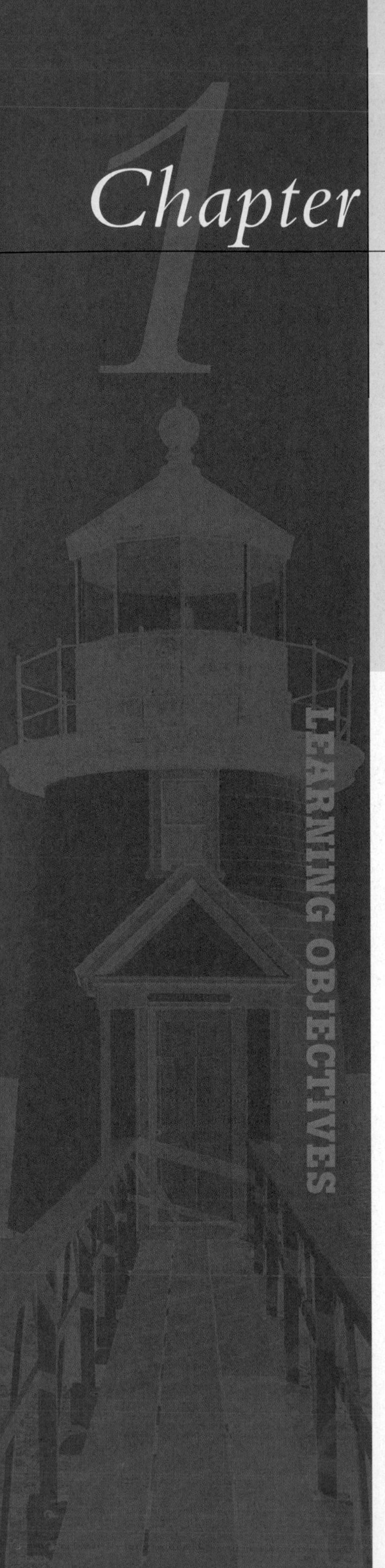

Chapter One

Managerial Accounting and the Business Environment

After studying Chapter 1, you should be able to:

1. Identify the major differences and similarities between financial and managerial accounting.
2. Understand the role of management accountants in an organization.
3. Understand the basic concepts underlying Just-In-Time (JIT), Total Quality Management (TQM), Process Reengineering, and the Theory of Constraints (TOC).
4. Understand the importance of upholding ethical standards.

BUSINESS FOCUS

Making Fact-Based Decisions in Real Time

Cisco Systems and Alcoa are on the leading edge of their industries and real-time management accounting is one of the keys to their success. Managers at these companies can drill down into the company's management accounting system to find the latest data on revenues, margins, order backlogs, expenses, and other data, by region, by business unit, by distribution channel, by salesperson, and so on. The Chief Financial Officer of Cisco, Larry Carter, says that with this kind of live information "you can empower all your management team to improve decision making." Richard Kelson, the Chief Financial Officer of Alcoa, says: "The earlier you get information, the easier it is to fix a problem." For example, with up-to-date data, managers at Alcoa saw softness in aerospace markets early enough to shift production from hard alloys that are used in aircraft to other products. John Chambers, the CEO of Cisco, says: "At any time in the quarter, first-line managers can look at margins and products and know exactly what the effect of their decisions will be."

Source: Thomas A. Stewart, "Making Decisions in Real Time," *Fortune*, June 26, 2000, pp. 332–333.

Managerial accounting is concerned with providing information to managers—that is, people *inside* an organization who direct and control its operations. In contrast, **financial accounting** is concerned with providing information to stockholders, creditors, and others who are *outside* an organization. Managerial accounting provides the essential data with which organizations are actually run. Financial accounting provides the scorecard by which a company's overall past performance is judged by outsiders.

Managerial accountants prepare a variety of reports. Some reports focus on how well managers or business units have performed—comparing actual results to plans and to benchmarks. Some reports provide timely, frequent updates on key indicators such as orders received, order backlog, capacity utilization, and sales. Other analytical reports are prepared as needed to investigate specific problems such as a decline in the profitability of a product line. And yet other reports analyze a developing business situation or opportunity. In contrast, financial accounting is oriented toward producing a limited set of specific prescribed annual and quarterly financial statements in accordance with generally accepted accounting principles.

Because it is manager oriented, any study of managerial accounting must be preceded by some understanding of what managers do, the information managers need, and the general business environment. Accordingly, the purpose of this chapter is to briefly examine these subjects.

The Work of Management and the Need for Managerial Accounting Information

Every organization—large and small—has managers. Someone must be responsible for making plans, organizing resources, directing personnel, and controlling operations. This is true of the Bank of America, the Peace Corps, the University of Illinois, the Catholic Church, and the Coca-Cola Corporation, as well as the local 7-Eleven convenience store. In this chapter, we will use a particular organization—Good Vibrations, Inc.—to illustrate the work of management. What we have to say about the management of Good Vibrations, Inc., however, is very general and can be applied to virtually any organization.

Good Vibrations, Inc., runs a chain of retail outlets that sell a full range of music CDs. The chain's stores are concentrated in Pacific Rim cities such as Sydney, Singapore, Hong Kong, Beijing, Tokyo, and Vancouver, British Columbia. The company has found that the best way to generate sales, and profits, is to create an exciting shopping environment. Consequently, the company puts a great deal of effort into planning the layout and decor of its stores—which are often quite large and extend over several floors in key downtown locations. Management knows that different types of clientele are attracted to different kinds of music. The international rock section is generally decorated with bold, brightly colored graphics, and the aisles are purposely narrow to create a crowded feeling much like one would experience at a popular nightclub on Friday night. In contrast, the classical music section is wood-paneled and fully sound insulated, with the rich, spacious feeling of a country club meeting room.

S

Managers at Good Vibrations, Inc., like managers everywhere, carry out three major activities—*planning, directing and motivating,* and *controlling.* **Planning** involves selecting a course of action and specifying how the action will be implemented. **Directing and motivating** involves mobilizing people to carry out plans and run routine operations. **Controlling** involves ensuring that the plan is actually carried out and is appropriately modified as circumstances change. Management accounting information plays a vital role in these basic management activities—but most particularly in the planning and control functions.

Planning

The first step in planning is to identify alternatives and then to select from among the alternatives the one that does the best job of furthering the organization's objectives. The basic objective of Good Vibrations, Inc., is to earn profits for the owners of the company by providing superior service at competitive prices in as many markets as possible. To further this objective, every year top management carefully considers a range of options, or alternatives, for expanding into new geographic markets. This year management is considering opening new stores in Shanghai, Los Angeles, and Auckland.

When making this and other choices, management must balance the opportunities against the demands made on the company's resources. Management knows from bitter experience that opening a store in a major new market is a big step that cannot be taken lightly. It requires enormous amounts of time and energy from the company's most experienced, talented, and busy professionals. When the company attempted to open stores in both Beijing and Vancouver in the same year, resources were stretched too thinly. The result was that neither store opened on schedule, and operations in the rest of the company suffered. Therefore, entering new markets is planned very, very carefully.

Among other data, top management looks at the sales volumes, profit margins, and costs of the company's established stores in similar markets. These data, supplied by the management accountant, are combined with projected sales volume data at the proposed new locations to estimate the profits that would be generated by the new stores. In general, virtually all important alternatives considered by management in the planning process have some effect on revenues or costs, and management accounting data are essential in estimating those effects.

After considering all of the alternatives, Good Vibrations, Inc.'s top management decided to open a store in the burgeoning Shanghai market in the third quarter of the year, but to defer opening any other new stores to another year. As soon as this decision was made, detailed plans were drawn up for all parts of the company that would be involved in the Shanghai opening. For example, the Personnel Department's travel budget was increased, since it would be providing extensive on-site training to the new personnel hired in Shanghai.

As in the Personnel Department example, the plans of management are often expressed formally in **budgets,** and the term *budgeting* is applied to generally describe this part of the planning process. Budgets are usually prepared under the direction of the **controller,** who is the manager in charge of the Accounting Department. Typically, budgets are prepared annually and represent management's plans in specific, quantitative terms. In addition to a travel budget, the Personnel Department will be given goals in terms of new hires, courses taught, and detailed breakdowns of expected expenses. Similarly, the manager of each store will be given a target for sales volume, profit, expenses, pilferage losses, and employee training. These data will be collected, analyzed, and summarized for management use in the form of budgets prepared by management accountants.

Directing and Motivating

In addition to planning for the future, managers must oversee day-to-day activities and keep the organization functioning smoothly. This requires the ability to motivate and effectively direct people. Managers assign tasks to employees, arbitrate disputes, answer questions, solve on-the-spot problems, and make many small decisions that affect customers and employees. In effect, directing is that part of the managers' work that deals with the routine and the here and now. Managerial accounting data, such as daily sales reports, are often used in this type of day-to-day decision making.

Controlling

In carrying out the **control** function, managers seek to ensure that the plan is being followed. **Feedback,** which signals whether operations are on track, is the key to effective control. In sophisticated organizations, this feedback is provided by detailed reports of various types. One of these reports, which compares budgeted to actual results, is called a **performance report.** Performance reports suggest where operations are not proceeding as planned and where some parts of the organization may require additional attention. For example, before the opening of the new Shanghai store in the third quarter of the year, the store's manager will be given sales volume, profit, and expense targets for the fourth quarter of the year. As the fourth quarter progresses, periodic reports will be made in which the actual sales volume, profit, and expenses are compared to the targets. If the actual results fall below the targets, top management is alerted that the Shanghai store requires more attention. Experienced personnel can be flown in to help the new manager, or top management may come to the conclusion that plans will have to be revised. As we shall see in following chapters, providing this kind of feedback to managers is one of the central purposes of managerial accounting.

The End Results of Managers' Activities

As a customer enters one of the Good Vibrations stores, the results of management's planning, directing and motivating, and controlling activities will be evident in the many details that make the difference between a pleasant and an irritating shopping experience. The store will be clean, fashionably decorated, and logically laid out. Featured artists' videos will be displayed on TV monitors throughout the store, and the background rock music will be loud enough to send older patrons scurrying for the classical music section. Popular CDs will be in stock, and the latest hits will be available for private listening on earphones. Specific titles will be easy to find. Regional music, such as CantoPop in Hong Kong, will be prominently featured. Checkout clerks will be alert, friendly, and efficient. In short, what the customer experiences doesn't simply happen; it is the result of the efforts of managers who must visualize and fit together the processes that are needed to get the job done.

The Planning and Control Cycle

The work of management can be summarized in a model such as the one shown in Exhibit 1–1. The model, which depicts the **planning and control cycle,** illustrates the smooth flow of management activities from planning through directing and motivating, controlling, and then back to planning again. All of these activities involve decision making, so it is depicted as the hub around which the other activities revolve.

Comparison of Financial and Managerial Accounting

LEARNING OBJECTIVE 1
Identify the major differences and similarities between financial and managerial accounting.

Financial accounting reports are prepared for the use of external parties such as shareholders and creditors, whereas managerial accounting reports are prepared for managers inside the organization. This contrast in basic orientation results in a number of major differences between financial and managerial accounting, even though both financial and managerial accounting often rely on the same underlying financial data. These differences are summarized in Exhibit 1–2.

As shown in Exhibit 1–2, in addition to the difference in who the reports are prepared for, financial and managerial accounting also differ in their emphasis between the past and the future, in the type of data provided to users, and in several other ways. These differences are discussed in the following paragraphs.

Emphasis on the Future

Concept 1–1

Since *planning* is such an important part of the manager's job, managerial accounting has a strong future orientation. In contrast, financial accounting primarily provides summaries of past financial transactions. These summaries may be useful in planning, but only to a point. The future is not simply a reflection of what has happened in the past. Changes are constantly taking place in economic conditions, customer needs and desires, competitive conditions, and so on. All of these changes demand that the manager's planning be based

Exhibit 1–1 The Planning and Control Cycle

Formulating long- and short-term plans (Planning)
Implementing plans (Directing and Motivating)
Measuring performance (Controlling)
Comparing actual to planned performance (Controlling)
Decision Making

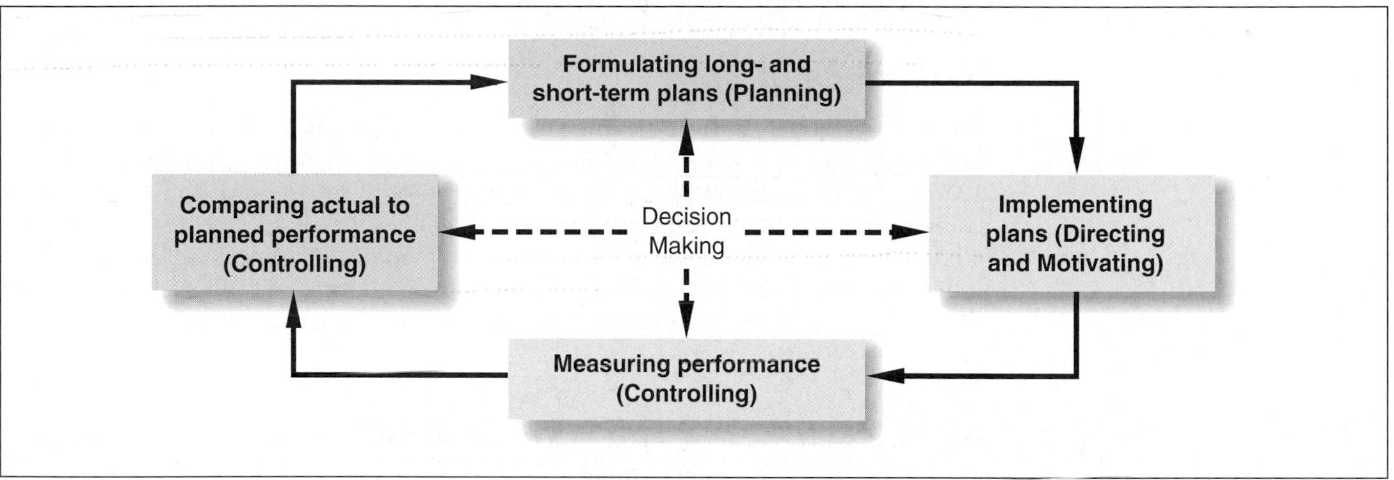

Exhibit 1–2 Comparison of Financial and Managerial Accounting

Accounting
• Recording
• Estimating
• Organizing
• Summarizing
Financial and Operational Data
Financial Accounting
• Reports to those outside the organization:
Owners
Lenders
Tax authorities
Regulators
• Emphasis is on summaries of financial consequences of past activities.
• Objectivity and verifiability of data are emphasized.
• Precision of information is required.
• Only summarized data for the entire organization are prepared.
• Must follow GAAP.
• Mandatory for external reports.
Managerial Accounting
• Reports to those inside the organization for:
Planning
Directing and motivating
Controlling
Performance evaluation
• Emphasis is on decisions affecting the future.
• Relevance is emphasized.
• Timeliness of information is required.
• Detailed segment reports about departments, products, customers, and employees are prepared.
• Need not follow GAAP.
• Not mandatory.

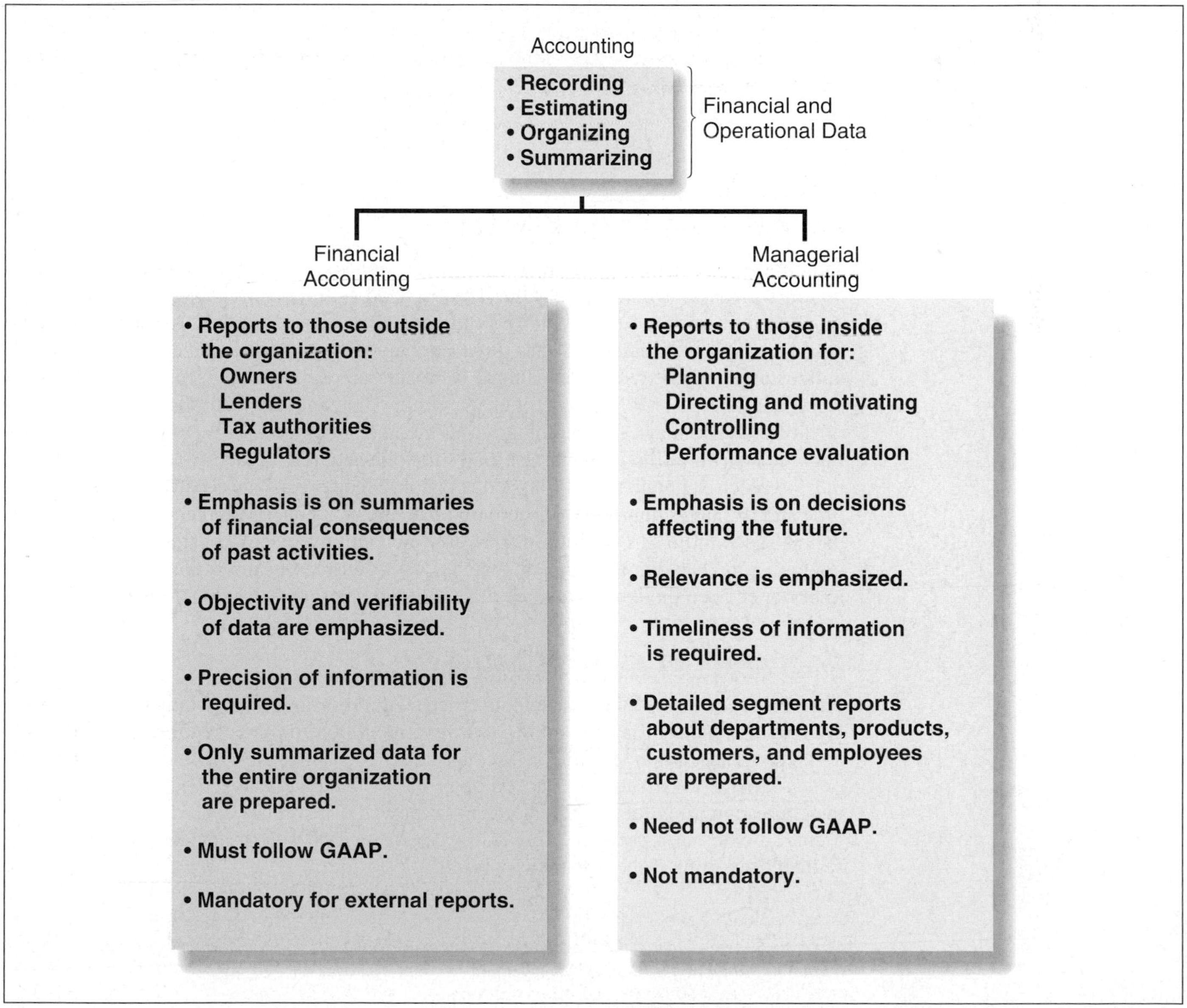

in large part on estimates of what will happen rather than on summaries of what has already happened.

Relevance of Data

Financial accounting data are expected to be objective and verifiable. However, for internal uses the manager wants information that is relevant even if it is not completely objective or verifiable. By relevant, we mean *appropriate for the problem at hand*. For example, it is difficult to verify estimated sales volumes for a proposed new store at Good Vibrations, Inc., but this is exactly the type of information that is most useful to managers in their decision making. The managerial accounting information system should be flexible enough to provide whatever data are relevant for a particular decision.

In Business

What Number Did You Have in Mind?

Caterpillar has long been at the forefront of management accounting practice. When asked by a manager for the cost of something, accountants at Caterpillar have been trained to ask "What are you going to use the cost for?" One management accountant at Caterpillar explains: "We want to make sure the information is formatted and the right elements are included. Do you need a variable cost, do you need a fully burdened cost, do you need overhead applied, are you just talking about discretionary cost? The cost that they really need depends on the decision they are making."

Source: Gary Siegel, "Practice Analysis: Adding Value," *Strategic Finance*, November 2000, pp. 89–90.

Less Emphasis on Precision

Timeliness is often more important than precision to managers. If a decision must be made, a manager would much rather have a good estimate now than wait a week for a more precise answer. A decision involving tens of millions of dollars does not have to be based on estimates that are precise down to the penny, or even to the dollar. In fact, one authoritative source recommends that, "as a general rule, no one needs more than three significant digits."[1] This means, for example, that if a company's sales are in the hundreds of millions of dollars, then nothing on an income statement needs to be more accurate than the nearest million dollars. Estimates that are accurate to the nearest million dollars may be precise enough to make a good decision. Since precision is costly in terms of both time and resources, managerial accounting places less emphasis on precision than does financial accounting. In addition, managerial accounting places considerable weight on nonmonetary data. For example, information about customer satisfaction is of tremendous importance even though it would be difficult to express such data in a monetary form.

Segments of an Organization

Financial accounting is primarily concerned with reporting for the company as a whole. By contrast, managerial accounting focuses much more on the parts, or **segments,** of a company. These segments may be product lines, sales territories, divisions, departments, or any other categorization of the company's activities that management finds useful. Financial accounting does require some breakdowns of revenues and costs by major segments in external reports, but this is a secondary emphasis. In managerial accounting, segment reporting is the primary emphasis.

---

[1] *Statements on Management Accounting, Statement Number 5B, Fundamentals of Reporting Information to Managers*, Institute of Management Accounting, Montvale, NJ, p. 6.

Generally Accepted Accounting Principles (GAAP)

Financial accounting statements prepared for external users must be prepared in accordance with generally accepted accounting principles (GAAP). External users must have some assurance that the reports have been prepared in accordance with some common set of ground rules. These common ground rules enhance comparability and help reduce fraud and misrepresentation, but they do not necessarily lead to the type of reports that would be most useful in internal decision making. For example, GAAP requires that land be stated at its historical cost on financial reports. However, if management is considering moving a store to a new location and then selling the land the store currently sits on, management would like to know the current market value of the land—a vital piece of information that is ignored under GAAP.

Managerial accounting is not bound by generally accepted accounting principles. Managers set their own ground rules concerning the content and form of internal reports. The only constraint is that the expected benefits from using the information should outweigh the costs of collecting, analyzing, and summarizing the data. Nevertheless, as we shall see in subsequent chapters, it is undeniably true that financial reporting requirements have heavily influenced management accounting practice.

Managerial Accounting—Not Mandatory

Financial accounting is mandatory; that is, it must be done. Various outside parties such as the Securities and Exchange Commission (SEC) and the tax authorities require periodic financial statements. Managerial accounting, on the other hand, is not mandatory. A company is completely free to do as much or as little as it wishes. No regulatory bodies or other outside agencies specify what is to be done, or, for that matter, whether anything is to be done at all. Since managerial accounting is completely optional, the important question is always, "Is the information useful?" rather than, "Is the information required?"

Expanding Role of Managerial Accounting

Managerial accounting has its roots in the industrial revolution of the 19th century. During this early period, most firms were tightly controlled by a few owner-managers who borrowed based on personal relationships and their personal assets. Since there were no external shareholders and little unsecured debt, there was little need for elaborate financial reports. In contrast, managerial accounting was relatively sophisticated and provided the essential information needed to manage the early large-scale production of textiles, steel, and other products.[2]

After the turn of the century, financial accounting requirements burgeoned because of new pressures placed on companies by capital markets, creditors, regulatory bodies, and federal taxation of income. Johnson and Kaplan state that "many firms needed to raise funds from increasingly widespread and detached suppliers of capital. To tap these vast reservoirs of outside capital, firms' managers had to supply audited financial reports. And because outside suppliers of capital relied on audited financial statements, independent accountants had a keen interest in establishing well-defined procedures for corporate financial reporting. The inventory costing procedures adopted by public accountants after the turn of the century had a profound effect on management accounting."[3]

As a consequence, for many decades, management accountants increasingly focused their efforts on ensuring that financial accounting requirements were met and financial

[2] A. D. Chandler, *The Visible Hand: The Managerial Revolution in American Business* (Cambridge, MA: Harvard University Press, 1977).

[3] H. Thomas Johnson and Robert S. Kaplan, *Relevance Lost: The Rise and Fall of Management Accounting* (Boston, MA: Harvard Business School Press, 1987), pp. 129–130.

reports were released on time. The practice of management accounting stagnated. In the early part of the century, as product lines expanded and operations became more complex, forward-looking companies such as Du Pont, General Motors, and General Electric saw a renewed need for management-oriented reports that was separate from financial reports.[4] But in most companies, management accounting practices up through the mid-1980s were largely indistinguishable from practices that were common prior to World War I. In recent years, however, new economic forces have led to many important innovations in management accounting. These new practices will be discussed in later chapters.

Organizational Structure

LEARNING OBJECTIVE 2
Understand the role of management accountants in an organization.

Since organizations are made up of people, management must accomplish its objectives by working *through* people. Presidents of companies like Good Vibrations, Inc., could not possibly execute all of their company's strategies alone; they must rely on other people. This is done by creating an organizational structure that permits *decentralization* of management responsibilities.

Decentralization

Decentralization is the delegation of decision-making authority throughout an organization by providing managers at various operating levels with the authority to make decisions relating to their area of responsibility. Some organizations are more decentralized than others. Because of Good Vibrations, Inc.'s geographic dispersion and the peculiarities of local markets, the company is highly decentralized.

Good Vibrations, Inc.'s president (also called chief executive officer or CEO) sets the broad strategy for the company and makes major strategic decisions such as opening stores in new markets, but much of the remaining decision-making authority is delegated to managers on various levels throughout the organization. These levels are as follows: The company has a number of retail stores, each of which has a store manager as well as a separate manager for each section such as international rock and classical/jazz. In addition, the company has support departments such as a central Purchasing Department and a Personnel Department. The organizational structure of the company is depicted in Exhibit 1–3.

The arrangement of boxes shown in Exhibit 1–3 is called an **organization chart.** The purpose of an organization chart is to show how responsibility has been divided among managers and to show formal lines of reporting and communication, or *chain of command.* Each box depicts an area of management responsibility, and the lines between the boxes show the lines of formal authority between managers. The chart tells us, for example, that the store managers are responsible to the operations vice president. In turn, the latter is responsible to the company president, who in turn is responsible to the board of directors. Following the lines of authority and communication on the organization chart, we can see that the manager of the Hong Kong store would ordinarily report to the operations vice president rather than directly to the president of the company.

Informal relationships and channels of communication often develop outside the formal reporting relationships on the organization chart as a result of personal contacts between managers. The informal structure does not appear on the organization chart, but it is often vital to effective operations.

Line and Staff Relationships

An organization chart also depicts *line* and *staff* positions in an organization. A person in a **line** position is *directly involved* in achieving the basic objectives of the organization. A

[4] H. Thomas Johnson, "Management Accounting in an Early Integrated Industrial: E. I. du Pont de Nemours Powder Company, 1903–1912," *Business History Review,* Summer 1975, pp. 186–187.

Exhibit 1–3 Organization Chart, Good Vibrations, Inc.

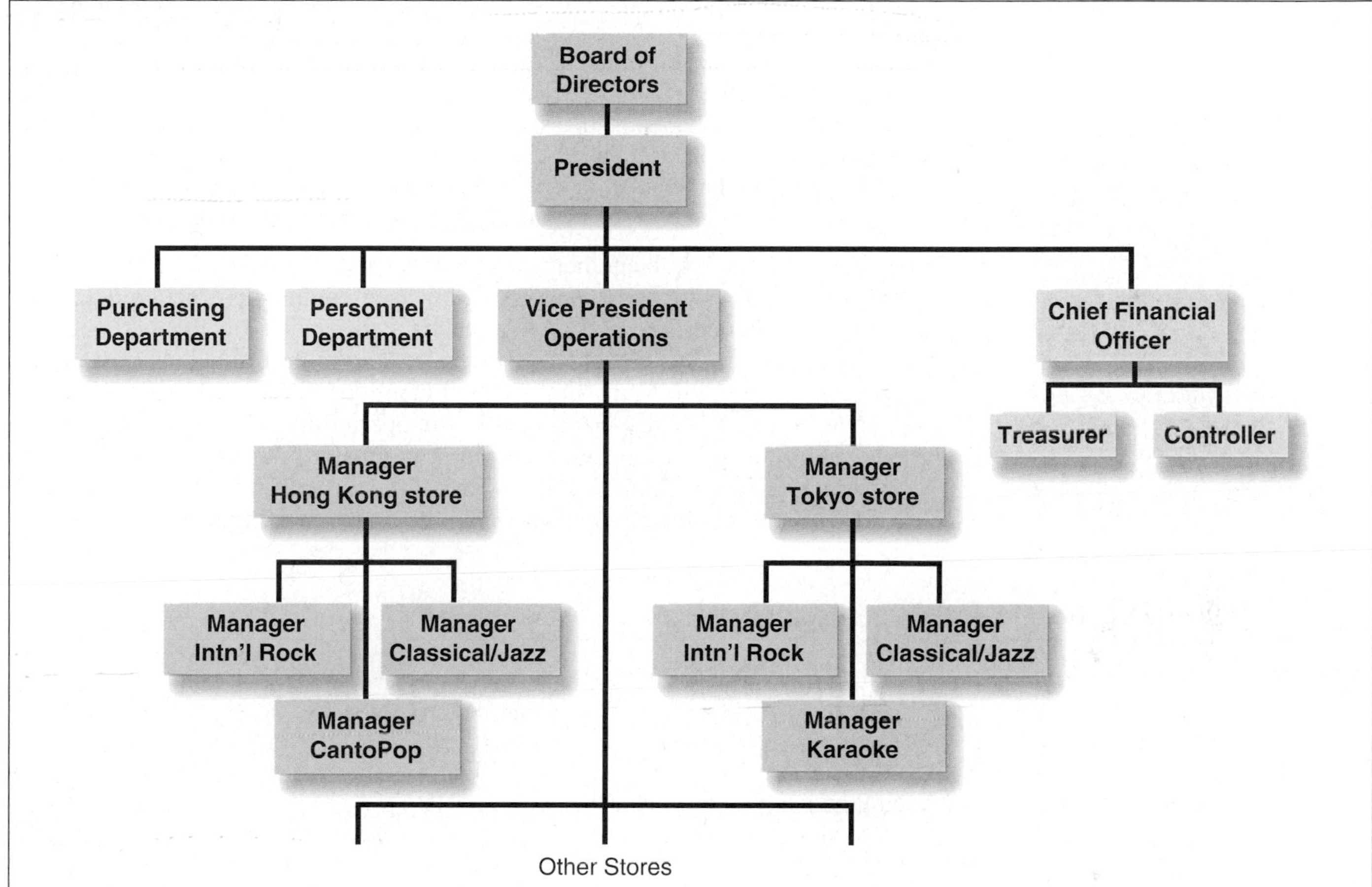

person in a **staff** position, by contrast, is only *indirectly* involved in achieving those basic objectives. Staff positions *support* or provide assistance to line positions or other parts of the organization, but they do not have direct authority over line positions. Refer again to the organization chart in Exhibit 1–3. Since the basic objective of Good Vibrations, Inc., is to sell recorded music at a profit, those managers whose areas of responsibility are directly related to the sales effort occupy line positions. These positions, which are shown in a darker color in the exhibit, include the managers of the various music departments in each store, the store managers, the operations vice president, and members of top management.

By contrast, the manager of the central Purchasing Department occupies a staff position, since the only function of the Purchasing Department is to support and serve the line departments by doing their purchasing for them. However, both line and staff managers have authority over the employees in their own departments.

The Chief Financial Officer

As previously mentioned, in the United States the manager of the accounting department is often known as the *controller*. The controller in turn reports to the *Chief Financial Officer (CFO)*, who usually comes from an accounting background. The **Chief Financial Officer** is the member of the top management team who is responsible for providing timely and relevant data to support planning and control activities and for preparing financial statements for external users. An effective CFO is considered a key member of the top management team whose advice is sought in all major decisions. The CFO is a highly paid professional who has command over the technical details of accounting and finance, who can provide leadership to other professionals in his or her department, who can analyze new and evolving situations, who can communicate technical data to others in a simple and clear manner, and who is able to work well with top managers from other disciplines.

It should be noted that few of the people who are trained as accountants and who work under the Chief Financial Officer in either the treasurer's office or the controller's office think of themselves as accountants. If asked, they are likely to identify themselves as working in finance. Management accounting is not about debits and credits or recording journal entries, although some knowledge of that is necessary. Management accounting is about helping managers to pursue the organization's goals. A recent report states that:

> Growing numbers of management accountants spend the bulk of their time as internal consultants or business analysts within their companies. Technological advances have liberated them from the mechanical aspects of accounting. They spend less time preparing standardized reports and more time analyzing and interpreting information. Many have moved from the isolation of accounting departments to be physically positioned in the operating departments with which they work. Management accountants work on cross-functional teams, have extensive face-to-face communications with people throughout their organizations, and are actively involved in decision making. . . . They are trusted advisors.[5]

In Business

Beyond the Numbers

Judy C. Lewent is the Chief Financial Officer (CFO) of Merck, a major pharmaceutical company. She is in charge of 750 people and is intimately involved in the company's most important strategic decisions. Cynthia Beach, vice president of global investment research at Goldman Sachs & Co., says this about Lewent: "From my standpoint, Merck is one of the best-managed [pharmaceutical] companies, and Judy is a key reason why." Merck's chairman, CEO, and president Raymond Gilmartin adds this about Lewent: "Many CFOs take as their prime directive the timely, accurate delivery of detailed financial data and analysis to top management. While the importance of these services cannot be overestimated, with Judy they are simply one of the many ways she contributes to the business. [Lewent and her organization] make decisions about which developmental-product projects to fund and how to structure our product franchises, acquisition possibilities, and licensing arrangements."

Source: Russ Banham, "Merck Grows from the Inside Out, Powered by the CFO's Joint Ventures," *CFO*, October 2000, pp. 69–70.

The Changing Business Environment

LEARNING OBJECTIVE 3
Understand the basic concepts underlying Just-In-Time (JIT), Total Quality Management (TQM), Process Reengineering, and the Theory of Constraints (TOC).

The last two decades have been a period of tremendous upheaval and change in the business environment, including the explosive growth of the Internet. Competition in many industries has become worldwide in scope, and the pace of innovation in products and services has accelerated. This has been good news for consumers, since intensified competition has generally led to lower prices, higher quality, and more choices. However, the last two decades have been a period of wrenching change for many businesses and their employees. Many managers have learned that cherished ways of doing business don't work anymore and that major changes must be made in how organizations are managed and in how work gets done. These changes are so great that some observers view them as a second industrial revolution.

[5] Gary Siegel Organization, *Counting More, Counting Less: Transformations in the Management Accounting Profession, The 1999 Practice Analysis of Management Accounting*, Institute of Management Accountants, Montvale, NJ, August 1999, p. 3.

This revolution is having a profound effect on the practice of managerial accounting—as we will see throughout the rest of the text. First, however, it is necessary to have an appreciation of the ways in which organizations are transforming themselves to become more competitive. Since the early 1980s, many companies have gone through several waves of improvement programs, starting with Just-In-Time (JIT) and passing on to Total Quality Management (TQM), Process Reengineering, and various other management programs—including in some companies the Theory of Constraints (TOC). When properly implemented, these improvement programs can enhance quality, reduce cost, increase output, eliminate delays in responding to customers, and ultimately increase profits. They have not, however, always been wisely implemented, and there is considerable controversy concerning the ultimate value of each of these programs. Nevertheless, the current business environment cannot be properly understood without some appreciation of what each of these approaches attempts to accomplish. Each is worthy of extended study, but we will discuss them only in the broadest terms. The details are best handled in operations management courses.

Concept 1–2

This section will close with a discussion of the role of international competition and the impact of the Internet on business.

Just-In-Time (JIT)

Traditionally, manufacturers have forecasted demand for their products into the future and then have attempted to smooth out production to meet that forecasted demand. At the same time, they have also attempted to keep everyone and everything as busy as possible producing output so as to maximize "efficiency" and (hopefully) reduce costs. Unfortunately, this approach has a number of major drawbacks including large inventories, long production times, high defect rates, product obsolescence, inability to meet delivery schedules, and (ironically) high costs. None of this is obvious—if it were, companies would long ago have abandoned this approach. Managers at Toyota are credited with the insight that an entirely new approach, called *Just-In-Time,* was needed.

When companies use the **Just-In-Time (JIT)** production and inventory control system, they purchase materials and produce units only as needed to meet actual customer demand. In a JIT system, inventories are reduced to the minimum and in some cases are zero. For example, the Memory Products Division of Stolle Corporation in Sidney, Ohio, slashed its work in process inventory from 10,000 units to 250 units by using JIT techniques.[6]

The JIT approach can be used in both merchandising and manufacturing companies. It has the most profound effects, however, on the operations of manufacturing companies, which maintain three classes of inventories—*raw materials, work in process,* and *finished goods*. **Raw materials** are the materials that are used to make a product. **Work in process** inventories consist of units of product that are only partially complete and will require further work before they are ready for sale to a customer. **Finished goods** inventories consist of units of product that have been completed but have not yet been sold to customers.

Traditionally, manufacturing companies have maintained large amounts of all three kinds of inventories to act as *buffers* so that operations can proceed smoothly even if there are unanticipated disruptions. Raw materials inventories provide insurance in case suppliers are late with deliveries. Work in process inventories are maintained in case a workstation is unable to operate due to a breakdown or other reason. Finished goods inventories are maintained to accommodate unanticipated fluctuations in demand.

While these inventories provide buffers against unforeseen events, they have a cost. In addition to the money tied up in the inventory, experts argue that the presence of inventories encourages inefficient and sloppy work, results in too many defects, and dramatically increases the amount of time required to complete a product.

[6] Nabil Hassan, Herbert E. Brown, Paula M. Sanders, and Nick Koumoutzis, "Stolle Puts World Class into Memory," *Management Accounting,* January 1993, pp. 22–25.

In Business — Chopping Inventories at Porsche

Industry insiders were writing off Porsche as an independent carmaker in the earlier 1990s. Sales in 1992 were down to less than 15,000 cars, one-fourth their 1986 peak, and losses had mounted to $133 million. That's when Wendelin Wiedeking became the top manager at the revered, but ailing, company.

Wiedeking hired two Japanese efficiency experts to help overcome Porsche's stubborn traditionalism. "They immediately tackled a wasteful inventory of parts stacked on shelves all over the three-story Stuttgart factory. One of the experts handed Wiedeking a circular saw. While astounded assembly workers watched, he moved down an aisle and chopped the top half off a row of shelves."

They proceeded to overhaul the assembly process, slashing the time required to build the new 911 Carrera model from 120 hours down to just 60 hours. They cut the time required to develop a new model from seven years to just three years. And a quality-control program has helped reduce the number of defective parts by a factor of 10. As a consequence of these, and other actions, the company's sales have more than doubled to about 34,000 cars, and earnings were about $55 million in the latest fiscal year.

Source: David Woodruff, "Porsche Is Back—And Then Some," *Business Week*, September 15, 1997, p. 57.

The JIT Concept Under ideal conditions, a company operating a Just-In-Time system would purchase *only* enough materials each day to meet that day's needs. Moreover, the company would have no goods still in process at the end of the day, and all goods completed during the day would have been shipped immediately to customers. As this sequence suggests, "just-in-time" means that raw materials are received *just in time* to go into production, manufactured parts are completed *just in time* to be assembled into products, and products are completed *just in time* to be shipped to customers.

Although few companies have been able to reach this ideal, many companies have been able to reduce inventories to only a fraction of their previous levels. The result has been a substantial reduction in ordering and warehousing costs, and much more efficient and effective operations.

How does a company avoid a buildup of parts and materials at various workstations and still ensure a smooth flow of goods when JIT is in use? In a JIT environment, the flow of goods is controlled by a *pull* approach. The pull approach can be explained as follows: At the final assembly stage, a signal is sent to the preceding workstation as to the exact amount of parts and materials that will be needed *over the next few hours* to assemble products to fill customer orders, and *only* that amount of parts and materials is provided. The same signal is sent back through each preceding workstation so that a smooth flow of parts and materials is maintained with no appreciable inventory buildup at any point. Thus, all workstations respond to the pull exerted by the final assembly stage, which in turn responds to customer orders. As one worker explained, "Under a JIT system you don't produce anything, anywhere, for anybody unless they *ask* for it somewhere *downstream*. Inventories are an evil that we're taught to avoid."

The pull approach described above can be contrasted to the *push* approach used in conventional manufacturing systems. In conventional systems, when a workstation completes its work, the partially completed goods are "pushed" forward to the next workstation regardless of whether that workstation is ready to receive them. The result is an unintentional stockpiling of partially completed goods that may not be completed for days or even weeks. This ties up funds and also results in operating inefficiencies. For one thing, it becomes very difficult to keep track of where everything is when so much is scattered all over the factory floor.

Another characteristic of conventional manufacturing systems is an emphasis on "keeping everyone busy" as an end in itself. This inevitably leads to excess inventories—particularly work in process inventories—for reasons that will be more fully explored in the later section on the Theory of Constraints. In JIT, the traditional emphasis on keeping everyone busy is abandoned in favor of producing only what customers actually want—even if that means some workers are idle.

Burgers Just In Time

In Business

McDonald's new Just-In-Time (JIT) system called "Made for You" is "plainly an answer to the charge that made-to-order food from rivals such as Burger King and Wendy's tastes fresher." McDonald's franchisees often cook burgers and other food in batches which then sit around, losing flavor and freshness. The objective of the new system, which costs about $25,000 to install in a restaurant, is to serve each customer with the freshest food possible within 90 seconds of ordering. To design the new "Made for You" system, McDonald's carefully studied JIT manufacturing systems like Toyota's.

"The moment a Big Mac is ordered, a computer screen in the kitchen tells one of the workers to start assembling it. Meanwhile, by monitoring the flow of orders, the computer also estimates future demand, indicating when to start cooking things (like fries) that cannot be squeezed into the 90-second slot.

"'Made for You' should help cut stock costs, and there may be some staff savings. But the proof of the pudding will, so to speak, be in the burgers."

Source: "McJITers," *The Economist,* April 4, 1998, p. 70.

PCs Just In Time

In Business

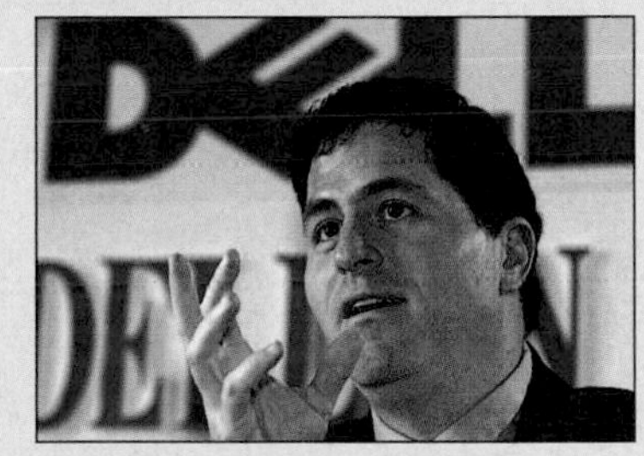

Dell Computer Corporation has finely tuned its Just-In-Time (JIT) system so that an order for a customized personal computer that comes in over the Internet at 9 A.M. can be on a delivery truck to the customer by 9 P.M. the following day. In addition, Dell's low-cost production system allows it to underprice its rivals by 10% to 15%. This combination has made Dell the envy of the personal computer industry and has enabled the company to grow at five times the industry rate.

How does the company's JIT system deliver lower costs? "While machines from Compaq and IBM can languish on dealer shelves for two months, Dell doesn't start ordering components and assembling computers until an order is booked. That may sound like no biggie, but the price of PC parts can fall rapidly in just a few months. By ordering right before assembly, Dell figures its parts, on average, are 60 days newer than those in an IBM or Compaq machine sold at the same time. That can translate into a 6% profit advantage in components alone."

Source: Gary McWilliams, "Whirlwind on the Web," *Business Week,* April 7, 1997, p. 134.

JIT Consequences Managers that attempted to implement the JIT approach found that it was necessary to make other major improvements in operations if inventories were to be significantly reduced. First, production would be held up and a deadline for shipping a product would be missed if a key part was missing or was found to be defective. So suppliers had to be able to deliver defect-free goods in just the right quantity and just when needed. This typically meant that the company would have to rely on a few, ultra-reliable suppliers that would be willing to make frequent deliveries in small lots just before the parts and materials would be needed in production. Second, the typical plant layout needed to be improved. Traditionally, similar machines were grouped together in a single location. All of the drill presses would be in one place, all of the lathes in another place, and so on. As a result, work in process had to be moved frequently over long distances—creating delays, difficulties in locating orders, and sometimes damage. In a JIT system, all of the machines required to make a single product or product line are typically brought together in one location—creating what is called a *focused factory* or a *manufacturing cell*. This improved plant layout allows workers to focus all of their efforts on one product from start to finish—creating a sense of ownership and pride in the product and minimizing handling and moving. One company was able to reduce the distance traveled by one product from three *miles* to just 300 feet. As the accompanying In Business box illustrates, an improved plant layout can dramatically increase *throughput*, which is the total volume of production through a facility during a period, and it can dramatically reduce **throughput time** (also known as **cycle time**), which is the time required to make a product.

In Business

Slashing Process Time

American Standard uses cell manufacturing to cut inventories and reduce manufacturing time. At its plant in Leeds, England, it used to take as long as three weeks to manufacture a vacuum pump and another week to process the paperwork for an order. Therefore, customers had to place orders a month in advance. "Today Leeds . . . has switched to manufacturing cells that do everything from lathing to assembly in quick sequence. The result is a breakthrough in speed. Manufacturing a pump now takes just six minutes."

Source: Shawn Tully, "Raiding a Company's Hidden Cash," *Fortune,* August 22, 1994, pp. 82–87.

Changing over production from one product to another, which involves *setups*, also creates problems for JIT. **Setups** require activities—such as moving materials, changing machine settings, setting up equipment, and running tests—that must be performed whenever production is switched over from making one item to another. For example, a company that makes side panels for DaimlerChrysler's PT Cruiser must prime and paint the steel panels with the color specified by DaimlerChrysler. Every time the color is changed, the spray paint reservoirs must be completely purged and cleaned. This may take hours and results in wasted paint. Because of the time and expense involved in such setups, many managers believe setups should be avoided and therefore items should be produced only in large batches. Think of this in terms of scheduling your classes. If you have to commute to school and pay for parking, would you rather have two classes more or less back-to-back on the same day or on different days? By scheduling your classes back-to-back on the same day, you will only have to commute and pay for parking once.

Managers follow the same reasoning when they schedule production. If the customer has ordered 400 units, most managers would rather produce all of them in one big batch and incur the setup costs once rather than in two batches of 200 units each, which incurs the setup costs twice. Indeed, because of setup costs, most companies have rules about the minimum size of a batch that can be run. If the customer orders just 25 units, managers will still run the order in a batch of 400 units and keep the other 375 units on hand in inventory in case someone orders the item later. The problem with this line of reasoning is that big batches result in large amounts of inventory—the exact opposite of what JIT attempts to accomplish. In JIT, this problem is attacked directly by reducing setup time so that it becomes insignificant. Simple techniques such as doing as much of the setup work as possible in advance off-line rather than waiting until production is shut down are often very effective in reducing setup time and costs. Reduced setup times make smaller batches more economical, which in turn makes it easier to respond quickly to the market with exactly the items that customers want.

Defective units create big problems in a JIT environment. If a completed order contains a defective unit, the company must ship the order with less than the promised quantity or it must restart the whole production process to make just one unit. At minimum, this creates a delay in shipping the order and may generate a ripple effect that delays other orders. For this and other reasons, defects cannot be tolerated in a JIT system. Companies that are deeply involved in JIT tend to become zealously committed to a goal of *zero defects.* Even though it may be next to impossible to attain the zero defect goal, companies have found that they can come very close. For example, Motorola, Allied Signal, and many other companies now measure defects in terms of the number of defects per *million* units of product.

In a traditional company, parts and materials are inspected for defects when they are received from suppliers, and quality inspectors inspect units as they progress along the production line. In a JIT system, the company's suppliers are responsible for the quality of incoming parts and materials. And instead of using quality inspectors, the company's production workers are directly responsible for spotting defective units. A worker who discovers a defect is supposed to punch an alarm button that stops the production flow line and sets off flashing lights. Supervisors and other workers then descend on the workstation to determine the cause of the defect and correct it before any further defective units are produced. This procedure ensures that problems are quickly identified and corrected, but it does require that defects are rare—otherwise there would be constant disruptions to the production process.

Workers on a JIT line must be multiskilled and flexible. They are often expected to operate all of the equipment in a manufacturing cell. In addition, they perform minor repairs and do maintenance work when they would otherwise be idle. In contrast, on a conventional assembly line a worker performs a single task all the time every day and all maintenance work is done by a specialized maintenance crew.

Benefits of a JIT System Many companies—large and small—have employed JIT with great success. Among the major companies using JIT are Bose, Goodyear, Westinghouse, General Motors, Hughes Aircraft, Ford Motor Company, Black and Decker, Chrysler, Borg-Warner, John Deere, Xerox, Tektronix, and Intel. The main benefits of JIT are the following:

1. Funds that were tied up in inventories can be used elsewhere.
2. Areas previously used to store inventories are made available for other, more productive uses.
3. Throughput time is reduced, resulting in greater potential output and quicker response to customers.
4. Defect rates are reduced, resulting in less waste and greater customer satisfaction.

As a result of benefits such as those cited above, more companies are embracing JIT each year. Most companies find, however, that simply reducing inventories is not enough. To remain competitive in an ever changing and ever more competitive business environment, companies must strive for *continuous improvement.*

The Downside of JIT

In Business

Just-In-Time (JIT) systems have many advantages, but they *are* vulnerable to unexpected disruptions in supply. A production line can quickly come to a halt if essential parts are unavailable. Toyota, the developer of JIT, found this out the hard way. One Saturday, a fire at Aisin Seiki Company's plant in Aichi Prefecture stopped the delivery of all brake parts to Toyota. By Tuesday, Toyota had to close down all of its Japanese assembly lines. By the time the supply of brake parts had been restored, Toyota had lost an estimated $15 billion in sales.

Source: "Toyota to Recalibrate 'Just-in-Time,'" *International Herald Tribune,* February 8, 1997, p. 9.

Total Quality Management (TQM)

The most popular approach to continuous improvement is known as *Total Quality Management.* There are two major characteristics of **Total Quality Management (TQM):** (1) a focus on serving customers and (2) systematic problem solving using teams made up of front-line workers. A variety of specific tools are available to aid teams in their problem solving. One of these tools, **benchmarking,** involves studying organizations that are among the best in the world at performing a particular task. For example, when Xerox wanted to improve its procedures for filling customer orders, it studied how the mail-order company L. L. Bean processes its customer orders.

In Business

Strawberries, Hepatitis, and Broken Air Conditioners

Auto companies spend huge amounts of money to fix problems in cars that are under warranty. General Motors (GM) spends $3.5 billion a year paying dealers to handle 22.5 *million* warranty claims. Not only does this cost GM considerable amounts of money, but every warranty claim represents a dissatisfied customer. Understandably, GM has made it a top priority to reduce warranty repairs by detecting problems early and eliminating them in the production process.

For help, GM managers turned to the Center for Disease Control (CDC). GM executives had been impressed when CDC doctors had traced a hepatitis outbreak in Michigan within a few days to a load of bad strawberries from Mexico. Borrowing methods from CDC, GM established a "warranty war room" in Warren, Michigan. A chart hangs on the wall in the warranty war room covered with colored dots. Red dots represent newly discovered outbreaks. Yellow dots represent problems for which a tentative solution has been identified. Green dots represent problems that have been eradicated—evidenced by 60 days of trouble-free production. With this new system, the root cause of a problem can usually be identified within 24 hours. This is important because GM makes about 25,000 cars and trucks a day. Quickly eradicating problems keeps more of them from showing up in dealer showrooms and customer garages.

As an example, hot air blowing out of air conditioners generated a surge of warranty claims. Within three days, GM engineers had isolated the problem to a compressor part that was sometimes defective. By working with the supplier, the cause was found to be a drilling machine that periodically clogged with metal shavings and made holes that were too big. Within days the equipment was modified to prevent this problem from recurring.

Source: Gregory L. White, "GM Takes Advice from Disease Sleuths to Debug Cars," *The Wall Street Journal*, April 8, 1999, pp. B1 & B4.

Perhaps the most important and pervasive TQM problem-solving tool is the *plan-do-check-act (PDCA) cycle,* which is also referred to as the Deming Wheel.[7] The **plan-do-check-act cycle** is a systematic, fact-based approach to continuous improvement. The basic elements of the PDCA cycle are illustrated in Exhibit 1–4. The PDCA cycle applies the scientific method to problem solving. In the Plan phase, the problem-solving team analyzes data to identify possible causes for the problem and then proposes a solution. In the Do phase, an experiment is conducted. In the Check phase, the results of the experiment are analyzed. And in the Act phase, if the results of the experiment are favorable, the plan is implemented. If the results of the experiment are not favorable, the team goes back to the original data and starts all over again.

Perhaps the most important feature of TQM is that "it improves productivity by encouraging the use of science in decision-making and discouraging counter-productive defensive behavior."[8]

Thousands of organizations have been involved in TQM and similar programs. Some of the more well-known companies are American Express, AT&T, Cadillac Motor Car,

---

[7] Dr. W. Edwards Deming, a pioneer in TQM, introduced many of the elements of TQM to Japanese industry after World War II. TQM was further refined and developed at Japanese companies such as Toyota.

[8] Karen Hopper Wruck and Michael C. Jensen, "Science, Specific Knowledge, and Total Quality Management," *Journal of Accounting and Economics* 18 (1994), pp. 247–287.

Exhibit 1–4 The Plan-Do-Check-Act Cycle

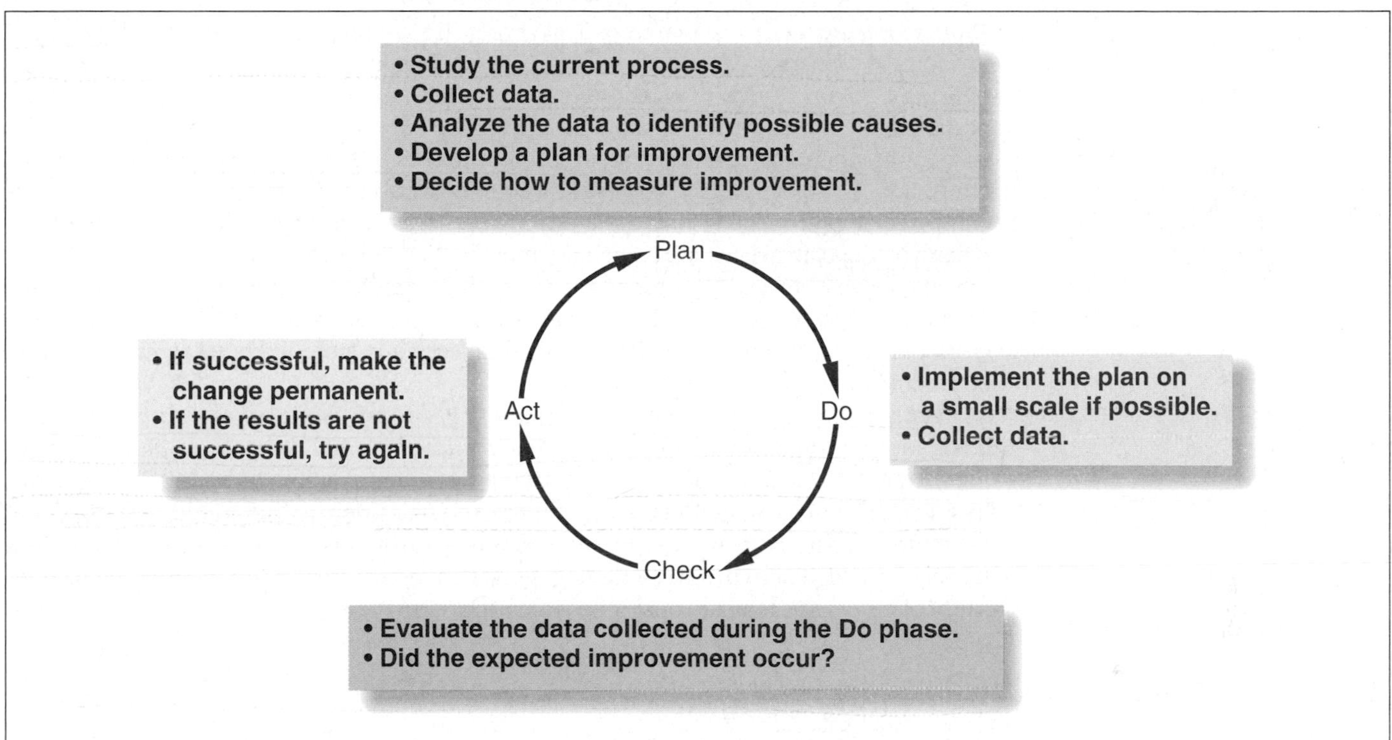

Corning, Dun & Bradstreet, Ericsson of Sweden, Federal Express, GTE Directories, First National Bank of Chicago, Florida Power and Light, General Electric, Hospital Corporation of America, IBM, Johnson & Johnson, KLM Royal Dutch Airlines, LTV, 3M, Milliken & Company, Motorola, Northern Telecom of Canada, Phillips of the Netherlands, Ritz Carlton Hotel, Texas Instruments, Westinghouse Electric, and Xerox. As this list illustrates, TQM is international in scope and is not confined to manufacturing. Indeed, a survey by the American Hospital Association of 3,300 hospitals found that 69% have launched quality-improvement programs. For example, Intermountain Healthcare's LDS Hospital in Salt Lake City is using total quality management techniques to reduce infection rates among surgery patients and the toxic side effects of chemotherapy.[9]

In sum, TQM provides tools and techniques for continuous improvement based on facts and analysis; and if properly implemented, it avoids counterproductive organizational infighting.

Dramatic Improvement

In Business

TQM is not just a big company phenomenon. Penril DataComm is a Maryland designer and producer of data communications equipment. Before embarking on TQM, defect rates were so high that the company was reworking or scrapping one-third of everything it made. Applying TQM techniques resulted in an 81% decrease in defects, an 83% decrease in failures in the first three months of use, and a 73% decrease in first-year warranty repairs. TQM is credited with taking the company "from the brink of financial disaster" to excellent financial health.

Source: "Poor Quality Nearly Short Circuits Electronics Company," *Productivity,* February 1993, pp. 1–3.

[9] Ron Wilson, "Excising Waste: Health-Care Providers Try Industrial Tactics in U.S. to Cut Costs," *The Wall Street Journal Europe,* November 10, 1993, p. 1 & 8.

Process Reengineering

Process Reengineering is a more radical approach to improvement than TQM. Instead of tweaking the existing system in a series of incremental improvements, in **Process Reengineering** a *business process* is diagrammed in detail, questioned, and then completely redesigned to eliminate unnecessary steps, to reduce opportunities for errors, and to reduce costs. A **business process** is any series of steps that are followed to carry out some task in a business. For example, the steps followed to make a large pineapple and Canadian bacon pizza at Godfather's Pizza are a business process. The steps followed by your bank when you deposit a check are a business process. While Process Reengineering is similar in some respects to TQM, its proponents view it as a more sweeping approach to change. One difference is that while TQM emphasizes a team approach involving people who work directly in the processes, Process Reengineering is more likely to be imposed from above and to use outside consultants.

Process Reengineering focuses on *simplification* and *elimination of wasted effort.* A central idea of Process Reengineering is that *all activities that do not add value to a product or service should be eliminated.* Activities that do not add value to a product or service that customers are willing to pay for are known as **non-value-added activities.** For example, moving large batches of work in process from one workstation to another is a non-value-added activity. To some degree, JIT involves Process Reengineering as does TQM. These management approaches often overlap.[10]

In Business

Design by Computer

One of the most time-consuming and expensive business processes is the design stage in product development, which has traditionally relied on paper and drafting tools. Dassault Systèmes has met the challenge of reengineering this process and has created Catia, the top-selling CAD/CAM software application to do it. CAD/CAM allows engineers to design and develop products on a computer. This eliminates huge amounts of paperwork and slashes the time required to design and develop a new product. Catia is used by nearly every aircraft manufacturer and was used by Boeing to design the 777. DaimlerChrysler used Catia to design the new Jeep Grand Cherokee. By debugging the production line on-screen, the company saved months and eliminated $800 million of costs.

Source: Howard Banks, "Virtually Perfect," *Forbes*, October 4, 1999, pp. 128–129.

Process Reengineering has been used by many companies to deal with a wide variety of problems. For example, the EMI Records Group was having difficulty filling orders for its most popular CDs. Retailers and recording stars were rebelling—it took the company as much as 20 days to deliver a big order for a hit CD, and then nearly 20% of the order would be missing. Small, incremental improvements would not have been adequate, so the company reengineered its entire distribution process with dramatic effects on on-time delivery and order fill rates.[11] Reynolds & Reynolds Co. of Dayton, Ohio, produces business forms. Filling an order for a customer used to take 90 separate steps. By reengineering, the number of steps was slashed to 20 and the time required to fill an order was cut from three weeks to one week.[12] Massachusetts General Hospital is even using Process Reengineering to standardize and improve surgical procedures.[13]

---

[10] Activity-based costing and activity-based management, both of which are discussed in Chapter 8, can be helpful in identifying areas in the company that could benefit from process reengineering.

[11] Glenn Rifkin, "EMI: Technology Brings the Music Giant a Whole New Spin," *Forbes ASAP,* February 27, 1995, pp. 32–38.

[12] William M. Bulkeley, "Pushing the Pace: The Latest Big Thing at Many Companies Is Speed, Speed, Speed," *The Wall Street Journal,* December 23, 1994, pp. A1 & A7.

[13] George Anders, "Required Surgery: Health Plans Force Even Elite Hospitals to Cut Costs Sharply," *The Wall Street Journal,* March 8, 1994, pp. A1 & A6.

Employee resistance is a recurrent problem in Process Reengineering. The cause of much of this resistance is the fear that people may lose their jobs. Workers reason that if Process Reengineering succeeds in eliminating non-value-added activities, there will be less work to do and management may be tempted to reduce the payroll. Process Reengineering, if carried out insensitively and without regard to such fears, can undermine morale and will ultimately fail to improve the bottom line (i.e., profits). As with other improvement projects, employees must be convinced that the end result of the improvement will be more secure, rather than less secure, jobs. Real improvement can have this effect if management uses the improvement to generate more business rather than to cut the workforce. If by improving processes the company is able to produce a better product at lower cost, the company will have the competitive strength to prosper. And a prosperous company is a much more secure employer than a company that is in trouble.

The Dark Side of Process Reengineering

In Business

Process Reengineering that is imposed from above and that results in disruptions and layoffs can lead to cynicism. Eileen Shapiro, a management consultant, says that "reengineering as often implemented can erode the bonds of trust that employees have toward their employers. Nevertheless, many companies reengineer at the same time that they issue mission statements proclaiming, 'Our employees are our most important asset,' or launch new initiatives to increase 'employee involvement.' As one senior executive, a veteran of reengineering, muttered recently while listening to his boss give a glowing speech about working conditions at their organization, 'I sure wish I worked for the company he is describing.'"

Source: Eileen Shapiro, "Theories Don't Pull Companies in Conflicting Directions. Managers Do," *Harvard Business Review,* March–April 1997, p. 142.

The Theory of Constraints (TOC)

A **constraint** is anything that prevents you from getting more of what you want. Every individual and every organization faces at least one constraint, so it is not difficult to find examples of constraints. You may not have enough time to study thoroughly for every subject *and* to go out with your friends on the weekend, so time is your constraint. United Airlines has only a limited number of loading gates available at its busy O'Hare hub, so its constraint is loading gates. Vail Resorts has only a limited amount of land to develop as homesites and commercial lots at its ski areas, so its constraint is land.

Since a constraint prevents you from getting more of what you want, the **Theory of Constraints (TOC)** maintains that effectively managing the constraint is a key to success. As an example, long waiting periods for surgery are a chronic problem in the National Health Service (NHS), the government-funded provider of health care in the United Kingdom. The diagram in Exhibit 1–5 illustrates a simplified version of the steps followed by a patient who is identified for surgery and eventually treated. The number of patients that can be processed through each step in a day is indicated in the exhibit. For example, up to 100 referrals from general practitioners can be processed in a day.

The constraint, or *bottleneck,* in the system is determined by the step that has the smallest capacity—in this case surgery. The total number of patients processed through the entire system cannot exceed 15 per day—the maximum number of patients that can be treated in surgery. No matter how hard managers, doctors, and nurses try to improve the processing rate elsewhere in the system, they will never succeed in driving down the wait lists until the capacity of surgery is increased. In fact, improvements elsewhere in the system—particularly before the constraint—are likely to result in even longer waiting times and more frustrated patients and health care providers. Thus, improvement efforts must be focused on the constraint to be effective. A business process, such as the process for serving surgery patients, is like a chain. If you want to increase the strength of a chain, what is the most effective way to do this? Should you concentrate your efforts on

Exhibit 1–5 Processing Surgery Patients at an NHS Facility (simplified)*

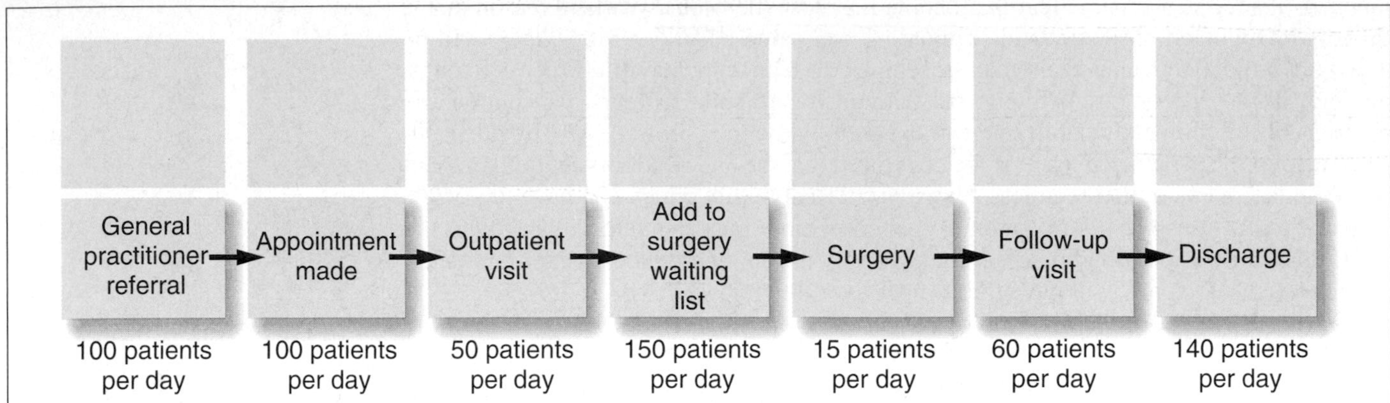

*This diagram originally appeared in the February 1999 issue of the U.K. magazine *Health Management.*

strengthening the strongest link, all the links, or the weakest link? Clearly, focusing your effort on the weakest link will bring the biggest benefit.

Continuing with this analogy, the procedure to follow to strengthen the chain is clear. First, identify the weakest link, which is the constraint. Second, don't place a greater strain on the system than the weakest link can handle—if you do, the chain will break. In the case of the NHS, waiting lists become unacceptably long. Third, concentrate improvement efforts on strengthening the weakest link. Find ways to increase the number of surgeries that can be performed in a day. Fourth, if the improvement efforts are successful, eventually the weakest link will improve to the point where it is no longer the weakest link. At that point, the new weakest link (i.e., the new constraint) must be identified, and improvement efforts must be shifted over to that link. This simple sequential process provides a powerful strategy for continuous improvement. The TOC approach is a perfect complement to other improvement tools such as TQM and process reengineering—it focuses improvement efforts where they are likely to be most effective.

In Business | **The Constraint Is the Key**

The Lessines plant of Baxter International makes medical products such as sterile bags. Management of the plant is acutely aware of the necessity to actively manage its constraints. For example, when materials are a constraint, management may go to a secondary vendor and purchase materials at a higher cost than normal. When a machine is the constraint, a weekend shift is often added on the machine. If a particular machine is chronically the constraint and management has exhausted the possibilities of using it more effectively, then additional capacity is purchased. For example, when the constraint was the plastic extruding machines, a new extruding machine was ordered. However, even before the machine arrived, management had determined that the constraint would shift to the blenders once the new extruding capacity was added. Therefore, a new blender was already being planned. By thinking ahead and focusing on the constraints, management is able to increase the plant's real capacity at the lowest possible cost.

Source: Eric Noreen, Debra Smith, and James Mackey, *The Theory of Constraints and Its Implications for Management Accounting* (Montvale, NJ: The IMA Foundation for Applied Research, Inc., 1995), p. 67.

International Competition

Over the last several decades, competition has become worldwide in many industries. This has been caused by reductions in tariffs, quotas, and other barriers to free trade; improvements in global transportation systems; and increasing sophistication in international markets. These factors work together to reduce the costs of conducting international trade and make it possible for foreign companies to compete on a more equal footing with local firms.

The movement toward freer trade has been most dramatic in the European Union (EU). The EU has grown from a very small free-trade zone involving a few basic commodities such as coal and steel in the late 1950s to a free-trade zone of over a dozen European nations involving almost unlimited movement of goods and services across national borders. This vast, largely unified market has a population of over 375 million, as compared with over 268 million in the United States and about 125 million in Japan. Many of the countries in the EU are adopting a common currency called the euro, which should make trading within the EU even easier. The euro will fully replace traditional currencies such as the French franc, the German mark, and the Italian lira in July 2002. The relatively new North American Free Trade Association (NAFTA) trading block, which consists of Canada, the United States, and Mexico, has a combined population in excess of 395 million.

Such reductions in trade barriers have made it easier for agile and aggressive companies to expand outside of their home markets. As a result, very few firms can afford to be complacent. A company may be very successful today in its local market relative to its local competitors, but tomorrow the competition may come from halfway around the globe. As a matter of survival, even firms that are presently doing very well in their home markets must become world-class competitors. On the bright side, the freer international movement of goods and services presents tremendous export opportunities for those companies that can transform themselves into world-class competitors. And, from the standpoint of consumers, heightened competition promises an even greater variety of goods, at higher quality and lower prices.

What does increased global competition imply for managerial accounting? It would be very difficult for a firm to become world-class if it plans, directs, and controls its operations and makes decisions using a second-class management accounting system. An excellent management accounting system will not by itself guarantee success, but a poor management accounting system can stymie the best efforts of people in an organization to make the firm truly competitive.

Throughout this text we will highlight the differences between obsolete management accounting systems that get in the way of success and well-designed management accounting systems that can enhance a firm's performance. It is noteworthy that elements of well-designed management accounting systems have originated in many countries. More and more, managerial accounting has become a discipline that is worldwide in scope.

E-Commerce

Widespread use of the Internet is a fairly new phenomenon, and the impact it will eventually have on business is far from settled. For a few brief months, it looked like dot.com startups would take over the business world—their stock market valuations reached astonishing heights. But, of course, the bubble burst and few of the startups are now in business. With the benefit of hindsight, it is now clear that the managers of the dot.com startups would have benefited from the use of many of the tools covered in this book, including cost concepts (Chapter 2), cost estimation (Chapter 5), cost-volume-profit analysis (Chapter 6), activity-based costing (Chapter 8), budgeting (Chapter 9), decision making (Chapter 13), and capital budgeting (Chapter 14). While applying these tools to a new company with little operational history would be difficult, it needs to be done. And the investors who plowed billions into dot.com startups only to see the money vanish would have been wise to pay attention to the tools covered in the chapters on the statement of cash flows (Chapter 16) and financial statement analysis (Chapter 17).

At the time of this writing, it is still not clear if a successful business model will emerge for Internet-based companies. It is generally believed that Amazon.com and eBay may have the best chances of building sustainable e-commerce businesses, but even Amazon.com has its detractors who believe it will never break even on a cash flow basis. If a successful e-commerce business model does emerge, it will be based on attracting enough profitable customers to cover the fixed expenses of the company as discussed in Chapter 6.

In Business

Global Forces

Traditionally, management accounting practices have differed significantly from one country to another. For example, Spain, Italy, and Greece have relied on less formal management accounting systems than other European countries. According to Professor Norman B. Macintosh, "In Greece and Italy the predominance of close-knit, private, family firms motivated by secrecy, tax avoidance, and largesse for family members along with lack of market competition (price fixing?) mitigated the development of MACS [management accounting and control systems]. Spain also followed this pattern and relied more on personal relationships and oral inquisitions than on hard data for control." At the same time, other Western European countries such as Germany, France, and the Netherlands developed relatively sophisticated formal management accounting systems emphasizing efficient operations. In the case of France, these were codified in law. In England, management accounting practice was influenced by economists, who emphasized the use of accounting data in decision making. The Nordic countries tended to import management accounting ideas from both Germany and from England.

A number of factors have been acting in recent years to make management accounting practices more similar within Europe and around the world. These forces include: intensified global competition, which makes it more difficult to continue sloppy practices; standardized information system software sold throughout the world by vendors such as SAP, PeopleSoft, Oracle, and Baan; the increasing significance and authority of multinational corporations; the global consultancy industry; the diffusion of information throughout academia; and the global use of market-leading textbooks.

Sources: Markus Granlund and Kari Lukka, "It's a Small World of Management Accounting Practices," *Journal of Management Accounting Research* 10, 1998, pp. 153–171; and Norman B. Macintosh, "Management Accounting in Europe: A View from Canada," *Management Accounting Research* 9, 1998, pp. 495–500.

Established brick-and-mortar companies like General Electric, Wells Fargo, American Airlines, and Wal-Mart will undoubtedly continue to expand into cyberspace—both for business-to-business transactions and for retailing. The Internet has important advantages over more conventional marketplaces for some kinds of transactions such as mortgage banking. The financial institution does not have to tie up staff filling out forms—that can be done directly by the consumer over the Internet. And data and funds can be sent back and forth electronically—no UPS delivery truck needs to drop by the consumer's home to deliver a check. However, it is unlikely that a successful blockbuster business will ever be built around the concept of selling low-value, low-margin, and bulky items like groceries over the Internet.

Professional Ethics

LEARNING OBJECTIVE 4
Understand the importance of upholding ethical standards.

In recent years, many concerns have been raised regarding ethical behavior in business and in public life. Allegations and scandals of unethical conduct have been directed toward managers in virtually all segments of society, including government, business, charitable organizations, and even religion. Although these allegations and scandals have received a lot of attention, it is doubtful that they represent a wholesale breakdown of the moral fiber of the nation. After all, hundreds of millions of transactions are conducted every day that remain untainted. Nevertheless, it is important to have an appreciation of what is and is not acceptable behavior in business and why. Fortunately, the Institute of Management Accountants (IMA) of the United States has developed a very useful ethical code called the *Standards of Ethical Conduct for Practitioners of Management Accounting and Financial Management.* Even though the standards were specifically developed for management accountants, they have much broader application.

Code of Conduct for Management Accountants

The IMA's Standards of Ethical Conduct for Practitioners of Management Accounting and Financial Management is presented in full in Exhibit 1–6. There are two parts to the standards. The first part provides general guidelines for ethical behavior. In a nutshell, the management accountant has ethical responsibilities in four broad areas: First, to maintain a high level of professional competence; second, to treat sensitive matters with confidentiality; third, to maintain personal integrity; and fourth, to be objective in all disclosures. The second part of the standards gives specific guidance concerning what should be done if an individual finds evidence of ethical misconduct within an organization. We recommend that you stop at this point and read the standards in Exhibit 1–6.

The ethical standards provide sound, practical advice for management accountants and managers. Most of the rules in the ethical standards are motivated by a very practical

Exhibit 1–6
Standards of Ethical Conduct for Practitioners of Management Accounting and Financial Management

Practitioners of management accounting and financial management have an obligation to the public, their profession, the organization they serve, and themselves, to maintain the highest standards of ethical conduct. In recognition of this obligation, the Institute of Management Accountants has promulgated the following standards of ethical conduct for practitioners of management accounting and financial management. Adherence to these standards, both domestically and internationally, is integral to achieving the Objectives of Management Accounting. Practitioners of management accounting and financial management shall not commit acts contrary to these standards nor shall they condone the commission of such acts by others within their organizations.

Competence. Practitioners of management accounting and financial management have a responsibility to:

- Maintain an appropriate level of professional competence by ongoing development of their knowledge and skills.
- Perform their professional duties in accordance with relevant laws, regulations, and technical standards.
- Prepare complete and clear reports and recommendations after appropriate analysis of relevant and reliable information.

Confidentiality. Practitioners of management accounting and financial management have a responsibility to:

- Refrain from disclosing confidential information acquired in the course of their work except when authorized, unless legally obligated to do so.
- Inform subordinates as appropriate regarding the confidentiality of information acquired in the course of their work and monitor their activities to assure the maintenance of that confidentiality.
- Refrain from using or appearing to use confidential information acquired in the course of their work for unethical or illegal advantage either personally or through third parties.

Integrity. Practitioners of management accounting and financial management have a responsibility to:

- Avoid actual or apparent conflicts of interest and advise all appropriate parties of any potential conflict.
- Refrain from engaging in any activity that would prejudice their ability to carry out their duties ethically.
- Refuse any gift, favor, or hospitality that would influence or would appear to influence their actions.
- Refrain from either actively or passively subverting the attainment of the organization's legitimate and ethical objectives.
- Recognize and communicate professional limitations or other constraints that would preclude responsible judgment or successful performance of an activity.
- Communicate unfavorable as well as favorable information and professional judgments or opinions.
- Refrain from engaging in or supporting any activity that would discredit the profession.

Exhibit 1–6
(concluded)

Objectivity. Practitioners of management accounting and financial management have a responsibility to:

- Communicate information fairly and objectively.
- Disclose fully all relevant information that could reasonably be expected to influence an intended user's understanding of the reports, comments, and recommendations presented.

Resolution of Ethical Conflict. In applying the standards of ethical conduct, practitioners of management accounting and financial management may encounter problems in identifying unethical behavior or in resolving an ethical conflict. When faced with significant ethical issues, practitioners of management accounting and financial management should follow the established policies of the organization bearing on the resolution of such conflict. If these policies do not resolve the ethical conflict, such practitioner should consider the following courses of action:

- Discuss such problems with the immediate superior except when it appears that the superior is involved, in which case the problem should be presented initially to the next higher managerial level. If a satisfactory resolution cannot be achieved when the problem is initially presented, submit the issues to the next higher managerial level.
- If the immediate superior is the chief executive officer, or equivalent, the acceptable reviewing authority may be a group such as the audit committee, executive committee, board of directors, board of trustees, or owners. Contact with levels above the immediate superior should be initiated only with the superior's knowledge, assuming the superior is not involved. Except where legally prescribed, communication of such problems to authorities or individuals not employed or engaged by the organization is not considered appropriate.
- Clarify relevant ethical issues by confidential discussion with an objective advisor (e.g., IMA Ethics Counseling Service) to obtain a better understanding of possible courses of action.
- Consult your own attorney as to legal obligations and rights concerning the ethical conflict.
- If the ethical conflict still exists after exhausting all levels of internal review, there may be no other recourse on significant matters than to resign from the organization and to submit an informative memorandum to an appropriate representative of the organization. After resignation, depending on the nature of the ethical conflict, it may also be appropriate to notify other parties.

*Institute of Management Accountants, formerly National Association of Accountants, *Statements on Management Accounting: Objectives of Management Accounting,* Statement No. 1B, New York, NY, June 17, 1982 as revised in 1997.

consideration—if these rules were not generally followed in business, then the economy would come to a screeching halt. Consider the following specific examples of the consequences of not abiding by the standards:

- Suppose employees could not be trusted with confidential information. Then top managers would be reluctant to distribute confidential information within the company. As a result, decisions would be based on incomplete information and operations would deteriorate.
- Suppose employees accepted bribes from suppliers. Then contracts would tend to go to suppliers who pay the highest bribes rather than to the most competent suppliers. Would you like to fly in an aircraft whose wings were made by the subcontractor who was willing to pay the highest bribe to a purchasing agent? What would happen to the airline industry if its safety record deteriorated due to shoddy workmanship on contracted parts and assemblies?
- Suppose the presidents of companies routinely lied in their annual reports to shareholders and grossly distorted financial statements. If the basic integrity of a company's financial statements could not be relied on, investors and creditors would have

little basis for making informed decisions. Suspecting the worst, rational investors would pay less for securities issued by companies. As a consequence, less funds would be available for productive investments and many firms might be unable to raise any funds at all. Ultimately, this would lead to slower economic growth, fewer goods and services, and higher prices.

As these examples suggest, if ethical standards were not generally adhered to, there would be undesirable consequences for everyone. Essentially, abandoning ethical standards would lead to a lower standard of living with lower-quality goods and services, less to choose from, and higher prices. In short, following ethical rules such as those in the Standards of Ethical Conduct for Practitioners of Management Accounting and Financial Management is not just a matter of being "nice"; it is absolutely essential for the smooth functioning of an advanced market economy.

Resisting the Flow

In Business

Jeff Henley, the executive vice president and CFO of Oracle Corporation, one of the world's leading software companies, has this to say about integrity: "You must have a strong sense of ethics. As a finance person you get pushed by people at times to do things that will make results look right but aren't necessarily right, so you've got to push back on people. But then remember the team. You aren't adding value unless you're in a business partnership."

Source: Kathy Williams and James Hart, "Getting Oracle Back to Basics," *Strategic Finance*, April 1999, pp. 36–41.

Character's the Thing

In Business

Personal character has become critically important to CEOs when hiring a CFO. A huge proportion (about 84%) of CEOs ranked personal integrity as second in importance only to technical expertise. The growing emphasis on character is partly driven by external pressures. The Securities and Exchange Commission is becoming more aggressive in going after companies that cook their books, and powerful shareholders are increasingly likely to demand that CFOs be beyond reproach. Moreover, CEOs agree that character is integral to the job. George Fellows, the CEO of Revlon, says: "Personal integrity is the cost of entry to this position." Frank Weise, the CEO of Toronto-based Cott Corp., agrees: "When you hire a CFO, you want that person to reek of integrity." Susan Landon, an executive recruiter with LAI Worldwide, adds: "In most executives, CEOs look for personal character; in a CFO, it is an absolute requirement."

Source: Julie Carrick Dalton, "What CEOs Want," *CFO*, July 1999, pp. 45–52.

Company Codes of Conduct

"Those who engage in unethical behavior often justify their actions with one or more of the following reasons: (1) the organization expects unethical behavior, (2) everyone else is unethical, and/or (3) behaving unethically is the only way to get ahead."[14]

To counter the first justification for unethical behavior, many companies have adopted formal ethical codes of conduct. These codes are generally broad-based statements of a company's responsibilities to its employees, its customers, its suppliers, and the communities in which the company operates. Codes rarely spell out specific do's and don'ts or suggest proper behavior in a specific situation. Instead, they give broad guidelines.

[14] Michael K. McCuddy, Karl E. Reichardt, and David Schroeder, "Ethical Pressures: Fact or Fiction?" *Management Accounting,* April 1993, pp. 57–61.

Unfortunately, the single-minded emphasis placed on short-term profits in some companies may make it seem like the only way to get ahead is to act unethically. When top managers say, in effect, that they will only be satisfied with bottom-line results and will accept no excuses, they are asking for trouble. See the accompanying In Business box "Taking a Chainsaw to Ethics" for a vivid example.

In Business

Taking a Chainsaw to Ethics

"Chainsaw" Al Dunlap earned a reputation as a no-nonsense executive specializing in turning around struggling companies. He is known to have proudly declared: "If you want a friend, buy a dog. I've got two." The dark side of his tactics came to light after the debacle at Sunbeam, which he took over as CEO and then left in disgrace two years later. For a while, Dunlap was able to show consistent improvements in quarterly earnings at Sunbeam, but only later did his methods for achieving this record come to light. John A. Byrne describes what happened:

> By the fourth quarter, as it became more difficult to meet the numbers, a new and rather menacing management technique was invented. It was called "tasking." Kersh [Sunbeam's CFO] and Dunlap would gather the top executives in the boardroom and ask each to run through the numbers for their businesses. If one area was lagging, someone else would be asked to make up the difference so Dunlap's forecasts to Wall Street would be met.
>
> "They would say, 'I don't care what your plan was. I don't care what you delivered last month," recalls Dixon Thayer, head of international sales. "We are going to task you with this number.' Russ [Kersh] would give you a revenue and profit number and say, . . . Your life depends on hitting that number.' These numbers got to be so outrageous they were ridiculous."
>
> In an effort to hang on to their jobs and their options, some Sunbeam managers began all sorts of game playing. Commissions were withheld from independent sales reps. Bills went unpaid. . . . As Sunbeam moved toward the holiday season, its struggle to make its numbers became more desperate. . . . [T]he company offered retailers major discounts to buy grills nearly six months before they were needed. The retailers did not have to pay for the grills or accept delivery of them for six months.
>
> In the often esoteric interpretations that are made in accounting, Kersh was rarely conservative or bashful about his creative competence during his tenure as Sunbeam's CFO. In a self-congratulatory tone, he would point to his chest and boast to fellow executives that he was "the biggest profit center" the company had. . . . At meetings, executives recalled, Dunlap would say: "If it weren't for Russ and the accounting team, we'd be nowhere." Several executives heard Dunlap shout to subordinates: "Make the [?@!] number. And Russ, you cover it with your ditty bag."

Deirdra DenDanto, then 26, a recently hired member of the company's internal audit department, challenged the company's questionable practices from the start, but there was little follow-up to her recommendations. She finally resigned after unsuccessfully attempting to send a warning memo to the board of directors. A few months later, the accounting ploys Dunlap had been using to bolster earnings came unraveled, leading to a dramatic boardroom ouster. The company's losses in that year totaled almost $1 billion and its stock crashed to $6, from an earlier price of $53. The company and its employees still suffer from the aftermath.

Source: John A. Byrne, "Chainsaw: He Anointed Himself America's Best CEO. But Al Dunlap Drove Sunbeam into the Ground," *Business Week*, October 18, 1999, pp. 128–149.

Codes of Conduct on the International Level

The *Guideline on Ethics for Professional Accountants,* issued in July 1990 by the International Federation of Accountants (IFAC), governs the activities of *all* professional accountants throughout the world, regardless of whether they are practicing as independent CPAs, employed in government service, or employed as internal accountants.[15] In addition to outlining ethical requirements in matters dealing with competence, objectivity, independence, and confidentiality, the IFAC's code also outlines the accountant's ethical responsibilities in matters relating to taxes, fees and commissions, advertising and solicitation, the handling of monies, and cross-border activities. Where cross-border activities are involved, the IFAC ethical requirements must be followed if these requirements are stricter than the ethical requirements of the country in which the work is being performed.[16]

In addition to professional and company codes of ethical conduct, accountants and managers in the United States are subject to the legal requirements of *The Foreign Corrupt Practices Act of 1977.* The Act requires that companies devise and maintain a system of internal controls sufficient to ensure that all transactions are properly executed and recorded. The Act specifically prohibits giving bribes, even if giving bribes is common practice in the country in which the company is doing business.

Are Women More Ethical than Men?

In Business

CMA Canada, the association of chartered management accountants in Canada, distributed questionnaires to Canadian business students that contained 28 questions involving ethical issues. For example, students were asked whether it would be acceptable or unacceptable to export a product that would be considered unsafe in Canada. The students responded on a six-point scale—with 1 being "acceptable" and 6 "unacceptable." Note that the scores are the students' perceptions of the acceptability of the action and not the "right" answer in any absolute sense. The average responses are revealing:

CMA Canada Business Student Survey
(1 = considered by student to be acceptable;
6 = considered by student to be unacceptable)

	Female	Male
Inflate an insurance claim?	5.09	4.18
Return worn clothing?	4.43	3.23
Purchase mismarked item for the incorrect price?	3.27	2.22
Sell a frequent flyer ticket?	3.39	2.69
Keep extra change given in error?	4.03	3.30
Misrepresent age to obtain a senior discount?	4.33	3.77
Misrepresent age to obtain a child discount?	3.95	3.33
Charge higher prices in a poorer area?	3.92	2.84
Use cheap foreign labor?	2.72	2.02
Sell an unsafe product overseas?	5.18	2.40
Charge a higher price after a tornado?	3.94	3.26
Sell an illegal pharmaceutical product?	4.64	3.99

Robert Dye, president and CEO of CMA Canada, emphasizes the importance of ethics in business: "Employees like to work for a company that they can trust. Customers like to deal with an ethically reliable business. Suppliers like to sell to firms with which they can have a real partnership. Communities are more likely to co-operate with organizations that deal honestly and fairly with them." If the business community is to function effectively, all of the players need to act ethically.

Source: Excerpted from a study by J. Fisher, "Ethics Check," appearing in *CMA Management* magazine (formerly *CMA Magazine*), April 1999, pp. 36–37, with permission of CMA Canada.

[15] A copy of this code can be obtained on the International Federation of Accountants' web site www.ifac.org.

[16] *Guideline on Ethics for Professional Accountants* (New York: International Federation of Accountants, July 1990), p. 23.

The Certified Management Accountant (CMA)

A management accountant who possesses the necessary qualifications and who possesses a rigorous professional exam earns the right to be known as a *Certified Management Accountant (CMA).* In addition to the prestige that accompanies a professional designation, CMAs are often given greater responsibilities and higher compensation than those who do not have such a designation. Information about becoming a CMA and the CMA program can be accessed on the Institute of Management Accountants' (IMA) web site www.imanet.org or by calling 1-800-638-4427.

To become a Certified Management Accountant, the following four steps must be completed:

1. File an Application for Admission and register for the CMA examination.
2. Pass all four parts of the CMA examination within a three-year period.
3. Satisfy the experience requirement of two continuous years of professional experience in management and/or financial accounting prior to or within seven years of passing the CMA examination.
4. Comply with the Standards of Ethical Conduct for Practitioners of Management Accounting and Financial Management.

In Business

How's the Pay?

In 1998 Roland Madison reported that, with normal progress in a larger corporation, a management accountant should be earning $45,000 within three to four years and after five to six years, $60,000. The salaries would be even higher now.

Source: Roland Mason, "How Do I Start My Career in Financial Management?" *imastudents.org magazine*, Winter 1998, pp. 16–20.

Summary

Managerial accounting assists managers in carrying out their responsibilities, which include planning, directing and motivating, and controlling.

Since managerial accounting is geared to the needs of the manager rather than to the needs of outsiders, it differs substantially from financial accounting. Managerial accounting is oriented more toward the future, places less emphasis on precision, emphasizes segments of an organization (rather than the organization as a whole), is not governed by generally accepted accounting principles, and is not mandatory.

Most organizations are decentralized to some degree. The organization chart depicts who works for whom in the organization and which units perform staff functions rather than line functions. Accountants perform a staff function—they support and provide assistance to others inside the organization.

The business environment in recent years has been characterized by increasing competition and a relentless drive for continuous improvement. Several approaches have been developed to assist organizations in meeting these challenges—including Just-In-Time (JIT), Total Quality Management (TQM), Process Reengineering, and the Theory of Constraints (TOC).

JIT emphasizes the importance of reducing inventories to the barest minimum possible. This reduces working capital requirements, frees up space, reduces throughput time, reduces defects, and eliminates waste.

TQM involves focusing on the customer, and it employs systematic problem solving using teams made up of front-line workers. Specific TQM tools include benchmarking and the plan-do-check-act (PDCA) cycle. By emphasizing teamwork, a focus on the customer, and facts, TQM can avoid the organizational infighting that might otherwise block improvement.

Process Reengineering involves completely redesigning a business process in order to eliminate non-value-added activities and to reduce opportunities for errors. Process Reengineering relies more on outside specialists than TQM and is more likely to be imposed by top management.

The Theory of Constraints emphasizes the importance of managing the organization's constraints. Since the constraint is whatever is holding back the organization, improvement efforts usually must be focused on the constraint in order to be really effective.

Ethical standards serve a very important practical function in an advanced market economy. Without widespread adherence to ethical standards, material living standards would fall. Ethics are the lubrication that keep a market economy functioning smoothly. The Standards of Ethical Conduct for Practitioners of Management Accounting and Financial Management provide sound, practical guidelines for resolving ethical problems that might arise in an organization.

Glossary

At the end of each chapter, a list of key terms for review is given, along with the definition of each term. (These terms are printed in boldface where they are defined in the chapter.) Carefully study each term to be sure you understand its meaning, since these terms are used repeatedly in the chapters that follow. The list for Chapter 1 follows.

Benchmarking A study of organizations that are among the best in the world at performing a particular task. (p. 18)

Budget A detailed plan for the future, usually expressed in formal quantitative terms. (p. 5)

Business process A series of steps that are followed in order to carry out some task in a business. (p. 20)

Chief Financial Officer The member of the top management team who is responsible for providing timely and relevant data to support planning and control activities and for preparing financial statements for external users. An effective CFO is a key member of the top management team whose advice is sought in all major decisions. (p. 11)

Constraint Anything that prevents an organization or individual from getting more of what it wants. (p. 21)

Control The process of instituting procedures and then obtaining feedback to ensure that all parts of the organization are functioning effectively and moving toward overall company goals. (p. 5)

Controller The manager in charge of the accounting department in an organization. (p. 5)

Controlling Ensuring that the plan is actually carried out and is appropriately modified as circumstances change. (p. 4)

Cycle time See *Throughput time*. (p. 16)

Decentralization The delegation of decision-making authority throughout an organization by providing managers at various operating levels with the authority to make key decisions relating to their area of responsibility. (p. 10)

Directing and motivating Mobilizing people to carry out plans and run routine operations. (p. 4)

Feedback Accounting and other reports that help managers monitor performance and focus on problems and/or opportunities that might otherwise go unnoticed. (p. 5)

Financial accounting The phase of accounting concerned with providing information to stockholders, creditors, and others outside the organization. (p. 4)

Finished goods Units of product that have been completed but have not yet been sold to customers. (p. 13)

Just-In-Time (JIT) A production and inventory control system in which materials are purchased and units are produced only as needed to meet actual customer demand. (p. 13)

Line A position in an organization that is directly related to the achievement of the organization's basic objectives. (p. 10)

Managerial accounting The phase of accounting concerned with providing information to managers for use in planning and controlling operations and in decision making. (p. 4)

Non-value-added activity An activity that consumes resources or takes time but that does not add value for which customers are willing to pay. (p. 20)

Organization chart A visual diagram of a firm's organizational structure that depicts formal lines of reporting, communication, and responsibility between managers. (p. 10)

Performance report A detailed report comparing budgeted data to actual data. (p. 6)

Plan-do-check-act (PDCA) cycle A systematic approach to continuous improvement that applies the scientific method to problem solving. (p. 18)

Planning Selecting a course of action and specifying how the action will be implemented. (p. 4)
Planning and control cycle The flow of management activities through planning, directing and motivating, and controlling, and then back to planning again. (p. 6)
Process Reengineering An approach to improvement that involves completely redesigning business processes in order to eliminate unnecessary steps, reduce errors, and reduce costs. (p. 20)
Raw materials Materials that are used to make a product. (p. 13)
Segment Any part of an organization that can be evaluated independently of other parts and about which the manager seeks financial data. Examples include a product line, a sales territory, a division, or a department. (p. 8)
Setup Activities that must be performed whenever production is switched over from making one type of item to another. (p. 16)
Staff A position in an organization that is only indirectly related to the achievement of the organization's basic objectives. Such positions are supportive in nature in that they provide service or assistance to line positions or to other staff positions. (p. 11)
Theory of Constraints (TOC) A management approach that emphasizes the importance of managing constraints. (p. 21)
Throughput time The time required to make a completed unit of product starting with raw materials. Throughput time is also known as cycle time. (p. 16)
Total Quality Management (TQM) An approach to continuous improvement that focuses on customers and using teams of front-line workers to systematically identify and solve problems. (p. 17)
Work in process Units of product that are only partially complete and will require further work before they are ready for sale to a customer. (p. 13)

Questions

1–1 What is the basic difference in orientation between financial and managerial accounting?
1–2 What are the three major activities of a manager?
1–3 Describe the four steps in the planning and control cycle.
1–4 What function does feedback play in the work of the manager?
1–5 Distinguish between line and staff positions in an organization.
1–6 What are the major differences between financial and managerial accounting?
1–7 In a Just-In-Time (JIT) system, what is meant by the pull approach to the flow of goods, as compared to the push approach used in conventional systems?
1–8 Identify the benefits that can result from reducing the setup time for a product.
1–9 What are the major benefits of a JIT system?
1–10 Explain how the plan-do-check-act cycle applies the scientific method to problem solving.
1–11 Why is Process Reengineering a more radical approach to improvement than Total Quality Management?
1–12 How can Process Reengineering undermine employee morale?
1–13 Where does the Theory of Constraints recommend that improvement efforts be focused?
1–14 Why is adherence to ethical standards important for the smooth functioning of an advanced market economy?

Exercises

EXERCISE 1–1 The Roles of Managers and Management Accountants [LO1, LO2]
Listed below are a number of terms that relate to organizations, the work of management, and the role of managerial accounting:

Budgets	Controller
Decentralization	Directing and motivating
Feedback	Financial accounting
Line	Managerial accounting
Nonmonetary data	Planning
Performance report	Staff
Precision	Chief Financial Officer

Choose the term or terms above that most appropriately complete the following statements.

1. ______ is concerned with providing information for the use of those who are inside the organization, whereas ______ is concerned with providing information for the use of those who are outside the organization.
2. ______ consists of identifying alternatives, selecting from among the alternatives the one that is best for the organization, and specifying what actions will be taken to implement the chosen alternative.
3. When ______, managers oversee day-to-day activities and keep the organization functioning smoothly.
4. The accounting and other reports coming to management that are used in controlling the organization are called ______.
5. The delegation of decision-making authority throughout an organization by allowing managers at various operating levels to make key decisions relating to their area of responsibility is called ______.
6. A position on the organization chart that is directly related to achieving the basic objectives of an organization is called a ______ position.
7. A ______ position provides service or assistance to other parts of the organization and does not directly achieve the basic objectives of the organization.
8. The manager in charge of the accounting department is generally known as the ______.
9. The plans of management are expressed formally in ______.
10. A detailed report to management comparing budgeted data to actual data for a specific time period is called a ______.
11. The ______ is the member of the top management team who is responsible for providing timely and relevant data to support planning and control activities and for preparing financial statements for external users.
12. Managerial accounting places less emphasis on ______ and more emphasis on ______ than financial accounting.

EXERCISE 1–2 The Business Environment [LO3]

Listed below are terms that relate to Just-In-Time, Total Quality Management, Process Reengineering, and the Theory of Constraints:

Constraint	Benchmarking
Total Quality Management	Process Reengineering
Just-In-Time	Nonconstraint
Non-value-added activities	Plan-Do-Check-Act cycle
Pull	Setup
Business process	

Choose the term or terms above that most appropriately complete the following statements.

1. A production system in which units are produced and materials are purchased only as needed to meet actual customer demand is called ______.
2. ______ involves studying the business processes of companies that are considered among the best in the world at performing a particular task.
3. In Just-In-Time, the flow of goods is controlled by what is described as a ______ approach to manufacturing.
4. The activities involved in getting equipment ready to produce a different product are called a ______.
5. ______ is an incremental approach to improvement, whereas ______ tends to be a more radical approach that involves completely redesigning business processes.
6. The ______ is a systematic, fact-based approach to continuous improvement that resembles the scientific method.
7. A ______ is any series of steps that are followed in order to carry out some task in a business.
8. In Process Reengineering, two objectives are to simplify and to eliminate ______.
9. The Theory of Constraints suggests that improvement efforts should be focused on the company's ______.
10. Increasing the rate of output of a ______ as the result of an improvement effort is unlikely to have much effect on profits.

EXERCISE 1–3 Ethics in Business [LO4]

Andy Morio was hired by a popular fast-food restaurant as an order-taker and cashier. Shortly after taking the job, he was shocked to overhear an employee bragging to a friend about shortchanging customers. He confronted the employee who then snapped back: "Mind your own business. Besides, everyone does it and the customers never miss the money." Andy didn't know how to respond to this aggressive stance.

Required:

What would be the practical consequences on the fast-food industry and on consumers if cashiers generally shortchanged customers at every opportunity?

Problems

PROBLEM 1–4 Preparing an Organization Chart [LO2]

Ridell University is a large private school located in the Midwest. The university is headed by a president who has five vice presidents reporting to him. These vice presidents are responsible for auxiliary services, admissions and records, academics, financial services (controller), and physical plant.

In addition, the university has managers who report to these vice presidents. These include managers for central purchasing, the university press, and the university bookstore, all of whom report to the vice president for auxiliary services; managers for computer services and for accounting and finance, who report to the vice president for financial services; and managers for grounds and custodial services and for plant and maintenance, who report to the vice president for physical plant.

The university has four colleges—business, humanities, fine arts, and engineering and quantitative methods—and a law school. Each of these units has a dean who is responsible to the academic vice president. Each college has several departments.

Required:

1. Prepare an organization chart for Ridell University.
2. Which of the positions on your chart would be line positions? Why would they be line positions? Which would be staff positions? Why?
3. Which of the positions on your chart would have need for accounting information? Explain.

PROBLEM 1–5 Ethics in Business [LO4]

Paul Sarver is the controller of a corporation whose stock is not listed on a national stock exchange. The company has just received a patent on a product that is expected to yield substantial profits in a year or two. At the moment, however, the company is experiencing financial difficulties; and because of inadequate working capital, it is on the verge of defaulting on a note held by its bank.

At the end of the most recent fiscal year, the company's president instructed Sarver not to record several invoices as accounts payable. Sarver objected since the invoices represented bona fide liabilities. However, the president insisted that the invoices not be recorded until after year-end, at which time it was expected that additional financing could be obtained. After several very strenuous objections—expressed to both the president and other members of senior management—Sarver finally complied with the president's instructions.

Required:

1. Did Sarver act in an ethical manner? Explain fully.
2. If the new product fails to yield substantial profits and the company becomes insolvent, can Sarver's actions be justified by the fact that he was following orders from a superior? Explain.

PROBLEM 1–6 Line and Staff Positions; Organization Chart [LO2]

The Association of Medical Personnel (AMP) is a membership/educational organization that serves a wide range of individuals who work for medical institutions including hospitals, clinics, and medical practices. The membership is composed of doctors, nurses, medical assistants, and professional administrators. The purpose of the organization is to provide individuals in the medical field with a professional organization that offers educational and training opportunities through local chapters, a monthly magazine (*AMP Review*), continuing education programs, seminars, self-study courses, and research publications.

AMP is governed by a board of directors who are members elected to these positions by the membership. The chairperson of the board is the highest ranking volunteer member and presides over the board; the board establishes policy for the organization. The policies are administered and

Exhibit A Partial Organization Chart for the Association of Medical Personnel

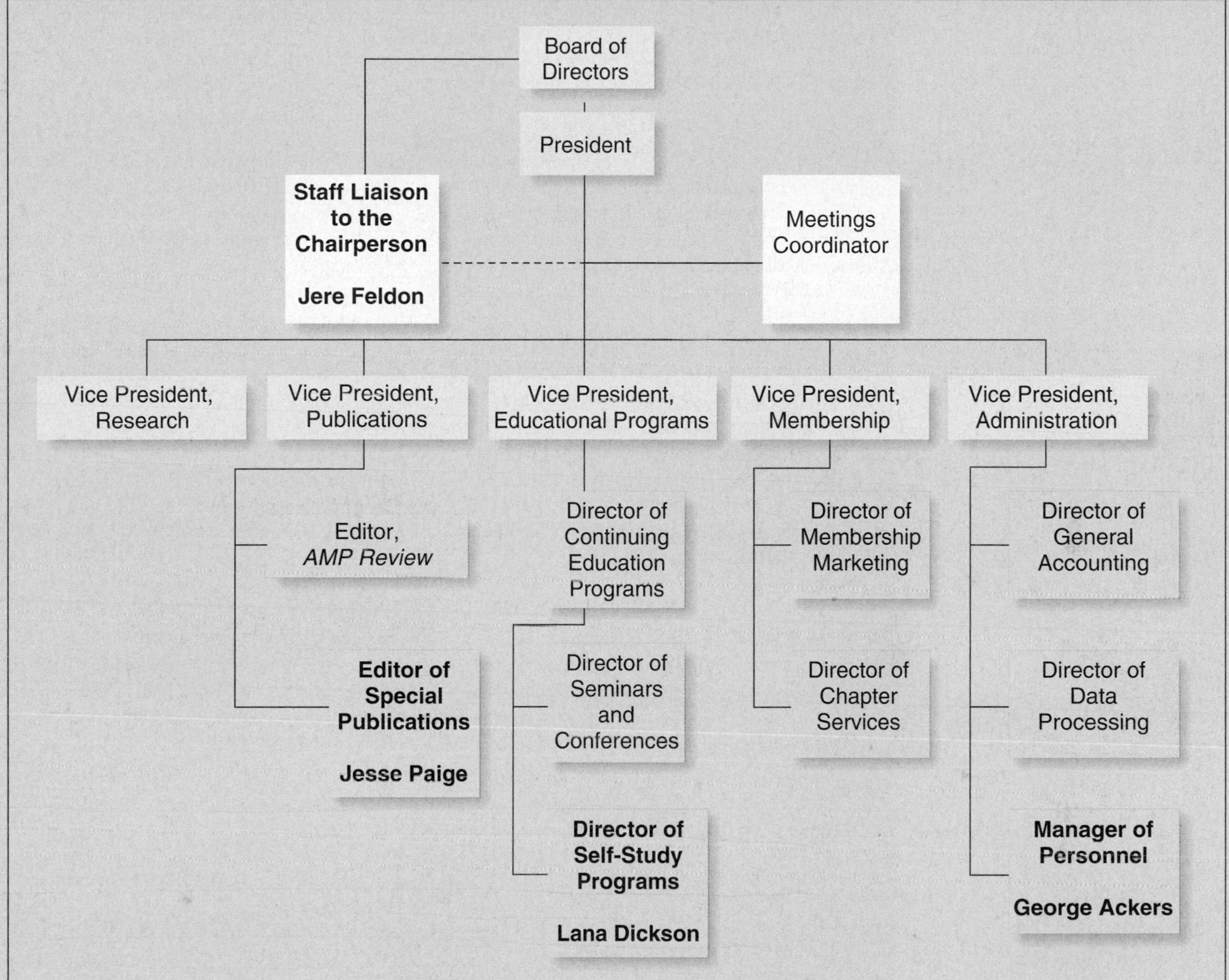

carried out by AMP's paid professional staff. The president's chief responsibility is to manage the operations of the professional staff. Like any organization, the professional staff of AMP is composed of line and staff positions. A partial organization chart of the AMP professional staff is shown in Exhibit A.

Four of the positions appearing in the organization chart are described below.

Jere Feldon, Staff Liaison to the Chairperson

Feldon is assigned to work with the chairperson of AMP by serving as an intermediary between the chairperson and the professional staff. All correspondence to the chairperson is funneled through Feldon. Feldon also works very closely with the president of AMP, especially on any matters that have to be brought to the attention of the chairperson and the board.

Lana Dickson, Director of Self-Study Programs

Dickson is responsible for developing and marketing the self-study programs offered by AMP. Self-study courses consist of cassette tapes and a workbook. Most of the courses are developed by outside contractors who work under her direction. Dickson relies on the director of membership marketing to assist her in marketing these courses.

Jesse Paige, Editor of Special Publications

Paige is primarily responsible for the publication and sale of any research monographs that are generated by the research department. In addition, he coordinates the publication of any special projects that may be prepared by any other AMP committees or departments. Paige also works with AMP's Publication Committee which sets policy on the types of publications that AMP should publish.

George Ackers, Manager of Personnel

Ackers works with all of the departments of AMP in hiring professional and clerical staff. The individual departments screen and interview prospective employees for professional positions, but Ackers is responsible for advertising open positions. Ackers plays a more active role in the hiring of clerical personnel by screening individuals before they are sent to the departments for interviews. In addition, Ackers coordinates the employee performance evaluation program and administers AMP's salary schedule and fringe benefit program.

Required:

1. Distinguish between line positions and staff positions in an organization by defining each. Include in your discussion the role, purpose, and importance of each.
2. Many times, conflicts will arise between line and staff managers in organizations. Discuss the characteristics of line and staff managers that may cause conflicts between the two.
3. For each of the four individuals identified by name in the text,
   a. Identify whether the individual's position is a line or staff position and explain why.
   b. Identify potential problems that could arise in each individual's position, either due to the type of position (i.e., line or staff) or to the location of the individual's position within the organization.

(CMA, adapted)

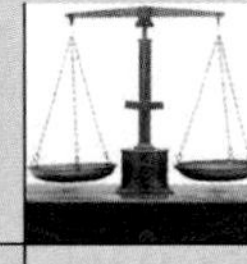

PROBLEM 1–7 Ethics in Business [LO4]

Consumers and attorneys general in more than 40 states accused a prominent nationwide chain of auto repair shops of misleading customers and selling them unnecessary parts and services, from brake jobs to front-end alignments. Lynn Sharpe Paine reported the situation as follows in "Managing for Organizational Integrity," *Harvard Business Review*, March-April, 1994:

> In the face of declining revenues, shrinking market share, and an increasingly competitive market . . . management attempted to spur performance of its auto centers. . . . The automotive service advisers were given product-specific sales quotas—sell so many springs, shock absorbers, alignments, or brake jobs per shift—and paid a commission based on sales. . . . [F]ailure to meet quotas could lead to a transfer or a reduction in work hours. Some employees spoke of the "pressure, pressure, pressure" to bring in sales.
>
> This pressure-cooker atmosphere created conditions under which employees felt that the only way to satisfy top management was by selling products and services to customers that they didn't really need.

Suppose all automotive repair businesses routinely followed the practice of attempting to sell customers unnecessary parts and services.

Required:

1. How would this behavior affect customers? How might customers attempt to protect themselves against this behavior?
2. How would this behavior probably affect profits and employment in the automotive service industry?

PROBLEM 1–8 Ethics in Business [LO4]

Adam Williams was recently hired as assistant controller of GroChem, Inc., which processes chemicals for use in fertilizers. Williams was selected for this position because of his past experience in chemical processing. During his first month on the job, Williams made a point of getting to know the people responsible for the plant operations and learning how things are done at GroChem.

During a conversation with the plant supervisor, Williams asked about the company procedures for handling toxic waste materials. The plant supervisor replied that he was not involved with the disposal of wastes and suggested that Williams might be wise to ignore this issue. This response strengthened Williams' determination to probe this area further to be sure that the company was not vulnerable to litigation.

Upon further investigation, Williams discovered evidence that GroChem was using a nearby residential landfill to dump toxic wastes. It appeared that some members of GroChem's management team were aware of this situation and may have been involved in arranging for this dumping; however, Williams was unable to determine whether his superior, the controller, was involved.

Uncertain how he should proceed, Williams began to consider his options by outlining the following three alternative courses of action:

- Seek the advice of his superior, the controller.
- Anonymously release the information to the local newspaper.
- Discuss the situation with an outside member of the board of directors with whom he is acquainted.

Required:

1. Discuss why Adam Williams has an ethical responsibility to take some action in the matter of GroChem, Inc., and the dumping of toxic wastes. Refer to the specific standards (competence, confidentiality, integrity, and/or objectivity) in the Standards of Ethical Conduct for Management Accountants to support your answer.
2. For each of the three alternative courses of action that Adam Williams has outlined, explain whether or not the action is appropriate according to the Standards of Ethical Conduct for Management Accountants.
3. Assume that Adam Williams sought the advice of his superior, the controller, and discovered that the controller was involved in the dumping of toxic wastes. Describe the steps that Williams should take to resolve this situation.

(CMA, adapted)

Group and Internet Exercises

GROUP EXERCISE 1–9 Ethics on the Job

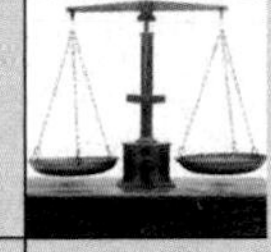

Ethical standards are very important in business, but they are not always followed. If you have ever held a job—even a summer job—describe the ethical climate in the organization where you worked. Did employees work a full day or did they arrive late and leave early? Did employees honestly report the hours they worked? Did employees use their employer's resources for their own purposes? Did managers set a good example? Did the organization have a code of ethics and were employees made aware of its existence? If the ethical climate in the organization you worked for was poor, what problems, if any, did it create?

INTERNET EXERCISE 1–10 Internet Exercise

As you know, the World Wide Web is a medium that is constantly evolving. Sites come and go, and change without notice. To enable periodic update of site addresses, this problem has been posted to the textbook website (www.mhhe.com/garrison10e). After accessing the site, enter the Student Center and select this chapter. Select and complete the Internet Exercise.

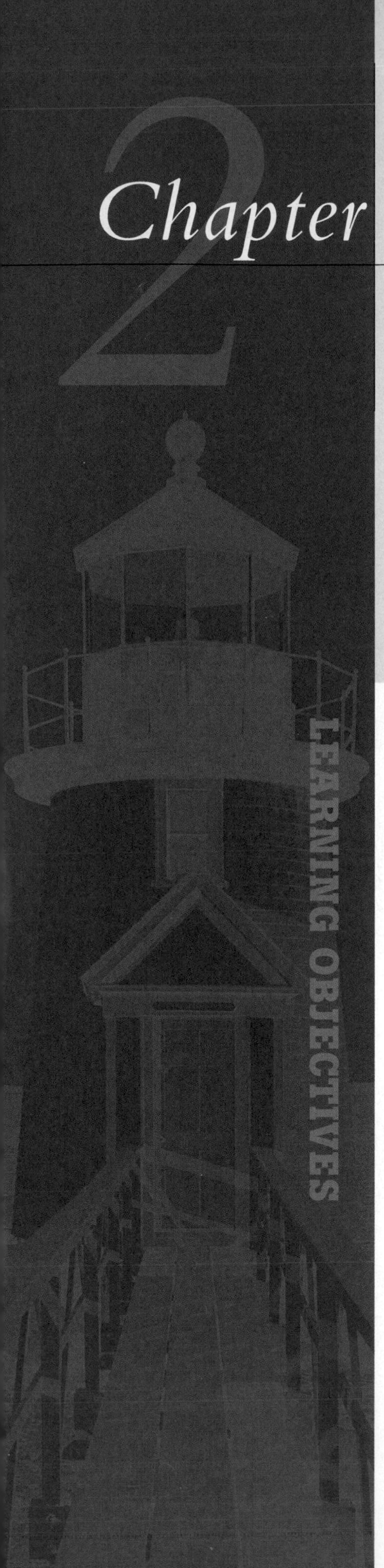

Chapter Two

Cost Terms, Concepts, and Classifications

After studying Chapter 2, you should be able to:

1. Identify and give examples of each of the three basic manufacturing cost categories.
2. Distinguish between product costs and period costs and give examples of each.
3. Prepare an income statement including calculation of the cost of goods sold.
4. Prepare a schedule of cost of goods manufactured.
5. Understand the differences between variable costs and fixed costs.
6. Understand the differences between direct and indirect costs.
7. Define and give examples of cost classifications used in making decisions: differential costs, opportunity costs, and sunk costs.
8. (Appendix 2A) Properly account for labor costs associated with idle time, overtime, and fringe benefits.
9. (Appendix 2B) Identify the four types of quality costs and explain how they interact.
10. (Appendix 2B) Prepare and interpret a quality cost report.

BUSINESS FOCUS

Costs Add Up

Understanding costs and how they behave is critical in business. Labor Ready is a company based in Tacoma, Washington, that was started in 1989 with an investment of $50,000. The company fills temporary manual labor jobs throughout the United States, Canada, and the UK—issuing over 6 million paychecks each year to more than half a million laborers. For example, the food vendors at the new Seattle Mariners' Safeco Field hire Labor Ready workers to serve soft drinks and food at baseball games. Employers are charged about $11 per hour for this service. Since Labor Ready pays its workers only about $6.50 per hour and offers no fringe benefits and has no national competitors, this business would appear to be a gold mine generating about $4.50 per hour in profit. However, the company must maintain 687 hiring offices, each employing a permanent staff of four to five persons. Those costs, together with payroll taxes, workmen's compensation insurance, and other administrative costs, result in a margin of only about 5%, or a little over 50¢ per hour. Costs add up—make sure you learn what costs are commonly encountered in practice.

Source: Catie Golding, "Short-Term Work, Long-Term Profits," *Washington CEO*, January 2000, pp. 10–12.

As explained in Chapter 1, the work of management focuses on (1) planning, which includes setting objectives and outlining how to attain these objectives; and (2) control, which includes the steps to take to ensure that objectives are realized. To carry out these planning and control responsibilities, managers need *information* about the organization. From an accounting point of view, this information often relates to the *costs* of the organization.

In managerial accounting, the term *cost* is used in many different ways. The reason is that there are many types of costs, and these costs are classified differently according to the immediate needs of management. For example, managers may want cost data to prepare external financial reports, to prepare planning budgets, or to make decisions. Each different use of cost data demands a different classification and definition of costs. For example, the preparation of external financial reports requires the use of historical cost data, whereas decision making may require predictions about future costs.

In this chapter, we discuss many of the possible uses of cost data and how costs are defined and classified for each use. Our first task is to explain how costs are classified for the purpose of preparing external financial reports—particularly in manufacturing companies. To set the stage for this discussion, we begin the chapter by defining some terms commonly used in manufacturing.

General Cost Classifications

Costs are associated with all types of organizations—business, nonbusiness, manufacturing, retail, and service. Generally, the kinds of costs that are incurred and the way in which these costs are classified depends on the type of organization involved. Managerial accounting is as applicable to one type of organization as to another. For this reason, we will consider in our discussion the cost characteristics of a variety of organizations—manufacturing, merchandising, and service.

Our initial focus in this chapter is on manufacturing companies, since their basic activities include most of the activities found in other types of business organizations. Manufacturing companies such as Texas Instruments, Ford, and Kodak are involved in acquiring raw materials, producing finished goods, marketing, distributing, billing, and almost every other business activity. Therefore, an understanding of costs in a manufacturing company can be very helpful in understanding costs in other types of organizations.

Concept 2–1

In this chapter, we develop cost concepts that apply to diverse organizations. For example, these cost concepts apply to fast-food outlets such as Kentucky Fried Chicken, Pizza Hut, and Taco Bell; movie studios such as Disney, Paramount, and United Artists; consulting firms such as Andersen Consulting and McKinsey; and your local hospital. The exact terms used in these industries may not be the same as those used in manufacturing, but the same basic concepts apply. With some slight modifications, these basic concepts also apply to merchandising companies such as Wal-Mart, The Gap, 7-Eleven, Nordstrom, and Tower Records that resell finished goods acquired from manufacturers and other sources. With that in mind, let us begin our discussion of manufacturing costs.

Manufacturing Costs

LEARNING OBJECTIVE 1
Identify and give examples of each of the three basic manufacturing cost categories.

Most manufacturing companies divide manufacturing costs into three broad categories: direct materials, direct labor, and manufacturing overhead. A discussion of each of these categories follows.

Direct Materials The materials that go into the final product are called **raw materials.** This term is somewhat misleading, since it seems to imply unprocessed natural resources like wood pulp or iron ore. Actually, raw materials refer to any materials that are used in the final product; and the finished product of one company can become the raw materials of another company. For example, the plastics produced by Du Pont are a raw material used by Compaq Computer in its personal computers. One study of 37 manufacturing industries found that materials costs averaged about 55% of sales revenues.[1]

Direct materials are those materials that become an integral part of the finished product and that can be physically and conveniently traced to it. This would include, for example, the seats Boeing purchases from subcontractors to install in its commercial aircraft. Also included is the tiny electric motor Panasonic uses in its CD players to make the CD spin.

Sometimes it isn't worth the effort to trace the costs of relatively insignificant materials to the end products. Such minor items would include the solder used to make electrical connections in a Sony TV or the glue used to assemble an Ethan Allen chair. Materials such as solder and glue are called **indirect materials** and are included as part of manufacturing overhead, which is discussed later in this section.

Direct Labor The term **direct labor** is reserved for those labor costs that can be easily (i.e., physically and conveniently) traced to individual units of product. Direct labor is sometimes called *touch labor,* since direct labor workers typically touch the product while it is being made. The labor costs of assembly-line workers, for example, would be direct labor costs, as would the labor costs of carpenters, bricklayers, and machine operators.

Labor costs that cannot be physically traced to the creation of products, or that can be traced only at great cost and inconvenience, are termed **indirect labor** and treated as part of manufacturing overhead, along with indirect materials. Indirect labor includes the labor costs of janitors, supervisors, materials handlers, and night security guards. Although the efforts of these workers are essential to production, it would be either impractical or impossible to accurately trace their costs to specific units of product. Hence, such labor costs are treated as indirect labor.

In some industries, major shifts are taking place in the structure of labor costs. Sophisticated automated equipment, run and maintained by skilled indirect workers, is increasingly replacing direct labor. Indeed, in the study cited above of 37 manufacturing industries, direct labor averaged only about 10% of sales revenues. In a few companies, direct labor has become such a minor element of cost that it has disappeared altogether as a separate cost category. More is said in later chapters about this trend and about the impact it is having on cost systems. However, the vast majority of manufacturing and service companies throughout the world continue to recognize direct labor as a separate cost category.

Manufacturing Overhead **Manufacturing overhead,** the third element of manufacturing cost, includes all costs of manufacturing except direct materials and direct labor. Manufacturing overhead includes items such as indirect materials; indirect labor; maintenance and repairs on production equipment; and heat and light, property taxes, depreciation, and insurance on manufacturing facilities. A company also incurs costs for heat and light, property taxes, insurance, depreciation, and so forth, associated with its selling and administrative functions, but these costs are not included as part of manufacturing overhead. Only those costs associated with *operating the factory* are included in the manufacturing overhead category. Several studies have found that manufacturing overhead averages about 16% of sales revenues.[2]

Various names are used for manufacturing overhead, such as *indirect manufacturing cost, factory overhead,* and *factory burden.* All of these terms are synonymous with *manufacturing overhead.*

[1] Germain Boer and Debra Jeter, "What's New About Modern Manufacturing? Empirical Evidence on Manufacturing Cost Changes," *Journal of Management Accounting Research*, Fall 1993, pp. 61–83.

[2] J. Miller, A. DeMeyer, and J. Nakane, *Benchmarking Global Manufacturing* (Homewood, IL: Richard D. Irwin), 1992, Chapter 2. The Boer and Jeter article cited above contains a similar finding concerning the magnitude of manufacturing overhead.

Manufacturing overhead combined with direct labor is called **conversion cost.** This term stems from the fact that direct labor costs and overhead costs are incurred to convert materials into finished products. Direct labor combined with direct materials is called **prime cost.**

Nonmanufacturing Costs

Generally, nonmanufacturing costs are subclassified into two categories:

1. Marketing or selling costs.
2. Administrative costs.

Marketing or selling costs include all costs necessary to secure customer orders and get the finished product into the hands of the customer. These costs are often called *order-getting and order-filling costs.* Examples of marketing costs include advertising, shipping, sales travel, sales commissions, sales salaries, and costs of finished goods warehouses.

Administrative costs include all executive, organizational, and clerical costs associated with the *general management* of an organization rather than with manufacturing, marketing, or selling. Examples of administrative costs include executive compensation, general accounting, secretarial, public relations, and similar costs involved in the overall, general administration of the organization *as a whole*.

In Business

Why Is Tuition So High?

Do you ever wonder why tuition costs are so high? Administrative costs can be crushing. *Forbes* magazine reports that an average of 2.5 administrators are employed for each faculty member in public colleges and 1.9 in private colleges. The worst case is Mississippi, which has four administrators for every teacher. The best case found in public colleges is Colorado, which "manages to get by with just under two administrators per teacher." Much of the administrative work results from "the mandates that accompany federal money, such as affirmative action, and the personnel needed to monitor compliance with those mandates."

Source: Peter Brimelow, "The Paper Chase," *Forbes*, May 17, 1999, pp. 78–79.

Product Costs versus Period Costs

LEARNING OBJECTIVE 2
Distinguish between product costs and period costs and give examples of each.

In addition to the distinction between manufacturing and nonmanufacturing costs, there are other ways to look at costs. For instance, they can also be classified as either *product costs* or *period costs.* To understand the difference between product costs and period costs, we must first refresh our understanding of the matching principle from financial accounting.

Generally, costs are recognized as expenses on the income statement in the period that benefits from the cost. For example, if a company pays for liability insurance in advance for two years, the entire amount is not considered an expense of the year in which the payment is made. Instead, one-half of the cost would be recognized as an expense each year. The reason is that both years—not just the first year—benefit from the insurance payment. The unexpensed portion of the insurance payment is carried on the balance sheet as an asset called prepaid insurance. You should be familiar with this type of *accrual* from your financial accounting coursework.

The *matching principle* is based on the accrual concept and states that *costs incurred to generate a particular revenue should be recognized as expenses in the same period that the revenue is recognized.* This means that if a cost is incurred to acquire or make something that will eventually be sold, then the cost should be recognized as an expense only when the sale takes place—that is, when the benefit occurs. Such costs are called *product costs.*

Dissecting the Value Chain

In Business

United Colors of Benetton, an Italian apparel company headquartered in Ponzano, is unusual in that it is involved in all activities in the "value chain" from clothing design through manufacturing, distribution, and ultimate sale to customers in Benetton retail outlets. Most companies are involved in only one or two of these activities. Looking at this company allows us to see how costs are distributed across the entire value chain. A recent income statement from the company contained the following data:

	Billions of Italian Lire	Percent of Net Sales
Net sales	2,768	100.0%
Cost of sales	1,721	62.2
Selling and general and administrative expenses:		
Payroll and related cost	166	6.0
Distribution and transport	57	2.1
Sales commissions	115	4.2
Advertising and promotion	120	4.3
Depreciation and amortization	42	1.5
Other expenses	275	9.9
Total selling and general and administrative expenses	775	28.0%

Even though this company spends large sums on advertising and runs its own shops, the cost of sales is still quite high in relation to the net sales—62% of net sales. And despite the company's lavish advertising campaigns, advertising and promotion costs amounted to only a little over 4% of net sales. (Note: One U.S. dollar was worth about 1,600 Italian lire at the time of this financial report.)

Product Costs

For financial accounting purposes, **product costs** include all the costs that are involved in acquiring or making a product. In the case of manufactured goods, these costs consist of direct materials, direct labor, and manufacturing overhead. Product costs are viewed as "attaching" to units of product as the goods are purchased or manufactured, and they remain attached as the goods go into inventory awaiting sale. So initially, product costs are assigned to an inventory account on the balance sheet. When the goods are sold, the costs are released from inventory as expenses (typically called cost of goods sold) and matched against sales revenue. Since product costs are initially assigned to inventories, they are also known as **inventoriable costs.**

We want to emphasize that product costs are not necessarily treated as expenses in the period in which they are incurred. Rather, as explained above, they are treated as expenses in the period in which the related products *are sold.* This means that a product cost such as direct materials or direct labor might be incurred during one period but not treated as an expense until a following period when the completed product is sold.

Period Costs

Period costs are all the costs that are not included in product costs. These costs are expensed on the income statement in the period in which they are incurred, using the usual rules of accrual accounting you have already learned in financial accounting. Period costs are not included as part of the cost of either purchased or manufactured goods. Sales commissions and office rent are good examples of period costs. Neither commissions nor office rent are included as part of the cost of purchased or manufactured goods. Rather,

Exhibit 2–1 Summary of Cost Terms

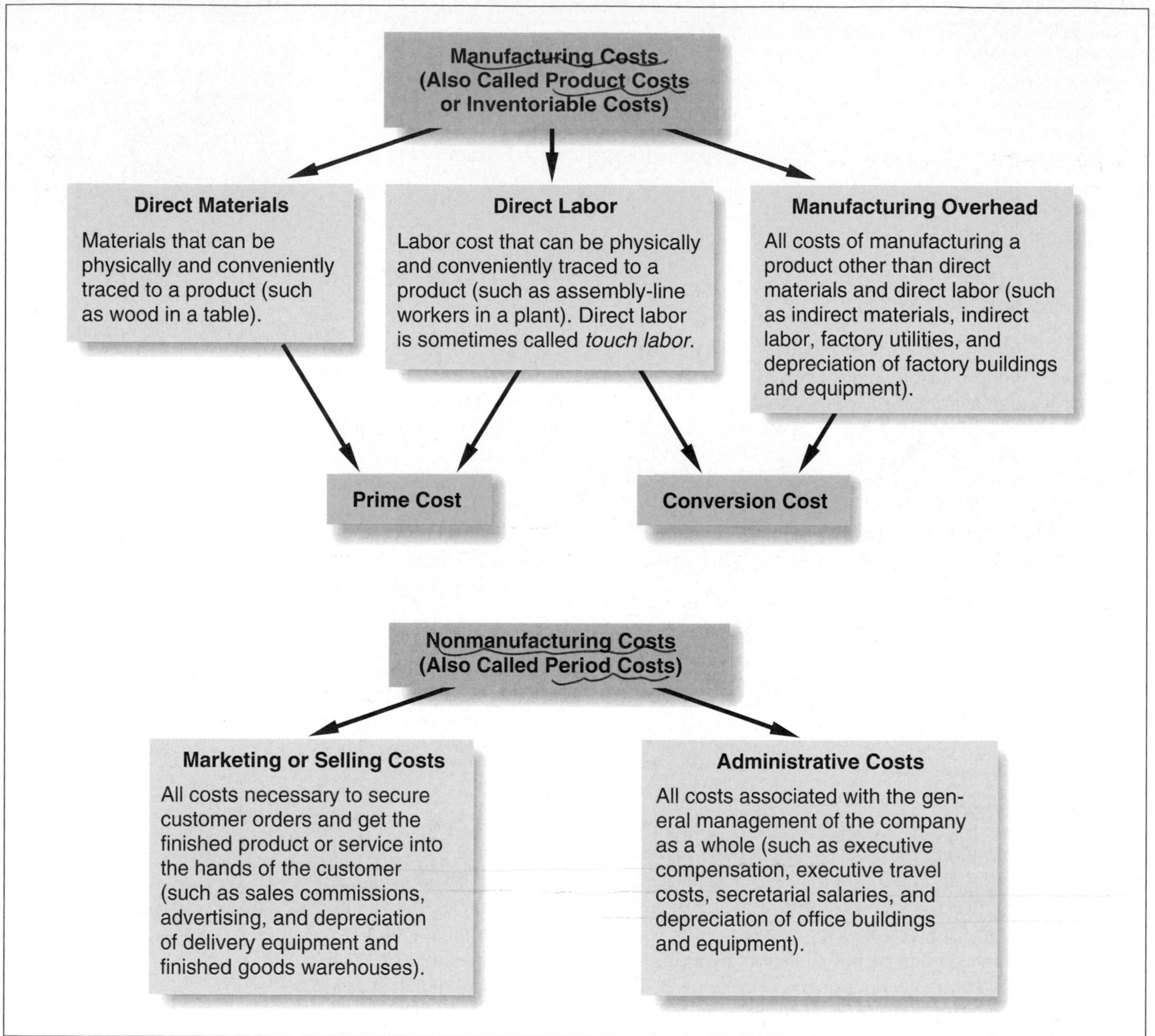

both items are treated as expenses on the income statement in the period in which they are incurred. Thus, they are said to be period costs.

As suggested above, *all selling and administrative expenses are considered to be period costs.* Therefore, advertising, executive salaries, sales commissions, public relations, and other nonmanufacturing costs discussed earlier would all be period costs. They will appear on the income statement as expenses in the period in which they are incurred.

Exhibit 2–1 contains a summary of the cost terms that we have introduced so far.

Cost Classifications on Financial Statements

In your prior accounting training, you learned that firms prepare periodic financial reports for creditors, stockholders, and others to show the financial condition of the firm and the firm's earnings performance over some specified interval. The reports you studied were probably those of merchandising companies, such as retail stores, which simply purchase goods from suppliers for resale to customers.

Concept 2–2

The financial statements prepared by a *manufacturing* company are more complex than the statements prepared by a merchandising company. Manufacturing companies are more complex organizations than merchandising companies because the manufacturing company must produce its goods as well as market them. The production process gives rise to many costs that do not exist in a merchandising company, and somehow these costs must be accounted for on the manufacturing company's financial statements. In this section, we focus our attention on how this accounting is carried out in the balance sheet and income statement.

The Balance Sheet

The balance sheet, or statement of financial position, of a manufacturing company is similar to that of a merchandising company. However, the inventory accounts differ between the two types of companies. A merchandising company has only one class of inventory—goods purchased from suppliers that are awaiting resale to customers. In contrast, manufacturing companies have three classes of inventories—*raw materials*, *work in process*, and *finished goods*. **Raw materials** are the materials that are used to make a product. **Work in process** consists of units of product that are only partially complete and will require further work before they are ready for sale to a customer. **Finished goods** consist of units of product that have been completed but have not yet been sold to customers. The overall inventory figure is usually broken down into these three classes of inventories in a footnote to the financial statements.

We will use two companies—Graham Manufacturing and Reston Bookstore—to illustrate the concepts discussed in this section. Graham Manufacturing is located in Portsmouth, New Hampshire, and makes precision brass fittings for yachts. Reston Bookstore is a small bookstore in Reston, Virginia, specializing in books about the Civil War.

The footnotes to Graham Manufacturing's Annual Report reveal the following information concerning its inventories:

Graham Manufacturing Corporation
Inventory Accounts

	Beginning Balance	Ending Balance
Raw Materials	$ 60,000	$ 50,000
Work in Process	90,000	60,000
Finished Goods	125,000	175,000
Total inventory accounts	$275,000	$285,000

Graham Manufacturing's raw materials inventory consists largely of brass rods and brass blocks. The work in process inventory consists of partially completed brass fittings. The finished goods inventory consists of brass fittings that are ready to be sold to customers.

In contrast, the inventory account at Reston Bookstore consists entirely of the costs of books the company has purchased from publishers for resale to the public. In merchandising companies like Reston, these inventories may be called *merchandise inventory.* The beginning and ending balances in this account appear as follows:

Reston Bookstore
Inventory Account

	Beginning Balance	Ending Balance
Merchandise Inventory	$100,000	$150,000

The Income Statement

LEARNING OBJECTIVE 3
Prepare an income statement including calculation of the cost of goods sold.

Exhibit 2–2 compares the income statements of Reston Bookstore and Graham Manufacturing. For purposes of illustration, these statements contain more detail about cost of goods sold than you will generally find in published financial statements.

At first glance, the income statements of merchandising and manufacturing firms like Reston Bookstore and Graham Manufacturing are very similar. The only apparent difference is in the labels of some of the entries in the computation of the cost of goods sold. In the exhibit, the computation of cost of goods sold relies on the following basic equation for inventory accounts:

Basic Equation for Inventory Accounts

$$\text{Beginning balance} + \text{Additions to inventory} = \text{Ending balance} + \text{Withdrawals from inventory}$$

The logic underlying this equation, which applies to any inventory account, is illustrated in Exhibit 2–3. At the beginning of the period, the inventory contains some beginning balance. During the period, additions are made to the inventory through purchases or other means. The sum of the beginning balance and the additions to the account is the total amount of inventory available. During the period, withdrawals are made from inventory. Whatever is left at the end of the period after these withdrawals is the ending balance.

Exhibit 2–2 Comparative Income Statements: Merchandising and Manufacturing Companies

MERCHANDISING COMPANY
Reston Bookstore

The cost of merchandise inventory purchased from outside suppliers during the period. → (Add: Purchases)

Sales		$1,000,000
Cost of goods sold:		
Beginning merchandise inventory	$100,000	
Add: Purchases	650,000	
Goods available for sale	750,000	
Deduct: Ending merchandise inventory	150,000	600,000
Gross margin		400,000
Less operating expenses:		
Selling expense	100,000	
Administrative expense	200,000	300,000
Net operating income		$ 100,000

MANUFACTURING COMPANY
Graham Manufacturing

The manufacturing costs associated with the goods that were finished during the period. (See Exhibit 2–4 for details.) → (Add: Cost of goods manufactured)

Sales		$1,500,000
Cost of goods sold:		
Beginning finished goods inventory	$125,000	
Add: Cost of goods manufactured	850,000	
Goods available for sale	975,000	
Deduct: Ending finished goods inventory	175,000	800,000
Gross margin		700,000
Less operating expenses:		
Selling expense	250,000	
Administrative expense	300,000	550,000
Net operating income		$ 150,000

ADD AS NEEDED ⇒

These concepts are applied to determine the cost of goods sold for a merchandising company like Reston Bookstore as follows:

Cost of Goods Sold in a Merchandising Company

$$\begin{matrix}\text{Beginning} \\ \text{merchandise} \\ \text{inventory}\end{matrix} + \text{Purchases} = \begin{matrix}\text{Ending} \\ \text{merchandise} \\ \text{inventory}\end{matrix} + \begin{matrix}\text{Cost of} \\ \text{goods sold}\end{matrix}$$

or

$$\begin{matrix}\text{Cost of} \\ \text{goods sold}\end{matrix} = \begin{matrix}\text{Beginning} \\ \text{merchandise} \\ \text{inventory}\end{matrix} + \text{Purchases} - \begin{matrix}\text{Ending} \\ \text{merchandise} \\ \text{inventory}\end{matrix}$$

To determine the cost of goods sold in a merchandising company like Reston Bookstore, we only need to know the beginning and ending balances in the Merchandise Inventory account and the purchases. Total purchases can be easily determined in a merchandising company by simply adding together all purchases from suppliers.

The cost of goods sold for a manufacturing company like Graham Manufacturing is determined as follows:

Cost of Goods Sold in a Manufacturing Company

$$\begin{matrix}\text{Beginning finished} \\ \text{goods inventory}\end{matrix} + \begin{matrix}\text{Cost of goods} \\ \text{manufactured}\end{matrix} = \begin{matrix}\text{Ending finished} \\ \text{goods inventory}\end{matrix} + \begin{matrix}\text{Cost of} \\ \text{goods sold}\end{matrix}$$

Exhibit 2–3 Inventory Flows

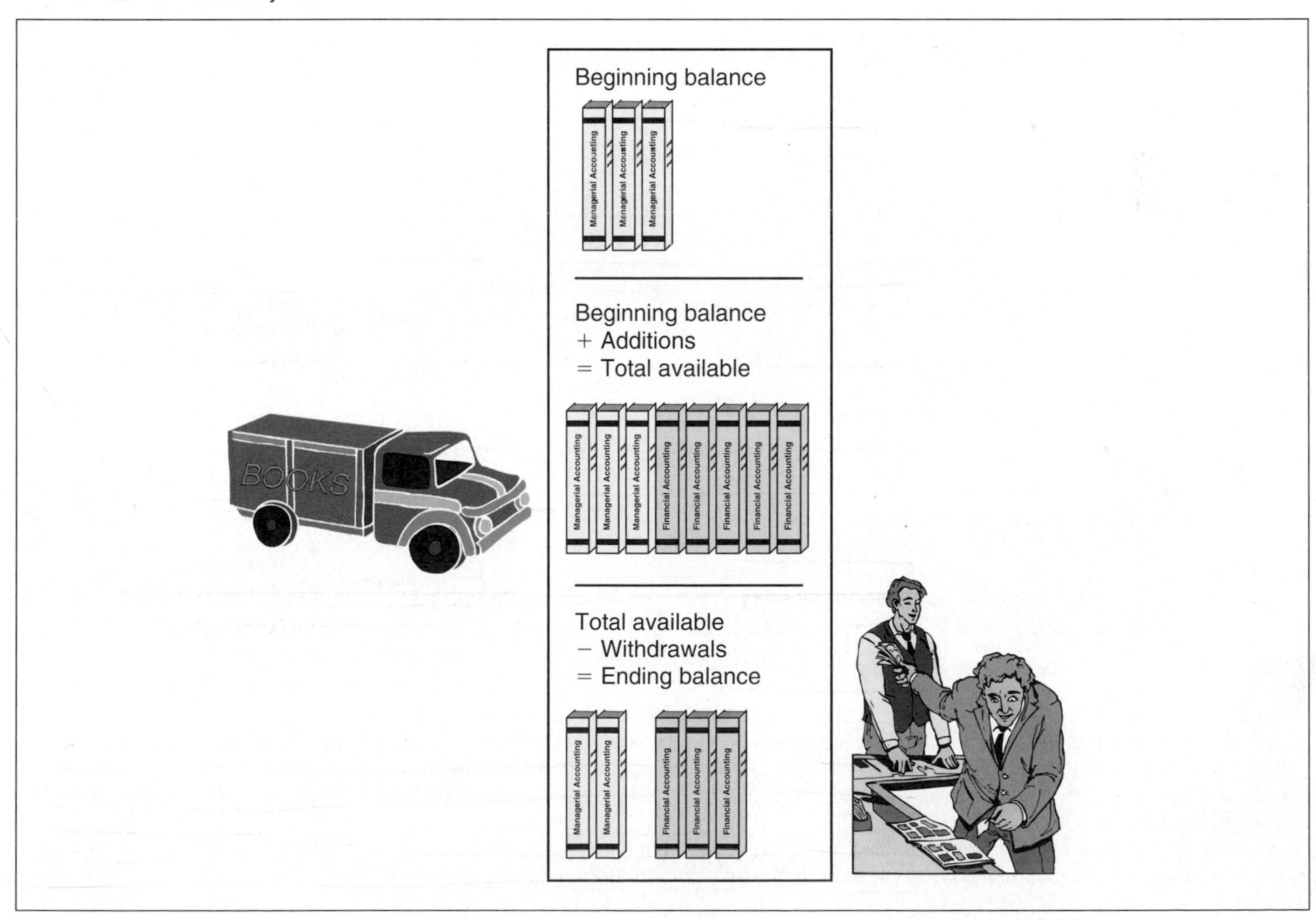

or

$$\text{Cost of goods sold} = \text{Beginning finished goods inventory} + \text{Cost of goods manufactured} - \text{Ending finished goods inventory}$$

To determine the cost of goods sold in a manufacturing company like Graham Manufacturing, we need to know the *cost of goods manufactured* and the beginning and ending balances in the Finished Goods inventory account. The **cost of goods manufactured** consists of the manufacturing costs associated with goods that were *finished* during the period. The cost of goods manufactured figure for Graham Manufacturing is derived in Exhibit 2–4, which contains a *schedule of cost of goods manufactured.*

Schedule of Cost of Goods Manufactured

LEARNING OBJECTIVE 4
Prepare a schedule of cost of goods manufactured.

At first glance, the **schedule of cost of goods manufactured** in Exhibit 2–4 appears complex and perhaps even intimidating. However, it is all quite logical. The schedule of cost of goods manufactured contains the three elements of product costs that we discussed earlier—direct materials, direct labor, and manufacturing overhead. The direct materials cost

Exhibit 2–4 Schedule of Cost of Goods Manufactured

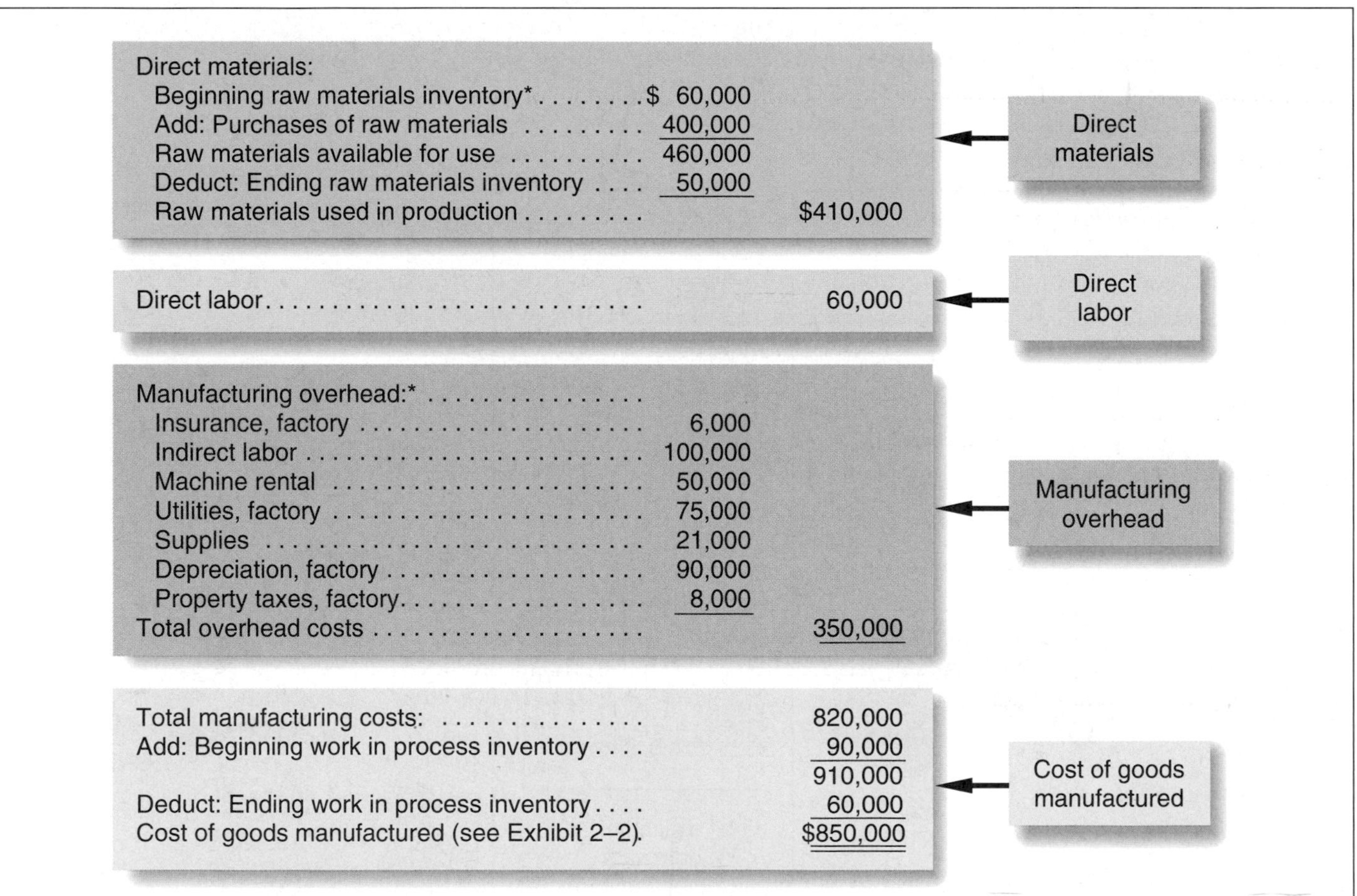

Direct materials:			
Beginning raw materials inventory*	$ 60,000		
Add: Purchases of raw materials	400,000		
Raw materials available for use	460,000		
Deduct: Ending raw materials inventory	50,000		
Raw materials used in production		$410,000	Direct materials
Direct labor		60,000	Direct labor
Manufacturing overhead:*			
Insurance, factory	6,000		
Indirect labor	100,000		
Machine rental	50,000		
Utilities, factory	75,000		Manufacturing overhead
Supplies	21,000		
Depreciation, factory	90,000		
Property taxes, factory	8,000		
Total overhead costs		350,000	
Total manufacturing costs		820,000	
Add: Beginning work in process inventory		90,000	
		910,000	Cost of goods manufactured
Deduct: Ending work in process inventory		60,000	
Cost of goods manufactured (see Exhibit 2–2)		$850,000	

*We assume in this example that the Raw Materials inventory account contains only direct materials and that indirect materials are carried in a separate Supplies account. Using a Supplies account for indirect materials is a common practice among companies. In Chapter 3, we discuss the procedure to be followed if *both* direct and indirect materials are carried in a single account.

†In Chapter 3 we will see that the manufacturing overhead section of the schedule of cost of goods manufactured can be considerably simplified by using what is called a *predetermined manufacturing overhead rate.*

is not simply the cost of materials purchased during the period—rather it is the cost of materials *used* during the period. The purchases of raw materials are added to the beginning balance to determine the cost of the materials available for use. The ending materials inventory is deducted from this amount to arrive at the cost of the materials used in production. The sum of the three cost elements—materials, direct labor, and manufacturing overhead—is the total manufacturing cost. This is *not* the same thing, however, as the cost of goods manufactured for the period. The subtle distinction between the total manufacturing cost and the cost of goods manufactured is very easy to miss. Some of the materials, direct labor, and manufacturing overhead costs incurred during the period relate to goods that are not yet completed. As stated above, the *cost of goods manufactured* consists of the manufacturing costs associated with the goods that were *finished* during the period. Consequently, adjustments need to be made to the total manufacturing cost of the period for the partially completed goods that were in process at the beginning and at the end of the period. The costs that relate to goods that are not yet completed are shown in the work in process inventory figures at the bottom of the schedule. Note that the beginning work in process inventory must be added to the manufacturing costs of the period, and the ending work in process inventory must be deducted, to arrive at the cost of goods manufactured.

Product Costs—A Closer Look

Earlier in the chapter, we defined product costs as those costs that are involved in either the purchase or the manufacture of goods. For manufactured goods, these costs consist of direct materials, direct labor, and manufacturing overhead. It will be helpful at this point to look briefly at the flow of costs in a manufacturing company. This will help us understand how product costs move through the various accounts and how they affect the balance sheet and the income statement.

Exhibit 2–5 illustrates the flow of costs in a manufacturing company. Raw materials purchases are recorded in the Raw Materials inventory account. When raw materials are used in production, their costs are transferred to the Work in Process inventory account as direct materials. Notice that direct labor cost and manufacturing overhead cost are added directly to Work in Process. Work in Process can be viewed most simply as an assembly line where workers are stationed and where products slowly take shape as they move from one end of the assembly line to the other. The direct materials, direct labor, and manufacturing overhead costs added to Work in Process in Exhibit 2–5 are the costs needed to complete these products as they move along this assembly line.

Notice from the exhibit that as goods are completed, their costs are transferred from Work in Process to Finished Goods. Here the goods await sale to customers. As goods are sold, their costs are transferred from Finished Goods to Cost of Goods Sold. At this point the various material, labor, and overhead costs required to make the product are finally treated as expenses. Until that point, these costs are in inventory accounts on the balance sheet.

Inventoriable Costs

As stated earlier, product costs are often called inventoriable costs. The reason is that these costs go directly into inventory accounts as they are incurred (first into Work in Process and then into Finished Goods), rather than going into expense accounts. Thus, they are termed *inventoriable costs. This is a key concept since such costs can end up on the balance sheet as assets if goods are only partially completed or are unsold at the end of a period.* To illustrate this point, refer again to Exhibit 2–5. At the end of the period, the materials, labor, and overhead costs that are associated with the units in the Work in Process and Finished Goods inventory accounts will appear on the balance sheet as part of the company's assets. As explained earlier, these costs will not become expenses until later when the goods are completed and sold.

Exhibit 2–5 Cost Flows and Classifications in a Manufacturing Company

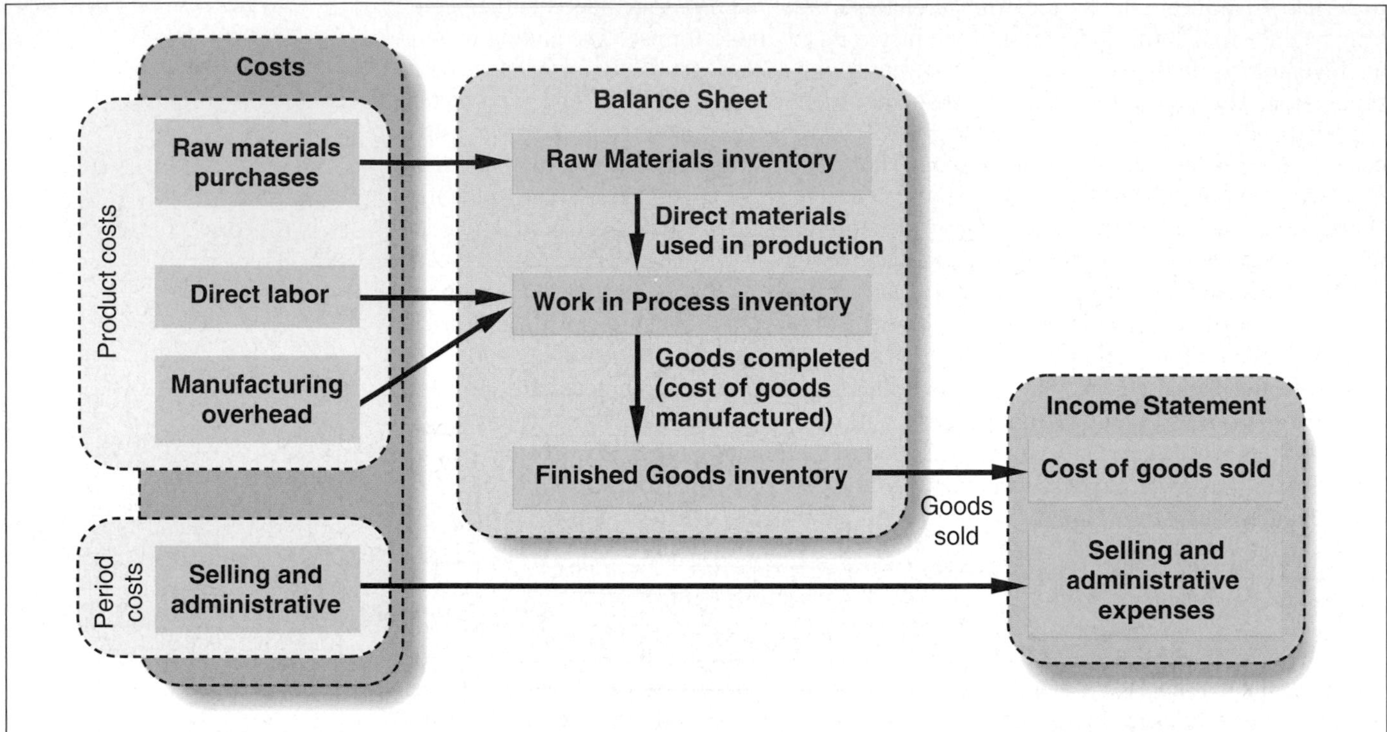

Selling and administrative expenses are not involved in the manufacture of a product. For this reason, they are not treated as product costs but rather as period costs that go directly into expense accounts as they are incurred, as shown in Exhibit 2–5.

An Example of Cost Flows

To provide an example of cost flows in a manufacturing company, assume that a company's annual insurance cost is $2,000. Three-fourths of this amount ($1,500) applies to factory operations, and one-fourth ($500) applies to selling and administrative activities. Therefore, $1,500 of the $2,000 insurance cost would be a product (inventoriable) cost and would be added to the cost of the goods produced during the year. This concept is illustrated in Exhibit 2–6, where $1,500 of insurance cost is added into Work in Process. As shown in the exhibit, this portion of the year's insurance cost will not become an expense until the goods that are produced during the year are sold—which may not happen until the following year or even later. Until the goods are sold, the $1,500 will remain as part of the asset, inventory (either as part of Work in Process or as part of Finished Goods), along with the other costs of producing the goods.

By contrast, the $500 of insurance cost that applies to the company's selling and administrative activities will be expensed immediately.

Thus far, we have been mainly concerned with classifications of manufacturing costs for the purpose of determining inventory valuations on the balance sheet and cost of goods sold on the income statement of external financial reports. However, costs are used for many other purposes, and each purpose requires a different classification of costs. We will consider several different purposes for cost classifications in the remaining sections of this chapter. These purposes and the corresponding cost classifications are summarized in Exhibit 2–7. To help keep the big picture in mind, we suggest that you refer back to this exhibit frequently as you progress through the rest of this chapter.

Exhibit 2–6 An Example of Cost Flows in a Manufacturing Company

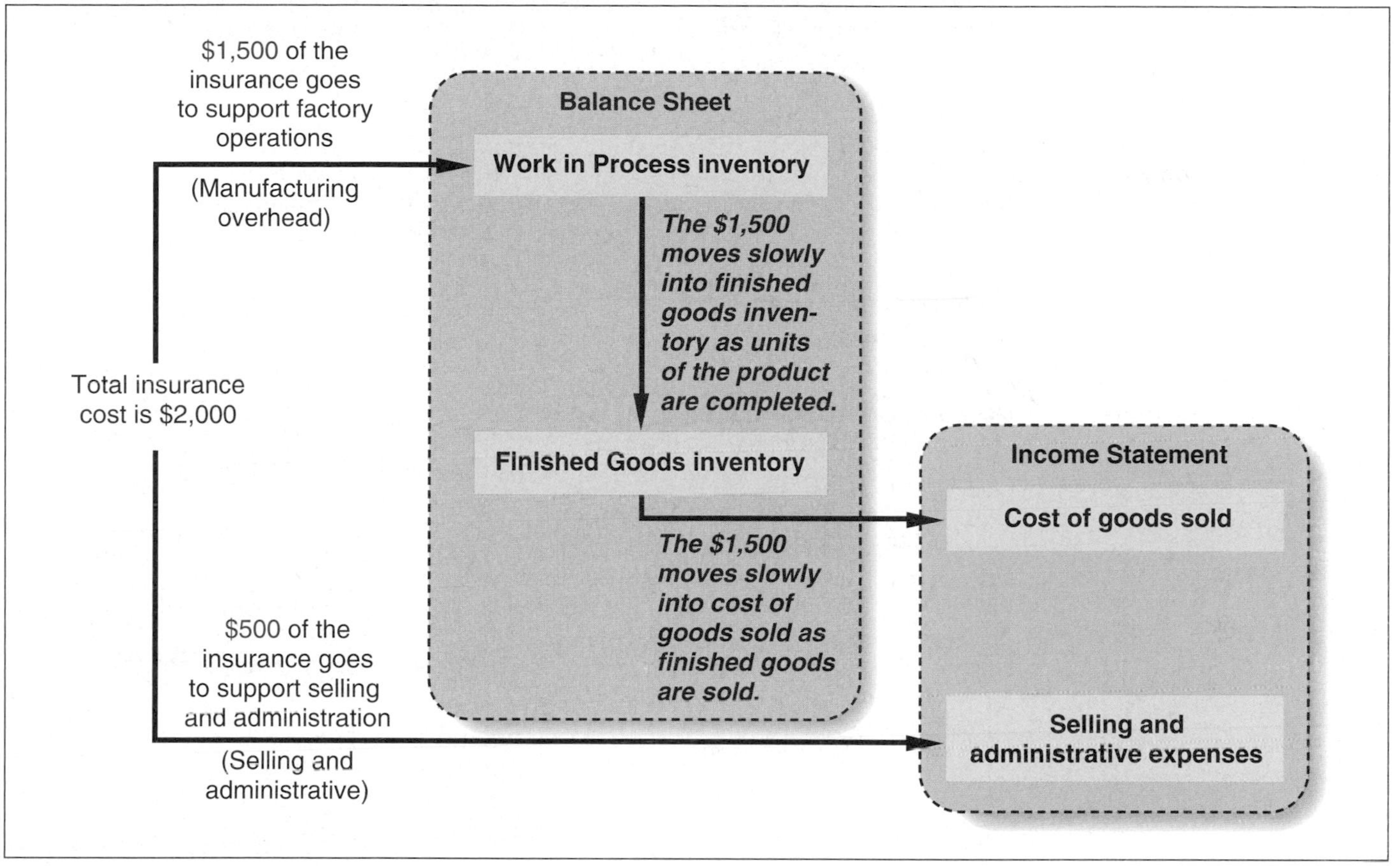

Product or Period Expense—Who Cares?

In Business

Whether a cost is considered a product or period cost can have an important impact on a company's financial statements. Consider the following excerpts from a conversation recorded on the Institute of Management Accountant's Ethics Hot-Line:

Caller: My problem basically is that my boss, the division general manager, wants me to put costs into inventory that I know should be expensed. . . .

Counselor: Have you expressed your doubts to your boss?

Caller: Yes, but he is basically a salesman and claims he knows nothing about GAAP. He just wants the "numbers" to back up the good news he keeps telling corporate [headquarters], which is what corporate demands. Also, he asks if I am ready to make the entries that I think are improper. It seems he wants to make it look like my idea all along. Our company had legal problems a few years ago with some government contracts, and it was the lower level people who were "hung out to dry" rather than the higher-ups who were really at fault.

Counselor: . . . What does he say when you tell him these matters need resolution?

Caller: He just says we need a meeting, but the meetings never solve anything. . . .

Counselor: Does your company have an ethics hot-line?

Caller: Yes, but my boss would view use of the hot-line as snitching or even whistle-blowing. . . .

Counselor: . . . If you might face reprisals for using the hot-line, perhaps you should evaluate whether or not you really want to work for a company whose ethical climate is one you are uncomfortable in.

Caller: I have already asked . . . for a transfer back to the corporate office.

Source: Curtis C. Verschoor, "Using a Hot-Line Isn't Whistle-Blowing," *Strategic Finance*, April 1999, pp. 27–28. Reprinted with permission from the IMA, Montvale, NJ, USA www.imanet.org.

Exhibit 2–7
Summary of Cost Classifications

Purpose of Cost Classification	Cost Classifications

Preparing external financial statements	• Product costs (inventoriable)
	  • Direct materials
	  • Direct labor
	  • Manufacturing overhead
	• Period costs (expensed)
	  • Nonmanufacturing costs
	    • Marketing or selling costs
	    • Administrative costs

Predicting cost behavior in response to changes in activity	• Variable cost (proportional to activity) • Fixed cost (constant in total)
Assigning costs to cost objects such as departments or products	• Direct cost (can be easily traced) • Indirect cost (cannot be easily traced; must be allocated)
Making decisions	• Differential cost (differs between alternatives) • Sunk cost (past cost not affected by a decision) • Opportunity cost (forgone benefit)
Cost of quality (Appendix)	• Prevention costs • Appraisal costs • Internal failure costs • External failure costs

Cost Classifications for Predicting Cost Behavior

LEARNING OBJECTIVE 5
Understand the differences between variable costs and fixed costs.

Quite frequently, it is necessary to predict how a certain cost will behave in response to a change in activity. For example, a manager at AT&T may want to estimate the impact a 5% increase in long-distance calls would have on the company's total electric bill or on the total wages the company pays its long-distance operators. **Cost behavior** refers to how a cost will react or respond to changes in the level of business activity. As the activity level rises and falls, a particular cost may rise and fall as well—or it may remain constant. For planning purposes, a manager must be able to anticipate which of these will happen; and if a cost can be expected to change, the manager must know by how much it will change. To help make such distinctions, costs are often categorized as variable or fixed.

Variable Cost

A **variable cost** is a cost that varies, in total, in direct proportion to changes in the level of activity. The activity can be expressed in many ways, such as units produced, units sold, miles driven, beds occupied, lines of print, hours worked, and so forth. A good example of a variable cost is direct materials. The cost of direct materials used during a period will vary, in total, in direct proportion to the number of units that are produced. To illustrate this idea, consider the Saturn Division of GM. Each auto requires one battery. As the output of autos increases and decreases, the number of batteries used will increase and decrease proportionately. If auto production goes up 10%, then the number of batteries used will also go up 10%. The concept of a variable cost is shown in graphic form in Exhibit 2–8.

It is important to note that when we speak of a cost as being variable, we mean the *total* cost rises and falls as the activity level rises and falls. This idea is presented below, assuming that a Saturn's battery costs $24:

Exhibit 2–8 Variable and Fixed Cost Behavior

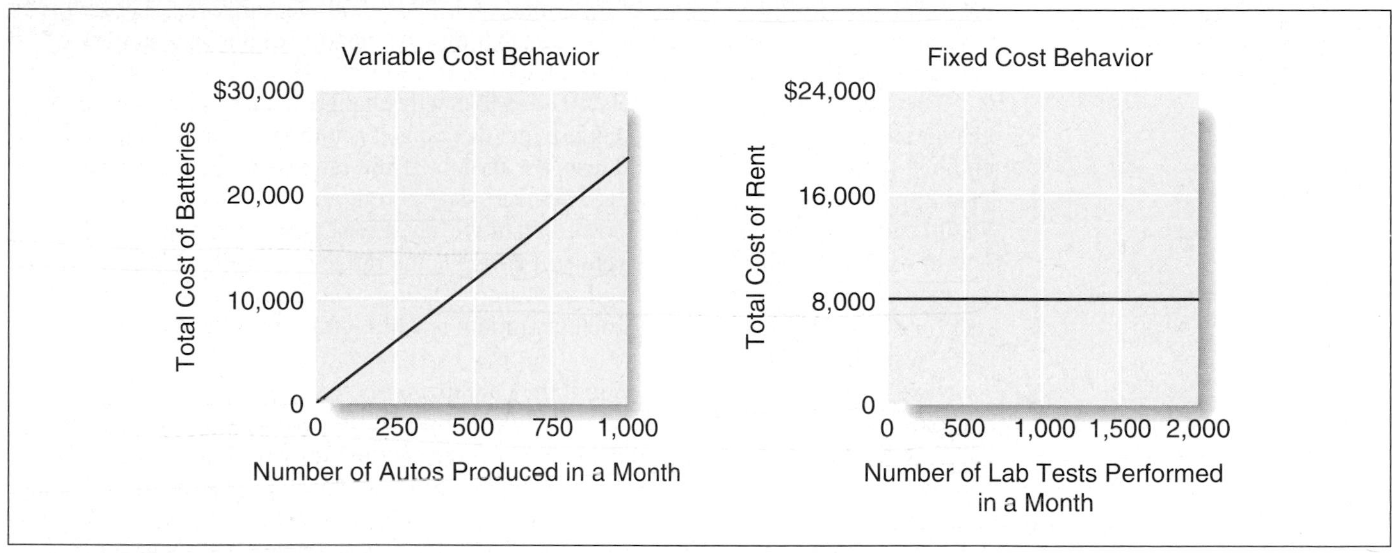

Number of Autos Produced	Cost per Battery	Total Variable Cost—Batteries
1	$24	$ 24
500	24	12,000
1,000	24	24,000

One interesting aspect of variable cost behavior is that a variable cost is constant if expressed on a *per unit* basis. Observe from the tabulation above that the per unit cost of batteries remains constant at $24 even though the total cost of the batteries increases and decreases with activity.

There are many examples of costs that are variable with respect to the products and services provided by a company. In a manufacturing company, variable costs include items such as direct materials and some elements of manufacturing overhead such as lubricants, shipping costs, and sales commissions. For the present we will also assume that direct labor is a variable cost, although as we shall see in Chapter 6, direct labor may act more like a fixed cost in many situations. In a merchandising company, variable costs include items such as cost of goods sold, commissions to salespersons, and billing costs. In a hospital, the variable costs of providing health care services to patients would include the costs of the supplies, drugs, meals, and perhaps nursing services.

When we say that a cost is variable, we ordinarily mean that it is variable with respect to the amount of goods or services the organization produces. However, costs can be variable with respect to other things. For example, the wages paid to employees at a Blockbuster Video outlet will depend on the number of hours the store is open and not strictly on the number of videos rented. In this case, we would say that wage costs are variable with respect to the hours of operation. Nevertheless, when we say that a cost is variable, we ordinarily mean it is variable with respect to the amount of goods and services produced. This could be how many Jeep Cherokees are produced, how many videos are rented, how many patients are treated, and so on.

Fixed Cost

A **fixed cost** is a cost that remains constant, in total, regardless of changes in the level of activity. Unlike variable costs, fixed costs are not affected by changes in activity. Consequently, as the activity level rises and falls, the fixed costs remain constant in total amount unless influenced by some outside force, such as a price change. Rent is a good example

of a fixed cost. Suppose the Mayo Clinic rents a machine for $8,000 per month that tests blood samples for the presence of leukemia cells. The $8,000 monthly rental cost will be sustained regardless of the number of tests that may be performed during the month. The concept of a fixed cost is shown in graphic form in Exhibit 2–8.

Very few costs are completely fixed. Most will change if there is a large enough change in activity. For example, suppose that the capacity of the leukemia diagnostic machine at the Mayo Clinic is 2,000 tests per month. If the clinic wishes to perform more than 2,000 tests in a month, it would be necessary to rent an additional machine, which would cause a jump in the fixed costs. When we say a cost is fixed, we mean it is fixed within some *relevant range*. The **relevant range** is the range of activity within which the assumptions about variable and fixed costs are valid. For example, the assumption that the rent for diagnostic machines is $8,000 per month is valid within the relevant range of 0 to 2,000 tests per month.

Fixed costs can create confusion if they are expressed on a per unit basis. This is because the average fixed cost per unit increases and decreases *inversely* with changes in activity. In the Mayo Clinic, for example, the average cost per test will fall as the number of tests performed increases. This is because the $8,000 rental cost will be spread over more tests. Conversely, as the number of tests performed in the clinic declines, the average cost per test will rise as the $8,000 rental cost is spread over fewer tests. This concept is illustrated in the table below:

Monthly Rental Cost	Number of Tests Performed	Average Cost per Test
$8,000.	10	$800
8,000.	500	16
8,000.	2,000	4

Note that if the Mayo Clinic performs only 10 tests each month, the rental cost of the equipment will average $800 per test. But if 2,000 tests are performed each month, the average cost will drop to only $4 per test. More will be said later about the problems created for both the accountant and the manager by this variation in unit costs.

Examples of fixed costs include straight-line depreciation, insurance, property taxes, rent, supervisory salaries, administrative salaries, and advertising.

A summary of both variable and fixed cost behavior is presented in Exhibit 2–9.

In Business

The Cost of a Call

Variable costs in some industries can be very low relative to fixed costs. For example, costs in the telecommunications industry are almost all fixed. The cost of physically transporting a call is now only about 7% of what customers pay and it costs more for the telephone company to bill for the call than it costs the telephone company to actually make the call.

Source: Scott Wooley, "Meltdown," *Forbes*, July 3, 2000, pp. 70–71.

Exhibit 2–9

Summary of Variable and Fixed Cost Behavior

	Behavior of the Cost (within the relevant range)	
Cost	**In Total**	**Per Unit**
Variable cost	Total variable cost increases and decreases in proportion to changes in the activity level.	Variable cost remains constant per unit.
Fixed cost	Total fixed cost is not affected by changes in the activity level within the relevant range.	Fixed cost per unit decreases as the activity level rises and increases as the activity level falls.

Cost Classifications for Assigning Costs to Cost Objects

LEARNING OBJECTIVE 6
Understand the differences between direct and indirect costs.

Costs are assigned to objects for a variety of purposes including pricing, profitability studies, and control of spending. A **cost object** is anything for which cost data are desired—including products, product lines, customers, jobs, and organizational subunits. For purposes of assigning costs to cost objects, costs are classified as either *direct* or *indirect.*

Direct Cost

A **direct cost** is a cost that can be easily and conveniently traced to the particular cost object under consideration. The concept of direct cost extends beyond just direct materials and direct labor. For example, if Reebok is assigning costs to its various regional and national sales offices, then the salary of the sales manager in its Tokyo office would be a direct cost of that office.

Indirect Cost

An **indirect cost** is a cost that cannot be easily and conveniently traced to the particular cost object under consideration. For example, a Campbell Soup factory may produce dozens of varieties of canned soups. The factory manager's salary would be an indirect cost of a particular variety such as chicken noodle soup. The reason is that the factory manager's salary is not caused by any one variety of soup but rather is incurred as a consequence of running the entire factory. *To be traced to a cost object such as a particular product, the cost must be caused by the cost object.* The factory manager's salary is called a *common cost* of producing the various products of the factory. A **common cost** is a cost that is incurred to support a number of costing objects but cannot be traced to them individually. A common cost is a particular type of indirect cost.

A particular cost may be direct or indirect, depending on the cost object. While the Campbell Soup factory manager's salary is an *indirect* cost of manufacturing chicken noodle soup, it is a *direct* cost of the manufacturing division. In the first case, the cost object is the chicken noodle soup product. In the second case, the cost object is the entire manufacturing division.

Cost Classifications for Decision Making

LEARNING OBJECTIVE 7
Define and give examples of cost classifications used in making decisions: differential costs, opportunity costs, and sunk costs.

Costs are an important feature of many business decisions. In making decisions, it is essential to have a firm grasp of the concepts *differential cost, opportunity cost,* and *sunk cost.*

Differential Cost and Revenue

Decisions involve choosing between alternatives. In business decisions, each alternative will have certain costs and benefits that must be compared to the costs and benefits of the other available alternatives. A difference in costs between any two alternatives is known as a **differential cost.** A difference in revenues between any two alternatives is known as **differential revenue.**

A differential cost is also known as an **incremental cost,** although technically an incremental cost should refer only to an increase in cost from one alternative to another; decreases in cost should be referred to as *decremental costs*. Differential cost is a broader term, encompassing both cost increases (incremental costs) and cost decreases (decremental costs) between alternatives.

The accountant's differential cost concept can be compared to the economist's marginal cost concept. In speaking of changes in cost and revenue, the economist employs the terms *marginal cost* and *marginal revenue.* The revenue that can be obtained from selling one more unit of product is called marginal revenue, and the cost involved in producing one more unit of product is called marginal cost. The economist's marginal concept is basically the same as the accountant's differential concept applied to a single unit of output.

Differential costs can be either fixed or variable. To illustrate, assume that Nature Way Cosmetics, Inc., is thinking about changing its marketing method from distribution through retailers to distribution by door-to-door direct sale. Present costs and revenues are compared to projected costs and revenues in the following table:

	Retailer Distribution (present)	Direct Sale Distribution (proposed)	Differential Costs and Revenues
Revenues (V)	$700,000	$800,000	$100,000
Cost of goods sold (V)	350,000	400,000	50,000
Advertising (F)	80,000	45,000	(35,000)
Commissions (V)	0	40,000	40,000
Warehouse depreciation (F)	50,000	80,000	30,000
Other expenses (F)	60,000	60,000	0
Total	540,000	625,000	85,000
Net operating income	$160,000	$175,000	$ 15,000

V = Variable; F = Fixed.

According to the above analysis, the differential revenue is $100,000 and the differential costs total $85,000, leaving a positive differential net operating income of $15,000 under the proposed marketing plan.

The decision of whether Nature Way Cosmetics should stay with the present retail distribution or switch to door-to-door direct selling could be made on the basis of the net operating incomes of the two alternatives. As we see in the above analysis, the net operating income under the present distribution method is $160,000, whereas the net operating income under door-to-door direct selling is estimated to be $175,000. Therefore, the door-to-door direct distribution method is preferred, since it would result in $15,000 higher net operating income. Note that we would have arrived at exactly the same conclusion by simply focusing on the differential revenues, differential costs, and differential net operating income, which also show a $15,000 advantage for the direct selling method.

In general, only the differences between alternatives are relevant in decisions. Those items that are the same under all alternatives and that are not affected by the decision can be ignored. For example, in the Nature Way Cosmetics example above, the "Other expenses" category, which is $60,000 under both alternatives, can be ignored, since it has no effect on the decision. If it were removed from the calculations, the door-to-door direct selling method would still be preferred by $15,000. This is an extremely important principle in management accounting that we will return to in later chapters.

In Business

Using Those Empty Seats

Many corporate jets fly with only one or two executives on board. Priscilla Blum wondered why some of the empty seats couldn't be used to fly cancer patients who need specialized treatment outside their home area. Flying on a regular commercial airline can be an expensive and grueling experience for cancer patients. Taking the initiative, she helped found the Corporate Angel Network, an organization that arranges free flights on some 1,500 jets from over 500 companies. Since the jets fly anyway, filling a seat with a cancer patient doesn't involve any significant incremental cost for the companies that donate the service. Since its founding in 1981, the Corporate Angel Network has arranged over 14,000 free flights.

Source: Scott McCormack, "Waste Not, Want Not," *Forbes*, July 26, 1999, p. 118.

Opportunity Cost

Opportunity cost is the potential benefit that is given up when one alternative is selected over another. To illustrate this important concept, consider the following examples:

Example 1

Vicki has a part-time job that pays her $200 per week while attending college. She would like to spend a week at the beach during spring break, and her employer has agreed to give her the time off, but without pay. The $200 in lost wages would be an opportunity cost of taking the week off to be at the beach.

Example 2

Suppose that Neiman Marcus is considering investing a large sum of money in land that may be a site for a future store. Rather than invest the funds in land, the company could invest the funds in high-grade securities. If the land is acquired, the opportunity cost will be the investment income that could have been realized if the securities had been purchased instead.

Example 3

Steve is employed with a company that pays him a salary of $30,000 per year. He is thinking about leaving the company and returning to school. Since returning to school would require that he give up his $30,000 salary, the forgone salary would be an opportunity cost of seeking further education.

Opportunity cost is not usually entered in the accounting records of an organization, but it is a cost that must be explicitly considered in every decision a manager makes. Virtually every alternative has some opportunity cost attached to it. In example 3 above, for instance, if Steve decides to stay at his job, there still is an opportunity cost involved: It is the greater income that could be realized in future years as a result of returning to school.

Sunk Cost

A **sunk cost** is a cost *that has already been incurred* and that cannot be changed by any decision made now or in the future. Since sunk costs cannot be changed by any decision, they are not differential costs. Therefore, they can and should be ignored when making a decision.

To illustrate a sunk cost, assume that a company paid $50,000 several years ago for a special-purpose machine. The machine was used to make a product that is now obsolete and is no longer being sold. Even though in hindsight the purchase of the machine may have been unwise, no amount of regret can undo that decision. And it would be folly to continue making the obsolete product in a misguided attempt to "recover" the original cost of the machine. In short, the $50,000 originally paid for the machine has already been incurred and cannot be a differential cost in any future decision. For this reason, such costs are said to be sunk and should be ignored in decisions.

Summary

In this chapter, we have looked at some of the ways in which managers classify costs. How the costs will be used—for preparing external reports, predicting cost behavior, assigning costs to cost objects, or decision making—will dictate how the costs will be classified.

For purposes of valuing inventories and determining expenses for the balance sheet and income statement, costs are classified as either product costs or period costs. Product costs are assigned to inventories and are considered assets until the products are sold. At the point of sale, product costs become cost of goods sold on the income statement. In contrast, following the usual accrual practices, period costs are taken directly to the income statement as expenses in the period in which they are incurred.

In a merchandising company, product cost is whatever the company paid for its merchandise. For external financial reports in a manufacturing company, product costs consist of all manufacturing costs. In both kinds of companies, selling and administrative costs are considered to be period costs and are expensed as incurred.

For purposes of predicting cost behavior—how costs will react to changes in activity—managers commonly classify costs into two categories—variable and fixed. Variable costs, in total, are strictly proportional to activity. Thus, the variable cost per unit is constant. Fixed costs, in total, remain at the same level for changes in activity that occur within the relevant range. Thus, the average fixed cost per unit decreases as the number of units increases.

For purposes of assigning costs to cost objects such as products or departments, costs are classified as direct or indirect. Direct costs can be conveniently traced to the cost objects. Indirect costs cannot be conveniently traced to cost objects.

For purposes of making decisions, the concepts of differential cost and revenue, opportunity cost, and sunk cost are of vital importance. Differential costs and revenues are the cost and revenue items that differ between alternatives. Opportunity cost is the benefit that is forgone when one alternative is selected over another. Sunk cost is a cost that occurred in the past and cannot be altered. Differential costs and opportunity costs should be carefully considered in decisions. Sunk cost is always irrelevant in decisions and should be ignored.

These various cost classifications are *different* ways of looking at costs. A particular cost, such as the cost of cheese in a taco served at Taco Bell, could be a manufacturing cost, a product cost, a variable cost, a direct cost, and a differential cost—all at the same time. Taco Bell can be considered to be a manufacturer of fast food. The cost of the cheese in a taco would be considered a manufacturing cost and, as such, it would be a product cost as well. In addition, the cost of cheese would be considered variable with respect to the number of tacos served and would be a direct cost of serving tacos. Finally, the cost of the cheese in a taco would be considered a differential cost of the taco.

Review Problem 1: Cost Terms

Many new cost terms have been introduced in this chapter. It will take you some time to learn what each term means and how to properly classify costs in an organization. Consider the following example: Porter Company manufactures furniture, including tables. Selected costs are given below:

1. The tables are made of wood that costs $100 per table.
2. The tables are assembled by workers, at a wage cost of $40 per table.
3. Workers assembling the tables are supervised by a factory supervisor who is paid $25,000 per year.
4. Electrical costs are $2 per machine-hour. Four machine-hours are required to produce a table.
5. The depreciation cost of the machines used to make the tables totals $10,000 per year.
6. The salary of the president of Porter Company is $100,000 per year.
7. Porter Company spends $250,000 per year to advertise its products.
8. Salespersons are paid a commission of $30 for each table sold.
9. Instead of producing the tables, Porter Company could rent its factory space out at a rental income of $50,000 per year.

Required:

Classify these costs according to the various cost terms used in the chapter. *Carefully study the classification of each cost.* If you don't understand why a particular cost is classified the way it is, reread the section of the chapter discussing the particular cost term. The terms *variable cost* and *fixed cost* refer to how costs behave with respect to the number of tables produced in a year.

Solution to Review Problem 1

				Product Cost			To Units of Product			
	Variable Cost	Fixed Cost	Period (selling and adminis-trative) Cost	Direct Materials	Direct Labor	Manufacturing Overhead	Direct	Indirect	Sunk Cost	Oppor-tunity Cost
1. Wood used in a table ($100 per table)	X			X			X			
2. Labor cost to assemble a table ($40 per table) . . .	X				X		X			

	Variable Cost	Fixed Cost	Period (selling and administrative) Cost	Product Cost: Direct Materials	Product Cost: Direct Labor	Product Cost: Manufacturing Overhead	To Units of Product: Direct	To Units of Product: Indirect	Sunk Cost	Opportunity Cost
3. Salary of the factory supervisor ($25,000 per year)		X				X		X		
4. Cost of electricity to produce tables ($2 per machine-hour)	X					X		X		
5. Depreciation of machines used to produce tables ($10,000 per year)		X				X		X	X*	
6. Salary of the company president ($100,000 per year)		X	X							
7. Advertising expense ($250,000 per year)		X	X							
8. Commissions paid to salespersons ($30 per table sold)	X		X							
9. Rental income forgone on factory space. . . .										X†

*This is a sunk cost, since the outlay for the equipment was made in a previous period.

†This is an opportunity cost, since it represents the potential benefit that is lost or sacrificed as a result of using the factory space to produce tables. Opportunity cost is a special category of cost that is not ordinarily recorded in an organization's accounting books. To avoid possible confusion with other costs, we will not attempt to classify this cost in any other way except as an opportunity cost.

Review Problem 2: Schedule of Cost of Goods Manufactured and Income Statement

The following information has been taken from the accounting records of Klear-Seal Company for last year:

Selling expenses	$ 140,000
Raw materials inventory, January 1	90,000
Raw materials inventory, December 31	60,000
Utilities, factory	36,000
Direct labor cost	150,000
Depreciation, factory.	162,000
Purchases of raw materials	750,000
Sales.	2,500,000
Insurance, factory	40,000
Supplies, factory	15,000
Administrative expenses.	270,000
Indirect labor.	300,000
Maintenance, factory	87,000
Work in process inventory, January 1.	180,000
Work in process inventory, December 31.	100,000
Finished goods inventory, January 1	260,000
Finished goods inventory, December 31	210,000

Management wants these data organized in a better format so that financial statements can be prepared for the year.

Required:

1. Prepare a schedule of cost of goods manufactured as in Exhibit 2–4.
2. Compute the cost of goods sold.
3. Using data as needed from (1) and (2) above, prepare an income statement.

Solution to Review Problem 2

1.

KLEAR-SEAL COMPANY
Schedule of Cost of Goods Manufactured
For the Year Ended December 31

Direct materials:		
Raw materials inventory, January 1	$ 90,000	
Add: Purchases of raw materials	750,000	
Raw materials available for use	840,000	
Deduct: Raw materials inventory, December 31	60,000	
Raw materials used in production		$ 780,000
Direct labor		150,000
Manufacturing overhead:		
Utilities, factory	36,000	
Depreciation, factory	162,000	
Insurance, factory	40,000	
Supplies, factory	15,000	
Indirect labor	300,000	
Maintenance, factory	87,000	
Total overhead costs		640,000
Total manufacturing costs		1,570,000
Add: Work in process inventory, January 1		180,000
		1,750,000
Deduct: Work in process inventory, December 31		100,000
Cost of goods manufactured		$1,650,000

2. The cost of goods sold would be computed as follows:

Finished goods inventory, January 1	$ 260,000
Add: Cost of goods manufactured	1,650,000
Goods available for sale	1,910,000
Deduct: Finished goods inventory, December 31	210,000
Cost of goods sold	$1,700,000

3.

KLEAR-SEAL COMPANY
Income Statement
For the Year Ended December 31

Sales		$2,500,000
Less cost of goods sold (above)		1,700,000
Gross margin		800,000
Less selling and administrative expenses:		
Selling expenses	$140,000	
Administrative expenses	270,000	
Total selling and administrative expenses		410,000
Net operating income		$ 390,000

Glossary

Administrative costs All executive, organizational, and clerical costs associated with the general management of an organization rather than with manufacturing, marketing, or selling. (p. 42)

Common costs A common cost is incurred to support a number of costing objects but cannot be traced to them individually. For example, the wage cost of the pilot of a 747 airliner is a common cost of all of the passengers on the aircraft. Without the pilot, there would be no flight and no passengers. But no part of the pilot's wage is caused by any one passenger taking the flight. (p. 55)

Conversion cost Direct labor cost plus manufacturing overhead cost. (p. 42)

Cost behavior The way in which a cost reacts or responds to changes in the level of business activity. (p. 52)

Cost object Anything for which cost data are desired. Examples of possible cost objects are products, product lines, customers, jobs, and organizational subunits such as departments or divisions of a company. (p. 55)

Cost of goods manufactured The manufacturing costs associated with the goods that were finished during the period. (p. 48)

Differential cost A difference in cost between any two alternatives. Also see *Incremental cost.* (p. 55)

Differential revenue The difference in revenue between any two alternatives. (p. 55)

Direct cost A cost that can be easily and conveniently traced to a specified cost object. (p. 55)

Direct labor Those factory labor costs that can be easily traced to individual units of product. Also called *touch labor.* (p. 41)

Direct materials Those materials that become an integral part of a finished product and can be conveniently traced into it. (p. 41)

Fixed cost A cost that remains constant, in total, regardless of changes in the level of activity within the relevant range. If a fixed cost is expressed on a per unit basis, it varies inversely with the level of activity. (p. 53)

Incremental cost An increase in cost between two alternatives. Also see *Differential cost.* (p. 55)

Indirect cost A cost that cannot be easily and conveniently traced to a specified cost object. (p. 55)

Indirect labor The labor costs of janitors, supervisors, materials handlers, and other factory workers that cannot be conveniently traced directly to particular products. (p. 41)

Indirect materials Small items of material such as glue and nails. These items may become an integral part of a finished product but are traceable to the product only at great cost or inconvenience. (p. 41)

Inventoriable costs Synonym for *product costs.* (p. 43)

Manufacturing overhead All costs associated with manufacturing except direct materials and direct labor. (p. 41)

Marketing or selling costs All costs necessary to secure customer orders and get the finished product or service into the hands of the customer. (p. 42)

Opportunity cost The potential benefit that is given up when one alternative is selected over another. (p. 57)

Period costs Costs that are taken directly to the income statement as expenses in the period in which they are incurred or accrued; such costs consist of selling (marketing) and administrative expenses. (p. 43)

Prime cost Direct materials cost plus direct labor cost. (p. 42)

Product costs All costs that are involved in the purchase or manufacture of goods. In the case of manufactured goods, these costs consist of direct materials, direct labor, and manufacturing overhead. Also see *Inventoriable costs.* (p. 43)

Raw materials Any materials that go into the final product. (p. 40)

Relevant range The range of activity within which assumptions about variable and fixed cost behavior are valid. (p. 54)

Schedule of cost of goods manufactured A schedule showing the direct materials, direct labor, and manufacturing overhead costs incurred for a period and assigned to Work in Process and completed goods. (p. 48)

Sunk cost Any cost that has already been incurred and that cannot be changed by any decision made now or in the future. (p. 57)

Variable cost A cost that varies, in total, in direct proportion to changes in the level of activity. A variable cost is constant per unit. (p. 52)

Appendix 2A: Further Classification of Labor Costs

LEARNING OBJECTIVE 8
Properly classify labor costs associated with idle time, overtime, and fringe benefits.

Idle time, overtime, and fringe benefits associated with direct labor workers pose particular problems in accounting for labor costs. Are these costs a part of the costs of direct labor or are they something else?

Idle Time

Machine breakdowns, materials shortages, power failures, and the like result in idle time. The labor costs incurred during idle time are ordinarily treated as a manufacturing overhead cost rather than as a direct labor cost. Most managers feel that such costs should be spread over all the production of a period rather than just the jobs that happen to be in process when breakdowns or other disruptions occur.

To give an example of how the cost of idle time is handled, assume that a press operator earns $12 per hour. If the press operator is paid for a normal 40-hour workweek but is idle for 3 hours during a given week due to breakdowns, labor cost would be allocated as follows:

Direct labor ($12 per hour × 37 hours)	$444
Manufacturing overhead (idle time: $12 per hour × 3 hours)	36
Total cost for the week	$480

Overtime Premium

The overtime premium paid to *all* factory workers (direct labor as well as indirect labor) is usually considered to be part of manufacturing overhead and is not assigned to any particular order. At first glance this may seem strange, since overtime is always spent working on some particular order. Why not charge that order for the overtime cost? The reason is that it would be considered unfair and arbitrary to charge an overtime premium against a particular order simply because the order *happened* to fall on the tail end of the daily production schedule.

To illustrate, assume that two batches of goods, order A and order B, each take three hours to complete. The production run on order A is scheduled early in the day, but the production run on order B isn't scheduled until late in the afternoon. By the time the run on order B is completed, two hours of overtime have been logged in. The necessity to work overtime was a result of the fact that total production exceeded the regular time available. Order B was no more responsible for the overtime than was order A. Therefore, managers feel that all production should share in the premium charge that resulted. This is considered a more equitable way of handling overtime premium in that it doesn't penalize one run simply because it happens to occur late in the day.

Let us again assume that a press operator in a plant earns $12 per hour. She is paid time and a half for overtime (time in excess of 40 hours a week). During a given week, she works 45 hours and has no idle time. Her labor cost for the week would be allocated as follows:

Direct labor ($12 per hour × 45 hours)	$540
Manufacturing overhead (overtime premium: $6 per hour × 5 hours)	30
Total cost for the week	$570

Observe from this computation that only the overtime premium of $6 per hour is charged to the overhead account—*not* the entire $18 earned for each hour of overtime work ($12 regular rate × 1.5 = $18).

Labor Fringe Benefits

Labor fringe benefits are made up of employment-related costs paid by the employer and include the costs of insurance programs, retirement plans, various supplemental unemployment benefits, and hospitalization plans. The employer also pays the employer's share of Social Security, Medicare, workers' compensation, federal employment tax, and state unemployment insurance. These costs often add up to as much as 30% to 40% of base pay.

Many firms treat all such costs as indirect labor by adding them in total to manufacturing overhead. Other firms treat the portion of fringe benefits that relates to direct labor as additional direct labor cost. This approach is conceptually superior, since the fringe benefits provided to direct labor workers clearly represent an added cost of their services.

Appendix 2B: Cost of Quality

A company may have a product with a high-quality design that uses high-quality components, but if the product is poorly assembled or has other defects, the company will have high warranty costs and dissatisfied customers. People who are dissatisfied with a product are unlikely to buy the product again. They are also likely to tell others about their bad experiences. One study found that "[c]ustomers who have bad experiences tell approximately 11 people about it."[1] This is the worst possible sort of advertising. To prevent such problems, companies have been expending a great deal of effort to reduce defects. The objective is to have high *quality of conformance.*

Quality of Conformance

LEARNING OBJECTIVE 9
Identify the four types of quality costs and explain how they interact.

A product that meets or exceeds its design specifications and is free of defects that mar its appearance or degrade its performance is said to have high **quality of conformance.** Note that if an economy car is free of defects, it can have a quality of conformance that is just as high as a defect-free luxury car. The purchasers of economy cars cannot expect their cars to be as opulently equipped as luxury cars, but they can and do expect them to be free of defects.

Preventing, detecting, and dealing with defects cause costs that are called *quality costs* or the *cost of quality.* The use of the term *quality cost* is confusing to some people. It does not refer to costs such as using a higher-grade leather to make a wallet or using 14K gold instead of gold-plating in jewelry. Instead, the term **quality cost** refers to all of the costs that are incurred to prevent defects or that result from defects in products.

The Quality Black Belt

In Business

GE has adopted the "Black Belt" quality control program developed by Motorola, Inc. Individuals selected to be Black Belts undergo intensive training for four months in statistical process control and other quality-control techniques. GE's CEO has made it clear to young managers that "they haven't much future at GE unless they are selected to be Black Belts. [With this program,] your customers are happy with you, you are not firefighting, you are not running in a reactive mode." GE hopes to save $7 to $10 billion over the next decade as a result of the Black Belt program.

Source: William M. Carley, "Charging Ahead: To Keep GE's Profits Rising, Welch Pushes Quality-Control Plan," *The Wall Street Journal*, January 13, 1997, pp. A1 and A6.

Quality costs can be broken down into four broad groups. Two of these groups—known as *prevention costs* and *appraisal costs*—are incurred in an effort to keep defective products from falling into the hands of customers. The other two groups of

[1] Christopher W. L. Hart, James L. Heskett, and W. Earl Sasser, Jr., "The Profitable Art of Service Recovery," *Harvard Business Review,* July–August 1990, p. 153.

Exhibit 2B–1
Typical Quality Costs

Prevention Costs	Internal Failure Costs
Systems development Quality engineering Quality training Quality circles Statistical process control activities Supervision of prevention activities Quality data gathering, analysis, and reporting Quality improvement projects Technical support provided to suppliers Audits of the effectiveness of the quality system	Net cost of scrap Net cost of spoilage Rework labor and overhead Reinspection of reworked products Retesting of reworked products Downtime caused by quality problems Disposal of defective products Analysis of the cause of defects in production Re-entering data because of keying errors Debugging software errors
Appraisal Costs	**External Failure Costs**
Test and inspection of incoming materials Test and inspection of in-process goods Final product testing and inspection Supplies used in testing and inspection Supervision of testing and inspection activities Depreciation of test equipment Maintenance of test equipment Plant utilities in the inspection area Field testing and appraisal at customer site	Cost of field servicing and handling complaints Warranty repairs and replacements Repairs and replacements beyond the warranty period Product recalls Liability arising from defective products Returns and allowances arising from quality problems Lost sales arising from a reputation for poor quality

costs—known as *internal failure costs* and *external failure costs*—are incurred because defects are produced despite efforts to prevent them. Examples of specific costs involved in each of these four groups are given in Exhibit 2B–1.

Several things should be noted about the quality costs shown in the exhibit. First, note that quality costs don't relate to just manufacturing; rather, they relate to all the activities in a company from initial research and development (R&D) through customer service. Second, note that the number of costs associated with quality is very large; therefore, total quality cost can be quite high unless management gives this area special attention. Finally, note how different the costs are in the four groupings. We will now look at each of these groupings more closely.

Prevention Costs

Generally, the most effective way to manage quality costs is to avoid having defects in the first place. It is much less costly to prevent a problem from ever happening than it is to find and correct the problem after it has occurred. **Prevention costs** support activities whose purpose is to reduce the number of defects. Companies employ many techniques to prevent defects including statistical process control, quality engineering, training, and a variety of tools from Total Quality Management.

Note from Exhibit 2B–1 that prevention costs include activities relating to quality circles and statistical process control. **Quality circles** consist of small groups of employees that meet on a regular basis to discuss ways to improve quality. Both management and workers are included in these circles. Quality circles are widely used and can be found in manufacturing companies, utilities, health care organizations, banks, and many other organizations.

Statistical process control is a technique that is used to detect whether a process is in or out of control. An out-of-control process results in defective units and may be caused by a miscalibrated machine or some other factor. In statistical process control, workers use charts to monitor the quality of units that pass through their workstations. With these charts, workers can quickly spot processes that are out of control and that are creating defects. Problems can be immediately corrected and further defects prevented rather than waiting for an inspector to catch the defects later.

Note also from the list of prevention costs in Exhibit 2B–1 that some companies provide technical support to their suppliers as a way of preventing defects. Particularly in just-in-time (JIT) systems, such support to suppliers is vital. In a JIT system, parts are delivered from suppliers just in time and in just the correct quantity to fill customer orders. There are no stockpiles of parts. If a defective part is received from a supplier, the part cannot be used and the order for the ultimate customer cannot be filled on time. Hence, every part received from a supplier must be free of defects. Consequently, companies that use JIT often require that their suppliers use sophisticated quality control programs such as statistical process control and that their suppliers certify that they will deliver parts and materials that are free of defects.

Simple Solutions

In Business

Very simple and inexpensive procedures can be used to prevent defects. Yamada Electric had a persistent problem assembling a simple push-button switch. The switch has two buttons, an on button and an off button, with a small spring under each button. Assembly is very simple. A worker inserts the small springs in the device and then installs the buttons. However, the worker sometimes forgets to put in one of the springs. When the customer discovers such a defective switch in a shipment from Yamada, an inspector has to be sent to the customer's plant to check every switch in the shipment. After each such incident, workers are urged to be more careful, and for a while quality improves. But eventually, someone forgets to put in a spring, and Yamada gets into trouble with the customer again. This chronic problem was very embarrassing to Yamada.

Shigeo Shingo, an expert on quality control, suggested a very simple solution. A small dish was placed next to the assembly station. At the beginning of each operation, two of the small springs are taken out of a parts box containing hundreds of springs and placed in the dish. The worker then assembles the switch. If a spring remains on the dish after assembling the switch, the worker immediately realizes a spring has been left out, and the switch is reassembled. This simple change in procedures completely eliminated the problem.

Source: Shigeo Shingo and Dr. Alan Robinson, editor-in-chief, *Modern Approaches to Manufacturing Improvement: The Shingo System,* (Cambridge, MA: Productivity Press, 1990), pp. 214–216.

Appraisal Costs

Any defective parts and products should be caught as early as possible in the production process. **Appraisal costs,** which are sometimes called *inspection costs,* are incurred to identify defective products *before* the products are shipped to customers. Unfortunately, performing appraisal activities doesn't keep defects from happening again, and most managers now realize that maintaining an army of inspectors is a costly (and ineffective) approach to quality control.

Professor John K. Shank of Dartmouth College has aptly stated, "The old-style approach was to say, 'We've got great quality. We have 40 quality control inspectors in the factory.' Then somebody realized that if you need 40 inspectors, it must be a lousy factory. So now the trick is to run a factory without any quality control inspectors; each employee is his or her own quality control person."[2]

[2] Robert W. Casey, "The Changing World of the CEO," *PPM World* 24, no. 2 (1990), p. 31.

Employees are increasingly being asked to be responsible for their own quality control. This approach, along with designing products to be easy to manufacture properly, allows quality to be built into products rather than relying on inspection to get the defects out.

Internal Failure Costs

Failure costs are incurred when a product fails to conform to its design specifications. Failure costs can be either internal or external. **Internal failure costs** result from identification of defects before they are shipped to customers. These costs include scrap, rejected products, reworking of defective units, and downtime caused by quality problems. In some companies, as little as 10% of the company's products make it through the production process without rework of some kind. Of course, the more effective a company's appraisal activities, the greater the chance of catching defects internally and the greater the level of internal failure costs. This is the price that is paid to avoid incurring external failure costs, which can be devastating.

External Failure Costs

External failure costs result when a defective product is delivered to a customer. As shown in Exhibit 2B–1, external failure costs include warranty repairs and replacements, product recalls, liability arising from legal action against a company, and lost sales arising from a reputation for poor quality. Such costs can decimate profits.

In the past, some managers have taken the attitude, "Let's go ahead and ship everything to customers, and we'll take care of any problems under the warranty." This attitude generally results in high external failure costs, customer ill will, and declining market share and profits.

Distribution of Quality Costs

A company's total quality cost is likely to be very high unless management gives this area special attention. Quality costs for U.S. companies range between 10% and 20% of total sales, whereas experts say that these costs should be more in the 2% to 4% range. How does a company reduce its total quality cost? The answer lies in how the quality costs are distributed. Refer to the graph in Exhibit 2B–2, which shows total quality costs as a function of the quality of conformance.

The graph shows that when the quality of conformance is low, total quality cost is high and that most of this cost consists of costs of internal and external failure. A low quality of conformance means that a high percentage of units are defective and hence the company must incur high failure costs. However, as a company spends more and more on prevention and appraisal, the percentage of defective units drops (the percentage of defect-free units increases). This results in lower costs of internal and external failure. Ordinarily, total quality cost drops rapidly as the quality of conformance increases. Thus, a company can reduce its total quality cost by focusing its efforts on prevention and appraisal. The cost savings from reduced defects usually swamp the costs of the additional prevention and appraisal efforts.

The graph in Exhibit 2B–2 has been drawn so that the total quality cost is minimized when the quality of conformance is less than 100%. However, some experts contend that the total quality cost is not minimized until the quality of conformance is 100% and there are no defects. Indeed, many companies have found that the total quality costs seem to keep dropping even when the quality of conformance approaches 100% and defect rates get as low as 1 in a million units. Others argue that total quality cost eventually increases as the quality of conformance increases. However, in most companies this does not seem to happen until the quality of conformance is very close to 100% and defect rates are very close to zero.

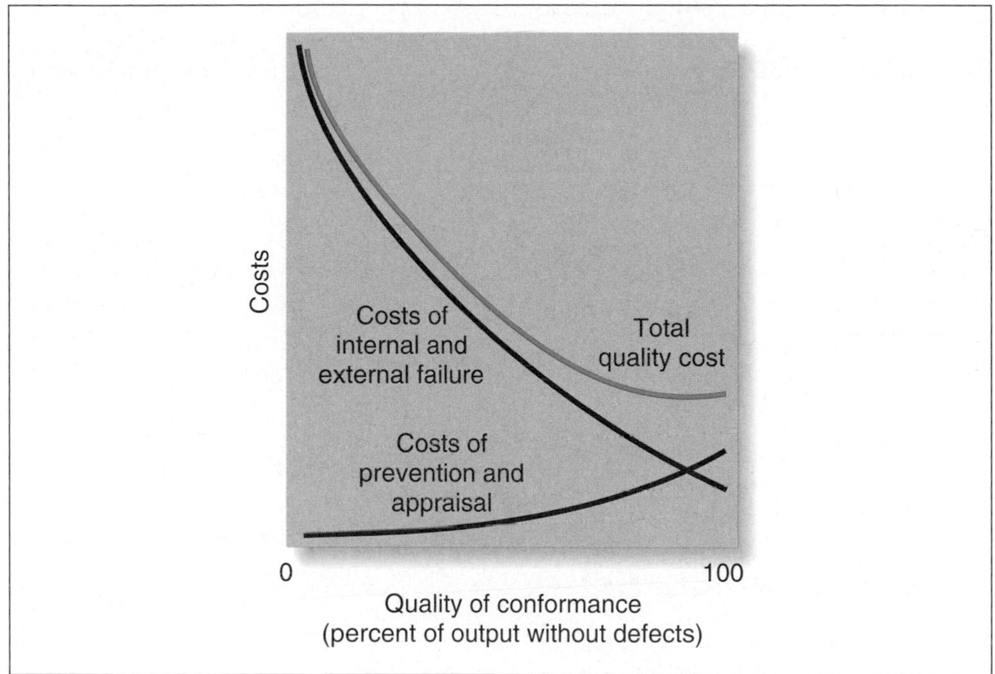

Exhibit 2B–2
Effect of Quality Costs on Quality of Conformance

As a company's quality program becomes more refined and as its failure costs begin to fall, prevention activities usually become more effective than appraisal activities. Appraisal can only find defects, whereas prevention can eliminate them. The best way to prevent defects from happening is to design processes that reduce the likelihood of defects and to continually monitor processes using statistical process control methods.

Quality Cost Reports

LEARNING OBJECTIVE 10
Prepare and interpret a quality cost report.

As an initial step in quality improvement programs, companies often construct a *quality cost report* that provides an estimate of the financial consequences of the company's current level of defects. A **quality cost report** details the prevention costs, appraisal costs, and costs of internal and external failures that arise from the company's current level of defective products and services. Managers are often shocked by the magnitude of these costs. A typical quality cost report is shown in Exhibit 2B–3.

Several things should be noted from the data in the exhibit. First, note that Ventura Company's quality costs are poorly distributed in both years, with most of the costs being traceable to either internal failure or external failure. The external failure costs are particularly high in Year 1 in comparison to other costs.

Second, note that the company increased its spending on prevention and appraisal activities in Year 2. As a result, internal failure costs went up in that year (from $2 million in Year 1 to $3 million in Year 2), but external failure costs dropped sharply (from $5.15 million in Year 1 to only $2 million in Year 2). Because of the increase in appraisal activity in Year 2, more defects were caught inside the company before they were shipped to customers. This resulted in more cost for scrap, rework, and so forth, but saved huge amounts in warranty repairs, warranty replacements, and other external failure costs.

Third, note that as a result of greater emphasis on prevention and appraisal, *total* quality cost decreased in Year 2. As continued emphasis is placed on prevention and appraisal in future years, total quality cost should continue to decrease. That is, future

Exhibit 2B–3 Quality Cost Report

Ventura Company
Quality Cost Report
For Years 1 and 2

	Year 2		Year 1	
	Amount	**Percent***	**Amount**	**Percent***
Prevention costs:				
Systems development	$ 400,000	0.80%	$ 270,000	0.54%
Quality training	210,000	0.42%	130,000	0.26%
Supervision of prevention activities	70,000	0.14%	40,000	0.08%
Quality improvement projects	320,000	0.64%	210,000	0.42%
Total	1,000,000	2.00%	650,000	1.30%
Appraisal costs:				
Inspection	600,000	1.20%	560,000	1.12%
Reliability testing	580,000	1.16%	420,000	0.84%
Supervision of testing and inspection	120,000	0.24%	80,000	0.16%
Depreciation of test equipment	200,000	0.40%	140,000	0.28%
Total	1,500,000	3.00%	1,200,000	2.40%
Internal failure costs:				
Net cost of scrap	900,000	1.80%	750,000	1.50%
Rework labor and overhead	1,430,000	2.86%	810,000	1.62%
Downtime due to defects in quality	170,000	0.34%	100,000	0.20%
Disposal of defective products	500,000	1.00%	340,000	0.68%
Total	3,000,000	6.00%	2,000,000	4.00%
External failure costs:				
Warranty repairs	400,000	0.80%	900,000	1.80%
Warranty replacements	870,000	1.74%	2,300,000	4.60%
Allowances	130,000	0.26%	630,000	1.26%
Cost of field servicing	600,000	1.20%	1,320,000	2.64%
Total	2,000,000	4.00%	5,150,000	10.30%
Total quality cost	$7,500,000	15.00%	$9,000,000	18.00%

*As a percentage of total sales. We assume that in each year sales totaled $50,000,000.

increases in prevention and appraisal costs should be more than offset by decreases in failure costs. Moreover, appraisal costs should also decrease as more effort is placed into prevention.

In Business

Fighting Bugs

Software bugs can have catastrophic consequences. Companies that sell products that rely on software know this, and fighting these particular defects can consume enormous resources. For example, it was once estimated that the cost of quality (i.e., the costs of preventing, detecting, and fixing bugs) at Raytheon Electronics Systems was almost 60% of the total costs of producing software for its products. That percentage has fallen to 15% due to new software management tools designed to prevent bugs from being written into the computer code in the first place.

Source: Otis Port, "Will Bugs Eat Up the U.S. Lead in Software?" *Business Week*, December 6, 1999, p. 118.

Exhibit 2B–4 Quality Cost Reports in Graphic Form

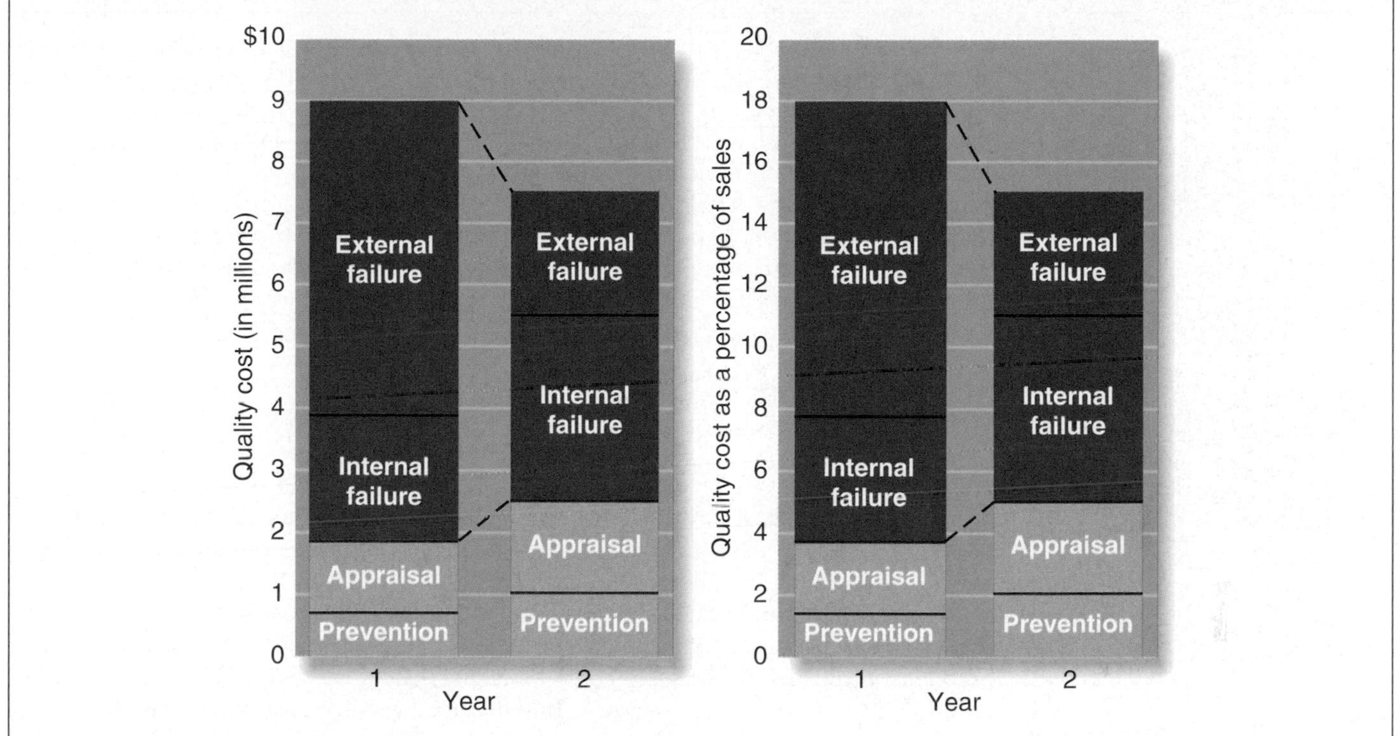

Quality Cost Reports in Graphic Form

As a supplement to the quality cost report shown in Exhibit 2B–3, companies frequently prepare quality cost information in graphic form. Graphic presentations include pie charts, bar graphs, trend lines, and so forth. The data for Ventura Company from Exhibit 2B–3 are presented in bar graph form in Exhibit 2B–4.

The first bar graph in Exhibit 2B–4 is scaled in terms of dollars of quality cost, and the second is scaled in terms of quality cost as a percentage of sales. In both graphs, the data are "stacked" upward. That is, appraisal costs are stacked on top of prevention costs, internal failure costs are stacked on top of the sum of prevention costs plus appraisal costs, and so forth. The percentage figures in the second graph show that total quality cost equals 18% of sales in Year 1 and 15% of sales in Year 2, the same as reported earlier in Exhibit 2B–3.

Data in graphic form help managers to see trends more clearly and to see the magnitude of the various costs in relation to each other. Such graphs are easily prepared using computer graphics and spreadsheet applications.

Uses of Quality Cost Information

A quality cost report has several uses. First, quality cost information helps managers see the financial significance of defects. Managers usually are not aware of the magnitude of their quality costs because these costs cut across departmental lines and are not normally tracked and accumulated by the cost system. Thus, when first presented with a quality cost report, managers often are surprised by the amount of cost attributable to poor quality.

Second, quality cost information helps managers identify the relative importance of the quality problems faced by the firm. For example, the quality cost report may show that scrap is a major quality problem or that the company is incurring huge warranty costs. With this information, managers have a better idea of where to focus efforts.

In Business | **Heads Up at Sola Optical**

Sola Optical, a manufacturer of ophthalmic spectacle lenses in Petaluma, California, prepared a cost of quality report similar to the one illustrated in this chapter. The company found that its cost of quality was about 20% of its revenues and about equal to its profits. The report demonstrated that relatively few dollars were spent on defect prevention, that appraisal costs were high, internal failure costs were extremely high, and external failure costs were quite low. This pattern occurred because the Quality Control Department used final inspection to assure only good products were shipped to customers. This resulted in high inspection, rework, and scrap costs, but few problems with defective products being sent to customers. "The Cost of Quality report was successful in alerting management to the magnitude of the costs and was a reasonable baseline against which to measure future performance."

Source: Richard K. Youde, "Cost-of-Quality Reporting: How We See It," *Management Accounting,* January 1992, pp. 34–38.

Third, quality cost information helps managers see whether their quality costs are poorly distributed. In general, quality costs should be distributed more toward prevention and appraisal activities and less toward failures.

Counterbalancing these uses, three limitations of quality cost information should be recognized. First, simply measuring and reporting quality costs does not solve quality problems. Problems can be solved only by taking action. Second, results usually lag behind quality improvement programs. Initially, total quality cost may even increase as quality control systems are designed and installed. Decreases in these costs may not begin to occur until the quality program has been in effect for a year or more. And third, the most important quality cost, lost sales arising from customer ill will, is usually omitted from the quality cost report because it is difficult to estimate.

Typically, during the initial years of a quality improvement program, the benefits of compiling a quality cost report outweigh the costs and limitations of the reports. As managers gain experience in balancing prevention and appraisal activities, the need for quality cost reports often diminishes.

International Aspects of Quality

Many of the tools used in quality management today were developed in Japan after World War II. In statistical process control, Japanese companies borrowed heavily from the work of W. Edwards Deming. However, Japanese companies are largely responsible for quality circles, JIT, the idea that quality is everyone's responsibility, and the emphasis on prevention rather than on inspection.

In the 1980s, quality reemerged as a pivotal factor in the market. Many companies now find that it is impossible to effectively compete without a very strong quality program in place. This is particularly true of companies that wish to compete in the European market.

The ISO 9000 Standards

The International Standards Organization (ISO), based in Geneva, Switzerland, has established quality control guidelines known as the **ISO 9000 standards.** Many companies and organizations in Europe will buy only from ISO 9000 standard-certified suppliers. This means that the suppliers must demonstrate to a certifying agency that:

1. A quality control system is in use, and the system clearly defines an expected level of quality.

2. The system is fully operational and is backed up with detailed documentation of quality control procedures.
3. The intended level of quality is being achieved on a sustained, consistent basis.

The key to receiving certification under the ISO 9000 standards is documentation. It's one thing for a company to say that it has a quality control system in operation, but it's quite a different thing to be able to document the steps in that system. Under ISO 9000, this documentation must be so detailed and precise that if all the employees in a company were suddenly replaced, the new employees could use the documentation to make the product exactly as it was made by the old employees. Even companies with good quality control systems find that it takes up to two years of painstaking work to develop this detailed documentation. But companies often find that compiling this documentation results in improvements in their quality systems.

The ISO 9000 standards have become an international measure of quality. Although the standards were developed to control the quality of goods sold in European countries, they have become widely accepted elsewhere as well. Companies in the United States that export to Europe often expect their own suppliers to comply with the ISO 9000 standards, since these exporters must document the quality of the materials going into their products as part of their own ISO 9000 certification.

The ISO program for certification of quality management programs is not limited to manufacturing companies. The American Institute of Certified Public Accountants was the first professional membership organization in the United States to win recognition under an ISO certification program.[3]

Consistency Pays

In Business

Over the years, E. I. du Pont de Nemours & Company has been a leader in quality control systems. Despite this emphasis on quality, for many years the engineers at one of Du Pont's plants were unable to control a high defect rate in the output from a molding press that makes plastic connectors for computers. As part of the documentation needed for certification under the ISO 9000 standards, workers on the press were required to detail in writing how they do their jobs. When engineers compared the workers' notes, they found that the workers were inconsistent in the way they calibrated probes that measure press temperature. As a result, the press temperature was often set incorrectly. When this problem was corrected, the defect rate for the press fell from 30% to only 8% of output.

Source: "Want EC Business? You Have Two Choices," *Business Week*, no. 3288 (October 19, 1992), p. 58.

Summary

Defects cause costs, which can be classified into prevention costs, appraisal costs, internal failure costs, and external failure costs. Prevention costs are incurred to keep defects from happening. Appraisal costs are incurred to ensure that defective products, once made, are not shipped to customers. Internal failure costs are incurred as a consequence of detecting defective products before they are shipped to customers. External failure costs are the consequences (in terms of repairs, servicing, and lost future business) of delivering defective products to customers. Most experts agree that management effort should be focused on preventing defects. Small investments in prevention can lead to dramatic reductions in appraisal costs and costs of internal and external failure.

Quality costs are summarized on a quality cost report. This report shows the type of quality costs being incurred and their significance and trends. The report helps managers understand the importance of quality costs, spot problem areas, and assess the way in which the quality costs are distributed.

[3] *The CPA Letter,* May 1998, p. 1.

Glossary

Appraisal costs Costs that are incurred to identify defective products before the products are shipped to customers. (p. 65)

External failure costs Costs that are incurred when a product or service that is defective is delivered to a customer. (p. 66)

Internal failure costs Costs that are incurred as a result of identifying defective products before they are shipped to customers. (p. 66)

ISO 9000 standards Quality control requirements issued by the International Standards Organization that relate to products sold in European countries. (p. 70)

Prevention costs Costs that are incurred to keep defects from occurring. (p. 64)

Quality circles Small groups of employees that meet on a regular basis to discuss ways of improving quality. (p. 64)

Quality cost Costs that are incurred to prevent defective products from falling into the hands of customers or that are incurred as a result of defective units. (p. 63)

Quality cost report A report that details prevention costs, appraisal costs, and the costs of internal and external failures. (p. 67)

Quality of conformance The degree to which a product or service meets or exceeds its design specifications and is free of defects or other problems that mar its appearance or degrade its performance. (p. 63)

Statistical process control A charting technique used to monitor the quality of work being done in a workstation for the purpose of immediately correcting any problems. (p. 64)

Questions

2–1 What are the three major elements of product costs in a manufacturing company?

2–2 Distinguish between the following: (a) direct materials, (b) indirect materials, (c) direct labor, (d) indirect labor, and (e) manufacturing overhead.

2–3 Explain the difference between a product cost and a period cost.

2–4 Describe how the income statement of a manufacturing company differs from the income statement of a merchandising company.

2–5 Of what value is the schedule of cost of goods manufactured? How does it tie into the income statement?

2–6 Describe how the inventory accounts of a manufacturing company differ from the inventory account of a merchandising company.

2–7 Why are product costs sometimes called inventoriable costs? Describe the flow of such costs in a manufacturing company from the point of incurrence until they finally become expenses on the income statement.

2–8 Is it possible for costs such as salaries or depreciation to end up as assets on the balance sheet? Explain.

2–9 What is meant by the term *cost behavior?*

2–10 "A variable cost is a cost that varies per unit of product, whereas a fixed cost is constant per unit of product." Do you agree? Explain.

2–11 How do fixed costs create difficulties in costing units of product?

2–12 Why is manufacturing overhead considered an indirect cost of a unit of product?

2–13 Define the following terms: differential cost, opportunity cost, and sunk cost.

2–14 Only variable costs can be differential costs. Do you agree? Explain.

2–15 (Appendix 2A) Mary Adams is employed by Acme Company. Last week she worked 34 hours assembling one of the company's products and was idle 6 hours due to material shortages. Acme's employees are engaged at their workstations for a normal 40-hour week. Ms. Adams is paid $15 per hour. Allocate her earnings between direct labor cost and manufacturing overhead cost.

2–16 (Appendix 2A) John Olsen operates a stamping machine on the assembly line of Drake Manufacturing Company. Last week Mr. Olsen worked 45 hours. His basic wage rate is $14 per hour, with time and a half for overtime (time worked in excess of 40 hours per week). Allocate Mr. Olsen's wages for the week between direct labor cost and manufacturing overhead cost.

2–17 (Appendix 2B) Costs associated with the quality of conformance can be broken down into four broad groups. What are these four groups and how do they differ?

2–18 (Appendix 2B) In their efforts to reduce the total cost of quality, should companies generally focus on decreasing prevention costs and appraisal costs?

2–19 (Appendix 2B) What is probably the most effective way to reduce a company's total quality costs?

2–20 (Appendix 2B) What are the main uses of quality cost reports?

2–21 (Appendix 2B) Why are managers often unaware of the magnitude of quality costs?

Exercises

EXERCISE 2–1 Using Cost Terms [LO2, LO5, LO7]

Following are a number of cost terms introduced in the chapter:

Period cost	Fixed cost
Variable cost	Prime cost
Opportunity cost	Conversion cost
Product cost	Sunk cost

Choose the cost term or terms above that most appropriately describe the costs identified in each of the following situations. A cost term can be used more than once.

1. Crestline Books, Inc., prints a small book titled *The Pocket Speller.* The paper going into the manufacture of the book would be called direct materials and classified as a ________ cost. In terms of cost behavior, the paper could also be described as a ________ cost with respect to the number of books printed.
2. Instead of compiling the words in the book, the author hired by the company could have earned considerable fees consulting with business organizations. The consulting fees forgone by the author would be called ________ cost.
3. The paper and other materials used in the manufacture of the book, combined with the direct labor cost involved, would be called ________ cost.
4. The salary of Crestline Books' president would be classified as a ________ cost, and the salary will appear on the income statement as an expense in the time period in which it is incurred.
5. Depreciation on the equipment used to print the book would be classified by Crestline Books as a ________ cost. However, depreciation on any equipment used by the company in selling and administrative activities would be classified as a ________ cost. In terms of cost behavior, depreciation would probably be classified as a ________ cost with respect to the number of books printed.
6. A ________ cost is also known as an inventoriable cost, since such costs go into the Work in Process inventory account and then into the Finished Goods inventory account before appearing on the income statement as part of cost of goods sold.
7. Taken together, the direct labor cost and manufacturing overhead cost involved in the manufacture of the book would be called ________ cost.
8. Crestline Books sells the book through agents who are paid a commission on each book sold. The company would classify these commissions as a ________ cost. In terms of cost behavior, commissions would be classified as a ________ cost.
9. Several hundred copies of the book were left over from the previous edition and are stored in a warehouse. The amount invested in these books would be called a ________ cost.
10. Costs can often be classified in several ways. For example, Crestline Books pays $4,000 rent each month on the building that houses its printing press. The rent would be part of manufacturing overhead. In terms of cost behavior, it would be classified as a ________ cost. The rent can also be classified as a ________ cost and as part of ________ cost.

EXERCISE 2–2 Classification of Costs as Period or Product Costs [LO2]

Suppose that you have been given a summer job at Fairwings Avionics, a company that manufactures sophisticated radar sets for commercial aircraft. The company, which is privately owned, has approached a bank for a loan to help finance its tremendous growth. The bank requires financial statements before approving such a loan. You have been asked to help prepare the financial statements and were given the following list of costs:

1. The cost of the memory chips used in a radar set.
2. Factory heating costs.

3. Factory equipment maintenance costs.
4. Training costs for new administrative employees.
5. The cost of the solder that is used in assembling the radar sets.
6. The travel costs of the company's salespersons.
7. Wages and salaries of factory security personnel.
8. The cost of air-conditioning executive offices.
9. Wages and salaries in the department that handles billing customers.
10. Depreciation on the equipment in the fitness room used by factory workers.
11. Telephone expenses incurred by factory management.
12. The costs of shipping completed radar sets to customers.
13. The wages of the workers who assemble the radar sets.
14. The president's salary.
15. Health insurance premiums for factory personnel.

Required:
Classify the above costs as either product (inventoriable) costs or period (noninventoriable) costs for purposes of preparing the financial statements for the bank.

EXERCISE 2–3 Classification of Costs as Fixed or Variable [LO5]
Below are a number of costs that might be incurred in a variety of organizations. Copy the list of costs onto your answer sheet, and then place an *X* in the appropriate column for each cost to indicate whether the cost involved would be variable or fixed with respect to the goods and services produced by the organization.

	Cost Behavior	
Cost	**Variable**	**Fixed**
1. Small glass plates used for lab tests in a hospital		
2. Straight-line depreciation of a building		
3. Top-management salaries		
4. Electrical costs of running machines		
5. Advertising of products and services		
6. Batteries used in manufacturing trucks		
7. Commissions to salespersons		
8. Insurance on a dentist's office		
9. Leather used in manufacturing footballs		
10. Rent on a medical center		

EXERCISE 2–4 Classification of Costs as Variable or Fixed and as Selling and Administrative or Product [LO2, LO5]
Below are listed various costs that are found in organizations.

1. The costs of turn signal switches used at the General Motors Saginaw, Michigan, plant. These are one of the parts installed in the steering columns assembled at the plant.
2. Interest expense on CBS's long-term debt.
3. Salespersons' commissions at Avon Products, a company that sells cosmetics door to door.
4. Insurance on one of Cincinnati Milacron's factory buildings.
5. The costs of shipping brass fittings from Graham Manufacturing's plant in New Hampshire to customers in California.
6. Depreciation on the bookshelves at Reston Bookstore.
7. The costs of X-ray film at the Mayo Clinic's radiology lab.
8. The cost of leasing an 800 telephone number at L. L. Bean. The monthly charge for the 800 number is independent of the number of calls taken.
9. The depreciation on the playground equipment at a McDonald's outlet.
10. The cost of mozzarella cheese used at a Pizza Hut outlet.

Required:
Classify each cost as either variable or fixed with respect to the volume of goods or services produced and sold by the organization. Also classify each cost as a selling and administrative cost or a product cost. Prepare your answer sheet as shown below:

	Cost Behavior			
Cost Item	**Variable**	**Fixed**	**Selling and Administrative Cost**	**Product Cost**

EXERCISE 2–5 (Appendix 2B) Classification of Quality Costs [LO9]

Below are listed several activities that are part of a company's quality control system:

a. Repairs of goods still under warranty.
b. Customer returns due to defects.
c. Statistical process control.
d. Disposal of spoiled goods.
e. Maintaining testing equipment.
f. Inspecting finished goods.
g. Downtime caused by quality problems.
h. Debugging errors in software.
i. Recalls of defective products.
j. Training quality engineers.
k. Re-entering data due to typing errors.
l. Inspecting materials received from suppliers.
m. Audits of the quality system.
n. Supervision of testing personnel.
o. Rework labor.

Required:

1. Classify the costs associated with each of these activities into one of the following categories: prevention cost, appraisal cost, internal failure cost, or external failure cost.
2. Which of the four types of costs listed in (1) above are incurred to keep poor quality of conformance from occurring? Which of the four types of costs are incurred because poor quality of conformance has occurred?

EXERCISE 2–6 Product Cost Flows; Product versus Period Costs [LO2, LO3]

Ryser Company was organized on May 1. On that date the company purchased 35,000 plastic emblems, each with a peel-off adhesive backing. The front of the emblems contained the company's name, accompanied by an attractive logo. Each emblem cost Ryser Company $2.

During May, 31,000 emblems were drawn from the Raw Materials inventory account. Of these, 1,000 were taken by the sales manager to an important sales meeting with prospective customers and handed out as an advertising gimmick. The remaining emblems drawn from inventory were affixed to units of the company's product that were being manufactured during May. Of the units of product having emblems affixed during May, 90% were completed and transferred from Work in Process to Finished Goods. Of the units completed during the month, 75% were sold and shipped to customers.

Required:

1. Determine the cost of emblems that would be in each of the following accounts at May 31:
   a. Raw Materials.
   b. Work in Process.
   c. Finished Goods.
   d. Cost of Goods Sold.
   e. Advertising Expense.
2. Specify whether each of the above accounts would appear on the balance sheet or on the income statement at May 31.

EXERCISE 2–7 Preparation of a Schedule of Cost of Goods Manufactured and Cost of Goods Sold [LO1, LO3, LO4]

The following cost and inventory data for the just completed year are taken from the accounting records of Eccles Company:

Costs incurred:	
Advertising expense	$100,000
Direct labor cost	90,000
Purchases of raw materials	132,000
Rent, factory building	80,000
Indirect labor	56,300
Sales commissions	35,000
Utilities, factory	9,000
Maintenance, factory equipment	24,000
Supplies, factory	700
Depreciation, office equipment	8,000
Depreciation, factory equipment	40,000

	Beginning of Year	End of Year
Inventories:		
Raw materials	$ 8,000	$10,000
Work in process	5,000	20,000
Finished goods	70,000	25,000

Required:
1. Prepare a schedule of cost of goods manufactured.
2. Prepare the cost of goods sold section of Eccles Company's income statement for the year.

EXERCISE 2–8 (Appendix 2A) Classification of Overtime Cost [LO8]

Several weeks ago you called Jiffy Plumbing Company to have some routine repair work done on the plumbing system in your home. The plumber came about two weeks later, at four o'clock in the afternoon, and spent two hours completing your repair work. When you received your bill from the company, it contained a $75 charge for labor—$30 for the first hour and $45 for the second.

When questioned about the difference in hourly rates, the company's service manager explained that the higher rate for the second hour contained a charge for an "overtime premium," since the union required that plumbers be paid time and a half for any work in excess of eight hours per day. The service manager further explained that the company was working overtime to "catch up a little" on its backlog of work orders, but still needed to maintain a "decent" profit margin on the plumbers' time.

Required:
1. Do you agree with the company's computation of the labor charge on your job?
2. Assume that the company pays its plumbers $20 per hour for the first eight hours worked in a day and $30 per hour for any additional time worked. Prepare computations to show how the cost of the plumber's time for the day (nine hours) should be allocated between direct labor cost and general overhead cost on the company's books.
3. Under what circumstances might the company be justified in charging an overtime premium for repair work on your home?

EXERCISE 2–9 (Appendix 2B) Using Quality Management Terms [LO9]

Listed below are terms relating to quality management.

Appraisal costs	Quality circles
Quality cost report	Prevention costs
Quality	External failure costs
Internal failure costs	Quality of conformance

Choose the term or terms that most appropriately complete the following statements. The terms can be used more than once. (Note that a blank can hold more than one word.)

1. When a product or service does not conform to customer expectations in terms of features or performance, it is viewed as being poor in ____________.
2. A product or service will have a low ____________ if it does not function the way its designers intended, or if it has many defects as a result of sloppy manufacture.
3. A company incurs ____________ and ____________ in an effort to keep poor quality of conformance from occurring.
4. A company incurs ____________ and ____________ because poor quality of conformance has occurred.
5. Of the four groups of costs associated with quality of conformance, ____________ are generally the most damaging to a company.
6. Inspection, testing, and other costs incurred to keep defective products from being shipped to customers are known as ____________.
7. ____________ are incurred in an effort to eliminate poor product design, defective manufacturing practices, and the providing of substandard service.
8. The costs relating to defects, rejected products, and downtime caused by quality problems are known as ____________.
9. When a product that is defective in some way is delivered to a customer, then ____________ are incurred.
10. Over time a company's total quality costs should decrease if it redistributes its quality costs by placing its greatest emphasis on ____________ and ____________.

11. In many companies, small groups of employees, known as ____________________, meet on a regular basis to discuss ways to improve the quality of output.
12. The way to ensure that management is aware of the costs associated with quality is to summarize such costs on a ____________________.

EXERCISE 2–10 (Appendix 2A) Classification of Labor Costs [LO8]
Fred Austin is employed by White Company. He works on the company's assembly line and assembles a component part for one of the company's products. Fred is paid $12 per hour for regular time, and he is paid time and a half (i.e., $18 per hour) for all work in excess of 40 hours per week.

Required:

1. Assume that during a given week Fred is idle for two hours due to machine breakdowns and that he is idle for four more hours due to material shortages. No overtime is recorded for the week. Allocate Fred's wages for the week between direct labor cost and manufacturing overhead cost.
2. Assume that during a following week Fred works a total of 50 hours. He has no idle time for the week. Allocate Fred's wages for the week between direct labor cost and manufacturing overhead cost.
3. Fred's company provides an attractive package of fringe benefits for its employees. This package includes a retirement program and a health insurance program. So far as direct labor workers are concerned, explain two ways that the company could handle the costs of fringe benefits in its cost records.

Problems

PROBLEM 2–11 Classification of Costs into Various Categories [LO1, LO2, LO5, LO7]
Several years ago Medex Company purchased a small building adjacent to its manufacturing plant in order to have room for expansion when needed. Since the company had no immediate need for the extra space, the building was rented out to another company for a rental revenue of $40,000 per year. The renter's lease will expire next month, and rather than renewing the lease, Medex Company has decided to use the building itself to manufacture a new product.

Direct materials cost for the new product will total $40 per unit. It will be necessary to hire a supervisor to oversee production. Her salary will be $2,500 per month. Workers will be hired to manufacture the new product, with direct labor cost amounting to $18 per unit. Manufacturing operations will occupy all of the building space, so it will be necessary to rent space in a warehouse nearby in order to store finished units of product. The rental cost will be $1,000 per month. In addition, the company will need to rent equipment for use in producing the new product; the rental cost will be $3,000 per month. The company will continue to depreciate the building on a straight-line basis, as in past years. Depreciation on the building is $10,000 per year.

Advertising costs for the new product will total $50,000 per year. Costs of shipping the new product to customers will be $10 per unit. Electrical costs of operating machines will be $2 per unit.

To have funds to purchase materials, meet payrolls, and so forth, the company will have to liquidate some temporary investments. These investments are presently yielding a return of $6,000 per year.

Required:
Prepare an answer sheet with the following column headings:

			Product Cost					
Name of the Cost	Variable Cost	Fixed Cost	Direct Materials	Direct Labor	Manufacturing Overhead	Period (selling and administrative) Cost	Opportunity Cost	Sunk Cost

List the different costs associated with the new product decision down the extreme left column (under Name of the Cost). Then place an *X* under each heading that helps to describe the type of cost involved. There may be *X*'s under several column headings for a single cost. (For example, a cost may be a fixed cost, a period cost, and a sunk cost; you would place an *X* under each of these column headings opposite the cost.)

PROBLEM 2–12 Classification of Costs as Variable or Fixed and Direct or Indirect [LO5, LO6]
Various costs associated with manufacturing operations are given below:

1. Plastic washers used in auto production.
2. Production superintendent's salary.
3. Laborers assembling a product.
4. Electricity for operation of machines.
5. Janitorial salaries.
6. Clay used in brick production.
7. Rent on a factory building.
8. Wood used in ski production.
9. Screws used in furniture production.
10. A supervisor's salary.
11. Cloth used in suit production.
12. Depreciation of cafeteria equipment.
13. Glue used in textbook production.
14. Lubricants for machines.
15. Paper used in textbook production.

Required:
Classify each cost as being either variable or fixed with respect to the number of units produced and sold. Also indicate whether each cost would typically be treated as a direct cost or an indirect cost with respect to units of product. Prepare your answer sheet as shown below:

	Cost Behavior		To Units of Product	
Cost Item	**Variable**	**Fixed**	**Direct**	**Indirect**
Example: Factory insurance		X		X

PROBLEM 2–13 (Appendix 2A) Classification of Labor Costs [LO8]
Lynn Bjorland is employed by Southern Laboratories, Inc., and is directly involved in preparing the company's leading antibiotic drug. Lynn's basic wage rate is $24 per hour. The company pays its employees time and a half (i.e., $36 per hour) for any work in excess of 40 hours per week.

Required:
1. Suppose that in a given week Lynn works 45 hours. Compute Lynn's total wages for the week. How much of this cost would the company allocate to direct labor cost? To manufacturing overhead cost?
2. Suppose in another week that Lynn works 50 hours but is idle for 4 hours during the week due to equipment breakdowns. Compute Lynn's total wages for the week. How much of this amount would be allocated to direct labor cost? To manufacturing overhead cost?
3. Southern Laboratories has an attractive package of fringe benefits that costs the company $8 for each hour of employee time (either regular time or overtime). During a particular week, Lynn works 48 hours but is idle for 3 hours due to material shortages. Compute Lynn's total wages and fringe benefits for the week. If the company treats all fringe benefits as part of manufacturing overhead cost, how much of Lynn's wages and fringe benefits for the week would be allocated to direct labor cost? To manufacturing overhead cost?
4. Refer to the data in (3) above. If the company treats that part of fringe benefits relating to direct labor as added direct labor cost, how much of Lynn's wages and fringe benefits for the week will be allocated to direct labor cost? To manufacturing overhead cost?

PROBLEM 2–14 (Appendix 2B) Quality Cost Report [LO9, LO10]
Yedder Enterprises was a pioneer in designing and producing precision surgical lasers. Yedder's product was brilliantly designed, but the manufacturing process was neglected by management with a consequence that quality problems have been chronic. When customers complained about defective units, Yedder would simply send out a repairperson or replace the defective unit with a new one. Recently, several competitors came out with similar products without Yedder's quality problems, and as a consequence Yedder's sales have declined.

To rescue the situation, Yedder embarked on an intensive campaign to strengthen its quality control at the beginning of the current year. These efforts met with some success—the downward slide in sales was reversed, and sales grew from $95 million last year to $100 million this year. To help monitor the company's progress, costs relating to quality and quality control were compiled for last year and for the first full year of the quality campaign this year. The costs, which do not include the lost sales due to a reputation for poor quality, appear below:

	For the Year (in thousands)	
	This Year	Last Year
Product recalls	$ 600	$3,500
Systems development	680	120
Inspection	2,770	1,700
Net cost of scrap	1,300	800
Supplies used in testing	40	30
Warranty repairs	2,800	3,300
Rework labor	1,600	1,400
Statistical process control	270	0
Customer returns of defective goods	200	3,200
Cost of testing equipment	390	270
Quality engineering	1,650	1,080
Downtime due to quality problems	1,100	600

Required:

1. Prepare a quality cost report for both this year and last year. Carry percentage computations to two decimal places.
2. Prepare a bar graph showing the distribution of the various quality costs by category.
3. Prepare a written evaluation to accompany the reports you have prepared in (1) and (2) above. This evaluation should discuss the distribution of quality costs in the company, changes in the distribution over the last year, and any other information you believe would be useful to management.

PROBLEM 2–15 Classification of Various Costs [LO2, LO5, LO6]

Listed below are several costs typically found in organizations.

1. Depreciation, executive jet.
2. Costs of shipping finished goods to customers.
3. Wood used in furniture manufacturing.
4. Sales manager's salary.
5. Electricity used in furniture manufacturing.
6. Secretary to the company president.
7. Aerosol attachment placed on a spray can produced by the company.
8. Billing costs.
9. Packing supplies for shipping products overseas.
10. Sand used in concrete manufacturing.
11. Supervisor's salary, factory.
12. Executive life insurance.
13. Sales commissions.
14. Fringe benefits, assembly-line workers.
15. Advertising costs.
16. Property taxes on finished goods warehouses.
17. Lubricants for machines.

Required:

Prepare an answer sheet with column headings as shown below. For each cost item, indicate whether it would be variable or fixed with respect to the number of units produced and sold; and then whether it would be a selling cost, an administrative cost, or a manufacturing cost. If it is a manufacturing cost, indicate whether it would typically be treated as a direct or indirect cost with respect to units of product. Three sample answers are provided for illustration.

				Manufacturing (product) Cost	
Cost Item	Variable or Fixed	Selling Cost	Administrative Cost	Direct	Indirect
Direct labor	V			X	
Executive salaries	F		X		
Factory rent	F				X

PROBLEM 2–16 Classification of Salary Cost as a Period or Product Cost [LO2]
You have just been hired by EduRom Company, which was organized on January 2 of the current year. The company manufactures and sells a variety of educational CDs for personal computers. It is your responsibility to supervise the employees who take orders from customers over the phone and to arrange for shipping orders via Federal Express, UPS, and other freight carriers.

The company is unsure how to classify your annual salary in its cost records. The company's cost analyst says that your salary should be classified as a manufacturing (product) cost; the controller says that it should be classified as a selling expense; and the president says that it doesn't matter which way your salary cost is classified.

Required:
1. Which viewpoint is correct? Why?
2. From the point of view of the reported net income for the year, is the president correct in saying that it doesn't matter which way your salary cost is classified? Explain.

PROBLEM 2–17 Classification of Various Costs [LO1, LO2, LO5, LO7]
Frieda Bronkowski has invented a new type of flyswatter. After giving the matter much thought, Frieda has decided to quit her $4,000 per month job with a computer firm and produce and sell the flyswatters full time. Frieda will rent a garage that will be used as a production plant. The rent will be $150 per month. Frieda will rent production equipment at a cost of $500 per month.

The cost of materials for each flyswatter will be $0.30. Frieda will hire workers to produce the flyswatters. They will be paid $0.50 for each completed unit. Frieda will rent a room in the house next door for use as her sales office. The rent will be $75 per month. She has arranged for the telephone company to attach a recording device to her home phone to get off-hours messages from customers. The device will increase her monthly phone bill by $20.

Frieda has some money in savings that is earning interest of $1,000 per year. These savings will be withdrawn and used for about a year to get the business going. To sell her flyswatters, Frieda will advertise heavily in the local area. Advertising costs will be $400 per month. In addition, Frieda will pay a sales commission of $0.10 for each flyswatter sold.

For the time being, Frieda does not intend to draw any salary from the new company.

Frieda has already paid the legal and filing fees to incorporate her business. These fees amounted to $600.

Required:
1. Prepare an answer sheet with the following column headings:

Name of the Cost	Variable Cost	Fixed Cost	Product Cost: Direct Materials	Product Cost: Direct Labor	Product Cost: Manufacturing Overhead	Period (selling and administrative) Cost	Opportunity Cost	Sunk Cost

List the different costs associated with the new company down the extreme left column (under Name of Cost). Then place an *X* under each heading that helps to describe the type of cost involved. There may be *X*'s under several column headings for a single cost. (That is, a cost may be a fixed cost, a period cost, and a sunk cost; you would place an *X* under each of these column headings opposite the cost.) Under the variable cost column, list only those costs that would be variable with respect to the number of flyswatters that are produced and sold.

2. All of the costs you have listed above, except one, would be differential costs between the alternatives of Frieda producing flyswatters or staying with the computer firm. Which cost is *not* differential? Explain.

PROBLEM 2–18 Cost Classification and Cost Behavior [LO2, LO5, LO6]
Heritage Company manufactures a beautiful bookcase that enjoys widespread popularity. The company has a backlog of orders that is large enough to keep production going indefinitely at the plant's full capacity of 4,000 bookcases per year. Annual cost data at full capacity follow:

Direct materials used (wood and glass)	$430,000
General office salaries	110,000
Factory supervision	70,000
Sales commissions	60,000
Depreciation, factory building.	105,000
Depreciation, office equipment.	2,000

Indirect materials, factory	18,000
Factory labor (cutting and assembly)	90,000
Advertising	100,000
Insurance, factory	6,000
General office supplies (billing)	4,000
Property taxes, factory	20,000
Utilities, factory	45,000

Required:

1. Prepare an answer sheet with the column headings shown below. Enter each cost item on your answer sheet, placing the dollar amount under the appropriate headings. As examples, this has been done already for the first two items in the list above. Note that each cost item is classified in two ways: first, as being either variable or fixed with respect to the number of units produced and sold; and second, as being either a selling and administrative cost or a product cost. (If the item is a product cost, it should also be classified as being either direct or indirect as shown.)

	Cost Behavior		Selling or Administrative	Product Cost	
Cost Item	**Variable**	**Fixed**	**Cost**	**Direct**	**Indirect***
Materials used	$430,000			$430,000	
General office salaries		$110,000	$110,000		

*To units of product.

2. Total the dollar amounts in each of the columns in (1) above. Compute the average product cost per bookcase.
3. Due to a recession, assume that production drops to only 2,000 bookcases per year. Would you expect the average product cost per bookcase to increase, decrease, or remain unchanged? Explain. No computations are necessary.
4. Refer to the original data. The president's next-door neighbor has considered making himself a bookcase and has priced the necessary materials at a building supply store. He has asked the president whether he could purchase a bookcase from the Heritage Company "at cost," and the president has agreed to let him do so.
   a. Would you expect any disagreement between the two men over the price the neighbor should pay? Explain. What price does the president probably have in mind? The neighbor?
   b. Since the company is operating at full capacity, what cost term used in the chapter might be justification for the president to charge the full, regular price to the neighbor and still be selling "at cost"? Explain.

PROBLEM 2–19 Schedule of Cost of Goods Manufactured; Income Statement; Cost Behavior [LO1, LO2, LO3, LO4, LO5]

Various cost and sales data for Medco, Inc., are given below for the just completed year:

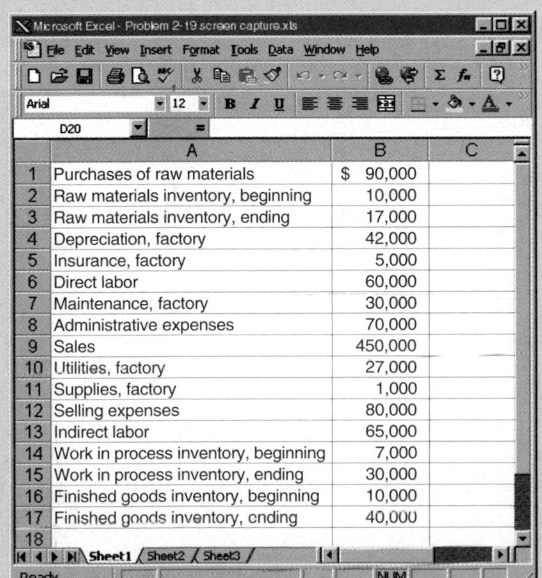

	A	B
1	Purchases of raw materials	$ 90,000
2	Raw materials inventory, beginning	10,000
3	Raw materials inventory, ending	17,000
4	Depreciation, factory	42,000
5	Insurance, factory	5,000
6	Direct labor	60,000
7	Maintenance, factory	30,000
8	Administrative expenses	70,000
9	Sales	450,000
10	Utilities, factory	27,000
11	Supplies, factory	1,000
12	Selling expenses	80,000
13	Indirect labor	65,000
14	Work in process inventory, beginning	7,000
15	Work in process inventory, ending	30,000
16	Finished goods inventory, beginning	10,000
17	Finished goods inventory, ending	40,000

Required:

1. Prepare a schedule of cost of goods manufactured.
2. Prepare an income statement.
3. Assume that the company produced the equivalent of 10,000 units of product during the year. What was the average cost per unit for direct materials? What was the average cost per unit for factory depreciation?
4. Assume that the company expects to produce 15,000 units of product during the coming year. What average cost per unit and what total cost would you expect the company to incur for direct materials at this level of activity? For factory depreciation? (In preparing your answer, assume that direct materials is a variable cost and that depreciation is a fixed cost; also assume that depreciation is computed on a straight-line basis.)
5. As the manager responsible for production costs, explain to the president any difference in the average costs per unit between (3) and (4) above.

PROBLEM 2–20 Schedule of Cost of Goods Manufactured; Income Statement [LO1, LO2, LO3, LO4]

Skyler Company was organized on November 1 of the previous year. After seven months of start-up losses, management had expected to earn a profit during June, the most recent month. Management was disappointed, however, when the income statement for June also showed a loss. June's income statement follows:

SKYLER COMPANY
Income Statement
For the Month Ended June 30

Sales		$600,000
Less operating expenses:		
Selling and administrative salaries	$ 35,000	
Rent on facilities	40,000	
Purchases of raw materials	190,000	
Insurance	8,000	
Depreciation, sales equipment	10,000	
Utilities costs	50,000	
Indirect labor	108,000	
Direct labor	90,000	
Depreciation, factory equipment	12,000	
Maintenance, factory	7,000	
Advertising	80,000	630,000
Net operating loss		$ (30,000)

After seeing the $30,000 loss for June, Skyler's president stated, "I was sure we'd be profitable within six months, but after eight months we're still spilling red ink. Maybe it's time for us to throw in the towel and accept one of those offers we've had for the company. To make matters worse, I just heard that Linda won't be back from her surgery for at least six more weeks."

Linda is the company's controller; in her absence, the statement above was prepared by a new assistant who has had little experience in manufacturing operations. Additional information about the company follows:

a. Only 80% of the rent on facilities applies to factory operations; the remainder applies to selling and administrative activities.

b. Inventory balances at the beginning and end of the month were as follows:

	June 1	June 30
Raw materials	$17,000	$42,000
Work in process	70,000	85,000
Finished goods	20,000	60,000

c. Some 75% of the insurance and 90% of the utilities cost apply to factory operations; the remaining amounts apply to selling and administrative activities.

The president has asked you to check over the above income statement and make a recommendation as to whether the company should continue operations.

Required:

1. As one step in gathering data for a recommendation to the president, prepare a schedule of cost of goods manufactured for June.
2. As a second step, prepare a new income statement for the month.
3. Based on your statements prepared in (1) and (2) above, would you recommend that the company continue operations?

PROBLEM 2–21 Schedule of Cost of Goods Manufactured; Income Statement; Cost Behavior [LO1, LO2, LO3, LO4, LO5]

The following selected account balances for the year ended December 31 are provided for Valenko Company:

Advertising expense	$215,000
Insurance, factory equipment	8,000
Depreciation, sales equipment	40,000
Rent, factory building	90,000
Utilities, factory	52,000
Sales commissions	35,000
Cleaning supplies, factory	6,000
Depreciation, factory equipment	110,000
Selling and administrative salaries	85,000
Maintenance, factory	74,000
Direct labor	?
Purchases of raw materials	260,000

Inventory balances at the beginning and end of the year were as follows:

	Beginning of Year	End of Year
Raw materials	$50,000	$40,000
Work in process	?	33,000
Finished goods	30,000	?

The total manufacturing costs for the year were $675,000; the goods available for sale totaled $720,000; and the cost of goods sold totaled $635,000.

Required:

1. Prepare a schedule of cost of goods manufactured and the cost of goods sold section of the company's income statement for the year.
2. Assume that the dollar amounts given above are for the equivalent of 30,000 units produced during the year. Compute the average cost per unit for direct materials used, and compute the average cost per unit for rent on the factory building.
3. Assume that in the following year the company expects to produce 50,000 units. What average cost per unit and total cost would you expect to be incurred for direct materials? For rent on the factory building? (In preparing your answer, you may assume that direct materials is a variable cost and that rent is a fixed cost.)
4. As the manager in charge of production costs, explain to the president the reason for any difference in unit costs between (2) and (3) above.

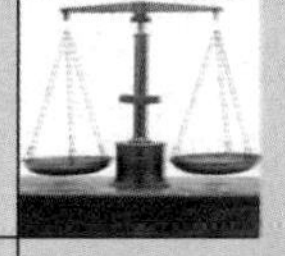

PROBLEM 2–22 Ethics and the Manager [LO2]

The top management of General Electronics, Inc., is well known for "managing by the numbers." With an eye on the company's desired growth in overall net profit, the company's CEO (chief executive officer) sets target profits at the beginning of the year for each of the company's divisions. The CEO has stated her policy as follows: "I won't interfere with operations in the divisions. I am available for advice, but the division vice presidents are free to do anything they want so long as they hit the target profits for the year."

In November, Stan Richart, the vice president in charge of the Cellular Telephone Technologies Division, saw that making the current year's target profit for his division was going to be very difficult. Among other actions, he directed that discretionary expenditures be delayed until the beginning of the new year. On December 30, he was angered to discover that a warehouse clerk had ordered $350,000 of cellular telephone parts earlier in December even though the parts weren't really needed by the assembly department until January or February. Contrary to common accounting practice, the General Electronics, Inc., Accounting Policy Manual states that such parts are to be recorded as an expense when delivered. To avoid recording the expense, Mr. Richart asked that the order be canceled, but the purchasing department reported that the parts had already been delivered and the supplier would not accept returns. Since the bill had not yet been paid, Mr. Richart asked the accounting department to correct the clerk's mistake by delaying recognition of the delivery until the bill is paid in January.

Required:

1. Are Mr. Richart's actions ethical? Explain why they are or are not ethical.
2. Do the general management philosophy and accounting policies at General Electronics encourage or discourage ethical behavior? Explain.

PROBLEM 2–23 (Appendix 2B) Analyzing a Quality Cost Report [LO10]

Bergen, Inc., produces telephone equipment at its Georgia plant. In recent years, the company's market share has been eroded by stiff competition from Asian and European competitors. Price and product quality are the two key areas in which companies compete in this market.

Two years ago, Jerry Holman, Bergen's president, decided to devote more resources to the improvement of product quality after learning that his company's products had been ranked fourth in product quality in a survey of telephone equipment users. He believed that Bergen could no longer afford to ignore the importance of product quality. Holman set up a task force that he headed to implement a formal quality improvement program. Included on this task force were representatives from engineering, sales, customer service, production, and accounting. This broad representation was needed because Holman believed that this was a companywide program, and that all employees should share the responsibility for its success.

After the first meeting of the task force, Sheila Haynes, manager of sales, asked Tony Reese, production manager, what he thought of the proposed program. Reese replied, "I have reservations. Quality is too abstract to be attaching costs to it and then to be holding you and me responsible for cost improvements. I like to work with goals that I can see and count! I'm nervous about having my annual bonus based on a decrease in quality costs; there are too many variables that we have no control over."

Bergen's quality improvement program has now been in operation for two years. The company's most recent quality cost report is shown below.

Bergen, Inc.
Quality Cost Report
(in thousands)

	Year 2	Year 1
Prevention costs:		
Machine maintenance	$ 160	$ 215
Training suppliers	15	5
Design reviews	95	20
Total	270	240
Appraisal costs:		
Incoming inspection	22	45
Final testing	94	160
Total	116	205
Internal failure costs:		
Rework	62	120
Scrap	40	68
Total	102	188
External failure costs:		
Warranty repairs	23	69
Customer returns	80	262
Total	103	331
Total quality cost	$ 591	$ 964
Total production cost	$4,510	$4,120

As they were reviewing the report, Haynes asked Reese what he now thought of the quality improvement program. "The work is really moving through the production department," Reese replied. "We used to spend time helping the customer service department solve their problems, but they are leaving us alone these days. I have no complaints so far, and I'm relieved to see that the new quality improvement hasn't adversely affected our bonuses. I'm anxious to see if it increases our bonuses in the future."

Required:

1. By analyzing the company's quality cost report, determine if Bergen, Inc.'s quality improvement program has been successful. *List specific evidence to support your answer.* Show percentage figures in two ways: first, as a percentage of total production cost; and second, as a percentage of total quality cost. Carry all computations to one decimal place.
2. Discuss why Tony Reese's current reaction to the quality improvement program is more favorable than his initial reaction.
3. Jerry Holman believed that the quality improvement program was essential and that Bergen, Inc., could no longer afford to ignore the importance of product quality. Discuss how Bergen, Inc., could measure the opportunity cost of not implementing the quality improvement program.

(CMA, adapted)

PROBLEM 2–24 Variable and Fixed Costs; Subtleties of Direct and Indirect Costs [LO5, LO6]

The Central Area Well-Baby Clinic provides a variety of health services to newborn babies and their parents. The clinic is organized into a number of departments, one of which is the Immunization Center. Listed below are a number of costs of the clinic and the Immunization Center.

Example: The cost of polio immunization tablets

a. The salary of the head nurse in the Immunization Center.
b. Costs of incidental supplies consumed in the Immunization Center, such as paper towels.
c. The cost of lighting and heating the Immunization Center.
d. The cost of disposable syringes used in the Immunization Center.
e. The salary of the Central Area Well-Baby Clinic's information systems manager.
f. The costs of mailing letters soliciting donations to the Central Area Well-Baby Clinic.
g. The wages of nurses who work in the Immunization Center.
h. The cost of medical malpractice insurance for the Central Area Well-Baby Clinic.
i. Depreciation on the fixtures and equipment in the Immunization Center.

Required:

For each cost listed above, indicate whether it is a direct or indirect cost of the Immunization Center, whether it is a direct or indirect cost of immunizing particular patients, and whether it is variable or fixed with respect to the number of immunizations administered. Use the form below for your answer.

		Direct or Indirect Cost of the Immunization Center		Direct or Indirect Cost of Particular Patients		Variable or Fixed with Respect to the Number of Immunizations Administered	
Item	Description	Direct	Indirect	Direct	Indirect	Variable	Fixed
Example:	The cost of polio immunization tablets	X		X		X	

PROBLEM 2–25 Working with Incomplete Data from the Income Statement and Schedule of Cost of Goods Manufactured [LO3, LO4]

Supply the missing data in the four cases below. Each case is independent of the others.

	Case 1	Case 2	Case 3	Case 4
Direct materials	$ 7,000	$ 9,000	$ 6,000	$ 8,000
Direct labor	2,000	4,000	?	3,000
Manufacturing overhead	10,000	?	7,000	21,000
Total manufacturing costs	?	25,000	18,000	?

	Case			
	1	2	3	4
Beginning work in process inventory . .	?	1,000	2,000	?
Ending work in process inventory	4,000	3,500	?	2,000
Cost of goods manufactured	$18,000	$?	$16,000	$?
Sales	$25,000	$40,000	$30,000	$50,000
Beginning finished goods inventory . . .	6,000	?	7,000	9,000
Cost of goods manufactured	?	?	?	31,500
Goods available for sale	?	?	?	?
Ending finished goods inventory	9,000	4,000	?	7,000
Cost of goods sold	?	26,500	18,000	?
Gross margin	?	?	?	?
Operating expenses	6,000	?	?	10,000
Net income	$?	$ 5,500	$ 3,000	$?

PROBLEM 2–26 Income Statement; Schedule of Cost of Goods Manufactured [LO1, LO2, LO3, LO4]

Hickey Company, a manufacturing firm, produces a single product. The following information has been taken from the company's production, sales, and cost records for the just completed year:

Production in units	30,000
Sales in units	?
Ending finished goods inventory in units	?
Sales in dollars	$650,000
Costs:	
Advertising	$ 50,000
Direct labor	80,000
Indirect labor	60,000
Raw materials purchased	160,000
Building rent (production uses 80% of the space; administrative and sales offices use the rest)	50,000
Utilities, factory	35,000
Royalty paid for use of production patent, $1 per unit produced	?
Maintenance, factory	25,000
Rent for special production equipment, $6,000 per year plus $0.10 per unit produced	?
Selling and administrative salaries	140,000
Other factory overhead costs	11,000
Other selling and administrative expenses	20,000

	Beginning of Year	End of Year
Inventories:		
Raw materials	$20,000	$10,000
Work in process	30,000	40,000
Finished goods	0	?

The finished goods inventory is being carried at the average unit production cost for the year. The selling price of the product is $25 per unit.

Required:

1. Prepare a schedule of cost of goods manufactured for the year.
2. Compute the following:
   a. The number of units in the finished goods inventory at the end of the year.
   b. The cost of the units in the finished goods inventory at the end of the year.
3. Prepare an income statement for the year.

Cases

CASE 2–27 Missing Data; Schedule of Cost of Goods Manufactured; Income Statement [LO1, LO2, LO3, LO4]

"I know I'm a pretty good scientist, but I guess I still have some things to learn about running a business," said Staci Morales, founder and president of Medical Technology, Inc. "Demand has been so strong for our heart monitor that I was sure we'd be profitable immediately, but just look at the gusher of red ink for the first quarter." The data to which Staci was referring are shown below:

MEDICAL TECHNOLOGY, INC.
Income Statement
For the Quarter Ended June 30

Sales (16,000 monitors)		$ 975,000
Less operating expenses:		
Selling and administrative salaries	$ 90,000	
Advertising	200,000	
Cleaning supplies, production	6,000	
Indirect labor cost	135,000	
Depreciation, office equipment	18,000	
Direct labor cost	80,000	
Raw materials purchased	310,000	
Maintenance, production	47,000	
Rental cost, facilities	65,000	
Insurance, production	9,000	
Utilities	40,000	
Depreciation, production equipment	75,000	
Travel, salespersons	60,000	1,135,000
Net operating loss		$ (160,000)

"At this rate we'll be out of business in a year," said Derek Louganis, the company's accountant. "But I've double-checked these figures, so I know they're right."

Medical Technology was organized on April 1 of the current year to produce and market a revolutionary new heart monitor. The company's accounting system was set up by Herb Steinbeck, an experienced accountant who recently left the company. The statement above was prepared by Louganis, his assistant.

"We may not last a year if the insurance company doesn't pay the $227,000 it owes us for the 4,000 monitors lost in the truck accident last week," said Staci. "The agent says our claim is inflated, but that's a lot of baloney."

Just after the end of the quarter, a truck carrying 4,000 monitors wrecked and burned, destroying the entire load. The monitors were part of the 20,000 units completed during the quarter ended June 30. They were in a warehouse awaiting sale at quarter-end and were sold and shipped on July 3 (this sale is *not* included on the income statement above). The trucking company's insurer is liable for the cost of the goods lost. Louganis has determined this cost as follows:

$$\frac{\text{Total costs for the quarter}}{\text{Monitors produced during the quarter}} = \$1{,}135{,}000/20{,}000 \text{ units} = \$56.75 \text{ per unit}$$

$$4{,}000 \text{ units} \times \$56.75 \text{ per unit} = \$227{,}000$$

The following additional information is available on the company's activities during the quarter ended June 30:

a. Inventories at the beginning and end of the quarter were as follows:

	Beginning of the Quarter	End of the Quarter
Raw materials	0	$40,000
Work in process	0	30,000
Finished goods	0	?

b. Eighty percent of the rental cost for facilities and 90% of the utilities cost relate to manufacturing operations. The remaining amounts relate to selling and administrative activities.

Required:

1. What conceptual errors, if any, were made in preparing the income statement above?
2. Prepare a schedule of cost of goods manufactured for the quarter.
3. Prepare a corrected income statement for the quarter. Your statement should show in detail how the cost of goods sold is computed.
4. Do you agree that the insurance company owes Medical Technology, Inc., $227,000? Explain your answer.

CASE 2–28 Inventory Computations from Incomplete Data [LO3, LO4]

While snoozing at the controls of his Pepper Six airplane, Dunse P. Sluggard leaned heavily against the door; suddenly, the door flew open and a startled Dunse tumbled out. As he parachuted to the ground, Dunse watched helplessly as the empty plane smashed into Operex Products' plant and administrative offices.

"The insurance company will never believe this," cried Mercedes Juliet, the company's controller, as she watched the ensuing fire burn the building to the ground. "The entire company is wiped out!"

"There's no reason to even contact the insurance agent," replied Ford Romero, the company's operations manager. "We can't file a claim without records, and all we have left is this copy of last year's annual report. It shows that raw materials at the beginning of this year (January 1) totaled $30,000, work in process totaled $50,000, and finished goods totaled $90,000. But what we need is a record of these inventories as of today, and our records are up in smoke."

"All except this summary page I was working on when the plane hit the building," said Mercedes. "It shows that our sales to date this year have totaled $1,350,000 and that manufacturing overhead cost has totaled $520,000."

"Hey! This annual report is more helpful than I thought," exclaimed Ford. "I can see that our gross margin rate has been 40% of sales for years. I can also see that direct labor cost is one-quarter of the manufacturing overhead cost."

"We may have a chance after all," cried Mercedes. "My summary sheet lists the sum of direct labor and direct materials at $510,000 for the year, and it says that our goods available for sale to customers this year has totaled $960,000 at cost. Now if we just knew the amount of raw materials purchased so far this year."

"I know that figure," yelled Ford. "It's $420,000! The purchasing agent gave it to me in our planning meeting yesterday."

"Fantastic," shouted Mercedes. "We'll have our claim ready before the day is over!"

To file a claim with the insurance company, Operex Products must determine the amount of cost in its inventories as of the date of the accident. You may assume that all of the materials used in production during the year were direct materials.

Required:

Determine the amount of cost in the raw materials, work in process, and finished goods inventories as of the date of the accident. (Hint: One way to proceed would be to reconstruct the various schedules and statements that would have been affected by the company's inventory accounts during the year.)

Group and Internet Exercises

GROUP EXERCISE 2–29 Implications of Mass Production

Management accounting systems tend to parallel the manufacturing systems they support and control. Traditional manufacturing systems emphasized productivity (average output per hour or per employee) and cost. This was the result of a competitive philosophy that was based on mass producing a few standard products and "meeting or beating competitors on price." If a firm is going to compete on price, it had better be a low-cost producer.

Firms achieved low unit cost for a fixed set of resources by maximizing the utilization of those resources. That is, traditional production strategies were based on the economies of mass production and maximizing output for a given productive capacity. The United States has experienced over 100 years of unprecedented economic prosperity in large part because innovators like Henry Ford applied these economic principles with a vengeance.

Competitors, never being completely satisfied with their present condition, were always looking for ways to lower the cost of a product or service even further to gain some temporary cost advantage. Additional productivity gains were achieved by standardizing work procedures, specializing work, and using machines to enhance the productivity of individual workers.

Required:

1. Henry Ford made a now-famous statement that the Model T "could be had in any color as long as it was black." Explain what he meant by this statement.
2. How would Henry Ford or any other manufacturer with a narrow product line gain even further efficiencies based on the traditional production model described above?
3. Are there any limits to lowering the cost of black Model Ts, black Bic pens, or any high-volume, commodity product? Explain.
4. Once understood, the economies of mass production were applied to most sectors of the American economy. Universities, hospitals, and airlines are prime examples. Describe how the concepts of mass production, standardization, and specialization have been applied to lower the costs of a university education. Of a stay in the hospital.

GROUP EXERCISE 2–30 If Big Is Good, Bigger Must Be Better

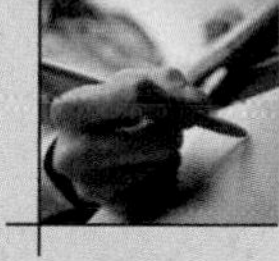

Steel production involves a large amount of fixed costs. Since competition is defined primarily in terms of price, American steel manufacturers (and many of their manufacturing and service industry counterparts) try to gain a competitive advantage by using economies of scale and investment in technology to increase productivity and drive unit costs lower. Their substantial fixed costs are the result of their size.

Required:

1. How are fixed costs and variable costs normally defined?
2. Give examples of fixed costs and variable costs for a steel company. What is the relevant measure of production activity?
3. Give examples of fixed and variable costs for a hospital, university, and auto manufacturer. What is the relevant measure of production or service activity for each of these organizations?
4. Using the examples of fixed and variable costs for steel companies from (2) above, explain the relationship between production output at a steel company and each of the following: total fixed costs, fixed cost per unit, total variable costs, variable cost per unit, total costs, and average unit cost.
5. With an *X* axis (horizontal axis) of tons produced and a *Y* axis (vertical axis) of total costs, graph total fixed costs, total variable costs, and total costs against tons produced.
6. With an *X* axis of tons produced and a *Y* axis of unit costs, graph fixed cost per unit, variable cost per unit, and total (or average) cost per unit against tons produced.
7. Explain how costs (total and per unit) behave with changes in demand once capacity has been set.

INTERNET EXERCISE 2–31 Internet Exercise

As you know, the World Wide Web is a medium that is constantly evolving. Sites come and go, and change without notice. To enable periodic update of site addresses, this problem has been posted to the textbook website (www.mhhe.com/garrison10e). After accessing the site, enter the Student Center and select this chapter. Select and complete the Internet Exercise.

Chapter Three

Systems Design: Job-Order Costing

LEARNING OBJECTIVES

After studying Chapter 3, you should be able to:

1. Distinguish between process costing and job-order costing and identify companies that would use each costing method.
2. Identify the documents used in a job-order costing system.
3. Compute predetermined overhead rates and explain why estimated overhead costs (rather than actual overhead costs) are used in the costing process.
4. Understand the flow of costs in a job-order costing system and prepare appropriate journal entries to record costs.
5. Apply overhead cost to Work in Process using a predetermined overhead rate.
6. Prepare schedules of cost of goods manufactured and cost of goods sold.
7. Prepare T-accounts to show the flow of costs in a job-order costing system.
8. Compute under- or overapplied overhead cost and prepare the journal entry to close the balance in Manufacturing Overhead to the appropriate accounts.
9. (Appendix 3A) Explain the implications of basing the predetermined overhead rate on activity at capacity rather than on estimated activity for the period.

Where's the Profit?

"Net profit participation" contracts in which writers, actors, and directors share in the net profits of movies are common in Hollywood. For example, Winston Groom, the author of the novel *Forrest Gump,* has a contract with Paramount Pictures Corp. that calls for him to receive 3% of the net profits on the movie. However, Paramount claims that *Forrest Gump* has yet to show any profits even though it has the third-highest gross receipts of any film in history. How can this be?

Movie studios assess a variety of overhead charges including a charge of about 15% on production costs for production overhead, a charge of about 30% of gross rentals for distribution overhead, and a charge for marketing overhead that amounts to about 10% of advertising costs. After all of these overhead charges and other hotly contested accounting practices, it is a rare film that shows a profit. Fewer than 5% of released films show a profit for net profit participation purposes. Examples of "money-losing" films include *Rain Man, Batman,* and *Who Framed Roger Rabbit?* as well as *Forrest Gump.* Disgruntled writers and actors are increasingly suing studios, claiming unreasonable accounting practices that are designed to cheat them of their share of profits. How do companies ordinarily assign overhead costs to their products since overhead costs consist of those costs that cannot be easily traced to products? We will answer that question in this chapter.

Source: Ross Engel and Bruce Ikawa, "Where's the Profit?" *Management Accounting*, January 1997, pp. 40–47.

BUSINESS FOCUS

As discussed in Chapter 2, product costing is the process of assigning costs to the products and services provided by a company. An understanding of this costing process is vital to managers, since the way in which a product or service is costed can have a substantial impact on reported net income, as well as on key management decisions.

The essential purpose of any managerial costing system should be to provide cost data to help managers plan, control, direct, and make decisions. Nevertheless, external financial reporting and tax reporting requirements often heavily influence how costs are accumulated and summarized on managerial reports. This is true of product costing.

In this chapter and in Chapter 4, we use an *absorption costing* approach to determine product costs. This was also the method that was used in Chapter 2. In **absorption costing,** *all* manufacturing costs, fixed and variable, are assigned to units of product—units are said to *fully absorb manufacturing costs.* The absorption costing approach is also known as the **full cost** approach. Later, in Chapter 7, we look at product costing from a different point of view called *variable costing,* which is often advocated as an alternative to absorption costing. Chapter 7 also discusses the strengths and weaknesses of the two approaches.

In one form or another, most countries—including the United States—require absorption costing for both external financial reporting and for tax reporting. In addition, the vast majority of companies throughout the world also use absorption costing for managerial accounting purposes. Since absorption costing is the most common approach to product costing, we discuss it first and then deal with alternatives in subsequent chapters.

Process and Job-Order Costing

LEARNING OBJECTIVE 1
Distinguish between process costing and job-order costing and identify companies that would use each costing method.

In computing the cost of a product or a service, managers are faced with a difficult problem. Many costs (such as rent) do not change much from month to month, whereas production may change frequently, with production going up in one month and then down in another. In addition to variations in the level of production, several different products or services may be produced in a given period in the same facility. Under these conditions, how is it possible to accurately determine the cost of a product or service? In practice, assigning costs to products and services involves an averaging of some type across time periods and across products. The way in which this averaging is carried out depends heavily on the type of production process involved. Two costing systems are commonly used in manufacturing and in many service companies; these two systems are known as *process costing* and *job-order costing.*

Process Costing

A **process costing system** is used in situations where the company produces many units of a single product (such as frozen orange juice concentrate) for long periods. Examples include producing paper at Weyerhaeuser, refining aluminum ingots at Reynolds Aluminum, mixing and bottling beverages at Coca-Cola, and making wieners at Oscar Meyer. All of these industries are characterized by an essentially homogeneous product that flows through the production process on a continuous basis.

The basic approach in process costing is to accumulate costs in a particular operation or department for an entire period (month, quarter, year) and then to divide this total cost by the number of units produced during the period. The basic formula for process costing is:

$$\frac{\text{Unit product cost}}{\text{(per gallon, pound, bottle)}} = \frac{\text{Total manufacturing cost}}{\text{Total units produced (gallons, pounds, bottles)}}$$

Since one unit of product (gallon, pound, bottle) is indistinguishable from any other unit of product, each unit is assigned the same average cost as any other unit produced during the period. This costing technique results in a broad, average unit cost figure that applies to homogeneous units flowing in a continuous stream out of the production process.

Job-Order Costing

A **job-order costing system** is used in situations where many *different* products are produced each period. For example, a Levi Strauss clothing factory would typically make many different types of jeans for both men and women during a month. A particular order might consist of 1,000 stonewashed men's blue denim jeans, style number A312, with a 32-inch waist and a 30-inch inseam. This order of 1,000 jeans is called a *batch* or a *job*. In a job-order costing system, costs are traced and allocated to jobs and then the costs of the job are divided by the number of units in the job to arrive at an average cost per unit.

Other examples of situations where job-order costing would be used include large-scale construction projects managed by Bechtel International, commercial aircraft produced by Boeing, greeting cards designed and printed at Hallmark, and airline meals prepared by LSG SkyChefs. All of these examples are characterized by diverse outputs. Each Bechtel project is unique and different from every other—the company may be simultaneously constructing a dam in Zaire and a bridge in Indonesia. Likewise, each airline orders a different type of meal from LSG SkyChefs' catering service.

S

Job-order costing is also used extensively in service industries. Hospitals, law firms, movie studios, accounting firms, advertising agencies, and repair shops, for example, all use a variation of job-order costing to accumulate costs for accounting and billing purposes. Although the detailed example of job-order costing provided in the following section deals with a manufacturing firm, the same basic concepts and procedures are used by many service organizations.

The record-keeping and cost assignment problems are more complex when a company sells many different products and services than when it has only a single product. Since the products are different, the costs are typically different. Consequently, cost records must be maintained for each distinct product or job. For example, an attorney in a large criminal law practice would ordinarily keep separate records of the costs of advising and defending each of her clients. And the Levi Strauss factory mentioned above would keep separate track of the costs of filling orders for particular styles, sizes, and colors of jeans. Thus, a job-order costing system requires more effort than a process-costing system.

In this chapter, we focus on the design of a job-order costing system. In the following chapter, we focus on process costing and also look more closely at the similarities and differences between the two costing methods.

Popularity of Costing Methods

In Business

Job-order costing appears to be the dominant product costing system in the United States. Of the manufacturing firms surveyed throughout the United States, 51.1% used job-order costing, 14.2% used process costing, and 10.6% used operation or hybrid costing. The other surveyed companies responded that they used standard costing (discussed in Chapter 8).

Source: Eun-Sup Shim and Joseph M. Larkin, "A Survey of Current Managerial Accounting Practices: Where Do We Stand," *Ohio CPA Journal*, February 1994, p. 21 (4 pages).

Job-Order Costing—An Overview

LEARNING OBJECTIVE 2
Identify the documents used in a job-order costing system.

To introduce job-order costing, we will follow a specific job as it progresses through the manufacturing process. This job consists of two experimental couplings that Yost Precision Machining has agreed to produce for Loops Unlimited, a manufacturer of roller coasters. The couplings connect the cars on the roller coaster and are a critical component in the performance and safety of the ride. Before we begin our discussion, recall from the previous chapter that companies generally classify manufacturing costs into three broad categories: (1) direct materials, (2) direct labor, and (3) manufacturing overhead. As we study the operation of a job-order costing system, we will see how each of these three types of costs is recorded and accumulated.

Managerial Accounting in Action

The Issue

Yost Precision Machining is a small company in Michigan that specializes in fabricating precision metal parts that are used in a variety of applications ranging from deep-sea exploration vehicles to the inertial triggers in automobile air bags. The company's top managers gather every morning at 8:00 A.M. in the company's conference room for the daily planning meeting. Attending the meeting this morning are: Jean Yost, the company's president; David Cheung, the marketing manager; Debbie Turner, the production manager; and Marcus White, the company controller. The president opened the meeting:

Jean: The production schedule indicates we'll be starting job 2B47 today. Isn't that the special order for experimental couplings, David?

David: That's right, Jean. That's the order from Loops Unlimited for two couplings for their new roller coaster ride for Magic Mountain.

Debbie: Why only two couplings? Don't they need a coupling for every car?

David: That's right. But this is a completely new roller coaster. The cars will go faster and will be subjected to more twists, turns, drops, and loops than on any other existing roller coaster. To hold up under these stresses, Loops Unlimited's engineers had to completely redesign the cars and couplings. They want to thoroughly test the design before proceeding to large-scale production. So they want us to make just two of these new couplings for testing purposes. If the design works, then we'll have the inside track on the order to supply couplings for the whole ride.

Jean: We agreed to take on this initial order at our cost just to get our foot in the door. Marcus, will there be any problem documenting our cost so we can get paid?

Marcus: No problem. The contract with Loops stipulates that they will pay us an amount equal to our cost of goods sold. With our job-order costing system, I can tell you that number on the day the job is completed.

Jean: Good. Is there anything else we should discuss about this job at this time? No? Well then let's move on to the next item of business.

Measuring Direct Materials Cost

Concept 3–1

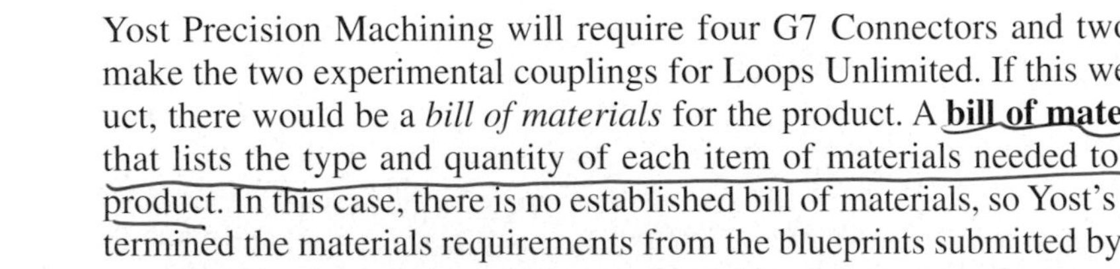

Yost Precision Machining will require four G7 Connectors and two M46 Housings to make the two experimental couplings for Loops Unlimited. If this were a standard product, there would be a *bill of materials* for the product. A **bill of materials** is a document that lists the type and quantity of each item of materials needed to complete a unit of product. In this case, there is no established bill of materials, so Yost's production staff determined the materials requirements from the blueprints submitted by the customer. Each coupling requires two connectors and one housing, so to make two couplings, four connectors and two housings are required.

When an agreement has been reached with the customer concerning the quantities, prices, and shipment date for the order, a *production order* is issued. The Production Department then prepares a *materials requisition form* similar to the form in Exhibit 3–1. The **materials requisition form** is a detailed source document that (1) specifies the type and quantity of materials to be drawn from the storeroom, and (2) identifies the job to which the costs of the materials are to be charged. The form is used to control the flow of materials into production and also for making entries in the accounting records.

The Yost Precision Machining materials requisition form in Exhibit 3–1 shows that the company's Milling Department has requisitioned two M46 Housings and four G7 Connectors for job 2B47. This completed form is presented to the storeroom clerk who

Exhibit 3–1
Materials Requisition Form

Materials Requistion Number 14873 Date March 2
Job Number to Be Charged 2B47
Department Milling

Description	Quantity	Unit Cost	Total Cost
M46 Housing	2	$124	$248
G7 Connector	4	103	412
			$660

Authorized Signature *Bill White*

then issues the necessary raw materials. The storeroom clerk is not allowed to release materials without such a form bearing an authorized signature.

Job Cost Sheet

After being notified that the production order has been issued, the Accounting Department prepares a *job cost sheet* similar to the one presented in Exhibit 3–2. A **job cost sheet** is a form prepared for each separate job that records the materials, labor, and overhead costs charged to the job.

After direct materials are issued, the Accounting Department records their costs directly on the job cost sheet. Note from Exhibit 3–2, for example, that the $660 cost for direct materials shown earlier on the materials requisition form has been charged to job 2B47 on its job cost sheet. The requisition number 14873 is also recorded on the job cost sheet to make it easier to identify the source document for the direct materials charge.

In addition to serving as a means for charging costs to jobs, the job cost sheet also serves as a key part of a firm's accounting records. The job cost sheets form a subsidiary ledger to the Work in Process account. They are detailed records for the jobs in process that add up to the balance in Work in Process.

Measuring Direct Labor Cost

Direct labor cost is handled in much the same way as direct materials cost. Direct labor consists of labor charges that are easily traced to a particular job. Labor charges that cannot be easily traced directly to any job are treated as part of manufacturing overhead. As discussed in the previous chapter, this latter category of labor costs is called *indirect labor* and includes tasks such as maintenance, supervision, and cleanup.

Relation of Direct Labor to Product Cost

In Business

How much direct labor is in the products you buy? Sometimes not very much. During a visit to the Massachusetts Institute of Technology, Chinese Prime Minister Zhu Rongji claimed that, of the $120 retail cost of a pair of athletic shoes made in China, only $2 goes to the Chinese workers who assemble them. The National Labor Committee based in New York estimates that the labor cost to assemble a $90 pair of Nike sneakers is only $1.20.

Source: Robert A. Senser, letter to the editor, *Business Week*, May 24, 1999, pp. 11–12.

Exhibit 3–2
Job Cost Sheet

JOB COST SHEET

Job Number 2B47 Date Initiated March 2

Date Completed ______

Department Milling Units Completed ______

Item Special order coupling

For Stock ______

Direct Materials		Direct Labor			Manufacturing Overhead		
Req. No.	Amount	Ticket	Hours	Amount	Hours	Rate	Amount
14873	$660	843	5	$45			

Cost Summary	
Direct Materials	$
Direct Labor	$
Manufacturing Overhead	$
Total Cost	$
Unit Product Cost	$

Units Shipped		
Date	Number	Balance

Workers use *time tickets* to record the time they spend on each job and task. A completed **time ticket** is an hour-by-hour summary of the employee's activities throughout the day. An example of an employee time ticket is shown in Exhibit 3–3. When working on a specific job, the employee enters the job number on the time ticket and notes the amount of time spent on that job. When not assigned to a particular job, the employee records the nature of the indirect labor task (such as cleanup and maintenance) and the amount of time spent on the task.

At the end of the day, the time tickets are gathered and the Accounting Department enters the direct labor-hours and costs on individual job cost sheets. (See Exhibit 3–2 for an example of how direct labor costs are entered on the job cost sheet.) The daily time tickets are source documents that are used as the basis for labor cost entries into the accounting records.

In Business

A More Productive Use of Time

Is it always worth the trouble to fill out labor time tickets? In a word, no. United Electric Controls, Inc., located in Waterton, Massachusetts, makes temperature and pressure sensors and controls. The manufacturing vice president decided he wanted employees to spend their time focusing on making products rather than on filling out labor time tickets. The company converted everyone into salaried workers and stopped producing labor reports.

Source: Richard L. Jenson, James W. Brackner, and Clifford Skousen, *Management Accounting in Support of* Manufacturing *Excellence*, 1996, The IMA Foundation for Applied Research, Inc., Montvale, New Jersey, p. 12.

Exhibit 3–3
Employee Time Ticket

Time Ticket No. 843 Date March 3
Employee Mary Holden Station 4

Started	Ended	Time Completed	Rate	Amount	Job Number
7:00	12:00	5.0	$9	$45	2B47
12:30	2:30	2.0	9	18	2B50
2:30	3:30	1.0	9	9	Maintenance
Totals		8.0		$72	

Supervisor *R.W. Pace*

The system we have just described is a manual method for recording and posting labor costs. Many companies now rely on computerized systems and no longer record labor time by hand on sheets of paper. One computerized approach uses bar codes to enter the basic data into the computer. Each employee and each job has a unique bar code. When an employee begins work on a job, he or she scans three bar codes using a hand-held device much like the bar code readers at grocery store check-out stands. The first bar code indicates that a job is being started; the second is the unique bar code on his or her identity badge; and the third is the unique bar code of the job itself. This information is fed automatically via an electronic network to a computer that notes the time and then records all of the data. When the employee completes the task, he or she scans a bar code indicating the task is complete, the bar code on his or her identity badge, and the bar code attached to the job. This information is relayed to the computer that again notes the time, and a time ticket is automatically prepared. Since all of the source data is already in computer files, the labor costs can be automatically posted to job cost sheets (or their electronic equivalents). Computers, coupled with technology such as bar codes, can eliminate much of the drudgery involved in routine bookkeeping activities while at the same time increasing timeliness and accuracy.

High Tech in the Fields

In Business

Advanced technology for recording data is even found in strawberry fields where the pay of workers is traditionally based on the amount of berries they pick. The Bob Jones Ranch in Oxnard, California, is using dime-sized metal buttons to record how many boxes of fruit each worker picks. The buttons, which are stuffed with microelectronics, are carried by the field workers. The buttons can be read in the field with a wand-like probe that immediately downloads data to a laptop computer. The information picked up by the probe includes the name of the worker; the type and quality of the crop; and the time, date, and location of the field being picked. Not only does the system supply the data needed to pay over 700 field workers but it also provides farm managers with information about which fields are most productive. Previously, two people were required every night to process the time tickets for the field workers.

Source: Mark Boslet, "Metal Buttons Carried by Crop Pickers Serve as Mini Databases for Farmers," *The Wall Street Journal*, May 31, 1994, p. A11A.

Application of Manufacturing Overhead

Manufacturing overhead must be included with direct materials and direct labor on the job cost sheet since manufacturing overhead is also a product cost. However, assigning

Concept 3–2

LEARNING OBJECTIVE 3
Compute predetermined overhead rates and explain why estimated overhead costs (rather than actual overhead costs) are used in the costing process.

manufacturing overhead to units of product can be a difficult task. There are three reasons for this.

1. Manufacturing overhead is an *indirect cost*. This means that it is either impossible or difficult to trace these costs to a particular product or job.
2. Manufacturing overhead consists of many different items ranging from the grease used in machines to the annual salary of the production manager.
3. Even though output may fluctuate due to seasonal or other factors, manufacturing overhead costs tend to remain relatively constant due to the presence of fixed costs.

Given these problems, about the only way to assign overhead costs to products is to use an allocation process. This allocation of overhead costs is accomplished by selecting an *allocation base* that is common to all of the company's products and services. An **allocation base** is a measure such as direct labor-hours (DLH) or machine-hours (MH) that is used to assign overhead costs to products and services.

The most widely used allocation bases are direct labor-hours and direct labor cost, with machine-hours and even units of product (where a company has only a single product) also used to some extent.

The allocation base is used to compute the **predetermined overhead rate** in the following formula:

$$\text{Predetermined overhead rate} = \frac{\text{Estimated total manufacturing overhead cost}}{\text{Estimated total units in the allocation base}}$$

Note that the predetermined overhead rate is based on estimates rather than actual results. This is because the *predetermined* overhead rate is computed *before* the period begins and is used to *apply* overhead cost to jobs throughout the period. The process of assigning overhead cost to jobs is called **overhead application.** The formula for determining the amount of overhead cost to apply to a particular job is:

$$\begin{matrix}\text{Overhead applied to} \\ \text{a particular job}\end{matrix} = \begin{matrix}\text{Predetermined} \\ \text{overhead rate}\end{matrix} \times \begin{matrix}\text{Amount of the allocation} \\ \text{base incurred by the job}\end{matrix}$$

For example, if the predetermined overhead rate is \$8 per direct labor-hour, then \$8 of overhead cost is *applied* to a job for each direct labor-hour incurred by the job. When the allocation base is direct labor-hours, the formula becomes:

$$\begin{matrix}\text{Overhead applied to} \\ \text{a particular job}\end{matrix} = \begin{matrix}\text{Predetermined} \\ \text{overhead rate}\end{matrix} \times \begin{matrix}\text{Actual direct labor-hours} \\ \text{charged to the job}\end{matrix}$$

Using the Predetermined Overhead Rate To illustrate the steps involved in computing and using a predetermined overhead rate, let's return to Yost Precision Machining. The company has estimated its total manufacturing overhead costs will be \$320,000 for the year and its total direct labor-hours will be 40,000. Its predetermined overhead rate for the year would be \$8 per direct labor-hour, as shown below:

$$\begin{aligned}\text{Predetermined overhead rate} &= \frac{\text{Estimated total manufacturing overhead cost}}{\text{Estimated total units in the allocation base}} \\ &= \frac{\$320{,}000}{40{,}000 \text{ direct labor-hours}} \\ &= \$8 \text{ per direct labor-hour}\end{aligned}$$

The job cost sheet in Exhibit 3–4 indicates that 27 direct labor-hours (i.e., DLHs) were charged to job 2B47. Therefore, a total of \$216 of manufacturing overhead cost would be applied to the job:

$$\begin{matrix}\text{Overhead applied to} \\ \text{job 2B47}\end{matrix} = \begin{matrix}\text{Predetermined} \\ \text{overhead rate}\end{matrix} \times \begin{matrix}\text{Actual direct labor-hours} \\ \text{charged to job 2B47}\end{matrix}$$

\$8 per DLH × 27 DLHs = \$216 of overhead applied to job 2B47

Exhibit 3–4
A Completed Job Cost Sheet

JOB COST SHEET

Job Number 2B47 | Date Initiated March 2
Date Completed March 8
Department Milling
Item Special order coupling | Units Completed 2
For Stock

Direct Materials		Direct Labor			Manufacturing Overhead		
Req. No.	Amount	Ticket	Hours	Amount	Hours	Rate	Amount
14873	$ 660	843	5	$ 45	27	$8/DLH	$216
14875	506	846	8	60			
14912	238	850	4	21			
	$1,404	851	10	54			
			27	$180			

Cost Summary		Units Shipped		
		Date	Number	Balance
Direct Materials	$1,404			
Direct Labor	$ 180	March 8	—	2
Manufacturing Overhead	$ 216			
Total Cost	$1,800			
Unit Product Cost	$ 900*			

*$1,800 ÷ 2 units = $900 per unit.

This amount of overhead has been entered on the job cost sheet in Exhibit 3–4. Note that this is *not* the actual amount of overhead caused by the job. There is no attempt to trace actual overhead costs to jobs—if that could be done, the costs would be direct costs, not overhead. The overhead assigned to the job is simply a share of the total overhead that was estimated at the beginning of the year. When a company applies overhead cost to jobs as we have done—that is, by multiplying actual activity times the predetermined overhead rate—it is called a **normal cost system.**

The overhead may be applied as direct labor-hours are charged to jobs, or all of the overhead can be applied at once when the job is completed. The choice is up to the company. If a job is not completed at year-end, however, overhead should be applied to value the work in process inventory.

The Need for a Predetermined Rate Instead of using a predetermined rate, a company could wait until the end of the accounting period to compute an actual overhead rate based on the *actual* total manufacturing costs and the *actual* total units in the allocation base for the period. However, managers cite several reasons for using predetermined overhead rates instead of actual overhead rates:

1. Managers would like to know the accounting system's valuation of completed jobs *before* the end of the accounting period. Suppose, for example, that Yost Precision Machining waits until the end of the year to compute its overhead rate. Then there

would be no way for managers to know the cost of goods sold for job 2B47 until the close of the year, even though the job was completed and shipped to the customer in March. The seriousness of this problem can be reduced to some extent by computing the actual overhead more frequently, but that immediately leads to another problem as discussed below.

2. If actual overhead rates are computed frequently, seasonal factors in overhead costs or in the allocation base can produce fluctuations in the overhead rates. For example, the costs of heating and cooling a production facility in Illinois will be highest in the winter and summer months and lowest in the spring and fall. If an overhead rate were computed each month or each quarter, the predetermined overhead rate would go up in the winter and summer and down in the spring and fall. Two identical jobs, one completed in winter and one completed in the spring, would be assigned different costs if the overhead rate were computed on a monthly or quarterly basis. Managers generally feel that such fluctuations in overhead rates and costs serve no useful purpose and are misleading.
3. The use of a predetermined overhead rate simplifies record keeping. To determine the overhead cost to apply to a job, the accounting staff at Yost Precision Machining simply multiplies the direct labor-hours recorded for the job by the predetermined overhead rate of $8 per direct labor-hour.

For these reasons, most companies use predetermined overhead rates rather than actual overhead rates in their cost accounting systems.

Choice of an Allocation Base for Overhead Cost

Ideally, the allocation base used in the predetermined overhead rate should be the *cost driver* of overhead cost. A **cost driver** is a factor, such as machine-hours, beds occupied, computer time, or flight-hours, that causes overhead costs. If a base is used to compute overhead rates that does not "drive" overhead costs, then the result will be inaccurate overhead rates and distorted product costs. For example, if direct labor-hours is used to allocate overhead, but in reality overhead has little to do with direct labor-hours, then products with high direct labor-hour requirements will shoulder an unrealistic burden of overhead and will be overcosted.

Most companies use direct labor-hours or direct labor cost as the allocation base for manufacturing overhead. However, as discussed in earlier chapters, major shifts are taking place in the structure of costs in many industries. In the past, direct labor accounted for up to 60% of the cost of many products, with overhead cost making up only a portion of the remainder. This situation has been changing—for two reasons. First, sophisticated automated equipment has taken over functions that used to be performed by direct labor workers. Since the costs of acquiring and maintaining such equipment are classified as overhead, this increases overhead while decreasing direct labor. Second, products are themselves becoming more sophisticated and complex and change more frequently. This increases the need for highly skilled indirect workers such as engineers. As a result of these two trends, direct labor is becoming less of a factor and overhead is becoming more of a factor in the cost of products in many industries.

In companies where direct labor and overhead costs have been moving in opposite directions, it would be difficult to argue that direct labor "drives" overhead costs. Accordingly, in recent years, managers in some companies have used *activity-based costing* principles to redesign their cost accounting systems. Activity-based costing is a costing technique that is designed to more accurately reflect the demands that products, customers, and other cost objects make on overhead resources. The activity-based approach is discussed in more detail in Chapter 8.

We hasten to add that although direct labor may not be an appropriate allocation base in some industries, in others it continues to be a significant driver of manufacturing overhead. The key point is that the allocation base used by the company should really drive, or cause, overhead costs, and direct labor is not always an appropriate allocation base.

The Potential for Inaccurate Product Costs

In Business

There was a time when direct labor was the predominant product cost, and the allocation of overhead was not as critical as it is today. However, as discussed in the chapter, cost structures have changed. Factory automation is now common. Forty-three percent of surveyed manufacturing firms indicated that their factories were either moderately or mostly automated. At the other end of the spectrum, only 5% of the firms reported a total lack of automation. Further, 91% of the surveyed firms manufacture more than one product. Not surprisingly, direct labor accounted for only 15% of product costs of the firms surveyed; direct materials and overhead accounted for 47% and 33%, respectively. [Source: Eun-Sup Shim and Joseph M. Larkin, "A Survey of Current Managerial Accounting Practices: Where Do We Stand," *Ohio CPA Journal*, February 1994, p. 21 (4 pages).]

Even so, the most recent surveys of managerial accounting practices indicate that 62% to 74% of manufacturing companies in the United States use direct labor as the primary or secondary allocation base for overhead. [Sources: Jeffrey R. Cohen and Laurence Paquette, "Management Accounting Practices: Perceptions of Controllers," *Journal of Cost Management* 5, no. 3, pp. 75–83. James R. Emore and Joseph A. Ness, "The Slow Pace of Meaningful Change in Cost Systems," *Journal of Cost Management* 4, no. 4, pp. 36–45.]

Companies that use direct labor to allocate overhead costs should consider whether direct labor does indeed drive overhead. If overhead is not actually caused by direct labor, product costs may be very misleading. And if product costs are distorted, decisions that rely on that data are likely to be less than ideal.

Computation of Unit Costs

With the application of Yost Precision Machining's $216 manufacturing overhead to the job cost sheet in Exhibit 3–4, the job cost sheet is complete except for two final steps. First, the totals for direct materials, direct labor, and manufacturing overhead are transferred to the Cost Summary section of the job cost sheet and added together to obtain the total cost for the job. Then the total cost ($1,800) is divided by the number of units (2) to obtain the unit cost ($900). As indicated earlier, *this unit cost is an average cost and should not be interpreted as the cost that would actually be incurred if another unit were produced*. Much of the actual overhead would not change at all if another unit were produced, so the incremental cost of an additional unit is something less than the average unit cost of $900.

The completed job cost sheet is now ready to be transferred to the Finished Goods inventory account, where it will serve as the basis for valuing unsold units in ending inventory and determining cost of goods sold.

Summary of Document Flows

The sequence of events discussed above is summarized in Exhibit 3–5. A careful study of the flow of documents in this exhibit will provide a good overview of the overall operation of a job-order costing system.

Managerial Accounting in Action

The Wrap-up

In the 8:00 A.M. daily planning meeting on March 9, Jean Yost, the president of Yost Precision Machining, once again drew attention to job 2B47, the experimental couplings:

Jean: I see job 2B47 is completed. Let's get those couplings shipped immediately to Loops Unlimited so they can get their testing program under way. Marcus, how much are we going to bill Loops for those two units?

Marcus: Just a second, let me check the job cost sheet for that job. Here it is. We agreed to sell the experimental units at cost, so we will be charging Loops Unlimited just $900 a unit.

Jean: Fine. Let's hope the couplings work out and we make some money on the big order later.

Exhibit 3–5 The Flow of Documents in a Job-Order Costing System

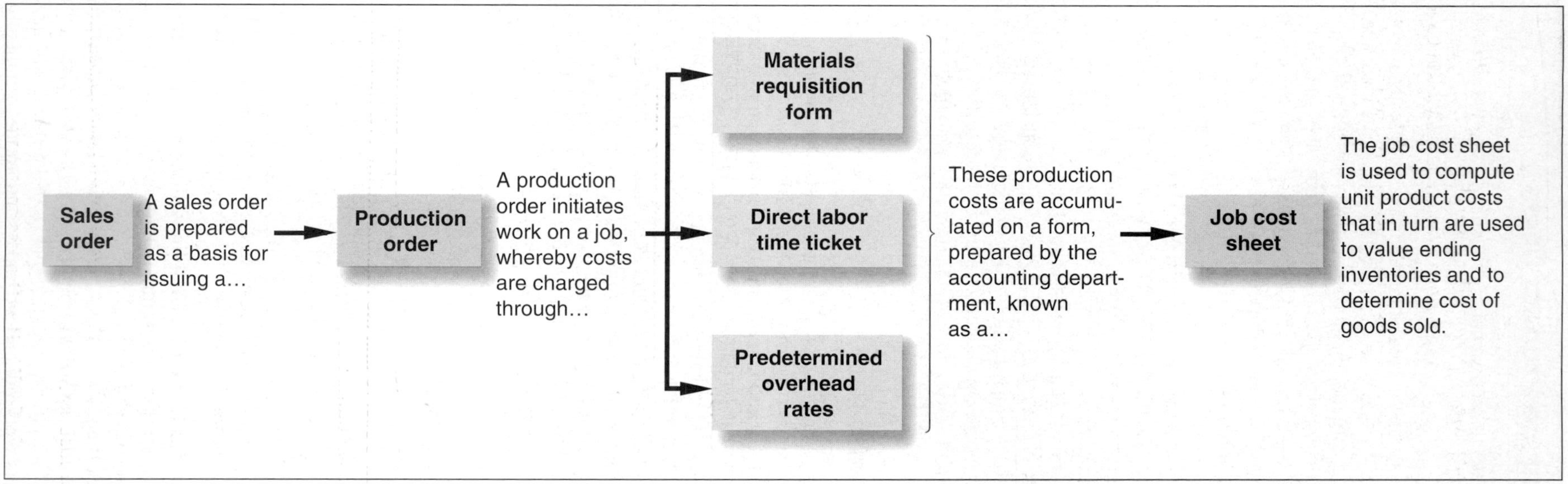

Sales order

A sales order is prepared as a basis for issuing a…

Production order

A production order initiates work on a job, whereby costs are charged through…

Materials requisition form

Direct labor time ticket

Predetermined overhead rates

These production costs are accumulated on a form, prepared by the accounting department, known as a…

Job cost sheet

The job cost sheet is used to compute unit product costs that in turn are used to value ending inventories and to determine cost of goods sold.

Job-Order Costing—The Flow of Costs

LEARNING OBJECTIVE 4
Understand the flow of costs in a job-order costing system and prepare appropriate journal entries to record costs.

We are now ready to take a more detailed look at the flow of costs through the company's formal accounting system. To illustrate, we shall consider a single month's activity for Rand Company, a producer of gold and silver commemorative medallions. Rand Company has two jobs in process during April, the first month of its fiscal year. Job A, a special minting of 1,000 gold medallions commemorating the invention of motion pictures, was started during March. By the end of March, $30,000 in manufacturing costs had been recorded for the job. Job B, an order for 10,000 silver medallions commemorating the fall of the Berlin Wall, was started in April.

The Purchase and Issue of Materials

On April 1, Rand Company had $7,000 in raw materials on hand. During the month, the company purchased an additional $60,000 in raw materials. The purchase is recorded in journal entry (1) below:

(1)

Raw Materials	60,000	
Accounts Payable		60,000

As explained in the previous chapter, Raw Materials is an asset account. Thus, when raw materials are purchased, they are initially recorded as an asset—not as an expense.

Issue of Direct and Indirect Materials During April, $52,000 in raw materials were requisitioned from the storeroom for use in production. These raw materials include both direct and indirect materials. Entry (2) records issuing the materials to the production departments.

(2)

Work in Process	50,000	
Manufacturing Overhead	2,000	
Raw Materials		52,000

The materials charged to Work in Process represent direct materials for specific jobs. As these materials are entered into the Work in Process account, they are also recorded on the appropriate job cost sheets. This point is illustrated in Exhibit 3–6, where $28,000 of the $50,000 in direct materials is charged to job A's cost sheet and the remaining $22,000 is charged to job B's cost sheet. (In this example, all data are presented in summary form and the job cost sheet is abbreviated.)

The $2,000 charged to Manufacturing Overhead in entry (2) represents indirect materials used in production during April. Observe that the Manufacturing Overhead account is separate from the Work in Process account. The purpose of the Manufacturing Overhead account is to accumulate all manufacturing overhead costs as they are incurred during a period.

Before leaving Exhibit 3–6 we need to point out one additional thing. Notice from the exhibit that the job cost sheet for job A contains a beginning balance of $30,000. We stated earlier that this balance represents the cost of work done during March that has been carried forward to April. Also note that the Work in Process account contains the same $30,000 balance. *The reason the $30,000 appears in both places is that the Work in Process account is a control account and the job cost sheets form a subsidiary ledger. Thus, the Work in Process account contains a summarized total of all costs appearing on the individual job cost sheets for all jobs in process at any given point in time.* (Since Rand Company had only job A in process at the beginning of April, job A's $30,000 balance on that date is equal to the balance in the Work in Process account.)

Exhibit 3–6
Raw Materials Cost Flows

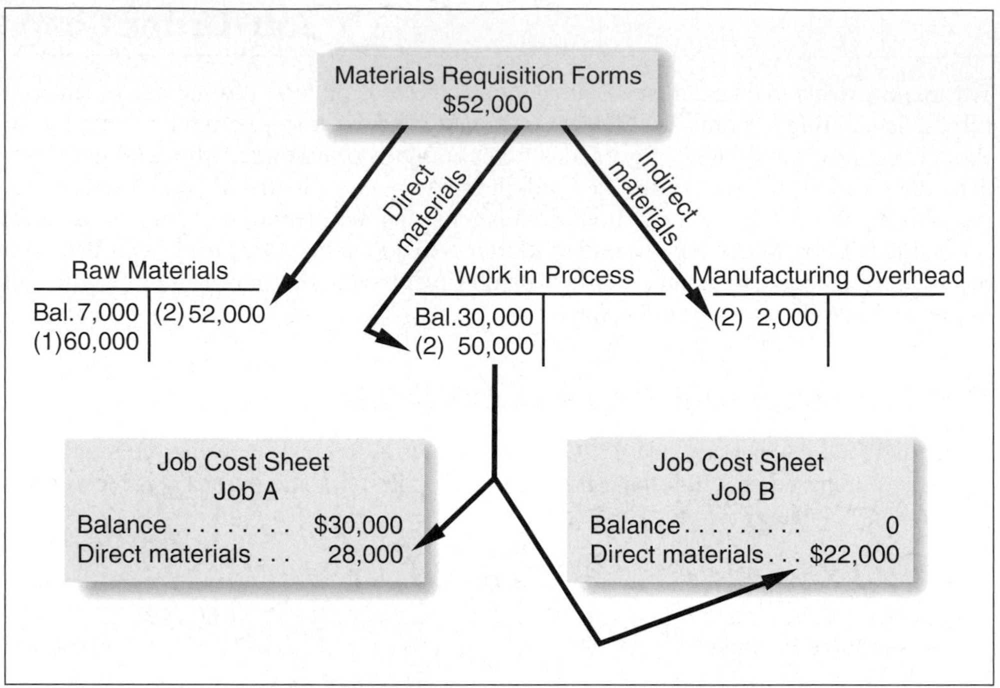

Issue of Direct Materials Only Sometimes the materials drawn from the Raw Materials inventory account are all direct materials. In this case, the entry to record the issue of the materials into production would be as follows:

Work in Process	XXX	
Raw Materials		XXX

Labor Cost

As work is performed each day in various departments of Rand Company, employee time tickets are filled out by workers, collected, and forwarded to the Accounting Department. In the Accounting Department, wages are computed and the resulting costs are classified as either direct or indirect labor. This costing and classification for April resulted in the following summary entry:

(3)

Work in Process	60,000	
Manufacturing Overhead	15,000	
Salaries and Wages Payable		75,000

Only direct labor is added to the Work in Process account. For Rand Company, this amounted to $60,000 for April.

At the same time that direct labor costs are added to Work in Process, they are also added to the individual job cost sheets, as shown in Exhibit 3–7. During April, $40,000 of direct labor cost was charged to job A and the remaining $20,000 was charged to job B.

The labor costs charged to Manufacturing Overhead represent the indirect labor costs of the period, such as supervision, janitorial work, and maintenance.

Manufacturing Overhead Costs

Recall that all costs of operating the factory other than direct materials and direct labor are classified as manufacturing overhead costs. These costs are entered directly into the Man-

Exhibit 3–7
Labor Cost Flows

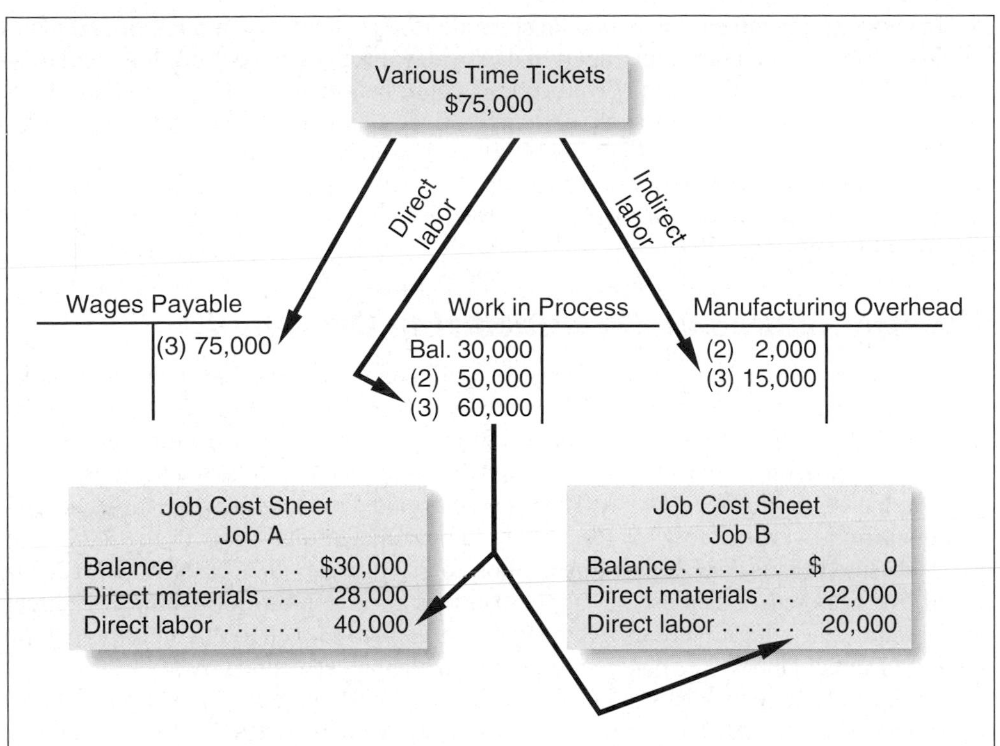

ufacturing Overhead account as they are incurred. To illustrate, assume that Rand Company incurred the following general factory costs during April:

Utilities (heat, water, and power)	$21,000
Rent on factory equipment	16,000
Miscellaneous factory costs	3,000
Total	$40,000

The following entry records the incurrence of these costs:

(4)

Manufacturing Overhead	40,000	
Accounts Payable		40,000

In addition, let us assume that during April, Rand Company recognized $13,000 in accrued property taxes and that $7,000 in prepaid insurance expired on factory buildings and equipment. The following entry records these items:

(5)

Manufacturing Overhead	20,000	
Property Taxes Payable		13,000
Prepaid Insurance		7,000

Finally, let us assume that the company recognized $18,000 in depreciation on factory equipment during April. The following entry records the accrual of this depreciation:

(6)

Manufacturing Overhead	18,000	
Accumulated Depreciation		18,000

In short, *all* manufacturing overhead costs are recorded directly into the Manufacturing Overhead account as they are incurred day by day throughout a period. It is important to understand that Manufacturing Overhead is a control account for many—perhaps thousands—of subsidiary accounts such as Indirect Materials, Indirect Labor, Factory Utilities, and so forth. As the Manufacturing Overhead account is debited for costs during a period, the various subsidiary accounts are also debited. In the example above and also in the assignment material for this chapter, we omit the entries to the subsidiary accounts for the sake of brevity.

The Application of Manufacturing Overhead

LEARNING OBJECTIVE 5
Apply overhead cost to Work in Process using a predetermined overhead rate.

Since actual manufacturing costs are charged to the Manufacturing Overhead control account rather than to Work in Process, how are manufacturing overhead costs assigned to Work in Process? The answer is, by means of the predetermined overhead rate. Recall from our discussion earlier in the chapter that a predetermined overhead rate is established at the beginning of each year. The rate is calculated by dividing the estimated total manufacturing overhead cost for the year by the estimated total units in the allocation base (measured in machine-hours, direct labor-hours, or some other base). The predetermined overhead rate is then used to apply overhead costs to jobs. For example, if direct labor-hours is the allocation base, overhead cost is applied to each job by multiplying the number of direct labor-hours charged to the job by the predetermined overhead rate.

To illustrate, assume that Rand Company has used machine-hours to compute its predetermined overhead rate and that this rate is \$6 per machine-hour. Also assume that during April, 10,000 machine-hours were worked on job A and 5,000 machine-hours were worked on job B (a total of 15,000 machine-hours). Thus, \$90,000 in overhead cost (15,000 machine-hours × \$6 per machine-hour = \$90,000) would be applied to Work in Process. The following entry records the application of Manufacturing Overhead to Work in Process:

(7)

Work in Process	90,000	
Manufacturing Overhead		90,000

The flow of costs through the Manufacturing Overhead account is shown in Exhibit 3–8.

The actual overhead costs in the Manufacturing Overhead account in Exhibit 3–8 are the costs that were added to the account in entries (2)–(6). Observe that the incurrence of these actual overhead costs [entries (2)–(6)] and the application of overhead to Work in Process [entry (7)] represent two separate and entirely distinct processes.

The Concept of a Clearing Account The Manufacturing Overhead account operates as a clearing account. As we have noted, actual factory overhead costs are debited to the accounts as they are incurred day by day throughout the year. At certain intervals during the year, usually when a job is completed, overhead cost is applied to the job by means of the predetermined overhead rate, and Work in Process is debited and Manufacturing Overhead is credited. This sequence of events is illustrated below:

Manufacturing Overhead
(a clearing account)

Actual overhead costs are charged to this account as they are incurred throughout the period.	Overhead is applied to Work in Process using the predetermined overhead rate.

As we emphasized earlier, the predetermined overhead rate is based entirely on estimates of what overhead costs are *expected* to be, and it is established before the year

Exhibit 3–8 The Flow of Costs in Overhead Application

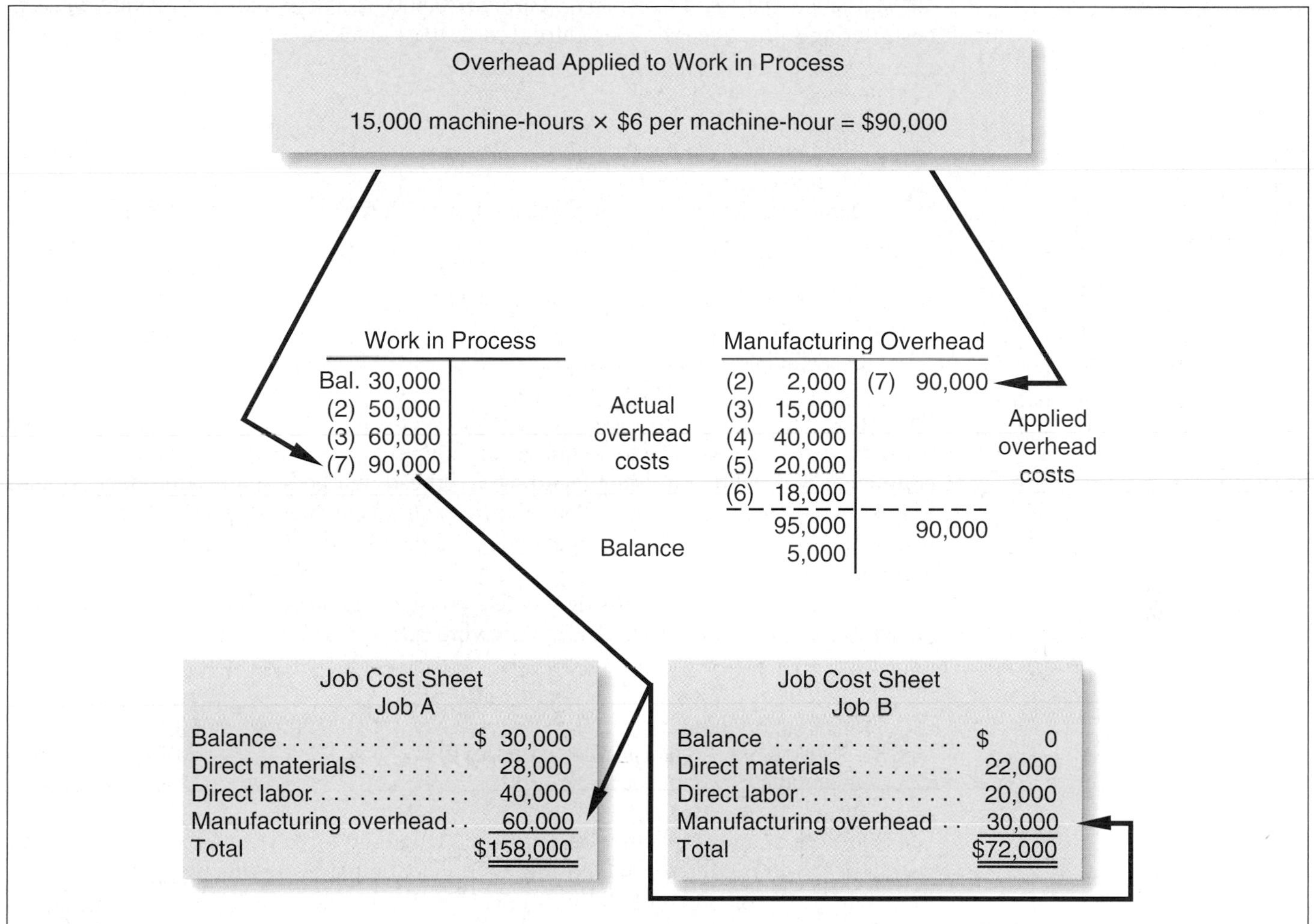

begins. As a result, the overhead cost applied during a year will almost certainly turn out to be more or less than the overhead cost that is actually incurred. For example, notice from Exhibit 3–8 that Rand Company's actual overhead costs for the period are $5,000 greater than the overhead cost that has been applied to Work in Process, resulting in a $5,000 debit balance in the Manufacturing Overhead account. We will reserve discussion of what to do with this $5,000 balance until the next section, Problems of Overhead Application.

For the moment, we can conclude by noting from Exhibit 3–8 that the cost of a completed job consists of the actual materials cost of the job, the actual labor cost of the job, and the overhead cost *applied* to the job. Pay particular attention to the following subtle but important point: *Actual overhead costs are not charged to jobs; actual overhead costs do not appear on the job cost sheet nor do they appear in the Work in Process account. Only the applied overhead cost, based on the predetermined overhead rate, appears on the job cost sheet and in the Work in Process account.* Study this point carefully.

Nonmanufacturing Costs

In addition to manufacturing costs, companies also incur marketing and selling costs. As explained in the previous chapter, these costs should be treated as period expenses and charged directly to the income statement. *Nonmanufacturing costs should not go into the*

Manufacturing Overhead account. To illustrate the correct treatment of nonmanufacturing costs, assume that Rand Company incurred $30,000 in selling and administrative salary costs during April. The following entry records these salaries:

(8)

Salaries Expense	30,000	
Salaries and Wages Payable		30,000

Assume that depreciation on office equipment during April was $7,000. The entry is as follows:

(9)

Depreciation Expense	7,000	
Accumulated Depreciation		7,000

Pay particular attention to the difference between this entry and entry (6) where we recorded depreciation on factory equipment. In journal entry (6), depreciation on factory equipment was debited to Manufacturing Overhead and is therefore a product cost. In journal entry (9) above, depreciation on office equipment is debited to Depreciation Expense. Depreciation on office equipment is considered to be a period expense rather than a product cost.

Finally, assume that advertising was $42,000 and that other selling and administrative expenses in April totaled $8,000. The following entry records these items:

(10)

Advertising Expense	42,000	
Other Selling and Administrative Expense	8,000	
Accounts Payable		50,000

Since the amounts in entries (8) through (10) all go directly into expense accounts, they will have no effect on the costing of Rand Company's production for April. The same will be true of any other selling and administrative expenses incurred during April, including sales commissions, depreciation on sales equipment, rent on office facilities, insurance on office facilities, and related costs.

Cost of Goods Manufactured

LEARNING OBJECTIVE 6
Prepare schedules of cost of goods manufactured and cost of goods sold.

When a job has been completed, the finished output is transferred from the production departments to the finished goods warehouse. By this time, the accounting department will have charged the job with direct materials and direct labor cost, and manufacturing overhead will have been applied using the predetermined rate. A transfer of costs is made within the costing system that *parallels* the physical transfer of the goods to the finished goods warehouse. The costs of the completed job are transferred out of the Work in Process account and into the Finished Goods account. The sum of all amounts transferred between these two accounts represents the cost of goods manufactured for the period.

In the case of Rand Company, let us assume that job A was completed during April. The following entry transfers the cost of job A from Work in Process to Finished Goods:

(11)

Finished Goods	158,000	
Work in Process		158,000

The $158,000 represents the completed cost of job A, as shown on the job cost sheet in Exhibit 3–8. Since job A was the only job completed during April, the $158,000 also represents the cost of goods manufactured for the month.

Job B was not completed by month-end, so its cost will remain in the Work in Process account and carry over to the next month. If a balance sheet is prepared at the end of April, the cost accumulated thus far on job B will appear as "Work in process inventory" in the assets section.

Cost of Goods Sold

As units in finished goods are shipped to fill customers' orders, their costs are transferred from the Finished Goods account into the Cost of Goods Sold account. If a complete job is shipped, as in the case where a job has been done to a customer's specifications, then it is a simple matter to transfer the entire cost appearing on the job cost sheet into the Cost of Goods Sold account. In most cases, however, only a portion of the units involved in a particular job will be immediately sold. In these situations, the unit cost must be used to determine how much product cost should be removed from Finished Goods and charged to Cost of Goods Sold.

For Rand Company, we will assume 750 of the 1,000 gold medallions in job A were shipped to customers by the end of the month for total sales revenue of $225,000. Since 1,000 units were produced and the total cost of the job from the job cost sheet was $158,000, the unit product cost was $158. The following journal entries would record the sale (all sales are on account):

(12)

Accounts Receivable	225,000	
Sales		225,000

(13)

Cost of Goods Sold	118,500	
Finished Goods		118,500
($158 per unit × 750 units = $118,500)		

With entry (13), the flow of costs through our job-order costing system is completed.

Summary of Cost Flows

LEARNING OBJECTIVE 7
Prepare T-accounts to show the flow of costs in a job-order costing system.

To pull the entire Rand Company example together, journal entries (1) through (13) are summarized in Exhibit 3–9. The flow of costs through the accounts is presented in T-account form in Exhibit 3–10.

Exhibit 3–11 presents a schedule of cost of goods manufactured and a schedule of cost of goods sold for Rand Company. Note particularly from Exhibit 3–11 that the manufacturing overhead cost on the schedule of cost of goods manufactured is the overhead applied to jobs during the month—not the actual manufacturing overhead costs incurred. The reason for this can be traced back to journal entry (7) and the T-account for Work in Process that appears in Exhibit 3–10. Under a normal costing system as illustrated in this chapter, applied—not actual—overhead costs are applied to jobs and thus to Work in Process inventory. Note also the cost of goods manufactured for the month ($158,000) agrees with the amount transferred from Work in Process to Finished Goods for the month as recorded earlier in entry (11). Also note that this $158,000 figure is used in computing the cost of goods sold for the month.

An income statement for April is presented in Exhibit 3–12. Observe that the cost of goods sold figure on this statement ($123,500) is carried down from Exhibit 3–11.

Exhibit 3–9
Summary of Rand Company Journal Entries

Account	Debit	Credit
(1)		
Raw Materials	60,000	
Accounts Payable		60,000
(2)		
Work in Process	50,000	
Manufacturing Overhead	2,000	
Raw Materials		52,000
(3)		
Work in Process	60,000	
Manufacturing Overhead	15,000	
Salaries and Wages Payable		75,000
(4)		
Manufacturing Overhead	40,000	
Accounts Payable		40,000
(5)		
Manufacturing Overhead	20,000	
Property Taxes Payable		13,000
Prepaid Insurance		7,000
(6)		
Manufacturing Overhead	18,000	
Accumulated Depreciation		18,000
(7)		
Work in Process	90,000	
Manufacturing Overhead		90,000
(8)		
Salaries Expense	30,000	
Salaries and Wages Payable		30,000
(9)		
Depreciation Expense	7,000	
Accumulated Depreciation		7,000
(10)		
Advertising Expense	42,000	
Other Selling and Administrative Expense	8,000	
Accounts Payable		50,000
(11)		
Finished Goods	158,000	
Work in Process		158,000
(12)		
Accounts Receivable	225,000	
Sales		225,000
(13)		
Cost of Goods Sold	118,500	
Finished Goods		118,500

Exhibit 3–10 Summary of Cost Flows—Rand Company

Accounts Receivable

	Debit		Credit
	XX*		
(12)	225,000		

Prepaid Insurance

	Debit		Credit
	XX		
		(5)	7,000

Raw Materials

	Debit		Credit
Bal.	7,000	(2)	52,000
(1)	60,000		
Bal.	15,000		

Work in Process

	Debit		Credit
Bal.	30,000	(11)	158,000
(2)	50,000		
(3)	60,000		
(7)	90,000		
Bal.	72,000		

Finished Goods

	Debit		Credit
Bal.	10,000	(13)	118,500
(11)	158,000		
Bal.	49,500		

Accumulated Depreciation

	Debit		Credit
			XX
		(6)	18,000
		(9)	7,000

Manufacturing Overhead

	Debit		Credit
(2)	2,000	(7)	90,000
(3)	15,000		
(4)	40,000		
(5)	20,000		
(6)	18,000		
Bal.	5,000		

Accounts Payable

	Debit		Credit
			XX
		(1)	60,000
		(4)	40,000
		(10)	50,000

Salaries and Wages Payable

	Debit		Credit
			XX
		(3)	75,000
		(8)	30,000

Property Taxes Payable

	Debit		Credit
			XX
		(5)	13,000

Capital Stock

	Debit		Credit
			XX

Retained Earnings

	Debit		Credit
			XX

Sales

	Debit		Credit
		(12)	225,000

Cost of Goods Sold

	Debit		Credit
(13)	118,500		

Salaries Expense

	Debit		Credit
(8)	30,000		

Depreciation Expense

	Debit		Credit
(9)	7,000		

Advertising Expense

	Debit		Credit
(10)	42,000		

Other Selling and Administrative Expense

	Debit		Credit
(10)	8,000		

Explanation of entries:

(1) Raw materials purchased.
(2) Direct and indirect materials issued into production.
(3) Direct and indirect factory labor cost incurred.
(4) Utilities and other factory costs incurred.
(5) Property taxes and insurance incurred on the factory.
(6) Depreciation recorded on factory assets.
(7) Overhead cost applied to Work in Process.
(8) Administrative salaries expense incurred.
(9) Depreciation recorded on office equipment.
(10) Advertising and other expense incurred.
(11) Cost of goods manufactured transferred into finished goods.
(12) Sale of job A recorded.
(13) Cost of goods sold recorded for job A.

*XX = Normal balance in the account (for example, Accounts Receivable normally carries a debit balance).

Exhibit 3–11
Schedules of Cost of Goods Manufactured and Cost of Goods Sold

Cost of Goods Manufactured		
Direct materials:		
Raw materials inventory, beginning	$ 7,000	
Add: Purchases of raw materials	60,000	
Total raw materials available	67,000	
Deduct: Raw materials inventory, ending	15,000	
Raw materials used in production	52,000	
Less indirect materials included in manufacturing overhead	2,000	$ 50,000
Direct labor		60,000
Manufacturing overhead applied to work in process		90,000
Total manufacturing costs		200,000
Add: Beginning work in process inventory		30,000
		230,000
Deduct: Ending work in process inventory		72,000
Cost of goods manufactured		$158,000
Cost of Goods Sold		
Finished goods inventory, beginning		$ 10,000
Add: Cost of goods manufactured		158,000
Goods available for sale		168,000
Deduct: Finished goods inventory, ending		49,500
Unadjusted cost of goods sold		118,500
Add: Underapplied overhead		5,000
Adjusted cost of goods sold		$123,500

*Note that the underapplied overhead is added to cost of goods sold. If overhead were overapplied, it would be deducted from costs of goods sold.

Exhibit 3–12
Income Statement

Rand Company
Income Statement
For the Month Ending April 30

Sales		$225,000
Less cost of goods sold ($118,500 + $5,000)		123,500
Gross margin		101,500
Less selling and administrative expenses:		
Salaries expense	$30,000	
Depreciation expense	7,000	
Advertising expense	42,000	
Other expense	8,000	87,000
Net operating income		$ 14,500

Problems of Overhead Application

We need to consider two complications relating to overhead application. These are (1) the computation of underapplied and overapplied overhead and (2) the disposition of any balance remaining in the Manufacturing Overhead account at the end of a period.

LEARNING OBJECTIVE 8
Compute under- or overapplied overhead cost and prepare the journal entry to close the balance in Manufacturing Overhead to the appropriate accounts.

Underapplied and Overapplied Overhead

Since the predetermined overhead rate is established before a period begins and is based entirely on estimated data, the overhead cost applied to Work in Process will generally differ from the amount of overhead cost actually incurred during a period. In the case of Rand Company, for example, the predetermined overhead rate of $6 per hour resulted in $90,000 of overhead cost being applied to Work in Process, whereas actual overhead costs for April proved to be $95,000 (see Exhibit 3–8). The difference between the overhead cost applied to Work in Process and the actual overhead costs of a period is termed either **underapplied** or **overapplied overhead.** For Rand Company, overhead was underapplied because the applied cost ($90,000) was $5,000 less than the actual cost ($95,000). If the situation had been reversed and the company had applied $95,000 in overhead cost to Work in Process while incurring actual overhead costs of only $90,000, then the overhead would have been overapplied.

What is the cause of underapplied or overapplied overhead? The causes can be complex, and a full explanation will have to wait for later chapters. Nevertheless, the basic problem is that the method of applying overhead to jobs using a predetermined overhead rate assumes that actual overhead costs will be proportional to the actual amount of the allocation base incurred during the period. If, for example, the predetermined overhead rate is $6 per machine-hour, then it is assumed that actual overhead costs incurred will be $6 for every machine-hour that is actually worked. There are at least two reasons why this may not be true. First, much of the overhead often consists of fixed costs that do not grow as the number of machine-hours incurred increases. Second, spending on overhead items may or may not be under control. If individuals who are responsible for overhead costs do a good job, those costs should be less than were expected at the beginning of the period. If they do a poor job, those costs will be more than expected. As we indicated above, however, a fuller explanation of the causes of underapplied and overapplied overhead will have to wait for later chapters.

To illustrate what can happen, suppose that two companies—Turbo Crafters and Black & Howell—have prepared the following estimated data for the coming year:

	Company	
	Turbo Crafters	**Black & Howell**
Predetermined overhead rate based on	Machine-hours	Direct materials cost
Estimated manufacturing overhead	$300,000 (a)	$120,000 (a)
Estimated machine-hours	75,000 (b)	—
Estimated direct materials cost	—	$ 80,000 (b)
Predetermined overhead rate, (a) ÷ (b).	$4 per machine-hour	150% of direct materials cost

Now assume that because of unexpected changes in overhead spending and changes in demand for the companies' products, the *actual* overhead cost and the *actual* activity recorded during the year in each company are as follows:

	Company	
	Turbo Crafters	**Black & Howell**
Actual manufacturing overhead costs	$290,000	$130,000
Actual machine-hours	68,000	—
Actual direct material costs	—	$ 90,000

Exhibit 3–13
Summary of Overhead Concepts

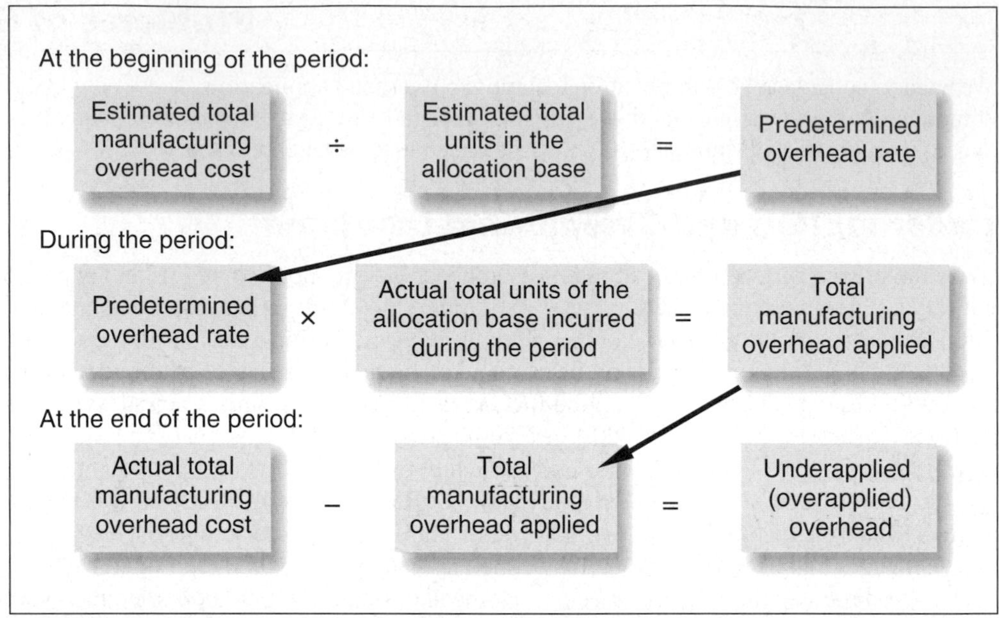

For each company, note that the actual data for both cost and activity differ from the estimates used in computing the predetermined overhead rate. This results in underapplied and overapplied overhead as follows:

	Company	
	Turbo Crafters	**Black & Howell**
Actual manufacturing overhead costs	$290,000	$130,000
Manufacturing overhead cost applied to Work in Process during the year:		
68,000 *actual* machine-hours × $4 per machine-hour	272,000	
$90,000 *actual* direct materials cost × 150% of direct materials cost		135,000
Underapplied (overapplied) overhead	$ 18,000	$ (5,000)

For Turbo Crafters, notice that the amount of overhead cost that has been applied to Work in Process ($272,000) is less than the actual overhead cost for the year ($290,000). Therefore, overhead is underapplied. Also notice that the original estimate of overhead in Turbo Crafters ($300,000) is not directly involved in this computation. Its impact is felt only through the $4 predetermined overhead rate that is used.

For Black & Howell, the amount of overhead cost that has been applied to Work in Process ($135,000) is greater than the actual overhead cost for the year ($130,000), and so overhead is overapplied.

A summary of the concepts discussed above is presented in Exhibit 3–13.

Disposition of Under- or Overapplied Overhead Balances

What disposition should be made of any under- or overapplied balance remaining in the Manufacturing Overhead account at the end of a period? Generally, any balance in the account is treated in one of two ways:

1. Closed out to Cost of Goods Sold.

2. Allocated between Work in Process, Finished Goods, and Cost of Goods Sold in proportion to the overhead applied during the current period in the ending balances of these accounts.[1]

The second method, which allocates the under- or overapplied overhead among ending inventories and Cost of Goods Sold, is equivalent to using an "actual" overhead rate and is for that reason considered by many to be more accurate than the first method. Consequently, if the amount of underapplied or overapplied overhead is material, many accountants would insist that the second method be used. In problem assignments we will always indicate which method you are to use for disposing of under- or overapplied overhead.

Closed Out to Cost of Goods Sold As mentioned above, closing out the balance in Manufacturing Overhead to Cost of Goods Sold is simpler than the allocation method. Returning to the example of Rand Company, the entry to close the $5,000 of underapplied overhead to Cost of Goods Sold would be as follows:

(14)

	Debit	Credit
Cost of Goods Sold	5,000	
Manufacturing Overhead		5,000

Note that since there is a debit balance in the Manufacturing Overhead account, Manufacturing Overhead must be credited to close out the account. This has the effect of increasing Cost of Goods Sold for April to $123,500:

Unadjusted cost of goods sold [from entry (13)]	$118,500
Add underapplied overhead [entry (14) above]	5,000
Adjusted cost of goods sold	$123,500

After this adjustment has been made, Rand Company's income statement for April will appear as was shown earlier in Exhibit 3–12.

Allocated between Accounts Allocation of under- or overapplied overhead between Work in Process, Finished Goods, and Cost of Goods Sold is more accurate than closing the entire balance into Cost of Goods Sold. The reason is that allocation assigns overhead costs to where they would have gone in the first place had it not been for the errors in the estimates going into the predetermined overhead rate.

Had Rand Company chosen to allocate the underapplied overhead among the inventory accounts and Cost of Goods Sold, it would first be necessary to determine the amount of overhead that had been applied during April to each of the accounts. The computations would have been as follows:

Overhead applied in work in process inventory, April 30	$30,000	33.33%
Overhead applied in finished goods inventory, April 30 ($60,000/1,000 units = $60 per unit) × 250 units	15,000	16.67%
Overhead applied in cost of goods sold, April ($60,000/1,000 units = $60 per unit) × 750 units	45,000	50.00%
Total overhead applied	$90,000	100.00%

Based on the above percentages, the underapplied overhead (i.e., the debit balance in Manufacturing Overhead) would be allocated as in the following journal entry:

	Debit	Credit
Work in Process (33.33% × $5,000)	1,666.50	
Finished Goods (16.67% × $5,000)	833.50	
Cost of Goods Sold (50.00% × $5,000)	2,500.00	
Manufacturing Overhead		5,000.00

[1] Some firms prefer to make the allocation on the basis of the total cost of direct materials, direct labor, and applied manufacturing overhead in each of the accounts at the end of the period. This method is not as accurate as allocating the balance in the Manufacturing Overhead account on the basis of just the overhead applied in each of the accounts during the current period.

Exhibit 3–14 A General Model of Cost Flows

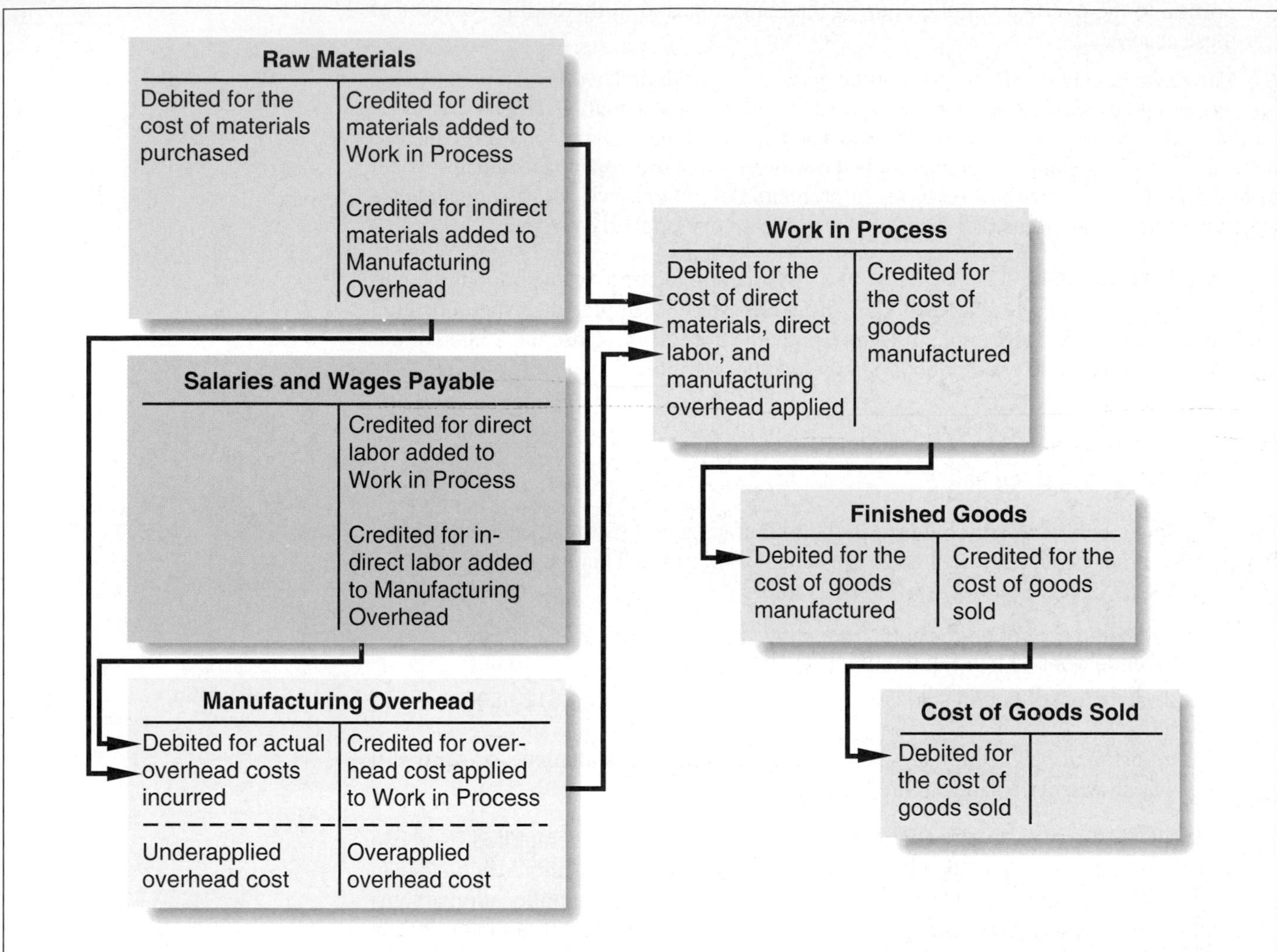

Note that the first step in the allocation was to determine the amount of overhead applied in each of the accounts. For Finished Goods, for example, the total amount of overhead applied to job A, $60,000, was divided by the total number of units in job A, 1,000 units, to arrive at the average overhead applied of $60 per unit. Since there were still 250 units from job A in ending finished goods inventory, the amount of overhead applied in the Finished Goods Inventory account was $60 per unit multiplied by 250 units or $15,000 in total.

If overhead had been overapplied, the entry above would have been just the reverse, since a credit balance would have existed in the Manufacturing Overhead account.

A General Model of Product Cost Flows

The flow of costs in a product costing system is presented in the form of a T-account model in Exhibit 3–14. This model applies as much to a process costing system as it does to a job-order costing system. This model can be very helpful in understanding how costs enter a system, flow through it, and finally end up as Cost of Goods Sold on the income statement.

Multiple Predetermined Overhead Rates

Our discussion in this chapter has assumed that there is a single predetermined overhead rate for an entire factory called a **plantwide overhead rate.** This is a fairly common practice—

particularly in smaller companies. But in larger companies, *multiple predetermined overhead rates* are often used. In a **multiple predetermined overhead rate** system each production department may have its own predetermined overhead rate. Such a system, while more complex, is considered to be more accurate, since it can reflect differences across departments in how overhead costs are incurred. For example, overhead might be allocated based on direct labor-hours in departments that are relatively labor intensive and based on machine-hours in departments that are relatively machine intensive. When multiple predetermined overhead rates are used, overhead is applied in each department according to its own overhead rate as a job proceeds through the department.

Enhancing the Accuracy of Product Costs

In Business

Only 34% of surveyed manufacturing firms reported that they used a single, plantwide overhead rate. The use of multiple overhead rates to obtain more accurate product costs was reported by 44% of the firms. The remaining 22% use activity-based costing—an even more complex, and presumably more accurate, approach to the allocation of overhead costs to products.

Source: Eun-Sup Shim and Joseph M. Larkin, "A Survey of Current Managerial Accounting Practices: Where Do We Stand," *Ohio CPA Journal*, February 1994, p. 21 (4 pages).

Job-Order Costing in Service Companies

We stated earlier in the chapter that job-order costing is also used in service organizations such as law firms, movie studios, hospitals, and repair shops, as well as in manufacturing companies. In a law firm, for example, each client represents a "job," and the costs of that job are accumulated day by day on a job cost sheet as the client's case is handled by the firm. Legal forms and similar inputs represent the direct materials for the job; the time expended by attorneys represents the direct labor; and the costs of secretaries, clerks, rent, depreciation, and so forth, represent the overhead.

In a movie studio such as Columbia Pictures, each film produced by the studio is a "job," and costs for direct materials (costumes, props, film, etc.) and direct labor (actors, directors, and extras) are accounted for and charged to each film's job cost sheet. A share of the studio's overhead costs, such as utilities, depreciation of equipment, wages of maintenance workers, and so forth, is also charged to each film. However, as discussed in the box at the very beginning of the chapter, the methods used by some studios to distribute overhead costs among movies are controversial and sometimes result in lawsuits.

In sum, the reader should be aware that job-order costing is a versatile and widely used costing method, and may be encountered in virtually any organization that provides diverse products or services.

Use of Information Technology

Earlier in the chapter we discussed how bar code technology can be used to record labor time—reducing the drudgery in that task and increasing accuracy. Bar codes have many other uses.

In a company with a well-developed bar code system, the manufacturing cycle begins with the receipt of a customer's order in electronic form. Until very recently, the order would have been received via electronic data interchange (EDI), which involves a network of computers linking organizations. An EDI network allows companies to electronically exchange business documents and other information that extend into all areas of business activity from ordering raw materials to shipping completed goods. EDI was developed in the 1980s and requires significant investments in programming and networking hardware. Recently, EDI has been challenged by a far cheaper web-based alternative—XML (Extensible Markup Language), an extension of HTML (Hypertext Markup Language). HTML uses codes to tell your web browser how to display information on your screen, but the computer doesn't know what the information is—it just displays it. XML provides additional tags that identify the kind of information that is being exchanged. For example, price data might be coded as <price> 14.95 <price>. When your computer reads this data and sees the tags <price> surrounding 14.95, your computer will immediately know that this is a price. XML tags can designate many different kinds of information—customer orders, medical records, bank statements, and so on—and the tags will indicate to your computer how to display, store, and retrieve the information. Office Depot is an early adopter of XML, which it is using to facilitate e-commerce with its big customers.

Once an order has been received via EDI or over the web in the form of an XML file, the computer draws up a list of required raw materials and sends out electronic purchase orders to suppliers. When materials arrive at the company's plant from the suppliers, bar codes that have been applied by the suppliers are scanned to update inventory records and to trigger payment for the materials. The bar codes are scanned again when the materials are requisitioned for use in production. At that point, the computer credits the Raw Materials inventory account for the amount and type of goods requisitioned and charges the Work in Process inventory account.

A unique bar code is assigned to each job. This bar code is scanned to update Work in Process records for labor and other costs incurred in the manufacturing process. When goods are completed, another scan is performed that transfers both the cost and quantity of goods from the Work in Process inventory account to the Finished Goods inventory account, or charges Cost of Goods Sold for goods ready to be shipped.

Goods ready to be shipped are packed into containers, which are bar coded with information that includes the customer number, the type and quantity of goods being shipped, and the order number. This bar code is then used for preparing billing information and for tracking the packed goods until placed on a carrier for shipment to the customer. Some customers require that the packed goods be bar coded with point-of-sale labels that can be scanned at retail check-out counters. These scans allow the retailer to update inventory records, verify price, and generate a customer receipt.

In Business

Using XML to Enhance Web Commerce

W.W. Grainger Inc. is in the unglamorous, but important, business of selling maintenance and repair supplies to organizations. For an effective web-based catalog, the company needs up-to-date, detailed product descriptions from its own suppliers. Grainger is using software from OnDisplay Inc. (www.ondisplay.com) to collect product descriptions from vendors' databases and to add XML tags. When Grainger's customers request product information on the web, this data can then be displayed in a standard format. This process cuts in half the amount of time required to post new product information to Grainger's web catalog.

If you would like to know more about XML, refer to the World Wide Web Consortium (W3C) web site www.w3c.org/xml.

Source: John J. Xenakis, *CFO*, October 1999, pp. 31–36.

In short, bar code technology is being integrated into all areas of business activity. When combined with EDI or XML, it eliminates a lot of clerical drudgery and allows companies to capture and exchange more data and to analyze and report information much more quickly and completely and with less error than with manual systems.

Managing Diversity with Technology

In Business

Andersen Windows of Bayport, Minnesota, has developed techniques that allow it to produce just about any window configuration that a customer might order. Andersen has installed hundreds of Macintosh-based systems for designing windows at distributors and retailers around the country. Beginning with a standard design from the company's catalog, this system allows a customer to "add, change, and strip away features until they've designed a window they're pleased with . . . The computer automatically checks the window specs for structural soundness, and then generates a price quote." Once the sale is made, the retailer's computer transmits the order with all of the necessary specifications to Andersen. At Andersen, the order is assigned a unique number and is tracked "in real time, using bar code technology, from the assembly line to the warehouse. This helps ensure that what the customer orders is what gets built and ultimately what gets shipped . . . Last year the company offered a whopping 188,000 different products, yet fewer than one in 200 van loads contained an order discrepancy."

Source: Justin Martin, "Are You as Good as You Think You Are?" *Fortune,* September 30, 1996, pp. 142–144.

Summary

Job-order costing and process costing are widely used to track costs. Job-order costing is used in situations where the organization offers many different products or services, such as in furniture manufacturing, hospitals, and legal firms. Process costing is used where units of product are homogeneous, such as in flour milling or cement production.

Materials requisition forms and labor time tickets are used to assign direct materials and direct labor costs to jobs in a job-costing system. Manufacturing overhead costs are assigned to jobs using a predetermined overhead rate. The predetermined overhead rate is determined before the period begins by dividing the estimated total manufacturing cost for the period by the estimated total allocation base for the period. The most frequently used allocation bases are direct labor-hours and machine-hours. Overhead is applied to jobs by multiplying the predetermined overhead rate by the actual amount of the allocation base used by the job.

Since the predetermined overhead rate is based on estimates, the actual overhead cost incurred during a period may be more or less than the amount of overhead cost applied to production. Such a difference is referred to as under- or overapplied overhead. The under- or overapplied overhead for a period can be either (1) closed out to Cost of Goods Sold or (2) allocated between Work in Process, Finished Goods, and Cost of Goods Sold. When overhead is underapplied, manufacturing overhead costs have been understated and therefore inventories and/or expenses must be adjusted upwards. When overhead is overapplied, manufacturing overhead costs have been overstated and therefore inventories and/or expenses must be adjusted downwards.

Review Problem: Job-Order Costing

Hogle Company is a manufacturing firm that uses job-order costing. On January 1, the beginning of its fiscal year, the company's inventory balances were as follows:

Raw materials	$20,000
Work in process	15,000
Finished goods	30,000

The company applies overhead cost to jobs on the basis of machine-hours worked. For the current year, the company estimated that it would work 75,000 machine-hours and incur $450,000 in manufacturing overhead cost. The following transactions were recorded for the year:

a. Raw materials were purchased on account, $410,000.
b. Raw materials were requisitioned for use in production, $380,000 ($360,000 direct materials and $20,000 indirect materials).

c. The following costs were incurred for employee services: direct labor, $75,000; indirect labor, $110,000; sales commissions, $90,000; and administrative salaries, $200,000.
d. Sales travel costs were $17,000.
e. Utility costs in the factory were $43,000.
f. Advertising costs were $180,000.
g. Depreciation was recorded for the year, $350,000 (80% relates to factory operations, and 20% relates to selling and administrative activities).
h. Insurance expired during the year, $10,000 (70% relates to factory operations, and the remaining 30% relates to selling and administrative activities).
i. Manufacturing overhead was applied to production. Due to greater than expected demand for its products, the company worked 80,000 machine-hours during the year.
j. Goods costing $900,000 to manufacture according to their job cost sheets were completed during the year.
k. Goods were sold on account to customers during the year at a total selling price of $1,500,000. The goods cost $870,000 to manufacture according to their job cost sheets.

Required:

1. Prepare journal entries to record the preceding transactions.
2. Post the entries in (1) above to T-accounts (don't forget to enter the beginning balances in the inventory accounts).
3. Is Manufacturing Overhead underapplied or overapplied for the year? Prepare a journal entry to close any balance in the Manufacturing Overhead account to Cost of Goods Sold. Do not allocate the balance between ending inventories and Cost of Goods Sold.
4. Prepare an income statement for the year.

Solution to Review Problem

		Account	Debit	Credit
1.	*a.*	Raw Materials	410,000	
		Accounts Payable		410,000
	b.	Work in Process	360,000	
		Manufacturing Overhead	20,000	
		Raw Materials		380,000
	c.	Work in Process	75,000	
		Manufacturing Overhead	110,000	
		Sales Commissions Expense	90,000	
		Administrative Salaries Expense	200,000	
		Salaries and Wages Payable		475,000
	d.	Sales Travel Expense	17,000	
		Accounts Payable		17,000
	e.	Manufacturing Overhead	43,000	
		Accounts Payable		43,000
	f.	Advertising Expense	180,000	
		Accounts Payable		180,000
	g.	Manufacturing Overhead	280,000	
		Depreciation Expense	70,000	
		Accumulated Depreciation		350,000
	h.	Manufacturing Overhead	7,000	
		Insurance Expense	3,000	
		Prepaid Insurance		10,000

i. The predetermined overhead rate for the year would be computed as follows:

$$\text{Predetermined overhead rate} = \frac{\text{Estimated total manufacturing overhead cost}}{\text{Estimated total units in the allocation base}}$$

$$= \frac{\$450{,}000}{75{,}000 \text{ machine-hours}}$$

$$= \$6 \text{ per machine-hour}$$

Based on the 80,000 machine-hours actually worked during the year, the company would have applied $480,000 in overhead cost to production: 80,000 machine-hours × $6 per machine-hour= $480,000. The following entry records this application of overhead cost:

	Account	Debit	Credit
	Work in Process	480,000	
	Manufacturing Overhead		480,000
j.	Finished Goods	900,000	
	Work in Process		900,000

k.	Accounts Receivable	1,500,000	
	Sales		1,500,000
	Cost of Goods Sold	870,000	
	Finished Goods		870,000

2.

Accounts Receivable

(k)	1,500,000		

Finished Goods

Bal.	30,000	(k)	870,000
(j)	900,000		
Bal.	60,000		

Accounts Payable

		(a)	410,000
		(d)	17,000
		(e)	43,000
		(f)	180,000

Sales

		(k)	1,500,000

Sales Commissions Expense

(c)	90,000		

Advertising Expense

(f)	180,000		

Raw Materials

Bal.	20,000	(b)	380,000
(a)	410,000		
Bal.	50,000		

Prepaid Insurance

		(h)	10,000

Salaries and Wages Payable

		(c)	475,000

Cost of Goods Sold

(k)	870,000		

Administrative Salary Expense

(c)	200,000		

Depreciation Expense

(g)	70,000		

Work in Process

Bal.	15,000	(j)	900,000
(b)	360,000		
(c)	75,000		
(i)	480,000		
Bal.	30,000		

Accumulated Depreciation

		(g)	350,000

Manufacturing Overhead

(b)	20,000	(i)	480,000
(c)	110,000		
(e)	43,000		
(g)	280,000		
(h)	7,000		
	460,000		480,000
		Bal.	20,000

Insurance Expense

(h)	3,000		

Sales Travel Expense

(d)	17,000		

3. Manufacturing overhead is overapplied for the year. The entry to close it out to Cost of Goods Sold is as follows:

Manufacturing Overhead	20,000	
Cost of Goods Sold		20,000

4.

HOGLE COMPANY
Income Statement
For the Year Ended December 31

Sales		$1,500,000
Less cost of goods sold ($870,000 − $20,000)		850,000
Gross margin		650,000
Less selling and administrative expenses:		
Commissions expense	$ 90,000	
Administrative salaries expense	200,000	
Sales travel expense	17,000	
Advertising expense	180,000	
Depreciation expense	70,000	
Insurance expense	3,000	560,000
Net operating income		$ 90,000

Glossary

Absorption costing A costing method that includes all manufacturing costs—direct materials, direct labor, and both variable and fixed overhead—as part of the cost of a finished unit of product. This term is synonymous with *full cost.* (p. 92)

Allocation base A measure of activity such as direct labor-hours or machine-hours that is used to assign costs to cost objects. (p. 98)

Bill of materials A document that shows the type and quantity of each major item of materials required to make a product. (94)

Cost driver A factor, such as machine-hours, beds occupied, computer time, or flight-hours, that causes overhead costs. (p. 100)

Full cost See *Absorption costing.* (p. 92)

Job cost sheet A form prepared for each job that records the materials, labor, and overhead costs charged to the job. (p. 95)

Job-order costing system A costing system used in situations where many different products, jobs, or services are produced each period. (p. 93)

Materials requisition form A detailed source document that specifies the type and quantity of materials that are to be drawn from the storeroom and identifies the job to which the costs of materials are to be charged. (p. 94)

Multiple predetermined overhead rates A costing system in which there are multiple overhead cost pools with a different predetermined rate for each cost pool, rather than a single predetermined overhead rate for the entire company. Frequently, each production department is treated as a separate overhead cost pool. (p. 117)

Normal cost system A costing system in which overhead costs are applied to jobs by multiplying a predetermined overhead rate by the actual amount of the allocation base incurred by the job. (p. 99)

Overapplied overhead A credit balance in the Manufacturing Overhead account that occurs when the amount of overhead cost applied to Work in Process is greater than the amount of overhead cost actually incurred during a period. (p. 113)

Overhead application The process of charging manufacturing overhead cost to job cost sheets and to the Work in Process account. (p. 98)

Plantwide overhead rate A single predetermined overhead rate that is used throughout a plant. (p. 116)

Predetermined overhead rate A rate used to charge overhead cost to jobs in production; the rate is established in advance for each period by use of estimates of total manufacturing overhead cost and of the total allocation base for the period. (p. 98)

Process costing system A costing system used in those manufacturing situations where a single, homogeneous product (such as cement or flour) is produced for long periods of time. (p. 92)

Time ticket A detailed source document that is used to record the amount of time an employee spends on various activities during a day. (p. 96)

Underapplied overhead A debit balance in the Manufacturing Overhead account that occurs when the amount of overhead cost actually incurred is greater than the amount of overhead cost applied to Work in Process during a period. (p. 113)

Appendix 3A: The Predetermined Overhead Rate and Capacity

LEARNING OBJECTIVE 9

Explain the implications of basing the predetermined overhead rate on activity at capacity rather than on estimated activity for the period.

Companies typically base their predetermined overhead rates on the estimated, or budgeted, amount of the allocation base for the upcoming period. This is the method that is used in the chapter, but it is a practice that has recently come under severe criticism.[1] An example will be very helpful in understanding why. Prahad Corporation manufactures music CDs for local recording studios. The company's CD duplicating machine is capable of

[1] Institute of Management Accountants, *Measuring the Cost of Capacity: Statements on Management Accounting, Statement Number 4Y,* March 31, 1996, Montvale, NJ; Thomas Klammer, ed., *Capacity Measurement and Improvement: A Manager's Guide to Evaluating and Optimizing Capacity Productivity* (Chicago: CAM-I, Irwin Professional Publishing, 1996); and C. J. McNair, "The Hidden Costs of Capacity," *The Journal of Cost Management* (Spring 1994), pp. 12–24.

producing a new CD every 10 seconds from a master CD. The company leases the CD duplicating machine for $180,000 per year, and this is the company's only manufacturing overhead. With allowances for setups and maintenance, the machine is theoretically capable of producing up to 900,000 CDs per year. However, due to weak retail sales of CDs, the company's commercial customers are unlikely to order more than 600,000 CDs next year. The company uses machine time as the allocation base for applying manufacturing overhead. These data are summarized below:

PRAHAD CORPORATION DATA	
Total manufacturing overhead cost	$180,000 per year
Allocation base: machine time per CD	10 seconds per CD
Capacity	900,000 CDs per year
Budgeted output for next year	600,000 CDs

If Prahad follows common practice and computes its predetermined overhead rate using estimated, or budgeted, figures, then its predetermined overhead rate for next year would be $0.03 per second of machine time computed as follows:

$$\text{Predetermined overhead rate} = \frac{\text{Estimated total manufacturing overhead cost}}{\text{Estimated total units in the allocation base}}$$

$$= \frac{\$180{,}000}{600{,}000 \text{ CDs} \times 10 \text{ seconds per CD}}$$

$$= \$0.03 \text{ per second}$$

Since each CD requires 10 seconds of machine time, each CD will be charged for $0.30 of overhead cost.

Critics charge that there are two problems with this procedure. First, if predetermined overhead rates are based on budgeted activity, then the unit product costs will fluctuate depending on the budgeted level of activity for the period. For example, if the budgeted output for the year was only 300,000 CDs, the predetermined overhead rate would be $0.06 per second of machine time or $0.60 per CD rather than $0.30 per CD. In general, if budgeted output falls, the overhead cost per unit will increase; it will appear that the CDs cost more to make. Managers may then be tempted to increase prices at the worst possible time—just as demand is falling.

Second, critics charge that under the traditional approach, products are charged for resources that they don't use. When the fixed costs of capacity are spread over estimated activity, the units that are produced must shoulder the costs of unused capacity. That is why the applied overhead cost per unit increases as the level of activity falls. The critics argue that products should be charged only for the capacity that they use; they should not be charged for the capacity they don't use. This can be accomplished by basing the predetermined overhead rate on capacity as follows:

$$\text{Predetermined overhead rate based on capacity} = \frac{\text{Estimated total manufacturing overhead cost at capacity}}{\text{Estimated total units in the allocation base at capacity}}$$

$$= \frac{\$180{,}000}{900{,}000 \text{ CDs} \times 10 \text{ seconds per CD}}$$

$$= \$0.02 \text{ per second}$$

Since the predetermined overhead rate is $0.02 per second, the overhead cost applied to each CD would be $0.20. This charge is constant and would not be affected by the level of activity during a period. If output falls, the charge would still be $0.20 per CD.

This method will almost certainly result in underapplied overhead. If actual output at Prahad Corporation is 600,000 CDs, then only $120,000 of overhead cost would be applied to products ($0.20 per CD × 600,000 CDs). Since the actual overhead cost is $180,000, there would be underapplied overhead of $60,000. In another departure from tradition, the critics suggest that the underapplied overhead that results from idle capacity should be separately disclosed on the income statement as the Cost of Unused Capacity—a period expense. Disclosing this cost as a lump sum on the income statement, rather than burying it in Cost of Goods Sold or ending inventories, makes it much more visible to managers.

Official pronouncements do not prohibit basing predetermined overhead rates on capacity for external reports.[2] Nevertheless, basing the predetermined overhead rate on estimated, or budgeted, activity is a long-established practice in industry, and some managers and accountants may object to the large amounts of underapplied overhead that would often result from using capacity to determine predetermined overhead rates. And some may insist that the underapplied overhead be allocated among Cost of Goods Sold and ending inventories—which would defeat the purpose of basing the predetermined overhead rate on capacity.

Questions

3–1 Why aren't actual overhead costs traced to jobs just as direct materials and direct labor costs are traced to jobs?

3–2 When would job-order costing be used in preference to process costing?

3–3 What is the purpose of the job cost sheet in a job-order costing system?

3–4 What is a predetermined overhead rate, and how is it computed?

3–5 Explain how a sales order, a production order, a materials requisition form, and a labor time ticket are involved in producing and costing products.

3–6 Explain why some production costs must be assigned to products through an allocation process. Name several such costs. Would such costs be classified as *direct* or as *indirect* costs?

3–7 Why do firms use predetermined overhead rates rather than actual manufacturing overhead costs in applying overhead to jobs?

3–8 What factors should be considered in selecting a base to be used in computing the predetermined overhead rate?

3–9 If a company fully allocates all of its overhead costs to jobs, does this guarantee that a profit will be earned for the period?

3–10 What account is credited when overhead cost is applied to Work in Process? Would you expect the amount applied for a period to equal the actual overhead costs of the period? Why or why not?

3–11 What is underapplied overhead? Overapplied overhead? What disposition is made of these amounts at the end of the period?

3–12 Provide two reasons why overhead might be underapplied in a given year.

3–13 What adjustment is made for underapplied overhead on the schedule of cost of goods sold? What adjustment is made for overapplied overhead?

3–14 Sigma Company applies overhead cost to jobs on the basis of direct labor cost. Job A, which was started and completed during the current period, shows charges of $5,000 for direct materials, $8,000 for direct labor, and $6,000 for overhead on its job cost sheet. Job B, which is still in process at year-end, shows charges of $2,500 for direct materials and $4,000 for direct labor. Should any overhead cost be added to job B at year-end? Explain.

3–15 A company assigns overhead cost to completed jobs on the basis of 125% of direct labor cost. The job cost sheet for job 313 shows that $10,000 in direct materials has been used on the job and that $12,000 in direct labor cost has been incurred. If 1,000 units were produced in job 313, what is the unit product cost?

3–16 What is a plantwide overhead rate? Why are multiple overhead rates, rather than a plantwide rate, used in some companies?

3–17 What happens to overhead rates based on direct labor when automated equipment replaces direct labor?

[2] Institute of Management Accountants, *Measuring the Cost of Capacity,* pp. 46–47.

Exercises

EXERCISE 3–1 Process Costing and Job-Order Costing [LO1]
Which would be more appropriate in each of the following situations—job-order costing or process costing?

a. A custom yacht builder.
b. A golf course designer.
c. A potato chip manufacturer.
d. A business consultant.
e. A plywood manufacturer.
f. A soft-drink bottler.
g. A film studio.
h. A firm that supervises bridge construction projects.
i. A manufacturer of fine custom jewelry.
j. A made-to-order garment factory.
k. A factory making one personal computer model.
l. A fertilizer factory.

EXERCISE 3–2 Journal Entries and T-Accounts [LO4, LO5, LO7]
Foley Company uses a job-order costing system. The following data relate to the month of October, the first month of the company's fiscal year:

a. Raw materials purchased on account, $210,000.
b. Raw materials issued to production, $190,000 (80% direct and 20% indirect).
c. Direct labor cost incurred, $49,000; and indirect labor cost incurred, $21,000.
d. Depreciation recorded on factory equipment, $105,000.
e. Other manufacturing overhead costs incurred during October, $130,000 (credit Accounts Payable).
f. The company applies manufacturing overhead cost to production on the basis of $4 per machine-hour. There were 75,000 machine-hours recorded for October.
g. Production orders costing $510,000 according to their job cost sheets were completed during October and transferred to Finished Goods.
h. Production orders that had cost $450,000 to complete according to their job cost sheets were shipped to customers during the month. These goods were sold at 50% above cost. The goods were sold on account.

Required:

1. Prepare journal entries to record the information given above.
2. Prepare T-accounts for Manufacturing Overhead and Work in Process. Post the relevant information above to each account. Compute the ending balance in each account, assuming that Work in Process has a beginning balance of $35,000.

EXERCISE 3–3 Applying Overhead with Various Bases [LO3, LO5, LO8]
Estimated cost and operating data for three companies for the upcoming year are given below:

	Company		
	A	B	C
Direct labor-hours	60,000	30,000	40,000
Machine-hours	25,000	90,000	18,000
Raw materials cost	$300,000	$160,000	$240,000
Manufacturing overhead cost	432,000	270,000	384,000

Predetermined overhead rates are computed using the following bases in the three companies:

Company	Overhead Rate Based on—
A	Direct labor-hours
B	Machine-hours
C	Raw materials cost

Required:

1. Compute the predetermined overhead rate to be used in each company.

2. Assume that Company A works on three jobs during the upcoming year. Direct labor-hours recorded by job are: job 308, 7,000 hours; job 309, 30,000 hours; and job 310, 21,000 hours. How much overhead cost will the company apply to Work in Process for the year? If actual costs are $420,000 for the year, will overhead be underapplied or overapplied? By how much?

EXERCISE 3–4 Varying Predetermined Overhead Rates [LO3, LO5]
Javadi Company makes a composting bin that is subject to wide seasonal variations in demand. Unit product costs are computed on a quarterly basis by dividing each quarter's manufacturing costs (materials, labor, and overhead) by the quarter's production in units. The company's estimated costs, by quarter, for the coming year are given below:

	Quarter			
	First	Second	Third	Fourth
Direct materials	$240,000	$120,000	$ 60,000	$180,000
Direct labor	96,000	48,000	24,000	72,000
Manufacturing overhead	228,000	204,000	192,000	216,000
Total manufacturing costs	$564,000	$372,000	$276,000	$468,000
Number of units to be produced	80,000	40,000	20,000	60,000
Estimated unit product cost	$7.05	$9.30	$13.80	$7.80

Management finds the variation in unit product costs to be confusing and difficult to work with. It has been suggested that the problem lies with manufacturing overhead, since it is the largest element of cost. Accordingly, you have been asked to find a more appropriate way of assigning manufacturing overhead cost to units of product. After some analysis, you have determined that the company's overhead costs are mostly fixed and therefore show little sensitivity to changes in the level of production.

Required:

1. The company uses a job-order costing system. How would you recommend that manufacturing overhead cost be assigned to production? Be specific, and show computations.
2. Recompute the company's unit product costs in accordance with your recommendations in (1) above.

EXERCISE 3–5 Departmental Overhead Rates [LO2, LO3, LO5]
Diewold Company has two departments, milling and assembly. The company uses a job-order cost system and computes a predetermined overhead rate in each department. The milling department bases its rate on machine-hours, and the assembly department bases its rate on direct labor cost. At the beginning of the year, the company made the following estimates:

	Department	
	Milling	Assembly
Direct labor-hours	8,000	75,000
Machine-hours	60,000	3,000
Manufacturing overhead cost	$510,000	$800,000
Direct labor cost	72,000	640,000

Required:

1. Compute the predetermined overhead rate to be used in each department.
2. Assume that the overhead rates you computed in (1) above are in effect. The job cost sheet for job 407, which was started and completed during the year, showed the following:

	Department	
	Milling	Assembly
Direct labor-hours	5	20
Machine-hours	90	4
Materials requisitioned	$800	$370
Direct labor cost	45	160

   Compute the total overhead cost applied to job 407.
3. Would you expect substantially different amounts of overhead cost to be charged to some jobs if the company used a plantwide overhead rate based on direct labor cost instead of using departmental rates? Explain. No computations are necessary.

EXERCISE 3–6 Applying Overhead; T-Accounts; Journal Entries [LO3, LO4, LO5, LO7, LO8]

Medusa Products is a manufacturing company that operates a job-order costing system. Overhead costs are applied to jobs on the basis of machine-hours. At the beginning of the year, management estimated that the company would incur $170,000 in manufacturing overhead costs for the year and work 85,000 machine-hours.

Required:

1. Compute the company's predetermined overhead rate.
2. Assume that during the year the company actually works only 80,000 machine-hours and incurs the following costs in the Manufacturing Overhead and Work in Process accounts:

Manufacturing Overhead

	Debit	Credit
(Utilities)	14,000	?
(Insurance)	9,000	
(Maintenance)	33,000	
(Indirect materials)	7,000	
(Indirect labor)	65,000	
(Depreciation)	40,000	

Work in Process

	Debit	Credit
(Direct materials)	530,000	
(Direct labor)	85,000	
(Overhead)	?	

Copy the data in the T-accounts above onto your answer sheet. Compute the amount of overhead cost that would be applied to Work in Process for the year, and make the entry in your T-accounts.

3. Compute the amount of under- or overapplied overhead for the year, and show the balance in your Manufacturing Overhead T-account. Prepare a journal entry to close out the balance in this account to Cost of Goods Sold.
4. Explain why the manufacturing overhead was underapplied or overapplied for the year.

EXERCISE 3–7 Applying Overhead; Journal Entries; Disposition of Underapplied or Overapplied Overhead [LO4, LO7, LO8]

The following information is taken from the accounts of FasGrow Company. The entries in the T-accounts are summaries of the transactions that affected those accounts during the year.

Manufacturing Overhead

	Debit	Credit	
(a)	380,000	410,000	(b)
		30,000	Bal.

Work in Process

	Debit	Credit	
Bal.	105,000	760,000	(c)
	210,000		
	115,000		
(b)	410,000		
Bal.	80,000		

Finished Goods

	Debit	Credit	
Bal.	160,000	820,000	(d)
(c)	760,000		
Bal.	100,000		

Cost of Goods Sold

	Debit	Credit
(d)	820,000	

The overhead that had been applied to production during the year is distributed among the ending balances in the accounts as follows:

Work in Process, ending	$ 32,800
Finished Goods, ending.	41,000
Cost of Goods Sold	336,200
Overhead Applied	$410,000

For example, of the $80,000 ending balance in Work in Process, $32,800 was overhead that had been applied during the year.

Required:

1. Identify the reasons for entries (a) through (d).
2. Assume that the company closes any balance in the Manufacturing Overhead account directly to Cost of Goods Sold. Prepare the necessary journal entry.
3. Assume instead that the company allocates any balance in the Manufacturing Overhead account to the other accounts in proportion to the overhead applied during the year that is in the ending balance in each account. Prepare the necessary journal entry, with supporting computations.

EXERCISE 3–8 Applying Overhead; Cost of Goods Manufactured [LO5, LO6, LO8]

The following cost data relate to the manufacturing activities of Black Company during the just completed year:

Manufacturing overhead costs:	
Property taxes, factory	$ 3,000
Utilities, factory	5,000
Indirect labor	10,000
Depreciation, factory	24,000
Insurance, factory	6,000
Total actual manufacturing overhead costs	$48,000
Other costs incurred:	
Purchases of raw materials	$32,000
Direct labor cost	40,000
Inventories:	
Raw materials, beginning	$ 8,000
Raw materials, ending	7,000
Work in process, beginning	6,000
Work in process, ending	7,500

The company uses a predetermined overhead rate to apply overhead cost to production. The rate for the year was $5 per machine-hour; a total of 10,000 machine-hours was recorded for the year.

Required:

1. Compute the amount of under- or overapplied overhead cost for the year.
2. Prepare a schedule of cost of goods manufactured for the year.

EXERCISE 3–9 Applying Overhead in a Service Company [LO2, LO3, LO5]

Pearson Architectural Design began operations on January 2. The following activity was recorded in the company's Work in Process account for the first month of operations:

Work in Process

Costs of subcontracted work	90,000	570,000	To completed projects
Direct staff costs	200,000		
Studio overhead	320,000		

Pearson Architectural Design is a service firm, so the names of the accounts it uses are different from the names used in manufacturing firms. Costs of Subcontracted Work is basically the same thing as Direct Materials; Direct Staff Costs is the same as Direct Labor; Studio Overhead is the same as Manufacturing Overhead; and Completed Projects is the same as Finished Goods. Apart from the difference in terms, the accounting methods used by the company are identical to the methods used by manufacturing companies.

Pearson Architectural Design uses a job-order costing system and applies studio overhead to Work in Process on the basis of direct staff costs. At the end of January, only one job was still in process. This job (the Krimmer Corporation Headquarters project) had been charged with $13,500 in direct staff costs.

Required:

1. Compute the predetermined overhead rate that was in use during January.

2. Complete the following job cost sheet for the partially completed Krimmer Corporation Headquarters project.

Job Cost Sheet
Krimmer Corporation Headquarters Project
As of January 31

Costs of subcontracted work	$?
Direct staff costs	?
Studio overhead	?
Total cost to January 31	$?

EXERCISE 3–10 Applying Overhead; Journal Entries; T-Accounts [LO3, LO4, LO5, LO7]

Custom Metal Works produces castings and other metal parts to customer specifications. The company uses a job-order costing system and applies overhead costs to jobs on the basis of machine-hours. At the beginning of the year, the company estimated that it would work 576,000 machine-hours and incur $4,320,000 in manufacturing overhead cost.

The company had no work in process at the beginning of the year. The company spent the entire month of January working on one large order—job 382, which was an order for 8,000 machined parts. Cost data for January follow:

a. Raw materials purchased on account, $315,000.
b. Raw materials requisitioned for production, $270,000 (80% direct and 20% indirect).
c. Labor cost incurred in the factory, $190,000, of which $80,000 was direct labor and $110,000 was indirect labor.
d. Depreciation recorded on factory equipment, $63,000.
e. Other manufacturing overhead costs incurred, $85,000 (credit Accounts Payable).
f. Manufacturing overhead cost was applied to production on the basis of 40,000 machine-hours actually worked during January.
g. The completed job was moved into the finished goods warehouse on January 31 to await delivery to the customer. (In computing the dollar amount for this entry, remember that the cost of a completed job consists of direct materials, direct labor, and *applied* overhead.)

Required:

1. Prepare journal entries to record items (a) through (f) above. Ignore item (g) for the moment.
2. Prepare T-accounts for Manufacturing Overhead and Work in Process. Post the relevant items from your journal entries to these T-accounts.
3. Prepare a journal entry for item (g) above.
4. Compute the unit product cost that will appear on the job cost sheet for job 382.

EXERCISE 3–11 Applying Overhead in a Service Company; Journal Entries [LO4, LO5, LO8]

Heritage Gardens uses a job-order costing system to track the costs of its landscaping projects. The company provides complete landscaping services—including garden design. The table below provides data concerning the three landscaping projects that were in progress during May. There was no work in process at the beginning of May.

	Project		
	Williams	Chandler	Nguyen
Designer-hours	200	80	120
Direct materials cost	$4,800	$1,800	$3,600
Direct labor cost	$2,400	$1,000	$1,500

Actual overhead costs were $16,000 for May. Overhead costs are applied to projects on the basis of designer-hours since most of the overhead is related to the costs of the garden design studio. The predetermined overhead rate is $45 per designer-hour. The Williams and Chandler projects were completed in May; the Nguyen project was not completed by the end of the month. No other jobs were in process during May.

Required:

1. Compute the amount of overhead cost that would have been charged to each project during May.

2. Prepare a journal entry showing the completion of the Williams and Chandler projects and the transfer of costs to the Completed Projects (i.e., Finished Goods) account.
3. What is the balance in the Work in Process account at the end of the month?
4. What is the balance in the Overhead account at the end of the month? What is this balance called?

EXERCISE 3–12 (Appendix 3A) Overhead Rates and Capacity Issues [LO3, LO5, LO8, LO9]

Estate Pension Services helps clients to set up and administer pension plans that are in compliance with tax laws and regulatory requirements. The firm uses a job-costing system in which overhead is applied to clients' accounts on the basis of professional staff hours charged to the accounts. Data concerning two recent years appear below:

	2002	2001
Estimated professional staff hours to be charged to clients' accounts	2,250	2,400
Estimated overhead cost	$144,000	$144,000
Professional staff hours available	3,000	3,000

"Professional staff hours available" is a measure of the capacity of the firm. Any hours available that are not charged to clients' accounts represent unused capacity.

Required:

1. Jennifer Miyami is an established client whose pension plan was set up many years ago. In both 2001 and 2002, only five hours of professional staff time were charged to Ms. Miyami's account. If the company bases its predetermined overhead rate on the estimated overhead cost and the estimated professional staff hours to be charged to clients, how much overhead cost would have been applied to Ms. Miyami's account in 2001? In 2002?
2. Suppose that the company bases its predetermined overhead rate on the estimated overhead cost and the estimated professional staff hours to be charged to clients as in (1) above. Also suppose that the actual professional staff hours charged to clients' accounts and the actual overhead costs turn out to be exactly as estimated in both years. By how much would the overhead be under- or overapplied in 2001? In 2002?
3. Refer back to the data concerning Ms. Miyami in (1) above. If the company bases its predetermined overhead rate on the estimated overhead cost and the professional staff hours available, how much overhead cost would have been applied to Ms. Miyami's account in 2001? In 2002?
4. Suppose that the company bases its predetermined overhead rate on the estimated overhead cost and the professional staff hours available as in (3) above. Also suppose that the actual professional staff hours charged to clients' accounts and the actual overhead costs turn out to be exactly as estimated in both years. By how much would the overhead be under- or overapplied in 2001? In 2002?

Problems

PROBLEM 3–13 Cost Flows; T-Accounts; Income Statement [LO3, LO5, LO6, LO7, LO8]

Fantastic Props, Inc., designs and fabricates movie props such as mock-ups of star-fighters and cybernetic robots. The company's balance sheet as of January 1, the beginning of the current year, appears below:

FANTASTIC PROPS, INC.
Balance Sheet
January 1

Assets

Current assets:		
Cash		$ 15,000
Accounts receivable		40,000
Inventories:		
Raw materials	$ 25,000	
Work in process	30,000	
Finished goods (props awaiting shipment)	45,000	100,000
Prepaid insurance		5,000

continued

Total current assets		160,000
Buildings and equipment	500,000	
Less accumulated depreciation	210,000	290,000
Total assets		$450,000
Liabilities and Stockholders' Equity		
Accounts payable		$ 75,000
Capital stock	$250,000	
Retained earnings	125,000	375,000
Total liabilities and stockholders' equity		$450,000

Since each prop is a unique design and may require anything from a few hours to a month or more to complete, Fantastic Props uses a job-order costing system. Overhead in the fabrication shop is charged to props on the basis of direct-labor cost. The company estimated that it would incur $80,000 in manufacturing overhead and $100,000 in direct labor cost during the year. The following transactions were recorded during the year:

a. Raw materials, such as wood, paints, and metal sheeting, were purchased on account, $80,000.
b. Raw materials were issued to production, $90,000; $5,000 of this amount was for indirect materials.
c. Payroll costs incurred and paid: direct labor, $120,000; indirect labor, $30,000; and selling and administrative salaries, $75,000.
d. Fabrication shop utilities costs incurred, $12,000.
e. Depreciation recorded for the year, $30,000 ($5,000 on selling and administrative assets; $25,000 on fabrication shop assets).
f. Prepaid insurance expired, $4,800 ($4,000 related to fabrication shop operations, and $800 related to selling and administrative activities).
g. Shipping expenses incurred, $40,000.
h. Other manufacturing overhead costs incurred, $17,000 (credit Accounts Payable).
i. Manufacturing overhead was applied to production. Overhead is applied on a basis of direct labor cost.
j. Movie props that cost $310,000 to produce according to their job cost sheets were completed.
k. Sales for the year totaled $450,000 and were all on account. The total cost to produce these movie props was $300,000 according to their job cost sheets.
l. Collections on account from customers, $445,000.
m. Payments on account to suppliers, $150,000.

Required:

1. Prepare a T-account for each account on the company's balance sheet, and enter the beginning balances.
2. Make entries directly into the T-accounts for the transactions given above. Create new T-accounts as needed. Determine an ending balance for each T-account.
3. Was manufacturing overhead underapplied or overapplied for the year? Assume that the company allocates any overhead balance between the Work in Process, Finished Goods, and Cost of Goods Sold accounts. Prepare a journal entry to show the allocation. (Round allocation percentages to one decimal place.)
4. Prepare an income statement for the year. (Do not prepare a schedule of cost of goods manufactured; all of the information needed for the income statement is available in the T-accounts.)

PROBLEM 3–14 Journal Entries; T-Accounts; Cost Flows [LO4, LO5, LO7]

Ravsten Company is a manufacturing firm that uses a job-order cost system. On January 1, the beginning of the current year, the company's inventory balances were as follows:

Raw materials	$16,000
Work in process	10,000
Finished goods	30,000

The company applies overhead cost to jobs on the basis of machine-hours. For the current year, the company estimated that it would work 36,000 machine-hours and incur $153,000 in manufacturing overhead cost. The following transactions were recorded for the year:

a. Raw materials purchased on account, $200,000.
b. Raw materials requisitioned for use in production, $190,000 (80% direct and 20% indirect).
c. The following costs were incurred for employee services:

Direct labor	$160,000
Indirect labor	27,000
Sales commissions	36,000
Administrative salaries	80,000

d. Heat, power, and water costs incurred in the factory, $42,000.
e. Prepaid insurance expired during the year, $10,000 (90% relates to factory operations, and 10% relates to selling and administrative activities).
f. Advertising costs incurred, $50,000.
g. Depreciation recorded for the year, $60,000 (85% relates to factory operations, and 15% relates to selling and administrative activities).
h. Manufacturing overhead cost was applied to production. The company recorded 40,000 machine-hours for the year.
i. Goods that cost $480,000 to manufacture according to their job cost sheets were transferred to the finished goods warehouse.
j. Sales for the year totaled $700,000 and were all on account. The total cost to manufacture these goods according to their job cost sheets was $475,000.

Required:

1. Prepare journal entries to record the transactions given above.
2. Prepare T-accounts for inventories, Manufacturing Overhead, and Cost of Goods Sold. Post relevant data from your journal entries to these T-accounts (don't forget to enter the opening balances in your inventory accounts). Compute an ending balance in each account.
3. Is Manufacturing Overhead underapplied or overapplied for the year? Prepare a journal entry to close any balance in the Manufacturing Overhead account to Cost of Goods Sold.
4. Prepare an income statement for the year. (Do not prepare a schedule of cost of goods manufactured; all of the information needed for the income statement is available in the journal entries and T-accounts you have prepared.)

PROBLEM 3–15 T-Accounts; Applying Overhead [LO5, LO7, LO8]

Durham Company's trial balance as of January 1, the beginning of the current year, is given below:

Cash	$ 8,000	
Accounts Receivable	13,000	
Raw Materials	7,000	
Work in Process	18,000	
Finished Goods	20,000	
Prepaid Insurance	4,000	
Plant and Equipment	230,000	
Accumulated Depreciation		$ 42,000
Accounts Payable		30,000
Capital Stock		150,000
Retained Earnings		78,000
Total	$300,000	$300,000

Durham Company manufactures items to customers' specifications and employs a job-order cost system. During the year, the following transactions took place:

a. Raw materials purchased on account, $45,000.
b. Raw materials requisitioned for use in production, $40,000 (80% direct and 20% indirect).
c. Factory utility costs incurred, $14,600.
d. Depreciation recorded on plant and equipment, $28,000. Three-fourths of the depreciation relates to factory equipment, and the remainder relates to selling and administrative equipment.
e. Costs for salaries and wages were incurred as follows:

Direct labor	$40,000
Indirect labor	18,000
Sales commissions	10,400
Administrative salaries	25,000

f. Prepaid insurance expired during the year, $3,000 (80% relates to factory operations, and 20% relates to selling and administrative activities).
g. Miscellaneous selling and administrative expenses incurred, $18,000.

h. Manufacturing overhead was applied to production. The company applies overhead on the basis of 150% of direct labor cost.
i. Goods that cost $130,000 to manufacture according to their job cost sheets were transferred to the finished goods warehouse.
j. Goods that had cost $120,000 to manufacture according to their job cost sheets were sold on account for $200,000.
k. Collections from customers during the year totaled $197,000.
l. Payments to suppliers on account during the year, $100,000; and payments to employees for salaries and wages, $90,000.

Required:

1. Prepare a T-account for each account in the company's trial balance, and enter the opening balances shown above.
2. Record the transactions above directly into the T-accounts. Prepare new T-accounts as needed. Key your entries to the letters (a) through (l) above. Find the ending balance in each account.
3. Is manufacturing overhead under- or overapplied for the year? Make an entry in the T-accounts to close any balance in the Manufacturing Overhead account to Cost of Goods Sold.
4. Prepare an income statement for the year. (Do not prepare a schedule of cost of goods manufactured; all of the information needed for the income statement is available in the journal entries and T-accounts you have prepared.)

PROBLEM 3–16 Comprehensive Problem [LO3, LO4, LO5, LO7, LO8]

Sovereign Millwork, Ltd., produces reproductions of antique residential moldings at a plant located in Manchester, England. Since there are hundreds of products, some of which are made only to order, the company uses a job-order costing system. On July 1, the start of the company's fiscal year, inventory account balances were as follows:

Raw Materials	£10,000
Work in Process	4,000
Finished Goods	8,000
Total	£22,000

The company applies overhead cost to jobs on the basis of machine-hours using the same principles followed by companies in the United States and elsewhere. For the fiscal year starting July 1, it was estimated that the plant would operate 45,000 machine-hours and incur £99,000 in manufacturing overhead cost. During the year, the following transactions were completed:

a. Raw materials purchased on account, £160,000.
b. Raw materials requisitioned for use in production, £140,000 (materials costing £120,000 were chargeable directly to jobs; the remaining materials were indirect).
c. Costs for employee services were incurred as follows:

Direct labor	£90,000
Indirect labor	60,000
Sales commissions	20,000
Administrative salaries	50,000

d. Prepaid insurance expired during the year, £18,000 (£13,000 of this amount related to factory operations, and the remainder related to selling and administrative activities).
e. Utility costs incurred in the factory, £10,000.
f. Advertising costs incurred, £15,000.
g. Depreciation recorded on equipment, £25,000. (£20,000 of this amount was on equipment used in factory operations; the remaining £5,000 was on equipment used in selling and administrative activities.)
h. Manufacturing overhead cost was applied to production, £ ? . (The company recorded 50,000 machine-hours of operating time during the year.)
i. Goods that had cost £310,000 to manufacture according to their job cost sheets were transferred into the finished goods warehouse.
j. Sales (all on account) to customers during the year totaled £498,000. These goods had cost £308,000 to manufacture according to their job cost sheets.

Required:

1. Prepare journal entries to record the transactions for the year.

2. Prepare T-accounts for inventories, Manufacturing Overhead, and Cost of Goods Sold. Post relevant data from your journal entries to these T-accounts (don't forget to enter the opening balances in your inventory accounts). Compute an ending balance in each account.
3. Is Manufacturing Overhead underapplied or overapplied for the year? Prepare a journal entry to close any balance in the Manufacturing Overhead account to Cost of Goods Sold.
4. Prepare an income statement for the year. (Do not prepare a schedule of cost of goods manufactured; all of the information needed for the income statement is available in the journal entries and T-accounts you have prepared.)

PROBLEM 3–17 T-Accounts; Overhead Rates; Journal Entries [LO2, LO3, LO4, LO5, LO7]

Kenworth Company uses a job-order costing system. Only three jobs—job 105, job 106, and job 107—were worked on during November and December. Job 105 was completed on December 10; the other two jobs were still in production on December 31, the end of the company's operating year. Data from the job cost sheets of the three jobs are given below:

	Job Cost Sheet		
	Job 105	**Job 106**	**Job 107**
November costs incurred:			
Direct materials.	$16,500	$ 9,300	$ 0
Direct labor	13,000	7,000	0
Manufacturing overhead.	20,800	11,200	0
December costs incurred:			
Direct materials.	0	8,200	21,300
Direct labor	4,000	6,000	10,000
Manufacturing overhead.	?	?	?

The following additional information is available:

a. Manufacturing overhead is applied to jobs on the basis of direct labor cost.
b. Balances in the inventory accounts at November 30 were as follows:

Raw Materials.	$40,000
Work in Process	?
Finished Goods	85,000

Required:

1. Prepare T-accounts for Raw Materials, Work in Process, Finished Goods, and Manufacturing Overhead. Enter the November 30 inventory balances given above; in the case of Work in Process, compute the November 30 balance and enter it into the Work in Process T-account.
2. Prepare journal entries for *December* as follows:
   a. Prepare an entry to record the issue of materials into production and post the entry to appropriate T-accounts. (In the case of direct materials, it is not necessary to make a separate entry for each job.) Indirect materials used during December totaled $4,000.
   b. Prepare an entry to record the incurrence of labor cost and post the entry to appropriate T-accounts. (In the case of direct labor cost, it is not necessary to make a separate entry for each job.) Indirect labor cost totaled $8,000 for December.
   c. Prepare an entry to record the incurrence of $19,000 in various actual manufacturing overhead costs for December (credit Accounts Payable). Post this entry to the appropriate T-accounts.
3. What apparent predetermined overhead rate does the company use to assign overhead cost to jobs? Using this rate, prepare a journal entry to record the application of overhead cost to jobs for December (it is not necessary to make a separate entry for each job). Post this entry to the appropriate T-accounts.
4. As stated earlier, job 105 was completed during December. Prepare a journal entry to show the transfer of this job off of the production line and into the finished goods warehouse. Post the entry to the appropriate T-accounts.
5. Determine the balance at December 31 in the Work in Process inventory account. How much of this balance consists of costs charged to job 106? Job 107?

PROBLEM 3–18 Predetermined Overhead Rate; Disposition of Under- or Overapplied Overhead [LO3, LO8]

Savallas Company is highly automated and uses computers to control manufacturing operations. The company has a job-order costing system in use and applies manufacturing overhead cost to products on the basis of computer-hours of activity. The following estimates were used in preparing the predetermined overhead rate at the beginning of the year:

Computer-hours	85,000
Manufacturing overhead cost	$1,530,000

During the year, a severe economic recession resulted in cutting back production and a buildup of inventory in the company's warehouse. The company's cost records revealed the following actual cost and operating data for the year:

Computer-hours	60,000
Manufacturing overhead cost	$1,350,000
Inventories at year-end:	
Raw materials	400,000
Work in process.	160,000
Finished goods	1,040,000
Cost of goods sold	2,800,000

Required:

1. Compute the company's predetermined overhead rate for the year.
2. Compute the under- or overapplied overhead for the year.
3. Assume the company closes any under- or overapplied overhead directly to Cost of Goods Sold. Prepare the appropriate entry.
4. Assume that the company allocates any under- or overapplied overhead to Work in Process, Finished Goods, and Cost of Goods Sold on the basis of the amount of overhead applied during the year that remains in each account at the end of the year. These amounts are $43,200 for Work in Process, $280,800 for Finished Goods, and $756,000 for Cost of Goods Sold. Prepare the journal entry to show the allocation.
5. How much higher or lower will net income be for the year if the under- or overapplied overhead is allocated rather than closed directly to Cost of Goods Sold?

PROBLEM 3–19 Schedule of Cost of Goods Manufactured; Overhead Analysis [LO3, LO5, LO6, LO7]

The Pacific Manufacturing Company operates a job-order cost system and applies overhead cost to jobs on the basis of direct labor cost. In computing an overhead rate for the year, the company's estimates were: manufacturing overhead cost, $126,000; and direct labor cost, $84,000. The company has provided the following data in the form of an Excel worksheet:

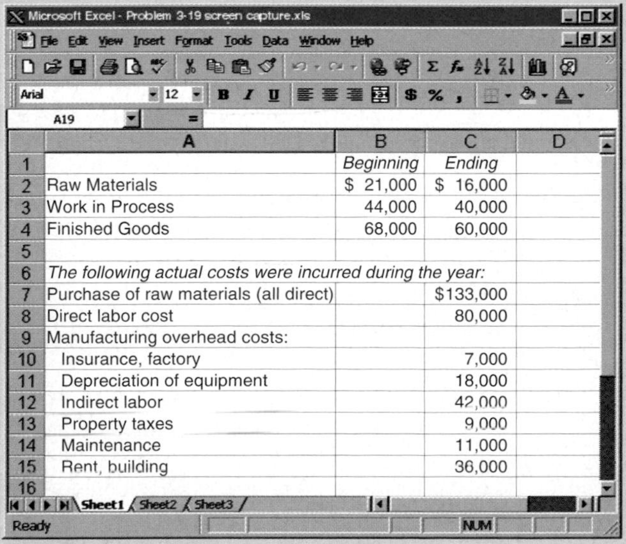

	A	B	C
1		*Beginning*	*Ending*
2	Raw Materials	$ 21,000	$ 16,000
3	Work in Process	44,000	40,000
4	Finished Goods	68,000	60,000
5			
6	*The following actual costs were incurred during the year:*		
7	Purchase of raw materials (all direct)		$133,000
8	Direct labor cost		80,000
9	Manufacturing overhead costs:		
10	Insurance, factory		7,000
11	Depreciation of equipment		18,000
12	Indirect labor		42,000
13	Property taxes		9,000
14	Maintenance		11,000
15	Rent, building		36,000
16			

Required:

1. *a.* Compute the predetermined overhead rate for the year.
   b. Compute the amount of under- or overapplied overhead for the year.
2. Prepare a schedule of cost of goods manufactured for the year.

3. Compute the cost of goods sold for the year. (Do not include any under- or overapplied overhead in your cost of goods sold figure.) What options are available for disposing of under- or overapplied overhead?
4. Job 137 was started and completed during the year. What price would have been charged to the customer if the job required $3,200 in materials and $4,200 in direct labor cost, and the company priced its jobs at 40% above cost to manufacture?
5. Direct labor made up $8,000 of the $40,000 ending Work in Process inventory balance. Supply the information missing below:

Direct materials	$?
Direct labor	8,000
Manufacturing overhead	?
Work in process inventory	$40,000

PROBLEM 3–20 Journal Entries; T-Accounts; Disposition of Underapplied or Overapplied Overhead; Income Statement [LO3, LO4, LO5, LO7, LO8]

Celestial Displays, Inc., puts together large-scale fireworks displays—primarily for Fourth of July celebrations sponsored by corporations and municipalities. The company assembles and orchestrates complex displays using pyrotechnic components purchased from suppliers throughout the world. The company has built a reputation for safety and for the awesome power and brilliance of its computer-controlled shows. Celestial Displays builds its own launch platforms and its own electronic controls. Because of the company's reputation, customers order shows up to a year in advance. Since each show is different in terms of duration and components used, Celestial Displays uses a job-order costing system.

Celestial Displays' trial balance as of January 1, the beginning of the current year, is given below:

Cash	$ 9,000	
Accounts Receivable	30,000	
Raw Materials	16,000	
Work in Process	21,000	
Finished Goods	38,000	
Prepaid Insurance	7,000	
Buildings and Equipment	300,000	
Accumulated Depreciation		$128,000
Accounts Payable		60,000
Salaries and Wages Payable		3,000
Capital Stock		200,000
Retained Earnings		30,000
Total	$421,000	$421,000

The company charges manufacturing overhead costs to jobs on the basis of direct labor-hours. (Each customer order for a complete fireworks display is a separate job.) Management estimated that the company would incur $135,000 in manufacturing overhead costs in the fabrication and electronics shops and would work 18,000 direct labor-hours during the year. The following transactions occurred during the year:

a. Raw materials, consisting mostly of skyrockets, mortar bombs, flares, wiring, and electronic components, were purchased on account, $820,000.
b. Raw materials were issued to production, $830,000 ($13,000 of this amount was for indirect materials, and the remainder was for direct materials).
c. Fabrication and electronics shop payrolls were accrued, $200,000 (70% direct labor and 30% indirect labor). A total of 20,800 direct labor-hours were worked during the year.
d. Sales and administrative salaries were accrued, $150,000.
e. The company prepaid additional insurance premiums of $38,000 during the year. Prepaid insurance expiring during the year was $40,000 (only $600 relates to selling and administrative; the other $39,400 relates to the fabrication and electronics shops because of the safety hazards involved in handling fireworks).
f. Marketing cost incurred, $100,000.
g. Depreciation charges for the year, $40,000 (70% relates to fabrication and electronics shop assets, and 30% relates to selling and administrative assets).

h. Property taxes accrued on the shop buildings, $12,600 (credit Accounts Payable).
i. Manufacturing overhead cost was applied to jobs.
j. Jobs completed during the year had a total production cost of $1,106,000 according to their job cost sheets.
k. Revenue (all on account), $1,420,000. Cost of Goods Sold (before any adjustment for underapplied or overapplied overhead), $1,120,000.
l. Cash collections on account from customers, $1,415,000.
m. Cash payments on accounts payable, $970,000. Cash payments to employees for salaries and wages, $348,000.

Required:

1. Prepare journal entries for the year's transactions.
2. Prepare a T-account for each account in the company's trial balance, and enter the opening balances given above. Post your journal entries to the T-accounts. Prepare new T-accounts as needed. Compute the ending balance in each account.
3. Is manufacturing overhead under- or overapplied for the year? Prepare the necessary journal entry to close the balance in the Manufacturing Overhead account to Cost of Goods Sold.
4. Prepare an income statement for the year. (Do not prepare a statement of cost of goods manufactured; all of the information needed for the income statement is available in the T-accounts.)

PROBLEM 3–21 Multiple Departments; Applying Overhead [LO3, LO5, LO8]

WoodGrain Technology makes home office furniture from fine hardwoods. The company uses a job-order costing system and predetermined overhead rates to apply manufacturing overhead cost to jobs. The predetermined overhead rate in the Preparation Department is based on machine-hours, and the rate in the Fabrication Department is based on direct materials cost. At the beginning of the year, the company's management made the following estimates for the year:

	Department	
	Preparation	Fabrication
Machine-hours	80,000	21,000
Direct labor-hours	35,000	65,000
Direct materials cost	$190,000	$400,000
Direct labor cost	280,000	530,000
Manufacturing overhead cost	416,000	720,000

Job 127 was started on April 1 and completed on May 12. The company's cost records show the following information on the job:

	Department	
	Preparation	Fabrication
Machine-hours	350	70
Direct labor-hours	80	130
Direct materials cost	$940	$1,200
Direct labor cost	710	980

Required:

1. Compute the predetermined overhead rate used during the year in the Preparation Department. Compute the rate used in the Fabrication Department.
2. Compute the total overhead cost applied to job 127.
3. What would be the total cost recorded for job 127? If the job contained 25 units, what would be the unit product cost?
4. At the end of the year, the records of WoodGrain Technology revealed the following *actual* cost and operating data for all jobs worked on during the year:

	Department	
	Preparation	Fabrication
Machine-hours	73,000	24,000
Direct labor-hours	30,000	68,000
Direct materials cost	$165,000	$420,000
Manufacturing overhead cost	390,000	740,000

What was the amount of underapplied or overapplied overhead in each department at the end of the year?

PROBLEM 3–22 Law Firm: Multiple Departments; Overhead Rates; Under- or Overapplied Overhead [LO3, LO5, LO8]

Winkle, Kotter, and Zale is a small law firm that contains 10 partners and 10 support persons. The firm employs a job-order costing system to accumulate costs chargeable to each client, and it is organized into two departments—the Research and Documents Department and the Litigation Department. The firm uses predetermined overhead rates to charge the costs of these departments to its clients. At the beginning of the current year, the firm's management made the following estimates for the year:

	Department	
	Research and Documents	Litigation
Research-hours	20,000	—
Direct attorney-hours	9,000	16,000
Materials and supplies	$ 18,000	$ 5,000
Direct attorney cost	430,000	800,000
Departmental overhead cost	700,000	320,000

The predetermined overhead rate in the Research and Documents Department is based on research-hours, and the rate in the Litigation Department is based on direct attorney cost.

The costs charged to each client are made up of three elements: materials and supplies used, direct attorney costs incurred, and an applied amount of overhead from each department in which work is performed on the case.

Case 618-3 was initiated on February 10 and completed on June 30. During this period, the following costs and time were recorded on the case:

	Department	
	Research and Documents	Litigation
Research-hours	18	—
Direct attorney-hours	9	42
Materials and supplies	$ 50	$ 30
Direct attorney cost	410	2,100

Required:

1. Compute the predetermined overhead rate used during the year in the Research and Documents Department. Compute the rate used in the Litigation Department.
2. Using the rates you computed in (1) above, compute the total overhead cost applied to case 618-3.
3. What would be the total cost charged to case 618-3? Show computations by department and in total for the case.
4. At the end of the year, the firm's records revealed the following *actual* cost and operating data for all cases handled during the year:

	Department	
	Research and Documents	Litigation
Research-hours	23,000	—
Direct attorney-hours	8,000	15,000
Materials and supplies	$ 19,000	$ 6,000
Direct attorney cost	400,000	725,000
Departmental overhead cost	770,000	300,000

Determine the amount of underapplied or overapplied overhead cost in each department for the year.

PROBLEM 3–23 (Appendix 3A) Predetermined Overhead Rate and Capacity [LO3, LO5, LO8, LO9]

Skid Road Recording, Inc., is a small audio recording studio located in Seattle. The company handles work for advertising agencies—primarily for radio ads—and has a few singers and bands as clients. Skid Road Recording handles all aspects of recording from editing to making a digital master from which CDs can be copied. The competition in the audio recording industry in Seattle has always been

tough, but it has been getting even tougher over the last several years. The studio has been losing customers to newer studios that are equipped with more up-to-date equipment and able to offer very attractive prices and excellent service. Summary data concerning the last two years of operations follow:

	2002	2001
Estimated hours of studio service	750	1,000
Estimated studio overhead cost	$90,000	$90,000
Actual hours of studio service provided	600	900
Actual studio overhead cost incurred	$90,000	$90,000
Hours of studio service at capacity	1,800	1,800

The company applies studio overhead to recording jobs on the basis of the hours of studio service provided. For example, 30 hours of studio time were required to record, edit, and master the *Slug Fest* music CD for a local band. All of the studio overhead is fixed, and the actual overhead cost incurred was exactly as estimated at the beginning of the year in both 2001 and 2002.

Required:

1. Skid Road Recording computes the predetermined overhead rate at the beginning of each year based on the estimated studio overhead and the estimated hours of studio service for the year. How much overhead would have been applied to the *Slug Fest* job if it had been done in 2001? In 2002? By how much would overhead have been under- or overapplied in 2001? In 2002?
2. The president of Skid Road Recording has heard that some companies in the industry have changed to a system of computing the predetermined overhead rate at the beginning of each year based on the estimated studio overhead for the year and the hours of studio service that could be provided at capacity. He would like to know what effect this method would have on job costs. How much overhead would have been applied using this method to the *Slug Fest* job if it had been done in 2001? In 2002? By how much would overhead have been under- or overapplied in 2001 using this method? In 2002?
3. How would you interpret the under- or overapplied overhead that results from using studio hours at capacity to compute the predetermined overhead rate?
4. What fundamental business problem is Skid Road Recording facing? Which method of computing the predetermined overhead rate is likely to be more helpful in facing this problem? Explain.

PROBLEM 3–24 T-Account Analysis of Cost Flows [LO3, LO6, LO8]

Selected ledger accounts for Rolm Company are given below for the just completed year:

Raw Materials

Bal. 1/1	30,000	Credits	?
Debits	420,000		
Bal. 12/31	60,000		

Manufacturing Overhead

Debits	385,000	Credits	?

Work in Process

Bal. 1/1	70,000	Credits	810,000
Direct materials	320,000		
Direct labor	110,000		
Overhead	400,000		
Bal. 12/31	?		

Factory Wages Payable

Debits	179,000	Bal. 1/1	10,000
		Credits	175,000
		Bal. 12/31	6,000

Finished Goods

Bal. 1/1	40,000	Credits	?
Debits	?		
Bal. 12/31	130,000		

Cost of Goods Sold

Debits	?		

Required:

1. What was the cost of raw materials put into production during the year?
2. How much of the materials in (1) above consisted of indirect materials?
3. How much of the factory labor cost for the year consisted of indirect labor?
4. What was the cost of goods manufactured for the year?
5. What was the cost of goods sold for the year (before considering under- or overapplied overhead)?
6. If overhead is applied to production on the basis of direct materials cost, what rate was in effect during the year?
7. Was manufacturing overhead under- or overapplied? By how much?
8. Compute the ending balance in the Work in Process inventory account. Assume that this balance consists entirely of goods started during the year. If $32,000 of this balance is direct materials cost, how much of it is direct labor cost? Manufacturing overhead cost?

PROBLEM 3–25 Plantwide versus Departmental Overhead Rates; Under- or Overapplied Overhead [LO3, LO5, LO8]

"Don't tell me we've lost another bid!" exclaimed Sandy Kovallas, president of Lenko Products, Inc. "I'm afraid so," replied Doug Martin, the operations vice president. "One of our competitors underbid us by about $10,000 on the Hastings job." "I just can't figure it out," said Kovallas. "It seems we're either too high to get the job or too low to make any money on half the jobs we bid any more. What's happened?"

Lenko Products manufactures specialized goods to customers' specifications and operates a job-order costing system. Manufacturing overhead cost is applied to jobs on the basis of direct labor cost. The following estimates were made at the beginning of the year:

	Department			
	Cutting	Machining	Assembly	Total Plant
Direct labor	$300,000	$200,000	$400,000	$ 900,000
Manufacturing overhead.	540,000	800,000	100,000	1,440,000

Jobs require varying amounts of work in the three departments. The Hastings job, for example, would have required manufacturing costs in the three departments as follows:

	Department			
	Cutting	Machining	Assembly	Total Plant
Direct materials.	$12,000	$ 900	$ 5,600	$18,500
Direct labor	6,500	1,700	13,000	21,200
Manufacturing overhead.	?	?	?	?

The company uses a plantwide overhead rate to apply manufacturing overhead cost to jobs.

Required:

1. Assuming use of a plantwide overhead rate:
   a. Compute the rate for the current year.
   b. Determine the amount of manufacturing overhead cost that would have been applied to the Hastings job.
2. Suppose that instead of using a plantwide overhead rate, the company had used a separate predetermined overhead rate in each department. Under these conditions:
   a. Compute the rate for each department for the current year.
   b. Determine the amount of manufacturing overhead cost that would have been applied to the Hastings job.
3. Explain the difference between the manufacturing overhead that would have been applied to the Hastings job using the plantwide rate in question 1(b) above and using the departmental rates in question 2(b).
4. Assume that it is customary in the industry to bid jobs at 150% of total manufacturing cost (direct materials, direct labor, and applied overhead). What was the company's bid price on the Hastings job? What would the bid price have been if departmental overhead rates had been used to apply overhead cost?
5. At the end of the year, the company assembled the following *actual* cost data relating to all jobs worked on during the year:

	Department			
	Cutting	Machining	Assembly	Total Plant
Direct materials	$760,000	$ 90,000	$410,000	$1,260,000
Direct labor	320,000	210,000	340,000	870,000
Manufacturing overhead	560,000	830,000	92,000	1,482,000

Compute the under- or overapplied overhead for the year (*a*) assuming that a plantwide overhead rate is used, and (*b*) assuming that departmental overhead rates are used.

PROBLEM 3–26 Comprehensive Problem: T-Accounts; Job-Order Cost Flows; Financial Statements [LO3, LO5, LO6, LO8]

Top-Products, Inc., produces goods to customers' orders and uses a job-order costing system. A trial balance for the company as of January 1, the beginning of the current year, is given below:

Cash	$ 18,000	
Accounts Receivable	40,000	
Raw Materials	25,000	
Work in Process	32,000	
Finished Goods	60,000	
Prepaid Insurance	5,000	
Plant and Equipment	400,000	
Accumulated Depreciation		$148,000
Accounts Payable		90,000
Salaries and Wages Payable		3,000
Capital Stock		250,000
Retained Earnings		89,000
Total	$580,000	$580,000

The company applies manufacturing overhead cost to jobs on the basis of direct labor cost. The following estimates were made at the beginning of the year for purposes of computing a predetermined overhead rate for the year: manufacturing overhead cost, $228,000; and direct labor cost, $190,000. Summarized transactions of the company for the year are given below:

a. Raw materials purchased on account, $180,000.
b. Raw materials requisitioned for use in production, $190,000 (all direct materials).
c. Utility costs incurred in the factory, $57,000.
d. Salary and wage costs were incurred as follows:

Direct labor	$200,000
Indirect labor	90,000
Selling and administrative salaries	120,000

e. Prepaid insurance expired during the year, $4,000 (75% related to factory operations, and 25% related to selling and administrative activities).
f. Property taxes incurred on the factory building, $16,000.
g. Advertising costs incurred, $150,000.
h. Depreciation recorded for the year, $50,000 (80% related to factory assets, and the remainder related to selling and administrative assets).
i. Other costs were incurred (credit Accounts Payable): for factory overhead, $30,000; and for miscellaneous selling and administrative expenses, $18,000.
j. Manufacturing overhead cost applied to jobs, $ __?__.
k. Cost of goods manufactured for the year, $635,000.
l. Sales for the year totaled $1,000,000 (all on account); the cost of goods sold was $ __?__. (The ending balance in the Finished Goods inventory account was $45,000.)
m. Cash collections from customers during the year, $950,000.
n. Cash payments during the year: to employees, $412,000; on accounts payable, $478,000.

Required:

1. Enter the company's transactions for the year directly into T-accounts. (Don't forget to enter the opening balances into the T-accounts.) Key your entries to the letters (a) through (n) above. Create new T-accounts as needed. Find the ending balance in each account.
2. Prepare a schedule of cost of goods manufactured.

3. Prepare a journal entry to close any balance in the Manufacturing Overhead account to Cost of Goods Sold. Prepare a schedule of cost of goods sold.
4. Prepare an income statement for the year. Ignore income taxes.
5. Job 316 was one of the many jobs started and completed during the year. The job required $2,400 in materials and $3,000 in direct labor cost. If the job contained 300 units and the company billed the job at 140% of the unit product cost on the job cost sheet, what price per unit would have been charged to the customer?

PROBLEM 3–27 Comprehensive Problem: Journal Entries; T-Accounts; Financial Statements [LO3, LO4, LO5, LO6, LO7, LO8]

Southworth Company uses a job-order cost system and applies manufacturing overhead cost to jobs on the basis of the cost of direct materials used in production. At the beginning of the current year, the following estimates were made for the purpose of computing the predetermined overhead rate: manufacturing overhead cost, $248,000; and direct materials cost, $155,000. The following transactions took place during the year (all purchases and services were acquired on account):

a. Raw materials purchased, $142,000.
b. Raw materials requisitioned for use in production (all direct materials), $150,000.
c. Utility bills incurred in the factory, $21,000.
d. Costs for salaries and wages were incurred as follows:

Direct labor	$216,000
Indirect labor	90,000
Selling and administrative salaries	145,000

e. Maintenance costs incurred in the factory, $15,000.
f. Advertising costs incurred, $130,000.
g. Depreciation recorded for the year, $50,000 (90% relates to factory assets, and the remainder relates to selling and administrative assets).
h. Rental cost incurred on buildings, $90,000 (80% of the space is occupied by the factory, and 20% is occupied by sales and administration).
i. Miscellaneous selling and administrative costs incurred, $17,000.
j. Manufacturing overhead cost was applied to jobs, $ __?__.
k. Cost of goods manufactured for the year, $590,000.
l. Sales for the year (all on account) totaled $1,000,000. These goods cost $600,000 to manufacture according to their job cost sheets.

The balances in the inventory accounts at the beginning of the year were as follows:

Raw Materials	$18,000
Work in Process	24,000
Finished Goods	35,000

Required:

1. Prepare journal entries to record the above data.
2. Post your entries to T-accounts. (Don't forget to enter the opening inventory balances above.) Determine the ending balances in the inventory accounts and in the Manufacturing Overhead account.
3. Prepare a schedule of cost of goods manufactured.
4. Prepare a journal entry to close any balance in the Manufacturing Overhead account to Cost of Goods Sold. Prepare a schedule of cost of goods sold.
5. Prepare an income statement for the year.
6. Job 218 was one of the many jobs started and completed during the year. The job required $3,600 in direct materials and 400 hours of direct labor time at a rate of $11 per hour. If the job contained 500 units and the company billed at 75% above the unit product cost on the job cost sheet, what price per unit would have been charged to the customer?

Cases

CASE 3–28 Incomplete Data; Review of Cost Flows [LO3, LO5, LO7, LO8]

After a dispute concerning wages, Orville Arson tossed an incendiary device into the Sparkle Company's record vault. Within moments, only a few charred fragments were readable from the company's factory ledger, as shown below:

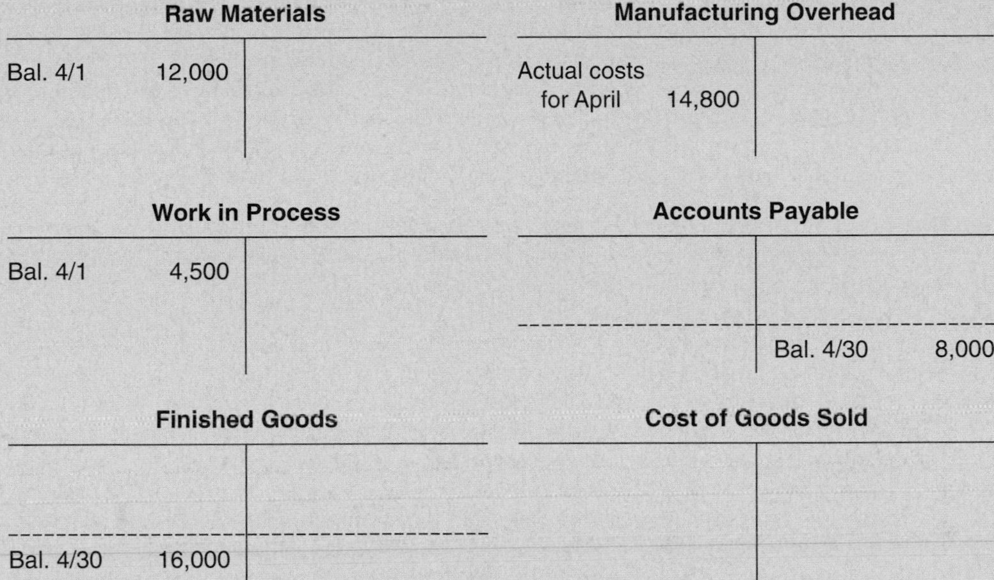

Sifting through ashes and interviewing selected employees has turned up the following additional information:

a. The controller remembers clearly that the predetermined overhead rate was based on an estimated 60,000 direct labor-hours to be worked over the year and an estimated $180,000 in manufacturing overhead costs.
b. The production superintendent's cost sheets showed only one job in process on April 30. Materials of $2,600 had been added to the job, and 300 direct labor-hours had been expended at $6 per hour.
c. The accounts payable are for raw material purchases only, according to the accounts payable clerk. He clearly remembers that the balance in the account was $6,000 on April 1. An analysis of canceled checks (kept in the treasurer's office) shows that payments of $40,000 were made to suppliers during April. (All materials used during April were direct materials.)
d. A charred piece of the payroll ledger shows that 5,200 direct labor-hours were recorded for the month. The personnel department has verified that there were no variations in pay rates among employees. (This infuriated Orville, who felt that his services were underpaid.)
e. Records maintained in the finished goods warehouse indicate that the finished goods inventory totaled $11,000 on April 1.
f. From another charred piece in the vault, you are able to discern that the cost of goods manufactured for April was $89,000.

Required:

Determine the following amounts:

1. Work in process inventory, April 30.
2. Raw materials purchased during April.
3. Overhead applied to work in process.
4. Cost of goods sold for April.
5. Over- or underapplied overhead for April.
6. Raw materials usage during April.
7. Raw materials inventory, April 30.

(Hint: A good way to proceed is to bring the fragmented T-accounts up-to-date through April 30 by posting whatever entries can be developed from the information provided.)

CASE 3–29 Ethics and the Manager [LO3, LO5, LO8]

Cristin Madsen has recently been transferred to the Appliances Division of Solequin Corporation. Shortly after taking over her new position as divisional controller, she was asked to develop the division's predetermined overhead rate for the upcoming year. The accuracy of the rate is of some importance, since it is used throughout the year and any overapplied or underapplied overhead is closed out to Cost of Goods Sold only at the end of the year. Solequin Corporation uses direct labor-hours in all of its divisions as the allocation base for manufacturing overhead.

To compute the predetermined overhead rate, Cristin divided her estimate of the total manufacturing overhead for the coming year by the production manager's estimate of the total direct labor-hours for the coming year. She took her computations to the division's general manager for approval but was quite surprised when he suggested a modification in the base. Her conversation with the general manager of the Appliances Division, Lance Jusic, went like this:

Madsen: Here are my calculations for next year's predetermined overhead rate. If you approve, we can enter the rate into the computer on January 1 and be up and running in the job-order costing system right away this year.

Jusic: Thanks for coming up with the calculations so quickly, and they look just fine. There is, however, one slight modification I would like to see. Your estimate of the total direct labor-hours for the year is 110,000 hours. How about cutting that to about 105,000 hours?

Madsen: I don't know if I can do that. The production manager says she will need about 110,000 direct labor-hours to meet the sales projections for next year. Besides, there are going to be over 108,000 direct labor-hours during the current year and sales are projected to be higher next year.

Jusic: Cristin, I know all of that. I would still like to reduce the direct labor-hours in the base to something like 105,000 hours. You probably don't know that I had an agreement with your predecessor as divisional controller to shave 5% or so off the estimated direct labor-hours every year. That way, we kept a reserve that usually resulted in a big boost to net income at the end of the fiscal year in December. We called it our Christmas bonus. Corporate headquarters always seemed as pleased as punch that we could pull off such a miracle at the end of the year. This system has worked well for many years, and I don't want to change it now.

Required:

1. Explain how shaving 5% off the estimated direct labor-hours in the base for the predetermined overhead rate usually results in a big boost in net income at the end of the fiscal year.
2. Should Cristin Madsen go along with the general manager's request to reduce the direct labor-hours in the predetermined overhead rate computation to 105,000 direct labor-hours?

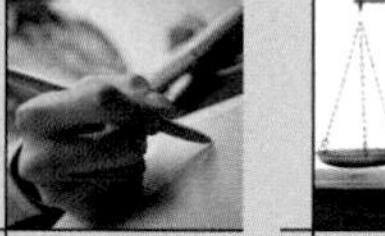
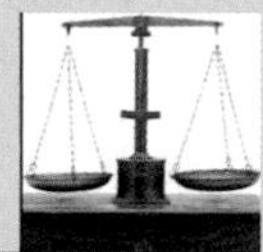

CASE 3–30 (Appendix 3A) Ethics; Predetermined Overhead Rate and Capacity [LO5, LO8, LO9]

Melissa Ostwerk, the new controller of TurboDrives, Inc., has just returned from a seminar on the choice of the activity level in the predetermined overhead rate. Even though the subject did not sound exciting at first, she found that there were some important ideas presented that should get a hearing at her company. After returning from the seminar, she arranged a meeting with the production manager, Jan Kingman, and the assistant production manager, Lonny Chan.

Melissa: I ran across an idea that I wanted to check out with both of you. It's about the way we compute predetermined overhead rates.

Jan: We're all ears.

Melissa: We compute the predetermined overhead rate by dividing the estimated total factory overhead for the coming year by the estimated total units produced for the coming year.

Lonny: We've been doing that as long as I've been with the company.

Jan: And it has been done that way at every other company I've worked at, except at most places they divide by direct labor-hours.

Melissa: We use units because it is simpler and we basically make one product with minor variations. But, there's another way to do it. Instead of dividing the estimated total factory overhead by the estimated total units produced for the coming year, we could divide by the total units produced at capacity.

Lonny: Oh, the Sales Department will love that. It will drop the costs on all the products. They'll go wild over there cutting prices.

Melissa: That is a worry, but I wanted to talk to both of you first before going over to Sales.

Jan: Aren't you always going to have a lot of underapplied overhead?

Melissa: That's correct, but let me show you how we would handle it. Here's an example based on our budget for next year.

Budgeted (estimated) production	80,000 units
Budgeted sales.	80,000 units
Capacity	100,000 units
Selling price	$70 per unit
Variable manufacturing cost	$18 per unit

Total manufacturing overhead cost (all fixed)	$2,000,000
Administrative and selling expenses (all fixed)	$1,950,000
Beginning inventories	0

Traditional approach to computation of the predetermined overhead rate:

$$\text{Predetermined overhead rate} = \frac{\text{Estimated total manufacturing overhead cost}}{\text{Estimated total amount of the allocation base}}$$

$$= \frac{\$2{,}000{,}000}{80{,}000 \text{ units}} = \$25 \text{ per unit}$$

Budgeted Income Statement

Revenue (80,000 units × $70 per unit)		$5,600,000
Cost of goods sold:		
Variable manufacturing		
(80,000 units × $18 per unit)	$1,440,000	
Manufacturing overhead applied		
(80,000 units × $25 per unit)	2,000,000	3,440,000
Gross margin		2,160,000
Administrative and selling expenses		1,950,000
Net operating income		$ 210,000

New approach to computation of the predetermined overhead rate using capacity in the denominator:

$$\text{Predetermined overhead rate} = \frac{\text{Estimated total manufacturing overhead cost at capacity}}{\text{Estimated total amount of the allocation base at capacity}}$$

$$= \frac{\$2{,}000{,}000}{100{,}000 \text{ units}} = \$20 \text{ per unit}$$

Budgeted Income Statement

Revenue (80,000 units × $70 per unit)		$5,600,000
Cost of goods sold:		
Variable manufacturing		
(80,000 units × $18 per unit)	$1,440,000	
Manufacturing overhead applied		
(80,000 units × $20 per unit)	1,600,000	3,040,000
Gross margin		2,560,000
Cost of unused capacity		
[(100,000 units − 80,000 units) × $20 per unit]		400,000
Administrative and selling expenses		1,950,000
Net operating income		$ 210,000

Jan: Whoa!! I don't think I like the looks of that "Cost of unused capacity." If that thing shows up on the income statement, someone from headquarters is likely to come down here looking for some people to lay off.

Lonny: I'm worried about something else, too. What happens when sales are not up to expectations? Can we pull the "hat trick"?

Melissa: I'm sorry, I don't understand.

Jan: Lonny's talking about something that happens fairly regularly. When sales are down and profits look like they are going to be lower than the president told the owners they were going to be, the president comes down here and asks us to deliver some more profits.

Lonny: And we pull them out of our hat.

Jan: Yeah, we just increase production until we get the profits we want.

Melissa: I still don't understand. You mean you increase sales?

Jan: Nope, we increase production. We're the production managers, not the sales managers.

Melissa: I get it. Since you have produced more, the sales force has more units they can sell.
Jan: Nope, the marketing people don't do a thing. We just build inventories and that does the trick.

Required:

In all of the questions below, assume that the predetermined overhead rate under the traditional method is \$25 per unit, and under the new method it is \$20 per unit. Also assume that under the traditional method any under- or overapplied overhead is taken directly to the income statement as an adjustment to Cost of Goods Sold.

1. Suppose actual production is 80,000 units. Compute the net operating incomes that would be realized under the traditional and new methods if actual sales are 75,000 units and everything else turns out as expected.
2. How many units would have to be produced under each of the methods in order to realize the budgeted net operating income of \$210,000 if actual sales are 75,000 units and everything else turns out as expected?
3. What effect does the new method based on capacity have on the volatility of net operating income?
4. Will the "hat trick" be easier or harder to perform if the new method based on capacity is used?
5. Do you think the "hat trick" is ethical?

CASE 3–31 Critical Thinking; Interpretation of Manufacturing Overhead Rates [LO3, LO5]

Sharpton Fabricators Company manufactures a variety of parts for the automotive industry. The company uses a job-order costing system with a plantwide predetermined overhead rate based on direct labor-hours. On December 10, 2002, the company's controller made a preliminary estimate of the predetermined overhead rate for 2003. The new rate was based on the estimated total manufacturing overhead cost of \$2,475,000 and the estimated 52,000 total direct labor-hours for 2003:

$$\text{Predetermined overhead rate} = \frac{\$2{,}475{,}000}{52{,}000 \text{ hours}}$$

$$= \$47.60 \text{ per direct labor-hour}$$

This new predetermined overhead rate was communicated to top managers in a meeting on December 11. The rate did not cause any comment because it was within a few pennies of the overhead rate that had been used during 2002. One of the subjects discussed at the meeting was a proposal by the production manager to purchase an automated milling machine center built by Central Robotics. The president of Sharpton Fabricators, Kevin Reynolds, agreed to meet with the regional sales representative from Central Robotics to discuss the proposal.

On the day following the meeting, Mr. Reynolds met with Jay Warner, Central Robotics' sales representative. The following discussion took place:

Reynolds: Larry Winter, our production manager, asked me to meet with you since he is interested in installing an automated milling machine center. Frankly, I am skeptical. You're going to have to show me this isn't just another expensive toy for Larry's people to play with.

Warner: That shouldn't be too difficult, Mr. Reynolds. The automated milling machine center has three major advantages. First, it is much faster than the manual methods you are using. It can process about twice as many parts per hour as your present milling machines. Second, it is much more flexible. There are some up-front programming costs, but once those have been incurred, almost no setup is required on the machines for standard operations. You just punch in the code of the standard operation, load the machine's hopper with raw material, and the machine does the rest.

Reynolds: Yeah, but what about cost? Having twice the capacity in the milling machine area won't do us much good. That center is idle much of the time anyway.

Warner: I was getting there. The third advantage of the automated milling machine center is lower cost. Larry Winters and I looked over your present operations, and we estimated that the automated equipment would eliminate the need for about 6,000 direct labor-hours a year. What is your direct labor cost per hour?

Reynolds: The wage rate in the milling area averages about \$21 per hour. Fringe benefits raise that figure to about \$30 per hour.

Warner: Don't forget your overhead.

Reynolds: Next year the overhead rate will be about \$48 per hour.

Warner: So including fringe benefits and overhead, the cost per direct labor-hour is about \$78.

Reynolds: That's right.

Warner: Since you can save 6,000 direct labor-hours per year, the cost savings would amount to about $468,000 a year.

Reynolds: That's pretty impressive, but you aren't giving away this equipment are you?

Warner: Several options are available, including leasing and outright purchase. Just for comparison purposes, our 60-month lease plan would require payments of only $300,000 per year.

Reynolds: Sold! When can you install the equipment?

Shortly after this meeting, Mr. Reynolds informed the company's controller of the decision to lease the new equipment, which would be installed over the Christmas vacation period. The controller realized that this decision would require a recomputation of the predetermined overhead rate for the year 2003 since the decision would affect both the manufacturing overhead and the direct labor-hours for the year. After talking with both the production manager and the sales representative from Central Robotics, the controller discovered that in addition to the annual lease cost of $300,000, the new machine would also require a skilled technician/programmer who would have to be hired at a cost of $45,000 per year to maintain and program the equipment. Both of these costs would be included in factory overhead. There would be no other changes in total manufacturing overhead cost, which is almost entirely fixed. The controller assumed that the new machine would result in a reduction of 6,000 direct labor-hours for the year from the levels that had initially been planned.

When the revised predetermined overhead rate for the year 2003 was circulated among the company's top managers, there was considerable dismay.

Required:

1. Recompute the predetermined rate assuming that the new machine will be installed. Explain why the new predetermined overhead rate is higher (or lower) than the rate that was originally estimated for the year 2000.
2. What effect (if any) would this new rate have on the cost of jobs that do not use the new automated milling machine?
3. Why would managers be concerned about the new overhead rate?
4. After seeing the new predetermined overhead rate, the production manager admitted that he probably wouldn't be able to eliminate all of the 6,000 direct labor-hours. He had been hoping to accomplish the reduction by not replacing workers who retire or quit, but that would not be possible. As a result, the real labor savings would be only about 2,000 hours—one worker. In the light of this additional information, evaluate the original decision to acquire the automated milling machine from Central Robotics.

Group and Internet Exercises

GROUP EXERCISE 3–32 Talk with a Controller

Look in the yellow pages or contact your local chamber of commerce or local chapter of the Institute of Certified Management Accountants to find the names of manufacturing companies in your area. Make an appointment to meet with the controller or chief financial officer of one of these companies.

Required:

Ask the following questions and write a brief report concerning what you found out.

1. Does the company use job-order costing, process costing, or some other method of determining product costs?
2. How is overhead assigned to products? What is the overhead rate? What is the basis of allocation? Is more than one overhead rate used?
3. Are product costs used in making any decisions? If so, what are those decisions and how are product costs used?
4. How are profits affected by changes in production volume? By changes in sales?
5. Has the company recently changed its cost system or is it considering changing its cost system? If so, why? What changes were made or what changes are being considered?

INTERNET EXERCISE 3–33 Internet Exercise

As you know, the World Wide Web is a medium that is constantly evolving. Sites come and go, and change without notice. To enable periodic update of site addresses, this problem has been posted to the textbook website (www.mhhe.com/garrison10e). After accessing the site, enter the Student Center and select this chapter. Select and complete the Internet exercise.

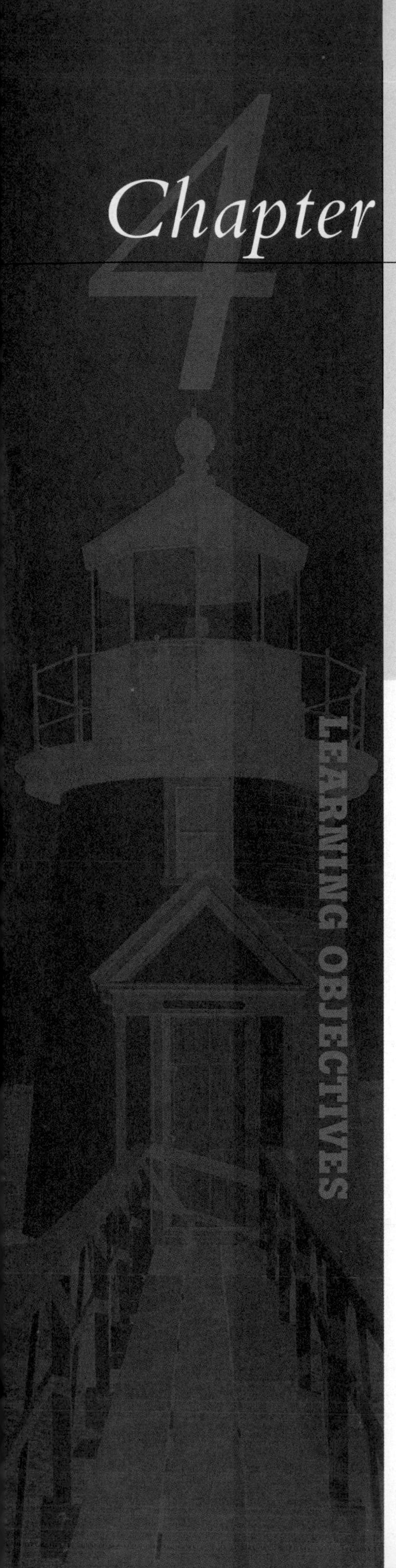

Chapter Four

Systems Design: Process Costing

After studying Chapter 4, you should be able to:

1. Record the flow of materials, labor, and overhead through a process costing system.
2. Compute the equivalent units of production using the weighted-average method.
3. Prepare a quantity schedule using the weighted-average method.
4. Compute the costs per equivalent unit using the weighted-average method.
5. Prepare a cost reconciliation using the weighted-average method.
6. (Appendix 4A) Compute the equivalent units of production using the FIFO method.
7. (Appendix 4A) Prepare a quantity schedule using the FIFO method.
8. (Appendix 4A) Compute the costs per equivalent unit using the FIFO method.
9. (Appendix 4A) Prepare a cost reconciliation using the FIFO method.

BUSINESS FOCUS

Costing Cream Soda

Using an old family recipe, Megan Harris started a company that produces cream soda. At first the company struggled, but as sales increased, the company expanded rapidly. Megan soon realized that to expand any further, it would be necessary to borrow money. The investment in additional equipment was too large for her to finance out of the company's current cash flows.

Megan was disappointed to find that few banks were willing to make a loan to such a small company, but she finally found a bank that would consider her loan application. However, Megan was informed that she would have to supply up-to-date financial statements with her loan application.

Megan had never bothered with financial statements before—she felt that as long as the balance in the company's checkbook kept increasing, the company was doing fine. She was puzzled how she was going to determine the value of the cream soda in the work in process and finished goods inventories. The valuation of the cream soda would affect both the cost of goods sold and the inventory balances of her company. Megan thought of perhaps using job-order costing, which had been used at her previous employer, but her company produces only one product. Raw ingredients are continually being mixed to make more cream soda, and more bottled cream soda is always coming off the end of the bottling line. Megan didn't see how she could use a job-order costing system since the job never really ended. Perhaps there was another way to account for the costs of producing the cream soda.

As explained in Chapter 3, a company can use either job-order costing or process costing. A job-order costing system is used in situations where many different jobs or products are worked on each period. Examples of industries that would typically use job-order costing include furniture manufacture, special-order printing, shipbuilding, and many types of service organizations.

By contrast, **process costing** is most commonly used in industries that produce essentially homogenous (i.e., uniform) products on a continuous basis, such as bricks, cornflakes, or paper. Process costing is particularly used in companies that convert basic raw materials into homogenous products, such as Reynolds Aluminum (aluminum ingots), Scott Paper (toilet paper), General Mills (flour), Exxon (gasoline and lubricating oils), Coppertone (sunscreens), and Kellogg (breakfast cereals). In addition, process costing is often used in companies with assembly operations, such as Panasonic (video monitors), Compaq (personal computers), General Electric (refrigerators), Toyota (automobiles), Amana (washing machines), and Sony (CD players). A form of process costing may also be used in utilities that produce gas, water, and electricity. As suggested by the length of this list, process costing is in very wide use.

Our purpose in this chapter is to explain how product costing works in a process costing system.

Comparison of Job-Order and Process Costing

In some ways process costing is very similar to job-order costing, and in some ways it is very different. In this section, we focus on these similarities and differences in order to provide a foundation for the detailed discussion of process costing that follows.

Similarities between Job-Order and Process Costing

Much of what was learned in Chapter 3 about costing and about cost flows applies equally well to process costing in this chapter. We are not throwing out all that we have learned about costing and starting from "scratch" with a whole new system. The similarities between job-order and process costing can be summarized as follows:

1. Both systems have the same basic purposes—to assign material, labor, and overhead cost to products and to provide a mechanism for computing unit product costs.
2. Both systems use the same basic manufacturing accounts, including Manufacturing Overhead, Raw Materials, Work in Process, and Finished Goods.
3. The flow of costs through the manufacturing accounts is basically the same in both systems.

As can be seen from this comparison, much of the knowledge that we have already acquired about costing is applicable to a process costing system. Our task now is to refine and extend this knowledge to process costing.

Differences between Job-Order and Process Costing

The differences between job-order and process costing arise from two factors. The first is that the flow of units in a process costing system is more or less continuous, and the second is that these units are indistinguishable from one another. Under process costing, it makes no sense to try to identify materials, labor, and overhead costs with a particular order from a customer (as we did with job-order costing), since each order is just one of many that are filled from a continuous flow of virtually identical units from the production line. Under process costing, we accumulate costs *by department,* rather than by order, and assign these costs uniformly to all units that pass through the department during a period.

Exhibit 4–1
Differences between Job-Order and Process Costing

Job-Order Costing	Process Costing
1. Many different jobs are worked on during each period, with each job having different production requirements.	1. A single product is produced either on a continuous basis or for long periods of time. All units of product are identical.
2. Costs are accumulated by individual job.	2. Costs are accumulated by department.
3. The *job cost sheet* is the key document controlling the accumulation of costs by a job.	3. The *department production report* is the key document showing the accumulation and disposition of costs by a department.
4. Unit costs are computed *by job* on the job cost sheet.	4. Unit costs are computed *by department* on the department production report.

A further difference between the two costing systems is that the job cost sheet is not used in process costing, since the focal point of process costing is on departments. Instead of using job cost sheets, a **production report** is prepared for each department in which work is done on products. The production report serves several functions. It provides a summary of the number of units moving through a department during a period, and it also provides a computation of unit costs. In addition, it shows what costs were charged to the department and what disposition was made of these costs. The department production report is the key document in a process costing system.

The major differences between job-order and process costing are summarized in Exhibit 4–1.

A Hybrid Approach

In Business

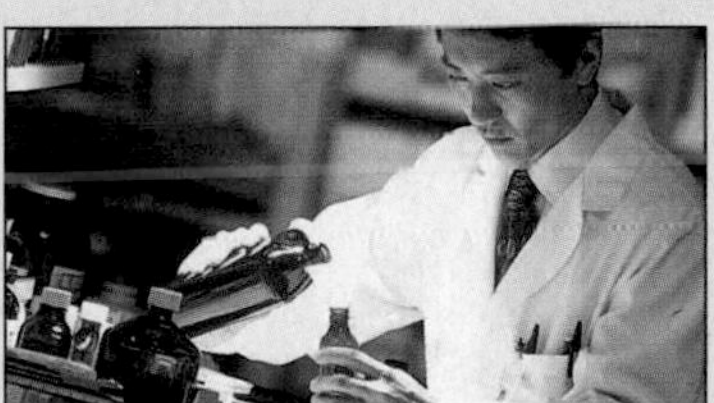

Managers of successful pharmacies understand product costs. Some pharmacies use a hybrid approach to costing drugs. For example, a hospital pharmacy may use process costing to develop the cost of formulating the base solution for parenterals (that is, drugs delivered by injection or through the blood stream) and then use job order costing to accumulate the additional costs incurred to create specific parenteral solutions. These additional costs include the ingredients added to the base solution and the time spent by the pharmacist to prepare the specific prescribed drug solution.

Source: "Pharmaceutical Care: Cost Estimation and Cost Management," *Drug Store News*, February 16, 1998, p. CP21, 5 p.

A Perspective of Process Cost Flows

Before presenting a detailed example of process costing, it will be helpful to see how manufacturing costs flow through a process costing system.

Processing Departments

A **processing department** is any location in an organization where work is performed on a product and where materials, labor, or overhead costs are added to the product. For example, a potato chip factory operated by Nalley's might have three processing departments—one for preparing potatoes, one for cooking, and one for inspecting and packaging. A brick factory might have two processing departments—one for mixing and molding clay into brick form and one for firing the molded brick. A company can have as many or as few processing departments as are needed to complete a product or service. Some products and

Exhibit 4–2 Sequential Processing Departments

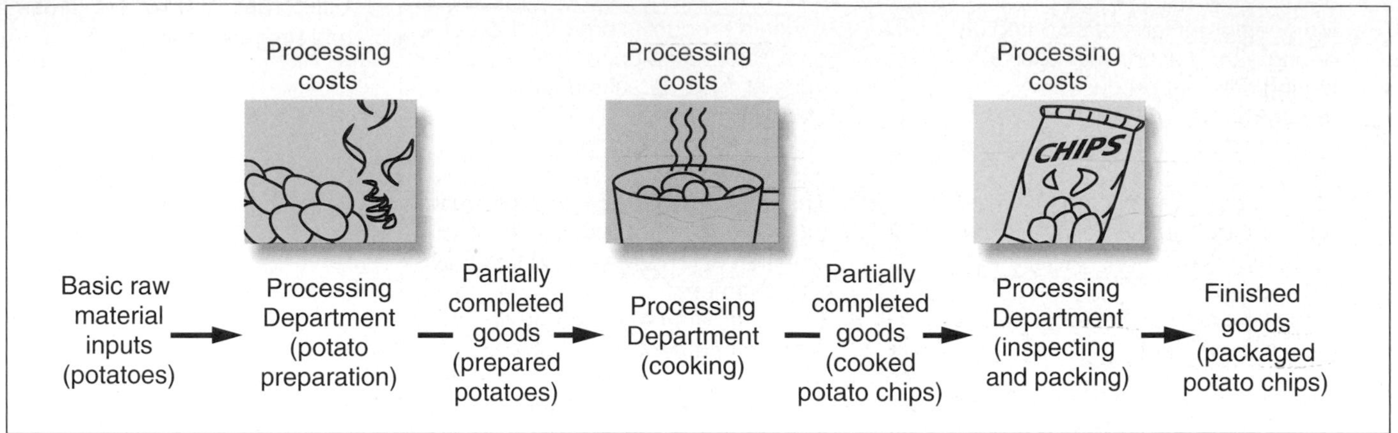

services may go through several processing departments, while others may go through only one or two. Regardless of the number of departments involved, all processing departments in a process costing system have two essential features. First, the activity performed in the processing department must be performed uniformly on all of the units passing through it. Second, the output of the processing department must be homogeneous.

The processing departments involved in making a product such as bricks or potato chips would probably be organized in a *sequential* pattern. By sequential processing, we mean that units flow in sequence from one department to another. An example of processing departments arranged in a sequential pattern is given in Exhibit 4–2, which illustrates a potato chip processing plant.

A different type of processing pattern, known as *parallel processing,* is used to make some products. Parallel processing is used in situations where, after a point, some units go through different processing departments than others. For example, petroleum refiners such as Exxon, Shell Oil, and BP separate crude oil into a number of intermediate products which then go through separate processes to create end products such as gasoline, heating oil, jet fuel, and lubricants.

An example of parallel processing is provided in Exhibit 4–3, which shows the process flows in a Coca-Cola™ bottling plant. In the first processing department, raw materials are mixed to make the basic concentrate. This concentrate can be used to make bottled Coke or it may be sold to restaurants and bars for use in soda fountains. Under the first option, the concentrate is sent on to the bottling department where it is mixed with carbonated water and then injected into sterile bottles and capped. In the final processing department, the bottles are inspected, labels are applied, and the bottles are packed in cartons. If the concentrate is to be sold for use in soda fountains, it is injected into large sterile metal cylinders, inspected, and packaged for shipping. This is just an example of one way in which parallel processing can be set up. The number of possible variations in parallel processing is virtually limitless.

In Business

Automating an Ancient Process

Honeytop Foods has transformed the preparation of naan, a flavored flatbread from India. Traditionally, dough is laboriously kneaded and shaped by hand and then slapped onto the inside wall of a ceramic oven, where it sticks and is baked at high heat. With the exception of one step, the 60-minute process is now automated. High-speed machinery is used to measure and mix the ingredients; roll, shape, and flame-bake the dough; and package the bread before it is refrigerated or frozen. Humans are still needed to perform the final shaping step, the outcome of which is a teardrop shape.

Source: "Naan Bread Revolution," *Food Manufacture,* February 2000, pp. 38–39.

Exhibit 4–3 Parallel Processing Departments

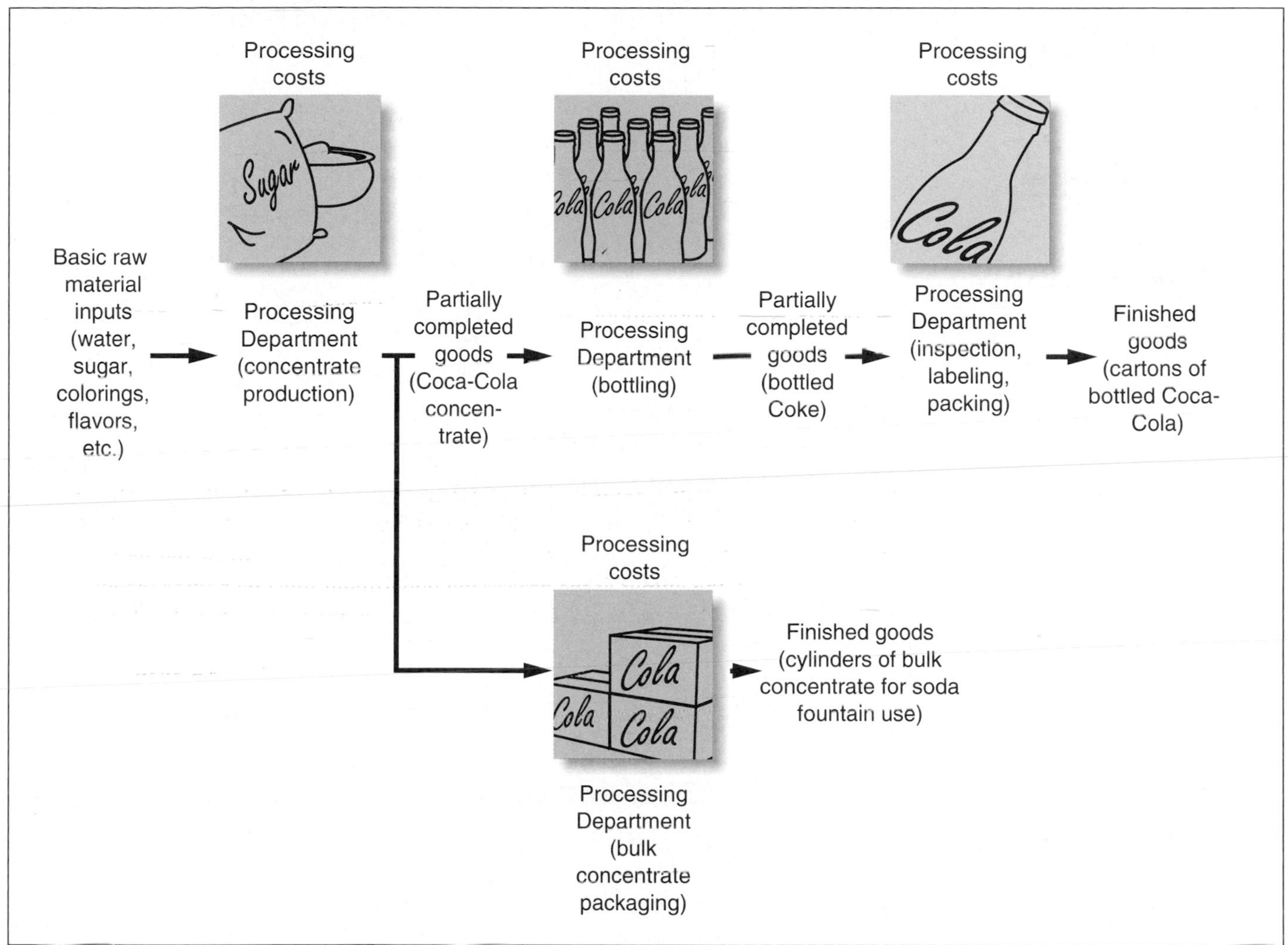

The Flow of Materials, Labor, and Overhead Costs

Cost accumulation is simpler in a process costing system than in a job-order costing system. In a process costing system, instead of having to trace costs to hundreds of different jobs, costs are traced to only a few processing departments.

A T-account model of materials, labor, and overhead cost flows in a process costing system is given in Exhibit 4–4. Several key points should be noted from this exhibit. First, note that a separate Work in Process account is maintained for *each processing department.* In contrast, in a job-order costing system there may be only a single Work in Process account for the entire company. Second, note that the completed production of the first processing department (Department A in the exhibit) is transferred to the Work in Process account of the second processing department (Department B), where it undergoes further work. After this further work, the completed units are then transferred to Finished Goods. (In Exhibit 4–4, we show only two processing departments, but there can be many such departments in a company.)

Finally, note that materials, labor, and overhead costs can be added in *any* processing department—not just the first. Costs in Department B's Work in Process account would consist of the materials, labor, and overhead costs incurred in Department B plus the costs attached to partially completed units transferred in from Department A (called **transferred-in costs**).

Exhibit 4–4 T-Account Model of Process Costing Flows

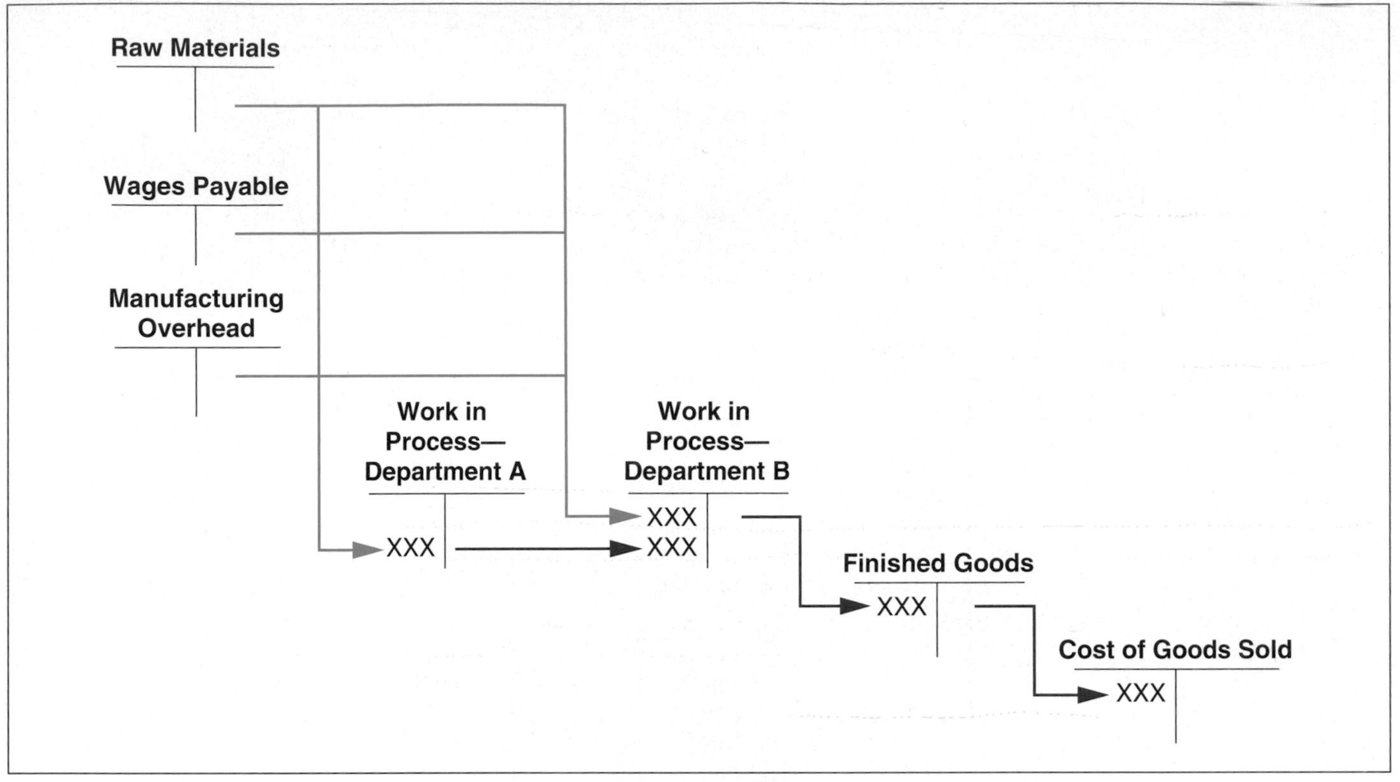

Materials, Labor, and Overhead Cost Entries

LEARNING OBJECTIVE 1
Record the flow of materials, labor, and overhead through a process costing system.

To complete our discussion of cost flows in a process costing system, in this section we show journal entries relating to materials, labor, and overhead costs at Megan's Classic Cream Soda, the company mentioned at the very beginning of this chapter. Megan's Classic Cream Soda has two processing departments—Formulation and Bottling. In the Formulation Department, the various ingredients are checked for quality and then mixed and injected with carbon dioxide to create bulk cream soda. In the Bottling Department, bottles are checked for defects, filled with cream soda, capped, visually inspected again for defects, and then packed for shipping.

Materials Costs As in job-order costing, materials are drawn from the storeroom using a materials requisition form. As stated earlier, materials can be added in any processing department, although it is not unusual for materials to be added only in the first processing department, with subsequent departments adding only labor and overhead costs as the partially completed units move along toward completion.

At Megan's Classic Cream Soda, some materials (i.e., water, flavors, sugar, and carbon dioxide) are added in the Formulating Department and some materials (i.e., bottles, caps, and packing materials) are added in the Bottling Department. The journal entry to record the materials used in the first processing department, the Formulating Department, is as follows:

Work in Process—Formulating	XXX	
Raw Materials		XXX

If other materials are subsequently added in another department, as at Megan's Classic Cream Soda, the entry is the following:

Work in Process—Bottling	XXX	
Raw Materials		XXX

Labor Costs In process costing, labor costs are traced to departments—not to individual jobs. The following journal entry will record the labor costs in the Formulating Department at Megan's Classic Cream Soda:

Work in Process—Formulating	XXX	
Salaries and Wages Payable		XXX

Overhead Costs In process costing, as in job-order costing, predetermined overhead rates are usually used. Each department has its own separate rate, which is computed as discussed in Chapter 2. Overhead cost is then applied to units of product as they move through the department. A journal entry such as the following records the cost for the Formulating Department:

Work in Process—Formulating	XXX	
Manufacturing Overhead		XXX

Completing the Cost Flows Once processing has been completed in a department, the units are transferred to the next department for further processing, as illustrated earlier in the T-accounts in Exhibit 4–4. The following journal entry is used to transfer the costs of partially completed units from the Formulating Department to the Bottling Department:

Work in Process—Bottling	XXX	
Work in Process—Formulating		XXX

After processing has been completed in the final department, the costs of the completed units are then transferred to the Finished Goods inventory account:

Finished Goods	XXX	
Work in Process—Bottling		XXX

Finally, when a customer's order is filled and units are sold, the cost of the units is transferred to Cost of Goods Sold:

Cost of Goods Sold	XXX	
Finished Goods		XXX

To summarize, the cost flows between accounts are basically the same in a process costing system as they are in a job-order costing system. The only noticeable difference at this point is that in a process costing system there is a separate Work in Process account for each department.

Managerial Accounting in Action

The Issue

Samantha Trivers, president of Double Diamond Skis, was worried about the future of her company. After a rocky start, the company had come out with a completely redesigned ski called The Ultimate made of exotic materials and featuring flashy graphics. Exhibit 4–5 illustrates how this ski is manufactured. The ski was a runaway best seller—particularly among younger skiers—and had provided the company with much-needed cash for two years. However, last year a dismal snowfall in the Rocky Mountains had depressed sales, and Double Diamond was once again short of cash. Samantha was worried that another bad ski season would force Double Diamond into bankruptcy.

Just before starting production of next year's model of The Ultimate, Samantha called Jerry Madison, the company controller, into her office to discuss the reports she would need in the coming year.

Samantha: Jerry, I am going to need more frequent cost information this year. I really have to stay on top of things.

Jerry: What do you have in mind?

Samantha: I'd like reports at least once a month that detail our production costs for each department and for each pair of skis.

Exhibit 4–5
The Production Process at Double Diamond Skis*

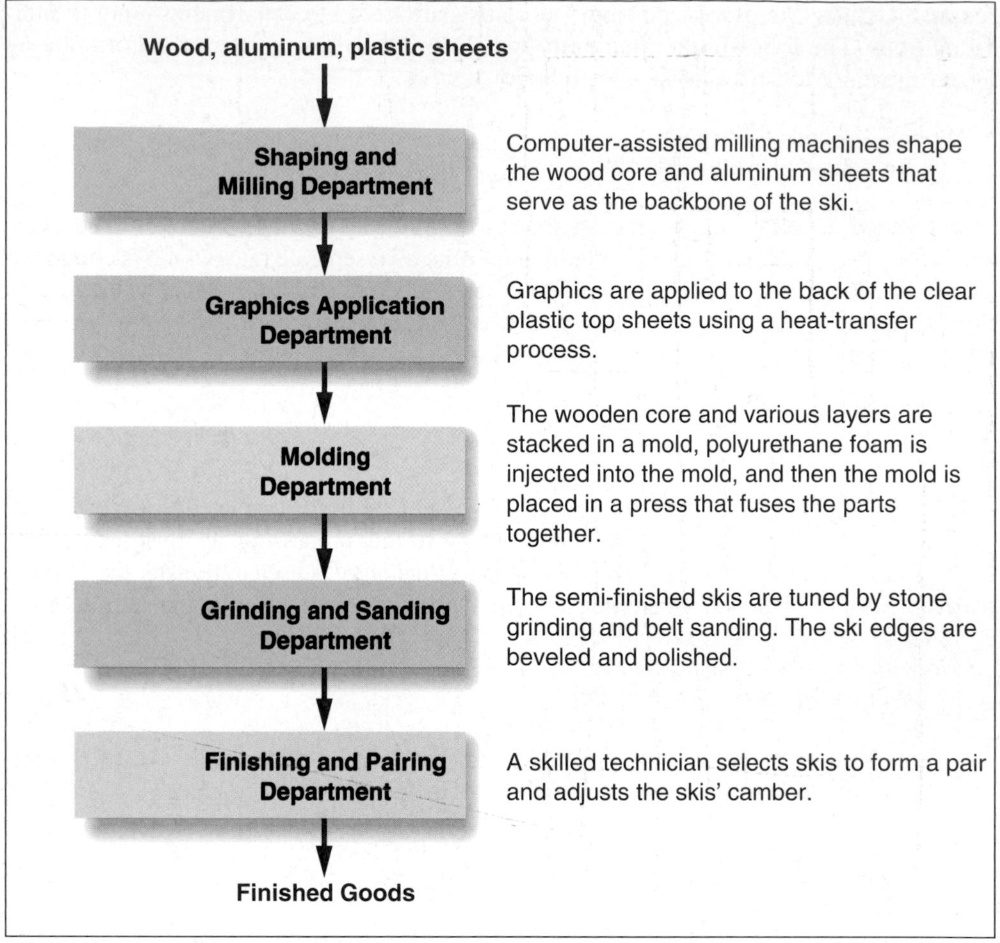

*Adapted from Bill Gout, Jesse James Doquilo, and Studio M D, "Capped Crusaders," *Skiing,* October 1993, pp. 138–44.

Jerry: That shouldn't be much of a problem. We already compile almost all of the necessary data for the annual report. The only complication is our work in process inventories. They haven't been a problem in our annual reports, since our fiscal year ends at a time when we have finished producing skis for the last model year and haven't yet started producing for the new model year. Consequently, there aren't any work in process inventories to value for the annual report. But that won't be true for monthly reports.

Samantha: I'm not sure why that is a problem, Jerry. But I'm confident you can figure out how to solve it.

Equivalent Units of Production

Concept 4–1

Jerry Madison, the controller of Double Diamond Skis, was concerned with the following problem: After materials, labor, and overhead costs have been accumulated in a department, the department's output must be determined so that unit costs can be computed. The difficulty is that a department usually has some partially completed units in its ending inventory. It does not seem reasonable to count these partially completed units as equivalent to fully completed units when counting the department's output. Therefore, Jerry will mathematically convert those partially completed units into an *equivalent* number of fully completed units. In process costing, this is done using the following formula:

$$\text{Equivalent units} = \text{Number of partially completed units} \times \text{Percentage completion}$$

As the formula states, **equivalent units** is defined to be the product of the number of partially completed units and the percentage completion of those units. The equivalent units is the number of complete units that could have been obtained from the materials and effort that went into the partially complete units.

For example, suppose the Molding Department at Double Diamond has 500 units in its ending work in process inventory that are 60% complete. These 500 partially complete units are equivalent to 300 fully complete units (500 × 60% = 300). Therefore, the ending work in process inventory would be said to contain 300 equivalent units. These equivalent units would be added to any units completed during the period to determine the period's output for the department—called the *equivalent units of production.*

Equivalent units of production for a period can be computed in two different ways. In this chapter, we discuss the *weighted-average method.* In Appendix 4A, the *FIFO method* is discussed. The **FIFO method** of process costing is a method in which equivalent units and unit costs relate only to work done during the current period. In contrast, the **weighted-average method** blends together units and costs from the current period with units and costs from the prior period. In the weighted-average method, the **equivalent units of production** for a department are the number of units transferred to the next department (or to finished goods) plus the equivalent units in the department's ending work in process inventory.

Weighted-Average Method

LEARNING OBJECTIVE 2
Compute the equivalent units of production using the weighted-average method.

Under the weighted-average method, a department's equivalent units are computed as follows:

Weighted-Average Method
(a separate calculation is made for each cost category in each processing department)

Equivalent units of production = Units transferred to the next department or to finished goods
+ Equivalent units in ending work in process inventory

We do not have to make an equivalent units calculation for units transferred to the next department. We can assume that they would not have been transferred unless they were 100% complete with respect to the work performed in the transferring department.

Consider the Shaping and Milling Department at Double Diamond. This department uses computerized milling machines to precisely shape the wooden core and metal sheets that will be used to form the backbone of the ski. (See Exhibit 4–5 for an overview of the production process at Double Diamond.) The following activity took place in the department in May, several months into the production of the new model of The Ultimate ski:

Shaping and Milling Department

		Percent Complete	
	Units	Materials	Conversion
Work in process, May 1	200	55%	30%
Units started into production during May	5,000		
Units completed during May and transferred to the next department	4,800	100%*	100%*
Work in process, May 31	400	40%	25%

*It is always assumed that units transferred out of a department are 100% complete with respect to the processing done in that department.

Note the use of the term *conversion* in the table on the previous page. **Conversion cost,** as defined in Chapter 2, is direct labor cost plus manufacturing overhead cost. In process costing, conversion cost is often—but not always—treated as a single element of product cost.

Also note that the May 1 beginning work in process was 55% complete with respect to materials costs and 30% complete with respect to conversion costs. This means that 55% of the materials costs required to complete the units in the department had already been incurred. Likewise, 30% of the conversion costs required to complete the units had already been incurred.

Since Double Diamond's work in process inventories are at different stages of completion in terms of the amounts of materials cost and conversion cost that have been added in the department, two equivalent unit figures must be computed. The equivalent units computations are shown in Exhibit 4–6.

Note from the computation in Exhibit 4–6 that units in the beginning work in process inventory are ignored. The weighted-average method is concerned only with the fact that there are 4,900 equivalent units for conversion cost in ending inventories and in units transferred to the next department—the method is not concerned with the additional fact that some of this work was accomplished in prior periods. This is a key point in the weighted-average method that is easy to overlook.

Computation of equivalent units of production is illustrated in Exhibit 4–7. Study this exhibit carefully before going on.

Exhibit 4–6
Equivalent Units of Production: Weighted-Average Method

Shaping and Milling Department	Materials	Conversion
Units transferred to the next department	4,800	4,800
Work in process, May 31:		
400 units × 40%	160	
400 units × 25%		100
Equivalent units of production	4,960	4,900

Production Report—Weighted-Average Method

The production report developed in this section contains the information requested by the president of Double Diamond Skis. The purpose of the production report is to summarize for management all of the activity that takes place in a department's Work in Process account for a period. This activity includes the units and costs that flow through the Work in Process account. As illustrated in Exhibit 4–8, a separate production report is prepared for each department.

Earlier, when we outlined the differences between job-order costing and process costing, we stated that the production report takes the place of a job cost sheet in a process costing system. The production report is a key management document. It has three separate (though highly interrelated) parts:

1. A quantity schedule, which shows the flow of units through the department and a computation of equivalent units.
2. A computation of costs per equivalent unit.
3. A reconciliation of all cost flows into and out of the department during the period.

We will use the data at the top of page 160 for the May operations of the Shaping and Milling Department of Double Diamond Skis to illustrate the production report. Keep in mind that this report is only one of the five reports that would be prepared for the company since the company has five processing departments.

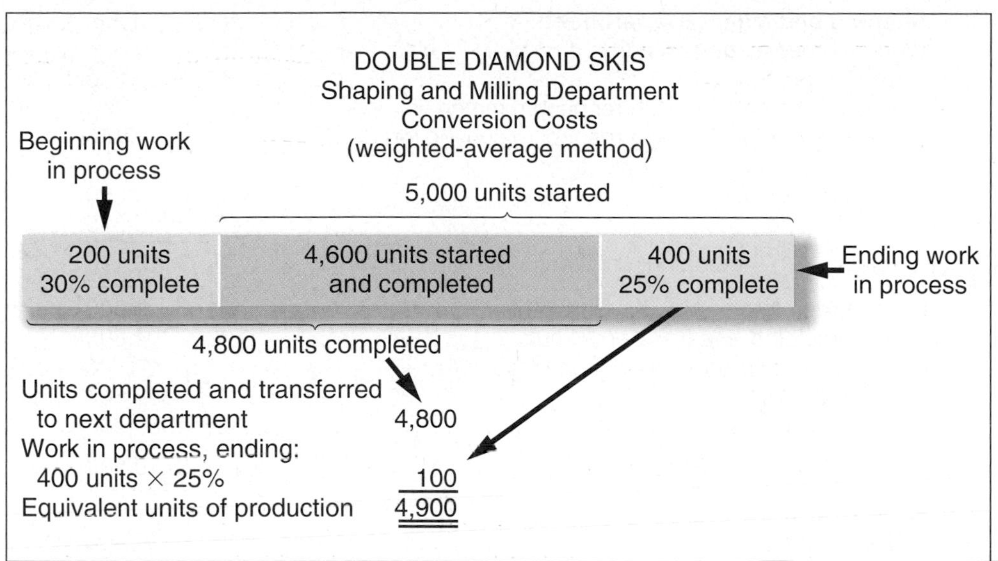

Exhibit 4–7
Visual Perspective of Equivalent Units of Production

Exhibit 4–8 The Position of the Production Report in the Flow of Costs

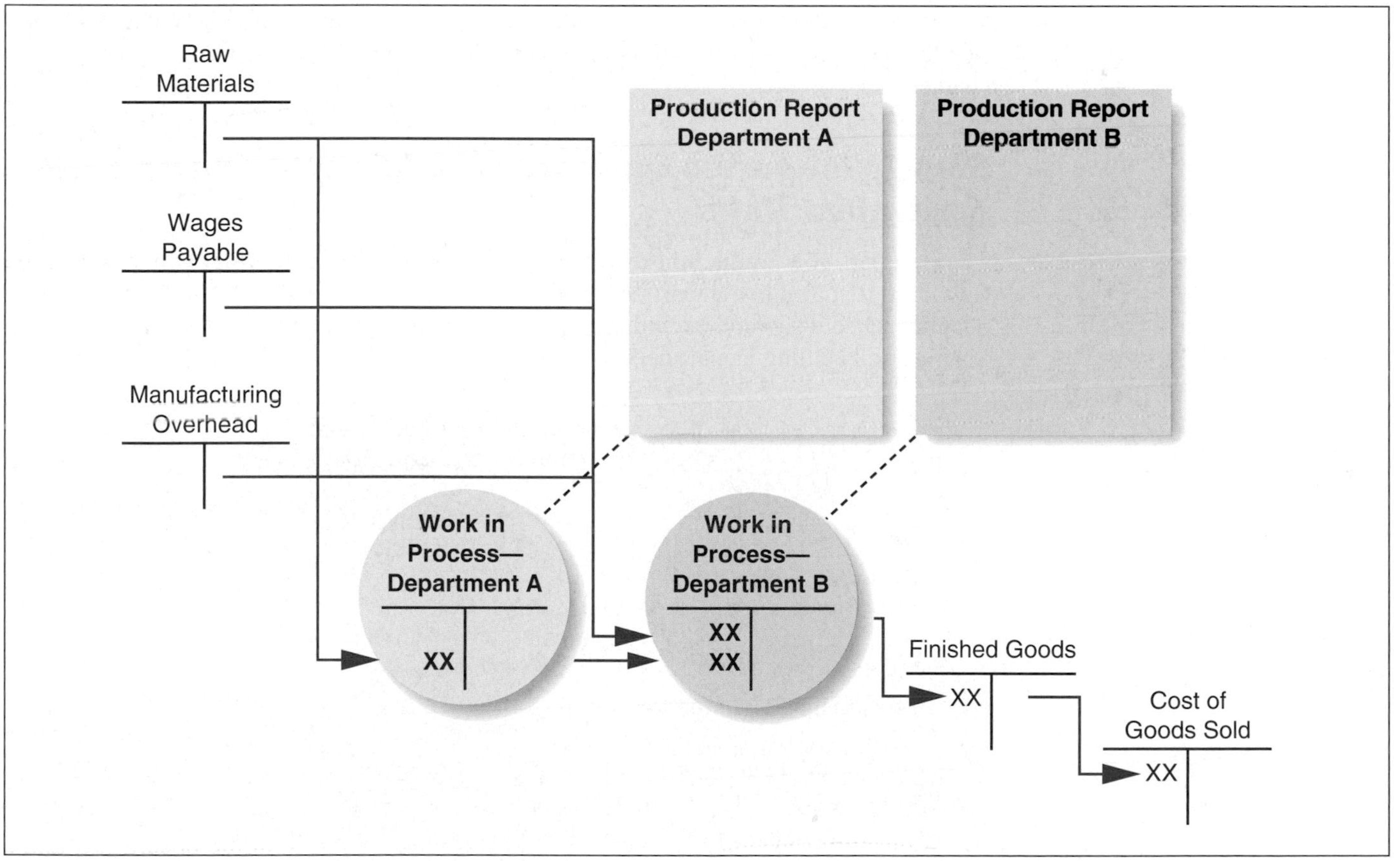

Raw Materials

Wages Payable

Manufacturing Overhead

Production Report Department A

Production Report Department B

Work in Process— Department A

XX

Work in Process— Department B

XX
XX

Finished Goods

XX

Cost of Goods Sold

XX

Shaping and Milling Department	
Work in process, beginning:	
Units in process	200
Stage of completion with respect to materials	55%
Stage of completion with respect to conversion	30%
Costs in the beginning inventory:	
Materials cost	$ 9,600
Conversion cost	5,575
Total cost in the beginning inventory	$ 15,175
Units started into production during May	5,000
Units completed and transferred out	4,800
Costs added to production during May:	
Materials cost	$368,600
Conversion cost	350,900
Total cost added in the department	$719,500
Work in process, ending:	
Units in process	400
Stage of completion with respect to materials	40%
Stage of completion with respect to conversion	25%

In this section, we show how a production report is prepared when the weighted-average method is used to compute equivalent units and unit costs. The preparation of a production report under the FIFO method is illustrated in Appendix 4A at the end of this chapter.

Step 1: Prepare a Quantity Schedule and Compute the Equivalent Units

LEARNING OBJECTIVE 3
Prepare a quantity schedule using the weighted-average method.

The first part of a production report consists of a **quantity schedule,** which shows the flow of units through a department and computation of equivalent units. To illustrate, a quantity schedule combined with a computation of equivalent units is given below for the Shaping and Milling Department of Double Diamond Skis.

Shaping and Milling Department
Quantity Schedule and Equivalent Units

	Quantity Schedule	Equivalent Units: Materials	Equivalent Units: Conversion
Units to be accounted for:			
Work in process, May 1 (materials 55% complete; conversion 30% complete)	200		
Started into production	5,000		
Total units to be accounted for	5,200		
Units accounted for as follows:			
Transferred to next department	4,800	4,800	4,800
Work in process, May 31 (materials 40% complete; conversion 25% complete)	400	160*	100†
Total units accounted for	5,200	4,960	4,900

*40% × 400 units = 160 equivalent units.
†25% × 400 units = 100 equivalent units.

The quantity schedule permits the manager to see at a glance how many units moved through the department during the period as well as to see the stage of completion of any in-process units. In addition to providing this information, the quantity schedule serves as an essential guide in preparing and tying together the remaining parts of a production report.

Step 2: Compute Costs per Equivalent Unit

LEARNING OBJECTIVE 4
Compute the costs per equivalent unit using the weighted-average method.

As stated earlier, the weighted-average method blends together the work that was accomplished in the prior period with the work that was accomplished in the current period. That is why it is called the weighted-average method; it averages together units and costs from both the prior and current periods by adding the cost in the beginning work in process inventory to the current period costs. These computations are shown below for the Shaping and Milling Department for May:

Shaping and Milling Department
Costs per Equivalent Unit

	Total Cost	Materials	Conversion	Whole Unit
Cost to be accounted for:				
Work in process, May 1	$ 15,175	$ 9,600	$ 5,575	
Cost added during the month in the Shaping and Milling Department.	719,500	368,600	350,900	
Total cost to be accounted for (a).	$734,675	$378,200	$356,475	
Equivalent units (Step 1 above) (b) . . .		4,960	4,900	
Cost per equivalent unit, (a) ÷ (b)		$76.25 +	$72.75 =	$149.00

The cost per equivalent unit (EU) that we have computed for the Shaping and Milling Department will be used to apply cost to units that are transferred to the next department, Graphics Application, and will also be used to compute the cost in the ending work in process inventory. For example, each unit transferred out of the Shaping and Milling Department to the Graphics Application Department will carry with it a cost of $149. Since the costs are passed on from department to department, the unit cost of the last department, Finishing and Pairing, will represent the final cost of a completed unit of product.

Step 3: Prepare a Cost Reconciliation

LEARNING OBJECTIVE 5
Prepare a cost reconciliation using the weighted-average method.

The purpose of a **cost reconciliation** is to show how the costs that have been charged to a department during a period are accounted for. Typically, the costs charged to a department will consist of the following:

1. Cost in the beginning work in process inventory.
2. Materials, labor, and overhead costs added during the period.
3. Cost (if any) transferred in from the preceding department.

In a production report, these costs are titled "Cost to be accounted for." They are accounted for in a production report by computing the following amounts:

1. Cost transferred out to the next department (or to Finished Goods).
2. Cost remaining in the ending work in process inventory.

In short, when a cost reconciliation is prepared, the "Cost to be accounted for" from step 2 is reconciled with the sum of the cost transferred out during the period plus the cost in the ending work in process inventory. This concept is shown graphically in Exhibit 4–9. Study this exhibit carefully before going on to the cost reconciliation below for the Shaping and Milling Department.

Example of a Cost Reconciliation To prepare a cost reconciliation, follow the quantity schedule line for line and show the cost associated with each group of units. This is done in Exhibit 4–10, where we present a completed production report for the Shaping and Milling Department.

Concept 4–2

Exhibit 4–9 Graphic Illustration of the Cost Reconciliation Part of a Production Report

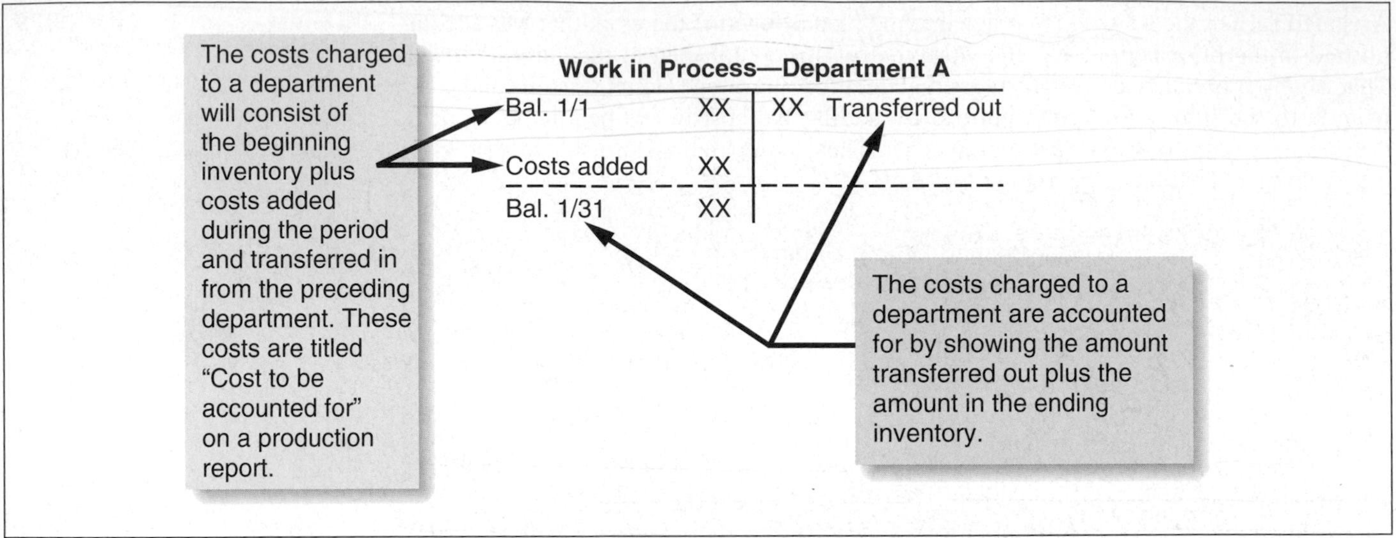

The quantity schedule in the exhibit shows that 200 units were in process on May 1 and that an additional 5,000 units were started into production during the month. Looking at the "Cost to be accounted for" in the middle part of the exhibit, notice that the units in process on May 1 had $15,175 in cost attached to them and that the Shaping and Milling Department added another $719,500 in cost to production during the month. Thus, the department has $734,675 ($15,175 + $719,500) in cost to be accounted for.

This cost is accounted for in two ways. As shown on the quantity schedule, 4,800 units were transferred to the Graphics Application Department, the next department in the production process. Another 400 units were still in process in the Shaping and Milling Department at the end of the month. Thus, part of the $734,675 "Cost to be accounted for" goes with the 4,800 units to the Graphics Application Department, and part of it remains with the 400 units in the ending work in process inventory in the Shaping and Milling Department.

Each of the 4,800 units transferred to the Graphics Application Department is assigned $149.00 in cost, for a total of $715,200. The 400 units still in process at the end of the month are assigned costs according to their stage of completion. To determine the stage of completion, we refer to the equivalent units computation and bring the equivalent units figures down to the cost reconciliation part of the report. We then assign costs to these units, using the cost per equivalent unit figures already computed.

After cost has been assigned to the ending work in process inventory, the total cost that we have accounted for ($734,675) agrees with the amount that we had to account for ($734,675). Thus, the cost reconciliation is complete.

Managerial Accounting in Action

The Wrap-Up

Jerry: Here's an example of the kind of report I can put together for you every month. This particular report is for the Shaping and Milling Department. It follows a fairly standard format for industries like ours and is called a production report. I hope this is what you have in mind.

Samantha: The quantity schedule makes sense to me. I can see we had a total of 5,200 units to account for in the department, and 4,800 of those were transferred to the next department while 400 were still in process at the end of the month. What are these "equivalent units"?

Jerry: That's the problem I mentioned earlier. The 400 units that are still in process are far from complete. When we compute the unit costs, it wouldn't make sense to count them as whole units.

Samantha: I suppose not. I see what you are driving at. Since those 400 units are only 25% complete with respect to our conversion costs, they should only be counted as 100 units when we compute the unit costs for conversion.

Exhibit 4–10 Production Report—Weighted-Average Method

DOUBLE DIAMOND SKIS
Shaping and Milling Department Production Report
(Weighted-Average Method)

Quantity Schedule and Equivalent Units

	Quantity Schedule		
Units to be accounted for:			
Work in process, May 1 (materials 55% complete; conversion 30% complete)	200		
Started into production	5,000		
Total units to be accounted for	5,200		
		Equivalent Units (EU)	
		Materials	**Conversion**
Units accounted for as follows:			
Transferred to next department	4,800	4,800	4,800
Work in process, May 31 (materials 40% complete; conversion 25% complete)	400	160*	100†
Total units accounted for	5,200	4,960	4,900

Costs per Equivalent Unit

	Total Cost	Materials		Conversion		Whole Unit
Cost to be accounted for:						
Work in process, May 1	$ 15,175	$ 9,600		$ 5,575		
Cost added in the department	719,500	368,600		350,900		
Total cost to be accounted for (a)	$734,675	$378,200		$356,475		
Equivalent units (b)		4,960		4,900		
Cost per EU, (a) ÷ (b)		$76.25	+	$72.75	=	$149.00

Cost Reconciliation

	Total Cost	Equivalent Units (above)	
		Materials	**Conversion**
Cost accounted for as follows:			
Transferred to the next department:			
4,800 units × $149.00 per unit	$715,200	4,800	4,800
Work in process, May 31:			
Materials, at $76.25 per EU	12,200	160	
Conversion, at $72.75 per EU	7,275		100
Total work in process, May 31	19,475		
Total cost accounted for	$734,675		

*40% × 400 units = 160 equivalent units.
†25% × 400 units = 100 equivalent units.
EU = Equivalent unit.

Jerry: That's right. Is the rest of the report clear?

Samantha: Yes, it does seem pretty clear, although I want to work the numbers through on my own to make sure I thoroughly understand the report.

Jerry: Does this report give you the information you wanted?

Samantha: Yes, it does. I can tell how many units are in process, how complete they are, what happened to them, and their costs. While I know the unit costs are averages and are heavily influenced by our volume, they still can give me some idea of how well we are doing on the cost side. Thanks, Jerry.

Operation Costing

The costing systems discussed in Chapters 3 and 4 represent the two ends of a continuum. On one end we have job-order costing, which is used by companies that produce many different items—generally to customers' specifications. On the other end we have process costing, which is used by companies that produce basically homogeneous products in large quantities. Between these two extremes there are many hybrid systems that include characteristics of both job-order and process costing. One of these hybrids is called *operation costing.*

Operation costing is used in situations where products have some common characteristics and also some individual characteristics. Shoes, for example, have common characteristics in that all styles involve cutting and sewing that can be done on a repetitive basis, using the same equipment and following the same basic procedures. Shoes also have individual characteristics—some are made of expensive leathers and others may be made using inexpensive synthetic materials. In a situation such as this, where products have some common characteristics but also must be handled individually to some extent, operation costing may be used to determine product costs.

As mentioned above, operation costing is a hybrid system that employs aspects of both job-order and process costing. Products are typically handled in batches when operation costing is in use, with each batch charged for its own specific materials. In this sense, operation costing is similar to job-order costing. However, labor and overhead costs are accumulated by operation or by department, and these costs are assigned to units as in process costing. If shoes are being produced, for example, each shoe is charged the same per unit conversion cost, regardless of the style involved, but it is charged with its specific materials cost. Thus, the company is able to distinguish between styles in terms of materials, but it is able to employ the simplicity of a process costing system for labor and overhead costs.

Examples of other products for which operation costing may be used include electronic equipment (such as semiconductors), textiles, clothing, and jewelry (such as rings, bracelets, and medallions). Products of this type are typically produced in batches, but they can vary considerably from model to model or from style to style in terms of the cost of raw material inputs. Therefore, an operation costing system is well suited for providing cost data.

Summary

Process costing is used in situations where homogeneous products or services are produced on a continuous basis. Costs flow through the manufacturing accounts in basically the same way in both job-order and process costing systems. A process costing system differs from a job-order system primarily in that costs are accumulated by department (rather than by job) and the department production report replaces the job cost sheet.

To compute unit costs in a department, the department's output in terms of equivalent units must be determined. In the weighted-average method, the equivalent units for a period are the sum of the units transferred out of the department during the period and the equivalent units in ending work in process inventory at the end of the period.

The activity in a department is summarized on a production report, which has three separate (though highly interrelated) parts. The first part is a quantity schedule, which includes a computation of equivalent units and shows the flow of units through a department during a period. The second part consists of a computation of costs per equivalent unit for materials, labor, and overhead as well as in total for the period. The third part consists of a cost reconciliation, which summarizes all cost flows through a department for a period.

Review Problem: Process Cost Flows and Reports

Luxguard Home Paint Company produces exterior latex paint, which it sells in one-gallon containers. The company has two processing departments—Base Fab and Finishing. White paint, which is used as a base for all the company's paints, is mixed from raw ingredients in the Base Fab Department. Pigments are then added to the basic white paint, the pigmented paint is squirted under pressure into one-gallon containers, and the containers are labeled and packed for shipping in the Finishing Department. Information relating to the company's operations for April follows:

a. Raw materials were issued for use in production: Base Fab Department, $851,000; and Finishing Department, $629,000.
b. Direct labor costs were incurred: Base Fab Department, $330,000; and Finishing Department, $270,000.
c. Manufacturing overhead cost was applied: Base Fab Department, $665,000; and Finishing Department, $405,000.
d. Basic white paint was transferred from the Base Fab Department to the Finishing Department, $1,850,000.
e. Paint that had been prepared for shipping was transferred from the Finishing Department to Finished Goods, $3,200,000.

Required:

1. Prepare journal entries to record items (a) through (e) above.
2. Post the journal entries from (1) above to T-accounts. The balance in the Base Fab Department's Work in Process account on April 1 was $150,000; the balance in the Finishing Department's Work in Process account was $70,000. After posting entries to the T-accounts, find the ending balance in each department's Work in Process account.
3. Prepare a production report for the Base Fab Department for April. The following additional information is available regarding production in the Base Fab Department during April:

Production data:	
Units (gallons) in process, April 1: materials 100% complete, labor and overhead 60% complete	30,000
Units (gallons) started into production during April	420,000
Units (gallons) completed and transferred to the Finishing Department	370,000
Units (gallons) in process, April 30: materials 50% complete, labor and overhead 25% complete	80,000
Cost data:	
Work in process inventory, April 1:	
Materials	$ 92,000
Labor	21,000
Overhead	37,000
Total cost of work in process	$ 150,000
Cost added during April:	
Materials	$ 851,000
Labor	330,000
Overhead	665,000
Total cost added during April	$1,846,000

Solution to Review Problem

1. a. Work in Process—Base Fab Department	851,000	
Work in Process—Finishing Department	629,000	
Raw Materials		1,480,000
b. Work in Process—Base Fab Department	330,000	
Work in Process—Finishing Department	270,000	
Salaries and Wages Payable		600,000

c.	Work in Process—Base Fab Department	665,000	
	Work in Process—Finishing Department	405,000	
	Manufacturing Overhead		1,070,000
d.	Work in Process—Finishing Department	1,850,000	
	Work in Process—Base Fab Department		1,850,000
e.	Finished Goods	3,200,000	
	Work in Process—Finishing Department		3,200,000

2.

Raw Materials

Bal.	XXX	(a)	1,480,000

Salaries and Wages Payable

		(b)	600,000

Work in Process—Base Fab Department

Bal.	150,000	(d)	1,850,000
(a)	851,000		
(b)	330,000		
(c)	665,000		
Bal.	146,000		

Manufacturing Overhead

(Various actual costs)		(c)	1,070,000

Work in Process—Finishing Department

Bal.	70,000	(e)	3,200,000
(a)	629,000		
(b)	270,000		
(c)	405,000		
(d)	1,850,000		
Bal.	24,000		

Finished Goods

Bal.	XXX		
(e)	3,200,000		

3.

LUXGUARD HOME PAINT COMPANY
Production Report—Base Fab Department
For the Month Ended April 30

Quantity Schedule and Equivalent Units

	Quantity Schedule
Units (gallons) to be accounted for:	
Work in process, April 1 (materials 100% complete, labor and overhead 60% complete)	30,000
Started into production	420,000
Total units to be accounted for	450,000

		Equivalent Units (EU)		
		Materials	Labor	Overhead
Units (gallons) accounted for as follows:				
Transferred to Finishing Department	370,000	370,000	370,000	370,000
Work in process, April 30 (materials 50% complete, labor and overhead 25% complete)	80,000	40,000*	20,000*	20,000*
Total units accounted for	450,000	410,000	390,000	390,000

Costs per Equivalent Unit

	Total Cost	Materials	Labor	Overhead	Whole Unit
Cost to be accounted for:					
Work in process, April 1.	$ 150,000	$ 92,000	$ 21,000	$ 37,000	
Cost added by the Base Fab Department.	1,846,000	851,000	330,000	665,000	
Total cost to be accounted for (a).	$1,996,000	$943,000	$351,000	$702,000	
Equivalent units of production (b)		410,000	390,000	390,000	
Cost per EU, (a) ÷ (b).		$2.30 +	$0.90 +	$1.80	= $5.00

Cost Reconciliation

	Total Cost	Equivalent Units (above)		
		Materials	Labor	Overhead
Cost accounted for as follows:				
Transferred to Finishing Department:				
370,000 units × $5.00 per unit	$1,850,000	370,000	370,000	370,000
Work in process, April 30:				
Materials, at $2.30 per EU	92,000	40,000		
Labor, at $0.90 per EU. . . .	18,000		20,000	
Overhead, at $1.80 per EU	36,000			20,000
Total work in process.	146,000			
Total cost accounted for	$1,996,000			

*Materials: 80,000 units × 50% = 40,000 EUs; labor and overhead: 80,000 units × 25% = 20,000 EUs.
EU = Equivalent unit.

Glossary

Conversion cost Direct labor cost plus manufacturing overhead cost. (p. 158)

Cost reconciliation The part of a department's production report that shows costs to be accounted for during a period and how those costs are accounted for. (p. 161)

Equivalent units The product of the number of partially completed units and their percentage of completion with respect to a particular cost. Equivalent units are the number of complete whole units one could obtain from the materials and effort contained in partially completed units. (p. 157)

Equivalent units of production (weighted-average method) The units transferred to the next department (or to finished goods) during the period plus the equivalent units in the department's ending work in process inventory. (p. 157)

FIFO method A method of accounting for cost flows in a process costing system in which equivalent units and unit costs relate only to work done during the current period. (p. 157)

Operation costing A hybrid costing system used when products are manufactured in batches and when the products have some common characteristics and some individual characteristics. This system handles materials the same as in job-order costing and labor and overhead the same as in process costing. (p. 164)

Process costing A costing method used in situations where essentially homogeneous products are produced on a continuous basis. (p. 150)

Processing department Any location in an organization where work is performed on a product and where materials, labor, or overhead costs are added to the product. (p. 151)

Production report A report that summarizes all activity in a department's Work in Process account during a period and that contains three parts: a quantity schedule and a computation of equivalent units, a computation of total and unit costs, and a cost reconciliation. (p. 151)

Quantity schedule The part of a production report that shows the flow of units through a department during a period and a computation of equivalent units. (p. 160)

Transferred-in cost The cost attached to products that have been received from a prior processing department. (p. 153)

Weighted-average method A method of process costing that blends together units and costs from both the current and prior periods. (p. 157)

Appendix 4A: FIFO Method

The FIFO method of process costing differs from the weighted-average method in two basic ways: (1) the computation of equivalent units, and (2) the way in which costs of beginning inventory are treated in the cost reconciliation report. The FIFO method is generally considered more accurate than the weighted-average method, but it is more complex. The complexity is not a problem for computers, but the FIFO method is a little more difficult to understand and to learn than the weighted-average method.

Equivalent Units—FIFO Method

LEARNING OBJECTIVE 6
Compute the equivalent units of production using the FIFO method.

The computation of equivalent units under the FIFO method differs from the computation under the weighted-average method in two ways.

First, the "units transferred out" figure is divided into two parts. One part consists of the units from the beginning inventory that were completed and transferred out, and the other part consists of the units that were both *started* and *completed* during the current period.

Second, full consideration is given to the amount of work expended during the current period on units in the *beginning* work in process inventory as well as on units in the ending inventory. Thus, under the FIFO method, it is necessary to convert both beginning and ending inventories to an equivalent units basis. For the beginning inventory, the equivalent units represent the work done to *complete* the units; for the ending inventory, the equivalent units represent the work done to bring the units to a stage of partial completion at the end of the period (the same as with the weighted-average method):

The formula for computing the equivalent units of production under the FIFO method is more complex than under the weighted-average method:

FIFO Method
(a separate calculation is made for each cost category in each processing department)

Equivalent units of production = Equivalent units to complete beginning inventory*
+ Units started and completed during the period
+ Equivalent units in ending work in process inventory

$$\text{*Equivalent units to complete beginning inventory} = \text{Units in beginning inventory} \times \left(100\% - \text{Percentage completion of beginning inventory}\right)$$

Or, the equivalent units of production can also be determined as follows:

Equivalent units of production = Units transferred out
+ Equivalent units in ending work in process inventory
− Equivalent units in beginning inventory

To illustrate the FIFO method, refer again to the data for the Shaping and Milling Department at Double Diamond Skis. The department completed and transferred 4,800 units

Exhibit 4A–1
Equivalent Units of Production: FIFO Method

	Materials	Conversion
Work in process, May 1:		
200 units × (100% − 55%)*	90	
200 units × (100% − 30%)*		140
Units started and completed in May	4,600†	4,600†
Work in process, May 31:		
400 units × 40%	160	
400 units × 25%		100
Equivalent units of production	4,850	4,840

*This is the work needed to complete the units in beginning inventory.
†5,000 units started − 400 units in ending work in process = 4,600 units started and completed. The FIFO method assumes that the units in beginning inventory are finished first.

to the next department, the Graphics Application Department, during May. Since 200 of these units came from the beginning inventory, the Shaping and Milling Department must have started and completed 4,600 units during May. The 200 units in the beginning inventory were 55% complete with respect to materials and only 30% complete with respect to conversion costs when the month started. Thus, to complete these units the department must have added another 45% of materials costs (100% − 55% = 45%) and another 70% of conversion costs (100% − 30% = 70%). Following this line of reasoning, the equivalent units for the department for May would be computed as shown in Exhibit 4A–1.

Comparison of Equivalent Units of Production under the Weighted-Average and FIFO Methods

Stop at this point and compare the data in Exhibit 4A–1 with the data in Exhibit 4–6 in the chapter, which shows the computation of equivalent units under the weighted-average method. Also refer to Exhibit 4A–2, which provides a visual comparison of the two methods.

The essential difference between the two methods is that the weighted-average method blends work and costs from the prior period with work and costs in the current period, whereas the FIFO method cleanly separates the two periods. To see this more clearly, consider the following comparison of the two calculations of equivalent units:

Shaping and Milling Department

	Materials	Conversion
Equivalent units—weighted-average method	4,960	4,900
Less equivalent units in beginning inventory:		
200 units × 55%	110	
200 units × 30%		60
Equivalent units of production—FIFO method	4,850	4,840

From the above, it is evident that the FIFO method removes the equivalent units that were already in beginning inventory from the equivalent units as defined using the weighted-average method. Thus, the FIFO method isolates the equivalent units due to work performed during the current period. The weighted-average method blends together the equivalent units already in beginning inventory with the equivalent units due to work performed in the current period.

Production Report—FIFO Method

The steps followed in preparing a production report under the FIFO method are the same as those discussed earlier for the weighted-average method. However, since the FIFO

Exhibit 4A–2 Visual Perspective of Equivalent Units of Production

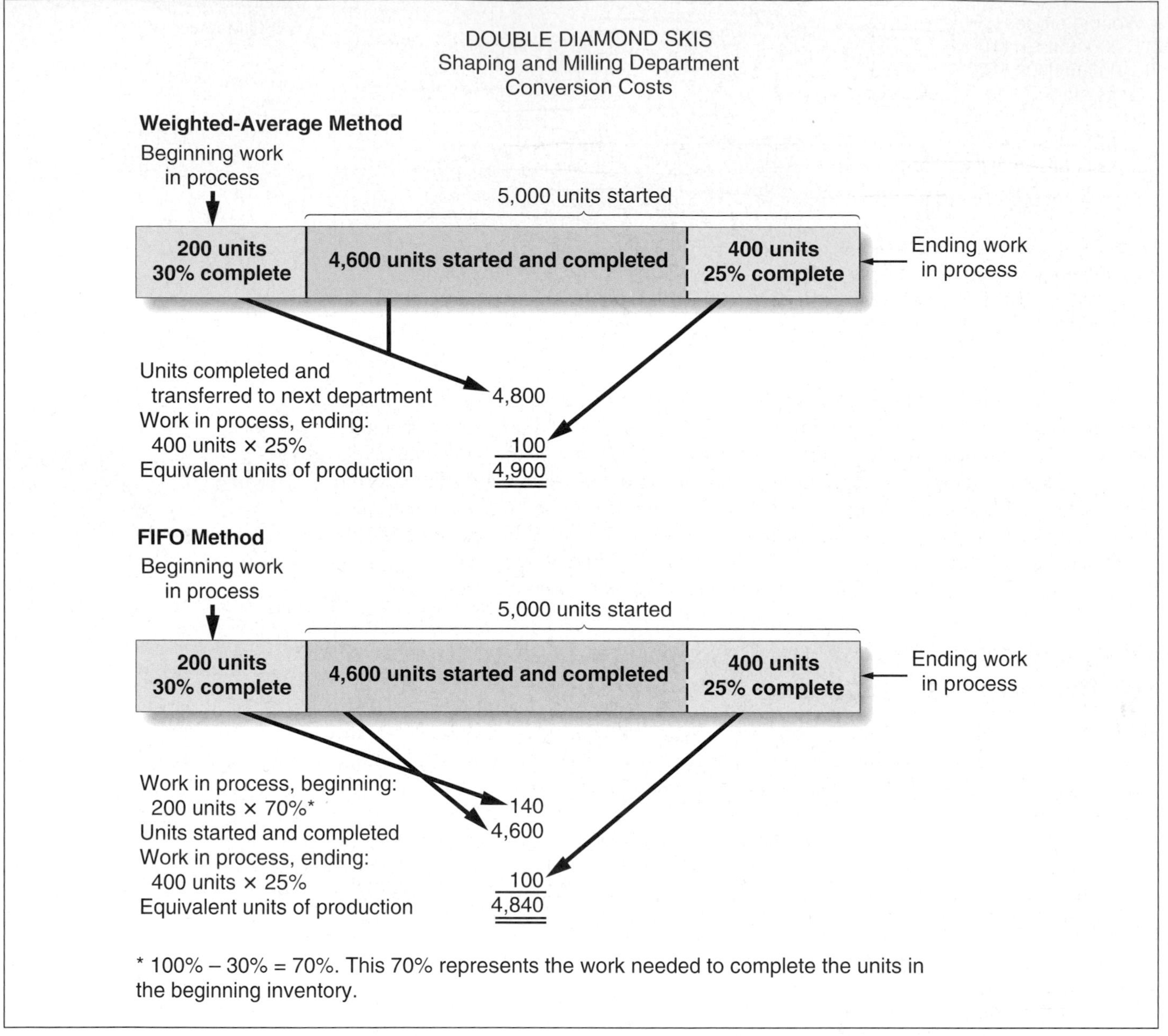

LEARNING OBJECTIVE 7
Prepare a quantity schedule using the FIFO method.

method makes a distinction between units in the beginning inventory and units started during the year, the cost reconciliation portion of the report is more complex under the FIFO method than it is under the weighted-average method. To illustrate the FIFO method, we will again use the data for Double Diamond Skis on page 160.

Step 1: Prepare a Quantity Schedule and Compute the Equivalent Units There is only one difference between a quantity schedule prepared under the FIFO method and one prepared under the weighted-average method. This difference relates to units transferred out. As explained earlier in our discussion of equivalent units, the FIFO method divides units transferred out into two parts. One part consists of the units in the beginning inventory, and the other part consists of the units started and completed during the current period. A quantity schedule showing this format for units transferred out is presented in Exhibit 4A–3, along with a computation of equivalent units for the month.

We explained earlier that in computing equivalent units under the FIFO method, we must first show the amount of work required *to complete* the units in the beginning

Exhibit 4A–3 Production Report—FIFO Method

DOUBLE DIAMOND SKIS
Shaping and Milling Department Production Report
(FIFO Method)

Quantity Schedule and Equivalent Units

	Quantity Schedule	Equivalent Units (EU)	
		Materials	Conversion
Units to be accounted for:			
Work in process, May 1 (materials 55% complete; conversion 30% complete)	200		
Started into production	5,000		
Total units to be accounted for	5,200		
Units accounted for as follows:			
Transferred to the next department:			
From the beginning inventory*	200	90	140
Started and completed this month†	4,600	4,600	4,600
Work in process, May 31 (materials 40% complete; conversion 25% complete)	400	160	100
Total units accounted for	5,200	4,850	4,840

Costs per Equivalent Unit

	Total Cost	Materials	Conversion	Whole Unit
Cost to be accounted for:				
Work in process, May 1	$ 15,175			
Cost added in the department (a)	719,500	$368,600	$350,900	
Total cost to be accounted for	$734,675			
Equivalent units (b)		4,850	4,840	
Cost per EU, (a) ÷ (b)		$76.00	+ $72.50	= $148.50

Cost Reconciliation

	Total Cost	Equivalent Units (above)	
		Materials	Conversion
Cost accounted for as follows:			
Transferred to the next department:			
From the beginning inventory:			
Cost in the beginning inventory	$ 15,175		
Cost to complete these units:			
Materials, at $76.00 per EU	6,840	90*	
Conversion, at $72.50 per EU	10,150		140*
Total cost from beginning inventory	32,165		
Units started and completed this month, at $148.50 per unit	683,100	4,600	4,600
Total cost transferred to the next department	715,265		
Work in process, May 31:			
Materials, at $76.00 per EU	12,160	160‡	
Conversion, at $72.50 per EU	7,250		100‡
Total work in process, May 31	19,410		
Total cost accounted for	$734,675		

*Materials: 200 units × (100% − 55%) = 90 EUs. Conversion: 200 units × (100% − 30%) = 140 EUs.
†5,000 units started − 400 units in ending work in process inventory = 4,600 units started and completed.
‡Materials: 400 units × 40% = 160 EUs. Conversion: 400 units × 25% = 100 EUs.
EU = Equivalent unit.

inventory. We then show the number of units started and completed during the period, and finally we show the amount of work *completed* on the units still in process at the end of the period. Carefully trace through these computations in Exhibit 4A–3.

LEARNING OBJECTIVE 8
Compute the costs per equivalent unit using the FIFO method.

Step 2: Compute the Costs per Equivalent Unit In computing unit costs under the FIFO method, we use only those costs that were incurred during the current period, and we ignore any costs in the beginning work in process inventory. Under the FIFO method, *unit costs relate only to work done during the current period.*

The costs per equivalent unit (EU) computed in Exhibit 4A–3 are used to cost units of product transferred to the next department; in addition, they are used to show the cost attached to partially completed units in the ending work in process inventory.

LEARNING OBJECTIVE 9
Prepare a cost reconciliation report using the FIFO method.

Step 3: Prepare a Cost Reconciliation The purpose of cost reconciliation is to show how the costs charged to a department during a period are accounted for. With the FIFO method, two cost elements are associated with the units in the beginning work in process inventory. The first element is the cost carried over from the prior period. The second element is the cost needed *to complete* these units. For the Shaping and Milling Department, $15,175 in cost was carried over from last month. In the cost reconciliation in Exhibit 4A–3, we add to this figure the $6,840 in materials cost and $10,150 in conversion cost needed to complete these units. Note from the exhibit that these materials and conversion cost figures are computed by multiplying the costs per equivalent unit for materials and conversion times the equivalent units of work needed *to complete* the items that were in the beginning inventory. (The equivalent units figures used in this computation are brought down from the "Equivalent units" portion of the production report.)

For units started and completed during the month, we simply multiply the number of units started and completed by the total cost per unit to determine the amount transferred out. This would be $683,100 (4,600 units × $148.50 per unit = $683,100) for the department.

Finally, the amount of cost attached to the ending work in process inventory is computed by multiplying the cost per equivalent unit figures for the month times the equivalent units for materials and conversion costs in the ending inventory. Once again, the equivalent units needed for this computation are brought down from the "Equivalent units" portion of the production report.

Exhibit 4A–4 summarizes the major similarities and differences between production reports prepared under the weighted-average and FIFO methods.

A Comparison of Costing Methods

In most situations, the weighted-average and FIFO methods will produce very similar unit costs. If there never are any ending inventories, as in an ideal JIT environment, the two methods will produce identical results. The reason for this is that without any ending inventories, no costs can be carried forward into the next period and the weighted-average method will base the unit costs on just the current period's costs—just as in the FIFO method. If there *are* ending inventories, either erratic input prices or erratic production levels would also be required to generate much of a difference in unit costs under the two methods. This is because the weighted-average method will blend the unit costs from the prior period with the unit costs of the current period. Unless these unit costs differ greatly, the blending will not make much difference.

Nevertheless, from the standpoint of cost control, the FIFO method is superior to the weighted-average method. Current performance should be measured in relation to costs of the current period only, and the weighted-average method mixes costs of the current period with costs of the prior period. Thus, under the weighted-average method, the manager's apparent performance in the current period is influenced by what happened in the prior period. This problem does not arise under the FIFO method, since it makes a clear distinction between costs of prior periods and costs incurred during the current period. For the same

Exhibit 4A–4
A Comparison of Production Report Content

Weighted-Average Method	FIFO Method
Quantity Schedule and Equivalent Units	
1. The quantity schedule includes all units transferred out in a single figure.	1. The quantity schedule separates the units transferred out into two parts. One part consists of units in the beginning inventory, and the other part consists of units started and completed during the current period.
2. In computing equivalent units, the units in the beginning inventory are treated as if they were started and completed during the current period.	2. Only work needed to *complete* units in the beginning inventory is included in the computation of equivalent units. Units started and completed during the current period are shown as a separate figure.
Total and Unit Costs	
1. The "Cost to be accounted for" part of the report is the same for both methods.	1. The "Cost to be accounted for" part of the report is the same for both methods.
2. Costs in the beginning inventory are added in with costs of the current period in computations of costs per equivalent unit.	2. Only costs of the current period are included in computations of costs per equivalent unit.
Cost Reconciliation	
1. All units transferred out are treated the same, regardless of whether they were part of the beginning inventory or started and completed during the period.	1. Units transferred out are divided into two groups: (a) units in the beginning inventory, and (b) units started and completed during the period.
2. Units in the ending inventory have cost applied to them in the same way under both methods.	2. Units in the ending inventory have cost applied to them in the same way under both methods.

reason, the FIFO method also provides more up-to-date cost data for decision-making purposes.

On the other hand, the weighted-average method is simpler to apply than the FIFO method, but computers can handle the additional calculations with ease once they have been appropriately programmed.

Questions

4–1 Under what conditions would it be appropriate to use a process costing system?

4–2 In what ways are job-order and process costing similar?

4–3 Costs are accumulated by job in a job-order costing system; how are costs accumulated in a process costing system?

4–4 What two essential features characterize any processing department in a process costing system?

4–5 Why is cost accumulation easier in a process costing system than it is in a job-order costing system?

4–6 How many Work in Process accounts are maintained in a company using process costing?

4–7 Assume that a company has two processing departments—Mixing and Firing. Prepare a journal entry to show a transfer of partially completed units from the Mixing Department to the Firing Department.

4–8 Assume again that a company has two processing departments—Mixing and Firing. Explain what costs might be added to the Firing Department's Work in Process account during a period.

4–9 What is meant by the term *equivalent units of production* when the weighted-average method is used?

4–10 What is a quantity schedule, and what purpose does it serve?

4–11 Under process costing, it is often suggested that a product is like a rolling snowball as it moves from department to department. Why is this an apt comparison?

4–12 Watkins Trophies, Inc., produces thousands of medallions made of bronze, silver, and gold. The medallions are identical except for the materials used in their manufacture. What costing system would you advise the company to use?

4–13 Give examples of companies that might use operation costing.

4–14 (Appendix 4A) How does the computation of equivalent units under the FIFO method differ from the computation of equivalent units under the weighted-average method?

4–15 (Appendix 4A) On the cost reconciliation part of the production report, the weighted-average method treats all units transferred out in the same way. How does this differ from the FIFO method of handling units transferred out?

4–16 (Appendix 4A) From the standpoint of cost control, why is the FIFO method superior to the weighted-average method?

Exercises

EXERCISE 4–1 Process Costing Journal Entries [LO1]

Schneider Brot is a bread-baking company located in Aachen, Germany, near the Dutch border. The company uses a process costing system for its single product—a popular pumpernickel bread. Schneider Brot has two processing departments—Mixing and Baking. The T-accounts below show the flow of costs through the two departments in April (all amounts are in the currency euros):

Work in Process—Mixing

Bal. 4/1	10,000	760,000	Transferred out
Direct materials	330,000		
Direct labor	260,000		
Overhead	190,000		

Work in Process—Baking

Bal. 4/1	20,000	980,000	Transferred out
Transferred in	760,000		
Direct labor	120,000		
Overhead	90,000		

Required:

Prepare journal entries showing the flow of costs through the two processing departments during April.

EXERCISE 4–2 Computation of Equivalent Units—Weighted-Average Method [LO2]

Lindex Company manufactures a product that goes through three departments. Information relating to activity in the first department during October is given below:

		Percent Completed	
	Units	Materials	Conversion
Work in process, October 1	50,000	90%	60%
Started into production.	390,000		
Completed and transferred to the next department	410,000		
Work in process, October 31	30,000	70%	50%

Required:

Compute the equivalent units for the first department for October, assuming that the company uses the weighted-average method for accounting for units and costs.

EXERCISE 4–3 (Appendix 4A) Computation of Equivalent Units—FIFO Method [LO6]
Refer to the data for Lindex Company in Exercise 4–2.

Required:
Compute the equivalent units of production for the first department for October assuming that the company uses the FIFO method for accounting for units and costs.

EXERCISE 4–4 Preparation of Quantity Schedule—Weighted-Average Method [LO3]
Societe Clemeau, a company located in Lyons, France, manufactures cement for the construction industry in the immediate area. Data relating to the kilograms of cement processed through the Mixing Department, the first department in the production process, are provided below for May:

	Kilograms of Cement	Percent Completed	
		Materials	Conversion
Work in process, May 1	80,000	80%	20%
Started into production during May	300,000	—	—
Work in process, May 31	50,000	40%	10%

WIP

Required:
1. Compute the number of kilograms of cement completed and transferred out of the Mixing Department during May.
2. Prepare a quantity schedule for the Mixing Department for May, assuming that the company uses the weighted-average method.

EXERCISE 4–5 (Appendix 4A) Preparation of Quantity Schedule—FIFO Method [LO7]
Refer to the data for Societe Clemeau in Exercise 4–4.

Required:
1. Compute the number of kilograms of cement completed and transferred out of the Mixing Department during May.
2. Prepare a quantity schedule for the Mixing Department for May assuming that the company uses the FIFO method.

EXERCISE 4–6 Quantity Schedule and Equivalent Units—Weighted-Average Method [LO2, LO3]
Gulf Fisheries, Inc., processes tuna for various distributors. Two departments are involved—Cleaning and Packing. Data relating to pounds of tuna processed in the Cleaning Department during May are given below:

	Pounds of Tuna	Percent Completed*
Work in process, May 1	30,000	55%
Started into processing during May	480,000	—
Work in process, May 31	20,000	90%

*Labor and overhead only.

All materials are added at the beginning of processing in the Cleaning Department.

Required:
Prepare a quantity schedule and a computation of equivalent units for May for the Cleaning Department, assuming that the company uses the weighted-average method of accounting for units.

EXERCISE 4–7 (Appendix 4A) Quantity Schedule and Equivalent Units—FIFO Method [LO6, LO7]
Refer to the data for Gulf Fisheries, Inc., in Exercise 4–6.

Required:
Prepare a quantity schedule and a computation of equivalent units for May for the Cleaning Department, assuming that the company uses the FIFO method of accounting for units.

EXERCISE 4–8 Quantity Schedule, Equivalent Units, and Cost per Equivalent Unit—Weighted-Average Method [LO2, LO3, LO4]
Kalox, Inc., manufactures an antacid product that passes through two departments. Data for May for the first department follow:

	Gallons	Materials	Labor	Overhead
Work in process, May 1	80,000	$ 68,600	$ 30,000	$ 48,000
Gallons started in process	760,000			
Gallons transferred out	790,000			
Work in process, May 31	50,000			
Cost added during May	—	907,200	370,000	592,000

The beginning work in process inventory was 80% complete with respect to materials and 75% complete with respect to processing. The ending work in process inventory was 60% complete with respect to materials and 20% complete with respect to processing.

Required:

1. Assume that the company uses the weighted-average method of accounting for units and costs. Prepare a quantity schedule and a computation of equivalent units for May's activity for the first department.
2. Determine the costs per equivalent unit for May.

EXERCISE 4–9 (Appendix 4A) Quantity Schedule, Equivalent Units, and Cost per Equivalent Unit—FIFO Method [LO6, LO7, LO8]

Refer to the data for Kalox, Inc., in Exercise 4–8.

Required:

1. Assume that the company uses the FIFO method of accounting for units and costs. Prepare a quantity schedule and a computation of equivalent units for May's activity for the first processing department.
2. Determine the costs per equivalent unit for May.

EXERCISE 4–10 Equivalent Units and Cost per Equivalent Unit—Weighted-Average Method [LO2, LO4]

Solex Company produces a high-quality insulation material that passes through two production processes. A quantity schedule for June for the first process follows:

	Quantity Schedule		
Units to be accounted for:			
Work in process, June 1 (materials 75% complete; conversion 40% complete)	60,000		
Started into production	280,000		
Total units to be accounted for	340,000		
		Equivalent Units	
		Materials	**Conversion**
Units accounted for as follows:			
Transferred to the next process	300,000	?	?
Work in process, June 30 (materials 50% complete; conversion 25% complete)	40,000	?	?
Total units accounted for	340,000	?	?

Costs in the beginning work in process inventory of the first processing department were: materials, $56,600; and conversion cost, $14,900. Costs added during June were: materials, $385,000; and conversion cost, $214,500.

Required:

1. Assume that the company uses the weighted-average method of accounting for units and costs. Determine the equivalent units for June for the first process.
2. Compute the costs per equivalent unit for June for the first process.

EXERCISE 4–11 Cost Reconciliation—Weighted-Average Method [LO5]

(This exercise should be assigned only if Exercise 4–10 is also assigned.) Refer to the data in Exercise 4–10 and to the equivalent units and costs per equivalent unit you have computed there.

Required:

Complete the following cost reconciliation for the first process:

	Total Cost	Equivalent Units Materials	Equivalent Units Conversion
Cost accounted for as follows:			
Transferred to the next process:			
______ units × ______ each	$?	?	?
Work in process, June 30:			
Materials, at ______ per EU	?	?	
Conversion, at ______ per EU	?		?
Total work in process, June 30	?		
Total cost accounted for	$?		

EXERCISE 4–12 (Appendix 4A) Quantity Schedule, Equivalent Units, Cost per Equivalent Unit—FIFO Method [LO6, LO7, LO8]

Refer to the data for Solex Company in Exercise 4–10. Assume that the company uses the FIFO cost method.

Required:

1. Prepare a quantity schedule and a computation of equivalent units for June for the first process.
2. Compute the costs per equivalent unit for June for the first process.

EXERCISE 4–13 (Appendix 4A) Cost Reconciliation—FIFO Method [LO9]

(This exercise should be assigned only if Exercise 4–12 is also assigned.) Refer to the data in Exercise 4–10 for Solex Company and to the equivalent units and costs per equivalent unit you computed in Exercise 4–12.

Required:

Complete the following cost reconciliation for the first process.

	Total Cost	Equivalent Units (EU) Materials	Equivalent Units (EU) Conversion
Cost accounted for as follows:			
Transferred to the next process:			
From the beginning inventory:			
Cost in the beginning inventory	$?		
Cost to complete these units:			
Materials, at ______ per EU.	?	?	
Conversion, at ______ per EU . . .	?		?
Total cost from beginning inventory	?		
Units started and completed this month:			
______ units × ______ each	?	?	?
Total cost transferred to the next process .	?		
Work in process, June 30:			
Materials, at ______ per EU	?	?	
Conversion, at ______ per EU	?		?
Total work in process, June 30	?		
Total cost accounted for	$?		

Problems

PROBLEM 4–14 Equivalent Units and Cost Reconciliation—Weighted-Average Method [LO2, LO5]

Rovex Company uses a process costing system and manufactures a single product. Activity for July has just been completed. A partially completed production report using the weighted-average method for July for the first processing department follows:

ROVEX COMPANY
Production Report
For the Month Ending July 31

Quantity Schedule and Equivalent Units

	Quantity Schedule			
Units to be accounted for:				
Work in process, July 1 (materials 100% complete, labor and overhead 80% complete)	10,000			
Started into production	100,000			
Total units to account for	110,000			
		Equivalent Units (EU)		
		Materials	**Labor**	**Overhead**
Units accounted for as follows:				
Transferred to the next department	95,000	?	?	?
Work in process, July 31 (materials 60% complete, labor and overhead 20% complete)	15,000	?	?	?
Total units accounted for	110,000	?	?	?

Costs per Equivalent Unit

	Total Cost	Materials		Labor		Overhead		Whole Unit
Cost to be accounted for:								
Work in process, July 1.	$ 8,700	$ 1,500		$ 1,800		$ 5,400		
Cost added by the department . . .	245,300	154,500		22,700		68,100		
Total cost (a).	$254,000	$156,000		$24,500		$73,500		
Equivalent units (b)		104,000		98,000		98,000		
Cost per EU (a) ÷ (b).		$1.50	+	$0.25	+	$0.75	=	$2.50

Cost Reconciliation
Cost accounted for as follows:
?

Required:

1. Prepare a schedule showing how the equivalent units were computed for the first processing department.
2. Complete the "Cost Reconciliation" part of the production report for the first processing department.

PROBLEM 4–15 Production Report—Weighted-Average Method [LO2, LO3, LO4, LO5]
Honeybutter, Inc., manufactures a product that goes through two departments prior to completion. The following information is available about work in the first department, the Mixing Department, during June.

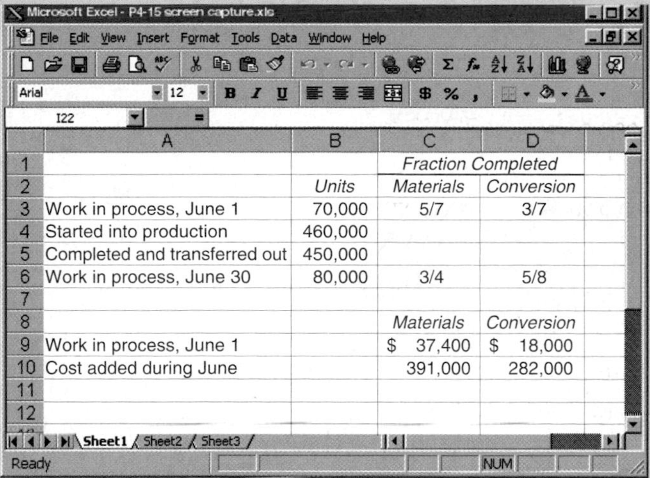

	A	B	C	D
1			*Fraction Completed*	
2		*Units*	*Materials*	*Conversion*
3	Work in process, June 1	70,000	5/7	3/7
4	Started into production	460,000		
5	Completed and transferred out	450,000		
6	Work in process, June 30	80,000	3/4	5/8
7				
8			*Materials*	*Conversion*
9	Work in process, June 1		$ 37,400	$ 18,000
10	Cost added during June		391,000	282,000
11				
12				

Required:

Prepare a production report for the Mixing Department for June assuming that the company uses the weighted-average method.

PROBLEM 4–16 (Appendix 4A) Basic Production Report—FIFO Method [LO6, LO7, LO8, LO9]

Refer to the data for the Mixing Department of Honeybutter, Inc., in Problem 4–15. Assume that the company uses the FIFO method rather than the weighted-average method in its process costing.

Required:

Prepare a production report for the Mixing Department for June.

PROBLEM 4–17 Step-by-Step Production Report—Weighted-Average Method [LO2, LO3, LO4, LO5]

The PVC Company manufactures a high-quality plastic pipe in two departments, Cooking and Molding. Materials are introduced at various points during work in the Cooking Department. After the cooking is completed, the materials are transferred into the Molding Department, in which pipe is formed.

Selected data relating to the Cooking Department during May are given below:

Production data:	
Pounds in process, May 1: materials 100% complete, conversion 90% complete	70,000
Pounds started into production during May	350,000
Pounds completed and transferred to Molding	?
Pounds in process, May 31: materials 75% complete, conversion 25% complete	40,000
Cost data:	
Work in process inventory, May 1:	
Materials cost	$ 86,000
Conversion cost	36,000
Cost added during May:	
Materials cost	447,000
Conversion cost	198,000

The company uses the weighted-average method.

Required:

Prepare a production report for the Cooking Department. Use the following three steps as a guide in preparing your report:

1. Prepare a quantity schedule and compute the equivalent units.
2. Compute the costs per equivalent unit for May.
3. Using the data from (1) and (2) above, prepare a cost reconciliation.

PROBLEM 4–18 (Appendix 4A) Step-by-Step Production Report—FIFO Method [LO6, LO7, LO8, LO9]

Reutter Company manufactures a single product and uses process costing. The company's product goes through two processing departments, Etching and Wiring. The following activity was recorded in the Etching Department during July:

Production data:		
Units in process, July 1: materials 60% complete, conversion 30% complete		60,000
Units started into production		510,000
Units completed and transferred to Wiring		?
Units in process, July 31: materials 80% complete, conversion 40% complete		70,000
Cost data:		
Work in process inventory, July 1:		
Materials cost	$ 27,000	
Conversion cost	13,000	$ 40,000
Cost added during July:		
Materials cost	468,000	
Conversion cost	357,000	825,000
Total cost		$865,000

Materials are added at several stages during the etching process. The company uses the FIFO method.

Required:

Prepare a production report for the Etching Department for July. Use the following three steps as a guide in preparing your report:

1. Prepare a quantity schedule and compute the equivalent units.
2. Compute the costs per equivalent unit for July.
3. Using the data from (1) and (2) above, prepare a cost reconciliation.

PROBLEM 4–19 Interpreting a Production Report—Weighted-Average Method [LO2, LO3, LO4]

Bell Computers, Ltd., located in Liverpool, England, assembles a standardized personal computer from parts it purchases from various suppliers. The production process consists of several steps, starting with assembly of the "mother" circuit board, which contains the central processing unit. This assembly takes place in the CPU Assembly Department. The company recently hired a new accountant who prepared the following partial production report for the department for May using the weighted-average method:

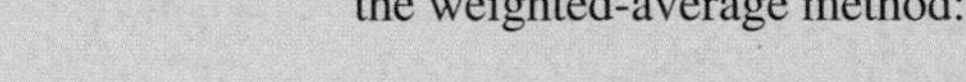

Quantity Schedule	
Units to be accounted for:	
Work in process, May 1 (materials 90% complete; conversion 80% complete)	5,000
Started into production	29,000
Total units	34,000
Units accounted for as follows:	
Transferred to next department	30,000
Work in process, May 31 (materials 75% complete; conversion 50% complete)	4,000
Total units	34,000

Total Cost	
Cost to be accounted for:	
Work in process, May 1	£ 13,400
Cost added in the department	87,800
Total cost	£101,200

Cost Reconciliation

Cost accounted for as follows:

Transferred to next department	£ 93,000
Work in process, May 31	8,200
Total cost	£101,200

The company's management would like some additional information about May's operation in the CPU Assembly Department. (The currency in England is the pound, which is denoted by the symbol £.)

Required:

1. How many units were started and completed during May?
2. What were the equivalent units for May for materials and conversion costs?
3. What were the costs per equivalent unit for May? The following additional data are available concerning the department's costs:

	Total	Materials	Conversion
Work in process, May 1	£13,400	£ 9,000	£ 4,400
Costs added during May	87,800	57,000	30,800

4. Verify the accountant's ending work in process inventory figure (£8,200) given in the report.
5. The new manager of the CPU Assembly Department was asked to estimate the incremental cost of processing an additional 1,000 units through the department. He took the unit cost for an equivalent whole unit you computed in (3) above and multiplied this figure by 1,000. Will this method yield a valid estimate of incremental cost? Explain.

PROBLEM 4–20 Preparation of Production Report from Analysis of Work in Process T-Account—Weighted-Average Method [LO2, LO3, LO4, LO5]

Brady Products manufactures a silicone paste wax that goes through three processing departments—Cracking, Blending, and Packing. All of the raw materials are introduced at the start of work in the Cracking Department, with conversion costs being incurred uniformly as cracking takes place. The Work in Process T-account for the Cracking Department for May follows:

Work in Process—Cracking Department

Inventory, May 1 (35,000 pounds, 4/5 complete)	63,700	Completed and transferred to Blending (_?_ pounds)	?
May costs added:			
Raw materials (280,000 pounds)	397,600		
Labor and overhead	189,700		
Inventory, May 31 (45,000 pounds, 2/3 complete)	?		

The May 1 work in process inventory consists of $43,400 in materials cost and $20,300 in labor and overhead cost. The company uses the weighted-average method to account for units and costs.

Required:

1. Prepare a production report for the Cracking Department for May.
2. What criticism can be made of the unit costs that you have computed on your production report if they are used to evaluate how well costs have been controlled?

PROBLEM 4–21 (Appendix 4A) Preparation of Production Report from Analysis of Work in Process T-Account—FIFO Method [LO6, LO7, LO8, LO9]

Hiko, Inc., manufactures a high-quality pressboard out of wood scraps and sawmill waste. The pressboard goes through two processing departments, Shredding and Forming. Activity in the Shredding Department during July is summarized in the department's Work in Process account below:

Work in Process—Shredding Department

Inventory, July 1 (10,000 pounds, 30% complete)	13,400	Completed and transferred to Forming (_?_ pounds)	?
July costs added:			
Wood materials (170,000 pounds)	139,400		
Labor and overhead	244,200		
Inventory, July 31 (20,000 pounds, 40% complete)	?		

The wood materials are all added at the beginning of work in the Shredding Department. The company uses the FIFO method.

Required:
Prepare a production report for the Shredding Department for July.

PROBLEM 4–22 Equivalent Units; Costing of Inventories; Journal Entries—Weighted-Average Method [LO1, LO2, LO4]
Zap Rap, Inc., is a manufacturer of audio CDs. The company's chief financial officer is trying to verify the accuracy of the December 31 work in process and finished goods inventories prior to closing books for the year. He strongly suspects that the year-end dollar balances are incorrect, but he believes that all the other data are accurate. The year-end balances shown on Zap Rap's books are as follows:

	Units	Costs
Work in process, Dec. 31 (materials 100% complete; conversion 50% complete)	30,000	$ 95,000
Finished goods, Dec. 31	50,000	201,000

There were no finished goods inventories at the beginning of the year. The company uses the weighted-average method of process costing. There is only one processing department.

A review of the company's inventory and cost records has disclosed the following data, all of which are accurate:

		Costs	
	Units	Materials	Conversion
Work in process, Jan. 1 (materials 100% complete; conversion 80% complete)	20,000	$ 22,000	$ 48,000
Started into production	800,000		
Costs added during the year		880,000	2,367,000
Units completed during the year	790,000		

Required:
1. Determine the equivalent units and the costs per equivalent unit for materials and overhead for the year.
2. Determine the amount of cost that should be assigned to the ending work in process and finished goods inventories.
3. Prepare the necessary correcting journal entry to adjust the work in process and finished goods inventories to the correct balances as of December 31.
4. Determine the cost of goods sold for the year, assuming that there is no under- or overapplied overhead.

(CPA, adapted)

PROBLEM 4–23 Comprehensive Process Costing Problem—Weighted-Average Method [LO1, LO2, LO3, LO4, LO5]
Nature's Way, Inc., keeps one of its production facilities busy making a perfume called Essence de la Vache. The perfume goes through two processing departments: Blending and Bottling.

The following incomplete Work in Process account is provided for the Blending Department for March:

Work in Process—Blending

March 1 bal. (40,000 ounces; materials 100% complete; labor and overhead 80% complete)	32,800	Completed and transferred to Bottling (760,000 ounces)	?
Raw materials	147,600		
Direct labor	73,200		
Overhead	481,000		
March 31 bal. (30,000 ounces; materials 60% complete; labor and overhead 40% complete)	?		

The $32,800 figure for the beginning inventory in the Blending Department consisted of the following cost elements: raw materials, $8,000; direct labor, $4,000; and overhead applied, $20,800.

Costs incurred during March in the Bottling Department were: materials used, $45,000; direct labor, $17,000; and overhead cost applied to production, $108,000.

The company uses the weighted-average method in its process costing.

Required:

1. Prepare journal entries to record the costs incurred in both the Blending Department and Bottling Department during March. Key your entries to items (a) through (g) below:
   a. Raw materials were issued for use in production.
   b. Direct labor costs were incurred.
   c. Manufacturing overhead costs for the entire factory were incurred, $596,000. (Credit Accounts Payable and use a single Manufacturing Overhead control account for the entire factory.)
   d. Manufacturing overhead was applied to production using a predetermined overhead rate.
   e. Units that were complete as to processing in the Blending Department were transferred to the Bottling Department, $722,000.
   f. Units that were complete as to processing in the Bottling Department were transferred to Finished Goods, $920,000.
   g. Completed units were sold on account for $1,400,000. The cost of goods sold was $890,000.
2. Post the journal entries from (1) above to T-accounts. The following account balances existed at the beginning of March. (The beginning balance in the Blending Department's Work in Process account is given above.)

Raw Materials	$198,600
Work in Process—Bottling Department.	49,000
Finished Goods	20,000

   After posting the entries to the T-accounts, find the ending balance in the inventory accounts and the manufacturing overhead account.
3. Prepare a production report for the Blending Department for March.

PROBLEM 4–24 Comprehensive Process Costing Problem—Weighted-Average Method [LO1, LO2, LO3, LO4, LO5]

Security Systems, Inc., makes a device that alerts a central dispatching office when activated and emits a radio signal that police can home in on. The device goes through two processing departments—the Assembly Department and the Testing and Packaging Department. The company has recently hired a new assistant accountant, who has prepared the following summary of activity in the Assembly Department for May using the weighted-average method.

Assembly Department costs:	
Work in process inventory, May 1: 8,000 units; materials 70% complete; labor and overhead 20% complete . . .	$ 49,000*
Materials cost added during May	422,000
Labor cost added during May	316,500
Overhead cost applied during May	200,000
Total departmental cost	$987,500

continued

Assembly Department costs assigned to:	
Units completed and transferred to the Testing and Packaging Department: 42,000 units at ? per unit	$?
Work in process inventory, May 31: 5,000 units; materials 60% complete; labor and overhead 20% complete	$
Total departmental costs assigned	$?

*Consists of materials, $28,000; labor, $6,000; and overhead, $15,000.

The new assistant accountant has calculated the cost per unit transferred to the Testing and Packaging Department to be $23.511, as follows:

$$\frac{\text{Total Assembly Department costs, \$987,500}}{\text{Units completed and transferred, 42,000}} = \$23.511$$

However, the assistant accountant is unsure whether he should use this unit cost figure to assign cost to the ending work in process inventory. In addition, the company's general ledger shows only $945,000 transferred to the Testing and Packaging Department, which does not agree with the $987,500 figure above.

The general ledger also shows the following costs incurred in the Testing and Packaging Department during May: materials used, $23,000; direct labor cost incurred, $57,000; and overhead cost applied, $42,000.

Required:

1. Prepare journal entries as follows to record activity in the company during May. Key your entries to the letters (a) through (g) below:
   a. Raw materials were issued to the two departments for use in production.
   b. Direct labor costs were incurred in the two departments.
   c. Manufacturing overhead costs were incurred, $254,000. (Credit Accounts Payable.) The company maintains a single Manufacturing Overhead control account for both departments.
   d. Manufacturing overhead cost was applied to production in each department using predetermined overhead rates.
   e. Units completed with respect to processing in the Assembly Department were transferred to the Testing and Packaging Department, $945,000.
   f. Units completed in the Testing and Packaging Department were transferred to finished goods, $1,080,000.
   g. Units were sold on account for $1,630,000. The cost of goods sold was $1,070,000.
2. Post the journal entries from (1) above to T-accounts. Balances in selected accounts on May 1 are given below:

Raw Materials	$460,000
Work in Process—Testing and Packaging Department	43,000
Finished Goods	30,000

   After posting the entries to the T-accounts, find the ending balance in the inventory accounts and the Manufacturing Overhead account.
3. Prepare a production report for the Assembly Department for May.

Cases

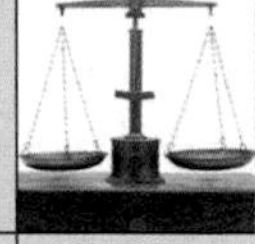

CASE 4–25 Ethics and the Manager; Understanding the Impact of Percentage Completion on Profit—Weighted-Average Method [LO2, LO4, LO5]

Thad Kostowski and Carol Lee are production managers in the Appliances Division of Mesger Corporation, which has several dozen plants scattered in locations throughout the world. Carol manages the plant located in Kansas City, Missouri, while Thad manages the plant in Roseville, Oregon. Production managers are paid a salary and get an additional bonus equal to 10% of their base salary if the entire division meets or exceeds its target profits for the year. The bonus is determined in March after the company's annual report has been prepared and issued to stockholders.

Late in February, Carol received a phone call from Thad that went like this:

Thad: How's it going, Carol?

Carol: Fine, Thad. How's it going with you?

Thad: Great! I just got the preliminary profit figures for the division for last year and we are within $62,500 of making the year's target profits. All we have to do is to pull a few strings, and we'll be over the top!

Carol: What do you mean?

Thad: Well, one thing that would be easy to change is your estimate of the percentage completion of your ending work in process inventories.

Carol: I don't know if I should do that, Thad. Those percentage completion numbers are supplied by Jean Jackson, my lead supervisor. I have always trusted her to provide us with good estimates. Besides, I have already sent the percentage completion figures to the corporate headquarters.

Thad: You can always tell them there was a mistake. Think about it, Carol. All of us managers are doing as much as we can to pull this bonus out of the hat. You may not want the bonus check, but the rest of us sure could use it.

The final processing department in Carol's production facility began the year with no work in process inventories. During the year, 270,000 units were transferred in from the prior processing department and 250,000 units were completed and sold. Costs transferred in from the prior department totaled $49,221,000. No materials are added in the final processing department. A total of $16,320,000 of conversion cost was incurred in the final processing department during the year.

Required:

1. Jean Jackson estimated that the units in ending inventory in the final processing department were 25% complete with respect to the conversion costs of the final processing department. If this estimate of the percentage completion is used, what would be the Cost of Goods Sold for the year?
2. Does Thad Kostowski want the estimated percentage completion to be increased or decreased? Explain why.
3. What percentage completion figure would result in increasing the reported net operating income by $62,500 over the net operating income that would be reported if the 25% figure were used?
4. Do you think Carol Lee should go along with the request to alter estimates of the percentage completion? Why or why not?

CASE 4–26 Production Report of Second Department—Weighted-Average Method [LO2, LO3, LO4, LO5]

Durall Company manufactures a plastic gasket that is used in automobile engines. The gaskets go through three processing departments: Mixing, Forming, and Stamping. The company's accountant (who is very inexperienced) has prepared a summary of production and costs for the Forming Department as follows for October:

Forming Department costs:	
Work in process inventory, October 1, 8,000 units; materials 100% complete; conversion costs 7/8 complete	$ 22,420*
Costs transferred in from the Mixing Department	81,480
Material added during October (added when processing is 50% complete in the Forming Department)	27,600
Conversion costs added during October	96,900
Total departmental costs	$228,400
Forming Department costs assigned to:	
Units completed and transferred to the Stamping Department, 100,000 units at $2.284 each	$228,400
Work in process inventory, October 31, 5,000 units, conversion costs 2/5 complete	—
Total departmental costs assigned	$228,400

*Consists of cost transferred in, $8,820; materials cost, $3,400; and conversion costs, $10,200.

After mulling over the data above, Durall's president commented, "I can't understand what's happening here. Despite a concentrated effort at cost reduction, our unit cost actually went up in the Forming Department last month. With that kind of performance, year-end bonuses are out of the question for the people in that department."

The company uses the weighted-average method in its process costing.

Required:

1. Prepare a revised production report for the Forming Department for October.
2. Explain to the president why the unit cost appearing on the report prepared by the accountant is so high.

CASE 4–27 (Appendix 4A) Production Report of Second Department—FIFO Method [LO6, LO7, LO8, LO9]

Refer to the data for Durall Company in the preceding case. Assume that the company uses the FIFO method to account for units and costs.

Required:

1. Prepare a production report for the Forming Department for October.
2. Assume that in order to remain competitive, the company undertook a major cost-cutting program during October. Would the effects of this cost-cutting program tend to show up more under the weighted-average method or under the FIFO method? Explain your answer.

Group and Internet Exercises

GROUP EXERCISE 4–28 Operation Costing

Operation costing combines characteristics of both job-order costing and process costing. It is used in those situations where the products have some common characteristics and also some individual characteristics. Examples of industries where operation costing may be appropriate include shoes, clothing, jewelry, and semiconductors.

Required:

Select one of the above products and research how the product is made. Construct a flowchart of the production process. Indicate which steps in the production process would use job-order costing and which steps would use process costing.

INTERNET EXERCISE 4–29

As you know, the World Wide Web is a medium that is constantly evolving. Sites come and go, and change without notice. To enable periodic update of site addresses, this problem has been posted to the textbook website (www.mhhe.com/garrison10e). After accessing the site, enter the Student Center and select this chapter. Select and complete the Internet exercise.

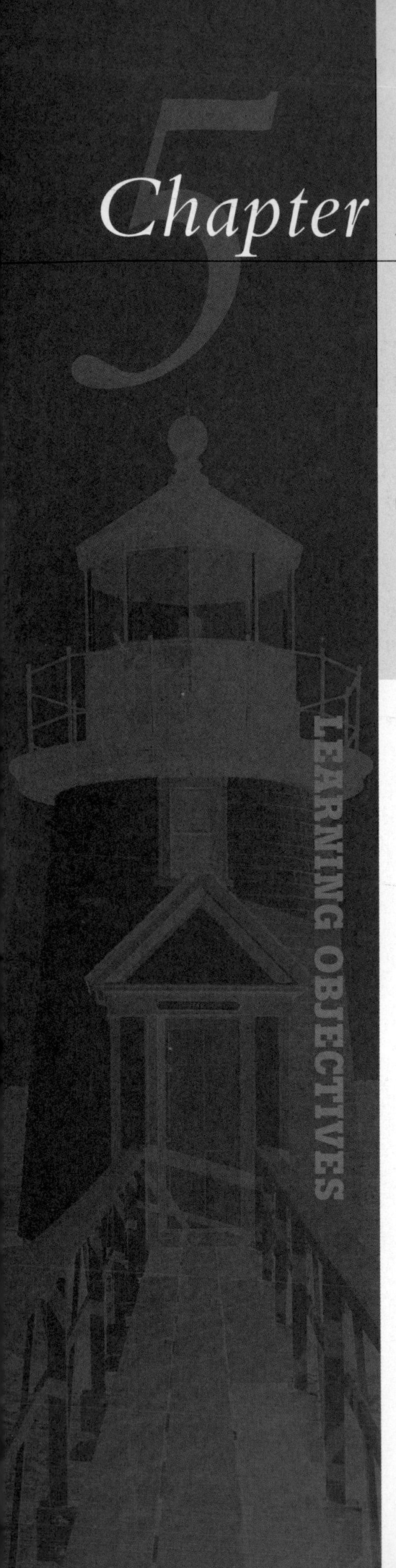

Chapter Five

Cost Behavior: Analysis and Use

After studying Chapter 5, you should be able to:

1. Understand how fixed and variable costs behave and how to use them to predict costs.
2. Use a scattergraph plot to diagnose cost behavior.
3. Analyze a mixed cost using the high-low method.
4. Prepare an income statement using the contribution format.
5. (Appendix 5A) Analyze a mixed cost using the least-squares regression method.

A Costly Mistake

After spending countless hours tracking down the hardware and fixtures he needed to restore his Queen Anne Victorian house, Stephen Gordon recognized an opportunity. He opened Restoration Hardware, Inc., a specialty store carrying antique hardware and fixtures. The company, based in Corte Madera, California, now sells fine furniture, lighting, hardware, home accessories, garden products, and gifts. The company's products, described by some as nostalgic, old-fashioned, and obscure, appeal to wealthy baby boomers. Customers can shop at one of the many Restoration Hardware stores, by catalog, or online at the company's website www.restorationhardware.com.

1998 was a year of phenomenal growth and change for Restoration Hardware. Twenty-four new stores were opened, increasing the total number in the chain to 65. The company's newly launched catalog business was an instant success. Net sales approached $200 million, an increase of almost 114% from the prior year. Gordon, chairman and CEO, took the company public.

The success enjoyed by the company in 1998 did not recur in 1999. Gordon believes his biggest mistake was a failure to consider cost behavior when making decisions to promote the company's products. The most popular furniture items in the store were discounted during the first quarter to encourage customer interest. The company spent $1 million to advertise this big sale, which was far more "successful" than Gordon had imagined. Sales for the first quarter increased by 84% to $60 million. However, much of the increase arose from sales of discounted goods. As a result, margins (that is, differences between sale prices and the cost of the goods that were sold) were lower than usual. Further, because the items placed on sale were larger and heavier than average, the costs to move them from the distribution centers to the stores were considerably higher. The company ended up reporting a loss of $2.7 million for the quarter.

BUSINESS FOCUS

Sources: Restoration Hardware website July 2000; Stephen Gordon, "My Biggest Mistake," *Inc.*, September 1999, p. 103; Heather Chaplin, "Past? Perfect," *American Demographics*, May 1999, pp. 68–69.

In our discussion of cost terms and concepts in Chapter 2, we stated that one way in which costs can be classified is by behavior. Cost behavior refers to how a cost will react or change as changes take place in the level of activity. An understanding of cost behavior is the key to many decisions in an organization. Managers who understand how costs behave are better able to predict what costs will be under various operating circumstances. Attempts at decision making without a thorough understanding of the costs involved—and how these costs may change with the activity level—can lead to disaster. For example, a decision to cut back production of a particular product line might result in far less cost savings than managers had assumed if they confuse fixed costs with variable costs—leading to a decline in profits. To avoid such problems, a manager must be able to accurately predict what costs will be at various activity levels. In this chapter, we shall find that the key to effective cost prediction lies in understanding cost behavior patterns.

We briefly review in this chapter the definitions of variable costs and fixed costs and then discuss the behavior of these costs in greater depth than we were able to do in Chapter 2. After this review and discussion, we turn our attention to the analysis of mixed costs. We conclude the chapter by introducing a new income statement format—called the contribution format—in which costs are organized by behavior rather than by the traditional functions of production, sales, and administration.

Types of Cost Behavior Patterns

Concept 5–1

In Chapter 2 we mentioned only variable and fixed costs. In this chapter we will discuss a third behavior pattern, generally known as a *mixed* or *semivariable* cost. All three cost behavior patterns—variable, fixed, and mixed—are found in most organizations. The relative proportion of each type of cost in an organization is known as its **cost structure**. For example, an organization might have many fixed costs but few variable or mixed costs. Alternatively, it might have many variable costs but few fixed or mixed costs. An organization's cost structure can have a significant impact on decisions. In this chapter we will concentrate on gaining a fuller understanding of the behavior of each type of cost. In the next chapter we will discuss more fully how cost structure impacts decisions.

In Business

Selling Online

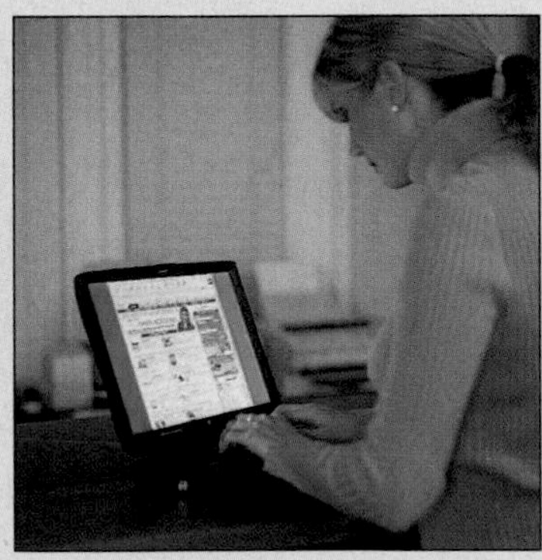

By making investments in technology, many firms have created radically different cost structures from traditional companies. John Labbett, the CFO of Onsale, an Internet auctioneer of discontinued computers, was previously employed at House of Fabrics, a traditional retailer. The two companies have roughly the same total revenues of about $250 million. However, House of Fabrics, with 5,500 employees, has a revenue per employee of about $90,000. At Onsale, with only 200 employees, the figure is $1.18 million per employee. Additionally, Internet companies like Onsale are often able to grow at very little cost. If demand grows, an Internet company just adds another computer server. If demand grows at a traditional retailer, the company may have to invest in a new building and additional inventory and may have to hire additional employees.

Source: George Donnelly, "New @ttitude," *CFO,* June 1999, pp. 42–54.

LEARNING OBJECTIVE 1
Understand how fixed and variable costs behave and how to use them to predict costs.

Variable Costs

We explained in Chapter 2 that a variable cost is a cost whose total dollar amount varies in direct proportion to changes in the activity level. If the activity level doubles, the total dollar amount of the variable cost also doubles. If the activity level increases by only 10%, then the total dollar amount of the variable cost increases by 10% as well.

We also found in Chapter 2 that a variable cost remains constant if expressed on a *per unit* basis. To provide an example, consider Nooksack Expeditions, a small company that provides daylong whitewater rafting excursions on rivers in the North Cascade Mountains. The company provides all of the necessary equipment and experienced guides, and it serves gourmet meals to its guests. The meals are purchased from an exclusive caterer for $30 a person for a daylong excursion. If we look at the cost of the meals on a *per person* basis, the cost remains constant at $30. This $30 cost per person will not change, regardless of how many people participate in a daylong excursion. The behavior of this variable cost, on both a per unit and a total basis, is tabulated as follows:

Number of Guests	Cost of Meals per Guest	Total Cost of Meals
250	$30	$ 7,500
500	30	15,000
750	30	22,500
1,000	30	30,000

The idea that a variable cost is constant per unit but varies in total with the activity level is crucial to an understanding of cost behavior patterns. We shall rely on this concept again and again in this chapter and in chapters ahead.

Exhibit 5–1 provides a graphic illustration of variable cost behavior. Note that the graph of the total cost of the meals slants upward to the right. This is because the total cost of the meals is directly proportional to the number of guests. In contrast, the graph of the per unit cost of meals is flat. This is because the cost of the meals per guest is constant at $30 per guest.

The Activity Base For a cost to be variable, it must be variable *with respect to something*. That "something" is its *activity base*. An **activity base** is a measure of whatever causes the incurrence of variable cost. In Chapter 3, we mentioned that an activity base is sometimes referred to as a *cost driver*. Some of the most common activity bases

Exhibit 5–1 Variable Cost Behavior

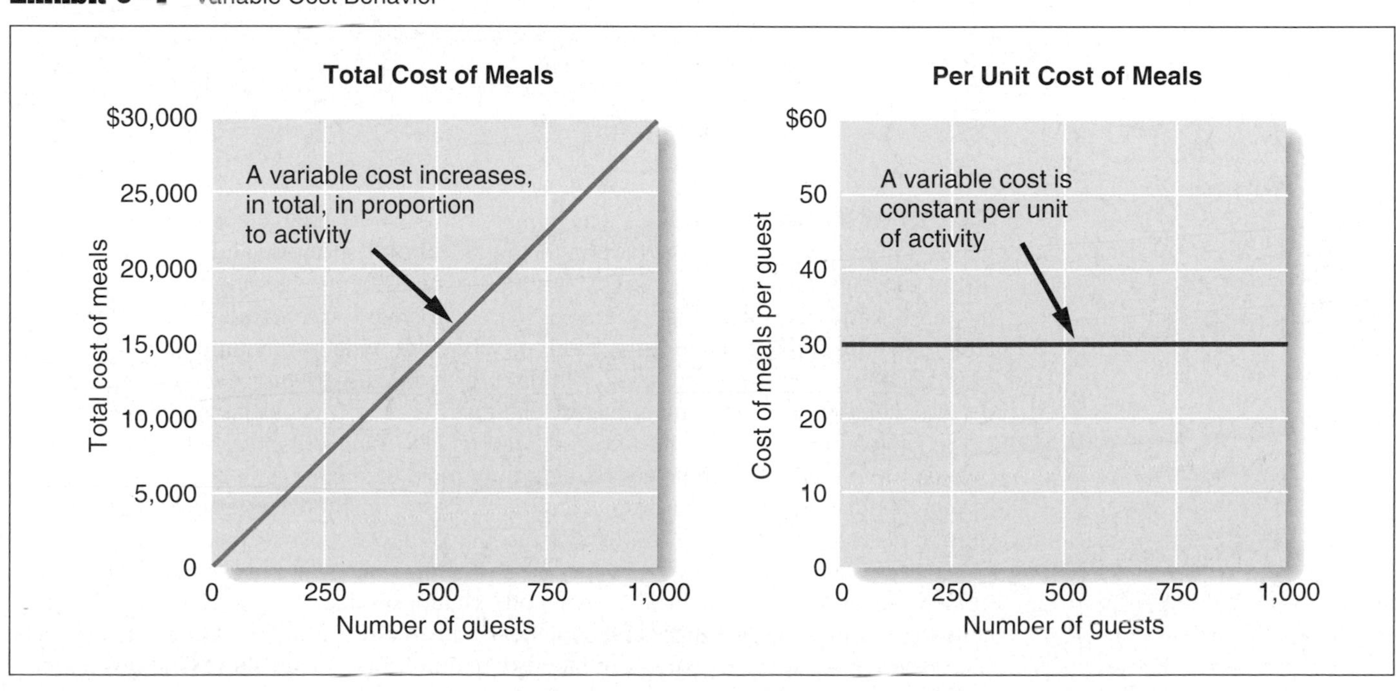

are direct labor-hours, machine-hours, units produced, and units sold. Other activity bases (cost drivers) might include the number of miles driven by salespersons, the number of pounds of laundry cleaned by a hotel, the number of calls handled by technical support staff at a software company, and the number of beds occupied in a hospital.

To plan and control variable costs, a manager must be well acquainted with the various activity bases within the firm. People sometimes get the notion that if a cost doesn't vary with production or with sales, then it is not really a variable cost. This is not correct. As suggested by the range of bases listed above, costs are caused by many different activities within an organization. Whether a cost is considered to be variable depends on whether it is caused by the activity under consideration. For example, if a manager is analyzing the cost of service calls under a product warranty, the relevant activity measure will be the number of service calls made. Those costs that vary in total with the number of service calls made are the variable costs of making service calls.

Nevertheless, unless stated otherwise, you can assume that the activity base under consideration is the total volume of goods and services provided by the organization. So, for example, if we ask whether direct materials at Ford is a variable cost, the answer is yes, since the cost of direct materials is variable with respect to Ford's total volume of output. We will specify the activity base only when it is something other than total output.

In Business

Really Haute Cuisine

Variable costs change in proportion to changes in activity. However, they can also vary from one situation to another due to other factors. For example, as the following discussion illustrates, the variable cost per passenger of airline meals varies considerably.

In August of 2000, the air-worthiness certification of the supersonic Concorde was suspended following a fatal crash after a take-off at Paris' Charles De Gaulle airport. Prior to that time, a New York to Paris round-trip ticket on Air France's supersonic Concorde had cost as much as $10,000. At this price, passengers expected something more than standard airline food. U.S. airlines spend an average of about $3.87 to feed a passenger. Air France budgeted $55 per passenger for the Concorde flight. However, even at $55 per passenger, the meals on the Concorde were undistinguished. Tired of complaints from passengers, the airline hired superstar chef Alain Ducasse to oversee the Concorde's food service. Ducasse struggled with tiny galleys, high-speed take-offs that made a mess of carefully arranged salads, and food that had to be reheated prior to serving. Ducasse demanded, and got, a budget of $90 per passenger from Air France to upgrade the meals on the Concorde.

Source: Shelly Branch, "A Chef's Trials on the Concorde," *The Wall Street Journal,* January 13, 2000, pp. B1 and B4.

Extent of Variable Costs The number and type of variable costs present in an organization will depend in large part on the organization's structure and purpose. A public utility like Florida Power and Light, with large investments in equipment, will tend to have few variable costs. Most of the costs are associated with its plant, and these costs tend to be insensitive to changes in levels of service provided. A manufacturing company like Black and Decker, by contrast, will often have many variable costs; these costs will be associated with both the manufacture and distribution of its products to customers.

A merchandising company like Wal-Mart or J. K. Gill will usually have a high proportion of variable costs in its cost structure. In most merchandising companies, the cost of merchandise purchased for resale, a variable cost, constitutes a very large component of total cost. Service companies, by contrast, have diverse cost structures. Some service companies, such as the Skippers restaurant chain, have fairly large variable costs because of the costs of their raw materials. On the other hand, service companies involved in consulting, auditing, engineering, dental, medical, and architectural activities have very large fixed costs in the form of expensive facilities and highly trained salaried employees.

Exhibit 5–2
Examples of Variable Costs

Type of Organization	Costs that Are Normally Variable with Respect to Volume of Output
Merchandising company	Cost of goods (merchandise) sold
Manufacturing company	Manufacturing costs: Direct materials Direct labor* Variable portion of manufacturing overhead: Indirect materials Lubricants Supplies Power
Both merchandising and manufacturing companies	Selling, general, and administrative costs: Commissions Clerical costs, such as invoicing Shipping costs
Service organizations	Supplies, travel, clerical

*Direct labor may or may not be variable in practice. See the discussion later in this chapter.

Some of the more frequently encountered variable costs are listed in Exhibit 5–2. This exhibit is not a complete listing of all costs that can be considered variable. Moreover, some of the costs listed in the exhibit may behave more like fixed than variable costs in some organizations. We will see some examples of this later in the chapter. Nevertheless, Exhibit 5–2 provides a useful listing of many of the costs that normally would be considered variable with respect to the volume of output.

True Variable versus Step-Variable Costs

Not all variable costs have exactly the same behavior pattern. Some variable costs behave in a *true variable* or *proportionately variable* pattern. Other variable costs behave in a *step-variable* pattern.

True Variable Costs Direct materials is a true or proportionately variable cost because the amount used during a period will vary in direct proportion to the level of production activity. Moreover, any amounts purchased but not used can be stored and carried forward to the next period as inventory.

Step-Variable Costs The wages of maintenance workers are often considered to be a variable cost, but this labor cost doesn't behave in quite the same way as the cost of direct materials. Unlike direct materials, the time of maintenance workers is obtainable only in large chunks. Moreover, any maintenance time not utilized cannot be stored as inventory and carried forward to the next period. If the time is not used effectively, it is gone forever. Furthermore, a maintenance crew can work at a fairly leisurely pace if pressures are light but intensify its efforts if pressures build up. For this reason, small changes in the level of production may have no effect on the number of maintenance people employed by the company.

A resource that is obtainable only in large chunks (such as maintenance workers) and whose costs increase or decrease only in response to fairly wide changes in activity is known as a **step-variable cost.** The behavior of a step-variable cost, contrasted with the behavior of a true variable cost, is illustrated in Exhibit 5–3.

Exhibit 5–3
True Variable versus Step-Variable Costs

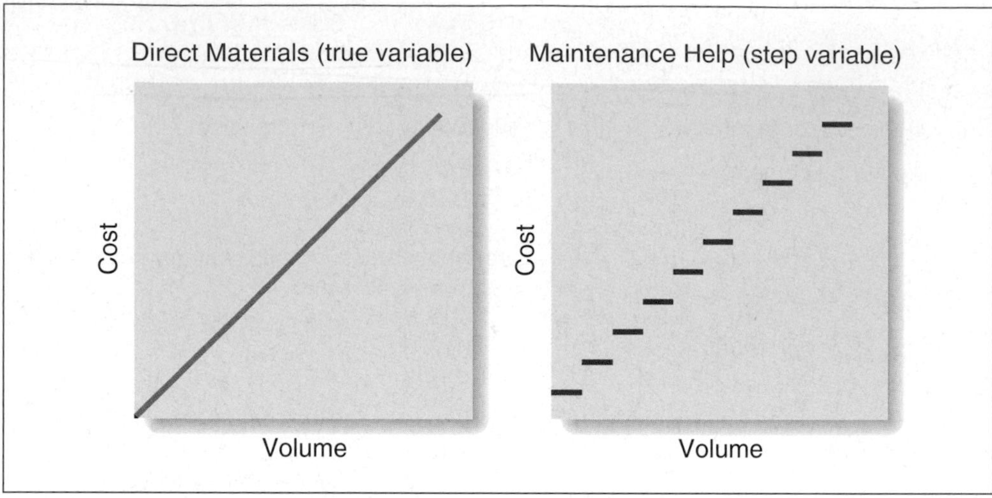

Notice that the need for maintenance help changes only with fairly wide changes in volume and that when additional maintenance time is obtained, it comes in large, indivisible chunks. Great care must be taken in working with these kinds of costs to prevent "fat" from building up in an organization. There may be a tendency to employ additional help more quickly than needed, and there is a natural reluctance to lay people off when volume declines.

The Linearity Assumption and the Relevant Range

In dealing with variable costs, we have assumed a strictly linear relationship between cost and volume, except in the case of step-variable costs. Economists correctly point out that many costs that the accountant classifies as variable actually behave in a *curvilinear* fashion. The behavior of a **curvilinear cost** is shown in Exhibit 5–4.

Although many costs are not strictly linear when plotted as a function of volume, a curvilinear cost can be satisfactorily approximated with a straight line within a narrow band of activity known as the *relevant range.* The **relevant range** is that range of activity within which the assumptions made about cost behavior by the manager are valid. For example, note that the dashed line in Exhibit 5–4 can be used as an approximation to the curvilinear cost with very little loss of accuracy within the shaded relevant range. However, outside of the relevant range this particular straight line is a poor approximation to the curvilinear cost relationship. Managers should always keep in mind that a particular assumption made about cost behavior may be very inappropriate if activity falls outside of the relevant range.

Fixed Costs

In our discussion of cost behavior patterns in Chapter 2, we stated that fixed costs remain constant in total dollar amount within the relevant range of activity. To continue the Nooksack Expeditions example, assume the company decides to rent a building for $500 per month to store its equipment. The *total* amount of rent paid is the same regardless of the number of guests the company takes on its expeditions during any given month. This cost behavior pattern is shown graphically in Exhibit 5–5.

Since fixed costs remain constant in total, the amount of fixed cost computed on a *per unit* basis becomes progressively smaller as the level of activity increases. If Nooksack Expeditions has only 250 guests in a month, the $500 fixed rental cost would amount to $2 per guest. If there are 1,000 guests, the fixed rental cost would amount to only 50 cents per guest. This aspect of the behavior of fixed costs is also displayed in Exhibit 5–5. Note

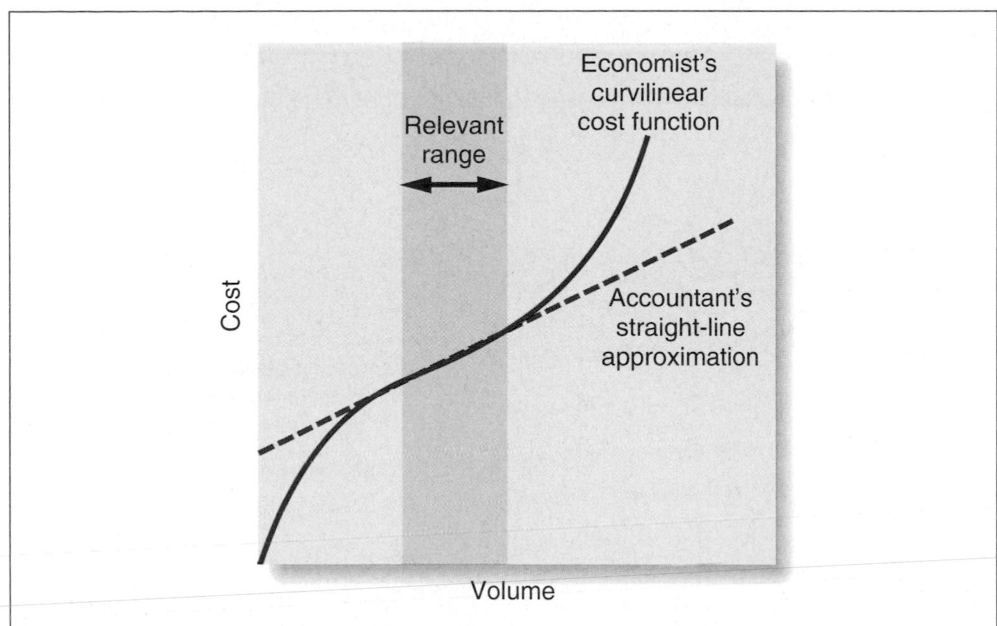

Exhibit 5–4
Curvilinear Costs and the Relevant Range

that as the number of guests increases, the average unit cost drops, but it drops at a decreasing rate. The first guests have the biggest impact on unit costs.

As we noted in Chapter 2, this aspect of fixed costs can be confusing, although it is necessary in some contexts to express fixed costs on an average per unit basis. We found in Chapter 3, for example, that unit product costs for use in *external* financial statements contain both variable and fixed elements. For *internal* uses, however, fixed costs should not be expressed on a per unit basis because of the potential confusion. For internal uses, fixed costs are most easily (and most safely) dealt with on a total basis rather than on a per unit basis.

Squeeze 'Em In

In Business

Airlines have long recognized that once a flight is scheduled, the variable cost of filling a seat with a passenger is very small. The costs of the cockpit flight crew, fuel, gate rentals, maintenance, aircraft depreciation, and so on, are all basically fixed with respect to the number of passengers who actually take a particular flight. The cost of the cabin flight crew is a step-variable cost—the number of flight attendants assigned to a flight will vary with the number of passengers on the flight. The only true variable costs are the costs of meals and a small increase in fuel consumption. Therefore, adding one passenger to a flight brings in additional revenue but has very little effect on total cost. Consequently, airlines have been stuffing more and more seats into their aircraft. Boeing 747s were configured originally with 9 seats across a row, but now they frequently have 10. One major airline has raised the number of seats in its fleet of DC-10 planes from 232 to nearly 300.

Source: Michael J. McCarthy, "Airline Squeeze Play: More Seats, Less Legroom," *The Wall Street Journal*, April 18, 1994, pp. B1 and B6.

Types of Fixed Costs

Fixed costs are sometimes referred to as capacity costs, since they result from outlays made for buildings, equipment, skilled professional employees, and other items needed to provide the basic capacity for sustained operations. For planning purposes, fixed costs can be viewed as being either *committed* or *discretionary*.

Exhibit 5–5 Fixed Cost Behavior

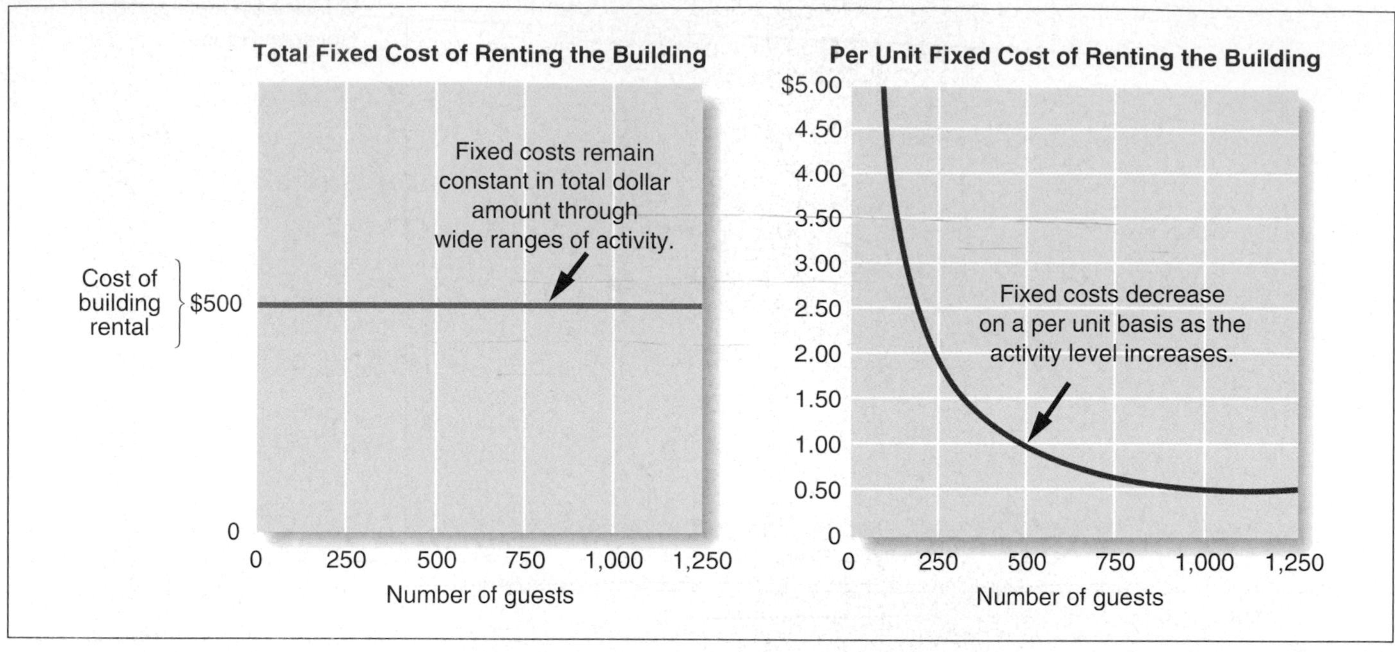

Committed Fixed Costs **Committed fixed costs** relate to the investment in facilities, equipment, and the basic organizational structure of a firm. Examples of such costs include depreciation of buildings and equipment, taxes on real estate, insurance, and salaries of top management and operating personnel.

The two key characteristics of committed fixed costs are that (1) they are long term in nature, and (2) they can't be significantly reduced even for short periods of time without seriously impairing the profitability or long-run goals of the organization. Even if operations are interrupted or cut back, the committed fixed costs will still continue largely unchanged. During a recession, for example, a firm won't usually discharge key executives or sell off key facilities. The basic organizational structure and facilities ordinarily are kept intact. The costs of restoring them later are likely to be far greater than any short-run savings that might be realized.

Since it is difficult to change a committed fixed cost once the commitment has been made, management should approach these decisions with particular care. Decisions to acquire major equipment or to take on other committed fixed costs involve a long planning horizon. Management should make such commitments only after careful analysis of the available alternatives. Once a decision is made to build a certain size facility, a firm becomes locked into that decision for many years to come. Decisions relating to committed fixed costs will be examined in Chapter 14.

In Business | **Sharing Office Space to Reduce Committed Fixed Costs**

Even committed fixed costs may be more flexible than they would appear at first glance. Doctors in private practice have been under enormous pressure in recent years to cut costs. Dr. Edward Betz of Encino, California, has reduced the committed fixed costs of maintaining his office by letting a urologist use the office on Wednesday afternoons and Friday mornings for $1,500 a month. Dr. Betz uses this time to work on paperwork at home and he makes up for the lost time in the office by treating some patients on Saturdays.

Source: Gloria Lau and Tim W. Ferguson, "Doc's Just an Employee Now," *Forbes,* May 18, 1998, pp. 162–172.

While not much can be done about committed fixed costs in the short run, management is generally very concerned about how these resources are *utilized.* The strategy of management must be to utilize the capacity of the organization as effectively as possible.

Discretionary Fixed Costs **Discretionary fixed costs** (often referred to as *managed fixed costs*) usually arise from *annual* decisions by management to spend in certain fixed cost areas. Examples of discretionary fixed costs include advertising, research, public relations, management development programs, and internships for students.

Basically, two key differences exist between discretionary fixed costs and committed fixed costs. First, the planning horizon for a discretionary fixed cost is fairly short term—usually a single year. By contrast, as we indicated earlier, committed fixed costs have a planning horizon that encompasses many years. Second, discretionary fixed costs can be cut for short periods of time with minimal damage to the long-run goals of the organization. For example, spending on management development programs can be reduced because of poor economic conditions. Although some unfavorable consequences may result from the cutback, it is doubtful that these consequences would be as great as those that would result if the company decided to economize during the year by laying off key personnel.

Whether a particular cost is regarded as committed or discretionary may depend on management's strategy. For example, during recessions when the level of home building is down, many construction companies lay off most of their workers and virtually disband operations. Other construction companies retain large numbers of employees on the payroll, even though the workers have little or no work to do. While these latter companies may be faced with short-term cash flow problems, it will be easier for them to respond quickly when economic conditions improve. And the higher morale and loyalty of their employees may give these companies a significant competitive advantage.

The most important characteristic of discretionary fixed costs is that management is not locked into a decision regarding such costs. They can be adjusted from year to year or even perhaps during the course of a year if circumstances demand such a modification.

The Trend toward Fixed Costs The trend in many industries is toward greater fixed costs relative to variable costs. Chores that used to be performed by hand have been taken over by machines. For example, grocery clerks at Safeway and Kroger used to key in prices by hand on cash registers. Now, most stores are equipped with barcode readers that enter price and other product information automatically. In general, competition has created pressure to give customers more value for their money—a demand that often can only be satisfied by automating business processes. For example, an H & R Block employee used to fill out tax returns for customers by hand and the advice given to a customer largely depended on the knowledge of that particular employee. Now, sophisticated computer software is used to complete tax returns, and the software provides the customer with tax planning and other advice tailored to the customer's needs based on the accumulated knowledge of many experts.

S

As machines take over more and more of the tasks that were performed by humans, the overall demand for human workers has not diminished. The demand for "knowledge" workers—those who work primarily with their minds rather than their muscles—has grown tremendously. And knowledge workers tend to be salaried, highly trained, and difficult to replace. As a consequence, the costs of compensating knowledge workers are often relatively fixed and are committed rather than discretionary costs.

Is Labor a Variable or a Fixed Cost? As the preceding discussion suggests, wages and salaries may be fixed or variable. The behavior of wage and salary costs will differ from one country to another, depending on labor regulations, labor contracts, and custom. In some countries, such as France, Germany, China, and Japan, management has little flexibility in adjusting the labor force to changes in business activity. In countries such as the United States and the United Kingdom, management typically has much greater latitude. However, even in these less restrictive environments, managers may choose to treat employee compensation as a fixed cost for several reasons.

First, many companies have become much more reluctant to adjust the work force in response to short-term fluctuations in sales. Most companies realize that their employees are a very valuable asset. More and more, highly skilled and trained employees are required to run a successful business, and these workers are not easy to replace. Trained workers who are laid off may never return, and layoffs undermine the morale of those workers who remain.

In addition, managers do not want to be caught with a bloated payroll in an economic downturn. Therefore, there is an increased reluctance to add workers when sales activity picks up. Many companies are turning to temporary and part-time workers to take up the slack when their permanent, full-time employees are unable to handle all of the demand for the company's products and services. In such companies, labor costs are a curious mixture of fixed and variable costs.

In Business

Labor Laws and Cost Behavior

The labor laws in the country in which the company operates often affect whether employee staff costs are fixed or variable. In Europe, banks have historically had very large numbers of branches, some of which serve very small villages. These branches are expensive to staff and maintain, and banks have argued that they are a drain on profits. In Denmark and the United Kingdom, the number of branches was cut by 34% and 22%, respectively, over a span of 10 years. In both cases, this led to a 15% reduction in staff employees. In contrast, countries with more restrictive labor laws that make it difficult to lay off workers have been unable to reduce staff or the number of branches significantly. For example, in Germany the number of branches was reduced by only 2% and the number of staff by only two-tenths of a percent during the same period.

Source: Charles Fleming, "Kinder Cuts: Continental Banks Seek to Expand Their Way Out of Retail Trouble," *The Wall Street Journal Europe,* March 11, 1997, pp. 1 and 8.

In Business

Employee for Life

Japanese law makes it difficult to lay off or fire workers or to hire away employees from competitors. Exemptions may be granted to the no-layoff rule—particularly for small companies—but this rule effectively ties an employee to a single company for life. As a result, labor is commonly regarded as a fixed cost in Japan. This reduces the ability of Japanese companies to adjust costs in response to peaks and valleys in the business cycle, but there are advantages to this system. "Since Japanese workers enjoy lifetime job guarantees, they see no downside risk in helping employers improve productivity. In fact, they embrace new technology because they know it will enhance their company's future and their own jobs."

Japan's lifetime employment system has another advantage. The really critical business assets are often people. In North America, key employees can easily be hired away by a competitor—taking with them investments in training and their knowledge about the company's innovations and plans. In contrast, the difficulty of hiring a competitor's employees in Japan safeguards those assets and arguably makes Japanese companies more willing to invest in training and in research and development.

The Japanese employment system has an important shock absorber. As much as 40% of workers' compensation is in the form of discretionary bonuses. If a company is doing poorly, these bonuses can be reduced or omitted.

Source: Eamonn Fingleton, "Jobs for Life: Why Japan Won't Give Them Up," *Fortune,* March 20, 1995, pp. 119–125.

Many major companies have undergone waves of downsizing in recent years in which large numbers of employees—particularly middle managers—have lost their jobs.

It may seem that this downsizing proves that even management salaries should be regarded as variable costs, but this would not be a valid conclusion. Downsizing has been the result of attempts to reengineer business processes and cut costs rather than a response to a decline in sales activity. This underscores an important, but subtle, point. Fixed costs can change—they just don't change in response to small changes in activity.

In sum, we cannot provide a clear-cut answer to the question "Is labor a variable or fixed cost?" It depends on how much flexibility management has and management's strategy. Nevertheless, we will assume in this text that, unless otherwise stated, direct labor is a variable cost. This assumption is more likely to be valid for companies in the United States than in countries where employment laws permit much less flexibility.

Fixed Costs and the Relevant Range

The concept of the relevant range, which was introduced in the discussion of variable costs, is also important in understanding fixed costs—particularly discretionary fixed costs. The levels of discretionary fixed costs are typically decided at the beginning of the year and depend on the support needs of planned programs such as advertising and training. The scope of these programs will depend, in turn, on the overall anticipated level of activity for the year. At very high levels of activity, programs are usually broadened or expanded. For example, if the company hopes to increase sales by 25%, it would probably plan for much larger advertising costs than if no sales increase were planned. So the *planned* level of activity might affect total discretionary fixed costs. However, once the total discretionary fixed costs have been budgeted, they are unaffected by the *actual* level of activity. For example, once the advertising budget has been decided on and has been spent, it will not be affected by how many units are actually sold. Therefore, the cost is fixed with respect to the *actual* number of units sold.

Discretionary fixed costs are easier to adjust than committed fixed costs. They also tend to be less "lumpy." Committed fixed costs consist of costs such as buildings, equipment, and the salaries of key personnel. It is difficult to buy half a piece of equipment or to hire a quarter of a product-line manager, so the step pattern depicted in Exhibit 5–6 is typical for such costs. The relevant range of activity for a fixed cost is the range of activity over which the graph of the cost is flat as in Exhibit 5–6. As a company expands its level of activity, it may outgrow its present facilities, or the key management team may

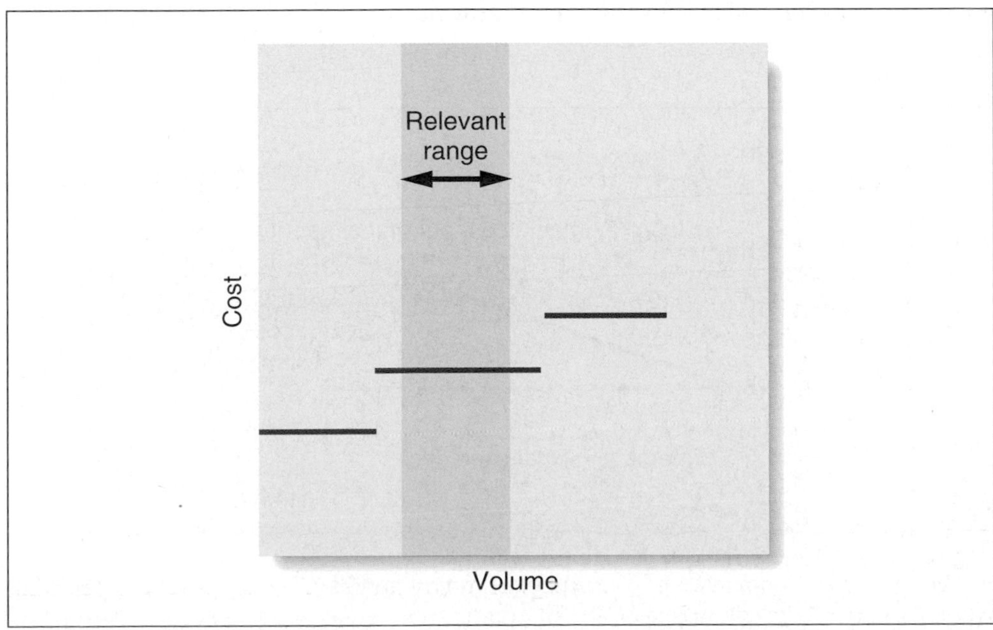

Exhibit 5–6
Fixed Costs and the Relevant Range

need to be expanded. The result, of course, will be increased committed fixed costs as larger facilities are built and as new management positions are created.

One reaction to the step pattern depicted in Exhibit 5–6 is to say that discretionary and committed fixed costs are really just step-variable costs. To some extent this is true, since almost *all* costs can be adjusted in the long run. There are two major differences, however, between the step-variable costs depicted earlier in Exhibit 5–3 and the fixed costs depicted in Exhibit 5–6.

The first difference is that the step-variable costs can often be adjusted quickly as conditions change, whereas once fixed costs have been set, they often can't be changed easily. A step-variable cost such as maintenance labor, for example, can be adjusted upward or downward by hiring and laying off maintenance workers. By contrast, once a company has signed a lease for a building, it is locked into that level of lease cost for the life of the contract.

The second difference is that the *width of the steps* depicted for step-variable costs is much narrower than the width of the steps depicted for the fixed costs in Exhibit 5–6. The width of the steps relates to volume or level of activity. For step-variable costs, the width of a step might be 40 hours of activity or less if one is dealing, for example, with maintenance labor cost. For fixed costs, however, the width of a step might be *thousands* or even *tens of thousands* of hours of activity. In essence, the width of the steps for step-variable costs is generally so narrow that these costs can be treated essentially as variable costs for most purposes. The width of the steps for fixed costs, on the other hand, is so wide that these costs must generally be treated as being entirely fixed within the relevant range.

Mixed Costs

A **mixed cost** is one that contains both variable and fixed cost elements. Mixed costs are also known as semivariable costs. To continue the Nooksack Expeditions example, the company must pay a license fee of $25,000 per year plus $3 per rafting party to the state's Department of Natural Resources. If the company runs 1,000 rafting parties this year, then the total fees paid to the state would be $28,000, made up of $25,000 in fixed cost plus $3,000 in variable cost. The behavior of this mixed cost is shown graphically in Exhibit 5–7.

Even if Nooksack fails to attract any customers, the company will still have to pay the license fee of $25,000. This is why the cost line in Exhibit 5–7 intersects the vertical cost axis at the $25,000 point. For each rafting party the company organizes, the total cost of the state fees will increase by $3. Therefore, the total cost line slopes upward as the variable cost element is added to the fixed cost element.

Exhibit 5–7
Mixed Cost Behavior

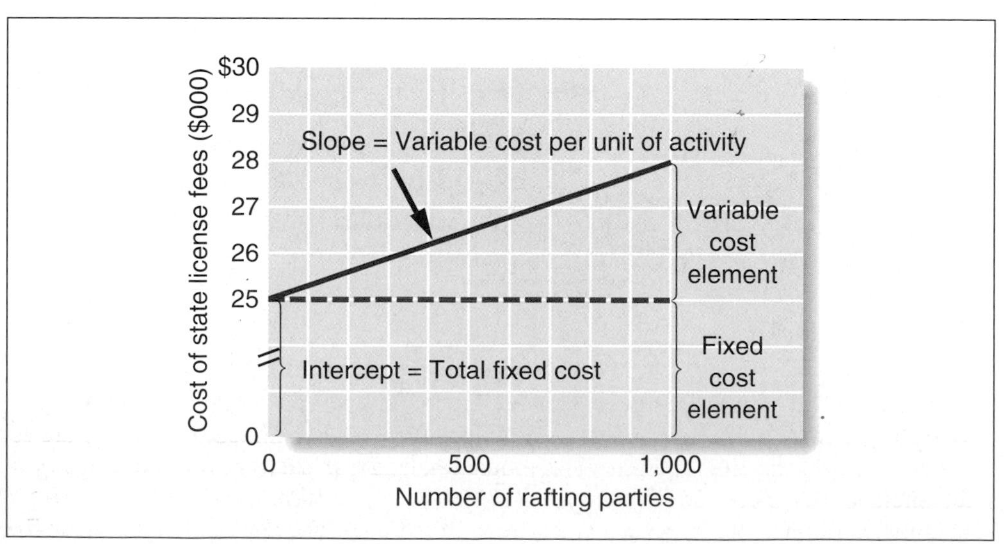

Since the mixed cost in Exhibit 5–7 is represented by a straight line, the following equation for a straight line can be used to express the relationship between mixed cost and the level of activity:

$$Y = a + bX$$

In this equation,

Y = The total mixed cost

a = The total fixed cost (the vertical intercept of the line)

b = The variable cost per unit of activity (the slope of the line)

X = The level of activity

Since the variable cost per unit equals the slope of the straight line, the steeper the slope, the higher the variable cost per unit.

In the case of the state fees paid by Nooksack Expeditions, the equation is written as follows:

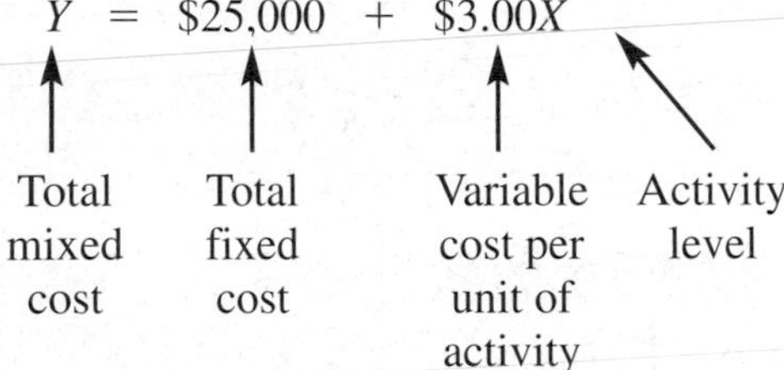

This equation makes it very easy to calculate what the total mixed cost would be for any level of activity within the relevant range. For example, suppose that the company expects to organize 800 rafting parties in the next year. Then the total state fees would be $27,400 calculated as follows:

$$\begin{aligned} Y &= \$25{,}000 + (\$3.00 \text{ per rafting party} \times 800 \text{ rafting parties}) \\ &= \$27{,}400 \end{aligned}$$

Cost Behavior in the U.S. and Japan

In Business

A total of 257 American and 40 Japanese manufacturing firms responded to a questionnaire concerning their management accounting practices. Among other things, the firms were asked whether they classified certain costs as variable, semivariable, or fixed. Some of the results are summarized in Exhibit 5–8. Note that firms do not all classify costs in the same way. For example, roughly 45% of the U.S. firms classify material-handling labor costs as variable, 35% as semivariable, and 20% as fixed. Also note that the Japanese firms are much more likely than U.S. firms to classify labor costs as fixed.

Source: NAA Tokyo Affiliate, "Management Accounting in the Advanced Management Surrounding—Comparative Study on Survey in Japan and U.S.A."

The Analysis of Mixed Costs

In practice, mixed costs are very common. For example, the cost of providing X-ray services to patients at the Harvard Medical School Hospital is a mixed cost. There are substantial fixed costs for equipment depreciation and for salaries for radiologists and technicians, but there are also variable costs for X-ray film, power, and supplies. At Southwest Airlines, maintenance costs are a mixed cost. The company must incur fixed

Exhibit 5–8
Percentages of Firms Classifying Specific Costs as Variable, Semivariable, or Fixed

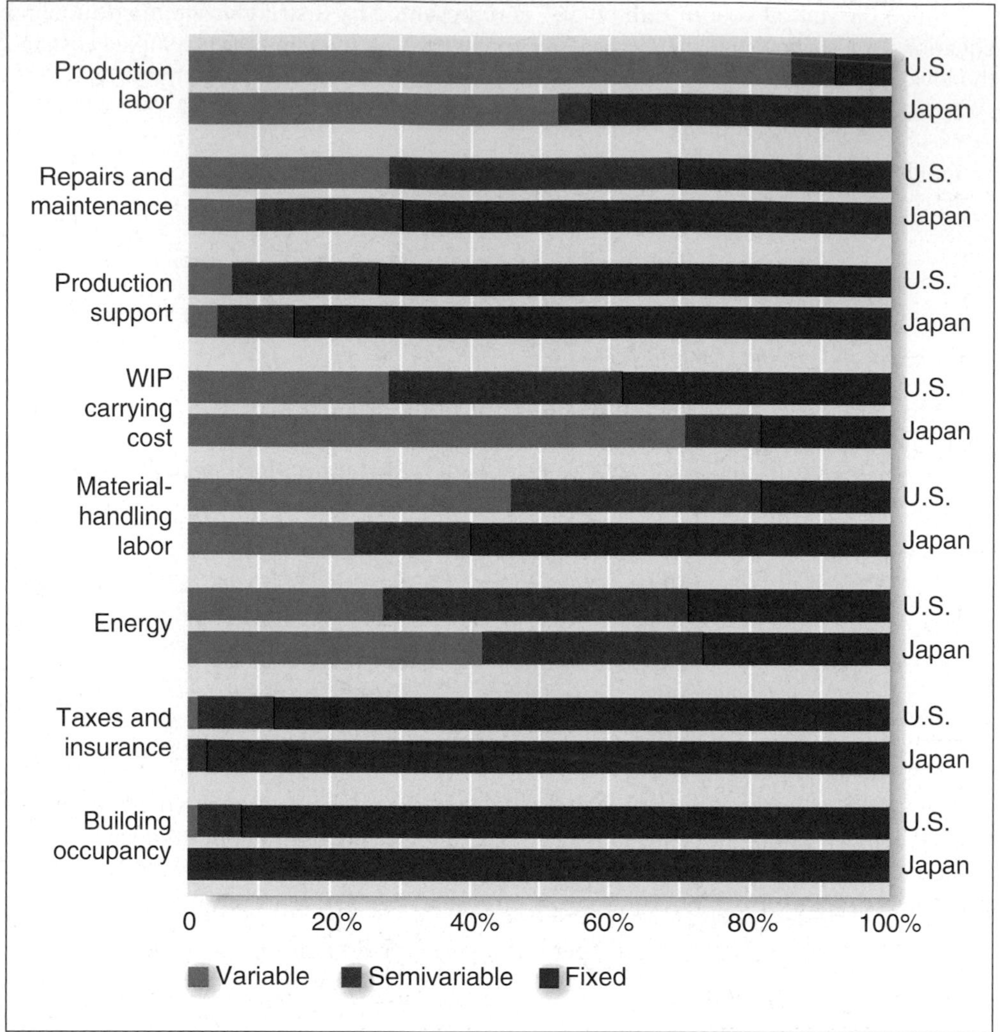

costs for renting maintenance facilities and for keeping skilled mechanics on the payroll, but the costs of replacement parts, lubricating oils, tires, and so forth, are variable with respect to how often and how far the company's aircraft are flown.

The fixed portion of a mixed cost represents the basic, minimum cost of just having a service *ready and available* for use. The variable portion represents the cost incurred for *actual consumption* of the service. The variable element varies in proportion to the amount of service that is consumed.

How does management go about actually estimating the fixed and variable components of a mixed cost? The most common methods used in practice and later in this text are *account analysis* and the *engineering approach.*

In **account analysis,** each account under consideration is classified as either variable or fixed based on the analyst's prior knowledge of how the cost in the account behaves. For example, direct materials would be classified as variable and a building lease cost would be classified as fixed because of the nature of those costs. The total fixed cost of an organization is the sum of the costs for the accounts that have been classified as fixed. The variable cost per unit is estimated by dividing the sum of the costs for the accounts that have been classified as variable by the total activity.

The **engineering approach** to cost analysis involves a detailed analysis of what cost behavior should be, based on an industrial engineer's evaluation of the production methods to be used, the materials specifications, labor requirements, equipment usage, efficiency of production, power consumption, and so on. For example, Pizza Hut might use

the engineering approach to estimate the cost of serving a particular take-out pizza. The cost of the pizza would be estimated by carefully costing the specific ingredients used to make the pizza, the power consumed to cook the pizza, and the cost of the container the pizza is delivered in. The engineering approach must be used in those situations where no past experience is available concerning activity and costs. In addition, it is sometimes used together with other methods to improve the accuracy of cost analysis.

Account analysis works best when analyzing costs at a fairly aggregated level, such as the cost of serving patients in the emergency room (ER) of Cook County General Hospital. The costs of drugs, supplies, forms, wages, equipment, and so on, can be roughly classified as variable or fixed and a mixed cost formula for the overall cost of the emergency room can be estimated fairly quickly. However, this method glosses over the fact that some of the accounts may have elements of both fixed and variable costs. For example, the cost of electricity for the ER is a mixed cost. Most of the electricity is used for heating and lighting and is a fixed cost. However, the consumption of electricity increases with activity in the ER since diagnostic equipment, operating theater lights, defibrillators, and so on, all consume electricity. The most effective way to estimate the fixed and variable elements of such a mixed cost may be to analyze past records of cost and activity data. These records should reveal whether electrical costs vary significantly with the number of patients and if so, by how much. The remainder of this section will be concerned with how to conduct such an analysis of past cost and activity data.

Managerial Accounting in Action

The Issue

Dr. Derek Chalmers, the chief executive officer of Brentline Hospital, motioned Kinh Nguyen, the chief financial officer of the hospital, into his office.

Derek: Kinh, come on in.

Kinh: What can I do for you?

Derek: Well for one, could you get the government to rescind the bookcase full of regulations against the wall over there?

Kinh: Sorry, that's a bit beyond my authority.

Derek: Just wishing, Kinh. Actually, I wanted to talk to you about our maintenance expenses. I don't usually pay attention to such things, but these expenses seem to be bouncing around a lot. Over the last half year or so they have been as low as $7,400 and as high as $9,800 per month.

Kinh: Actually, that's a pretty normal variation in those expenses.

Derek: Well, we budgeted a constant $8,400 a month. Can't we do a better job of predicting what these costs are going to be? And how do we know when we've spent too much in a month? Shouldn't there be some explanation for these variations?

Kinh: Now that you mention it, we are in the process of tightening up our budgeting process. Our first step is to break all of our costs down into fixed and variable components.

Derek: How will that help?

Kinh: Well, that will permit us to predict what the level of costs will be. Some costs are fixed and shouldn't change much. Other costs go up and down as our activity goes up and down. The trick is to figure out what is driving the variable component of the costs.

Derek: What about the maintenance costs?

Kinh: My guess is that the variations in maintenance costs are being driven by our overall level of activity. When we treat more patients, our equipment is used more intensively, which leads to more maintenance expense.

Derek: How would you measure the level of overall activity? Would you use patient-days?

Kinh: I think so. Each day a patient is in the hospital counts as one patient-day. The greater the number of patient-days in a month, the busier we are. Besides, our budgeting is all based on projected patient-days.

Derek: Okay, so suppose you are able to break the maintenance costs down into fixed and variable components. What will that do for us?

Kinh: Basically, I will be able to predict what maintenance costs should be as a function of the number of patient-days.

Derek: I can see where that would be useful. We could use it to predict costs for budgeting purposes.

Kinh: We could also use it as a benchmark. Based on the actual number of patient-days for a period, I can predict what the maintenance costs should have been. We can compare this to the actual spending on maintenance.

Derek: Sounds good to me. Let me know when you get the results.

Diagnosing Cost Behavior with a Scattergraph Plot

LEARNING OBJECTIVE 2
Use a scattergraph plot to diagnose cost behavior.

Kinh Nguyen began his analysis of maintenance costs by collecting cost and activity data for a number of recent months. Those data are displayed below:

Month	Activity Level: Patient-Days	Maintenance Cost Incurred
January	5,600	$7,900
February	7,100	8,500
March.	5,000	7,400
April	6,500	8,200
May	7,300	9,100
June.	8,000	9,800
July	6,200	7,800

The first step in analyzing the cost and activity data should be to plot the data on a scattergraph. This plot will immediately reveal any nonlinearities or other problems with the data. The scattergraph of maintenance costs versus patient-days at Brentline Hospital is reproduced in the first panel of Exhibit 5–9. Two things should be noted about this scattergraph:

1. The total maintenance cost, *Y*, is plotted on the vertical axis. Cost is known as the **dependent variable,** since the amount of cost incurred during a period depends on the level of activity for the period. (That is, as the level of activity increases, total cost will also ordinarily increase.)
2. The activity, *X* (patient-days in this case), is plotted on the horizontal axis. Activity is known as the **independent variable,** since it causes variations in the cost.

From the scattergraph, it is evident that maintenance costs do increase with the number of patient-days. In addition, the scattergraph reveals that the relation between maintenance costs and patient-days is approximately *linear*. In other words, the points lie more or less along a straight line. Such a straight line has been drawn using a ruler in the second panel of Exhibit 5–9. Cost behavior is said to be **linear** whenever a straight line is a reasonable approximation for the relation between cost and activity. Note that the data points do not fall exactly on the straight line. This will almost always happen in practice; the relation is seldom perfectly linear.

Note that the straight line in Exhibit 5–9 has been drawn through the point representing 7,300 patient-days and a total maintenance cost of $9,100. Drawing the straight line through one of the data points allows the analyst to make a quick-and-dirty estimate of variable and fixed costs. The vertical intercept where the straight line crosses the *Y* axis—in this case, about $3,300—is the rough estimate of the fixed cost. The variable cost can be quickly estimated by subtracting the estimated fixed cost from the total cost at the point lying on the straight line.

Total maintenance cost for 7,300 patient-days (a point falling on the straight line).	$9,100
Less estimated fixed cost (the vertical intercept)	3,300
Estimated total variable cost for 7,300 patient-days	$5,800

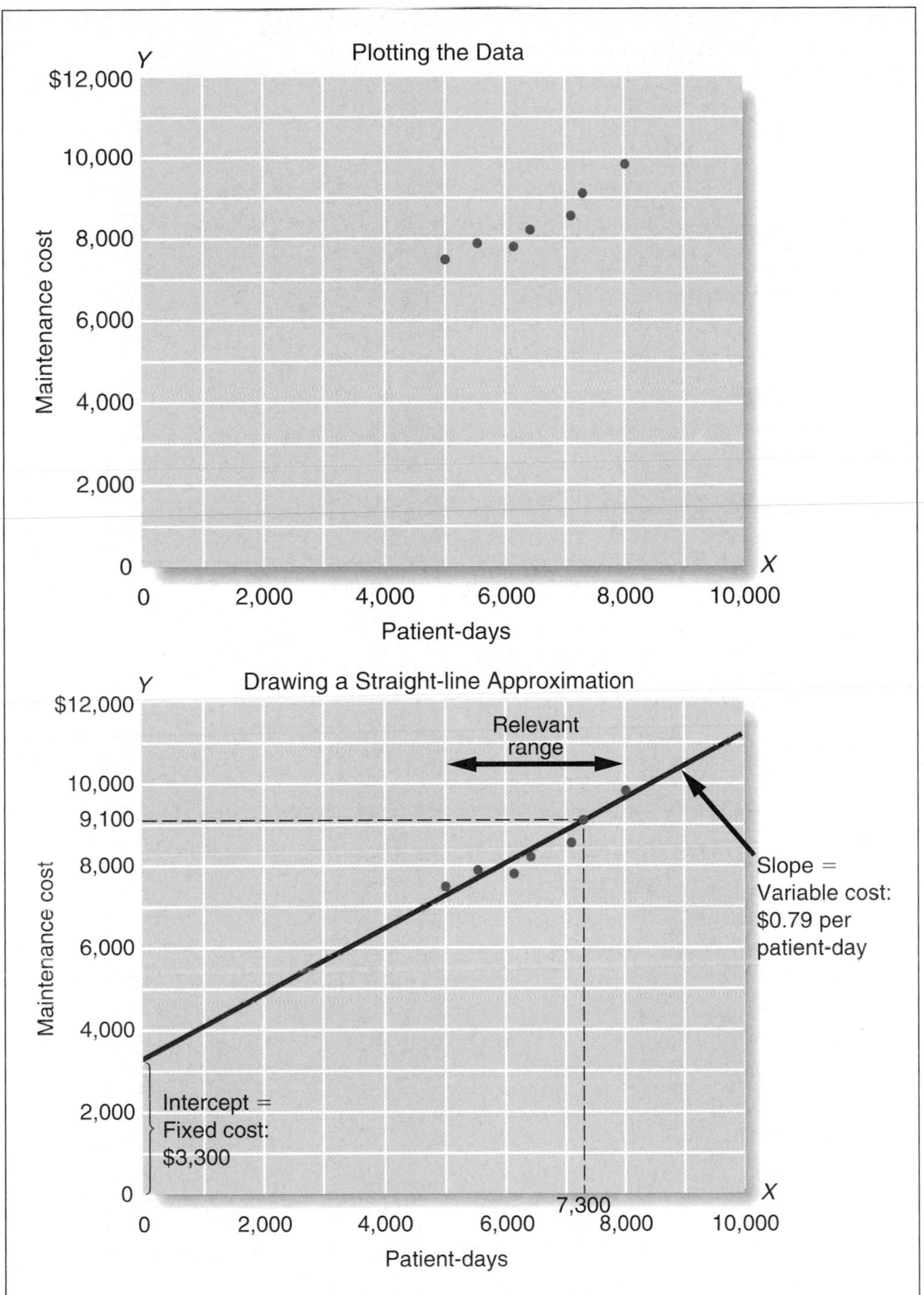

Exhibit 5–9
Scattergraph Method of Cost Analysis

The average variable cost per unit at 7,300 patient-days is computed as follows:

$$\begin{aligned}\text{Variable cost per unit} &= \$5{,}800 \div 7{,}300 \text{ patient-days}\\ &= \$0.79 \text{ per patient-day (rounded)}\end{aligned}$$

Combining the estimate of the fixed cost and the estimate of the variable cost per patient-day, we can write the relation between cost and activity as follows:

$$Y = \$3{,}300 + \$0.79X$$

where X is the number of patient-days.

We hasten to add that this *is* a quick-and-dirty method of estimating the fixed and variable cost elements of a mixed cost; it is seldom used in practice when significant matters

Exhibit 5–10
More than One Relevant Range

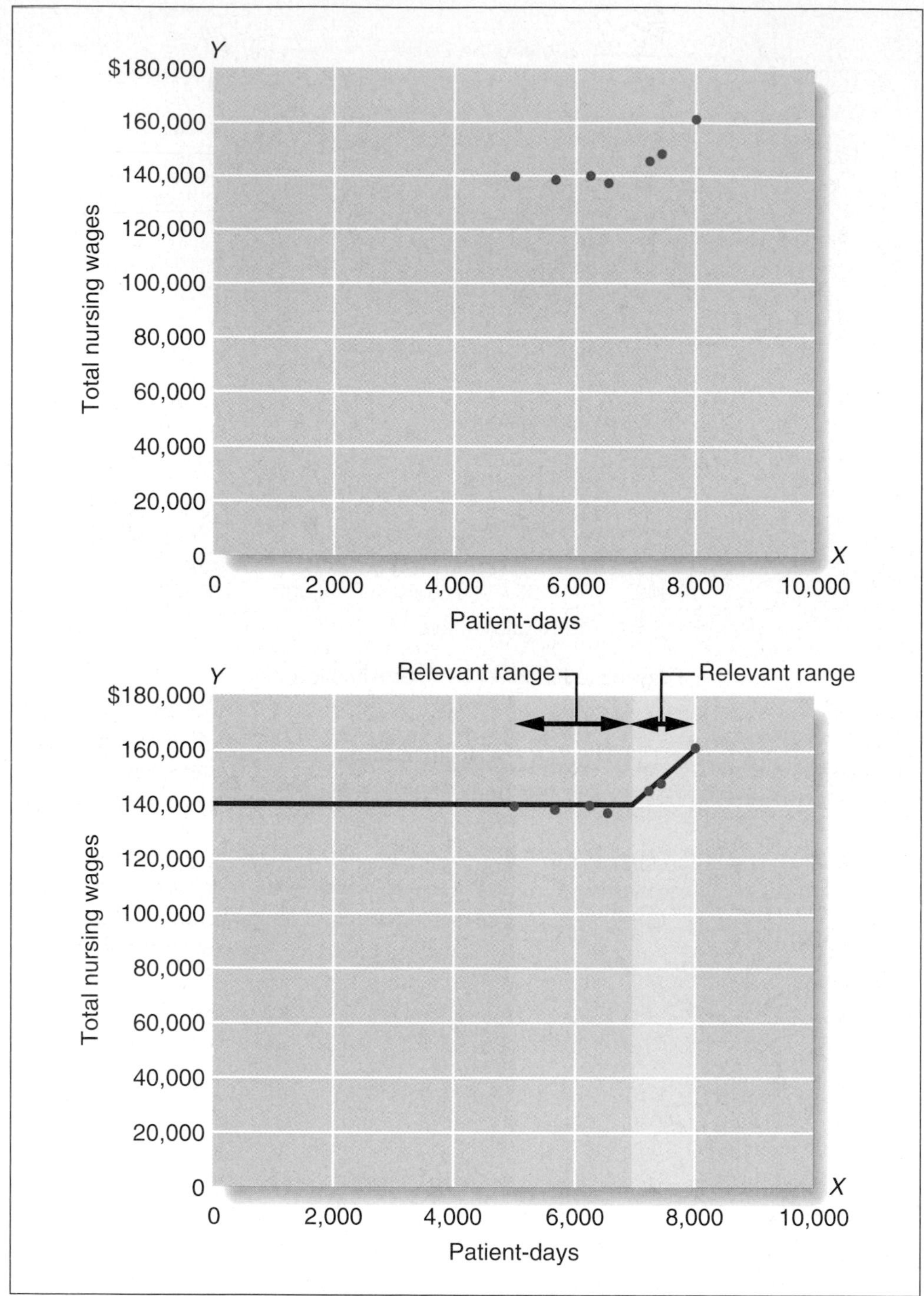

are at stake. However, setting aside the estimates of the fixed and variable cost elements, plotting the data on a scattergraph is an essential diagnostic step that is too often overlooked. Suppose, for example, we had been interested in the relation between total nursing wages and the number of patient-days at the hospital. The permanent, full-time nursing staff can handle up to 7,000 patient-days in a month. Beyond that level of activity, part-time nurses must be called in to help out. The cost and activity data for nurses are plotted on the scattergraph in Exhibit 5–10. Looking at that scattergraph, it is evident that two straight lines would do a much better job of fitting the data than a single straight line. Up to 7,000 patient-days, total nursing wages are essentially a fixed cost. Above 7,000 patient-days, total nursing wages are a mixed cost. This happens because, as stated above, the

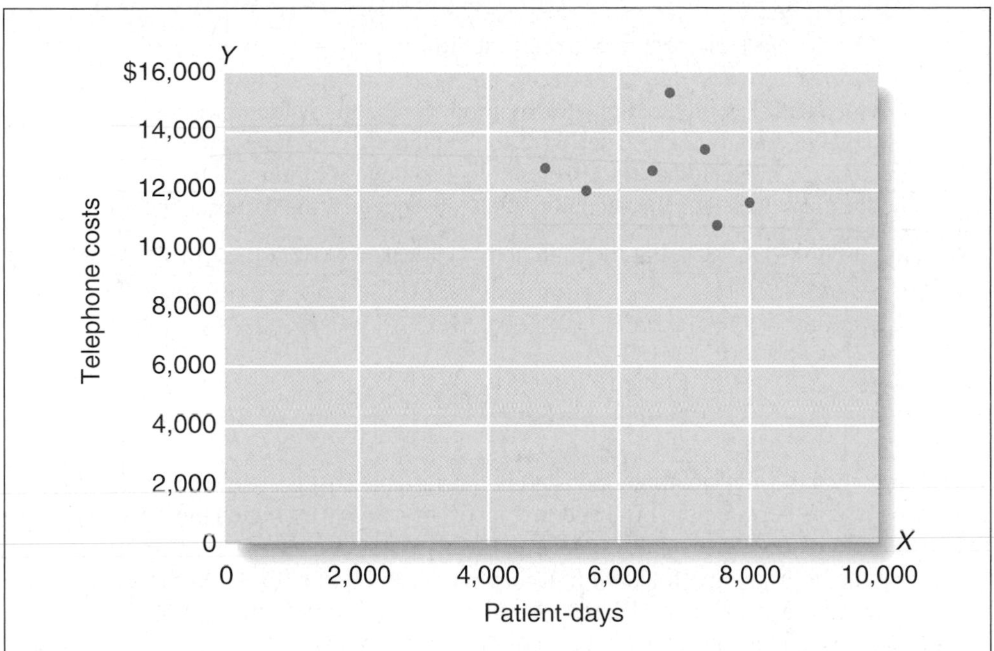

Exhibit 5–11
A Diagnostic Scattergraph Plot

permanent, full-time nursing staff can handle up to 7,000 patient-days in a month. Above that level, part-time nurses are called in to help, which adds to the cost. Consequently, two straight lines (and two equations) would be used to represent total nursing wages—one for the relevant range of 5,600 to 7,000 patient-days and one for the relevant range of 7,000 to 8,000 patient-days.

As another example, suppose that Brentline Hospital management is interested in the relation between the hospital's telephone costs and patient-days. Patients are billed directly for their use of telephones, so those costs do not appear on the hospital's cost records. The telephone costs of concern to management are the charges for the staff's use of telephones. The data for this cost are plotted in Exhibit 5–11. It is evident from that plot that while the telephone costs do vary from month to month, they are not related to patient-days. Something other than patient-days is driving the telephone bills. Therefore, it would not make sense to analyze this cost any further by attempting to estimate a variable cost per patient-day for telephone costs. Plotting the data helps the cost analyst to diagnose such situations.

The High-Low Method

LEARNING OBJECTIVE 3
Analyze a mixed cost using the high-low method.

In addition to the quick-and-dirty method described in the preceding section, more precise methods are available for estimating fixed and variable costs. However, it must be emphasized that fixed and variable costs should be computed only if a scattergraph plot confirms that the relation is approximately linear. In the case of maintenance costs at Brentline Hospital, the relation does appear to be linear. In the case of telephone costs, there isn't any clear relation between telephone costs and patient-days, so there is no point in estimating how much of the cost varies with patient-days.

Assuming that the scattergraph plot indicates a linear relation between cost and activity, the fixed and variable cost elements of a mixed cost can be estimated using the *high-low method* or the *least-squares regression method*. The high-low method is based on the rise-over-run formula for the slope of a straight line. As discussed above, if the relation between cost and activity can be represented by a straight line, then the slope of the straight line is equal to the variable cost per unit of activity. Consequently, the following formula from high school algebra can be used to estimate the variable cost.

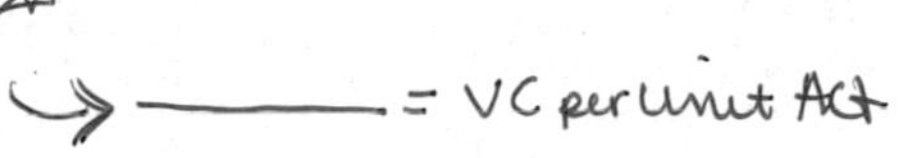

$$\text{Variable cost} = \text{Slope of the line} = \frac{\text{Rise}}{\text{Run}} = \frac{Y_2 - Y_1}{X_2 - X_1}$$

To analyze mixed costs with the **high-low method,** you begin by identifying the period with the lowest level of activity and the period with the highest level of activity. The period with the lowest activity is selected as the first point in the above formula and the period with the highest activity is selected as the second point. Consequently, the formula becomes:

$$\frac{\text{Variable}}{\text{cost}} = \frac{Y_2 - Y_1}{X_2 - X_1} = \frac{\text{Cost at the high activity level} - \text{Cost at the low activity level}}{\text{High activity level} - \text{Low activity level}}$$

or

$$\text{Variable cost} = \frac{\text{Change in cost}}{\text{Change in activity}}$$

Therefore, when the high-low method is used, the variable cost is estimated by dividing the difference in cost between the high and low levels of activity by the change in activity between those two points.

Using the high-low method, we first identify the periods with the highest and lowest *activity*—in this case, June and March. We then use the activity and cost data from these two periods to estimate the variable cost component as follows:

	Patient-Days	Maintenance Cost Incurred
High activity level (June)	8,000	$9,800
Low activity level (March)	5,000	7,400
Change	3,000	$2,400

$$\frac{\text{Variable}}{\text{cost}} = \frac{\text{Change in cost}}{\text{Change in activity}} = \frac{\$2{,}400}{3{,}000 \text{ patient-days}} = \$0.80 \text{ per patient-day}$$

Having determined that the variable rate for maintenance cost is 80 cents per patient-day, we can now determine the amount of fixed cost. This is done by taking total cost at *either* the high or the low activity level and deducting the variable cost element. In the computation below, total cost at the high activity level is used in computing the fixed cost element:

$$\begin{aligned} \text{Fixed cost element} &= \text{Total cost} - \text{Variable cost element} \\ &= \$9{,}800 - (\$0.80 \text{ per patient-day} \times 8{,}000 \text{ patient-days}) \\ &= \$3{,}400 \end{aligned}$$

Both the variable and fixed cost elements have now been isolated. The cost of maintenance can be expressed as $3,400 per month plus 80 cents per patient-day.

The cost of maintenance can also be expressed in terms of the equation for a straight line as follows:

$$Y = \$3{,}400 + \$0.80X$$

↑ Total maintenance cost (Y)

↑ Total patient-days (X)

The data used in this illustration are shown graphically in Exhibit 5–12. Notice that a straight line has been drawn through the points corresponding to the low and high levels of activity. In essence, that is what the high-low method does—it draws a straight line through those two points.

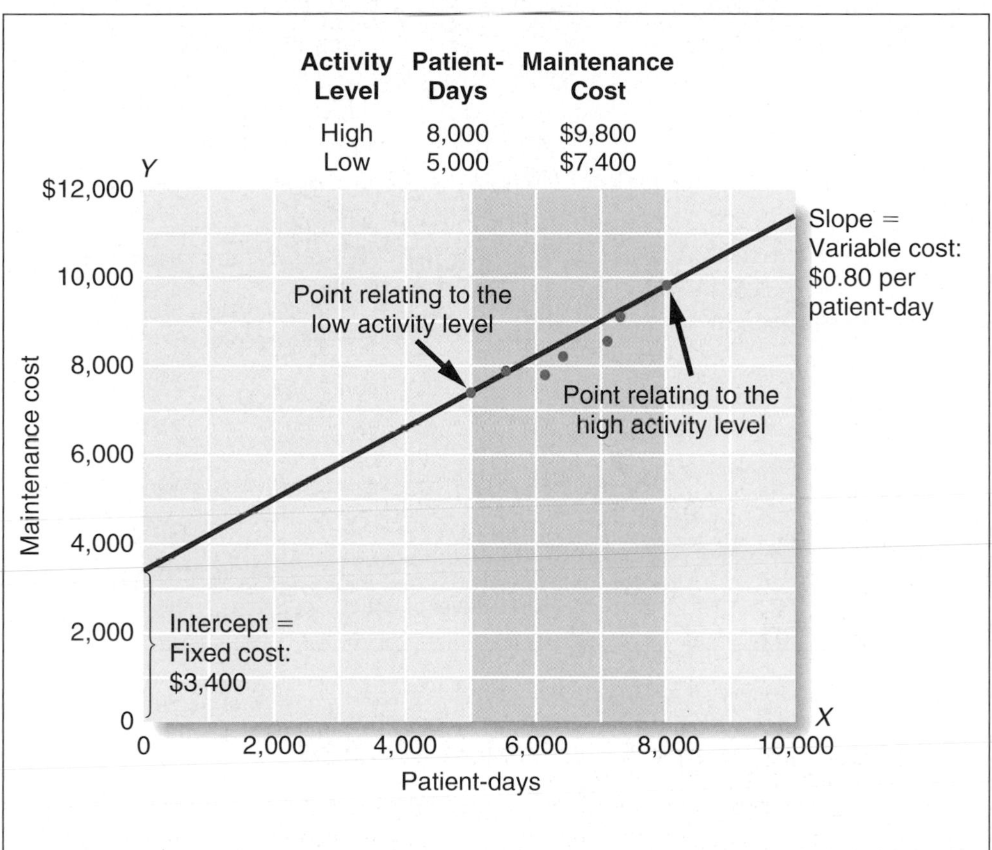

Exhibit 5–12
High-Low Method of Cost Analysis

Sometimes the high and low levels of activity don't coincide with the high and low amounts of cost. For example, the period that has the highest level of activity may not have the highest amount of cost. Nevertheless, the highest and lowest levels of *activity* are always used to analyze a mixed cost under the high-low method. The reason is that the analyst would like to use data that reflect the greatest possible variation in activity.

The high-low method is very simple to apply, but it suffers from a major (and sometimes critical) defect—it utilizes only two data points. Generally, two points are not enough to produce accurate results in cost analysis work. Additionally, periods in which the activity level is unusually low or unusually high will tend to produce inaccurate results. A cost formula that is estimated solely using data from these unusual periods may seriously misrepresent the true cost relationship that holds during normal periods. Such a distortion is evident in Exhibit 5–12. The straight line should probably be shifted down somewhat so that it is closer to more of the data points. For these reasons, other methods of cost analysis that utilize a greater number of points will generally be more accurate than the high-low method. If a manager chooses to use the high-low method, he or she should do so with a full awareness of the method's limitations.

Fortunately, modern computer software makes it very easy to use sophisticated statistical methods, such as *least-squares regression,* that use all of the data and that are capable of providing much more information than just the estimates of variable and fixed costs. The details of these statistical methods are beyond the scope of this text, but the basic approach is discussed below. Nevertheless, even if the least-squares regression approach is used, it is always a good idea to plot the data in a scattergraph. By simply looking at the scattergraph, you can quickly verify whether it makes sense to fit a straight line to the data using least-squares regression or some other method.

Exhibit 5–13
The Concept of Least-Squares Regression

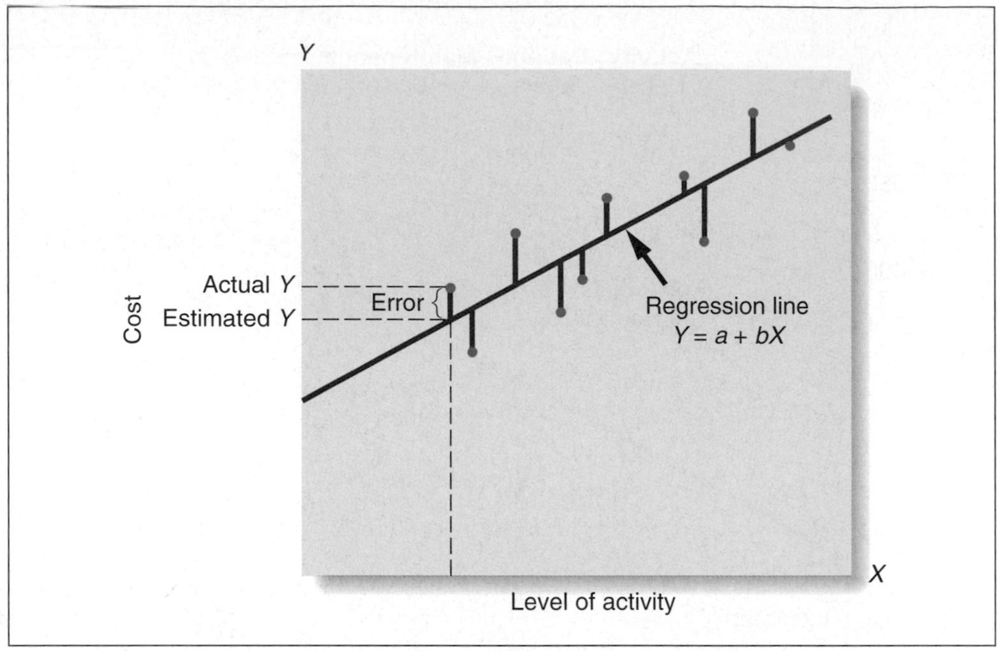

The Least-Squares Regression Method

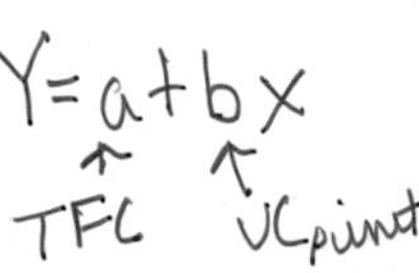

The **least-squares regression method** is a method of separating a mixed cost into its fixed and variable components that uses all of the data. A *regression line* of the form $Y = a + bX$ is fitted to the data, where a represents the total fixed cost and b represents the variable cost per unit of activity. The basic idea underlying the least-squares regression method is illustrated in Exhibit 5–13 using hypothetical data points. Notice from the exhibit that the deviations from the plotted points to the regression line are measured vertically on the graph. These vertical deviations are called the regression errors and are the key to understanding what least-squares regression does. There is nothing mysterious about the least-squares regression method. It simply computes the regression line that minimizes the sum of these squared errors. The formulas that accomplish this are fairly complex and involve numerous calculations, but the principle is simple.

Fortunately, computers are adept at carrying out the computations required by the least-squares regression formulas. The data—the observed values of X and Y—are entered into the computer, and software does the rest. In the case of the Brentline Hospital maintenance cost data, we used a statistical software package on a personal computer to calculate the following least-squares regression estimates of the total fixed cost (a) and the variable cost per unit of activity (b):

$$a = \$3{,}431$$

$$b = \$0.759$$

Therefore, using the least-squares regression method, the fixed element of the maintenance cost is \$3,431 per month and the variable portion is 75.9 cents per patient-day.

In terms of the linear equation $Y = a + bX$, the cost formula can be written as

$$Y = \$3{,}431 + \$0.759X$$

where activity (X) is expressed in patient-days.

While we used statistical software to calculate the values of a and b in this example, the estimates can also be computed using a spreadsheet application such as Microsoft® Excel. In Appendix 5A to this chapter, we show how this can be done.

In addition to estimates of the intercept (fixed cost) and slope (variable cost per unit), least-squares regression software ordinarily provides a number of other very useful statistics. One of these statistics is the R^2, which is a measure of "goodness of fit." The $\mathbf{R^2}$

tells us the percentage of the variation in the dependent variable (cost) that is explained by variation in the independent variable (activity). The R^2 varies from 0% to 100%, and the higher the percentage, the better. In the case of the Brentline Hospital maintenance cost data, the R^2 is 0.90, which indicates that 90% of the variation in maintenance costs is explained by the variation in patient-days. This is reasonably high and is an indication of a good fit. On the other hand, a low R^2 would be an indication of a poor fit. You should always plot the data in a scattergraph, but it is particularly important to check the data visually when the R^2 is low. A quick look at the scattergraph can reveal that there is little real relation between the cost and the activity or that the relation is something other than a simple straight line. In such cases, additional analysis would be required.

Managerial Accounting in Action

The Wrap-Up

After completing the analysis of maintenance costs, Kinh Nguyen met with Dr. Derek Chalmers to discuss the results.

Kinh: We used least-squares regression analysis to estimate the fixed and variable components of maintenance costs. According to the results, the fixed cost per month is $3,431 and the variable cost per patient-day is 75.9 cents.

Derek: Okay, so if we plan for 7,800 patient-days next month, what is your estimate of the maintenance costs?

Kinh: That will take just a few seconds to figure out. [Kinh wrote the following calculations on a pad of paper.]

Fixed costs	$3,431
Variable costs:	
7,800 patient-days × $0.759 per patient-day	5,920
Total expected maintenance costs	$9,351

Derek: Nine thousand three hundred and fifty *one* dollars; isn't that a bit *too* precise?

Kinh: Sure. I don't really believe the maintenance costs will be exactly this figure. However, based on the information we have, this is the best estimate we can come up with.

Derek: Don't let me give you a hard time. Even though it is an estimate, it will be a lot better than just guessing like we have done in the past. Thanks. I hope to see more of this kind of analysis.

Managing Power Consumption

In Business

The Tata Iron Steel Company Ltd. is one of the largest companies in India. Because of the unreliable electrical supply in India, the company is faced with frequent power shortages and must carefully manage its power consumption—allocating scarce power to the most profitable uses. Estimating the power requirements of each processing station in the steel mill was the first step in building a model to better manage power consumption. Management used simple least-squares regression to estimate the fixed and variable components of the power load. Total power consumption was the dependent variable and tons of steel processed was the independent variable. The fixed component estimated from the least-squares regression was the fixed power consumption (in KWHs) per month and the variable component was the power consumption (again in KWHs) per ton of steel processed.

Source: "How Tata Steel Optimized Its Results," *The Management Accountant* (India), May 1996, pp. 372–376.

Multiple Regression Analysis

In the discussion thus far, we have assumed that a single factor such as patient-days drives the variable cost component of a mixed cost. This assumption is acceptable for many mixed costs, but in some situations there may be more than one causal factor driving the variable cost element. For example, shipping costs may depend on both the number of units shipped *and* the weight of the units. In a situation such as this, *multiple regression* is necessary. **Multiple regression** is an analytical method that is used when the dependent variable (i.e., cost) is caused by more than one factor. Although adding more factors, or variables, makes the computations more complex, the principles involved are the same as in the simple least-squares regressions discussed above.

The Contribution Format

LEARNING OBJECTIVE 4
Prepare an income statement using the contribution format.

Once the manager has separated costs into fixed and variable elements, what is done with the data? We have already answered this question somewhat by showing how a cost formula can be used to predict costs. To answer this question more fully will require most of the remainder of this text, since much of what the manager does requires an understanding of cost behavior. One immediate and very significant application of the ideas we have developed, however, is found in a new income statement format known as the **contribution approach.** The unique thing about the contribution approach is that it provides the manager with an income statement geared directly to cost behavior.

Why a New Income Statement Format?

An income statement prepared using the *traditional approach*, as illustrated in Chapter 2, is not organized in terms of cost behavior. Rather, it is organized in a "functional" format—emphasizing the functions of production, administration, and sales in the classification and presentation of cost data. No attempt is made to distinguish between the behavior of costs included under each functional heading. Under the heading "Administrative expense," for example, one can expect to find both variable and fixed costs lumped together.

Although an income statement prepared in the functional format may be useful for external reporting purposes, it has serious limitations when used for internal purposes. Internally, the manager needs cost data organized in a format that will facilitate planning, control, and decision-making. As we shall see in chapters ahead, these tasks are much easier when cost data are available in a fixed and variable format. The contribution approach to the income statement has been developed in response to this need.

The Contribution Approach

Concept 5–2

Exhibit 5–14 illustrates the contribution approach to the income statement with a simple example based on assumed data, along with the traditional approach discussed in Chapter 2.

Notice that the contribution approach separates costs into fixed and variable categories, first deducting variable expenses from sales to obtain what is known as the *contribution margin.* The **contribution margin** is the amount remaining from sales revenues after variable expenses have been deducted. This amount *contributes* toward covering fixed expenses and then toward profits for the period.

The contribution approach to the income statement is used as an internal planning and decision-making tool. Its emphasis on costs by behavior facilitates cost-volume-profit analysis, such as we shall be doing in the next chapter. The approach is also very useful in appraising management performance, in segmented reporting of profit data, and in budgeting. Moreover, the contribution approach helps managers organize data pertinent to all kinds of special decisions such as product-line analysis, pricing, use of scarce resources, and make or buy analysis. All of these topics are covered in later chapters.

Exhibit 5–14 Comparison of the Contribution Income Statement with the Traditional Income Statement (the data are given)

Traditional Approach (costs organized by function)

Sales		$12,000
Less cost of goods sold		6,000*
Gross margin		6,000
Less operating expenses:		
Selling	$3,100*	
Administrative	1,900*	5,000
Net operating income		$ 1,000

Contribution Approach (costs organized by behavior)

Sales		$12,000
Less variable expenses:		
Variable production	$2,000	
Variable selling	600	
Variable administrative	400	3,000
Contribution margin		9,000
Less fixed expenses:		
Fixed production	4,000	
Fixed selling	2,500	
Fixed administrative	1,500	8,000
Net operating income		$ 1,000

*Contains both variable and fixed expenses. This is the income statement for a manufacturing company; thus, when the income statement is placed in the contribution format, the "cost of goods sold" figure is divided between variable production costs and fixed production costs. If this were the income statement for a *merchandising* company (which simply purchases completed goods from a supplier), then the cost of goods sold would be *all* variable.

Summary

As we shall see in later chapters, the ability to predict how costs will respond to changes in activity is critical for making decisions, for controlling operations, and for evaluating performance. Three major classifications of costs were discussed in this chapter—variable, fixed, and mixed. Mixed costs consist of a mixture of variable and fixed elements and a mixed cost can be expressed in equation form as $Y = a + bX$, where X is the activity, Y is the cost, a is the fixed cost element, and b is the variable cost per unit of activity. Several methods are available to estimate the fixed and variable cost components of a mixed cost using past records of cost and activity. If the relation between cost and activity appears to be linear based on a scattergraph plot, then the variable and fixed components of the mixed cost can be estimated using the quick-and-dirty method, the high-low method, or the least-squares regression method. The quick-and-dirty method is based on drawing a straight line and then using the slope and the intercept of the straight line to estimate the variable and fixed cost components of the mixed cost. The high-low method implicitly draws a straight line through the points of lowest activity and highest activity. In most situations, the least-squares regression method should be used in preference to both the quick-and-dirty and the high-low methods. Computer software is widely available for using the least-squares method and a variety of useful statistics are automatically produced by most software packages along with estimates of the intercept (fixed cost) and slope (variable cost per unit). Nevertheless, even when least-squares regression is used, the data should be plotted to confirm that the relationship is really a straight line.

Managers use costs organized by behavior as a basis for many decisions. To facilitate this use, the income statement can be prepared in a contribution format. The contribution format classifies costs on the income statement by cost behavior (i.e., variable versus fixed) rather than by the functions of production, administration, and sales.

Review Problem 1: Cost Behavior

Neptune Rentals offers a boat rental service. Consider the following costs of the company over the relevant range of 5,000 to 8,000 hours of operating time for its boats:

	Hours of Operating Time			
	5,000	6,000	7,000	8,000
Total costs:				
Variable costs	$ 20,000	$?	$?	$?
Fixed costs	168,000	?	?	?
Total costs	$188,000	$?	$?	$?
Cost per hour:				
Variable cost	$?	$?	$?	$?
Fixed cost	?	?	?	?
Total cost per hour	$?	$?	$?	$?

Required:
Compute the missing amounts, assuming that cost behavior patterns remain unchanged within the relevant range of 5,000 to 8,000 hours.

Solution to Review Problem 1

The variable cost per hour can be computed as follows:

$$\$20,000 \div 5,000 \text{ hours} = \$4 \text{ per hour}$$

Therefore, in accordance with the behavior of variable and fixed costs, the missing amounts are as follows:

	Hours of Operating Time			
	5,000	6,000	7,000	8,000
Total costs:				
Variable costs	$ 20,000	$ 24,000	$ 28,000	$ 32,000
Fixed costs	168,000	168,000	168,000	168,000
Total costs	$188,000	$192,000	$196,000	$200,000
Cost per hour:				
Variable cost	$ 4.00	$ 4.00	$ 4.00	$ 4.00
Fixed cost	33.60	28.00	24.00	21.00
Total cost per hour	$ 37.60	$ 32.00	$ 28.00	$ 25.00

Observe that the total variable costs increase in proportion to the number of hours of operating time, but that these costs remain constant at $4 if expressed on a per hour basis.

In contrast, the total fixed costs do not change with changes in the level of activity. They remain constant at $168,000 within the relevant range. With increases in activity, however, the fixed costs decrease on a per hour basis, dropping from $33.60 per hour when the boats are operated 5,000 hours a period to only $21.00 per hour when the boats are operated 8,000 hours a period. *Because of this troublesome aspect of fixed costs, they are most easily (and most safely) dealt with on a total basis, rather than on a unit basis, in cost analysis work.*

Review Problem 2: High-Low Method

The administrator of Azalea Hills Hospital would like a cost formula linking the costs involved in admitting patients to the number of patients admitted during a month. The admitting department's costs and the number of patients admitted during the immediately preceding eight months are given in the table on the following page:

Month	Number of Patients Admitted	Admitting Department Costs
May	1,800	$14,700
June.	1,900	15,200
July	1,700	13,700
August	1,600	14,000
September.	1,500	14,300
October	1,300	13,100
November	1,100	12,800
December	1,500	14,600

Required:

1. Use the high-low method to establish the fixed and variable components of admitting costs.
2. Express the fixed and variable components of admitting costs as a cost formula in the linear equation form $Y = a + bX$.

Solution to Review Problem 2

1. The first step in the high-low method is to identify the periods of the lowest and highest activity. Those periods are November (1,100 patients admitted) and June (1,900 patients admitted).

   The second step is to compute the variable cost per unit using those two points:

Month	Number of Patients Admitted	Admitting Department Costs
High activity level (June)	1,900	$15,200
Low activity level (November)	1,100	12,800
Change	800	$ 2,400

$$\text{Variable cost} = \frac{\text{Change in cost}}{\text{Change in activity}} = \frac{\$2{,}400}{800 \text{ patients admitted}} = \$3 \text{ per patient admitted}$$

   The third step is to compute the fixed cost element by deducting the variable cost element from the total cost at either the high or low activity. In the computation below, the high point of activity is used:

$$\begin{aligned}\text{Fixed cost element} &= \text{Total cost} - \text{Variable cost element}\\ &= \$15{,}200 - (\$3 \text{ per patient admitted} \times 1{,}900 \text{ patients admitted})\\ &= \$9{,}500\end{aligned}$$

2. The cost formula expressed in the linear equation form is $Y = \$9{,}500 + \$3X$.

Glossary

Account analysis A method for analyzing cost behavior in which each account under consideration is classified as either variable or fixed based on the analyst's prior knowledge of how the cost in the account behaves. (p. 202)

Activity base A measure of whatever causes the incurrence of a variable cost. For example, the total cost of X-ray film in a hospital will increase as the number of X-rays taken increases. Therefore, the number of X-rays is an activity base for explaining the total cost of X-ray film. (p. 191)

Committed fixed costs Those fixed costs that are difficult to adjust and that relate to the investment in facilities, equipment, and the basic organizational structure of a firm. (p. 196)

Contribution approach An income statement format that is geared to cost behavior in that costs are separated into variable and fixed categories rather than being separated according to the functions of production, sales, and administration. (p. 212)

Contribution margin The amount remaining from sales revenues after all variable expenses have been deducted. (p. 212)

Cost structure The relative proportion of fixed, variable, and mixed costs found within an organization. (p. 190)

Curvilinear costs A relationship between cost and activity that is a curve rather than a straight line. (p. 194)

Dependent variable A variable that reacts or responds to some causal factor; total cost is the dependent variable, as represented by the letter Y, in the equation $Y = a + bX$. (p. 204)

Discretionary fixed costs Those fixed costs that arise from annual decisions by management to spend in certain fixed cost areas, such as advertising and research. (p. 197)

Engineering approach A detailed analysis of cost behavior based on an industrial engineer's evaluation of the inputs that are required to carry out a particular activity and of the prices of those inputs. (p. 202)

High-low method A method of separating a mixed cost into its fixed and variable elements by analyzing the change in cost between the high and low levels of activity. (p. 208)

Independent variable A variable that acts as a causal factor; activity is the independent variable, as represented by the letter X, in the equation $Y = a + bX$. (p. 204)

Least-squares regression method A method of separating a mixed cost into its fixed and variable elements by fitting a regression line that minimizes the sum of the squared errors. (p. 210)

Linear cost behavior Cost behavior is said to be linear whenever a straight line is a reasonable approximation for the relation between cost and activity. (p. 204)

Mixed cost A cost that contains both variable and fixed cost elements. (p. 200)

Multiple regression An analytical method required in those situations where variations in a dependent variable are caused by more than one factor. (p. 212)

R^2 A measure of goodness of fit in least-squares regression analysis. It is the percentage of the variation in the dependent variable that is explained by variation in the independent variable. (p. 210)

Relevant range The range of activity within which assumptions about variable and fixed cost behavior are valid. (p. 194)

Scattergraph method A method of separating a mixed cost into its fixed and variable elements. Under this method, a regression line is fitted to an array of plotted points by drawing a line with a straight-edge. (p. 204)

Step-variable cost The cost of a resource (such as the cost of a maintenance worker) that is obtainable only in large chunks and that increases and decreases only in response to fairly wide changes in the activity level. (p. 193)

Appendix 5A: Least-Squares Regression Using Microsoft® Excel

LEARNING OBJECTIVE 5
Analyze a mixed cost using the least-squares regression method.

The least-squares regression method for estimating a linear relationship is based on the equation for a straight line:

$$Y = a + bX$$

As explained in the chapter, least-squares regression selects the values for the intercept a and the slope b that minimize the sum of the squared errors. The following formulas, which are derived in statistics and calculus texts, accomplish that objective:

$$b = \frac{n(\Sigma XY - (\Sigma X)(\Sigma Y)}{n(\Sigma X^2) - (\Sigma X)^2}$$

$$a = \frac{(\Sigma Y) - b(\Sigma X)}{n}$$

where:

X = The level of activity (independent variable)

Y = The total mixed cost (dependent variable)

a = The total fixed cost (the vertical intercept of the line)

b = The variable cost per unit of activity (the slope of the line)

n = Number of observations

Σ = Sum across all n observations

Exhibit 5A–1 The Least-Squares Regression Worksheet for Brentline Hospital

Microsoft Excel - Appendix 5A.xls

	A	B	C	D	E
1		*Patient*	*Maintenance*		
2		*Days*	*Costs*		
3	*Month*	*X*	*Y*		
4	January	5,600	$7,900		
5	February	7,100	8,500		
6	March	5,000	7,400		
7	April	6,500	8,200		
8	May	7,300	9,100		
9	June	8,000	9,800		
10	July	6,200	7,800		
11					
12	Intercept	$3,431			
13	Slope	$0.759			
14	RSQ	0.90			
15					

Least-squares regression

Ready NUM

Carrying out the calculations required by the formulas is tedious at best. Fortunately, statistical software packages are widely available that perform the calculations automatically. Spreadsheet software, such as Microsoft® Excel, can also be used to do least-squares regression—although it requires a little more work than specialized statistical packages do.

To illustrate how Excel can be used to calculate the intercept a, the slope b, and the R^2, we will use the Brentline Hospital data for maintenance costs on page 204. The worksheet in Exhibit 5A–1 contains the data and the calculations.

As you can see, the X values (the independent variable) have been entered in cells B4 through B10. The Y values (the dependent variable) have been entered in cells C4 through C10. The slope, intercept, and R^2 are computed using the Excel functions INTERCEPT, SLOPE, and RSQ. In each case, you must specify the range of cells for the Y values and for the X values. In the above worksheet, cell B12 contains the formula =INTERCEPT(C4:C10,B4:B10); cell B13 contains the formula =SLOPE(C4:C10,B4:B10); and cell B14 contains the formula =RSQ(C4:C10,B4:B10).

According to the calculations carried out by Excel, the fixed maintenance cost (the intercept) is $3,431 per month and the variable cost (the slope) is $0.759 per patient-day. Therefore, the cost formula for maintenance cost is:

$$Y = a + bX$$

$$Y = \$3{,}431 + \$0.759X$$

Note that the R^2 (i.e., RSQ) is 0.90, which—as previously discussed—is quite good and indicates that 90% of the variation in maintenance costs is explained by the variation in patient-days.

Exhibit 5A–2
A Scattergraph Plot of the Brentline Hospital Data

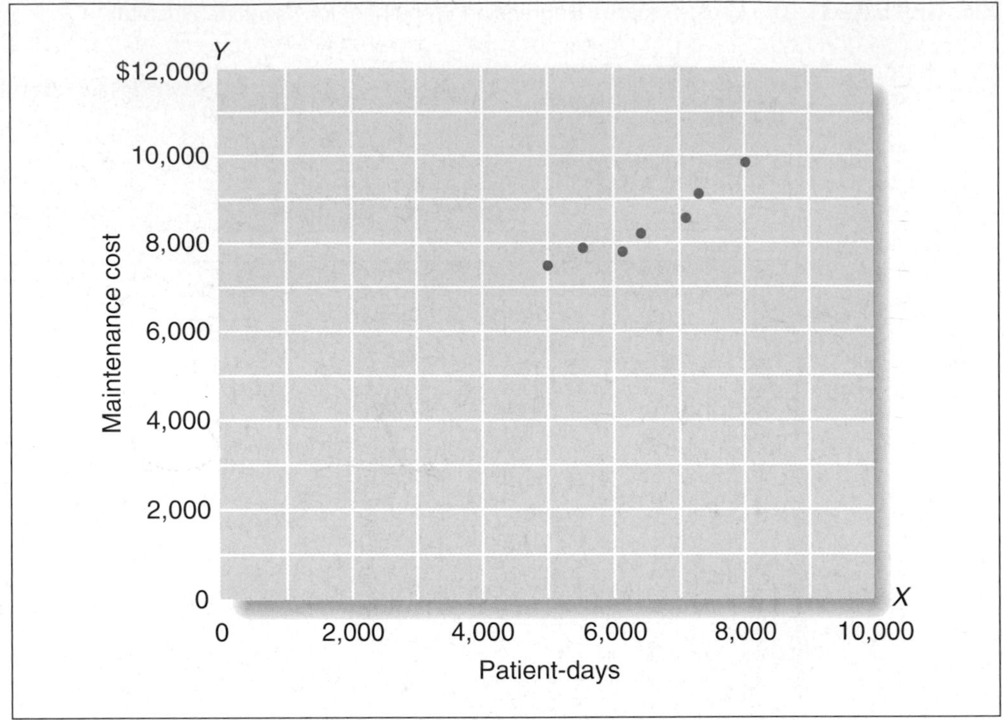

Plotting the data is easy in Excel. Select the range of values that you would like to plot—in this case, cells B4:C10. Then select the Chart Wizard tool on the toolbar and make the appropriate choices in the various dialogue boxes that appear. When you are finished, you should have a scattergraph that looks something like the plot in Exhibit 5A–2. Note that the relation between cost and activity is approximately linear, so it is reasonable to fit a straight line to the data as we have implicitly done with the least-squares regression.

Questions

5–1 Distinguish between (*a*) a variable cost, (*b*) a fixed cost, and (*c*) a mixed cost.

5–2 What effect does an increase in volume have on—
- *a.* Unit fixed costs?
- *b.* Unit variable costs?
- *c.* Total fixed costs?
- *d.* Total variable costs?

5–3 Define the following terms: (*a*) cost behavior and (*b*) relevant range.

5–4 What is meant by an *activity base* when dealing with variable costs? Give several examples of activity bases.

5–5 Distinguish between (*a*) a variable cost, (*b*) a mixed cost, and (*c*) a step-variable cost. Chart the three costs on a graph, with activity plotted horizontally and cost plotted vertically.

5–6 Managers often assume a strictly linear relationship between cost and volume. How can this practice be defended in light of the fact that many costs are curvilinear?

5–7 Distinguish between discretionary fixed costs and committed fixed costs.

5–8 Classify the following fixed costs as normally being either committed or discretionary:
- *a.* Depreciation on buildings.
- *b.* Advertising.
- *c.* Research.
- *d.* Long-term equipment leases.
- *e.* Pension payments to the firm's retirees.
- *f.* Management development and training.

5–9 Does the concept of the relevant range apply to fixed costs? Explain.

5–10 What is the major disadvantage of the high-low method?

5–11 What is meant by a regression line? Give the general formula for a regression line. Which term represents the variable cost? The fixed cost?

5–12 What is meant by the term *least-squares regression?*

5–13 What is the difference between ordinary least-squares regression analysis and multiple regression analysis?

5–14 What is the difference between the contribution approach to the income statement and the traditional approach to the income statement?

5–15 What is the contribution margin?

Exercises

EXERCISE 5–1 High-Low Method; Scattergraph Analysis [LO2, LO3]

Zerbel Company, a wholesaler of large, custom-built air conditioning units for commercial buildings, has noticed considerable fluctuation in its shipping expense from month to month, as shown below:

Month	Units Shipped	Total Shipping Expense
January	4	$2,200
February	7	3,100
March	5	2,600
April	2	1,500
May	3	2,200
June	6	3,000
July	8	3,600

Required:

1. Using the high-low method, estimate the cost formula for shipping expense.
2. The president has no confidence in the high-low method and would like you to "check out" your results using the scattergraph method. Do the following:
   a. Prepare a scattergraph, using the data given above. Plot cost on the vertical axis and activity on the horizontal axis. Fit a straight line to your plotted points using a ruler.
   b. Using your scattergraph, estimate the approximate variable cost per unit shipped and the approximate fixed cost per month with the quick-and-dirty method.
3. What factors, other than the number of units shipped, are likely to affect the company's shipping expense? Explain.

EXERCISE 5–2 (Appendix 5A) Least-Squares Regression [LO5]

Refer to the data for Zerbel Company in Exercise 5–1.

Required:

1. Using the least-squares regression method, estimate the cost formula for shipping expense.
2. If you also completed Exercise 5–1, prepare a simple table comparing the variable and fixed cost elements of shipping expense as computed under the quick-and-dirty scattergraph method, the high-low method, and the least-squares regression method.

EXERCISE 5–3 High-Low Method; Predicting Cost [LO1, LO3]

The number of X-rays taken and X-ray costs over the last nine months in Beverly Hospital are given below:

Month	X-Rays Taken	X-Ray Costs
January	6,250	$28,000
February	7,000	29,000
March	5,000	23,000
April	4,250	20,000
May	4,500	22,000
June	3,000	17,000
July	3,750	18,000
August	5,500	24,000
September	5,750	26,000

Required:

1. Using the high-low method, estimate the cost formula for X-ray costs.
2. Using the cost formula you derived above, what X-ray costs would you expect to be incurred during a month in which 4,600 X-rays are taken?

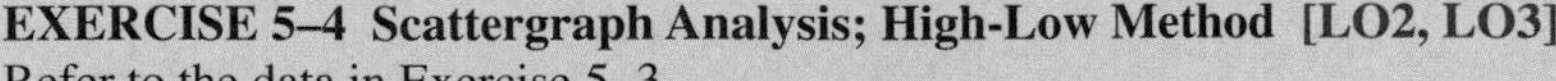

EXERCISE 5–4 Scattergraph Analysis; High-Low Method [LO2, LO3]

Refer to the data in Exercise 5–3.

Required:

1. Prepare a scattergraph using the data from Exercise 5–3. Plot cost on the vertical axis and activity on the horizontal axis. Using a ruler, fit a line to your plotted points.
2. Using the quick-and-dirty method, what is the approximate monthly fixed cost for X-rays? The approximate variable cost per X-ray taken?
3. Scrutinize the points on your graph, and explain why the high-low method would or would not yield an accurate cost formula in this situation.

EXERCISE 5–5 Cost Behavior; Contribution Income Statement [LO1, LO4]

Parker Company manufactures and sells a single product. A partially completed schedule of the company's total and per unit costs over a relevant range of 60,000 to 100,000 units produced and sold each year is given below:

	Units Produced and Sold		
	60,000	80,000	100,000
Total costs:			
Variable costs	$150,000	?	?
Fixed costs	360,000	?	?
Total costs	$510,000	?	?
Cost per unit:			
Variable cost	?	?	?
Fixed cost	?	?	?
Total cost per unit	?	?	?

Required:

1. Complete the schedule of the company's total and unit costs above.
2. Assume that the company produces and sells 90,000 units during a year. The selling price is $7.50 per unit. Prepare an income statement in the contribution format for the year.

EXERCISE 5–6 Scattergraph Analysis [LO2]

The data below have been taken from the cost records of the Atlanta Processing Company. The data relate to the cost of operating one of the company's processing facilities at various levels of activity:

Month	Units Processed	Total Cost
January	8,000	$14,000
February	4,500	10,000
March	7,000	12,500
April	9,000	15,500
May	3,750	10,000
June	6,000	12,500
July	3,000	8,500
August	5,000	11,500

Required:

1. Prepare a scattergraph by plotting the above data on a graph. Plot cost on the vertical axis and activity on the horizontal axis. Fit a line to your plotted points using a ruler.
2. Using the quick-and-dirty method, what is the approximate monthly fixed cost? The approximate variable cost per unit processed? Show your computations.

EXERCISE 5–7 High-Low Method; Predicting Cost [LO1, LO3]
Resort Inns, Inc., has a total of 2,000 rooms in its nationwide chain of motels. On average, 70% of the rooms are occupied each day. The company's operating costs are $21 per occupied room per day at this occupancy level, assuming a 30-day month. This $21 figure contains both variable and fixed cost elements. During October, the occupancy rate dropped to only 45%. A total of $792,000 in operating cost was incurred during October.

Required:
1. Estimate the variable cost per occupied room per day.
2. Estimate the total fixed operating costs per month.
3. Assume that the occupancy rate increases to 60% during November. What total operating costs would you expect the company to incur during November?

EXERCISE 5–8 Cost Behavior; High-Low Method [LO1, LO3]
Speedy Parcel Service operates a fleet of delivery trucks in a large metropolitan area. A careful study by the company's cost analyst has determined that if a truck is driven 120,000 miles during a year, the average operating cost is 11.6 cents per mile. If a truck is driven only 80,000 miles during a year, the average operating cost increases to 13.6 cents per mile.

Required:
1. Using the high-low method, estimate the variable and fixed cost elements of the annual cost of truck operation.
2. Express the variable and fixed costs in the form $Y = a + bX$.
3. If a truck were driven 100,000 miles during a year, what total cost would you expect to be incurred?

EXERCISE 5–9 Contribution Format Income Statement [LO4]
Haaki Shop, Inc., is a large retailer of water sports equipment. An income statement for the company's surfboard department for a recent quarter is presented below:

THE HAAKI SHOP, INC.
Income Statement—Surfboard Department
For the Quarter Ended May 31

Sales		$800,000
Less cost of goods sold		300,000
Gross margin		500,000
Less operating expenses:		
Selling expenses	$250,000	
Administrative expenses	160,000	410,000
Net operating income		$ 90,000

The surfboards sell, on the average, for $400 each. The department's variable selling expenses are $50 per surfboard sold. The remaining selling expenses are fixed. The administrative expenses are 25% variable and 75% fixed. The company purchases its surfboards from a supplier at a cost of $150 per surfboard.

Required:
1. Prepare an income statement for the quarter using the contribution approach.
2. What was the contribution toward fixed expenses and profits from each surfboard sold during the quarter? (State this figure in a single dollar amount per surfboard.)

EXERCISE 5–10 (Appendix 5A) Least-Squares Regression [LO1, LO5]
One of Varic Company's products goes through a glazing process. The company has observed glazing costs as follows over the last six weeks (the numbers have been simplified for ease of computation):

Week	Units Produced	Total Glazing Cost
1	8	$270
2	5	200
3	10	310
4	4	190
5	6	240
6	9	290

For planning purposes, the company's management must know the amount of variable glazing cost per unit and the total fixed glazing cost per week.

Required:

1. Using the least-squares regression method, estimate the variable and fixed elements of the glazing cost.
2. Express the cost data in (1) above in the form $Y = a + bX$.
3. If the company processes seven units next week, what would be the expected total glazing cost?

Problems

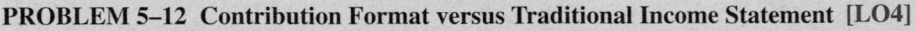

PROBLEM 5–11 Cost Behavior; High-Low Method; Contribution Income Statement [LO1, LO3, LO4]

Frankel Ltd., a British merchandising firm, is the exclusive distributor of a product that is gaining rapid market acceptance. The company's revenues and expenses (in British pounds) for the last three months are given below:

FRANKEL LTD.
Comparative Income Statement
For the Three Months Ended June 30

	April	May	June
Sales in units	3,000	3,750	4,500
Sales revenue	£420,000	£525,000	£630,000
Less cost of goods sold	168,000	210,000	252,000
Gross margin	252,000	315,000	378,000
Less operating expenses:			
Shipping expense	44,000	50,000	56,000
Advertising expense	70,000	70,000	70,000
Salaries and commissions	107,000	125,000	143,000
Insurance expense	9,000	9,000	9,000
Depreciation expense	42,000	42,000	42,000
Total operating expenses	272,000	296,000	320,000
Net operating income (loss)	£ (20,000)	£ 19,000	£ 58,000

(Note: Frankel Ltd.'s income statement has been recast in the functional format common in the United States. The British currency is the pound, denoted by £.)

Required:

1. Identify each of the company's expenses (including cost of goods sold) as either variable, fixed, or mixed.
2. Using the high-low method, separate each mixed expense into variable and fixed elements. State the cost formula for each mixed expense.
3. Redo the company's income statement at the 4,500-unit level of activity using the contribution format.

PROBLEM 5–12 Contribution Format versus Traditional Income Statement [LO4]

House of Organs, Inc., purchases organs from a well-known manufacturer and sells them at the retail level. The organs sell, on the average, for $2,500 each. The average cost of an organ from the manufacturer is $1,500.

House of Organs, Inc., has always kept careful records of its costs. The costs that the company incurs in a typical month are presented below in the form of a spreadsheet:

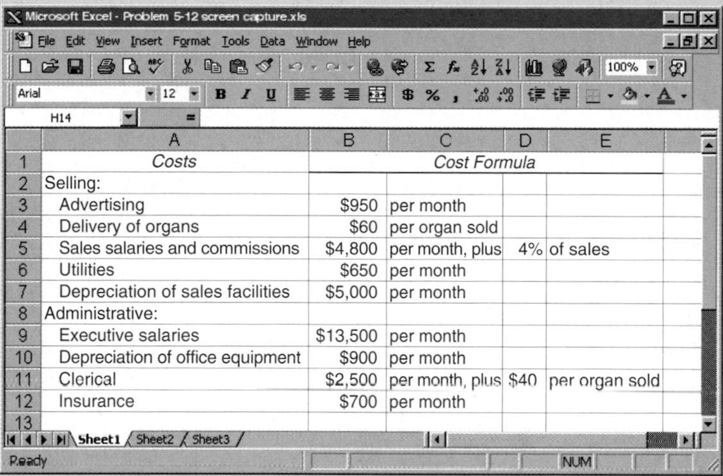

Microsoft Excel - Problem 5-12 screen capture.xls

	A	B	C	D	E
1	*Costs*	*Cost Formula*			
2	Selling:				
3	Advertising	$950	per month		
4	Delivery of organs	$60	per organ sold		
5	Sales salaries and commissions	$4,800	per month, plus	4%	of sales
6	Utilities	$650	per month		
7	Depreciation of sales facilities	$5,000	per month		
8	Administrative:				
9	Executive salaries	$13,500	per month		
10	Depreciation of office equipment	$900	per month		
11	Clerical	$2,500	per month, plus	$40	per organ sold
12	Insurance	$700	per month		
13					

During November, the company sold and delivered 60 organs.

Required:

1. Prepare an income statement for November using the traditional format with costs organized by function.
2. Redo (1) above, this time using the contribution format with costs organized by behavior. Show costs and revenues on both a total and a per unit basis down through contribution margin.
3. Refer to the income statement you prepared in (2) above. Why might it be misleading to show the fixed costs on a per unit basis?

PROBLEM 5–13 (Appendix 5A) Scattergraph; Cost Behavior; Least-Squares Regression Method [LO1, LO2, LO5]

Amanda King has just been appointed director of recreation programs for Highland Park, a rapidly growing community in Connecticut. In the past, the city has sponsored a number of softball leagues in the summer months. From the city's cost records, Amanda has found the following total costs associated with the softball leagues over the last five years:

Number of Leagues	Total Cost
5	$13,000
2	7,000
4	10,500
6	14,000
3	10,000

Each league requires its own paid supervisor and paid umpires as well as printed schedules and other copy work. Therefore, Amanda knows that some variable costs are associated with the leagues. She would like to know the amount of variable cost per league and the total fixed cost per year associated with the softball program. This information would help her for planning purposes.

Required:

1. Using the least-squares regression method, estimate the variable cost per league and the total fixed cost per year for the softball program.
2. Express the cost data derived in (1) above in the linear equation form $Y = a + bX$.
3. Assume that Amanda would like to expand the softball program during the coming year to involve a total of seven leagues. Compute the expected total cost for the softball program. Can you see any problem with using the cost formula from (2) above to derive this total cost figure? Explain.
4. Prepare a scattergraph, and fit a regression line to the plotted points using the cost formula expressed in (2) above.

PROBLEM 5–14 Identifying Cost Behavior Patterns [LO1]

A number of graphs displaying cost behavior patterns that might be found in a company's cost structure are shown on the following page. The vertical axis on each graph represents total cost and the horizontal axis represents the level of activity (volume).

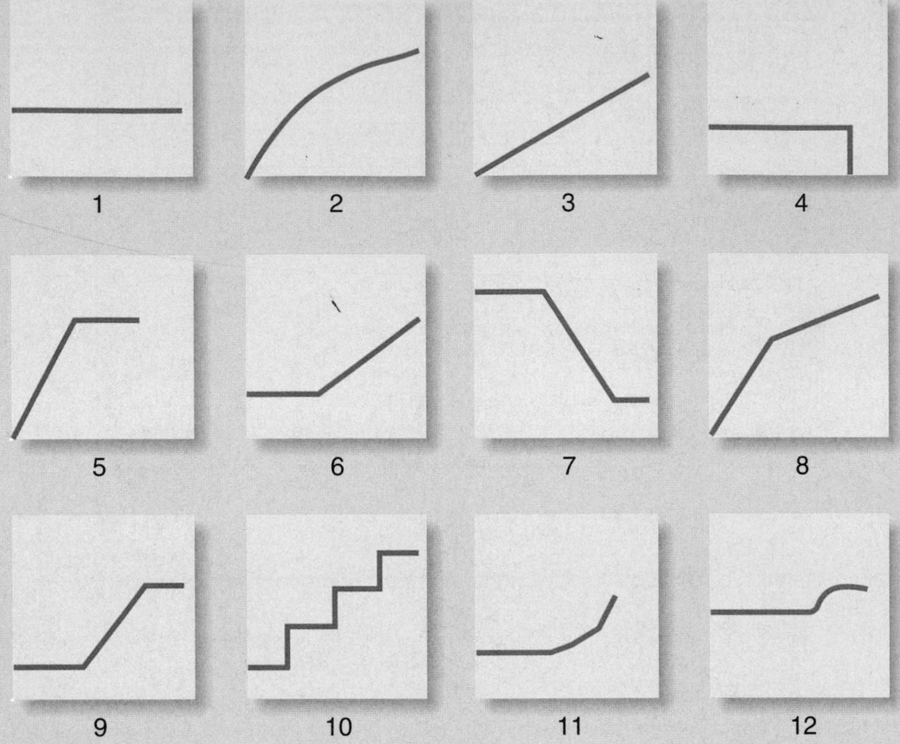

Required:

1. For each of the following situations, identify the graph that illustrates the cost pattern involved. Any graph may be used more than once.
   a. Electricity bill—a flat fixed charge, plus a variable cost after a certain number of kilowatt-hours are used.
   b. City water bill, which is computed as follows:

First 1,000,000 gallons or less	$1,000 flat fee
Next 10,000 gallons	0.003 per gallon used
Next 10,000 gallons	0.006 per gallon used
Next 10,000 gallons	0.009 per gallon used
Etc.	Etc.

   c. Depreciation of equipment, where the amount is computed by the straight-line method. When the depreciation rate was established, it was anticipated that the obsolescence factor would be greater than the wear and tear factor.
   d. Rent on a factory building donated by the city, where the agreement calls for a fixed fee payment unless 200,000 labor-hours or more are worked, in which case no rent need be paid.
   e. Cost of raw materials, where the cost starts at $7.50 per unit and then decreases by 5 cents per unit for each of the first 100 units purchased, after which it remains constant at $2.50 per unit.
   f. Salaries of maintenance workers, where one maintenance worker is needed for every 1,000 hours of machine-hours or less (that is, 0 to 1,000 hours requires one maintenance worker, 1,001 to 2,000 hours requires two maintenance workers, etc.).
   g. Cost of raw material used.
   h. Rent on a factory building donated by the county, where the agreement calls for rent of $100,000 less $1 for each direct labor-hour worked in excess of 200,000 hours, but a minimum rental payment of $20,000 must be paid.
   i. Use of a machine under a lease, where a minimum charge of $1,000 is paid for up to 400 hours of machine time. After 400 hours of machine time, an additional charge of $2 per hour is paid up to a maximum charge of $2,000 per period.
2. How would a knowledge of cost behavior patterns such as those above be of help to a manager in analyzing the cost structure of his or her firm?

(CPA, adapted)

PROBLEM 5–15 High-Low Method; Predicting Cost [LO1, LO3]

Golden Company's total overhead costs at various levels of activity are presented below:

Month	Machine-Hours	Total Overhead Costs
March	50,000	$194,000
April.	40,000	170,200
May	60,000	217,800
June	70,000	241,600

Assume that the overhead costs above consist of utilities, supervisory salaries, and maintenance. The breakdown of these costs at the 40,000 machine-hour level of activity is as follows:

Utilities (variable)	$ 52,000
Supervisory salaries (fixed)	60,000
Maintenance (mixed)	58,200
Total overhead costs	$170,200

The company wants to break down the maintenance cost into its basic variable and fixed cost elements.

Required:

1. As shown above, overhead costs in June amounted to $241,600. Estimate how much of this consisted of maintenance cost. (Hint: To do this, it may be helpful to first determine how much of the $241,600 consisted of utilities and supervisory salaries. Think about the behavior of variable and fixed costs within the relevant range!)
2. Using the high-low method, estimate a cost formula for maintenance.
3. Express the company's total overhead costs in the linear equation form $Y = a + bX$.
4. What total overhead costs would you expect to be incurred at an operating activity level of 45,000 machine-hours?

PROBLEM 5–16 High-Low Method; Predicting Cost [LO1, LO3]

Echeverria SA is an Argentinian manufacturing company whose total factory overhead costs fluctuate somewhat from year to year according to the number of machine-hours worked in its production facility. These costs (in Argentinian pesos) at high and at low levels of activity over recent years are given below:

	Level of Activity	
	Low	High
Machine-hours	60,000	80,000
Total factory overhead costs.	274,000 pesos	312,000 pesos

The factory overhead costs above consist of indirect materials, rent, and maintenance. The company has analyzed these costs at the 60,000 machine-hours level of activity as follows:

Indirect materials (variable)	90,000 pesos
Rent (fixed).	130,000
Maintenance (mixed)	54,000
Total factory overhead costs	274,000 pesos

For planning purposes, the company wants to break down the maintenance cost into its variable and fixed cost elements.

Required:

1. Estimate how much of the factory overhead cost of 312,000 pesos at the high level of activity above consists of maintenance cost. (Hint: To do this, it may be helpful to first determine how much of the 312,000 pesos cost consists of indirect materials and rent. Think about the behavior of variable and fixed costs.)
2. Using the high-low method of cost analysis, estimate a cost formula for maintenance.
3. What *total* overhead costs would you expect the company to incur at an operating level of 65,000 machine-hours?

PROBLEM 5–17 High-Low Method; Cost of Goods Manufactured [LO1, LO3]

NuWay, Inc., manufactures a single product. Selected data from the company's cost records for two recent months are given below:

	Level of Activity	
	July—Low	**October—High**
Number of units produced	9,000	12,000
Cost of goods manufactured	$285,000	$390,000
Work in process inventory, beginning. . . .	14,000	22,000
Work in process inventory, ending	25,000	15,000
Direct materials cost per unit	15	15
Direct labor cost per unit	6	6
Manufacturing overhead cost, total	?	?

The company's manufacturing overhead cost consists of both variable and fixed cost elements. In order to have data available for planning, management wants to determine how much of the overhead cost is variable with units produced and how much of it is fixed per year.

Required:

1. For both July and October, estimate the amount of manufacturing overhead cost added to production. The company had no under- or overapplied overhead in either month. (Hint: A useful way to proceed might be to construct a schedule of cost of goods manufactured.)
2. Using the high-low method of cost analysis, estimate a cost formula for manufacturing overhead. Express the variable portion of the formula in terms of a variable rate per unit of product.
3. If 9,500 units are produced during a month, what would be the cost of goods manufactured? (Assume that the company's beginning work in process inventory for the month is $16,000 and that its ending work in process inventory is $19,000. Also assume that there is no under- or overapplied overhead cost for the month.)

PROBLEM 5–18 High-Low and Scattergraph Analysis [LO2, LO3]

Sebolt Wire Company heats copper ingots to very high temperatures by placing the ingots in a large heat coil. The heated ingots are then run through a shaping machine that shapes the soft ingot into wire. Due to the long heat-up time, the coil is never turned off. When an ingot is placed in the coil, the temperature is raised to an even higher level, and then the coil is allowed to drop to the "waiting" temperature between ingots. Management needs to know the variable cost of power involved in heating an ingot and the fixed cost of power during "waiting" periods. The following data on ingots processed and power costs are available:

Month	Ingots	Power Cost
January	110	$5,500
February.	90	4,500
March	80	4,400
April	100	5,000
May	130	6,000
June	120	5,600
July.	70	4,000
August	60	3,200
September	50	3,400
October	40	2,400

Required:

1. Using the high-low method, estimate a cost formula for power cost. Express the formula in the form $Y = a + bX$.
2. Prepare a scattergraph by plotting ingots processed and power cost on a graph. Fit a straight line to the plotted points, and estimate a cost formula for power cost using the quick-and-dirty method.

PROBLEM 5–19 (Appendix 5A) Least-Squares Regression Method [LO5]

Refer to the data for Sebolt Wire Company in Problem 5–18.

Required:

1. Using the least-squares regression method, estimate a cost formula for power cost. (Round the variable cost to two decimal places and the fixed cost to the nearest whole dollar.)

2. Prepare a table showing the total fixed cost per month and the variable cost per ingot under each of the three methods used in problems 5–18 and 5–19. Then comment on the accuracy and usefulness of the data derived by each method.

PROBLEM 5–20 Scattergraph Analysis [LO2]

In the past, Big Piney Resort has had great difficulty in predicting its costs at various levels of activity through the year. The reason is that the company has never attempted to study its cost structure by analyzing cost behavior patterns. The president has now become convinced that such an analysis is necessary if the company is to maintain its profits and its competitive position. Accordingly, an analysis of cost behavior patterns has been undertaken.

The company has managed to identify variable and fixed costs in all areas of its operation except for food services. Costs in this area do not seem to exhibit either a strictly variable or a strictly fixed pattern. Food costs over the past several months, along with the number of meals served, are given below:

Month	Number of Meals Served (000)	Total Food Cost
January	4	$18,000
February	5	21,000
March	6	24,000
April	10	33,000
May	12	35,000
June	11	33,000
July	9	30,000
August	8	27,000
September	7	26,000

The president believes that the costs above contain a mixture of variable and fixed cost elements. He has assigned you the responsibility of determining whether this is correct.

Required:

1. Prepare a scattergraph using the data given above. Place cost on the vertical axis and activity (meals served) on the horizontal axis. Using a ruler, fit a straight line to the plotted points.
2. Is the president correct in assuming that food costs contain both variable and fixed cost elements? If so, what is the approximate total fixed cost and the approximate variable cost per meal served? (You may use the quick-and-dirty method of estimating variable and fixed costs.)

PROBLEM 5–21 (Appendix 5A) Least-Squares Regression Method [LO5]

Refer to the data for Big Piney Resort in Problem 5–20.

Required:

1. Using the least-squares regression method, estimate the variable and fixed cost elements in total food cost. (Since "Number of meals served" is in thousands of meals, the variable cost you compute will also be in thousands of meals. It can be left in this form, or you can convert your variable cost to a per meal basis by dividing it by 1,000.)
2. From the data determined in (1) above, express the cost formula for food in linear equation form.

PROBLEM 5–22 (Appendix 5A) Least-Squares Regression Analysis; Contribution Income Statement [LO4, LO5]

Alden Company has decided to use the contribution approach to the income statement internally for planning purposes. The company has analyzed its expenses and developed the following cost formulas:

Cost	Cost Formula
Cost of goods sold	$20 per unit sold
Advertising expense	$170,000 per quarter
Sales commissions	5% of sales
Administrative salaries	$80,000 per quarter
Shipping expense	?
Depreciation expense	$50,000 per quarter

Management has concluded that shipping expense is a mixed cost, containing both variable and fixed cost elements. Units sold and the related shipping expense over the last eight quarters are given below:

Quarter	Units Sold (000)	Shipping Expense
Year 1:		
First	16	$160,000
Second	18	175,000
Third	23	210,000
Fourth	19	180,000
Year 2:		
First	17	170,000
Second	20	190,000
Third	25	230,000
Fourth	22	205,000

Management would like a cost formula derived for shipping expense so that a budgeted income statement using the contribution approach can be prepared for the next quarter.

Required:

1. Using the least-squares regression method, estimate a cost formula for shipping expense. (Since the Units Sold above are in thousands of units, the variable cost you compute will also be in thousands of units. It can be left in this form, or you can convert your variable cost to a per unit basis by dividing it by 1,000.)
2. In the first quarter of Year 3, the company plans to sell 21,000 units at a selling price of $50 per unit. Prepare an income statement for the quarter using the contribution format.

Cases

CASE 5–23 Analysis of Mixed Costs in a Pricing Decision [LO1, LO2, LO3, LO5]

Jasmine Lee owns a catering company that serves food and beverages at exclusive parties and business functions. Lee's business is seasonal, with a heavy schedule during the summer months and holidays and a lighter schedule at other times.

One of the major events that Lee's customers request is a cocktail party. She offers a standard cocktail party and has estimated the cost per guest for this party as follows:

Food and beverages	$17.00
Labor (0.5 hour @ $10.00 per hour)	5.00
Overhead (0.5 hour @ $18.63 per hour)	9.32
Total cost per guest	$31.32

This standard cocktail party lasts three hours and Lee hires one worker for every six guests, which is one-half hour of labor per guest. These workers are hired only as needed and are paid only for the hours they actually work.

Lee ordinarily charges $45 per guest. She is confident about her estimates of the costs of foods and beverages and labor, but is not as comfortable with the estimate of overhead cost. The $18.63 overhead cost per labor-hour was determined by dividing total overhead expenses for the last 12 months by total labor-hours for the same period. Monthly data concerning overhead costs and labor-hours appear below:

Month	Labor Hours	Overhead Expenses
January	1,500	$ 44,000
February	1,680	47,200
March	1,800	48,000
April	2,520	51,200
May	2,700	53,600
June	3,300	56,800
July	3,900	59,200
August	4,500	61,600
September	4,200	60,000
October	2,700	54,400
November	1,860	49,600
December	3,900	58,400
Total	34,560	$644,000

Lee has received a request to bid on a 120-guest fund-raising cocktail party to be given next month by an important local charity. (The party would last the usual three hours.) She would really like to win this contract; the guest list for this charity event includes many prominent individuals she would like to land as future clients. Lee is confident that these potential customers would be favorably impressed by her company's services at the charity event.

Required:

1. Estimate the contribution to profit of a standard 120-guest cocktail party if Lee charges her usual price of $45 per guest. (In other words, by how much would her overall profit increase?)
2. How low could Lee bid for the charity event, in terms of a price per guest, and still not lose money on the event itself?
3. The individual who is organizing the charity's fund-raising event has indicated that he has already received a bid under $42 from another catering company. Do you think Lee should bid below her normal $45 per guest price for the charity event? Why or why not?

(CMA, adapted)

CASE 5–24 (Appendix 5A) Analysis of Mixed Costs, Job-Cost System, and Activity-Based Costing [LO1, LO2, LO5]

Ruedi Bärlach PLC, a company located in Gümligen, Switzerland, manufactures custom-designed high-precision industrial tools. The company has a traditional job-cost system in which direct labor and direct materials costs are assigned directly to jobs, but factory overhead is applied using direct labor-hours as a base. Management uses this job cost data for valuing cost of goods sold and inventories for external reports. For internal decision-making, management has largely ignored this cost data since direct labor costs are basically fixed and management believes overhead costs actually have little to do with direct labor-hours. Recently, management has become interested in activity-based costing (ABC) as a way of estimating job costs and other costs for decision-making purposes.

Management assembled a cross-functional team to design a prototype ABC system. Electrical costs were among the first factory overhead costs investigated by the team. Electricity is used to provide light, to power equipment, and to heat the building in the winter. The ABC team proposed allocating electrical costs to jobs based on machine-hours since running the machines consumes significant amounts of electricity. Data assembled by the team concerning actual direct labor-hours, machine-hours, and electrical costs over a recent eight-week period have been entered into the spreadsheet that appears below. (The Swiss currency is the Swiss franc, which is denoted by SFr.)

	A	B	C	D
1		Direct Labor-Hours	Machine-Hours	Electrical Costs
2	Week 1	8,910	7,700	SFr 84,600
3	Week 2	8,920	8,600	81,800
4	Week 3	8,870	8,600	81,000
5	Week 4	8,840	8,500	80,800
6	Week 5	8,990	7,600	79,400
7	Week 6	8,940	7,100	82,800
8	Week 7	8,870	6,000	73,100
9	Week 8	8,910	6,800	80,800
10	Total	71,250	60,900	SFr 644,300

To help assess the effect of the proposed change to machine-hours as the allocation base, the above eight-week totals were converted to annual figures by multiplying them by six.

	Direct Labor-Hours	Machine-Hours	Electrical Costs
Estimated annual total (eight-week total above × 6)	427,500	365,400	SFr 3,865,800

Required:

1. Assume that the estimated annual totals from the above table are used to compute the company's predetermined overhead rate. What would be the predetermined overhead rate for electrical costs if the allocation base is direct labor-hours? machine-hours?

2. Management intends to bid on a job for a set of custom tools for a watchmaker that would require 30 direct labor-hours and 25 machine-hours. How much electrical cost would be charged to this job using the predetermined overhead rate computed in part (1) above if the allocation base is direct labor-hours? machine-hours?
3. Prepare a scattergraph in which you plot direct labor-hours on the horizontal axis and electrical costs on the vertical axis. Prepare another scattergraph in which you plot machine-hours on the horizontal axis and electrical costs on the vertical axis. Do you agree with the ABC team that machine-hours is a better allocation base for electrical costs than direct labor-hours? Why?
4. Using machine-hours as the measure of activity and the least-squares regression method, estimate the fixed and variable components of electrical costs.
5. How much electrical cost do you think would actually be caused by the custom tool job for the watchmaker in part (2) above? Explain.
6. What factors, apart from direct labor-hours and machine-hours, are likely to affect consumption of electrical power in the company?

CASE 5–25 Scattergraph Analysis; Selection of an Activity Base [LO2]

Mapleleaf Sweepers of Toronto manufactures replacement rotary sweeper brooms for the large sweeper trucks that clear leaves and snow from city streets. The business is to some degree seasonal, with the largest demand during and just preceding the fall and winter months. Since there are so many different kinds of sweeper brooms used by its customers, Mapleleaf Sweepers makes all of its brooms to order.

The company has been analyzing its overhead accounts to determine fixed and variable components for planning purposes. Below are data for the company's janitorial labor costs over the last nine months. (Cost data are in Canadian dollars.)

	Number of Units Produced	Number of Janitorial Workdays	Janitorial Labor Cost
January	115	21	$3,840
February	109	19	3,648
March	102	23	4,128
April	76	20	3,456
May	69	23	4,320
June	108	22	4,032
July	77	16	2,784
August	71	14	2,688
September	127	21	3,840

The number of workdays varies from month to month due to the number of weekdays, holidays, days of vacation, and sick leave taken in the month. The number of units produced in a month varies depending on demand and the number of workdays in the month.

There are two janitors who each work an eight-hour shift each workday. They each can take up to 10 days of paid sick leave each year. Their wages on days they call in sick and their wages during paid vacations are charged to miscellaneous overhead rather than to the janitorial labor cost account.

Required:

1. Prepare a scattergraph and plot the janitorial labor cost and units produced. (Place cost on the vertical axis and units produced on the horizontal axis.)
2. Prepare a scattergraph and plot the janitorial labor cost and number of workdays. (Place cost on the vertical axis and the number of workdays on the horizontal axis.)
3. Which measure of activity—number of units produced or janitorial workdays—should be used as the activity base for explaining janitorial labor cost?

CASE 5–26 (Appendix 5A) Least-Squares Regression; Scattergraph; Comparison of Activity Bases [LO2, LO5]

The Hard Rock Mining Company is developing cost formulas to have data available for management planning and decision-making purposes. The company's cost analyst has concluded that utilities cost is a mixed cost, and he is attempting to find a base with which the cost might be closely correlated. The controller has suggested that tons mined might be a good base to use in developing a cost formula. The production superintendent disagrees; she thinks that direct labor-hours would be a better base. The cost analyst has decided to try both bases and has assembled the following information:

Quarter	Tons Mined (000)	Direct Labor-Hours (000)	Utilities Cost
Year 1:			
First	15	5	$ 50,000
Second	11	3	45,000
Third	21	4	60,000
Fourth	12	6	75,000
Year 2:			
First	18	10	100,000
Second	25	9	105,000
Third	30	8	85,000
Fourth	28	11	120,000

Required:

1. Using tons mined as the independent (*X*) variable:
   a. Determine a cost formula for utilities cost using the least-squares regression method. (The variable cost you compute will be in thousands of tons. It can be left in this form, or you can convert your variable cost to a per ton basis by dividing it by 1,000.)
   b. Prepare a scattergraph and plot the tons mined and utilities cost. (Place cost on the vertical axis and tons mined on the horizontal axis.) Fit a regression line to the plotted points using the cost formula determined in (*a*) above.
2. Using direct labor-hours as the independent (*X*) variable, repeat the computations in (*a*) and (*b*) above.
3. Would you recommend that the company use tons mined or direct labor-hours as a base for planning utilities cost?

Group and Internet Exercises

GROUP EXERCISE 5–27 Variable and Fixed Costs in Practice

Form a team to investigate how an organization in your area handles variable and fixed costs. Find a local organization that you are interested in. It may be in any industry and can be a business, a not-for-profit organization, or a part of the government. Research the organization on the Web and in periodicals to find out as much as you can about what the organization does and its finances. Make an appointment to meet with the controller or with another top manager in the organization who is familiar with the financial side of the organization. After meeting with that individual, write a memo in which you discuss the following issues.

Required:

1. Does the organization make any attempt to formally distinguish between variable and fixed costs in planning and controlling operations? If not, why not?
2. If the organization does formally distinguish between variable and fixed costs, how are variable and fixed costs estimated? What activity bases are used? How are these activity bases selected? What method does the company use for estimating the variable cost per unit of activity? How often are these estimates made? Does the company prepare scattergraphs of past cost and activity data?
3. If the organization does formally distinguish between variable and fixed costs, how does this help managers in planning and controlling operations?

INTERNET EXERCISE 5–28

As you know, the World Wide Web is a medium that is constantly evolving. Sites come and go, and change without notice. To enable periodic update of site addresses, this problem has been posted to the textbook website (www.mhhe.com/garrison10e). After accessing the site, enter the Student Center and select this chapter. Select and complete the Internet Exercise.

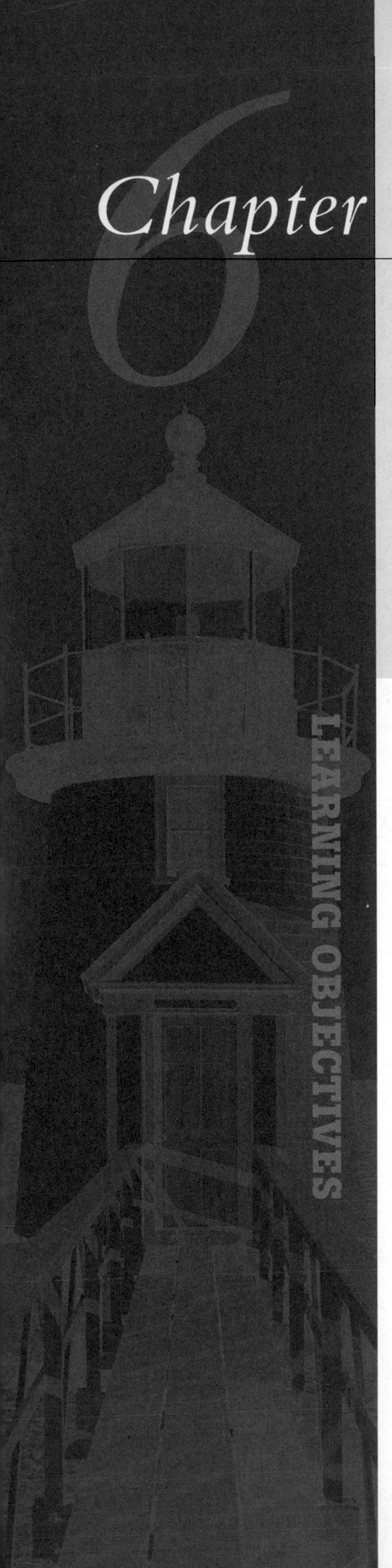

Chapter Six

Cost-Volume-Profit Relationships

After studying Chapter 6, you should be able to:

1. Explain how changes in activity affect contribution margin and net operating income.
2. Prepare and interpret a cost-volume-profit (CVP) graph.
3. Use the contribution margin ratio (CM ratio) to compute changes in contribution margin and net operating income resulting from changes in sales volume.
4. Show the effects on contribution margin of changes in variable costs, fixed costs, selling price, and volume.
5. Compute the break-even point.
6. Determine the level of sales needed to achieve a desired target profit.
7. Compute the margin of safety and explain its significance.
8. Compute the degree of operating leverage at a particular level of sales and explain how the degree of operating leverage can be used to predict changes in net operating income.
9. Compute the break-even point for a multiple product company and explain the effects of shifts in the sales mix on contribution margin and the break-even point.

BUSINESS FOCUS

Forget the Theater—Make Money on Cable TV

"Several years ago, Hollywood experienced a phenomenon known as the 'straight-to-cable' era. What this phrase referred to was a well used (and abused!) movie-making principle that hinted that if anyone (and many times it really was just *anyone*) could produce a movie (quality was never an issue) for under a million dollars, it'd automatically turn a profit from the sale of its cable TV rights. In essence, the 'movie' would bypass the theaters all together [*sic*] and still turn a profit. From a business standpoint, what this money-making scheme illustrates is [that] every product has a break-even point. Make more money than this and you turn a profit. Make less than this, and, well, you get the picture (pardon the pun)."

Source: Ben Chiu, "The Last Big-Budget Combat Sim," *Computer Games*, June 1999, p. 40.

Cost-volume-profit (CVP) analysis is one of the most powerful tools that managers have at their command. It helps them understand the interrelationship between cost, volume, and profit in an organization by focusing on interactions among the following five elements:

1. Prices of products.
2. Volume or level of activity.
3. Per unit variable costs.
4. Total fixed costs.
5. Mix of products sold.

Because CVP analysis helps managers understand the interrelationships among cost, volume, and profit, it is a vital tool in many business decisions. These decisions include, for example, what products to manufacture or sell, what pricing policy to follow, what marketing strategy to employ, and what type of productive facilities to acquire. To help understand the role of CVP analysis in business decisions, consider the case of Acoustic Concepts, Inc., a company founded by Prem Narayan.

Managerial Accounting in Action

The Issue

Prem, who was a graduate student in engineering at the time, started Acoustic Concepts to market a radical new speaker he had designed for automobile sound systems. The speaker, called the Sonic Blaster, uses an advanced microprocessor chip to boost amplification to awesome levels. Prem contracted with a Taiwanese electronics manufacturer to produce the speaker. With seed money provided by his family, Prem placed an order with the manufacturer and ran advertisements in auto magazines.

The Sonic Blaster was an almost immediate success, and sales grew to the point that Prem moved the company's headquarters out of his apartment and into rented quarters in a neighboring industrial park. He also hired a receptionist, an accountant, a sales manager, and a small sales staff to sell the speakers to retail stores. The accountant, Bob Luchinni, had worked for several small companies where he had acted as a business advisor as well as accountant and bookkeeper. The following discussion occurred soon after Bob was hired:

Prem: Bob, I've got a lot of questions about the company's finances that I hope you can help answer.

Bob: We're in great shape. The loan from your family will be paid off within a few months.

Prem: I know, but I am worried about the risks I've taken on by expanding operations. What would happen if a competitor entered the market and our sales slipped? How far could sales drop without putting us into the red? Another question I've been trying to resolve is how much our sales would have to increase in order to justify the big marketing campaign the sales staff is pushing for.

Bob: Marketing always wants more money for advertising.

Prem: And they are always pushing me to drop the selling price on the speaker. I agree with them that a lower price will boost our volume, but I'm not sure the increased volume will offset the loss in revenue from the lower price.

Bob: It sounds like these questions all are related in some way to the relationships among our selling prices, our costs, and our volume. We shouldn't have a problem coming up with some answers. I'll need a day or two, though, to gather some data.

Prem: Why don't we set up a meeting for three days from now? That would be Thursday.

Bob: That'll be fine. I'll have some preliminary answers for you as well as a model you can use for answering similar questions in the future.

Prem: Good. I'll be looking forward to seeing what you come up with.

The Basics of Cost-Volume-Profit (CVP) Analysis

Bob Luchinni's preparation for the Thursday meeting begins where our study of cost behavior in the preceding chapter left off—with the contribution income statement. The contribution income statement emphasizes the behavior of costs and therefore is extremely helpful to a manager in judging the impact on profits of changes in selling price, cost, or volume. Bob will base his analysis on the following contribution income statement he prepared last month:

Acoustic Concepts, Inc.
Contribution Income Statement
For the Month of June

	Total	Per Unit
Sales (400 speakers)	$100,000	$250
Less variable expenses	60,000	150
Contribution margin	40,000	$100
Less fixed expenses	35,000	
Net operating income	$ 5,000	

Notice that sales, variable expenses, and contribution margin are expressed on a per unit basis as well as in total on this contribution income statement. The per unit figures will be very helpful in the work we will be doing in the following pages. Note that this contribution income statement has been prepared for management's use inside the company and would not ordinarily be made available to those outside the company.

Contribution Margin

LEARNING OBJECTIVE 1
Explain how changes in activity affect contribution margin and net operating income.

As explained in the previous chapter, contribution margin is the amount remaining from sales revenue after variable expenses have been deducted. Thus, it is the amount available to cover fixed expenses and then to provide profits for the period. Notice the sequence here—contribution margin is used *first* to cover the fixed expenses, and then whatever remains goes toward profits. If the contribution margin is not sufficient to cover the fixed expenses, then a loss occurs for the period. To illustrate with an extreme example, assume that by the middle of a particular month Acoustic Concepts has been able to sell only one speaker. If the company does not sell any more speakers during the month, the company's income statement will appear as follows:

	Total	Per Unit
Sales (1 speaker)	$ 250	$250
Less variable expenses	150	150
Contribution margin	100	$100
Less fixed expenses	35,000	
Net operating loss	$(34,900)	

For each additional speaker that the company is able to sell during the month, $100 more in contribution margin will become available to help cover the fixed expenses. If a second speaker is sold, for example, then the total contribution margin will increase by $100 (to a total of $200) and the company's loss will decrease by $100, to $34,800:

	Total	Per Unit
Sales (2 speakers)	$ 500	$250
Less variable expenses	300	150
Contribution margin	200	$100
Less fixed expenses	35,000	
Net operating loss	$(34,800)	

If enough speakers can be sold to generate $35,000 in contribution margin, then all of the fixed costs will be covered and the company will have managed to at least *break even* for the month—that is, to show neither profit nor loss but just cover all of its costs. To reach the break-even point, the company will have to sell 350 speakers in a month, since each speaker sold yields $100 in contribution margin:

	Total	Per Unit
Sales (350 speakers)	$87,500	$250
Less variable expenses	52,500	150
Contribution margin	35,000	$100
Less fixed expenses	35,000	
Net operating income	$ 0	

Computation of the break-even point is discussed in detail later in the chapter; for the moment, note that the **break-even point** is the level of sales at which profit is zero.

In Business

Will eToys Make It?

The company eToys, which sells toys over the Internet, lost $190 million in 1999 on sales of $151 million. One big cost was advertising. eToys spent about $37 on advertising for each $100 of sales. (Other e-tailers were spending even more—in some cases, up to $460 on advertising for each $100 in sales!)

eToys does have some advantages relative to bricks-and-mortar stores such as Toys "R" Us. eToys has much lower inventory costs since it need only keep on hand one or two of a slow-moving item, whereas a traditional store has to fully stock its shelves. And bricks-and-mortar retail spaces in malls and elsewhere do cost money—on average, about 7% of sales. However, e-tailers such as eToys have their own set of disadvantages. Customers "pick and pack" their own items at a bricks-and-mortar outlet, but e-tailers have to pay employees to carry out this task. This costs eToys about $33 for every $100 in sales. And the technology to sell over the net does not come free. eToys paid about $29 on its website and related technology for every $100 in sales. However, many of these costs of selling over the net are fixed. Toby Lenk, the CEO of eToys, estimates that the company will pass its break-even point somewhere between $750 and $900 million in sales—representing less than 1% of the market for toys.

Source: Erin Kelly, "The Last e-Store on the Block," *Fortune,* September 18, 2000, pp. 214–220.

Once the break-even point has been reached, net income will increase by the unit contribution margin for each additional unit sold. For example, if 351 speakers are sold in a month, then we can expect that the net income for the month will be $100, since the company will have sold 1 speaker more than the number needed to break even:

	Total	Per Unit
Sales (351 speakers)	$87,750	$250
Less variable expenses	52,650	150
Contribution margin	35,100	$100
Less fixed expenses	35,000	
Net operating income	$ 100	

If 352 speakers are sold (2 speakers above the break-even point), then we can expect that the net operating income for the month will be $200, and so forth. To know what the profits will be at various levels of activity, therefore, it is not necessary for a manager to prepare a whole series of income statements. To estimate the profit at any point above the break-even point, the manager can simply take the number of units to be sold over the break-even point and multiply that number by the unit contribution margin. The result represents the anticipated profits for the period. Or, to estimate the effect of a planned increase in sales on profits, the manager can simply multiply the increase in units sold by the unit contribution margin. The result will be the expected increase in profits. To illustrate, if Acoustic Concepts is currently selling 400 speakers per month and plans to increase sales to 425 speakers per month, the anticipated impact on profits can be computed as follows:

Increased number of speakers to be sold	25
Contribution margin per speaker	×$100
Increase in net operating income	$2,500

These calculations can be verified as follows:

	Sales Volume			
	400 Speakers	425 Speakers	Difference 25 Speakers	Per Unit
Sales	$100,000	$106,250	$6,250	$250
Less variable expenses	60,000	63,750	3,750	150
Contribution margin	40,000	42,500	2,500	$100
Less fixed expenses	35,000	35,000	0	
Net operating income	$ 5,000	$ 7,500	$2,500	

To summarize these examples, if there were no sales, the company's loss would equal its fixed expenses. Each unit that is sold reduces the loss by the amount of the unit contribution margin. Once the break-even point has been reached, each additional unit sold increases the company's profit by the amount of the unit contribution margin.

CVP Relationships in Graphic Form

The relations among revenue, cost, profit, and volume can be expressed graphically by preparing a **cost-volume-profit (CVP) graph.** A CVP graph highlights CVP relationships over wide ranges of activity and can give managers a perspective that can be obtained in no other way. To help explain his analysis to Prem Narayan, Bob Luchinni decided to prepare a CVP graph for Acoustic Concepts.

LEARNING OBJECTIVE 2
Prepare and interpret a cost-volume-profit (CVP) graph.

Preparing the CVP Graph In a CVP graph (sometimes called a *break-even chart*), unit volume is commonly represented on the horizontal (*X*) axis and dollars on the vertical (*Y*) axis. Preparing a CVP graph involves three steps. These steps are keyed to the graph in Exhibit 6–1:

1. Draw a line parallel to the volume axis to represent total fixed expenses. For Acoustic Concepts, total fixed expenses are $35,000.
2. Choose some volume of sales and plot the point representing total expenses (fixed and variable) at the activity level you have selected. In Exhibit 6–1, Bob Luchinni chose a volume of 600 speakers. Total expenses at that activity level would be as follows:

Fixed expenses	$35,000
Variable expenses (600 speakers × $150 per speaker)	90,000
Total expenses	$125,000

   After the point has been plotted, draw a line through it back to the point where the fixed expenses line intersects the dollars axis.
3. Again choose some volume of sales and plot the point representing total sales dollars at the activity level you have selected. In Exhibit 6–1, Bob Luchinni again chose a volume of 600 speakers. Sales at that activity level total $150,000 (600 speakers × $250 per speaker). Draw a line through this point back to the origin.

The interpretation of the completed CVP graph is given in Exhibit 6–2. The anticipated profit or loss at any given level of sales is measured by the vertical distance between the total revenue line (sales) and the total expenses line (variable expenses plus fixed expenses).

The break-even point is where the total revenue and total expenses lines cross. The break-even point of 350 speakers in Exhibit 6–2 agrees with the break-even point computed earlier.

Exhibit 6–1
Preparing the CVP Graph

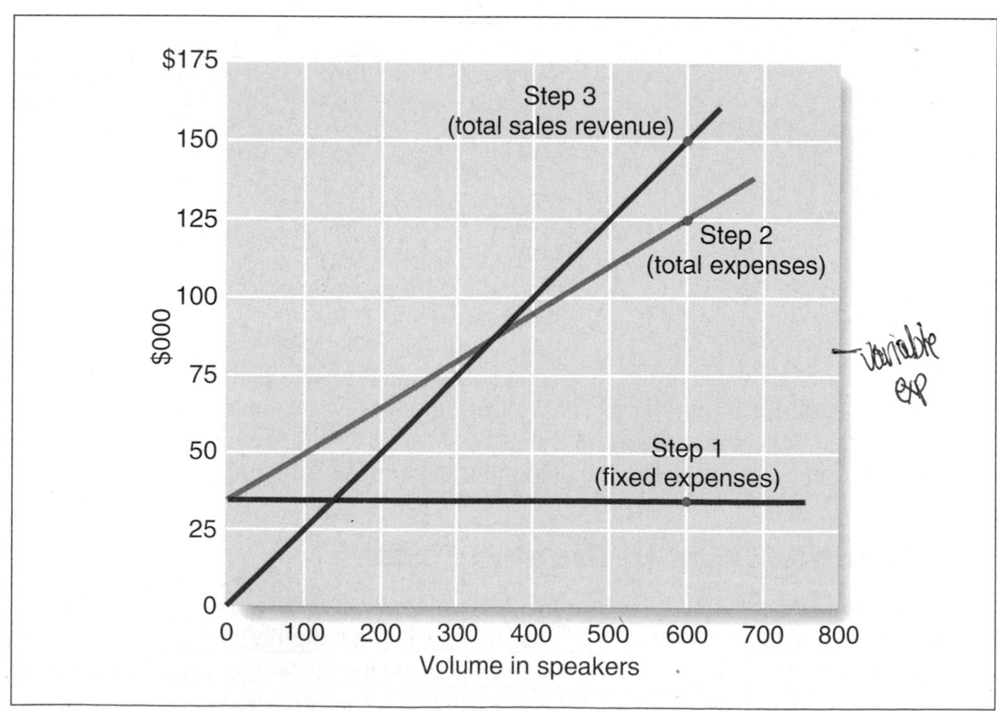

As discussed earlier, when sales are below the break-even point—in this case, 350 units—the company suffers a loss. Note that the loss (represented by the vertical distance between the total expense and total revenue lines) gets worse as sales decline. When sales are above the break-even point, the company earns a profit and the size of the profit (represented by the vertical distance between the total revenue and total expense lines) increases as sales increase.

Buying Your Groceries Online

In Business

Online grocers such as Peapod.com (www.peapod.com), Webvan (www.webvan.com), Streamline.com (www.streamline.com), HomeRuns.com (www.homeruns.com), Netgrocer.com (www.netgrocer.com), and HomeGrocer.com (www.homegrocer.com) have interesting cost structures. Large investments in fixed costs are necessary to create appealing web pages and for bricks-and-mortar infrastructure such as warehouses and delivery vans. Variable costs come in at least two varieties. One kind of variable cost is related to the number of deliveries made. These variable costs include fuel, maintenance, and depreciation on vehicles. The other kind of variable cost is related to the amount of groceries ordered by a customer.

With the cost structure in this industry, and the low margins prevalent in the grocery business, it is very difficult for online grocers to break even. For example, HomeRuns.com's president Tom Furber says that the Somerville, Massachusetts-based grocer needs 8,000 orders in a week to break even. In a good week, it may get less than a third that many orders.

Source: Timothy J. Mullaney and David Leonhardt, "A Hard Sell Online? Guess Again," *Business Week*, July 12, 1999, pp. 142–143.

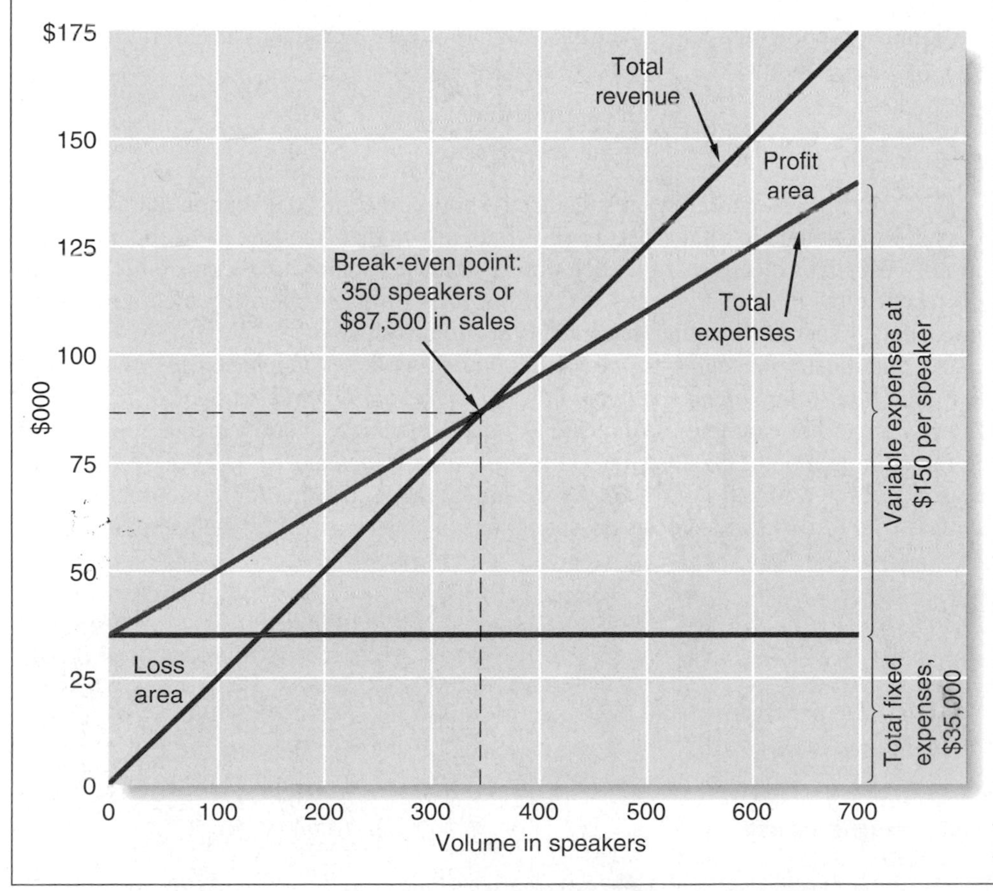

Exhibit 6–2
The Completed CVP Graph

Contribution Margin Ratio (CM Ratio)

LEARNING OBJECTIVE 3
Use the contribution margin ratio (CM ratio) to compute changes in contribution margin and net operating income resulting from changes in sales volume.

In the previous section, we explored how cost-volume-profit relations can be visualized. In this section we will see how the *contribution margin ratio* can be used in cost-volume-profit calculations. As the first step, we have added a column to Acoustic Concepts' contribution income statement in which sales revenues, variable expenses, and contribution margin are expressed as a percentage of sales:

	Total	Per Unit	Percent of Sales
Sales (400 speakers)	$100,000	$250	100%
Less variable expenses	60,000	150	60%
Contribution margin	40,000	$100	40%
Less fixed expenses	35,000		
Net operating income	$ 5,000		

The contribution margin as a percentage of total sales is referred to as the **contribution margin ratio (CM ratio).** This ratio is computed as follows:

$$\text{CM ratio} = \frac{\text{Contribution margin}}{\text{Sales}}$$

For Acoustic Concepts, the computations are:

$$\text{CM ratio} = \frac{\text{Total contribution margin}}{\text{Total sales}} = \frac{\$40{,}000}{\$100{,}000} = 40\%$$

In a company such as Acoustic Concepts that has only one product, the CM ratio can also be computed as follows:

$$\text{CM ratio} = \frac{\text{Unit contribution margin}}{\text{Unit selling price}} = \frac{\$100}{\$250} = 40\%$$

The CM ratio is extremely useful since it shows how the contribution margin will be affected by a change in total sales. To illustrate, notice that Acoustic Concepts has a CM ratio of 40%. This means that for each dollar increase in sales, total contribution margin will increase by 40 cents ($1 sales × CM ratio of 40%). Net operating income will also increase by 40 cents, assuming that fixed costs do not change.

As this illustration suggests, *the impact on net operating income of any given dollar change in total sales can be computed in seconds by simply applying the CM ratio to the dollar change.* For example, if Acoustic Concepts plans a $30,000 increase in sales during the coming month, the contribution margin should increase by $12,000 ($30,000 increased sales × CM ratio of 40%). As we noted above, net operating income will also increase by $12,000 if fixed costs do not change. This is verified by the following table:

	Sales Volume			Percent
	Present	Expected	Increase	of Sales
Sales	$100,000	$130,000	$30,000	100%
Less variable expenses	60,000	78,000*	18,000	60%
Contribution margin	40,000	52,000	12,000	40%
Less fixed expenses	35,000	35,000	0	
Net operating income	$ 5,000	$ 17,000	$12,000	

*$130,000 expected sales ÷ $250 per unit = 520 units. 520 units × $150 per unit = $78,000.

Some managers prefer to work with the CM ratio rather than the unit contribution margin. The CM ratio is particularly valuable in situations where trade-offs must be made between more dollar sales of one product versus more dollar sales of another. Generally speaking, when trying to increase sales, products that yield the greatest amount of contribution margin per dollar of sales should be emphasized.

Some Applications of CVP Concepts

LEARNING OBJECTIVE 4
Show the effects on contribution margin of changes in variable costs, fixed costs, selling price, and volume.

Bob Luchinni, the accountant at Acoustic Concepts, wanted to demonstrate to the company's president Prem Narayan how the concepts developed on the preceding pages can be used in planning and decision making. Bob gathered the following basic data:

	Per Unit	Percent of Sales
Selling price	$250	100%
Less variable expenses	150	60%
Contribution margin	$100	40%

Recall that fixed expenses are $35,000 per month. Bob Luchinni will use these data to show the effects of changes in variable costs, fixed costs, sales price, and sales volume on the company's profitability in a variety of situations.

Change in Fixed Cost and Sales Volume Acoustic Concepts is currently selling 400 speakers per month (monthly sales of $100,000). The sales manager feels that a $10,000 increase in the monthly advertising budget would increase monthly sales by $30,000 to a total of 520 units. Should the advertising budget be increased? The following table shows the effect of the proposed change in the monthly advertising budget:

	Current Sales	Sales with Additional Advertising Budget	Difference	Percent of Sales
Sales	$100,000	$130,000	$30,000	100%
Less variable expenses	60,000	78,000*	18,000	60%
Contribution margin	40,000	52,000	12,000	40%
Less fixed expenses	35,000	45,000†	10,000	
Net operating income	$ 5,000	$ 7,000	$ 2,000	

*520 units × $150 per unit = $78,000.
†$35,000 plus additional $10,000 monthly advertising budget = $45,000.

Assuming no other factors need to be considered, the increase in the advertising budget should be approved since it would lead to an increase in net operating income of $2,000. There are two shorter ways to present this solution. The first alternative solution follows:

Alternative Solution 1

Expected total contribution margin:	
$130,000 × 40% CM ratio	$52,000
Present total contribution margin:	
$100,000 × 40% CM ratio	40,000
Incremental contribution margin	12,000
Change in fixed expenses:	
Less incremental advertising expense	10,000
Increased net operating income	$ 2,000

Concept 6–1

Since in this case only the fixed costs and the sales volume change, the solution can be presented in an even shorter format, as follows:

Alternative Solution 2

Incremental contribution margin:	
$30,000 × 40% CM ratio	$12,000
Less incremental advertising expense	10,000
Increased net operating income	$ 2,000

Notice that this approach does not depend on a knowledge of previous sales. Also notice that it is unnecessary under either shorter approach to prepare an income statement. Both of the solutions above involve an **incremental analysis**—they consider only those items of revenue, cost, and volume that will change if the new program is implemented. Although in each case a new income statement could have been prepared, the incremental approach is simpler and more direct and focuses attention on the specific items involved in the decision.

Change in Variable Costs and Sales Volume Refer to the original data. Recall that Acoustic Concepts is currently selling 400 speakers per month. Management is considering the use of higher-quality components, which would increase variable costs (and thereby reduce the contribution margin) by $10 per speaker. However, the sales manager predicts that the higher overall quality would increase sales to 480 speakers per month. Should the higher-quality components be used?

The $10 increase in variable costs will decrease the unit contribution margin by $10—from $100 down to $90.

Solution

Expected total contribution margin with higher-quality components:	
480 speakers × $90 per speaker	$43,200
Present total contribution margin:	
400 speakers × $100 per speaker	40,000
Increase in total contribution margin	$ 3,200

According to this analysis, the higher-quality components should be used. Since fixed costs will not change, the $3,200 increase in contribution margin shown above should result in a $3,200 increase in net operating income.

Change in Fixed Cost, Sales Price, and Sales Volume Refer to the original data and recall again that the company is currently selling 400 speakers per month. To increase sales, the sales manager would like to cut the selling price by $20 per speaker and increase the advertising budget by $15,000 per month. The sales manager argues that if these two steps are taken, unit sales will increase by 50% to 600 speakers per month. Should the changes be made?

A decrease of $20 per speaker in the selling price will cause the unit contribution margin to decrease from $100 to $80.

Solution

Expected total contribution margin with lower selling price:	
600 speakers × $80 per speaker	$48,000
Present total contribution margin:	
400 speakers × $100 per speaker	40,000
Incremental contribution margin	8,000
Change in fixed expenses:	
Less incremental advertising expense	15,000
Reduction in net operating income	$ (7,000)

According to this analysis, the changes should not be made. The same solution can be obtained by preparing comparative income statements as follows:

	Present 400 Speakers per Month		Expected 600 Speakers per Month		
	Total	Per Unit	Total	Per Unit	Difference
Sales	$100,000	$250	$138,000	$230	$38,000
Less variable expenses . . .	60,000	150	90,000	150	30,000
Contribution margin	40,000	$100	48,000	$ 80	8,000
Less fixed expenses	35,000		50,000*		15,000
Net operating income (loss)	$ 5,000		$ (2,000)		$ (7,000)

*35,000 + Additional monthly advertising budget of $15,000 = $50,000.

Notice that the effect on net operating income is the same as that obtained by the incremental analysis above.

Change in Variable Cost, Fixed Cost, and Sales Volume Refer to the original data. As before, the company is currently selling 400 speakers per month. The sales manager would like to pay a sales commission of $15 per speaker sold, rather than pay salespersons' flat salaries that now total $6,000 per month. The sales manager is confident that the change will increase monthly sales by 15% to 460 speakers per month. Should the change be made?

Solution

Changing the sales staff from a salaried basis to a commission basis will affect both fixed and variable expenses. Fixed expenses will decrease by $6,000, from $35,000 to $29,000. Variable expenses will increase by $15, from $150 to $165, and the unit contribution margin will decrease from $100 to $85.

Expected total contribution margin with sales staff on commissions:	
460 speakers × $85 per speaker.	$39,100
Present total contribution margin:	
400 speakers × $100 per speaker.	40,000
Decrease in total contribution margin	(900)
Change in fixed expenses:	
Add salaries avoided if a commission is paid.	6,000
Increase in net operating income.	$ 5,100

According to this analysis, the changes should be made. Again, the same answer can be obtained by preparing comparative income statements:

	Present 400 Speakers per Month		Expected 460 Speakers per Month		Difference: Increase (or Decrease) in Net Operating Income
	Total	Per Unit	Total	Per Unit	
Sales	$100,000	$250	$115,000	$250	$15,000
Less variable expenses . . .	60,000	150	75,900	165	(15,900)
Contribution margin	40,000	$100	39,100	$ 85	(900)
Less fixed expenses	35,000		29,000		6,000
Net operating income	$ 5,000		$ 10,100		$ 5,100

Change in Regular Sales Price Refer to the original data where Acoustic Concepts is currently selling 400 speakers per month. The company has an opportunity to make a bulk sale of 150 speakers to a wholesaler if an acceptable price can be worked out. This sale would not disturb the company's regular sales and would not affect the company's total fixed expenses. What price per speaker should be quoted to the wholesaler if Acoustic Concepts wants to increase its monthly profits by $3,000?

Solution

Variable cost per speaker	$150
Desired profit per speaker:	
$3,000 ÷ 150 speakers.	20
Quoted price per speaker	$170

Notice that fixed expenses are not included in the computation. This is because fixed expenses are not affected by the bulk sale, so all of the additional revenue that is in excess of variable costs increases the profits of the company.

Importance of the Contribution Margin

As stated in the introduction to the chapter, CVP analysis can be used to help find the most profitable combination of variable costs, fixed costs, selling price, and sales volume. The above examples show that the effect of a decision on the contribution margin is often critical. We have seen that profits can sometimes be improved by reducing the contribution margin if fixed costs can be reduced by a greater amount. More commonly, however, we have seen that the way to improve profits is to increase the total contribution margin figure. Sometimes this can be done by reducing the selling price and thereby increasing volume; sometimes it can be done by increasing the fixed costs (such as advertising) and thereby increasing volume; and sometimes it can be done by trading off variable and fixed costs with appropriate changes in volume. Many other combinations of factors are possible.

The size of the unit contribution margin (and the size of the CM ratio) is very important. For example, the greater the unit contribution margin, the greater is the amount that a company will be willing to spend to increase unit sales. This explains in part why companies with high unit contribution margins (such as auto manufacturers) advertise so heavily, while companies with low unit contribution margins (such as dishware manufacturers) tend to spend much less for advertising.

In short, the effect on the contribution margin holds the key to many decisions.

Break-Even Analysis

Concept 6–2

CVP analysis is sometimes referred to simply as break-even analysis. This is unfortunate because break-even analysis is only one element of CVP analysis—although an important element. Break-even analysis is designed to answer questions such as those asked by Prem Narayan, the president of Acoustic Concepts, concerning how far sales could drop before the company begins to lose money.

Break-Even Computations

LEARNING OBJECTIVE 5
Compute the break-even point.

Earlier in the chapter we defined the break-even point to be the level of sales at which the company's profit is zero. The break-even point can be computed using either the *equation method* or the *contribution margin method*—the two methods are equivalent.

The Equation Method The **equation method** centers on the contribution approach to the income statement illustrated earlier in the chapter. The format of this income statement can be expressed in equation form as follows:

$$\text{Profits} = (\text{Sales} - \text{Variable expenses}) - \text{Fixed expenses}$$

Rearranging this equation slightly yields the following equation, which is widely used in CVP analysis:

$$\text{Sales} = \text{Variable expenses} + \text{Fixed expenses} + \text{Profits}$$

At the break-even point, profits are zero. Therefore, the break-even point can be computed by finding that point where sales just equal the total of the variable expenses plus the fixed expenses. For Acoustic Concepts, the break-even point in unit sales, Q, can be computed as follows:

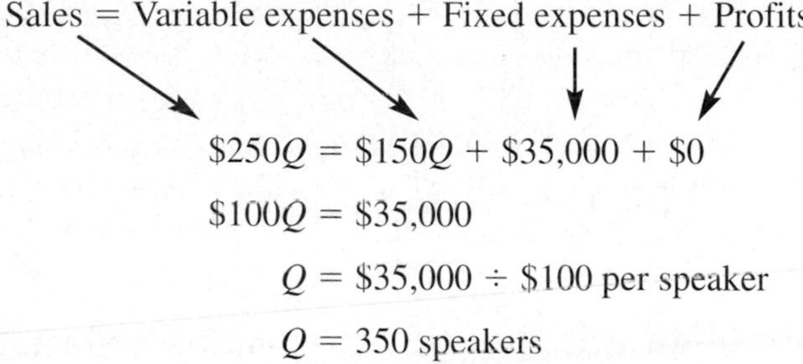

$$\$250Q = \$150Q + \$35{,}000 + \$0$$

$$\$100Q = \$35{,}000$$

$$Q = \$35{,}000 \div \$100 \text{ per speaker}$$

$$Q = 350 \text{ speakers}$$

where:

Q = Number (quantity) of speakers sold

\$250 = Unit sales price

\$150 = Unit variable expenses

\$35,000 = Total fixed expenses

The break-even point in sales dollars can be computed by multiplying the break-even level of unit sales by the selling price per unit:

$$350 \text{ speakers} \times \$250 \text{ per speaker} = \$87{,}500$$

The break-even in total sales dollars, X, can also be directly computed as follows:

$$\text{Sales} = \text{Variable expenses} + \text{Fixed expenses} + \text{Profits}$$

$$X = 0.60X + \$35{,}000 + \$0$$

$$0.40X = \$35{,}000$$

$$X = \$35{,}000 \div 0.40$$

$$X = \$87{,}500$$

where:

X = Total sales dollars

0.60 = Variable expenses as a percentage of sales

\$35,000 = Total fixed expenses

Firms often have data available only in percentage form, and the approach we have just illustrated must then be used to find the break-even point. Notice that use of percentages in the equation yields a break-even point in sales dollars rather than in units sold. The break-even point in units sold is the following:

$$\$87{,}500 \div \$250 \text{ per speaker} = 350 \text{ speakers}$$

In Business

Buying on the Go—A Dot.com Tale

Star CD is a company set up by two young engineers, George Searle and Humphrey Chen, to allow customers to order music CDs on their cell phones. Suppose you hear a cut from a CD on your car radio that you would like to own. Pick up your cell phone, punch "*CD," enter the radio station's frequency, and the time you heard the song, and the CD will soon be on its way to you.

Star CD charges about $17 for a CD, including shipping. The company pays its supplier about $13, leaving a contribution margin of $4 per CD. Because of the fixed costs of running the service, Searle expects the company to lose $1.5 million on sales of $1.5 million in its first year of operations. That assumes the company sells in excess of 88,000 CDs.

What is the company's break-even point? Working backwards, the company's fixed expenses would appear to be about $1,850,000 per year. Since the contribution margin per CD is $4, the company would have to sell over 460,000 CDs per year just to break even!

Source: Peter Kafka, "Play It Again," *Forbes,* July 26, 1999, p. 94.

The Contribution Margin Method The **contribution margin method** is actually just a shortcut version of the equation method already described. The approach centers on the idea discussed earlier that each unit sold provides a certain amount of contribution margin that goes toward covering fixed costs. To find how many units must be sold to break even, divide the total fixed costs by the unit contribution margin:

$$\text{Break-even point in units sold} = \frac{\text{Fixed expenses}}{\text{Unit contribution margin}}$$

Each speaker generates a contribution margin of $100 ($250 selling price, less $150 variable expenses). Since the total fixed expenses are $35,000, the break-even point is computed as follows:

$$\frac{\text{Fixed expenses}}{\text{Unit contribution margin}} = \frac{\$35{,}000}{\$100 \text{ per speaker}} = 350 \text{ speakers}$$

A variation of this method uses the CM ratio instead of the unit contribution margin. The result is the break-even in total sales dollars rather than in total units sold.

$$\text{Break-even point in total sales dollars} = \frac{\text{Fixed expenses}}{\text{CM ratio}}$$

In the Acoustic Concepts example, the calculations are as follows:

$$\frac{\text{Fixed expenses}}{\text{CM ratio}} = \frac{\$35{,}000}{0.40} = \$87{,}500$$

This approach, based on the CM ratio, is particularly useful in those situations where a company has multiple product lines and wishes to compute a single break-even point for the company as a whole. More is said on this point in a later section titled The Concept of Sales Mix.

Target Profit Analysis

LEARNING OBJECTIVE 6
Determine the level of sales needed to achieve a desired target profit.

CVP formulas can be used to determine the sales volume needed to achieve a target profit. Suppose that Prem Narayan of Acoustic Concepts would like to earn a target profit of $40,000 per month. How many speakers would have to be sold?

The CVP Equation One approach is to use the equation method. Instead of solving for the unit sales where profits are zero, you instead solve for the unit sales where profits are $40,000.

$$
\begin{aligned}
\text{Sales} &= \text{Variable expenses} + \text{Fixed expenses} + \text{Profits} \\
\$250Q &= \$150Q + \$35{,}000 + \$40{,}000 \\
\$100Q &= \$75{,}000 \\
Q &= \$75{,}000 \div \$100 \text{ per speaker} \\
Q &= 750 \text{ speakers}
\end{aligned}
$$

where:

$$
\begin{aligned}
Q &= \text{Number of speakers sold} \\
\$250 &= \text{Unit sales price} \\
\$150 &= \text{Unit variable expenses} \\
\$35{,}000 &= \text{Total fixed expenses} \\
\$40{,}000 &= \text{Target profit}
\end{aligned}
$$

Thus, the target profit can be achieved by selling 750 speakers per month, which represents \$187,500 in total sales (\$250 per speaker × 750 speakers).

Thrift Shop Publishing

In Business

Hesh Kestin failed in his attempt at publishing an English-language newspaper in Israel in the 1980s. His conclusion: "Never start a business with too many people or too much furniture." Kestin's newest venture is *The American,* a Sunday-only newspaper for overseas Americans. His idea is to publish *The American* on the one day of the week that the well-established *International Herald Tribune* (circulation, 190,000 copies) does not publish. But following what he learned from his first failed venture, he is doing it on a shoestring.

In contrast to the Paris-based *International Herald Tribune* with its eight-story office tower and staff of 250, Kestin has set up business in a small clapboard building on Long Island. Working at desks purchased from a thrift shop, Kestin's staff of 12 assembles the tabloid from stories pulled off wire services. The result of this frugality is that *The American*'s break-even point is only 14,000 copies. Sales topped 20,000 copies just two months after the paper's first issue.

Source: Jerry Useem, "American Hopes to Conquer the World—from Long Island," *Inc,* December 1996, p. 23.

Sports
Arts
Money
Postcard
THE AMERICAN
CAREFUL WHERE YOU DOUBLE CLICK
The Cold War is over, but the CIA still needs a few good spooks. Trouble is, they're hard to find.
RESPECT ME, I'M A ROBOT
KIDS
SPEED THRILLS
SPIES WANTED
Concierge

The Contribution Margin Approach A second approach involves expanding the contribution margin formula to include the target profit:

$$
\begin{aligned}
\text{Unit sales to attain the target profit} &= \frac{\text{Fixed expenses} + \text{Target profit}}{\text{Unit contribution margin}} \\
&= \frac{\$35{,}000 + \$40{,}000}{\$100 \text{ per speaker}} \\
&= 750 \text{ speakers}
\end{aligned}
$$

This approach gives the same answer as the equation method since it is simply a shortcut version of the equation method. Similarly, the dollar sales needed to attain the target profit can be computed as follows:

$$
\begin{aligned}
\text{Dollar sales to attain target profit} &= \frac{\text{Fixed expenses} + \text{Target profit}}{\text{CM ratio}} \\
&= \frac{\$35{,}000 + \$40{,}000}{0.40} \\
&= \$187{,}500
\end{aligned}
$$

The Margin of Safety

LEARNING OBJECTIVE 7
Compute the margin of safety and explain its significance.

The **margin of safety** is the excess of budgeted (or actual) sales over the break-even volume of sales. It states the amount by which sales can drop before losses begin to be incurred. The higher the margin of safety, the lower the risk of not breaking even. The formula for its calculation is:

$$\text{Margin of safety} = \text{Total budgeted (or actual) sales} - \text{Break-even sales}$$

The margin of safety can also be expressed in percentage form. This percentage is obtained by dividing the margin of safety in dollar terms by total sales:

$$\text{Margin of safety percentage} = \frac{\text{Margin of safety in dollars}}{\text{Total budgeted (or actual) sales}}$$

The calculations for the margin of safety for Acoustic Concepts are as follows:

Sales (at the current volume of 400 speakers) (a)	$100,000
Break-even sales (at 350 speakers)	87,500
Margin of safety (in dollars) (b)	$ 12,500
Margin of safety as a percentage of sales, (b) ÷ (a).	12.5%

This margin of safety means that at the current level of sales and with the company's current prices and cost structure, a reduction in sales of $12,500, or 12.5%, would result in just breaking even.

In a single-product firm like Acoustic Concepts, the margin of safety can also be expressed in terms of the number of units sold by dividing the margin of safety in dollars by the selling price per unit. In this case, the margin of safety is 50 speakers ($12,500 ÷ $250 per speaker = 50 speakers).

In Business

Soup Nutsy

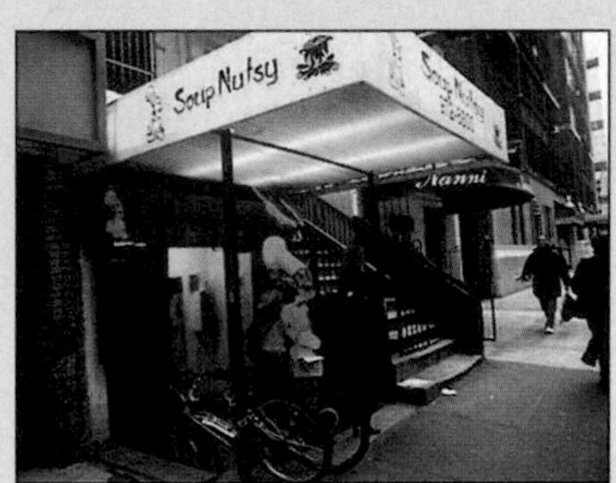

Pak Melwani and Kumar Hathiramani, former silk merchants from Bombay, opened a soup store in Manhattan after watching a *Seinfeld* episode featuring the "soup Nazi." The episode parodied a real-life soup vendor, Ali Yeganeh, whose loyal customers put up with hour-long lines and "snarling customer service." Melwani and Hathiramani approached Yeganeh about turning his soup kitchen into a chain, but they were gruffly rebuffed. Instead of giving up, the two hired a French chef with a repertoire of 500 soups and opened a store called Soup Nutsy. For $6 per serving, Soup Nutsy offers 12 homemade soups each day, such as sherry crab bisque and Thai coconut shrimp. Melwani and Hathiramani report that in their first year of operation, they netted $210,000 on sales of $700,000. They report that it costs about $2 per serving to make the soup. So their variable expense ratio is one-third ($2 cost ÷ $6 selling price). If so, what are their fixed expenses? We can answer that question using the equation approach as follows:

$$\text{Sales} = \text{Variable expenses} + \text{Fixed expenses} + \text{Profits}$$

$$\$700{,}000 = \left(\frac{1}{3} \times \$700{,}000\right) + \text{Fixed expenses} + \$210{,}000$$

$$\text{Fixed expenses} = \$700{,}000 - \left(\frac{1}{3} \times \$700{,}000\right) - \$210{,}000$$

$$= \$256{,}667$$

With this information, you can determine that Soup Nutsy's break-even point is about $385,000 of sales. This gives the store a comfortable margin of safety of 45% of sales.

Source: Silva Sansoni, "The Starbucks of Soup?" *Forbes*, July 7, 1997, pp. 90–91.

Managerial Accounting in Action

The Wrap Up

It is Thursday morning, and Prem Narayan and Bob Luchinni are discussing the results of Bob's analysis.

Prem: Bob, everything you have shown me is pretty clear. I can see what impact some of the sales manager's suggestions would have on our profits. Some of those suggestions are quite good and some are not so good. I also understand that our break-even is 350 speakers, so we have to make sure we don't slip below that level of sales. What really bothers me is that we are only selling 400 speakers a month now. What did you call the 50-speaker cushion?

Bob: That's the margin of safety.

Prem: Such a small cushion makes me very nervous. What can we do to increase the margin of safety?

Bob: We have to increase total sales or decrease the break-even point or both.

Prem: And to decrease the break-even point, we have to either decrease our fixed expenses or increase our unit contribution margin?

Bob: Exactly.

Prem: And to increase our unit contribution margin, we have to either increase our selling price or decrease the variable cost per unit?

Bob: Correct.

Prem: So what do you suggest?

Bob: Well, the analysis doesn't tell us which of these to do, but it does indicate we have a potential problem here.

Prem: If you don't have any immediate suggestions, I would like to call a general meeting next week to discuss ways we can work on increasing the margin of safety. I think everyone will be concerned about how vulnerable we are to even small downturns in sales.

Bob: I agree. This is something everyone will want to work on.

CVP Considerations in Choosing a Cost Structure

As stated in the preceding chapter, cost structure refers to the relative proportion of fixed and variable costs in an organization. An organization often has some latitude in trading off between these two types of costs. For example, fixed investments in automated equipment can reduce variable labor costs. In this section, we discuss the choice of a cost structure. We focus on the impact of cost structure on profit stability, in which *operating leverage* pays a key role.

Cost Structure and Profit Stability

When a manager has some latitude in trading off between fixed and variable costs, which cost structure is better—high variable costs and low fixed costs, or the opposite? No single answer to this question is possible; there may be advantages either way, depending on the specific circumstances. To show what we mean by this statement, refer to the income statements given below for two blueberry farms. Bogside Farm depends on migrant workers to pick its berries by hand, whereas Sterling Farm has invested in expensive berry-picking machines. Consequently, Bogside Farm has higher variable costs, but Sterling Farm has higher fixed costs:

	Bogside Farm		Sterling Farm	
	Amount	Percent	Amount	Percent
Sales	$100,000	100%	$100,000	100%
Less variable expenses	60,000	60%	30,000	30%
Contribution margin	40,000	40%	70,000	70%
Less fixed expenses	30,000		60,000	
Net operating income.	$ 10,000		$ 10,000	

In Business

Cost Structure in an E-Business

Career Central (recently renamed Cruel World), is an employment agency located in Palo Alto, California, on the outskirts of Silicon Valley. The company was founded in June 1996 by Jeffrey Hyman, an MBA from Northwestern University, who was dissatisfied with his own job search in the San Francisco Bay area.

Jobseekers pay nothing to register on the company's website. They provide detailed information about their experience, salary expectations, willingness to travel, geographic preferences, and so on. Employers pay. For a fee of $2,995 per search, employers submit their specifications to a Career Central staffer who searches the database for possible matches. When a possible candidate for the job is found, he or she is sent an e-mail describing the job opening. If the jobseeker is interested, Career Central prints out the individual's resume and sends it to the potential employer. Career Central promises to deliver the names of at least 10 qualified, interested candidates within five business days of a search request.

Note that the potential employer does not directly search the database of jobseekers. Hyman feels that this is a critical aspect of the business plan. He wants to encourage professionals who are already employed, but who might be interested in a better job, to register at the Career Central website. If potential employers could directly access the database, confidentiality would be compromised. For example, the human resources department of a jobseeker's own company might tap into the database and discover that the jobseeker is looking for another job. At best, this would be embarrassing. By having a Career Central staffer handle all database searches, confidentiality for jobseekers is assured. However, this confidentiality comes at a high price. More calls from potential employers require more staffers to handle the calls. Hence, Career Central has added a layer of variable costs to its cost structure, which has decreased the contribution margin per search and increased the level of sales at which the break-even point will occur.

Source: Jerry Useem, *Inc.*, December 1998, pp. 71–83.

The question as to which farm has the better cost structure depends on many factors, including the long-run trend in sales, year-to-year fluctuations in the level of sales, and the attitude of the owners toward risk. If sales are expected to be above $100,000 in the future, then Sterling Farm probably has the better cost structure. The reason is that its CM ratio is higher, and its profits will therefore increase more rapidly as sales increase. To illustrate, assume that each farm experiences a 10% increase in sales without any increase in fixed costs. The new income statements would be as follows:

	Bogside Farm		Sterling Farm	
	Amount	**Percent**	**Amount**	**Percent**
Sales	$110,000	100%	$110,000	100%
Less variable expenses	66,000	60%	33,000	30%
Contribution margin	44,000	40%	77,000	70%
Less fixed expenses	30,000		60,000	
Net operating income	$ 14,000		$ 17,000	

Sterling Farm has experienced a greater increase in net operating income due to its higher CM ratio even though the increase in sales was the same for both farms.

What if sales drop below $100,000 from time to time? What are the break-even points of the two farms? What are their margins of safety? The computations needed to answer these questions are carried out below using the contribution margin method:

	Bogside Farm	Sterling Farm
Fixed expenses	$ 30,000	$ 60,000
Contribution margin ratio	÷ 40%	÷ 70%
Break-even in total sales dollars	$ 75,000	$ 85,714

continued

Total current sales (a)	$100,000	$100,000
Break-even sales	75,000	85,714
Margin of safety in sales dollars (b)	$ 25,000	$ 14,286
Margin of safety as a percentage of sales, (b) ÷ (a)	25.0%	14.3%

This analysis makes it clear that Bogside Farm is less vulnerable to downturns than Sterling Farm. We can identify two reasons why it is less vulnerable. First, due to its lower fixed expenses, Bogside Farm has a lower break-even point and a higher margin of safety, as shown by the computations above. Therefore, it will not incur losses as quickly as Sterling Farm in periods of sharply declining sales. Second, due to its lower CM ratio, Bogside Farm will not lose contribution margin as rapidly as Sterling Farm when sales fall off. Thus, Bogside Farm's income will be less volatile. We saw earlier that this is a drawback when sales increase, but it provides more protection when sales drop.

To summarize, without knowing the future, it is not obvious which cost structure is better. Both have advantages and disadvantages. Sterling Farm, with its higher fixed costs and lower variable costs, will experience wider swings in net income as changes take place in sales, with greater profits in good years and greater losses in bad years. Bogside Farm, with its lower fixed costs and higher variable costs, will enjoy greater stability in net operating income and will be more protected from losses during bad years, but at the cost of lower net operating income in good years.

Operating Leverage

A lever is a tool for multiplying force. Using a lever, a massive object can be moved with only a modest amount of force. In business, *operating leverage* serves a similar purpose. **Operating leverage** is a measure of how sensitive net operating income is to percentage changes in sales. Operating leverage acts as a multiplier. If operating leverage is high, a small percentage increase in sales can produce a much larger percentage increase in net operating income.

LEARNING OBJECTIVE 8
Compute the degree of operating leverage at a particular level of sales and explain how the degree of operating leverage can be used to predict changes in net operating income.

Operating leverage can be illustrated by returning to the data given above for the two blueberry farms. We previously showed that a 10% increase in sales (from $100,000 to $110,000 in each farm) results in a 70% increase in the net operating income of Sterling Farm (from $10,000 to $17,000) and only a 40% increase in the net operating income of Bogside Farm (from $10,000 to $14,000). Thus, for a 10% increase in sales, Sterling Farm experiences a much greater percentage increase in profits than does Bogside Farm. Therefore, Sterling Farm has greater operating leverage than Bogside Farm.

The **degree of operating leverage** at a given level of sales is computed by the following formula:

$$\text{Degree of operating leverage} = \frac{\text{Contribution margin}}{\text{Net operating income}}$$

The degree of operating leverage is a measure, at a given level of sales, of how a percentage change in sales volume will affect profits. To illustrate, the degree of operating leverage for the two farms at a $100,000 sales level would be computed as follows:

$$\text{Bogside Farm: } \frac{\$40{,}000}{\$10{,}000} = 4$$

$$\text{Sterling Farm: } \frac{\$70{,}000}{\$10{,}000} = 7$$

Since the degree of operating leverage for Bogside Farm is 4, the farm's net operating income grows four times as fast as its sales. Similarly, Sterling Farm's net operating income grows seven times as fast as its sales. Thus, if sales increase by 10%, then we can expect the net operating income of Bogside Farm to increase by four times this amount, or by

40%, and the net operating income of Sterling Farm to increase by seven times this amount, or by 70%.

	(1) Percent Increase in Sales	(2) Degree of Operating Leverage	(3) Percent Increase in Net Operating Income (1) × (2)
Bogside Farm	10%	4	40%
Sterling Farm.	10%	7	70%

What is responsible for the higher operating leverage at Sterling Farm? The only difference between the two farms is their cost structure. If two companies have the same total revenue and same total expense but different cost structures, then the company with the higher proportion of fixed costs in its cost structure will have higher operating leverage. Referring back to the original example on page 249, when both farms have sales of $100,000 and total expenses of $90,000, one-third of Bogside Farm's costs are fixed but two-thirds of Sterling Farm's costs are fixed. As a consequence, Sterling's degree of operating leverage is higher than Bogside's.

The degree of operating leverage is not a constant; it is greatest at sales levels near the break-even point and decreases as sales and profits rise. This can be seen from the tabulation below, which shows the degree of operating leverage for Bogside Farm at various sales levels. (Data used earlier for Bogside Farm are shown in color.)

Sales.	$75,000	$80,000	$100,000	$150,000	$225,000
Less variable expenses	45,000	48,000	60,000	90,000	135,000
Contribution margin (a)	30,000	32,000	40,000	60,000	90,000
Less fixed expenses	30,000	30,000	30,000	30,000	30,000
Net operating income (b)	$ 0	$ 2,000	$ 10,000	$ 30,000	$ 60,000
Degree of operating leverage, (a) ÷ (b).	∞	16	4	2	1.5

Thus, a 10% increase in sales would increase profits by only 15% (10% × 1.5) if the company were operating at a $225,000 sales level, as compared to the 40% increase we computed earlier at the $100,000 sales level. The degree of operating leverage will continue to decrease the farther the company moves from its break-even point. At the break-even point, the degree of operating leverage is infinitely large ($30,000 contribution margin ÷ $0 net operating income = ∞).

In Business

Fan Appreciation

Operating leverage can be a good thing when business is booming but can turn the situation ugly when sales slacken. Jerry Colangelo, the managing partner of the Arizona Diamondbacks professional baseball team, spent over $100 million to sign six free agents—doubling the team's payroll cost—on top of the costs of operating and servicing the debt on the team's new stadium. With annual expenses of about $100 million, the team needs to average 40,000 fans per game to just break even.

Faced with a financially risky situation, Colangelo decided to raise ticket prices by 12%. And he did it during Fan Appreciation Weekend! Attendance for the season dropped by 15%, turning what should have been a $20 million profit into a loss of over $10 million for the year. Note that a drop in attendance of 15% did not cut profit by just 15%—that's the magic of operating leverage at work.

Source: Mary Summers, "Bottom of the Ninth, Two Out," *Forbes,* November 1, 1999, pp. 69–70.

A manager can use the degree of operating leverage to quickly estimate what impact various percentage changes in sales will have on profits, without the necessity of preparing detailed income statements. As shown by our examples, the effects of operating leverage can be dramatic. If a company is near its break-even point, then even small percentage increases in sales can yield large percentage increases in profits. *This explains why management will often work very hard for only a small increase in sales volume.* If the degree of operating leverage is 5, then a 6% increase in sales would translate into a 30% increase in profits.

Structuring Sales Commissions

Companies generally compensate salespeople by paying them either a commission based on sales or a salary plus a sales commission. Commissions based on sales dollars can lead to lower profits in a company. To illustrate, consider Pipeline Unlimited, a producer of surfing equipment. Salespeople for the company sell the company's product to retail sporting goods stores throughout North America and the Pacific Basin. Data for two of the company's surfboards, the XR7 and Turbo models, appear below:

	Model	
	XR7	Turbo
Selling price	$100	$150
Less variable expenses	75	132
Contribution margin.	$ 25	$ 18

Which model will salespeople push hardest if they are paid a commission of 10% of sales revenue? The answer is the Turbo, since it has the higher selling price and hence the larger commission. On the other hand, from the standpoint of the company, profits will be greater if salespeople steer customers toward the XR7 model since it has the higher contribution margin.

To eliminate such conflicts, commissions can be based on contribution margin rather than on selling price alone. If this is done, there is no need to worry about the mix of products the salespersons sell because they will want to sell the mix of products that will maximize contribution margin. Providing that fixed costs are not affected by the sales mix, maximizing the contribution margin will also maximize the company's profit. In effect, by maximizing their own compensation, salespersons will also maximize the company's profit.

The Concept of Sales Mix

Before concluding our discussion of CVP concepts, we need to consider the impact of changes in *sales mix* on a company's profit.

LEARNING OBJECTIVE 9
Compute the break-even point for a multiple product company and explain the effects of shifts in the sales mix on contribution margin and the break-even point.

The Definition of Sales Mix

The term **sales mix** refers to the relative proportions in which a company's products are sold. The idea is to achieve the combination, or mix, that will yield the greatest amount of profits. Most companies have many products, and often these products are not equally profitable. Hence, profits will depend to some extent on the company's sales mix. Profits will be greater if high-margin rather than low-margin items make up a relatively large proportion of total sales.

Changes in the sales mix can cause interesting (and sometimes confusing) variations in a company's profits. A shift in the sales mix from high-margin items to low-margin items can cause total profits to decrease even though total sales may increase. Conversely, a shift in the sales mix from low-margin items to high-margin items can cause the reverse effect—total profits may increase even though total sales decrease. It is one thing to achieve a particular sales volume; it is quite a different thing to sell the most profitable mix of products.

In Business | **Kodak: Going Digital**

Kodak dominates the film industry in the U.S., selling two out of every three rolls of film. It also processes 40% of all film dropped off for developing. Unfortunately for Kodak, this revenue stream is threatened by digital cameras, which do not use film at all. To counter this threat, Kodak is moving into the digital market with its own line of digital cameras and various services, but sales of digital products undeniably cut into the company's film business. "Chief Financial Officer Robert Brust has 'stress-tested' profit models based on how quickly digital cameras may spread. If half of homes go digital by 2005, . . . Kodak's sales would rise 10% a year—but profits would go up only 8% a year. Cost cuts couldn't come fast enough to offset a slide in film sales and the margin pressure from selling cheap digital cameras." The sales mix is moving in the wrong direction, given the company's current cost structure and competitive prices.

Source: Bruce Upbin, "Kodak's Digital Moment," *Forbes,* August 21, 2000, pp. 106–112.

Sales Mix and Break-Even Analysis

If a company sells more than one product, break-even analysis is somewhat more complex than discussed earlier in the chapter. The reason is that different products will have different selling prices, different costs, and different contribution margins. Consequently, the break-even point will depend on the mix in which the various products are sold. To illustrate, consider Sound Unlimited, a small company that imports CD-ROMs from France for use in personal computers. At present, the company distributes the following CDs to retail computer stores: the Le Louvre CD, a multimedia free-form tour of the famous art museum in Paris; and the Le Vin CD, which features the wines and wine-growing regions of France. Both multimedia products have sound, photos, video clips, and sophisticated software. The company's September sales, expenses, and break-even point are shown in Exhibit 6–3.

As shown in the exhibit, the break-even point is $60,000 in sales. This is computed by dividing the fixed costs by the company's *overall* CM ratio of 45%. The sales mix is currently 20% for the Le Louvre CD and 80% for the Le Vin CD. If this sales mix does not change, then at the break-even total sales of $60,000, the sales of the Le Louvre CD would be $12,000 (20% of $60,000) and the sales of the Le Vin CD would be $48,000 (80% of $60,000). As shown in Exhibit 6–3, at these levels of sales, the company would indeed break even. But $60,000 in sales represents the break-even point for the company only so long as the sales mix does not change. *If the sales mix changes, then the break-even point will also change.* This is illustrated by the results for October in which the sales mix shifted away from the more profitable Le Vin CD (which has a 50% CM ratio) toward the less profitable Le Louvre CD (which has only a 25% CM ratio). These results appear in Exhibit 6–4.

Although sales have remained unchanged at $100,000, the sales mix is exactly the reverse of what it was in Exhibit 6–3, with the bulk of the sales now coming from the less profitable Le Louvre CD. Notice that this shift in the sales mix has caused both the overall CM ratio and total profits to drop sharply from the prior month—the overall CM ratio has dropped from 45% in September to only 30% in October, and net operating income has dropped from $18,000 to only $3,000. In addition, with the drop in the overall CM ratio, the company's break-even point is no longer $60,000 in sales. Since the company is now realizing less average contribution margin per dollar of sales, it takes more sales to cover the same amount of fixed costs. Thus, the break-even point has increased from $60,000 to $90,000 in sales per year.

Exhibit 6–3 Multiple-Product Break-Even Analysis

SOUND UNLIMITED
Contribution Income Statement
For the Month of September

	Le Louvre CD		Le Vin CD		Total	
	Amount	**Percent**	**Amount**	**Percent**	**Amount**	**Percent**
Sales	$20,000	100%	$80,000	100%	$100,000	100%
Less variable expenses	15,000	75%	40,000	50%	55,000	55%
Contribution margin	$ 5,000	25%	$40,000	50%	45,000	45%
Less fixed expenses					27,000	
Net operating income					$ 18,000	

Computation of the break-even point:

$$\frac{\text{Fixed expenses}}{\text{Overall CM ratio}} = \frac{\$27{,}000}{0.45} = \$60{,}000$$

Verification of the break-even:

	Le Louvre CD	Le Vin CD	Total
Current dollar sales	$20,000	$80,000	$100,000
Percentage of total dollar sales	20%	80%	100%
Sales at break-even	$12,000	$48,000	$60,000

	Le Louvre CD		Le Vin CD		Total	
	Amount	**Percent**	**Amount**	**Percent**	**Amount**	**Percent**
Sales	$12,000	100%	$48,000	100%	$ 60,000	100%
Less variable expenses	9,000	75%	24,000	50%	33,000	55%
Contribution margin	$ 3,000	25%	$24,000	50%	27,000	45%
Less fixed expenses					27,000	
Net operating income					$ 0	

Exhibit 6–4 Multiple-Product Break-Even Analysis: A Shift in Sales Mix (see Exhibit 6–3)

SOUND UNLIMITED
Contribution Income Statement
For the Month of October

	Le Louvre CD		Le Vin CD		Total	
	Amount	**Percent**	**Amount**	**Percent**	**Amount**	**Percent**
Sales	$80,000	100%	$20,000	100%	$100,000	100%
Less variable expenses	60,000	75%	10,000	50%	70,000	70%
Contribution margin	$20,000	25%	$10,000	50%	30,000	30%
Less fixed expenses					27,000	
Net operating income					$ 3,000	

Computation of the break-even point:

$$\frac{\text{Fixed expenses}}{\text{Overall CM ratio}} = \frac{\$27{,}000}{0.30} = \$90{,}000$$

In preparing a break-even analysis, some assumption must be made concerning the sales mix. Usually the assumption is that it will not change. However, if the sales mix is expected to change, then these factors must be explicitly considered in any CVP computations.

In Business

Benefiting from a Shift in Sales Mix

Roger Maxwell grew up near a public golf course where he learned the game and worked as a caddie. After attending Oklahoma State on a golf scholarship, he became a golf pro and eventually rose to become vice president at Marriott, responsible for Marriott's golf courses in the United States. Sensing an opportunity to serve a niche market, Maxwell invested his life savings in opening his own golfing superstore, In Celebration of Golf (ICOG), in Scottsdale, Arizona. Maxwell says, "I'd rather sacrifice profit up front for sizzle . . . [P]eople are bored by malls. They're looking for something different." Maxwell has designed his store to be a museum-like mecca for golfing fanatics. For example, maintenance work is done in a replica of a turn-of-the-century club maker's shop.

Maxwell's approach seems to be working. In the second year of operation, Maxwell projected a profit of $81,000 on sales of $2.4 million as follows:

	Projected	Percent of Sales
Sales	$2,400,000	100%
Cost of sales	1,496,000	62⅓%
Other variable expenses	296,000	12⅓%
Contribution margin	608,000	25⅓%
Fixed expenses	527,000	
Net operating income	$ 81,000	

Happily for Maxwell, sales for the year were even better than expected—reaching $3.0 million. In the absence of any other changes, the net income should have been approximately $233,000, computed as follows:

	Projected	Percent of Sales
Sales	$3,000,000	100%
Cost of sales	1,870,000	62⅓%
Other variable expenses	370,000	12⅓%
Contribution margin	760,000	25⅓%
Fixed expenses	527,000	
Net operating income	$ 233,000	

However, net income for the year was actually $289,000—apparently because of a favorable shift in the sales mix toward higher margin items. A 25% increase in sales over the projections at the beginning of the year resulted in a 356% increase in net income. That's leverage!

Source: Edward O. Welles, "Going for the Green," *Inc.*, July 1996, pp. 68–75.

Assumptions of CVP Analysis

A number of assumptions underlie CVP analysis:

1. Selling price is constant. The price of a product or service will not change as volume changes.

2. Costs are linear and can be accurately divided into variable and fixed elements. The variable element is constant per unit, and the fixed element is constant in total over the entire relevant range.
3. In multiproduct companies, the sales mix is constant.
4. In manufacturing companies, inventories do not change. The number of units produced equals the number of units sold.

While some of these assumptions may be violated in practice, the violations are usually not serious enough to call into question the basic validity of CVP analysis. For example, in most multiproduct companies, the sales mix is constant enough so that the results of CVP analysis are reasonably valid.

Perhaps the greatest danger lies in relying on simple CVP analysis when a manager is contemplating a large change in volume that lies outside of the relevant range. For example, a manager might contemplate increasing the level of sales far beyond what the company has ever experienced before. However, even in these situations a manager can adjust the model as we have done in this chapter to take into account anticipated changes in selling prices, fixed costs, and the sales mix that would otherwise violate the assumptions. For example, in a decision that would affect fixed costs, the change in fixed costs can be explicitly taken into account as illustrated earlier in the chapter in the Acoustic Concepts example on page 241.

Summary

CVP analysis involves finding the most favorable combination of variable costs, fixed costs, selling price, sales volume, and mix of products sold. Trade-offs are possible between types of costs, as well as between costs and selling price, and between selling price and sales volume. Sometimes these trade-offs are desirable, and sometimes they are not. CVP analysis provides the manager with a powerful tool for identifying those courses of action that will improve profitability.

The concepts developed in this chapter represent a *way of thinking* rather than a mechanical set of procedures. That is, to put together the optimum combination of costs, selling price, and sales volume, the manager must be trained to think in terms of the unit contribution margin, the break-even point, the CM ratio, the sales mix, and the other concepts developed in this chapter.

Review Problem: CVP Relationships

Voltar Company manufactures and sells a telephone answering machine. The company's contribution format income statement for the most recent year is given below:

	Total	Per Unit	Percent of Sales
Sales (20,000 units)	$1,200,000	$60	100%
Less variable expenses	900,000	45	? %
Contribution margin	300,000	$15	? %
Less fixed expenses	240,000		
Net operating income	$ 60,000		

Management is anxious to improve the company's profit performance and has asked for an analysis of a number of items.

Required:

1. Compute the company's CM ratio and variable expense ratio.
2. Compute the company's break-even point in both units and sales dollars. Use the equation method.
3. Assume that sales increase by $400,000 next year. If cost behavior patterns remain unchanged, by how much will the company's net operating income increase? Use the CM ratio to determine your answer.

4. Refer to the original data. Assume that next year management wants the company to earn a minimum profit of $90,000. How many units will have to be sold to meet this target profit figure?
5. Refer to the original data. Compute the company's margin of safety in both dollar and percentage form.
6. *a.* Compute the company's degree of operating leverage at the present level of sales.
   b. Assume that through a more intense effort by the sales staff the company's sales increase by 8% next year. By what percentage would you expect net operating income to increase? Use the operating leverage concept to obtain your answer.
   c. Verify your answer to (*b*) by preparing a new income statement showing an 8% increase in sales.
7. In an effort to increase sales and profits, management is considering the use of a higher-quality speaker. The higher-quality speaker would increase variable costs by $3 per unit, but management could eliminate one quality inspector who is paid a salary of $30,000 per year. The sales manager estimates that the higher-quality speaker would increase annual sales by at least 20%.
   a. Assuming that changes are made as described above, prepare a projected income statement for next year. Show data on a total, per unit, and percentage basis.
   b. Compute the company's new break-even point in both units and dollars of sales. Use the contribution margin method.
   c. Would you recommend that the changes be made?

Solution to Review Problem

1.

$$\text{CM ratio} = \frac{\text{Contribution margin}}{\text{Selling price}} = \frac{\$15}{\$60} = 25\%$$

$$\text{Variable expense ratio} = \frac{\text{Variable expense}}{\text{Selling price}} = \frac{\$45}{\$60} = 75\%$$

2.

$$\text{Sales} = \text{Variable expenses} + \text{Fixed expenses} + \text{Profits}$$

$$\$60Q = \$45Q + \$240{,}000 + \$0$$

$$\$15Q = \$240{,}000$$

$$Q = \$240{,}000 \div \$15 \text{ per unit}$$

$$Q = 16{,}000 \text{ units; or at } \$60 \text{ per unit, } \$960{,}000$$

Alternative solution:

$$X = 0.75X + \$240{,}000 + \$0$$

$$0.25X = \$240{,}000$$

$$X = \$240{,}000 \div 0.25$$

$$X = \$960{,}000\text{; or at } \$60 \text{ per unit, } 16{,}000 \text{ units}$$

3.

Increase in sales	$400,000
Multiply by the CM ratio	× 25%
Expected increase in contribution margin	$ 100,000

Since the fixed expenses are not expected to change, net operating income will increase by the entire $100,000 increase in contribution margin computed above.

4. Equation method:

$$\text{Sales} = \text{Variable expenses} + \text{Fixed expenses} + \text{Profits}$$

$$\$60Q = \$45Q + \$240{,}000 + \$90{,}000$$

$$\$15Q = \$330{,}000$$

$$Q = \$330{,}000 \div \$15 \text{ per unit}$$

$$Q = 22{,}000 \text{ units}$$

Contribution margin method:

$$\frac{\text{Fixed expenses} + \text{Target profit}}{\text{Contribution margin per unit}} = \frac{\$240{,}000 + \$90{,}000}{\$15 \text{ per unit}} = 22{,}000 \text{ units}$$

5. Margin of safety in dollars = Total sales − Break-even sales

$$= \$1{,}200{,}000 - \$960{,}000 = \$240{,}000$$

$$\text{Margin of safety percentage} = \frac{\text{Margin of safety in dollars}}{\text{Total sales}} = \frac{\$240{,}000}{\$1{,}200{,}000} = 20\%$$

6. *a.* $$\text{Degree of operating leverage} = \frac{\text{Contribution margin}}{\text{Net operating income}} = \frac{\$300{,}000}{\$60{,}000} = 5$$

b.

Expected increase in sales.	8%
Degree of operating leverage.	× 5
Expected increase in net operating income	40%

c. If sales increase by 8%, then 21,600 units (20,000 × 1.08 = 21,600) will be sold next year. The new income statement will be as follows:

	Total	Per Unit	Percent of Sales
Sales (21,600 units)	$1,296,000	$60	100%
Less variable expenses.	972,000	45	75%
Contribution margin.	324,000	$15	25%
Less fixed expenses	240,000		
Net operating income	$ 84,000		

Thus, the $84,000 expected net operating income for next year represents a 40% increase over the $60,000 net operating income earned during the current year:

$$\frac{\$84{,}000 - \$60{,}000}{\$60{,}000} = \frac{\$24{,}000}{\$60{,}000} = 40\% \text{ increase}$$

Note from the income statement above that the increase in sales from 20,000 to 21,600 units has resulted in increases in *both* total sales and total variable expenses. It is a common error to overlook the increase in variable expenses when preparing a projected income statement.

7. *a.* A 20% increase in sales would result in 24,000 units being sold next year: 20,000 units × 1.20 = 24,000 units.

	Total	Per Unit	Percent of Sales
Sales (24,000 units)	$1,440,000	$60	100%
Less variable expenses.	1,152,000	48*	80%
Contribution margin.	288,000	$12	20%
Less fixed expenses	210,000†		
Net operating income	$ 78,000		

*$45 + $3 = $48; $48 ÷ $60 = 80%.

†$240,000 − $30,000 = $210,000.

Note that the change in per unit variable expenses results in a change in both the per unit contribution margin and the CM ratio.

b. $$\text{Break-even point in unit sales} = \frac{\text{Fixed expenses}}{\text{Contribution margin per unit}}$$

$$= \frac{\$210{,}000}{\$12 \text{ per unit}} = 17{,}500 \text{ units}$$

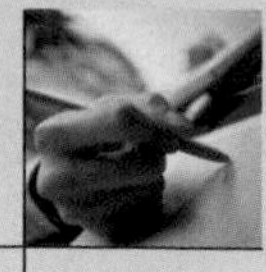

EXERCISE 6–3 Break-Even and Target Profit Analysis [LO4, LO5, LO6]

Reveen Products sells camping equipment. One of the company's products, a camp lantern, sells for $90 per unit. Variable expenses are $63 per lantern, and fixed expenses associated with the lantern total $135,000 per month.

Required:

1. Compute the company's break-even point in number of lanterns and in total sales dollars.
2. If the variable expenses per lantern increase as a percentage of the selling price, will it result in a higher or a lower break-even point? Why? (Assume that the fixed expenses remain unchanged.)
3. At present, the company is selling 8,000 lanterns per month. The sales manager is convinced that a 10% reduction in the selling price will result in a 25% increase in the number of lanterns sold each month. Prepare two contribution income statements, one under present operating conditions, and one as operations would appear after the proposed changes. Show both total and per unit data on your statements.
4. Refer to the data in (3) above. How many lanterns would have to be sold at the new selling price to yield a minimum net operating income of $72,000 per month?

EXERCISE 6–4 Operating Leverage [LO4, LO8]

Superior Door Company sells prehung doors to home builders. The doors are sold for $60 each. Variable costs are $42 per door, and fixed costs total $450,000 per year. The company is currently selling 30,000 doors per year.

Required:

1. Prepare a contribution format income statement for the company at the present level of sales and compute the degree of operating leverage.
2. Management is confident that the company can sell 37,500 doors next year (an increase of 7,500 doors, or 25%, over current sales). Compute the following:
   a. The expected percentage increase in net operating income for next year.
   b. The expected total dollar net operating income for next year. (Do not prepare an income statement; use the degree of operating leverage to compute your answer.)

EXERCISE 6–5 Multiproduct Break-Even Analysis [LO9]

Okabee Enterprises sells two products, Model A100 and Model B900. Monthly sales and the contribution margin ratios for the two products follow:

	Product		
	Model A100	Model B900	Total
Sales	$700,000	$300,000	$1,000,000
Contribution margin ratio	60%	70%	?

The company's fixed expenses total $598,500 per month.

Required:

1. Prepare an income statement for the company as a whole. Use the format shown in Exhibit 6–3.
2. Compute the break-even point for the company based on the current sales mix.
3. If sales increase by $50,000 per month, by how much would you expect net operating income to increase? What are your assumptions?

EXERCISE 6–6 Break-Even Analysis; Target Profit; Margin of Safety; CM Ratio [LO1, LO3, LO5, LO6, LO7]

Pringle Company sells a single product. The company's sales and expenses for a recent month follow:

	Total	Per Unit
Sales	$600,000	$40
Less variable expenses	420,000	28
Contribution margin	180,000	$12
Less fixed expenses	150,000	
Net operating income	$ 30,000	

Required:

1. What is the monthly break-even point in units sold and in sales dollars?

2. Without resorting to computations, what is the total contribution margin at the break-even point?
3. How many units would have to be sold each month to earn a minimum target profit of $18,000? Use the contribution margin method. Verify your answer by preparing a contribution income statement at the target level of sales.
4. Refer to the original data. Compute the company's margin of safety in both dollar and percentage terms.
5. What is the company's CM ratio? If monthly sales increase by $80,000 and there is no change in fixed expenses, by how much would you expect monthly net operating income to increase?

EXERCISE 6–7 Break-Even and Target Profit Analysis [LO3, LO4, LO5, LO6]
Super Sales Company is the exclusive distributor for a revolutionary bookbag. The product sells for $60 per unit and has a CM ratio of 40%. The company's fixed expenses are $360,000 per year.

Required:
1. What are the variable expenses per unit?
2. Using the equation method:
   a. What is the break-even point in units and in sales dollars?
   b. What sales level in units and in sales dollars is required to earn an annual profit of $90,000?
   c. Assume that through negotiation with the manufacturer the Super Sales Company is able to reduce its variable expenses by $3 per unit. What is the company's new break-even point in units and in sales dollars?
3. Repeat (2) above using the contribution margin method.

EXERCISE 6–8 Missing Data; Basic CVP Concepts [LO1, LO9]
Fill in the missing amounts in each of the eight case situations below. Each case is independent of the others. (Hint: One way to find the missing amounts would be to prepare a contribution income statement for each case, enter the known data, and then compute the missing items.)

a. Assume that only one product is being sold in each of the four following case situations:

Case	Units Sold	Sales	Variable Expenses	Contribution Margin per Unit	Fixed Expenses	Net Operating Income (Loss)
1	9,000	$270,000	$162,000	$?	$ 90,000	$?
2	?	350,000	?	15	170,000	40,000
3	20,000	?	280,000	6	?	35,000
4	5,000	160,000	?	?	82,000	(12,000)

b. Assume that more than one product is being sold in each of the four following case situations:

Case	Sales	Variable Expenses	Average Contribution Margin (Percent)	Fixed Expenses	Net Operating Income (Loss)
1.....	$450,000	$?	40	$?	$65,000
2.....	200,000	130,000	?	60,000	?
3.....	?	?	80	470,000	90,000
4.....	300,000	90,000	?	?	(15,000)

Problems

PROBLEM 6–9 Basics of CVP Analysis; Cost Structure [LO1, LO3, LO4, LO5, LO6]
Memofax, Inc., produces memory enhancement kits for fax machines. Sales have been very erratic, with some months showing a profit and some months showing a loss. The company's income statement for the most recent month is given below:

Sales (13,500 units at $20 per unit)	$270,000
Less variable expenses	189,000
Contribution margin....................	81,000
Less fixed expenses	90,000
Net operating loss......................	$ (9,000)

Required:

1. Compute the company's CM ratio and its break-even point in both units and dollars.
2. The sales manager feels that an $8,000 increase in the monthly advertising budget, combined with an intensified effort by the sales staff, will result in a $70,000 increase in monthly sales. If the sales manager is right, what will be the effect on the company's monthly net operating income or loss? (Use the incremental approach in preparing your answer.)
3. The president is convinced that a 10% reduction in the selling price, combined with an increase of $35,000 in the monthly advertising budget, will cause unit sales to double. What will the new income statement look like if these changes are adopted?
4. Refer to the original data. The company's advertising agency thinks that a new package would help sales. The new package being proposed would increase packaging costs by $0.60 per unit. Assuming no other changes, how many units would have to be sold each month to earn a profit of $4,500?
5. Refer to the original data. By automating certain operations, the company could slash its variable expenses in half. However, fixed costs would increase by $118,000 per month.
   a. Compute the new CM ratio and the new break-even point in both units and dollars.
   b. Assume that the company expects to sell 20,000 units next month. Prepare two income statements, one assuming that operations are not automated and one assuming that they are.
   c. Would you recommend that the company automate its operations? Explain.

PROBLEM 6–10 Basic CVP Analysis; Graphing [LO1, LO2, LO4, LO5]

Shirts Unlimited operates a chain of shirt stores around the country. The stores carry many styles of shirts that are all sold at the same price. To encourage sales personnel to be aggressive in their sales efforts, the company pays a substantial sales commission on each shirt sold. Sales personnel also receive a small basic salary.

The following worksheet contains cost and revenue data for Store 36. These data are typical of the company's many outlets:

Microsoft Excel - Problem 6-10 screen capture.xls

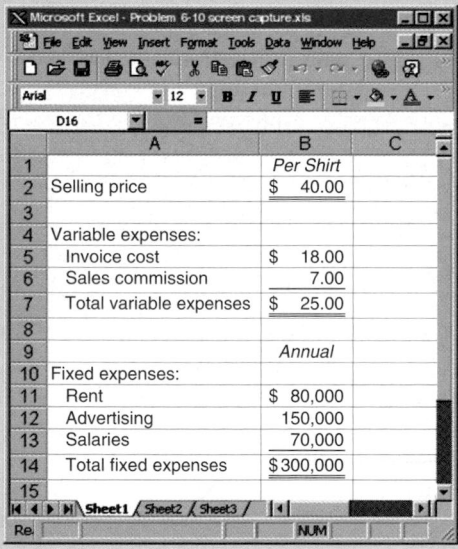

	A	B	C
1		*Per Shirt*	
2	Selling price	$ 40.00	
3			
4	Variable expenses:		
5	Invoice cost	$ 18.00	
6	Sales commission	7.00	
7	Total variable expenses	$ 25.00	
8			
9		*Annual*	
10	Fixed expenses:		
11	Rent	$ 80,000	
12	Advertising	150,000	
13	Salaries	70,000	
14	Total fixed expenses	$300,000	
15			

Shirts Unlimited is a fairly new organization. The company has asked you, as a member of its planning group, to assist in some basic analysis of its stores and company policies.

Required:

1. Calculate the annual break-even point in dollar sales and in unit sales for Store 36.
2. Prepare a CVP graph showing cost and revenue data for Store 36 from a zero level of activity up to 30,000 shirts sold each year. Clearly indicate the break-even point on the graph.
3. If 19,000 shirts are sold in a year, what would be Store 36's net operating income or loss?
4. The company is considering paying the store manager of Store 36 an incentive commission of $3 per shirt (in addition to the salespersons' commissions). If this change is made, what will be the new break-even point in dollar sales and in unit sales?
5. Refer to the original data. As an alternative to (4) above, the company is considering paying the store manager a $3 commission on each shirt sold in excess of the break-even point. If this change is made, what will be the store's net operating income or loss if 23,500 shirts are sold in a year?

6. Refer to the original data. The company is considering eliminating sales commissions entirely in its stores and increasing fixed salaries by $107,000 annually.
   a. If this change is made, what will be the new break-even point in dollar sales and in unit sales in Store 36?
   b. Would you recommend that the change be made? Explain.

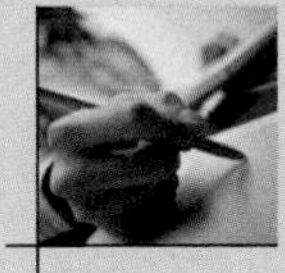

PROBLEM 6–11 Sales Mix; Multiproduct Break-Even Analysis [LO9]
Marlin Company has been operating for only a few months. The company sells three products—sinks, mirrors, and vanities. Budgeted sales by product and in total for the coming month are shown below:

	Product							
	Sinks		Mirrors		Vanities		Total	
Percentage of total sales	48%		20%		32%		100%	
Sales.	$240,000	100%	$100,000	100%	$160,000	100%	$500,000	100%
Less variable expenses	72,000	30	80,000	80	88,000	55	240,000	48
Contribution margin	$168,000	70%	$ 20,000	20%	$ 72,000	45%	260,000	52%
Less fixed expenses							223,600	
Net operating income							$ 36,400	

$$\text{Break-even point in dollar sales} = \frac{\text{Fixed expenses}}{\text{CM ratio}} = \frac{\$223{,}600}{0.52} = \$430{,}000$$

As shown by these data, net operating income is budgeted at $36,400 for the month, and break-even sales at $430,000.

Assume that actual sales for the month total $500,000 as planned. Actual sales by product are: sinks, $160,000; mirrors, $200,000; and vanities, $140,000.

Required:

1. Prepare a contribution income statement for the month based on actual sales data. Present the income statement in the format shown above.
2. Compute the break-even sales for the month, based on your actual data.
3. Considering the fact that the company met its $500,000 sales budget for the month, the president is shocked at the results shown on your income statement in (1) above. Prepare a brief memo for the president explaining why both the operating results and break-even sales are different from what was budgeted.

PROBLEM 6–12 Basic CVP Analysis [LO1, LO3, LO4, LO5, LO8]
Stratford Company distributes a lightweight lawn chair that sells for $15 per unit. Variable costs are $6 per unit, and fixed costs total $180,000 annually.

Required:

Answer the following independent questions:

1. What is the product's CM ratio?
2. Use the CM ratio to determine the break-even point in sales dollars.
3. The company estimates that sales will increase by $45,000 during the coming year due to increased demand. By how much should net operating income increase?
4. Assume that the operating results for last year were as follows:

Sales	$360,000
Less variable expenses	144,000
Contribution margin	216,000
Less fixed expenses.	180,000
Net operating income	$ 36,000

   a. Compute the degree of operating leverage at the current level of sales.
   b. The president expects sales to increase by 15% next year. By how much should net income increase?

5. Refer to the original data. Assume that the company sold 28,000 units last year. The sales manager is convinced that a 10% reduction in the selling price, combined with a $70,000 increase

in advertising expenditures, would cause annual sales in units to increase by 50%. Prepare two contribution income statements, one showing the results of last year's operations and one showing what the results of operations would be if these changes were made. Would you recommend that the company do as the sales manager suggests?

6. Refer to the original data. Assume again that the company sold 28,000 units last year. The president feels that it would be unwise to change the selling price. Instead, he wants to increase the sales commission by $2 per unit. He thinks that this move, combined with some increase in advertising, would cause annual sales to double. By how much could advertising be increased with profits remaining unchanged? Do not prepare an income statement; use the incremental analysis approach.

PROBLEM 6–13 Break-Even Analysis; Pricing [LO1, LO4, LO5]

Detmer Holdings AG of Zurich, Switzerland, has just introduced a new fashion watch for which the company is trying to find an optimal selling price. Marketing studies suggest that the company can increase sales by 5,000 units for each SFr2 per unit reduction in the selling price. (SFr2 denotes 2 Swiss francs.) The company's present selling price is SFr90 per unit, and variable expenses are SFr60 per unit. Fixed expenses are SFr840,000 per year. The present annual sales volume (at the SFr90 selling price) is 25,000 units.

Required:

1. What is the present yearly net operating income or loss?
2. What is the present break-even point in units and in Swiss franc sales?
3. Assuming that the marketing studies are correct, what is the *maximum* profit that the company can earn yearly? At how many units and at what selling price per unit would the company generate this profit?
4. What would be the break-even point in units and in Swiss franc sales using the selling price you determined in (3) above (i.e., the selling price at the level of maximum profits)? Why is this break-even point different from the break-even point you computed in (2) above?

PROBLEM 6–14 Changes in Fixed and Variable Costs; Break-Even and Target Profit Analysis [LO4, LO5, LO6]

Novelties, Inc., produces and sells highly faddish products directed toward the preteen market. A new product has come onto the market that the company is anxious to produce and sell. Enough capacity exists in the company's plant to produce 30,000 units each month. Variable costs to manufacture and sell one unit would be $1.60, and fixed costs would total $40,000 per month.

The Marketing Department predicts that demand for the product will exceed the 30,000 units that the company is able to produce. Additional production capacity can be rented from another company at a fixed cost of $2,000 per month. Variable costs in the rented facility would total $1.75 per unit, due to somewhat less efficient operations than in the main plant. The product would sell for $2.50 per unit.

Required:

1. Compute the monthly break-even point for the new product in units and in total dollar sales. Show all computations in good form.
2. How many units must be sold each month to make a monthly profit of $9,000?
3. If the sales manager receives a bonus of 15 cents for each unit sold in excess of the break-even point, how many units must be sold each month to earn a return of 25% on the monthly investment in fixed costs?

PROBLEM 6–15 Interpretive Questions on the CVP Graph [LO2, LO5]

A CVP graph, as illustrated on the next page, is a useful technique for showing relationships between costs, volume, and profits in an organization.

Required:

1. Identify the numbered components in the CVP graph.
2. State the effect of each of the following actions on line 3, line 9, and the break-even point. For line 3 and line 9, state whether the action will cause the line to:

    Remain unchanged.
    Shift upward.
    Shift downward.
    Have a steeper slope (i.e., rotate upward).
    Have a flatter slope (i.e., rotate downward).
    Shift upward *and* have a steeper slope.

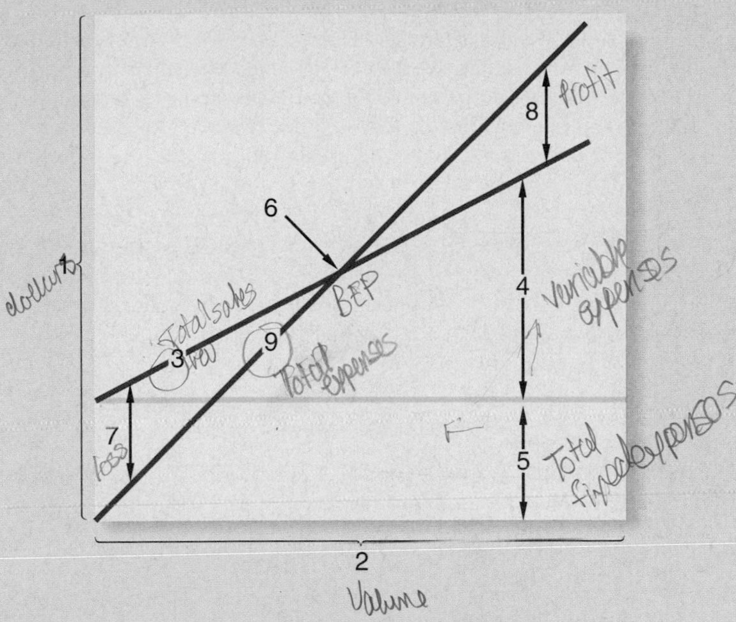

Shift upward *and* have a flatter slope.
Shift downward *and* have a steeper slope.
Shift downward *and* have a flatter slope.

In the case of the break-even point, state whether the action will cause the break-even point to:
Remain unchanged.
Increase.
Decrease.
Probably change, but the direction is uncertain.

Treat each case independently.

x. *Example.* Fixed costs are increased by $20,000 each period.
Answer (see choices above): Line 3: Shift upward.
Line 9: Remain unchanged.
Break-even point: Increase.

a. The unit selling price is decreased from $30 to $27.
b. The per unit variable costs are increased from $12 to $15.
c. The total fixed costs are reduced by $40,000.
d. Five thousand fewer units are sold during the period than were budgeted.
e. Due to purchasing a robot to perform a task that was previously done by workers, fixed costs are increased by $25,000 per period, and variable costs are reduced by $8 per unit.
f. As a result of a decrease in the cost of materials, both unit variable costs and the selling price are decreased by $3.
g. Advertising costs are increased by $50,000 per period, resulting in a 10% increase in the number of units sold.
h. Due to paying salespersons a commission rather than a flat salary, fixed costs are reduced by $21,000 per period, and unit variable costs are increased by $6.

PROBLEM 6–16 Break-Even and Target Profit Analysis [LO5, LO6]

The Marbury Stein Shop sells steins from all parts of the world. The owner of the shop, Clint Marbury, is thinking of expanding his operations by hiring local college students, on a commission basis, to sell steins at the local college. The steins will bear the school emblem.

These steins must be ordered from the manufacturer three months in advance, and because of the unique emblem of each college, they cannot be returned. The steins would cost Mr. Marbury $15 each with a minimum order of 200 steins. Any additional steins would have to be ordered in increments of 50.

Since Mr. Marbury's plan would not require any additional facilities, the only costs associated with the project would be the cost of the steins and the cost of sales commissions. The selling price of the steins would be $30 each. Mr. Marbury would pay the students a commission of $6 for each stein sold.

Required:

1. To make the project worthwhile in terms of his own time, Mr. Marbury would require a $7,200 profit for the first six months of the venture. What level of sales in units and dollars would be required to meet this target net operating income figure? Show all computations.
2. Assume that the venture is undertaken and an order is placed for 200 steins. What would be Mr. Marbury's break-even point in units and in sales dollars? Show computations, and explain the reasoning behind your answer.

PROBLEM 6–17 Sales Mix; Break-Even Analysis; Margin of Safety [LO7, LO9]
Puleva Milenario SA, a company located in Toledo, Spain, manufactures and sells two models of luxuriously finished cutlery—Alvaro and Bazan. Present revenue, cost, and sales data on the two products appear below. All currency amounts are stated in terms of Spanish pesetas (e.g., 400 ptas represents 400 Spanish pesetas).

	Alvaro	Bazan
Selling price per unit	400 ptas	600 ptas
Variable expenses per unit	240 ptas	120 ptas
Number of units sold monthly	200 units	80 units

Fixed expenses are 66,000 ptas per month.

Required:

1. Assuming the sales mix above, do the following:
   a. Prepare a contribution income statement showing both Peseta and Percent columns for each product and for the company as a whole.
   b. Compute the break-even point in pesetas for the company as a whole and the margin of safety in both pesetas and percent of sales.
2. The company has developed another product, Cano, that the company plans to sell for 800 ptas each. At this price, the company expects to sell 40 units per month of the product. The variable expenses would be 600 ptas per unit. The company's fixed expenses would not change.
   a. Prepare another contribution income statement, including the Cano product (sales of the other two products would not change).
   b. Compute the company's new break-even point in pesetas for the company as a whole and the new margin of safety in both pesetas and percent of sales.
3. The president of the company was puzzled by your analysis. He did not understand why the break-even point has gone up even though there has been no increase in fixed costs and the addition of the new product has increased the total contribution margin. Explain to the president what has happened.

PROBLEM 6–18 Various CVP Questions: Break-Even Point; Cost Structure; Target Sales [LO1, LO3, LO4, LO5, LO6, LO8]
Tyrene Products manufactures recreational equipment. One of the company's products, a skateboard, sells for $37.50. The skateboards are manufactured in an antiquated plant that relies heavily on direct labor workers. Thus, variable costs are high, totaling $22.50 per skateboard.

Over the past year the company sold 40,000 skateboards, with the following operating results:

Sales (40,000 skateboards)	$1,500,000
Less variable expenses	900,000
Contribution margin	600,000
Less fixed expenses	480,000
Net operating income	$ 120,000

Management is anxious to maintain and perhaps even improve its present level of income from the skateboards.

Required:

1. Compute (*a*) the CM ratio and the break-even point in skateboards, and (*b*) the degree of operating leverage at last year's level of sales.
2. Due to an increase in labor rates, the company estimates that variable costs will increase by $3 per skateboard next year. If this change takes place and the selling price per skateboard remains constant at $37.50, what will be the new CM ratio and the new break-even point in skateboards?

3. Refer to the data in (2) above. If the expected change in variable costs takes place, how many skateboards will have to be sold next year to earn the same net operating income ($120,000) as last year?
4. Refer again to the data in (2) above. The president has decided that the company may have to raise the selling price on the skateboards. If Tyrene Products wants to maintain *the same CM ratio as last year,* what selling price per skateboard must it charge next year to cover the increased labor costs?
5. Refer to the original data. The company is considering the construction of a new, automated plant to manufacture the skateboards. The new plant would slash variable costs by 40%, but it would cause fixed costs to increase by 90%. If the new plant is built, what would be the company's new CM ratio and new break-even point in skateboards?
6. Refer to the data in (5) above.
   a. If the new plant is built, how many skateboards will have to be sold next year to earn the same net operating income ($120,000) as last year?
   b. Assume that the new plant is constructed and that next year the company manufactures and sells 40,000 skateboards (the same number as sold last year). Prepare a contribution income statement, and compute the degree of operating leverage.
   c. If you were a member of top management, would you have been in favor of constructing the new plant? Explain.

PROBLEM 6–19 Graphing; Incremental Analysis; Operating Leverage [LO2, LO4, LO5, LO6, LO8]

Teri Hall has recently opened Sheer Elegance, Inc., a store specializing in fashionable stockings. Ms. Hall has just completed a course in managerial accounting, and she believes that she can apply certain aspects of the course to her business. She is particularly interested in adopting the cost-volume-profit (CVP) approach to decision making. Thus, she has prepared the following analysis:

Sales price per pair of stockings	$2.00
Variable expense per pair of stockings	0.80
Contribution margin per pair of stockings	$1.20
Fixed expenses per year:	
Building rental	$12,000
Equipment depreciation	3,000
Selling	30,000
Administrative	15,000
Total fixed expenses	$60,000

Required:

1. How many pairs of stockings must be sold to break even? What does this represent in total dollar sales?
2. Prepare a CVP graph for the store from a zero level of activity up to 70,000 pairs of stockings sold each year. Indicate the break-even point on the graph.
3. How many pairs of stockings must be sold to earn a $9,000 target profit for the first year?
4. Ms. Hall now has one full-time and one part-time salesperson working in the store. It will cost her an additional $8,000 per year to convert the part-time position to a full-time position. Ms. Hall believes that the change would bring in an additional $20,000 in sales each year. Should she convert the position? Use the incremental approach. (Do not prepare an income statement.)
5. Refer to the original data. Actual operating results for the first year are as follows:

Sales	$125,000
Less variable expenses	50,000
Contribution margin	75,000
Less fixed expenses	60,000
Net operating income	$ 15,000

   a. What is the store's degree of operating leverage?
   b. Ms. Hall is confident that with some effort she can increase sales by 20% next year. What would be the expected percentage increase in net operating income? Use the degree of operating leverage concept to compute your answer.

2. In an effort to make next year profitable, the president is considering two proposals prepared by members of her staff:
   a. The sales manager would like to reduce the unit selling price by 25%. He is certain that this would fill the plant to capacity.
   b. The executive vice president would like to *increase* the unit selling price by 25%, increase the sales commissions to 12% of sales, and increase advertising by $90,000. Based on experience in another company, he is confident this would trigger a 50% increase in unit sales.

   Prepare two contribution income statements, one showing what profits would be under the sales manager's proposal and one showing what profits would be under the vice president's proposal. On each statement, include both Total and Per Unit columns (do not show per unit data for the fixed costs).
3. Refer to the original data. The president thinks it would be unwise to change the selling price. Instead, she wants to use less costly materials in manufacturing units of product, thereby reducing costs by $1.73 per unit. How many units would have to be sold next year to earn a target profit of $59,000 for the year?
4. Refer to the original data. Alpine, Inc.'s advertising agency thinks that the problem lies in inadequate promotion. By how much can advertising be increased and still allow the company to earn a target return of 4.5% on sales of 60,000 units?
5. Refer to the original data. The company has been approached by an overseas distributor who wants to purchase 15,000 units on a special price basis. There would be no sales commission on these units. However, shipping costs would be increased by 80%, and variable administrative costs would be reduced by 50%. Alpine, Inc., would have to pay a foreign import duty of $3,150 on behalf of the overseas distributor in order to get the goods into the country. Given these data, what unit price would have to be quoted on the 15,000 units by Alpine, Inc., to allow the company to earn a profit of $18,000 on total operations? Regular business would not be disturbed by this special order.

CASE 6–23 Break-Evens for Individual Products in a Multiproduct Company [LO5, LO9]

Jasmine Park encountered her boss, Bubba Gompers, at the pop machine in the lobby. Bubba is the vice president of marketing at Down South Lures Corporation. Jasmine was puzzled by some calculations she had been doing, so she asked him:

Jasmine: "Bubba, I'm not sure how to go about answering the questions that came up at the meeting with the president yesterday."

Bubba: "What's the problem?"

Jasmine: "The president wanted to know the break-even for each of the company's products, but I am having trouble figuring them out."

Bubba: "I'm sure you can handle it, Jasmine. And, by the way, I need your analysis on my desk tomorrow morning at 8:00 sharp so I can look at it before the follow-up meeting at 9:00."

Down South Lures makes three fishing lures in its manufacturing facility in Alabama. Data concerning these products appear below.

	Frog	Minnow	Worm
Normal annual sales volume	100,000	200,000	300,000
Unit selling price	$2.00	$1.40	$0.80
Variable cost per unit	$1.20	$0.80	$0.50

Total fixed expenses for the entire company are $282,000 per year.

All three products are sold in highly competitive markets, so the company is unable to raise its prices without losing unacceptable numbers of customers.

The company has no work in process or finished goods inventories due to an extremely effective just-in-time manufacturing system.

Required:

1. What is the company's overall break-even in total sales dollars?
2. Of the total fixed costs of $282,000, $18,000 could be avoided if the Frog lure product were dropped, $96,000 if the Minnow lure product were dropped, and $60,000 if the Worm lure product were dropped. The remaining fixed costs of $108,000 consist of common fixed costs such as administrative salaries and rent on the factory building that could be avoided only by going out of business entirely.
   a. What is the break-even quantity of each product?

b. If the company sells exactly the break-even quantity of each product, what will be the overall profit of the company? Explain this result.

CASE 6–24 Break-Even Analysis with Step Fixed Costs [LO5, LO6]

The Cardiac Care Department at St. Andrew's General Hospital has a capacity of 70 beds and operates 24 hours a day year-around. The measure of activity in the department is patient-days, where one patient-day represents one patient occupying a bed for one day. The average revenue per patient-day is $240 and the average variable cost per patient-day is $90. The fixed cost of the department (not including personnel costs) is $1,370,000.

The only personnel directly employed by the Cardiac Care Department are aides, nurses, and supervising nurses. The hospital has minimum staffing requirements for the department based on total annual patient-days in Cardiac Care. Hospital requirements, beginning at the minimum expected level of activity, follow:

Annual Patient-Days	Aides	Nurses	Supervising Nurses
10,000–12,000	7	15	3
12,001–13,750	8	15	3
13,751–16,500	9	16	4
16,501–18,250	10	16	4
18,251–20,750	10	17	5
20,751–23,000	11	18	5

These staffing levels represent full-time equivalents, and it should be assumed that the Cardiac Care Department always employs only the minimum number of required full-time equivalent personnel.

Average annual salaries for each class of employee are: aides, $18,000; nurses, $29,000; and supervising nurses, $38,000.

Required:

1. Compute the total fixed costs (including the salaries of aides, nurses, and supervising nurses) in the Cardiac Care Department for each level of activity shown above (i.e., total fixed costs at the 10,000–12,000 patient-day level of activity, total fixed costs at the 12,001–13,750 patient-day level of activity, etc.).
2. Compute the minimum number of patient-days required for the Cardiac Care Department to break even.
3. Determine the minimum number of patient-days required for the Cardiac Care Department to earn an annual "profit" of $360,000.

(CPA, adapted)

CASE 6–25 Cost Structure; Break-Even Point; Target Profits [LO4, LO5, LO6]

Marston Corporation manufactures disposable thermometers that are sold to hospitals through a network of independent sales agents located in the United States and Canada. These sales agents sell a variety of products to hospitals in addition to Marston's disposable thermometer. The sales agents are currently paid an 18% commission on sales, and this commission rate was used when Marston's management prepared the following budgeted income statement for the upcoming year.

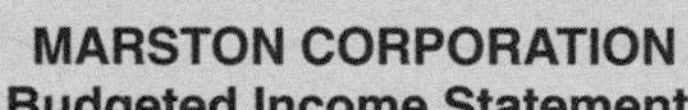
MARSTON CORPORATION
Budgeted Income Statement

Sales		$30,000,000
Cost of goods sold:		
Variable	$17,400,000	
Fixed	2,800,000	20,200,000
Gross profit		9,800,000
Selling and administrative expenses:		
Commissions	5,400,000	
Fixed advertising expense	800,000	
Fixed administrative expense	3,200,000	9,400,000
Net operating income		$ 400,000

Since the completion of the above statement, Marston's management has learned that the independent sales agents are demanding an increase in the commission rate to 20% of sales for the

Required:

1. What is the maximum seating capacity of the stadium or arena in which the sport is played? During the past year, what was the average attendance at the games? On average, what percentage of the stadium or arena capacity was filled?
2. The number of seats sold often depends on the opponent. The attendance for a game with a traditional rival (e.g., Nebraska vs. Colorado, University of Washington vs. Washington State, or Texas vs. Texas A&M) is usually substantially above the average. Also, games against conference foes may draw larger crowds than other games. As a consequence, the number of tickets sold for a game is somewhat predictable. What implications does this have for the nature of the costs of putting on a game? Are most of the costs really fixed with respect to the number of tickets sold?
3. Estimate the variable cost per ticket sold.
4. Estimate the total additional revenue that would be generated in an average game if all of the tickets were sold at their normal prices. Estimate how much profit is lost because these tickets are not sold.
5. Estimate the ancillary revenue (parking and concessions) per ticket sold. Estimate how much profit is lost in an average game from these sources of revenue as a consequence of not having a sold-out game.
6. Estimate how much additional profit would be generated for your college if every game were sold out for the entire season.

GROUP EXERCISE 6–28 Airline Cost Structure

Airlines provide an excellent illustration of the concept of operating leverage, the sensitivity of a firm's operating profits to changes in demand, and the opportunities and risks presented by such a cost structure. The Uniform System of Accounts required by the Department of Transportation for airlines operating in the United States contains the following cost categories:

- Fuel and oil.
- Flying operations labor (flight crews—pilots, copilots, navigators, and flight engineers).
- Passenger service labor (flight attendants).
- Aircraft traffic and servicing labor (personnel servicing aircraft and handling passengers at gates, baggage, and cargo).
- Promotions and sales labor (reservations and sales agents, advertising and publicity).
- Maintenance labor (maintenance of flight equipment and ground property and equipment).
- Maintenance materials and overhead.
- Ground property and equipment (landing fees and rental expenses and depreciation for ground property and equipment).
- Flight equipment (rental expenses and depreciation on aircraft frames and engines).
- General overhead (administrative personnel, utilities, insurance, communications, etc.).

Required:

1. Which of the above costs are likely to be affected if an airline adds an airport to its network?
2. Which of the above costs are likely to be affected if an airline schedules one more flight out of an airport that the airline already serves?
3. Which of the above costs are likely to be variable with respect to the number of passengers who actually fly on a particular scheduled flight?
4. Are airline profits likely to be affected very much by their load factors? Why? (The load factor refers to the percentage of scheduled seats filled by paying passengers.)

GROUP EXERCISE 6–29 The Economics of Higher Education

The "baby bust" of the 1960s and early 1970s resulted in the number of college-age 18- and 19-year-olds contracting sharply from 1980 to 1993. The number of graduating high school seniors peaked in 1979 and declined to a low of 6.9 million in 1992, a drop of nearly 40%. Throughout the eighties, tuition at private and public universities rose at an average of 9% per year, a figure far above the rise in household family incomes. Then, the demographics began to reverse themselves: the number of 18- and 19-year-olds began to increase in 1996 and will continue until they peak in 2010 at about 9.3 million for nearly a 33% increase in the college-eligible population. The four-year cost of attending a private college now often exceeds $100,000—including room and board.

Required:

1. If tuition and room and board costs increase at the rate of 9% per year, what will four years' tuition at a private college cost in 10 years? How affordable will a college education be at this level?

2. What is the cost of adding an extra student to a typical class? Explain this in terms of the cost structure of a university.
3. After two decades of almost uninterrupted expansion, the "baby bust" enrollment drop left many colleges with considerable underutilized capacity. What impact will increasing enrollment and economies of scale have on costs and tuition?
4. Which colleges do you expect will be helped the most by increasing enrollments—public or private?

INTERNET EXERCISE 6–30

As you know, the World Wide Web is a medium that is constantly evolving. Sites come and go, and change without notice. To enable periodic update of site addresses, this problem has been posted to the textbook website (www.mhhe.com/garrison10e). After accessing the site, enter the Student Center and select this chapter. Select and complete the Internet exercise.

Chapter Seven

Variable Costing: A Tool for Management

LEARNING OBJECTIVES

After studying Chapter 7, you should be able to:

1. Explain how variable costing differs from absorption costing and compute unit product costs under each method.
2. Prepare income statements using both variable and absorption costing.
3. Reconcile variable costing and absorption costing net operating incomes and explain why the two amounts differ.
4. Understand the advantages and disadvantages of both variable and absorption costing.

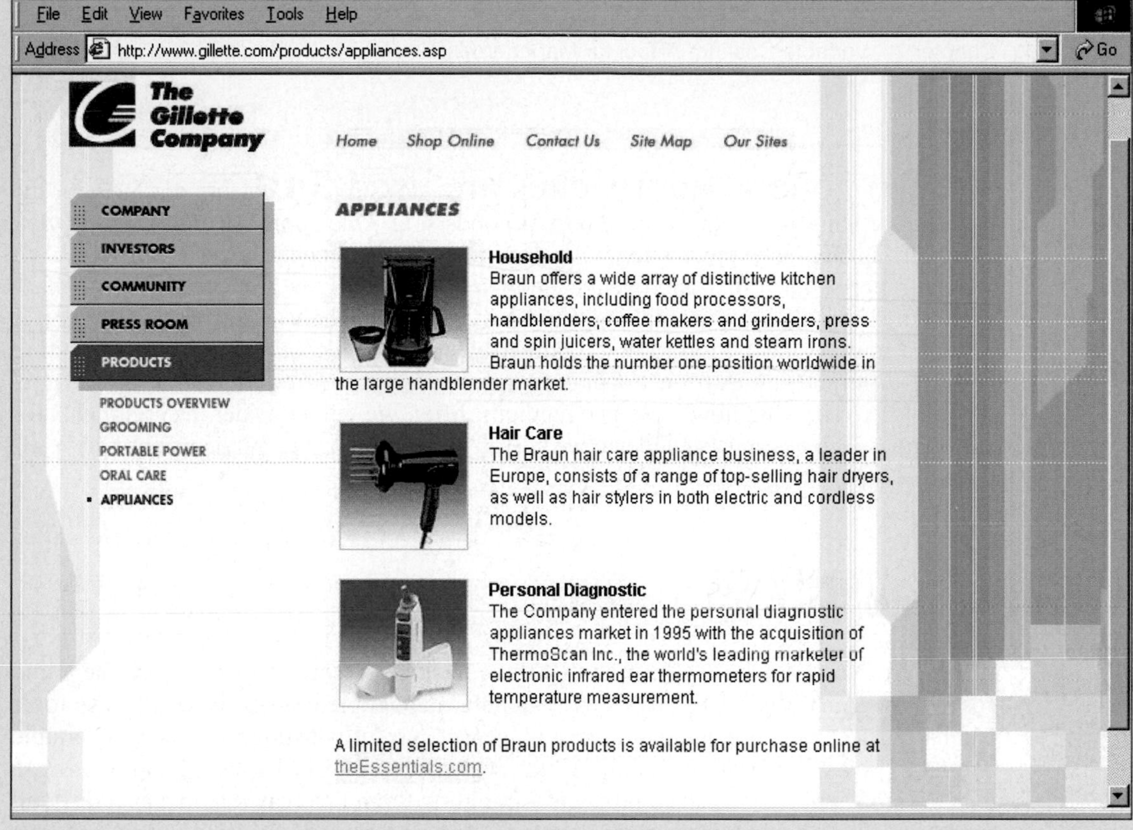

File Edit View Favorites Tools Help
Address http://www.gillette.com/products/appliances.asp
Go
The Gillette Company
Home Shop Online Contact Us Site Map Our Sites
COMPANY
INVESTORS
COMMUNITY
PRESS ROOM
PRODUCTS
PRODUCTS OVERVIEW
GROOMING
PORTABLE POWER
ORAL CARE
APPLIANCES
APPLIANCES
Household
Braun offers a wide array of distinctive kitchen appliances, including food processors, handblenders, coffee makers and grinders, press and spin juicers, water kettles and steam irons. Braun holds the number one position worldwide in the large handblender market.
Hair Care
The Braun hair care appliance business, a leader in Europe, consists of a range of top-selling hair dryers, as well as hair stylers in both electric and cordless models.
Personal Diagnostic
The Company entered the personal diagnostic appliances market in 1995 with the acquisition of ThermoScan Inc., the world's leading marketer of electronic infrared ear thermometers for rapid temperature measurement.
A limited selection of Braun products is available for purchase online at theEssentials.com.

The House of Cards at Gillette

Alfred M. Zeien was the successful CEO of Gillette Co. for eight years, leading the company to earnings growth rates of 15% to 20% per year. However, as his successor as CEO discovered, some of this profit growth was an illusion based on building inventories. William H. Steele, an analyst with Bank of America Securities, alleges: "There is no question Gillette was making its numbers (in part) by aggressively selling to the trade, and building inventories." Within a three-year period, Gillette's inventories of finished goods had increased by over 40% (to $1.3 billion) even though Gillette's sales had barely increased.

How can building inventories increase profits without any increase in sales? As we will discover in this chapter, absorption costing—the most widely used method of determining product costs—can be used to manipulate profits in just this way.

Source: William C. Symonds, "The Big Trim at Gillette," *Business Week,* November 8, 1999, p. 42.

Two general approaches are used for costing products for the purposes of valuing inventories and cost of goods sold. One approach, called *absorption costing,* was discussed in Chapter 3. Absorption costing is generally used for external financial reports. The other approach, called *variable costing,* is preferred by some managers for internal decision making and must be used when an income statement is prepared in the contribution format. Ordinarily, absorption costing and variable costing produce different figures for net operating income, and the difference can be quite large. In addition to showing how these two methods differ, we will consider the arguments for and against each costing method and we will show how management decisions can be affected by the costing method chosen.

Overview of Absorption and Variable Costing

LEARNING OBJECTIVE 1
Explain how variable costing differs from absorption costing and compute unit product costs under each method.

In the last two chapters, we learned that the contribution format income statement and cost-volume-profit (CVP) analysis are valuable management tools. Both of these tools emphasize cost behavior and require that managers carefully distinguish between variable and fixed costs. Absorption costing, which was discussed in Chapters 2 and 3, assigns both variable and fixed costs to products—mingling them in a way that makes it difficult for managers to distinguish between them. In contrast, variable costing focuses on *cost behavior*—clearly separating fixed from variable costs. One of the strengths of variable costing is that it harmonizes fully with both the contribution approach and the CVP concepts discussed in the preceding chapter.

Absorption Costing

In Chapter 3, we learned that **absorption costing** treats *all* costs of production as product costs, regardless of whether they are variable or fixed. The cost of a unit of product under the absorption costing method therefore consists of direct materials, direct labor, and *both* variable and fixed overhead. Thus, absorption costing allocates a portion of fixed manufacturing overhead cost to each unit of product, along with the variable manufacturing costs. Because absorption costing includes all costs of production as product costs, it is frequently referred to as the **full cost** method.

Variable Costing

Under **variable costing,** only those costs of production that vary with output are treated as product costs. This would usually include direct materials, direct labor, and the variable portion of manufacturing overhead. Fixed manufacturing overhead is not treated as a product cost under this method. Rather, fixed manufacturing overhead is treated as a period cost and, like selling and administrative expenses, it is charged off in its entirety against revenue each period. Consequently, the cost of a unit of product in inventory or in cost of goods sold under the variable costing method does not contain any fixed overhead cost.

Variable costing is sometimes referred to as **direct costing** or **marginal costing.** The term *direct costing* was popular for many years, but it is slowly disappearing from day-to-day use. The term *variable costing* is more descriptive of the way in which product costs are computed when a contribution income statement is prepared.

To complete this summary comparison of absorption and variable costing, we need to consider briefly the handling of selling and administrative expenses. These expenses are never treated as product costs, regardless of the costing method in use. Thus, under either absorption or variable costing, both variable and fixed selling and administrative expenses are always treated as period costs and deducted from revenues as incurred.

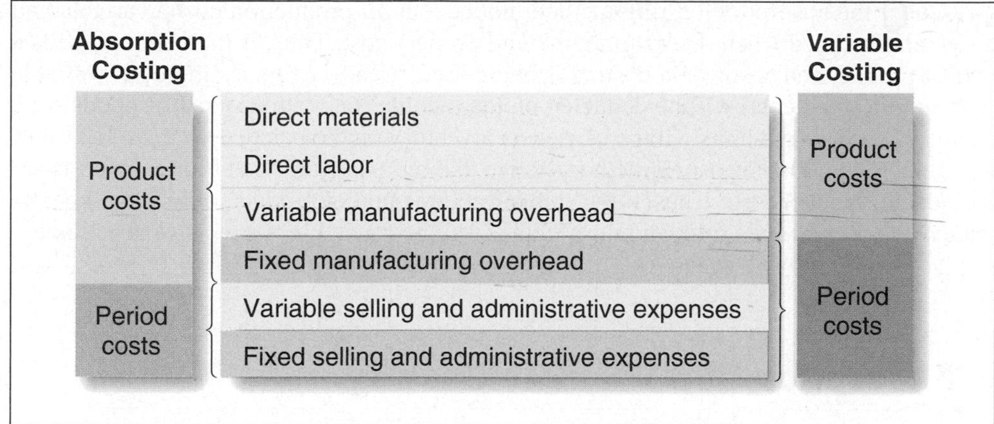

Exhibit 7–1
Cost Classifications—Absorption versus Variable Costing

The concepts discussed so far in this section are illustrated in Exhibit 7–1, which shows the classification of costs under both absorption and variable costing.

Unit Cost Computations

Concept 7–1

To illustrate the computation of unit product costs under both absorption and variable costing, consider Boley Company, a small company that produces a single product and has the following cost structure:

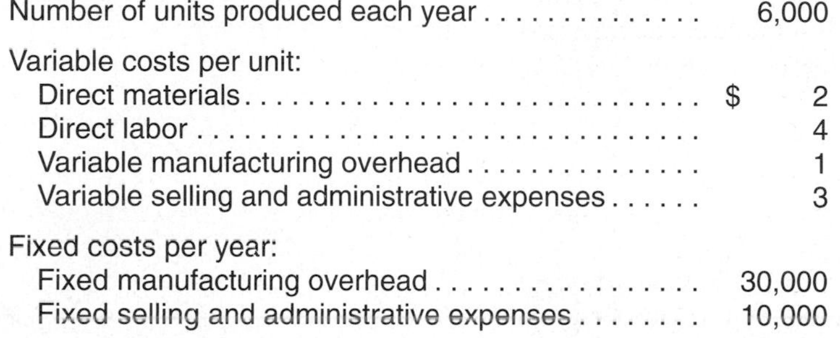

Number of units produced each year	6,000
Variable costs per unit:	
Direct materials	$ 2
Direct labor	4
Variable manufacturing overhead	1
Variable selling and administrative expenses	3
Fixed costs per year:	
Fixed manufacturing overhead	30,000
Fixed selling and administrative expenses	10,000

Required:

1. Compute the unit product cost under absorption costing.
2. Compute the unit product cost under variable costing.

Solution

Absorption Costing	
Direct materials	$ 2
Direct labor	4
Variable manufacturing overhead	1
Total variable production cost	7
Fixed manufacturing overhead ($30,000 ÷ 6,000 units of product)	5
Unit product cost	$12

Variable Costing	
Direct materials	$ 2
Direct labor	4
Variable manufacturing overhead	1
Unit product cost	$ 7

(The $30,000 fixed manufacturing overhead will be charged off in total against income as a period expense along with selling and administrative expenses.)

Under the absorption costing method, notice that *all* production costs, variable and fixed, are included when determining the unit product cost. Thus, if the company sells a unit of product and absorption costing is being used, then $12 (consisting of $7 variable cost and $5 fixed cost) will be deducted on the income statement as cost of goods sold. Similarly, any unsold units will be carried as inventory on the balance sheet at $12 each.

Under the variable costing method, notice that only the variable production costs are included in product costs. Thus, if the company sells a unit of product, only $7 will be deducted as cost of goods sold, and unsold units will be carried in the balance sheet inventory account at only $7 each.

Income Comparison of Absorption and Variable Costing

LEARNING OBJECTIVE 2
Prepare income statements using both variable and absorption costing.

Income statements prepared under the absorption and variable costing approaches are shown in Exhibit 7–2. In preparing these statements, we use the data for Boley Company presented earlier, along with other information about the company as given below:

Units in beginning inventory	0
Units produced	6,000
Units sold	5,000
Units in ending inventory	1,000
Selling price per unit	$ 20
Selling and administrative expenses:	
Variable per unit	3
Fixed per year	10,000

	Absorption Costing	Variable Costing
Unit product cost:		
Direct materials	$ 2	$ 2
Direct labor	4	4
Variable manufacturing overhead	1	1
Fixed manufacturing overhead ($30,000 ÷ 6,000 units)	5	—
Unit product cost	$12	$ 7

Several points can be made from the financial statements in Exhibit 7–2:

1. Under the absorption costing method, if inventories increase then some of the fixed manufacturing costs of the current period will not appear on the income statement as part of cost of goods sold. Instead, these costs are deferred to a future period and are carried on the balance sheet as part of the inventory count. Such a deferral of costs is known as **fixed manufacturing overhead cost deferred in inventory.** The process involved can be explained by referring to the data for Boley Company. During the current period, Boley Company produced 6,000 units but sold only 5,000 units, thus leaving 1,000 unsold units in the ending inventory. Under the absorption costing method, each unit produced was assigned $5 in fixed overhead cost (see the unit cost computations above). Therefore, each of the 1,000 units going into inventory at the end of the period has $5 in fixed manufacturing overhead cost attached to it, or a total of $5,000 for the 1,000 units. *This fixed manufacturing overhead cost of the current period is deferred in inventory to the next period, when, hopefully, these units will be taken out of inventory and sold.* The deferral of $5,000 of fixed manufacturing overhead costs can be clearly seen by analyzing the ending inventory under the absorption costing method:

Variable manufacturing costs: 1,000 units × $7 per unit	$ 7,000
Fixed manufacturing overhead costs: 1,000 units × $5 per unit	5,000
Total inventory value	$12,000

Exhibit 7–2
Comparison of Absorption and Variable Costing—Boley Company

Absorption Costing		
Sales (5,000 units × $20 per unit)		$100,000
Less cost of goods sold:		
Beginning inventory	$ 0	
Add cost of goods manufactured (6,000 units × $12 per unit).	72,000	
Goods available for sale	72,000	
Less ending inventory (1,000 units × $12 per unit).	12,000	
Cost of goods sold		60,000
Gross margin		40,000
Less selling and administrative expenses (5,000 units × $3 variable per unit + $10,000 fixed)		25,000
Net operating income		$ 15,000
Variable Costing		
Sales ($5,000 units × $20 per unit)		$100,000
Less variable expenses:		
Variable cost of goods sold:		
Beginning inventory.	$ 0	
Add variable manufacturing costs (6,000 units × $7 per unit).	42,000	
Goods available for sale	42,000	
Less ending inventory (1,000 units × $7 per unit).	7,000	
Variable cost of goods sold	35,000	
Variable selling and administrative expenses (5,000 units × $3 per unit)	15,000	50,000
Contribution margin		50,000
Less fixed expenses:		
Fixed manufacturing overhead	30,000	
Fixed selling and administrative expenses.	10,000	40,000
Net operating income		$ 10,000

Note the difference in ending inventories. Fixed manufacturing overhead cost at $5 per unit is included under the absorption approach. This explains the difference in ending inventory and in net operating income (1,000 units × $5 per unit = $5,000).

In summary, under absorption costing, of the $30,000 in fixed manufacturing overhead costs incurred during the period, only $25,000 (5,000 units sold × $5 per unit) has been included in cost of goods sold. The remaining $5,000 (1,000 units *not* sold × $5 per unit) has been deferred in inventory to the next period.

2. Under the variable costing method, the entire $30,000 in fixed manufacturing overhead costs has been treated as an expense of the current period (see the bottom portion of the variable costing income statement).
3. The ending inventory figure under the variable costing method is $5,000 lower than it is under the absorption costing method. The reason is that under variable costing, only the variable manufacturing costs are assigned to units of product and therefore included in inventory:

Concept 7–2

Variable manufacturing costs: 1,000 units × $7 per unit	$7,000

The $5,000 difference in ending inventories explains the difference in net operating income reported between the two costing methods. Net operating income is $5,000 *higher* under absorption costing since, as explained above, $5,000 of fixed manufacturing overhead cost has been deferred in inventory to the next period under that costing method.

4. The absorption costing income statement makes no distinction between fixed and variable costs; therefore, it is not well suited for CVP computations, which are important for good planning and control. To generate data for CVP analysis, it would be necessary to spend considerable time reworking and reclassifying costs on the absorption statement.
5. The variable costing approach to costing units of product works very well with the contribution approach to the income statement, since both concepts are based on the idea of classifying costs by behavior. The variable costing data in Exhibit 7–2 could be used immediately in CVP computations.

Essentially, the difference between the absorption costing method and the variable costing method centers on timing. Advocates of variable costing say that fixed manufacturing costs should be expensed immediately in total, whereas advocates of absorption costing say that fixed manufacturing costs should be charged against revenues bit by bit as units of product are sold. Any units of product not sold under absorption costing result in fixed costs being inventoried and carried forward *as assets* to the next period. We will defer discussing the arguments presented by each side in this dispute until after we have a better understanding of the two methods. Nevertheless, as we shall see in the following discussion of Emerald Isle Knitters, the use of absorption costing can sometimes produce strange effects on income statements.

In Business

Direct Labor—A Fixed Cost in China

The Shanghai Bund Steel Works (SBSW) of the Peoples' Republic of China is a large state-owned enterprise. In recent years, state-owned companies such as SBSW have been given a great deal of autonomy, providing that they meet their financial and nonfinancial targets. However, in state-owned enterprises, management has very little freedom to adjust the work force—eliminating jobs would create political problems. Therefore, for internal management purposes, SBSW treats labor cost as a fixed cost that is part of fixed manufacturing overhead.

Source: Yau Shiu Wing Joseph, *Management Accounting* (UK), October 1996, pp. 52–54.

Extended Comparison of Income Data

Managerial Accounting in Action

The Issue

Mary O'Meara is the owner and manager of Emerald Isle Knitters, Ltd., located in the Republic of Ireland. The company is very small, with only 10 employees. Mary started the company three years ago with cash loaned to her by a local bank. The company manufactures a traditional wool fisherman's sweater from a pattern Mary learned from her grandmother. Like most apparel manufacturers, Emerald Isle Knitters sells its product to department stores and clothing store chains rather than to retail customers.

The sweater was an immediate success, and the company sold all of the first year's production. However, in the second year of operations, one of the company's major customers canceled its order due to bankruptcy, and the company ended the year with large stocks of unsold sweaters. The third year of operations was a great year in contrast to that disastrous second year. Sales rebounded dramatically, and all of the unsold production carried over from the second year was sold by the end of the third year.

Shortly after the close of the third year, Mary met with her accountant Sean MacLafferty to discuss the results for the year. (Note: All of the company's business is transacted using the euro, denoted by €, as the currency. The euro is the new common currency of many member countries of the European Union.)

Mary: Sean, the results for this year look a lot better than for last year, but I am frankly puzzled why this year's results aren't even better than the income statement shows.

Sean: I know what you mean. The net operating income for this year is just €90,000. Last year it was €30,000. That is a huge improvement, but it seems that profits this year should have been even higher and profits last year should have been much less. We were in big trouble last year. I was afraid we might not even break even—yet we showed a healthy €30,000 profit. Somehow it doesn't seem quite right.

Mary: I wondered about that €30,000 profit last year, but I didn't question it since it was the only good news I had gotten for quite some time.

Sean: In case you're wondering, I didn't invent that profit last year just to make you feel better. Our auditor required that I follow certain accounting rules in preparing those reports for the bank. This may sound heretical, but we *could* use different rules for our own internal reports.

Mary: Wait a minute, rules are rules—especially in accounting.

Sean: Yes and no. For our internal reports, it might be better to use different rules than we use for the reports we send to the bank.

Mary: As I said, rules are rules. Still, I'm willing to listen if you want to show me what you have in mind.

Sean: It's a deal.

Immediately after the meeting with Mary, Sean put together the data and financial reports that appear in Exhibit 7–3. To make the principles clearer, Sean simplified the data so that the illustrations all use round figures.

Exhibit 7–3 Absorption and Variable Costing Statements—Emerald Isle Knitters, Ltd.

Basic Data				
Selling price per unit sold	€ 20			
Variable manufacturing cost per unit produced	7			
Fixed manufacturing overhead costs per year	150,000			
Variable selling and administrative expenses per unit sold	1			
Fixed selling and administrative expenses per year	90,000			

	Year 1	**Year 2**	**Year 3**	**Three Years Together**
Units in beginning inventory	0	0	5,000	0
Units produced	25,000	25,000	25,000	75,000
Units sold	25,000	20,000	30,000	75,000
Units in ending inventory	0	5,000	0	0

Unit Product Costs	**Year 1**	**Year 2**	**Year 3**
Under variable costing (variable manufacturing costs only)	€ 7	€ 7	€ 7
Under absorption costing:			
Variable manufacturing costs	€ 7	€ 7	€ 7
Fixed manufacturing overhead costs (€150,000 spread over the number of units produced in each year)	6	6	6
Total absorption cost per unit	€13	€13	€13

continued

Exhibit 7–3 *concluded*

	Year 1		Year 2		Year 3		Three Years Together	
Absorption Costing								
Sales		€500,000		€400,000		€600,000		€1,500,000
Less cost of goods sold:								
Beginning inventory	€ 0		€ 0		€ 65,000		€ 0	
Add cost of goods manufactured (25,000 units × €13 per unit)	325,000		325,000		325,000		975,000	
Goods available for sale	325,000		325,000		390,000		975,000	
Less ending inventory (5,000 units × €13 per unit)	0		65,000		0		0	
Cost of goods sold		325,000		260,000		390,000		975,000
Gross margin		175,000		140,000		210,000		525,000
Less selling and administrative expenses		115,000*		110,000*		120,000*		345,000
Net operating income		€ 60,000		€ 30,000		€ 90,000		€ 180,000

*The selling and administrative expenses are computed as follows:

Year 1: 25,000 units × €1 per unit variable + €90,000 fixed = €115,000.

Year 2: 20,000 units × €1 per unit variable + €90,000 fixed = €110,000.

Year 3: 30,000 units × €1 per unit variable + €90,000 fixed = €120,000.

	Year 1		Year 2		Year 3		Three Years Together	
Variable Costing								
Sales		€500,000		€400,000		€600,000		€1,500,000
Less variable expenses:								
Variable cost of goods sold:								
Beginning inventory	€ 0		€ 0		€ 35,000		€ 0	
Add variable manufacturing costs (25,000 units × €7 per unit)	175,000		175,000		175,000		525,000	
Goods available for sale	175,000		175,000		210,000		525,000	
Less ending inventory (5,000 units × €7 per unit)	0		35,000		0		0	
Variable cost of goods sold	175,000*		140,000*		210,000*		525,000	
Variable selling and administrative expenses (€1 per unit sold)	25,000	200,000	20,000	160,000	30,000	240,000	75,000	600,000
Contribution margin		300,000		240,000		360,000		900,000
Less fixed expenses:								
Fixed manufacturing overhead	150,000		150,000		150,000		450,000	
Fixed selling and administrative expenses	90,000	240,000	90,000	240,000	90,000	240,000	270,000	720,000
Net operating income		€ 60,000		€ 0		€120,000		€ 180,000

*The variable cost of goods sold could have been computed more simply as follows:

Year 1: 25,000 units sold × €7 per unit = €175,000.

Year 2: 20,000 units sold × €7 per unit = €140,000.

Year 3: 30,000 units sold × €7 per unit = €210,000.

LEARNING OBJECTIVE 3
Reconcile variable costing and absorption costing net operating incomes and explain why the two amounts differ.

The basic data appear at the top of Exhibit 7–3, and the absorption costing income statements as reported to the bank for the last three years appear at the top of the exhibit on page 286. Sean decided to try using the variable costing approach to see what effect that might have on net operating income. The variable costing income statements for the last three years appear in the last part of Exhibit 7–3 on page 286.

Note that Emerald Isle Knitters maintained a steady rate of production of 25,000 sweaters per year. However, sales varied from year to year. In Year 1, production and sales were equal. In Year 2, production exceeded sales due to the canceled order. In Year 3, sales recovered and exceeded production. As a consequence, inventories did not change during Year 1, inventories increased during Year 2, and inventories decreased during Year 3. The change in inventories during the year is the key to understanding how absorption costing differs from variable costing. Note that when inventories increase in Year 2, absorption costing net operating income exceeds variable costing net operating income. When inventories decrease in Year 3, the opposite occurs—variable costing net operating income exceeds absorption costing net operating income. And when inventories do not change as in Year 1, there is no difference in net operating income between the two methods. Why is this? The reasons are discussed below and are briefly summarized in Exhibit 7–4.

1. When production and sales are equal, as in Year 1 for Emerald Isle Knitters, net operating income will generally be the same regardless of whether absorption or variable costing is used. The reason is as follows: The *only* difference that can exist between absorption and variable costing net operating income is the amount of fixed manufacturing overhead recognized as expense on the income statement. When everything that is produced in the year is sold, all of the fixed manufacturing overhead assigned to units of product under absorption costing becomes part of the year's cost of goods sold. Under variable costing, the total fixed manufacturing overhead flows directly to the income statement as an expense. So under either method, when production equals sales (and hence inventories do not change), all the fixed manufacturing overhead incurred during the year flows through to the income statement as expense. And therefore, the net operating income under the two methods is the same.
2. When production exceeds sales, the net operating income reported under absorption costing will generally be greater than the net operating income reported under

Exhibit 7–4
Comparative Income Effects—Absorption and Variable Costing

Relation between Production and Sales for the Period	Effect on Inventories	Relation between Absorption and Variable Costing Net Operating Incomes
Production = Sales	No change in inventories	Absorption costing net operating income = Variable costing net operating income
Production > Sales	Inventories increase	Absorption costing net operating income > Variable costing net operating income*
Production < Sales	Inventories decrease	Absorption costing net operating income < Variable costing net operating income†

*Net operating income is higher under absorption costing, since fixed manufacturing overhead cost is *deferred* in inventory under absorption costing as inventories increase.
†Net operating income is lower under absorption costing, since fixed manufacturing overhead cost is *released* from inventory under absorption costing as inventories decrease.

Exhibit 7–5
Reconciliation of Variable Costing and Absorption Costing—Net Operating Income Data from Exhibit 7–3

	Year 1	Year 2	Year 3
Variable costing net operating income	€60,000	€ 0	€120,000
Add fixed manufacturing overhead costs deferred in inventory under absorption costing (5,000 units ×€6 per unit)	0	30,000	0
Deduct fixed manufacturing overhead costs released from inventory under absorption costing (5,000 units × €6 per unit)	0	0	(30,000)
Absorption costing net operating income	€60,000	€30,000	€ 90,000

variable costing (see Year 2 in Exhibit 7–3). This occurs because under absorption costing, part of the fixed manufacturing overhead costs of the current period is deferred in inventory. In Year 2, for example, €30,000 of fixed manufacturing overhead costs (5,000 units × €6 per unit) has been applied to units in ending inventory. These costs are excluded from cost of goods sold.

Under variable costing, however, *all* of the fixed manufacturing overhead costs of Year 2 have been charged immediately against income as a period cost. As a result, the net operating income for Year 2 under variable costing is €30,000 *lower* than it is under absorption costing. Exhibit 7–5 contains a reconciliation of the variable costing and absorption costing net operating incomes.

3. When production is less than sales, the net operating income reported under the absorption costing approach will generally be less than the net operating income reported under the variable costing approach (see Year 3 in Exhibit 7–3). This happens because inventories are drawn down and fixed manufacturing overhead costs that were previously deferred in inventory under absorption costing are released and charged against income (known as **fixed manufacturing overhead cost released from inventory**). In Year 3, for example, the €30,000 in fixed manufacturing overhead costs deferred in inventory under the absorption approach from Year 2 to Year 3 is released from inventory because these units were sold. As a result, the cost of goods sold for Year 3 contains not only all of the fixed manufacturing overhead costs for Year 3 (since all that was produced in Year 3 was sold in Year 3) but €30,000 of fixed manufacturing overhead costs from Year 2 as well.

   By contrast, under variable costing only the fixed manufacturing overhead costs of Year 3 have been charged against Year 3. The result is that net operating income under variable costing is €30,000 *higher* than it is under absorption costing. Exhibit 7–5 contains a reconciliation of the variable costing and absorption costing net operating income figures for Year 3.
4. Over an *extended* period of time, the net operating income figures reported under absorption costing and variable costing will tend to be the same. The reason is that over the long run sales can't exceed production, nor can production much exceed sales. The shorter the time period, the more the net operating income figures will tend to differ.

Effect of Changes in Production on Net Operating Income

In the Emerald Isle Knitters example in the preceding section, production was constant and sales fluctuated over the three-year period. Since sales fluctuated, the data Sean MacLafferty presented in Exhibit 7–3 allowed us to see the effect of changes in sales on net operating income under both variable and absorption costing.

To further investigate the differences between variable and absorption costing, Sean next put together the hypothetical example in Exhibit 7–6. In this hypothetical example, sales are constant and production fluctuates (the opposite of Exhibit 7–3). The purpose of Exhibit 7–6 is to illustrate for Mary O'Meara the effect of changes in *production* on net operating income under both variable and absorption costing.

Variable Costing

Net operating income is *not* affected by changes in production under variable costing. Notice from Exhibit 7–6 that net operating income is the same for all three years under variable costing, although production exceeds sales in one year and is less than sales in another year. In short, a change in production has no impact on net operating income when variable costing is used.

Absorption Costing

Net operating income *is* affected by changes in production under absorption costing. As shown in Exhibit 7–6, net operating income under absorption costing goes up in Year 2, in response to the increase in production for that year, and then goes down in Year 3, in response to the drop in production for that year. Note particularly that net operating income goes up and down between these two years *even though the same number of units is sold in each year.* The reason for this effect can be traced to fixed manufacturing overhead costs that shift between periods under the absorption costing method as a result of changes in inventory.

As shown in Exhibit 7–6, production exceeds sales in Year 2, resulting in an increase of 10,000 units in inventory. Each unit produced during Year 2 has €6 in fixed manufacturing overhead costs attached to it (see the unit cost computations at the top of Exhibit 7–6). Therefore, €60,000 (10,000 units × €6 per unit) of the fixed manufacturing overhead costs of Year 2 are not charged against that year but rather are added to the inventory account (along with the variable manufacturing costs). The net operating income of Year

Exhibit 7–6 Sensitivity of Costing Methods to Changes in Production—Hypothetical Data

Basic Data			
Selling price per unit sold			€ 25
Variable manufacturing cost per unit produced			10
Fixed manufacturing overhead costs per year			300,000
Variable selling and administrative expenses per unit sold			1
Fixed selling and administrative expenses per year			200,000
	Year 1	**Year 2**	**Year 3**
Units in beginning inventory	0	0	10,000
Units produced	40,000	50,000	30,000
Units sold	40,000	40,000	40,000
Units in ending inventory	0	10,000	0
Unit Product Costs			
Under variable costing (variable manufacturing costs only)	€10.00	€10.00	€10.00
Under absorption costing			
Variable manufacturing costs	€10.00	€10.00	€10.00
Fixed manufacturing overhead costs (€300,000 total spread over the number of units produced in each year)	7.50	6.00	10.00
Total absorption cost per unit	€17.50	€16.00	€20.00

continued

Exhibit 7–6 *concluded*

	Year 1		Year 2		Year 3	
Absorption Costing						
Sales (40,000 units)		€1,000,000		€1,000,000		€1,000,000
Less cost of goods sold:						
Beginning inventory	€ 0		€ 0		€160,000	
Add cost of goods manufactured	700,000*		800,000*		600,000*	
Goods available for sale	700,000		800,000		760,000	
Less ending inventory	0		160,000†		0	
Cost of goods sold		700,000		640,000		760,000
Gross margin		300,000		360,000		240,000
Less selling and administrative expenses (40,000 units × €1 per unit + €200,000)		240,000		240,000		240,000
Net operating income		€ 60,000		€ 120,000		€ 0

*Cost of goods manufactured:

Year 1: 40,000 units × €17.50 per unit = €700,000.

Year 2: 50,000 units × €16.00 per unit = €800,000.

Year 3: 30,000 units × €20.00 per unit = €600,000.

†Ending inventory, Year 2: 10,000 units × €16 per unit = €160,000.

	Year 1		Year 2		Year 3	
Variable Costing						
Sales (40,000 units)		€1,000,000		€1,000,000		€1,000,000
Less variable expenses:						
Variable cost of goods sold:						
Beginning inventory	€ 0		€ 0		€100,000	
Add variable manufacturing costs at €10 per unit produced	400,000		500,000		300,000	
Goods available for sale	400,000		500,000		400,000	
Less ending inventory	0		100,000*		0	
Variable cost of goods sold	400,000		400,000		400,000	
Variable selling and administrative expenses	40,000	440,000	40,000	440,000	40,000	440,000
Contribution margin		560,000		560,000		560,000
Less fixed expenses:						
Fixed manufacturing overhead	300,000		300,000		300,000	
Fixed selling and administrative expenses	200,000	500,000	200,000	500,000	200,000	500,000
Net operating income		€ 60,000		€ 60,000		€ 60,000

*Ending inventory, Year 2: 10,000 units × €10 per unit = €100,000.

Exhibit 7–7
Reconciliation of Variable Costing and Absorption Costing—Net Operating Income Data from Exhibit 7–6

	Year 1	Year 2	Year 3
Variable costing net operating income	€60,000	€ 60,000	€60,000
Add fixed manufacturing overhead costs deferred in inventory under absorption costing (10,000 units × €6 per unit)	0	60,000	0
Deduct fixed manufacturing overhead costs released from inventory under absorption costing (10,000 units × €6 per unit)	0	0	(60,000)
Absorption costing net operating income	€60,000	€120,000	€ 0

2 rises sharply, because of the deferral of these costs in inventories, even though the same number of units is sold in Year 2 as in the other years.

The reverse effect occurs in Year 3. Since sales exceed production in Year 3, that year is forced to cover all of its own fixed manufacturing overhead costs as well as the fixed manufacturing overhead costs carried forward in inventory from Year 2. A substantial drop in net operating income during Year 3 results from the release of fixed manufacturing overhead costs from inventories despite the fact that the same number of units is sold in that year as in the other years.

The variable costing and absorption costing net operating incomes are reconciled in Exhibit 7–7. This exhibit shows that the differences in net operating income can be traced to the effects of changes in inventories on absorption costing net operating income. Under absorption costing, fixed manufacturing overhead costs are deferred in inventory when inventories increase and are released from inventory when inventories decrease.

Chainsaw Al Dunlap's Legacy at Sunbeam

In Business

Albert J. Dunlap, who relished his nickname "chainsaw Al," left Sunbeam Corp. under a cloud after three years as CEO. Dunlap was hired to turn around Sunbeam with his well-known cost-cutting and disregard for the sensibilities of existing employees. Three years later, Dunlap had been fired by the board of directors amid well-publicized concerns about his aggressive accounting practices. In addition to questionable accounting practices, Dunlap left a legacy of excess inventories. Dunlap's successors complain that eliminating those excess inventories has required the company to keep production levels well under capacity. Since Sunbeam, like almost all other companies, uses absorption costing to prepare its external financial reports, liquidating these excess inventories depresses the company's profits.

Source: Martha Brannigan, "Sunbeam Reports a $60.7 Million Loss Amid a Continued Excess Inventory," *The Wall Street Journal,* Tuesday, June 8, 1999, p. B10.

Managerial Accounting in Action

The Wrap-Up

After checking all of his work, Sean discussed his results with Mary.

Sean: I have some calculations I would like to show you.

Mary: Will this take long? I only have a few minutes before I have to meet with the buyer from Neiman Marcus.

Sean: Well, we can at least get started. These exhibits should help explain why our net operating income didn't increase this year as much as you thought it should have.

Mary: This first exhibit (i.e., Exhibit 7–3) looks like it just summarizes our income statements for the last three years.

Sean: Not exactly. There are actually two sets of income statements on this exhibit. The absorption costing income statements are the ones I originally prepared and we submitted to the bank. Below the absorption costing income statements are another set of income statements.

Mary: Those are the ones labeled variable costing.

Sean: That's right. You can see that the net operating incomes are the same for the two sets of income statements in our first year of operations, but they differ for the other two years.

Mary: I'll say! The variable costing statements indicate that we just broke even in the second year instead of earning a €30,000 profit. And the increase in net operating income between the second and third years is €120,000 instead of just €60,000. I don't know how you came up with two different net operating income figures, but the variable costing net operating income seems to be much closer to the truth. The second year was almost a disaster. We barely sold enough sweaters to cover all of our fixed costs.

Sean: You and I both know that, but the accounting rules view the situation a little differently. If we produce more than we sell, the accounting rules require that we take some of the fixed production cost and assign it to the units that end up in inventories at year-end.

Mary: You mean that instead of appearing on the income statement as an expense, some of the fixed production costs wind up on the balance sheet as inventories?

Sean: Precisely.

Mary: I thought accountants were conservative. Since when was it conservative to call an expense an asset?

Sean: We accountants have been debating whether fixed production costs are an asset or an expense for over 50 years.

Mary: It must have been a *fascinating* debate.

Sean: I have to admit that it ranks right up there with watching grass grow in terms of excitement level.

Mary: I don't know what the arguments are, but I can tell you for sure that we don't make any money by just producing sweaters. If I understand what you have shown me, I can increase my net operating income under absorption costing by simply making more sweaters—we don't have to sell them.

Sean: Correct.

Mary: So all I have to do to enjoy the lifestyle of the rich and famous is to hire every unemployed knitter in Ireland to make sweaters I can't sell.

Sean: We would have a major cash flow problem, but our net operating income would certainly go up.

Mary: Well, if the banks want us to use absorption costing so be it. I don't know why they would want us to report that way, but if that's what they want, that's what they'll get. Is there any reason why we can't use this variable costing method inside the company? The statements are easier to understand, and the net operating income figures make more sense to me. Can't we do both?

Sean: I don't see why not. Making the adjustment from one method to the other is very simple.

Mary: Good. Let's talk about this some more after I get back from the meeting with Neiman Marcus.

Choosing a Costing Method

LEARNING OBJECTIVE 4
Understand the advantages and disadvantages of both variable and absorption costing.

The Impact on the Manager

Like Mary O'Meara, opponents of absorption costing argue that shifting fixed manufacturing overhead cost between periods can be confusing and can lead to misinterpretations and even to faulty decisions. Look again at the data in Exhibit 7–6; a manager might wonder why net operating income went up substantially in Year 2 under absorption costing when sales remained the same as in the prior year. Was it a result of lower selling costs, more efficient operations, or was some other factor involved? The manager is unable to tell, looking simply at the absorption costing income statement. Then in Year 3, net operating income drops sharply, even though the same number of units is sold as in the other two years. Why would income rise in one year and then drop in the next? The figures seem erratic and contradictory and can lead to confusion and a loss of confidence in the integrity of the financial data.

By contrast, the variable costing income statements in Exhibit 7–6 are clear and easy to understand. Sales remain constant over the three-year period covered in the exhibit, so both contribution margin and net operating income also remain constant. The statements are consistent with what the manager would expect to happen under the circumstances, so they tend to generate confidence rather than confusion.

To avoid mistakes when absorption costing is used, readers of financial statements should be alert to changes in inventory levels. Under absorption costing, if inventories increase, fixed manufacturing overhead costs are deferred in inventories and net operating income is elevated. If inventories decrease, fixed manufacturing overhead costs are released from inventories and net operating income is depressed. Thus, fluctuations in net operating income can be due to changes in inventories rather than to changes in sales when absorption costing is used.

Absorption costing used

The Perverse Effects of Absorption Costing at Nissan

In Business

Jed Connelly, the top American executive at Nissan North America, admits: "We had a lot of excess production that we had to force on the market." Nissan liked to run its factories at capacity, regardless of how well the cars were selling, because under its bookkeeping rules (presumably absorption costing), the factories would then generate a profit. As a consequence, Nissan dealers had to slash prices and offer big rebates to move its cars. According to *Fortune* magazine, "Years of discounting and distress sales seriously undercut the value of the Nissan brand. While Toyota stood for quality, customers came to Nissan to get a better deal."

Source: Alex Taylor III, "The Man Who Wants to Change Japan Inc.," *Fortune,* December 20, 1999, pp. 189–198.

CVP Analysis and Absorption Costing

Absorption costing is widely used for both internal and external reports. Many firms use the absorption approach exclusively because of its focus on *full* costing of units of product. A weakness of the method, however, is its inability to dovetail well with CVP analysis.

To illustrate, refer again to Exhibit 7–3. Let us compute the break-even point for Emerald Isle Knitters. To obtain the break-even point, we divide total fixed costs by the contribution margin per unit:

Selling price per unit	€ 20
Variable costs per unit (production and selling)	8
Contribution margin per unit	€ 12
Fixed manufacturing overhead costs	€150,000
Fixed selling and administrative costs	90,000
Total fixed costs	€240,000

$$\frac{\text{Total fixed costs}}{\text{Contribution margin per unit}} = \frac{€240{,}000}{€12 \text{ per unit}} = 20{,}000 \text{ units}$$

The break-even point is 20,000 units. Notice from Exhibit 7–3 that in Year 2 the firm sold exactly 20,000 units, the break-even volume. Under the contribution approach, using variable costing, the firm does break even in Year 2, showing zero net operating income. *Under absorption costing, however, the firm shows a positive net operating income of €30,000 for Year 2.* How can this be? How can absorption costing produce a positive net operating income when the firm sold exactly the break-even volume of units?

The answer lies in the fact that €30,000 in fixed manufacturing overhead costs were deferred in inventory during Year 2 under absorption costing and therefore did not appear as charges against income. By deferring these fixed manufacturing overhead costs in inventory, the income statement shows a profit even though the company sold exactly the break-even volume of units. Absorption costing runs into similar kinds of difficulty in other areas of CVP analysis, which assumes that variable costing is being used.

Decision Making

A basic problem with absorption costing is that fixed manufacturing overhead costs appear to be variable with respect to the number of units sold, but they are not. For example, in Exhibit 7–3, the absorption unit product cost is €13, but the variable portion of this cost is only €7. Since the product costs are stated in terms of a per unit figure, managers may mistakenly believe that if another unit is produced, it will cost the company €13.

The misperception that absorption unit product costs are variable can lead to many managerial problems, including inappropriate pricing decisions and decisions to drop products that are in fact profitable. These problems with absorption costing product costs will be discussed more fully in later chapters.

External Reporting and Income Taxes

Practically speaking, absorption costing is required for external reports in the United States. A company that attempts to use variable costing on its external financial reports runs the risk that its auditors may not accept the financial statements as conforming to generally accepted accounting principles (GAAP).[1] Tax law on this issue is clear-cut. Under the Tax Reform Act of 1986, a form of absorption costing must be used when filling out income tax forms.

Even if a company must use absorption costing for its external reports, a manager can, as Mary O'Meara suggests, use variable costing statements for internal reports. No particular accounting problems are created by using *both* costing methods—the variable costing method for internal reports and the absorption costing method for external reports. As we demonstrated earlier in Exhibits 7–5 and 7–7, the adjustment from variable costing net operating income to absorption costing net operating income is a simple one that can be easily made at year-end.

Top executives are typically evaluated based on the earnings reported to shareholders on the external financial reports. This creates a problem for top executives who might otherwise favor using variable costing for internal reports. They may feel that since they are evaluated based on absorption costing reports, decisions should also be based on absorption costing data.

[1] The situation is actually slightly ambiguous concerning whether absorption costing is strictly required. Michael Schiff, "Variable Costing: A Closer Look," *Management Accounting,* February 1987, pp. 36–39, and Eric W. Noreen and Robert M. Bowen, "Tax Incentives and the Decision to Capitalize or Expense Manufacturing Overhead," *Accounting Horizons,* March 1989, pp. 29–42, argue that official pronouncements do not actually prohibit variable costing. And both articles provide examples of companies that expense significant elements of their fixed manufacturing costs on their external reports. Nevertheless, the reality is that most accountants believe that absorption costing is required for external reporting and a manager who argues otherwise is likely to be unsuccessful.

Absorption Costing Around the World

In Business

Absorption costing is the norm for external financial reports around the world. After the fall of communism, accounting methods were changed in Russia to bring them into closer agreement with accounting methods used in the West. One result was the adoption of absorption costing.

Source: Adolf J. H. Enthoven, "Russia's Accounting Moves West," *Strategic Finance,* July 1999, pp. 32–37.

Advantages of Variable Costing and the Contribution Approach

As stated earlier, even if the absorption approach is used for external reporting purposes, variable costing, together with the contribution margin format income statement, is an appealing alternative for internal reports. The advantages of variable costing can be summarized as follows:

1. The data that are required for CVP analysis can be taken directly from a contribution margin format income statement. These data are not available on a conventional income statement based on absorption costing.
2. Under variable costing, the profit for a period is not affected by changes in inventories. Other things remaining the same (i.e., selling prices, costs, sales mix, etc.), profits move in the same direction as sales when variable costing is in use.
3. Managers often assume that unit product costs are variable costs. This is a problem under absorption costing, since unit product costs are a combination of both fixed and variable costs. Under variable costing, unit product costs do not contain fixed costs.
4. The impact of fixed costs on profits is emphasized under the variable costing and contribution approach. The total amount of fixed costs appears explicitly on the income statement. Under absorption costing, the fixed costs are mingled together with the variable costs and are buried in cost of goods sold and in ending inventories.
5. Variable costing data make it easier to estimate the profitability of products, customers, and other segments of the business. With absorption costing, profitability is obscured by arbitrary allocations of fixed costs. These issues will be discussed in later chapters.
6. Variable costing ties in with cost control methods such as standard costs and flexible budgets, which will be covered in later chapters.
7. Variable costing net operating income is closer to net cash flow than absorption costing net operating income. This is particularly important for companies having cash flow problems.

With all of these advantages, one might wonder why absorption costing continues to be used almost exclusively for external reporting and why it is the predominant choice for internal reports as well. This is partly due to tradition, but absorption costing is also attractive to many accountants and managers because they believe it better matches costs with revenues. Advocates of absorption costing argue that *all* manufacturing costs must be assigned to products in order to properly match the costs of producing units of product with the revenues from the units when they are sold. The fixed costs of depreciation, taxes, insurance, supervisory salaries, and so on, are just as essential to manufacturing products as are the variable costs.

Advocates of variable costing argue that fixed manufacturing costs are not really the costs of any particular unit of product. These costs are incurred to have the *capacity* to make products during a particular period and will be incurred even if nothing is made during the period. Moreover, whether a unit is made or not, the fixed manufacturing costs will be exactly the same. Therefore, variable costing advocates argue that fixed manufacturing costs are not part of the costs of producing a particular unit of product and thus the matching principle dictates that fixed manufacturing costs should be charged to the current period.

At any rate, absorption costing is the generally accepted method for preparing mandatory external financial reports and income tax returns. Probably because of the cost and possible confusion of maintaining two separate costing systems—one for external reporting and one for internal reporting—most companies use absorption costing for both external and internal reports.

Variable Costing and the Theory of Constraints

The Theory of Constraints (TOC), which was introduced in Chapter 1, focuses on managing the constraints in a company as the key to improving profits. For reasons that will be discussed in Chapter 13, this requires careful identification of the variable costs of each product. Consequently, companies involved in TOC use a form of variable costing. One difference is that in the TOC approach, direct labor is generally considered to be a fixed cost. As discussed in earlier chapters, in many companies direct labor is not really a variable cost. Even though direct labor workers may be paid on an hourly basis, many companies have a commitment—sometimes enforced in labor contracts or by law—to guarantee workers a minimum number of paid hours. In TOC companies, there are two additional reasons to consider direct labor to be a fixed cost.

First, direct labor is not usually the constraint. In the simplest cases, the constraint is a machine. In more complex cases, the constraint is a policy (such as a poorly designed compensation scheme for salespersons) that prevents the company from using its resources more effectively. If direct labor is not the constraint, there is no reason to increase it. Hiring more direct labor would increase costs without increasing the output of salable products and services.

Second, TOC emphasizes continuous improvement to maintain competitiveness. Without committed and enthusiastic employees, sustained continuous improvement is virtually impossible. Since layoffs often have devastating effects on employee morale, managers involved in TOC are extremely reluctant to lay off employees.

For these reasons, most managers in TOC companies regard direct labor as a committed fixed cost rather than as a variable cost. Hence, in the modified form of variable costing used in TOC companies, direct labor is not usually included as a part of product costs.

Impact of JIT Inventory Methods

As discussed in this chapter, variable and absorption costing will produce different net operating income figures whenever the number of units produced is different from the number of units sold—in other words, whenever there is a change in the number of units in inventory. We have also learned that the absorption costing net operating income figure can be erratic, sometimes moving in a direction that is opposite from the movement in sales.

When companies use just-in-time (JIT) methods, these problems are reduced. The erratic movement of net operating income under absorption costing and the difference in net operating income between absorption and variable costing occur because of changes in the number of units in inventory. Under JIT, goods are produced to customers' orders and the goal is to eliminate finished goods inventories entirely and reduce work in process inventory to almost nothing. If there is very little inventory, then changes in inventories will be very small and both variable and absorption costing will show basically the same net operating income figure. In that case, absorption costing net operating income will move in the same direction as movements in sales.

Of course, the cost of a unit of product will still be different between variable and absorption costing, as explained earlier in the chapter. But when JIT is used, the differences in net operating income will largely disappear.

Summary

Variable and absorption costing are alternative methods of determining unit product costs. Under variable costing, only those production costs that vary with output are treated as product costs. This includes direct materials, variable overhead, and ordinarily direct labor. Fixed manufacturing overhead is treated as a period cost and charged off against revenue as it is incurred, the same as selling and administrative expenses. By contrast, absorption costing treats fixed manufacturing overhead as a product cost, along with direct materials, direct labor, and variable overhead.

Since absorption costing treats fixed manufacturing overhead as a product cost, a portion of fixed manufacturing overhead is assigned to each unit as it is produced. If units of product are unsold at the end of a period, then the fixed manufacturing overhead cost attached to the units is carried with them into the inventory account and deferred to the next period. When these units are later sold, the fixed manufacturing overhead cost attached to them is released from the inventory account and charged against revenues as a part of cost of goods sold. Thus, under absorption costing, it is possible to defer a portion of the fixed manufacturing overhead cost of one period to the next period through the inventory account.

Unfortunately, this shifting of fixed manufacturing overhead cost between periods can cause net operating income to fluctuate erratically and can result in confusion and unwise decisions on the part of management. To guard against mistakes when they interpret income statement data, managers should be alert to any changes that may have taken place in inventory levels or in unit product costs during the period.

Practically speaking, variable costing can't be used externally for either financial reporting or income tax purposes. However, it may be used internally for planning purposes. The variable costing approach dovetails well with CVP concepts that are often indispensable in profit planning and decision making.

Review Problem: Contrasting Variable and Absorption Costing

Dexter Company produces and sells a single product, a wooden hand loom for weaving small items such as scarves. Selected cost and operating data relating to the product for two years are given below:

Selling price per unit	$ 50	
Manufacturing costs:		
Variable per unit produced:		
Direct materials	11	
Direct labor	6	
Variable overhead	3	
Fixed per year	120,000	
Selling and administrative costs:		
Variable per unit sold	5	
Fixed per year	70,000	
	Year 1	**Year 2**
Units in beginning inventory	0	2,000
Units produced during the year	10,000	6,000
Units sold during the year	8,000	8,000
Units in ending inventory	2,000	0

Required:

1. Assume that the company uses absorption costing.
   a. Compute the unit product cost in each year.
   b. Prepare an income statement for each year.
2. Assume that the company uses variable costing.
   a. Compute the unit product cost in each year.
   b. Prepare an income statement for each year.
3. Reconcile the variable costing and absorption costing net operating incomes.

Solution to Review Problem

1. *a.* Under absorption costing, all manufacturing costs, variable and fixed, are included in unit product costs:

	Year 1	Year 2
Direct materials	$11	$11
Direct labor	6	6
Variable manufacturing overhead	3	3
Fixed manufacturing overhead		
($120,000 ÷ 10,000 units)	12	
($120,000 ÷ 6,000 units)		20
Unit product cost	$32	$40

b. The absorption costing income statements follow:

	Year 1		Year 2	
Sales (8,000 units × $50 per unit)		$400,000		$400,000
Less cost of goods sold:				
Beginning inventory	$ 0		$ 64,000	
Add cost of goods manufactured				
(10,000 units × $32 per unit)	320,000			
(6,000 units × $40 per unit)			240,000	
Goods available for sale	320,000		304,000	
Less ending inventory (2,000 units × $32 per unit; 0 units)	64,000	256,000	0	304,000
Gross margin		144,000		96,000
Less selling and administrative expenses		110,000*		110,000*
Net operating income		$ 34,000		$ (14,000)

*Selling and administrative expenses:

Variable (8,000 units × $5 per unit)	$ 40,000
Fixed per year	70,000
Total	$110,000

2. *a.* Under variable costing, only the variable manufacturing costs are included in unit product costs:

	Year 1	Year 2
Direct materials	$11	$11
Direct labor	6	6
Variable manufacturing overhead	3	3
Unit product cost	$20	$20

b. The variable costing income statements follow. Notice that the variable cost of goods sold is computed in a simpler, more direct manner than in the examples provided earlier. On a variable costing income statement, either approach to computing the cost of goods sold followed in this chapter is acceptable.

	Year 1		Year 2	
Sales (8,000 units × $50 per unit)		$400,000		$400,000
Less variable expenses:				
Variable cost of goods sold (8,000 units × $20 per unit)	$160,000		$160,000	
Variable selling and administrative expenses (8,000 units × $5 per unit)	40,000		40,000	
Contribution margin		200,000		200,000
Less fixed expenses:				
Fixed manufacturing overhead	120,000		120,000	

continued

Fixed selling and administrative expenses	70,000	190,000	70,000	190,000
Net operating income		$ 10,000		$ 10,000

3. The reconciliation of the variable and absorption costing net operating incomes follows:

	Year 1	Year 2
Variable costing net operating income	$10,000	$10,000
Add fixed manufacturing overhead costs deferred in inventory under absorption costing (2,000 units × $12 per unit)	24,000	
Deduct fixed manufacturing overhead costs released from inventory under absorption costing (2,000 units × $12 per unit)		24,000
Absorption costing net operating income	$34,000	$(14,000)

Glossary

Absorption costing A costing method that includes all manufacturing costs—direct materials, direct labor, and both variable and fixed manufacturing overhead—in unit product costs. Absorption costing is also referred to as the *full cost* method. (p. 280)

Direct costing Another term for variable costing. See *Variable costing.* (p. 280)

Fixed manufacturing overhead cost deferred in inventory The portion of the fixed manufacturing overhead cost of a period that goes into inventory under the absorption costing method as a result of production exceeding sales. (p. 282)

Fixed manufacturing overhead cost released from inventory The portion of the fixed manufacturing overhead cost of a *prior* period that becomes an expense of the current period under the absorption costing method as a result of sales exceeding production. (p. 288)

Full cost See *Absorption costing.* (p. 280)

Marginal costing Another term for variable costing. See *Variable costing.* (p. 280)

Variable costing A costing method that includes only variable manufacturing costs—direct materials, direct labor, and variable manufacturing overhead—in unit product costs. Also see *Marginal costing* or *Direct costing.* (p. 280)

Questions

7–1 What is the basic difference between absorption costing and variable costing?

7–2 Are selling and administrative expenses treated as product costs or as period costs under variable costing?

7–3 Explain how fixed manufacturing overhead costs are shifted from one period to another under absorption costing.

7–4 What arguments can be advanced in favor of treating fixed manufacturing overhead costs as product costs?

7–5 What arguments can be advanced in favor of treating fixed manufacturing overhead costs as period costs?

7–6 If production and sales are equal, which method would you expect to show the higher net operating income, variable costing or absorption costing? Why?

7–7 If production exceeds sales, which method would you expect to show the higher net operating income, variable costing or absorption costing? Why?

7–8 If fixed manufacturing overhead costs are released from inventory under absorption costing, what does this tell you about the level of production in relation to the level of sales?

7–9 Parker Company had $5,000,000 in sales and reported a $300,000 loss in its annual report to stockholders. According to a CVP analysis prepared for management's use, $5,000,000 in sales is the break-even point for the company. Did the company's inventory level increase, decrease, or remain unchanged? Explain.

7–10 Under absorption costing, how is it possible to increase net operating income without increasing sales?

7–11 How is the use of variable costing limited?

7–12 How does the use of JIT inventory methods reduce or eliminate the difference in reported net operating income between absorption and variable costing?

Exercises

EXERCISE 7–1 Variable and Absorption Costing Unit Product Costs and Income Statements [LO1, LO2]

Maxwell Company manufactures and sells a single product. The following costs were incurred during the company's first year of operations:

Variable costs per unit:	
Production:	
Direct materials	$ 18
Direct labor	7
Variable manufacturing overhead	2
Variable selling and administrative	5
Fixed costs per year:	
Fixed manufacturing overhead	$160,000
Fixed selling and administrative expenses	110,000

During the year, the company produced 20,000 units and sold 16,000 units. The selling price of the company's product is $50 per unit.

Required:

1. Assume that the company uses the absorption costing method:
   a. Compute the unit product cost.
   b. Prepare an income statement for the year.
2. Assume that the company uses the variable costing method:
   a. Compute the unit product cost.
   b. Prepare an income statement for the year.

EXERCISE 7–2 Variable Costing Income Statements; Reconciliation [LO2, LO3]

Morey Company was organized just one year ago. The results of the company's first year of operations are shown below (absorption costing basis):

MOREY COMPANY
Income Statement

Sales (40,000 units at $33.75 per unit)		$1,350,000
Less cost of goods sold:		
Beginning inventory	$ 0	
Add cost of goods manufactured (50,000 units at $21 per unit)	1,050,000	
Goods available for sale	1,050,000	
Less ending inventory (10,000 units at $21 per unit)	210,000	840,000
Gross margin		510,000
Less selling and administrative expenses		420,000
Net operating income		$ 90,000

The company's selling and administrative expenses consist of $300,000 per year in fixed expenses and $3 per unit sold in variable expenses. The company's $21 unit product cost given above is computed as follows:

Direct materials	$10
Direct labor	4
Variable manufacturing overhead	2
Fixed manufacturing overhead ($250,000 ÷ 50,000 units)	5
Unit product cost	$21

Required:

1. Redo the company's income statement in the contribution format using variable costing.
2. Reconcile any difference between the net operating income figure on your variable costing income statement and the net operating income figure on the absorption costing income statement above.

EXERCISE 7–3 Variable and Absorption Costing Unit Product Costs [LO1]

Shastri Bicycle of Bombay, India, produces an inexpensive, yet rugged, bicycle for use on the city's crowded streets that it sells for 500 rupees. (Indian currency is denominated in rupees, denoted by R.) Selected data for the company's operations last year follow:

Units in beginning inventory	0
Units produced	10,000
Units sold	8,000
Units in ending inventory	2,000
Variable costs per unit:	
Direct materials	R120
Direct labor	140
Variable manufacturing overhead	50
Variable selling and administrative	20
Fixed costs:	
Fixed manufacturing overhead	R600,000
Fixed selling and administrative	400,000

Required:

1. Assume that the company uses absorption costing. Compute the unit product cost for one bicycle.
2. Assume that the company uses variable costing. Compute the unit product cost for one bicycle.

EXERCISE 7–4 Variable Costing Income Statement; Explanation of Difference in Net Operating Income [LO2]

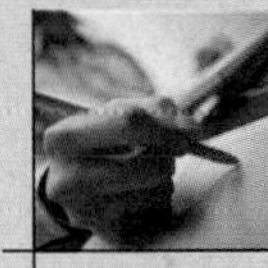

Refer to the data in Exercise 7–3 for Shastri Bicycle. An income statement prepared under the absorption costing method by the company's accountant appears below:

Sales (8,000 units × R500 per unit)		R4,000,000
Costs of goods sold:		
Beginning inventory	R 0	
Add cost of goods manufactured (10,000 units × R _?_ per unit)	3,700,000	
Goods available for sale	3,700,000	
Less ending inventory (2,000 units × R _?_ per unit)	740,000	2,960,000
Gross margin		1,040,000
Less selling and administrative expenses:		
Variable selling and administrative	160,000	
Fixed selling and administrative	400,000	560,000
Net operating income		R480,000

Required:

1. Determine how much of the ending inventory of R740,000 above consists of fixed manufacturing overhead cost deferred in inventory to the next period.
2. Prepare an income statement for the year using the variable costing method. Explain the difference in net operating income between the two costing methods.

EXERCISE 7–5 Variable Costing Unit Product Cost and Income Statement; Break-Even [LO1, LO2]

CompuDesk, Inc., makes an oak desk specially designed for personal computers. The desk sells for $200. Data for last year's operations follow:

Units in beginning inventory	0
Units produced	10,000
Units sold	9,000
Units in ending inventory	1,000
Variable costs per unit:	
Direct materials	$ 60
Direct labor	30
Variable manufacturing overhead	10
Variable selling and administrative	20
Total variable cost per unit	$ 120
Fixed costs:	
Fixed manufacturing overhead	$300,000
Fixed selling and administrative	450,000
Total fixed costs	$750,000

Required:

1. Assume that the company uses variable costing. Compute the unit product cost for one computer desk.
2. Assume that the company uses variable costing. Prepare an income statement for the year using the contribution format.
3. What is the company's break-even point in terms of units sold?

EXERCISE 7–6 Absorption Costing Unit Product Cost and Income Statement [LO1, LO2]
Refer to the data in Exercise 7–5 for CompuDesk. Assume in this exercise that the company uses absorption costing.

Required:

1. Compute the unit product cost for one computer desk.
2. Prepare an income statement for the year in good form.

EXERCISE 7–7 Inferring Method; Unit Product Cost [LO1, LO4]
Amcor, Inc., produces and sells a single product. The following costs relate to its production and sale:

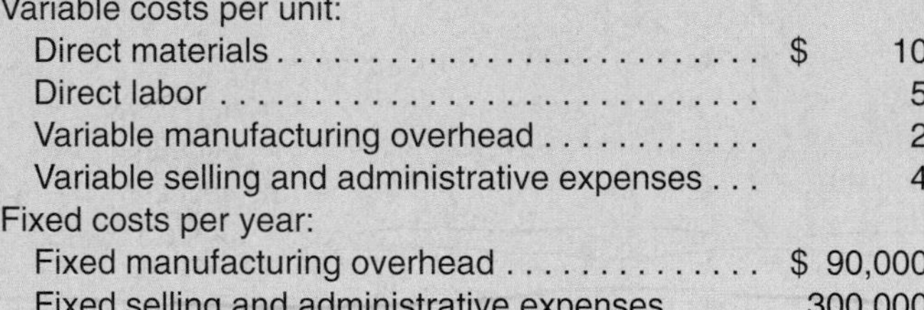

Variable costs per unit:	
Direct materials	$ 10
Direct labor	5
Variable manufacturing overhead	2
Variable selling and administrative expenses	4
Fixed costs per year:	
Fixed manufacturing overhead	$ 90,000
Fixed selling and administrative expenses	300,000

During the last year, 30,000 units were produced and 25,000 units were sold. The Finished Goods inventory account at the end of the year shows a balance of $85,000 for the 5,000 unsold units.

Required:

1. Is the company using absorption costing or variable costing to cost units in the Finished Goods inventory account? Show computations to support your answer.
2. Assume that the company wishes to prepare financial statements for the year to issue to its stockholders.
   a. Is the $85,000 figure for Finished Goods inventory the correct figure to use on these statements for external reporting purposes? Explain.
   b. At what dollar amount *should* the 5,000 units be carried in inventory for external reporting purposes?

Problems

PROBLEM 7–8 Variable Costing Income Statement; Reconciliation [LO2, LO3]
During Denton Company's first two years of operations, the company reported net operating income as follows (absorption costing basis):

	Year 1	Year 2
Sales (at $50 per unit)	$1,000,000	$1,500,000
Less cost of goods sold:		
Beginning inventory	0	170,000
Add cost of goods manufactured (at $34 per unit)	850,000	850,000
Goods available for sale	850,000	1,020,000
Less ending inventory (at $34 per unit)	170,000	0
Cost of goods sold	680,000	1,020,000
Gross margin	320,000	480,000
Less selling and administrative expenses*	310,000	340,000
Net operating income	$ 10,000	$ 140,000

*$3 per unit variable; $250,000 fixed each year.

The company's $34 unit product cost is computed as follows:

Direct materials	$ 8
Direct labor	10
Variable manufacturing overhead	2
Fixed manufacturing overhead ($350,000 ÷ 25,000 units)	14
Unit product cost	$34

Production and cost data for the two years are given below:

	Year 1	Year 2
Units produced	25,000	25,000
Units sold	20,000	30,000

Required:

1. Prepare an income statement for each year in the contribution format using variable costing.
2. Reconcile the absorption costing and variable costing net operating income figures for each year.

PROBLEM 7–9 Variable and Absorption Costing Unit Product Costs and Income Statements; Explanation of Difference in Net Operating Income [LO1, LO2, LO3]

Wiengot Antennas, Inc., produces and sells a unique type of TV antenna. The company has just opened a new plant to manufacture the antenna, and the following cost and revenue data have been provided for the first month of the plant's operation in the form of a worksheet.

Microsoft Excel - Problem 7-9 screen capture.xls

	A	B
1	Beginning inventory	0
2	Units produced	40,000
3	Units sold	35,000
4	Selling price per unit	$ 60
5		
6	Selling and administrative expenses:	
7	Variable per unit	$ 2
8	Fixed (total)	560,000
9	Manufacturing costs:	
10	Direct materials cost per unit	15
11	Direct labor cost per unit	7
12	Variable manufacturing overhead cost per unit	2
13	Fixed manufacturing overhead cost (total)	640,000

Since the new antenna is unique in design, management is anxious to see how profitable it will be and has asked that an income statement be prepared for the month.

Required:

1. Assume that the company uses absorption costing.
   a. Determine the unit product cost.
   b. Prepare an income statement for the month.
2. Assume that the company uses the contribution approach with variable costing.
   a. Determine the unit product cost.
   b. Prepare an income statement for the month.
3. Explain the reason for any difference in the ending inventory under the two costing methods and the impact of this difference on reported net operating income.

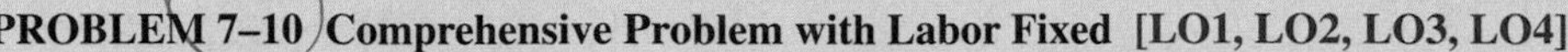

PROBLEM 7–10 Comprehensive Problem with Labor Fixed [LO1, LO2, LO3, LO4]
Advance Products, Inc., has just organized a new division to manufacture and sell specially designed tables using select hardwoods for personal computers. The company's new plant is highly automated and thus requires high monthly fixed costs, as shown in the schedule below:

Manufacturing costs:	
Variable costs per unit:	
Direct materials	$ 86
Variable manufacturing overhead	4
Fixed manufacturing overhead costs (total)	240,000
Selling and administrative costs:	
Variable	15% of sales
Fixed (total)	$160,000

Advance Products regards all of its workers as full-time employees and the company has a long-standing no-layoff policy. Furthermore, production is highly automated. Accordingly, the company has included in its fixed manufacturing overhead all of its labor costs.

During the first month of operations, the following activity was recorded:

Units produced	4,000
Units sold	3,200
Selling price per unit	$ 250

Required:

1. Compute the unit product cost under:
   a. Absorption costing.
   b. Variable costing.
2. Prepare an income statement for the month using absorption costing.
3. Prepare an income statement for the month using variable costing.
4. Assume that in order to continue operations, the company must obtain additional financing. As a member of top management, which of the statements that you have prepared in (2) and (3) above would you prefer to take with you as you negotiate with the bank? Why?
5. Reconcile the absorption costing and variable costing net operating income figures in (2) and (3) above for the month.

PROBLEM 7–11 Preparation and Reconciliation of Variable Costing Statements [LO1, LO2, LO3, LO4]
Linden Company manufactures and sells a single product. Cost data for the product follow:

Variable costs per unit:	
Direct materials	$ 6
Direct labor	12
Variable factory overhead	4
Variable selling and administrative	3
Total variable costs per unit	$25
Fixed costs per month:	
Fixed manufacturing overhead	$240,000
Fixed selling and administrative	180,000
Total fixed cost per month	$420,000

The product sells for $40 per unit. Production and sales data for May and June, the first two months of operations, are as follows:

	Units Produced	Units Sold
May	30,000	26,000
June	30,000	34,000

Income statements prepared by the Accounting Department, using absorption costing, are presented below:

	May	June
Sales	$1,040,000	$1,360,000
Less cost of goods sold:		
Beginning inventory	0	120,000
Add cost of goods manufactured	900,000	900,000
Goods available for sale	900,000	1,020,000
Less ending inventory	120,000	0
Cost of goods sold	780,000	1,020,000
Gross margin	260,000	340,000
Less selling and administrative expenses	258,000	282,000
Net operating income	$ 2,000	$ 58,000

Required:

1. Determine the unit product cost under:
   a. Absorption costing.
   b. Variable costing.
2. Prepare income statements for May and June using the contribution approach with variable costing.
3. Reconcile the variable costing and absorption costing net operating income figures.
4. The company's Accounting Department has determined the break-even point to be 28,000 units per month, computed as follows:

$$\frac{\text{Fixed cost per month}}{\text{Unit contribution margin}} = \frac{\$420{,}000}{\$15 \text{ per unit}} = 28{,}000 \text{ units}$$

   Upon receiving this figure, the president commented, "There's something peculiar here. The controller says that the break-even point is 28,000 units per month. Yet we sold only 26,000 units in May, and the income statement we received showed a $2,000 profit. Which figure do we believe?" Prepare a brief explanation of what happened on the May income statement.

PROBLEM 7–12 Absorption and Variable Costing; Production Constant, Sales Fluctuate [LO1, LO2, LO3, LO4]

Sandi Scott obtained a patent on a small electronic device and organized Scott Products, Inc., in order to produce and sell the device. During the first month of operations, the device was very well received on the market, so Ms. Scott looked forward to a healthy profit from sales. For this reason, she was surprised to see a loss for the month on her income statement. This statement was prepared by her accounting service, which takes great pride in providing its clients with timely financial data. The statement follows:

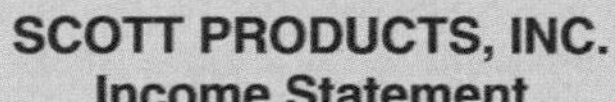

SCOTT PRODUCTS, INC.
Income Statement

Sales (40,000 units)		$200,000
Less variable expenses:		
Variable cost of goods sold*	$80,000	
Variable selling and administrative expenses	30,000	110,000
Contribution margin		90,000
Less fixed expenses:		
Fixed manufacturing overhead	75,000	
Fixed selling and administrative expenses	20,000	95,000
Net operating loss		$ (5,000)

*Consists of direct materials, direct labor, and variable manufacturing overhead.

Ms. Scott is discouraged over the loss shown for the month, particularly since she had planned to use the statement to encourage investors to purchase stock in the new company. A friend, who is a CPA, insists that the company should be using absorption costing rather than variable costing. He argues that if absorption costing had been used, the company would probably have reported a nice profit for the month.

Selected cost data relating to the product and to the first month of operations follow:

Units produced	50,000
Units sold	40,000
Variable costs per unit:	
Direct materials	$1.00
Direct labor	0.80
Variable manufacturing overhead	0.20
Variable selling and administrative expenses	0.75

Required:

1. Complete the following:
   a. Compute the unit product cost under absorption costing.
   b. Redo the company's income statement for the month using absorption costing.
   c. Reconcile the variable and absorption costing net operating income figures.
2. Was the CPA correct in suggesting that the company really earned a "profit" for the month? Explain.
3. During the second month of operations, the company again produced 50,000 units but sold 60,000 units. (Assume no change in total fixed costs.)
   a. Prepare an income statement for the month using variable costing.
   b. Prepare an income statement for the month using absorption costing.
   c. Reconcile the variable costing and absorption costing net operating income figures.

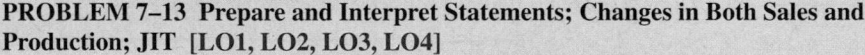

PROBLEM 7–13 Prepare and Interpret Statements; Changes in Both Sales and Production; JIT [LO1, LO2, LO3, LO4]

Memotec, Inc., manufactures and sells a unique electronic part. Operating results for the first three years of activity were as follows (absorption costing basis):

	Year 1	Year 2	Year 3
Sales	$1,000,000	$800,000	$1,000,000
Cost of goods sold:			
Beginning inventory	0	0	280,000
Add cost of goods manufactured	800,000	840,000	760,000
Goods available for sale	800,000	840,000	1,040,000
Less ending inventory	0	280,000	190,000
Cost of goods sold	800,000	560,000	850,000
Gross margin	200,000	240,000	150,000
Less selling and administrative expenses	170,000	150,000	170,000
Net operating income (loss)	$ 30,000	$ 90,000	$ (20,000)

Sales dropped by 20% during Year 2 due to the entry of several foreign competitors into the market. Memotec had expected sales to remain constant at 50,000 units for the year; production was set at 60,000 units in order to build a buffer of protection against unexpected spurts in demand. By the start of Year 3, management could see that spurts in demand were unlikely and that the inventory was excessive. To work off the excessive inventories, Memotec cut back production during Year 3, as shown below:

	Year 1	Year 2	Year 3
Production in units	50,000	60,000	40,000
Sales in units	50,000	40,000	50,000

Additional information about the company follows:

a. The company's plant is highly automated. Variable manufacturing costs (direct materials, direct labor, and variable manufacturing overhead) total only $4 per unit, and fixed manufacturing costs total $600,000 per year.

b. Fixed manufacturing costs are applied to units of product on the basis of each year's production. (That is, a new fixed overhead rate is computed each year, as in Exhibit 7–6).
c. Variable selling and administrative expenses are $2 per unit sold. Fixed selling and administrative expenses total $70,000 per year.
d. The company uses a FIFO inventory flow assumption.

Memotec's management can't understand why profits tripled during Year 2 when sales dropped by 20%, and why a loss was incurred during Year 3 when sales recovered to previous levels.

Required:

1. Prepare a new income statement for each year using the contribution approach with variable costing.
2. Refer to the absorption costing income statements above.
   a. Compute the unit product cost in each year under absorption costing. (Show how much of this cost is variable and how much is fixed.)
   b. Reconcile the variable costing and absorption costing net operating income figures for each year.
3. Refer again to the absorption costing income statements. Explain why net operating income was higher in Year 2 than it was in Year 1 under the absorption approach, in light of the fact that fewer units were sold in Year 2 than in Year 1.
4. Refer again to the absorption costing income statements. Explain why the company suffered a loss in Year 3 but reported a profit in Year 1, although the same number of units was sold in each year.
5. *a.* Explain how operations would have differed in Year 2 and Year 3 if the company had been using JIT inventory methods.
   b. If JIT had been in use during Year 2 and Year 3, what would the company's net operating income (or loss) have been in each year under absorption costing? Explain the reason for any differences between these income figures and the figures reported by the company in the statements above.

PROBLEM 7–14 Incentives Created by Absorption Costing; Ethics and the Manager [LO2, LO4]

Aristotle Constantinos, the manager of DuraProducts' Australian Division, is trying to decide what production schedule to set for the last quarter of the year. The Australian Division had planned to sell 100,000 units during the year, but current projections indicate sales will be only 78,000 units in total. By September 30 the following activity had been reported:

	Units
Inventory, January 1	0
Production	72,000
Sales	60,000
Inventory, September 30	12,000

Demand has been soft, and the sales forecast for the last quarter is only 18,000 units.

The division can rent warehouse space to store up to 30,000 units. The division should maintain a minimum inventory level of at least 1,500 units. Mr. Constantinos is aware that production must be at least 6,000 units per quarter in order to retain a nucleus of key employees. Maximum production capacity is 45,000 units per quarter.

Due to the nature of the division's operations, fixed manufacturing overhead is a major element of product cost.

Required:

1. Assume that the division is using variable costing. How many units should be scheduled for production during the last quarter of the year? (The basic formula for computing the required production for a period in a company is: Expected sales + Desired ending inventory − Beginning inventory = Required production.) Show computations and explain your answer. Will the number of units scheduled for production affect the division's reported profit for the year? Explain.
2. Assume that the division is using absorption costing and that the divisional manager is given an annual bonus based on the division's net operating income. If Mr. Constantinos wants to maximize his division's net operating income for the year, how many units should be scheduled for production during the last quarter? [See the formula in (1) above.] Show computations and explain your answer.

3. Identify the ethical issues involved in the decision Mr. Constantinos must make about the level of production for the last quarter of the year.

PROBLEM 7–15 Variable Costing Income Statements; Sales Constant; Production Varies; JIT Impact [LO1, LO2, LO3, LO4]

"Can someone explain to me what's wrong with these statements?" asked Cheri Reynolds, president of Milex Corporation. "They just don't make sense. We sold the same number of units this year as we did last year, yet our profits have tripled! Who messed up the calculations?"

The statements to which Ms. Reynolds was referring are shown below (absorption costing basis):

	Year 1	Year 2
Sales (40,000 units each year)	$1,250,000	$1,250,000
Less cost of goods sold	840,000	720,000
Gross margin	410,000	530,000
Less selling and administrative expenses	350,000	350,000
Net operating income	$ 60,000	$ 180,000

In the first year, the company produced and sold 40,000 units; in the second year, the company again sold 40,000 units, but it increased production to 50,000 units, as shown below:

	Year 1	Year 2
Production in units	40,000	50,000
Sales in units	40,000	40,000
Variable production cost per unit	$ 6	$ 6
Fixed manufacturing overhead costs (total)	$600,000	$600,000

Milex Corporation produces a single product. Fixed manufacturing overhead costs are applied to the product on the basis of each year's production. (Thus, a new fixed manufacturing overhead rate is computed each year, as in Exhibit 7–6.) Variable selling and administrative expenses are $2 per unit sold.

Required:

1. Compute the unit product cost for each year under:
   a. Absorption costing.
   b. Variable costing.
2. Prepare an income statement for each year, using the contribution approach with variable costing.
3. Reconcile the variable costing and absorption costing net operating income figures for each year.
4. Explain to the president why the net operating income for Year 2 was higher than for Year 1 under absorption costing, although the same number of units was sold in each year.
5. *a.* Explain how operations would have differed in Year 2 if the company had been using JIT inventory methods and inventories had been eliminated.
   b. If JIT had been in use during Year 2 and ending inventories were zero, what would the company's net operating income have been under absorption costing? Explain the reason for any difference between this income figure and the figure reported by the company in the statements above.

Cases

CASE 7–16 Ethics and the Manager; Absorption Costing Income Statements [LO2, LO4]

Michael Lee was hired as chief executive officer (CEO) in late November by the board of directors of Hunter Electronics, a company that produces a state-of-the-art CD-ROM drive for personal computers. The previous CEO had been fired by the board due to a series of questionable business practices including prematurely recording revenues on products that had not yet been shipped to customers.

Michael felt that his first priority on the job was to restore employee morale—which had suffered during the previous CEO's reign. He was particularly anxious to build a sense of trust between himself and the company's employees. His second priority was to prepare the budget for the coming year, which the board of directors wanted to review in their December 15 meeting.

After hammering out the details in meetings with key managers, Michael was able to put together a budget that he felt the company could realistically meet during the coming year. That budget appears below:

Basic Budget Data

Units in beginning inventory	0
Units produced	200,000
Units sold	200,000
Units in ending inventory	0
Variable costs per unit:	
Direct materials	$ 50
Direct labor	40
Variable manufacturing overhead	20
Variable selling and administrative	10
Total variable cost per unit	$120
Fixed costs:	
Fixed manufacturing overhead	$ 8,400,000
Fixed selling and administrative	3,600,000
Total fixed costs	$12,000,000

HUNTER ELECTRONICS
Budgeted Income Statement
(absorption method)

Sales (200,000 units)		$40,000,000
Cost of goods sold:		
Beginning inventory	$ 0	
Add cost of goods manufactured (200,000 × $152 per unit)	30,400,000	
Goods available for sale	30,400,000	
Less ending inventory	0	30,400,000
Gross margin		9,600,000
Less selling and administrative expenses:		
Variable selling and administrative	2,000,000	
Fixed selling and administrative	3,600,000	5,600,000
Net operating income		$ 4,000,000

While the board of directors did not oppose the budget, they made it clear that the budget was not as ambitious as they had hoped. The most influential member of the board stated that "managers should have to really stretch to meet profit goals." After some discussion, the board decided to set a profit goal of $4,800,000 for the coming year. To provide strong incentives and a win-win situation, the board agreed to pay out bonuses to top managers of $200,000 if this profit goal were met. Michael's share of the bonus pool would be $50,000. The bonus would be all-or-nothing. If actual net operating income turned out to be $4,800,000 or more, the bonus would be paid. Otherwise, no bonus would be allowed.

Required:

1. Assuming that the company does not build up its inventory (i.e., production equals sales) and its selling price and cost structure remain the same, how many units of the CD-ROM drive would have to be sold to meet the target net operating income of $4,800,000?
2. Verify your answer to (1) above by constructing a revised budget and budgeted income statement that yields a net operating income of $4,800,000. Use the absorption costing method.
3. Unfortunately, by October of the next year it had become clear that the company would not be able to make the $4,800,000 target profit. In fact, it looked like the company would wind up the year as originally planned, with sales of 200,000 units, no ending inventories, and a profit of $4,000,000.

   Several managers who were reluctant to lose their year-end bonuses approached Michael and suggested that the company could still show a profit of $4,800,000. The managers argued that at the present rate of sales, there was enough capacity to produce tens of thousands of additional CD-ROM drives for the warehouse. Overtime costs might have to be incurred, but all of this additional cost would be assigned to the CD-ROM drives in ending inventory.

If sales are 200,000 units for the year and the selling price and cost structure remain the same, how many units would have to be produced to show a profit of at least $4,800,000 under absorption costing? (Round your answer up to the nearest whole unit.)

4. Verify your answer to (3) above by constructing an income statement. Use the absorption costing method.
5. Do you think Michael Lee should approve the plan to build ending inventories in order to attain the target profit?
6. What advice would you give to the board of directors concerning how they determine bonuses in the future?

CASE 7–17 Absorption and Variable Costing; Uneven Production; Break-Even Analysis; JIT Impact [LO2, LO3, LO4]

"I thought that new, automated plant was supposed to make us more efficient and therefore more profitable," exclaimed Marla Warner, president of Visic Company. "Just look at these monthly income statements for the second quarter. Sales have risen steadily month by month, but income is going in the opposite direction, and we even show a loss for June! Can someone explain what's happening?"

The statements to which Ms. Warner was referring are given below:

VISIC COMPANY
Monthly Income Statements
For the Second Quarter

	April	May	June
Sales (at $25)	$1,500,000	$1,625,000	$1,750,000
Less cost of goods sold:			
Beginning inventory	70,000	280,000	350,000
Cost applied to production:			
Variable manufacturing costs (at $6 per unit)	450,000	420,000	300,000
Fixed manufacturing overhead	600,000	560,000	400,000
Cost of goods manufactured	1,050,000	980,000	700,000
Goods available for sale	1,120,000	1,260,000	1,050,000
Less ending inventory	280,000	350,000	70,000
Cost of goods sold	840,000	910,000	980,000
Underapplied (or overapplied) overhead cost	(40,000)	—	160,000
Adjusted cost of goods sold	800,000	910,000	1,140,000
Gross margin	700,000	715,000	610,000
Less selling and administrative expenses	620,000	665,000	710,000
Net operating income (loss)	$ 80,000	$ 50,000	$ (100,000)

"Fixed costs associated with the new plant are very high," replied Brian Hauber, the controller. "We're just following good absorption costing, as we have for years."

"Maybe the costing method *is* the problem," responded Teri Carlyle, the financial vice president. "A management development seminar I just attended suggested that the contribution approach, with variable costing, is the best way to report profit data to management."

Production and sales data for the second quarter follow:

	April	May	June
Production in units	75,000	70,000	50,000
Sales in units	60,000	65,000	70,000

Additional information about the company's operations is given below:

a. Five thousand units were in inventory on April 1.
b. Fixed manufacturing overhead costs total $1,680,000 per quarter and are incurred evenly throughout the quarter. This fixed manufacturing overhead cost is applied to units of product on the basis of a budgeted production volume of 70,000 units per month.

c. Variable selling and administrative expenses are $9 per unit sold. The remainder of the selling and administrative expenses on the statements above are fixed.
d. The company uses a FIFO inventory flow assumption. Work in process inventories are insignificant and can be ignored.

"We had to build inventory early in the year in anticipation of a strike in June," said Mr. Hauber. "Since the union settled without a strike, we then had to cut back production in June in order to work off the excess inventories. The income statements you have are completely accurate."

Required:

1. Prepare an income statement for each month using the contribution approach with variable costing.
2. Compute the monthly break-even point in units under variable costing.
3. Explain to Ms. Warner why profits have moved erratically over the three-month period shown in the absorption costing income statements above and why profits have not been more closely related to changes in sales volume.
4. Reconcile the variable costing and absorption costing net operating income (loss) figures for each month. Show all computations, and show how you have derived each figure used in your reconciliation.
5. Assume that the company had decided to introduce JIT inventory methods at the beginning of June. (Sales and production during April and May were as shown above.)
   a. How many units would have been produced during June under JIT?
   b. Starting with the next quarter (July, August, and September), would you expect any difference between the net operating income reported under absorption costing and under variable costing? Explain why there would or would not be any difference.
   c. Refer to your computations in (2) above. How would JIT help break-even analysis "make sense" under absorption costing?

CASE 7–18 The Case of the Perplexed President; JIT Impact [LO2, LO3, LO4]

John Ovard, president of Mylar, Inc., was looking forward to receiving the company's second quarter income statement. He knew that the sales budget of 20,000 units sold had been met during the second quarter and that this represented a 25% increase in sales over the first quarter. He was especially happy about the increase in sales, since Mylar was about to approach its bank for additional loan money for expansion purposes. He anticipated that the strong second-quarter results would be a real plus in persuading the bank to extend the additional credit.

For this reason, Mr. Ovard was shocked when he received the second-quarter income statement below, which showed a substantial drop in net operating income from the first quarter.

MYLAR, INC.
Income Statements
For the First Two Quarters

	First Quarter		Second Quarter	
Sales		$1,600,000		$2,000,000
Less cost of goods sold:				
Beginning inventory	$ 210,000		$ 490,000	
Add cost of goods manufactured	1,400,000		980,000	
Goods available for sale	1,610,000		1,470,000	
Less ending inventory	490,000		70,000	
Cost of goods sold	1,120,000		1,400,000	
Add underapplied overhead	0	1,120,000	240,000	1,640,000
Gross margin		480,000		360,000
Less selling and administrative expenses		310,000		330,000
Net operating income		$ 170,000		$ 30,000

Mr. Ovard was certain there had to be an error somewhere and immediately called the controller into his office to find the problem. The controller stated, "That net operating income figure is correct, John. I agree that sales went up during the second quarter, but the problem is in production. You see, we budgeted to produce 20,000 units each quarter, but a strike in one of our supplier's plants forced us to cut production back to only 14,000 units in the second quarter. That's what caused the drop in net operating income."

Mr. Ovard was angered by the controller's explanation. "I call you in here to find out why income dropped when sales went up, and you talk about production! So what if production was off? What does that have to do with the sales that we made? If sales go up, then income ought to go up. If your statements can't show a simple thing like that, then we're due for some changes in your area!"

Budgeted production and sales for the year, along with actual production and sales for the first two quarters, are given below:

	Quarter			
	First	Second	Third	Fourth
Budgeted sales (units)	16,000	20,000	20,000	24,000
Actual sales (units)	16,000	20,000	—	—
Budgeted production (units)	20,000	20,000	20,000	20,000
Actual production (units)	20,000	14,000	—	—

The company's plant is heavily automated, so fixed manufacturing overhead costs total $800,000 per quarter. Variable manufacturing costs are $30 per unit. The fixed manufacturing overhead cost is applied to units of product at the rate of $40 per unit (based on the budgeted production shown above). Any under- or overapplied overhead is taken directly to cost of goods sold for the quarter.

The company had 3,000 units in inventory to start the first quarter and uses the FIFO inventory flow assumption. Variable selling and administrative expenses are $5 per unit sold.

Required:

1. What characteristic of absorption costing caused the drop in net operating income for the second quarter and what could the controller have said to explain the problem more fully?
2. Prepare income statements for each quarter using the contribution approach, with variable costing.
3. Reconcile the absorption costing and the variable costing net operating income figures for each quarter.
4. Identify and discuss the advantages and disadvantages of using the variable costing method for internal reporting purposes.
5. Assume that the company had introduced JIT inventory methods at the beginning of the second quarter. (Sales and production during the first quarter were as shown above.)
   a. How many units would have been produced during the second quarter under JIT?
   b. Starting with the third quarter, would you expect any difference between the net operating income reported under absorption costing and under variable costing? Explain why there would or would not be any difference.

Group and Internet Exercises

GROUP EXERCISE 7–19 Who Needs Customers? I Can Make Money without Them
Tough times always seem to bring out the worst in people. When companies are desperate to stay in business or to report more favorable earnings to Wall Street, some managers just can't seem to resist the temptation to manipulate reported profits. Unfortunately, inventory is sometimes a tempting source of such manipulations. It is important to know how such earnings distortions can occur, whether they result from intentional actions or innocent miscalculations.

Required:

1. What product cost concept is the basis for inventory valuation and cost of goods sold determination for external financial reporting purposes?
2. Explain the concept of "phantom" or "illusory" profits. Excluding inflation and changes in the selling prices of products, how could a firm with the same sales as last year report significantly higher profits without cutting any costs? Could a firm with sales below the break-even point report profits? Explain.
3. Are all such "fictitious" profits an attempt to distort profits and mislead investors and creditors? If not, under what economic conditions would this most likely occur?
4. Could the reverse situation occur? That is, could lower accounting profits be reported even though the firm is not economically worse off? Under what economic conditions would this most likely occur?

GROUP EXERCISE 7–20 Changing Cost Structures and Product Costing
As firms automate their operations with advanced manufacturing technology and information technology, cost structures are becoming more fixed with higher proportions of overhead.

Required:

1. What implications does this trend hold for arguments favoring absorption costing? What implications does this trend hold for arguments favoring variable costing?
2. If absorption costing continues to be used for external financial reporting, what impact will inventory buildups or inventory liquidations have on future reported earnings compared with the effects they have had on past reported earnings?
3. Most firms evaluate and compensate top management, in part, on the basis of net operating income. Would top management have a preference for basing its evaluations on variable costing or full absorption costing? Explain.

INTERNET EXERCISE 7–21
As you know, the World Wide Web is a medium that is constantly evolving. Sites come and go, and change without notice. To enable periodic update of site addresses, this problem has been posted to the textbook website (www.mhhe.com/garrison10e). After accessing the site, enter the Student Center and select this chapter. Select and complete the Internet Exercise.

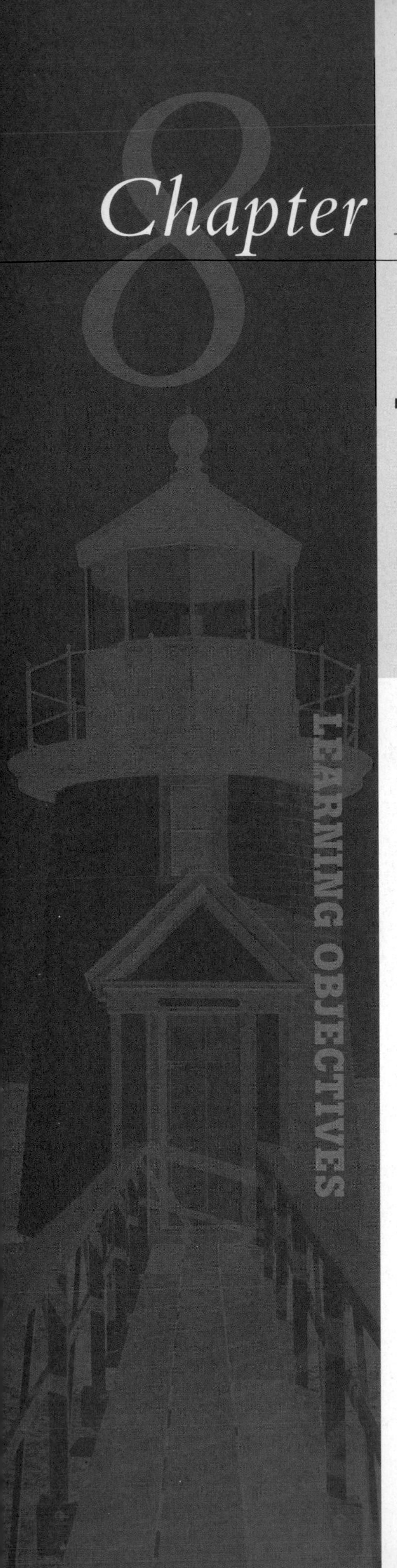

Chapter Eight

Activity-Based Costing: A Tool to Aid Decision Making

After studying Chapter 8, you should be able to:

1. Understand activity-based costing and how it differs from a traditional costing system.
2. Assign costs to cost pools using a first-stage allocation.
3. Compute activity rates for cost pools.
4. Assign costs to a cost object using a second-stage allocation.
5. Prepare a report showing activity-based costing margins from an activity view.
6. (Appendix 8A) Prepare an action analysis report using activity-based costing data and interpret the report.

Bank of America Focuses on Profitability

Some companies track how much their customers spend on their products and how much it costs to serve these customers. Profitable customers are carefully nurtured. Unprofitable customers may be let go.

For example, "Bank of America calculates its profits every month on each of its more than 75 million accounts . . . By wading through all that data . . . BofA is able to zero in on the 10% of households that are most profitable. It assigns a financial adviser to track about 300 accounts at a time. Their job: to answer questions, coordinate the bank's efforts to sell more services, and—perhaps most important—watch for warning flags that these lucrative customers may be moving their business elsewhere . . . . The heavy intervention seems to be working . . . [C]ustomer defections are down, and account balances in the top 10% have grown . . . "

Source: Paul C. Judge, "What've You Done for Us Lately?" *Business Week,* September 14, 1998, pp. 140–146.

The cost accounting systems described in Chapters 2, 3, and 4 were designed primarily to provide unit product costs for external reporting purposes. Variable costing, which was described in Chapter 7, is intended to provide managers with product costs and other information for decisions that do not affect fixed costs and capacity. Another method called *activity-based costing* has been embraced by a wide variety of organizations including American Express, The Association of Neurological Surgeons, Cambridge Hospital Community Health Network, Carrier Corporation, Dana Corporation, Dialysis Clinic, GE Medical Systems, Hallmark, Harris Semi-Conductor, ITT Automotive North America, Maxwell Appliance Controls, Pillsbury, Tampa Electric Company, and the U.S. Postal Service. **Activity-based costing (ABC)** is a costing method that is designed to provide managers with cost information for strategic and other decisions that potentially affect capacity and therefore "fixed" costs. Activity-based costing is ordinarily used as a supplement to, rather than as a replacement for, the company's usual costing system. Most organizations that use activity-based costing have two costing systems—the official costing system that is used for preparing external financial reports and the activity-based costing system that is used for internal decision making and for managing activities.

In practice, activity-based costing comes in many "flavors." Consultants emphasize different aspects of activity-based costing, and companies interpret activity-based costing differently. Since so much variation occurs in practice, we focus our attention in this chapter on what we consider to be "the best practice"—those techniques that provide managers with the most useful information for making strategic decisions. We will assume that the ABC system is used as a supplement to, rather than as a replacement for, the company's formal cost accounting system. The cost accounting methods described in Chapters 2, 3, and 4 would continue to be used to determine product costs for external financial reports. Activity-based costing would be used to determine product and other costs for special management reports. To keep the discussion simple, we gloss over some of the relatively unimportant details that can add enormously to the complexity of activity-based costing. Even so, you are likely to find this chapter especially challenging.

In Business

ABC in the Public Sector

Robin Cooper and Robert S. Kaplan report that: "The U.S. Veterans Affairs Department has identified the cost of the 10 activities performed to process death benefits and uses this information to monitor and improve the underlying cost structure for performing this function. The U.S. Immigration and Naturalization Service (INS) uses its ABC cost information to set fees for all its outputs, including administering citizenship exams and issuing permanent work permits (green cards)." The City of Indianapolis made ABC a cornerstone of its privatization efforts and its drive to provide more services at lower cost to citizens. As the mayor of the city, Stephen Goldsmith, explained: "Introducing competition and privatization to government services requires real cost information. You can't compete out if you are using fake money." When city workers became aware of the costs of carrying out activities such as filling potholes in streets and were faced with the possible transfer of such tasks to the private sector, they became highly motivated to reduce costs. Instead of going out to fill potholes with a five- or six-man repair crew, plus a supervisor, they started doing the same job with a three- or four-man crew without a supervisor. The number of politically appointed supervisors, which had stood at 36 for 75 employees, was slashed by half.

Source: Robert S. Kaplan and Robin Cooper, *Cost & Effect: Using Integrated Cost Systems to Drive Profitability and Performance,* Harvard Business School Press, Boston, 1998, pp. 245–250.

In the traditional cost accounting systems described in Chapters 2, 3, and 4, the objective is to value inventories and cost of goods sold for external financial reports in accordance with generally accepted accounting principles (GAAP). In activity-based costing, the objective is to understand overhead and the profitability of products and customers and to manage overhead. As a consequence of these differences in objectives, "best practice" activity-based costing differs in a number of ways from traditional cost accounting.

LEARNING OBJECTIVE 1
Understand activity-based costing and how it differs from a traditional costing system.

In activity-based costing:

1. Nonmanufacturing as well as manufacturing costs may be assigned to products.
2. Some manufacturing costs may be excluded from product costs.
3. A number of overhead cost pools are used, each of which is allocated to products and other costing objects using its own unique measure of activity.
4. The allocation bases often differ from those used in traditional costing systems.
5. The overhead rates, or *activity rates,* may be based on the level of activity at capacity rather than on the budgeted level of activity.

As we will see later in the chapter, these differences from traditional cost accounting systems can dramatically impact the apparent costs of products and the profitability of products and customers. But first, we will briefly discuss the reasons for these departures from traditional cost accounting practices.

How Costs Are Treated under Activity-Based Costing

Nonmanufacturing Costs and Activity-Based Costing

In traditional cost accounting, only manufacturing costs are assigned to products. Selling, general, and administrative expenses are treated as period expenses and are not assigned to products. However, many of these nonmanufacturing costs are also part of the costs of producing, selling, distributing, and servicing products. For example, commissions paid to salespersons, shipping costs, and warranty repair costs can be easily traced to individual products. In this chapter, we will use the term *overhead* to refer to nonmanufacturing costs as well as to indirect manufacturing costs. In activity-based costing, products are assigned all of the overhead costs—nonmanufacturing as well as manufacturing—that they can reasonably be supposed to have caused. In essence, we will be determining the entire cost of a product rather than just its manufacturing cost. The focus in Chapters 2, 3, and 4 was on determining just the manufacturing cost of a product.

Manufacturing Costs and Activity-Based Costing

In traditional cost accounting, *all* manufacturing costs are assigned to products—even manufacturing costs that are not caused by the products. For example, a portion of the factory security guard's wages would be allocated to each product even though the guard's wages are totally unaffected by which products are made or not made during a period. In activity-based costing, a cost is assigned to a product only if there is good reason to believe that the cost would be affected by decisions concerning the product.

Plantwide Overhead Rate Our discussion in Chapter 3 assumed that a single overhead rate, called a *plantwide overhead rate,* was being used throughout an entire factory and that the allocation base was direct labor-hours or machine-hours. This simple approach to overhead assignment can result in distorted unit product costs when it is used for decision-making purposes.

When cost systems were developed in the 1800s, cost and activity data had to be collected by hand and all calculations were done with paper and pen. Consequently, the emphasis was on simplicity. Companies often established a single overhead cost pool for an entire facility or department as described in Chapter 3. Direct labor was the obvious choice as an allocation base for overhead costs. Direct labor-hours were already being recorded for purposes of determining wages and direct labor time spent on tasks was often closely monitored. In the labor-intensive production processes of that time, direct labor was a large component of product costs—larger than it is today. Moreover, managers believed direct labor and overhead costs were highly correlated. (Two variables, such as direct labor and overhead costs, are highly correlated if they tend to move together.) And finally, most companies produced a very limited variety of products that required similar resources to produce, so in fact there was probably little difference in the overhead costs attributable to different products. Under these conditions, it was not cost-effective to use a more elaborate costing system.

Conditions have changed. Many companies now sell a large variety of products and services that consume significantly different overhead resources. Consequently, a costing system that assigns essentially the same overhead cost to every product may no longer be adequate. Additionally, many managers now believe that overhead costs and direct labor are no longer highly correlated and that other factors drive overhead costs.

On an economywide basis, direct labor and overhead costs have been moving in opposite directions for a long time. As a percentage of total cost, direct labor has been declining, whereas overhead has been increasing.[1] Many tasks that used to be done by hand are now done with largely automated equipment—a component of overhead. Furthermore, product diversity has increased. Companies are creating new products and services at an ever-accelerating rate that differ in volume, batch size, and complexity. Managing and sustaining this product diversity requires many more overhead resources such as production schedulers and product design engineers, and many of these overhead resources have no obvious connection with direct labor. Finally, computers, bar code readers, and other technology have dramatically reduced the costs of collecting and manipulating data—making more complex (and accurate) costing systems such as activity-based costing much less expensive to build and maintain.

Nevertheless, direct labor remains a viable base for applying overhead to products in some companies—particularly for external reports. Direct labor is an appropriate allocation base for overhead when overhead costs and direct labor are highly correlated. And indeed, most companies throughout the world continue to base overhead allocations on direct labor or machine-hours. However, if factorywide overhead costs do not move in tandem with factorywide direct labor or machine-hours, some other means of assigning overhead costs must be found or product costs will be distorted.

Departmental Overhead Rates Rather than use a plantwide overhead rate, many companies have a system in which each department has its own overhead rate. The nature of the work performed in a department will determine the department's allocation base. For example, overhead costs in a machining department may be allocated on the basis of the machine-hours incurred in that department. In contrast, the overhead costs in an assembly department may be allocated on the basis of direct labor-hours incurred in that department.

Unfortunately, even departmental overhead rates will not correctly assign overhead costs in situations where a company has a range of products that differ in volume, batch size, or complexity of production.[2] The reason is that the departmental approach usually relies on volume as the factor in allocating overhead cost to products. For example, if the machining department's overhead is applied to products on the basis of machine-hours, it is assumed that the department's overhead costs are caused by, and are directly proportional to, machine-hours. However, the department's overhead costs are probably more

---

[1] Germain Böer provides some data concerning these trends in "Five Modern Management Accounting Myths," *Management Accounting,* January 1994, pp. 22–27. Data maintained by the U.S. Department of Commerce show that since 1849, on average, material cost has been fairly constant at 55% of sales. Labor cost has always been less important than direct materials and has declined steadily from 23% of sales in 1849 to about 10% in 1987. Overhead has grown from about 18% of sales in 1947 to about 33% of sales 50 years later.

[2] See Robin Cooper and Robert S. Kaplan, "How Cost Accounting Distorts Product Costs," *Management Accounting,* April 1988, pp. 20–27.

complex than this and are caused by a variety of factors, including the range of products processed in the department, the number of batch setups that are required, the complexity of the products, and so on. Activity-based costing is a technique that is designed to reflect these diverse factors more accurately when costing products. It attempts to accomplish this goal by identifying the major *activities* such as batch setups, purchase order processing, and so on, that consume overhead resources and thus cause costs. An **activity** is any event that causes the consumption of overhead resources. The costs of carrying out these activities are assigned to the products that cause the activities.

ABC Changes the Focus

In Business

Euclid Engineering makes parts and components for the big automobile manufacturers. As a result of its ABC study, Euclid's managers "discovered that the company was spending more in launching new products than on direct labor expenses to produce existing products. Product development and launch expenses were 10% of expenses, whereas direct labor costs were only 9%. Of course, in the previous direct labor cost system, all attention had been focused on reducing direct labor costs . . . . Product development and launch costs were blended into the factory overhead rate applied to products based on direct labor cost. Now Euclid's managers realized that they had a major cost reduction opportunity by attacking the product launch cost directly."

The new information produced by the ABC study also helped Euclid in its relations with customers. The detailed breakdown of the costs of design and engineering activities helped customers to make trade-offs, with the result that they would often ask that certain activities whose costs exceeded their benefits be skipped.

Source: Robert S. Kaplan and Robin Cooper, *Cost & Effect: Using Integrated Cost Systems to Drive Profitability and Performance* (Boston: Harvard Business School Press, 1998), pp. 219–222.

The Costs of Idle Capacity in Activity-Based Costing

In traditional cost accounting, predetermined overhead rates are computed by dividing budgeted overhead costs by a measure of budgeted activity such as budgeted direct labor-hours. This practice results in applying the costs of unused, or idle, capacity to products, and it results in unstable unit product costs as discussed in Appendix 3A. If budgeted activity falls, the overhead rate increases because the fixed components of overhead are spread over a smaller base, resulting in increased unit product costs.

In contrast to traditional cost accounting, in activity-based costing, products are charged for the costs of capacity they use—not for the costs of capacity they don't use. In other words, the costs of idle capacity are not charged to products. This results in more stable unit costs and is consistent with the objective of assigning only those costs to products that are actually caused by the products. Instead of assigning the costs of idle capacity to products, in activity-based costing these costs are considered to be period costs that flow through to the income statement as an expense of the current period. This treatment highlights the cost of idle capacity rather than burying it in inventory and cost of goods sold.

Designing an Activity-Based Costing (ABC) System

Concept 8–1

Experts agree on several essential characteristics of any successful implementation of activity-based costing. First, the initiative to implement activity-based costing must be strongly supported by top management. Second, the design and implementation of an ABC system should be the responsibility of a cross-functional team rather than of the accounting department. The team should include representatives from each area that will use the data provided by the ABC system. Ordinarily, this would include representatives from marketing, production, engineering, and top management as well as technically trained accounting staff. An outside consultant who specializes in activity-based costing may serve as an advisor to the team.

The reason for insisting on strong top-management support and a multifunction team approach is rooted in the fact that it is difficult to implement changes in organizations unless those changes have the full support of those who are affected. Activity-based costing changes "the rules of the game" since it changes some of the key measures that managers use for their decision making and for evaluating individuals' performance. Unless the managers who are directly affected by the changes in the rules have a say, resistance will be inevitable. In addition, designing a good ABC system requires intimate knowledge of many parts of the organization's overall operations. This knowledge can only come from the people who are familiar with those operations.

Top managers must support the initiative for two reasons. First, without leadership from top management, some managers may not see any reason to change. Second, if top managers do not support the ABC system and continue to play the game by the old rules, their subordinates will quickly get the message that ABC is not important and they will abandon the ABC initiative. Time after time, when accountants have attempted to implement an ABC system on their own without top-management support and active cooperation from other managers, the results have been ignored.

Managerial Accounting in Action

The Issue

Classic Brass, Inc., makes finely machined brass fittings for a variety of applications including stanchions, cleats, and helms for luxury yachts. The president of the company, John Towers, recently attended a management conference at which activity-based costing was discussed. Following the conference, he called a meeting of the top managers in the company to discuss what he had learned. Attending the meeting were the production manager Susan Ritcher, the marketing manager Tom Olafson, and the accounting manager Mary Goodman.

John: I'm glad we could all get together this morning. I just attended a conference that dealt with some issues that we have all been wondering about for some time.

Susan: Did anyone at the conference explain why my equipment always breaks down at the worst possible moment?

John: Sorry Susan, I guess it must be bad karma.

Tom: Did the conference tell you why we've been losing all those bids lately on our high-volume routine work?

John: Tom, you probably weren't expecting this answer, but, yes, there may be a simple reason why we've been losing those bids.

Tom: Let me guess. We've been losing the bids because we have more competition.

John: Yes, the competition has a lot to do with it. But Tom, we may have been shooting ourselves in the foot.

Tom: How so? I don't know about anyone else, but my salespeople have been hustling like crazy to get more business for the company.

Susan: Wait a minute Tom, my production people have been turning in tremendous improvements in defect rates, on-time delivery, and so on.

John: Whoa everybody. Calm down. I don't think anyone is to blame for losing the bids. Tom, when you talk with our customers, what reasons do they give for taking their business to our competitors? Is it a problem with the quality of our products or our on-time delivery?

Tom: No, they don't have any problem with our products or with our service—our customers readily admit we're among the best in the business.

Susan: Darn right!

John: Then what's the problem?

Tom: Price. The competition is undercutting our prices on the high-volume work.

John: Why are our prices too high?

Tom: Our prices aren't too high. Theirs are too low. Our competitors must be pricing below their cost.

John: Tom, why do you think that?

Tom: Well, if we charged the prices on high-volume work that our competitors are quoting, we'd be pricing below *our* cost, and I know we are just as efficient as any competitor.

Susan: Tom, why would our competitors price below their cost?

Tom: They are out to grab market share.

Susan: Does that make any sense? What good does more market share do if they are pricing below their cost?

John: I think Susan has a point, Tom. Mary, you're the expert with the numbers. Can you suggest another explanation?

Mary: I was afraid you would ask that. Those unit product cost figures our department reports to you are primarily intended to be used to value inventories and to determine cost of goods sold for our external financial statements. I am awfully uncomfortable about using them for bidding. In fact, I have mentioned this several times, but no one was interested.

John: Now I'm interested. Mary, are you telling us that the product cost figures we have been using for bidding are wrong? Perhaps the competition isn't pricing below our cost—we just don't know what our cost is?

Mary: Yes, that could be the problem. I just wish someone had listened earlier.

John: Does everyone agree with Mary that this is a problem we should work on?

Tom: Sure, if it means we can win more bids.

John: Okay, I want each of you to appoint one of your top people to a special team to investigate how we cost products.

Susan: Isn't this something Mary can handle with her staff?

John: Perhaps she could, but you know more about your operations than she does and besides, I want to make sure you agree with the results of the study and use them. Mary, do you agree?

Mary: Absolutely.

Getting Even

In Business

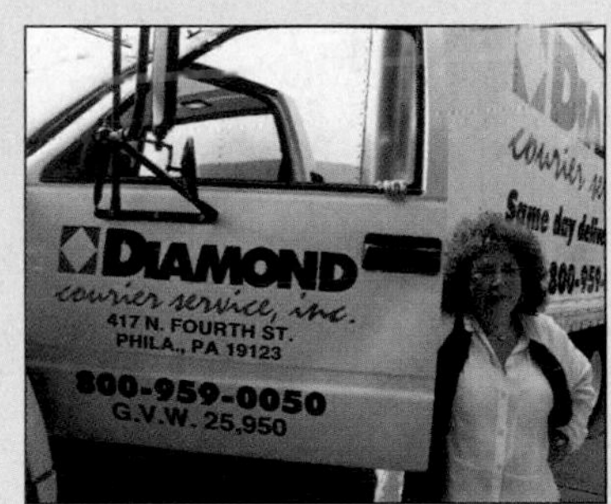

Diamond Courier of Philadelphia was started by Claudia Post shortly after having been fired as a salesperson for another courier service. Her downtown bicycle messenger service grew quickly—reaching $1 million in sales within 17 months. Seeing opportunities to sell other services, she added truck deliveries, airfreight services, a parts-distribution service, and a legal service that served subpoenas and prepared court filings. Within three years of beginning operations, Diamond Courier had $3.1 million in annual sales and employed about 40 bike messengers and 25 back-office staffers in addition to providing work for about 50 independent drivers.

The company had one problem—it was losing money. Post had to sell her jewelry in order to meet the payroll and pay bills. With the help of an adviser, Post took a serious look at the profitability of each of the company's lines of business. Post had assumed that if she charged a competitive rate, kept clients happy, and increased sales, she would make money. However, an ABC analysis of her overhead costs indicated that the average cost of a bike delivery—including overhead—was $9.24, but she was charging only $4.69. "The bicycle division, which she thought of as Diamond's core business, generated just 10% of total sales and barely covered its own direct-labor and insurance costs. Worse, the division created more logistical and customer-service nightmares than any other single business, thereby generating a disproportionate share of overhead costs." Since smaller, focused competitors were charging as little as $3 per delivery, there was little alternative except to drop the bicycle messenger business and concentrate on the other, more profitable, lines of business. A similar analysis led her to also close the airfreight and parts-distribution businesses. At last report, Diamond Courier has regained a good chunk of the lost sales of $400,000 from closing these lines of business and is now operating profitably.

S

Source: Susan Greco, "Are We Making Money Yet?" *Inc.*, July 1996, pp. 52–61.

Exhibit 8–1
The Activity-Based Costing Model

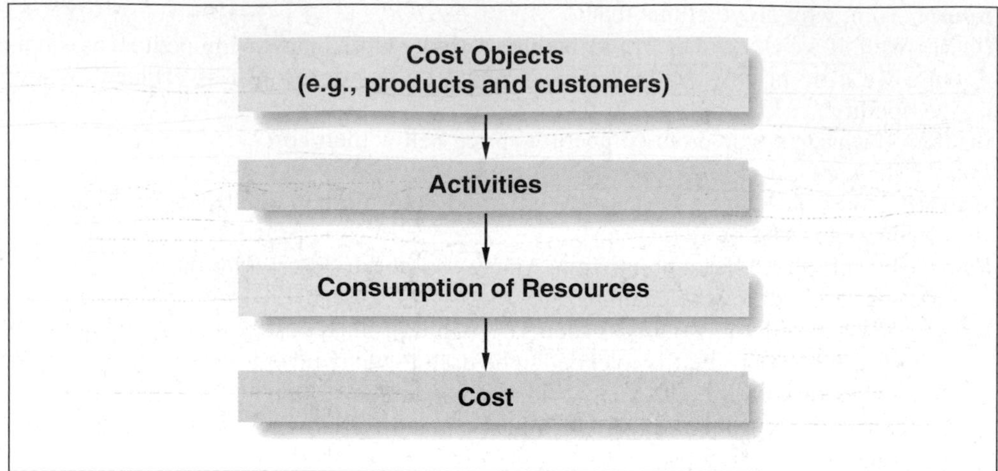

After studying the existing cost accounting system at Classic Brass and reviewing articles in professional and trade journals, the special team decided to implement an activity-based costing (ABC) system. Like most other ABC implementations, the new ABC system would supplement, rather than replace, the existing cost accounting system, which would continue to be used for external financial reports. The new ABC system would be used to prepare special reports for management decisions such as bidding on new business.

The accounting manager drew the chart appearing in Exhibit 8–1 to explain the general structure of the ABC model. Cost objects such as products generate activities. For example, a customer order for a brass cupholder requires the activity of preparing a production order. Such an activity consumes resources. A production order uses a sheet of paper and takes time to fill out. And consumption of resources causes costs. The greater the number of sheets used to fill out production orders and the greater the amount of time devoted to filling out such orders, the greater the cost. Activity-based costing attempts to trace through these relationships to identify how products and customers affect costs.

As in most other companies, the ABC team at Classic Brass felt that the company's traditional cost accounting system adequately measured the direct material and direct labor costs of products since these costs are directly traced to products. Therefore, the ABC study would be concerned solely with the other costs of the company—manufacturing overhead and selling, general, and administrative costs.

The team felt it was important to carefully plan how it would go about implementing the new ABC system at Classic Brass. Accordingly, the implementation process was broken down into the following six basic steps:

Steps for Implementing Activity-Based Costing:

1. Identify and define activities and activity cost pools.
2. Wherever possible, directly trace costs to activities and cost objects.
3. Assign costs to activity cost pools.
4. Calculate activity rates.
5. Assign costs to cost objects using the activity rates and activity measures.
6. Prepare management reports.

Step 1: Identify and Define Activities and Activity Cost Pools

The first major step in implementing an ABC system is to identify the activities that will form the foundation for the system. This can be difficult, time-consuming, and involves a great deal of judgment. A common procedure is for the individuals on the ABC implementation team to interview people who work in overhead departments and ask them to describe their major activities. Ordinarily, this results in a very long list of activities.

Is E-Tailing Really Easier?

In Business

The company art.com™ sells prints and framed prints over the web. An ABC study identified the following 12 activities carried out in the company:

1. Service customers
2. Website optimization
3. Merchandise inventory selection and management
4. Purchasing and receiving
5. Customer acquisition and retention—paid-for marketing
6. Customer acquisition and retention—revenue share marketing (affiliate group)
7. Sustain information system
8. Sustain business—administration
9. Sustain business—production
10. Maintain facility—administrative
11. Maintain facility—production
12. Sustain business—executive

For example, the activity "merchandise inventory selection and management" involves scanning, describing, classifying, and linking each inventory item to search options. "Staff must carefully manage each change to the database, which is similar to adding and removing inventory items from the shelf of a store. They annotate added inventory items and upload them into the system, as well as remove obsolete and discontinued items. . . . The number of inventory items for an e-tailer is typically much greater than for a brick-and-mortar [store], which is a competitive advantage, but experience shows managing a large inventory consumes substantial resources."

Source: Thomas L. Zeller, David R. Kublank, and Philip G. Makris, " How art.com™ Uses ABC to Succeed," *Strategic Finance*, March 2001, pp. 25–31. Reprinted with permission from the IMA, Montvale, NJ, USA, www.imanet.org.

The length of such lists of activities poses a problem. On the one hand, the greater the number of activities tracked in the ABC system, the more accurate the costs are likely to be. On the other hand, it is costly to design, implement, maintain, and use a complex system involving large numbers of activities. Consequently, the original lengthy list of activities is usually reduced to a handful by combining similar activities. For example, several actions may be involved in handling and moving raw materials—from receiving raw materials on the loading dock to sorting them into the appropriate bins in the storeroom. All of these activities might be combined into a single activity called material handling.

A useful way to think about activities and how to combine them is to organize them into five general levels: *unit-level, batch-level, product-level, customer-level,* and *organization-sustaining* activities. These levels are described as follows:[3]

1. **Unit-level activities** are performed each time a unit is produced. The costs of unit-level activities should be proportional to the number of units produced. For example, providing power to run processing equipment would be a unit-level activity since power tends to be consumed in proportion to the number of units produced.
2. **Batch-level activities** are performed each time a batch is handled or processed, regardless of how many units are in the batch. For example, tasks such as placing purchase orders, setting up equipment, and arranging for shipments to customers are batch-level activities. They are incurred once for each batch (or customer order). Costs at the batch level depend on the number of batches processed rather than on the number of units produced, the number of units sold, or other measures of volume. For example, the cost of setting up a machine for batch processing is the same regardless of whether the batch contains one or thousands of items.
3. **Product-level activities** relate to specific products and typically must be carried out regardless of how many batches are run or units of product are produced or sold. For

[3] Robin Cooper, "Cost Classification in Unit-Based and Activity-Based Manufacturing Cost Systems," *Journal of Cost Management*, Fall 1990, pp. 4–14.

example, activities such as designing a product, advertising a product, and maintaining a product manager and staff are all product-level activities.

4. **Customer-level activities** relate to specific customers and include activities such as sales calls, catalog mailings, and general technical support that are not tied to any specific product.
5. **Organization-sustaining activities** are carried out regardless of which customers are served, which products are produced, how many batches are run, or how many units are made. This category includes activities such as heating the factory, cleaning executive offices, providing a computer network, arranging for loans, preparing annual reports to shareholders, and so on.

When combining activities in an ABC system, activities should be grouped together at the appropriate level. Batch-level activities should not be combined with unit-level activities or product-level activities with batch-level activities and so on. In general, it is best to combine only those activities that are highly correlated with each other within a level. Activities are correlated with each other if they tend to move in tandem. For example, the number of customer orders received is likely to be highly correlated with the number of completed customer orders shipped, so these two batch-level activities (receiving and shipping orders) can usually be combined with little loss of accuracy.

At Classic Brass, the ABC team, in consultation with top managers, selected the following *activity cost pools* and *activity measures*:

Activity Cost Pools at Classic Brass

Activity Cost Pool	Activity Measure
Customer orders	Number of customer orders
Product design.	Number of product designs
Order size	Machine-hours
Customer relations	Number of active customers
Other	Not applicable

An **activity cost pool** is a "bucket" in which costs are accumulated that relate to a single activity measure in the ABC system. For example, the *Customer Orders* cost pool will be assigned all costs of resources that are consumed by taking and processing customer orders, including costs of processing paperwork and any costs involved in setting up machines for specific orders. The measure of activity for this cost pool is simply the number of customer orders received. This is a batch-level activity, since each order generates work that occurs regardless of whether the order is for one unit or 1,000 units. The number of customer orders received is an example of an *activity measure.* An **activity measure** is an allocation base in an activity-based costing system. The term *cost driver* is also used to refer to an activity measure. The activity measure should "drive" the cost being allocated.

Activity measures are often very rough measures of resource consumption. Probably the least accurate type of activity measure is known as a *transaction driver*. **Transaction drivers** are simple counts of the number of times an activity occurs such as the number of bills sent out to customers. This activity measure is satisfactory when all bills take about the same amount of time to prepare. However, if some bills are simple to prepare and others are very complex, a more accurate type of activity measure known as a *duration driver* may be used. **Duration drivers** are measures of the amount of time required to perform an activity such as the time spent preparing individual bills. In general, duration drivers are more accurate measures of the consumption of resources than transaction drivers, but they take more effort to record. For that reason, transaction drivers are often used in practice.

The *Product Design* cost pool will be assigned all costs of resources consumed by designing products. The activity measure for this cost pool is the number of products designed. This is a product-level activity, since the amount of design work on a new product does not depend on the number of units ultimately ordered or batches ultimately run.

The *Order Size* cost pool will be assigned all costs of resources consumed as a consequence of the number of units produced, including the costs of miscellaneous factory supplies, power to run machines, and some equipment depreciation. This is a unit-level activity since each unit requires some of these resources. The activity measure for this cost pool is machine-hours.

The *Customer Relations* cost pool will be assigned all costs associated with maintaining relations with customers, including the costs of sales calls and the costs of entertaining customers. The activity measure for this cost pool is the number of customers the company has on its active customer list. The Customer Relations cost pool represents a customer-level activity.

The *Other* cost pool will be assigned all overhead costs that are not associated with customer orders, product design, the size of the orders, or customer relations. These costs mainly consist of organization-sustaining costs and the costs of unused, idle capacity. These costs *will not* be assigned to products since they represent resources that are *not* consumed by products.

It is unlikely that any other company would use exactly the same activity cost pools and activities that were selected by Classic Brass. Because of the amount of judgment involved, the number and definitions of the activity cost pools and activity measures used by companies vary considerably.

The Mechanics of Activity-Based Costing

After the ABC system had been designed, the team was ready to begin the process of actually computing the costs of products, customers, and other objects of interest.

Step 2: Whenever Possible, Directly Trace Overhead Costs to Activities and Cost Objects

The second step in implementing an ABC system is to directly trace as many overhead costs as possible to the ultimate cost objects. At Classic Brass, the ultimate cost objects are products, customer orders, and customers. The company's annual manufacturing overhead and selling, general, and administrative costs are listed in Exhibit 8–2. In the ABC system at Classic Brass all of these costs are considered to be "overhead" and will be assigned to cost objects where appropriate.

One of these overhead costs—shipping—can be traced directly to customer orders. Classic Brass is directly billed for each customer order it ships, so it is a simple matter to trace these costs to the customer orders. Customers do not pay these actual shipping costs;

Exhibit 8–2
Annual Overhead Costs (both Manufacturing and Nonmanufacturing) at Classic Brass

Production Department:		
Indirect factory wages	$500,000	
Factory equipment depreciation	300,000	
Factory utilities	120,000	
Factory building lease	80,000	$1,000,000
Shipping costs*		40,000
General Administrative Department:		
Administrative wages and salaries	400,000	
Office equipment depreciation	50,000	
Administrative building lease	60,000	510,000
Marketing Department:		
Marketing wages and salaries	250,000	
Selling expenses	50,000	300,000
Total overhead costs		$1,850,000

*Shipping costs can be traced directly to customer orders.

instead they pay a standard shipping charge that can differ substantially from the actual bill that Classic Brass receives from the freight company.

No other overhead costs can be directly traced to products, customer orders, or customers. Consequently, the remainder of the overhead costs are assigned to cost objects using the ABC system.

In Business

The Virtual Bakery

Super Bakery, Inc., founded by former Pittsburgh Steelers running back Franco Harris, supplies donuts and other baked goods to schools, hospitals, and other institutions. The company is a virtual corporation—only the core, strategic functions of the business are performed inside the company. The remaining support activities are outsourced to a network of external companies. Super Bakery's products are sold by independent brokers, and the company contracts out baking, warehousing, and shipping. What does Super Bakery itself do? The company's master baker develops products, and the company formulates and produces its own dry mixes from ingredients it has purchased. The contracted bakeries simply add water to the mix and follow the baking instructions. Super Bakery maintains four regional sales managers, and a small office staff processes orders and handles bookkeeping and accounting.

As much as possible, actual costs are traced to individual customer accounts. The remaining costs of the company are assigned to customer accounts using the following activity cost pools and activity measures:

Activity Cost Pool	Activity Measure
Advertising, trade shows, and bonds.	Projected number of cases sold
Order department.	Number of orders
Sales management.	Time spent in each sales territory
Research and development (R&D).	Hours of R&D for each product line

Since the independent sales brokers are paid a flat 5% commission on sales, they have little incentive to make sure that the sales are actually profitable to Super Bakery. To make sales, brokers tend to heavily discount prices. Consequently, Super Bakery's regional sales managers must approve all price discounts and they use the ABC data to evaluate the profitability of the deals proposed by the brokers.

Source: Tim R. V. Davis and Bruce L. Darling, "ABC in a Virtual Corporation," *Management Accounting,* October 1996, pp. 18–26.

Step 3: Assign Costs to Activity Cost Pools

LEARNING OBJECTIVE 2
Assign costs to cost pools using a first-stage allocation.

Most overhead costs are originally classified in the company's basic accounting system according to the departments in which they are incurred. For example, salaries, supplies, rent, and so forth incurred by the marketing department are charged to that department. In some cases, some or all of these costs can be directly traced to one of the activity cost pools in the ABC system—the third step in implementing activity-based costing. For example, if the ABC system has an activity called *purchase order processing,* then all of the costs of the purchasing department could probably be traced to that activity. To the extent possible, costs should be traced directly to the activity cost pools. However, it is quite common for an overhead department to be involved in several of the activities that are tracked in the ABC system. In such situations, the costs of the department are divided among the activity cost pools via an allocation process called *first-stage allocation.* The **first-stage allocation** in an ABC system is the process by which overhead costs are assigned to activity cost pools.

The immediate problem is to figure out how to divide, for example, the $500,000 of indirect factory wages at Classic Brass shown in Exhibit 8–2 among the various activity cost pools in the ABC system. The point of activity-based costing is to determine the resources consumed by cost objects. Since indirect factory worker time is a resource, we need some way of estimating the amount of indirect factory worker time that is consumed by each activity in the ABC system. Often, the best way to get this kind of information is to ask the people who are directly involved. Members of the ABC team interview indirect factory workers (e.g., supervisors, engineers, quality inspectors, etc.) and ask them what percentage of time they spend dealing with customer orders, with product design, with processing units of product (i.e., order size), and with customer relations. These interviews are conducted with considerable care. Those who are interviewed must thoroughly understand what the activities encompass and what is expected of them in the interview. In addition, departmental managers are interviewed to determine how the nonpersonnel costs should be distributed across the activity cost pools. In each case the key question is, "What percentage of the available resource is consumed by this activity?" For example, the production manager would be asked, "What percentage of the available machine capacity is consumed as a consequence of the number of units processed (i.e., size of orders)?"

The results of the interviews at Classic Brass are displayed in Exhibit 8–3. For example, factory equipment depreciation is distributed 20% to Customer Orders, 60% to Order Size, and 20% to the Other cost pool. The resource in this instance is machine time. According to the estimate made by the production manager, 60% of the total available time was used to actually process units to fill orders. Each customer order requires setting up, which also requires machine time. This activity consumes 20% of the total available machine time and is entered under the Customer Orders column. The remaining 20% of available machine time represents idle time and is entered under the Other column.

Exhibit 8–3 and many of the other exhibits in this chapter are presented in the form of Excel spreadsheets. All of the calculations required in activity-based costing can be done by hand. Nevertheless, setting up the activity-based costing system on a spreadsheet or using special ABC software can save a lot of work—particularly in situations involving many activity cost pools and in organizations that periodically update their ABC systems.

We will not go into the details of how all of the percentages in Exhibit 8–3 were determined. However, note that 100% of the factory building lease has been assigned to the Other cost pool. Classic Brass has a single production facility. It has no plans to expand or to sublease any excess space. The cost of this production facility is treated as an organization-sustaining cost since there is no way to avoid even a portion of this cost if a particular product or customer were to be dropped. (Remember that organization-sustaining costs are assigned to the Other cost pool and are not allocated to products.) In contrast, some companies have separate facilities for manufacturing specific products. The costs of these separate facilities could be directly traced to the specific products.

Once the percentage distributions in Exhibit 8–3 have been established, it is a simple matter to allocate costs to the activity cost pools. The results of this first-stage allocation are displayed in Exhibit 8–4. Each cost is allocated across the activity cost pools by multiplying it by the percentages in Exhibit 8–3. For example, the indirect factory wages of $500,000 are multiplied by the 25% entry under Customer Orders in Exhibit 8–3 to arrive at the $125,000 entry under Customer Orders in Exhibit 8–4. Similarly, the indirect factory wages of $500,000 are multiplied by the 40% entry under Product Design in Exhibit 8–3 to arrive at the $200,000 entry under Product Design in Exhibit 8–4. All of the entries in Exhibit 8–4 are computed in this way.

Concept 8–2

Now that the first-stage allocations to the activity cost pools have been completed, the fourth step is to compute the activity rates.

Step 4: Calculate Activity Rates

LEARNING OBJECTIVE 3
Compute activity rates for cost pools.

The activity rates that will be used for assigning overhead costs to products and customers are computed in Exhibit 8–5. The ABC team determined the total activity for each cost pool that would be required to produce the company's present product mix and to serve its present customers. These numbers are listed in Exhibit 8–5. For example, the ABC team found that 200 new product designs are required each year to serve the company's present customers. The activity rates are computed by dividing the *total* cost for each

Exhibit 8–3
Results of Interviews: Distribution of Resource Consumption across Activity Cost Pools

Microsoft Excel - ABC model-Classic Brass.XLS

	Activity Cost Pools					
	Customer Orders	Product Design	Order Size	Customer Relations	Other	Totals
Production Department:						
Indirect factory wages	25%	40%	20%	10%	5%	100%
Factory equipment depreciation	20%	0%	60%	0%	20%	100%
Factory utilities	0%	10%	50%	0%	40%	100%
Factory building lease	0%	0%	0%	0%	100%	100%
Shipping costs*	NA	NA	NA	NA	NA	NA
General Administrative Department:						
Administrative wages and salaries	15%	5%	10%	30%	40%	100%
Office equipment depreciation	30%	0%	0%	25%	45%	100%
Administrative building lease	0%	0%	0%	0%	100%	100%
Marketing Department:						
Marketing wages and salaries	20%	10%	0%	60%	10%	100%
Selling expenses	10%	0%	0%	70%	20%	100%

*Shipping costs are not included in this and subsequent tables because they are directly traced to customer orders rather than being allocated using the ABC system. NA = Not applicable.

Exhibit 8–4
First-Stage Allocations to Activity Cost Pools

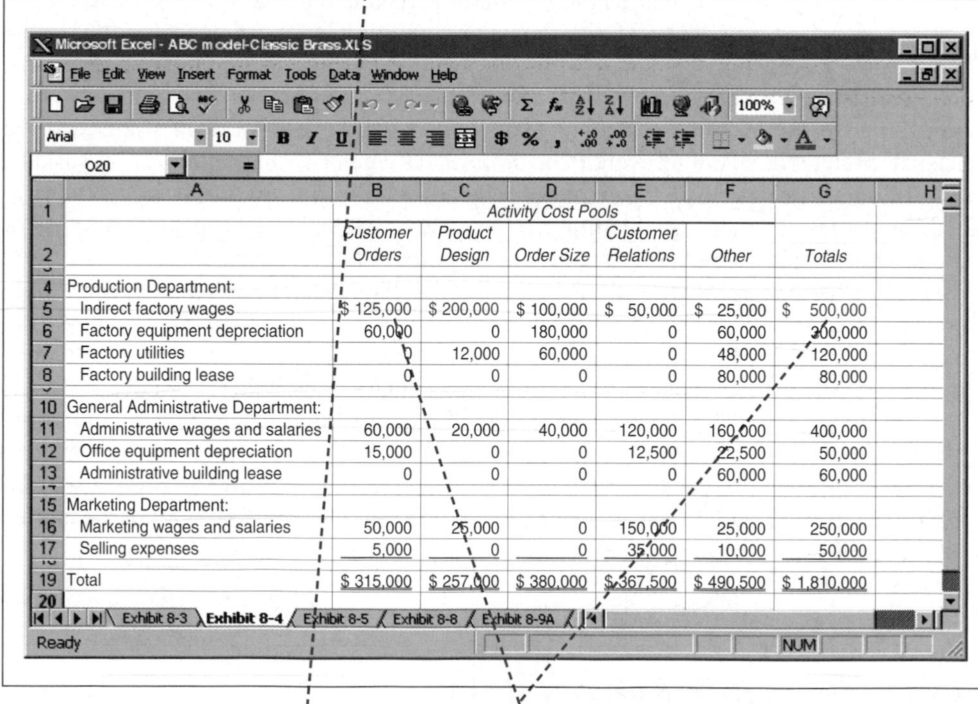

Microsoft Excel - ABC model-Classic Brass.XLS

	Activity Cost Pools					
	Customer Orders	Product Design	Order Size	Customer Relations	Other	Totals
Production Department:						
Indirect factory wages	$ 125,000	$ 200,000	$ 100,000	$ 50,000	$ 25,000	$ 500,000
Factory equipment depreciation	60,000	0	180,000	0	60,000	300,000
Factory utilities	0	12,000	60,000	0	48,000	120,000
Factory building lease	0	0	0	0	80,000	80,000
General Administrative Department:						
Administrative wages and salaries	60,000	20,000	40,000	120,000	160,000	400,000
Office equipment depreciation	15,000	0	0	12,500	22,500	50,000
Administrative building lease	0	0	0	0	60,000	60,000
Marketing Department:						
Marketing wages and salaries	50,000	25,000	0	150,000	25,000	250,000
Selling expenses	5,000	0	0	35,000	10,000	50,000
Total	$ 315,000	$ 257,000	$ 380,000	$ 367,500	$ 490,500	$ 1,810,000

Exhibit 8–3 shows that Customer Orders consume 25% of the resources represented by the $500,000 of indirect factory wages.

$$25\% \times \$500{,}000 = \$125{,}000$$

Other entries in the table are computed in a similar fashion.

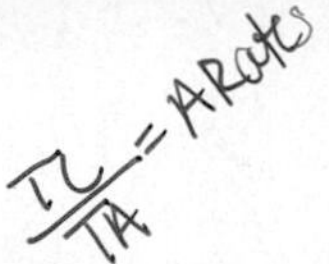

activity by its *total* activity. For example, the $315,000 total annual cost for the Customer Orders cost pool is divided by the total of 1,000 customer orders per year to arrive at the activity rate of $315 per customer order. Similarly, the $257,000 *total* cost for the Product Design cost pool is divided by the *total* number of designs (i.e., 200 product designs) to determine the activity rate of $1,285 per design. Note that activity rates are not computed for the *Other* category of costs. This is because the Other cost pool consists of organization-sustaining costs and costs of idle capacity that are not allocated to products and customers. Overall profits must be large enough to cover these unallocated costs. Also note that the activity rates represent *average* costs. For example, the average cost of a customer order is $315.

The entries in Exhibit 8–5 indicate that on average a customer order consumes resources that cost $315; a product design consumes resources that cost $1,285; a unit of product consumes resources that cost $19 per machine-hour; and maintaining relations with a customer consumes resources that cost $3,675. Note that these are *average* figures. Some members of the ABC design team at Classic Brass argued that it would be unfair to charge all new products the same $1,285 product design cost regardless of how much design time they actually require. After discussing the pros and cons, the team concluded that it would not be worth the effort at the present time to keep track of actual design time spent on each new product. They felt that the benefits of increased accuracy would not be great enough to justify the higher cost of implementing and maintaining the more detailed costing system. Similarly, some team members were uncomfortable assigning the same $3,675 cost to each customer. Some customers are undemanding—ordering standard products well in advance of their needs. Others are very demanding and consume large amounts of marketing and administrative staff time. These are generally customers who order customized products, who tend to order at the last minute, and who change their minds. While everyone agreed with this observation, the data that would be required to measure individual customers' demands on resources was not currently available. Rather than delay implementation of the ABC system, the team decided to defer such refinements to a later date.

Concept 8–2

Before proceeding further, it would be helpful to get a better idea of the overall process of assigning costs to products and other cost objects in an ABC system. Exhibit 8–6 provides a visual perspective of the ABC system at Classic Brass. We recommend

Exhibit 8–5 Computation of Activity Rates

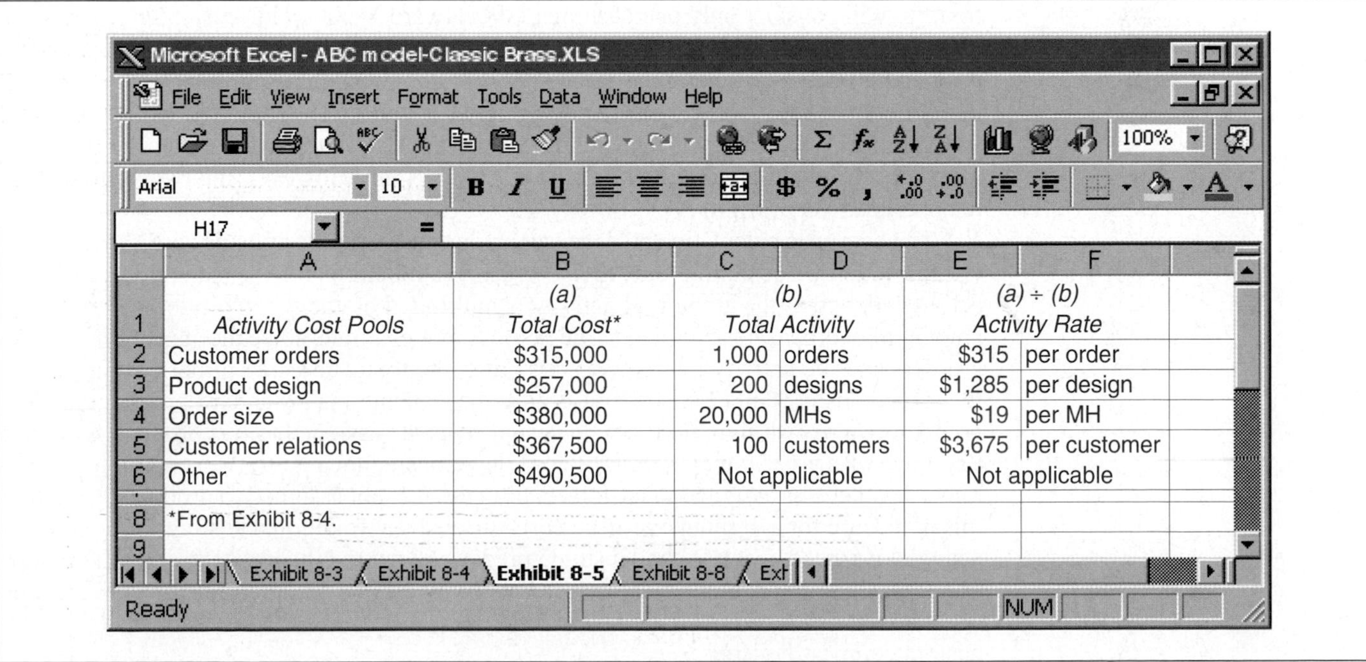

Microsoft Excel - ABC model-Classic Brass.XLS

	A	B	C	D	E	F
1	*Activity Cost Pools*	*(a)* *Total Cost**	*(b)* *Total Activity*		*(a) ÷ (b)* *Activity Rate*	
2	Customer orders	$315,000	1,000	orders	$315	per order
3	Product design	$257,000	200	designs	$1,285	per design
4	Order size	$380,000	20,000	MHs	$19	per MH
5	Customer relations	$367,500	100	customers	$3,675	per customer
6	Other	$490,500	Not applicable		Not applicable	
8	*From Exhibit 8-4.					
9						

Exhibit 8-3 | Exhibit 8-4 | **Exhibit 8-5** | Exhibit 8-8 | Ext

Ready NUM

Exhibit 8–6 The Activity-Based Costing Model at Classic Brass

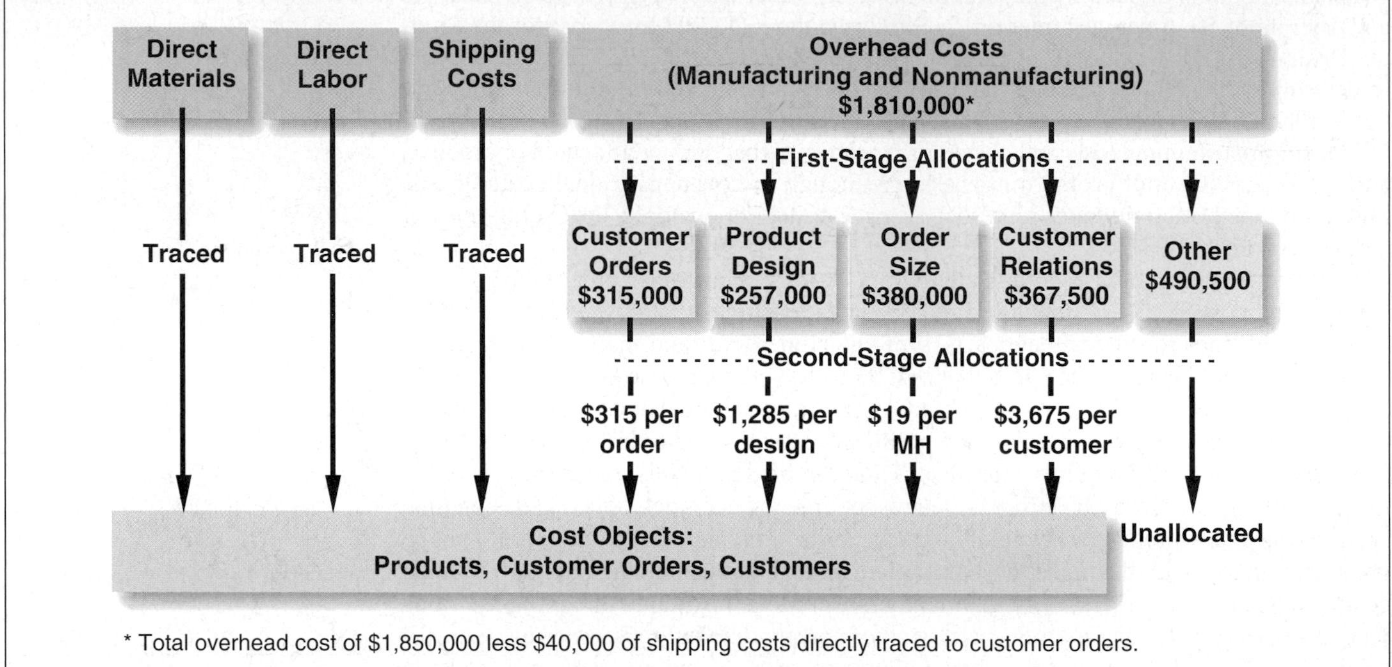

* Total overhead cost of $1,850,000 less $40,000 of shipping costs directly traced to customer orders.

that you carefully go over this exhibit. In particular, note that the Other category, which contains organization-sustaining costs and costs of idle capacity, is not allocated to products or customers.

Step 5: Assign Costs to Cost Objects

LEARNING OBJECTIVE 4
Assign costs to a cost object using a second-stage allocation.

The fifth step in the implementation of activity-based costing is called *second-stage allocation.* In the **second-stage allocation,** activity rates are used to apply costs to products and customers. At Classic Brass, the ABC system might be used to apply activity costs to all of the company's products, customer orders, and customers. For purposes of illustration, we will consider only one customer—Windward Yachts. This customer ordered two different products—stanchions and a compass housing. The stanchions are a standard product that does not require any design work. In contrast, the compass housing is a custom product that requires extensive designing. Data concerning these two products appear in Exhibit 8–7. Direct materials and direct labor costs are the same under the old traditional cost accounting system and the new ABC system. However, the two systems handle overhead very differently.

The overhead calculations for the stanchions and compass housings are carried out in Exhibit 8–8. Let's examine the ABC overhead calculations for the stanchions. For each activity cost pool, the amount of activity is multiplied by the activity rate to arrive at the amount of overhead cost applied to the product. For example, since the stanchions involve 2 orders and the activity rate is $315 per order, the total Customer Order cost applied to the stanchions is $630 (2 × $315). Because the stanchion is a standard product that does not require a new design, no Product Design costs are assigned to this product. Also note that none of the Customer Relations costs have been allocated to the stanchions. A customer-level cost is assigned to customers directly; it is not assigned to products. Note how this procedure for assigning overhead costs differs from traditional costing. Instead of just a single overhead cost pool and a single predetermined overhead rate based on direct labor or machine-hours, now there are several cost pools and predetermined overhead rates.

The same procedure is followed in Exhibit 8–8 to determine the overhead cost for the custom compass housing.

Exhibit 8–7
Data Concerning the Products Ordered by Windward Yachts

Standard Stanchions
1. This is a standard design that does not require any new design resources.
2. Four hundred units were ordered during the year, comprising two separate orders.
3. Each stanchion required 0.5 machine-hours, for a total of 200 machine-hours.
4. The selling price per unit was $34, for a total of $13,600.
5. Direct materials for 400 units totaled $2,110.
6. Direct labor for 400 units totaled $1,850.
7. Shipping costs for the two orders totaled $180.

Custom Compass Housing
1. This is a custom product that requires new design resources.
2. There was only one order for a single unit during the year.
3. The compass housing required 4 machine-hours.
4. The selling price was $650.
5. Direct materials were $13.
6. Direct labor was $50.
7. Shipping costs were $25.

Exhibit 8–8 Computation of Overhead Costs

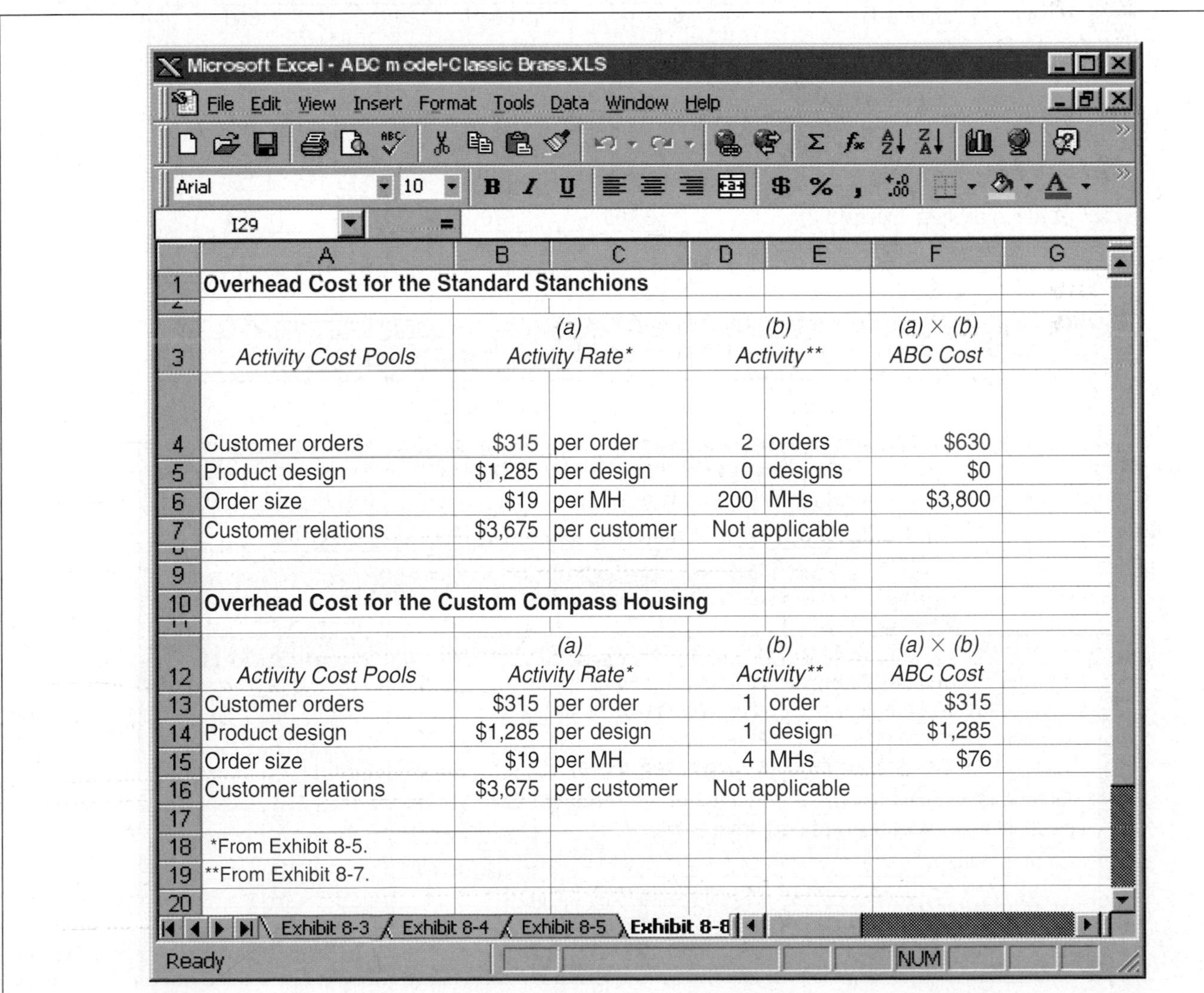

Microsoft Excel - ABC model-Classic Brass.XLS

	A	B	C	D	E	F
1	**Overhead Cost for the Standard Stanchions**					
3	*Activity Cost Pools*	*(a) Activity Rate**		*(b) Activity***		*(a) × (b) ABC Cost*
4	Customer orders	$315	per order	2	orders	$630
5	Product design	$1,285	per design	0	designs	$0
6	Order size	$19	per MH	200	MHs	$3,800
7	Customer relations	$3,675	per customer	Not applicable		
10	**Overhead Cost for the Custom Compass Housing**					
12	*Activity Cost Pools*	*(a) Activity Rate**		*(b) Activity***		*(a) × (b) ABC Cost*
13	Customer orders	$315	per order	1	order	$315
14	Product design	$1,285	per design	1	design	$1,285
15	Order size	$19	per MH	4	MHs	$76
16	Customer relations	$3,675	per customer	Not applicable		
18	*From Exhibit 8-5.					
19	**From Exhibit 8-7.					

Exhibit 8-3 / Exhibit 8-4 / Exhibit 8-5 / Exhibit 8-8

Ready

Step 6: Prepare Management Reports

LEARNING OBJECTIVE 5
Prepare a report showing activity-based costing margins from an activity view.

In Exhibit 8–9, the overhead costs computed in Exhibit 8–8 are combined with direct materials, direct labor, and shipping cost data. For each of the products, these combined costs are deducted from sales to arrive at product margins. Under the ABC system, the stanchions show a profit of $5,030, whereas the compass housing shows a loss of $1,114.

Note from Exhibit 8–9 that the new ABC system also includes a profitability analysis of Windward Yachts, the customer that ordered the stanchions and the custom compass

Exhibit 8–9 Product and Customer Margins—Activity-Based Costing System (Activity View)

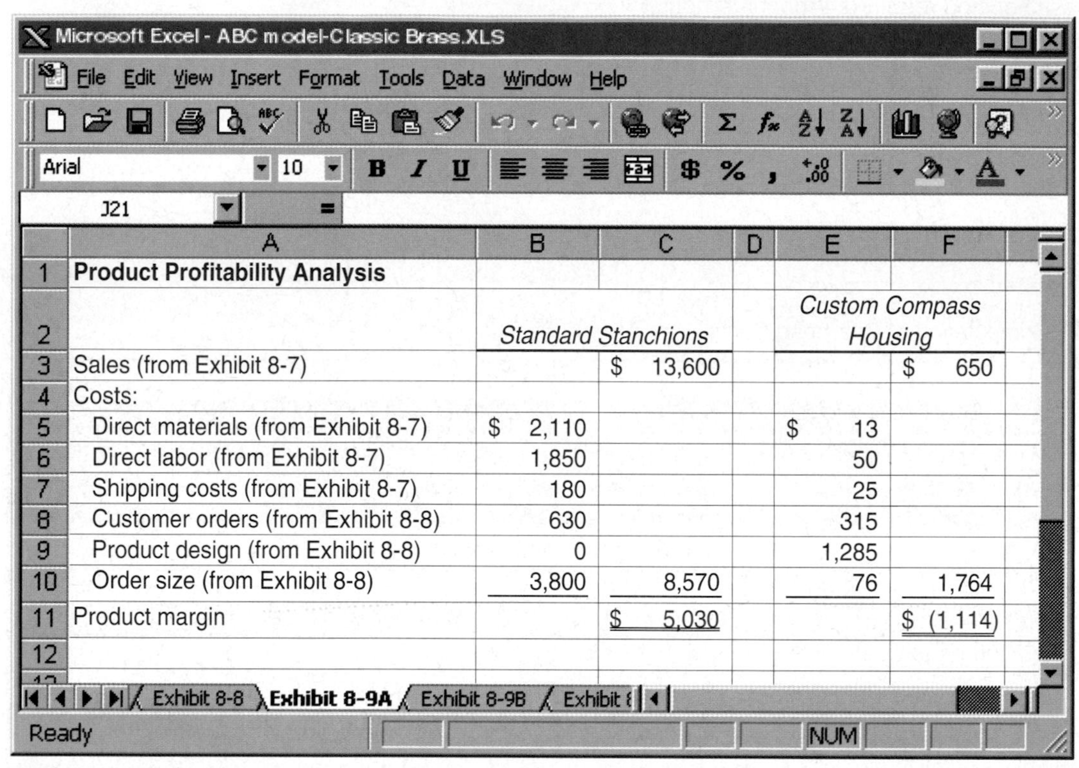

Product Profitability Analysis		Standard Stanchions		Custom Compass Housing
Sales (from Exhibit 8-7)		$ 13,600		$ 650
Costs:				
Direct materials (from Exhibit 8-7)	$ 2,110		$ 13	
Direct labor (from Exhibit 8-7)	1,850		50	
Shipping costs (from Exhibit 8-7)	180		25	
Customer orders (from Exhibit 8-8)	630		315	
Product design (from Exhibit 8-8)	0		1,285	
Order size (from Exhibit 8-8)	3,800	8,570	76	1,764
Product margin		$ 5,030		$ (1,114)

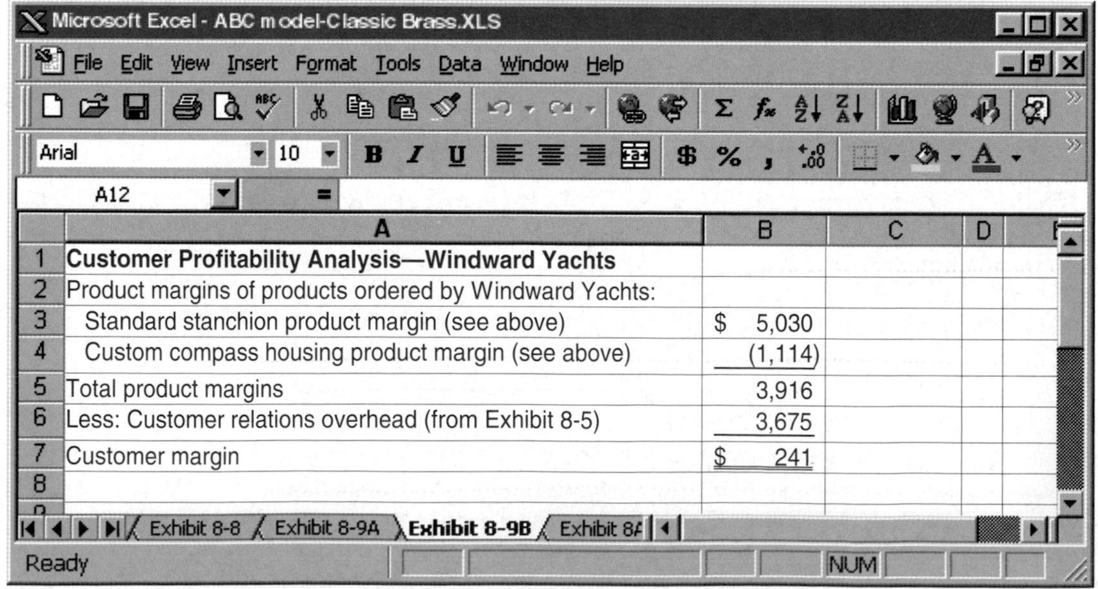

Customer Profitability Analysis—Windward Yachts	
Product margins of products ordered by Windward Yachts:	
Standard stanchion product margin (see above)	$ 5,030
Custom compass housing product margin (see above)	(1,114)
Total product margins	3,916
Less: Customer relations overhead (from Exhibit 8-5)	3,675
Customer margin	$ 241

housing. Such customer analyses can be easily accomplished by adding together the product margins for each of the products a customer has ordered and then subtracting the average charge of $3,675 for Customer Relations.

ABC at the Bank

In Business

First Tennessee National Corporation, a regional bank holding company, used activity-based costing to analyze the profitability of its certificates of deposit (CDs). The bank found that 30% of its CD customers were responsible for 88% of the overall profit generated from CDs, while another 30% of its customers were losing the bank money. "This situation was corrected through a combination of higher minimum balances, new products, and process redesign."

Source: Robert B. Sweeney and James W. Mays, "ABM," *Management Accounting*, March 1997, pp. 20–26.

Comparison of Traditional and ABC Product Costs

Now that the product margins have been computed using activity-based costing, it would be interesting to compare them to the product margins computed using the company's traditional cost system.

Product Margins Computed Using the Traditional Cost System

The costs of the two products ordered by Windward Yachts are computed under the company's traditional cost accounting system in Exhibit 8–10. The company's traditional system uses a plantwide predetermined overhead rate based on machine-hours. Since the total manufacturing overhead cost is $1,000,000 (see Exhibit 8–2) and the total machine time is 20,000 machine-hours (see Exhibit 8–5), the predetermined manufacturing overhead rate for the company is $50 per machine-hour ($1,000,000 ÷ 20,000 machine-hours = $50 per machine-hour). From Exhibit 8–10, we see that when this predetermined manufacturing overhead rate is used to determine product costs, the stanchions show a loss of $360, whereas the compass housing shows a profit of $387.

The Differences between ABC and Traditional Product Costs

The costs of the products under the new ABC system are dramatically different from the costs computed using the old traditional costing system. The stanchions, which looked unprofitable under the traditional cost system, appear to be very profitable under the ABC system in Exhibit 8–9. And the compass housing, which looked profitable under the old cost system, appears to be unprofitable under the new costing system.

There are two major reasons for these changes in apparent profitability. First, under the old cost system the costs of designing products were spread across all products without regard to whether they actually required design work. Under the new ABC system, these costs are assigned only to products that actually require design work. Consequently, under the ABC system, design costs have been shifted from standard products like stanchions, which do not require any design work, to custom products like the compass housing.

Second, the Customer Orders costs, which are batch-level costs, were applied on the basis of machine-hours, a unit-level base, under the old cost system. Therefore, under the old cost system, high-volume products absorbed the bulk of these batch-level costs even

Exhibit 8–10
Product Margins—Traditional Cost Accounting System

	Standard Stanchions		Custom Compass Housing	
Sales (from Exhibit 8–7)		$13,600		$650
Cost:				
Direct materials (from Exhibit 8–7)	$ 2,110		$ 13	
Direct labor (from Exhibit 8–7)	1,850		50	
Manufacturing overhead (see below)	10,000	13,960	200	263
Product margin*		$ (360)		$387

In the traditional costing system used at Classic Brass, manufacturing overhead is applied based on machine-hours. The predetermined rate is $50 per machine-hour, determined as follows:

$$\text{Predetermined manufacturing overhead rate} = \frac{\text{Total estimated manufacturing overhead}}{\text{Total estimated machine-hours}}$$

$$= \frac{\$1{,}000{,}000}{20{,}000 \text{ machine-hours}} = \$50 \text{ per machine-hour}$$

Referring back to Exhibit 8–7, the standard stanchions require 200 machine-hours in total and the custom compass housing requires 4 machine-hours. Therefore, $10,000 (200 machine-hours × $50 per machine-hour) of manufacturing overhead would be charged to the standard stanchions and $200 (4 machine-hours × $50 per machine-hour) to the custom compass housing.

*In a traditional costing system, the product margins do not include any nonmanufacturing costs such as shipping costs.

though they caused no more of these costs than low-volume products that are ordered as frequently. Under the new cost system, these batch-level costs are assigned as a lump-sum to each customer order. Consequently, the new cost system shifts these costs from high-volume orders like the stanchions to low-volume orders like the compass housing.

When there are batch-level or product-level costs, activity-based costing will ordinarily shift costs from high-volume products produced in large batches to low-volume products produced in small batches. This cost shifting will usually have a greater impact on the *per unit* costs of low-volume products than on the per unit costs of high-volume products. For example, suppose that a total of $100 in batch-level cost is shifted from a high-volume, 100-unit product to a low-volume, 1-unit product. This shifting of cost will decrease the cost of the high-volume product by $1 per unit, on average, but will increase the cost of the low-volume product by $100 for the single unit. In sum, implementing activity-based costing will typically shift costs from high-volume to low-volume products, but the effects will be much more dramatic on the per unit costs of the low-volume products. The per unit costs of the low-volume products will increase far more than the per unit costs of the high-volume products will decrease.

It is important to remember another major difference between the costs of products as computed under the new ABC system at Classic Brass and product costs as computed under the old traditional cost system. Under a traditional system, only manufacturing costs are assigned to products. Under the new ABC system at Classic Brass, nonmanufacturing costs are assigned to products as well as the manufacturing costs. In addition, the organization-sustaining manufacturing costs and the costs of idle capacity are *not* assigned to products under the ABC system, whereas they *are* assigned to products under the old traditional costing system. For these reasons, the term *product cost* in this chapter has a different meaning than it had in Chapters 2, 3, and 4. In the context of an ABC system like the one implemented at Classic Brass, product costs include the costs of *all* resources consumed by the product, whether they are manufacturing costs or not.

Costing Can Be a Grim Business

In Business

S

The Hospice of Central Kentucky (HCK) provides all medical needs to terminally ill patients, including nursing care, medical equipment, medications, and palliative treatments so that patients can be at home with their families during their last days. HCK was being squeezed by increasing costs, without any compensating increases in reimbursements from insurance companies. As the first step in negotiating a better reimbursement plan, management decided to use ABC to get a better understanding of its costs. The following activity rates were computed:

Activity Cost Pool	Total Cost	Total Activity	Activity Rate
Prereferral	$ 24,611	74 referrals*	$332.58 per referral
Referral	10,873	74 referrals*	$146.93 per referral
Admission	1,960	46 admissions	$42.61 per admission
Post-admission	3,649	46 admissions	$79.33 per admission
Post-death	1,476	46 deaths	$32.09 per death
Bereavement	12,670	46 deaths	$275.43 per death
Medical services	5,588	2,080 service calls	$2.69 per service call
Reception	8,597	3,200 calls	$2.69 per call
Accounting/finance	13,566	5,553 patient-days*	$2.44 per patient-day
Management	17,107	5,553 patient-days*	$3.08 per patient-day
Information systems	6,191	5,553 patient-days*	$1.11 per patient-day
Billing	2,899	192 billings	$15.10 per billing
Volunteer services	3,378	75 volunteers	$45.04 per volunteer
Total	$112,565		

*Referrals and patient-days are weighted by the stage of the disease. For example, the actual number of patient-days is 3,593, but a day for a patient whose death is imminent is counted as equivalent to three patient-days for a patient in slow decline due to the more intensive care such patients receive.

The ABC system was then used to estimate the average cost per patient-day for patients in various stages of their diseases:

Stage of Disease	Cost per Patient-Day
Slow decline	$27.39
Rapid decline	$29.84
Imminent death	$62.88
Death	$381.57

This was a definite eye-opener for the hospice's management. The hospice's old cost system did not distinguish between costs at various stages of a disease and indeed would have given an answer of a flat $31.33 per patient-day ($112,565 ÷ 3,593 unweighted patient-days), regardless of the stage of the disease. This new information helped management to negotiate more favorable reimbursement rates from insurance companies.

Source: Sidney J. Baxendale and Victoria Dornbusch, "Activity-Based Costing for a Hospice," *Strategic Finance*, March 2000, pp. 65–70. Reprinted with permission from the IMA, Montvale, NJ, USA, www.imanet.org.

Managerial Accounting in Action

The Wrap-Up

The ABC design team presented the results of its work in a meeting attended by all of the top managers of Classic Brass, including the president John Towers, the production manager Susan Richter, the marketing manager Tom Olafson, and the accounting manager Mary Goodman. The ABC team brought with them to the meeting copies of the chart showing the ABC design (Exhibit 8–6), the tables showing the product margins for the

stanchions and compass housing under the company's old cost accounting system (Exhibit 8–10), and the tables showing the ABC analysis of the same products (Exhibit 8–9). After the formal presentation by the ABC team, the following discussion took place:

John: I would like to personally thank the ABC team for all of the work they have done and for an extremely interesting presentation. I am now beginning to wonder about a lot of the decisions we have made in the past using our old cost accounting system.

Mary: I hope I don't have to remind anyone that I have been warning everyone for quite some time about this problem.

John: No, you don't have to remind us, Mary. I guess we just didn't understand the problem before.

John: Tom, why did we accept this order for standard stanchions in the first place if our old cost accounting system was telling us it was a big money loser?

Tom: Windward Yachts, the company that ordered the stanchions, has asked us to do a lot of custom work like the compass housing in the past. To get that work, we felt we had to accept their orders for money-losing standard products.

John: According to this ABC analysis, we had it all backwards. We are losing money on the custom products and making a fistful on the standard products.

Susan: I never did believe we were making a lot of money on the custom jobs. You ought to see all of the problems they create for us in production.

Tom: I hate to admit it, but the custom jobs always seem to give us headaches in marketing, too.

John: Why don't we just stop soliciting custom work? This seems like a no-brainer to me. If we are losing money on custom jobs like the compass housing, why not suggest to our customers that they go elsewhere for that kind of work?

Tom: Wait a minute, we would lose a lot of sales.

Susan: So what, we would save a lot more costs.

Mary: Maybe yes, maybe no. Some of the costs would not disappear if we were to drop all of those products.

Tom: Like what?

Mary: Well Tom, part of your salary is included in the costs of the ABC model.

Tom: Where? I don't see anything listed that looks like my salary.

Mary: Tom, when the ABC team interviewed you they asked you what percentage of your time was spent in handling customer orders and how much was spent dealing with new product design issues. Am I correct?

Tom: Sure, but what's the point?

Mary: I believe you said that about 10% of your time is spent dealing with new products. As a consequence, 10% of your salary was allocated to the Product Design cost pool. If we were to drop all of the products requiring design work, would you be willing to take a 10% pay cut?

Tom: I trust you're joking.

Mary: Do you see the problem? Just because 10% of your time is spent on custom products doesn't mean that the company would save 10% of your salary if the custom products were dropped. Before we take a drastic action like dropping the custom products, we should identify which costs are really relevant.

John: I think I see what you are driving at. We wouldn't want to drop a lot of products just to find that our costs really haven't changed much. It is true that dropping the products would free up resources like Tom's time, but we had better be sure we have some good use for those resources *before* we take such an action.

As this discussion among the managers of Classic Brass illustrates, caution should be exercised before taking an action based on an ABC analysis such as the one in Exhibit 8–9. The product and customer margins computed in that exhibit are a useful starting point for further analysis, but managers need to know what costs are really affected before taking any action such as dropping a product or customer or changing the prices of products or services. The appendix to this chapter shows how an *action analysis report* can be constructed to help managers make such decisions. An **action analysis report** provides more detail about costs and how they might adjust to changes in activity than the ABC analysis presented in Exhibit 8–9.

Culling the Customer List

In Business

FedEx is now classifying its customers as the good, the bad, and the ugly based on their profitability. "At FedEx, customers who spend a lot with little service and marketing investment get different treatment than, say, those who spend just as much but cost more to keep. The 'good' can expect a phone call if their shipping volume falters, which can head off defections before they occur. As for the 'bad'—those who spend but are expensive to the company—FedEx is turning them into profitable customers, in many cases, by charging higher shipping prices. And the 'ugly'? . . . 'We just don't market to them anymore.'"

Source: Paul C. Judge, "What've You Done for Us Lately?" *Business Week*, September 14, 1998, pp. 137–146.

Targeting Process Improvements

Activity-based costing can be used to identify areas that would benefit from process improvements. Indeed, managers often cite this as the major benefit of activity-based costing.[4] **Activity-based management (ABM)** is used in conjunction with activity-based costing to improve processes and reduce costs. Activity-based management is used in organizations as diverse as manufacturing companies, hospitals, and the U.S. Marine Corps.[5] When "forty percent of the cost of running a hospital involves storing, collecting and moving information," there is obviously a great deal of room for eliminating waste and for improvement.[6]

The first step in any improvement program is to decide what to improve. The theory of constraints approach discussed in Chapter 1 is a powerful tool for targeting the area in an organization whose improvement will yield the greatest benefit. Activity-based management provides another approach. The activity rates computed in activity-based costing can provide valuable clues concerning where there is waste and scope for improvement in an organization. For example, managers at Classic Brass were surprised at the high cost of customer orders. Some customer orders are for less than $100 worth of products, and yet it costs, on average, $315 to process an order according to the activity rates calculated in Exhibit 8–5. This seemed like an awful lot of money for an activity that adds no value to the product. As a consequence, the customer order processing activity was targeted for improvement using TQM and process reengineering as discussed in Chapter 1.

Benchmarking provides a systematic approach to identifying the activities with the greatest room for improvement. For example, the Marketing Resources Group of US WEST, the telephone company, performed an ABC analysis of the activities carried out in the Accounting Department.[7] Managers computed the activity rates for the activities of the Accounting Department and then compared these rates to the costs of carrying out the same activities in other companies. Two benchmarks were used: (1) a sample of FORTUNE 100 companies, which are the largest 100 companies in the United States; and (2) a sample of "world-class" companies that had been identified by a consultant as having the best accounting practices in the world. These comparisons appear on the next page:

---

[4] Dan Swenson, "The Benefits of Activity-Based Cost Management to the Manufacturing Industry," *Journal of Management Accounting Research* 7 (Fall 1995), pp. 168–180.

[5] Julian Freeman, "Marines Embrace Continuous Improvement: Highlight of CAM-I's Meeting," *Management Accounting*, February 1997, p. 64.

[6] Kambiz Foroohar, "Rx: Software," *Forbes*, April 7, 1997, p. 114.

[7] Steve Coburn, Hugh Grove, and Cynthia Fukami, "Benchmarking with ABCM," *Management Accounting*, January 1995, pp. 56–60.

Activity	Activity Measure	US WEST Cost	FORTUNE 100 Benchmark	World-Class Benchmark
Processing accounts receivable	Number of invoices processed	$3.80 per invoice	$15.00 per invoice	$4.60 per invoice
Processing accounts payable	Number of invoices processed	$8.90 per invoice	$7.00 per invoice	$1.80 per invoice
Processing payroll checks	Number of checks processed	$7.30 per check	$5.00 per check	$1.72 per check
Managing customer credit	Number of customer accounts	$12.00 per account	$16.00 per account	$5.60 per account

It is clear from this analysis that US WEST does a good job of processing accounts receivable. Its average cost per invoice is $3.80, whereas the cost in other companies that are considered world class is even higher—$4.60 per invoice. On the other hand, the cost of processing payroll checks is significantly higher at US WEST than at benchmark companies. The cost per payroll check at US WEST is $7.30 versus $5.00 at FORTUNE 100 companies and $1.72 at world-class companies. This suggests that it may be possible to wring some waste out of this activity using TQM, process reengineering, or some other method.

In Business

Disciplining the Software Development Process

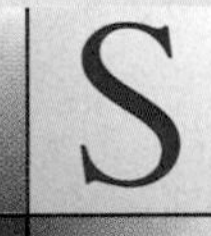

Tata Consultancy Services (TCS) of India is the largest consulting organization in India, serving both Indian and international clients. The company used activity-based management to identify problem areas in its software development business. An early finding was that "quality assurance, testing, and error correction activities made up a significant chunk of the overall effort required to build a system, and this cost had to be kept under control to improve productivity and profitability." The company already had in place a Quality Management System that helped identify the types of errors that were occurring and the corrective action that would be required, but no costs were attached to these errors and actions. The activity-based management system provided this cost information, which allowed managers to set better priorities and to monitor the costs of error-detection and error-correction activities.

As another example of the usefulness of the system, 54 person-days in one software development project at TCS were charged to the activity "Waiting for client feedback"—a non-value-added activity. Investigation revealed that the client was taking a long time to review the Graphical User Interface (GUI) designed by TCS. The client was showing the GUI to various end users—often resulting in contradictory suggestions. The solution was to draw up guidelines for the GUI with the client, which were enforced. "As a result of this corrective action, subsequent client feedback was well within the time schedule. Most of our screens were accepted because they conformed to standards . . . ."

Source: Maha S. Mahalingam, Bala V. Balachandran, and Farooq C. Kohli, "Activity-Based Management for Systems Consulting Industry," *Journal of Cost Management*, May/June 1999, pp. 4–15.

Activity-Based Costing and External Reports

Since activity-based costing generally provides more accurate product costs than traditional costing methods, why isn't it used for external reports? Some companies *do* use activity-based costing in their external reports, but most do not. There are a number of reasons for this. First, external reports are less detailed than internal reports prepared for decision making. On the external reports, individual product costs are not reported. Cost of goods sold and inventory valuations are disclosed, but there is no breakdown of these accounts by product. If some products are undercosted and some are overcosted, the errors tend to cancel each other when the product costs are added together.

Second, it is often very difficult to make changes in a company's accounting system. The official cost accounting systems in most large companies are usually embedded in complex computer programs that have been modified in-house over the course of many years. It is extremely difficult to make changes in such computer programs without causing numerous bugs.

Third, an ABC system such as the one described in this chapter does not conform to generally accepted accounting principles (GAAP). As discussed in Chapter 2, product costs computed for external reports must include all of the manufacturing costs and only manufacturing costs; but in an ABC system as described in this chapter, product costs exclude some manufacturing costs and include some nonmanufacturing costs. It is possible to adjust the ABC data at the end of the period to conform to GAAP, but that requires more work.

Fourth, auditors are likely to be uncomfortable with allocations that are based on interviews with the company's personnel. Such subjective data can be easily manipulated by management to make earnings and other key variables look more favorable.

For all of these reasons, most companies confine their ABC efforts to special studies for management, and they do not attempt to integrate activity-based costing into their formal cost accounting systems.

The Limitations of Activity-Based Costing

Implementing an activity-based costing system is a major project that requires substantial resources. And once implemented, an activity-based costing system is more costly to maintain than a traditional direct labor-based costing system—data concerning numerous activity measures must be collected, checked, and entered into the system. The benefits of increased accuracy may not outweigh these costs.

Activity-based costing produces numbers, such as product margins, that are at odds with the numbers produced by traditional costing systems. But managers are accustomed to using traditional costing systems to run their operations and traditional costing systems are often used in performance evaluations. Essentially, activity-based costing changes the rules of the game. It is a fact of human nature that changes in organizations, particularly those that alter the rules of the game, inevitably face resistance. This underscores the importance of top management support and the full participation of line managers, as well as the accounting staff, in any activity-based costing initiative. If activity-based costing is viewed as an accounting initiative that does not have the full support of top management, it is doomed to failure.

In practice, most managers insist on fully allocating all costs to products, customers, and other costing objects in an activity-based costing system—including the costs of idle capacity and organization-sustaining costs. This results in overstated costs and understated margins and mistakes in pricing and other critical decisions.

Activity-based costing data can easily be misinterpreted and must be used with care when used in making decisions. Costs assigned to products, customers, and other cost objects are only *potentially* relevant. Before making any significant decisions using activity-based costing data, managers must identify which costs are really relevant for the decision at hand. See the appendix to this chapter for more details.

As discussed in the previous section, reports generated by the best activity-based costing systems do not conform to generally accepted accounting principles. Consequently, an organization involved in activity-based costing should have two cost systems—one for internal use and one for preparing external reports. This is costlier than maintaining just one system and may cause confusion about which system is to be believed and relied on.

In Business

Sometimes ABC Isn't the Best Solution

Bertch Cabinet Mfg., Inc., makes high-quality wooden cabinets, marble tops, and mirrors for bathrooms and kitchens. The company experimented with activity-based costing (ABC) but found that it was too difficult to set up and maintain such a complex costing system. For example, 21 separate operations are required to make a single raised panel cabinet door. The costs of keeping track of each of these operations would far exceed any conceivable benefit. Instead of building a complex ABC system, Bertch Cabinet adopted a variation of variable costing used in the Theory of Constraints. This simpler system required far less effort to build and maintain, and it was much easier to understand. In the Bertch Cabinet Mfg. variable costing system, 70% of the direct labor cost was classified as variable and the rest as fixed.

Source: John B. MacArthur, "From Activity-Based Costing to Throughput Accounting," *Management Accounting,* April 1996, pp. 30–38.

Summary

Traditional cost accounting methods suffer from several defects that can result in distorted costs for decision-making purposes. All manufacturing costs—even those that are not caused by any specific product—are allocated to products. And nonmanufacturing costs that are caused by products are not assigned to products. Traditional methods also allocate the costs of idle capacity to products. In effect, products are charged for resources that they don't use. And finally, traditional methods tend to place too much reliance on unit-level allocation bases such as direct labor and machine-hours. This results in overcosting high-volume products and undercosting low-volume products and can lead to mistakes when making decisions.

Activity-based costing estimates the costs of the resources consumed by cost objects such as products and customers. The approach taken in activity-based costing assumes that cost objects generate activities that in turn consume costly resources. Activities form the link between costs and cost objects. Activity-based costing is concerned with overhead—both manufacturing overhead and selling, general, and administrative overhead. The accounting for direct labor and direct material is usually unaffected.

To build an ABC system, companies typically choose a small set of activities that summarize much of the work performed in overhead departments. Associated with each activity is an activity cost pool. To the extent possible, overhead costs are directly traced to these activity cost pools. The remaining overhead costs are assigned to the activity cost pools in the first-stage allocation. Interviews with managers often form the basis for these allocations.

An activity rate is computed for each cost pool by dividing the costs assigned to the cost pool by the measure of activity for the cost pool. Activity rates provide useful information to managers concerning the costs of carrying out overhead activities. A particularly high cost for an activity may trigger efforts to improve the way the activity is carried out in the organization.

In the second-stage allocation, the activity rates are used to apply costs to cost objects such as products and customers. The costs computed under activity-based costing are often quite different from the costs generated by a company's traditional cost accounting system. While the ABC system is almost certainly more accurate, managers should nevertheless exercise caution before making decisions based on the ABC data. Some of the costs may not be avoidable and hence would not be relevant.

Review Problem: Activity-Based Costing

Ferris Corporation makes a single product—a fire-resistant commercial filing cabinet—that it sells to office furniture distributors. The company has a simple ABC system that it uses for internal decision making. The company has two overhead departments whose costs are listed on the next page:

Manufacturing overhead	$500,000
Selling and administrative overhead	300,000
Total overhead costs	$800,000

The company's ABC system has the following activity cost pools and activity measures:

Activity Cost Pool	Activity Measure
Assembling units	Number of units
Processing orders	Number of orders
Supporting customers	Number of customers
Other	Not applicable

Costs assigned to the "Other" activity cost pool have no activity measure; they consist of the costs of unused capacity and organization-sustaining costs—neither of which are assigned to products, orders, or customers.

Ferris Corporation distributes the costs of manufacturing overhead and of selling and administrative overhead to the activity cost pools based on employee interviews, the results of which are reported below:

Distribution of Resource Consumption Across Activity Cost Pools

	Assembling Units	Processing Orders	Supporting Customers	Other	Total
Manufacturing overhead	50%	35%	5%	10%	100%
Selling and administrative overhead	10%	45%	25%	20%	100%
Total activity	1,000 units	250 orders	100 customers		

Required:

1. Perform the first-stage allocation of overhead costs to the activity cost pools as in Exhibit 8–4.
2. Compute activity rates for the activity cost pools as in Exhibit 8–5.
3. OfficeMart is one of Ferris Corporation's customers. Last year, OfficeMart ordered filing cabinets four different times. OfficeMart ordered a total of 80 filing cabinets during the year. Construct a table as in Exhibit 8–8 showing the overhead costs of these 80 units and four orders.
4. The selling price of a filing cabinet is $595. The cost of direct materials is $180 per filing cabinet, and direct labor is $50 per filing cabinet. What is the product margin on the 80 filing cabinets ordered by OfficeMart? How profitable is OfficeMart as a customer? See Exhibit 8–9 for an example of how to complete this report.

Solution to Review Problem

1. The first-stage allocation of costs to the activity cost pools appears below:

	Activity Cost Pools				
	Assembling Units	Processing Orders	Supporting Customers	Other	Total
Manufacturing overhead	$250,000	$175,000	$ 25,000	$ 50,000	$500,000
Selling and administrative overhead	30,000	135,000	75,000	60,000	300,000
Total cost	$280,000	$310,000	$100,000	$110,000	$800,000

2. The activity rates for the activity cost pools are:

Activity Cost Pools	(a) Total Cost	(b) Total Activity	(a) ÷ (b) Activity Rate
Assembling units	$280,000	1,000 units	$280 per unit
Processing orders	$310,000	250 orders	$1,240 per order
Supporting customers	$100,000	100 customers	$1,000 per customer

3. The overhead cost for the four orders of a total of 80 filing cabinets would be computed as follows:

Activity Cost Pools	(a) Activity Rate	(b) Activity	(a) × (b) ABC Cost
Assembling units	$280 per unit	80 units	$22,400
Processing orders	$1,240 per order	4 orders	$4,960
Supporting customers	$1,000 per customer	Not applicable	

4. The product and customer margins can be computed as follows:

Filing Cabinet Product Margin		
Sales ($595 per unit × 80 units)		$47,600
Cost:		
Direct materials ($180 per unit × 80 units).	$14,400	
Direct labor ($50 per unit × 80 units)	4,000	
Volume-related overhead (above)	22,400	
Order-related overhead (above)	4,960	45,760
Product margin.		$ 1,840

Customer Profitability Analysis—OfficeMart	
Product margin (above)	$ 1,840
Less: Customer support overhead (above)	1,000
Customer margin	$ 840

Glossary

Action analysis report A report showing what costs have been assigned to a cost object, such as a product or customer, and how difficult it would be to adjust the cost if there is a change in activity. (p. 336)

Activity An event that causes the consumption of overhead resources in an organization. (p. 319)

Activity-based costing (ABC) A costing method based on activities that is designed to provide managers with cost information for strategic and other decisions that potentially affect capacity and therefore fixed costs. (p. 316)

Activity-based management (ABM) A management approach that focuses on managing activities as a way of eliminating waste and reducing delays and defects. (p. 337)

Activity cost pool A "bucket" in which costs are accumulated that relate to a single activity measure in the activity-based costing system. (p. 324)

Activity measure An allocation base in an activity-based costing system; ideally, a measure of the amount of activity that drives the costs in an activity cost pool. (p. 324)

Batch-level activities Activities that are performed each time a batch of goods is handled or processed, regardless of how many units are in a batch. The amount of resource consumed depends on the number of batches run rather than on the number of units in the batch. (p. 323)

Customer-level activities Activities that are carried out to support customers but that are not related to any specific product. (p. 324)

Duration driver A measure of the amount of time required to perform an activity. (p. 324)

First-stage allocation The process by which overhead costs are assigned to activity cost pools in an activity-based costing system. (p. 326)

Organization-sustaining activities Activities that are carried out regardless of which customers are served, which products are produced, how many batches are run, or how many units are made. (p. 324)

Product-level activities Activities that relate to specific products that must be carried out regardless of how many units are produced and sold or batches run. (p. 323)

Second-stage allocation The process by which activity rates are used to apply costs to products and customers in activity-based costing. (p. 330)

Transaction driver A simple count of the number of times an activity occurs. (p. 324)

Unit-level activities Activities that arise as a result of the total volume of goods and services that are produced and that are performed each time a unit is produced. (p. 323)

Appendix 8A: ABC Action Analysis

LEARNING OBJECTIVE 6
Prepare an action analysis report using activity-based costing data and interpret the report.

A conventional ABC analysis, such as the one presented in Exhibit 8–9 in the chapter, has several important limitations. Referring back to that exhibit, recall that the custom compass housing shows a negative product margin of $1,114. Because of this apparent loss, managers were considering dropping this product. However, as the discussion among the managers revealed, it is unlikely that all of the $1,764 cost of the product would be avoided if the product were dropped. Some of these costs would continue even if the product were totally eliminated. *Before* taking action, it is vital to identify which costs would be avoided and which costs would continue. Only those costs that can be avoided are relevant in the decision. Moreover, many of the costs are managed costs that would require explicit management action to eliminate. If the custom compass housing product were eliminated, the direct materials cost would be avoided without any explicit management action—the materials simply wouldn't be ordered. On the other hand, if the custom compass housing product were dropped, explicit management action would be required to eliminate the salaries of overhead workers that have been assigned to the product.

Simply shifting these managed costs to other products would not solve anything. These costs would have to be eliminated or the resources *shifted to the constraint* to have any benefit to the company. Eliminating the cost is obviously beneficial. Redeploying the resource is only beneficial if the resource is shifted to the constraint in the process. If the resource is redeployed to a work center that is not a constraint, it would have the effect of increasing the excess capacity in that work center—which has no direct benefit to the company.

In addition, if some overhead costs need to be eliminated as a result of dropping a product, specific managers must be held responsible for eliminating those costs or the reductions are unlikely to occur. If no one is specifically held responsible for eliminating the costs, they will almost certainly continue to be incurred. Without external pressure, managers usually avoid cutting costs in their areas of responsibility. The action analysis report developed in this appendix is intended to help top managers identify what costs are relevant in a decision and to place responsibility for the elimination of the costs on the appropriate managers.

Activity Rates—Action Analysis Report

Constructing an action analysis report begins with the results of the first-stage allocation, which is reproduced as Exhibit 8A–1. In contrast to the conventional ABC analysis covered in the chapter, the calculation of the activity rates for an action analysis report is a bit more involved. In addition to computing an overall activity rate for each activity cost pool, an activity rate is computed for each cell in Exhibit 8A–1. The computations of activity rates for the action analysis are carried out in Exhibit 8A–2. For example, the $125,000 cost of indirect factory wages for the Customer Orders cost pool is divided by the total activity for that cost pool—1,000 orders—to arrive at the activity rate of $125 per customer order for indirect factory wages. Similarly, the $200,000 cost of indirect factory wages for the Product Design cost pool is divided by the total activity for that cost pool—200 designs—to arrive at the activity rate of $1,000 per design for indirect factory wages. Note that the totals at the bottom of Exhibit 8A–2 agree with the overall activity rates in Exhibit 8–5 in the chapter. Exhibit 8A–2, which shows the activity rates for the action analysis report, contains more detail than Exhibit 8–5, which contains the activity rates for the conventional ABC analysis.

Assignment of Overhead Costs to Products—Action Analysis Report

Similarly, computing the overhead costs to be assigned to products for an action analysis report involves more detail than for a conventional ABC analysis. The computations for Classic Brass are carried out in Exhibit 8A–3. For example, the activity rate of $125 per

Exhibit 8A–1 First-Stage Allocations to Activity Cost Pools

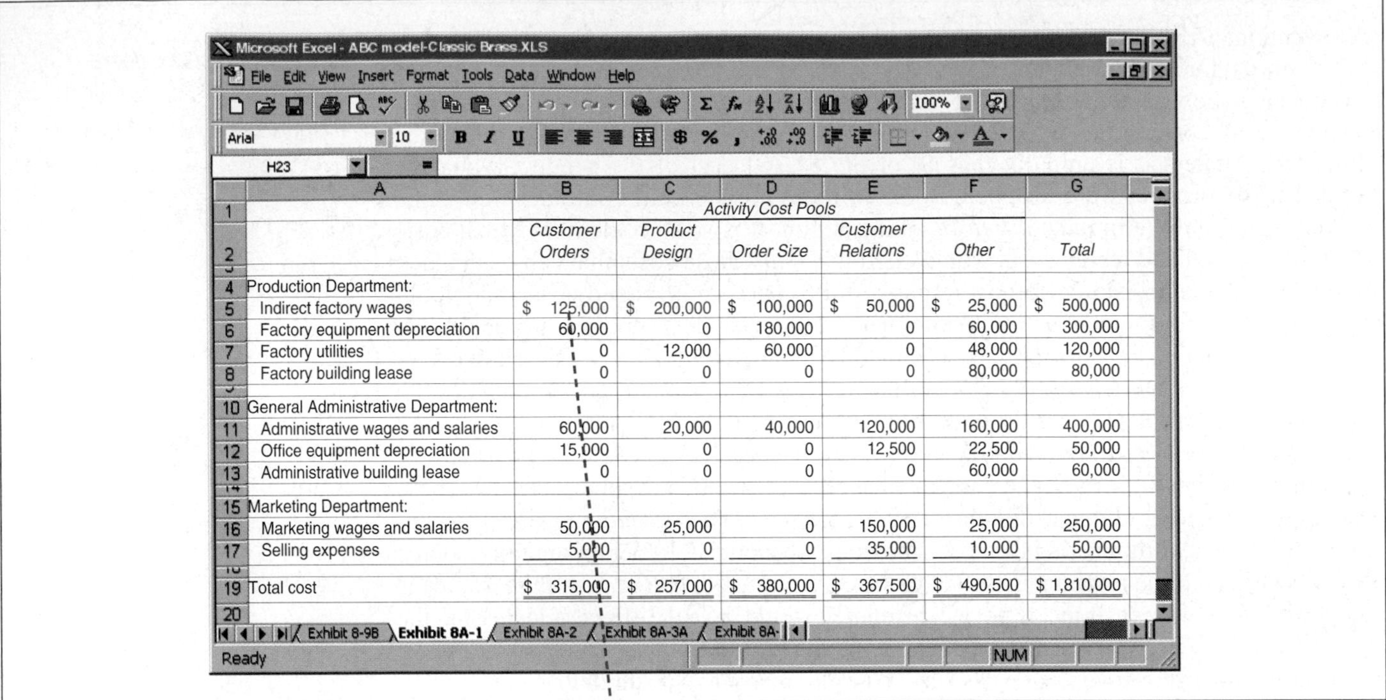

	Activity Cost Pools					
	Customer Orders	Product Design	Order Size	Customer Relations	Other	Total
Production Department:						
Indirect factory wages	$ 125,000	$ 200,000	$ 100,000	$ 50,000	$ 25,000	$ 500,000
Factory equipment depreciation	60,000	0	180,000	0	60,000	300,000
Factory utilities	0	12,000	60,000	0	48,000	120,000
Factory building lease	0	0	0	0	80,000	80,000
General Administrative Department:						
Administrative wages and salaries	60,000	20,000	40,000	120,000	160,000	400,000
Office equipment depreciation	15,000	0	0	12,500	22,500	50,000
Administrative building lease	0	0	0	0	60,000	60,000
Marketing Department:						
Marketing wages and salaries	50,000	25,000	0	150,000	25,000	250,000
Selling expenses	5,000	0	0	35,000	10,000	50,000
Total cost	$ 315,000	$ 257,000	$ 380,000	$ 367,500	$ 490,500	$ 1,810,000

Exhibit 8A–2 Computation of the Activity Rates for the Action Analysis Report

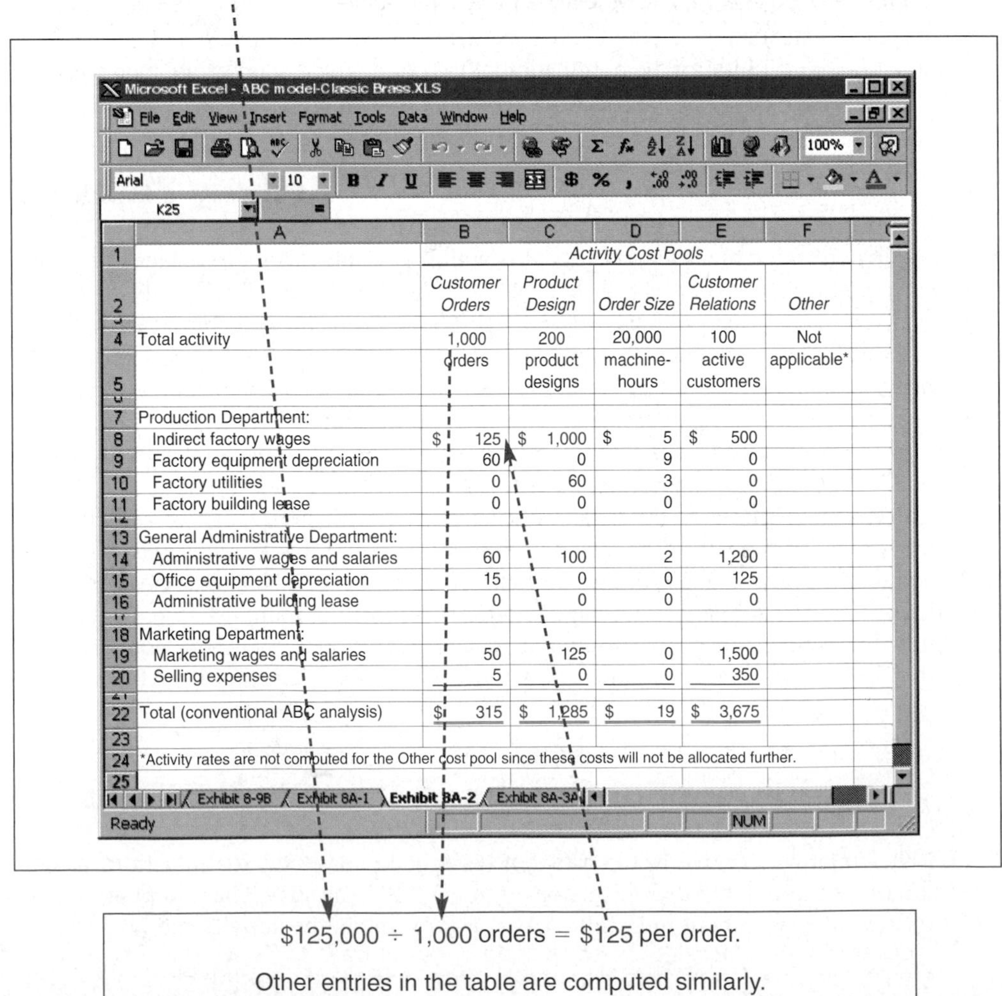

	Activity Cost Pools				
	Customer Orders	Product Design	Order Size	Customer Relations	Other
Total activity	1,000 orders	200 product designs	20,000 machine-hours	100 active customers	Not applicable*
Production Department:					
Indirect factory wages	$ 125	$ 1,000	$ 5	$ 500	
Factory equipment depreciation	60	0	9	0	
Factory utilities	0	60	3	0	
Factory building lease	0	0	0	0	
General Administrative Department:					
Administrative wages and salaries	60	100	2	1,200	
Office equipment depreciation	15	0	0	125	
Administrative building lease	0	0	0	0	
Marketing Department:					
Marketing wages and salaries	50	125	0	1,500	
Selling expenses	5	0	0	350	
Total (conventional ABC analysis)	$ 315	$ 1,285	$ 19	$ 3,675	

*Activity rates are not computed for the Other cost pool since these costs will not be allocated further.

$125,000 ÷ 1,000 orders = $125 per order.

Other entries in the table are computed similarly.

Exhibit 8A–3

Action Analysis Cost Matrices

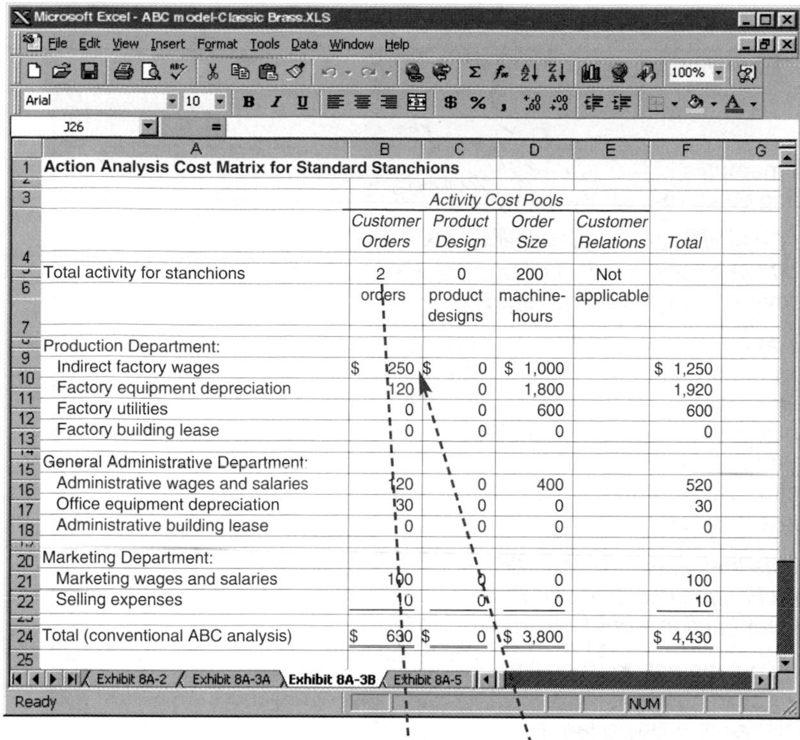

Action Analysis Cost Matrix for Standard Stanchions

	Activity Cost Pools				
	Customer Orders	*Product Design*	*Order Size*	*Customer Relations*	*Total*
Total activity for stanchions	2 orders	0 product designs	200 machine-hours	Not applicable	
Production Department:					
Indirect factory wages	$ 250	$ 0	$ 1,000		$ 1,250
Factory equipment depreciation	120	0	1,800		1,920
Factory utilities	0	0	600		600
Factory building lease	0	0	0		0
General Administrative Department:					
Administrative wages and salaries	120	0	400		520
Office equipment depreciation	30	0	0		30
Administrative building lease	0	0	0		0
Marketing Department:					
Marketing wages and salaries	100	0	0		100
Selling expenses	10	0	0		10
Total (conventional ABC analysis)	$ 630	$ 0	$ 3,800		$ 4,430

From Exhibit 8A–2, the activity rate for indirect factory wages for the Customer Orders cost pool is $125 per order.

$125 per order × 2 orders = $250

Other entries in the table are computed in a similar way.

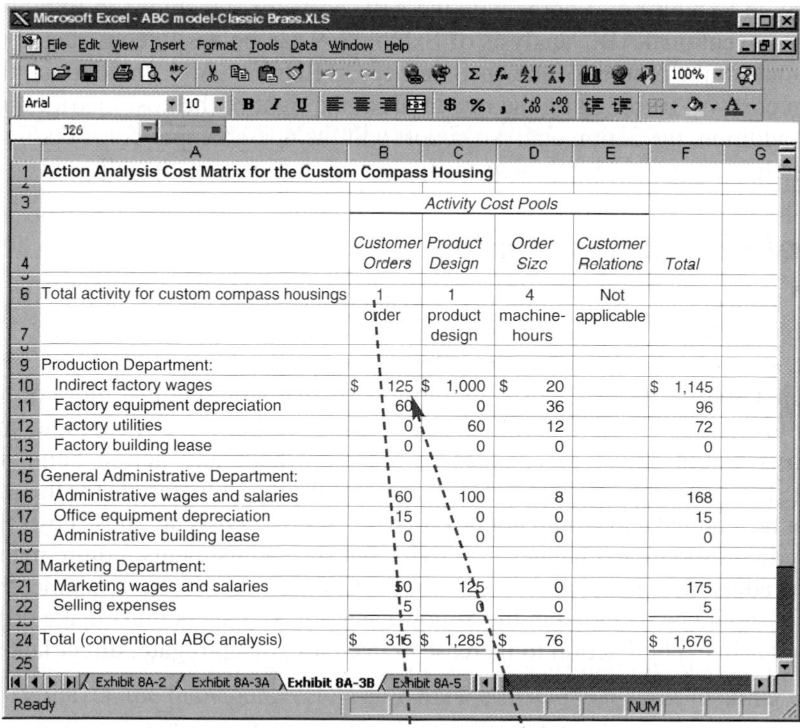

Action Analysis Cost Matrix for the Custom Compass Housing

	Activity Cost Pools				
	Customer Orders	*Product Design*	*Order Size*	*Customer Relations*	*Total*
Total activity for custom compass housings	1 order	1 product design	4 machine-hours	Not applicable	
Production Department:					
Indirect factory wages	$ 125	$ 1,000	$ 20		$ 1,145
Factory equipment depreciation	60	0	36		96
Factory utilities	0	60	12		72
Factory building lease	0	0	0		0
General Administrative Department:					
Administrative wages and salaries	60	100	8		168
Office equipment depreciation	15	0	0		15
Administrative building lease	0	0	0		0
Marketing Department:					
Marketing wages and salaries	50	125	0		175
Selling expenses	5	0	0		5
Total (conventional ABC analysis)	$ 316	$ 1,285	$ 76		$ 1,676

From Exhibit 8A–2, the activity rate for indirect factory wages for the Customer Orders cost pool is $125 per order.

$125 per order × 1 order = $125

Other entries in the table are computed in a similar way.

Exercises

EXERCISE 8–1 Cost Hierarchy [LO1]

Green Glider Corporation makes golf carts that it sells directly to golf courses throughout the world. Several basic models are available, which are modified to suit the needs of each particular golf course. A golf course located in the Pacific Northwest, for example, would typically specify that its golf carts come equipped with retractable rain-proof covers. In addition, each customer (i.e., golf course) customizes its golf carts with its own color scheme and logo. The company typically makes all of the golf carts for a customer before starting work on the next customer's golf carts. Below are listed a number of activities and costs at Green Glider Corporation:

a. The purchasing department orders the specific color of paint specified by the customer from the company's supplier.
b. A steering wheel is installed in a golf cart.
c. An outside attorney draws up a new generic sales contract for the company limiting Green Glider's liability in case of accidents that involve its golf carts.
d. The company's paint shop makes a stencil for a customer's logo.
e. A sales representative visits an old customer to check on how the company's golf carts are working out and to try to make a new sale.
f. The accounts receivable department prepares the bill for a completed order.
g. Electricity is used to heat and light the factory and the administrative offices.
h. A golf cart is painted.
i. The company's engineer modifies the design of a model to eliminate a potential safety problem.
j. The marketing department has a catalogue printed and then mails copies to golf course managers.
k. Completed golf carts are individually tested on the company's test track.
l. A new model golf cart is shipped to the leading golfing trade magazine to be evaluated for the magazine's annual rating of golf carts.

Required:

Classify each of the costs or activities above as unit-level, batch-level, product-level, customer-level, or organization-sustaining. In this case, customers are golf courses, products are models of the golf cart, a batch is a specific order from a customer, and units are individual golf carts.

EXERCISE 8–2 Activity Measures [LO1]

Listed below are various activities that you have observed at Morales Corporation, a manufacturing company. Each activity has been classified as unit-level, batch-level, product-level, customer-level, or organization-sustaining.

Activity	Activity Classification	Examples of Activity Measures
a. Materials are moved from the receiving dock to the assembly area by a material-handling crew	Batch-level	
b. Direct labor workers assemble various products	Unit-level	
c. Diversity training is provided to all employees in the company	Organization-sustaining	
d. A product is designed by a cross-functional team	Product-level	
e. Equipment is set up to process a batch	Batch-level	
f. A customer is billed for all products delivered during the month	Customer-level	

Required:

Complete the above table by listing examples of activity measures for each activity.

EXERCISE 8–3 Cost Hierarchy and Activity Measures [LO1]

Listed below are various activities that you have observed at Companhia de Textils, S.A., a manufacturing company located in Brazil. The company makes a variety of products in its plant outside Sao Paulo.

a. Preventive maintenance is performed on general-purpose production equipment.
b. Products are assembled by hand.
c. Reminder notices are sent to customers who are late in making payments.
d. Purchase orders are issued for materials to be used in production.
e. Modifications are made to product designs.
f. New employees are hired by the personnel office.
g. Machine settings are changed between batches of different products.
h. Parts inventories are maintained in the storeroom. (Each product requires its own unique parts.)
i. Insurance costs are incurred on the company's facilities.

Required:

1. Classify each of the activities as either unit-level, batch-level, product-level, customer-level, or organization-sustaining.
2. Where possible, name one or more activity measures that could be used to assign costs generated by the activity to products or customers.

EXERCISE 8–4 First-Stage Allocations [LO2]

The operations vice president of First Bank of Eagle, Kristin Wu, has been interested in investigating the efficiency of the bank's operations. She has been particularly concerned about the costs of handling routine transactions at the bank and would like to compare these costs at the bank's various branches. If the branches with the most efficient operations can be identified, their methods can be studied and then replicated elsewhere. While the bank maintains meticulous records of wages and other costs, there has been no attempt thus far to show how those costs are related to the various services provided by the bank. Ms. Wu has asked your help in conducting an activity-based costing study of bank operations. In particular, she would like to know the cost of opening an account, the cost of processing deposits and withdrawals, and the cost of processing other customer transactions.

The Avon branch of First Bank of Eagle has submitted the following cost data for last year:

Teller wages	$150,000
Assistant branch manager salary	70,000
Branch manager salary	85,000
Total	$305,000

Virtually all of the other costs of the branch—rent, depreciation, utilities, and so on—are organization-sustaining costs that cannot be meaningfully assigned to individual customer transactions such as depositing checks.

In addition to the cost data above, the employees of the Avon branch have been interviewed concerning how their time was distributed last year across the activities included in the activity-based costing study. The results of those interviews appear below:

	Distribution of Resource Consumption Across Activities				
	Opening Accounts	Processing Deposits and Withdrawals	Processing Other Customer Transactions	Other Activities	Totals
Teller wages	0%	75%	15%	10%	100%
Assistant branch manager salary	10%	15%	25%	50%	100%
Branch manager salary . . .	0%	0%	20%	80%	100%

Required:

Prepare the first-stage allocation for Ms. Wu as illustrated in Exhibit 8–4.

EXERCISE 8–5 Computing and Interpreting Activity Rates [LO3]

(This exercise is a continuation of Exercise 8–4; it should be assigned *only* if Exercise 8–4 is also assigned.) The manager of the Avon branch of First Bank of Eagle has provided the following data concerning the transactions of the branch during the past year:

Activity	Total Activity at the Avon Branch
Opening accounts	200 accounts opened
Processing deposits and withdrawals	50,000 deposits and withdrawals
Processing other customer transactions	1,000 other customer transactions

The lowest costs reported by other branches for these activities are displayed below:

Activity	Lowest Cost Among All First Bank of Eagle Branches
Opening accounts	$24.35 per account opened
Processing deposits and withdrawals	$2.72 per deposit or withdrawal
Processing other customer transactions	$48.90 per other customer transaction

Required:

1. Using the first-stage allocation from Exercise 8–4 and the above data, compute the activity rates for the activity-based costing system. (Use Exhibit 8–5 as a guide.) Round all computations to the nearest whole cent.
2. What do these results suggest to you concerning operations at the Avon branch?

EXERCISE 8–6 Second-Stage Allocation to an Order [LO4]

Transvaal Mining Tools Ltd. of South Africa makes specialty tools used in the mining industry. The company uses an activity-based costing system for internal decision-making purposes. The company has four activity cost pools as listed below:

Activity Cost Pool	Activity Measure	Activity Rate
Order size	Number of direct labor-hours	R 17.60 per direct labor-hour*
Customer orders	Number of customer orders	R 360 per customer order
Product testing	Number of testing hours	R 79 per testing hour
Selling	Number of sales calls	R 1,494 per sales call

*(The currency in South Africa is the rand, denoted here by R.)

The managing director of the company would like information concerning the cost of a recently completed order for hard-rock drills. The order required 150 direct labor-hours, 18 hours of product testing, and three sales calls.

Required:

Prepare a report showing the overhead cost of the order for hard-rock drills according to the activity-based costing system. (Use Exhibit 8–8 as a guide.) What is the total overhead cost assigned to the order?

EXERCISE 8–7 (Appendix 8A) Second-Stage Allocation to an Order Using the Action Analysis Approach [LO4, LO6]

This exercise should be assigned in conjunction with Exercise 8–6.

The results of the first-stage allocation of the activity-based costing system at Transvaal Mining Tools Ltd., in which the activity rates were computed, appear below:

	Order Size	Customer Orders	Product Testing	Selling
Manufacturing:				
Indirect labor	R 9.60	R 231.00	R 36.00	R 0.00
Factory depreciation	7.00	0.00	18.00	0.00
Factory utilities	0.20	0.00	1.00	0.00
Factory administration	0.00	46.00	24.00	12.00
General selling and administrative:				
Wages and salaries	0.80	72.00	0.00	965.00
Depreciation	0.00	11.00	0.00	36.00
Taxes and insurance	0.00	0.00	0.00	49.00
Selling expenses	0.00	0.00	0.00	432.00
Total overhead cost	R 17.60	R 360.00	R 79.00	R 1,494.00

Required:

1. Using Exhibit 8A–3 as a guide, prepare a report showing the overhead cost of the order for hard-rock drills discussed in Exercise 8–6. What is the total overhead cost of the order?
2. Explain the two different perspectives this report gives to managers concerning the nature of the overhead costs involved in the order. (Hint: Look at the row and column totals of the report you have prepared.)

EXERCISE 8–8 Second-Stage Allocation and Margin Calculations [LO4, LO5]
Theatre Seating, Inc., makes high quality adjustable seats for theaters. The company's activity-based costing system has four activity cost pools, which are listed below along with their activity measures and activity rates:

Activity Cost Pool	Activity Measure	Activity Rate
Volume	Number of direct labor-hours	$12 per direct labor-hour
Batch processing	Number of batches	$96 per batch
Order processing	Number of orders	$284 per order
Customer service	Number of customers	$2,620 per customer

The company just completed a single order from CineMax Entertainment Corporation for 2,400 custom seats. The order was produced in four batches. Each seat required 0.8 direct labor-hour. The selling price was $137.95 per seat, the direct materials cost was $112.00 per seat, and the direct labor cost was $14.40 per seat. This was the only order from CineMax Entertainment for the year.

Required:
1. Using Exhibit 8–9 as a guide, prepare a report showing the product margin for this order. Ignore the customer service costs.
2. Again using Exhibit 8–9 as a guide, prepare a report showing the customer margin on sales to CineMax Entertainment for the year.

EXERCISE 8–9 (Appendix 8A) Second-Stage Allocations and Margin Calculations Using the Action Analysis Approach [LO4, LO6]
Refer to the data for Theatre Seating, Inc., in Exercise 8–8 and the following additional details concerning the activity rates:

	Activity Rates			
	Volume	Batch Processing	Order Processing	Customer Service
Production overhead:				
Indirect labor	$ 1.80	$72.00	$ 18.00	$ 0.00
Factory equipment depreciation . .	7.35	3.25	0.00	0.00
Factory administration	2.10	7.00	28.00	268.00
General selling & administrative:				
Wages and salaries	0.50	13.00	153.00	1,864.00
Depreciation	0.00	0.75	6.00	26.00
Marketing expenses	0.25	0.00	79.00	462.00
Total activity rate	$12.00	$96.00	$284.00	$2,620.00

Management has provided their ease of adjustment codes for purposes of preparing action analyses.

	Ease of Adjustment Codes
Direct materials	Green
Direct labor	Yellow
Production overhead:	
Indirect labor	Yellow
Factory equipment depreciation	Red
Factory administration	Red
General selling and administrative:	
Wages and salaries	Red
Depreciation	Red
Marketing expenses	Yellow

Required:
1. Using Exhibit 8A–5 as a guide, prepare an action analysis report on the order from CineMax Entertainment. Ignore the customer service costs.
2. Management would like an action analysis report for the customer similar to those prepared for products, but it is unsure of how this can be done. The customer service cost of $2,620

could be deducted directly from the product margin for the order, but this would obscure how much of the customer service cost consists of Green, Yellow, and Red costs. Prepare a report that clearly shows the adjustability of the various costs.

EXERCISE 8–10 Comprehensive Activity-Based Costing Exercise [LO2, LO3, LO4, LO5]
Silicon Optics has supplied the following data for use in its activity-based costing system:

Overhead Costs	
Wages and salaries	$350,000
Other overhead costs	200,000
Total overhead costs	$550,000

Activity Cost Pool	Activity Measure	Total Activity
Volume	Number of direct labor-hours	10,000 DLHs
Order processing	Number of orders	500 orders
Customer support	Number of customers	100 customers
Other	These costs are not allocated to products or customers	Not applicable

	Distribution of Resource Consumption Across Activity Cost Pools				
	Volume	Order Processing	Customer Support	Other	Total
Wages and salaries	30%	35%	25%	10%	100%
Other overhead costs	25%	15%	20%	40%	100%

During the year, Silicon Optics completed an order for a special optical switch for a new customer, Indus Telecom. This customer did not order any other products during the year. Data concerning that order follow:

Data Concerning the Indus Telecom Order	
Selling price	$295 per unit
Units ordered	100 units
Direct materials	$264 per unit
Direct labor-hours	0.5 DLH per unit
Direct labor rate	$25 per DLH

Required:

1. Using Exhibit 8–4 as a guide, prepare a report showing the first-stage allocations of overhead costs to the activity cost pools.
2. Using Exhibit 8–5 as a guide, compute the activity rates for the activity cost pools.
3. Using Exhibit 8–8 as a guide, prepare a report showing the overhead costs for the order from Indus Telecom. Do not include customer support costs at this point in the analysis.
4. Using Exhibit 8–9 as a guide, prepare a report showing the product margin for the order and the customer margin for Indus Telecom.

EXERCISE 8–11 (Appendix 8A) Comprehensive Activity-Based Costing Exercise [LO2, LO3, LO4, LO6]
Refer to the data for Silicon Optics in Exercise 8–10.

Required:

1. Using Exhibit 8–4 as a guide, prepare a report showing the first-stage allocations of overhead costs to the activity cost pools.
2. Using Exhibit 8A–2 as a guide, compute the activity rates for the activity cost pools.
3. Using Exhibit 8A–3 as a guide, prepare a report showing the overhead costs for the order from Indus Telecom. Do not include customer support costs at this point in the analysis.
4. Using Exhibit 8–9 as a guide, prepare an activity analysis report showing the product margin for the order and the customer margin for Indus Telecom.
5. Using Exhibit 8A–5 as a guide, prepare an action analysis report showing the product margin for the order and the customer margin for Indus Telecom. Direct materials should be coded as

a Green cost, direct labor and wages and salaries as Yellow costs, and other overhead costs as a Red cost.

6. Using Exhibit 8A–5 as a guide, prepare an action analysis report showing the customer margin for Indus Telecom. Direct materials should be coded as a Green cost, direct labor and wages and salaries as Yellow costs, and other overhead costs as a Red cost.
7. What action, if any, do you recommend as a result of the above analyses?

EXERCISE 8–12 Calculating and Interpreting Activity-Based Costing Data [LO1, LO3, LO4]

Sven's Cookhouse is a popular restaurant located on Lake Union in Seattle. The owner of the restaurant has been trying to better understand costs at the restaurant and has hired a student intern to conduct an activity-based costing study. The intern, in consultation with the owner, identified three major activities. She then completed the first-stage allocations of costs to the activity cost pools, using data from last month's operations. The results appear below:

Activity Cost Pool	Activity Measure	Total Cost	Total Activity
Serving a party of diners	Number of parties served	$12,000	5,000 parties
Serving a diner	Number of diners served	$90,000	12,000 diners
Serving a drink	Number of drinks ordered	$26,000	10,000 drinks

The above costs include all of the costs of the restaurant except for organization-sustaining costs such as rent, property taxes, and top-management salaries. A group of diners who ask to sit at the same table are counted as a party. Some costs, such as the costs of cleaning linen, are the same whether one person is at a table or the table is full. Other costs, such as washing dishes, depend on the number of diners served.

Prior to the activity-based costing study, the owner knew very little about the costs of the restaurant. He knew that the total cost for the month (including organization-sustaining costs) was $180,000 and that 12,000 diners had been served. Therefore, the average cost per diner was $15.

Required:

1. According to the activity-based costing system, what is the total cost of serving each of the following parties of diners?
   a. A party of four diners who order three drinks in total.
   b. A party of two diners who do not order any drinks.
   c. A lone diner who orders two drinks.
2. Convert the total costs you computed in (1) above to costs per diner. In other words, what is the average cost per diner for serving each of the following parties of diners?
   a. A party of four diners who order three drinks in total.
   b. A party of two diners who do not order any drinks.
   c. A lone diner who orders two drinks.
3. Why do the costs per diner for the three different parties differ from each other and from the overall average cost of $15.00 per diner?

Problems

PROBLEM 8–13 Activity-Based Costing as an Alternative to Traditional Product Costing [LO1, LO3, LO4]

This chapter emphasizes the use of activity-based costing in internal decisions. However, a modified form of activity-based costing can also be used to develop product costs for external financial reports. For this purpose, product costs include all manufacturing overhead costs and exclude all nonmanufacturing costs. This problem illustrates such a costing system.

Erte, Inc., manufactures two models of high-pressure steam valves, the XR7 model and the ZD5 model. Data regarding the two products follow:

Product	Direct Labor-Hours	Annual Production	Total Direct Labor-Hours
XR7	0.2 DLHs per unit	20,000 units	4,000 DLHs
ZD5	0.4 DLHs per unit	40,000 units	16,000 DLHs
			20,000 DLHs

Additional information about the company follows:

a. Product XR7 requires $35 in direct materials per unit, and product ZD5 requires $25.
b. The direct labor rate is $20 per hour.
c. The company has always used direct labor-hours as the base for applying manufacturing overhead cost to products. Manufacturing overhead totals $1,480,000 per year.
d. Product XR7 is more complex to manufacture than product ZD5 and requires the use of a special milling machine.
e. Because of the special work required in (d) above, the company is considering the use of activity-based costing to apply overhead cost to products. Three activity cost pools have been identified and the first-stage allocations have been completed. Data concerning these activity cost pools appear below:

			Total Activity		
Activity Cost Pool	**Activity Measure**	**Total Cost**	**XR7**	**ZD5**	**Total**
Machine setups	Number of setups	$ 180,000	150	100	250
Special milling	Machine-hours	300,000	1,000	0	1,000
General factory	Direct labor-hours	1,000,000	4,000	16,000	20,000
		$1,480,000			

Required:

1. Assume that the company continues to use direct labor-hours as the base for applying overhead cost to products.
   a. Compute the predetermined overhead rate.
   b. Determine the unit product cost of each product.
2. Assume that the company decides to use activity-based costing to apply overhead cost to products.
   a. Compute the activity rate for each activity cost pool. Also compute the amount of overhead cost that would be applied to each product.
   b. Determine the unit product cost of each product.
3. Explain why overhead cost shifted from the high-volume product to the low-volume product under activity-based costing.

PROBLEM 8–14 Activity-Based Costing and Bidding on Jobs [LO1, LO2, LO3, LO4]

Denny Asbestos Removal Company is in the business of removing potentially toxic asbestos insulation and related products from buildings. The company's estimator has been involved in a long-simmering dispute with the on-site work supervisors. The on-site supervisors claim that the estimator does not take enough care in distinguishing between routine work such as removal of asbestos insulation around heating pipes in older homes and nonroutine work such as removing asbestos-contaminated ceiling plaster in industrial buildings. The on-site supervisors believe that nonroutine work is far more expensive than routine work and should bear higher customer charges. The estimator sums up his position in this way: "My job is to measure the area to be cleared of asbestos. As directed by top management, I simply multiply the square footage by $4,000 per thousand square feet to determine the bid price. Since our average cost is only $3,000 per thousand square feet, that leaves enough cushion to take care of the additional costs of nonroutine work that shows up. Besides, it is difficult to know what is routine or not routine until you actually start tearing things apart."

Partly to shed light on this controversy, the company initiated an activity-based costing study of all of its costs. Data from the activity-based costing system follow:

Activity Cost Pool	Activity Measure	Total Activity
Job size.	Thousands of square feet	500 thousand square feet
Estimating and job setup	Number of jobs	200 jobs*
Working on nonroutine jobs	Number of nonroutine jobs	25 nonroutine jobs
Other (costs of idle capacity and organization-sustaining costs)	Not applicable; these costs are not allocated to jobs	

*The total number of jobs includes nonroutine jobs as well as routine jobs. Nonroutine jobs as well as routine jobs require estimating and setup work.

Wages and salaries	$ 200,000
Disposal fees	600,000
Equipment depreciation	80,000
On-site supplies	60,000
Office expenses	190,000
Licensing and insurance	370,000
Total cost	$1,500,000

Distribution of Resource Consumption Across Activity Cost Pools

	Job Size	Estimating and Job Setup	Working on Nonroutine Jobs	Other	Total
Wages and salaries	40%	10%	35%	15%	100%
Disposal fees	70%	0%	30%	0%	100%
Equipment depreciation	50%	0%	40%	10%	100%
On-site supplies	55%	15%	20%	10%	100%
Office expenses	10%	40%	30%	20%	100%
Licensing and insurance	50%	0%	40%	10%	100%

Required:

1. Using Exhibit 8–4 as a guide, perform the first-stage allocation of costs to the activity cost pools.
2. Using Exhibit 8–5 as a guide, compute the activity rates for the activity cost pools.
3. Using the activity rates you have computed, determine the total cost and the average cost per thousand square feet of each of the following jobs according to the activity-based costing system.
   a. A routine 2,000-square-foot asbestos removal job.
   b. A routine 4,000-square foot asbestos removal job.
   c. A nonroutine 2,000-square-foot asbestos removal job.
4. Given the results you obtained in (3) above, do you agree with the estimator that the company's present policy for bidding on jobs is adequate?

PROBLEM 8–15 Second Stage Allocations and Product Margins [LO4, LO5]

AnimPix, Inc., is a small company that creates computer-generated animations for films and television. Much of the company's work consists of short commercials for television, but the company also does realistic computer animations for special effects in movies.

The young founders of the company have become increasingly concerned with the economics of the business—particularly since many competitors have sprung up recently in the local area. To help understand the company's cost structure, an activity-based costing system has been designed. Three major activities are carried out in the company: animation concept, animation production, and contract administration. The animation concept activity is carried out at the contract proposal stage when the company bids on projects. This is an intensive activity that involves individuals from all parts of the company in creating storyboards and prototype stills to be shown to the prospective client. After the client has accepted a project, the animation goes into production and contract administration begins. Technical staff do almost all of the work involved in animation production, whereas the administrative staff is largely responsible for contract administration. The activity cost pools and their activity measures and rates are listed below:

Activity Cost Pool	Activity Measure	Activity Rate
Animation concept	Number of proposals	$6,000 per proposal
Animation production	Minutes of animation	$7,700 per minute of animation
Contract administration	Number of contracts	$6,600 per contract

These activity rates include all of the costs of the company, except for the costs of idle capacity and organization-sustaining costs. There are no direct labor or direct materials costs.

Preliminary analysis using these activity rates has indicated that the local commercials segment of the market may be unprofitable. This segment is highly competitive. Producers of local commercials may ask several companies like AnimPix to bid, which results in an unusually low ratio of accepted contracts to bids. Furthermore, the animation sequences tend to be much shorter for local commercials than for other work. Since animation work is billed at standard rates according to the running time of the completed animation, the revenues from these short projects tend to be below average. Data concerning activity in the local commercials market appear below:

Activity Measure	Local Commercials
Number of proposals	20
Minutes of animation	12
Number of contracts	8

The total sales for local commercials amounted to $240,000.

Required:

1. Using Exhibit 8–8 as a guide, determine the cost of the local commercials market. (Think of the local commercials market as a product.)
2. Using Exhibit 8–9 as a guide, prepare a report showing the product margin of the local commercials market. (Remember, this company has no direct materials or direct labor costs.)
3. What would you recommend to management concerning the local commercials market?

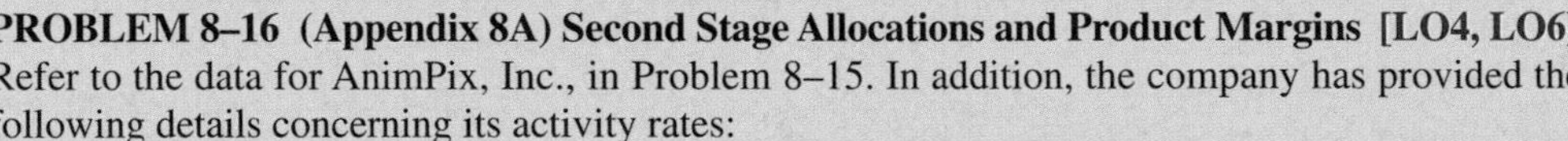

PROBLEM 8–16 (Appendix 8A) Second Stage Allocations and Product Margins [LO4, LO6]
Refer to the data for AnimPix, Inc., in Problem 8–15. In addition, the company has provided the following details concerning its activity rates:

	Activity Rates		
	Animation Concept	Animation Production	Contract Administration
Technical staff salaries	$3,500	$5,000	$1,800
Animation equipment depreciation	600	1,500	0
Administrative wages and salaries	1,400	200	4,600
Supplies costs	300	600	100
Facility costs	200	400	100
Total	$6,000	$7,700	$6,600

Management has provided the following ease of adjustment codes for the various costs:

	Ease of Adjustment Code
Technical staff salaries	Red
Animation equipment depreciation	Red
Administrative wages and salaries	Yellow
Supplies costs	Green
Facility costs	Red

These codes created some controversy. In particular, some administrators objected to coding their own salaries Yellow, while the technical staff salaries were coded Red. However, the founders of the firm overruled these objections by pointing out that "our technical staff is our most valuable asset. Good animators are extremely difficult to find, and they would be the last to go if we had to cut back."

Required:

1. Using Exhibit 8A–3 as a guide, determine the cost of the local commercials market. (Think of the local commercials market as a product.)
2. Using Exhibit 8A–5 as a guide, prepare an action analysis report concerning the local commercials market. (This company has no direct materials or direct labor costs.)
3. What would you recommend to management concerning the local commercials market?

PROBLEM 8–17 Activity-Based Costing as an Alternative to Traditional Product Costing [LO1, LO3, LO4]
This chapter emphasizes the use of activity-based costing in internal decisions. However, a modified form of activity-based costing can also be used to develop product costs for external financial reports. For this purpose, product costs include all manufacturing overhead costs and exclude all nonmanufacturing costs. This problem illustrates such a costing system.

Rehm Company manufactures a product that is available in both a deluxe model and a regular model. The company has manufactured the regular model for years. The deluxe model was introduced several years ago to tap a new segment of the market. Since introduction of the deluxe model, the company's profits have steadily declined, and management has become increasingly concerned about the accuracy of its costing system. Sales of the deluxe model have been increasing rapidly.

Manufacturing overhead is assigned to products on the basis of direct labor-hours. For the current year, the company has estimated that it will incur $6,000,000 in manufacturing overhead cost and produce 15,000 units of the deluxe model and 120,000 units of the regular model. The deluxe model requires 1.6 hours of direct labor time per unit, and the regular model requires 0.8 hour. Material and labor costs per unit are as follows:

	Model	
	Deluxe	Regular
Direct materials	$154	$112
Direct labor	16	8

Required:

1. Using direct labor-hours as the base for assigning manufacturing overhead cost to products, compute the predetermined overhead rate. Using this rate and other data from the problem, determine the unit product cost of each model.
2. Management is considering using activity-based costing to apply manufacturing overhead costs to products for external financial reports. The activity-based costing system would have the following four activity cost pools:

Activity Cost Pool	Activity Measure	Estimated Overhead Costs
Purchase orders	Number of purchase orders	$ 252,000
Scrap/rework orders	Number of scrap/rework orders	648,000
Product testing	Number of tests	1,350,000
Machine related	Machine-hours	3,750,000
Total overhead cost		$6,000,000

	Expected Activity		
Activity Measure	Deluxe	Regular	Total
Number of purchase orders	400	800	1,200
Number of scrap/rework orders	500	400	900
Number of tests	6,000	9,000	15,000
Machine-hours	20,000	30,000	50,000

   Using Exhibit 8 5 as a guide, compute the predetermined overhead rates (i.e., activity rates) for each of the four activity cost pools.
3. Using the predetermined overhead rates computed in part (2) above, do the following:
   a. Compute the total amount of manufacturing overhead cost that would be applied to each model using the activity-based costing system. After these totals have been computed, determine the amount of manufacturing overhead cost per unit for each model.
   b. Compute the unit product cost of each model (materials, labor, and manufacturing overhead).
4. From the data you have developed in (1) through (3) above, identify factors that may account for the company's declining profits.

PROBLEM 8–18 (Appendix 8A) Activity Rates and Activity-Based Management [LO2, LO3, LO6]

Chefs de Vitesse SA is a French company that provides passenger and crew meals to airlines operating out of the two international airports of Paris—Orly and Charles de Gaulle (CDG). The operations at Orly and CDG are managed separately, and top management believes that greater sharing of information between the two operations should lead to improvements in operations.

To better compare the two operations, an activity-based costing system has been designed with the active participation of the managers at both Orly and CDG. The activity-based costing system is based on the following activity cost pools and activity measures:

Activity Cost Pool	Activity Measure
Meal preparation	Number of meals
Flight-related activities	Number of flights
Customer service	Number of customers
Other (costs of idle capacity and organization-sustaining costs)	Not applicable

The operation at CDG airport serves 500,000 meals annually on 4,000 flights for 8 different airlines. (Each airline is considered one customer.) The annual cost of running the CDG airport operation, excluding only the costs of raw materials for meals, totals €2,650,000. (The currency in France is the euro, denoted here by €.)

Annual Cost of the CDG Operation	
Cooks and delivery personnel wages	€ 1,800,000
Kitchen supplies	100,000
Chef salaries	200,000
Equipment depreciation	50,000
Administrative wages and salaries	180,000
Building costs	320,000
Total cost	€ 2,650,000

To help determine the activity rates, employees were interviewed and asked how they divided their time among the four major activities. The results of the interviews at CDG are displayed below:

Distribution of Resource Consumption Across Activity Cost Pools at the CDG Operation

	Meal Preparation	Flight Related	Customer Service	Other	Total
Cooks and delivery personnel wages	70%	25%	0%	5%	100%
Kitchen supplies	90%	0%	0%	10%	100%
Chef salaries	35%	15%	40%	10%	100%
Equipment depreciation	70%	0%	0%	30%	100%
Administrative wages and salaries	0%	25%	45%	30%	100%
Building costs	0%	0%	0%	100%	100%

Required:

1. Using Exhibit 8A–1 as a guide, perform the first-stage allocation of costs to the activity cost pools.
2. Using Exhibit 8A–2 as a guide, compute the activity rates for the activity cost pools.
3. The Orly operation has already concluded its activity-based costing study and has reported the following costs of carrying out activities at Orly:

	Meal Preparation	Flight Related	Customer Service
Cooks and delivery personnel wages	€ 2.63	€ 135.50	€ 0
Kitchen supplies	0.19	0.00	0
Chef salaries	0.18	12.00	10,500
Equipment depreciation	0.05	0.00	0
Administrative wages and salaries	0.00	9.65	8,765
Building costs	0.00	0.00	0
Total cost	€ 3.05	€ 157.15	€ 19,265

Comparing the activity rates for the CDG operation you computed in (2) above to the activity rates for Orly, do you have any suggestions for the top management of Chefs de Vitesse SA?

PROBLEM 8–19 Evaluating the Profitability of Services [LO2, LO3, LO4, LO5]

Gore Range Carpet Cleaning is a small, family-owned business operating out of Eagle-Vail, Colorado. For its services, the company has always charged a flat fee per 100 square feet of carpet cleaned. The current fee is $22.95 per 100 square feet. However, there is some question about whether the company is actually making any money on jobs for some customers—particularly those located on more remote ranches that require considerable travel time. The owner's daughter, home for the summer from college, has suggested investigating this question using activity-based costing. After some discussion, a simple system consisting of four activity cost pools seemed to be adequate. The activity cost pools and their activity measures appear on the next page:

Activity Cost Pool	Activity Measure	Activity for the Year
Cleaning carpets	Square feet cleaned (00s)	10,000 hundred square feet
Travel to jobs	Miles driven	50,000 miles
Job support	Number of jobs	1,800 jobs
Other (costs of idle capacity and organization-sustaining costs)	None	Not applicable

The total cost of operating the company for the year is $340,000, which includes the following costs:

Wages	$140,000
Cleaning supplies	25,000
Cleaning equipment depreciation	10,000
Vehicle expenses	30,000
Office expenses	60,000
President's compensation	75,000
Total cost	$340,000

Resource consumption is distributed across the activities as follows:

	Distribution of Resource Consumption Across Activity Cost Pools				
	Cleaning Carpets	Travel to Jobs	Job Support	Other	Total
Wages	75%	15%	0%	10%	100%
Cleaning supplies	100%	0%	0%	0%	100%
Cleaning equipment depreciation	70%	0%	0%	30%	100%
Vehicle expenses	0%	80%	0%	20%	100%
Office expenses	0%	0%	60%	40%	100%
President's compensation	0%	0%	30%	70%	100%

Job support consists of receiving calls from potential customers at the home office, scheduling jobs, billing, resolving issues, and so on.

Required:

1. Using Exhibit 8–4 as a guide, prepare the first-stage allocation of costs to the activity cost pools.
2. Using Exhibit 8–5 as a guide, compute the activity rates for the activity cost pools.
3. The company recently completed a 600-square-foot carpet-cleaning job at the Lazy Bee Ranch—a 52-mile round-trip journey from the company's offices in Eagle-Vail. Using Exhibit 8–8 as a guide, compute the cost of this job using the activity-based costing system.
4. The revenue from the Lazy Bee Ranch was $137.70 (600 square feet at $22.95 per 100 square feet). Using Exhibit 8–9 as a guide, prepare a report showing the margin from this job. (Think of the job as a product.)
5. What do you conclude concerning the profitability of the Lazy Bee Ranch job? Explain.
6. What advice would you give the president concerning pricing jobs in the future?

PROBLEM 8–20 (Appendix 8A) Evaluating the Profitability of Services Using an Action Analysis [LO2, LO3, LO4, LO6]

Refer to the data for Gore Range Carpet Cleaning in Problem 8–19.

Required:

1. Using Exhibit 8A–1 as a guide, prepare the first-stage allocation of costs to the activity cost pools.
2. Using Exhibit 8A–2 as a guide, compute the activity rates for the activity cost pools.
3. The company recently completed a 600-square-foot carpet-cleaning job at the Lazy Bee Ranch—a 52-mile round-trip journey from the company's offices in Eagle-Vail. Using Exhibit 8–8A as a guide, compute the cost of this job using the activity-based costing system.
4. The revenue from the Lazy Bee Ranch was $137.70 (600 square feet at $22.95 per 100 square feet). Using Exhibit 8A–5 as a guide, prepare an action analysis report of the Lazy Bee Ranch job. The president of Gore Range Carpet Cleaning considers all of the company's costs to be

Green costs except for office expenses, which are coded Yellow, and his own compensation, which is coded Red. The people who do the actual carpet cleaning are all trained part-time workers who are paid only for work actually done.

5. What do you conclude concerning the profitability of the Lazy Bee Ranch job? Explain.
6. What advice would you give the president concerning pricing jobs in the future?

PROBLEM 8–21 Activity-Based Costing as an Alternative to Traditional Product Costing [LO1, LO3, LO4]

This chapter emphasizes the use of activity-based costing in internal decisions. However, a modified form of activity-based costing can also be used to develop product costs for external financial reports. For this purpose, product costs include all manufacturing overhead costs and exclude all nonmanufacturing costs. This problem illustrates such a costing system.

For many years, Gorski Company manufactured a single product called a mono-circuit. Then, three years ago, the company automated a portion of its plant and at the same time introduced a second product called a bi-circuit that has become increasingly popular. The bi-circuit product is a more complex product than the mono-circuit, requiring two hours of direct labor time per unit to manufacture, and extensive machining in the automated portion of the plant. In addition, it requires numerous inspections to ensure that high quality is maintained. The mono-circuit requires only one hour of direct labor time per unit, only a small amount of machining, and few quality control checks. Manufacturing overhead costs are assigned to the products on the basis of direct labor-hours.

Despite the growing popularity of the company's new bi-circuit, profits have declined steadily. Management is beginning to believe that the company's costing system may be faulty. Unit costs for materials and labor for the two products follow:

	Mono-Circuit	Bi-Circuit
Direct materials	$40	$80
Direct labor ($18 per hour)	18	36

Management estimates that the company will incur $3,000,000 in manufacturing overhead costs during the current year and that 40,000 units of the mono-circuit and 10,000 units of the bi-circuit will be produced and sold.

Required:

1. Compute the predetermined overhead rate assuming that the company continues to apply manufacturing overhead cost to products on the basis of direct labor-hours. Using this rate and other data from the problem, determine the unit product cost of each product.
2. Management is considering using activity-based costing to apply manufacturing overhead cost to products for external financial reports. Some preliminary work has been done and the data that have been collected are displayed below in the form of an Excel spreadsheet.

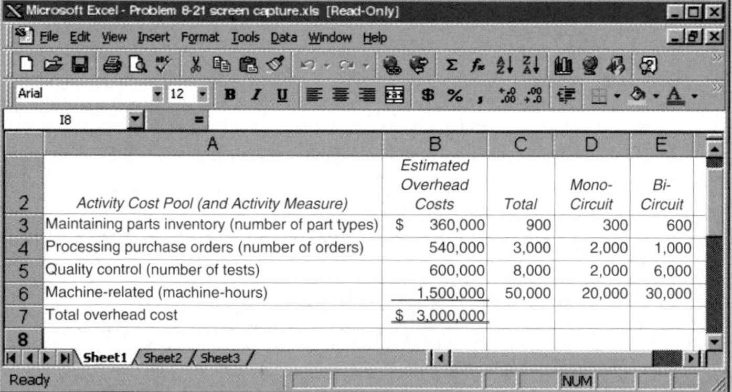

	A	B	C	D	E
2	Activity Cost Pool (and Activity Measure)	Estimated Overhead Costs	Total	Mono-Circuit	Bi-Circuit
3	Maintaining parts inventory (number of part types)	$ 360,000	900	300	600
4	Processing purchase orders (number of orders)	540,000	3,000	2,000	1,000
5	Quality control (number of tests)	600,000	8,000	2,000	6,000
6	Machine-related (machine-hours)	1,500,000	50,000	20,000	30,000
7	Total overhead cost	$ 3,000,000			
8					

Determine the predetermined manufacturing overhead rate (i.e., activity rate) for each of the four activity cost pools.

3. Using predetermined manufacturing overhead rates you computed in part (2) above, do the following:
   a. Determine the total amount of manufacturing overhead cost that would be applied to each product using the activity-based costing system. After these totals have been computed, determine the amount of manufacturing overhead cost per unit of each product.
   b. Compute the unit product cost of each product.

4. Look at the data you have computed in parts (1) through (3) above. In terms of manufacturing overhead cost, what factors make the bi-circuit more costly to produce than the mono-circuit? Is the bi-circuit as profitable as the company thinks it is? Explain.

Cases

CASE 8–22* Activity-Based Costing as an Alternative to Traditional Product Costing [LO1, LO3, LO4, LO5]

This chapter emphasizes the use of activity-based costing in internal decisions. However, a modified form of activity-based costing can also be used to develop product costs for external financial reports. For this purpose, product costs include all manufacturing overhead costs and exclude all nonmanufacturing costs. This problem illustrates such a costing system.

"Two dollars of gross margin per briefcase? That's ridiculous!" roared Roy Thurmond, president of FirstLine Cases, Inc. "Why do we go on producing those standard briefcases when we're able to make over $11 per unit on our specialty items? Maybe it's time to get out of the standard line and focus the whole plant on specialty work."

Mr. Thurmond was referring to a summary of unit costs and revenues that he had just received from the company's accounting department:

	Standard Briefcases	Specialty Briefcases
Selling price per unit	$26.25	$42.50
Unit manufacturing cost	24.25	31.40
Gross margin per unit	$ 2.00	$11.10

FirstLine Cases produces briefcases from leather, fabric, and synthetic materials in a single plant. The basic product is a standard briefcase that is made from leather lined with fabric. The standard briefcase is a high-quality item and has sold well for many years.

Last year, the company decided to expand its product line and produce specialty briefcases for special orders. These briefcases differ from the standard in that they vary in size, they contain the finest leather and synthetic materials, and they are imprinted with the buyer's name. To reduce labor costs on the specialty briefcases, automated machines do most of the cutting and stitching. These machines are used to a much lesser degree in the production of standard briefcases.

"I agree that the specialty business is looking better and better," replied Beth Mersey, the company's marketing manager. "And there seems to be plenty of demand out there, particularly since the competition hasn't been able to touch our price. Did you know that Velsun Company, our biggest competitor, charges over $50 a unit for its specialty items? Now that's what I call gouging the customer!"

A breakdown of the manufacturing cost for each of FirstLine Cases' products is given below:

	Standard Briefcases	Specialty Briefcases
Units produced each month	10,000	2,500
Direct materials:		
Leather	$ 8.00	$12.00
Fabric	2.00	1.00
Synthetic	0	7.00
Total materials	10.00	20.00
Direct labor (0.5 DLH and 0.4 DLH @ $12.00 per DLH)	6.00	4.80
Manufacturing overhead (0.5 DLH and 0.4 DLH @ $16.50 per DLH)	8.25	6.60
Total cost per unit	$24.25	$31.40

* Adapted from Harold P. Roth and Imogene Posey, "Management Accounting Case Study: CarryAll Company," *Management Accounting Campus Report*, Institute of Management Accountants, Fall 1991, p. 9. Used by permission from the IMA, Montvale, NJ, USA, www.imanet.org.

Manufacturing overhead is applied to products on the basis of direct labor-hours. The rate of \$16.50 per hour was determined by dividing the total manufacturing overhead cost for a month by the direct labor-hours:

$$\text{Predetermined overhead rate} = \frac{\text{Manufacturing overhead}}{\text{Direct labor-hours}}$$

$$= \frac{\$99{,}000}{6{,}000 \text{ DLHs}} = \$16.50 \text{ per DLH}$$

The following additional information is available about the company and its products:

a. Standard briefcases are produced in batches of 1,000 units, and specialty briefcases are produced in batches of 100 units. Thus, the company does 10 setups for the standard items each month and 25 setups for the specialty items. A setup for the standard items requires one hour of time, whereas a setup for the specialty items requires two hours of time.

b. All briefcases are inspected to ensure that quality standards are met. A total of 200 hours of inspection time is spent on the standard briefcases and 400 hours of inspection time is spent on the specialty briefcases each month.

c. A standard briefcase requires 0.5 hour of machine time, and a specialty briefcase requires 1.2 hours of machine time.

d. The company is considering the use of activity-based costing as an alternative to its traditional costing system for computing unit product costs. Since these unit product costs will be used for external financial reporting, all manufacturing overhead costs are to be allocated to products and nonmanufacturing costs are to be excluded from product costs. The activity-based costing system has already been designed and costs have been allocated to the activity cost pools. The activity cost pools and activity measures are detailed below:

Activity Cost Pool	Activity Measure	Estimated Overhead Cost
Purchasing	Number of orders	\$15,000
Material handling	Number of receipts	16,000
Production orders and setups	Setup-hours	6,000
Inspection	Inspection-hours	18,000
Frame assembly	Assembly-hours	12,000
Machine-related	Machine-hours	32,000
		\$99,000

	Expected Activity		
Activity Measure	**Standard Briefcases**	**Specialty Briefcases**	**Total**
Number of orders:			
Leather	50	10	60
Fabric	70	20	90
Synthetic material	0	150	150
Number of receipts:			
Leather	70	10	80
Fabric	85	20	105
Synthetic material	0	215	215
Setup-hours	?	?	?
Inspection-hours	200	400	600
Assembly-hours	700	800	1,500
Machine-hours	?	?	?

Required:

1. Using activity-based costing, determine the amount of manufacturing overhead cost that should be applied to each standard briefcase and each specialty briefcase.
2. Using the data computed in (1) above and other data from the case as needed, determine the unit product cost of each product line from the perspective of activity-based costing.
3. Within the limitations of the data that have been provided, evaluate the president's concern about the profitability of the two product lines. Would you recommend that the company shift its resources entirely to the production of specialty briefcases? Explain.

4. Beth Mersey stated that "the competition hasn't been able to touch our price on specialty business." Why do you suppose the competition hasn't been able to touch FirstLine Cases' price?

CASE 8–23 (Appendix 8A) Comprehensive Activity-Based Costing Case [LO1, LO2, LO3, LO4, LO6]

Victorian Windows is a small company that builds specialty wooden windows for local builders. For years the company has relied on a simple costing system based on direct labor-hours (DLHs) for determining the costs of its products. However, the company's president became interested in activity-based costing after reading an article about it in a trade journal. An activity-based costing design team was put together, and within a few months a simple system consisting of four activity cost pools had been designed. The activity cost pools and their activity measures appear below:

Activity Cost Pool	Activity Measure	Total Activity for the Year
Making windows	Direct labor-hours	80,000 DLHs
Processing orders	Number of orders	1,000 orders
Customer relations	Number of customers	200 customers
Other (costs of idle capacity and organization-sustaining costs)	None	Not applicable

The Processing Orders activity includes order taking, job setup, job scheduling, and so on. Direct materials and direct labor are directly assigned to jobs in both the traditional and activity-based costing systems. The total overhead cost (both nonmanufacturing and manufacturing) for the year is $1,180,000 and includes the following costs:

Manufacturing overhead costs:		
Indirect factory wages	$240,000	
Production equipment depreciation	250,000	
Other factory costs	110,000	$ 600,000
Selling and administrative expenses:		
Administrative wages and salaries	240,000	
Office expenses	60,000	
Marketing expenses	280,000	580,000
Total overhead cost		$1,180,000

Based largely on interviews with employees, the distribution of resource consumption across the activities has been estimated as follows:

	Distribution of Resource Consumption Across Activities				
	Making Windows	Processing Orders	Customer Relations	Other	Total
Indirect factory wages	25%	50%	10%	15%	100%
Production equipment depreciation	80%	0%	0%	20%	100%
Other factory costs	40%	0%	0%	60%	100%
Administrative wages and salaries	0%	25%	35%	40%	100%
Office expenses	0%	20%	30%	50%	100%
Marketing expenses	0%	0%	75%	25%	100%

Management of the company is particularly interested in measuring the profitability of two customers. One of the customers, Avon Construction, is a low-volume purchaser. The other, Lynx Builders, is a relatively high-volume purchaser. Details of these two customers' orders for the year appear below:

	Avon Construction	Lynx Builders
Number of orders during the year	2 orders	3 orders
Total direct labor-hours	250 DLHs	1,500 DLHs
Total sales	$9,995	$54,995
Total direct materials	$3,400	$17,200
Total direct labor cost	$4,500	$27,000

Required:

1. The company's traditional costing system applies manufacturing overhead to jobs strictly on the basis of direct labor-hours. Using this traditional approach, carry out the following steps:
   a. Compute the predetermined manufacturing overhead rate.
   b. Compute the total margin for all of the windows ordered by Avon Construction according to the traditional costing system. Do the same for Lynx Builders.
2. Using activity-based costing, carry out the following steps:
   a. Using Exhibit 8–4 as a guide, perform the first-stage allocation of costs to the activity cost pools.
   b. Using Exhibit 8A–2 as a guide, compute the activity rates for the activity cost pools.
   c. Compute the overhead costs of serving each of the two customers. (You will need to construct a table like Exhibit 8A–3 for each customer. However, unlike Exhibit 8A–3, you should fill in the column for Customer Relations as well as the other columns. Exhibit 8A–3 was constructed for a product; in this case we are interested in a customer.)
   d. Management has provided the following ease of adjustment codes to use in action analysis reports:

	Ease of Adjustment Code
Direct materials	Green
Direct labor	Yellow
Indirect factory wages	Yellow
Production equipment depreciation	Yellow
Other factory costs	Yellow
Administrative wages and salaries	Red
Office expenses	Yellow
Marketing expenses	Yellow

   Using Exhibit 8A–5 as a guide, prepare an action analysis report showing the margin on business with Avon Construction. Repeat for Lynx Builders.
3. Does Victorian Windows appear to be losing money on either customer? Do the traditional and activity-based costing systems agree concerning the profitability of the customers? If they do not agree, which costing system do you believe? Why?

CASE 8–24 Activity-Based Costing and Pricing [LO1, LO3, LO4]

This chapter emphasizes the use of activity-based costing in internal decisions. However, a modified form of activity-based costing can also be used to develop product costs for external financial reports. For this purpose, product costs include all manufacturing overhead costs and exclude all nonmanufacturing costs. This problem illustrates such a costing system.

Coffee Bean, Inc. (CBI), is a processor and distributor of a variety of blends of coffee. The company buys coffee beans from around the world and roasts, blends, and packages them for resale. CBI currently has 40 different coffees that it offers to gourmet shops in one-pound bags. The major cost of the coffee is raw materials. However, the company's predominantly automated roasting, blending, and packing process requires a substantial amount of manufacturing overhead. The company uses relatively little direct labor.

Some of CBI's coffees are very popular and sell in large volumes, while a few of the newer blends have very low volumes. CBI prices its coffee at manufacturing cost plus a markup of 30%. If CBI's prices for certain coffees are significantly higher than market, adjustments are made to bring CBI's prices more into alignment with the market since customers are somewhat price conscious.

For the coming year, CBI's budget includes estimated manufacturing overhead cost of $3,000,000. CBI assigns manufacturing overhead to products on the basis of direct labor-hours. The expected direct labor cost totals $600,000, which represents 50,000 hours of direct labor time. Based on the sales budget and expected raw materials costs, the company will purchase and use $6,000,000 of raw materials (mostly coffee beans) during the year.

The expected costs for direct materials and direct labor for one-pound bags of two of the company's coffee products appear below.

	Mona Loa	Malaysian
Direct materials	$4.20	$3.20
Direct labor (0.025 hours per bag)	0.30	0.30

CBI's controller believes that the company's traditional costing system may be providing misleading cost information. To determine whether or not this is correct, the controller has prepared an analysis of the year's expected manufacturing overhead costs, as shown in the following table:

Activity Cost Pool	Activity Measure	Expected Activity for the Year	Expected Cost for the Year
Purchasing	Purchase orders	1,710 orders	$ 513,000
Material handling	Number of setups	1,800 setups	720,000
Quality control.	Number of batches	600 batches	144,000
Roasting	Roasting hours	96,100 roasting hours	961,000
Blending	Blending hours	33,500 blending hours	402,000
Packaging.	Packaging hours	26,000 packaging hours	260,000
Total manufacturing overhead cost			$3,000,000

Data regarding the expected production of Mona Loa and Malaysian coffee are presented below. There will be no raw materials inventory for either of these coffees at the beginning of the year.

	Mona Loa	Malaysian
Expected sales	100,000 pounds	2,000 pounds
Batch size.	10,000 pounds	500 pounds
Setups	3 per batch	3 per batch
Purchase order size	20,000 pounds	500 pounds
Roasting time per 100 pounds	1.0 hour	1.0 hour
Blending time per 100 pounds	0.5 hour	0.5 hour
Packaging time per 100 pounds.	0.1 hour	0.1 hour

Required:

1. Using direct labor-hours as the base for assigning manufacturing overhead cost to products, do the following:
   a. Determine the predetermined overhead rate that will be used during the year.
   b. Determine the unit product cost of one pound of the Mona Loa coffee and one pound of the Malaysian coffee.
   c. Determine the selling price of one pound of the Mona Loa coffee and one pound of the Malaysian coffee using the company's 30% markup.
2. Using activity-based costing as the basis for assigning manufacturing overhead cost to products, do the following:
   a. Determine the total amount of manufacturing overhead cost assigned to the Mona Loa coffee and to the Malaysian coffee for the year.
   b. Using the data developed in (2a) above, compute the amount of manufacturing overhead cost per pound of the Mona Loa coffee and the Malaysian coffee. Round all computations to the nearest whole cent.
   c. Determine the unit product cost of one pound of the Mona Loa coffee and one pound of the Malaysian coffee.
3. Write a brief memo to the president of CBI explaining what you have found in (1) and (2) above and discussing the implications to the company of using direct labor as the base for assigning manufacturing overhead cost to products.

(CMA, adapted)

CASE 8–25 Contrasting Activity-Based Costing and Traditional Costing [LO1, LO3, LO4, LO5]

This chapter emphasizes the use of activity-based costing in internal decisions. However, a modified form of activity-based costing can also be used to develop product costs for external financial reports. For this purpose, product costs include all manufacturing overhead costs and exclude all nonmanufacturing costs. This problem illustrates such a costing system.

"Wow! Is that B-10 model ever a loser! It's time to cut back its production and shift our resources toward the new C-20 model," said Rory Moncur, executive vice president of Hammer Products, Inc. "Just look at this statement I've received from accounting. The C-20 is generating twice as much in profits as the B-10, and it has only about one-fifth as much in sales. I'm convinced that our future depends on the C-20." The year-end statement to which Rory was referring follows:

	Total	Model B-10	Model C-20
Sales	$14,500,000	$12,000,000	$2,500,000
Cost of goods sold	9,000,000	7,200,000	1,800,000
Gross margin	5,500,000	4,800,000	700,000
Less selling and administrative expenses	4,900,000	4,600,000	300,000
Net operating income	$ 600,000	$ 200,000	$ 400,000
Number of units produced and sold		60,000	10,000
Net operating income per unit		$3.33	$40.00

"The numbers sure look that way," replied Connie Collins, the company's sales manager. "But why isn't the competition more excited about the C-20? I know we've only been producing the model for three years, but I'm surprised that more of our competitors haven't recognized what a cash cow it is."

"I think it's our new automated plant," replied Rory. "Now it takes only one direct labor-hour to produce a unit of the B-10 and one-and-a-half direct labor-hours to produce a unit of the C-20. That's considerably less than it used to take us."

"I agree that automation is wonderful," replied Connie. "I suppose that's how we're able to hold down the price of the C-20. Borst Company in Germany tried to bring out a C-20 but discovered they couldn't touch our price. But Borst is killing us on the B-10 by undercutting our price with some of our best customers. I suppose they'll pick up all of our B-10 business if we move out of that market. But who cares? We don't even have to advertise the C-20; it just seems to sell itself."

"My only concern about automation is how our manufacturing overhead rate has shot up," said Rory. "Our total manufacturing overhead cost is $3,600,000. That comes out to be a hefty amount per direct labor-hour, but old Fred down in accounting has been using labor-hours as the base for computing overhead rates for years and doesn't want to change. I don't suppose it matters so long as costs get assigned to products."

"I've never understood that debit and credit stuff," replied Connie. "But I think you've got a problem in production. I had lunch with Joanne yesterday and she complained about how complex the C-20 is to produce. Apparently they have to do a lot of setups, special soldering, and other work on the C-20 just to keep production moving. And they have to inspect every single unit."

"It'll have to wait," said Rory. "I'm writing a proposal to the board of directors to phase out the B-10. We've got to increase our bottom line or we'll all be looking for jobs."

Required:

1. Compute the predetermined overhead rate based on direct labor-hours that the company used during the year. (There was no under- or overapplied overhead for the year.)
2. Materials and labor costs per unit for the two products are as follows:

	B-10	C-20
Direct materials	$60	$90
Direct labor	12	18

   Using these data and the rate computed in (1) above, determine the unit product cost of each product under the company's old traditional costing system.
3. Assume that the company's $3,600,000 in manufacturing overhead cost can be assigned to six activity cost pools, as follows:

Activity Cost Pool (and Activity Measure)	Estimated Overhead Costs	Expected Activity Total	B-10	C-20
Machine setups (number of setups)	$ 416,000	3,200	2,000	1,200
Quality control (number of inspections)	720,000	18,000	8,000	10,000
Purchase orders (number of orders)	180,000	2,400	1,680	720
Soldering (number of solder joints)	900,000	400,000	120,000	280,000
Shipments (number of shipments)	264,000	1,200	800	400
Machine related (machine-hours)	1,120,000	140,000	60,000	80,000
	$3,600,000			

   Given these data, would you support a recommendation to expand sales of the C-20? Explain your position.

4. From the data you have prepared in (3) above, why do you suppose the C-20 "just seems to sell itself"?
5. If you were president of Hammer Products, Inc., what strategy would you follow from this point forward to improve the company's overall profits?

Group and Internet Exercises

GROUP EXERCISE 8–26 The Problems with Traditional Costing Systems

Many managers realize that the methods they use to cost their products or services suffer from fundamental problems. But should they change from traditional product costing methods based on direct labor-hours to activity-based costing (ABC) methods? It is important first of all to understand the limitations of existing product costing systems in the current competitive environment, which is typified by a diverse product line with many low-volume complex products.

Required:

1. How does the cost structure of many manufacturing firms today differ from their cost structure of 20 years ago?
2. Why can't traditional product costing systems account for costs of product diversity? Volume diversity? Product complexity?

GROUP EXERCISE 8–27 The Impact of Changing Cost Systems on Product Costs

A manufacturing company is thinking of changing its method of computing product costs for the purposes of making decisions. Under the company's conventional direct labor-based costing system, manufacturing overhead costs are applied to products on the basis of direct labor-hours. Under the proposed activity-based costing (ABC) system, manufacturing overhead costs would be applied to products using a variety of activity measures at the unit, batch, and product levels.

Required:

For each of the following products, indicate the impact on the product's apparent unit cost of switching from a conventional direct labor-based costing system to an activity-based costing system.

1. A low-volume product that is produced in small batches.
2. A high-volume product that is produced in large batches with automated equipment and that requires very few direct labor-hours per unit.
3. A high-volume product that requires little machine work but a lot of direct labor.

GROUP EXERCISE 8–28 Dividing the Bill

You and your friends go to a restaurant as a group. At the end of the meal, the issue arises of how the bill for the group should be shared. One alternative is to figure out the cost of what each individual consumed and divide up the bill accordingly. Another alternative is to split the bill equally among the individuals.

Required:

Which system for dividing the bill is more equitable? Which system is easier to use? How does this issue relate to the material covered in this chapter?

INTERNET EXERCISE 8–29

As you know, the World Wide Web is a medium that is constantly evolving. Sites come and go, and change without notice. To enable periodic update of site addresses, this problem has been posted to the textbook website (www.mhhe.com/garrison10e). After accessing the site, enter the Student Center and select this chapter. Select and complete the Internet Exercise.

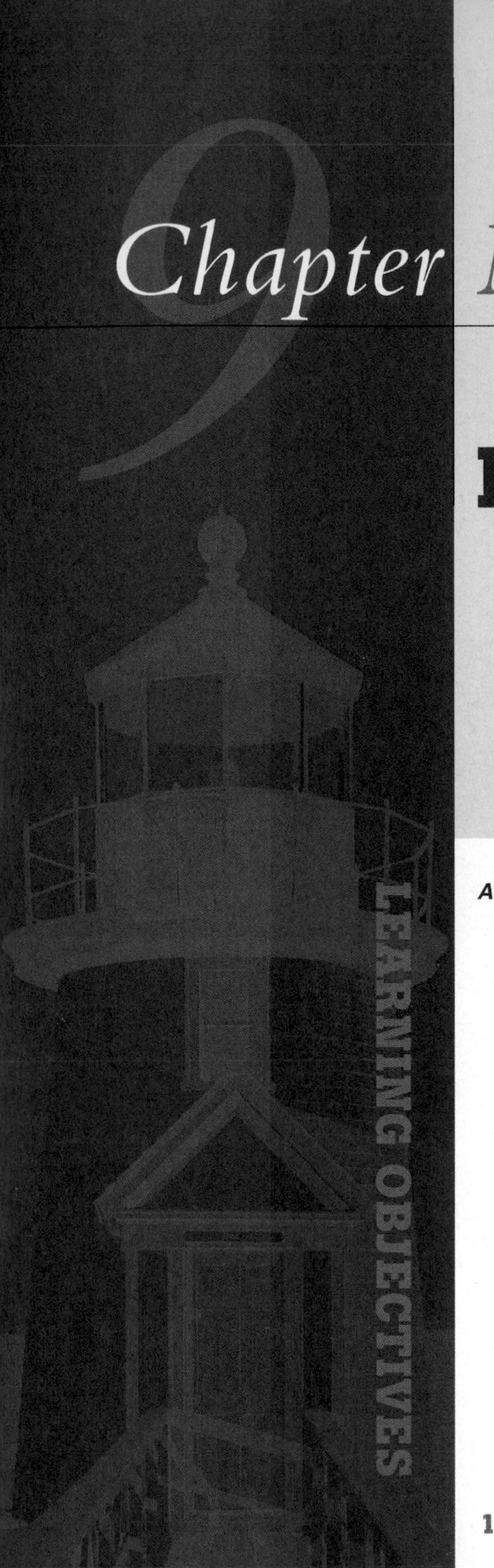

Chapter Nine

Profit Planning

After studying Chapter 9, you should be able to:

1. Understand why organizations budget and the processes they use to create budgets.

2. Prepare a sales budget, including a schedule of expected cash receipts.

3. Prepare a production budget.

4. Prepare a direct materials budget, including a schedule of expected cash disbursements for purchases of materials.

5. Prepare a direct labor budget.

6. Prepare a manufacturing overhead budget.

7. Prepare a selling and administrative expense budget.

8. Prepare a cash budget.

9. Prepare a budgeted income statement.

10. Prepare a budgeted balance sheet.

Budgeting—A Basic Survival Skill

Budgets are perhaps even more important in small service organizations than they are in large manufacturing companies. The accounting firm of Carter, Young, Lankford & Roach, P.C. in Nashville, Tennessee, is typical of many small firms that must keep a constant eye on their cash flows. Because of high fixed costs, small changes in revenues or a client that is delinquent in paying bills can have potentially disastrous effects on the firm's cash flows.

Lucy Carter, the managing partner of the firm, uses a formal budget for keeping cash flow on an even keel. She says, "I don't know how small CPA firms can survive without a budget in this business climate." The formal budget is based on estimated client billings (i.e., revenues) for the coming year. The annual budget is broken down into months, and each month the budget is compared to the actual financial results of the month. If the actuals fall short of the budget, adjustments may be necessary. For example, because of shortfalls in billings in one year, the firm reduced its staff by three staff accountants and added a part-time staff accountant. Because of the critical nature of client billings, Carter's staff prepares daily reports on billings that indicate how well actual billings compare to the budgeted billings on a month-to-date basis. (See the firm's website www.cylr.com for details about its services and partners.)

Source: Gene R. Barrett, "How Small CPA Firms Manage Their Cash," *Journal of Accountancy,* August 1993, pp. 56–59.

In this chapter, we focus on the steps taken by businesses to achieve their desired levels of profits—a process that can be called *profit planning.* We shall see that profit planning is accomplished through the preparation of a number of budgets, which, when brought together, form an integrated business plan known as the *master budget.* The master budget is an essential management tool that communicates management's plans throughout the organization, allocates resources, and coordinates activities.

The Basic Framework of Budgeting

LEARNING OBJECTIVE 1
Understand why organizations budget and the processes they use to create budgets.

A **budget** is a detailed plan for acquiring and using financial and other resources over a specified time period. It represents a plan for the future expressed in formal quantitative terms. The act of preparing a budget is called *budgeting.* The use of budgets to control a firm's activities is known as *budgetary control.*

The **master budget** is a summary of a company's plans that sets specific targets for sales, production, distribution, and financing activities. It generally culminates in a cash budget, a budgeted income statement, and a budgeted balance sheet. In short, it represents a comprehensive expression of management's plans for the future and how these plans are to be accomplished.

Personal Budgets

Nearly everyone budgets to some extent, even though many of the people who use budgets do not recognize what they are doing as budgeting. For example, most people make estimates of their income and plan expenditures for food, clothing, housing, and so on. As a result of this planning, people restrict their spending to some predetermined, allowable amount. While they may not be conscious of the fact, these people clearly go through a budgeting process. Income is estimated, expenditures are planned, and spending is restricted in accordance with the plan. Individuals also use budgets to forecast their future financial condition for purposes such as purchasing a home, financing college education, or setting aside funds for retirement. These budgets may exist only in the mind of the individual, but they are budgets nevertheless.

The budgets of a business or other organization serve much the same functions as the budgets prepared informally by individuals. Business budgets tend to be more detailed and to involve more work, but they are similar to the budgets prepared by individuals in most other respects. Like personal budgets, they assist in planning and controlling expenditures; they also assist in predicting operating results and financial condition in future periods.

Difference between Planning and Control

The terms *planning* and *control* are often confused, and occasionally these terms are used in such a way as to suggest that they mean the same thing. Actually, planning and control are two quite distinct concepts. **Planning** involves developing objectives and preparing various budgets to achieve those objectives. **Control** involves the steps taken by management to increase the likelihood that the objectives set down at the planning stage are attained and that all parts of the organization are working together toward that goal. To be completely effective, a good budgeting system must provide for *both* planning and control. Good planning without effective control is time wasted.

Advantages of Budgeting

Companies realize many benefits from a budgeting program. Among these benefits are the following:

1. Budgets provide a means of *communicating* management's plans throughout the organization.
2. Budgets force managers to *think about* and plan for the future. In the absence of the necessity to prepare a budget, many managers would spend all of their time dealing with daily emergencies.
3. The budgeting process provides a means of *allocating resources* to those parts of the organization where they can be used most effectively.
4. The budgeting process can uncover potential *bottlenecks* before they occur.
5. Budgets *coordinate* the activities of the entire organization by *integrating* the plans of the various parts. Budgeting helps to ensure that everyone in the organization is pulling in the same direction.
6. Budgets define goals and objectives that can serve as *benchmarks* for evaluating subsequent performance.

Bringing Order Out of Chaos

In Business

S

Consider the following situation encountered by one of the authors at a mortgage banking firm: For years, the company operated with virtually no system of budgets whatever. Management contended that budgeting wasn't well suited to the firm's type of operation. Moreover, management pointed out that the firm was already profitable. Indeed, outwardly the company gave every appearance of being a well-managed, smoothly operating organization. A careful look within, however, disclosed that day-to-day operations were far from smooth, and often approached chaos. The average day was nothing more than an exercise in putting out one brush fire after another. The Cash account was always at crisis levels. At the end of a day, no one ever knew whether enough cash would be available the next day to cover required loan closings. Departments were uncoordinated, and it was not uncommon to find that one department was pursuing a course that conflicted with the course pursued by another department. Employee morale was low, and turnover was high. Employees complained bitterly that when a job was well done, nobody ever knew about it.

The company was bought out by a new group of stockholders who required that an integrated budgeting system be established to control operations. Within one year's time, significant changes were evident. Brush fires were rare. Careful planning virtually eliminated the problems that had been experienced with cash, and departmental efforts were coordinated and directed toward predetermined overall company goals. Although the employees were wary of the new budgeting program initially, they became "converted" when they saw the positive effects that it brought about. The more efficient operations caused profits to jump dramatically. Communication increased throughout the organization. When a job was well done, everybody knew about it. As one employee stated, "For the first time, we know what the company expects of us."

Responsibility Accounting

Most of what we say in this chapter and in the next three chapters is concerned with *responsibility accounting*. The basic idea behind **responsibility accounting** is that a manager should be held responsible for those items—and *only* those items—that the manager can actually control to a significant extent. Each line item (i.e., revenue or cost) in the budget is made the responsibility of a manager, and that manager is held responsible for subsequent deviations between budgeted goals and actual results. In effect, responsibility accounting *personalizes* accounting information by looking at costs from a *personal control* standpoint. This concept is central to any effective profit planning and control system. Someone must be held responsible for each cost or else no one will be responsible, and the cost will inevitably grow out of control.

Being held responsible for costs does not mean that the manager is penalized if the actual results do not measure up to the budgeted goals. However, the manager should take the initiative to correct any unfavorable discrepancies, should understand the source of significant favorable or unfavorable discrepancies, and should be prepared to explain the reasons for discrepancies to higher management. The point of an effective responsibility system is to make sure that nothing "falls through the cracks," that the organization reacts quickly and appropriately to deviations from its plans, and that the organization learns from the feedback it gets by comparing budgeted goals to actual results. The point is *not* to penalize individuals for missing targets.

In Business

A Little Coordination Please!

Budgeting plays an important role in coordinating activities in large organizations. Jerome York, the chief financial officer at IBM, discovered at one budget meeting that "the division that makes AS/400 workstations planned to churn out 10,000 more machines than the marketing division was promising to sell. He asked nicely that the two divisions agree on how many they would sell for the sake of consistency (and to cut down on the inventory problem). The rival executives said it couldn't be done. Mr. York got tougher, saying it could. Ultimately, it was."

Source: Laurie Hays, "Blue Blood: IBM's Finance Chief, Ax in Hand, Scours Empire for Costs to Cut," *The Wall Street Journal,* January 26, 1994, pp. A1, A6.

Choosing a Budget Period

Operating budgets ordinarily cover a one-year period corresponding to the company's fiscal year. Many companies divide their budget year into four quarters. The first quarter is then subdivided into months, and monthly budgets are developed. These near-term figures can often be established with considerable accuracy. The last three quarters may be carried in the budget at quarterly totals only. As the year progresses, the figures for the second quarter are broken down into monthly amounts, then the third-quarter figures are broken down, and so forth. This approach has the advantage of requiring periodic review and reappraisal of budget data throughout the year.

In Business

Heading Off a Crisis

S

The Repertory Theatre of St. Louis is a not-for-profit professional theater that is supported by contributions from donors and by ticket sales. Financially, the theater appeared to be doing well. However, a five-year budget revealed that within a few years, expenses would exceed revenues and the theater would be facing a financial crisis. Realistically, additional contributions from donors would not fill the gap. Cutting costs would not work because of the theater's already lean operations; cutting costs even more would jeopardize the quality of the theater's productions. Raising ticket prices was ruled out due to competitive pressures and to the belief that this would be unpopular with many donors. The solution was to build a second mainstage performing space that would allow the theater to put on more performances and thereby sell more tickets. By developing a long-range budget, the management of The Repertory Theatre of St. Louis was able to identify in advance a looming financial crisis and to develop a solution that would avert the crisis in time.

Source: Lawrence P. Carr, ed., "The Repertory Theatre of St. Louis (B): Strategic Budgeting," *Cases from Management Accounting Practice: Volumes 10 and 11,* Institute of Management Accountants, Montvale, NJ, 1997.

Continuous or *perpetual budgets* are used by a significant number of organizations. A **continuous or perpetual budget** is a 12-month budget that rolls forward one month (or quarter) as the current month (or quarter) is completed. In other words, one month (or quarter) is added to the end of the budget as each month (or quarter) comes to a close.

This approach keeps managers focused on the future at least one year ahead. Advocates of continuous budgets argue that with this approach there is less danger that managers will become too narrowly focused on short-term results.

In this chapter, we will look at one-year operating budgets. However, using basically the same techniques, operating budgets can be prepared for periods that extend over many years. It may be difficult to accurately forecast sales and required data much beyond a year, but even rough estimates can be invaluable in uncovering potential problems and opportunities that would otherwise be overlooked. For example, as just described in the box on page 376, as a result of preparing a five-year budget, management at The Repertory Theatre of St. Louis was able to identify an impending financial crisis.

The Self-Imposed Budget

The success of a budget program will be determined in large part by the way in which the budget is developed. In the most successful budget programs, managers with cost control responsibilities actively participate in preparing their own budgets. This is in contrast to the approach in which budgets are imposed from above. The participative approach to preparing budgets is particularly important if the budget is to be used to control and evaluate a manager's performance. If a budget is imposed on a manager from above, it will probably generate resentment and ill will rather than cooperation and commitment.

This budgeting approach in which managers prepare their own budget estimates—called a *self-imposed budget*—is generally considered to be the most effective method of budget preparation. A **self-imposed budget** or **participative budget** is a budget that is prepared with the full cooperation and participation of managers at all levels. Exhibit 9–1 illustrates this approach to budget preparation.

Exhibit 9–1 The Initial Flow of Budget Data in a Participative Budgeting System

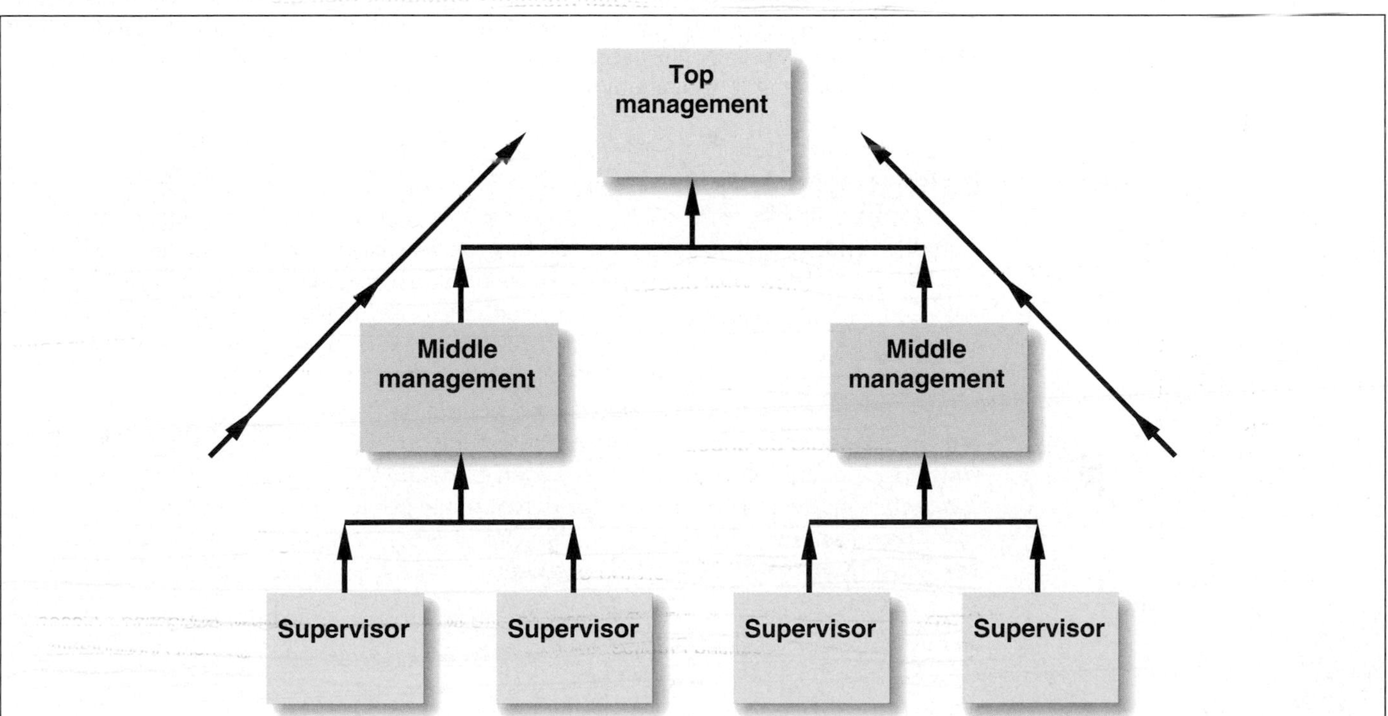

The initial flow of budget data in a participative system is from lower levels of responsibility to higher levels of responsibility. Each person with responsibility for cost control will prepare his or her own budget estimates and submit them to the next higher level of management. These estimates are reviewed and consolidated as they move upward in the organization.

A number of advantages are commonly cited for such self-imposed budgets:

1. Individuals at all levels of the organization are recognized as members of the team whose views and judgments are valued by top management.
2. Budget estimates prepared by front-line managers can be more accurate and reliable than estimates prepared by top managers who are more remote from day-to-day activities and who have less intimate knowledge of markets and operating conditions.
3. Motivation is generally higher when an individual participates in setting his or her own goals than when the goals are imposed from above. Self-imposed budgets create commitment.
4. If a manager is not able to meet the budget and it has been imposed from above, the manager can always say that the budget was unreasonable or unrealistic to start with and, therefore, was impossible to meet. With a self-imposed budget, this excuse is not available.

Once self-imposed budgets are prepared, are they subject to any kind of review? The answer is yes. Budget estimates prepared by lower-level managers should be scrutinized by higher levels of management. Without such a review, self-imposed budgets may be too loose and allow too much "budgetary slack." The result will be inefficiency and waste. Therefore, before budgets are accepted, they must be carefully reviewed by immediate superiors. If changes from the original budget seem desirable, the items in question are discussed and modified as necessary.

In essence, all levels of an organization should work together to produce the budget. Since top management is generally unfamiliar with detailed, day-to-day operations, it should rely on subordinates to provide detailed budget data. On the other hand, top management has an overall strategic perspective that is also vital. Each level of responsibility in an organization should contribute in the way that it best can in a *cooperative* effort to develop an integrated budget.

To be successful, a self-imposed approach to setting budgets requires that all managers understand and agree with the organization's strategy. Otherwise, the budgets proposed by the lower-level managers will lack coherent direction. We will discuss in greater detail in the following chapter how a company can go about formulating its strategy and then communicating it throughout the organization.

In Business

Cutting Slack in Ireland

A study of budgeting in four Irish businesses provides some interesting insights into controlling budgetary slack. It appears that one of the best ways to control budgetary slack is to have management accountants who fully understand the operational side of the business. As one operating manager put it, "Finance [i.e., management accountants] understand my budget completely. There is no slack or opportunity for slack." In contrast, budgetary slack was greatest in a subsidiary of a company headquartered in North America whose management accountants least understood the operating side of the business and yet always insisted that the budget be met. In fact, in this particular organization, corporate headquarters had previously ordered the Irish subsidiary midway through a year to deliver additional cost savings to make up for poor performance elsewhere in the corporation. Not surprisingly, the managers of the Irish subsidiary now routinely pad their budgets in case this happens again.

Source: Paul Pendergast, "Budget Padding: Is It a Job for the Finance Police?" *Management Accounting* (UK), November 1997, pp. 44–46.

We have described an ideal budgetary process that involves self-imposed budgets prepared by the managers who are directly responsible for revenues and costs. Most companies deviate from this ideal. Typically, top managers initiate the budget process by issuing broad guidelines in terms of overall target profits or sales. Lower-level managers are directed to prepare budgets that meet those targets. The difficulty is that the targets set by top managers may be unrealistically high or may allow too much slack. If the targets are too high and employees know they are unrealistic, motivation will suffer. If the targets allow too much slack, waste will occur. And unfortunately top managers are often not in a position to know whether the targets they have set are appropriate. Admittedly, however, a pure self-imposed budgeting system may lack sufficient strategic direction and lower-level managers may be tempted to build into their budgets a great deal of budgetary slack. Nevertheless, because of the motivational advantages of self-imposed budgets, top managers should be cautious about setting inflexible targets.

Human Factors in Budgeting

The success of a budget program also depends on (1) the degree to which top management accepts the budget program as a vital part of the company's activities, and (2) the way in which top management uses budgeted data.

If a budget program is to be successful, it must have the complete acceptance and support of the persons who occupy key management positions. If lower or middle management personnel sense that top management is lukewarm about budgeting, or if they sense that top management simply tolerates budgeting as a necessary evil, then their own attitudes will reflect a similar lack of enthusiasm. Budgeting is hard work, and if top management is not enthusiastic about and committed to the budget program, then it is unlikely that anyone else in the organization will be either.

In administering the budget program, it is particularly important that top management not use the budget as a club to pressure employees or as a way to find someone to blame if something goes wrong. Using budgets in such negative ways will breed hostility, tension, and mistrust rather than greater cooperation and productivity. Unfortunately, the budget is too often used as a pressure device and great emphasis is placed on "meeting the budget" under all circumstances.

Rather than being used as a weapon, the budget should be used as a positive instrument to assist in establishing goals, in measuring operating results, and in isolating areas that are in need of extra effort or attention. Any misgivings that employees have about a budget program can be overcome by meaningful involvement at all levels and by proper use of the program over time. Administration of a budget program requires a great deal of insight and sensitivity on the part of management. The budget program should be designed to be a positive aid in achieving both individual and company goals.

Management must keep clearly in mind that the human aspect of budgeting is of key importance. It is easy to become preoccupied with the technical aspects of the budget to the exclusion of the human aspects. Indeed, the use of budget data in a rigid and inflexible manner is often the greatest single complaint of persons whose performance is evaluated using budgets. Management should remember that the purposes of the budget are to motivate employees and to coordinate efforts. Preoccupation with the dollars and cents in the budget, or being rigid and inflexible, can only lead to frustration of these purposes.

Who Cares About Budgets?

In Business

Towers Perrin, a consulting firm, reports that the bonuses of more than two out of three corporate managers are based on meeting targets set in annual budgets. "Under this arrangement, managers at the beginning of a year all too often argue that their targets should be lowered because of tough business conditions, when in fact conditions are better than projected. If their arguments are successful, they can easily surpass the targets."

Source: Ronald Fink and Towers Perrin, "Riding the Bull: The 2000 Compensation Survey," *CFO*, June 2000, pp. 45–60.

In establishing a budget, how challenging should budget targets be? In practice, companies typically set their budgets either at a "stretch" level or a "highly achievable" level.

A stretch-level budget is one that has only a small chance of being met and in fact may be met less than half the time by even the most capable managers. A highly achievable budget is one that is challenging, but which can be met through hard work. Managers usually prefer highly achievable budgets. Such budgets are generally coupled with bonuses that are given when budget targets are met, along with added bonuses when these targets are exceeded. Highly achievable budgets are believed to build a manager's confidence and to generate greater commitment to the budget program.

Zero-Based Budgeting

In the traditional approach to budgeting, the manager starts with last year's budget and adds to it (or subtracts from it) according to anticipated needs. This is an incremental approach to budgeting in which the previous year's budget is taken for granted as a baseline.

Zero-based budgeting is an alternative approach that is sometimes used—particularly in the governmental and not-for-profit sectors of the economy. Under a **zero-based budget,** managers are required to justify *all* budgeted expenditures, not just changes in the budget from the previous year. The baseline is zero rather than last year's budget.

A zero-based budget requires considerable documentation. In addition to all of the schedules in the usual master budget, the manager must prepare a series of "decision packages" in which all of the activities of the department are ranked according to their relative importance and the cost of each activity is identified. Higher-level managers can then review the decision packages and cut back in those areas that appear to be less critical or whose costs do not appear to be justified.

Nearly everyone would agree that zero-based budgeting is a good idea. The only issue is the frequency with which a zero-based review is carried out. Under zero-based budgeting, the review is performed every year. Critics of zero-based budgeting charge that properly executed zero-based budgeting is too time-consuming and too costly to justify on an annual basis. In addition, it is argued that annual reviews soon become mechanical and that the whole purpose of zero-based budgeting is then lost.

Whether or not a company should use an annual review is a matter of judgment. In some situations, annual zero-based reviews may be justified; in other situations, they may not because of the time and cost involved. However, most managers would at least agree that on occasion zero-based reviews can be very helpful.

The Budget Committee

A standing **budget committee** will usually be responsible for overall policy matters relating to the budget program and for coordinating the preparation of the budget itself. This committee generally consists of the president; vice presidents in charge of various functions such as sales, production, and purchasing; and the controller. Difficulties and disputes between segments of the organization in matters relating to the budget are resolved by the budget committee. In addition, the budget committee approves the final budget and receives periodic reports on the progress of the company in attaining budgeted goals.

Disputes can (and do) erupt over budget matters. Because budgets allocate resources, the budgeting process to a large extent determines which departments get more resources and which get relatively less. Also, the budget sets the benchmarks by which managers and their departments will be at least partially evaluated. Therefore, it should not be surprising that managers take the budgeting process very seriously and invest considerable energy and even emotion in ensuring that their interests, and those of their departments, are protected. Because of this, the budgeting process can easily degenerate into an interoffice brawl in which the ultimate goal of working together toward common goals is forgotten.

Running a successful budgeting program that avoids interoffice battles requires considerable interpersonal skills in addition to purely technical skills. But even the best interpersonal skills will fail if, as discussed earlier, top management uses the budget process inappropriately as a club or as a way to find blame.

The Politics of Budgeting

In Business

Budgeting is often an intensely political process in which managers jockey for resources and relaxed goals for the upcoming year. One group of consultants describes the process in this way: Annual budgets "have a particular urgency in that they provide the standard and most public framework against which managers are assessed and judged. It is, therefore, not surprising that budget-setting is taken seriously . . . Often budgets are a means for managers getting what they want. A relaxed budget will secure a relatively easy twelve months, a tight one means that their names will constantly be coming up in the monthly management review meeting. Far better to shift the burden of cost control and financial discipline to someone else. Budgeting is an intensely political exercise conducted with all the sharper managerial skills not taught at business school, such as lobbying and flattering superiors, forced haste, regretted delay, hidden truth, half-truths, and lies."

Source: Michael Morrow, ed., *Activity-Based Management* (New York: Woodhead-Faulkner), p. 91.

The Master Budget: An Overview

The master budget consists of a number of separate but interdependent budgets. Exhibit 9–2 provides an overview of the various parts of the master budget and how they are related.

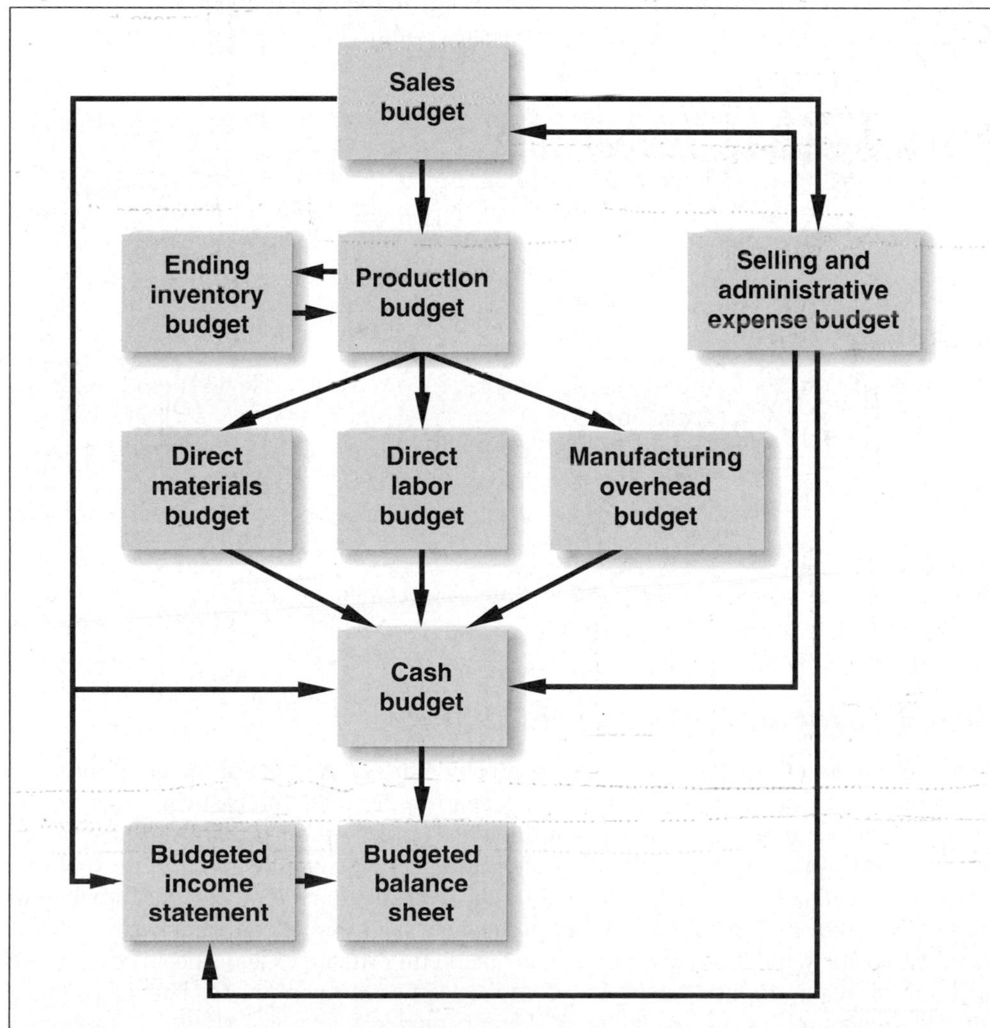

Exhibit 9–2
The Master Budget Interrelationships

Concept 9–1

The Sales Budget A **sales budget** is a detailed schedule showing the expected sales for the budget period; typically, it is expressed in both dollars and units of product. An accurate sales budget is the key to the entire budgeting process. All of the other parts of the master budget are dependent on the sales budget in some way, as illustrated in Exhibit 9–2. Thus, if the sales budget is sloppily done, then the rest of the budgeting process is largely a waste of time.

The sales budget will help determine how many units will have to be produced. Thus, the production budget is prepared after the sales budget. The production budget in turn is used to determine the budgets for manufacturing costs including the direct materials budget, the direct labor budget, and the manufacturing overhead budget. These budgets are then combined with data from the sales budget and the selling and administrative expense budget to determine the cash budget. In essence, the sales budget triggers a chain reaction that leads to the development of the other budgets.

As shown in Exhibit 9–2, the selling and administrative expense budget is both dependent on and a determinant of the sales budget. This reciprocal relationship arises because sales will in part be determined by the funds committed for advertising and sales promotion.

The Cash Budget Once the operating budgets (sales, production, and so on) have been established, the cash budget and other financial budgets can be prepared. A **cash budget** is a detailed plan showing how cash resources will be acquired and used over some specified time period. Observe from Exhibit 9–2 that all of the operating budgets have an impact on the cash budget. In the case of the sales budget, the impact comes from the planned cash receipts to be received from sales. In the case of the other budgets, the impact comes from the planned cash expenditures within the budgets themselves.

In Business

The Importance of Ownership

Jack Stack, the president and CEO of Springfield Manufacturing, advises managers to accept the sales forecasts made by salespeople. He says that the forecasts should be substantiated, but that the forecasts should be accepted even when the manager disagrees with the forecasts. He admits that accepting a sales forecast that you disagree with can be very difficult, but he says that you have to do it. Why?

> Because if you don't, you let your salespeople off the hook. You take away their ownership of the forecast. It's not theirs anymore; it's yours—and so is the responsibility for hitting it. Oh, sure, your salespeople will go out and do their jobs, but something will be missing . . . . The pride, the desire to win that makes them dig deep down and pull off the big play when you need it. What you lose is passion—which is, ironically, the one thing you must have to achieve a reliable forecast.

Source: Jack Stack, "A Passion for Forecasting," *Inc.*, November 1997, pp. 37–38.

Sales Forecasting—A Critical Step

The sales budget is usually based on the company's *sales forecast*. Sales from prior years are commonly used as a starting point in preparing the sales forecast. In addition, the manager may examine the company's unfilled back orders, the company's pricing policy and marketing plans, trends in the industry, and general economic conditions. Sophisticated statistical tools may be used to analyze the data and to build models that are helpful in predicting key factors influencing the company's sales. Some companies use sophisticated computer simulations to enhance their marketing strategies and sales forecasts. We will not, however, go into the details of how sales forecasts are made. This is a subject that is more appropriately covered in marketing courses.

Virtual Customers

In Business

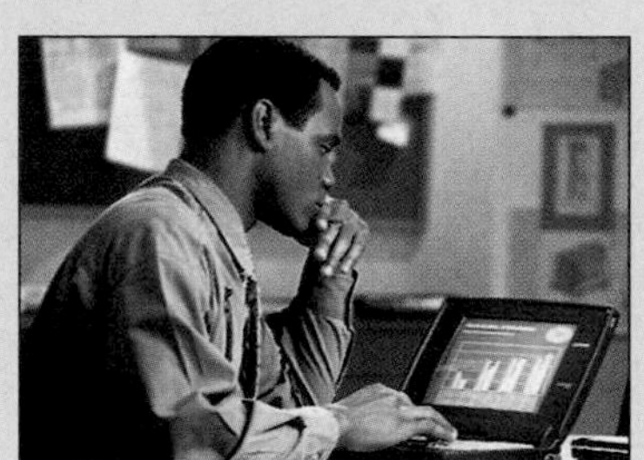

Some companies are turning to elaborate computer simulations for help in forecasting sales. In one emerging approach, software designers create a "virtual economy" containing "virtual people." "These 'people,' constructed of bits of computer code, are endowed with ages, incomes, domiciles, genders and buying habits. [For example, some people] buy a new music CD as soon as it hits the stores; others, only after a certain number of their neighbors own it or a certain number of radio stations have played it. All these assumptions are based on real data . . . " The computer model may contain millions of these virtual people who then react—sometimes in unpredictable ways—to advertising, sales promotions, new product offerings, and so on. Managers can use such a model to plan their marketing strategy and to forecast sales.

Source: Rita Koselka, "Playing the Game of Life," *Forbes*, April 7, 1997, pp. 100–108.

Preparing the Master Budget

Managerial Accounting in Action

The Issue

Tom Wills is the majority stockholder and chief executive officer of Hampton Freeze, Inc., a company he started in 2001. The company makes premium popsicles using only natural ingredients and featuring exotic flavors such as tangy tangerine and minty mango. The company's business is highly seasonal, with most of the sales occurring in spring and summer.

In 2002, the company's second year of operations, a major cash crunch in the first and second quarters almost forced the company into bankruptcy. In spite of this cash crunch, 2002 turned out to be overall a very successful year in terms of both cash flow and net income. Partly as a result of that harrowing experience, Tom decided toward the end of 2002 to hire a professional financial manager. Tom interviewed several promising candidates for the job and settled on Larry Giano, who had considerable experience in the packaged foods industry. In the job interview, Tom questioned Larry about the steps he would take to prevent a recurrence of the 2002 cash crunch:

Tom: As I mentioned earlier, we are going to wind up 2002 with a very nice profit. What you may not know is that we had some very big financial problems this year.

Larry: Let me guess. You ran out of cash sometime in the first or second quarter.

Tom: How did you know?

Larry: Most of your sales are in the second and third quarter, right?

Tom: Sure, everyone wants to buy popsicles in the spring and summer, but nobody wants them when the weather turns cold.

Larry: So you don't have many sales in the first quarter?

Tom: Right.

Larry: And in the second quarter, which is the spring, you are producing like crazy to fill orders?

Tom: Sure.

Larry: Do your customers, the grocery stores, pay you the day you make your deliveries?

Tom: Are you kidding? Of course not.

Larry: So in the first quarter, you don't have many sales. In the second quarter, you are producing like crazy, which eats up cash, but you aren't paid by your customers until long after you have paid your employees and suppliers. No wonder you had a cash problem. I see this pattern all the time in food processing because of the seasonality of the business.

Tom: So what can we do about it?

Larry: The first step is to predict the magnitude of the problem before it occurs. If we can predict early in the year what the cash shortfall is going to be, we can go to the bank and arrange for credit before we really need it. Bankers tend to be leery of panicky people who show up begging for emergency loans. They are much more likely to make the loan if you look like you know what you are doing, you have done your homework, and you are in control of the situation.

Tom: How can we predict the cash shortfall?

Larry: You can put together a cash budget. While you're at it, you might as well do a master budget. You'll find it is well worth the effort.

Tom: I don't like budgets. They are too confining. My wife budgets everything at home, and I can't spend what I want.

Larry: Can I ask a personal question?

Tom: What?

Larry: Where did you get the money to start this business?

Tom: Mainly from our family's savings. I get your point. We wouldn't have had the money to start the business if my wife hadn't been forcing us to save every month.

Larry: Exactly. I suggest you use the same discipline in your business. It is even more important here because you can't expect your employees to spend your money as carefully as you would.

Tom: I'm sold. Welcome aboard.

With the full backing of Tom Wills, Larry Giano set out to create a master budget for the company for the year 2003. In his planning for the budgeting process, Larry drew up the following list of documents that would be a part of the master budget:

1. A sales budget, including a schedule of expected cash collections.
2. A production budget (a merchandise purchases budget would be used in a merchandising company).
3. A direct materials budget, including a schedule of expected cash disbursements for raw materials.
4. A direct labor budget.
5. A manufacturing overhead budget.
6. An ending finished goods inventory budget.
7. A selling and administrative expense budget.
8. A cash budget.
9. A budgeted income statement.
10. A budgeted balance sheet.

Larry felt it was important to have everyone's cooperation in the budgeting process, so he asked Tom to call a companywide meeting in which the budgeting process would be explained. At the meeting there was initially some grumbling, but Tom was able to convince nearly everyone of the necessity for planning and getting better control over spending. It helped that the cash crisis earlier in the year was still fresh in everyone's minds. As much as some people disliked the idea of budgets, they liked their jobs even more.

In the months that followed, Larry worked closely with all of the managers involved in the master budget, gathering data from them and making sure that they understood and fully supported the parts of the master budget that would affect them. In subsequent years, Larry hoped to turn the whole budgeting process over to the managers and to take a more advisory role.

The interdependent documents that Larry Giano prepared for Hampton Freeze are Schedules 1 through 10 of his company's master budget. In this section, we will study these schedules.

LEARNING OBJECTIVE 2
Prepare a sales budget, including a schedule of expected cash receipts.

The Sales Budget

The sales budget is the starting point in preparing the master budget. As shown earlier in Exhibit 9–2, all other items in the master budget, including production, purchases, inventories, and expenses, depend on it in some way.

Schedule 1

Microsoft Excel - Hampton Freeze.xls

	A	B	C	D	E	F
1		HAMPTON FREEZE, INC.				
2		Sales Budget				
3		For the Year Ended December 31, 2003				
4						
5		*Quarter*				
6		*1*	*2*	*3*	*4*	*Year*
7	Budgeted sales in cases	10,000	30,000	40,000	20,000	100,000
8	Selling price per case	$ 20.00	$ 20.00	$ 20.00	$ 20.00	$ 20.00
9	Total sales	$ 200,000	$ 600,000	$ 800,000	$ 400,000	$ 2,000,000
10						
11	Percentage of sales collected in the period of the sale			70%		
12	Percentage of sales collected in the period after the sale			30%		
13		70%	30%			
14		Schedule of Expected Cash Collections				
15	Accounts receivable, beginning balance[1]	$ 90,000				$ 90,000
16	First-quarter sales[2]	140,000	$ 60,000			200,000
17	Second-quarter sales[3]		420,000	$ 180,000		600,000
18	Third-quarter sales[4]			560,000	$ 240,000	800,000
19	Fourth-quarter sales[5]	-	-	-	280,000	280,000
20	Total cash collections[6]	$ 230,000	$ 480,000	$ 740,000	$ 520,000	$ 1,970,000

Schedule 1 / Schedule 2 / Schedule 3 / Schedule 4 / Schedule 5 / Schedul

[1]Cash collections from last year's fourth-quarter sales. See the beginning-of-year balance sheet on page 397.

[2]$200,000 × 70%; $200,000 × 30%.

[3]$600,000 × 70%; $600,000 × 30%.

[4]$800,000 × 70%; $800,000 × 30%.

[5]$400,000 × 70%.

[6]Uncollected fourth-quarter sales appear as accounts receivable on the company's end-of-year balance sheet (see Schedule 10 on page 398).

The sales budget is constructed by multiplying the budgeted sales in units by the selling price. Schedule 1 above contains the sales budget for Hampton Freeze for the year 2003, by quarters. Notice from the schedule that the company plans to sell 100,000 cases of popsicles during the year, with sales peaking in the third quarter.

A schedule of expected cash collections, such as the one that appears in Schedule 1 for Hampton Freeze, is prepared after the sales budget. This schedule will be needed later to prepare the cash budget. Cash collections consist of collections on sales made to customers in prior periods plus collections on sales made in the current budget period. At Hampton Freeze, experience has shown that 70% of sales are collected in the quarter in which the sale is made and the remaining 30% are collected in the following quarter. For example, 70% of the first quarter sales of $200,000 (or $140,000) is collected during the first quarter and 30% (or $60,000) is collected during the second quarter.

The Production Budget

LEARNING OBJECTIVE 3
Prepare a production budget.

The production budget is prepared after the sales budget. The **production budget** lists the number of units that must be produced during each budget period to meet sales needs and to provide for the desired ending inventory. Production needs can be determined as follows:

Budgeted sales in units	XXXX
Add desired ending inventory	XXXX
Total needs	XXXX
Less beginning inventory	XXXX
Required production	XXXX

Note that production requirements for a quarter are influenced by the desired level of the ending inventory. Inventories should be carefully planned. Excessive inventories tie up funds and create storage problems. Insufficient inventories can lead to lost sales or crash production efforts in the following period. At Hampton Freeze, management believes that an ending inventory equal to 20% of the next quarter's sales strikes the appropriate balance.

Schedule 2 contains the production budget for Hampton Freeze. The first row in the production budget contains the budgeted sales, which have been taken directly from the sales budget (Schedule 1). The total needs for the first quarter are determined by adding together the budgeted sales of 10,000 cases for the quarter and the desired ending inventory of 6,000 cases. As discussed above, the ending inventory is intended to provide some cushion in case problems develop in production or sales increase unexpectedly. Since the budgeted sales for the second quarter are 30,000 cases and management would like the ending inventory in each quarter to be equal to 20% of the following quarter's sales, the desired ending inventory is 6,000 cases (20% of 30,000 cases). Consequently, the total needs for the first quarter are 16,000 cases. However, since the company already has 2,000 cases in beginning inventory, only 14,000 cases need to be produced in the first quarter.

Pay particular attention to the Year column to the right of the production budget in Schedule 2. In some cases (e.g., budgeted sales, total needs, and required production), the amount listed for the year is the sum of the quarterly amounts for the item. In other cases (e.g., desired inventory of finished goods and beginning inventory of finished goods), the amount listed for the year is not simply the sum of the quarterly amounts. From the stand-

Schedule 2

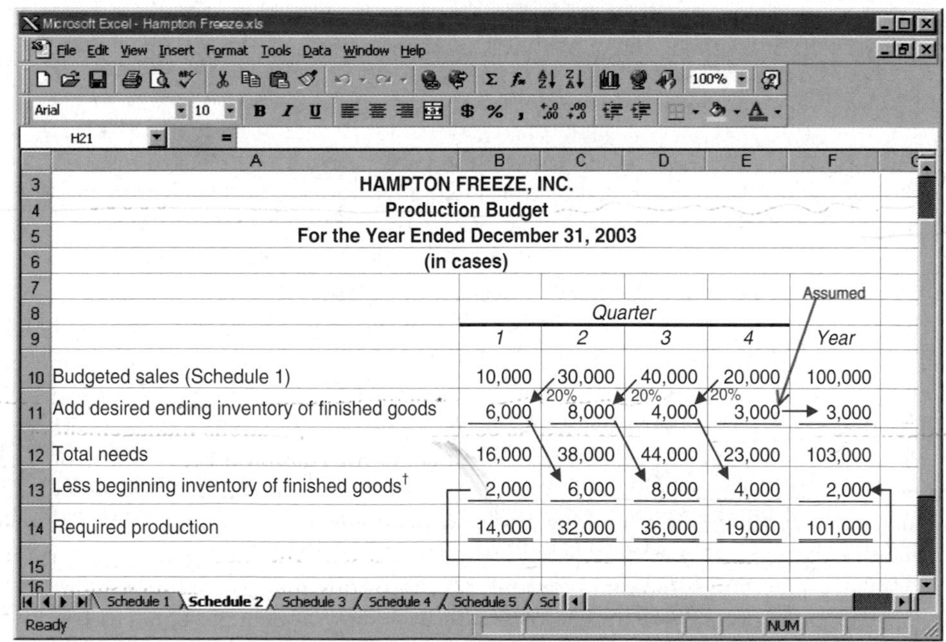

HAMPTON FREEZE, INC.
Production Budget
For the Year Ended December 31, 2003
(in cases)

	Quarter 1	2	3	4	Year
Budgeted sales (Schedule 1)	10,000	30,000	40,000	20,000	100,000
Add desired ending inventory of finished goods*	6,000	8,000	4,000	3,000	3,000
Total needs	16,000	38,000	44,000	23,000	103,000
Less beginning inventory of finished goods†	2,000	6,000	8,000	4,000	2,000
Required production	14,000	32,000	36,000	19,000	101,000

*Twenty percent of the next quarter's sales. The ending inventory of 3,000 cases is assumed.

†The beginning inventory in each quarter is the same as the prior quarter's ending inventory.

point of the entire year, the beginning inventory of finished goods is the same as the beginning inventory of finished goods for the first quarter—it is *not* the sum of the beginning inventories of finished goods for all quarters. Similarly, from the standpoint of the entire year, the ending inventory of finished goods is the same as the ending inventory of finished goods for the fourth quarter—it is *not* the sum of the ending inventories of finished goods for all four quarters. It is important to pay attention to such distinctions in all of the schedules that follow.

Inventory Purchases—Merchandising Firm

Hampton Freeze prepares a production budget, since it is a *manufacturing* firm. If it were a *merchandising* firm, it would prepare a **merchandise purchases budget** instead showing the amount of goods to be purchased from its suppliers during the period. The merchandise purchases budget has the same basic format as the production budget, as shown below:

Budgeted cost of goods sold (in units or in dollars)	XXXXX
Add desired ending merchandise inventory.	XXXXX
Total needs.	XXXXX
Less beginning merchandise inventory	XXXXX
Required purchases (in units or in dollars).	XXXXX

Concept 9–2

A merchandising firm would prepare an inventory purchases budget such as the one above for each item carried in stock.

The Direct Materials Budget

LEARNING OBJECTIVE 4
Prepare a direct materials budget, including a schedule of expected cash disbursements for purchases of materials.

Returning to Hampton Freeze after the production requirements have been computed, a *direct materials budget* can be prepared. The **direct materials budget** details the raw materials that must be purchased to fulfill the production budget and to provide for adequate inventories. The required purchases of raw materials are computed as follows:

Raw materials needed to meet the production schedule	XXXXX
Add desired ending inventory of raw materials	XXXXX
Total raw materials needs	XXXXX
Less beginning inventory of raw materials.	XXXXX
Raw materials to be purchased	XXXXX

Preparing a budget of this kind is one step in a company's overall **material requirements planning (MRP).** MRP is an operations management tool that uses a computer to help manage materials and inventories. The objective of MRP is to ensure that the right materials are on hand, in the right quantities, and at the right time to support the production budget. The detailed operation of MRP is covered in most operations management books.

Schedule 3 contains the direct materials budget for Hampton Freeze. The only raw material included in that budget is high fructose sugar, which is the major ingredient in popsicles other than water. The remaining raw materials are relatively insignificant and are included in variable manufacturing overhead. As with finished goods, management would like to maintain some minimum inventories of raw materials as a cushion. In this case, management would like to maintain ending inventories of sugar equal to 10% of the following quarter's production needs.

The first line in the direct materials budget contains the required production for each quarter, which is taken directly from the production budget (Schedule 2). Looking at the first quarter, since the production schedule calls for production of 14,000 cases of popsicles and each case requires 15 pounds of sugar, the total production needs are for 210,000

Schedule 3

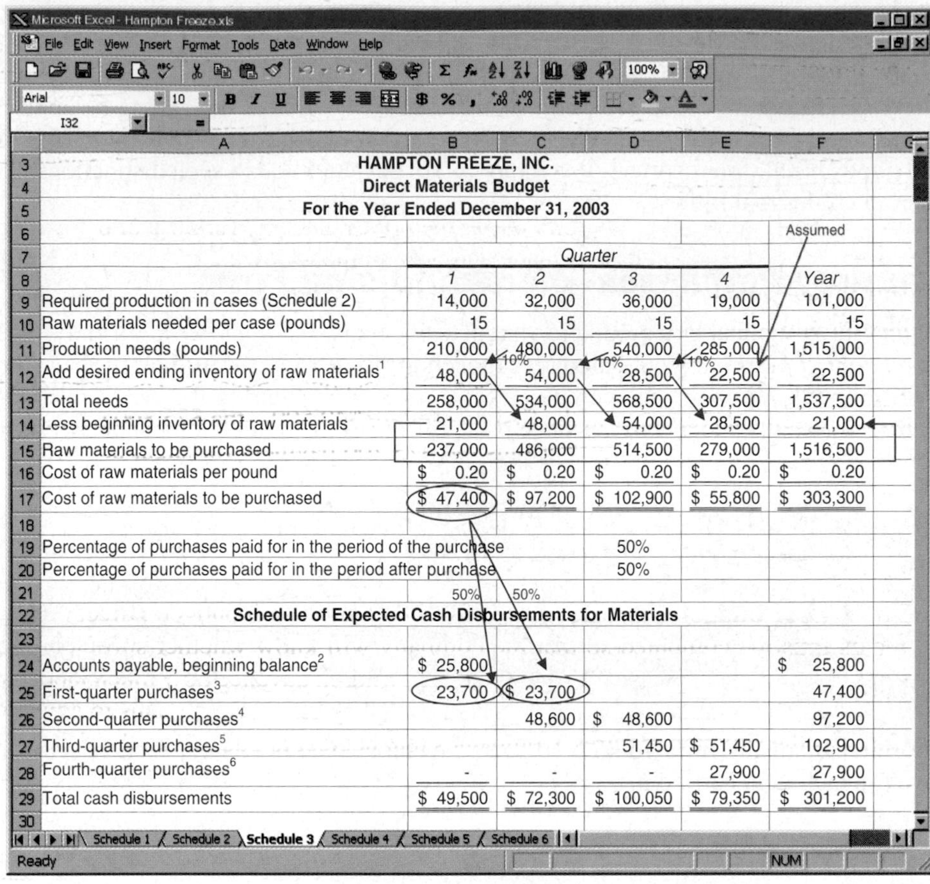

HAMPTON FREEZE, INC.					
Direct Materials Budget					
For the Year Ended December 31, 2003					
					Assumed
	Quarter				
	1	2	3	4	Year
Required production in cases (Schedule 2)	14,000	32,000	36,000	19,000	101,000
Raw materials needed per case (pounds)	15	15	15	15	15
Production needs (pounds)	210,000	480,000	540,000	285,000	1,515,000
Add desired ending inventory of raw materials[1]	48,000	54,000	28,500	22,500	22,500
Total needs	258,000	534,000	568,500	307,500	1,537,500
Less beginning inventory of raw materials	21,000	48,000	54,000	28,500	21,000
Raw materials to be purchased	237,000	486,000	514,500	279,000	1,516,500
Cost of raw materials per pound	$ 0.20	$ 0.20	$ 0.20	$ 0.20	$ 0.20
Cost of raw materials to be purchased	$ 47,400	$ 97,200	$ 102,900	$ 55,800	$ 303,300
Percentage of purchases paid for in the period of the purchase			50%		
Percentage of purchases paid for in the period after purchase			50%		
Schedule of Expected Cash Disbursements for Materials					
Accounts payable, beginning balance[2]	$ 25,800				$ 25,800
First-quarter purchases[3]	23,700	$ 23,700			47,400
Second-quarter purchases[4]		48,600	$ 48,600		97,200
Third-quarter purchases[5]			51,450	$ 51,450	102,900
Fourth-quarter purchases[6]	-	-	-	27,900	27,900
Total cash disbursements	$ 49,500	$ 72,300	$ 100,050	$ 79,350	$ 301,200

[1]Ten percent of the next quarter's production needs. For example, the second-quarter production needs are 480,000 pounds. Therefore, the desired ending inventory for the first quarter would be 10% × 480,000 pounds = 48,000 pounds. The ending inventory of 22,500 pounds for the quarter is assumed.

[2]Cash payments for last year's fourth-quarter material purchases. See the beginning-of-year balance sheet on page 397.

[3]$47,500 × 50%; $47,500 × 50%.

[4]$97,200 × 50%; $97,200 × 50%.

[5]$102,900 × 50%; $102,900 × 50%.

[6]$55,800 × 50%. Unpaid fourth-quarter purchases appear as accounts payable on the company's end-of-year balance sheet.

pounds of sugar (14,000 cases × 15 pounds per case). In addition, management wants to have ending inventories of 48,000 pounds of sugar, which is 10% of the following quarter's needs of 480,000 pounds. Consequently, the total needs are for 258,000 pounds (210,000 pounds for the current quarter's production plus 48,000 pounds for the desired ending inventory). However, since the company already has 21,000 pounds in beginning inventory, only 237,000 pounds of sugar (258,000 pounds − 21,000 pounds) will need to be purchased. Finally, the cost of the raw materials purchases is determined by multiplying the amount of raw material to be purchased by the cost per unit of the raw material. In this case, since 237,000 pounds of sugar will have to be purchased during the first quarter and sugar costs $0.20 per pound, the total cost will be $47,400 (237,000 pounds × $0.20 per pound).

As with the production budget, the amounts listed under the Year column are not always just the sum of the quarterly amounts. The desired ending inventory of raw materials for the year is the same as the desired ending inventory of raw materials for the fourth quarter. Likewise, the beginning inventory of raw materials for the year is the same as the beginning inventory of raw materials for the first quarter.

The direct materials budget is usually accompanied by a schedule of expected cash disbursements for raw materials. This schedule is needed to prepare the overall cash budget. Disbursements for raw materials consist of payments for purchases on account in prior periods plus any payments for purchases in the current budget period. Schedule 3 contains such a schedule of cash disbursements. Ordinarily, companies do not immediately pay their suppliers. At Hampton Freeze, the policy is to pay for 50% of purchases in the quarter in which the purchase is made and 50% in the following quarter, so while the company intends to purchase $47,400 worth of sugar in the first quarter, the company will only pay for half, $23,700, in the first quarter and the other half will be paid in the second quarter. The company will also pay $25,800 for sugar acquired in the previous quarter, but not yet paid for. This is the beginning balance in the accounts payable. Therefore, the total cash disbursements for sugar in the first quarter are $49,500—the $25,800 payment for sugar acquired in the previous quarter plus the $23,700 payment for sugar acquired during the first quarter.

The Direct Labor Budget

LEARNING OBJECTIVE 5
Prepare a direct labor budget.

The **direct labor budget** is also developed from the production budget. Direct labor requirements must be computed so that the company will know whether sufficient labor time is available to meet production needs. By knowing in advance how much labor time will be needed throughout the budget year, the company can develop plans to adjust the labor force as the situation requires. Companies that neglect to budget run the risk of facing labor shortages or having to hire and lay off workers at awkward times. Erratic labor policies lead to insecurity, low morale, and inefficiency.

The direct labor budget for Hampton Freeze is shown in Schedule 4. The first line in the direct labor budget consists of the required production for each quarter, which is taken directly from the production budget (Schedule 2). The direct labor requirement for each quarter is computed by multiplying the number of units to be produced in that quarter by the number of direct labor-hours required to make a unit. For example, 14,000 cases are to be produced in the first quarter and each case requires 0.40 direct labor-hour, so a total of 5,600 direct labor-hours (14,000 cases × 0.40 direct labor-hour per case) will be required in the first quarter. The direct labor requirements can then be translated into budgeted direct labor costs. How this is done will depend on the company's labor policy. In Schedule 4, the management of Hampton Freeze has assumed that the direct labor force will be adjusted as the work requirements change from quarter to quarter. In that case, the direct labor cost is computed by simply multiplying the direct labor-hour requirements by the direct labor rate per hour. For example, the direct labor cost in the first quarter is $84,000 (5,600 direct labor-hours × $15 per direct labor-hour).

However, many companies have employment policies or contracts that prevent them from laying off and rehiring workers as needed. Suppose, for example, that Hampton Freeze has 25 workers who are classified as direct labor and each of them is guaranteed at least 480 hours of pay each quarter at a rate of $15 per hour. In that case, the minimum direct labor cost for a quarter would be as follows:

25 workers × 480 hours per worker × $15 per hour = $180,000

Note that in Schedule 4 the direct labor costs for the first and fourth quarters would have to be increased to a $180,000 level if Hampton Freeze's labor policy did not allow it to adjust the work force at will.

The Manufacturing Overhead Budget

LEARNING OBJECTIVE 6
Prepare a manufacturing overhead budget.

The **manufacturing overhead budget** provides a schedule of all costs of production other than direct materials and direct labor. Schedule 5 shows the manufacturing overhead budget for Hampton Freeze. At Hampton Freeze the manufacturing overhead is separated into

Schedule 4

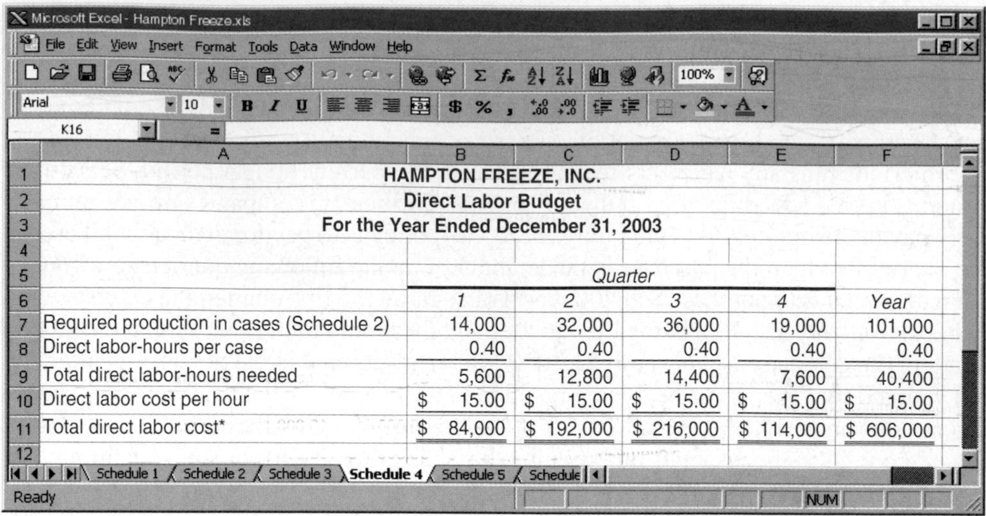

HAMPTON FREEZE, INC.
Direct Labor Budget
For the Year Ended December 31, 2003

	Quarter				
	1	2	3	4	Year
Required production in cases (Schedule 2)	14,000	32,000	36,000	19,000	101,000
Direct labor-hours per case	0.40	0.40	0.40	0.40	0.40
Total direct labor-hours needed	5,600	12,800	14,400	7,600	40,400
Direct labor cost per hour	$ 15.00	$ 15.00	$ 15.00	$ 15.00	$ 15.00
Total direct labor cost*	$ 84,000	$ 192,000	$ 216,000	$ 114,000	$ 606,000

*This schedule assumes that the direct labor work force will be fully adjusted to the total direct labor-hours needed each quarter.

variable and fixed components. The variable component is $4 per direct labor-hour and the fixed component is $60,600 per quarter. Because the variable component of the manufacturing overhead depends on direct labor, the first line in the manufacturing overhead budget consists of the budgeted direct labor-hours from the direct labor budget (Schedule 4). The budgeted direct labor-hours in each quarter are multiplied by the variable rate to determine the variable component of manufacturing overhead. For example, the variable manufacturing overhead for the first quarter is $22,400 (5,600 direct labor-hours × $4.00 per direct labor-hour). This is added to the fixed manufacturing overhead for the quarter to determine the total manufacturing overhead for the quarter. For example, the total manufacturing overhead for the first quarter is $83,000 ($22,400 + $60,600).

A few words about fixed costs and the budgeting process are in order. In most cases, fixed costs are the costs of supplying capacity to do things like make products, process purchase orders, handle customer calls, and so on. The amount of capacity that will be required depends on the expected level of activity for the period. If the expected level of activity is greater than the company's current capacity, then fixed costs may have to be increased. Or, if the expected level is appreciably below the company's current capacity, then it may be desirable to decrease fixed costs if that is possible. However, once the level of the fixed costs has been determined in the budget, the costs really are fixed. The time to adjust fixed costs is during the budgeting process. To determine the appropriate level of fixed costs at budget time, an activity-based costing system can be very helpful. It can help answer questions like, "How many clerks will we need to hire to process the anticipated number of purchase orders next year?" For simplicity, we assume in all of the budgeting examples in this book that the appropriate levels of fixed costs have already been determined for the budget with the aid of activity-based costing or some other method.

The last line of Schedule 5 for Hampton Freeze shows its budgeted cash disbursements for manufacturing overhead. Since some of the overhead costs are not cash outflows, the total budgeted manufacturing overhead costs must be adjusted to determine the cash disbursements for manufacturing overhead. At Hampton Freeze, the only significant noncash manufacturing overhead cost is depreciation, which is $15,000 per quarter. These noncash depreciation charges are deducted from the total budgeted manufacturing overhead to determine the expected cash disbursements. Hampton Freeze pays all overhead costs involving cash disbursements in the quarter incurred. Note that the company's predetermined overhead rate for the year will be $10 per direct labor-hour, which is determined by dividing the total budgeted manufacturing overhead for the year by the total budgeted direct labor-hours for the year.

Schedule 5

HAMPTON FREEZE, INC.					
Manufacturing Overhead Budget					
For the Year Ended December 31, 2003					
	Quarter				
	1	*2*	*3*	*4*	*Year*
Budgeted direct labor-hours (Schedule 4)	5,600	12,800	14,400	7,600	40,400
Variable overhead rate	$ 4.00	$ 4.00	$ 4.00	$ 4.00	$ 4.00
Variable manufacturing overhead	$ 22,400	$ 51,200	$ 57,600	$ 30,400	$ 161,600
Fixed manufacturing overhead	60,600	60,600	60,600	60,600	242,400
Total manufacturing overhead	83,000	111,800	118,200	91,000	404,000
Less depreciation	15,000	15,000	15,000	15,000	60,000
Cash disbursement for manufacturing overhead	$ 68,000	$ 96,800	$ 103,200	$ 76,000	$ 344,000
Total manufacturing overhead (a)					$ 404,000
Budgeted direct labor-hours (b)					40,400
Predetermined overhead rate for the year (a) ÷ (b)					$ 10.00

The Ending Finished Goods Inventory Budget

After completing Schedules 1–5, Larry Giano had all of the data he needed to compute unit product costs. This computation was needed for two reasons: first, to determine cost of goods sold on the budgeted income statement; and second, to know what amount to put on the balance sheet inventory account for unsold units. The carrying cost of the unsold units is computed on the **ending finished goods inventory budget.**

Larry Giano considered using variable costing in preparing Hampton Freeze's budget statements, but he decided to use absorption costing instead since the bank would very likely require that absorption costing be used. He also knew that it would be easy to convert the absorption costing financial statements to a variable costing basis later. At this point, the primary concern was to determine what financing, if any, would be required in the year 2003 and then to arrange for that financing from the bank.

The unit product cost computations are shown in Schedule 6. For Hampton Freeze, the absorption costing unit product cost is $13 per case of popsicles—consisting of $3 of direct materials, $6 of direct labor, and $4 of manufacturing overhead. The manufacturing overhead is applied to units of product on the basis of direct labor-hours at the rate of $10 per direct labor-hour. The budgeted carrying cost of the expected ending inventory is $39,000.

The Selling and Administrative Expense Budget

LEARNING OBJECTIVE 7
Prepare a selling and administrative expense budget.

The **selling and administrative expense budget** lists the budgeted expenses for areas other than manufacturing. In large organizations, this budget would be a compilation of many smaller, individual budgets submitted by department heads and other persons responsible for selling and administrative expenses. For example, the marketing manager in a large organization would submit a budget detailing the advertising expenses for each budget period.

Schedule 7 contains the selling and administrative expense budget for Hampton Freeze. Like the manufacturing overhead budget, the selling and administrative budget is divided into variable and fixed cost components. In the case of Hampton Freeze, the variable selling and administrative expense is $1.80 per case. Consequently, budgeted sales in cases for each quarter are entered at the top of the schedule. These data are taken from the sales budget (Schedule 1). The budgeted variable selling and administrative expenses are determined by multiplying the budgeted sales in cases by the variable selling and administrative expense per case. For example, the budgeted variable selling and administrative

Schedule 6

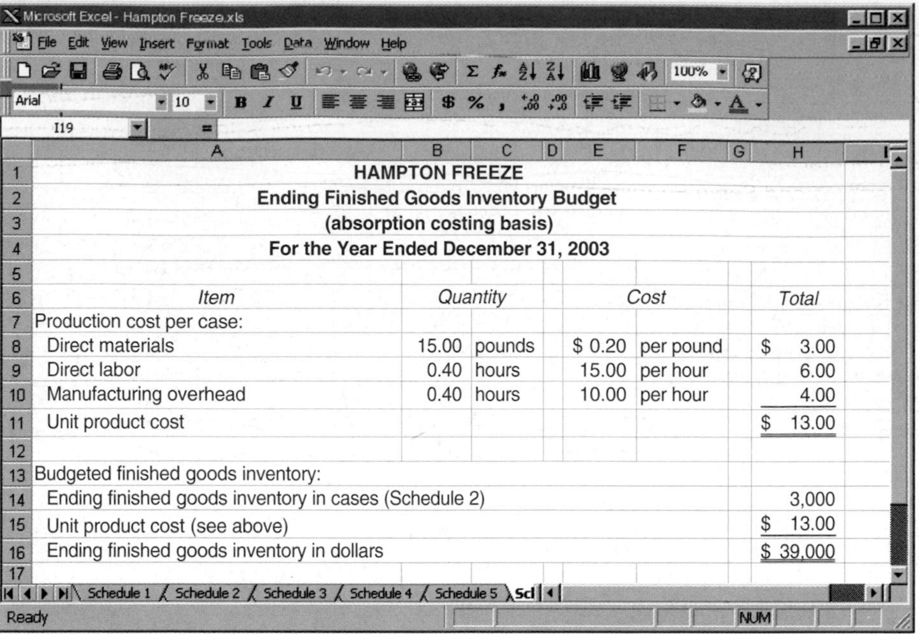

HAMPTON FREEZE
Ending Finished Goods Inventory Budget
(absorption costing basis)
For the Year Ended December 31, 2003

Item	*Quantity*		*Cost*		*Total*
Production cost per case:					
Direct materials	15.00	pounds	$ 0.20	per pound	$ 3.00
Direct labor	0.40	hours	15.00	per hour	6.00
Manufacturing overhead	0.40	hours	10.00	per hour	4.00
Unit product cost					$ 13.00
Budgeted finished goods inventory:					
Ending finished goods inventory in cases (Schedule 2)					3,000
Unit product cost (see above)					$ 13.00
Ending finished goods inventory in dollars					$ 39,000

Schedule 7

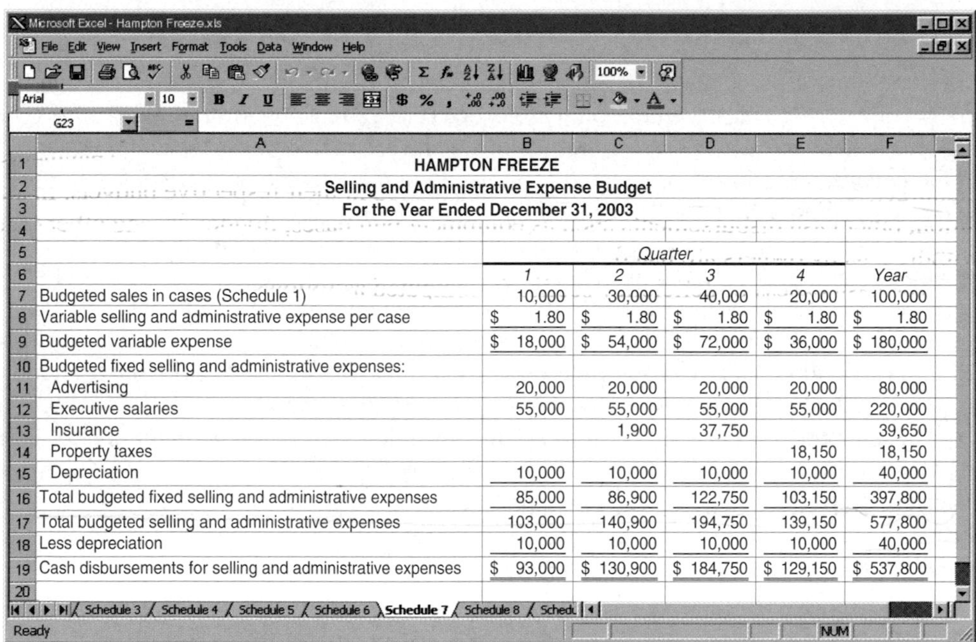

HAMPTON FREEZE
Selling and Administrative Expense Budget
For the Year Ended December 31, 2003

	Quarter				
	1	*2*	*3*	*4*	*Year*
Budgeted sales in cases (Schedule 1)	10,000	30,000	40,000	20,000	100,000
Variable selling and administrative expense per case	$ 1.80	$ 1.80	$ 1.80	$ 1.80	$ 1.80
Budgeted variable expense	$ 18,000	$ 54,000	$ 72,000	$ 36,000	$ 180,000
Budgeted fixed selling and administrative expenses:					
Advertising	20,000	20,000	20,000	20,000	80,000
Executive salaries	55,000	55,000	55,000	55,000	220,000
Insurance		1,900	37,750		39,650
Property taxes				18,150	18,150
Depreciation	10,000	10,000	10,000	10,000	40,000
Total budgeted fixed selling and administrative expenses	85,000	86,900	122,750	103,150	397,800
Total budgeted selling and administrative expenses	103,000	140,900	194,750	139,150	577,800
Less depreciation	10,000	10,000	10,000	10,000	40,000
Cash disbursements for selling and administrative expenses	$ 93,000	$ 130,900	$ 184,750	$ 129,150	$ 537,800

expense for the first quarter is $18,000 (10,000 cases × $1.80 per case). The fixed selling and administrative expenses (all given data) are then added to the variable selling and administrative expenses to arrive at the total budgeted selling and administrative expenses. Finally, to determine the cash disbursements for selling and administrative items, the total budgeted selling and administrative expense is adjusted by adding back any noncash selling and administrative expenses (in this case, just depreciation).

The Cash Budget

LEARNING OBJECTIVE 8
Prepare a cash budget.

As illustrated in Exhibit 9–2, the cash budget pulls together much of the data developed in the preceding steps. It is a good idea to restudy Exhibit 9–2 to get the big picture firmly in mind before moving on.

Concentrating on the Cash Flow

In Business

Burlington Northern Santa Fe (BNSF) operates the second largest railroad in the United States. The company's senior vice president, CFO, and treasurer is Tom Hunt, who reports that "As a general theme, we've become very cash-flow-oriented." After the merger of the Burlington Northern and Santa Fe railroads, the company went through a number of years in which they were investing heavily and consequently had negative cash flows. To keep on top of the company's cash position, Hunt has a cash forecast prepared every month. "Everything falls like dominoes from free cash flow," Hunt says. "It provides us with alternatives. Right now, the alternative of choice is buying back our own stock . . . [b]ut it could be increasing dividends or making acquisitions. All those things are not even on the radar screen if you don't have free cash flow."

Source: Randy Myers, "Cash Crop: The 2000 Working Capital Survey," *CFO*, August 2000, pp. 59–82.

The cash budget is composed of four major sections:

1. The receipts section.
2. The disbursements section
3. The cash excess or deficiency section.
4. The financing section.

The receipts section consists of a listing of all of the cash inflows, except for financing, expected during the budget period. Generally, the major source of receipts will be from sales.

The disbursements section consists of all cash payments that are planned for the budget period. These payments will include raw materials purchases, direct labor payments, manufacturing overhead costs, and so on, as contained in their respective budgets. In addition, other cash disbursements such as equipment purchases, dividends, and other cash withdrawals by owners are listed.

The cash excess or deficiency section is computed as follows:

Cash balance, beginning	XXXX
Add receipts	XXXX
Total cash available	XXXX
Less disbursements	XXXX
Excess (deficiency) of cash available over disbursements	XXXX

If there is a cash deficiency during any budget period, the company will need to borrow funds. If there is a cash excess during any budget period, funds borrowed in previous periods can be repaid or the excess funds can be invested.

The financing section details the borrowings and repayments projected to take place during the budget period. It also includes interest payments that will be due on money borrowed.[1]

Generally speaking, the cash budget should be broken down into time periods that are as short as feasible. Considerable fluctuations in cash balances may be hidden by looking at a longer time period. While a monthly cash budget is most common, many firms budget cash on a weekly or even daily basis. Larry Giano has prepared a quarterly cash budget for Hampton Freeze that can be further refined as necessary. This budget appears in

[1] The format for the statement of cash flows, which is discussed in Chapter 16, may also be used for the cash budget.

Schedule 8

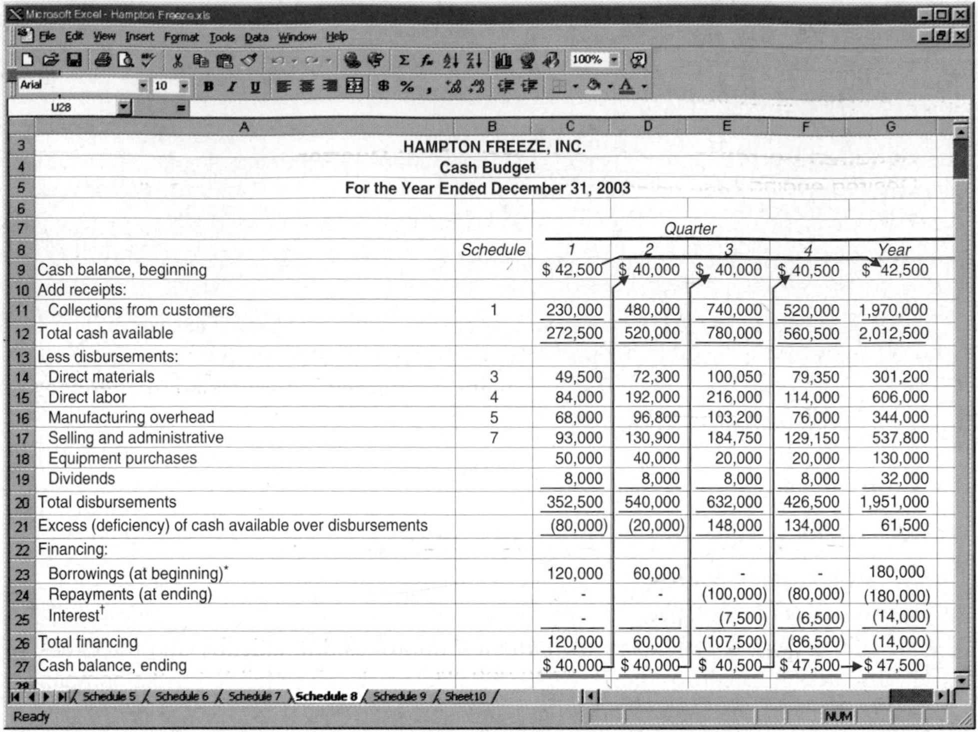

HAMPTON FREEZE, INC.
Cash Budget
For the Year Ended December 31, 2003

	Schedule	Quarter 1	2	3	4	Year
Cash balance, beginning		$ 42,500	$ 40,000	$ 40,000	$ 40,500	$ 42,500
Add receipts:						
Collections from customers	1	230,000	480,000	740,000	520,000	1,970,000
Total cash available		272,500	520,000	780,000	560,500	2,012,500
Less disbursements:						
Direct materials	3	49,500	72,300	100,050	79,350	301,200
Direct labor	4	84,000	192,000	216,000	114,000	606,000
Manufacturing overhead	5	68,000	96,800	103,200	76,000	344,000
Selling and administrative	7	93,000	130,900	184,750	129,150	537,800
Equipment purchases		50,000	40,000	20,000	20,000	130,000
Dividends		8,000	8,000	8,000	8,000	32,000
Total disbursements		352,500	540,000	632,000	426,500	1,951,000
Excess (deficiency) of cash available over disbursements		(80,000)	(20,000)	148,000	134,000	61,500
Financing:						
Borrowings (at beginning)*		120,000	60,000	-	-	180,000
Repayments (at ending)		-	-	(100,000)	(80,000)	(180,000)
Interest†		-	-	(7,500)	(6,500)	(14,000)
Total financing		120,000	60,000	(107,500)	(86,500)	(14,000)
Cash balance, ending		$ 40,000	$ 40,000	$ 40,500	$ 47,500	$ 47,500

*The company requires a minimum cash balance of $40,000. Therefore, borrowing must be sufficient to cover the cash deficiency of $80,000 in quarter 1 and to provide for the minimum cash balance of $40,000. All borrowings and repayments of principal are in round $1,000 amounts.

†The interest payments relate only to the principal being repaid at the time it is repaid. For example, the interest in quarter 3 relates only to the interest due on the $100,000 principal being repaid from quarter 1 borrowing: $100,000 × 10% per year × ¾ year = $7,500. The interest paid in quarter 4 is computed as follows:

$20,000 × 10% per year × 1 year	$2,000
$60,000 × 10% per year × ¾ year	4,500
Total interest paid	$6,500

Schedule 8. The cash budget builds on the earlier schedules and on some additional data that are provided below:

- The beginning cash balance is $42,500.
- Management plans to spend $130,000 during the year on equipment purchases: $50,000 in the first quarter; $40,000 in the second quarter; $20,000 in the third quarter; and $20,000 in the fourth quarter.
- The board of directors has approved cash dividends of $8,000 per quarter.
- Management would like to have a cash balance of at least $40,000 at the beginning of each quarter for contingencies.
- Assume Hampton Freeze will be able to get agreement from a bank for an open line of credit. This would enable the company to borrow at an interest rate of 10% per year. All borrowing and repayments would be in round $1,000 amounts. All borrowing would occur at the beginning of quarters and all repayments would be made at the end of quarters. Interest would be due when repayments are made and only on the amount of principal that is repaid.

The cash budget is prepared one quarter at a time, starting with the first quarter. Larry began the cash budget by entering the beginning balance of cash for the first quarter of $42,500—a number that is given above. Receipts—in this case, just the $230,000 in cash collections from customers—are added to the beginning balance to arrive at the total cash available of $272,500. Since the total disbursements are $352,500 and the total cash available is only $272,500, there is a shortfall of $80,000. Since management would like to have a beginning cash balance of at least $40,000 for the second quarter, the company will need to borrow $120,000.

Required Borrowings at the End of the First Quarter	
Desired ending cash balance	$ 40,000
Plus deficiency of cash available over disbursements	80,000
Required borrowings	$120,000

The second quarter of the cash budget is handled similarly. Note that the ending cash balance for the first quarter is brought forward as the beginning cash balance for the second quarter. Also note that additional borrowing is required in the second quarter because of the continued cash shortfall.

Required Borrowings at the End of the Second Quarter	
Desired ending cash balance	$40,000
Plus deficiency of cash available over disbursements	20,000
Required borrowings	$60,000

In the third quarter, the cash flow situation improves dramatically and the excess of cash available over disbursements is $148,000. This makes it possible for the company to repay part of its loan from the bank, which now totals $180,000. How much can be repaid? The total amount of the principal *and* interest that can be repaid is determined as follows:

Total Maximum Feasible Loan Payments at the End of the Third Quarter	
Excess of cash available over disbursements	$148,000
Less desired ending cash balance	40,000
Maximum feasible principal and interest payment	$108,000

The next step—figuring out the exact amount of the loan payment—is tricky since interest must be paid on the principal amount that is repaid. In this case, the principal amount that is repaid must be less than $108,000, so we know that we would be paying off part of the loan that was taken out at the beginning of the first quarter. Since the repayment would be made at the end of the third quarter, interest would have accrued for three quarters. So the interest owed would be ¾ of 10%, or 7.5%. Either a trial-and-error or an algebraic approach will lead to the conclusion that the maximum principal repayment that can be made is $100,000.[2] The interest payment would be 7.5% of this amount, or $7,500—making the total payment $107,500.

In the fourth quarter, all of the loan and accumulated interest are paid off. If all loans are not repaid at the end of the year and budgeted financial statements are prepared, then interest must be accrued on the unpaid loans. This interest will not appear on the cash budget (since it has not yet been paid), but it will appear as interest expense on the budgeted income statement and as a liability on the budgeted balance sheet.

As with the production and raw materials budgets, the amounts under the Year column in the cash budget are not always the sum of the amounts for the four quarters. In particular, the beginning cash balance for the year is the same as the beginning cash

[2] The algebraic approach to determining the amount that can be repaid on the loan follows:
Let X be the amount of the principal repayment. Then $10\% \times 3/4 \times X$ is the amount of interest owed on that principal amount. Since the company can afford to pay at most $108,000 to the bank, the sum of the principal repayment and the interest payment cannot exceed $108,000.

$$X + 10\% \times 3/4 \times X \leq \$108{,}000, \text{ or}$$

$$X \leq \$100{,}465$$

Since all repayments must be in round $1,000 amounts, the appropriate principal repayment is $100,000.

balance for the first quarter and the ending cash balance for the year is the same as the ending cash balance for the fourth quarter. Also note the beginning cash balance in any quarter is the same as the ending cash balance for the previous quarter.

In Business | Flying without a Plan

Harlan Accola turned his interests in flying and photography into a business by selling aerial photos of farms and homes. Sales were so good that what started out as a way to finance a hobby soon became a full-scale business. He paid an outside accountant to prepare financial statements, which he admits he didn't understand. "I didn't think it was important. I thought a financial statement was just something you had to give to the bank to keep your loan OK. So I took it, looked at the bottom line, and tossed it into a desk drawer."

Accola's casual approach worked for a while. However, within a few years he had lost control of his cash flows. Unpaid creditors were hounding him, and the Internal Revenue Service was demanding overdue taxes. The bank, alarmed by the cash flow situation, demanded to be repaid the $240,000 loan it had extended to the company. Accola confesses that "I thought if I made enough sales, everything else would take care of itself. But I confused profits with cash flow." The good news is that the company recovered from its near-brush with bankruptcy, instituted formal financial planning procedures, and is now very successful.

Source: Jay Finnegan, "Everything according to Plan," *Inc.*, March 1995, pp. 78–85.

The Budgeted Income Statement

LEARNING OBJECTIVE 9
Prepare a budgeted income statement.

A budgeted income statement can be prepared from the data developed in Schedules 1–8. *The budgeted income statement is one of the key schedules in the budget process.* It shows the company's planned profit for the upcoming budget period, and it stands as a benchmark against which subsequent company performance can be measured.

Schedule 9 contains the budgeted income statement for Hampton Freeze.

Schedule 9

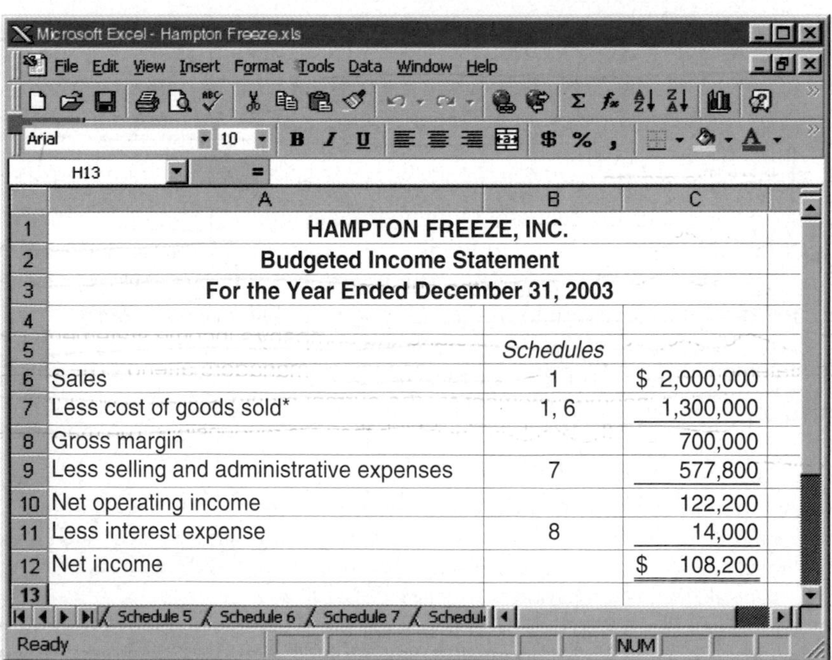

HAMPTON FREEZE, INC.		
Budgeted Income Statement		
For the Year Ended December 31, 2003		
	Schedules	
Sales	1	$ 2,000,000
Less cost of goods sold*	1, 6	1,300,000
Gross margin		700,000
Less selling and administrative expenses	7	577,800
Net operating income		122,200
Less interest expense	8	14,000
Net income		$ 108,200

*100,000 cases sold × $13 per case = $1,300,000.

The Budgeted Balance Sheet

LEARNING OBJECTIVE 10
Prepare a budgeted balance sheet.

The budgeted balance sheet is developed by beginning with the current balance sheet and adjusting it for the data contained in the other budgets. Hampton Freeze's budgeted balance sheet is presented in Schedule 10. Some of the data on the budgeted balance sheet have been taken from the company's previous end-of-year balance sheet for 2002 which appears below:

HAMPTON FREEZE, INC.
Balance Sheet
December 31, 2002

Assets		
Current assets:		
Cash	$ 42,500	
Accounts receivable	90,000	
Raw materials inventory (21,000 pounds)	4,200	
Finished goods inventory (2,000 cases)	26,000	
Total current assets		$162,700
Plant and equipment:		
Land	80,000	
Buildings and equipment	700,000	
Accumulated depreciation	(292,000)	
Plant and equipment, net		488,000
Total assets		$650,700
Liabilities and Stockholders' Equity		
Current liabilities:		
Accounts payable (raw materials)		$ 25,800
Stockholders' equity:		
Common stock, no par	$175,000	
Retained earnings	449,900	
Total stockholders' equity		624,900
Total liabilities and stockholders' equity		$650,700

The Great Huddle

In Business

Springfield Remanufacturing Corporation (SRC) rebuilds used engines. SRC was a failing division of International Harvester when it was purchased by Jack Stack and a group of employees. Mr. Stack, the CEO of the company, likens a successful business to a winning team on the playing field. He argues that in order to win:

- All team players must know the rules of the game.
- All team players must follow the action and know how to keep score.
- All team players must have a stake in the outcome.

At SRC, every employee is taught to understand the company's income statement, balance sheet, and statement of cash flows. Each Wednesday all managers attend "The Great Huddle" in which a projected income statement for the current month is filled in on a blank form. Managers report and discuss the numbers for which they are responsible. The managers then return to their departments and hold a series of "huddles" with employees in which the projected income statement is discussed and actions (called new plays) are planned. Employees are given a stake in the outcome by receiving bonuses if certain overall financial goals are met. In addition, an employee stock ownership program (ESOP) encourages employees to take a direct financial stake in the company.

The company has been very successful. Over the six years since leaving International Harvester, a share of stock in the company that was originally worth $63 has grown in value to $26,250.

Source: Olen L. Greer, Stevan K. Olson, and Mary Callison, "The Key to Real Teamwork: Understanding Numbers," *Management Accounting,* May 1992, pp. 39–44.

In Business — Automating the Budgeting Process

A number of companies, including Texaco, Fujitsu, Sprint, Nationwide Financial Services, Nortel Networks, Owens Corning, and Xilinx have been attempting to reengineer and automate the budgeting process. The goal is to eliminate the conventional iterative budgeting process that often finds preliminary budgets being passed up and down the management hierarchy many times before final agreement is reached—wasting much time and resulting in budgets that often don't reconcile. Apart from the tremendous technical challenges of integrating diverse budgets from many different operations, automation faces a high behavioral hurdle. As Greg Vesey of Texaco states, "Planning is the most political of all processes to fall under the finance function." Consequently, as many as half of all automation efforts fail. Companies such as National Semiconductor Corp. have given up entirely and have returned to their old budgeting methods.

Source: Russ Banham, "The Revolution in Planning," *CFO*, August 1999, pp. 46–56.

Summary

This chapter presents an overview of the budgeting process and shows how the various operating budgets relate to each other. The sales budget forms the foundation for profit planning. Once the sales budget has been set, the production budget and the selling and administrative budget can be prepared since they depend on how many units are to be sold. The production budget determines how many units are to be produced, so after it is prepared, the various manufacturing cost budgets can be prepared. All of these various budgets feed into the cash budget and the budgeted income statement and balance sheet. There are many connections between these various parts of the master budget. For example, the schedule of expected cash collections, which is completed in connection with the sales budget, provides data for both the cash budget and the budgeted balance sheet.

The material in this chapter is just an introduction to budgeting and profit planning. In later chapters, we will see how budgets are used to control day-to-day operations and how they are used in performance evaluation.

Review Problem: Budget Schedules

Mylar Company manufactures and sells a product that has seasonal variations in demand, with peak sales coming in the third quarter. The following information concerns operations for Year 2—the coming year—and for the first two quarters of Year 3:

a. The company's single product sells for $8 per unit. Budgeted sales in units for the next six quarters are as follows:

	Year 2 Quarter				Year 3 Quarter	
	1	2	3	4	1	2
Budgeted sales in units.......	40,000	60,000	100,000	50,000	70,000	80,000

b. Sales are collected in the following pattern: 75% in the quarter the sales are made, and the remaining 25% in the following quarter. On January 1, Year 2, the company's balance sheet showed $65,000 in accounts receivable, all of which will be collected in the first quarter of the year. Bad debts are negligible and can be ignored.

c. The company desires an ending inventory of finished units on hand at the end of each quarter equal to 30% of the budgeted sales for the next quarter. On December 31, Year 1, the company had 12,000 units on hand.

d. Five pounds of raw materials are required to complete one unit of product. The company requires an ending inventory of raw materials on hand at the end of each quarter equal to 10% of the production needs of the following quarter. On December 31, Year 1, the company had 23,000 pounds of raw materials on hand.

e. The raw material costs $0.80 per pound. Purchases of raw material are paid for in the following pattern: 60% paid in the quarter the purchases are made, and the remaining 40% paid in the following quarter. On January 1, Year 2, the company's balance sheet showed $81,500 in accounts payable for raw material purchases, all of which will be paid for in the first quarter of the year.

Required:

Prepare the following budgets and schedules for the year, showing both quarterly and total figures:

1. A sales budget and a schedule of expected cash collections.
2. A production budget.
3. A direct materials purchases budget and a schedule of expected cash payments for material purchases.

Solution to Review Problem

1. The sales budget is prepared as follows:

	Year 2 Quarter				
	1	2	3	4	Year
Budgeted sales in units . . .	40,000	60,000	100,000	50,000	250,000
Selling price per unit.	× $8	× $8	× $8	× $8	× $8
Total sales.	$320,000	$480,000	$800,000	$400,000	$2,000,000

Based on the budgeted sales above, the schedule of expected cash collections is prepared as follows:

	Year 2 Quarter				
	1	2	3	4	Year
Accounts receivable, beginning balance	$ 65,000				$ 65,000
First-quarter sales ($320,000 × 75%, 25%).	240,000	$ 80,000			320,000
Second-quarter sales ($480,000 × 75%, 25%)		360,000	$120,000		480,000
Third-quarter sales ($800,000 × 75%, 25%)			600,000	$200,000	800,000
Fourth-quarter sales ($400,000 × 75%).				300,000	300,000
Total cash collections	$305,000	$440,000	$720,000	$500,000	$1,965,000

2. Based on the sales budget in units, the production budget is prepared as follows:

	Year 2 Quarter					Year 3 Quarter	
	1	2	3	4	Year	1	2
Budgeted sales (units).	40,000	60,000	100,000	50,000	250,000	70,000	80,000
Add desired ending inventory of finished goods*	18,000	30,000	15,000	21,000†	21,000	24,000	
Total needs	58,000	90,000	115,000	71,000	271,000	94,000	
Less beginning inventory of finished goods	12,000	18,000	30,000	15,000	12,000	21,000	
Required production	46,000	72,000	85,000	56,000	259,000	73,000	

*30% of the following quarter's budgeted sales in units.

†30% of the budgeted Year 3 first-quarter sales.

3. Based on the production budget figures, raw materials will need to be purchased as follows during the year:

	Year 2 Quarter					Year 3 Quarter
	1	2	3	4	Year 2	1
Required production (units)	46,000	72,000	85,000	56,000	259,000	73,000
Raw materials needed per unit (pounds)	× 5	× 5	× 5	× 5	× 5	× 5
Production needs (pounds)	230,000	360,000	425,000	280,000	1,295,000	365,000
Add desired ending inventory of raw materials (pounds)* . . .	36,000	42,500	28,000	36,500†	36,500	
Total needs (pounds)	266,000	402,500	453,000	316,500	1,331,500	
Less beginning inventory of raw materials (pounds)	23,000	36,000	42,500	28,000	23,000	
Raw materials to be purchased (pounds).	243,000	366,500	410,500	288,500	1,308,500	

*Ten percent of the following quarter's production needs in pounds.

†Ten percent of the Year 3 first-quarter production needs in pounds.

2. What are the behavioral implications of the way Cadence and Cross went about preparing the master budget?

(CMA, adapted)

PROBLEM 9–9 Schedules of Expected Cash Collections and Disbursements [LO2, LO4, LO8]

Calgon Products, a distributor of organic beverages, needs a cash budget for September. The following information is available:

a. The cash balance at the beginning of September is $9,000.
b. Actual sales for July and August and expected sales for September are as follows:

	July	August	September
Cash sales	$ 6,500	$ 5,250	$ 7,400
Sales on account	20,000	30,000	40,000
Total sales	$26,500	$35,250	$47,400

Sales on account are collected over a three-month period in the following ratio: 10% collected in the month of sale, 70% collected in the month following sale, and 18% collected in the second month following sale. The remaining 2% is uncollectible.

c. Purchases of inventory will total $25,000 for September. Twenty percent of a month's inventory purchases are paid for during the month of purchase. The accounts payable remaining from August's inventory purchases total $16,000, all of which will be paid in September.
d. Selling and administrative expenses are budgeted at $13,000 for September. Of this amount, $4,000 is for depreciation.
e. Equipment costing $18,000 will be purchased for cash during September, and dividends totaling $3,000 will be paid during the month.
f. The company must maintain a minimum cash balance of $5,000. An open line of credit is available from the company's bank to bolster the cash position as needed.

Required:

1. Prepare a schedule of expected cash collections for September.
2. Prepare a schedule of expected cash disbursements during September for inventory purchases.
3. Prepare a cash budget for September. Indicate in the financing section any borrowing that will be needed during September.

PROBLEM 9–10 Production and Purchases Budgets [LO3, LO4]

Tonga Toys manufactures and distributes a number of products to retailers. One of these products, Playclay, requires three pounds of material A135 in the manufacture of each unit. The company is now planning raw materials needs for the third quarter—July, August, and September. Peak sales of Playclay occur in the third quarter of each year. To keep production and shipments moving smoothly, the company has the following inventory requirements:

a. The finished goods inventory on hand at the end of each month must be equal to 5,000 units plus 30% of the next month's sales. The finished goods inventory on June 30 is budgeted to be 17,000 units.
b. The raw materials inventory on hand at the end of each month must be equal to one-half of the following month's production needs for raw materials. The raw materials inventory on June 30 for material A135 is budgeted to be 64,500 pounds.
c. The company maintains no work in process inventories.

A sales budget for Playclay for the last six months of the year follows.

	Budgeted Sales in Units
July	40,000
August	50,000
September	70,000
October	35,000
November	20,000
December	10,000

Required:

1. Prepare a production budget for Playclay for the months July, August, September, and October.
2. Examine the production budget that you prepared. Why will the company produce more units than it sells in July and August and less units than it sells in September and October?

3. Prepare a budget showing the quantity of material A135 to be purchased for July, August, and September and for the quarter in total.

PROBLEM 9–11 Direct Materials and Direct Labor Budgets [LO4, LO5]
The production department of Priston Company has submitted the following forecast of units to be produced by quarter for the upcoming fiscal year.

	1st Quarter	2nd Quarter	3rd Quarter	4th Quarter
Units to be produced	6,000	7,000	8,000	5,000

In addition, the beginning raw materials inventory for the 1st Quarter is budgeted to be 3,600 pounds and the beginning accounts payable for the 1st Quarter is budgeted to be $11,775.

Each unit requires three pounds of raw material that costs $2.50 per pound. Management desires to end each quarter with an inventory of raw materials equal to 20% of the following quarter's production needs. The desired ending inventory for the 4th Quarter is 3,700 pounds. Management plans to pay for 70% of raw material purchases in the quarter acquired and 30% in the following quarter. Each unit requires 0.50 direct labor-hour and direct labor-hour workers are paid $12 per hour.

Required:

1. Prepare the company's direct materials budget and schedule of expected cash disbursements for materials for the upcoming fiscal year.
2. Prepare the company's direct labor budget for the upcoming fiscal year, assuming that the direct labor work force is adjusted each quarter to match the number of hours required to produce the forecasted number of units produced.

PROBLEM 9–12 Direct Labor and Manufacturing Overhead Budgets [LO5, LO6]
The Production Department of Harveton Corporation has submitted the following forecast of units to be produced by quarter for the upcoming fiscal year.

	1st Quarter	2nd Quarter	3rd Quarter	4th Quarter
Units to be produced	16,000	15,000	14,000	15,000

Each unit requires 0.80 direct labor-hours and direct labor-hour workers are paid $11.50 per hour.

In addition, the variable manufacturing overhead rate is $2.50 per direct labor-hour. The fixed manufacturing overhead is $90,000 per quarter. The only noncash element of manufacturing overhead is depreciation, which is $34,000 per quarter.

Required:

1. Prepare the company's direct labor budget for the upcoming fiscal year, assuming that the direct labor work force is adjusted each quarter to match the number of hours required to produce the forecasted number of units produced.
2. Prepare the company's manufacturing overhead budget.

PROBLEM 9–13 Cash Budget; Income Statement; Balance Sheet [LO2, LO4, LO8, LO9, LO10]
The balance sheet of Phototec, Inc., a distributor of photographic supplies, as of May 31 is given below:

PHOTOTEC, INC.
Balance Sheet
May 31

Assets	
Cash	$ 8,000
Accounts receivable	72,000
Inventory	30,000
Buildings and equipment, net of depreciation	500,000
Total assets	$610,000
Liabilities and Stockholders' Equity	
Accounts payable, suppliers	$ 90,000
Note payable	15,000
Capital stock, no par	420,000
Retained earnings	85,000
Total liabilities and stockholders' equity	$610,000

Phototec, Inc., has not budgeted previously, and for this reason it is limiting its master budget planning horizon to just one month ahead—namely, June. The company has assembled the following budgeted data relating to June:

a. Sales are budgeted at $250,000. Of these sales, $60,000 will be for cash; the remainder will be credit sales. One-half of a month's credit sales are collected in the month the sales are made, and the remainder is collected in the month following. All of the May 31 accounts receivable will be collected in June.
b. Purchases of inventory are expected to total $200,000 during June. These purchases will all be on account. Forty percent of all inventory purchases are paid for in the month of purchase; the remainder is paid in the following month. All of the May 31 accounts payable to suppliers will be paid during June.
c. The June 30 inventory balance is budgeted at $40,000.
d. Operating expenses for June are budgeted at $51,000, exclusive of depreciation. These expenses will be paid in cash. Depreciation is budgeted at $2,000 for the month.
e. The note payable on the May 31 balance sheet will be paid during June. The company's interest expense for June (on all borrowing) will be $500, which will be paid in cash.
f. New warehouse equipment costing $9,000 will be purchased for cash during June.
g. During June, the company will borrow $18,000 from its bank by giving a new note payable to the bank for that amount. The new note will be due in one year.

Required:

1. Prepare a cash budget for June. Support your budget with schedules showing budgeted cash receipts from sales and budgeted cash payments for inventory purchases.
2. Prepare a budgeted income statement for June. Use the income statement format as shown in Schedule 9.
3. Prepare a budgeted balance sheet as of June 30.

PROBLEM 9–14 Schedule of Expected Cash Collections; Cash Budget [LO2, LO8]

Jodi Horton, president of Crestline Products, has just approached the company's bank with a request for a $30,000, 90-day loan. The purpose of the loan is to assist the company in acquiring inventories in support of peak April sales. Since the company has had some difficulty in paying off its loans in the past, the loan officer has asked for a cash budget to help determine whether the loan should be made. The following data are available for the months April–June, during which the loan will be used:

a. On April 1, the start of the loan period, the cash balance will be $26,000. Accounts receivable on April 1 will total $151,500, of which $141,000 will be collected during April and $7,200 will be collected during May. The remainder will be uncollectible.
b. Past experience shows that 20% of a month's sales are collected in the month of sale, 75% in the month following sale, and 4% in the second month following sale. The other 1% represents bad debts that are never collected. Budgeted sales and expenses for the period follow:

	April	May	June
Sales	$200,000	$300,000	$250,000
Merchandise purchases	120,000	180,000	150,000
Payroll	9,000	9,000	8,000
Lease payments	15,000	15,000	15,000
Advertising	70,000	80,000	60,000
Equipment purchases	8,000	—	—
Depreciation	10,000	10,000	10,000

c. Merchandise purchases are paid in full during the month following purchase. Accounts payable for merchandise purchases on March 31, which will be paid during April, total $108,000.
d. In preparing the cash budget, assume that the $30,000 loan will be made in April and repaid in June. Interest on the loan will total $1,200.

Required:

1. Prepare a schedule of expected cash collections for April, May, and June and for the three months in total.
2. Prepare a cash budget, by month and in total, for the three-month period.
3. If the company needs a minimum cash balance of $20,000 to start each month, can the loan be repaid as planned? Explain.

PROBLEM 9–15 Behavioral Aspects of Budgeting; Ethics and the Manager [LO1]
Granger Stokes, managing partner of the venture capital firm of Halston and Stokes, was dissatisfied with the top management of PrimeDrive, a manufacturer of computer disk drives. Halston and Stokes had invested $20 million in PrimeDrive, and the return on their investment had been below par for several years. In a tense meeting of the board of directors of PrimeDrive, Stokes exercised his firm's rights as the major equity investor in PrimeDrive and fired PrimeDrive's chief executive officer (CEO). He then quickly moved to have the board of directors of PrimeDrive appoint himself as the new CEO.

Stokes prided himself on his hard-driving management style. At the first management meeting, he asked two of the managers to stand and fired them on the spot, just to show everyone who was in control of the company. At the budget review meeting that followed, he ripped up the departmental budgets that had been submitted for his review and yelled at the managers for their "wimpy, do nothing targets." He then ordered everyone to submit new budgets calling for at least a 40% increase in sales volume and announced that he would not accept excuses for results that fell below budget.

Keri Kalani, an accountant working for the production manager at PrimeDrive, discovered toward the end of the year that her boss had not been scrapping defective disk drives that had been returned by customers. Instead, he had been shipping them in new cartons to other customers to avoid booking losses. Quality control had deteriorated during the year as a result of the push for increased volume, and returns of defective TRX drives were running as high as 15% of the new drives shipped. When she confronted her boss with her discovery, he told her to mind her own business. And then, in the way of a justification for his actions, he said, "All of us managers are finding ways to hit Stokes' targets."

Required:

1. Is Granger Stokes using budgets as a planning and control tool?
2. What are the behavioral consequences of the way budgets are being used at PrimeDrive?
3. What, if anything, do you think Keri Kalani should do?

PROBLEM 9–16 Integration of Sales, Production, and Purchases Budgets [LO2, LO3, LO4]
Crydon, Inc., manufactures an advanced swim fin for scuba divers. Management is now preparing detailed budgets for the third quarter, July through September, and has assembled the following information to assist in the budget preparation:

a. The Marketing Department has estimated sales as follows for the remainder of the year (in pairs of swim fins):

July	6,000	October	4,000
August.	7,000	November	3,000
September	5,000	December	3,000

The selling price of the swim fins is $50 per pair.

b. All sales are on account. Based on past experience, sales are expected to be collected in the following pattern:

40% in the month of sale
50% in the month following sale
10% uncollectible

The beginning accounts receivable balance (excluding uncollectible amounts) on July 1 will be $130,000.

c. The company maintains finished goods inventories equal to 10% of the following month's sales. The inventory of finished goods on July 1 will be 600 pairs.

d. Each pair of swim fins requires 2 pounds of geico compound. To prevent shortages, the company would like the inventory of geico compound on hand at the end of each month to be equal to 20% of the following month's production needs. The inventory of geico compound on hand on July 1 will be 2,440 pounds.

e. Geico compound costs $2.50 per pound. Crydon pays for 60% of its purchases in the month of purchase; the remainder is paid for in the following month. The accounts payable balance for geico compound purchases will be $11,400 on July 1.

Required:

1. Prepare a sales budget, by month and in total, for the third quarter. (Show your budget in both pairs of swim fins and dollars.) Also prepare a schedule of expected cash collections, by month and in total, for the third quarter.

2. Prepare a production budget for each of the months July through October.
3. Prepare a materials purchases budget for geico compound, by month and in total, for the third quarter. Also prepare a schedule of expected cash payments for geico compound, by month and in total, for the third quarter.

PROBLEM 9–17 Cash Budget with Supporting Schedules [LO2, LO4, LO8]
Janus Products, Inc., is a merchandising company that sells binders, paper, and other school supplies. The company is planning its cash needs for the third quarter. In the past, Janus Products has had to borrow money during the third quarter to support peak sales of back-to-school materials, which occur during August. The following information has been assembled to assist in preparing a cash budget for the quarter:

a. Budgeted monthly income statements for July–October are as follows:

	July	August	September	October
Sales	$40,000	$70,000	$50,000	$45,000
Cost of goods sold	24,000	42,000	30,000	27,000
Gross margin	16,000	28,000	20,000	18,000
Less operating expenses:				
Selling expense	7,200	11,700	8,500	7,300
Administrative expense*	5,600	7,200	6,100	5,900
Total expenses	12,800	18,900	14,600	13,200
Net income	$ 3,200	$ 9,100	$ 5,400	$ 4,800

*Includes $2,000 depreciation each month.

b. Sales are 20% for cash and 80% on credit.
c. Credit sales are collected over a three-month period with 10% collected in the month of sale, 70% in the month following sale, and 20% in the second month following sale. May sales totaled $30,000, and June sales totaled $36,000.
d. Inventory purchases are paid for within 15 days. Therefore, 50% of a month's inventory purchases are paid for in the month of purchase. The remaining 50% is paid in the following month. Accounts payable for inventory purchases at June 30 total $11,700.
e. The company maintains its ending inventory levels at 75% of the cost of the merchandise to be sold in the following month. The merchandise inventory at June 30 is $18,000.
f. Land costing $4,500 will be purchased in July.
g. Dividends of $1,000 will be declared and paid in September.
h. The cash balance on June 30 is $8,000; the company must maintain a cash balance of at least this amount at all times.
i. The company can borrow from its bank as needed to bolster the Cash account. Borrowings and repayments must be in multiples of $1,000. All borrowings take place at the beginning of a month, and all repayments are made at the end of a month. The annual interest rate is 12%. Compute interest on whole months ($1/12$, $2/12$, and so on).

Required:

1. Prepare a schedule of expected cash collections from sales for each of the months July, August, and September and for the quarter in total.
2. Prepare the following for merchandise inventory:
    a. An inventory purchases budget for each of the months July, August, and September.
    b. A schedule of expected cash disbursements for inventory for each of the months July, August, and September and for the quarter in total.
3. Prepare a cash budget for the third quarter, by month as well as for the quarter in total. Show borrowings from the company's bank and repayments to the bank as needed to maintain the minimum cash balance.

PROBLEM 9–18 Cash Budget with Supporting Schedules [LO2, LO4, LO7, LO8]
The president of Univax, Inc., has just approached the company's bank seeking short-term financing for the coming year, Year 2. Univax is a distributor of commercial vacuum cleaners. The bank has stated that the loan request must be accompanied by a detailed cash budget that shows the quarters in which financing will be needed, as well as the amounts that will be needed and the quarters in which repayments can be made.

To provide this information for the bank, the president has directed that the following data be gathered from which a cash budget can be prepared:

a. Budgeted sales and merchandise purchases for Year 2, as well as actual sales and purchases for the last quarter of Year 1, are as follows:

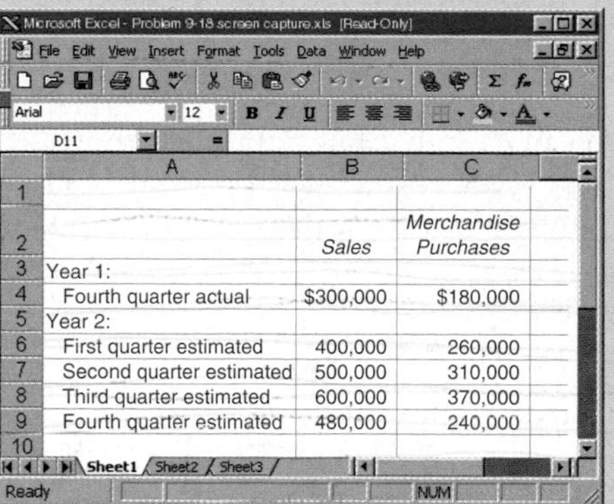

	Sales	Merchandise Purchases
Year 1:		
Fourth quarter actual	$300,000	$180,000
Year 2:		
First quarter estimated	400,000	260,000
Second quarter estimated	500,000	310,000
Third quarter estimated	600,000	370,000
Fourth quarter estimated	480,000	240,000

b. The company typically collects 33% of a quarter's sales before the quarter ends and another 65% in the following quarter. The remainder is uncollectible. This pattern of collections is now being experienced in the actual data for the Year 1 fourth quarter.

c. Some 20% of a quarter's merchandise purchases are paid for within the quarter. The remainder is paid in the following quarter.

d. Operating expenses for Year 2 are budgeted quarterly at $90,000 plus 12% of sales. Of the fixed amount, $20,000 each quarter is depreciation.

e. The company will pay $10,000 in cash dividends each quarter.

f. Land purchases will be made as follows during the year: $80,000 in the second quarter and $48,500 in the third quarter.

g. The Cash account contained $20,000 at the end of Year 1. The company must maintain a minimum cash balance of at least $18,000.

h. Any borrowing will take place at the beginning of a quarter, and any repayments will be made at the end of a quarter at an annual interest rate of 10%. Interest is paid only when principal is repaid. All borrowings and all repayments of principal must be in round $1,000 amounts. Interest payments can be in any amount.

i. At present, the company has no loans outstanding.

Required:

1. Prepare the following, by quarter and in total, for Year 2:
   a. A schedule of expected cash collections on sales.
   b. A schedule of budgeted cash disbursements for merchandise purchases.
2. Compute the expected cash disbursements for operating expenses, by quarter and in total, for Year 2.
3. Using the data from (1) and (2) above and other data as needed, prepare a cash budget for Year 2, by quarter and in total for the year. Show clearly on your budget the quarter(s) in which borrowing will be needed and the quarter(s) in which repayments can be made, as requested by the company's bank.

PROBLEM 9–19 Completing a Master Budget [LO2, LO4, LO7, LO8, LO9, LO10]

Nordic Company, a merchandising company, prepares its master budget on a quarterly basis. The following data have been assembled to assist in preparation of the master budget for the second quarter.

a. As of March 31 (the end of the prior quarter), the company's balance sheet showed the following account balances:

Cash	$ 9,000	
Accounts Receivable	48,000	
Inventory	12,600	
Buildings and Equipment (net)	214,100	
Accounts Payable		$ 18,300
Capital Stock		190,000
Retained Earnings		75,400
	$283,700	$283,700

b. Actual sales for March and budgeted sales for April–July are as follows:

March (actual)	$60,000
April	70,000
May	85,000
June.	90,000
July	50,000

c. Sales are 20% for cash and 80% on credit. All payments on credit sales are collected in the month following sale. The accounts receivable at March 31 are a result of March credit sales.

d. The company's gross profit rate is 40% of sales. (In other words, cost of goods sold is 60% of sales.)

e. Monthly expenses are budgeted as follows: salaries and wages, $7,500 per month; shipping, 6% of sales; advertising, $6,000 per month; other expenses, 4% of sales. Depreciation, including depreciation on new assets acquired during the quarter, will be $6,000 for the quarter.

f. At the end of each month, inventory is to be on hand equal to 30% of the following month's cost of goods sold.

g. Half of a month's inventory purchases are paid for in the month of purchase and half in the following month.

h. Equipment purchases during the quarter will be as follows: April, $11,500; and May, $3,000.

i. Dividends totaling $3,500 will be declared and paid in June.

j. The company must maintain a minimum cash balance of $8,000. An open line of credit is available at a local bank. All borrowing is done at the beginning of a month, and all repayments are made at the end of a month. Borrowings and repayments of principal must be in multiples of $1,000. Interest is paid only at the time of payment of principal. The annual interest rate is 12%. (Figure interest on whole months, e.g., 1/12, 2/12.)

Required:

Using the data above, complete the following statements and schedules for the second quarter:

1. Schedule of expected cash collections:

	April	May	June	Total
Cash sales	$14,000			
Credit sales.	48,000			
Total collections	$62,000			

2. *a.* Inventory purchases budget:

	April	May	June	Total
Budgeted cost of goods sold	$42,000*	$51,000		
Add desired ending inventory. . . .	15,300†			
Total needs	57,300			
Less beginning inventory	12,600			
Required purchases	$44,700			

*$70,000 sales × 60% = $42,000.

†$51,000 × 30% = $15,300.

b. Schedule of cash disbursements for purchases:

	April	May	June	Total
For March purchases	$18,300			$18,300
For April purchases.	22,350	$22,350		44,700
For May purchases.				
For June purchases				
Total cash disbursements for purchases	$40,650			

3. Schedule of cash disbursements for operating expenses:

	April	May	June	Total
Salaries and wages	$7,500			
Shipping	4,200			
Advertising	6,000			
Other expenses	2,800			
Total cash disbursements for operating expenses	$20,500			

4. Cash budget:

	April	May	June	Total
Cash balance, beginning	$ 9,000			
Add cash collections	62,000			
Total cash available	71,000			
Less disbursements:				
For inventory purchases	40,650			
For operating expenses	20,500			
For equipment purchases	11,500			
For dividends	—			
Total disbursements	72,650			
Excess (deficiency) of cash	(1,650)			
Financing				
Etc.				

5. Prepare an income statement for the quarter ending June 30 as shown in Schedule 9 in the chapter.
6. Prepare a balance sheet as of June 30.

PROBLEM 9–20 Completing a Master Budget [LO2, LO4, LO7, LO8, LO9, LO10]
The following data relate to the operations of Picanuy Corporation, a wholesale distributor of consumer goods:

Current assets as of December 31:	
Cash	$ 6,000
Accounts receivable	36,000
Inventory	9,800
Buildings and equipment, net	110,885
Accounts payable	32,550
Capital stock	100,000
Retained earnings	30,135

a. Gross profit is 30% of sales. (In other words, cost of goods sold is 70% of sales.)
b. Actual and budgeted sales data:

December (actual)	$60,000
January	70,000
February	80,000
March	85,000
April	55,000

c. Sales are 40% for cash and 60% on credit. Credit sales are collected in the month following sale. The accounts receivable at December 31 are the result of December credit sales.
d. At the end of each month, inventory is to be on hand equal to 20% of the following month's budgeted cost of goods sold.
e. One-quarter of a month's inventory purchases is paid for in the month of purchase; the other three-quarters is paid for in the following month. The accounts payable at December 31 are the result of December purchases of inventory.

f. Monthly expenses are as follows: salaries and wages, $12,000; rent, $1,800; other expenses (excluding depreciation), 8% of sales. Assume that these expenses are paid monthly. Depreciation is $2,400 for the quarter and includes depreciation on new assets acquired during the quarter.
g. Equipment will be acquired for cash: $3,000 in January and $8,000 in February.
h. The company must maintain a minimum cash balance of $5,000. An open line of credit is available at a local bank. All borrowing is done at the beginning of a month, and all repayments are made at the end of a month; borrowing must be in multiples of $1,000. The annual interest rate is 12%. Interest is paid only at the time of repayment of principal; figure interest on whole months (1/12, 2/12, and so forth).

Required:
Using the data above:

1. Complete the following schedule:

Schedule of Expected Cash Collections

	January	February	March	Quarter
Cash sales	$28,000			
Credit sales	36,000			
Total collections	$64,000			

2. Complete the following:

Inventory Purchases Budget

	January	February	March	Quarter
Budgeted cost of goods sold	$49,000*			
Add desired ending inventory	11,200†			
Total needs	60,200			
Less beginning inventory	9,800			
Required purchases	$50,400			

*$70,000 sales × 70% = $49,000.
†$80,000 × 70% × 20% = $11,200.

Schedule of Expected Cash Disbursements—Purchases

	January	February	March	Quarter
December purchases	$32,550*			$32,550
January purchases	12,600	$37,800		50,400
February purchases				
March purchases				
Total disbursements	$45,150			

*Beginning balance of the accounts payable.

3. Complete the following:

Schedule of Expected Cash Disbursements—Operating Expenses

	January	February	March	Quarter
Salaries and wages	$12,000			
Rent	1,800			
Other expenses	5,600			
Total disbursements	$19,400			

4. Complete the following cash budget:

Cash Budget

	January	February	March	Quarter
Cash balance, beginning	$ 6,000			
Add cash collections	64,000			
Total cash available	70,000			

Cash Budget (concluded)

	January	February	March	Quarter
Less cash disbursements:				
For inventory	45,150			
For operating expenses	19,400			
For equipment	3,000			
Total cash disbursements	67,550			
Excess (deficiency) of cash	2,450			
Financing				
Etc.				

5. Prepare an income statement for the quarter ended March 31. (Use the format as shown in Schedule 9 in the text to prepare your income statement.)
6. Prepare a balance sheet as of March 31.

PROBLEM 9–21 Integrated Operating Budgets [LO3, LO4, LO5, LO6]

The East Division of Kensic Company manufactures a vital component that is used in one of Kensic's major product lines. The East Division has been experiencing some difficulty in coordinating activities between its various departments, which has resulted in some shortages of the component at critical times. To overcome the shortages, the manager of East Division has decided to initiate a monthly budgeting system that is integrated between departments.

The first budget is to be for the second quarter of the current year. To assist in developing the budget figures, the divisional controller has accumulated the following information:

Sales. Sales through the first three months of the current year were 30,000 units. Actual sales in units for January, February, and March, and planned sales in units over the next five months, are given below:

January (actual)	6,000
February (actual)	10,000
March (actual)	14,000
April (planned)	20,000
May (planned)	35,000
June (planned)	50,000
July (planned)	45,000
August (planned)	30,000

In total, the East Division expects to produce and sell 250,000 units during the current year.

Direct Material. Two different materials are used in the production of the component. Data regarding these materials are given below:

Direct Material	Units of Direct Materials per Finished Component	Cost per Unit	Inventory at March 31
No. 208	4 pounds	$5.00	46,000 pounds
No. 311	9 feet	2.00	69,000 feet

Material No. 208 is sometimes in short supply. Therefore, the East Division requires that enough of the material be on hand at the end of each month to provide for 50% of the following month's production needs. Material No. 311 is easier to get, so only one-third of the following month's production needs must be on hand at the end of each month.

Direct Labor. The East Division has three departments through which the components must pass before they are completed. Information relating to direct labor in these departments is given below:

Department	Direct Labor-Hours per Finished Component	Cost per Direct Labor-Hour
Shaping	0.25	$18.00
Assembly	0.70	16.00
Finishing	0.10	20.00

Direct labor is adjusted to the workload each month.

Manufacturing Overhead. East Division manufactured 32,000 components during the first three months of the current year. The actual variable overhead costs incurred during this three-month period are shown below. East Division's controller believes that the variable overhead costs incurred during the last nine months of the year will be at the same rate per component as experienced during the first three months.

Utilities	$ 57,000
Indirect labor	31,000
Supplies	16,000
Other	8,000
Total variable overhead	$112,000

The actual fixed manufacturing overhead costs incurred during the first three months amounted to $1,170,000. The East Division has planned fixed manufacturing overhead costs for the entire year as follows:

Supervision	$ 872,000
Property taxes	143,000
Depreciation	2,910,000
Insurance	631,000
Other	72,000
Total fixed manufacturing overhead	$4,628,000

Finished Goods Inventory. The desired monthly ending inventory of completed components is 20% of the next month's estimated sales. The East Division has 4,000 units in the finished goods inventory on March 31.

Required:

1. Prepare a production budget for the East Division for the second quarter ending June 30. Show computations by month and in total for the quarter.
2. Prepare a direct materials purchases budget in units and in dollars for each type of material for the second quarter ending June 30. Again show computations by month and in total for the quarter.
3. Prepare a direct labor budget in hours and in dollars for the second quarter ending June 30. This time it is *not* necessary to show monthly figures; show quarterly totals only.
4. Assume that the company plans to produce a total of 250,000 units for the year. Prepare a manufacturing overhead budget for the nine-month period ending December 31. (Do not compute a predetermined overhead rate.) Again, it is *not* necessary to show monthly figures.

(CMA, adapted)

PROBLEM 9–22 Cash Budget for One Month [LO2, LO4, LO6, LO8]

The treasurer of Househall Company, Ltd., states, "Our monthly financial budget shows me our cash surplus or deficiency and assures me that an unexpected cash shortage will not occur."

A cash budget is now being prepared for May. The following information has been gathered to assist in preparing the budget:

a. Budgeted sales and production requirements are as follows:

Budgeted sales	$650,000
Production requirements:	
Raw materials to be used	301,000
Direct labor cost	85,000

The raw materials inventory is budgeted to increase by $6,000 during the month; other inventories will not change.

b. Customers are allowed a 2% cash discount on accounts paid within 10 days after the end of the month of sale. Only 50% of the payments made in the month following sale fall within the discount period.

c. Accounts receivable outstanding at April 30 were as follows:

Month	Sales	Accounts Receivable at April 30	Percentage of Sales Uncollected at April 30	Percentage to Be Collected in May
January	$340,000	$ 8,500	2½	?
February	530,000	31,800	6	?
March	470,000	47,000	10	?
April	550,000	550,000	100	?

Bad debts are negligible. All January receivables outstanding will have been collected by the end of May, and the collection pattern since the time of sale will be the same in May as in previous months.

d. Raw materials purchases are paid for in the month following purchase, and $320,000 in accounts payable for purchases was outstanding at the end of April.

e. Accrued wages on April 30 were $11,000. All May payroll amounts will be paid within the month of May.

f. Budgeted operating expenses and overhead costs for May are as follows:

Overhead and other charges:		
Indirect labor	$34,000	
Real estate taxes	1,500	
Depreciation	25,000	
Utilities	1,500	
Wage benefits	9,000	
Fire insurance	1,500	
Amortization of patents	5,000	
Spoilage of materials in the warehouse	1,500	$79,000
Sales salaries		45,000
Administrative salaries		15,000

g. Real estate taxes are paid in August each year.

h. Utilities are billed and paid within the month.

i. The $9,000 monthly charge above for "Wage benefits" includes the following:

Unemployment insurance (payable monthly)	$1,350
Canada pension plan (payable monthly)	820
Holiday pay, which represents 1/12 of the annual cost (May holidays will require $2,040)	1,100
Company pension fund, including 1/12 of a $10,800 adjustment that was paid in January	5,000
Group insurance (payable quarterly, with the last payment having been made in February)	730

j. Fire insurance premiums were paid in January, in advance.

k. Shipping costs for May will be $1,000, all payable during the month.

l. The cash balance on April 30 was $5,750.

Required:

1. Prepare a schedule showing expected cash collections for May.
2. Prepare a cash budget for May in good form.
3. Comment briefly on the treasurer's statement quoted at the beginning of the problem.

(CMA, adapted)

Cases

CASE 9–23 Evaluating a Company's Budget Procedures [LO1]

Tom Emory and Jim Morris strolled back to their plant from the administrative offices of Ferguson & Son Mfg. Company. Tom is manager of the machine shop in the company's factory; Jim is manager of the equipment maintenance department.

The men had just attended the monthly performance evaluation meeting for plant department heads. These meetings had been held on the third Tuesday of each month since Robert Ferguson, Jr., the president's son, had become plant manager a year earlier.

As they were walking, Tom Emory spoke: "Boy, I hate those meetings! I never know whether my department's accounting reports will show good or bad performance. I'm beginning to expect the worst. If the accountants say I saved the company a dollar, I'm called 'Sir,' but if I spend even a little too much—boy, do I get in trouble. I don't know if I can hold on until I retire."

Tom had just been given the worst evaluation he had ever received in his long career with Ferguson & Son. He was the most respected of the experienced machinists in the company. He had been with Ferguson & Son for many years and was promoted to supervisor of the machine shop when the company expanded and moved to its present location. The president (Robert Ferguson, Sr.) had often stated that the company's success was due to the high quality of the work of machinists like Tom. As supervisor, Tom stressed the importance of craftsmanship and told his workers that he wanted no sloppy work coming from his department.

When Robert Ferguson, Jr., became the plant manager, he directed that monthly performance comparisons be made between actual and budgeted costs for each department. The departmental budgets were intended to encourage the supervisors to reduce inefficiencies and to seek cost reduction opportunities. The company controller was instructed to have his staff "tighten" the budget slightly whenever a department attained its budget in a given month; this was done to reinforce the plant manager's desire to reduce costs. The young plant manager often stressed the importance of continued progress toward attaining the budget; he also made it known that he kept a file of these performance reports for future reference when he succeeded his father.

Tom Emory's conversation with Jim Morris continued as follows:

Emory: I really don't understand. We've worked so hard to get up to budget, and the minute we make it they tighten the budget on us. We can't work any faster and still maintain quality. I think my men are ready to quit trying. Besides, those reports don't tell the whole story. We always seem to be interrupting the big jobs for all those small rush orders. All that setup and machine adjustment time is killing us. And quite frankly, Jim, you were no help. When our hydraulic press broke down last month, your people were nowhere to be found. We had to take it apart ourselves and got stuck with all that idle time.

Morris: I'm sorry about that, Tom, but you know my department has had trouble making budget, too. We were running well behind at the time of that problem, and if we'd spent a day on that old machine, we would never have made it up. Instead we made the scheduled inspections of the forklift trucks because we knew we could do those in less than the budgeted time.

Emory: Well, Jim, at least you have some options. I'm locked into what the scheduling department assigns to me and you know they're being harassed by sales for those special orders. Incidentally, why didn't your report show all the supplies you guys wasted last month when you were working in Bill's department?

Morris: We're not out of the woods on that deal yet. We charged the maximum we could to other work and haven't even reported some of it yet.

Emory: Well, I'm glad you have a way of getting out of the pressure. The accountants seem to know everything that's happening in my department, sometimes even before I do. I thought all that budget and accounting stuff was supposed to help, but it just gets me into trouble. It's all a big pain. I'm trying to put out quality work; they're trying to save pennies.

Required:

1. Identify the problems that appear to exist in Ferguson & Son Mfg. Company's budgetary control system and explain how the problems are likely to reduce the effectiveness of the system.
2. Explain how Ferguson & Son Mfg. Company's budgetary control system could be revised to improve its effectiveness.

(CMA, adapted)

CASE 9–24 Cash Budget for a Growing Company [LO2, LO4, LO6, LO8]

Roller, Ltd., of Melbourne, Australia, is the exclusive distributor in Australia and the South Pacific of a popular brand of in-line skates manufactured in Mexico. The company is in the process of putting together its cash budget for the second quarter—April, May, and June—of next year. The president of the company suspects that some financing will be required in the second quarter because sales are expanding and the company intends to make several major equipment purchases in that quarter. The president is confident that the company will be able to meet or exceed the following budgeted sales figures (all in Australian dollars) next year:

January	$158,000	July	$190,000
February	160,000	August.	192,000
March	164,000	September	210,000
April.	172,000	October.	230,000
May.	176,000	November	260,000
June	184,000	December	180,000

The following additional information will be used in formulating the cash budget:

a. All of the company's sales are on credit terms. The company collects 30% of its billings in the month after the sale and the remaining 70% in the second month after the sale. Uncollectible accounts are negligible.

b. The cost of sales is 75% of sales. Because of the shipping time from Mexico, the company orders skates from the manufacturer one month in advance of their expected sale. Roller, Ltd., desires to maintain little or no inventory.

c. The company orders the skates on credit terms from the manufacturer. The company pays half of the bill in the month after it orders the skates and the other half in the second month after it places the order.

d. Operating expenses, other than cost of sales, are budgeted to be $178,800 for the year. The composition of these expenses is given below. All of these expenses are incurred evenly throughout the year except for the property taxes. Property taxes are paid in four equal installments in the last month of each quarter.

Salaries and wages	$120,000
Advertising and promotion	12,000
Property taxes	18,000
Insurance	4,800
Utilities	6,000
Depreciation.	18,000
Total operating expenses.	$178,800

e. Income tax payments are made by the company in the first month of each quarter based on the taxable income for the prior quarter. The income tax payment due in April is $16,000.

f. Because of expanding sales, the company plans to make equipment purchases of $22,300 in April and $29,000 in May. These purchases will not affect depreciation for the year.

g. The company has a policy of maintaining an end-of-month cash balance of $20,000. Cash is borrowed or invested monthly, as needed, to maintain this balance. All borrowing is done at the beginning of the month, and all investments and repayments are made at the end of the month. As of March 31, there are no investments of excess cash and no outstanding loans.

h. The annual interest rate on loans from the bank is 12%. Compute interest on whole months (1/12, 2/12, and so forth). The company will pay off any loans, including accumulated interest, at the end of the second quarter if sufficient cash is available.

Required:

1. Prepare a cash budget for Roller, Ltd., by month and in total for the second quarter.
2. Discuss why cash budgeting is particularly important for an expanding company like Roller, Ltd.

CASE 9–25 Master Budget with Supporting Schedules [LO2, LO4, LO8, LO9, LO10]

You have just been hired as a management trainee by Cravat Sales Company, a nationwide distributor of a designer's silk ties. The company has an exclusive franchise on the distribution of the ties, and sales have grown so rapidly over the last few years that it has become necessary to add new members to the management team. You have been given direct responsibility for all planning and budgeting. Your first assignment is to prepare a master budget for the next three months, starting April 1. You are anxious to make a favorable impression on the president and have assembled the information below.

The company desires a minimum ending cash balance each month of $10,000. The ties are sold to retailers for $8 each. Recent and forecasted sales in units are as follows:

January (actual)	20,000	June	60,000
February (actual)	24,000	July	40,000
March (actual).	28,000	August.	36,000
April.	35,000	September.	32,000
May.	45,000		

The large buildup in sales before and during June is due to Father's Day. Ending inventories are supposed to equal 90% of the next month's sales in units. The ties cost the company $5 each.

Purchases are paid for as follows: 50% in the month of purchase and the remaining 50% in the following month. All sales are on credit, with no discount, and payable within 15 days. The company has found, however, that only 25% of a month's sales are collected by month-end. An additional 50% is collected in the month following, and the remaining 25% is collected in the second month following. Bad debts have been negligible.

The company's monthly operating expenses are given below:

Variable:	
Sales commissions	$1 per tie
Fixed:	
Wages and salaries	$22,000
Utilities	14,000
Insurance expired	1,200
Depreciation	1,500
Miscellaneous	3,000

All operating expenses are paid during the month, in cash, with the exception of depreciation and insurance expired. Land will be purchased during May for $25,000 cash. The company declares dividends of $12,000 each quarter, payable in the first month of the following quarter. The company's balance sheet at March 31 is given below:

Assets	
Cash	$ 14,000
Accounts receivable ($48,000 February sales; $168,000 March sales)	216,000
Inventory (31,500 units)	157,500
Unexpired insurance	14,400
Fixed assets, net of depreciation	172,700
Total assets	$574,600
Liabilities and Stockholders' Equity	
Accounts payable, purchases	$ 85,750
Dividends payable	12,000
Capital stock, no par	300,000
Retained earnings	176,850
Total liabilities and stockholders' equity	$574,600

The company can borrow money from its bank at 12% annual interest. All borrowing must be done at the beginning of a month, and repayments must be made at the end of a month. Repayments of principal must be in round $1,000 amounts. Borrowing (and payments of interest) can be in any amount.

Interest is computed and paid at the end of each quarter on all loans outstanding during the quarter. Round all interest payments to the nearest whole dollar. Compute interest on whole months ($\frac{1}{12}$, $\frac{2}{12}$, and so forth). The company wishes to use any excess cash to pay loans off as rapidly as possible.

Required:

Prepare a master budget for the three-month period ending June 30. Include the following detailed budgets:

1. *a.* A sales budget by month and in total.
   b. A schedule of expected cash collections from sales and accounts receivable, by month and in total.
   c. A purchases budget in units and in dollars. Show the budget by month and in total.
   d. A schedule of budgeted cash disbursements for purchases, by month and in total.
2. A cash budget. Show the budget by month and in total.
3. A budgeted income statement for the three-month period ending June 30. Use the contribution approach.
4. A budgeted balance sheet as of June 30.

Group and Internet Exercises

GROUP EXERCISE 9–26 Financial Pressures Hit Higher Education
In the late eighties and early nineties, public universities found that they were no longer immune to the financial stress faced by their private sister institutions and the rest of Corporate America. Budget cuts were in the air across the land. When the budget ax hit, the cuts often came without warning and their size was sometimes staggering. State support for some institutions dropped by 40% or more. Most university administrators had only experienced budget increases, never budget cuts. Also, the budget setbacks usually occurred at the most inopportune time—during the school year when contractual commitments with faculty and staff had been signed, programs had been planned, and students were enrolled and taking classes.

Required:

1. Should the administration be "fair" to all affected and institute a round of across-the-board cuts whenever the state announces another subsidy reduction?
2. If not across-the-board cutbacks in programs, then would you recommend more focused reductions, and if so, what priorities would you establish for bringing spending in line with revenues?
3. Since these usually are not one-time-only cutbacks, how would you manage continuous, long-term reductions in budgets extending over a period of years?
4. Should the decision-making process be top-down (centralized with top administrators) or bottom-up (participative)? Why?
5. How should issues such as protect-your-turf mentality, resistance to change, and consensus building be dealt with?

INTERNET EXERCISE 9–27 Internet Exercise
As you know, the World Wide Web is a medium that is constantly evolving. Sites come and go, and change without notice. To enable periodic update of site addresses, this problem has been posted to the textbook website (www.mhhe.com/garrison10e). After accessing the site, enter the Student Center and select this chapter. Select and complete the Internet Exercise.

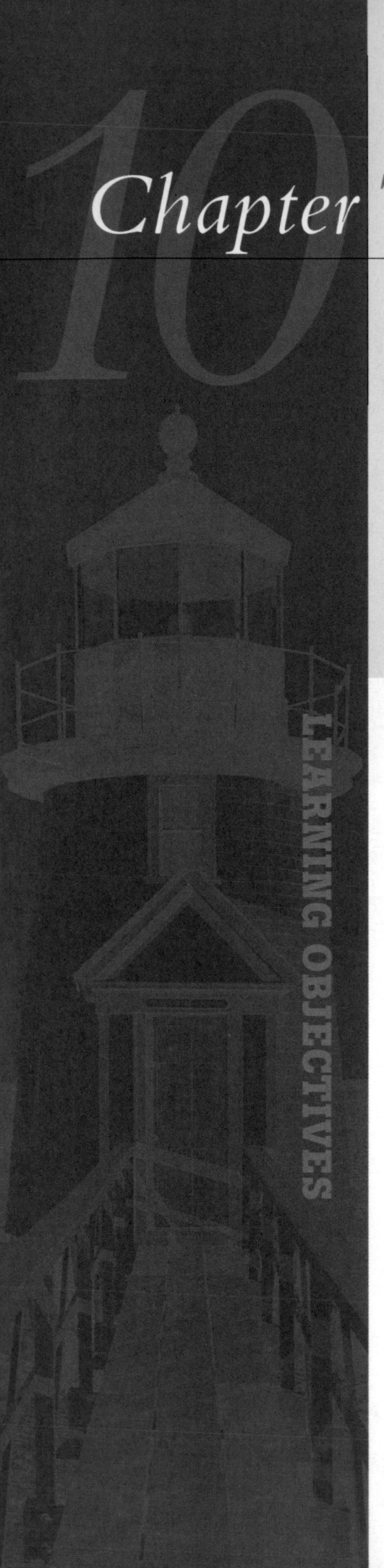

Chapter Ten

Standard Costs and the Balanced Scorecard

After studying Chapter 10, you should be able to:

1. Explain how direct materials standards and direct labor standards are set.
2. Compute the direct materials price and quantity variances and explain their significance.
3. Compute the direct labor rate and efficiency variances and explain their significance.
4. Compute the variable manufacturing overhead spending and efficiency variances.
5. Understand how a balanced scorecard fits together and how it supports a company's strategy.
6. Compute the delivery cycle time, the throughput time, and the manufacturing cycle efficiency (MCE).
7. (Appendix 10A) Prepare journal entries to record standard costs and variances.

The Business End of Visual Effects

BUSINESS FOCUS

Special effects, such as the computer-generated action shots of dinosaurs in the movie *Jurassic Park,* are expensive to produce. A single visual effect, lasting three to seven seconds, can cost up to $50,000. And a high-profile film may contain hundreds of these shots.

With over 30 visual-effects companies in the United States, competition is fierce. Since visual effects are produced under fixed-price contracts, visual-effects companies must carefully estimate their costs. And once a bid has been accepted, costs must be zealously monitored to make sure they do not spin out of control. Buena Vista Visual Effects, a part of Walt Disney Studios, uses a standard cost system to estimate and control costs. A "storyboard" is created for each special-effects shot. The storyboard sketches the visual effect, details the length of the shot (measured in frames—24 frames equal one second of film), and describes the work that will need to be done to create the effect. A detailed budget is then prepared using standard costs. For example, a shot may require a miniature model maker working full time for 12 weeks at a specified weekly wage. As the job progresses, this standard cost is compared to actual costs and significant cost overruns are investigated. Management attention is directed to significant variances.

Source: Ray Scalice, "Lights! Cameras! . . . Accountants?" *Management Accounting,* June 1996, pp. 42–46.

In this chapter we begin our study of management control and performance measures. Quite often, these terms carry with them negative connotations—we may have a tendency to think of performance measurement as something to be feared. And indeed, performance measurements can be used in very negative ways—to cast blame and to punish. However, that is not the way they should be used. As explained in the following quotation, performance measurement serves a vital function in both personal life and in organizations:

> Imagine you want to improve your basketball shooting skill. You know that practice will help, so you [go] to the basketball court. There you start shooting toward the hoop, but as soon as the ball gets close to the rim your vision goes blurry for a second, so that you cannot observe where the ball ended up in relation to the target (left, right, in front, too far back, inside the hoop?). It would be pretty difficult to improve under those conditions. . . . (And by the way, how long would [shooting baskets] sustain your interest if you couldn't observe the outcome of your efforts?)
>
> Or imagine someone engaging in a weight loss program. A normal step in such programs is to purchase a scale to be able to track one's progress: Is this program working? Am I losing weight? A positive answer would be encouraging and would motivate me to keep up the effort, while a negative answer might lead me to reflect on the process: Am I working on the right diet and exercise program? Am I doing everything I am supposed to?, etc. Suppose you don't want to set up a sophisticated measurement system and decide to forgo the scale. You would still have some idea of how well you are doing from simple methods such as clothes feeling looser, a belt that fastens at a different hole, or simply via observation in a mirror! Now, imagine trying to sustain a weight loss program without *any* feedback on how well you are doing.
>
> In these . . . examples, availability of quantitative measures of performance can yield two types of benefits: First, performance feedback can help improve the "production process" through a better understanding of what works and what doesn't; e.g., shooting this way works better than shooting that way. Secondly, feedback on performance can sustain motivation and effort, because it is encouraging and/or because it suggests that more effort is required for the goal to be met.[1]

In the same way, performance measurement can be helpful in an organization. It can provide feedback concerning what works and what does not work, and it can help motivate people to sustain their efforts.

Our study of performance measurement begins in this chapter with the lowest levels in the organization. We work our way up the organizational ladder in subsequent chapters. In this chapter we see how various measures are used to control operations and to evaluate performance. Even though we are starting with the lowest levels in the organization, keep in mind that performance measures should be derived from the organization's overall strategy. For example, a company like Sony that bases its strategy on rapid introduction of innovative consumer products should use different performance measures than a company like Federal Express where on-time delivery, customer convenience, and low cost are key competitive advantages. Sony may want to keep close track of the percentage of revenues from products introduced within the last year; whereas Federal Express may want to closely monitor the percentage of packages delivered on time. Later in this chapter when we discuss the *balanced scorecard,* we will have more to say concerning the role of strategy in the selection of performance measures. But first we will see how *standard costs* are used by managers to help control costs.

Companies in highly competitive industries like Federal Express, Southwest Airlines, Dell Computer, Shell Oil, and Toyota must be able to provide high-quality goods and services at low cost. If they do not, they will perish. Stated in the starkest terms, managers must obtain inputs such as raw materials and electricity at the lowest possible prices and must use them as effectively as possible—while maintaining or increasing the quality of

---

[1] Soumitra Dutta and Jean-François Manzoni, *Process Reengineering, Organizational Change and Performance Improvement* (New York: McGraw-Hill, 1999), Chapter IV.

the output. If inputs are purchased at prices that are too high or more input is used than is really necessary, higher costs will result.

How do managers control the prices that are paid for inputs and the quantities that are used? They could examine every transaction in detail, but this obviously would be an inefficient use of management time. For many companies, the answer to this control problem lies at least partially in *standard costs.*

Standard Costs—Management by Exception

A *standard* is a benchmark or "norm" for measuring performance. Standards are found everywhere. Your doctor evaluates your weight using standards that have been set for individuals of your age, height, and gender. The food we eat in restaurants must be prepared under specified standards of cleanliness. The buildings we live in must conform to standards set in building codes. Standards are also widely used in managerial accounting where they relate to the *quantity* and *cost* of inputs used in manufacturing goods or providing services.

Managers—often assisted by engineers and accountants—set quantity and cost standards for each major input such as raw materials and labor time. *Quantity standards* specify how much of an input should be used to make a product or provide a service. *Cost (price) standards* specify how much should be paid for each unit of the input. Actual quantities and actual costs of inputs are compared to these standards. If either the quantity or the cost of inputs departs significantly from the standards, managers investigate the discrepancy. The purpose is to find the cause of the problem and then eliminate it so that it does not recur. This process is called **management by exception.**

In our daily lives, we operate in a management by exception mode most of the time. Consider what happens when you sit down in the driver's seat of your car. You put the key in the ignition, you turn the key, and your car starts. Your expectation (standard) that the car will start is met; you do not have to open the car hood and check the battery, the connecting cables, the fuel lines, and so on. If you turn the key and the car does not start, then you have a discrepancy (variance). Your expectations are not met, and you need to investigate why. Note that even if the car starts after a second try, it would be wise to investigate anyway. The fact that the expectation was not met should be viewed as an opportunity to uncover the cause of the problem rather than as simply an annoyance. If the underlying cause is not discovered and corrected, the problem may recur and become much worse.

This basic approach to identifying and solving problems is exploited in the *variance analysis cycle,* which is illustrated in Exhibit 10–1. The cycle begins with the preparation of standard cost performance reports in the accounting department. These reports highlight the *variances,* which are the differences between actual results and what should have occurred according to the standards. The variances raise questions. Why did this variance occur? Why is this variance larger than it was last period? The significant variances are investigated to discover their root causes. Corrective actions are taken. And then next period's operations are carried out. The cycle then begins again with the preparation of a new standard cost performance for the latest period. The emphasis should be on flagging problems for attention, finding their root causes, and then taking corrective action. The goal is to improve operations—not to find blame.

Who Uses Standard Costs?

Manufacturing, service, food, and not-for-profit organizations all make use of standards to some extent. Auto service centers like Firestone and Sears, for example, often set specific labor time standards for the completion of certain work tasks, such as installing a carburetor or doing a valve job, and then measure actual performance against these standards. Fast-food outlets such as McDonald's have exacting standards for the quantity of

Exhibit 10–1
The Variance Analysis Cycle

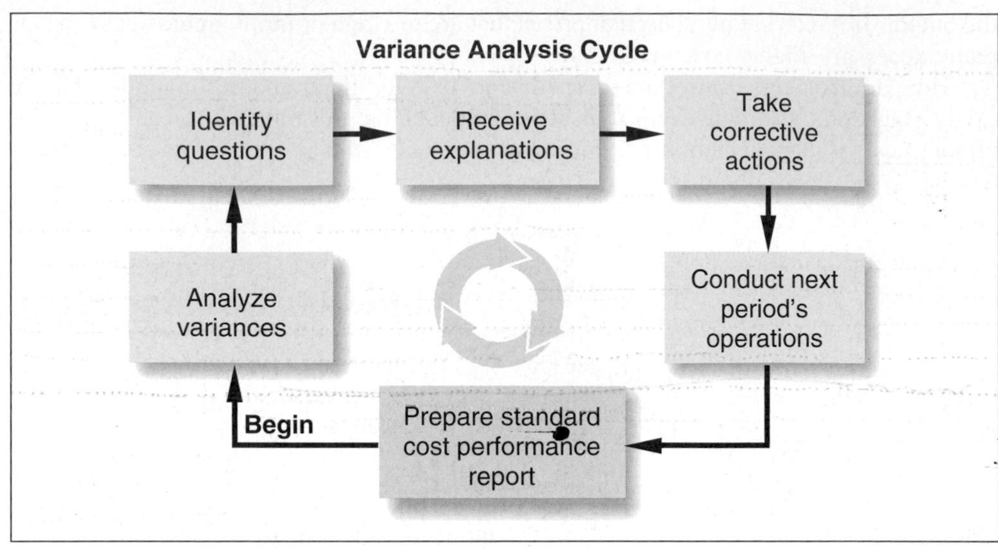

meat going into a sandwich, as well as standards for the cost of the meat. Hospitals have standard costs (for food, laundry, and other items) for each occupied bed per day, as well as standard time allowances for certain routine activities, such as laboratory tests. In short, you are likely to run into standard costs in virtually any line of business that you enter.

In Business

Standard Costing at Parker Brass

The Brass Products Division at Parker Hannifin Corporation, known as Parker Brass, is a world-class manufacturer of tube and brass fittings, valves, hose, and hose fittings. Management at the company uses variances from its standard costing system to target problem areas for improvement. If a production variance exceeds 5% of sales, the responsible manager is required to explain the variance and to propose a plan of action to correct the detected problems. In the past, variances were reported at the end of the month—often several weeks after a particular job had been completed. Now, a variance report is generated the day after a job is completed and summary variance reports are prepared weekly. These more frequent reports permit managers to take more timely action.

Source: David Johnsen and Parvez Sopariwala, "Standard Costing Is Alive and Well at Parker Brass," *Management Accounting Quarterly*, Winter 2000, pp. 12–20.

Manufacturing companies often have highly developed standard costing systems in which standards relating to materials, labor, and overhead are developed in detail for each separate product. These standards are listed on a **standard cost card** that provides the manager with a great deal of information concerning the inputs that are required to produce a unit and their costs. In the following section, we provide a detailed example of the setting of standard costs and the preparation of a standard cost card.

Setting Standard Costs

Setting price and quantity standards requires the combined expertise of all persons who have responsibility over input prices and over the effective use of inputs. In a manufacturing setting, this might include accountants, purchasing managers, engineers, production supervisors, line managers, and production workers. Past records of purchase prices and of input usage can be helpful in setting standards. However, the standards should be designed to encourage efficient *future* operations, not a repetition of *past* inefficient operations.

Ideal versus Practical Standards

Should standards be attainable all of the time, should they be attainable only part of the time, or should they be so tight that they become, in effect, "the impossible dream"? Opinions among managers vary, but standards tend to fall into one of two categories—either ideal or practical.

Ideal standards are those that can be attained only under the best circumstances. They allow for no machine breakdowns or other work interruptions, and they call for a level of effort that can be attained only by the most skilled and efficient employees working at peak effort 100% of the time. Some managers feel that such standards have a motivational value. These managers argue that even though employees know they will rarely meet the standard, it is a constant reminder of the need for ever-increasing efficiency and effort. Few firms use ideal standards. Most managers feel that ideal standards tend to discourage even the most diligent workers. Moreover, variances from ideal standards are difficult to interpret. Large variances from the ideal are normal and it is difficult to "manage by exception."

Practical standards are defined as standards that are "tight but attainable." They allow for normal machine downtime and employee rest periods, and they can be attained through reasonable, though highly efficient, efforts by the average worker. Variances from such a standard represent deviations that fall outside of normal operating conditions and signal a need for management attention. Furthermore, practical standards can serve multiple purposes. In addition to signaling abnormal conditions, they can also be used in forecasting cash flows and in planning inventory. By contrast, ideal standards cannot be used in forecasting and planning; they do not allow for normal inefficiencies, and therefore they result in unrealistic planning and forecasting figures.

Throughout the remainder of this chapter, we will assume the use of practical rather than ideal standards.

Managerial Accounting in Action

The Issue

The Colonial Pewter Company was organized a year ago. The company's only product at present is a reproduction of an 18th century pewter bookend. The bookend is made largely by hand, using traditional metal-working tools. Consequently, the manufacturing process is labor intensive and requires a high level of skill.

Colonial Pewter has recently expanded its work force to take advantage of unexpected demand for the bookends as gifts. The company started with a small cadre of experienced pewter workers but has had to hire less experienced workers as a result of the expansion. The president of the company, J. D. Wriston, has called a meeting to discuss production problems. Attending the meeting are Tom Kuchel, the production manager; Janet Warner, the purchasing manager; and Terry Sherman, the corporate controller.

J. D.: I've got a feeling that we aren't getting the production we should out of our new people.

Tom: Give us a chance. Some of the new people have been with the company for less than a month.

Janet: Let me add that production seems to be wasting an awful lot of material—particularly pewter. That stuff is very expensive.

Tom: What about the shipment of defective pewter you bought a couple of months ago—the one with the iron contamination? That caused us major problems.

Janet: That's ancient history. How was I to know it was off-grade? Besides, it was a great deal.

J. D.: Calm down everybody. Let's get the facts before we start sinking our fangs into each other.

Tom: I agree. The more facts the better.

J. D.: Okay, Terry, it's your turn. Facts are the controller's department.

Terry: I'm afraid I can't provide the answers off the top of my head, but it won't take me too long to set up a system that can routinely answer questions relating to worker productivity, material waste, and input prices.

J. D.: How long is "not too long"?
Terry: I will need all of your cooperation, but how about a week from today?
J. D.: That's okay with me. What about everyone else?
Tom: Sure.
Janet: Fine with me.
J. D.: Let's mark it on our calendars.

Setting Direct Materials Standards

LEARNING OBJECTIVE 1
Explain how direct materials standards and direct labor standards are set.

Terry Sherman's first task was to prepare price and quantity standards for the company's only significant raw material, pewter ingots. The **standard price per unit** for direct materials should reflect the final, delivered cost of the materials, net of any discounts taken. After consulting with purchasing manager Janet Warner, Terry prepared the following documentation for the standard price of a pound of pewter in ingot form:

Purchase price, top-grade pewter ingots, in 40-pound ingots	$ 3.60
Freight, by truck, from the supplier's warehouse	0.44
Receiving and handling	0.05
Less purchase discount	(0.09)
Standard price per pound	$ 4.00

Notice that the standard price reflects a particular grade of material (top grade), purchased in particular lot sizes (40-pound ingots), and delivered by a particular type of carrier (truck). Allowances have also been made for handling and discounts. If everything proceeds according to these expectations, the net cost of a pound of pewter should therefore be $4.00.

The **standard quantity per unit** for direct materials should reflect the amount of material required for each unit of finished product, as well as an allowance for unavoidable waste, spoilage, and other normal inefficiencies. After consulting with the production manager, Tom Kuchel, Terry Sherman prepared the following documentation for the standard quantity of pewter in a pair of bookends:

Material requirements as specified in the bill of materials for a pair of bookends, in pounds	2.7
Allowance for waste and spoilage, in pounds.	0.2
Allowance for rejects, in pounds.	0.1
Standard quantity per pair of bookends, in pounds	3.0

A **bill of materials** is a list that shows the quantity of each type of material in a unit of finished product. It is a handy source for determining the basic material input per unit, but it should be adjusted for waste and other factors, as shown above, when determining the standard quantity per unit of product. "Waste and spoilage" in the table above refers to materials that are wasted as a normal part of the production process or that spoil before they are used. "Rejects" refers to the direct material contained in units that are defective and must be scrapped.

Although it is common to recognize allowances for waste, spoilage, and rejects when setting standard costs, this practice is now coming into question. Those involved in TQM (total quality management) and similar improvement programs argue that no amount of waste or defects should be tolerated. If allowances for waste, spoilage, and rejects are built into the standard cost, the levels of those allowances should be periodically reviewed and reduced over time to reflect improved processes, better training, and better equipment.

Once the price and quantity standards have been set, the standard cost of material per unit of finished product can be computed as follows:

$$3.0 \text{ pounds per unit} \times \$4.00 \text{ per pound} = \$12 \text{ per unit}$$

This $12 cost figure will appear as one item on the product's standard cost card.

Standards in the Spanish Royal Tobacco Factory

In Business

Standards have been used for centuries in commercial enterprises. For example, the Spanish Royal Tobacco Factory in Seville used standards to control costs in the 1700s. The Royal Tobacco Factory had a monopoly over snuff and cigar production in Spain and was the largest industrial building in Europe. Employee theft of tobacco was a particular problem, due to its high value. Careful records were maintained of the amount of tobacco leaf issued to each worker, the number of cigars expected to be made based on standards, and the actual production. The worker was not paid if the actual production was less than expected. To minimize theft, tobacco was weighed after each production step to determine the amount of wastage.

Source: Salvador Carmona, Mahmoud Ezzamel, and Fernando Gutiérrez, "Control and Cost Accounting Practices in the Spanish Royal Tobacco Factory," *Accounting, Organizations, and Society* 22, no. 5, 1997, pp. 411–446.

Setting Direct Labor Standards

Direct labor price and quantity standards are usually expressed in terms of a labor rate and labor-hours. The **standard rate per hour** for direct labor includes not only wages earned but also fringe benefits and other labor costs. Using last month's wage records and in consultation with the production manager, Terry Sherman determined the standard rate per hour at the Colonial Pewter Company as follows:

Basic wage rate per hour	$10
Employment taxes at 10% of the basic rate	1
Fringe benefits at 30% of the basic rate	3
Standard rate per direct labor-hour	$14

Many companies prepare a single standard rate for all employees in a department. This standard rate reflects the expected "mix" of workers, even though the actual wage rates may vary somewhat from individual to individual due to differing skills or seniority. A single standard rate simplifies the use of standard costs and also permits the manager to monitor the use of employees within departments. More is said on this point a little later. According to the standard computed above, the direct labor rate for Colonial Pewter should average $14 per hour.

The standard direct labor time required to complete a unit of product (called the **standard hours per unit**) is perhaps the single most difficult standard to determine. One approach is to divide each operation performed on the product into elemental body movements (such as reaching, pushing, and turning over). Standard times for such movements are available in reference works. These standard times can be applied to the movements and then added together to determine the total standard time allowed per operation. Another approach is for an industrial engineer to do a time and motion study, actually clocking the time required for certain tasks. As stated earlier, the standard time should include allowances for breaks, personal needs of employees, cleanup, and machine downtime.

After consulting with the production manager, Terry Sherman prepared the following documentation for the standard hours per unit:

Basic labor time per unit, in hours	1.9
Allowance for breaks and personal needs	0.1
Allowance for cleanup and machine downtime	0.3
Allowance for rejects	0.2
Standard labor-hours per unit of product	2.5

Once the rate and time standards have been set, the standard labor cost per unit of product can be computed as follows:

2.5 hours per unit × $14 per hour = $35 per unit

This $35 per unit standard labor cost appears along with direct materials on the standard cost card of the product.

In Business

Watching the Pennies

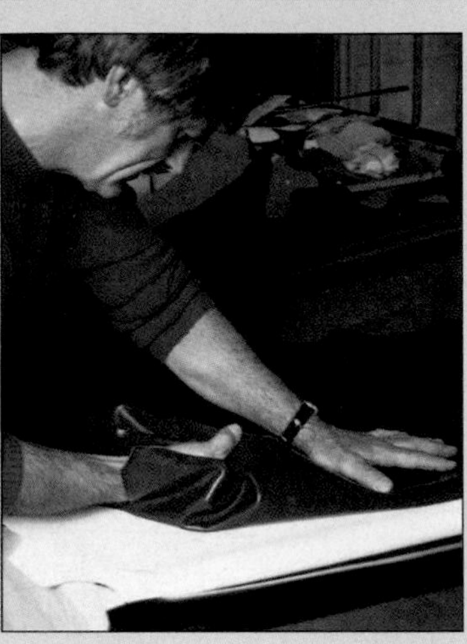

Industrie Natuzzi SpA, founded and run by Pasquale Natuzzi, produces handmade leather furniture for the world market in Santaeramo Del Colle in southern Italy. Natuzzi is export-oriented and has about 25% of the U.S. leather furniture market. The company's furniture is handmade by craftsmen, each of whom has a computer terminal that is linked to a sophisticated computer network. The computer provides precise instructions on how to accomplish a particular task and keeps track of how quickly the craftsman completes the task. If the craftsman beats the standard time to complete the task, the computer adds a bonus to the craftsman's pay.

The company's computers know exactly how much thread, screws, foam, leather, labor, and so on, is required for every model. "Should the price of Argentinean hides or German dyes rise one day, employees in Santaeramo enter the new prices into the computer, and the costs for all sofas with that leather and those colors are immediately recalculated. 'Everything has to be clear for me,' says Natuzzi. 'Why this penny? Where is it going?'"

Source: Richard C. Morais, "A Methodical Man," *Forbes,* August 11, 1997, pp. 70–72.

Setting Variable Manufacturing Overhead Standards

As with direct labor, the price and quantity standards for variable manufacturing overhead are usually expressed in terms of rate and hours. The rate represents *the variable portion of the predetermined overhead rate* discussed in Chapter 3; the hours represent whatever hours base is used to apply overhead to units of product (usually machine-hours or direct labor-hours, as we learned in Chapter 3). At Colonial Pewter, the variable portion of the predetermined overhead rate is $3 per direct labor-hour. Therefore, the standard variable manufacturing overhead cost per unit is computed as follows:

2.5 hours per unit × $3 per hour = $7.50 per unit

This $7.50 per unit cost for variable manufacturing overhead appears along with direct materials and direct labor on the standard cost card in Exhibit 10–2. Observe that the **standard cost per unit** is computed by multiplying the standard quantity or hours by the standard price or rate.

Are Standards the Same as Budgets?

Standards and budgets are very similar. The major distinction between the two terms is that a standard is a *unit* amount, whereas a budget is a *total* amount. The standard cost for

Exhibit 10–2
Standard Cost Card—Variable Production Cost

Inputs	(1) Standard Quantity or Hours	(2) Standard Price or Rate	(3) Standard Cost (1) × (2)
Direct materials	3.0 pounds	$ 4.00	$12.00
Direct labor	2.5 hours	14.00	35.00
Variable manufacturing overhead	2.5 hours	3.00	7.50
Total standard cost per unit			$54.50

materials at Colonial Pewter is $12 per pair of bookends. If 1,000 pairs of bookends are to be made during a budgeting period, then the budgeted cost of materials would be $12,000. In effect, *a standard can be viewed as the budgeted cost for one unit of product.*

A General Model for Variance Analysis

An important reason for separating standards into two categories—price and quantity—is that different managers are usually responsible for buying and for using inputs and these two activities occur at different points in time. In the case of raw materials, for example, the purchasing manager is responsible for the price, and this responsibility is exercised at the time of purchase. In contrast, the production manager is responsible for the amount of the raw material used, and this responsibility is exercised when the materials are used in production, which may be many weeks or months after the purchase date. It is important, therefore, that we cleanly separate discrepancies due to deviations from price standards from those due to deviations from quantity standards. Differences between *standard* prices and *actual* prices and *standard* quantities and *actual* quantities are called **variances.** The act of computing and interpreting variances is called *variance analysis.*

Price and Quantity Variances

A general model for computing standard cost variances for variable costs is presented in Exhibit 10–3. This model isolates price variances from quantity variances and shows how each of these variances is computed.[2] We will be using this model throughout the chapter to compute variances for direct materials, direct labor, and variable manufacturing overhead.

Three things should be noted from Exhibit 10–3. First, note that a price variance and a quantity variance can be computed for all three variable cost elements—direct materials, direct labor, and variable manufacturing overhead—even though the variance is not called by the same name in all cases. For example, a price variance is called a *materials price variance* in the case of direct materials but a *labor rate variance* in the case of direct labor and an *overhead spending variance* in the case of variable manufacturing overhead.

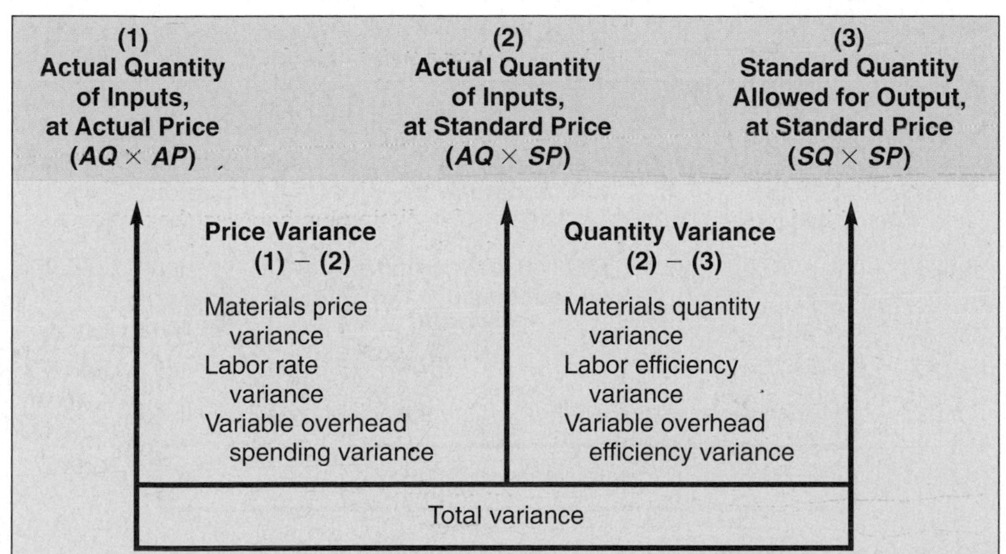

Exhibit 10–3
A General Model for Variance Analysis—Variable Production Costs

[2] Variance analysis of fixed costs is reserved until the next chapter.

Second, note that even though a price variance may be called by different names, it is computed in exactly the same way regardless of whether one is dealing with direct materials, direct labor, or variable manufacturing overhead. The same is true of the quantity variance.

Third, the inputs represent the actual quantity of direct materials, direct labor, and variable manufacturing overhead used; the output represents the good production of the period, expressed in terms of the *standard quantity* (or the *standard hours*) *allowed for the actual output* (see column 3 in Exhibit 10–3). By **standard quantity allowed** or **standard hours allowed,** we mean the amount of direct materials, direct labor, or variable manufacturing overhead *that should have been used* to produce the actual output of the period. This could be more or could be less than the actual materials, labor, or overhead, depending on the efficiency or inefficiency of operations. The standard quantity allowed is computed by multiplying the actual output in units by the standard input allowed per unit.

With this general model as a foundation, we will now examine the price and quantity variances in more detail.

Using Standard Costs—Direct Materials Variances

LEARNING OBJECTIVE 2
Compute the direct materials price and quantity variances and explain their significance.

Concept 10–1

After determining Colonial Pewter Company's standard costs for direct materials, direct labor, and variable manufacturing overhead, Terry Sherman's next step was to compute the company's variances for June, the most recent month. As discussed in the preceding section, variances are computed by comparing standard costs to actual costs. To facilitate this comparison, Terry referred to the standard cost data contained in Exhibit 10–2. This exhibit shows that the standard cost of direct materials per unit of product is as follows:

3.0 pounds per unit × $4.00 per pound = $12 per unit

Colonial Pewter's purchasing records for June showed that 6,500 pounds of pewter were purchased at a cost of $3.80 per pound. This cost figure included freight and handling and was net of the quantity discount. All of the material purchased was used during June to manufacture 2,000 pairs of pewter bookends. Using these data and the standard costs from Exhibit 10–2, Terry computed the price and quantity variances shown in Exhibit 10–4.

Exhibit 10–4
Variance Analysis—Direct Materials

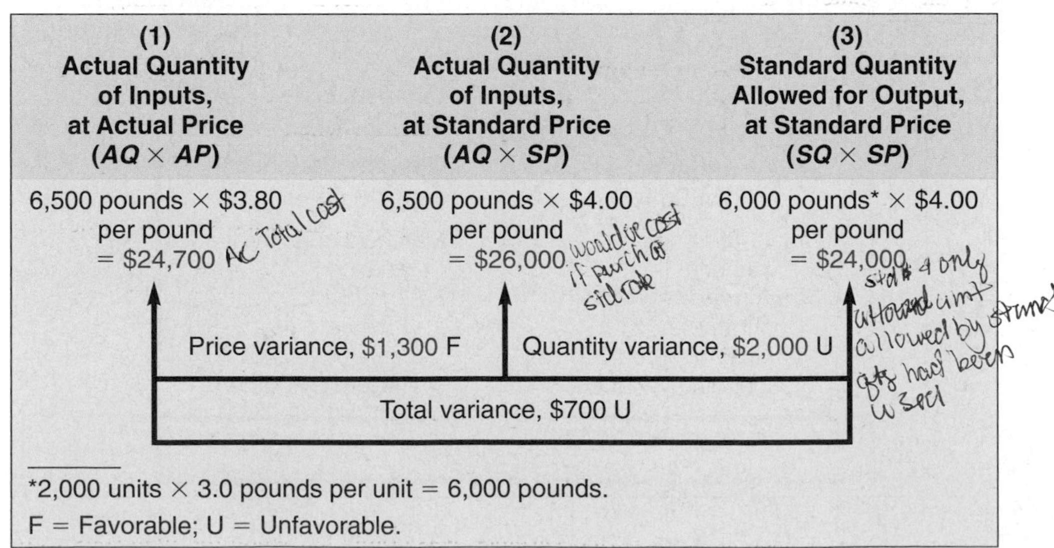

The three arrows in Exhibit 10–4 point to three different total cost figures. The first, $24,700, refers to the actual total cost of the pewter that was purchased during June. The second, $26,000, refers to what the pewter would have cost if it had been purchased at the standard price of $4.00 a pound rather than the actual price of $3.80 a pound. The difference between these two figures, $1,300 ($26,000 − $24,700), is the price variance. It exists because the actual purchase price was $0.20 per pound less than the standard purchase price. Since 6,500 pounds were purchased, the total amount of the variance is $1,300 ($0.20 per pound × 6,500 pounds). This variance is labeled favorable (denoted by F), since the actual purchase price was less than the standard purchase price. A price variance is labeled unfavorable (denoted by U) if the actual price exceeds the standard price.

The third arrow in Exhibit 10–4 points to $24,000—the cost if the pewter had been purchased at the standard price *and* only the amount allowed by the standard quantity had been used. The standards call for 3 pounds of pewter per unit. Since 2,000 units were produced, 6,000 pounds of pewter should have been used. This is referred to as the standard quantity allowed for the output. If this 6,000 pounds of pewter had been purchased at the standard price of $4.00 per pound, the company would have spent $24,000. The difference between this figure, $24,000, and the figure at the end of the middle arrow in Exhibit 10–4, $26,000, is the quantity variance of $2,000.

To understand this quantity variance, note that the actual amount of pewter used in production was 6,500 pounds. However, the standard amount of pewter allowed for the actual output is 6,000 pounds. Therefore, too much pewter was used to produce the actual output—by a total of 500 pounds. To express this in dollar terms, the 500 pounds is multiplied by the standard price of $4.00 per pound to yield the quantity variance of $2,000. Why is the standard price, rather than the actual price, of the pewter used in this calculation? The production manager is ordinarily responsible for the quantity variance. If the actual price were used in the calculation of the quantity variance, the production manager would be held responsible for the efficiency or inefficiency of the purchasing manager. Apart from being unfair, fruitless arguments between the production manager and purchasing manager would occur every time the actual price of an input was above its standard price. To avoid these arguments, the standard price is used when computing the quantity variance.

The quantity variance in Exhibit 10–4 is labeled unfavorable (denoted by U). This is because more pewter was used to produce the actual output than the standard allows. A quantity variance is labeled unfavorable if the actual quantity exceeds the standard quantity and is labeled favorable if the actual quantity is less than the standard quantity.

The computations in Exhibit 10–4 reflect the fact that all of the material purchased during June was also used during June. How are the variances computed if a different amount of material is purchased than is used? To illustrate, assume that during June the company purchased 6,500 pounds of materials, as before, but that it used only 5,000 pounds of material during the month and produced only 1,600 units. In this case, the price variance and quantity variance would be as shown in Exhibit 10–5.

Most companies compute the materials price variance when materials are *purchased* rather than when they are used in production. There are two reasons for this practice. First, delaying the computation of the price variance until the materials are used would result in less timely variance reports. Second, by computing the price variance when the materials are purchased, the materials can be carried in the inventory accounts at their standard cost. This greatly simplifies bookkeeping. (See Appendix 10A at the end of the chapter for an explanation of how the bookkeeping works in a standard costing system.)

Note from the exhibit that the price variance is computed on the entire amount of material purchased (6,500 pounds), as before, whereas the quantity variance is computed only on the portion of this material used in production during the month (5,000 pounds). What about the other 1,500 pounds of material that were purchased during the period, but that have not yet been used? When those materials are used in future periods, a quantity variance will be computed. However, a price variance will not be computed when the materials are finally used since the price variance was computed when the materials were

Exhibit 10–5
Variance Analysis—Direct Materials, When the Amount Purchased Differs from the Amount Used

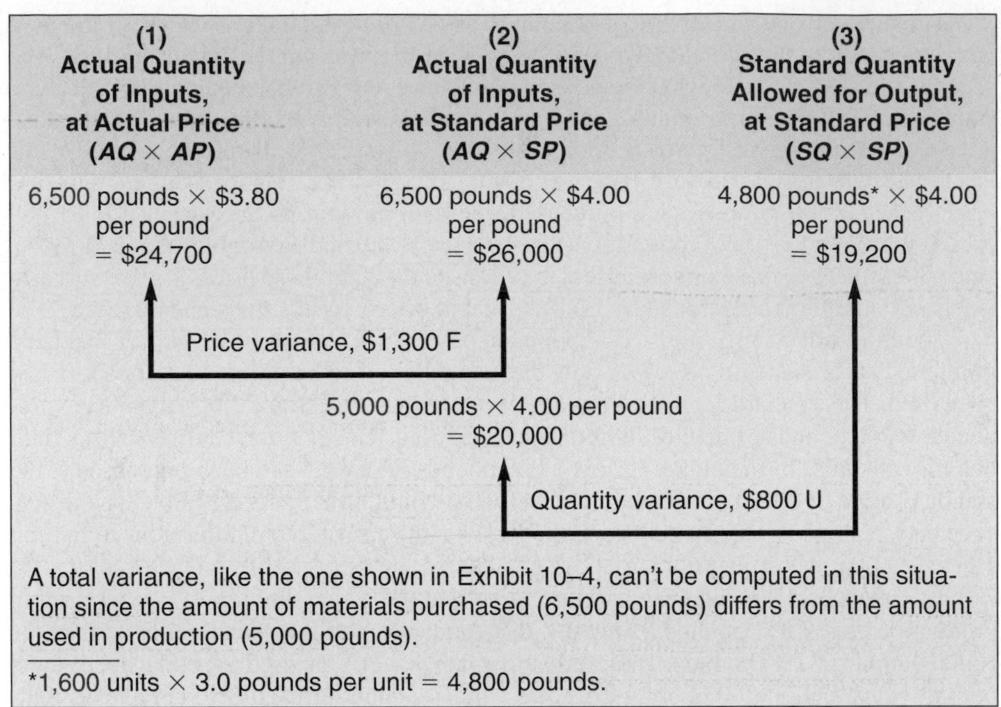

purchased. The situation illustrated in Exhibit 10–5 is common for companies that purchase materials well in advance of when they are used in production.

Materials Price Variance—A Closer Look

A **materials price variance** measures the difference between what is paid for a given quantity of materials and what should have been paid according to the standard that has been set. From Exhibit 10–4, this difference can be expressed by the following formula:

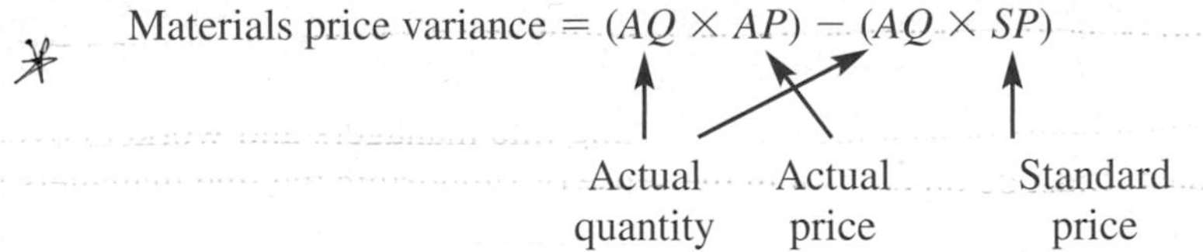

Materials price variance = (AQ × AP) − (AQ × SP)
Actual quantity
Actual price
Standard price

The formula can be factored into simpler form as follows:

$$\text{Materials price variance} = AQ(AP - SP)$$

Some managers prefer this simpler formula, since it permits variance computations to be made very quickly. Using the data from Exhibit 10–4 in this formula, we have the following:

$$6{,}500 \text{ pounds } (\$3.80 \text{ per pound} - \$4.00 \text{ per pound}) = \$1{,}300 \text{ F}$$

Notice that the answer is the same as that yielded in Exhibit 10–4. Also note that using this formula approach, a negative variance is always labeled as favorable (F) and a positive variance is always labeled as unfavorable (U). This will be true of all variance formulas in this and later chapters.

Variance reports are often issued in a tabular format. An example of such a report follows, along with an explanation for the materials price variance that has been provided by the purchasing manager.

COLONIAL PEWTER COMPANY
Performance Report—Purchasing Department

Item Purchased	(1) Quantity Purchased	(2) Actual Price	(3) Standard Price	(4) Difference in Price (2) − (3)	(5) Total Price Variance (1) × (4)	Explanation
Pewter.	6,500 pounds	\$3.80	\$4.00	\$0.20	\$1,300 F	Bargained for an especially good price.

F = Favorable; U = Unfavorable.

Isolation of Variances At what point should variances be isolated and brought to the attention of management? The answer is, the earlier the better. The sooner deviations from standard are brought to the attention of management, the sooner problems can be evaluated and corrected.

Once a performance report has been prepared, what does management do with the price variance data? The most significant variances should be viewed as "red flags," calling attention to the fact that an exception has occurred that will require some explanation and perhaps follow-up effort. Normally, the performance report itself will contain some explanation of the reason for the variance, as shown above. In the case of Colonial Pewter Company, the purchasing manager, Janet Warner, said that the favorable price variance resulted from bargaining for an especially good price.

Responsibility for the Variance Who is responsible for the materials price variance? Generally speaking, the purchasing manager has control over the price paid for goods and is therefore responsible for any price variances. Many factors influence the prices paid for goods, including how many units are ordered in a lot, how the order is delivered, whether the order is a rush order, and the quality of materials purchased. A deviation in any of these factors from what was assumed when the standards were set can result in a price variance. For example, purchase of second-grade materials rather than top-grade materials may result in a favorable price variance, since the lower-grade materials would generally be less costly (but perhaps less suitable for production).

However, someone other than the purchasing manager could be responsible for a materials price variance. Production may be scheduled in such a way, for example, that the purchasing manager must request express delivery. In these cases, the production manager should be held responsible for the resulting price variances.

A word of caution is in order. Variance analysis should not be used as an excuse to conduct witch hunts or as a means of beating line managers and workers over the head. The emphasis must be on control in the sense of *supporting* the line managers and *assisting* them in meeting the goals that they have participated in setting for the company. In short, the emphasis should be positive rather than negative. Excessive dwelling on what has already happened, particularly in terms of trying to find someone to blame, can destroy morale and kill any cooperative spirit.

Materials Quantity Variance—A Closer Look

The **materials quantity variance** measures the difference between the quantity of materials used in production and the quantity that should have been used according to the standard that has been set. Although the variance is concerned with the physical usage of materials, it is generally stated in dollar terms to help gauge its importance, as shown in Exhibit 10–4. The formula for the materials quantity variance is as follows:

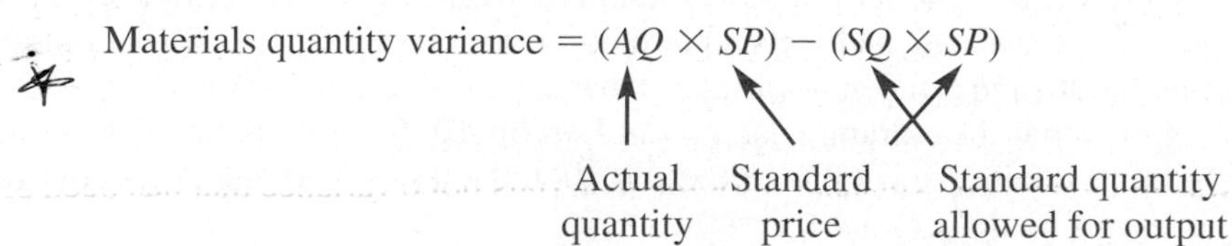

Again, the formula can be factored into simpler terms:

$$\text{Materials quantity variance} = SP(AQ - SQ)$$

Using the data from Exhibit 10–4 in the formula, we have the following:

$4.00 per pound (6,500 pounds − 6,000 pounds*) = $2,000 U

*2,000 units × 3.0 pounds per unit = 6,000 pounds.

The answer, of course, is the same as that yielded in Exhibit 10–4.

The data might appear as follows if a formal performance report were prepared:

COLONIAL PEWTER COMPANY
Performance Report—Production Department

Type of Materials	(1) Standard Price	(2) Actual Quantity	(3) Standard Quantity Allowed	(4) Difference in Quantity (2) − (3)	(5) Total Quantity Variance (1) × (4)	Explanation
Pewter	$4.00	6,500 pounds	6,000 pounds	500 pounds	$2,000 U	Low quality materials unsuitable for production.

F = Favorable; U = Unfavorable.

The materials quantity variance is best isolated when materials are placed into production. Materials are drawn for the number of units to be produced, according to the standard bill of materials for each unit. Any additional materials are usually drawn with an excess materials requisition slip, which is different in color from the normal requisition slips. This procedure calls attention to the excessive usage of materials *while production is still in process* and provides an opportunity to correct any developing problem.

Excessive usage of materials can result from many factors, including faulty machines, inferior quality of materials, untrained workers, and poor supervision. Generally speaking, it is the responsibility of the production department to see that material usage is kept in line with standards. There may be times, however, when the *purchasing* department may be responsible for an unfavorable materials quantity variance. If the purchasing department obtains inferior quality materials in an effort to economize on price, the materials may be unsuitable for use and may result in excessive waste. Thus, purchasing rather than production would be responsible for the quantity variance. At Colonial Pewter, the production manager, Tom Kuchel, claimed that low quality materials were the cause of the unfavorable materials quantity variance for June.

Using Standard Costs—Direct Labor Variances

LEARNING OBJECTIVE 3
Compute the direct labor rate and efficiency variances and explain their significance.

Concept 10–2

Terry Sherman's next step in determining Colonial Pewter's variances for June was to compute the direct labor variances for the month. Recall from Exhibit 10–2 that the standard direct labor cost per unit of product is $35, computed as follows:

2.5 hours per unit × $14.00 per hour = $35 per unit

During June, the company paid its direct labor workers $74,250, including employment taxes and fringe benefits, for 5,400 hours of work. This was an average of $13.75 per hour. Using these data and the standard costs from Exhibit 10–2, Terry computed the direct labor rate and efficiency variances that appear in Exhibit 10–6.

Notice that the column headings in Exhibit 10–6 are the same as those used in the prior two exhibits, except that in Exhibit 10–6 the terms *hours* and *rate* are used in place of the terms *quantity* and *price*.

Exhibit 10–6 Variance Analysis—Direct Labor

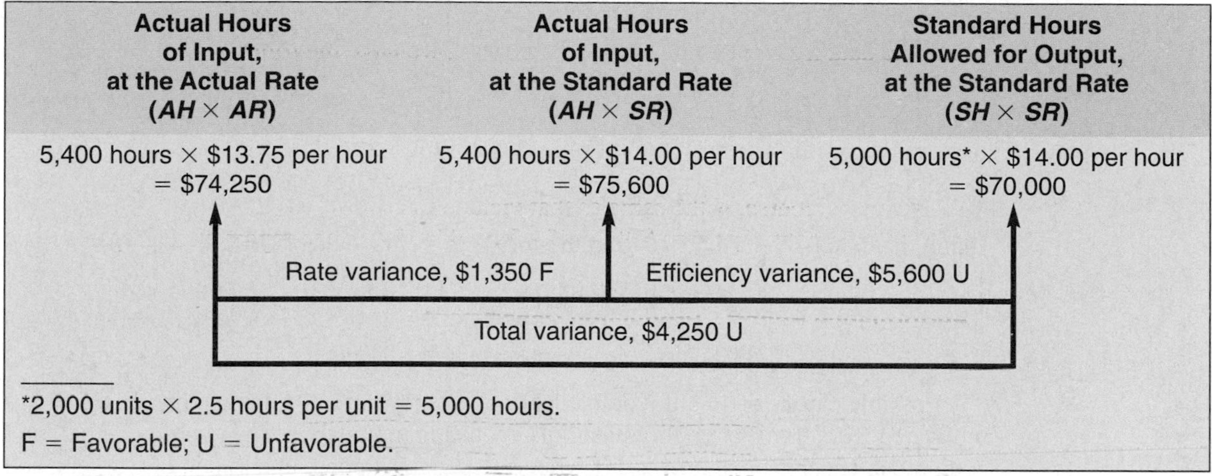

Labor Rate Variance—A Closer Look

As explained earlier, the price variance for direct labor is commonly termed a **labor rate variance.** This variance measures any deviation from standard in the average hourly rate paid to direct labor workers. The formula for the labor rate variance is expressed as follows:

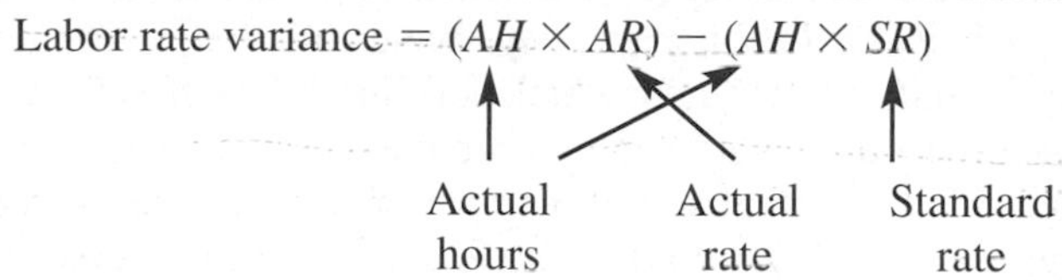

Labor rate variance = (AH × AR) − (AH × SR)
Actual hours
Actual rate
Standard rate

The formula can be factored into simpler form as follows:

$$\text{Labor rate variance} = AH(AR - SR)$$

Using the data from Exhibit 10–6 in the formula, the labor rate variance can be computed as follows:

$$5{,}400 \text{ hours } (\$13.75 \text{ per hour} - \$14.00 \text{ per hour}) = \$1{,}350 \text{ F}$$

In most firms, the rates paid to workers are quite predictable. Nevertheless, rate variances can arise through the way labor is used. Skilled workers with high hourly rates of pay may be given duties that require little skill and call for low hourly rates of pay. This will result in an unfavorable labor rate variance, since the actual hourly rate of pay will exceed the standard rate specified for the particular task. In contrast, a favorable rate variance would result when workers who are paid at a rate lower than specified in the standard are assigned to the task. However, the lower paid workers may not be as efficient. Finally, overtime work at premium rates will result in an unfavorable rate variance if the overtime premium is charged to the direct labor account.

Who is responsible for controlling the labor rate variance? Since rate variances generally arise as a result of how labor is used, production supervisors bear responsibility for seeing that labor rate variances are kept under control.

Labor Efficiency Variance—A Closer Look

The quantity variance for direct labor, more commonly called the **labor efficiency variance,** measures the productivity of labor time. No variance is more closely watched by management, since it is widely believed that increasing the productivity of direct labor time is vital to reducing costs. The formula for the labor efficiency variance is expressed as follows:

$$\text{Labor efficiency variance} = (AH \times SR) - (SH \times SR)$$

Actual hours — Standard rate — Standard hours allowed for output

Factored into simpler terms, the formula is as follows:

$$\text{Labor efficiency variance} = SR(AH - SH)$$

Using the data from Exhibit 10–6 in the formula, we have the following:

$14.00 per hour (5,400 hours − 5,000 hours*) = $5,600 U

*2,000 units × 2.5 hours per unit = 5,000 hours.

Possible causes of an unfavorable labor efficiency variance include poorly trained or motivated workers; poor quality materials, requiring more labor time in processing; faulty equipment, causing breakdowns and work interruptions; poor supervision of workers; and inaccurate standards. The managers in charge of production would generally be responsible for control of the labor efficiency variance. However, purchasing could be held responsible if the acquisition of poor materials resulted in excessive labor processing time.

Another important cause of an unfavorable labor efficiency variance may be insufficient demand for the company's products. Managers in some companies argue that it is difficult, and perhaps unwise, to constantly adjust the work force in response to changes in the amount of work that needs to be done. In such companies, the direct labor work force is essentially fixed in the short run. If demand is insufficient to keep everyone busy, workers are not laid off. In this case, if demand falls below the level needed to keep everyone busy, an unfavorable labor efficiency variance will often be recorded.

If customer orders are insufficient to keep the workers busy, the work center manager has two options—either accept an unfavorable labor efficiency variance or build inventory.[3] A central lesson of just-in-time (JIT) is that building inventory with no immediate prospect of sale is a bad idea. Inventory—particularly work in process inventory—leads to high defect rates, obsolete goods, and generally inefficient operations. As a consequence, when the work force is basically fixed in the short term, managers must be cautious about how labor efficiency variances are used. Some managers advocate dispensing with labor efficiency variances entirely in such situations—at least for the purposes of motivating and controlling workers on the shop floor.

Using Standard Costs—Variable Manufacturing Overhead Variances

LEARNING OBJECTIVE 4
Compute the variable manufacturing overhead spending and efficiency variances.

The final step in Terry Sherman's analysis of Colonial Pewter's variances for June was to compute the variable manufacturing overhead variances. The variable portion of manufacturing overhead can be analyzed using the same basic formulas that are used to analyze direct materials and direct labor. Recall from Exhibit 10–2 that the standard variable manufacturing overhead is $7.50 per unit of product, computed as follows:

2.5 hours per unit × $3.00 per hour = $7.50 per unit

Colonial Pewter's cost records showed that the total actual variable manufacturing overhead cost for June was $15,390. Recall from the earlier discussion of the direct labor variances that 5,400 hours of direct labor time were recorded during the month and that the company produced 2,000 pairs of bookends. Terry's analysis of this overhead data appears in Exhibit 10–7.

3 For further discussion, see Eliyahu M. Goldratt and Jeff Cox, *The Goal,* 2nd rev. ed. (Croton-on-Hudson, NY: North River Press, 1992).

Exhibit 10–7 Variance Analysis—Variable Manufacturing Overhead

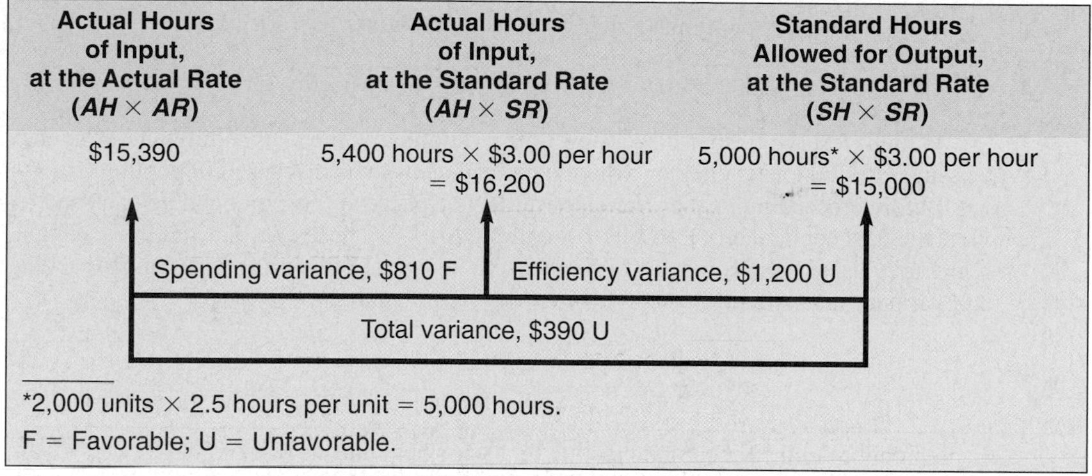

Notice the similarities between Exhibits 10–6 and 10–7. These similarities arise from the fact that direct labor-hours are being used as a base for allocating overhead cost to units of product; thus, the same hourly figures appear in Exhibit 10–7 for variable manufacturing overhead as in Exhibit 10–6 for direct labor. The main difference between the two exhibits is in the standard hourly rate being used, which in this company is much lower for variable manufacturing overhead than for direct labor.

Manufacturing Overhead Variances—A Closer Look

The formula for the **variable overhead spending variance** is expressed as follows:

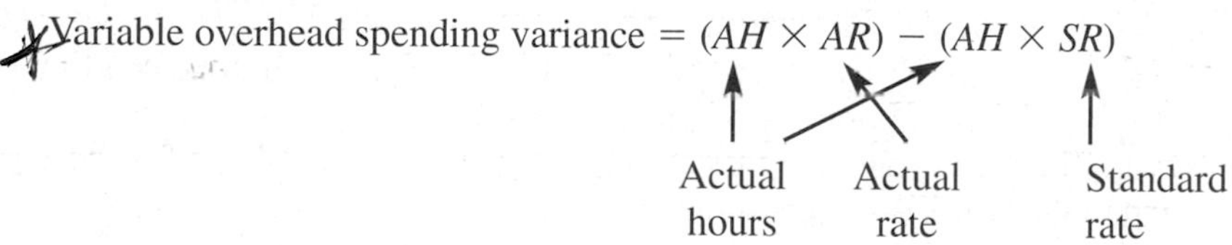

Variable overhead spending variance = (AH × AR) − (AH × SR)
Actual hours
Actual rate
Standard rate

Or, factored into simpler terms:

$$\text{Variable overhead spending variance} = AH(AR - SR)$$

Using the data from Exhibit 10–7 in the formula, the variable overhead spending variance can be computed as follows:

5,400 hours ($2.85 per hour* − $3.00 per hour) = $810 F

*$15,390 ÷ 5,400 hours = $2.85 per hour.

The formula for the **variable overhead efficiency variance** is expressed as follows:

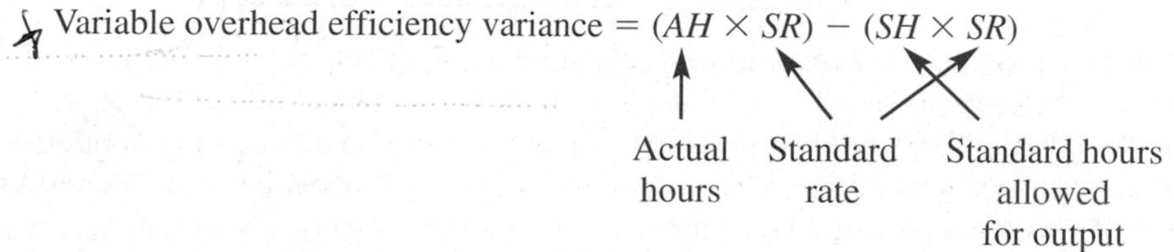

Or, factored into simpler terms:

$$\text{Variable overhead efficiency variance} = SR(AH - SH)$$

Again using the data from Exhibit 10–7, the variance could be computed as follows:

$3.00 per hour (5,400 hours − 5,000 hours*) = $1,200 U

*2,000 units × 2.5 hours per unit = 5,000 hours.

We will reserve further discussion of the variable overhead spending and efficiency variances until the next chapter, where overhead analysis is discussed in depth.

Before proceeding further, we suggest that you pause at this point and go back and review the data contained in Exhibits 10–2 through 10–7. These exhibits and the accompanying text discussion provide a comprehensive, integrated illustration of standard setting and variance analysis.

Managerial Accounting in Action

The Wrap-Up

In preparation for the scheduled meeting to discuss her analysis of Colonial Pewter's standard costs and variances, Terry distributed Exhibits 10–2 through 10–7 to the management group of Colonial Pewter. This included J. D. Wriston, the president of the company; Tom Kuchel, the production manager; and Janet Warner, the purchasing manager. J. D. Wriston opened the meeting with the following question:

J. D.: Terry, I think I understand the report you distributed, but just to make sure, would you mind summarizing the highlights of what you found?

Terry: As you can see, the biggest problems are the unfavorable materials quantity variance of $2,000 and the unfavorable labor efficiency variance of $5,600.

J. D.: Tom, you're the production boss. What do you think is responsible for the unfavorable labor efficiency variance?

Tom: It pretty much has to be the new production workers. Our experienced workers shouldn't have much problem meeting the standard of 2.5 hours per unit. We all knew that there would be some inefficiency for a while as we brought new people on board.

J. D.: No one is disputing that, Tom. However, $5,600 is a lot of money. Is this problem likely to go away very soon?

Tom: I hope so. If we were to contrast the last two weeks of June with the first two weeks, I'm sure we would see some improvement.

J. D.: I don't want to beat up on you, Tom, but this is a significant problem. Can you do something to accelerate the training process?

Tom: Sure. I could pair up each of the new guys with one of our old-timers and have them work together for a while. It would slow down our older guys a bit, but I'll bet the new workers would learn a lot.

J. D.: Let's try it. Now, what about that $2,000 unfavorable materials quantity variance?

Tom: Are you asking me?

J. D.: Well, I would like someone to explain it.

Tom: Don't look at me. It's that iron-contaminated pewter that Janet bought on her "special deal."

Janet: We got rid of that stuff months ago.

J. D.: Hold your horses. We're not trying to figure out who to blame here. I just want to understand what happened. If we can understand what happened, maybe we can fix it.

Terry: Tom, are the new workers generating a lot of scrap?

Tom: Yeah, I guess so.

J. D.: I think that could be part of the problem. Can you do anything about it?

Tom: I can watch the scrap real closely for a few days to see where it's being generated. If it is the new workers, I can have the old-timers work with them on the problem when I team them up.

J. D.: Good. Let's reconvene in a few weeks and see what has happened. Hopefully, we can get those unfavorable variances under control.

Structure of Performance Reports

On the preceding pages we have learned that performance reports are used in a standard cost system to communicate variance data to management. Exhibit 10–8 provides an example of how these reports can be integrated in a responsibility reporting system.

Note from the exhibit that the performance reports *start at the bottom and build upward,* with managers at each level receiving information on their own performance as well as information on the performance of each manager under them in the chain of responsibility. This variance information flows upward from level to level in a pyramid fashion, with the president finally receiving a summary of all activities in the organization. If the manager at a particular level (such as the production superintendent) wants to

Exhibit 10–8 Upward Flow of Performance Reports

President's Report
The president's performance report summarizes all company data. The president can trace the variances downward through the company as needed to determine where top management time should be spent.

Responsibility center:	Budget	Actual	Variance
Sales manager	X	X	X
Production superintendent	$26,000	$29,000	$3,000 U
Engineering head	X	X	X
Personnel supervisor	X	X	X
Controller	X	X	X
	$54,000	$61,000	$7,000 U

Production Superintendent
The performance of each department head is summarized for the production superintendent. The totals on the superintendent's performance report are then passed upward to the next level of responsibility.

Responsibility center:	Budget	Actual	Variance
Cutting department	X	X	X
Machining department	X	X	X
Finishing department	$11,000	$12,500	$1,500 U
Packaging department	X	X	X
	$26,000	$29,000	$3,000 U

Finishing Department Head
The performance report of each supervisor is summarized on the performance report of the department head. The department totals are then passed upward to the production superintendent.

Responsibility center:	Budget	Actual	Variance
Sanding operation	X	X	X
Wiring operation	$ 5,000	$ 5,800	$ 800 U
Assembly operation	X	X	X
	$11,000	$12,500	$1,500 U

Wiring Operation Supervisor
The supervisor of each operation receives a performance report. The totals on these reports are then communicated upward to the next higher level of responsibility.

Variable costs:	Budget	Actual	Variance
Direct materials	X	X	X
Direct labor	X	X	X
Manufacturing overhead	X	X	X
	$ 5,000	$ 5,800	$ 800 U

Exhibit 10–12
Examples of Performance Measures for Balanced Scorecards

Customer Perspective	
Performance Measure	**Desired Change**
Customer satisfaction as measured by survey results	+
Number of customer complaints	−
Market share	+
Product returns as a percentage of sales	−
Percentage of customers retained from last period	+
Number of new customers	+

Internal Business Processes Perspective	
Performance Measure	**Desired Change**
Percentage of sales from new products	+
Time to introduce new products to market	−
Percentage of customer calls answered within 20 seconds	+
On-time deliveries as a percentage of all deliveries	+
Work in process inventory as a percentage of sales	−
Unfavorable standard cost variances	−
Defect-free units as a percentage of completed units	+
Delivery cycle time*	−
Throughput time*	−
Manufacturing cycle efficiency*	+
Quality costs†	−
Setup time	−
Time from call by customer to repair of product	−
Percent of customer complaints settled on first contact	+
Time to settle a customer claim	−

Learning and Growth Perspective	
Performance Measure	**Desired Change**
Suggestions per employee	+
Value-added employee‡	+
Employee turnover	−
Hours of in-house training per employee	+

*Explained later in this chapter.
†See Appendix 2B, Cost of Quality.
‡Value-added is revenue less externally purchased materials, supplies, and services.

Exhibit 10–12 lists some examples of performance measures that can be found on the balanced scorecards of companies. However, few companies, if any, would use all of these performance measures, and almost all companies would add other performance measures. Managers should carefully select the performance measures for their company's balanced scorecard, keeping the following points in mind. First and foremost, the performance measures should be consistent with, and follow from, the company's strategy. If the performance measures are not consistent with the company's strategy, people will find themselves working at cross-purposes. Second, the scorecard should not have too many performance measures. This can lead to a lack of focus and confusion.

While the entire organization will have an overall balanced scorecard, each responsible individual will have his or her own personal scorecard as well. This scorecard should consist of items the individual can personally influence that relate directly to the performance measures on the overall balanced scorecard. The performance measures on this personal scorecard should not be overly influenced by actions taken by others in the company or by events that are outside of the individual's control. And, using the performance measure should not lead employees to take actions that are counter to the organization's objectives.

With those broad principles in mind, we will now take a look at how a company's strategy affects its balanced scorecard.

When Improvement Isn't Better

In Business

Mark Graham Brown, a performance-measurement consultant, warns managers to focus on the right metrics when measuring performance. He relates the following story: "A fast-food chain gave lip service to many objectives, but what senior managers watched most rigorously was how much chicken its restaurants had to throw away . . . What happened? As one restaurant operator explained, it was easy to hit your . . . targets: just don't cook any chicken until somebody orders it. Customers might have to wait 20 minutes for their meal, and would probably never come back—but you'd sure make your numbers. Moral: a measurement may look good on paper, but you need to ask what behavior it will drive."

Source: "Using Measurement to Boost Your Unit's Performance," *Harvard Management Update*, October 1998.

A Company's Strategy and the Balanced Scorecard

Returning to the performance measures in Exhibit 10–11, each company must decide which customers to target and what internal business processes are crucial to attracting and retaining those customers. Different companies, having different strategies, will target different customers with different kinds of products and services. Take the automobile industry as an example. BMW stresses engineering and handling; Volvo, safety; Jaguar, luxury detailing; Corvette, racy styling; and Toyota, reliability. Because of these differences in emphases, a one-size-fits-all approach to performance measurement won't work even within this one industry. Performance measures must be tailored to the specific strategy of each company.

Suppose, for example, that Jaguar's strategy is to offer distinctive, richly finished luxury automobiles to wealthy individuals who prize handcrafted, individualized products. Part of Jaguar's strategy might be to create such a large number of options for details, such as leather seats, interior and exterior color combinations, and wooden dashboards, that each car becomes virtually one of a kind. For example, instead of just offering tan or blue leather seats in standard cowhide, the company may offer customers the choice of an almost infinite palette of colors in any of a number of different exotic leathers. For such a system to work effectively, Jaguar would have to be able to deliver a completely customized car within a reasonable amount of time—and without incurring more cost for this customization than the customer is willing to pay. Exhibit 10–13 suggests how Jaguar might reflect this strategy in its balanced scorecard.

If the balanced scorecard is correctly constructed, the performance measures should be linked together on a cause-and-effect basis. Each link can then be read as a hypothesis in the form "If we improve this performance measure, then this other performance measure should also improve." Starting from the bottom of Exhibit 10–13, we can read the links between performance measures as follows. If employees acquire the skills to install new options more effectively, then the company can offer more options and the options can be installed in less time. If more options are available and they are installed in less time, then customer surveys should show greater satisfaction with the range of options available. If customer satisfaction improves, then the number of cars sold should increase.

Direct material: 6 ounces at $0.50 per ounce	$ 3
Direct labor: 1.8 hours at $10 per hour	18
Variable manufacturing overhead: 1.8 hours at $5 per hour	9
Total standard variable cost per unit	$30

During June, 2,000 units were produced. The costs associated with June's operations were as follows:

Material purchased: 18,000 ounces at $0.60 per ounce	$10,800
Material used in production: 14,000 ounces	—
Direct labor: 4,000 hours at $9.75 per hour	39,000
Variable manufacturing overhead costs incurred	20,800

Required:
Compute the materials, labor, and variable manufacturing overhead variances.

Solution to the Review Problem

Materials Variances

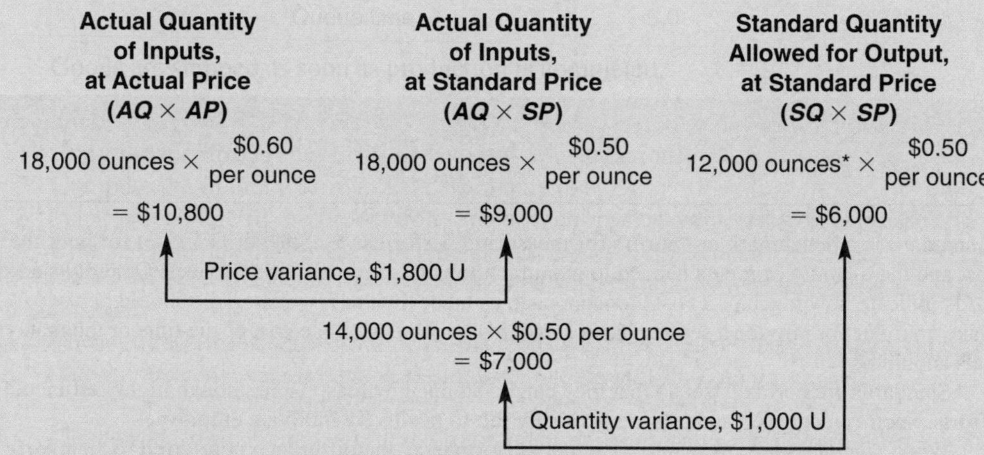

*2,000 units × 6 ounces per unit = 12,000 ounces.

Using the formulas in the chapter, the same variances would be computed as follows:

$$\text{Materials price variance} = AQ(AP - SP)$$

$$18{,}000 \text{ ounces } (\$0.60 \text{ per ounce} - \$0.50 \text{ per ounce}) = \$1{,}800 \text{ U}$$

$$\text{Materials quantity variance} = SP(AQ - SQ)$$

$$\$0.50 \text{ per ounce } (14{,}000 \text{ ounces} - 12{,}000 \text{ ounces}) = \$1{,}000 \text{ U}$$

Labor Variances

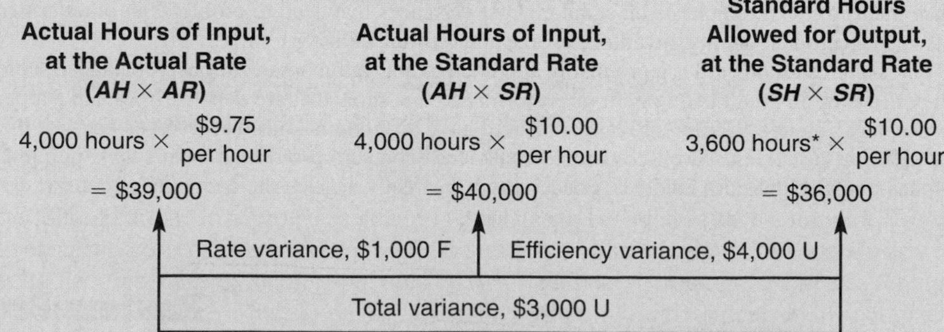

*2,000 units × 1.8 hours per unit = 3,600 hours.

Using the formulas in the chapter, the same variances would be computed as:

Labor rate variance = $AH(AR - SR)$

4,000 hours ($9.75 per hour − $10.00 per hour) = $1,000 F

Labor efficiency variance = $SR(AH - SH)$

$10.00 per hour (4,000 hours − 3,600 hours) = $4,000 U

Variable Manufacturing Overhead Variances

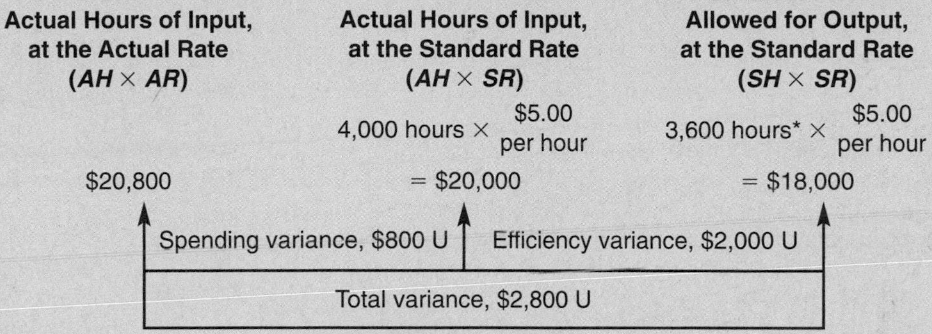

*2,000 units × 1.8 hours per unit = 3,600 hours.

Using the formulas in the chapter, the same variances would be computed as follows:

Variable overhead spending variance = $AH(AR - SR)$
4,000 hours ($5.20 per hour* − $5.00 per hour) = $800 U

*$20,800 ÷ 4,000 hours = $5.20 per hour

Variable overhead efficiency variance = $SR(AH - SH)$
$5.00 per hour (4,000 hours − 3,600 hours) = $2,000 U

Glossary

Balanced scorecard An integrated set of performance measures that is derived from and supports the organization's strategy. (p. 445)

Bill of materials A listing of the quantity of each type of material required to make a unit of product. (p. 428)

Delivery cycle time The amount of time required from receipt of an order from a customer to shipment of the completed goods. (p. 453)

Ideal standards Standards that allow for no machine breakdowns or other work interruptions and that require peak efficiency at all times. (p. 427)

Labor efficiency variance A measure of the difference between the actual hours taken to complete a task and the standard hours allowed, multiplied by the standard hourly labor rate. (p. 437)

Labor rate variance A measure of the difference between the actual hourly labor rate and the standard rate, multiplied by the number of hours worked during the period. (p. 437)

Management by exception A system of management in which standards are set for various operating activities, with actual results then compared to these standards. Any differences that are deemed significant are brought to the attention of management as "exceptions." (p. 425)

Manufacturing cycle efficiency (MCE) Process (value-added) time as a percentage of throughput time. (p. 453)

Materials price variance A measure of the difference between the actual unit price paid for an item and the standard price, multiplied by the quantity purchased. (p. 434)

Materials quantity variance A measure of the difference between the actual quantity of materials used in production and the standard quantity allowed, multiplied by the standard price per unit of materials. (p. 435)

Practical standards Standards that allow for normal machine downtime and other work interruptions and that can be attained through reasonable, though highly efficient, efforts by the average worker. (p. 427)

Standard cost card A detailed listing of the standard amounts of materials, labor, and overhead that should go into a unit of product, multiplied by the standard price or rate that has been set for each cost element. (p. 426)

Standard cost per unit The standard cost of a unit of product as shown on the standard cost card; it is computed by multiplying the standard quantity or hours by the standard price or rate for each cost element. (p. 430)

Standard hours allowed The time that should have been taken to complete the period's output as computed by multiplying the actual number of units produced by the standard hours per unit. (p. 432)

Standard hours per unit The amount of labor time that should be required to complete a single unit of product, including allowances for breaks, machine downtime, cleanup, rejects, and other normal inefficiencies. (p. 429)

Standard price per unit The price that should be paid for a single unit of materials, including allowances for quality, quantity purchased, shipping, receiving, and other such costs, net of any discounts allowed. (p. 428)

Standard quantity allowed The amount of materials that should have been used to complete the period's output as computed by multiplying the actual number of units produced by the standard quantity per unit. (p. 432)

Standard quantity per unit The amount of materials that should be required to complete a single unit of product, including allowances for normal waste, spoilage, rejects, and similar inefficiencies. (p. 428)

Standard rate per hour The labor rate that should be incurred per hour of labor time, including employment taxes, fringe benefits, and other such labor costs. (p. 429)

Throughput time The amount of time required to turn raw materials into completed products. (p. 453)

Variable overhead efficiency variance The difference between the actual activity (direct labor-hours, machine-hours, or some other base) of a period and the standard activity allowed, multiplied by the variable part of the predetermined overhead rate. (p. 439)

Variable overhead spending variance The difference between the actual variable overhead cost incurred during a period and the standard cost that should have been incurred based on the actual activity of the period. (p. 439)

Variance The difference between standard prices and quantities on the one hand and actual prices and quantities on the other hand. (p. 431)

Appendix 10A: General Ledger Entries to Record Variances

LEARNING OBJECTIVE 7
Prepare journal entries to record standard costs and variances.

Although standard costs and variances can be computed and used by management without being formally entered into the accounting records, many organizations prefer to make formal entries. Formal entry tends to give variances a greater emphasis than informal, off-the-record computations. This emphasis gives a clear signal of management's desire to keep costs within the limits that have been set. In addition, formal use of standard costs simplifies the bookkeeping process enormously. Inventories and cost of goods sold can be valued at their standard costs—eliminating the need to keep track of the actual cost of each unit.

Direct Materials Variances

To illustrate the general ledger entries needed to record standard cost variances, we will return to the data contained in the review problem at the end of the chapter. The entry to record the purchase of direct materials would be as follows:

Raw Materials (18,000 ounces at $0.50 per ounce)	9,000	
Materials Price Variance (18,000 ounces at $0.10 per ounce U)	1,800	
Accounts Payable (18,000 ounces at $0.60 per ounce) . . .		10,800

Notice that the price variance is recognized when purchases are made, rather than when materials are actually used in production. This permits the price variance to be isolated immediately, and it also permits the materials to be carried in the inventory account at standard cost. As direct materials are later drawn from inventory and used in production, the quantity variance is isolated as follows:

Work in Process (12,000 ounces at $0.50 per ounce)	6,000	
Materials Quantity Variance (2,000 ounces U at $0.50 per ounce)	1,000	
Raw Materials (14,000 ounces at $0.50 per ounce)		7,000

Thus, direct materials are added to the Work in Process account at the standard cost of the materials that should have been used to produce the actual output.

Notice that both the price variance and the quantity variance above are unfavorable and are debit entries. If these variances had been favorable, they would have appeared as credit entries.

Direct Labor Variances

Referring again to the cost data in the review problem at the end of the chapter, the general ledger entry to record the incurrence of direct labor cost would be:

Work in Process (3,600 hours at $10.00 per hour)	36,000	
Labor Efficiency Variance (400 hours U at $10.00 per hour) . . .	4,000	
Labor Rate Variance (4,000 hours at $0.25 per hour F) . . .		1,000
Wages Payable (4,000 hours at $9.75 per hour)		39,000

Thus, as with direct materials, direct labor costs enter into the Work in Process account at standard, both in terms of the rate and in terms of the hours allowed for the actual production of the period.

Variable Manufacturing Overhead Variances

Variable manufacturing overhead variances usually are not recorded in the accounts separately but rather are determined as part of the general analysis of overhead, which is discussed in the next chapter.

Cost Flows in a Standard Cost System

The flows of costs through the company's accounts are illustrated in Exhibit 10A–1. Note that entries into the various inventory accounts are made at standard cost—not actual cost. The differences between actual and standard costs are entered into special accounts that accumulate the various standard cost variances. Ordinarily, these standard cost variance accounts are closed out to Cost of Goods Sold at the end of the period. Unfavorable variances increase Cost of Goods Sold, and favorable variances decrease Cost of Goods Sold.

Exhibit 10A–1 Cost Flows in a Standard Cost System*

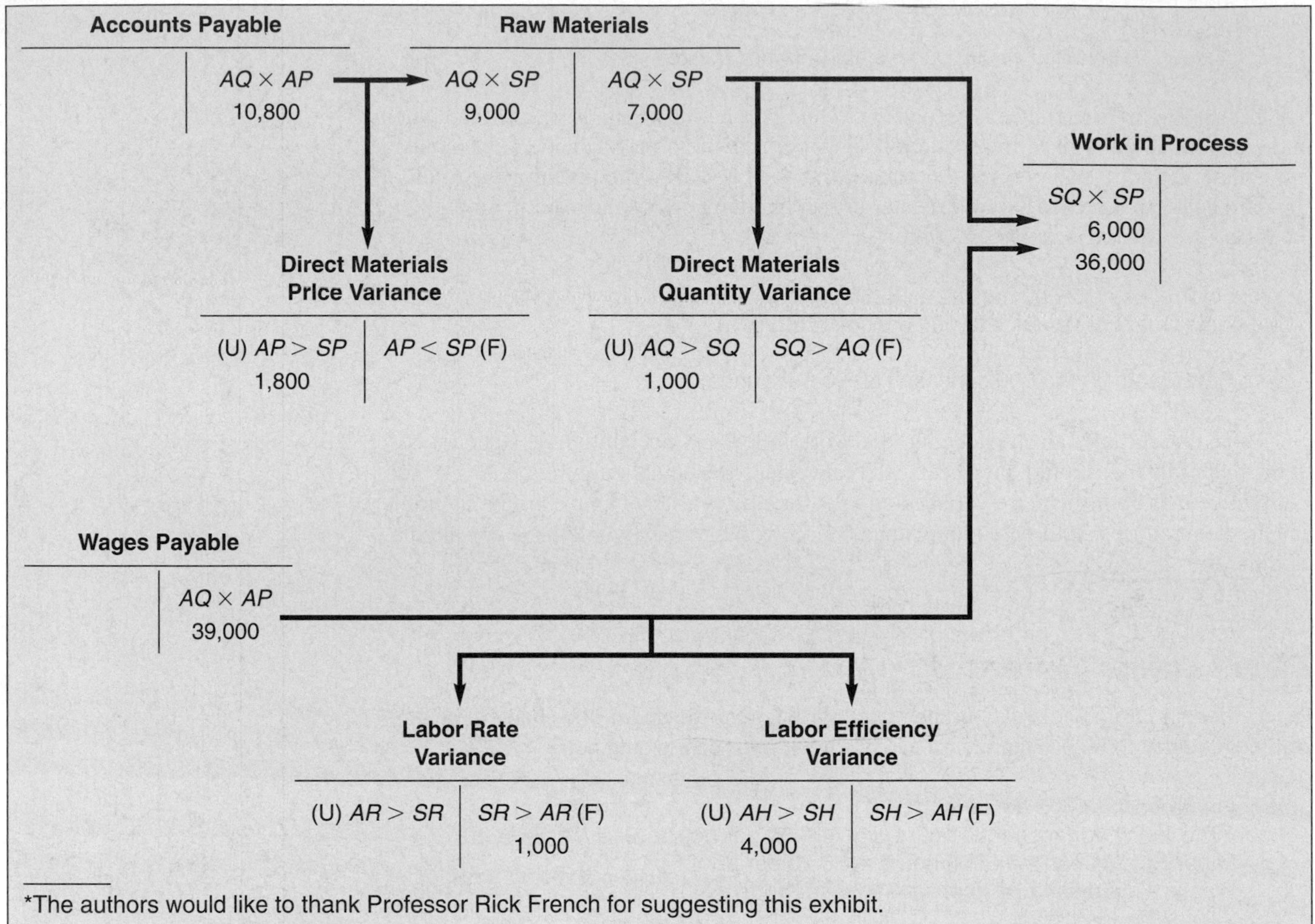

*The authors would like to thank Professor Rick French for suggesting this exhibit.

Questions

10–1 What is a quantity standard? What is a price standard?

10–2 Distinguish between ideal and practical standards.

10–3 If employees are chronically unable to meet a standard, what effect would you expect this to have on their productivity?

10–4 What is the difference between a standard and a budget?

10–5 What is meant by the term *variance?*

10–6 What is meant by the term *management by exception?*

10–7 Why are separate price and quantity variances computed?

10–8 Who is generally responsible for the materials price variance? The materials quantity variance? The labor efficiency variance?

10–9 The materials price variance can be computed at what two different points in time? Which point is better? Why?

10–10 An examination of the cost records of the Chittenden Furniture Company reveals that the materials price variance is favorable but that the materials quantity variance is unfavorable by a substantial amount. What might this indicate?

10–11 What dangers lie in using standards as punitive tools?

10–12 "Our workers are all under labor contracts; therefore, our labor rate variance is bound to be zero." Discuss.

10–13 What effect, if any, would you expect poor quality materials to have on direct labor variances?

10–14 If variable manufacturing overhead is applied to production on the basis of direct labor-hours and the direct labor efficiency variance is unfavorable, will the variable overhead efficiency variance be favorable or unfavorable, or could it be either? Explain.

10–15 What is a statistical control chart, and how is it used?

10–16 Why can undue emphasis on labor efficiency variances lead to excess work in process inventories?

10–17 Why does the balanced scorecard differ from company to company?

10–18 Why does the balanced scorecard include financial performance measures as well as measures of how well internal business processes are doing?

10–19 What is the difference between the delivery cycle time and the throughput time? What four elements make up the throughput time? Into what two classes can these four elements be placed?

10–20 If a company has a manufacturing cycle efficiency (MCE) of less than 1, what does it mean? How would you interpret an MCE of 0.40?

10–21 (Appendix 10A) What are the advantages of making formal journal entries in the accounting records for variances?

Exercises

EXERCISE 10–1 Setting Standards; Preparing a Standard Cost Card [LO1]

Svenska Pharmicia, a Swedish pharmaceutical company, makes an anticoagulant drug. The main ingredient in the drug is a raw material called Alpha SR40. Information concerning the purchase and use of Alpha SR40 follows:

Purchase of Alpha SR40: The raw material Alpha SR40 is purchased in 2-kilogram containers at a cost of 3,000 Kr per kilogram. (The Swedish currency is the krona, which is abbreviated as Kr.) A discount of 2% is offered by the supplier for payment within 10 days and Svenska Pharmicia takes all discounts. Shipping costs, which Svenska Pharmicia must pay, amount to 1,000 Kr for an average shipment of ten 2-kilogram containers.

Use of Alpha SR40: The bill of materials calls for 6 grams of Alpha SR40 per capsule of the anticoagulant drug. (A kilogram equals 1,000 grams.) About 4% of all Alpha SR40 purchased is rejected as unsuitable before being used to make the anticoagulant drug. In addition, after the addition of Alpha SR40, about 1 out of every 26 capsules is rejected at final inspection, due to defects of one sort or another in the capsule.

Required:

1. Compute the standard purchase price for one gram of Alpha SR40.
2. Compute the standard quantity of Alpha SR40 (in grams) per capsule that passes final inspection. (Carry computations to two decimal places.)
3. Using the data from (1) and (2) above, prepare a standard cost card showing the standard cost of Alpha SR40 per capsule of the anticoagulant drug.

EXERCISE 10–2 Material Variances [LO2]

Harmon Household Products, Inc., manufactures a number of consumer items for general household use. One of these products, a chopping board, requires an expensive hardwood. During a recent month, the company manufactured 4,000 chopping boards using 11,000 board feet of hardwood. The hardwood cost the company $18,700.

The company's standards for one chopping board are 2.5 board feet of hardwood, at a cost of $1.80 per board foot.

Required:

1. What cost for wood should have been incurred to make 4,000 chopping blocks? How much greater or less is this than the cost that was incurred?
2. Break down the difference computed in (1) above into a materials price variance and a materials quantity variance.

EXERCISE 10–3 Material and Labor Variances [LO2, LO3]

Topper Toys has developed a new toy called the Brainbuster. The company has a standard cost system to help control costs and has established the following standards for the Brainbuster toy:

Direct materials: 8 diodes per toy at $0.30 per diode
Direct labor: 1.2 hours per toy at $7 per hour

During August, the company produced 5,000 Brainbuster toys. Production data on the toy for August follow:

Direct materials: 70,000 diodes were purchased for use in production at a cost of $0.28 per diode. Some 20,000 of these diodes were still in inventory at the end of the month.
Direct labor: 6,400 direct labor-hours were worked at a cost of $48,000.

Required:

1. Compute the following variances for August:
   a. Direct materials price and quantity variances.
   b. Direct labor rate and efficiency variances.
2. Prepare a brief explanation of the significance and possible causes of each variance.

EXERCISE 10–4 Labor and Variable Overhead Variances [LO3, LO4]
Hollowell Audio, Inc., manufactures military-specification compact discs. The company uses standards to control its costs. The labor standards that have been set for one disc are as follows:

Standard Hours	Standard Rate per Hour	Standard Cost
24 minutes	$6.00	$2.40

During July, 8,500 hours of direct labor time were recorded to make 20,000 discs. The direct labor cost totaled $49,300 for the month.

Required:

1. What direct labor cost should have been incurred to make the 20,000 discs? By how much does this differ from the cost that was incurred?
2. Break down the difference in cost from (1) above into a labor rate variance and a labor efficiency variance.
3. The budgeted variable manufacturing overhead rate is $4 per direct labor-hour. During July, the company incurred $39,100 in variable manufacturing overhead cost. Compute the variable overhead spending and efficiency variances for the month.

EXERCISE 10–5 Material and Labor Variances [LO2, LO3]
Sonne Company produces a perfume called Whim. The direct materials and direct labor standards for one bottle of Whim are given below:

	Standard Quantity or Hours	Standard Price or Rate	Standard Cost
Direct materials	7.2 ounces	$2.50 per ounce	$18
Direct labor	0.4 hours	$10.00 per hour	$ 4

During the most recent month, the following activity was recorded:

a. Twenty thousand ounces of material were purchased at a cost of $2.40 per ounce.
b. All of the material was used to produce 2,500 bottles of Whim.
c. Nine hundred hours of direct labor time were recorded at a total labor cost of $10,800.

Required:

1. Compute the direct materials price and quantity variances for the month.
2. Compute the direct labor rate and efficiency variances for the month.

EXERCISE 10–6 Material Variances [LO2]
Refer to the data in Exercise 10–5. Assume that instead of producing 2,500 bottles of Whim during the month, the company produced only 2,000 bottles using 16,000 ounces of material. (The rest of the material purchased remained in inventory.)

Required:
Compute the direct materials price and quantity variances for the month.

EXERCISE 10–7 Working Backwards from Labor Variances [LO3]
The Worldwide Credit Card, Inc., uses standards to control the labor time involved in opening mail from card holders and recording the enclosed remittances. Incoming mail is gathered into batches, and a standard time is set for opening and recording each batch. The labor standards relating to one batch are given on the following page:

	Standard Hours	Standard Rate	Standard Cost
Per batch.	2.5	$6	$15

The record showing the time spent last week in opening batches of mail has been misplaced. However, the batch supervisor recalls that 168 batches were received and opened during the week, and the controller recalls the following variance data relating to these batches:

Total labor variance	$330 U
Labor rate variance	150 F

Required:

1. Determine the number of actual labor-hours spent opening batches during the week.
2. Determine the actual hourly rate paid to employees for opening batches last week.

(Hint: A useful way to proceed would be to work from known to unknown data either by using the variance formulas or by using the columnar format shown in Exhibit 10–6.)

EXERCISE 10–8 Measures of Internal Business Process Performance [LO6]

Lipex, Ltd., of Birmingham, England, is interested in cutting the amount of time between when a customer places an order and when the order is completed. For the first quarter of the year, the following data were reported:

Inspection time.	0.5 days
Process time	2.8 days
Wait time	16.0 days
Queue time	4.0 days
Move time	0.7 days

Required:

1. Compute the throughput time, or velocity of production.
2. Compute the manufacturing cycle efficiency (MCE) for the quarter.
3. What percentage of the throughput time was spent in non-value-added activities?
4. Compute the delivery cycle time.
5. If by use of JIT all queue time can be eliminated in production, what will be the new MCE?

EXERCISE 10–9 (Appendix 10A) Material and Labor Variances; Journal Entries [LO2, LO3, LO7]

Aspen Products, Inc., began production of a new product on April 1. The company uses a standard cost system and has established the following standards for one unit of the new product:

	Standard Quantity	Standard Price or Rate	Standard Cost
Direct materials	3.5 feet	$6 per foot	$21
Direct labor	0.4 hours	$10 per hour	$4

During April, the following activity was recorded relative to the new product:

a. Purchased 7,000 feet of material at a cost of $5.75 per foot.
b. Used 6,000 feet of material to produce 1,500 units of the new product.
c. Worked 725 direct labor-hours on the new product at a cost of $8,120.

Required:

1. For materials:
   a. Compute the direct materials price and quantity variances.
   b. Prepare journal entries to record the purchase of materials and the use of materials in production.
2. For direct labor:
   a. Compute the direct labor rate and efficiency variances.
   b. Prepare journal entries to record the incurrence of direct labor cost for the month.
3. Post the entries you have prepared to the T-accounts below:

Raw Materials

	Debit	Credit
	?	?
Bal.	?	

Accounts Payable

Debit	Credit
	40,250

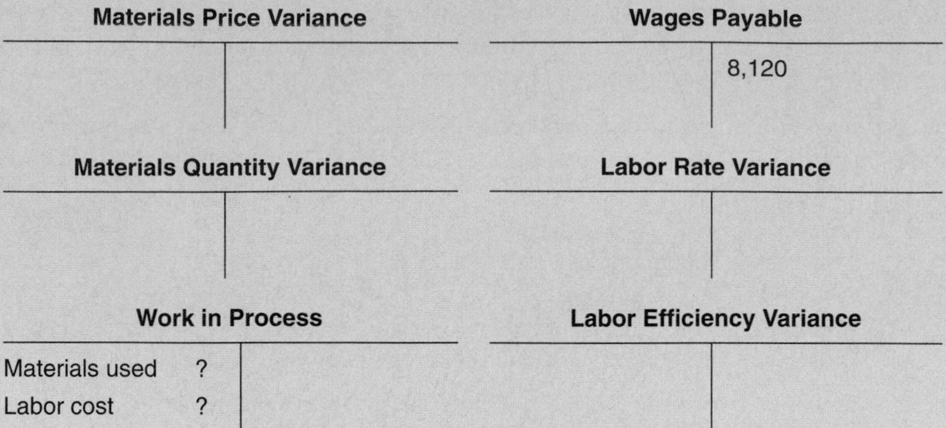

Materials Price Variance

Wages Payable

	8,120

Materials Quantity Variance

Labor Rate Variance

Work in Process

Materials used ?	
Labor cost ?	

Labor Efficiency Variance

Problems

PROBLEM 10–10 Basic Variance Analysis [LO2, LO3, LO4]

Barberry, Inc., manufactures a product called Fruta. The company uses a standard cost system and has established the following standards for one unit of Fruta:

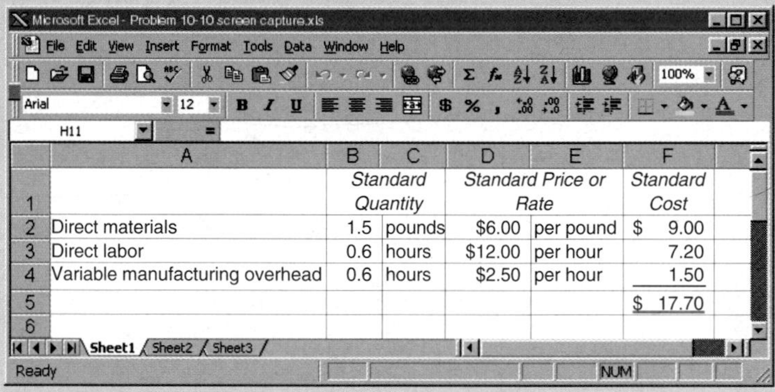

	A	B	C	D	E	F
1		*Standard Quantity*		*Standard Price or Rate*		*Standard Cost*
2	Direct materials	1.5	pounds	$6.00	per pound	$ 9.00
3	Direct labor	0.6	hours	$12.00	per hour	7.20
4	Variable manufacturing overhead	0.6	hours	$2.50	per hour	1.50
5						$ 17.70
6						

During June, the company recorded this activity relative to production of Fruta:

a. The company produced 3,000 units during June.
b. A total of 8,000 pounds of material were purchased at a cost of $46,000.
c. There was no beginning inventory of materials on hand to start the month; at the end of the month, 2,000 pounds of material remained in the warehouse unused.
d. The company employs 10 persons to work on the production of Fruta. During June, each worked an average of 160 hours at an average rate of $12.50 per hour.
e. Variable manufacturing overhead is assigned to Fruta on the basis of direct labor-hours. Variable manufacturing overhead costs during June totaled $3,600.

The company's management is anxious to determine the efficiency of the activities surrounding the production of Fruta.

Required:

1. For materials used in the production of Fruta:
   a. Compute the price and quantity variances.
   b. The materials were purchased from a new supplier who is anxious to enter into a long-term purchase contract. Would you recommend that the company sign the contract? Explain.
2. For labor employed in the production of Fruta:
   a. Compute the rate and efficiency variances.
   b. In the past, the 10 persons employed in the production of Fruta consisted of 4 senior workers and 6 assistants. During June, the company experimented with five senior workers and five assistants. Would you recommend that the new labor mix be continued? Explain.
3. Compute the variable overhead spending and efficiency variances. What relation can you see between this efficiency variance and the labor efficiency variance?

PROBLEM 10–11 Variance Analysis in a Hospital [LO2, LO3, LO4]

"What's going on in that lab?" asked Derek Warren, chief administrator for Cottonwood Hospital, as he studied the prior month's reports. "Every month the lab teeters between a profit and a loss. Are we going to have to increase our lab fees again?"

"We can't," replied Lois Ankers, the controller. "We're getting *lots* of complaints about the last increase, particularly from the insurance companies and governmental health units. They're now paying only about 80% of what we bill. I'm beginning to think the problem is on the cost side."

To determine if lab costs are in line with other hospitals, Mr. Warren has asked you to evaluate the costs for the past month. Ms. Ankers has provided you with the following information:

a. Two basic types of tests are performed in the lab—smears and blood tests. During the past month, 2,700 smears and 900 blood tests were performed in the lab.
b. Small glass plates are used in both types of tests. During the past month, the hospital purchased 16,000 plates at a cost of $38,400. This cost is net of a 4% quantity discount. A total of 2,000 of these plates were still on hand unused at the end of the month; no plates were on hand at the beginning of the month.
c. During the past month, 1,800 hours of labor time were used in performing smears and blood tests. The cost of this labor time was $18,450.
d. Variable overhead cost last month in the lab for utilities and supplies totaled $11,700.

Cottonwood Hospital has never used standard costs. By searching industry literature, however, you have determined the following nationwide averages for hospital labs:

Plates: Three plates are required per lab test. These plates cost $2.50 each and are disposed of after the test is completed.

Labor: Each smear should require 0.3 hours to complete, and each blood test should require 0.6 hours to complete. The average cost of this lab time is $12 per hour.

Overhead: Overhead cost is based on direct labor-hours. The average rate of variable overhead is $6 per hour.

Mr. Warren would like a complete analysis of the cost of plates, labor, and variable overhead in the lab for the last month so that he can determine if costs in the lab are indeed out of line.

Required:

1. Compute the materials price variance for the plates purchased last month, and compute a materials quantity variance for the plates used last month.
2. For labor cost in the lab:
   a. Compute a labor rate variance and a labor efficiency variance.
   b. In most hospitals, three-fourths of the workers in the lab are certified technicians and one-fourth are assistants. In an effort to reduce costs, Cottonwood Hospital employs only one-half certified technicians and one-half assistants. Would you recommend that this policy be continued? Explain.
3. Compute the variable overhead spending and efficiency variances. Is there any relation between the variable overhead efficiency variance and the labor efficiency variance? Explain.

PROBLEM 10–12 (Appendix 10A) Comprehensive Variance Analysis; Journal Entries [LO2, LO3, LO4, LO7]

Vermont Mills, Inc., is a large producer of men's and women's clothing. The company uses standard costs for all of its products. The standard costs and actual costs for a recent period are given below for one of the company's product lines (per unit of product):

	Standard Cost	Actual Cost
Direct materials:		
Standard: 4.0 yards at $3.60 per yard	$14.40	
Actual: 4.4 yards at $3.35 per yard.		$14.74
Direct labor:		
Standard: 1.6 hours at $4.50 per hour	7.20	
Actual: 1.4 hours at $4.85 per hour		6.79
Variable manufacturing overhead:		
Standard: 1.6 hours at $1.80 per hour	2.88	
Actual: 1.4 hours at $2.15 per hour		3.01
Total cost per unit.	$24.48	$24.54

During this period, the company produced 4,800 units of product. A comparison of standard and actual costs for the period on a total cost basis is given below:

Actual costs: 4,800 units at $24.54	$117,792
Standard costs: 4,800 units at $24.48	117,504
Difference in cost—unfavorable.	$ 288

There was no inventory of materials on hand to start the period. During the period, 21,120 yards of materials were purchased, all of which were used in production.

Required:

1. For direct materials:
   a. Compute the price and quantity variances for the period.
   b. Prepare journal entries to record all activity relating to direct materials for the period.
2. For direct labor:
   a. Compute the rate and efficiency variances.
   b. Prepare a journal entry to record the incurrence of direct labor cost for the period.
3. Compute the variable manufacturing overhead spending and efficiency variances.
4. On seeing the $288 total cost variance, the company's president stated, "This variance of $288 is only 0.2% of the $117,504 standard cost for the period. It's obvious that our costs are well under control." Do you agree? Explain.
5. State possible causes of each variance that you have computed.

PROBLEM 10–13 Comprehensive Variance Analysis [LO2, LO3, LO4]
Portland Company's Ironton Plant produces precast ingots for industrial use. Carlos Santiago, who was recently appointed general manager of the Ironton Plant, has just been handed the plant's income statement for October. The statement is shown below:

	Budgeted	Actual
Sales (5,000 ingots)	$250,000	$250,000
Less variable expenses:		
Variable cost of goods sold*	80,000	96,390
Variable selling expenses	20,000	20,000
Total variable expenses	100,000	116,390
Contribution margin	150,000	133,610
Less fixed expenses:		
Manufacturing overhead	60,000	60,000
Selling and administrative	75,000	75,000
Total fixed expenses	135,000	135,000
Net operating income (loss)	$ 15,000	$ (1,390)

*Contains direct materials, direct labor, and variable manufacturing overhead.

Mr. Santiago was shocked to see the loss for the month, particularly since sales were exactly as budgeted. He stated, "I sure hope the plant has a standard cost system in operation. If it doesn't, I won't have the slightest idea of where to start looking for the problem."

The plant does use a standard cost system, with the following standard variable cost per ingot:

	Standard Quantity or Hours	Standard Price or Rate	Standard Cost
Direct materials	4.0 pounds	$2.50 per pound	$10.00
Direct labor	0.6 hours	$9.00 per hour	5.40
Variable manufacturing overhead	0.3 hours*	$2.00 per hour	0.60
Total standard variable cost			$16.00

*Based on machine-hours.

Mr. Santiago has determined that during October the plant produced 5,000 ingots and incurred the following costs:

a. Purchased 25,000 pounds of materials at a cost of $2.95 per pound. There were no raw materials in inventory at the beginning of the month.
b. Used 19,800 pounds of materials in production. (Finished goods and work in process inventories are insignificant and can be ignored.)
c. Worked 3,600 direct labor-hours at a cost of $8.70 per hour.
d. Incurred a total variable manufacturing overhead cost of $4,320 for the month. A total of 1,800 machine-hours was recorded.

It is the company's policy to close all variances to cost of goods sold on a monthly basis.

Required:

1. Compute the following variances for October:
   a. Direct materials price and quantity variances.
   b. Direct labor rate and efficiency variances.
   c. Variable manufacturing overhead spending and efficiency variances.
2. Summarize the variances that you computed in (1) above by showing the net overall favorable or unfavorable variance for October. What impact did this figure have on the company's income statement?
3. Pick out the two most significant variances that you computed in (1) above. Explain to Mr. Santiago possible causes of these variances.

PROBLEM 10–14 Measures of Internal Business Process Performance [LO6]

MacIntyre Fabrications, Ltd., of Aberdeen, Scotland, has recently begun a continuous improvement campaign in conjunction with a move toward JIT production and purchasing. Management has developed new performance measures as part of this campaign. The following operating data have been gathered over the last four months:

	Month			
	1	**2**	**3**	**4**
Throughput time, or velocity	?	?	?	?
Manufacturing cycle efficiency	?	?	?	?
Delivery cycle time	?	?	?	?
Percentage of on-time deliveries	72%	73%	78%	85%
Total sales (units)	10,540	10,570	10,550	10,490

Management would like to know the company's throughput time, manufacturing cycle efficiency, and delivery cycle time. The data to compute these measures have been gathered and appear below:

	Month			
	1	**2**	**3**	**4**
Move time per unit, in days	0.5	0.5	0.4	0.5
Process time per unit, in days	0.6	0.5	0.5	0.4
Wait time per order before start of production, in days	9.6	8.7	5.3	4.7
Queue time per unit, in days	3.6	3.6	2.6	1.7
Inspection time per unit, in days	0.7	0.7	0.4	0.3

As part of its continuous improvement program, the company is planning to move toward a JIT purchasing and production system.

Required:

1. For each month, compute the following operating performance measures:
   a. The throughput time, or velocity of production.
   b. The manufacturing cycle efficiency (MCE).
   c. The delivery cycle time.
2. Using the performance measures given in the problem and those you computed in (1) above, identify whether the trend over the four months is generally favorable, generally unfavorable, or mixed. What areas apparently require improvement and how might they be improved?
3. Refer to the move time, process time, and so forth, given above for month 4.
   a. Assume that in month 5 the move time, process time, and so forth, are the same as for month 4, except that through the implementation of JIT, the company is able to completely eliminate the queue time during production. Compute the new throughput time and MCE.

b. Assume that in month 6 the move time, process time, and so forth, are the same as for month 4, except that the company is able to completely eliminate both the queue time during production and the inspection time. Compute the new throughput time and MCE.

PROBLEM 10–15 Setting Standards [LO1]

L'Essence is a small cosmetics company located in the perfume center of Grasse in southern France. The company plans to introduce a new body oil, called Energique, for which it needs to develop a standard product cost. The following information is available on the production of Energique:

a. The Energique base is made by mixing select lanolin and alcohol. Some loss in volume occurs for both the lanolin and the alcohol during the mixing process. As a result, each 100-liter batch of Energique base requires 100 liters of lanolin and 8 liters of alcohol.
b. After the base has been prepared, a highly concentrated lilac powder is added to impart a pleasing scent. Only 200 grams of the powder are added to each 100-liter batch. The addition of the lilac powder does not affect the total liquid volume.
c. Both the lanolin and the lilac powder are subject to some contamination from naturally occurring materials. For example, the lilac powder often contains some traces of insects that are not detected and removed when the lilac petals are processed. Occasionally such contaminants interact in ways that result in an unacceptable product with an unpleasant odor. About one 100-liter batch in twenty-one is rejected as unsuitable for sale for this reason and is thrown away.
d. It takes a worker two hours to process one 100-liter batch of Energique. Employees work an eight-hour day, including two hours per day for lunch, rest breaks, and cleanup.

Required:

1. Determine the standard quantity for each of the raw materials needed to produce an acceptable 100-liter batch of Energique.
2. Determine the standard labor time to produce an acceptable 100-liter batch of Energique.
3. The standard prices for the materials and the labor in euros (€) appear below:

Lanolin	€16 per liter
Alcohol	€2 per liter
Lilac powder	€1 per gram
Direct labor cost	€12 per hour

Prepare a standard cost card for materials and labor for one acceptable 100-liter batch of Energique.

(CMA, adapted)

PROBLEM 10–16 Variance Analysis with Multiple Lots [LO2, LO3]

Ricardo Shirts, Inc., manufactures short- and long-sleeved men's shirts for large stores. Ricardo produces a single-quality shirt in lots to each customer's order and attaches the store's label to each shirt. The standard direct costs for a dozen long-sleeved shirts include:

Direct materials:	24 yards at $0.65 per yard	$15.60
Direct labor:	3 hours at $7.25 per hour	21.75

During April, Ricardo worked on three orders for long-sleeved shirts. Job cost records for the month disclose the following:

Lot	Units in Lot (dozens)	Materials Used (yards)	Hours Worked
30	1,000	24,100	2,980
31	1,700	40,440	5,130
32	1,200	28,825	2,890

The following additional information is available:

a. Ricardo purchased 95,000 yards of material during April at a cost of $66,500.
b. Direct labor cost incurred amounted to $80,740 during April.
c. There was no work in process at April 1. During April, lots 30 and 31 were completed. At April 30, lot 32 was 100% complete with respect to materials but only 80% complete with respect to labor.

Required:

1. Compute the materials price variance for April, and show whether the variance was favorable or unfavorable.
2. Determine the materials quantity variance for April in both yards and dollars:
   a. For the company in total.
   b. For each lot worked on during the month.
3. Compute the labor rate variance for April, and show whether the variance was favorable or unfavorable.
4. Determine the labor efficiency variance for April in both hours and dollars:
   a. For the company in total.
   b. For each lot worked on during the month.
5. In what situations might it be better to express variances in units (hours, yards, and so on) rather than in dollars? In dollars rather than in units?

(CPA, adapted)

PROBLEM 10–17 Materials and Labor Variances; Computations from Incomplete Data [LO1, LO2, LO3]

Topaz Company produces a single product. The company has set standards as follows for materials and labor:

	Direct Materials	Direct Labor
Standard quantity or hours per unit	? pounds	2.5 hours
Standard price or rate................	? per pound	$9 per hour
Standard cost per unit	?	$22.50

During the past month, the company purchased 6,000 pounds of direct materials at a cost of $16,500. All of this material was used in the production of 1,400 units of product. Direct labor cost totaled $28,500 for the month. The following variances have been computed:

Materials quantity variance	$1,200 U
Total materials variance	300 F
Labor efficiency variance................	4,500 F

Required:

1. For direct materials:
   a. Compute the standard price per pound for materials.
   b. Compute the standard quantity allowed for materials for the month's production.
   c. Compute the standard quantity of materials allowed per unit of product.
2. For direct labor:
   a. Compute the actual direct labor cost per hour for the month.
   b. Compute the labor rate variance.

(Hint: In completing the problem, it may be helpful to move from known to unknown data either by using the variance formulas or by using the columnar format shown in Exhibits 10–4 and 10–6.)

PROBLEM 10–18 Comprehensive Variance Analysis [LO1, LO2, LO3, LO4]

Vitalite, Inc., produces a number of products, including a body-wrap kit. Standard variable costs relating to a single kit are given below:

	Standard Quantity or Hours	Standard Price or Rate	Standard Cost
Direct materials........................	?	$6 per yard	$?
Direct labor...........................	?	?	?
Variable manufacturing overhead..........	?	$2 per hour	?
Total standard cost per kit................			$42

During August, 500 kits were manufactured and sold. Selected information relating to the month's production is given below:

	Materials Used	Direct Labor	Variable Manufacturing Overhead
Total standard cost*	$?	$8,000	$1,600
Actual costs incurred	10,000	?	1,620
Materials price variance	?		
Materials quantity variance	600 U		
Labor rate variance		?	
Labor efficiency variance		?	
Variable overhead spending variance			?
Variable overhead efficiency variance			?

*For the month's production.

The following additional information is available for August's production of kits:

Actual direct labor-hours	900
Overhead is based on	Direct labor-hours
Difference between standard and actual cost per kit produced during August	$0.14 U

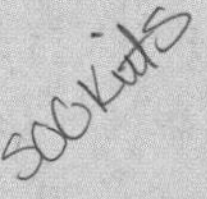

Required:

1. What was the total standard cost of the materials used during August?
2. How many yards of material are required at standard per kit?
3. What was the materials price variance for August?
4. What is the standard direct labor rate per hour?
5. What was the labor rate variance for August? The labor efficiency variance?
6. What was the variable overhead spending variance for August? The variable overhead efficiency variance?
7. Complete the standard cost card for one kit shown at the beginning of the problem.

PROBLEM 10–19 (Appendix 10A) Comprehensive Variance Analysis with Incomplete Data; Journal Entries [LO2, LO3, LO4, LO7]

Topline Surf Boards manufactures a single product. The standard cost of one unit of this product is as follows:

Direct materials: 6 feet at $1	$ 6.00
Direct labor: 1 hour at $4.50	4.50
Variable manufacturing overhead: 1 hour at $3	3.00
Total standard variable cost per unit	$13.50

During October, 6,000 units were produced. Selected cost data relating to the month's production follow:

Material purchased: 60,000 feet at $0.95 per foot	$57,000
Material used in production: 38,000 feet	—
Direct labor: __?__ hours at $ __?__ per hour	27,950
Variable manufacturing overhead cost incurred	20,475
Variable manufacturing overhead efficiency variance	1,500 U

There was no beginning inventory of raw materials. The variable manufacturing overhead rate is based on direct labor-hours.

Required:

1. For direct materials:
   a. Compute the price and quantity variances for October.
   b. Prepare journal entries to record activity for October.
2. For direct labor:
   a. Compute the rate and efficiency variances for October.
   b. Prepare a journal entry to record labor activity for October.
3. For variable manufacturing overhead:
   a. Compute the spending variance for October, and verify the efficiency variance given above.

b. If manufacturing overhead is applied to production on the basis of direct labor-hours, is it possible to have a favorable direct labor efficiency variance and an unfavorable variable overhead efficiency variance? Explain.

4. State possible causes of each variance that you have computed.

PROBLEM 10–20 Variance Analysis and Measures of Internal Business Process Performance [LO2, LO3, LO4, LO6]

PC Deco is a small company that makes an attractive and popular solid wood computer desk. Based on the recommendations of the plant manager and the purchasing agent, the president of the company, Tom Hanson, had approved changing over to a JIT production and purchasing system. He was, however, very unhappy with the latest monthly standard cost variance report for the plant.

Tom opened the first management meeting of the month with the following challenge: "I thought JIT was supposed to make us more efficient, but just look at last month's efficiency report. The labor efficiency variance was $50,000 unfavorable. That's nearly five times higher than it's ever been before! If you add on the $29,000 unfavorable materials price variance, that's over $79,000 down the drain in a single month! What's going on here?"

"We knew when we adopted JIT that our material costs would go up somewhat," replied Beth Chin, the company's purchasing agent. "But we've negotiated long-term contracts with our very best suppliers, and they're making defect-free deliveries three times a day. In a few months we'll be able to offset all of our higher purchasing costs by completely vacating the warehouse we had been renting."

"And I know our labor efficiency variance looks bad," responded Jose Martin, the plant manager, "but it doesn't tell the whole story. We eliminated the inspection and maintenance positions and turned them all into direct labor workers. And with JIT flow lines and our new equipment, we've never been more efficient in the plant."

"How can you say you're efficient when you took 35,000 direct labor-hours to produce just 20,000 desks last month?" asked Tom Hanson. "That works out to be 1.75 hours per desk, but according to the standard cost card, you should be able to produce a desk in just 1.5 hours. Do you call that efficient?"

"There are several reasons for that," answered Jose, "but the biggest reason is that we don't want to make desks just to keep everyone busy. Under the JIT approach, we start production only when we have an order."

"Well, you've got an order now!" roared Tom Hanson, "I've been looking at these reports for nearly 20 years, and I know inefficiency when I see it. Let's get things back under control!"

After leaving Tom Hanson's office, Jose has approached you for help in explaining to the president why the efficiency report is at odds with the actual progress in the plant. Working with Jose, you have gathered the following information:

a. The standard cost card for the desks is given below:

	Standard Quantity or Hours	Standard Price or Rate	Standard Cost
Direct materials	15 board feet	$ 2.00 per board foot	$30.00
Direct labor	1.5 hours	10.00 per hour	15.00
Variable manufacturing overhead . .	1.5 hours	4.00 per hour	6.00
Total standard cost			$51.00

b. During June, the most recent month, the company purchased 290,000 board feet of material at a cost of $2.10 per board foot. All of this material was used in the production of 20,000 desks during the month.

c. The company maintains a stable work force. Persons who previously were inspectors and on the maintenance crew have been reassigned as direct labor workers. During June, 35,000 hours were logged by direct labor workers. The average pay rate was $9.80 per hour.

d. Variable manufacturing overhead cost is applied on the basis of direct labor-hours. During June, the company incurred $118,000 in variable manufacturing overhead costs.

e. The following operating data have been gathered:

Processing: As workers have become more familiar with the new equipment and procedures, average processing time per unit has declined over the last three months from 1.6 hours in April, to 1.5 hours in May, to 1.3 hours in June.

Inspection: Workers are now directly responsible for quality control, which accounts for the following changes in inspection time per unit over the last three months: April, 0.3 hours; May, 0.2 hours; and June, 0.1 hours.

Movement of goods: With the change to JIT flow lines, goods now move shorter distances between work stations. Move time per unit over the past three months has been: April, 3.2 hours; May, 2.7 hours; and June, 1.2 hours.

Queue time: Better coordination of production with demand has resulted in less queue time as goods move along the production line. The average queue time per unit for the last three months has been: April, 14.9 hours; May, 10.6 hours; and June, 3.9 hours.

Required:

1. Compute the materials price and quantity variances using traditional variance analysis. Is the decrease in waste apparent in this computation? Explain. If the company wants to compute the materials price variance, what should be done to make this computation more appropriate?
2. Compute the direct labor rate and efficiency variances using traditional variance analysis. Do you agree with Tom Hanson that the efficiency variance is still appropriate as a measure of performance for the company? Explain why you do or do not agree.
3. Compute the variable manufacturing overhead spending and efficiency variances using traditional variance analysis. Would you expect that a correlation still exists between direct labor and the incurrence of variable manufacturing overhead cost in the company? Explain, using data from your variance computations to support your position.
4. Compute the following for April, May, and June:
   a. The throughput time per unit.
   b. The manufacturing cycle efficiency (MCE).
5. Which performance measure do you think is more appropriate in this situation—the labor efficiency variance or throughput time per unit and manufacturing cycle efficiency?

PROBLEM 10–21 Perverse Effects of Some Performance Measures [LO5]

There is often more than one way to improve a performance measure. Unfortunately, some of the actions taken by managers to make their performance look better may actually harm the organization. For example, suppose the marketing department is held responsible only for increasing the performance measure "total revenues." Increases in total revenues may be achieved by working harder and smarter, but they can also usually be achieved by simply cutting prices. The increase in volume from cutting prices almost always results in greater total revenues; however, it does not always lead to greater total profits. Those who design performance measurement systems need to keep in mind that managers who are under pressure to perform may take actions to improve performance measures that have negative consequences elsewhere.

Required:

For each of the following situations, describe actions that managers might take to show improvement in the performance measure but which do not actually lead to improvement in the organization's overall performance.

1. Concerned with the slow rate at which new products are brought to market, top management of a consumer electronics company introduces a new performance measure—speed-to-market. The research and development department is given responsibility for this performance measure, which measures the average amount of time a product is in development before it is released to the market for sale.
2. The CEO of a telephone company has been under public pressure from city officials to fix the large number of public pay phones that do not work. The company's repair people complain that the problem is vandalism and damage caused by theft of coins from coin boxes—particularly in high-crime areas in the city. The CEO says she wants the problem solved and has pledged to city officials that there will be substantial improvement by the end of the year. To ensure that this is done, she makes the managers in charge of installing and maintaining pay phones responsible for increasing the percentage of public pay phones that are fully functional.
3. A manufacturing company has been plagued by the chronic failure to ship orders to customers by the promised date. To solve this problem, the production manager has been given the responsibility of increasing the percentage of orders shipped on time. When a customer calls in an order, the production manager and the customer agree to a delivery date. If the order is not completed by that date, it is counted as a late shipment.
4. Concerned with the productivity of employees, the board of directors of a large multinational corporation has dictated that the manager of each subsidiary will be held responsible for increasing the revenue per employee of his or her subsidiary.

PROBLEM 10–22 Measures of Internal Business Process Performance [LO6]

Exeter Corporation has recently begun a continuous improvement campaign. As a consequence, there have been many changes in operating procedures. Progress has been slow, particularly in trying to develop new performance measures for the factory.

Management has been gathering the following data over the past four months:

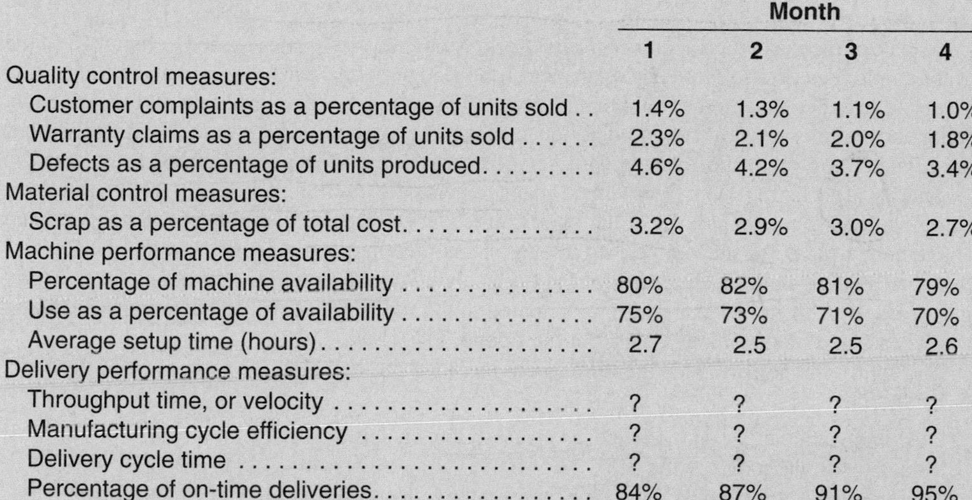

	Month 1	2	3	4
Quality control measures:				
Customer complaints as a percentage of units sold	1.4%	1.3%	1.1%	1.0%
Warranty claims as a percentage of units sold	2.3%	2.1%	2.0%	1.8%
Defects as a percentage of units produced	4.6%	4.2%	3.7%	3.4%
Material control measures:				
Scrap as a percentage of total cost	3.2%	2.9%	3.0%	2.7%
Machine performance measures:				
Percentage of machine availability	80%	82%	81%	79%
Use as a percentage of availability	75%	73%	71%	70%
Average setup time (hours)	2.7	2.5	2.5	2.6
Delivery performance measures:				
Throughput time, or velocity	?	?	?	?
Manufacturing cycle efficiency	?	?	?	?
Delivery cycle time	?	?	?	?
Percentage of on-time deliveries	84%	87%	91%	95%

The president has attended conferences at which the importance of throughput time, manufacturing cycle efficiency, and delivery cycle time were stressed, but no one at the company is sure how they are computed. The data to compute these measures have been gathered and appear below:

	Month 1	2	3	4
Wait time per order before start of production, in days	16.7	15.2	12.3	9.6
Inspection time per unit, in days	0.1	0.3	0.6	0.8
Process time per unit, in days	0.6	0.6	0.6	0.6
Queue time per unit, in days	5.6	5.7	5.6	5.7
Move time per unit, in days	1.4	1.3	1.3	1.4

As part of its continuous improvement program, the company is planning to move toward a JIT purchasing and production system.

Required:

1. For each month, compute the following operating performance measures:
   a. The throughput time, or velocity of production.
   b. The manufacturing cycle efficiency (MCE).
   c. The delivery cycle time.
2. Using the performance measures given in the problem and those you computed in (1) above, do the following:
   a. Identify the areas where the company seems to be improving.
   b. Identify the areas where the company seems to be deteriorating or stagnating.
   c. Explain why you think some specific areas are improving while others are not.
3. Refer to the move time, process time, and so forth, given above for month 4.
   a. Assume that in month 5 the move time, process time, and so forth, are the same as for month 4, except that through the implementation of JIT, the company is able to completely eliminate the queue time during production. Compute the new throughput time and MCE.
   b. Assume that in month 6 the move time, process time, and so forth, are the same as for month 4, except that the company is able to completely eliminate both the queue time during production and the inspection time. Compute the new throughput time and MCE.

PROBLEM 10–23 Building a Balanced Scorecard [LO5]

Deer Creek ski resort was for many years a small, family-owned resort serving day skiers from nearby towns. Deer Creek was recently acquired by Mountain Associates, a major ski resort operator with destination resorts in several western states. The new owners have plans to upgrade the

   b. How many pounds of material B were used in production last week? How many pounds should have been used at standard?
   c. What is the standard quantity of material B per batch?
   d. What was the price variance for material B?
   e. Prepare journal entries to record all activity relating to material B during the week.
4. For direct labor:
   a. What were the standard hours allowed for last week's production?
   b. What are the standard hours per batch?
   c. What was the direct labor rate variance?
   d. Prepare a journal entry to record all activity relating to direct labor during the week.
5. In terms of materials and labor, compute the standard cost of one batch of syrup.

CASE 10–29 Balanced Scorecard [LO5]

Weierman Department Store is located in the downtown area of a medium-sized city in the American Midwest. While the store had been profitable for many years, it is facing increasing competition from large national chains that have set up stores in the city's suburbs. Recently the downtown area has been undergoing revitalization, and the owners of Weierman Department Store are somewhat optimistic that profitability can be restored.

In an attempt to accelerate the return to profitability, the management of Weierman Department Store is in the process of designing a balanced scorecard for the company. Management believes the company should focus on two key problems. First, customers are taking longer and longer to pay the bills they incur on the department store's charge card and they have far more bad debts than are normal for the industry. If this problem were solved, the company would have more cash to make much needed renovations. Investigation has revealed that much of the problem with late payments and unpaid bills is apparently due to disputed bills that are the result of incorrect charges on the customer bills. These incorrect charges usually occur because salesclerks enter data incorrectly on the charge account slip. Second, the company has been incurring large losses on unsold seasonal apparel. Such items are ordinarily resold at a loss to discount stores that specialize in such distress items.

The meeting in which the balanced scorecard approach was discussed was disorganized and ineffectively led—possibly because no one other than one of the vice presidents had read anything about how to put a balanced scorecard together. Nevertheless, a number of potential performance measures were suggested by various managers. These potential performance measures are listed below:

Performance measures suggested by various managers:

- Total sales revenue.
- Percentage of salesclerks trained to correctly enter data on charge account slips.
- Customer satisfaction with accuracy of charge account bills from monthly customer survey.
- Sales per employee.
- Travel expenses for buyers for trips to fashion shows.
- Average age of accounts receivables.
- Courtesy shown by junior staff members to senior staff members based on surveys of senior staff.
- Unsold inventory at the end of the season as a percentage of total cost of sales.
- Sales per square foot of floor space.
- Percentage of suppliers making just-in-time deliveries.
- Quality of food in the staff cafeteria based on staff surveys.
- Written-off accounts receivables (bad debts) as a percentage of sales.
- Percentage of charge account bills containing errors.
- Percentage of employees who have attended the city's cultural diversity workshop.
- Total profit.
- Profit per employee.

Required:

1. As someone with more knowledge of the balanced scorecard than almost anyone else in the company, you have been asked to build an integrated balanced scorecard. In your scorecard, use only performance measures suggested by the managers above. You do not have to use all of the performance measures suggested by the managers, but you should build a balanced scorecard that reveals a strategy for dealing with the problems with accounts receivable and with unsold merchandise. Construct the balanced scorecard following the format used in Exhibit 10–13. Do not be particularly concerned with whether a specific performance measure

falls within the learning and growth, internal business process, customer, or financial perspective. However, clearly show the causal links between the performance measures with arrows and whether the performance measures should show increases or decreases.

2. Assume that the company adopts your balanced scorecard. After operating for a year, there are improvements in some performance measures but not in others. What should management do next?
3. *a.* Suppose that customers express greater satisfaction with the accuracy of their charge account bills but the performance measures for the average age of receivables and for bad debts do not improve. Explain why this might happen.
   b. Suppose that the performance measures for the average age of accounts receivable, bad debts, and unsold inventory improve, but total profits do not. Explain why this might happen. Assume in your answer that the explanation lies within the company.

Group and Internet Exercises

GROUP EXERCISE 10–30 Standards in an Auto Repair Shop

Make an appointment to meet with the manager of an auto repair shop that uses standards. In most cases, this would be an auto repair shop that is affiliated with a national chain such as Firestone or Sears or the service department of a new-car dealer.

Required:

At the scheduled meeting, find out the answers to the following questions:

1. How are standards set?
2. Are standards practical or ideal?
3. How are the standards used?
4. Is the actual time taken to complete a task compared to the standard time?
5. What are the consequences of unfavorable variances? Of favorable variances?
6. Do the standards and variances create any potential problems?

GROUP EXERCISE 10–31 Standards in Practice

Identify a company in your local area that is likely to use standards such as a commercial bakery, commercial printer, chain restaurant, or manufacturer. After verifying that the company uses standards, make an appointment to meet with the manager, controller, or chief financial officer of the organization.

Required:

At the scheduled meeting, find out the answers to the following questions:

1. How are standards set?
2. Are standards practical or ideal?
3. How are the standards used?
4. What are the consequences of unfavorable variances? Of favorable variances?
5. Do the standards and variances create any potential problems?

INTERNET EXERCISE 10–32 Internet Exercise

As you know, the World Wide Web is a medium that is constantly evolving. Sites come and go, and change without notice. To enable periodic update of site addresses, this problem has been posted to the textbook website (www.mhhe.com/garrison10e). After accessing the site, enter the Student Center and select this chapter. Select and complete the Internet Exercise.

Chapter Eleven

Flexible Budgets and Overhead Analysis

After studying Chapter 11, you should be able to:

1. Prepare a flexible budget and explain the advantages of the flexible budget approach over the static budget approach.
2. Prepare a performance report for both variable and fixed overhead costs using the flexible budget approach.
3. Use the flexible budget to prepare a variable overhead performance report containing only a spending variance.
4. Use the flexible budget to prepare a variable overhead performance report containing both a spending and an efficiency variance.
5. Compute the predetermined overhead rate and apply overhead to products in a standard cost system.
6. Compute and interpret the fixed overhead budget and volume variances.

How Much Is Too Much?

Dr. Salinas had just been unexpectedly appointed director of Providence Medical Center. The previous director, who had instituted tight budgetary controls, was extremely unpopular with the hospital's staff, which led to his sacking by the hospital's board of directors. Dr. Salinas suspected that he had been chosen for the job because of his popularity rather than any innate management ability. He thought of himself as a physician rather than as a manager.

Shortly after taking over as director, the hospital's lab supervisor came storming into Dr. Salinas' office, threw a computer-generated report on Dr. Salinas' desk, and angrily stated: "Here, look at this report. It says we spent too much money in the Lab Department. We spent 5% more than had been authorized in the annual budget. Well, of course we did! Practically every department in the hospital asked for more tests than they had predicted at budget time! What are we supposed to do, refuse to run tests as soon as we run over budget?" Dr. Salinas responded: "Of course not. You have to run the tests. However, we also have to keep some control over our spending. On the other hand, I agree it isn't fair to hold you to the original budget. I don't see the solution right now, but I will work on it."

Controlling overhead costs is a major preoccupation of managers in business, in government, and in not-for-profit organizations. Overhead is a major cost, if not *the* major cost, in many organizations. It costs Microsoft very little to download copies of its software onto hard disks and to provide purchasers with software manuals; almost all of Microsoft's costs are in research and development and marketing—elements of overhead. Or consider Disney World. The only direct cost of serving a particular guest is the cost of the food the guest consumes at the park; virtually all of the other costs of running the amusement park are overhead. Boeing has huge amounts of overhead in the form of engineering salaries, buildings, insurance, administrative salaries, and marketing costs.

In Business

Focus on Overhead Costs

Overhead costs now account for as much as 66% of the costs incurred by companies in service industries and up to 37% of the total costs of manufacturers. Consequently, overhead reduction is a recurring theme in many organizations. However, the extent of the reductions must be considered in light of competitive pressures to improve services to customers and product quality. Managers must take care not to cut costs that add value to the organization.

Source: Nick Develin, "Unlocking Overhead Value," *Management Accounting*, December 1999, pp. 22–34.

Controlling overhead costs poses special problems. Costs like direct materials and direct labor are usually easier to understand, and therefore to control, than overhead, which can include everything from the disposable coffee cup in the visitor's waiting area to the president's salary. Overhead is usually made up of many separate costs—many of which may be small. This makes it impractical to control them in the same way that costs such as direct materials and direct labor are controlled. And some overhead costs are variable, some are fixed, and some are a mixture of fixed and variable. These particular problems can be largely overcome by the use of flexible budgets. In this chapter, we study flexible budgets in detail and learn how they can be used to control costs. We also expand the study of overhead variances that we started in Chapter 10.

Flexible Budgets

Characteristics of a Flexible Budget

LEARNING OBJECTIVE 1
Prepare a flexible budget and explain the advantages of the flexible budget approach over the static budget approach.

The budgets that we studied in Chapter 9 were *static budgets.* A **static budget** is prepared at the beginning of the budgeting period and is valid for only the planned level of activity. A static budget approach is suitable for planning purposes, but it is inadequate for evaluating how well costs are controlled. If the actual activity during a period differs from what was planned, it would be misleading to simply compare actual costs to the static budget. If activity is higher than expected, variable costs should be higher than expected; and if activity is lower than expected, variable costs should be lower than expected.

Flexible budgets take into account changes in costs that should occur as a consequence of changes in activity. A **flexible budget** provides estimates of what costs should be for any level of activity within a specified range. When a flexible budget is used in performance evaluation, actual costs are compared to what the *costs should have been for the actual level of activity during the period* rather than to the budgeted costs from the original budget. This is a very important distinction—particularly for variable costs. If adjustments for the level of activity are not made, it is very difficult to interpret discrepancies between budgeted and actual costs.

Exhibit 11–1

RICK'S HAIRSTYLING Static Budget For the Month Ended March 31	
Budgeted number of client-visits	5,000
Budgeted variable overhead costs:	
Hairstyling supplies (@$1.20 per client-visit)	$ 6,000
Client gratuities (@$4.00 per client-visit)	20,000
Electricity (@$0.20 per client-visit)	1,000
Total variable overhead cost	27,000
Budgeted fixed overhead costs:	
Support staff wages and salaries	8,000
Rent	12,000
Insurance	1,000
Utilities other than electricity	500
Total fixed overhead cost	21,500
Total budgeted overhead cost	$48,500

Deficiencies of the Static Budget

To illustrate the difference between a static budget and a flexible budget, we will consider the case of Rick's Hairstyling, an upscale hairstyling salon located in Beverly Hills that is owned and managed by Rick Manzi. The salon has very loyal customers—many of whom are associated with the film industry. Despite the glamour associated with his salon, Rick is a very shrewd businessman. Recently he has been attempting to get better control over his overhead, and at the urging of his accounting and business adviser Victoria Kho, he has begun to prepare monthly budgets. Victoria Kho is a certified public accountant and certified management accountant in independent practice who specializes in small service-oriented businesses like Rick's Hairstyling.

At the end of February, Rick carefully prepared the March budget for overhead items that appears in Exhibit 11–1. Rick believes that the number of customers served in a month is the best way to measure the overall level of activity in his salon. Rick refers to these visits as client-visits. A customer who comes into the salon and has his or her hair styled is counted as one client-visit. After some discussion with Victoria Kho, Rick identified three major categories of variable overhead costs—hairstyling supplies, client gratuities, and electricity—and four major categories of fixed costs—support staff wages and salaries, rent, insurance, and utilities other than electricity. Client gratuities consist of flowers, candies, and glasses of champagne that Rick gives to his customers while they are in the salon. Rick considers electricity to be a variable cost, since almost all of the electricity in the salon is consumed in running blow-dryers, curling irons, and other hairstyling equipment.

To develop the budget for variable overhead, Rick estimated that the average cost per client-visit should be $1.20 for hairstyling supplies, $4.00 for client gratuities, and $0.20 for electricity. Based on his estimate of 5,000 client-visits in March, Rick budgeted for $6,000 ($1.20 per client-visit × 5,000 client-visits) in hairstyling supplies, $20,000 ($4.00 per client-visit × 5,000 client-visits) in client gratuities, and $1,000 ($0.20 per client-visit × 5,000 client-visits) in electricity.

The budget for fixed overhead items was based on Rick's records of how much he had spent on these items in the past. The budget included $8,000 for support staff wages and salaries, $12,000 for rent, $1,000 for insurance, and $500 for utilities other than electricity.

At the end of March, Rick prepared a report comparing actual to budgeted costs. That report appears in Exhibit 11–2. The problem with that report, as Rick immediately realized,

Exhibit 11–2

RICK'S HAIRSTYLING
Static Budget Performance Report
For the Month Ended March 31

	Actual	Budgeted	Variance
Client-visits	5,200	5,000	200 F
Variable overhead costs:			
Hairstyling supplies	$ 6,400	$ 6,000	$ 400 U*
Client gratuities	22,300	20,000	2,300 U*
Electricity	1,020	1,000	20 U*
Total variable overhead cost	29,720	27,000	2,720 U*
Fixed overhead costs:			
Support staff wages and salaries	8,100	8,000	100 U
Rent	12,000	12,000	0
Insurance	1,000	1,000	0
Utilities other than electricity	470	500	30 F
Total fixed overhead cost	21,570	21,500	70 U
Total overhead cost	$51,290	$48,500	$2,790 U*

*The cost variances for variable costs and for total overhead are useless for evaluating how well costs were controlled since they have been derived by comparing actual costs at one level of activity to budgeted costs at a different level of activity.

is that it compares costs at one level of activity (5,200 client-visits) to costs at a different level of activity (5,000 client-visits). Since Rick had 200 more client-visits than expected, his variable costs *should* be higher than budgeted. The static budget performance report confuses control over activity and control over costs. From Rick's standpoint, the increase in activity was good and should be counted as a favorable variance, but the increase in activity has an apparently negative impact on the costs in the report. Rick knew that something would have to be done to make the report more meaningful, but he was unsure of what to do. So he made an appointment to meet with Victoria Kho to discuss the next step.

Managerial Accounting in Action

The Issue

Victoria: How is the budgeting going?

Rick: Pretty well. I didn't have any trouble putting together the overhead budget for March. I also made out a report comparing the actual costs for March to the budgeted costs, but that report isn't giving me what I really want to know.

Victoria: Because your actual level of activity didn't match your budgeted activity?

Rick: Right. I know the level of activity shouldn't affect my fixed costs, but we had a lot more client-visits than I had expected and that had to affect my variable costs.

Victoria: So you want to know whether the actual costs are justified by the actual level of activity you had in March?

Rick: Precisely.

Victoria: If you leave your reports and data with me, I can work on it later today, and by tomorrow I'll have a report to show to you. Actually, I have a styling appointment for later this week. Why don't I move my appointment up to tomorrow, and I will bring along the analysis so we can discuss it.

Rick: That's great.

How a Flexible Budget Works

The basic idea of the flexible budget approach is that a budget does not have to be static. Depending on the actual level of activity, a budget can be adjusted to show what costs

Exhibit 11–3 Illustration of the Flexible Budgeting Concept

RICK'S HAIRSTYLING
Flexible Budget
For the Month Ended March 31

Budgeted number of client-visits 5,000

Overhead Costs	Cost Formula (per client-visit)	Activity (in client-visits) 4,900	5,000	5,100	5,200
Variable overhead costs:					
Hairstyling supplies	$1.20	$ 5,880	$ 6,000	$ 6,120	$ 6,240
Client gratuities	4.00	19,600	20,000	20,400	20,800
Electricity (variable)	0.20	980	1,000	1,020	1,040
Total variable overhead cost	$5.40	26,460	27,000	27,540	28,080
Fixed overhead costs:					
Support staff wages and salaries		8,000	8,000	8,000	8,000
Rent		12,000	12,000	12,000	12,000
Insurance		1,000	1,000	1,000	1,000
Utilities other than electricity		500	500	500	500
Total fixed overhead cost		21,500	21,500	21,500	21,500
Total overhead cost		$47,960	$48,500	$49,040	$49,580

should be for that specific level of activity. To illustrate how flexible budgets work, Victoria prepared the report in Exhibit 11–3. It shows how overhead costs can be expected to change, depending on the monthly level of activity. Within the activity range of 4,900 to 5,200 client-visits, the fixed costs are expected to remain the same. For the variable overhead costs, Victoria multiplied Rick's per-client costs ($1.20 for hairstyling supplies, $4.00 for client gratuities, and $0.20 for electricity) by the appropriate number of client-visits in each column. For example, the $1.20 cost of hairstyling supplies was multiplied by 4,900 client-visits to give the total cost of $5,880 for hairstyling supplies at that level of activity.

Concept 11–1

Using the Flexible Budgeting Concept in Performance Evaluation

LEARNING OBJECTIVE 2
Prepare a performance report for both variable and fixed overhead costs using the flexible budget approach.

To get a better idea of how well Rick's variable overhead costs were controlled in March, Victoria applied the flexible budgeting concept to create a new performance report. (Exhibit 11–4.) Using the flexible budget approach, Victoria constructed a budget based on the *actual* number of client-visits for the month. The budget is prepared by multiplying the actual level of activity by the cost formula for each of the variable cost categories. For example, using the $1.20 per client-visit for hairstyling supplies, the total cost for this item *should be* $6,240 for 5,200 client-visits ($1.20 × 5,200). Since the actual cost for hairstyling supplies was $6,400, the unfavorable variance was $160.

Contrast the performance report in Exhibit 11–4 with the static budget approach in Exhibit 11–2. The variance for hairstyling supplies was $400 unfavorable using the static budget approach. In that exhibit, apples were being compared to oranges in the case of the variable cost items. Actual costs at one level of activity were being compared to budgeted costs at a different level of activity. Because actual activity was higher by 200 client-visits than budgeted activity, the total cost of hairstyling supplies *should* have been $240 ($1.20 per client-visit × 200 client-visits) higher than budgeted. As a result, $240 of the $400 "unfavorable" variance in the static budget performance report in Exhibit 11–2 was spurious.

Exhibit 11–4

RICK'S HAIRSTYLING
Flexible Budget Performance Report
For the Month Ended March 31

Budgeted number of client-visits 5,000
Actual number of client-visits 5,200

Overhead Costs	**Cost Formula (per client-visit)**	**Actual Costs Incurred for 5,200 Client-Visits**	**Budget Based on 5,200 Client-Visits**	**Variance**
Variable overhead costs:				
Hairstyling supplies	$1.20	$ 6,400	$ 6,240	$ 160 U
Client gratuities	4.00	22,300	20,800	1,500 U
Electricity (variable)	0.20	1,020	1,040	20 F
Total variable overhead cost	$5.40	29,720	28,080	1,640 U
Fixed overhead costs:				
Support staff wages and salaries		8,100	8,000	100 U
Rent		12,000	12,000	0
Insurance		1,000	1,000	0
Utilities other than electricity		470	500	30 F
Total fixed overhead cost		21,570	21,500	70 U
Total overhead cost		$51,290	$49,580	$1,710 U

In contrast, the flexible budget performance report in Exhibit 11–4 provides a more valid assessment of performance. Apples are compared to apples. Actual costs are compared to what costs should have been at the actual level of activity. When this is done, we see that the variance is $160 unfavorable rather than $400 unfavorable as it was in the original static budget performance report. In some cases, as with electricity in Rick's report, an unfavorable variance may be transformed into a favorable variance when an increase in activity is properly taken into account in a performance report.

Managerial Accounting in Action

The Wrap-Up

The following discussion took place the next day at Rick's salon.

Victoria: Let me show you what I've got. [Victoria shows the report contained in Exhibit 11–4.] All I did was multiply the costs per client-visit by the number of client-visits you actually had in March for the variable costs. That allowed me to come up with a better benchmark for what the variable costs should have been.

Rick: That's what you labeled the "budget based on 5,200 client-visits"?

Victoria: That's right. Your original budget was based on 5,000 client-visits, so it understated what the variable overhead costs should be when you actually serve 5,200 customers.

Rick: That's clear enough. These variances aren't quite as shocking as the variances on my first report.

Victoria: Yes, but you still have an unfavorable variance of $1,500 for client gratuities.

Rick: I know how that happened. In March there was a big Democratic Party fund-raising dinner that I forgot about when I prepared the March budget. Everyone in the film industry was there.

Victoria: Even Arnold Schwarzeneger?

Rick: Well, all the Democrats were there. At any rate, to fit all of our regular clients in, we had to push them through here pretty fast. Everyone still got top-rate service, but I felt pretty bad about not being able to spend as much time with each customer. I wanted to give my customers a little extra something to compensate them for the less personal service, so I ordered a lot of flowers which I gave away by the bunch.

Victoria: With the prices you charge, Rick, I am sure the gesture was appreciated.

Rick: One thing bothers me about the report. Why are some of my actual fixed costs different from what I budgeted? Doesn't fixed mean that they are not supposed to change?

Victoria: We call these costs *fixed* because they shouldn't be affected by *changes in the level of activity.* However, that doesn't mean that they can't change for other reasons. For example, your utilities bill, which includes natural gas for heating, varies with the weather.

Rick: I can see that. March was warmer than normal, so my utilities bill was lower than I had expected.

Victoria: The use of the term *fixed* also suggests to people that the cost can't be controlled, but that isn't true. It is often easier to control fixed costs than variable costs. For example, it would be fairly easy for you to change your insurance bill by adjusting the amount of insurance you carry. It would be much more difficult for you to have much of an impact on the variable electric bill, which is a necessary part of serving customers.

Rick: I think I understand, but it *is* confusing.

Victoria: Just remember that a cost is called variable if it is proportional to activity; it is called fixed if it does not depend on the level of activity. However, fixed costs can change for reasons having nothing to do with changes in the level of activity. And controllability has little to do with whether a cost is variable or fixed. Fixed costs are often more controllable than variable costs.

Focus on Opportunities

In Business

Legendary management guru Peter F. Drucker cautions managers that "almost without exception, the first page of the [monthly] report presents the areas in which results fall below expectations or in which expenditures exceed the budget. It focuses on problems. Problems cannot be ignored. But . . . enterprises have to focus on opportunities. That requires a small but fundamental procedural change: a new first page to the monthly report, one that precedes the page that shows the problems. The new page should focus on where results are better than expected. As much time should be spent on that new first page as traditionally was spent on the problem page."

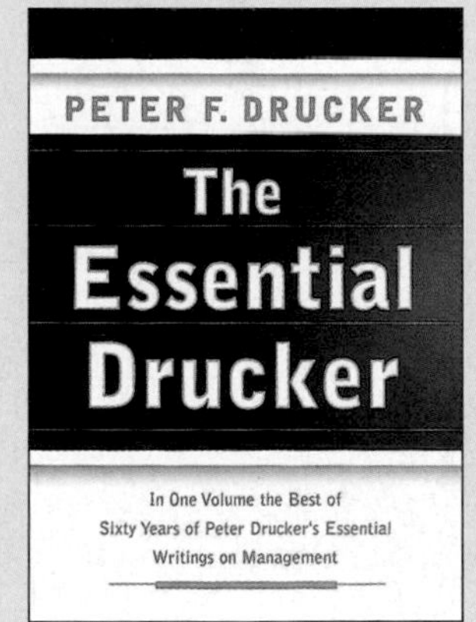

Source: Peter F. Drucker, "Change Leaders," *Inc.*, June 1999, pp. 65–72.

Using the flexible budget approach, Rick Manzi now has a much better way of assessing whether overhead costs are under control. The analysis is not so simple, however, in companies that provide a variety of products and services. The number of units produced or customers served may not be an adequate measure of overall activity. For example, does it make sense to count a Sony floppy diskette, worth only a few dollars, as equivalent to a large-screen Sony TV? If the number of units produced is used as a measure of overall activity, then the floppy diskette and the large-screen TV would be counted as equivalent. Clearly, the number of units produced (or customers served) may not be appropriate as an overall measure of activity when the organization has a variety of products or services; a common denominator may be needed.

The Measure of Activity—A Critical Choice

What should be used as the measure of activity when the company produces a variety of products and services? At least three factors are important in selecting an activity base for an overhead flexible budget:

1. The activity base and variable overhead costs should be causally related. Changes in the activity base should cause, or at least be highly correlated with, changes in the variable overhead costs in the flexible budget. Ideally, the variable overhead costs in the flexible budget should vary in direct proportion to changes in the activity base. For example, in a carpentry shop specializing in handmade wood furniture, the costs of miscellaneous supplies such as glue, wooden dowels, and sandpaper can be expected to vary with the number of direct labor-hours. Direct labor-hours would therefore be a good measure of activity to use in a flexible budget for the costs of such supplies.
2. The activity base should not be expressed in dollars or other currency. For example, direct labor cost is usually a poor choice for an activity base in flexible budgets. Changes in wage rates affect the activity base but do not usually result in a proportionate change in overhead. For example, we would not ordinarily expect to see a 5% increase in the consumption of glue in a carpentry shop if the workers receive a 5% increase in pay. Therefore, it is normally best to use physical rather than financial measures of activity in flexible budgets.
3. The activity base should be simple and easily understood. A base that is not easily understood will probably result in confusion and misunderstanding. It is difficult to control costs if people don't understand the reports or do not accept them as valid.

Variable Overhead Variances—A Closer Look

Concept 11–2

A special problem arises when the flexible budget is based on *hours* of activity (such as direct labor-hours) rather than on units of product or number of customers served. The problem relates to whether actual hours or standard hours should be used to develop the flexible budget on the performance report.

The Problem of Actual versus Standard Hours

The nature of the problem can best be seen through a specific example. MicroDrive Corporation makes precision computer disk-drive motors for military applications. Data concerning the company's variable manufacturing overhead costs are shown in Exhibit 11–5.

MicroDrive Corporation uses machine-hours as the activity base in its flexible budget because its managers believe most of the overhead costs are driven by machine-hours. Based on the budgeted production of 25,000 motors and the standard of 2 machine-hours per motor, the budgeted level of activity was 50,000 machine-hours. However, actual production for the year was only 20,000 motors, and 42,000 hours of machine time were used to produce these motors. According to the standard, only 40,000 hours of machine time should have been used (40,000 hours = 2 hours per motor × 20,000 motors).

In preparing an overhead performance report for the year, MicroDrive could use the 42,000 machine-hours actually worked during the year *or* the 40,000 machine-hours that should have been worked according to the standard. If the actual hours are used, only a spending variance will be computed. If the standard hours are used, both a spending *and* an efficiency variance will be computed. Both of these approaches are illustrated in the following sections.

LEARNING OBJECTIVE 3
Use the flexible budget to prepare a variable overhead performance report containing only a spending variance.

Spending Variance Alone

If MicroDrive Corporation bases its overhead performance report on the 42,000 machine-hours actually worked during the year, then the performance report will show only a

Exhibit 11–5
MicroDrive Corporation Data

Budgeted production	25,000 motors
Actual production	20,000 motors
Standard machine-hours per motor	2 machine-hours per motor
Budgeted machine-hours (2 × 25,000)	50,000 machine-hours
Standard machine-hours allowed for the actual production (2 × 20,000)	40,000 machine-hours
Actual machine-hours	42,000 machine-hours
Variable overhead costs per machine-hour:	
Indirect labor	$0.80 per machine-hour
Lubricants	0.30 per machine-hour
Power	0.40 per machine-hour
Actual total variable overhead costs:	
Indirect labor	$36,000
Lubricants	11,000
Power	24,000
Total actual variable overhead cost	$71,000

Exhibit 11–6

MICRODRIVE CORPORATION
Variable Overhead Performance Report
For the Year Ended December 31

Budget allowances are based on 42,000 machine-hours actually worked.

Comparing the budget to actual overhead cost yields only a spending variance.

Budgeted machine-hours	50,000
Actual machine-hours	42,000
Standard machine-hours allowed	40,000

Overhead Costs	**Cost Formula (per machine-hour)**	**Actual Costs Incurred 42,000 Machine-Hours (*AH* × *AR*)**	**Budget Based on 42,000 Machine-Hours (*AH* × *SR*)**	**Spending Variance**
Variable overhead costs:				
Indirect labor	$0.80	$36,000	$33,600*	$2,400 U
Lubricants	0.30	11,000	12,600	1,600 F
Power	0.40	24,000	16,800	7,200 U
Total variable overhead cost	$1.50	$71,000	$63,000	$8,000 U

*42,000 machine-hours × $0.80 per machine-hour = $33,600. Other budget allowances are computed in the same way.

spending variance for variable overhead. A performance report prepared in this way is shown in Exhibit 11–6.

The formula for the spending variance was introduced in the preceding chapter. That formula is:

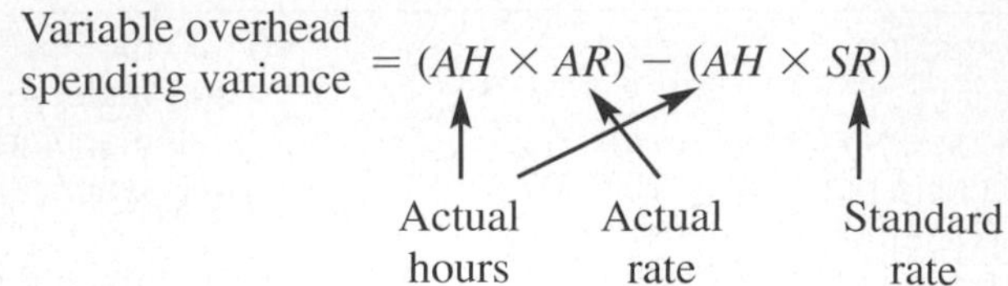

Variable overhead spending variance = (AH × AR) − (AH × SR)
Actual hours
Actual rate
Standard rate

Or, in factored form:

$$\text{Variable overhead spending variance} = AH\,(AR - SR)$$

The report in Exhibit 11–6 is structured around the first, or unfactored, format.

Interpreting the Spending Variance The variable overhead spending variance is useful only if the cost driver for variable overhead really is the actual hours worked. Then the flexible budget based on the actual hours worked is a valid benchmark that tells us how much *should* have been spent in total on variable overhead items during the period. The actual overhead costs would be larger than this benchmark, resulting in an unfavorable variance, if either (1) the variable overhead items cost more to purchase than the standards allow or (2) more variable overhead items were used than the standards allow. So the spending variance includes both price and quantity variances. In principle, these variances could be separately reported, but this is seldom done. Ordinarily, the price element in this variance will be small, so the variance will mainly be influenced by how efficiently variable overhead resources such as production supplies are used.

Both Spending and Efficiency Variances

LEARNING OBJECTIVE 4
Use the flexible budget to prepare a variable overhead performance report containing both a spending and an efficiency variance.

If management of MicroDrive Corporation wants both a spending and an efficiency variance for variable overhead, then it should compute budget allowances for *both* the 40,000 machine-hour and the 42,000 machine-hour levels of activity. A performance report prepared in this way is shown in Exhibit 11–7.

Note from Exhibit 11–7 that the spending variance is the same as the spending variance shown in Exhibit 11–6. The performance report in Exhibit 11–7 has simply been expanded to include an efficiency variance as well. Together, the spending and efficiency variances make up the total variance.

Interpreting the Efficiency Variance Like the variable overhead spending variance, the variable overhead efficiency variance is useful only if the cost driver for variable overhead really is the actual hours worked. Then any increase in hours actually worked should result in additional variable overhead costs. Consequently, if too many hours are used to create the actual output, this is likely to result in an increase in variable overhead. The variable overhead efficiency variance is an estimate of the effect on variable overhead costs of inefficiency in the use of the base (i.e., hours). In a sense, the term *variable overhead efficiency variance* is a misnomer. It seems to suggest that it measures the efficiency with which variable overhead resources are used. It does not. It is an estimate of the indirect effect on variable overhead costs of inefficiency in the use of the activity base.

Recall from the preceding chapter that the variable overhead efficiency variance is a function of the difference between the actual hours incurred and the hours that should have been used to produce the period's output:

$$\text{Variable overhead efficiency variance} = (AH \times SR) - (SH \times SR)$$

Actual hours | Standard rate | Standard hours allowed for output

Exhibit 11–7

MICRODRIVE CORPORATION
Variable Overhead Performance Report
For the Year Ended December 31

Budget allowances are based on 40,000 machine-hours—the time it *should have taken* to produce the year's output of 20,000 motors—as well as on the 42,000 *actual* machine-hours worked.

This approach yields both a spending and an efficiency variance.

Budgeted machine-hours	50,000
Actual machine-hours	42,000
Standard machine-hours allowed	40,000

Overhead Costs	Cost Formula (per machine-hour)	(1) Actual Costs Incurred 42,000 Machine-Hours (*AH* × *AR*)	(2) Budget Based on 42,000 Machine-Hours (*AH* × *SR*)	(3) Budget Based on 40,000 Machine-Hours (*SH* × *SR*)	(4) Total Variance (1) − (3)	Breakdown of the Total Variance: Spending Variance (1) − (2)	Breakdown of the Total Variance: Efficiency Variance (2) − (3)
Variable overhead costs:							
Indirect labor	$0.80	$36,000	$33,600*	$32,000	$ 4,000 U	$2,400 U	$1,600 U
Lubricants	0.30	11,000	12,600	12,000	1,000 F	1,600 F	600 U
Power	0.40	24,000	16,800	16,000	8,000 U	7,200 U	800 U
Total variable overhead cost	$1.50	$71,000	$63,000	$60,000	$11,000 U	$8,000 U	$3,000 U

*42,000 machine-hours × $0.80 per machine-hour = $33,600. Other budget allowances are computed in the same way.

Or, in factored form:

$$\text{Variable overhead efficiency variance} = SR(AH - SH)$$

If more hours are worked than are allowed at standard, then the overhead efficiency variance will be unfavorable. However, as discussed above, the inefficiency is not in the use of overhead *but rather in the use of the base itself.*

This point can be illustrated by looking again at Exhibit 11–7. Two thousand more machine-hours were used during the period than should have been used to produce the period's output. Each of these hours presumably required the incurrence of $1.50 of variable overhead cost, resulting in an unfavorable variance of $3,000 (2,000 hours × $1.50 = $3,000). Although this $3,000 variance is called an overhead efficiency variance, it could better be called a machine-hours efficiency variance, since it results from using too many machine-hours rather than from inefficient use of overhead resources. However, the term *overhead efficiency variance* is so firmly ingrained in practice that a change is unlikely. Even so, be careful to interpret the variance with a clear understanding of what it really measures.

Control of the Efficiency Variance Who is responsible for control of the overhead efficiency variance? Since the variance really reflects efficiency in the utilization of the base underlying the flexible budget, whoever is responsible for control of this base is responsible for control of the variance. If the base is direct labor-hours, then the supervisor responsible for the use of labor time will be responsible for any overhead efficiency variance.

Activity-Based Costing and the Flexible Budget

It is unlikely that all of the variable overhead in a complex organization is driven by a single factor such as the number of units produced or the number of labor-hours or machine-hours. Activity-based costing provides a way of recognizing a variety of overhead cost drivers and thereby increasing the accuracy of the costing system. In activity-based costing, each overhead cost pool has its own measure of activity. The actual spending in each overhead cost pool can be independently evaluated using the techniques discussed in this chapter. The only difference is that the cost formulas for variable overhead costs will be stated in terms of different kinds of activities instead of all being stated in terms of units or a common measure of activity such as direct labor-hours or machine-hours. If done properly, activity-based costing can greatly enhance the usefulness of overhead performance reports by recognizing multiple causes of overhead costs. But the usefulness of overhead performance reports depends on how carefully the reports are done. In particular, managers must take care to separate the variable from the fixed costs in the flexible budgets.[1]

In Business

Pools within Pools

Caterpillar, Inc., a manufacturer of heavy equipment and a pioneering company in the development and use of activity-based costing, separates its overhead costs into three large pools—the logistics cost pool, the manufacturing cost pool, and the general cost pool. In turn, these three cost pools are subdivided into scores of activity centers, with each center having its own flexible budget from which variable and fixed overhead rates are developed. "The many manufacturing cost center rates are the unique elements that set Caterpillar's system apart from simple cost systems."

Source: Lou F. Jones, "Product Costing at Caterpillar," *Management Accounting* 72, no. 8, p. 39.

Overhead Rates and Fixed Overhead Analysis

The detailed analysis of fixed overhead differs considerably from the analysis of variable overhead, simply because of the difference in the nature of the costs. To provide a background for our discussion, we will first briefly review the need for, and computation of, predetermined overhead rates. This review will be helpful, since the predetermined overhead rate plays a major role in fixed overhead analysis. We will then show how fixed overhead variances are computed and make some observations about their usefulness to managers.

Flexible Budgets and Overhead Rates

LEARNING OBJECTIVE 5
Compute the predetermined overhead rate and apply overhead to products in a standard cost system.

Fixed costs come in large, indivisible pieces that by definition do not change with changes in the level of activity within the relevant range. This creates a problem in product costing, since a given amount of fixed overhead cost spread over a small number of

[1] See Mak and Roush, "Managing Activity Costs with Flexible Budgeting and Variance Analysis," *Accounting Horizons,* September 1996, pp. 141–146, for an insightful discussion of activity-based costing and overhead variance analysis.

units will result in a higher cost per unit than if the same amount of cost is spread over a large number of units. Consider the data in the following table:

Month	(1) Total Fixed Overhead Cost	(2) Number of Units Produced	(3) Average Fixed Cost per Unit (1) ÷ (2)
January	$6,000	1,000	$6.00
February	6,000	1,500	4.00
March	6,000	800	7.50

Notice that the large number of units produced in February results in a low unit cost ($4.00), whereas the small number of units produced in March results in a high unit cost ($7.50). This problem arises only in connection with the fixed portion of overhead, since by definition the variable portion of overhead remains constant on a per unit basis, rising and falling in total proportionately with changes in the activity level. Most managers feel that the fixed portion of unit cost should be stabilized so that a single unit cost figure can be used throughout the year. As we learned in Chapter 3, this stability can be accomplished through use of the predetermined overhead rate.

Throughout the remainder of this chapter, we will be analyzing the fixed overhead costs of MicroDrive Corporation. To assist us in that task, the flexible budget of the company—including fixed costs—is displayed in Exhibit 11–8. Note that the total fixed overhead costs amount to $300,000 within the range of activity in the flexible budget.

Denominator Activity The formula that we used in Chapter 3 to compute the predetermined overhead rate was:

$$\text{Predetermined overhead rate} = \frac{\text{Estimated total manufacturing overhead cost}}{\text{Estimated total units in the base (MH, DLH, etc.)}}$$

The estimated total units in the base in the formula for the predetermined overhead rate is called the **denominator activity.** Recall from our discussion in Chapter 3 that once an estimated activity level (denominator activity) has been chosen, it remains unchanged throughout the year, even if the actual activity turns out to be different from what was

Exhibit 11–8

MICRODRIVE CORPORATION
Flexible Budgets at Various Levels of Activity

Overhead Costs	Cost Formula (per machine-hour)	Activity (in machine-hours) 40,000	45,000	50,000	55,000
Variable overhead costs:					
Indirect labor	$0.80	$ 32,000	$ 36,000	$ 40,000	$ 44,000
Lubricants	0.30	12,000	13,500	15,000	16,500
Power	0.40	16,000	18,000	20,000	22,000
Total variable overhead cost	$1.50	60,000	67,500	75,000	82,500
Fixed overhead costs:					
Depreciation		100,000	100,000	100,000	100,000
Supervisory salaries		160,000	160,000	160,000	160,000
Insurance		40,000	40,000	40,000	40,000
Total fixed overhead cost		300,000	300,000	300,000	300,000
Total overhead cost		$360,000	$367,500	$375,000	$382,500

estimated. The reason for not changing the denominator is to maintain stability in the amount of overhead applied to each unit of product regardless of when it is produced during the year.

In Business

Know Your Costs

Understanding the difference between fixed and variable costs can be critical. Kennard T. Wing, of OMG Center for Collaborative Learning, reports that a large health care system made the mistake of classifying all its costs as variable. As a consequence, when volume dropped, managers felt that costs should be cut proportionately and more than 1,000 people were laid off—even though "the workload of most of them had no direct relation to patient volume. The result was that morale of the survivors plummeted and within a year the system was scrambling to replace not only those it had let go, but many others who had quit. The point is, the accounting systems we design and implement really do affect management decisions in significant ways. A system built on a bad model of the business will either not be used or, if used, will lead to bad decisions."

Source: Kennard T. Wing, "Using Enhanced Cost Models in Variance Analysis for Better Control and Decision Making," *Management Accounting Quarterly*, Winter 2000, pp. 27–35.

Computing the Overhead Rate When we discussed predetermined overhead rates in Chapter 3, we didn't explain how the estimated total manufacturing cost was determined. This figure can be derived from the flexible budget. Once the denominator level of activity has been chosen, the flexible budget can be used to determine the total amount of overhead cost that should be incurred at that level of activity. The predetermined overhead rate can then be computed using the following variation on the basic formula for the predetermined overhead rate:

$$\text{Predetermined overhead rate} = \frac{\text{Overhead from the flexible budget at the denominator level of activity}}{\text{Denominator level of activity}}$$

To illustrate, refer to MicroDrive Corporation's flexible budget for manufacturing overhead in Exhibit 11–8. Suppose that the budgeted activity level for the year is 50,000 machine-hours and that this will be used as the denominator activity in the formula for the predetermined overhead rate. The numerator in the formula is the estimated total overhead cost of $375,000 when the activity is 50,000 machine-hours. This figure is taken from the flexible budget in Exhibit 11–8. Thus, the predetermined overhead rate for MicroDrive Corporation will be computed as follows:

$$\frac{\$375{,}000}{50{,}000 \text{ MHs}} = \$7.50 \text{ per machine-hour (MH)}$$

Or the company can break its predetermined overhead rate down into variable and fixed elements rather than using a single combined figure:

$$\text{Variable element: } \frac{\$75{,}000}{50{,}000 \text{ MHs}} = \$1.50 \text{ per MH}$$

$$\text{Fixed element: } \frac{\$300{,}000}{50{,}000 \text{ MHs}} = \$6 \text{ per MH}$$

For every standard machine-hour of operation, work in process will be charged with $7.50 of overhead, of which $1.50 will be variable overhead and $6.00 will be fixed overhead. If a disk-drive motor should take two machine-hours to complete, then its cost will include $3 of variable overhead and $12 of fixed overhead, as shown on the following standard cost card:

Standard Cost Card—Per Motor

Direct materials (assumed)	$14
Direct labor (assumed)	6
Variable overhead (2 MHs at $1.50 per MH)	3
Fixed overhead (2 MHs at $6 per MH)	12
Total standard cost per motor	$35

In sum, the flexible budget provides the estimated overhead cost needed to compute the predetermined overhead rate. Thus, the flexible budget plays a key role in determining the amount of fixed and variable overhead cost that will be charged to units of product.

Overhead Application in a Standard Cost System

To understand the fixed overhead variances, it is necessary first to understand how overhead is applied to work in process in a standard cost system. In Chapter 3, recall that we applied overhead to work in process on the basis of actual hours of activity (multiplied by the predetermined overhead rate). This procedure was correct, since at the time we were dealing with a normal cost system.[2] However, we are now dealing with a standard cost system. In such a system, overhead is applied to work in process on the basis of the *standard hours allowed for the output of the period* rather than on the basis of the actual number of hours worked. This point is illustrated in Exhibit 11–9. In a standard cost system, every unit of product moving along the production line bears the same amount of overhead cost, regardless of how much time it actually takes to process a particular unit.

The Fixed Overhead Variances

LEARNING OBJECTIVE 6
Compute and interpret the fixed overhead budget and volume variances.

To illustrate the computation of fixed overhead variances, we will refer again to the data for MicroDrive Corporation.

Denominator activity in machine-hours	50,000
Budgeted fixed overhead costs	$300,000
Fixed portion of the predetermined overhead rate (computed earlier)	$6

Exhibit 11–9
Applied Overhead Costs: Normal Cost System versus Standard Cost System

Normal Cost System Manufacturing Overhead		Standard Cost System Manufacturing Overhead	
Actual overhead costs incurred.	Applied overhead costs: Actual hours × Predetermined overhead rate.	Actual overhead costs incurred.	Applied overhead costs: Standard hours allowed for output × Predetermined overhead rate.
Under- or overapplied overhead		Under- or overapplied overhead	

[2] Normal cost systems are discussed on page 99 in Chapter 3.

Let us assume that the following actual operating results were recorded for the year:

Actual machine-hours	42,000
Standard machine-hours allowed*	40,000
Actual fixed overhead costs:	
Depreciation	$100,000
Supervisory salaries	172,000
Insurance	36,000
Total actual fixed overhead cost	$308,000

*For the actual production of the year.

From these data, two variances can be computed for fixed overhead—a *budget variance* and a *volume variance.* The variances are shown in Exhibit 11–10.

Notice from the exhibit that overhead has been applied to work in process on the basis of 40,000 standard hours allowed for the output of the year rather than on the basis of 42,000 actual hours worked. As stated earlier, this keeps unit costs from being affected by variations in efficiency.

The Budget Variance—A Closer Look

The **budget variance** is the difference between the actual fixed overhead costs incurred during the period and the original budgeted fixed overhead costs for the period. It can be computed as shown in Exhibit 11–10 or by using the following formula:

$$\text{Budget variance} = \text{Actual fixed overhead cost} - \text{Budgeted fixed overhead cost}$$

Applying this formula to MicroDrive Corporation, the budget variance would be as follows:

$$\$308{,}000 - \$300{,}000 = \$8{,}000\text{ U}$$

The variances computed for the fixed costs at Rick's Hairstyling in Exhibit 11–4 are all budget variances, since they represent the difference between the actual fixed overhead cost and the budgeted fixed overhead cost.

An expanded overhead performance report for MicroDrive Corporation appears in Exhibit 11–11. This report now includes the budget variances for fixed overhead as well as the spending variances for variable overhead that were in Exhibit 11–6.

The budget variances for fixed overhead can be very useful, since they represent the difference between how much *should* have been spent (according to the budget) and how much was actually spent. For example, supervisory salaries has a $12,000 unfavorable

Exhibit 11–10
Computation of the Fixed Overhead Variances

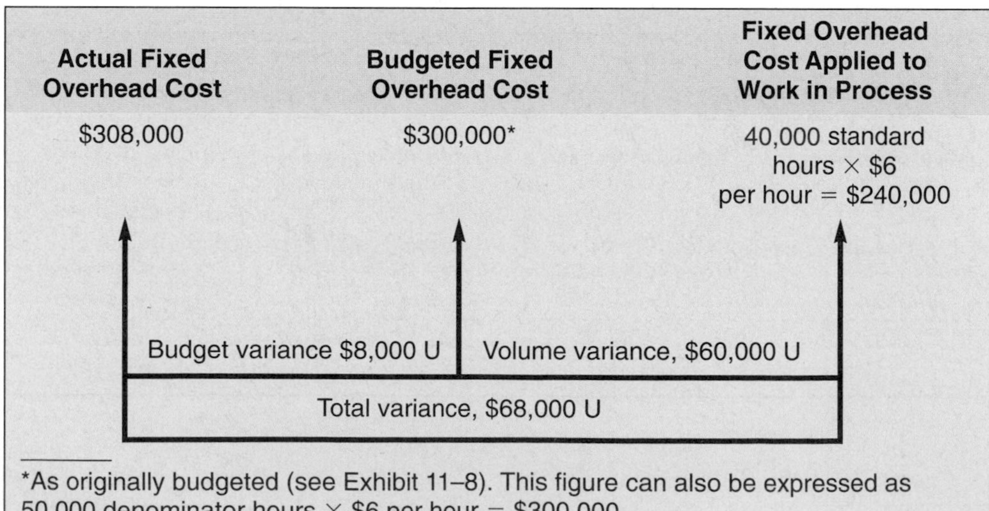

*As originally budgeted (see Exhibit 11–8). This figure can also be expressed as 50,000 denominator hours × $6 per hour = $300,000.

variance. There should be some explanation for this large variance. Was it due to an increase in salaries? Was it due to overtime? Was another supervisor hired? If so, why was another supervisor hired?—this was not included in the budget when activity for the year was planned.

The Volume Variance—A Closer Look

The **volume variance** is a measure of utilization of facilities. The variance arises whenever the standard hours allowed for the output of a period are different from the denominator activity level that was planned when the period began. It can be computed as shown in Exhibit 11–10 or using the following formula:

$$\text{Volume variance} = \text{Fixed portion of the predetermined overhead rate} \times \left(\text{Denominator hours} - \text{Standard hours allowed}\right)$$

Applying this formula to MicroDrive Corporation, the volume variance would be computed as follows:

$$\$6 \text{ per MH } (50{,}000 \text{ MHs} - 40{,}000 \text{ MHs}) = \$60{,}000 \text{ U}$$

Note that this computation agrees with the volume variance as shown in Exhibit 11–10. As stated earlier, the volume variance is a measure of utilization of facilities. An unfavorable variance, as above, means that the company operated at an activity level *below* that planned for the period. A favorable variance would mean that the company operated at an activity level *greater* than that planned for the period.

It is important to note that the volume variance does not measure over- or underspending. A company normally would incur the same dollar amount of fixed overhead cost regardless of whether the period's activity was above or below the planned (denominator) level. In short, the volume variance is an activity-related variance. It is explainable only by activity and is controllable only through activity.

Exhibit 11–11
Fixed Overhead Costs on the Overhead Performance Report

MICRODRIVE CORPORATION
Overhead Performance Report
For the Year Ended December 31

Budgeted machine-hours	50,000
Actual machine-hours	42,000
Standard machine-hours allowed	40,000

Overhead Costs	Cost Formula (per machine-hour)	Actual Costs 42,000 Machine-Hours	Budget Based on 42,000 Machine-Hours	Spending or Budget Variance
Variable overhead costs:				
Indirect labor	$0.80	$ 36,000	$ 33,600	$ 2,400 U
Lubricants	0.30	11,000	12,600	1,600 F
Power	0.40	24,000	16,800	7,200 U
Total variable overhead cost	$1.50	71,000	63,000	8,000 U
Fixed overhead costs:				
Depreciation		100,000	100,000	0
Supervisory salaries		172,000	160,000	12,000 U
Insurance		36,000	40,000	4,000 F
Total fixed overhead cost		308,000	300,000	8,000 U
Total overhead cost		$379,000	$363,000	$16,000 U

To summarize:

1. If the denominator activity and the standard hours allowed for the output of the period are the same, then there is no volume variance.
2. If the denominator activity is greater than the standard hours allowed for the output of the period, then the volume variance is unfavorable, signifying an underutilization of available facilities.
3. If the denominator activity is less than the standard hours allowed for the output of the period, then the volume variance is favorable, signifying a higher utilization of available facilities than was planned.

Graphic Analysis of Fixed Overhead Variances

Graphic analysis can provide insights into the budget and volume variances. A graph containing these variances is presented in Exhibit 11–12.

As shown in the graph, fixed overhead cost is applied to work in process at the predetermined rate of $6 for each standard hour of activity. (The applied-cost line is the upward-sloping line on the graph.) Since a denominator level of 50,000 machine-hours was used in computing the $6 rate, the applied-cost line crosses the budget-cost line at exactly the 50,000 machine-hours point. If the denominator hours and the standard hours allowed for the output are the same, there can be no volume variance. It is only when the standard hours differ from the denominator hours that a volume variance can arise.

In the case at hand, the standard hours allowed for the actual output (40,000 hours) are less than the denominator hours (50,000 hours). The result is an unfavorable volume variance, since less cost was applied to production than was originally budgeted. If the situation had been reversed and the standard hours allowed for the actual output had exceeded the denominator hours, then the volume variance on the graph would have been favorable.

Exhibit 11–12
Graphic Analysis of Fixed Overhead Variances

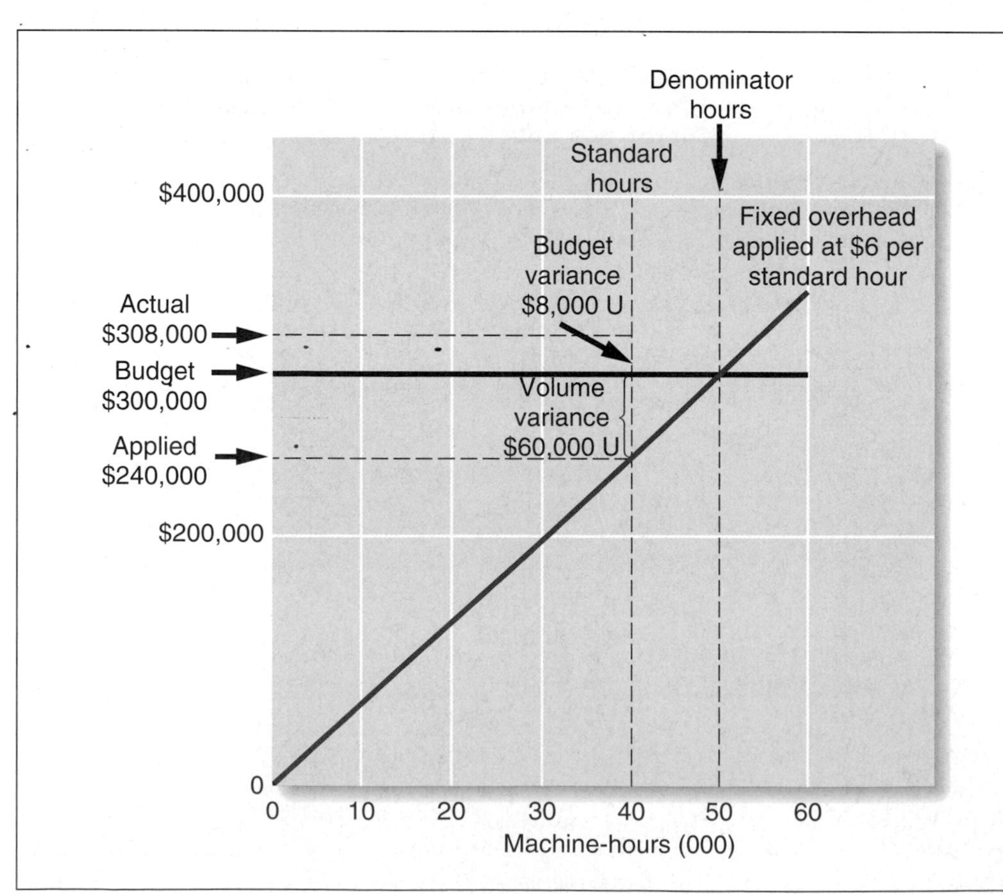

Cautions in Fixed Overhead Analysis

A volume variance for fixed overhead arises because when applying the costs to work in process, we act *as if* the fixed costs were variable and depended on activity. This point can be seen from the graph in Exhibit 11–12. Notice from the graph that the fixed overhead costs are applied to work in process at a rate of $6 per hour *as if* they were variable. Treating these costs as if they were variable is necessary for product costing purposes, but some real dangers lurk here. Managers can easily be misled into thinking of the fixed costs as if they were *in fact* variable.

Keep clearly in mind that fixed overhead costs come in large, indivisible pieces. Expressing fixed costs on a unit or per hour basis, though necessary for product costing for external reports, is artificial. Increases or decreases in activity in fact have no effect on total fixed costs within the relevant range of activity. Even though fixed costs are expressed on a unit or per hour basis, they are *not* proportional to activity. In a sense, the volume variance is the error that occurs as a result of treating fixed costs as variable costs in the costing system.

Overhead Variances and Under- or Overapplied Overhead Cost

Four variances relating to overhead cost have been computed for MicroDrive Corporation in this chapter. These four variances are as follows:

Variable overhead spending variance (p. 491)	$ 8,000 U
Variable overhead efficiency variance (p. 491)	3,000 U
Fixed overhead budget variance (p. 496)	8,000 U
Fixed overhead volume variance (p. 496)	60,000 U
Total overhead variance	$79,000 U

Recall from Chapter 3 that under- or overapplied overhead is the difference between the amount of overhead applied to products and the actual overhead costs incurred during a period. Basically, the overhead variances we have computed in this chapter break the under- or overapplied overhead down into variances that can be used by managers for control purposes. *The sum of the overhead variances equals the under- or overapplied overhead cost for a period.*

Furthermore, in a standard cost system, unfavorable variances are equivalent to underapplied overhead and favorable variances are equivalent to overapplied overhead. Unfavorable variances occur because more was spent on overhead than the standards allow. Underapplied overhead occurs when more was spent on overhead than was applied to products during the period. But in a standard costing system, the standard amount of overhead allowed is exactly the same amount of overhead applied to products. Therefore, in a standard costing system, unfavorable variances and underapplied overhead are the same thing, as are favorable variances and overapplied overhead.

For MicroDrive Corporation, the total overhead variance was $79,000 unfavorable. Therefore, its overhead cost was underapplied by $79,000 for the year. To solidify this point in your mind, *carefully study the review problem at the end of the chapter!* This review problem provides a comprehensive summary of overhead analysis, including the computation of under- or overapplied overhead cost in a standard cost system.

Summary

When analyzing overhead costs, it is vital to distinguish between variable overhead and fixed overhead. Variable overhead costs vary in total in proportion to changes in activity whereas total fixed costs do not change within the relevant range. This distinction is important when constructing flexible budgets and when computing variances for overhead.

A flexible budget shows what costs should be for various levels of activity. The flexible budget amount for a specific level of activity is determined differently depending on whether a cost is variable or fixed. If a cost is variable, the flexible budget amount is computed by multiplying the cost per unit of activity by the level of activity specified for the flexible budget. If a cost is fixed, the original total budgeted fixed cost is used as the flexible budget amount.

The two variances for variable overhead discussed in the chapter are the variable overhead spending and variable overhead efficiency variances. These variances were also covered in the previous chapter.

Two variances for fixed overhead are covered in the chapter. One—the budget variance—is quite simple; the other is considerably more complex. The budget variance is the difference between the actual total fixed overhead cost incurred and the total amount of fixed overhead cost that was originally budgeted. The volume variance is the difference between the amount of fixed overhead cost applied to inventory and the total amount of fixed overhead cost that was originally budgeted. The budget variance is a straightforward measure of the degree to which fixed overhead spending was under control. The volume variance is a consequence of treating a fixed cost as if it were variable and is more difficult to interpret meaningfully.

The sum of all four overhead variances equals the overhead over- or underapplied for the period. Unfavorable variances are equivalent to underapplied overhead and favorable variances are equivalent to overapplied overhead.

Review Problem: Overhead Analysis

(This problem provides a comprehensive review of Chapter 11, including the computation of under- or overapplied overhead and its breakdown into the four overhead variances.)

Data for the manufacturing overhead of Aspen Company are given below:

Overhead Costs	Cost Formula (per machine-hour)	Machine-Hours 5,000	6,000	7,000
Variable overhead costs:				
Supplies	$0.20	$ 1,000	$ 1,200	$ 1,400
Indirect labor	0.30	1,500	1,800	2,100
Total variable overhead cost	$0.50	2,500	3,000	3,500
Fixed overhead costs:				
Depreciation		4,000	4,000	4,000
Supervision		5,000	5,000	5,000
Total fixed overhead cost		9,000	9,000	9,000
Total overhead cost		$11,500	$12,000	$12,500

Five hours of machine time are required per unit of product. The company has set denominator activity for the coming period at 6,000 machine-hours (or 1,200 units). The computation of the predetermined overhead rate would be as follows:

$$\text{Total: } \frac{\$12{,}000}{6{,}000 \text{ MHs}} = \$2.00 \text{ per machine-hour}$$

$$\text{Variable element: } \frac{\$3{,}000}{6{,}000 \text{ MHs}} = \$0.50 \text{ per machine-hour}$$

$$\text{Fixed element: } \frac{\$9{,}000}{6{,}000 \text{ MHs}} = \$1.50 \text{ per machine-hour}$$

Assume the following *actual* results for the period:

Number of units produced	1,300 units
Actual machine-hours	6,800 machine-hours

Standard machine-hours allowed*	6,500 machine-hours
Actual variable overhead cost.	\$4,200
Actual fixed overhead cost	\$9,400

*1,300 units × 5 machine-hours per unit.

Therefore, the company's Manufacturing Overhead account would appear as follows at the end of the period:

Manufacturing Overhead

	Debit	Credit	
Actual overhead costs	13,600*	13,000†	Applied overhead costs
Underapplied overhead	600		

*\$4,200 variable + \$9,400 fixed = \$13,600.

†6,500 standard machine-hours × \$2 per machine-hour = \$13,000. In a standard cost system, overhead is applied on the basis of standard hours, not actual hours.

Required:

Analyze the \$600 underapplied overhead in terms of:

1. A variable overhead spending variance.
2. A variable overhead efficiency variance.
3. A fixed overhead budget variance.
4. A fixed overhead volume variance.

Solution to Review Problem

Variable Overhead Variances

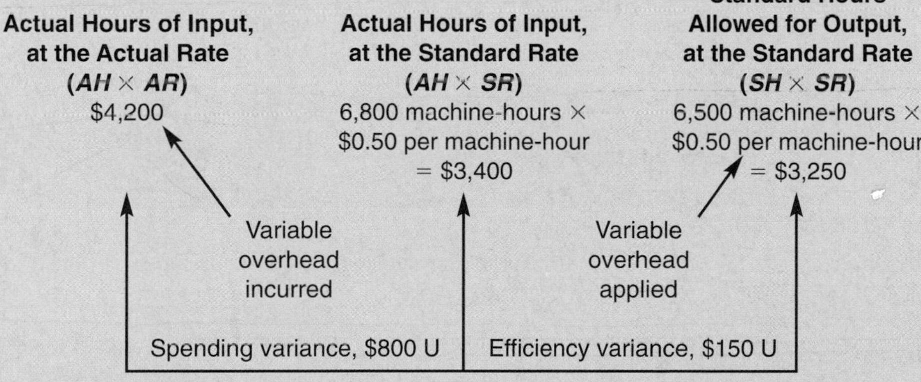

These same variances in the alternative format would be as follows:

Variable overhead spending variance:

$$\text{Spending variance} = (AH \times AR) - (AH \times SR)$$

$$(\$4{,}200^*) - (6{,}800 \text{ machine-hours} \times \$0.50 \text{ per machine-hour}) = \$800 \text{ U}$$

*$AH \times AR$ equals the total actual cost for the period.

Variable overhead efficiency variance:

$$\text{Efficiency variance} = SR(AH - SH)$$

$$\$0.50 \text{ per machine-hour } (6{,}800 \text{ machine-hours} - 6{,}500 \text{ machine-hours}) = \$150 \text{ U}$$

Fixed Overhead Variances

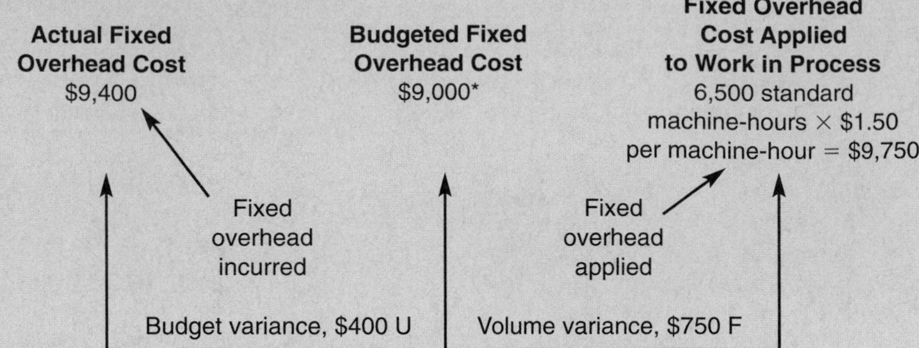

*Can be expressed as: 6,000 denominator machine-hours × $1.50 per machine-hour = $9,000.

These same variances in the alternative format would be as follows:

Fixed overhead budget variance:

$$\text{Budget variance} = \text{Actual fixed overhead cost} - \text{Budgeted fixed overhead cost}$$

$$\$9{,}400 - \$9{,}000 = \$400\text{ U}$$

Fixed overhead volume variance:

$$\text{Volume variance} = \text{Fixed portion of the predetermined overhead rate} \times (\text{Denominator hours} - \text{Standard hours})$$

$$\$1.50\text{ per machine-hour }(6{,}000\text{ machine-hours} - 6{,}500\text{ machine-hours}) = \$750\text{ F}$$

Summary of Variances A summary of the four overhead variances is given below:

Variable overhead:	
Spending variance	$800 U
Efficiency variance	150 U
Fixed overhead:	
Budget variance	400 U
Volume variance	750 F
Underapplied overhead	$600

Notice that the $600 summary variance figure agrees with the underapplied balance in the company's Manufacturing Overhead account. This agreement verifies the accuracy of our variance analysis.

Glossary

Budget variance A measure of the difference between the actual fixed overhead costs incurred during the period and budgeted fixed overhead costs as contained in the flexible budget. (p. 496)

Denominator activity The activity figure used to compute the predetermined overhead rate. (p. 493)

Flexible budget A budget that is designed to cover a range of activity and that can be used to develop budgeted costs at any point within that range to compare to actual costs incurred. (p. 482)

Static budget A budget created at the beginning of the budgeting period that is valid only for the planned level of activity. (p. 482)

Volume variance The variance that arises whenever the standard hours allowed for the output of a period are different from the denominator activity level that was used to compute the predetermined overhead rate. (p. 497)

Questions

11–1 What is a static budget?
11–2 What is a flexible budget and how does it differ from a static budget?
11–3 Name three criteria that should be considered in choosing an activity base on which to construct a flexible budget.
11–4 In comparing budgeted data with actual data in a performance report for variable overhead, what variance(s) will be produced if the budgeted data are based on actual hours worked? On both actual hours worked and standard hours allowed?
11–5 What is meant by the term *standard hours allowed?*
11–6 How does the variable manufacturing overhead spending variance differ from the materials price variance?
11–7 Why is the term *overhead efficiency variance* a misnomer?
11–8 In what way is the flexible budget involved in product costing?
11–9 What is meant by the term *denominator level of activity?*
11–10 Why do we apply overhead to work in process on the basis of standard hours allowed in Chapter 11 when we applied it on the basis of actual hours in Chapter 3? What is the difference in costing systems between the two chapters?
11–11 In a standard cost system, what two variances are computed for fixed manufacturing overhead?
11–12 What does the fixed overhead budget variance measure?
11–13 Under what circumstances would you expect the volume variance to be favorable? Unfavorable? Does the variance measure deviations in spending for fixed overhead items? Explain.
11–14 What is the danger in expressing fixed costs on a per unit basis?
11–15 Under- or overapplied overhead can be broken down into what four variances?
11–16 If factory overhead is overapplied for August, would you expect the total of the overhead variances to be favorable or unfavorable?

Exercises

EXERCISE 11–1 Preparing a Flexible Budget [LO1]
An incomplete flexible budget for overhead is given below for AutoPutz, Gmbh, a German company that owns and operates a large automatic carwash facility near Köln. The German currency is the euro, which is denoted by €.

AUTOPUTZ, GMBH
Flexible Budget

Overhead Costs	Cost Formula (per car)	Activity (cars) 7,000	8,000	9,000
Variable overhead costs:				
Cleaning supplies	?	?	€ 6,000	?
Electricity	?	?	4,800	?
Maintenance	?	?	1,200	?
Total variable overhead costs	?	?	?	?
Fixed overhead costs:				
Operator wages		?	10,000	?
Depreciation		?	20,000	?
Rent		?	8,000	?
Total fixed overhead costs		?	?	?
Total overhead costs		?	?	?

Required:
Fill in the missing data in the flexible budget.

EXERCISE 11–2 Using a Flexible Budget [LO1]
Refer to the data in Exercise 11–1. AutoPutz, Gmbh's owner-manager would like to prepare a budget for August assuming an activity level of 8,200 cars.

Required:
Prepare a static budget for August. Use Exhibit 11–1 in the chapter as your guide.

EXERCISE 11–3 Flexible Budget Performance Report [LO2]
Refer to the data in Exercise 11–1. AutoPutz, Gmbh's actual level of activity during August was 8,300 cars, although the owner had constructed his static budget for the month assuming the level of activity would be 8,200 cars. The actual overhead costs incurred during August are given below:

	Actual Costs Incurred for 8,300 Cars
Variable overhead costs:	
Cleaning supplies	€ 6,350
Electricity	4,865
Maintenance	1,600
Fixed overhead costs:	
Operator wages	10,050
Depreciation	20,200
Rent	8,000

Required:
Prepare a flexible budget performance report for both the variable and fixed overhead costs for August. Use Exhibit 11–4 in the chapter as your guide.

EXERCISE 11–4 Prepare a Flexible Budget [LO1]
The cost formulas for Swan Company's manufacturing overhead costs are given below. The costs cover a range of 8,000 to 10,000 machine-hours.

Overhead Costs	Cost Formula
Supplies	$0.20 per machine-hour
Indirect labor	$10,000 plus $0.25 per machine-hour
Utilities	$0.15 per machine-hour
Maintenance	$7,000 plus $0.10 per machine-hour
Depreciation	$8,000

Required:
Prepare a flexible budget in increments of 1,000 machine-hours. Include all costs in your flexible budget.

EXERCISE 11–5 Variable Overhead Performance Report [LO3]
The variable portion of Whaley Company's flexible budget for manufacturing overhead is given below:

	Cost Formula (per machine-	Machine-Hours		
Overhead Costs	hour)	10,000	18,000	24,000
Utilities	$1.20	$12,000	$21,600	$ 28,800
Supplies	0.30	3,000	5,400	7,200
Maintenance	2.40	24,000	43,200	57,600
Rework time	0.60	6,000	10,800	14,400
Total variable overhead costs	$4.50	$45,000	$81,000	$108,000

During a recent period, the company recorded 16,000 machine-hours of activity. The variable overhead costs incurred were as follows:

Utilities	$20,000
Supplies	4,700
Maintenance	35,100
Rework time	12,300

The budgeted activity for the period had been 18,000 machine-hours.

Required:

1. Prepare a variable overhead performance report for the period. Indicate whether variances are favorable (F) or unfavorable (U). Show only a spending variance on your report.
2. Discuss the significance of the variances. Might some variances be the result of others? Explain.

EXERCISE 11–6 Variable Overhead Performance Report with Both Spending and Efficiency Variances [LO4]

The check-clearing office of San Juan Bank is responsible for processing all checks that come to the bank for payment. Managers at the bank believe that variable overhead costs are essentially proportional to the number of labor-hours worked in the office, so labor-hours are used as the activity base for budgeting and for performance reports for variable overhead costs in the department. Data for October, the most recent month, appear below:

Budgeted labor-hours	865
Actual labor-hours	860
Standard labor-hours allowed for the actual number of checks processed	880

	Cost Formula (per labor-hour)	Actual Costs Incurred in October
Variable overhead costs:		
Office supplies	$0.15	$ 146
Staff coffee lounge	0.05	124
Indirect labor	3.25	2,790
Total variable overhead cost	$3.45	$3,060

Required:

Prepare a variable overhead performance report for October for the check-clearing office that includes both spending and efficiency variances. Use Exhibit 11–7 as a guide.

EXERCISE 11–7 Predetermined Overhead Rate; Overhead Variances [LO4, LO5, LO6]

Weller Company's flexible budget for manufacturing overhead (in condensed form) follows:

	Cost Formula (per machine-hour)	Machine-Hours		
Overhead Costs		**8,000**	**9,000**	**10,000**
Variable costs	$1.05	$ 8,400	$ 9,450	$10,500
Fixed costs		24,800	24,800	24,800
Total overhead costs		$33,200	$34,250	$35,300

The following information is available for a recent period:

a. The denominator activity of 8,000 machine-hours was chosen to compute the predetermined overhead rate.

b. At the 8,000 standard machine-hours level of activity, the company should produce 3,200 units of product.

c. The company's actual operating results were as follows:

Number of units produced	3,500
Actual machine-hours	8,500
Actual variable overhead costs	$9,860
Actual fixed overhead costs	$25,100

Required:

1. Compute the predetermined overhead rate and break it down into variable and fixed cost elements.
2. What were the standard hours allowed for the year's output?
3. Compute the variable overhead spending and efficiency variances and the fixed overhead budget and volume variances.

EXERCISE 11–8 Predetermined Overhead Rates [LO5]

Operating at a normal level of 24,000 direct labor-hours, Trone Company produces 8,000 units of product. The direct labor wage rate is $12.60 per hour. Two pounds of raw materials go into each unit of product at a cost of $4.20 per pound. A flexible budget is used to plan and control overhead costs:

Flexible Budget Data

Overhead Costs	Cost Formula (per direct labor-hour)	Direct Labor-Hours 20,000	22,000	24,000
Variable costs	$1.60	$ 32,000	$ 35,200	$ 38,400
Fixed costs		84,000	84,000	84,000
Total overhead costs		$116,000	$119,200	$122,400

Required:

1. Using 24,000 direct labor-hours as the denominator activity, compute the predetermined overhead rate and break it down into fixed and variable elements.
2. Complete the standard cost card below for one unit of product:

Direct materials, 2 pounds at $4.20 per pound	$8.40
Direct labor, ?	?
Variable overhead, ?	?
Fixed overhead, ?	?
Total standard cost per unit	$?

EXERCISE 11–9 Using Fixed Overhead Variances [LO6]

The standard cost card for the single product manufactured by Prince Company is given below:

Standard Cost Card—Per Unit

Direct materials, 3.5 feet at $4 per foot	$14.00
Direct labor, 0.8 direct labor-hours at $9 per direct labor-hour	7.20
Variable overhead, 0.8 direct labor-hours at $2.50 per direct labor-hour	2.00
Fixed overhead, 0.8 direct labor-hours at $6 per direct labor-hour	4.80
Total standard cost per unit	$28.00

Last year, the company produced 10,000 units of product and worked 8,200 actual direct labor-hours. Manufacturing overhead cost is applied to production on the basis of direct labor-hours. Selected data relating to the company's fixed manufacturing overhead cost for the year are shown below:

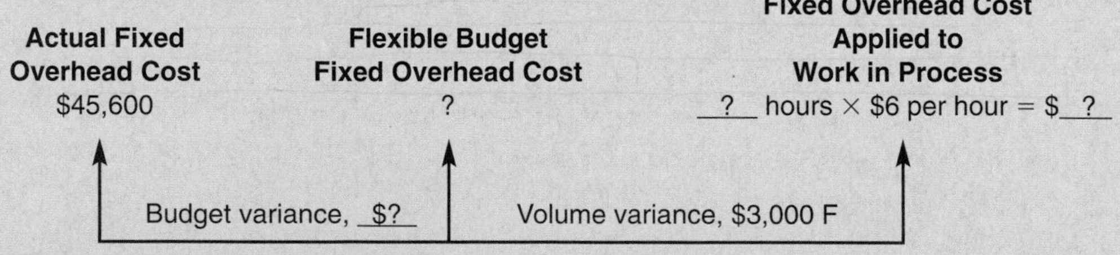

Required:

1. What were the standard hours allowed for the year's production?
2. What was the amount of fixed overhead cost contained in the flexible budget for the year?
3. What was the budget variance for the year?
4. What denominator activity level did the company use in setting the predetermined overhead rate for the year?

EXERCISE 11–10 Relations Among Fixed Overhead Variances [LO5, LO6]

Selected information relating to the fixed overhead costs of Westwood Company for a recent period is given on the following page:

Activity:	
Number of units produced	9,500
Standard machine-hours allowed per unit	2
Denominator activity (machine-hours)	20,000
Costs:	
Actual fixed overhead costs incurred	$79,000
Budget variance	$1,000 F

Overhead cost is applied to products on the basis of machine-hours.

Required:

1. What was the fixed portion of the predetermined overhead rate?
2. What were the standard machine-hours allowed for the period's production?
3. What was the volume variance?

EXERCISE 11–11 Fixed Overhead Variances [LO6]

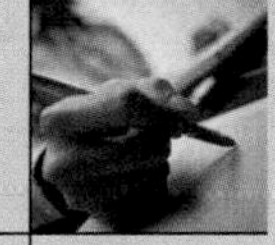

Selected operating information on three different companies for a recent period is given below:

	Company		
	X	Y	Z
Full-capacity direct labor-hours	20,000	9,000	10,000
Budgeted direct labor-hours*	19,000	8,500	8,000
Actual direct labor-hours	19,500	8,000	9,000
Standard direct labor-hours allowed for actual output	18,500	8,250	9,500

*Denominator activity for computing the predetermined overhead rate.

Required:

For each company, state whether the volume variance would be favorable or unfavorable; also, explain in each case *why* the volume variance would be favorable or unfavorable.

Problems

PROBLEM 11–12 Preparing an Overhead Performance Report [LO2]

Shipley Company has had a comprehensive budgeting system in operation for several years. Feelings vary among the managers as to the value and benefit of the system. The line supervisors are very happy with the reports being prepared on their performance, but upper management often expresses dissatisfaction over the reports being prepared on various phases of the company's operations. A typical manufacturing overhead performance report for a recent period is shown below:

SHIPLEY COMPANY
Overhead Performance Report—Milling Department
For the Quarter Ended June 30

	Actual	Budget	Variance
Machine-hours	25,000	30,000	
Variable overhead:			
Indirect labor	$ 20,000	$ 22,500	$2,500 F
Supplies	5,400	6,000	600 F
Utilities	27,000	30,000	3,000 F
Rework time	14,000	15,000	1,000 F
Total variable costs	66,400	73,500	7,100 F
Fixed overhead:			
Maintenance	61,900	60,000	1,900 U
Inspection	90,000	90,000	—
Total fixed costs	151,900	150,000	1,900 U
Total overhead costs	$218,300	$223,500	$5,200 F

After receiving a copy of this performance report, the supervisor of the Milling Department stated, "No one can complain about my department; our variances have been favorable for over a year now. We've saved the company thousands of dollars by our excellent cost control."

The budget data above are for the original planned level of activity for the quarter.

Required:

1. The production superintendent is uneasy about the performance reports being prepared and would like you to evaluate their usefulness to the company.
2. What changes, if any, should be made in the overhead performance report to give the production superintendent better insight into how well the supervisor is controlling costs?
3. Prepare a new overhead performance report for the quarter, incorporating any changes you suggested in (2) above.

PROBLEM 11–13 Comprehensive Standard Cost Variances [LO4, LO5, LO6]

Dresser Company uses a standard cost system and sets predetermined overhead rates on the basis of direct labor-hours. The following data are taken from the company's budget for the current year:

Denominator activity (direct labor-hours)	9,000
Variable manufacturing overhead cost at 9,000 direct labor-hours	$34,200
Fixed manufacturing overhead cost	$63,000

The standard cost card for the company's only product is given below:

Direct materials, 4 pounds at $2.60 per pound	$10.40
Direct labor, 2 direct labor-hours at $9 per direct labor-hour	18.00
Overhead, 120% of direct labor cost	21.60
Standard cost per unit	$50.00

During the year, the company produced 4,800 units of product and incurred the following costs:

Materials purchased, 30,000 pounds at $2.50 per pound	$75,000
Materials used in production (in pounds)	20,000
Direct labor cost incurred, 10,000 direct labor-hours at $8.60 per direct labor-hour	$86,000
Variable manufacturing overhead cost incurred	$35,900
Fixed manufacturing overhead cost incurred	$64,800

Required:

1. Redo the standard cost card in a clearer, more usable format by detailing the variable and fixed overhead cost elements.
2. Prepare an analysis of the variances for materials and labor for the year.
3. Prepare an analysis of the variances for variable and fixed overhead for the year.
4. What effect, if any, does the choice of a denominator activity level have on standard unit costs? Is the volume variance a controllable variance from a spending point of view? Explain.

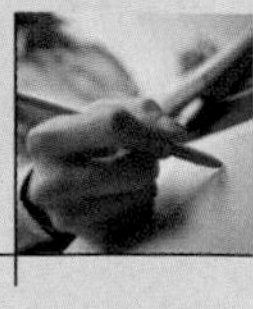

PROBLEM 11–14 Applying the Flexible Budget Approach [LO2]

The KGV Blood Bank, a private charity partly supported by government grants, is located on the Caribbean island of St. Lucia. The Blood Bank has just finished its operations for September, which was a particularly busy month due to a powerful hurricane that hit neighboring islands, causing many injuries. The hurricane largely bypassed St. Lucia, but residents of St. Lucia willingly donated their blood to help people on other islands. As a consequence, the blood bank collected and processed over 25% more blood than had been originally planned for the month.

A report prepared by a government official comparing actual costs to budgeted costs for the Blood Bank appears below. (The currency on St. Lucia is the East Caribbean dollar.) Continued support from the government depends on the Blood Bank's ability to demonstrate control over its costs.

KGV BLOOD BANK
Cost Control Report
For the Month Ended September 30

	Actual	Budget	Variance
Liters of blood collected	780	600	180 F
Variable costs:			
Medical supplies	$ 9,252	$ 7,110	$2,142 U
Lab tests	10,782	8,610	2,172 U
Refreshments for donors	1,186	960	226 U
Administrative supplies	189	150	39 U
Total variable costs	21,409	16,830	4,579 U
Fixed costs:			
Staff salaries	13,200	13,200	—
Equipment depreciation	2,100	1,900	200 U
Rent	1,500	1,500	—
Utilities	324	300	24 U
Total fixed costs	17,124	16,900	224 U
Total costs	$38,533	$33,730	$4,803 U

The managing director of the Blood Bank was very unhappy with this report, claiming that his costs were higher than expected due to the emergency on the neighboring islands. He also pointed out that the additional costs had been fully covered by payments from grateful recipients on the other islands. The government official who prepared the report countered that all of the figures had been submitted by the blood bank to the government; he was just pointing out that actual costs were a lot higher than promised in the budget.

Required:

1. Prepare a new performance report for September using the flexible budget approach. (Note: Even though some of these costs might be classified as direct costs rather than as overhead, the flexible budget approach can still be used to prepare a flexible budget performance report.)
2. Do you think any of the variances in the report you prepared should be investigated? Why?

PROBLEM 11–15 Comprehensive Standard Cost Variances [LO4, LO6]

"It certainly is nice to see that small variance on the income statement after all the trouble we've had lately in controlling manufacturing costs," said Linda White, vice president of Molina Company. "The $12,250 overall manufacturing variance reported last period is well below the 3% limit we have set for variances. We need to congratulate everybody on a job well done."

The company produces and sells a single product. The standard cost card for the product follows:

Standard Cost Card—Per Unit

Direct materials, 4 yards at $3.50 per yard	$14
Direct labor, 1.5 direct labor-hours at $12 per direct labor-hour	18
Variable overhead, 1.5 direct labor-hours at $2 per direct labor-hour	3
Fixed overhead, 1.5 direct-labor hours at $6 per direct labor-hour	9
Standard cost per unit	$44

The following additional information is available for the year just completed:

a. The company manufactured 20,000 units of product during the year.
b. A total of 78,000 yards of material was purchased during the year at a cost of $3.75 per yard. All of this material was used to manufacture the 20,000 units. There were no beginning or ending inventories for the year.
c. The company worked 32,500 direct labor-hours during the year at a cost of $11.80 per hour.
d. Overhead cost is applied to products on the basis of direct labor-hours. Data relating to manufacturing overhead costs follow:

Denominator activity level (direct labor-hours)	25,000
Budgeted fixed overhead costs (from the flexible budget)	$150,000
Actual fixed overhead costs	$148,000
Actual variable overhead costs	$68,250

Required:

1. Compute the direct materials price and quantity variances for the year.
2. Compute the direct labor rate and efficiency variances for the year.
3. For manufacturing overhead, compute the following:
   a. The variable overhead spending and efficiency variances for the year.
   b. The fixed overhead budget and volume variances for the year.
4. Total the variances you have computed, and compare the net amount with the $12,250 mentioned by the vice president. Do you agree that everyone should be congratulated for a job well done? Explain.

PROBLEM 11–16 Applying Overhead; Overhead Variances [LO4, LO5, LO6]
Highland Shortbread, Ltd., of Aberdeen, Scotland, produces a single product and uses a standard cost system to help control costs. Manufacturing overhead is applied to production on the basis of machine-hours. According to the company's flexible budget, the following overhead costs should be incurred at an activity level of 18,000 machine-hours (the denominator activity level chosen for the year):

Variable manufacturing overhead costs	£ 31,500
Fixed manufacturing overhead costs	72,000
Total manufacturing overhead costs	£103,500

During the year, the following operating results were recorded:

Actual machine-hours worked	15,000
Standard machine-hours allowed	16,000
Actual variable manufacturing overhead cost incurred	£26,500
Actual fixed manufacturing overhead cost incurred	£70,000

At the end of the year, the company's Manufacturing Overhead account contained the following data:

Manufacturing Overhead

Actual costs	96,500	92,000	Applied costs
	4,500		

Management would like to determine the cause of the £4,500 underapplied overhead.

Required:

1. Compute the predetermined overhead rate for the year. Break it down into variable and fixed cost elements.
2. Show how the £92,000 "Applied costs" figure in the Manufacturing Overhead account was computed.
3. Analyze the £4,500 underapplied overhead figure in terms of the variable overhead spending and efficiency variances and the fixed overhead budget and volume variances.
4. Explain the meaning of each variance that you computed in (3) above.

PROBLEM 11–17 Comprehensive Problem: Flexible Budget; Overhead Performance Report [LO1, LO2, LO3, LO4]
Elgin Company has recently introduced budgeting as an integral part of its corporate planning process. An inexperienced member of the accounting staff was given the assignment of constructing a flexible budget for manufacturing overhead costs and prepared it in the format that follows:

Percentage of Capacity	**80%**	**100%**
Machine-hours	40,000	50,000
Utilities	$ 41,000	$ 49,000
Supplies	4,000	5,000
Indirect labor	8,000	10,000

continued

Maintenance	37,000	41,000
Supervision	10,000	10,000
Total manufacturing overhead costs	$100,000	$115,000

The company assigns overhead costs to production on the basis of machine-hours. The cost formulas used to prepare the budgeted figures above are relevant over a range of 80% to 100% of capacity in a month. The managers who will be working under these budgets have control over both fixed and variable manufacturing overhead costs.

Required:

1. Redo the company's flexible budget, presenting it in better format. Show the budgeted costs at 80%, 90%, and 100% levels of capacity. (Use the high-low method to separate fixed and variable costs.)
2. Express the flexible budget prepared in (1) above in cost formula form using a single cost formula to express all overhead costs.
3. During May, the company operated at 86% of capacity in terms of actual machine-hours recorded in the factory. Actual manufacturing overhead costs incurred during the month were as follows:

Utilities	$ 42,540
Supplies	6,450
Indirect labor	9,890
Maintenance	35,190
Supervision	10,000
Total actual manufacturing overhead costs	$104,070

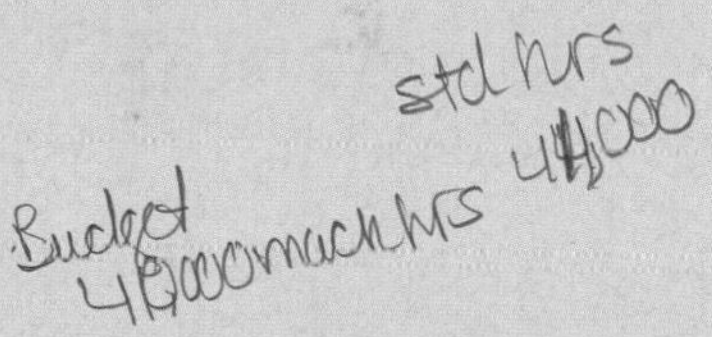

Fixed costs had no budget variances. Prepare an overhead performance report for May. Include both fixed and variable costs in your report (in separate sections). Structure your report so that it shows only a spending variance for overhead. The company originally budgeted to work 40,000 machine-hours during the month; standard hours allowed for the month's production totaled 41,000 machine-hours.

4. Explain possible causes of the spending variance for supplies.
5. Compute an efficiency variance for *total* variable overhead cost, and explain the nature of the variance.

PROBLEM 11–18 Evaluting an Overhead Performance Report [LO2, LO4]

Ronald Davis, superintendent of Mason Company's Milling Department, is very happy with his performance report for the past month. The report follows:

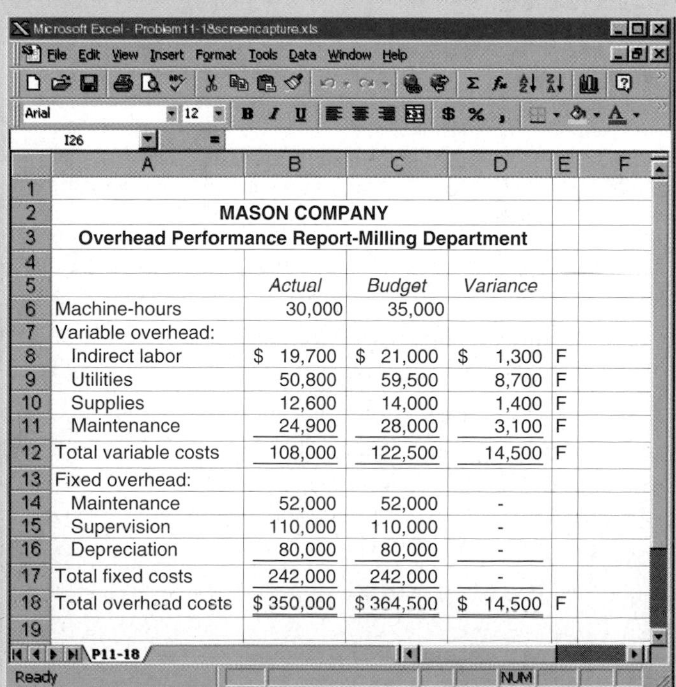

MASON COMPANY
Overhead Performance Report-Milling Department

	Actual	Budget	Variance	
Machine-hours	30,000	35,000		
Variable overhead:				
Indirect labor	$ 19,700	$ 21,000	$ 1,300	F
Utilities	50,800	59,500	8,700	F
Supplies	12,600	14,000	1,400	F
Maintenance	24,900	28,000	3,100	F
Total variable costs	108,000	122,500	14,500	F
Fixed overhead:				
Maintenance	52,000	52,000	-	
Supervision	110,000	110,000	-	
Depreciation	80,000	80,000	-	
Total fixed costs	242,000	242,000	-	
Total overhead costs	$ 350,000	$ 364,500	$ 14,500	F

Upon receiving a copy of this report, John Arnold, the production manager, commented, "I've been getting these reports for months now, and I still can't see how they help me assess efficiency and cost control in that department. I agree that the budget for the month was 35,000 machine-hours, but that represents 17,500 units of product, since it should take two hours to produce one unit. The department produced only 14,000 units during the month, and took 30,000 machine-hours to do it. Why do all the variances turn up favorable?"

Required:

1. In answer to Mr. Arnold's question, why are all the variances favorable? Evaluate the performance report.
2. Prepare a new overhead performance report that will help Mr. Arnold assess efficiency and cost control in the Milling Department. (Hint: Exhibit 11–7 may be helpful in structuring your report; however, include both variable and fixed costs in the report.)

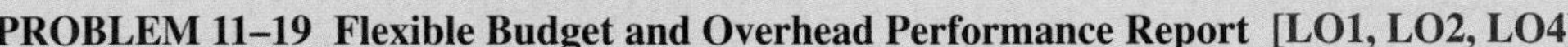

PROBLEM 11–19 Flexible Budget and Overhead Performance Report [LO1, LO2, LO4]
Durrant Company has had great difficulty in controlling manufacturing overhead costs. At a recent convention, the president heard about a control device for overhead costs known as a flexible budget, and he has hired you to implement this budgeting program in Durrant Company. After some effort, you have developed the following cost formulas for the company's Machining Department. These costs are based on a normal operating range of 10,000 to 20,000 machine-hours per month:

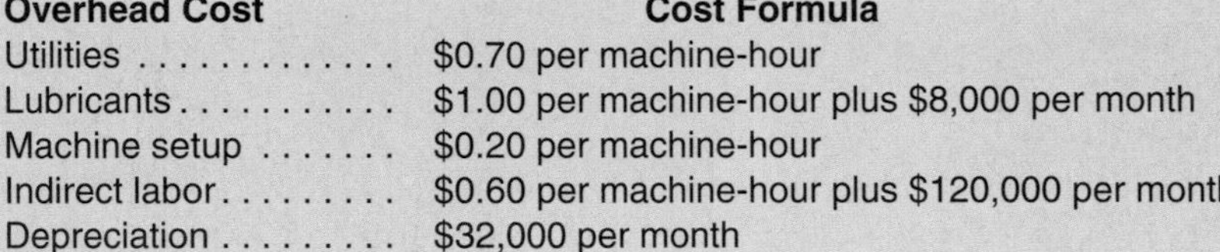

Overhead Cost	Cost Formula
Utilities	$0.70 per machine-hour
Lubricants	$1.00 per machine-hour plus $8,000 per month
Machine setup	$0.20 per machine-hour
Indirect labor	$0.60 per machine-hour plus $120,000 per month
Depreciation	$32,000 per month

During March, the first month after your preparation of the above data, the Machining Department worked 18,000 machine-hours and produced 9,000 units of product. The actual manufacturing overhead costs of this production were as follows:

Utilities	$ 12,000
Lubricants	24,500
Machine setup	4,800
Indirect labor	132,500
Depreciation	32,000
Total manufacturing overhead costs	$205,800

Fixed costs had no budget variances. The department had originally been budgeted to work 20,000 machine-hours during March.

Required:

1. Prepare a flexible budget for the Machining Department in increments of 5,000 hours. Include both variable and fixed costs in your budget.
2. Prepare an overhead performance report for the Machining Department for the month of March. Include both variable and fixed costs in the report (in separate sections). Show only a spending variance on the report.
3. What additional information would you need to compute an overhead efficiency variance for the department?

PROBLEM 11–20 Flexible Budgets and Overhead Analysis [LO1, LO4, LO5, LO6]
Rowe Company manufactures a variety of products in several departments. Budgeted costs for the company's Finishing Department have been set as follows:

Variable costs:	
Direct materials	$ 600,000
Direct labor	450,000
Indirect labor	30,000
Utilities	50,000
Maintenance	20,000
Total variable costs	1,150,000

continued

Fixed costs:	
Supervisory salaries	60,000
Insurance	5,000
Depreciation	190,000
Equipment rental	45,000
Total fixed costs	300,000
Total budgeted costs	$1,450,000
Budgeted direct labor-hours	50,000

After careful study, the company has determined that operating activity in the Finishing Department is best measured by direct labor-hours. The cost formulas used to develop the budgeted costs above are valid over a relevant range of 40,000 to 60,000 direct labor-hours per year.

Required:

1. Prepare a manufacturing overhead flexible budget in good form for the Finishing Department. Make your budget in increments of 10,000 hours. (The company does not include direct materials and direct labor costs in the flexible budget.)
2. Assume that the company computes predetermined overhead rates by department. Compute the rates, variable and fixed, that will be used to apply Finishing Department overhead costs to production.
3. Suppose that during the year the following actual activity and costs are recorded in the Finishing Department:

Actual direct labor-hours worked	46,000
Standard direct labor-hours allowed for the output of the year	45,000
Actual variable manufacturing overhead cost incurred	$89,700
Actual fixed manufacturing overhead cost incurred	$296,000

a. A T-account for manufacturing overhead costs in the Finishing Department is given below. Determine the amount of applied overhead cost for the year, and compute the under- or overapplied overhead.

Manufacturing Overhead

Actual costs	385,700	

b. Analyze the under- or overapplied overhead in terms of the variable overhead spending and efficiency variances and the fixed overhead budget and volume variances.

PROBLEM 11–21 Variable Overhead Performance Report [LO4]

Ronson Products, Ltd., an Australian company, has the following cost formulas (expressed in Australian dollars) for variable overhead costs in one of its machine shops:

Variable Overhead Cost	Cost Formula (per machine-hour)
Supplies	$0.70
Power	1.20
Lubrication	0.50
Wearing tools	3.10
Total	$5.50

During July, the machine shop was scheduled to work 3,200 machine-hours and to produce 16,000 units of product. The standard machine time per unit of product is 0.2 hours. A severe storm during the month forced the company to close for several days, which reduced the level of output for the month. Actual results for July were as follows:

Actual machine-hours worked	2,700
Actual number of units produced	14,000

Actual costs for July were as follows:

Variable Overhead Cost	Total Actual Cost	Per Machine-Hour
Supplies.	$ 1,836	$0.68
Power	3,348	1.24
Lubrication.	1,485	0.55
Wearing tools.	8,154	3.02
Total.	$14,823	$5.49

Required:
Prepare an overhead performance report for the machine shop for July. Use column headings in your report as shown below:

Overhead Costs	Cost Formula (per MH)	Actual Costs Incurred, 2,700 MHs	Budget Based on ? MHs	Budget Based on ? MHs	Total Variance	Breakdown of the Total Variance: Spending Variance	Breakdown of the Total Variance: Efficiency Variance

PROBLEM 11–22 Selection of a Denominator; Overhead Analysis; Standard Cost Card [LO4, LO5, LO6]
The condensed flexible budget for manufacturing overhead of the Scott Company is given below:

Overhead Costs	Cost Formula (per DLH)	Direct Labor-Hours: 30,000	40,000	50,000
Variable overhead costs.	$2.50	$ 75,000	$100,000	$125,000
Fixed overhead costs.		320,000	320,000	320,000
Total overhead costs		$395,000	$420,000	$445,000

The company produces a single product that requires 2.5 direct labor-hours to complete. The direct labor wage rate is $10 per hour. Three yards of raw material are required for each unit of product, at a cost of $5 per yard.

Demand for the company's product differs widely from year to year. Expected activity for this year is 50,000 direct labor-hours; normal activity is 40,000 direct labor-hours per year.

Required:
1. Assume that the company chooses 40,000 direct labor-hours as the denominator level of activity. Compute the predetermined overhead rate, breaking it down into fixed and variable cost elements.
2. Assume that the company chooses 50,000 direct labor-hours as the denominator level of activity. Repeat the computations in (1) above.
3. Complete two standard cost cards as outlined below. Each card should relate to a single unit of product.

Denominator Activity: 40,000 DLHs	
Direct materials, 3 yards at $5 per yard	$15.00
Direct labor, ?	?
Variable overhead, ?	?
Fixed overhead, ?	?
Total standard cost per unit	$?

Denominator Activity: 50,000 DLHs	
Direct materials, 3 yards at $5 per yard	$15.00
Direct labor, ?	?
Variable overhead, ?	?
Fixed overhead, ?	?
Total standard cost per unit	$?

4. Assume that 48,000 actual hours are worked during the year, and that 18,500 units are produced. Actual manufacturing overhead costs for the year are as follows:

Variable overhead costs	$124,800
Fixed overhead costs	321,700
Total overhead costs	$446,500

a. Compute the standard hours allowed for the year's production.

b. Compute the missing items from the Manufacturing Overhead account below. Assume that the company uses 40,000 direct labor-hours (normal activity) as the denominator activity figure in computing overhead rates, as you have used in (1) above.

Manufacturing Overhead

Actual costs	446,500	?
	?	?

c. Analyze your under- or overapplied overhead balance in terms of variable overhead spending and efficiency variances and fixed overhead budget and volume variances.

5. Looking at the variances that you have computed, what appears to be the major disadvantage of using normal activity rather than expected actual activity as a denominator in computing the predetermined overhead rate? What advantages can you see to offset this disadvantage?

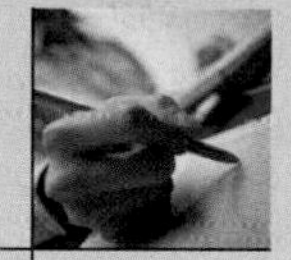

PROBLEM 11–23 Applying Overhead; Overhead Variances [LO4, LO5, LO6]

Wymont Company produces a single product that requires a large amount of labor time. Overhead cost is applied on the basis of direct labor-hours. The company's condensed flexible budget for manufacturing overhead is given below:

Overhead Costs	Cost Formula (per DLH)	Direct Labor-Hours 24,000	30,000	36,000
Variable overhead costs	$2	$ 48,000	$ 60,000	$ 72,000
Fixed overhead costs		180,000	180,000	180,000
Total overhead costs		$228,000	$240,000	$252,000

The company's product requires 4 feet of direct material that has a standard cost of $3 per foot. The product requires 1.5 hours of direct labor time. The standard labor rate is $12 per hour.

During the year, the company had planned to operate at a denominator activity level of 30,000 direct labor-hours and to produce 20,000 units of product. Actual activity and costs for the year were as follows:

Number of units produced	22,000
Actual direct labor-hours worked	35,000
Actual variable overhead cost incurred	$63,000
Actual fixed overhead cost incurred	$181,000

Required:

1. Compute the predetermined overhead rate for the year. Break the rate down into variable and fixed elements.
2. Prepare a standard cost card for the company's product; show the details for all manufacturing costs on your standard cost card.
3. *a.* Compute the standard direct labor-hours allowed for the year's production.
   b. Complete the following Manufacturing Overhead T-account for the year:

Manufacturing Overhead

?	?
?	?

4. Determine the reason for the under- or overapplied overhead from (3) above by computing the variable overhead spending and efficiency variances and the fixed overhead budget and volume variances.
5. Suppose the company had chosen 36,000 direct labor-hours as the denominator activity rather than 30,000 hours. State which, if any, of the variances computed in (4) above would have changed, and explain how the variance(s) would have changed. No computations are necessary.

PROBLEM 11–24 Standard Cost Card; Fixed Overhead Analysis; Graphing [LO5, LO6]
For the current year, Eastwood Company chose a denominator activity level of 15,000 direct labor-hours. According to the company's flexible budget, the following manufacturing overhead costs should be incurred at this activity level:

Variable manufacturing overhead costs.	$18,000
Fixed manufacturing overhead costs.	$135,000

The company manufactures a single product that requires 2.5 hours to complete. The direct labor rate is $14 per hour. The product requires 4 pounds of raw materials; this material has a standard cost of $8 per pound. Overhead is applied to production on the basis of direct labor-hours.

Required:
1. Compute the predetermined overhead rate for the year. Break the rate down into variable and fixed cost elements.
2. Prepare a standard cost card for one unit of product using the following format:

Direct materials, 4 pounds at $8.00 per pound.	$32.00
Direct labor, ?	?
Variable manufacturing overhead, ?.	?
Fixed manufacturing overhead, ?.	?
Standard cost per unit	$?

3. Prepare a graph with cost on the vertical (Y) axis and direct labor-hours on the horizontal (X) axis. Plot a line on your graph from a zero level of activity to 20,000 direct labor-hours for each of the following costs:
   a. Budgeted fixed overhead cost (in total).
   b. Applied fixed overhead cost applied at the hourly rate computed in (1) above.
4. Assume that during the year the company's actual activity is as follows:

Number of units produced	5,600
Actual direct labor-hours worked	14,500
Actual fixed manufacturing overhead cost incurred.	$137,400

   a. Compute the fixed overhead budget and volume variances for the year.
   b. Show the volume variance on the graph you prepared in (3) above.
5. Disregard the data in (4) above. Assume instead that the company's actual activity for the year is as follows:

Number of units produced	6,200
Actual direct labor-hours worked	15,800
Actual fixed manufacturing overhead costs incurred	$137,400

   a. Compute the fixed overhead budget and volume variances for the year.
   b. Show the volume variance on the graph you prepared in (3) above.

PROBLEM 11–25 Activity-Based Costing and the Flexible Budget Approach [LO2]
The Munchkin Theater is a nonprofit organization devoted to staging theater productions of plays for children in Toronto, Canada. The theater has a very small full-time professional administrative staff. Through a special arrangement with the actors' union, actors and directors rehearse without pay and are paid only for actual performances.

The costs of 2002's operations appear below. During 2002, The Munchkin Theater had five different productions—each of which was performed 12 times.

THE MUNCHKIN THEATER
Cost Report
For the Year Ended 31 December 2002

Number of productions	5
Number of performances of each production	12
Total number of performances	60
Actual costs incurred:	
Actors and directors' wages	$144,000
Stagehands' wages	27,000
Ticket booth personnel and ushers' wages	10,800
Scenery, costumes, and props	43,000
Theater hall rent	45,000
Printed programs	10,500
Publicity	13,000
Administrative expenses	43,200
Total	$336,500

Some of the costs vary with the number of productions, some with the number of performances, and some are relatively fixed and depend on neither the number of productions nor the number of performances. The costs of scenery, costumes, props, and publicity vary with the number of productions. It doesn't make any difference how many times Peter the Rabbit is performed, the cost of the scenery is the same. Likewise, the cost of publicizing a play with posters and radio commercials is the same whether there are 10, 20, or 30 performances of the play. On the other hand, the wages of the actors, directors, stagehands, ticket booth personnel, and ushers vary with the number of performances. The greater the number of performances, the higher the wage costs will be. Similarly, the costs of renting the hall and printing the programs will vary with the number of performances. Administrative expenses are more difficult to pin down, but the best estimate is that approximately 75% of these costs are fixed, 15% depend on the number of productions staged, and the remaining 10% depend on the number of performances.

At the end of 2002, the board of directors of the theater authorized changing the theater's program in 2003 to four productions, with 16 performances each. Actual costs for 2003 were higher than the costs for 2002. (Grants from donors and ticket sales were also correspondingly higher.) Data concerning 2003's operations appear below:

THE MUNCHKIN THEATER
Cost Report
For the Year Ended 31 December 2003

Number of productions	4
Number of performances of each production	16
Total number of performances	64
Actual costs incurred:	
Actors and directors' wages	$148,000
Stagehands' wages	28,600
Ticket booth personnel and ushers' wages	12,300
Scenery, costumes, and props	39,300
Theater hall rent	49,600
Printed programs	10,950
Publicity	12,000
Administrative expenses	41,650
Total	$342,400

Even though many of the costs above may be considered direct costs rather than overhead, the flexible budget approach covered in the chapter can be used to evaluate how well these costs are controlled. The principles are the same whether a cost is a direct cost or is overhead.

Required:

1. Use the actual results from 2002 to estimate the cost formulas for the flexible budget for The Munchkin Theater. Keep in mind that the theater has two measures of activity—the number of productions and the number of performances.

2. Prepare a performance report for 2003 using the flexible budget approach and both measures of activity. Assume inflation was insignificant. (Note: To evaluate administrative expenses, first determine the flexible budget amounts for the three elements of administrative expenses. Then compare the total of the three elements to the actual administrative expense of $41,650.)
3. If you were on the board of directors of the theater, would you be pleased with how well costs were controlled during 2003? Why or why not?
4. The cost formulas provide figures for the average cost per production and average cost per performance. How accurate do you think these figures would be for predicting the cost of a new production or of an additional performance of a particular production?

Cases

CASE 11–26 Ethics and the Manager [LO2]

Lance Prating is the controller of the Colorado Springs manufacturing facility of Advance Macro, Incorporated. Among the many reports that must be filed with corporate headquarters is the annual overhead performance report. The report covers an entire fiscal year, which ends on December 31, and is due at corporate headquarters shortly after the beginning of the new year. Prating does not like putting work off to the last minute, so just before Christmas he put together a preliminary draft of the overhead performance report. Some adjustments would later be required for the few transactions that occur between Christmas and New Year's Day. A copy of the preliminary draft report, which Prating completed on December 21, follows:

COLORADO SPRINGS MANUFACTURING FACILITY
Overhead Performance Report
December 21 Preliminary Draft

Budgeted machine-hours.	100,000
Actual machine-hours	90,000

Overhead Costs	Cost Formula (per machine-hour)	Actual Costs for 90,000 Machine-Hours	Budget Based on 90,000 Machine-Hours	Spending or Budget Variance
Variable overhead costs:				
Power	$0.03	$ 2,840	$ 2,700	$ 140 U
Supplies.	0.86	79,060	77,400	1,660 U
Abrasives.	0.34	32,580	30,600	1,980 U
Total variable overhead cost	$1.23	114,480	110,700	3,780 U
Fixed overhead costs:				
Depreciation		228,300	226,500	1,800 U
Supervisory salaries		187,300	189,000	1,700 F
Insurance.		23,000	23,000	—
Industrial engineering		154,000	160,000	6,000 F
Factory building lease		46,000	46,000	—
Total fixed overhead cost		638,600	644,500	5,900 F
Total overhead cost.		$753,080	$755,200	$2,120 F

Tab Kapp, the general manager at the Colorado Springs facility, asked to see a copy of the preliminary draft report at 4:45 P.M. on December 23. Prating carried a copy of the report to Kapp's office where the following discussion took place:

Kapp: Ouch! Almost all of the variances on the report are unfavorable. The only thing that looks good at all are the favorable variances for supervisory salaries and for industrial engineering. How did we have an unfavorable variance for depreciation?

Prating: Do you remember that milling machine that broke down because the wrong lubricant was used by the machine operator?

Kapp: Only vaguely.

Prating: It turned out we couldn't fix it. We had to scrap the machine and buy a new one.

Kapp: This report doesn't look good. I was raked over the coals last year when we had just a few unfavorable variances.

Prating: I'm afraid the final report is going to look even worse.

Kapp: Oh?

Prating: The line item for industrial engineering on the report is for work we hired Sanchez Engineering to do for us on a contract basis. The original contract was for $160,000, but we asked them to do some additional work that was not in the contract. Under the terms of the contract, we have to reimburse Sanchez Engineering for the costs of the additional work. The $154,000 in actual costs that appear on the preliminary draft report reflects only their billings up through December 21. The last bill they had sent us was on November 28, and they completed the project just last week. Yesterday I got a call from Maria over at Sanchez and she said they would be sending us a final bill for the project before the end of the year. The total bill, including the reimbursements for the additional work, is going to be . . .

Kapp: I am not sure I want to hear this.

Prating: $176,000.

Kapp: Ouch! Ouch! Ouch!

Prating: The additional work we asked them to do added $16,000 to the cost of the project.

Kapp: No way can I turn in a performance report with an overall unfavorable variance. They'll kill me at corporate headquarters. Call up Maria at Sanchez and ask her not to send the bill until after the first of the year. We have to have that $6,000 favorable variance for industrial engineering on the performance report.

Required:

What should Lance Prating do? Explain.

CASE 11–27 Integrative Case; Working Backwards from Variance Data [LO3, LO5, LO6]

You have recently accepted a position with Bork Company, the manufacturer of an unusual product that is popular with some people. As part of your duties, you review the variances that are reported for each period and make a presentation on the variances to the company's executive committee.

Earlier this morning you received the variances for the most recent period. After reviewing the variances and organizing the data for your presentation, you accidentally placed the material on top of some papers that were going to the shredder. In the middle of lunch you suddenly realized your mistake and dashed from the executive lunchroom to the shredding room. There you found the operator busily feeding your pages through the machine. You managed to pull only part of one page from the feeding chute, which contains the following information:

Standard Cost Card—Per Unit

Direct materials, 2 yards at $16 per yard	$32.00
Direct labor, 3 direct labor-hours at $5 per direct labor-hour	15.00
Variable overhead, 3 direct labor-hours at $3 per direct labor-hour.	9.00
Fixed overhead, 3 direct labor-hours at $8 per direct labor-hour.	24.00
Standard cost per unit	$80.00

	Total Standard Cost*	Variances Reported: Price or Rate	Spending or Budget	Quantity or Efficiency	Volume
Direct materials	$608,000	$11,600 F		$32,000 U	
Direct labor	285,000	8,540 U		20,000 U	
Variable manufacturing overhead	171,000		$3,700 F	?†	
Fixed manufacturing overhead	456,000		1,500 F		$24,000 U

*Applied to Work in Process during the period.

†Entry obliterated by the shredder.

You recall that manufacturing overhead cost is applied to production on the basis of direct labor-hours and that all of the materials purchased during the period were used in production. Since the company uses JIT to control work flows, work in process inventories are insignificant and can be ignored.

At lunch your supervisor said how pleased she was with your work and that she was looking forward to your presentation that afternoon. You realize that to avoid looking like a bungling fool you must somehow generate the necessary "backup" data for the variances before the executive committee meeting starts in one hour.

Required:

1. How many units were produced last period? (You'll have to think a bit to derive this figure from the data.)
2. How many yards of direct materials were purchased and used in production?
3. What was the actual cost per yard of material?
4. How many actual direct labor-hours were worked during the period?
5. What was the actual rate per direct labor-hour?
6. How much actual variable manufacturing overhead cost was incurred during the period?
7. What is the total fixed manufacturing overhead cost in the company's flexible budget?
8. What were the denominator hours for last period?

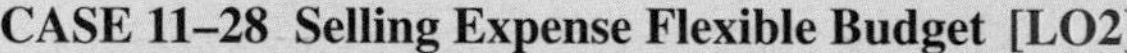

CASE 11–28 Selling Expense Flexible Budget [LO2]

Mark Fletcher, president of SoftGro Inc., was looking forward to seeing the performance reports for November because he knew the company's sales for the month had exceeded budget by a considerable margin. SoftGro, a distributor of educational software packages, had been growing steadily for approximately two years. Fletcher's biggest challenge at this point was to ensure that the company did not lose control of expenses during this growth period. When Fletcher received the November reports, he was dismayed to see the large unfavorable variance in the company's monthly selling expense report that is presented below:

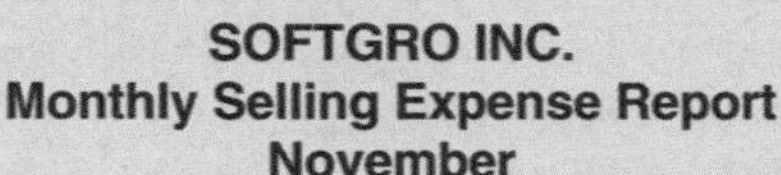

SOFTGRO INC.
Monthly Selling Expense Report
November

		November		
	Annual Budget	Budget	Actual	Variance
Unit sales	2,000,000	280,000	310,000	30,000 F
Dollar sales	$80,000,000	$11,200,000	$12,400,000	$1,200,000 F
Orders processed	54,000	6,500	5,800	700 U
Salespersons per month	90	90	96	6 U
Expenses:				
Advertising	$19,800,000	$ 1,650,000	$ 1,660,000	$ 10,000 U
Staff salaries	1,500,000	125,000	125,000	—
Sales salaries	1,296,000	108,000	115,400	7,400 U
Commissions	3,200,000	448,000	496,000	48,000 U
Per diem expense	1,782,000	148,500	162,600	14,100 U
Office expense	4,080,000	340,000	358,400	18,400 U
Shipping expense	6,750,000	902,500	976,500	74,000 U
Total expenses	$38,408,000	$ 3,722,000	$ 3,893,900	$ 171,900 U

Fletcher called in the company's new controller, Susan Porter, to discuss the implications of the variances reported for November and to plan a strategy for improving performance. Porter suggested that the reporting format that the company had been using might not be giving Fletcher a true picture of the company's operations and proposed that SoftGro implement flexible budgeting for reporting purposes. Porter offered to redo the monthly selling expense report for November using flexible budgeting so that Fletcher could compare the two reports and see the advantages of flexible budgeting.

After some analysis, Porter derived the following data about the company's selling expenses:

a. The total compensation paid to the sales force consists of both a monthly base salary and a commission. The commission varies with sales dollars.

b. Sales office expense is a mixed cost with the variable portion related to the number of orders processed. The fixed portion of office expense is $3,000,000 annually and is incurred uniformly throughout the year.
c. Subsequent to the adoption of the annual budget for the current year, SoftGro decided to open a new sales territory. As a consequence, approval was given to hire six additional salespersons effective November 1. Porter decided that these additional six people should be recognized in her revised report.
d. Per diem reimbursement to the sales force, while a fixed amount per day, is variable with the number of salespersons and the number of days spent traveling. SoftGro's original budget was based on an average sales force of 90 persons throughout the year with each salesperson traveling 15 days per month.
e. The company's shipping expense is a mixed cost with the variable portion, $3 per unit, dependent on the number of units sold. The fixed portion is incurred uniformly throughout the year.

Using the data above, Porter believed she would be able to redo the November report and present it to Fletcher for his review.

Required:
1. Describe the benefits of flexible budgeting, and explain why Susan Porter would propose that SoftGro use flexible budgeting in this situation.
2. Prepare a revised monthly selling expense report for November that would permit Mark Fletcher to more clearly evaluate SoftGro's control over selling expenses. The report should have a line for *each* selling expense item showing the appropriate budgeted amount, the actual selling expense, and the variance for November.

(CMA, adapted)

CASE 11–29 Comprehensive Variance Analysis; Incomplete Data [LO4, LO5, LO6]

Each of the cases below is independent. Each company uses a standard cost system and each company's flexible budget for manufacturing overhead is based on standard machine-hours.

	Company	
Item	**X**	**Y**
1. Denominator activity in machine-hours	18,000	?
2. Standard machine-hours allowed for units produced	?	28,000
3. Actual machine-hours worked	?	27,500
4. Flexible budget variable overhead per machine-hour	$ 1.60	$?
5. Flexible budget fixed overhead (total)	?	?
6. Actual variable overhead cost	30,000	55,275
7. Actual fixed overhead cost	72,500	134,600
8. Variable overhead cost applied to production*	31,200	?
9. Fixed overhead cost applied to production*	?	126,000
10. Variable overhead spending variance	?	?
11. Variable overhead efficiency variance	800 U	1,000 F
12. Fixed overhead budget variance	500 U	?
13. Fixed overhead volume variance	?	9,000 U
14. Variable portion of the predetermined overhead rate	?	?
15. Fixed portion of the predetermined overhead rate	?	?
16. Underapplied (or overapplied) overhead	?	?

*Based on standard machine-hours allowed for units produced.

Required:
Compute the unknown amounts. (Hint: One way to proceed would be to use the format for variance analysis found in Exhibit 11–7 for variable overhead and in Exhibit 11-10 for fixed overhead.)

Group and Internet Exercises

GROUP EXERCISE 11–30 Choice of Denominator Activity Level

American Widget, Inc., makes a number of high-volume standard products that are sold in highly competitive markets. As a result, its cost system stresses cost control. American uses a standard cost system and updates standards on a regular and timely basis. Until recently, expected annual capacity was the basis for determining predetermined factory overhead rates. This rate was used for internal planning and reporting and performance evaluation purposes, as well as for inventory valuation.

Recently, John Phillips, controller, has proposed changing the basis for internal planning and reporting from expected annual capacity to practical capacity. Since practical capacity remains relatively constant unless there is a plant expansion or purchase of new manufacturing machinery, Phillips believes this change would facilitate planning and budgeting.

Phillips has held one meeting with department managers and presented them with their new annual budgets prepared on the basis of the new, proposed practical capacity standard. There was little discussion. Later, a member of the cost accounting staff pointed out that the new standard for fixed manufacturing costs would be tighter than the old standard.

Required:

1. If the new annual budgets for American Widget reflect the implementation of tighter standards based on practical capacity:
   a. What negative behavioral implications for employees and department managers could occur as a result of this change?
   b. What could American Widget management do to reduce the negative behavioral effects?
2. Explain how tight cost standards within an organization could have positive behavioral effects.
3. Identify the individuals who should participate in setting standards and describe the benefits to an organization of their participation in the standard-setting process.

(CMA, adapted)

GROUP EXERCISE 11–31 Analyzing Your College's Budget

Obtain a copy of your college or university's budget and actual results for the most recently completed year.

Required:

1. Determine the major assumptions used in the last budget (e.g., number of students; tuition per student; number of employees; increases in wages, salaries, benefits; changes in occupancy costs; etc.).
2. Compare the budgeted revenue amounts with the actual results. Try to determine the reasons for any differences.
3. Compare budgeted expenses with the actual results using the basic approach shown in Exhibit 11–4. Try to determine the reasons for any differences.

INTERNET EXERCISE 11–32

As you know, the World Wide Web is a medium that is constantly evolving. Sites come and go, and change without notice. To enable periodic update of site addresses, this problem has been posted to the textbook website (www.mhhe.com/garrison10e). After accessing the site, enter the Student Center and select this chapter. Select and complete the Internet Exercise.

Chapter Twelve

Segment Reporting and Decentralization

After studying Chapter 12, you should be able to:

1. Prepare a segmented income statement using the contribution format, and explain the difference between traceable fixed costs and common fixed costs.

2. Compute return on investment (ROI) and show how changes in sales, expenses, and assets affect ROI.

3. Compute residual income and understand the strengths and weaknesses of this method of measuring performance.

4. (Appendix 12A) Determine the range, if any, within which a negotiated transfer price should fall.

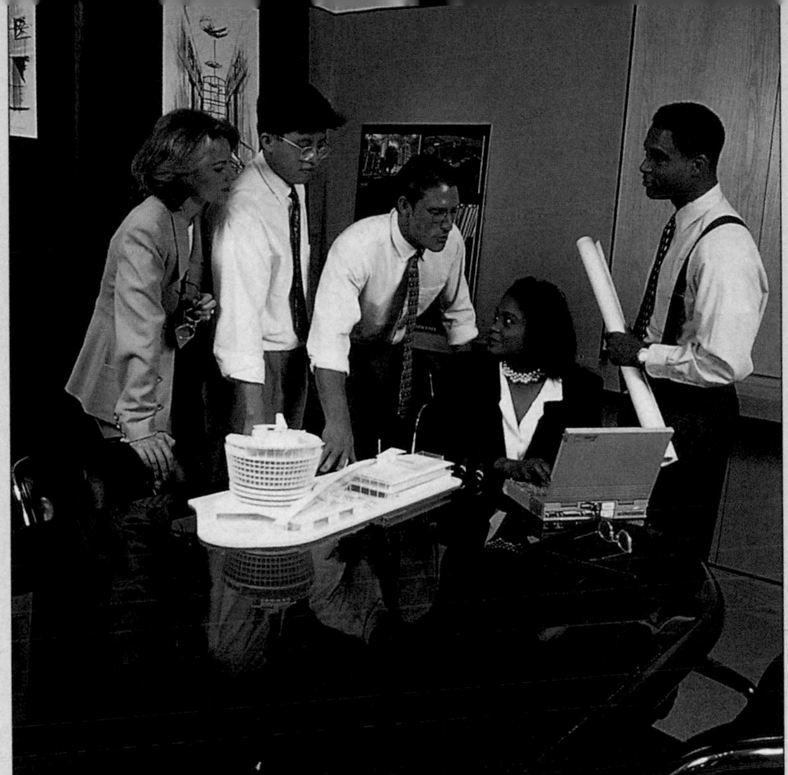

Tracing Changes the Picture

E & A Company (the name has been changed to conceal the company's true identity) provides a wide range of engineering and architectural consulting services to both government and industry. For many years, the company pooled all operating costs and allocated them to its three branch offices on the basis of labor cost. When it abandoned this practice and started tracing costs such as rent directly to the offices, while at the same time assigning other costs on a more appropriate basis, the reported profits of one branch office doubled, the reported profits of another branch office changed from a loss to a profit, and the reported profits of the third branch office changed from a profit to a loss.

Source: Beth M. Chaffman and John Talbott, "Activity-Based Costing in a Service Organization," *CMA* 64, no. 10, p. 18.

Once an organization grows beyond a few people, it becomes impossible for the top manager to make decisions about everything. For example, the CEO of the Hyatt Hotel chain cannot be expected to decide whether a particular hotel guest at the Hyatt Hotel on Maui should be allowed to check out later than the normal checkout time. To some degree, managers have to delegate decisions to those who are at lower levels in the organization. However, the degree to which decisions are delegated varies from organization to organization.

Decentralization in Organizations

A **decentralized organization** is one in which decision making is not confined to a few top executives but rather is spread throughout the organization, with managers at various levels making key operating decisions relating to their sphere of responsibility. Decentralization is a matter of degree, since all organizations are decentralized to some extent out of necessity. At one extreme, a strongly decentralized organization is one in which even the lowest-level managers and employees are empowered to make decisions. At the other extreme, in a strongly centralized organization, lower-level managers have little freedom to make a decision. Although most organizations fall somewhere between these two extremes, there is a pronounced trend toward more and more decentralization.

Advantages and Disadvantages of Decentralization

Decentralization has many benefits, including:

1. Top management is relieved of much day-to-day problem solving and is left free to concentrate on strategy, on higher-level decision making, and on coordinating activities.
2. Decentralization provides lower-level managers with vital experience in making decisions. Without such experience, they would be ill-prepared to make decisions when they are promoted into higher-level positions.
3. Added responsibility and decision-making authority often result in increased job satisfaction. Responsibility, and the authority that goes with it, makes the job more interesting and provides greater incentives for people to put out their best efforts.
4. Lower-level managers generally have more detailed and up-to-date information about local conditions than top managers. Therefore, the decisions of lower-level managers are often based on better information.
5. It is difficult to evaluate a manager's performance if the manager is not given much latitude in what he or she can do.

Decentralization has four major disadvantages:

1. Lower-level managers may make decisions without fully understanding the "big picture." While top-level managers typically have less detailed information about local operations than the lower-level managers, they usually have more information about the company as a whole and should have a better understanding of the company's strategy.
2. In a truly decentralized organization, there may be a lack of coordination among autonomous managers. This problem can be reduced by clearly defining the company's strategy and communicating it effectively throughout the organization.
3. Lower-level managers may have objectives that are different from the objectives of the entire organization. For example, some managers may be more interested in

increasing the sizes of their departments than in increasing the profits of the company.[1] To some degree, this problem can be overcome by designing performance evaluation systems that motivate managers to make decisions that are in the best interests of the company.

4. In a strongly decentralized organization, it may be more difficult to effectively spread innovative ideas. Someone in one part of the organization may have a terrific idea that would benefit other parts of the organization, but without strong central direction the idea may not be shared with, and adopted by, other parts of the organization.

Decentralization and Segment Reporting

Effective decentralization requires *segmental reporting*. In addition to the companywide income statement, reports are needed for individual segments of the organization. A **segment** is a part or activity of an organization about which managers would like cost, revenue, or profit data. Examples of segments include divisions of a company, sales territories, individual stores, service centers, manufacturing plants, marketing departments, individual customers, and product lines. A company's operations can be segmented in many ways. For example, a grocery store chain like Safeway or Kroger can segment its business by geographic region, by individual store, by the nature of the merchandise (i.e., green groceries, canned goods, paper goods), by brand name, and so on. In this chapter, we learn how to construct income statements for such business segments. These segmented income statements are useful in analyzing the profitability of segments and in measuring the performance of segment managers.

Cost, Profit, and Investment Centers

Decentralized companies typically categorize their business segments into cost centers, profit centers, and investment centers—depending on the responsibilities of the managers of the segments.[2]

Cost Center A **cost center** is a business segment whose manager has control over costs but not over revenue or investment funds. Service departments such as accounting, finance, general administration, legal, personnel, and so on, are usually considered to be cost centers. In addition, manufacturing facilities are often considered to be cost centers. The managers of cost centers are expected to minimize cost while providing the level of services or the amount of products demanded by the other parts of the organization. For example, the manager of a production facility would be evaluated at least in part by comparing actual costs to how much the costs should have been for the actual number of units produced during the period. Standard cost variances and flexible budget variances, such

1 There is a similar problem with top-level managers as well. The shareholders of the company have, in effect, decentralized it by delegating their decision-making authority to the top managers. Unfortunately, top managers may abuse that trust by spending too much company money on palatial offices, rewarding themselves and their friends too generously, and so on. The issue of how to ensure that top managers act in the best interests of the owners of the company continues to puzzle experts. To a large extent, the owners rely on performance evaluation using return on investment and residual income measures as discussed later in the chapter and on bonuses and stock options. The stock market is also an important disciplining mechanism. If top managers squander the company's resources, the price of the company's stock will almost surely fall—resulting in a loss of prestige, bonuses, and possibly a job.

2 Some companies classify business segments that are responsible mainly for generating revenue, such as an insurance sales office, as *revenue centers.* Other companies would consider this to be just another type of profit center, since costs of some kind (salaries, rent, utilities) are usually deducted from the revenues in the segment's income statement.

as those discussed in Chapters 10 and 11, are often used to evaluate the performance of cost centers.

Profit Center In contrast to a cost center, a **profit center** is any business segment whose manager has control over both cost and revenue. Like a cost center, however, a profit center generally does not have control over investment funds. For example, the manager in charge of one of the Six Flags amusement parks would be responsible for both the revenues and costs, and hence the profits, of the amusement park but may not have control over major investments in the park. Profit center managers are often evaluated by comparing actual profit to targeted or budgeted profit. Segmented income statements, such as those developed in this chapter, should be used to evaluate profit center managers.

In Business

Meeting Targets the Wrong Way

Putting too much emphasis on meeting financial targets can lead to undesirable behavior. Michael C. Jensen reports "I once watched the management of a manufacturing company struggle to reach their year-end targets. In late fall, they announced a price increase of 10% effective January 2. Now it may be that a price increase was needed, but it was not in line with the competition, nor was it likely that January 2, of all dates, was the best time for the increase. A price increase on January 2, would, however, cause customers to order before year-end and thereby help managers reach their targets." The short-term boost in sales comes at the cost of lost future sales and possible customer ill will.

Source: Michael C. Jensen, "Why Pay People to Lie?" *The Wall Street Journal*, January 8, 2001, p. A32.

In Business

Putting Too Much Pressure on Meeting Targets

Business Week reports that the CEO of Tyco International, Ltd., puts unrelenting pressure on his managers to deliver growth. "Each year, [the CEO] sets targets for how much each manager must increase his or her unit's earnings in the coming year. The targets are coupled with a powerful incentive system. If they meet or exceed these targets, managers are promised a bonus that can be many times their salary. But if they fall even a bit short, the bonus plummets." This sounds good, but "to many accounting experts, the sort of all-or-nothing bonus structure set up at Tyco is a warning light. If top executives set profit targets too high or turn a blind eye to how managers achieve them, the incentives for managers to cut corners is enormous. Indeed, a blue-ribbon panel of accounting experts who were trying to improve corporate auditing standards several years ago in the wake of such well-known corporate failures as Phar-Mor and Leslie Fay identified just such extreme incentives as a red flag. 'If you're right under the target, there's a tremendous economic interest to accelerate earnings," says David F. Larcker, a professor of accounting at the Wharton School. 'If you're right over it, there is an incentive to push earnings into the next period.'"

Source: William C. Symonds, Diane Brady, Geoffrey Smith, and Lorraine Woellert, "Tyco: Aggressive or Out of Line?" *Business Week*, November 1, 1999, pp. 160–165.

Investment Center An **investment center** is any segment of an organization whose manager has control over cost, revenue, and investments in operating assets. For example, the vice president of the Truck Division at General Motors would have a great deal of discretion over investments in the division. The vice president of the Truck Division would be responsible for initiating investment proposals, such as funding research into more fuel-efficient engines for sport-utility vehicles. Once the proposal has been approved by the top level of managers at General Motors and the board of directors, the vice president of the Truck Division would then be responsible for making sure that the investment pays off. Investment center managers are usually evaluated using return on investment or residual income measures as discussed later in the chapter.

Insuring the Bottom Line

In Business

S

Insurance companies have begun to offer managers a radical way to avoid some of the risk of having to report bad financial results. For example, the Reliance Group has created a product called Enterprise Earnings Protection Insurance that covers any operating earnings shortfall due to events beyond management's control. If a company buys an insurance policy guaranteeing $5 million in profits, but it posted only a $3 million profit, then Reliance would have to make up the difference of $2 million. Reliance reports that a company may have to pay as little as 5% of its estimated profit to ensure against a 20% shortfall.

Source: Diane Brady, "Is Your Bottom Line Covered?" *Business Week*, February 8, 1999, pp. 85–86.

Responsibility Centers

LEARNING OBJECTIVE 1
Prepare a segmented income statement using the contribution format, and explain the difference between traceable fixed costs and common fixed costs.

Responsibility center is broadly defined as any part of an organization whose manager has control over cost, revenue, or investment funds. Cost centers, profit centers, and investment centers are *all* known as responsibility centers.

A partial organization chart for Superior Foods Corporation, a company in the snack food and beverage industry, appears in Exhibit 12–1. This partial organization chart indicates how the various business segments of the company are classified in terms of responsibility. Note that the departments and work centers that do not generate significant revenues by themselves are classified as cost centers. These are staff departments such as finance, legal, and personnel, and operating units such as the bottling plant, warehouse, and beverage distribution center. The profit centers are business segments that generate revenues and include the beverage, salty snacks, and confections product segments. The vice president of operations oversees allocation of investment funds across the product segments and is responsible for revenues and costs and so is treated as an investment center. And finally, corporate headquarters is an investment center, since it is responsible for all revenues, costs, and investments.

Segment Reporting and Profitability Analysis

A different kind of income statement is required for evaluating the performance of a profit or investment center—one that emphasizes segments rather than the performance of the company as a whole. This point is illustrated in the following discussion.

Managerial Accounting in Action

The Issue

SoftSolutions, Inc., is a rapidly growing computer software company founded by Lori Saffer, who had previously worked in a large software company, and Marjorie Matsuo, who had previously worked in the hotel industry as a general manager. They formed the company to develop and market user-friendly accounting and operations software designed specifically for hotels. They quit their jobs, pooled their savings, hired several programmers, and got down to work.

The first sale was by far the most difficult. No hotel wanted to be the first to use an untested product from an unknown company. After overcoming this obstacle with persistence, good luck, dedication to customer service, and a very low introductory price, the company's sales burgeoned.

The company quickly developed similar business software for other specialized markets and then branched out into clip art and computer games. Within four years of its

Exhibit 12–1 Business Segments Classified as Cost, Profit, and Investment Centers

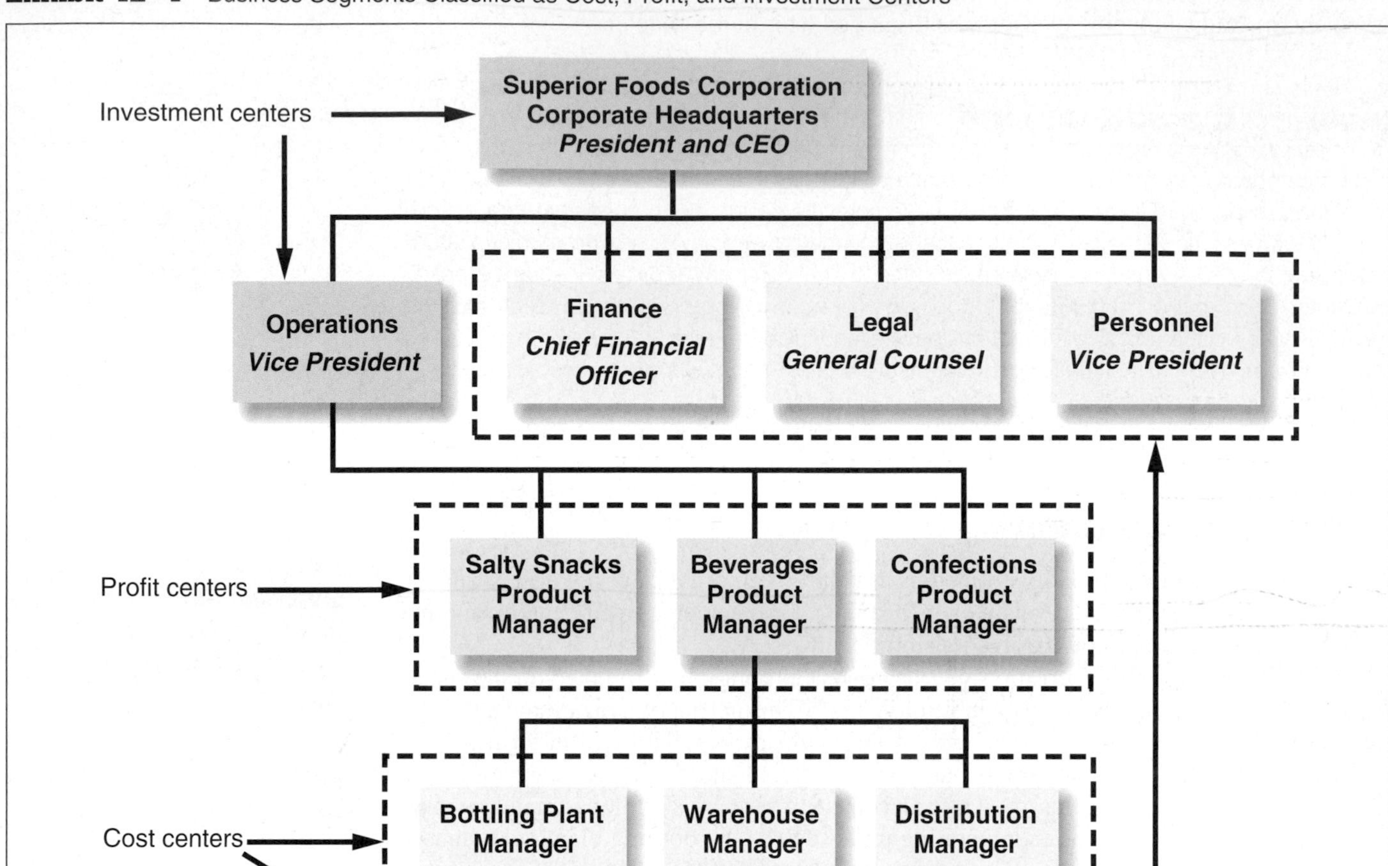

founding, the organization had grown to the point where Saffer and Matsuo were no longer able to personally direct all of the company's activities. Decentralization had become a necessity.

Accordingly, the company was split into two divisions—Business Products and Consumer Products. By mutual consent, Matsuo took the title president and Saffer took the title vice president of the Business Products Division. Chris Worden, a programmer who had spearheaded the drive into the clip art and computer games markets, was designated vice president of the Consumer Products Division.

Almost immediately, the issue arose of how best to evaluate the performance of the divisions. Matsuo called a meeting to consider this issue and asked Saffer, Worden, and the controller, Bill Carson, to attend. The following discussion took place at that meeting:

Marjorie Matsuo: We need to find a better way to measure the performance of the divisions.

Chris Worden: I agree. Consumer Products has been setting the pace in this company for the last two years, and we should be getting more recognition.

Lori Saffer: Chris, we are delighted with the success of the Consumer Products Division.

Chris Worden: I know. But it is hard to figure out just how successful we are with the present accounting reports. All we have are sales and cost of goods sold figures for the division.

Bill Carson: What's the matter with those figures? They are prepared using generally accepted accounting principles.

Chris Worden: The sales figures are fine. However, cost of goods sold includes some costs that really aren't the costs of our division, and it excludes some costs that are. Let's take a simple example. Everything we sell in the Consumer Products Division has to pass through the automatic bar-coding machine, which applies a unique bar code to the product.

Lori Saffer: We know. Every item we ship must have a unique identifying bar code. That's true for items from the Business Products Division as well as for items from the Consumer Products Division.

Chris Worden: That's precisely the point. Whether an item comes from the Business Products Division or the Consumer Products Division, it must pass through the automatic bar-coding machine after the software has been packaged. How much of the cost of the automatic bar coder would be saved if we didn't have any consumer products?

Marjorie Matsuo: Since we have only one automatic bar coder and we would need it anyway to code the business products, I guess none of the cost would be saved.

Chris Worden: That's right. And since none of the cost could be saved even if the entire Consumer Products Division were eliminated, how can we logically say that some of the cost of the automatic bar coder is a cost of the Consumer Products Division?

Lori Saffer: Just a minute, Chris, are you saying that my Business Products Division should be charged with the entire cost of the automatic bar coder?

Chris Worden: No, that's not what I am saying.

Marjorie Matsuo: But Chris, I don't see how we can have sensible performance reports without making someone responsible for costs like the cost of the automatic bar coder. Bill, as our accounting expert, what do you think?

Bill Carson: I have some ideas for handling issues like the automatic bar coder. The best approach would probably be for me to put together a draft performance report. We can discuss it at the next meeting when everyone has something concrete to look at.

Marjorie Matsuo: Okay, let's see what you come up with.

Bill Carson, the controller of SoftSolutions, realized that segmented income statements would be required to more appropriately evaluate the performance of the two divisions. To construct the segmented reports, he would have to carefully segregate costs that are attributable to the segments from costs that are not. Since most of the disputes over costs would be about fixed costs such as the automatic bar-coding machine, he knew he would also have to separate fixed from variable costs. Under the conventional absorption costing income statement prepared for the entire company, variable and fixed production costs were being commingled in the cost of goods sold.

Largely for these reasons, Bill Carson decided to use the contribution format income statement discussed in earlier chapters. Recall that when the contribution format is used: (1) the cost of goods sold consists only of the variable manufacturing costs; (2) variable and fixed costs are listed in separate sections; and (3) a contribution margin is computed. When such a statement is segmented as in this chapter, fixed costs are broken down further into what are called traceable and common costs as discussed later. This breakdown allows a *segment margin* to be computed for each segment of the company. The segment margin is a valuable tool for assessing the long-run profitability of a segment and is also a much better tool for evaluating performance than the usual absorption costing reports.

Levels of Segmented Statements

A portion of the segmented report Bill Carson prepared is shown in Exhibit 12–2. The contribution format income statement for the entire company appears at the very top of the exhibit under the column labeled Total Company. Immediately to the right of this column are two columns—one for each of the two divisions. We can see that the divisional segment margin is $60,000 for the Business Products Division and $40,000 for the Consumer Products Division. This is the portion of the report that was specifically requested by the company's divisional managers. They wanted to know how much each of their divisions was contributing to the company's profits.

Exhibit 12–2

SoftSolutions, Inc.—Segmented Income Statements in the Contribution Format

Segments Defined as Divisions

		Divisions	
	Total Company	Business Products Division	Consumer Products Division
Sales	$500,000	$300,000	$200,000
Less variable expenses:			
Variable cost of goods sold	180,000	120,000	60,000
Other variable expenses	50,000	30,000	20,000
Total variable expenses	230,000	150,000	80,000
Contribution margin	270,000	150,000	120,000
Less traceable fixed expenses	170,000	90,000	80,000*
Divisional segment margin	100,000	$ 60,000	$ 40,000
Less common fixed expenses not traceable to the individual divisions	85,000		
Net operating income	$ 15,000		

Segments Defined as Product Lines of the Consumer Products Division

		Product Line	
	Consumer Products Division	Clip Art	Computer Games
Sales	$200,000	$ 75,000	$125,000
Less variable expenses:			
Variable cost of goods sold	60,000	20,000	40,000
Other variable expenses	20,000	5,000	15,000
Total variable expenses	80,000	25,000	55,000
Contribution margin	120,000	50,000	70,000
Less traceable fixed expenses	70,000	30,000	40,000
Product-line segment margin	50,000	$ 20,000	$ 30,000
Less common fixed expenses not traceable to the individual product lines	10,000		
Divisional segment margin	$ 40,000		

Segments Defined as Sales Channels for One Product Line, Computer Games, of the Consumer Products Division

		Sales Channels	
	Computer Games	Retail Stores	Catalog Sales
Sales	$125,000	$100,000	$ 25,000
Less variable expenses:			
Variable cost of goods sold	40,000	32,000	8,000
Other variable expenses	15,000	5,000	10,000
Total variable expenses	55,000	37,000	18,000
Contribution margin	70,000	63,000	7,000
Less traceable fixed expenses	25,000	15,000	10,000
Sales-channel segment margin	45,000	$ 48,000	$ (3,000)
Less common fixed expenses not traceable to the individual sales channels	15,000		
Product-line segment margin	$ 30,000		

*Notice that this $80,000 in traceable fixed expense is divided into two parts when the Consumer Products Division is broken down into product lines—$70,000 traceable and $10,000 common. The reasons for this are discussed later in the section "Traceable Costs Can Become Common Costs."

However, segmented income statements can be prepared for activities at many levels in a company. To provide more information to the company's divisional managers, Bill Carson has further segmented the divisions according to their major product lines. In the case of the Consumer Products Division, the product lines are clip art and computer games. Going even further, Bill Carson has segmented each of the product lines according to how they are sold—in retail computer stores or by catalog sales. In Exhibit 12–2, this further segmentation is illustrated for the computer games product line. Notice that as we go from one segmented statement to another, we look at smaller and smaller pieces of the company. While not shown in Exhibit 12–2, Bill Carson also prepared segmented income statements for the major product lines in the Business Products Division.

Substantial benefits are received from a series of statements such as those contained in Exhibit 12–2. By carefully examining trends and results in each segment, a manager is able to gain considerable insight into the company's operations viewed from many different angles. And advanced computer-based information systems are making it easier and easier to construct such statements and to keep them continuously current.

Putting Segments on Trial

In Business

Segment margins should be regularly examined. Management guru Peter F. Drucker urges managers to "put every product, every service, every process, every market, every distribution channel, every customer, and every end use on trial for its life. And the change leader does so on a regular schedule. The question . . . is 'If we did not do this already, would we, knowing what we now know, go into it?'"

Source: Peter F. Drucker, "Change Leaders," *Inc.*, June 1999, p. 66.

Sales and Contribution Margin

To prepare an income statement for a particular segment, variable expenses are deducted from sales to yield the contribution margin for the segment. It is important to keep in mind that the contribution margin tells us what happens to profits as volume changes—holding a segment's capacity and fixed costs constant. The contribution margin is especially useful in decisions involving temporary uses of capacity such as special orders. Decisions concerning the most effective uses of existing capacity often involve only variable costs and revenues, which of course are the very elements involved in contribution margin. Such decisions will be discussed in detail in Chapter 13.

Traceable and Common Fixed Costs

The most puzzling aspect of Exhibit 12–2 is probably the treatment of fixed costs. The report has two kinds of fixed costs—traceable and common. Only the *traceable fixed costs* are charged to the segments in the segmented income statements in the report. If a cost is not traceable to a segment, then it is not assigned to the segment.

A **traceable fixed cost** of a segment is a fixed cost that is incurred because of the existence of the segment—if the segment had never existed, the fixed cost would not have been incurred; and if the segment were eliminated, the fixed cost would disappear. Examples of traceable fixed costs include the following:

- The salary of the Fritos product manager at PepsiCo is a *traceable* fixed cost of the Fritos business segment of PepsiCo.
- The maintenance cost for the building in which Boeing 747s are assembled is a *traceable* fixed cost of the 747 business segment of Boeing.
- The liability insurance at Disney World is a *traceable* fixed cost of the Disney World business segment of the Disney Corporation.

A **common fixed cost** is a fixed cost that supports the operations of more than one segment, but is not traceable in whole or in part to any one segment. Even if a segment were entirely eliminated, there would be no change in a true common fixed cost. For example:

- The salary of the CEO of General Motors is a *common* fixed cost of the various divisions of General Motors.
- The cost of lighting and heating a Safeway or Kroger grocery store is a *common* fixed cost of the various departments—groceries, produce, bakery, meat, etc.—in the store.
- The cost of the automatic bar-coding machine at SoftSolutions is a *common* fixed cost of the Consumer Products Division and of the Business Products Division.
- The cost of the receptionist's salary at an office shared by a number of doctors is a *common* fixed cost of the doctors. The cost is traceable to the office, but not to any one of the doctors individually.

Identifying Traceable Fixed Costs The distinction between traceable and common fixed costs is crucial in segment reporting, since traceable fixed costs are charged to the segments, whereas common fixed costs should not be charged to segments. In an actual situation, it is sometimes hard to determine whether a cost should be classified as traceable or common.

The general guideline is to treat as traceable costs *only those costs that would disappear over time if the segment itself disappeared.* For example, if the Consumer Products Division were sold or discontinued, it would no longer be necessary to pay the division manager's salary. Therefore the division manager's salary should be classified as a traceable fixed cost of the division. On the other hand, the president of the company undoubtedly would continue to be paid even if the Consumer Products Division were dropped. In fact, he or she might even be paid more if dropping the division was a good idea. Therefore, the president's salary is common to both divisions and should not be charged to either division.

Activity-Based Costing Some costs are easy to identify as traceable costs. For example, the costs of advertising Crest toothpaste on television are clearly traceable to Crest. A more difficult situation arises when a building, machine, or other resource is shared by two or more segments. For example, assume that a multiproduct company leases warehouse space that is used for storing the full range of its products. Would the lease cost of the warehouse be a traceable or a common cost of the products? Managers familiar with activity-based costing might argue that the lease cost is traceable and should be assigned to the products according to how much space the products use in the warehouse. In like manner, these managers would argue that order processing costs, sales support costs, and other selling, general, and administrative (SG&A) expenses should also be charged to segments according to the segments' consumption of SG&A resources.

To illustrate, consider Holt Corporation, a company that manufactures concrete pipe for industrial uses. The company has three products—9-inch pipe, 12-inch pipe, and 18-inch pipe. Space is leased in a large warehouse on a yearly basis as needed. The lease cost of this space is $4 per square foot per year. The 9-inch pipe occupies 1,000 square feet of space, the 12-inch pipe occupies 4,000 square feet, and the 18-inch pipe occupies 5,000 square feet. The company also has an order processing department that incurred $150,000 in order processing costs last year. Management believes that order processing costs are driven by the number of orders placed by customers in a year. Last year 2,500 orders were placed, of which 1,200 were for 9-inch pipe, 800 were for 12-inch pipe, and 500 were for 18-inch pipe. Given these data, the following costs would be assigned to each product using the activity-based costing approach:

Warehouse space cost:	
9-inch pipe: $4 per square foot × 1,000 square feet	$ 4,000
12-inch pipe: $4 per square foot × 4,000 square feet	16,000
18-inch pipe: $4 per square foot × 5,000 square feet	20,000
Total cost assigned	$ 40,000

Order processing costs:	
$150,000 ÷ 2,500 orders = $60 per order	
9-inch pipe: $60 per order × 1,200 orders	$ 72,000
12-inch pipe: $60 per order × 800 orders	48,000
18-inch pipe: $60 per order × 500 orders	30,000
Total cost assigned	$150,000

This method of assigning costs combines the strength of activity-based costing with the power of the contribution approach and greatly enhances the manager's ability to measure the profitability and performance of segments. However, managers must still ask themselves if the costs would in fact disappear over time if the segment itself disappeared. In the case of Holt Corporation, it is clear that the $20,000 in warehousing costs for the 18-inch pipe would be eliminated if 18-inch pipes were no longer being produced. The company would simply rent less warehouse space the following year. However, suppose the company owns the warehouse. Then it is not so clear that $20,000 of the cost of the warehouse would really disappear if the 18-inch pipes were discontinued as a product. The company might be able to sublease the space, or use it for other products, but then again the space might simply be empty while the costs of the warehouse continue to be incurred.

In assigning costs to segments, the key point is to resist the temptation to allocate costs (such as depreciation of corporate facilities) that are clearly common and that will continue regardless of whether the segment exists or not. *Any allocation of common costs to segments will reduce the value of the segment margin as a guide to long-run segment profitability and segment performance.* This point will be discussed at length later in the chapter.

Traceable Costs Can Become Common Costs

Fixed costs that are traceable to one segment may be a common cost of another segment. For example, an airline might want a segmented income statement that shows the segment margin for a particular flight from Los Angeles to Paris further broken down into first-class, business-class, and economy-class segment margins. The airline must pay a substantial landing fee at Charles DeGaulle airport in Paris. This fixed landing fee is a traceable cost of the flight, but it is a common cost of the first-class, business-class, and economy-class segments. Even if the first-class cabin is empty, the entire landing fee must be paid. So the landing fee is not a traceable cost of the first-class cabin. But on the other hand, paying the fee is necessary in order to have any first-class, business-class, or economy-class passengers. So the landing fee is a common cost of these three classes.

The dual nature of some of the fixed costs can be seen in Exhibit 12–3. Notice from the diagram that when segments are defined as divisions, the Consumer Products Division has $80,000 in traceable fixed expenses. However, when we drill down to the product lines, only $70,000 of the $80,000 cost that was traceable to the Consumer Products Division is traceable to the product lines. Notice that the other $10,000 then becomes a common cost of the two product lines of the Consumer Products Division.

Why would $10,000 of traceable fixed cost become a common cost when the division is divided into product lines? The $10,000 is the monthly salary of the manager of the Consumer Products Division. This salary is a traceable cost of the division as a whole, but it is a common cost of the division's product lines. The manager's salary is a necessary cost of having the two product lines, but even if one of the product lines were discontinued entirely, the manager's salary would probably not be cut. Therefore, none of the manager's salary can really be traced to the individual products.

The $70,000 traceable fixed cost of the product lines consists of the costs of product-specific advertising. A total of $30,000 was spent on advertising clip art and $40,000 was spent on advertising computer games. These costs can clearly be traced to the individual product lines.

Exhibit 12–3
Reclassification of Traceable Fixed Expenses from Exhibit 12–2

		Segment	
	Total Company	Business Products Division	Consumer Products Division
Contribution margin.	$270,000	$150,000	$120,000
Less traceable fixed expenses	170,000	90,000	80,000

		Segment	
	Consumer Products Division	Clip Art	Computer Games
Contribution margin.	$120,000	$50,000	$70,000
Less traceable fixed expenses	70,000	30,000	40,000
Product-line segment margin	50,000	$20,000	$30,000
Less common fixed expenses.	10,000		
Divisional segment margin	$ 40,000		

Segment Margin

Observe from Exhibit 12–2 that the **segment margin** is obtained by deducting the traceable fixed costs of a segment from the segment's contribution margin. It represents the margin available after a segment has covered all of its own costs. *The segment margin is the best gauge of the long-run profitability of a segment,* since it includes only those costs that are caused by the segment. If a segment can't cover its own costs, then that segment probably should not be retained (unless it has important side effects on other segments). Notice from Exhibit 12–2, for example, that Catalog Sales has a negative segment margin. This means that the segment is not covering its own costs; it is generating more costs than it collects in revenue. Retention or elimination of product lines and other segments is covered in more depth in Chapter 13.

From a decision-making point of view, the segment margin is most useful in major decisions that affect capacity such as dropping a segment. By contrast, as we noted earlier, the contribution margin is most useful in decisions relating to short-run changes in volume, such as pricing special orders that involve utilization of existing capacity.

In Business

Segment Information Makes Profits Rise

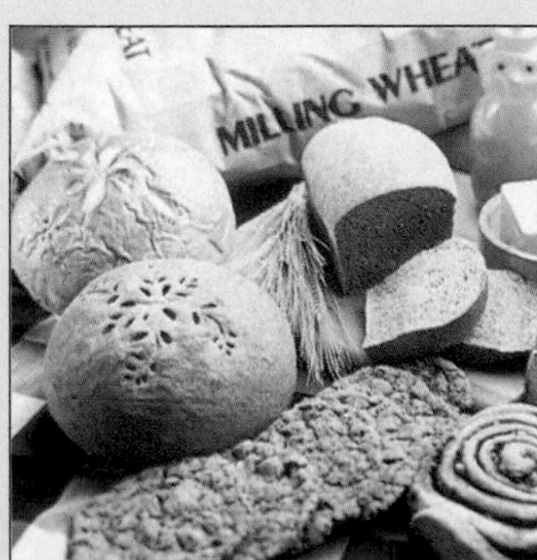

Great Harvest bakeries use freshly milled Montana whole wheat to make soft-crust specialty breads. The company was founded by Pete and Laura Wakeman and is headquartered in Dillon, Montana. Great Harvest encourages each of its over 100 franchised bakeries to experiment with new approaches to business management, customer service, and marketing and uses several methods to spread the best innovations throughout the system. Staffers at the headquarters in Dillon "provide franchisees with a **top 10 list** of the 10 best-performing bakeries in 14 statistical and financial categories. . . . Got a problem controlling labor expenses at your store? Call up the bakery owners who've got that figured out and get their advice." In addition, bakery owners who join the Numbers Club agree to open their books to the other owners in the club. "Franchisees can spot other owners whose situations might be similar to theirs (same size bakery and market, say, or the same level of owner's labor)—and who appear to have found better solutions to problems. They can identify the perfectly useful peer—and call him or her up."

Source: Michael Hopkins, "Zen and the Art of the Self-Managing Company," *Inc.*, November 2000, pp. 54–63.

Daily Segment Feedback Fuels Innovation

In Business

Steve Briley, the department manager of Cracking Plant 3B at Texas Eastman Company's chemical plant in Longview, Texas, created an innovative daily performance report to help guide his department. Instead of relying on rules and orders to run operations, Briley turned his department into a minicompany called the "Threebee Company" and made his employees the "owners"—complete with official-looking stock certificates. An income statement for the company was issued at the beginning of each day to the owners. The daily income statement assigned revenues to the output of the previous day and costs to the inputs used in the department that day. Briley promised that he would reward the department with a new kitchen if the daily profit hit an ambitious goal after 90 days. This approach was very successful—for a variety of reasons. First, the daily income statement provided rapid, easily understood feedback to the workers in the department. If they did something that increased—or decreased—profit such as changing operating temperatures, they would know the next day. Second, this approach empowered employees to make decisions quickly in response to changes in the operating environment. For example, if a critical machine broke down, workers now knew the lost output would have a tremendous impact on profits and would take immediate steps to get the machine working. Third, the daily income statement helped employees make trade-offs and set priorities. After some experience with the income statement, they realized what problems were important in terms of their impact on profits.

Source: Robert S. Kaplan and Robin Cooper, *Cost & Effect: Using Integrated Cost Systems to Drive Profitability and Performance*, Harvard Business School Press, 1998, pp. 64–71.

Managerial Accounting in Action

The Wrap-Up

Shortly after Bill Carson, the SoftSolutions, Inc., controller, completed the draft segmented income statement, he sent copies to the other managers and scheduled a meeting in which the report could be explained. The meeting was held on the Monday following the first meeting; and Marjorie Matsuo, Lori Saffer, and Chris Worden were all in attendance.

Lori Saffer: I think these segmented income statements are fairly self-explanatory. However, there is one thing I wonder about.

Bill Carson: What's that?

Lori Saffer: What is this common fixed expense of $85,000 listed under the total company? And who is going to be responsible for it if neither Chris nor I have responsibility?

Bill Carson: The $85,000 of common fixed expenses represents expenses like general administrative salaries and the costs of common production equipment such as the automatic bar-coding machine. Marjorie, do you want to respond to the question about responsibility for these expenses?

Marjorie Matsuo: Sure. Since I'm the president of the company, I'm responsible for those costs. Some things can be delegated, others cannot be. It wouldn't make any sense for either you or Chris to make decisions about the bar coder, since it affects both of you. That's an important part of my job—making decisions about resources that affect all parts of the organization. This report makes it much clearer who is responsible for what. I like it.

Chris Worden: So do I—my division's segment margin is higher than the net operating income for the entire company.

Marjorie Matsuo: Don't get carried away, Chris. Let's not misinterpret what this report means. The segment margins *have* to be big to cover the common costs of the company. We can't let the big segment margins lull us into a sense of complacency. If we use these reports, we all have to agree that our objective is to increase all of the segment margins over time.

Lori Saffer: I'm willing to give it a try.

Chris Worden: The reports make sense to me.

Marjorie Matsuo: So be it. Then the first item of business would appear to be a review of catalog sales of computer games, where we appear to be losing money. Chris, could you brief us on this at our next meeting?

Chris Worden: I'd be happy to. I have been suspecting for some time that our catalog sales strategy could be improved.

Marjorie Matsuo: We look forward to hearing your analysis. Meeting's adjourned.

There Is More Than One Way to Segment a Company

SoftSolutions segmented its sales by division, by product line within each division, and by sales channel. An organization can be segmented in many ways. For example, two different ways of segmenting the sales of the General Electric Company are displayed in Exhibit 12–4. In the first diagram, the company's sales are segmented by geographic region.

Exhibit 12–4 General Electric Company's Revenues Segmented by Geographic Region and Products

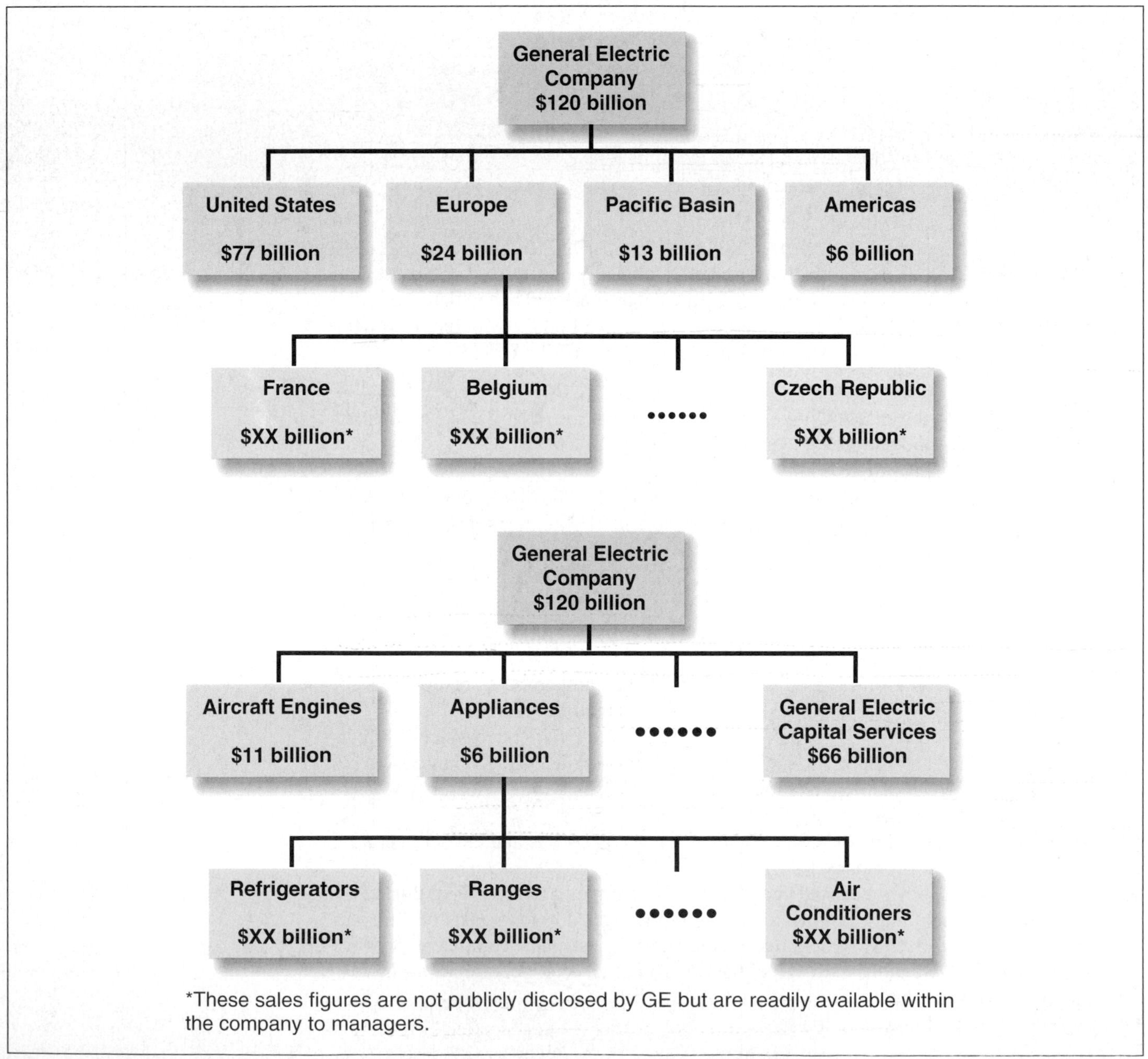

*These sales figures are not publicly disclosed by GE but are readily available within the company to managers.

In the second diagram, they are segmented by products. Note that each of the diagrams could be continued, providing progressively more detailed segment data. For example, the sales in France could be broken down by major product line, then by product. Similar breakdowns could be done of General Electric's costs and segment margins, although that would require substantial additional analytical work to identify the segments to which various costs should be assigned.

Segment breakdowns such as those shown in Exhibit 12–4 give a company's managers the ability to look at the company from many different directions. With the increasing availability of companywide databases and sophisticated management information system software, detailed segmental reports of revenues, costs, and margins are becoming much easier to do.

What's in a Segment?

In Business

S

In 1995, Continental Airlines could figure out the profitability of a specific route on a monthly basis—for example, Houston to Los Angeles—but management did not know the profitability of a particular flight on that route. The company's new Chief Financial Officer (CFO), Larry Kellner, placed top priority on developing a flight profitability system (FPS) that would break out the profit (or loss) for each individual flight. Once completed, the FPS revealed such money-losing flights as two December flights that left Houston for London within a four-hour period with only about 30 passengers each. "If those flights are blurred in with the whole month of December, they just don't jump off the page," says Kellner. With the data on the profitability of individual flights, Continental was able to design more appropriate schedules.

Source: Tim Reason, "Making Continental Airlines' Turnaround Permanent Meant Installing Some High-Flying IT Systems," *CFO*, October 2000, pp. 61–64.

Segmented Financial Information on External Reports

The Financial Accounting Standards Board (FASB) now requires that companies in the United States include segmented financial and other data in their annual reports and that the segmented reports prepared for external users *must use the same methods and definitions that the companies use in internal segmented reports that are prepared to aid in making operating decisions.* This is a very unusual requirement. Companies are not ordinarily required to report the same data to external users that are reported internally for decision-making purposes. This may seem like a reasonable requirement for the FASB to make, but it has some serious drawbacks. First, segmented data are often highly sensitive and companies are reluctant to release such data to the public for the simple reason that their competitors will then have access to the data. Second, companies must reconcile their segmented financial statements, which need not be prepared under GAAP, to their consolidated financial statements, which must be prepared under GAAP. It is important to realize that the segmented income statement illustrated in this chapter does not conform to GAAP. For example, statements prepared in accordance with GAAP do not distinguish between fixed and variable costs and between traceable and common costs. To avoid the complications of the reconciliation between non-GAAP segment earnings and GAAP consolidated earnings, it is likely that at least some managers will choose to construct their segmented financial statements so as to be within GAAP. This will result in more occurrences of the problems discussed in the following section.

Hindrances to Proper Cost Assignment

For segment reporting to accomplish its intended purposes, costs must be properly assigned to segments. If the purpose is to determine the profits being generated by a particular division, then all of the costs attributable to that division—and only those

Exhibit 12–5 Business Functions Making Up the Value Chain

Research and Development	Product Design	Manufacturing	Marketing	Distribution	Customer Service

costs—should be assigned to it. Unfortunately, three practices greatly hinder proper cost assignment: (1) omission of some costs in the assignment process, (2) the use of inappropriate methods for allocating costs among segments of a company, and (3) the assignment of costs to segments when they are really common costs.

Omission of Costs

The costs assigned to a segment should include all costs attributable to that segment from the company's entire *value chain.* The **value chain,** which is illustrated in Exhibit 12–5, consists of the major business functions that add value to a company's products and services. All of these functions, from research and development, through product design, manufacturing, marketing, distribution, and customer service, are required to bring a product or service to the customer and generate revenues.

However, as discussed in Chapters 2, 3, and 7, only manufacturing costs are included in product costs for financial reporting purposes. Consequently, when trying to determine product profitability for internal decision-making purposes, some companies deduct only manufacturing costs from product revenues. As a result, such companies omit from their profitability analysis part or all of the "upstream" costs in the value chain, which consist of research and development and product design, and the "downstream" costs, which consist of marketing, distribution, and customer service. Yet these nonmanufacturing costs are just as essential in determining product profitability as are the manufacturing costs. These upstream and downstream costs, which are usually titled *Selling, General, and Administrative (SG&A)* on the income statement, can represent half or more of the total costs of an organization. If either the upstream or downstream costs are omitted in profitability analysis, then the product is undercosted and management may unwittingly develop and maintain products that in the long run result in losses rather than profits for the company.

Inappropriate Methods for Allocating Costs among Segments

Cross-subsidization, or cost distortion, occurs when costs are improperly assigned among a company's segments. Cross-subsidization can occur in two ways; first, when companies fail to trace costs directly to segments in those situations where it is feasible to do so; and second, when companies use inappropriate bases to allocate costs.

Failure to Trace Costs Directly Costs that can be traced directly to a specific segment of a company should not be allocated to other segments. Rather, such costs should be charged directly to the responsible segment. For example, the rent for a branch office of an insurance company should be charged directly against the branch office rather than included in a companywide overhead pool and then spread throughout the company.

Inappropriate Allocation Base Some companies allocate costs to segments using arbitrary bases such as sales dollars or cost of goods sold. For example, under the sales dollars approach, costs are allocated to the various segments according to the percentage of company sales generated by each segment. Thus, if a segment generates 20% of total company sales, it would be allocated 20% of the company's SG&A expenses as its "fair share." This same basic procedure is followed if costs of goods sold or some other measure is used as the allocation base.

For this approach to be valid, the allocation base must actually drive the overhead cost. (Or at least the allocation base should be highly correlated with the cost driver of the overhead cost.) For example, when sales dollars is used as the allocation base for SG&A expenses, it is implicitly assumed that SG&A expenses change in proportion to changes in total sales. If that is not true, the SG&A expenses allocated to segments will be misleading.

Stopping the Bickering

In Business

AT&T Power Systems, a subsidiary of AT&T, makes electronic power supplies and components for the data processing and telecommunications industries. Independent business units (i.e., segments) at AT&T Power Systems are evaluated as profit centers, however, "more time was being spent debating the appropriate overhead-allocation scheme than was being spent on strategies to increase contribution margins." If, in fact, no cause-and-effect relation exists between an overhead expense and the activity in any particular segment, then any allocation of this overhead expense to the segments is completely arbitrary and can be endlessly debated by segment managers. Consequently, a change was made to evaluate the segments on the basis of just contribution margin and controllable expenses—eliminating arbitrary allocations of overhead from the performance measure.

Source: Richard L. Jenson, James W. Brackner, and Clifford R. Skousen, *Managerial Accounting in Support of Manufacturing Excellence*, The IMA Foundation for Applied Research, Inc., Montvale, NJ, 1996, pp. 97–101.

Arbitrarily Dividing Common Costs among Segments

The third business practice that leads to distorted segment costs is the practice of assigning nontraceable costs to segments. For example, some companies allocate the costs of the corporate headquarters building to products on segment reports. However, in a multiproduct company, no single product is likely to be responsible for any significant amount of this cost. Even if a product were eliminated entirely, there would usually be no significant effect on any of the costs of the corporate headquarters building. In short, there is no cause-and-effect relation between the cost of the corporate headquarters building and the existence of any one product. As a consequence, any allocation of the cost of the corporate headquarters building to the products must be arbitrary.

Common costs like the costs of the corporate headquarters building are necessary, of course, to have a functioning organization. The common practice of arbitrarily allocating these costs to segments is often justified on the grounds that "someone" has to "cover the common costs." While it is undeniably true that the common costs must be covered, arbitrarily allocating common costs to segments does not ensure that this will happen. In fact, adding a share of common costs to the real costs of a segment may make an otherwise profitable segment appear to be unprofitable. If a manager erroneously eliminates the segment, the revenues will be lost, the real costs of the segment will be saved, but the common costs will still be there. The net effect will be to reduce the profits of the company as a whole and make it even more difficult to "cover the common costs."

In sum, the way many companies handle segment reporting results in cost distortion. This distortion results from three practices—the failure to trace costs directly to a specific segment when it is feasible to do so, the use of inappropriate bases for allocating costs, and the allocation of common costs to segments. These practices are widespread. One study found that 60% of the companies surveyed made no attempt to assign SG&A costs to segments on a cause-and-effect basis.[3]

---

[3] James R. Emore and Joseph A. Ness, "The Slow Pace of Meaningful Change in Cost Systems," *Journal of Cost Management* 4, no. 4, p. 39.

In Business

Slippery Profits

Segment profits can be seriously distorted by arbitrary allocations of common fixed costs. Steven Spielberg, the legendary movie producer and director, learned this lesson early in his career. Spielberg's contract with Columbia Pictures for *Close Encounters of the Third Kind* stipulated that he would receive 17.5% of the profits from the film. But even though the film grossed over $300 million at the box office, he ended up with only about $5 million. "Spielberg was discovering the first rule of Hollywood accounting: Even the biggest hits show very little 'profit' after overhead, interest and distribution fees are generously factored in . . . So he went to Universal and to Warner Bros. and negotiated the basic deal that he still uses today: a cut of the revenues so that he makes out even if the film doesn't make any money or if the studio inflates the costs; some control over the accounting so profits show up as profits; and half the earnings." With such a deal, Spielberg is believed to have made over $250 million from *Jurassic Park.*

Source: Randall Lane, "I Want Gross," *Forbes,* September 26, 1994, pp. 104–108.

Rate of Return for Measuring Managerial Performance

LEARNING OBJECTIVE 2
Compute return on investment (ROI) and show how changes in sales, expenses, and assets affect ROI.

When a company is truly decentralized, segment managers are given a great deal of autonomy. Profit and investment centers are virtually independent businesses, with their managers having about the same control over decisions as if they were in fact running their own independent firms. With this autonomy, fierce competition often develops among managers, with each striving to make his or her segment the "best" in the company.

Competition between investment centers is particularly keen for investment funds. How do top managers in corporate headquarters go about deciding who gets new investment funds as they become available, and how do these managers decide which investment centers are most profitably using the funds that have already been entrusted to their care? One of the most popular ways of making these judgments is to measure the rate of return that investment center managers are able to generate on their assets. This rate of return is called the *return on investment (ROI).*

The Return on Investment (ROI) Formula

The **return on investment (ROI)** is defined as net operating income divided by average operating assets:

$$\text{ROI} = \frac{\text{Net operating income}}{\text{Average operating assets}}$$

There are some issues about how to measure net operating income and average operating assets, but this formula seems clear enough. The higher the return on investment (ROI) of a business segment, the greater the profit generated per dollar invested in the segment's operating assets.

Net Operating Income and Operating Assets Defined

Note that *net operating income,* rather than net income, is used in the ROI formula. **Net operating income** is income before interest and taxes and is sometimes referred to as EBIT (earnings before interest and taxes). Net operating income is used in the formula because the base (i.e., denominator) consists of *operating assets.* Thus, to be consistent we use net operating income in the numerator.

Operating assets include cash, accounts receivable, inventory, plant and equipment, and all other assets held for productive use in the organization. Examples of assets that would not be included in the operating assets category (i.e., examples of nonoperating assets) would include land held for future use, an investment in another company, or a building rented to someone else. The operating assets base used in the formula is typically computed as the average of the operating assets between the beginning and the end of the year.

Concept 12–1

Plant and Equipment: Net Book Value or Gross Cost?

Determining the dollar amount of plant and equipment that should be included in the operating assets base is a major issue in ROI computations. To illustrate the problem, assume that a company reports the following amounts for plant and equipment on its balance sheet:

Plant and equipment	$3,000,000
Less accumulated depreciation	900,000
Net book value	$2,100,000

What dollar amount of plant and equipment should the company include in its operating assets in computing ROI? One widely used approach is to include only the plant and equipment's *net book value*—that is, the plant's original cost less accumulated depreciation ($2,100,000 in the example above). A second approach is to ignore depreciation and include the plant's entire *gross cost* in the operating assets base ($3,000,000 in the example above). Both of these approaches are used in actual practice, even though they will obviously yield very different operating asset and ROI figures.

The following arguments can be raised for using net book value to measure operating assets and for using gross cost to measure operating assets in ROI computations:

Arguments for Using Net Book Value to Measure Operating Assets in ROI Computations:

1. The net book value method is consistent with how plant and equipment are reported on the balance sheet (i.e., cost less accumulated depreciation to date).
2. The net book value method is consistent with the computation of operating income, which includes depreciation as an operating expense.

Arguments for Using Gross Cost to Measure Operating Assets in ROI Computations:

1. The gross cost method eliminates both the age of equipment and the method of depreciation as factors in ROI computations. (Under the net book value method, ROI will tend to increase over time as net book value declines due to depreciation.)
2. The gross cost method does not discourage replacement of old, worn-out equipment. (Under the net book value method, replacing fully depreciated equipment with new equipment can have a dramatic, adverse effect on ROI.)

Managers generally view consistency as the most important consideration. As a result, a majority of companies use the net book value approach in ROI computations. In this text, we will also use the net book value approach unless a specific exercise or problem directs otherwise.

Controlling the Rate of Return

When we first defined the return on investment, we used the following formula:

$$\text{ROI} = \frac{\text{Net operating income}}{\text{Average operating assets}}$$

We can modify this formula slightly by introducing sales as follows:

$$\text{ROI} = \frac{\text{Net operating income}}{\text{Sales}} \times \frac{\text{Sales}}{\text{Average operating assets}}$$

These two equations are equivalent because the sales terms cancel out in the second equation. The first term on the right-hand side of the equation is the *margin,* which is defined as follows:

$$\text{Margin} = \frac{\text{Net operating income}}{\text{Sales}}$$

Margin is a measure of management's ability to control operating expenses in relation to sales. The lower the operating expenses per dollar of sales, the higher the margin earned.

The second term on the right-hand side of the equation is *turnover*, which is defined as follows:

$$\text{Turnover} = \frac{\text{Sales}}{\text{Average operating assets}}$$

Turnover is a measure of the sales that are generated for each dollar invested in operating assets.

The following alternative form of the ROI formula, which we will use most frequently, combines margin and turnover:

$$\text{ROI} = \text{Margin} \times \text{Turnover}$$

Which formula for ROI should be used—the original one stated in terms of net operating income and average operating assets or this one stated in terms of margin and turnover? Either can be used—they will always give the same answer. However, the margin and turnover formulation provides some additional insights.

Some managers tend to focus too much on margin and ignore turnover. To some degree at least, the margin can be a valuable indicator of a manager's performance. Standing alone, however, it overlooks one very crucial area of a manager's responsibility—the investment in operating assets. Excessive funds tied up in operating assets, which depresses turnover, can be just as much of a drag on profitability as excessive operating expenses, which depresses margin. One of the advantages of ROI as a performance measure is that it forces the manager to control the investment in operating assets as well as to control expenses and the margin.

Du Pont pioneered the ROI concept and recognized the importance of looking at both margin and turnover in assessing the performance of a manager. The ROI formula is now widely used as the key measure of the performance of an investment center. The ROI formula blends together many aspects of the manager's responsibilities into a single figure that can be compared to the returns of competing investment centers, the returns of other firms in the industry, and to the past returns of the investment center itself.

Du Pont also developed the diagram that appears in Exhibit 12–6. This exhibit helps managers understand how they can control ROI. An investment center manager can increase ROI in basically three ways:

1. Increase sales.
2. Reduce expenses.
3. Reduce assets.

To illustrate how the rate of return can be improved by each of these three actions, consider how the manager of the Monthaven Burger Grill is evaluated. Burger Grill is a small chain of upscale casual restaurants that has been rapidly adding outlets via franchising. The Monthaven franchise is owned by a group of local surgeons who have little time to devote to management and little expertise in business matters. Therefore, they delegate operating decisions—including decisions concerning investment in operating assets such as inventories—to a professional manager they have hired. The manager is evaluated largely based on the ROI the franchise generates.

Exhibit 12–6 Elements of Return on Investment (ROI)

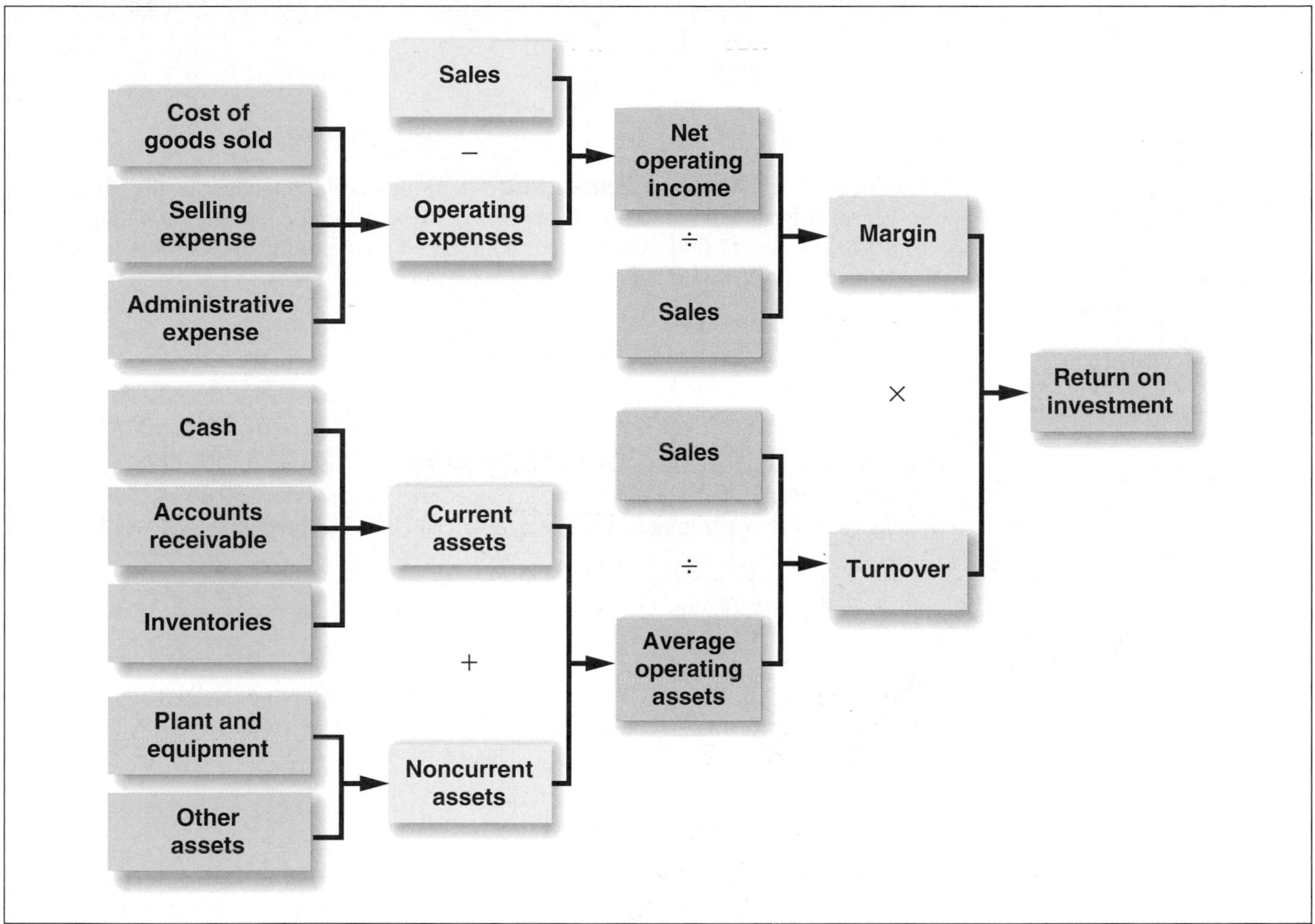

The following data represent the results of operations for the most recent month:

Net operating income	$ 10,000
Sales	100,000
Average operating assets	50,000

The rate of return generated by the Monthaven Burger Grill investment center is as follows:

$$\text{ROI} = \text{Margin} \times \text{Turnover}$$

$$\frac{\text{Net operating income}}{\text{Sales}} \times \frac{\text{Sales}}{\text{Average operating assets}}$$

$$\frac{\$10{,}000}{\$100{,}000} \times \frac{\$100{,}000}{\$50{,}000}$$

$$10\% \times 2 = 20\%$$

As we stated above, to improve the ROI figure, the manager can (1) increase sales, (2) reduce expenses, or (3) reduce the operating assets.

Approach 1: Increase Sales Assume that the manager of the Monthaven Burger Grill is able to increase sales from $100,000 to $110,000. Assume further that either because of good cost control or because some costs in the company are fixed, the net operating income increases even more rapidly, going from $10,000 to $12,000 per period. Assume that the operating assets remain constant. Then the new ROI will be:

$$\text{ROI} = \frac{\$12{,}000}{\$110{,}000} \times \frac{\$110{,}000}{\$50{,}000}$$

$$10.91\% \times 2.2 = 24\% \text{ (as compared to 20\% above)}$$

Approach 2: Reduce Expenses Assume that the manager of the Monthaven Burger Grill is able to reduce expenses by $1,000 so that net operating income increases from $10,000 to $11,000. Assume that both sales and operating assets remain constant. Then the new ROI would be:

$$\text{ROI} = \frac{\$11{,}000}{\$100{,}000} \times \frac{\$100{,}000}{\$50{,}000}$$

$$11\% \times 2 = 22\% \text{ (as compared to 20\% above)}$$

Approach 3: Reduce Operating Assets Assume that the manager of the Monthaven Burger Grill is able to reduce operating assets from $50,000 to $40,000, but that sales and net operating income remain unchanged. Then the new ROI would be:

$$\text{ROI} = \frac{\$10{,}000}{\$100{,}000} \times \frac{\$100{,}000}{\$40{,}000}$$

$$10\% \times 2.5 = 25\% \text{ (as compared to 20\% above)}$$

A clear understanding of these three approaches to improving the ROI figure is critical to the effective management of an investment center. We will now look at each approach in more detail.

Increase Sales

When first looking at the ROI formula, one is inclined to think that the sales figure is neutral, since it appears as the denominator in the margin computation and as the numerator in the turnover computation. We *could* cancel out the sales figure, but we don't do so for two reasons. First, this would tend to draw attention away from the fact that the rate of return is a function of *two* variables, margin and turnover. And second, it would tend to conceal the fact that a change in sales can affect both the margin and the turnover in an organization. A change in sales can affect the *margin* if expenses increase or decrease at a different rate than sales. For example, a company may be able to keep a tight control on its costs as its sales go up, with the result that net operating income increases more rapidly than sales and increases the margin. Or a company may have fixed expenses that remain constant as sales go up, resulting in an increase in the net operating income and in the margin. Either (or both) of these factors could have been responsible for the increase in the margin percentage from 10% to 10.91% illustrated in approach 1 above.

Further, a change in sales can affect the *turnover* if sales either increase or decrease without a proportionate increase or decrease in the operating assets. In the first approach above, for example, sales increased from $100,000 to $110,000, but the operating assets remained unchanged. As a result, the turnover increased from 2 to 2.2 for the period.

Reduce Expenses

Often the easiest route to increased profitability and to a stronger ROI figure is to simply cut the "fat" out of an organization through a concerted effort to control expenses. When margins begin to be squeezed, this is generally the first line of attack by a manager. Discretionary fixed costs (i.e., fixed costs that arise from annual decisions by management) usually come under scrutiny first, and various programs are either curtailed or eliminated in an effort to cut costs. Managers must be careful, however, not to cut out muscle and bone along with the fat. Also, they must remember that frequent cost cutting binges can destroy morale. Most managers now agree that it is best to stay "lean and mean" all of the time.

Reduce Operating Assets

Managers have always been sensitive to the need to control sales, operating expenses, and operating margins. However, they have not always been equally sensitive to the need to control investment in operating assets. Firms that have adopted the ROI approach to measuring managerial performance report that one of the first reactions of investment center managers is to trim their investment in operating assets. Managers soon realize that an excessive investment in operating assets reduces turnover and hurts the ROI. As these managers reduce their investment in operating assets, funds are released that can be used elsewhere in the organization.

How can an investment center manager control the investment in operating assets? One approach is to eliminate unneeded inventory. JIT purchasing and JIT manufacturing have been extremely helpful in reducing inventories of all types. Another approach is to devise various methods of speeding up the collection of receivables. For example, many firms now employ the lockbox technique by which customers in distant states send their payments directly to post office boxes in their area. The funds are received and deposited by a local bank on behalf of the payee firm. This speeds up the collection process, since the payments are not delayed in the postal system. As a result of the speedup in collection, the accounts receivable balance is reduced and the asset turnover is increased.

ROI and the Balanced Scorecard

Simply exhorting managers to increase ROI is not sufficient. Managers who are told to increase ROI will naturally wonder how this is to be accomplished. The Du Pont scheme, which is illustrated in Exhibit 12–6, provides managers with *some* guidance. Generally speaking, ROI can be increased by increasing sales, decreasing costs, and/or decreasing investments in operating assets. However, it may not be obvious to managers *how* they are supposed to increase sales, decrease costs, and decrease investments in a way that is consistent with the company's strategy. For example, a manager who is given inadequate guidance may cut back on investments that are critical to implementing the company's strategy.

For that reason, as discussed in Chapter 10, when managers are evaluated based on ROI, a balanced scorecard approach is advised. And indeed, ROI, or residual income (discussed below), is typically included as one of the financial performance measures on a company's balanced scorecard. As briefly discussed in Chapter 10, the balanced scorecard provides a way of communicating a company's strategy to managers throughout the organization. The scorecard indicates *how* the company intends to improve its financial performance. A well-constructed balanced scorecard should answer questions like: "What internal business processes should be improved?" and "Which customer should be targeted and how will they be attracted and retained at a profit?" In short, a well-constructed balanced scorecard can provide managers with a road map that indicates how the company intends to increase its ROI. In the absence of such a road map of the company's strategy, managers may have difficulty understanding what they are supposed to do to increase ROI and they may work at cross-purposes rather than in harmony with the overall strategy of the company.

Criticisms of ROI

Although ROI is widely used in evaluating performance, it is not a perfect tool. The method is subject to the following criticisms:

1. Just telling managers to increase ROI may not be enough. Managers may not know how to increase ROI; they may increase ROI in a way that is inconsistent with the company's strategy; or they may take actions that increase ROI in the short run but harm the company in the long run (such as cutting back on research and development). This is

why ROI is best used as part of a balanced scorecard as discussed above. A balanced scorecard can provide concrete guidance to managers, making it more likely that actions taken are consistent with the company's strategy and reducing the likelihood that short-run performance will be enhanced at the expense of long-term performance.

2. A manager who takes over a business segment typically inherits many committed costs over which the manager has no control. These committed costs may be relevant in assessing the performance of the business segment as an investment but make it difficult to fairly assess the performance of the manager relative to other managers.
3. As discussed in the next section, a manager who is evaluated based on ROI may reject investment opportunities that are profitable for the whole company but that would have a negative impact on the manager's performance evaluation.

Residual Income—Another Measure of Performance

LEARNING OBJECTIVE 3
Compute residual income and understand the strengths and weaknesses of this method of measuring performance.

Another approach to measuring an investment center's performance focuses on a concept known as *residual income.* **Residual income** is the net operating income that an investment center earns above the minimum required return on its operating assets. **Economic Value Added (EVA®)** is an adaptation of residual income that has recently been adopted by many companies.[4] Under EVA, companies often modify their accounting principles in various ways. For example, funds used for research and development are often treated as investments rather than as expenses under EVA.[5] These complications are best dealt with in a more advanced course; in this text we will focus on the basics and will not draw any distinction between residual income and EVA.

When residual income or EVA is used to measure performance, the objective is to maximize the total amount of residual income or EVA, not to maximize ROI. If the objective were to maximize ROI, then every company should divest all of its products except the single product with the highest ROI. A wide variety of organizations have embraced some version of residual income or EVA, including Bausch & Lomb, Best Buy, Boise Cascade, Coca-Cola, Dun and Bradstreet, Eli Lilly, Federated Mogul, Georgia-Pacific, Guidant Corporation, Hershey Foods, Husky Injection Molding, J.C. Penney, Kansas City Power & Light, Olin, Quaker Oats, Silicon Valley Bank, Sprint, Toys R Us, Tupperware, and the United States Postal Service. In addition, financial institutions such as Credit Suisse First Boston now use EVA—and its allied concept, market value added—to evaluate potential investments in other companies.

For purposes of illustration, consider the following data for an investment center—the Ketchican Division of Alaskan Marine Services Corporation.

ALASKAN MARINE SERVICES CORPORATION
Ketchican Division
Basic Data for Performance Evaluation

Average operating assets	$100,000
Net operating income	$20,000
Minimum required rate of return	15%

[4] The basic idea underlying residual income and economic value added has been around for over 100 years. In recent years, economic value added has been popularized and trademarked by the consulting firm Stern, Stewart & Co.

[5] Over 100 different adjustments could be made for deferred taxes, LIFO reserves, provisions for future liabilities, mergers and acquisitions, gains or losses due to changes in accounting rules, operating leases, and other accounts, but most companies make only a few. For further details, see John O'Hanlon and Ken Peasnell, "Wall Street's Contribution to Management Accounting: the Stern Stewart EVA® Financial Management System," *Management Accounting Research* 9, 1998, pp. 421–444.

Alaskan Marine Services Corporation has long had a policy of evaluating investment center managers based on ROI, but it is considering a switch to residual income. The controller of the company, who is in favor of the change to residual income, has provided the following table that shows how the performance of the division would be evaluated under each of the two methods:

ALASKAN MARINE SERVICES CORPORATION
Ketchican Division

	Alternative Performance Measures	
	ROI	**Residual Income**
Average operating assets (a)	$100,000	$100,000
Net operating income (b)	$ 20,000	$ 20,000
ROI, (b) ÷ (a)	20%	
Minimum required return (15% × $100,000)		15,000
Residual income		$ 5,000

The reasoning underlying the residual income calculation is straightforward. The company is able to earn a rate of return of at least 15% on its investments. Since the company has invested $100,000 in the Ketchican Division in the form of operating assets, the company should be able to earn at least $15,000 (15% × $100,000) on this investment. Since the Ketchican Division's net operating income is $20,000, the residual income above and beyond the minimum required return is $5,000. If residual income is adopted as the performance measure to replace ROI, the manager of the Ketchican Division would be evaluated based on the growth in residual income from year to year.

Flocking to EVA

In Business

According to *Fortune* magazine, "Managers who run their businesses according to the precepts of EVA have hugely increased the value of their companies. Investors who know about EVA, and know which companies are employing it, have grown rich. Little wonder that highly regarded major corporations—Coca-Cola, AT&T, Quaker Oats, Briggs & Stratton, CSX, and many others—are flocking to the concept . . . Here's how [former] Coca-Cola CEO Roberto Goizueta, a champion wealth creator, explained it: 'We raise capital to make concentrate, and sell it at an operating profit. Then we pay the cost of capital. Shareholders pocket the difference.'"

Source: Shawn Tully, "The Real Key to Creating Wealth," *Fortune*, September 20, 1993, pp. 38–50.

Motivation and Residual Income

Concept 12–2

One of the primary reasons why the controller of Alaskan Marine Services Corporation would like to switch from ROI to residual income has to do with how managers view new investments under the two performance measurement schemes. The residual income approach encourages managers to make investments that are profitable for the entire company but that would be rejected by managers who are evaluated by the ROI formula.

To illustrate this problem with ROI, suppose that the manager of the Ketchican Division is considering purchasing a computerized diagnostic machine to aid in servicing marine diesel engines. The machine would cost $25,000 and is expected to generate additional operating income of $4,500 a year. From the standpoint of the company, this would be a good investment since it promises a rate of return of 18% ($4,500 ÷ $25,000), which is in excess of the company's minimum required rate of return of 15%.

If the manager of the Ketchican Division is evaluated based on residual income, she would be in favor of the investment in the diagnostic machine as shown below:

ALASKAN MARINE SERVICES CORPORATION
Ketchican Division
Performance Evaluated Using Residual Income

	Present	New Project	Overall
Average operating assets	$100,000	$25,000	$125,000
Net operating income	$ 20,000	$ 4,500	$ 24,500
Minimum required return	15,000	3,750*	18,750
Residual income	$ 5,000	$ 750	$ 5,750

*$25,000 × 15% = $3,750.

Since the project would increase the residual income of the Ketchican Division, the manager would want to invest in the new diagnostic machine.

Now suppose that the manager of the Ketchican Division is evaluated based on ROI. The effect of the diagnostic machine on the division's ROI is computed below:

ALASKAN MARINE SERVICES CORPORATION
Ketchican Division
Performance Evaluated Using ROI

	Present	New Project	Overall
Average operating assets (a)	$100,000	$25,000	$125,000
Net operating income (b)	$20,000	$4,500	$24,500
ROI, (b) ÷ (a)	20%	18%	19.6%

The new project reduces the division's ROI from 20% to 19.6%. This happens because the 18% rate of return on the new diagnostic machine, while above the company's 15% minimum rate of return, is below the division's present ROI of 20%. Therefore, the new diagnostic machine would drag the division's ROI down even though it would be a good investment from the standpoint of the company as a whole. If the manager of the division is evaluated based on ROI, she will be reluctant to even propose such an investment.

In Business

Quaker Oats Goes on a Diet

Quaker Oats provides an example of how use of EVA can change the way a company operates. Prior to adopting EVA, "its businesses had one overriding goal—increasing quarterly earnings. To do it, they guzzled capital. They offered sharp price discounts at the end of each quarter, so plants ran overtime turning out huge shipments of Gatorade, Rice-A-Roni, 100% Natural Cereal, and other products. Managers led the late rush, since their bonuses depended on raising operating profits each quarter . . . Pumping up sales requires many warehouses (capital) to hold vast temporary inventories (more capital). But who cared? Quaker's operating businesses paid no charge for capital in internal accounting, so they barely noticed. It took EVA to spotlight the problem . . . One plant has trimmed inventories from $15 million to $9 million, even though it is producing much more, and Quaker has closed five of 15 warehouses, saving $6 million a year in salaries and capital costs."

Source: Shawn Tully, "The Real Key to Creating Wealth," *Fortune*, September 20, 1993, pp. 38–50.

Basically, a manager who is evaluated based on ROI will reject any project whose rate of return is below the division's current ROI even if the rate of return on the project is above the minimum required rate of return for the entire company. In contrast, any project whose rate of return is above the minimum required rate of return for the company will result in an increase in residual income. Since it is in the best interests of the company as a whole to accept any project whose rate of return is above the minimum required rate of return, managers who are evaluated based on residual income will tend to make better decisions concerning investment projects than managers who are evaluated based on ROI.

Divisional Comparison and Residual Income

The residual income approach has one major disadvantage. It can't be used to compare the performance of divisions of different sizes. You would expect larger divisions to have more residual income than smaller divisions, not necessarily because they are better managed but simply because they are bigger.

As an example, consider the following residual income computations for Division X and Division Y:

	Division	
	X	Y
Average operating assets (a)	$1,000,000	$250,000
Net operating income	$ 120,000	$ 40,000
Minimum required return: 10% × (a)	100,000	25,000
Residual income	$ 20,000	$ 15,000

Observe that Division X has slightly more residual income than Division Y, but that Division X has $1,000,000 in operating assets as compared to only $250,000 in operating assets for Division Y. Thus, Division X's greater residual income is probably more a result of its size than the quality of its management. In fact, it appears that the smaller division is better managed, since it has been able to generate nearly as much residual income with only one-fourth as much in operating assets to work with. This problem can be reduced by focusing on the percentage change in residual income from year to year rather than on the absolute amount of the residual income.

Reacting to the Use of EVA

In Business

One study found that, relative to companies that did not adopt EVA, a sample of companies adopting Economic Value Added as a performance measure "(1) increased their dispositions of assets and decreased their new investment, (2) increased their payouts to shareholders through share repurchases, and (3) used their assets more intensively. These actions are consistent with the strong rate of return discipline associated with the capital charge in residual income-based measures."

Source: James S. Wallace, "Adopting Residual Income-Based Compensation Plans: Do You Get What You Pay For?" *Journal of Accounting and Economics* 24, 1997, pp. 275–300.

Summary

For purposes of evaluating performance, business units are classified as cost centers, profit centers, and investment centers. Cost centers are commonly evaluated using standard cost and flexible budget variances as discussed in prior chapters. Profit centers and investment centers are evaluated using the techniques discussed in this chapter.

Segmented income statements provide information for evaluating the profitability and performance of divisions, product lines, sales territories, and other segments of a company. Under the contribution approach covered in this chapter, variable costs and fixed costs are clearly distinguished from each other and only those costs that are traceable to a segment are assigned to the segment. A cost is considered traceable to a segment only if the cost is caused by the segment and could be avoided by eliminating the segment. Fixed common costs are not allocated to segments. The segment margin consists of revenues, less variable expenses, less traceable fixed expenses of the segment.

Return on investment (ROI) and residual income and its cousin EVA are widely used to evaluate the performance of investment centers. ROI suffers from the underinvestment problem—managers are reluctant to invest in projects whose returns that exceed the company's required rate of return but would drag down the manager's ROI. The residual income and EVA approaches solve this problem by giving managers full credit for any returns in excess of the company's required rate of return.

Review Problem 1: Segmented Statements

The business staff of the legal firm Frampton, Davis & Smythe has constructed the following report which breaks down the firm's overall results for last month in terms of its two main business segments—family law and commercial law:

	Total	Family Law	Commercial Law
Revenues from clients	$1,000,000	$400,000	$600,000
Less variable expenses	220,000	100,000	120,000
Contribution margin	780,000	300,000	480,000
Less traceable fixed expenses	670,000	280,000	390,000
Segment margin	110,000	20,000	90,000
Less common fixed expenses	60,000	24,000	36,000
Net operating income	$ 50,000	$ (4,000)	$ 54,000

However, this report is not quite correct. The common fixed expenses such as the managing partner's salary, general administrative expenses, and general firm advertising have been allocated to the two segments based on revenues from clients.

Required:

1. Redo the segment report, eliminating the allocation of common fixed expenses. Show both Amount and Percent columns for the firm as a whole and for each of the segments. Would the firm be better off financially if the family law segment were dropped? (Note: Many of the firm's commercial law clients also use the firm for their family law requirements such as drawing up wills.)
2. The firm's advertising agency has proposed an ad campaign targeted at boosting the revenues of the family law segment. The ad campaign would cost $20,000, and the advertising agency claims that it would increase family law revenues by $100,000. The managing partner of Frampton, Davis & Smythe believes this increase in business could be accommodated without any increase in fixed expenses. What effect would this ad campaign have on the family law segment margin and on overall net operating income of the firm?

Solution to Review Problem 1

1. The corrected segmented income statement appears below:

	Total		Family Law		Commercial Law	
	Amount	Percent	Amount	Percent	Amount	Percent
Revenues from clients	$1,000,000	100%	$400,000	100%	$600,000	100%
Less variable expenses	220,000	22%	100,000	25%	120,000	20%
Contribution margin	780,000	78%	300,000	75%	480,000	80%
Less traceable fixed expenses	670,000	67%	280,000	70%	390,000	65%
Segment margin	110,000	11%	$ 20,000	5%	$ 90,000	15%
Less common fixed expenses	60,000	6%				
Net operating income	$ 50,000	5%				

No, the firm would not be financially better off if the family law practice were dropped. The family law segment is covering all of its own costs and is contributing $20,000 per month to covering the common fixed expenses of the firm. While the segment margin as a percent of sales is much lower for family law than for commercial law, it is still profitable. Moreover, family law may be a service that the firm must provide to its commercial clients in order to remain competitive.

2. The ad campaign would be expected to add $55,000 to the family law segment as follows:

Increased revenues from clients	$100,000
Family law contribution margin ratio.	× 75%
Incremental contribution margin	75,000
Less cost of the ad campaign.	20,000
Increased segment margin.	$ 55,000

Since there would be no increase in fixed expenses (including common fixed expenses), the increase in overall net operating income should also be $55,000.

Review Problem 2: Return on Investment (ROI) and Residual Income

The Magnetic Imaging Division of Medical Diagnostics, Inc., has reported the following results for last year's operations:

Sales.	$25 million
Net operating income	3 million
Average operating assets.	10 million

Required:

1. Compute the margin, turnover, and ROI for the Magnetic Imaging Division.
2. Top management of Medical Diagnostics, Inc., has set a minimum required rate of return on average operating assets of 25%. What is the Magnetic Imaging Division's residual income for the year?

Solution to Review Problem 2

1. The required calculations appear below:

$$\text{Margin} = \frac{\text{Net operating income, \$3,000,000}}{\text{Sales, \$25,000,000}}$$

$$= 12\%$$

$$\text{Turnover} = \frac{\text{Sales, \$25,000,000}}{\text{Average operating assets, \$10,000,000}}$$

$$= 2.5$$

$$\text{ROI} = \text{Margin} \times \text{Turnover}$$
$$= 12\% \times 2.5$$
$$= 30\%$$

2. The residual income for the Magnetic Imaging Division is computed as follows:

Average operating assets.	$10,000,000
Net operating income	$ 3,000,000
Minimum required return (25% × $10,000,000).	2,500,000
Residual income.	$ 500,000

Glossary

Common fixed cost A fixed cost that supports more than one business segment, but is not traceable in whole or in part to any one of the business segments. (p. 534)

Cost center A business segment whose manager has control over cost but has no control over revenue or the use of investment funds. (p. 527)

Cross-subsidization Improper assignment of costs among a company's segments; also called *cost distortion.* (p. 540)

Decentralized organization An organization in which decision making is not confined to a few top executives but rather is spread throughout the organization. (p. 526)

Economic Value Added (EVA) A concept similar to residual income in which a variety of adjustments may be made to GAAP financial statements for performance evaluation purposes. (p. 548)

Investment center A business segment whose manager has control over cost, revenue, and the use of investment funds. (p. 528)

Margin Net operating income divided by sales. (p. 544)

Net operating income Income before interest and income taxes have been deducted. (p. 542)

Operating assets Cash, accounts receivable, inventory, plant and equipment, and all other assets held for productive use in an organization. (p. 542)

Profit center A business segment whose manager has control over cost and revenue but has no control over the use of investment funds. (p. 528)

Residual income The net operating income that an investment center earns above the required return on its operating assets. (p. 548)

Responsibility center Any business segment whose manager has control over cost, revenue, or the use of investment funds. (p. 529)

Return on investment (ROI) Net operating income divided by average operating assets. It also equals margin multiplied by turnover. (p. 542)

Segment Any part or activity of an organization about which the manager seeks cost, revenue, or profit data. (p. 527)

Segment margin The amount computed by deducting the traceable fixed costs of a segment from the segment's contribution margin. It represents the margin available after a segment has covered all of its own traceable costs. (p. 536)

Traceable fixed cost A fixed cost that is incurred because of the existence of a particular business segment. (p. 533)

Turnover The amount of sales generated in an investment center for each dollar invested in operating assets. It is computed by dividing sales by the average operating assets figure. (p. 544)

Value chain The major business functions that add value to a company's products and services such as research and development, product design, manufacturing, marketing, distribution, and customer service. (p. 540)

Appendix 12A: Transfer Pricing

Business segments often supply goods and services to other business segments within the same company. For example, the truck division of Toyota supplies trucks to other Toyota divisions to use in their operations. When the divisions are evaluated based on their profit, return on investment, or residual income, a price must be established for such a transfer—otherwise, the division that produces the good or service will receive no credit. The price in such a situation is called a *transfer price*. A **transfer price** is the price charged when one segment of a company provides goods or services to another segment of the company. For example, most companies in the oil industry, such as Exxon, Shell, and Texaco, have petroleum refining and retail sales divisions that are evaluated on the basis of ROI or residual income. The petroleum refining division processes crude oil into gasoline, kerosene, lubricants, and other end products. The retail sales division takes gasoline and other products from the refining division and sells them through the company's chain of service stations. Each product has a price for transfers within the company. Suppose the transfer price for gasoline is $0.80 a gallon. Then the refining division gets credit for $0.80 a gallon of revenue on its segment report and the retailing division must deduct $0.80 a gallon as an expense on its segment report. Clearly, the refining division would like the transfer price to be as high as possible, whereas the retailing division would like the transfer price to be as low as possible. However, the transaction has no direct effect on the entire company's reported profit. It is like taking money out of one pocket and putting it into the other.

Managers are intensely interested in how transfer prices are set, since transfer prices can have a dramatic effect on the apparent profitability of a division. Three common approaches are used to set transfer prices:

1. Allow the managers involved in the transfer to negotiate their own transfer price.
2. Set transfer prices at cost using:
   a. Variable cost.
   b. Full (absorption) cost.
3. Set transfer prices at the market price.

We will consider each of these transfer pricing methods in turn, beginning with negotiated transfer prices. Throughout the discussion we should keep in mind that *the fundamental objective in setting transfer prices is to motivate the managers to act in the best interests of the overall company.* In contrast, **suboptimization** occurs when managers do not act in the best interests of the overall company or even in the best interests of their own segment.

Negotiated Transfer Prices

LEARNING OBJECTIVE 4
Determine the range, if any, within which a negotiated transfer price should fall.

A **negotiated transfer price** results from discussions between the selling and buying divisions. Negotiated transfer prices have several important advantages. First, this approach preserves the autonomy of the divisions and is consistent with the spirit of decentralization. Second, the managers of the divisions are likely to have much better information about the potential costs and benefits of the transfer than others in the company.

When negotiated transfer prices are used, the managers who are involved in a proposed transfer within the company meet to discuss the terms and conditions of the transfer. They may decide not to go through with the transfer, but if they do, they must agree to a transfer price. Generally speaking, we cannot predict the exact transfer price they will agree to. However, we can confidently predict two things: (1) the selling division will agree to the transfer only if the profits of the selling division increase as a result of the transfer, and (2) the buying division will agree to the transfer only if the profits of the buying division also increase as a result of the transfer. This may seem obvious, but it is an important point.

Clearly, if the transfer price is below the selling division's cost, a loss will occur on the transaction and the selling division will refuse to agree to the transfer. Likewise, if the transfer price is set too high, it will be impossible for the buying division to make any profit on the transferred item. For any given proposed transfer, the transfer price has both a lower limit (determined by the situation of the selling division) and an upper limit (determined by the situation of the buying division). The actual transfer price agreed to by the two division managers can fall anywhere between those two limits. These limits determine the **range of acceptable transfer prices**—the range of transfer prices within which the profits of both divisions participating in a transfer would increase.

An example will help us to understand negotiated transfer prices. Harris & Louder, Ltd., owns fast-food restaurants and snack food and beverage manufacturers in the United Kingdom. One of the restaurants, Pizza Maven, serves a variety of beverages along with pizzas. One of the beverages is ginger beer, which is served on tap. Harris & Louder has just purchased a new division, Imperial Beverages, that produces ginger beer. The managing director of Imperial Beverages has approached the managing director of Pizza Maven about purchasing Imperial Beverages ginger beer for sale at Pizza Maven restaurants rather than its usual brand of ginger beer. Managers at Pizza Maven agree that the quality of Imperial Beverages' ginger beer is comparable to the quality of their regular brand. It is just a question of price. The basic facts are as follows:

Imperial Beverages:	
Ginger beer production capacity per month	10,000 barrels
Variable cost per barrel of ginger beer	£8 per barrel
Fixed costs per month	£70,000
Selling price of Imperial Beverages ginger beer on the outside market	£20 per barrel
Pizza Maven:	
Purchase price of regular brand of ginger beer	£18 per barrel
Monthly consumption of ginger beer	2,000 barrels

The Selling Division's Lowest Acceptable Transfer Price The selling division, Imperial Beverages, will be interested in a proposed transfer only if its profit increases. Clearly, the transfer price must not fall below the variable cost per barrel of £8. In addition, if Imperial Beverages has insufficient capacity to fill the Pizza Maven order, then it would have to give up some of its regular sales. Imperial Beverages would expect to be compensated for the contribution margin on these lost sales. In sum, if the transfer has no effect on fixed costs, then from the selling division's standpoint, the transfer price must cover both the variable costs of producing the transferred units and any opportunity costs from lost sales.

Seller's perspective:

$$\text{Transfer price} \geq \begin{matrix}\text{Variable cost}\\ \text{per unit}\end{matrix} + \frac{\text{Total contribution margin on lost sales}}{\text{Number of units transferred}}$$

The Buying Division's Highest Acceptable Transfer Price The buying division, Pizza Maven, will be interested in the proposal only if its profit increases. In cases like this where a buying division has an outside supplier, the buying division's decision is simple. Buy from the inside supplier if the price is less than the price offered by the outside supplier.

Purchaser's perspective:

$$\text{Transfer price} \leq \text{Cost of buying from outside supplier}$$

We will consider several different hypothetical situations and see what the range of acceptable transfer prices would be in each situation.

Selling Division with Idle Capacity Suppose that Imperial Beverages has sufficient idle capacity to satisfy the demand for ginger beer from Pizza Maven without cutting into sales of ginger beer to its regular customers. To be specific, let's suppose that Imperial Beverages is selling only 7,000 barrels of ginger beer a month on the outside market. That leaves unused capacity of 3,000 barrels a month—more than enough to satisfy Pizza Maven's requirement of 2,000 barrels a month. What range of transfer prices, if any, would make both divisions better off with the transfer of 2,000 barrels a month?

1. The selling division, Imperial Beverages, will be interested in the proposal only if:

$$\text{Transfer price} \geq \begin{matrix}\text{Variable cost}\\ \text{per unit}\end{matrix} + \frac{\text{Total contribution margin on lost sales}}{\text{Number of units transferred}}$$

   Since Imperial Beverages has ample idle capacity, there are no lost outside sales. And since the variable cost per unit is £8, the lowest acceptable transfer price as far as the selling division is concerned is also £8.

$$\text{Transfer price} \geq £8 + \frac{£0}{2{,}000} = £8$$

2. The buying division, Pizza Maven, can buy similar ginger beer from an outside vendor for £18. Therefore, Pizza Maven would be unwilling to pay more than £18 per barrel for Imperial Beverages' ginger beer.

$$\text{Transfer price} \leq \text{Cost of buying from outside supplier} = £18$$

3. Combining the requirements of both the selling division and the buying division, the acceptable range of transfer prices in this situation is:

$$£8 \leq \text{Transfer price} \leq £18$$

Assuming that the managers understand their own businesses and that they are cooperative, they should be able to agree on a transfer price within this range.

Selling Division with No Idle Capacity Suppose that Imperial Beverages has *no* idle capacity; it is selling 10,000 barrels of ginger beer a month on the outside market at £20 per barrel. To fill the order from Pizza Maven, Imperial Beverages would have to divert 2,000 barrels from its regular customers. What range of transfer prices, if any, would make both divisions better off transferring the 2,000 barrels within the company?

1. The selling division, Imperial Beverages, will be interested in the proposal only if:

$$\text{Transfer price} \geq \begin{matrix}\text{Variable cost}\\ \text{per unit}\end{matrix} + \frac{\text{Total contribution margin on lost sales}}{\text{Number of units transferred}}$$

Since Imperial Beverages has no idle capacity, there *are* lost outside sales. The contribution margin per barrel on these outside sales is £12 (£20 − £8).

$$\text{Transfer price} \geq £8 + \frac{(£20 - £8) \times 2{,}000}{2{,}000} = £8 + (£20 - £8) = £20$$

Thus, as far as the selling division is concerned, the transfer price must at least cover the revenue on the lost sales, which is £20 per barrel. This makes sense since the cost of producing the 2,000 barrels is the same whether they are sold on the inside market or on the outside. The only difference is that the selling division loses the revenue of £20 per barrel if it transfers the barrels to Pizza Maven.

2. As before, the buying division, Pizza Maven, would be unwilling to pay more than the £18 per barrel it is already paying for similar ginger beer from its regular supplier.

$$\text{Transfer price} \leq \text{Cost of buying from outside supplier} = £18$$

3. Therefore, the selling division would insist on a transfer price of at least £20. But the buying division would refuse any transfer price above £18. It is impossible to satisfy both division managers simultaneously; there can be no agreement on a transfer price and no transfer will take place. Is this good? The answer is yes. From the standpoint of the entire company, the transfer doesn't make sense. Why give up sales of £20 to save costs of £18?

   Basically, the transfer price is a mechanism for dividing between the two divisions any profit the entire company earns as a result of the transfer. If the company loses money on the transfer, there will be no profit to divide up, and it will be impossible for the two divisions to come to an agreement. On the other hand, if the company makes money on the transfer, there will be a potential profit to share, and it will always be possible for the two divisions to find a mutually agreeable transfer price that increases the profits of both divisions. If the pie is bigger, it is always possible to divide it up in such a way that everyone has a bigger piece.

Selling Division Has Some Idle Capacity Suppose now that Imperial Beverages is selling 9,000 barrels of ginger beer a month on the outside market. Pizza Maven can only sell one kind of ginger beer on tap. It cannot buy 1,000 barrels from Imperial Beverages and 1,000 barrels from its regular supplier; it must buy all of its ginger beer from one source.

To fill the entire 2,000-barrel a month order from Pizza Maven, Imperial Beverages would have to divert 1,000 barrels from its regular customers who are paying £20 per barrel. The other 1,000 barrels can be made using idle capacity. What range of transfer prices, if any, would make both divisions better off transferring the 2,000 barrels within the company?

1. As before, the selling division, Imperial Beverages, will insist on a transfer price that at least covers its variable cost and opportunity cost:

$$\text{Transfer price} \geq \frac{\text{Variable cost}}{\text{per unit}} + \frac{\text{Total contribution margin on lost sales}}{\text{Number of units transferred}}$$

   Since Imperial Beverages does not have enough idle capacity to fill the entire order for 2,000 barrels, there *are* lost outside sales. The contribution margin per barrel on the 1,000 barrels of lost outside sales is £12 (£20 − £8).

$$\text{Transfer price} \geq £8 + \frac{(£20 - £8) \times 1{,}000}{2{,}000} = £8 + £6 = £14$$

   Thus, as far as the selling division is concerned, the transfer price must cover the variable cost of £8 plus the average opportunity cost of lost sales of £6.

2. As before, the buying division, Pizza Maven, would be unwilling to pay more than the £18 per barrel it pays its regular supplier.

$$\text{Transfer price} \leq \text{Cost of buying from outside suppliers} = £18$$

3. Combining the requirements for both the selling and buying divisions, the range of acceptable transfer prices is:

$$£14 \leq \text{Transfer price} \leq £18$$

   Again, assuming that the managers understand their own businesses and that they are cooperative, they should be able to agree on a transfer price within this range.

No Outside Supplier If Pizza Maven has no outside supplier for the ginger beer, the highest price the buying division would be willing to pay depends on how much the buying division expects to make on the transferred units—excluding the transfer price. If, for example, Pizza Maven expects to earn £30 per barrel of ginger beer after paying its own expenses, then it should be willing to pay up to £30 per barrel to Imperial Beverages. Remember, however, that this assumes Pizza Maven cannot buy ginger beer from other sources.

Evaluation of Negotiated Transfer Prices As discussed earlier, if a transfer within the company would result in higher overall profits for the company, there is always a range of transfer prices within which both the selling and buying division would also have higher profits if they agree to the transfer. Therefore, if the managers understand their own businesses and are cooperative, then they should always be able to agree on a transfer price if it is in the best interests of the company that they do so.

Unfortunately, not all managers understand their own businesses and not all managers are cooperative. As a result, negotiations often break down even when it would be in the managers' own best interests to come to an agreement. Sometimes that is the fault of the way managers are evaluated. If managers are pitted against each other rather than against their own past performance or reasonable benchmarks, a noncooperative atmosphere is almost guaranteed. Nevertheless, it must be admitted that even with the best performance evaluation system, some people by nature are not cooperative.

Possibly because of the fruitless and protracted bickering that often accompanies disputes over transfer prices, most companies rely on some other means of setting transfer prices. Unfortunately, as we will see below, all of the alternatives to negotiated transfer prices have their own serious drawbacks.

Transfers at the Cost to the Selling Division

Many companies set transfer prices at either the variable cost or full (absorption) cost incurred by the selling division. Although the cost approach to setting transfer prices is relatively simple to apply, it has some major defects.

First, the use of cost—particularly full cost—as a transfer price can lead to bad decisions and thus suboptimization. Return to the example involving the ginger beer. The full cost of ginger beer can never be less than £15 per barrel (£8 per barrel variable cost + £7 per barrel fixed cost at capacity). What if the cost of buying the ginger beer from an outside supplier is less than £15—for example, £14 per barrel? If the transfer price were bureaucratically set at full cost, then Pizza Maven would never want to buy ginger beer from Imperial Beverages, since it could buy its ginger beer from the outside supplier at less cost. However, from the standpoint of the company as a whole, ginger beer should be transferred from Imperial Beverages to Pizza Maven whenever Imperial Beverages has idle capacity. Why? Because when Imperial Beverages has idle capacity, it only costs the company £8 in variable cost to produce a barrel of ginger beer, but it costs £14 per barrel to buy from outside suppliers.

Second, if cost is used as the transfer price, the selling division will never show a profit on any internal transfer. The only division that shows a profit is the division that makes the final sale to an outside party.

A third problem with cost-based prices is that they may not provide incentives to control costs. If the actual costs of one division are simply passed on to the next, then there is little incentive for anyone to work to reduce costs. This problem can be overcome by using standard costs rather than actual costs for transfer prices.

Despite these shortcomings, cost-based transfer prices are commonly used in practice. Advocates argue that they are easily understood and convenient to use.

ABC-Based Transfer Prices

In Business

Teva Pharmaceutical Industries Ltd. of Israel rejected the negotiated transfer price approach because senior executives believed that this approach would lead to endless, nonproductive arguments. Instead, the company uses activity-based costing to set its transfer prices. Marketing divisions are charged for unit-level costs based on the actual quantities of each product they acquire. In addition, they are charged batch-level costs based on the actual number of batches their orders require. Product-level and facility-level costs are charged to the marketing divisions annually in lump sums—the details will be covered in Chapter 16. Essentially, Teva Pharmaceutical Industries sets its transfer prices at carefully computed variable costs. As long as Teva Pharmaceutical Industries has unused capacity, this system sends the marketing managers the correct signals about how much it really costs the company to produce each product. With this information, the marketing managers are much better equipped to make pricing and other decisions regarding the products.

Source: Robert S. Kaplan, Dan Weiss, and Eyal Desheh, "Transfer Pricing with ABC," *Management Accounting,* May 1997, pp. 20–28.

Transfers at Market Price

Some form of competitive **market price** (i.e., the price charged for an item on the open market) is often regarded as the best approach to the transfer pricing problem—particularly if transfer price negotiations routinely become bogged down.

The market price approach is designed for situations in which there is an *outside market* for the transferred product or service; the product or service is sold in its present form to outside customers. If the selling division has no idle capacity, the market price in the outside market is the perfect choice for the transfer price. The reason for this is that if the selling division can sell a transferred item on the outside market instead, then the real cost of the transfer as far as the company is concerned is the opportunity cost of the lost revenue on the outside sale. Whether the item is transferred internally or sold on the outside market, the production costs are exactly the same. If the market price is used as the transfer price, the selling division manager will not lose anything by making the transfer, and the buying division manager will get the correct signal about how much it really costs the company for the transfer to take place.

While the market price works beautifully when the selling division has no idle capacity, difficulties occur when the selling division has idle capacity. Recalling once again the ginger beer example, the outside market price for the ginger beer produced by Imperial Beverages is £20 per barrel. However, Pizza Maven can purchase all of the ginger beer it wants from outside suppliers for £18 per barrel. Why would Pizza Maven ever buy from Imperial Beverages if Pizza Maven is forced to pay Imperial Beverages' market price? In some market price-based transfer pricing schemes, the transfer price would be lowered to £18, the outside vendor's market price, and Pizza Maven would be directed to buy from Imperial Beverages as long as Imperial Beverages is willing to sell. This scheme can work reasonably well, but a drawback is that managers at Pizza Maven will regard the cost of ginger beer as £18 rather than the £8, which is the real cost to the company when the selling division has idle capacity. Consequently, the managers of Pizza Maven will make pricing and other decisions based on an incorrect cost.

Unfortunately, none of the possible solutions to the transfer pricing problem are perfect—not even market-based transfer prices.

Divisional Autonomy and Suboptimization

How much autonomy should be granted to divisions in setting their own transfer prices and in making decisions concerning whether to sell internally or to sell outside? Should the divisional heads have complete authority to make these decisions, or should top corporate management step in if it appears that a decision is about to be made that would result in suboptimization? For example, if the selling division has idle capacity and divisional managers are unable to agree on a transfer price, should top corporate management step in and *force* a settlement?

Efforts should always be made, of course, to bring disputing managers together, but if a manager flatly refuses to change his or her position in a dispute, *then this decision should be respected* even if it results in suboptimization. This is simply the price that is paid for divisional autonomy. If top management steps in and forces the decisions in difficult situations, then the purposes of decentralization are defeated and the company simply becomes a centralized operation with decentralization of only minor decisions and responsibilities. In short, if a division is to be viewed as an autonomous unit with independent profit responsibility, then it must have control over its own destiny—even to the extent of having the right to make bad decisions.

We should note, however, that if a division consistently makes bad decisions, the results will sooner or later reduce its profit and rate of return, and the divisional manager may find that he or she has to defend the division's performance. Even so, the manager's right to get into an embarrassing situation must be respected if decentralization is to operate successfully. Divisional autonomy and independent profit responsibility are thought to lead to much greater success and profitability than closely controlled, centrally administered operations. Part of the price of this success is occasional suboptimization due to pettiness, bickering, or just plain stubbornness.

Furthermore, one of the major reasons for decentralizing is that top managers cannot know enough about every detail of operations to make every decision themselves. To impose the correct transfer price, top managers would have to know details about the outside market, variable costs, and capacity utilization. If top managers have all of this information, it is not clear why they decentralized in the first place.

International Aspects of Transfer Pricing

The objectives of transfer pricing change when a multinational corporation is involved and the goods and services being transferred cross international borders. The objectives of international transfer pricing, as compared to domestic transfer pricing, are summarized in Exhibit 12A–1.[6]

[6] The exhibit is adapted from Wagdy M. Abdallah, "Guidelines for CEOs in Transfer Pricing Policies," *Management Accounting* 70, no. 3, p. 61.

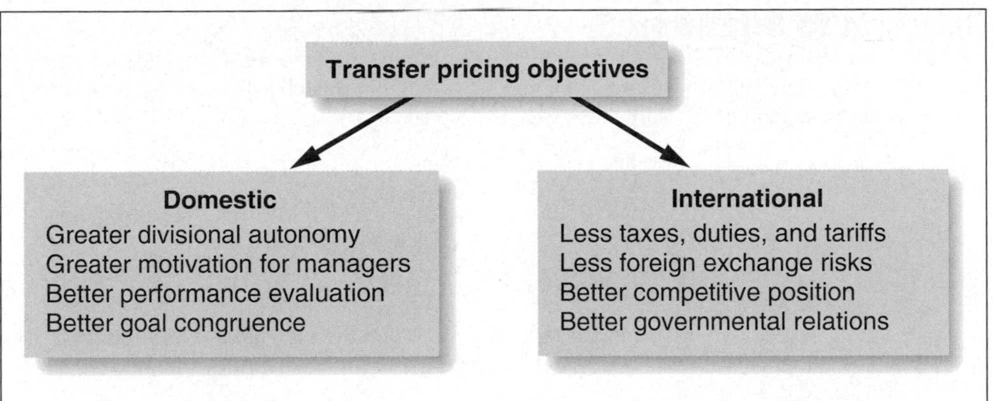

Exhibit 12A–1
Domestic and International Transfer Pricing Objectives

As shown in the exhibit, the objectives of international transfer pricing focus on minimizing taxes, duties, and foreign exchange risks, along with enhancing a company's competitive position and improving its relations with foreign governments. Although domestic objectives such as managerial motivation and divisional autonomy are always important, they often become secondary when international transfers are involved. Companies will focus instead on charging a transfer price that will slash its total tax bill or that will strengthen a foreign subsidiary.

For example, charging a low transfer price for parts shipped to a foreign subsidiary may reduce customs duty payments as the parts cross international borders, or it may help the subsidiary to compete in foreign markets by keeping the subsidiary's costs low. On the other hand, charging a high transfer price may help a multinational corporation draw profits out of a country that has stringent controls on foreign remittances, or it may allow a multinational corporation to shift income from a country that has high income tax rates to a country that has low rates.

Review Problem 3: Transfer Pricing

Situation A

Collyer Products, Inc., has a Valve Division that manufactures and sells a standard valve as follows:

Capacity in units	100,000
Selling price to outside customers	$30
Variable costs per unit	$16
Fixed costs per unit (based on capacity)	$9

The company has a Pump Division that could use this valve in one of its pumps. The Pump Division is currently purchasing 10,000 valves per year from an overseas supplier at a cost of $29 per valve.

Required:

1. Assume that the Valve Division has ample idle capacity to handle all of the Pump Division's needs. What is the acceptable range, if any, for the transfer price between the two divisions?
2. Assume that the Valve Division is selling all of the valves that it can produce to outside customers. What is the acceptable range, if any, for the transfer price between the two divisions?
3. Assume again that the Valve Division is selling all of the valves that it can produce to outside customers. Also assume that $3 in variable expenses can be avoided on transfers within the company, due to reduced selling costs. What is the acceptable range, if any, for the transfer price between the two divisions?

Solution to Situation A

1. Since the Valve Division has idle capacity, it does not have to give up any outside sales to take on the Pump Division's business. Applying the formula for the lowest acceptable transfer price from the viewpoint of the selling division, we get:

$$\text{Transfer price} \geq \begin{array}{c}\text{Variable cost}\\ \text{per unit}\end{array} + \frac{\text{Total contribution margin on lost sales}}{\text{Number of units transferred}}$$

$$\text{Transfer price} \geq \$16 + \frac{\$0}{10{,}000} = \$16$$

The Pump Division would be unwilling to pay more that \$29, the price it is currently paying an outside supplier for its valves. Therefore, the transfer price must fall within the range:

$$\$16 \leq \text{Transfer price} \leq \$29$$

2. Since the Valve Division is selling all of the valves that it can produce on the outside market, it would have to give up some of these outside sales to take on the Pump Division's business. Thus, the Valve Division has an opportunity cost, which is the total contribution margin on lost sales:

$$\text{Transfer price} \geq \begin{array}{c}\text{Variable cost}\\ \text{per unit}\end{array} + \frac{\text{Total contribution margin on lost sales}}{\text{Number of units transferred}}$$

$$\text{Transfer price} \geq \$16 + \frac{(\$30 - \$16) \times 10{,}000}{10{,}000} = \$16 + \$14 = \$30$$

Since the Pump Division can purchase valves from an outside supplier at only \$29 per unit, no transfers will be made between the two divisions.

3. Applying the formula for the lowest acceptable price from the viewpoint of the selling division, we get:

$$\text{Transfer price} \geq \begin{array}{c}\text{Variable cost}\\ \text{per unit}\end{array} + \frac{\text{Total contribution margin on lost sales}}{\text{Number of units transferred}}$$

$$\text{Transfer price} \geq (\$16 - \$3) + \frac{(\$30 - \$16) \times 10{,}000}{10{,}000} = \$13 + \$14 = \$27$$

In this case, the transfer price must fall within the range:

$$\$27 \leq \text{Transfer price} \leq \$29$$

Situation B

Refer to the original data in situation A above. Assume that the Pump Division needs 20,000 special high-pressure valves per year. The Valve Division's variable costs to manufacture and ship the special valve would be \$20 per unit. To produce these special valves, the Valve Division would have to reduce its production and sales of regular valves from 100,000 units per year to 70,000 units per year.

Required:
As far as the Valve Division is concerned, what is the lowest acceptable transfer price?

Solution to Situation B

To produce the 20,000 special valves, the Valve Division will have to give up sales of 30,000 regular valves to outside customers. Applying the formula for the lowest acceptable price from the viewpoint of the selling division, we get:

$$\text{Transfer price} \geq \begin{array}{c}\text{Variable cost}\\ \text{per unit}\end{array} + \frac{\text{Total contribution margin on lost sales}}{\text{Number of units transferred}}$$

$$\text{Transfer price} \geq \$20 + \frac{(\$30 - \$16) \times 30{,}000}{20{,}000} = \$20 + \$21 = \$41$$

Glossary (Appendix 12A)

Market price The price being charged for an item on the open market. (p. 559)

Negotiated transfer price A transfer price agreed on between buying and selling divisions. (p. 555)

Range of acceptable transfer prices The range of transfer prices within which the profits of both the selling division and the buying division would increase as a result of a transfer. (p. 555)

Suboptimization An overall level of profitability that is less than a segment or a company is capable of earning. (p. 555)

Transfer price The price charged when one division or segment provides goods or services to another division or segment of an organization. (p. 554)

Questions

12–1 What is meant by the term *decentralization?*

12–2 What benefits result from decentralization?

12–3 Distinguish between a cost center, a profit center, and an investment center.

12–4 Define a segment of an organization. Give several examples of segments.

12–5 How does the contribution approach assign costs to segments of an organization?

12–6 Distinguish between a traceable cost and a common cost. Give several examples of each.

12–7 Explain how the segment margin differs from the contribution margin.

12–8 Why aren't common costs allocated to segments under the contribution approach?

12–9 How is it possible for a cost that is traceable to a segment to become a common cost if the segment is divided into further segments?

12–10 What is meant by the terms *margin* and *turnover* in ROI calculations?

12–11 What are the three basic approaches to improving return on investment (ROI)?

12–12 What is meant by residual income?

12–13 In what way can the use of ROI as a performance measure for investment centers lead to bad decisions? How does the residual income approach overcome this problem?

12–14 (Appendix 12A) What is meant by the term *transfer price,* and why are transfer prices needed?

12–15 (Appendix 12A) From the standpoint of a selling division that has idle capacity, what is the minimum acceptable transfer price for an item?

12–16 (Appendix 12A) From the standpoint of a selling division that has *no* idle capacity, what is the minimum acceptable transfer price for an item?

12–17 (Appendix 12A) What are the advantages and disadvantages of cost-based transfer prices?

12–18 (Appendix 12A) If a market price for a product can be determined, why isn't it always the best transfer price?

Exercises

EXERCISE 12–1 Basic Segmented Income Statement [LO1]

Caltec, Inc., produces and sells recordable CD and DVD packs. Revenue and cost information relating to the products follow:

	Product	
	CD	DVD
Selling price per pack	$ 8.00	$ 25.00
Variable expenses per pack	3.20	17.50
Traceable fixed expenses per year	138,000	45,000

Common fixed expenses in the company total $105,000 annually. Last year the company produced and sold 37,500 CD packs and 18,000 DVD packs.

Required:

Prepare an income statement for the year segmented by product lines. Show both Amount and Percent columns for the company as a whole and for each of the products. Carry percentage computations to one decimal place.

EXERCISE 12–2 Working with a Segmented Income Statement [LO1]

Marple Associates is a consulting firm that specializes in information systems for construction and landscaping companies. The firm has two offices—one in Houston and one in Dallas. The firm classifies the direct costs of consulting jobs as variable costs. A segmented income statement for the company's most recent year is given below:

	Total Company		Segment: Houston		Segment: Dallas	
Sales	$750,000	100.0%	$150,000	100%	$600,000	100%
Less variable expenses	405,000	54.0	45,000	30	360,000	60
Contribution margin	345,000	46.0	105,000	70	240,000	40
Less traceable fixed expenses	168,000	22.4	78,000	52	90,000	15
Office segment margin	177,000	23.6	$27,000	18%	$150,000	25%
Less common fixed expenses not traceable to segments	120,000	16.0				
Net operating income	$ 57,000	7.6%				

Required:

1. By how much would the company's net operating income increase if Dallas increased its sales by $75,000 per year? Assume no change in cost behavior patterns.
2. Refer to the original data. Assume that sales in Houston increase by $50,000 next year and that sales in Dallas remain unchanged. Assume no change in fixed costs.
   a. Prepare a new segmented income statement for the company using the format above. Show both amounts and percentages.
   b. Observe from the income statement you have prepared that the CM ratio for Houston has remained unchanged at 70% (the same as in the data above) but that the segment margin ratio has changed. How do you explain the change in the segment margin ratio?

EXERCISE 12–3 Working with a Segmented Income Statement [LO1]

Refer to the data in Exercise 12–2. Assume that Dallas' sales by major market are as follows:

	Dallas		Market: Construction Clients		Market: Landscaping Clients	
Sales	$600,000	100%	$400,000	100%	$200,000	100%
Less variable expenses	360,000	60	260,000	65	100,000	50
Contribution margin	240,000	40	140,000	35	100,000	50
Less traceable fixed expenses	72,000	12	20,000	5	52,000	26
Market segment margin	168,000	28	$120,000	30%	$48,000	24%
Less common fixed expenses not traceable to markets	18,000	3				
Office segment margin	$150,000	25%				

The company would like to initiate an intensive advertising campaign in one of the two markets during the next month. The campaign would cost $8,000. Marketing studies indicate that such a campaign would increase sales in the construction market by $70,000 or increase sales in the landscaping market by $60,000.

Required:

1. In which of the markets would you recommend that the company focus its advertising campaign? Show computations to support your answer.
2. In Exercise 12–2, Dallas shows $90,000 in traceable fixed expenses. What happened to the $90,000 in this exercise?

EXERCISE 12–4 Common Costs [LO1]

You have a client who operates a large upscale grocery store that has a full range of departments. The management has encountered difficulty in using accounting data as a basis for decisions as to possible changes in departments operated, products, marketing methods, and so forth. List several overhead costs, or costs not applicable to a particular department, and explain how the existence of such costs (sometimes called *common costs*) complicates and limits the use of accounting data in making decisions in such a store.

(CPA, adapted)

EXERCISE 12–5 Segmented Income Statement [LO1]
Bovine Company, a wholesale distributor of DVDs, has been experiencing losses for some time, as shown by its most recent monthly income statement below:

Sales	$1,500,000
Less variable expenses	588,000
Contribution margin	912,000
Less fixed expenses	945,000
Net operating loss	$ (33,000)

In an effort to isolate the problem, the president has asked for an income statement segmented by geographic market. Accordingly, the Accounting Department has developed the following data:

	Geographic Market		
	South	Central	North
Sales	$400,000	$600,000	$500,000
Variable expenses as a percentage of sales	52%	30%	40%
Traceable fixed expenses	$240,000	$330,000	$200,000

Required:
1. Prepare an income statement segmented by geographic market, as desired by the president. Show both Amount and Percent columns for the company as a whole and for each geographic market. Carry percentage computations to one decimal place.
2. The company's sales manager believes that sales in the Central geographic market could be increased by 15% if advertising were increased by $25,000 each month. Would you recommend the increased advertising? Show computations to support your answer.

EXERCISE 12–6 Return on Investment (ROI) Relations [LO2]
Provide the missing data in the following tabulation:

	Division		
	Fab	Consulting	IT
Sales	$800,000	$?	$?
Net operating income	72,000	?	40,000
Average operating assets	?	130,000	?
Margin	?	4%	8%
Turnover	?	5	?
Return on investment (ROI)	18%	?	20%

EXERCISE 12–7 Computing and Interpreting Return on Investment (ROI) [LO2]
Selected operating data on the two divisions of York Company are given below:

	Division	
	Eastern	Western
Sales	$1,000,000	$1,750,000
Average operating assets	500,000	500,000
Net operating income	90,000	105,000
Property, plant, and equipment	250,000	200,000

Required:
1. Compute the rate of return for each division using the return on investment (ROI) formula stated in terms of margin and turnover.
2. So far as you can tell from the available data, which divisional manager seems to be doing the better job? Why?

EXERCISE 12–8 Return on Investment (ROI) and Residual Income Relations [LO2, LO3]
A family friend has asked your help in analyzing the operations of three anonymous companies. Supply the missing data in the tabulation below:

	Company		
	A	B	C
Sales	$400,000	$750,000	$600,000
Net operating income	?	45,000	?
Average operating assets	160,000	?	150,000
Return on investment (ROI)	20%	18%	?
Minimum required rate of return:			
Percentage	15%	?	12%
Dollar amount	$?	$ 50,000	$?
Residual income	?	?	6,000

EXERCISE 12–9 Contrasting Return on Investment (ROI) and Residual Income [LO2, LO3]
Rains Nickless Ltd. of Australia has two divisions that operate in Perth and Darwin. Selected data on the two divisions follow:

	Division	
	Perth	Darwin
Sales	$9,000,000	$20,000,000
Net operating income	630,000	1,800,000
Average operating assets	3,000,000	10,000,000

Required:
1. Compute the return on investment (ROI) for each division.
2. Assume that the company evaluates performance by use of residual income and that the minimum required return for any division is 16%. Compute the residual income for each division.
3. Is the Darwin Division's greater residual income an indication that it is better managed? Explain.

EXERCISE 12–10 Evaluating New Investments Using Return on Investment (ROI) and Residual Income [LO2, LO3]
Selected sales and operating data for three divisions of three different companies are given below:

	Division A	Division B	Division C
Sales	$6,000,000	$10,000,000	$8,000,000
Average operating assets	1,500,000	5,000,000	2,000,000
Net operating income	300,000	900,000	180,000
Minimum required rate of return	15%	18%	12%

Required:
1. Compute the return on investment (ROI) for each division, using the formula stated in terms of margin and turnover.
2. Compute the residual income for each division.
3. Assume that each division is presented with an investment opportunity that would yield a rate of return of 17%.
   a. If performance is being measured by ROI, which division or divisions will probably accept the opportunity? Reject? Why?
   b. If performance is being measured by residual income, which division or divisions will probably accept the opportunity? Reject? Why?

EXERCISE 12–11 (Appendix 12A) Transfer Pricing Basics [LO4]
Nelcro Company's Electrical Division produces a high-quality transformer. Sales and cost data on the transformer follow:

Selling price per unit on the outside market	$40
Variable costs per unit	$21
Fixed costs per unit (based on capacity)	$9
Capacity in units	60,000

Nelcro Company has a Motor Division that would like to begin purchasing this transformer from the Electrical Division. The Motor Division is currently purchasing 10,000 transformers each year from another company at a cost of $38 per transformer. Nelcro Company evaluates its division managers on the basis of divisional profits.

Required:

1. Assume that the Electrical Division is now selling only 50,000 transformers each year to outside customers.
   a. From the standpoint of the Electrical Division, what is the lowest acceptable transfer price for transformers sold to the Motor Division?
   b. From the standpoint of the Motor Division, what is the highest acceptable transfer price for transformers acquired from the Electrical Division?
   c. If left free to negotiate without interference, would you expect the division managers to voluntarily agree to the transfer of 10,000 transformers from the Electrical Division to the Motor Division? Why or why not?
   d. From the standpoint of the entire company, should a transfer take place? Why or why not?
2. Assume that the Electrical Division is now selling all of the transformers it can produce to outside customers.
   a. From the standpoint of the Electrical Division, what is the lowest acceptable transfer price for transformers sold to the Motor Division?
   b. From the standpoint of the Motor Division, what is the highest acceptable transfer price for transformers acquired from the Electrical Division?
   c. If left free to negotiate without interference, would you expect the division managers to voluntarily agree to the transfer of 10,000 transformers from the Electrical Division to the Motor Division? Why or why not?
   d. From the standpoint of the entire company, should a transfer take place? Why or why not?

EXERCISE 12–12 (Appendix 12A) Transfer Pricing from Viewpoint of the Entire Company [LO4]

Division A manufactures picture tubes for TVs. The tubes can be sold either to Division B of the same company or to outside customers. Last year, the following activity was recorded in Division A:

Selling price per tube	$175
Production cost per tube.	$130
Number of tubes:	
Produced during the year	20,000
Sold to outside customers.	16,000
Sold to Division B	4,000

Sales to Division B were at the same price as sales to outside customers. The tubes purchased by Division B were used in a TV set manufactured by that division. Division B incurred $300 in additional cost per TV and then sold the TVs for $600 each.

Required:

1. Prepare income statements for last year for Division A, Division B, and the company as a whole.
2. Assume that Division A's manufacturing capacity is 20,000 tubes per year. Next year, Division B wants to purchase 5,000 tubes from Division A, rather than only 4,000 tubes as in last year. (Tubes of this type are not available from outside sources.) From the standpoint of the company as a whole, should Division A sell the 1,000 additional tubes to Division B, or should it continue to sell them to outside customers? Explain.

EXERCISE 12–13 (Appendix 12A) Transfer Pricing Situations [LO4]

In each of the cases below, assume that Division X has a product that can be sold either to outside customers or to Division Y of the same company for use in its production process. The managers of the divisions are evaluated based on their divisional profits.

	Case	
	A	B
Division X:		
Capacity in units	100,000	100,000
Number of units being sold to outside customers.	100,000	80,000
Selling price per unit to outside customers.	$50	$35

continued

Variable costs per unit	$30	$20
Fixed costs per unit (based on capacity)	$8	$6
Division Y:		
Number of units needed for production	20,000	20,000
Purchase price per unit now being paid to an outside supplier	$47	$34

Required:

1. Refer to the data in case A above. Assume that $2 per unit in variable selling costs can be avoided on intracompany sales. If the managers are free to negotiate and make decisions on their own, will a transfer take place? If so, within what range will the transfer price fall? Explain.
2. Refer to the data in case B above. In this case there will be no reduction in variable selling costs on intracompany sales. If the managers are free to negotiate and make decisions on their own, will a transfer take place? If so, within what range will the transfer price fall? Explain.

Problems

PROBLEM 12–14 Segment Reporting and Decision-Making [LO1]
The most recent monthly income statement for Reston Company is given below:

RESTON COMPANY
Income Statement
For the Month Ended May 31

Sales	$900,000	100.0%
Less variable expenses	408,000	45.3
Contribution margin	492,000	54.7
Less fixed expenses	465,000	51.7
Net operating income	$ 27,000	3.0%

Management is disappointed with the company's performance and is wondering what can be done to improve profits. By examining sales and cost records, you have determined the following:

a. The company is divided into two sales territories—Central and Eastern. The Central Territory recorded $400,000 in sales and $208,000 in variable expenses during May. The remaining sales and variable expenses were recorded in the Eastern Territory. Fixed expenses of $160,000 and $130,000 are traceable to the Central and Eastern Territories, respectively. The rest of the fixed expenses are common to the two territories.
b. The company sells two products—Awls and Pows. Sales of Awls and Pows totaled $100,000 and $300,000, respectively, in the Central Territory during May. Variable expenses are 25% of the selling price for Awls and 61% for Pows. Cost records show that $60,000 of the Central Territory's fixed expenses are traceable to Awls and $54,000 to Pows, with the remainder common to the two products.

Required:

1. Prepare segmented income statements, first showing the total company broken down between sales territories and then showing the Central Territory broken down by product line. Show both Amount and Percent columns for the company in total and for each segment. Round percentage computations to one decimal place.
2. Look at the statement you have prepared showing the total company segmented by sales territory. What points revealed by this statement should be brought to the attention of management?
3. Look at the statement you have prepared showing the Central Territory segmented by product lines. What points revealed by this statement should be brought to the attention of management?

PROBLEM 12–15 Basic Segmented Statement; Activity-Based Cost Assignment [LO1]
Vega Foods, Inc., has recently purchased a small mill that it intends to operate as one of its subsidiaries. The newly acquired mill has three products that it offers for sale—wheat cereal, pancake

mix, and flour. Each product sells for $10 per package. Materials, labor, and other variable production costs are $3.00 per bag of wheat cereal, $4.20 per bag of pancake mix, and $1.80 per bag of flour. Sales commissions are 10% of sales for any product. All other costs are fixed.

The mill's income statement for the most recent month is given below:

	Total Company		Product Line		
			Wheat Cereal	Pancake Mix	Flour
Sales	$600,000	100.0%	$200,000	$300,000	$100,000
Less expenses:					
Materials, labor, and other	204,000	34.0	60,000	126,000	18,000
Sales commissions	60,000	10.0	20,000	30,000	10,000
Advertising	123,000	20.5	48,000	60,000	15,000
Salaries	66,000	11.0	34,000	21,000	11,000
Equipment depreciation	30,000	5.0	10,000	15,000	5,000
Warehouse rent	12,000	2.0	4,000	6,000	2,000
General administration	90,000	15.0	30,000	30,000	30,000
Total expenses	585,000	97.5	206,000	288,000	91,000
Net operating income (loss)	$ 15,000	2.5%	$ (6,000)	$ 12,000	$ 9,000

The following additional information is available about the company:

a. The same equipment is used to mill and package all three products. In the above income statement, equipment depreciation has been allocated on the basis of sales dollars. An analysis of the use of the equipment indicates that it is used 40% of the time to make wheat cereal, 50% of the time to make pancake mix, and 10% of the time to make flour.
b. All three products are stored in the same warehouse. In the above income statement, the warehouse rent has been allocated on the basis of sales dollars. The warehouse contains 24,000 square feet of space, of which 8,000 square feet are used for wheat cereal, 14,000 square feet are used for pancake mix, and 2,000 square feet are used for flour. The warehouse space costs the company $0.50 per square foot to rent.
c. The general administration costs relate to the administration of the company as a whole. In the above income statement, these costs have been divided equally among the three product lines.
d. All other costs are traceable to the product lines.

Vega Foods' management is anxious to improve the mill's 2.5% margin on sales.

Required:

1. Prepare a new segmented income statement for the month, using the contribution approach. Show both Amount and Percent columns for the company as a whole and for each product line. Adjust the allocation of equipment depreciation and warehouse rent as indicated by the additional information provided.
2. After seeing the income statement in the main body of the problem, management has decided to eliminate the wheat cereal, since it is not returning a profit, and to focus all available resources on promoting the pancake mix.
   a. Based on the statement you have prepared, do you agree with the decision to eliminate the wheat cereal? Explain.
   b. Based on the statement you have prepared, do you agree with the decision to focus all available resources on promoting the pancake mix? Explain. (You may assume that an ample market is available for all three products.)
3. What additional points would you bring to the attention of management that might help to improve profits?

PROBLEM 12–16 Restructuring a Segmented Income Statement [LO1]

Brabant NV of the Netherlands is a wholesale distributor of Dutch cheeses that it sells throughout the European Community. Unfortunately, the company's profits have been declining, which has caused considerable concern. To help understand the condition of the company, the managing director of the company has requested that the monthly income statement be segmented by sales territory. Accordingly, the company's accounting department has prepared the following statement for March, the most recent month. (The Dutch currency is the euro which is designated by €.)

	Sales Territory		
	Southern Europe	Middle Europe	Northern Europe
Sales	€300,000	€800,000	€700,000
Less territorial expenses (traceable):			
Cost of goods sold	93,000	240,000	315,000
Salaries	54,000	56,000	112,000
Insurance	9,000	16,000	14,000
Advertising	105,000	240,000	245,000
Depreciation	21,000	32,000	28,000
Shipping	15,000	32,000	42,000
Total territorial expenses	297,000	616,000	756,000
Territorial income (loss) before corporate expenses	3,000	184,000	(56,000)
Less corporate expenses:			
Advertising (general)	15,000	40,000	35,000
General administrative	20,000	20,000	20,000
Total corporate expenses	35,000	60,000	55,000
Net operating income (loss)	€(32,000)	€124,000	€(111,000)

Cost of goods sold and shipping expenses are both variable; other costs are all fixed. Brabant NV purchases cheeses at auction and from farmers' cooperatives, and it distributes them in the three territories listed above. Each of the three sales territories has its own manager and sales staff. The cheeses vary widely in profitability; some have a high margin and some have a low margin. (Certain cheeses, after having been aged for long periods, are the most expensive and carry the highest margins.)

Required:

1. List any disadvantages or weaknesses that you see to the statement format illustrated above.
2. Explain the basis that is apparently being used to allocate the corporate expenses to the territories. Do you agree with these allocations? Explain.
3. Prepare a new segmented income statement for May using the contribution approach. Show a Total column as well as data for each territory. Include percentages on your statement for all columns. Carry percentages to one decimal place.
4. Analyze the statement that you prepared in (3) above. What points that might help to improve the company's performance would you be particularly anxious to bring to the attention of management?

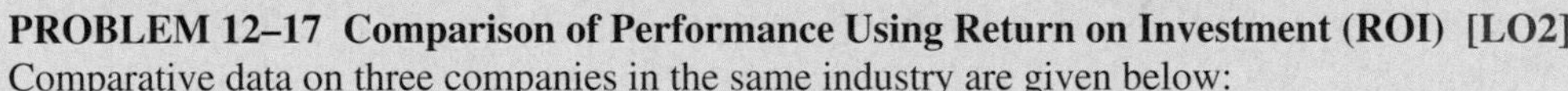

PROBLEM 12–17 Comparison of Performance Using Return on Investment (ROI) [LO2]
Comparative data on three companies in the same industry are given below:

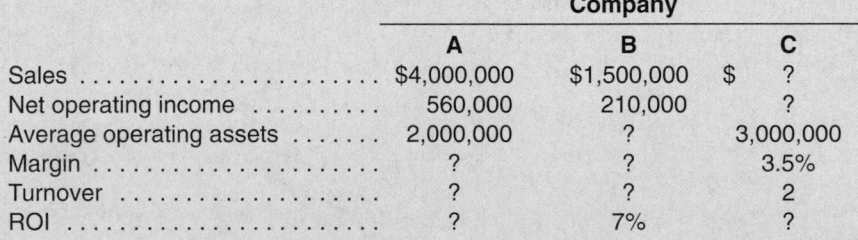

	Company		
	A	B	C
Sales	$4,000,000	$1,500,000	$?
Net operating income	560,000	210,000	?
Average operating assets	2,000,000	?	3,000,000
Margin	?	?	3.5%
Turnover	?	?	2
ROI	?	7%	?

Required:

1. What advantages can you see in breaking down the ROI computation into two separate elements, margin and turnover?
2. Fill in the missing information above, and comment on the relative performance of the three companies in as much detail as the data permit. Make *specific recommendations* on steps to be taken to improve the return on investment, where needed.

(Adapted from National Association of Accountants, *Research Report No. 35,* p. 34)

PROBLEM 12–18 Return on Investment (ROI) and Residual Income [LO2, LO3]
"I know headquarters wants us to add on that new product line," said Fred Halloway, manager of Kirsi Products' East Division. "But I want to see the numbers before I make a move. Our division has led the company for three years, and I don't want any letdown."

Kirsi Products is a decentralized company with four autonomous divisions. The divisions are evaluated on a basis of the return that they are able to generate on invested assets, with year-end bonuses given to divisional managers who have the highest ROI figures. Operating results for the company's East Division for last year are given below:

Sales	$21,000,000
Less variable expenses	$13,400,000
Contribution margin	7,600,000
Less fixed expenses	5,920,000
Net operating income	$ 1,680,000
Divisional operating assets	$ 5,250,000

The company had an overall return on investment (ROI) of 18% last year (considering all divisions). The company's East Division has an opportunity to add a new product line that would require an investment of $3,000,000. The cost and revenue characteristics of the new product line per year would be as follows:

Sales	$9,000,000
Variable expenses	65% of sales 5,850,000
Fixed expenses	$2,520,000

Required:

1. Compute the East Division's ROI for last year; also compute the ROI as it will appear if the new product line is added.
2. If you were in Fred Halloway's position, would you be inclined to accept or reject the new product line? Explain.
3. Why do you suppose headquarters is anxious for the East Division to add the new product line?
4. Suppose that the company views a return of 15% on invested assets as being the minimum that any division should earn and that performance is evaluated by the residual income approach.
   a. Compute the East Division's residual income for last year; also compute the residual income as it will appear if the new product line is added.
   b. Under these circumstances, if you were in Fred Halloway's position would you accept or reject the new product line? Explain.

PROBLEM 12–19 Return on Investment (ROI) and Residual Income [LO2, LO3]
Financial data for Bridger, Inc., for last year appear below:

BRIDGER, INC.
Balance Sheet

	Ending Balance	Beginning Balance
Assets		
Cash	$ 130,000	$ 125,000
Accounts receivable	480,000	340,000
Inventory	490,000	570,000
Plant and equipment, net	820,000	845,000
Investment in Brier Company	430,000	400,000
Land (undeveloped)	250,000	250,000
Total assets	$2,600,000	$2,530,000
Liabilities and Stockholders' Equity		
Accounts payable	$ 340,000	$ 380,000
Long-term debt	1,000,000	1,000,000
Stockholders' equity	1,260,000	1,150,000
Total liabilities and stockholders' equity	$2,600,000	$2,530,000

BRIDGER, INC.
Income Statement

Sales		$4,180,000
Less operating expenses		3,553,000
Net operating income		627,000
Less interest and taxes:		
Interest expense	$120,000	
Tax expense	200,000	320,000
Net operating income		$ 307,000

The company paid dividends of $197,000 last year. The "Investment in Brier Company" on the balance sheet represents an investment in the stock of another company.

Required:

1. Compute the company's margin, turnover, and return on investment (ROI) for last year.
2. The board of directors of Bridger, Inc., has set a minimum required return of 20%. What was the company's residual income last year?

PROBLEM 12–20 (Appendix 12A) Basic Transfer Pricing [LO4]

In cases 1–3 below, assume that Division A has a product that can be sold either to Division B of the same company or to outside customers. The managers of both divisions are evaluated based on their own division's return on investment (ROI). The managers are free to decide if they will participate in any internal transfers. All transfer prices are negotiated. Treat each case independently.

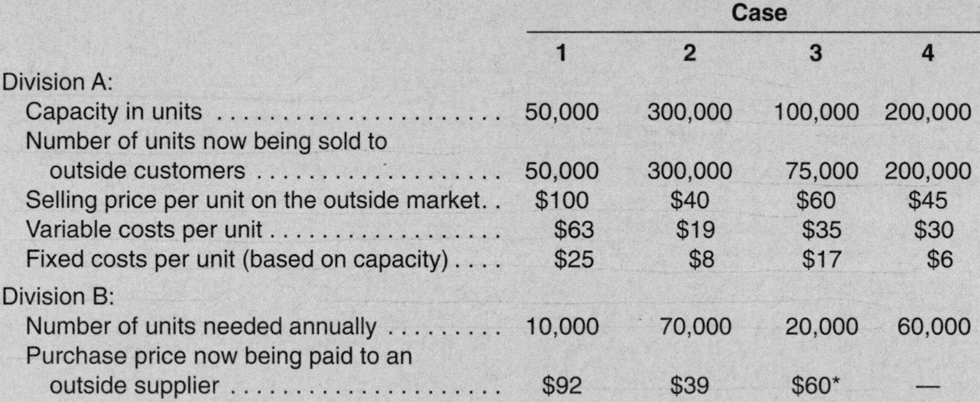

	Case			
	1	2	3	4
Division A:				
Capacity in units	50,000	300,000	100,000	200,000
Number of units now being sold to outside customers	50,000	300,000	75,000	200,000
Selling price per unit on the outside market	$100	$40	$60	$45
Variable costs per unit	$63	$19	$35	$30
Fixed costs per unit (based on capacity)	$25	$8	$17	$6
Division B:				
Number of units needed annually	10,000	70,000	20,000	60,000
Purchase price now being paid to an outside supplier	$92	$39	$60*	—

*Before any quantity discount.

Required:

1. Refer to case 1 above. A study has indicated that Division A can avoid $5 per unit in variable costs on any sales to Division B. Will the managers agree to a transfer and if so, within what range will the transfer price be? Explain.
2. Refer to case 2 above. Assume that Division A can avoid $4 per unit in variable costs on any sales to Division B.
   a. Would you expect any disagreement between the two divisional managers over what the transfer price should be? Explain.
   b. Assume that Division A offers to sell 70,000 units to Division B for $38 per unit and that Division B refuses this price. What will be the loss in potential profits for the company as a whole?
3. Refer to case 3 above. Assume that Division B is now receiving a 5% quantity discount from the outside supplier.
   a. Will the managers agree to a transfer? If so, within what range will the transfer price be?
   b. Assume that Division B offers to purchase 20,000 units from Division A at $52 per unit. If Division A accepts this price, would you expect its ROI to increase, decrease, or remain unchanged? Why?
4. Refer to case 4 above. Assume that Division B wants Division A to provide it with 60,000 units of a *different* product from the one that Division A is now producing. The new product would require $25 per unit in variable costs and would require that Division A cut back production of its present product by 30,000 units annually. What is the lowest acceptable transfer price from Division A's perspective?

PROBLEM 12–21 (Appendix 12A) Transfer Pricing with an Outside Market [LO4]
Galati Products, Inc., has just purchased a small company that specializes in the manufacture of electronic tuners that are used as a component part of TV sets. Galati Products, Inc., is a decentralized company, and it will treat the newly acquired company as an autonomous division with full profit responsibility. The new division, called the Tuner Division, has the following revenue and costs associated with each tuner that it manufactures and sells:

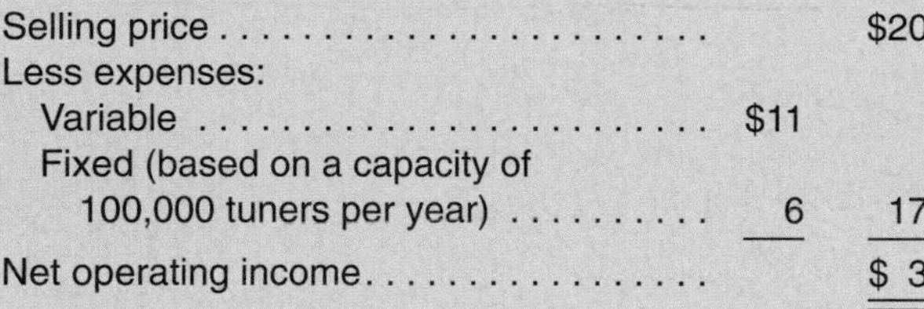

Selling price		$20
Less expenses:		
Variable	$11	
Fixed (based on a capacity of 100,000 tuners per year)	6	17
Net operating income		$ 3

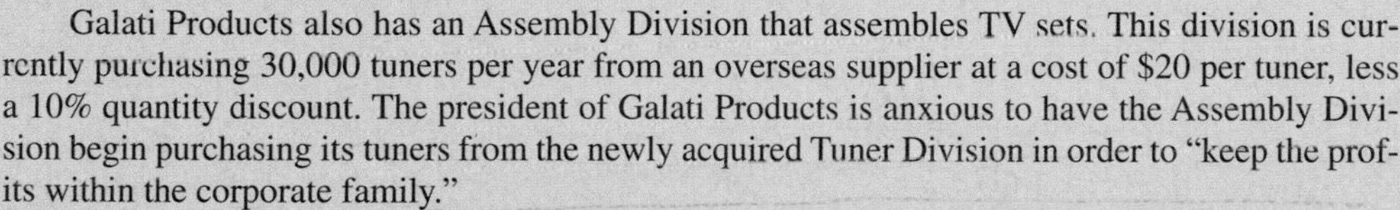

Galati Products also has an Assembly Division that assembles TV sets. This division is currently purchasing 30,000 tuners per year from an overseas supplier at a cost of $20 per tuner, less a 10% quantity discount. The president of Galati Products is anxious to have the Assembly Division begin purchasing its tuners from the newly acquired Tuner Division in order to "keep the profits within the corporate family."

Required:

For (1) through (2) below, assume that the Tuner Division can sell all of its output to outside TV manufacturers at the normal $20 price.

1. Are the managers of the Tuner and Assembly Divisions likely to voluntarily agree to a transfer price for 30,000 tuners each year? Why or why not?
2. If the Tuner Division meets the price that the Assembly Division is currently paying to its overseas supplier and sells 30,000 tuners to the Assembly Division each year, what will be the effect on the profits of the Tuner Division, the Assembly Division, and the company as a whole?

For (3) through (6) below, assume that the Tuner Division is currently selling only 60,000 tuners each year to outside TV manufacturers at the stated $20 price.

3. Are the managers of the Tuner and Assembly Divisions likely to voluntarily agree to a transfer price for 30,000 tuners each year? Why or why not?
4. Suppose that the Assembly Division's overseas supplier drops its price (net of the quantity discount) to only $16 per tuner. Should the Tuner Division meet this price? Explain. If the Tuner Division does *not* meet this price, what will be the effect on the profits of the company as a whole?
5. Refer to (4) above. If the Tuner Division refuses to meet the $16 price, should the Assembly Division be required to purchase from the Tuner Division at a higher price for the good of the company as a whole? Explain.
6. Refer to (4) above. Assume that due to inflexible management policies, the Assembly Division is required to purchase 30,000 tuners each year from the Tuner Division at $20 per tuner. What will be the effect on the profits of the company as a whole?

PROBLEM 12–22 Multiple Segmented Income Statements [LO1]

Severo S.A. of Sao Paulo, Brazil, is organized into two divisions. The company's segmented income statement (in terms of the Brazilian currency Real) for last month is given below:

		Divisions	
	Total Company	**Cloth**	**Leather**
Sales	R3,500,000	R2,000,000	R1,500,000
Less variable expenses	1,721,000	960,000	761,000
Contribution margin	1,779,000	1,040,000	739,000
Less traceable fixed expenses:			
Advertising	612,000	300,000	312,000
Administration	427,000	210,000	217,000
Depreciation	229,000	115,000	114,000
Total traceable fixed expenses	1,268,000	625,000	643,000
Divisional segment margin	511,000	R 415,000	R 96,000
Less common fixed expenses	390,000		
Net operating income	R 121,000		

Top management can't understand why the Leather Division has such a low segment margin when its sales are only 25% less than sales in the Cloth Division. As one step in isolating the problem, management has directed that the Leather Division be further segmented into product lines. The following information is available on the product lines in the Leather Division:

	Leather Division Product Lines		
	Garments	**Shoes**	**Handbags**
Sales	R500,000	R700,000	R300,000
Traceable fixed expenses:			
Advertising	80,000	112,000	120,000
Administration	30,000	35,000	42,000
Depreciation	25,000	56,000	33,000
Variable expenses as a percentage of sales	65%	40%	52%

Analysis shows that R110,000 of the Leather Division's administration expenses are common to the product lines.

Required:

1. Prepare a segmented income statement for the Leather Division with segments defined as product lines. Use the contribution approach. Show both Amount and Percent columns for the division in total and for each product line. Carry percentage figures to one decimal place.
2. Management is surprised by the handbag product line's poor showing and would like to have the product line segmented by market. The following information is available about the markets in which the handbag line is sold:

	Handbag Markets	
	Domestic	**Foreign**
Sales	R200,000	R100,000
Traceable fixed expenses:		
Advertising	40,000	80,000
Variable expenses as a percentage of sales	43%	70%

   All of handbag product line's administration expenses and depreciation are common to the markets in which the product is sold. Prepare a segmented income statement for the handbag product line with segments defined as markets. Again use the contribution approach and show both Amount and Percent columns.
3. Refer to the statement prepared in (1) above. The sales manager wants to run a special promotional campaign on one of the product lines over the next month. A marketing study indicates that such a campaign would increase sales of the garment product line by R200,000 or sales of the shoes product line by R145,000. The campaign would cost R30,000. Show computations to determine which product line should be chosen.

PROBLEM 12–23 Segment Reporting; Activity-Based Cost Assignment [LO1]

"Rats! We're still in the red," said Jana Andrews, executive vice president of the Ashland Company. "I know," said Steve Clark, the controller. "Just look at this income statement for March. We've got to forget about Districts A and B and focus on District C." The statement to which Mr. Clark was referring is shown below:

	Total Company	Districts A	B	C
Sales @ $20 per unit	$1,000,000	$300,000	$500,000	$200,000
Less cost of goods sold @ $9 per unit	450,000	135,000	225,000	90,000
Gross margin	550,000	165,000	275,000	110,000
Less operating expenses:				
Marketing expenses:				
Shipping	51,250	11,250	25,000	15,000
Warehouse rent	80,000	24,000	40,000	16,000
Sales commissions	60,000	18,000	30,000	12,000

continued

Sales salaries	30,000	12,000	10,000	8,000
District advertising	75,000	20,000	25,000	30,000
National advertising*	115,000	34,500	57,500	23,000
Total marketing expenses	411,250	119,750	187,500	104,000
Administrative expenses:				
District management salaries	40,000	12,000	15,000	13,000
Central office administrative expenses*	100,000	30,000	50,000	20,000
Total administrative expenses	140,000	42,000	65,000	33,000
Total operating expenses	551,250	161,750	252,500	137,000
Net operating income (loss)	$ (1,250)	$ 3,250	$ 22,500	$ (27,000)

*Allocated on the basis of sales dollars.

The company is a retail organization that sells a single product. The product is sold in three districts, as shown above. Additional information on the company follows:

a. The sales and administrative offices are centrally located, being about the same distance from each district.
b. Each district specifies on the sales order what shipping method is to be used (by truck, rail, or air). All goods are shipped from a central warehouse. Shipping is a variable cost, and it is traceable to the districts; differences in amounts above are reflective of the different shipping methods used.
c. All salespersons are paid a base salary of $2,000 per month, plus a commission of 6% of sales. There are 6 salespersons in District A, 5 in District B, and 4 in District C.
d. Each district manager must arrange his or her own district's advertising program. The national advertising is provided by the central office.
e. The variable costs of processing orders, which have been included in the "Central office administrative expenses" above, amount to $25,000. During March, District A had 3,000 orders, District B had 1,500 orders, and District C had 500 orders. The remainder of the "Central office administrative expenses" are fixed and relate to general administrative assistance provided to all parts of the organization.
f. The warehouse contains 160,000 square feet of storage space. District A uses 60,000 square feet, District B uses 80,000 square feet, and District C uses 20,000 square feet.

Required:

1. Garth Hansen, the president, has asked that the company's income statement be redone using the contribution format, which he heard about at a recent industry convention. Prepare the income statement as requested by Mr. Hansen. Show both an Amount and a Percent column for the company in total and for each district. (Carry computations to one decimal place.)
2. Compute the contribution margin per order for each district. What problems does this computation suggest?
3. The manager of District B would like to spend an extra $25,000 next month in a special promotional campaign. If sales increase by $100,000 as a result, would the expenditure be justified? No additional warehouse space would be required.
4. Analyze the data in the statement you prepared in (1) above. What points should be brought to the attention of management?

PROBLEM 12–24 Return on Investment (ROI) and Residual Income; Decentralization [LO2, LO3]

Lawton Industries has manufactured prefabricated houses for over 20 years. The houses are constructed in sections to be assembled on customers' lots.

Lawton expanded into the kit housing market several years ago when it acquired Presser Company, one of its suppliers. In this market, various types of lumber are precut into the appropriate lengths, banded into packages, and shipped to customers' lots in the form of a kit for assembly. Lawton decided to maintain Presser's separate identity and therefore established the Presser Division as an investment center of Lawton.

Lawton uses ROI as a performance measure. Management bonuses are based in part on ROI. All investments in operating assets are expected to earn a minimum rate of return of 15%.

Presser's ROI has ranged from 19% to 22%, since it was acquired by Lawton. During the past year, Presser had an investment opportunity that had an estimated rate of return of 18%. Presser's management decided against the investment because it believed the investment would decrease the division's overall ROI.

Last year's income statement for the Presser Division is given below. The division's operating assets employed were $15,500,000 at the end of the year, which represents a 24% increase over the previous year-end balance. (Several purchases of new equipment were made during the year.)

PRESSER DIVISION
Divisional Income Statement

Sales		$35,000,000
Cost of goods sold		24,600,000
Gross margin		10,400,000
Less operating expenses:		
Selling expenses	$5,700,000	
Administrative expenses	1,900,000	7,600,000
Net operating income		$ 2,800,000

Required:

1. Calculate the following performance measures for the Presser Division:
   a. ROI. (Remember, ROI is based on the *average* operating assets, computed from the beginning-of-year and end-of-year balances.) State the ROI in terms of margin and turnover.
   b. Residual income.
2. Would the management of Presser Division have been more likely to accept the investment opportunity with an ROI of 18% if residual income were used as a performance measure instead of ROI? Explain.
3. The Presser Division is a separate investment center within Lawton Industries. Identify the items Presser Division must be free to control if it is to be evaluated fairly by either the ROI or residual income performance measures.

(CMA, adapted)

PROBLEM 12–25 Return on Investment (ROI) Analysis [LO2]
The income statement for Westex, Inc., for its most recent period is given below:

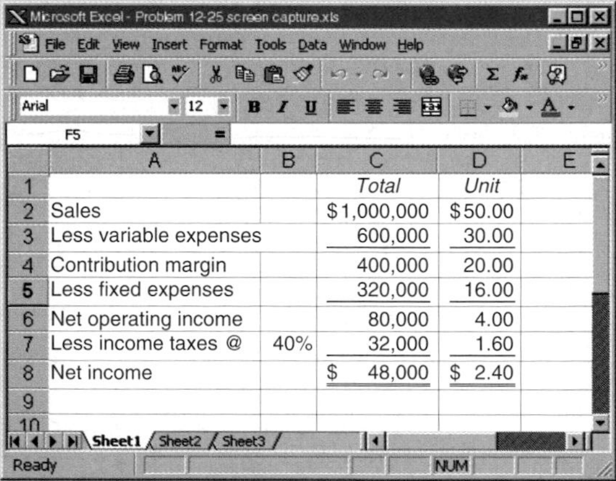

	A	B	C	D
1			*Total*	*Unit*
2	Sales		$1,000,000	$50.00
3	Less variable expenses		600,000	30.00
4	Contribution margin		400,000	20.00
5	Less fixed expenses		320,000	16.00
6	Net operating income		80,000	4.00
7	Less income taxes @	40%	32,000	1.60
8	Net income		$ 48,000	$ 2.40

The company had average operating assets of $500,000 during the period.

Required:

1. Compute the company's return on investment (ROI) for the period using the ROI formula stated in terms of margin and turnover.

For each of the following questions, indicate whether the margin and turnover will increase, decrease, or remain unchanged as a result of the events described, and then compute the new ROI figure. Consider each question separately, starting in each case from the original ROI computed in (1) above.

2. The company achieves a cost savings of $10,000 per period by using less costly materials.

3. Using just-in-time (JIT), the company is able to reduce the average level of inventory by $100,000. (The released funds are used to pay off bank loans.)
4. Sales are increased by $100,000; operating assets remain unchanged.
5. The company issues bonds and uses the proceeds to purchase $125,000 in machinery and equipment at the beginning of the period. Interest on the bonds is $15,000 per period. Sales remain unchanged. The new, more efficient equipment reduces production costs by $5,000 per period.
6. The company invests $180,000 of cash (received on accounts receivable) in a plot of land that is to be held for possible future use as a plant site.
7. Obsolete items of inventory carried on the records at a cost of $20,000 are scrapped and written off as a loss.

PROBLEM 12–26 (Appendix 12A) Cost Volume Profit Analysis; Return on Investment (ROI); Transfer Pricing [LO2, LO4]

The Bearing Division of Timkin Company produces a small bearing that is used by a number of companies as a component part in the manufacture of their products. Timkin Company operates its divisions as autonomous units, giving its divisional managers great discretion in pricing and other decisions. Each division is expected to generate a return on its operating assets of at least 12%. The Bearing Division has operating assets of $300,000. The bearings are sold for $4 each. Variable costs are $2.50 per bearing, and fixed costs total $234,000 each period. The division's capacity is 200,000 bearings each period.

Required:

1. How many bearings must be sold each period for the division to obtain the desired rate of return on its assets?
   a. What is the margin earned at this sales level?
   b. What is the turnover at this sales level?
2. The divisional manager is considering two ways of increasing the ROI figure:
   a. Market studies suggest that an increase in price to $4.25 per bearing would result in sales of 160,000 units each period. The decrease in units sold would allow the division to reduce its investment in assets by $10,000, due to the lower level of inventories and receivables that would be needed to support sales. Compute the margin, turnover, and ROI if these changes are made.
   b. Other market studies suggest that a reduction in price to $3.75 per bearing would result in sales of 200,000 units each period. However, this would require an increase in total assets of $10,000, due to the somewhat larger inventories and receivables that would be carried. Compute the margin, turnover, and ROI if these changes are made.
3. Refer to the original data. Assume that the normal volume of sales is 180,000 bearings each period at a price of $4 per bearing. Another division of Timkin Company is currently purchasing 20,000 bearings each period from an overseas supplier at $3.25 per bearing. The manager of the Bearing Division says that this price is "ridiculous" and refuses to meet it, since doing so would result in a loss of $0.42 per bearing for her division:

Selling price		$3.25
Cost per bearing:		
Variable cost.	$2.50	
Fixed cost ($234,000 ÷ 200,000 bearings)	1.17	3.67
Loss per bearing		$(0.42)

You may assume that sales to the other division would require an increase of $25,000 in the total assets carried by the Bearing Division. Would you recommend that the Bearing Division meet the $3.25 price and start selling 20,000 bearings per period to the other division? Support your answer with ROI computations.

PROBLEM 12–27 (Appendix 12A) Market-Based Transfer Price [LO4]

Damico Company's Board Division manufactures an electronic control board that is widely used in high-end DVD players. The cost per control board is as follows:

Variable cost per board	$120
Fixed cost per board	30*
Total cost per board.	$150

*Based on a capacity of 800,000 boards per year.

Part of the Board Division's output is sold to outside manufacturers of DVD players, and part is sold to Damico Company's Consumer Products Division, which produces a DVD player under the Damico name. The Board Division charges a selling price of $190 per control board for all sales, both internally and externally.

The costs, revenues, and net operating income associated with the Consumer Products Division's DVD player are given below:

Selling price per player		$580
Less variable costs per player:		
Cost of the control board	$190	
Variable cost of other parts	230	
Total variable costs		420
Contribution margin		160
Less fixed costs per player		85*
Net operating income per player		$ 75

*Based on a capacity of 200,000 DVD players per year.

The Consumer Products Division has an order from an overseas distributor for 5,000 DVD players. The distributor wants to pay only $400 per DVD player.

Required:

1. Assume that the Consumer Products Division has enough idle capacity to fill the 5,000-unit order. Is the division likely to accept the $400 price, or to reject it? Explain.
2. Assume that both the Board Division and the Consumer Products Division have idle capacity. Under these conditions, would rejecting the $400 price be an advantage to the company as a whole, or would it result in the loss of potential profits? Show computations to support your answer.
3. Assume that the Board Division is operating at capacity and could sell all of its control boards to outside manufacturers of DVD players. Assume, however, that the Consumer Products Division has enough idle capacity to fill the 5,000-unit order. Under these conditions, compute the dollar advantage or disadvantage to the Consumer Products Division of accepting the order at the $400 price.
4. What conclusions do you draw concerning the use of market price as a transfer price in intracompany transactions?

PROBLEM 12–28 (Appendix 12A) Negotiated Transfer Price [LO4]

Pella Company has several independent divisions. The company's Compressor Division produces a high-quality compressor that is sold to various users. The division's income statement for the most recent month, in which 500 compressors were sold, is given below:

	Total	Unit
Sales	$125,000	$250
Less cost of goods sold	75,000	150
Gross margin	50,000	100
Less selling and administrative expenses	30,000	60
Divisional net operating income	$ 20,000	$ 40

As shown above, it costs the division $150 to produce a compressor. This figure consists of the following costs:

Direct materials	$ 50
Direct labor	60
Manufacturing overhead (50% fixed)	40
Total cost	$150

The division has fixed selling and administrative expenses of $25,000 per month and variable selling and administrative expenses of $10 per compressor.

Another division of Pella Company, the Home Products Division, uses compressors as a component part of air-conditioning systems that it installs. The Home Products Division has asked the

Compressor Division to sell it 40 compressors each month of a somewhat different design. The Compressor Division has estimated the following cost for each of the new compressors:

Direct materials	$ 60
Direct labor	90
Manufacturing overhead (two-thirds fixed)	75
Total cost	$225

In order to produce the new compressors, the Compressor Division would have to reduce production of its present compressors by 100 units per month. However, all variable selling and administrative expenses could be avoided on the intracompany business. Total fixed overhead costs would not change. Assume direct labor is a variable cost.

Required:

1. Determine the lowest acceptable transfer price from the perspective of the Compressor Division for the new compressor.
2. Suppose the Home Products Division has found an outside supplier that will provide the new compressors for only $350 each. If the Compressor Division meets this price, what will be the effect on the profits of the company as a whole?

Cases

CASE 12–29 Service Organization; Segment Reporting [LO1]

The American Association of Acupuncturists is a professional association for acupuncturists that has 10,000 members. The association operates from a central headquarters but has local chapters throughout North America. The association's monthly journal, *American Acupuncture,* features recent developments in the field. The association also publishes special reports and books, and it sponsors courses that qualify members for the continuing professional education credit required by state certification boards. The association's statement of revenues and expenses for the current year is presented below:

AMERICAN ASSOCIATION OF ACUPUNCTURISTS
Statement of Revenues and Expenses
For the Year Ended December 31

Revenues	$970,000
Less expenses:	
Salaries	440,000
Occupancy costs	120,000
Distributions to local chapters	210,000
Printing	82,000
Mailing	24,000
Continuing education instructors' fees	60,000
General and administrative	27,000
Total expenses	963,000
Excess of revenues over expenses	$ 7,000

The board of directors of the association has requested that you construct a segmented statement of operations that shows the financial contribution of each of the association's four major programs—membership service, journal, books and reports, and continuing education. The following data have been gathered to aid you:

a. Membership dues are $60 per year, of which $15 covers a one-year subscription to the association's journal. The other $45 pays for general membership services.
b. One-year subscriptions to *American Acupuncture* are sold to nonmembers and libraries at $20 per subscription. A total of 1,000 of these subscriptions were sold last year. In addition to subscriptions, the journal generated $50,000 in advertising revenues. The costs per journal subscription, for members as well as nonmembers, were $4 for printing and $1 for mailing.
c. A variety of technical reports and professional books were sold for a total of $70,000 during the year. Printing costs for these materials totaled $25,000, and mailing costs totaled $8,000.

goodness for these segmented statements. It's pretty obvious that we should cut back production of line A. Pass the word, and concentrate all of our B4 chip inventory on production of line B."

Required:

1. Prepare a new income statement segmented by product lines, using the contribution approach. Show both Amount and Percent columns for the company in total and for each of the product lines. (Carry percentages to one decimal place.)
2. Do you agree with Mr. Aiken's decision to cut back production of line A? Why or why not?
3. Assume that the company's executive committee is considering the elimination of line C, due to its poor showing. If you were serving on this committee, what points would you make for or against elimination of the line?
4. Line C is sold in both a home and a foreign market, with sales and cost data as follows:

	Home Market	Foreign Market
Sales.	$300,000	$50,000
Traceable fixed costs:		
Selling	$10,000	$40,000

The fixed production costs of line C are considered to be common to the markets in which the product is sold. Variable expense relationships in the markets are the same as those shown in the main body of the problem for line C.

a. Prepare a segmented income statement showing line C segmented by markets. Show both Amount and Percent columns for line C in total and for both of the markets.

b. What points revealed by this statement would you be particularly anxious to bring to the attention of management?

Group and Internet Exercises

GROUP EXERCISE 12–32 College Segment Reports

Obtain a copy of your college or university's most recent financial report prepared for internal use.

Required:

1. Does the financial report break down the results into major segments such as schools, academic departments, intercollegiate sports, and so on? Can you determine the financial contribution (i.e., revenues less expenses) of each segment from the report?
2. If the report attempts to show the financial contribution of each major segment, does the report follow the principles for segment reporting in this chapter? If not, what principles are violated and what harm, if any, can occur as a result from violating those principles?

INTERNET EXERCISE 12–33

As you know, the World Wide Web is a medium that is constantly evolving. Sites come and go, and change without notice. To enable periodic update of site addresses, this problem has been posted to the textbook website (www.mhhe.com/garrison10e). After accessing the site, enter the Student Center and select this chapter. Select and complete the Internet Exercise.

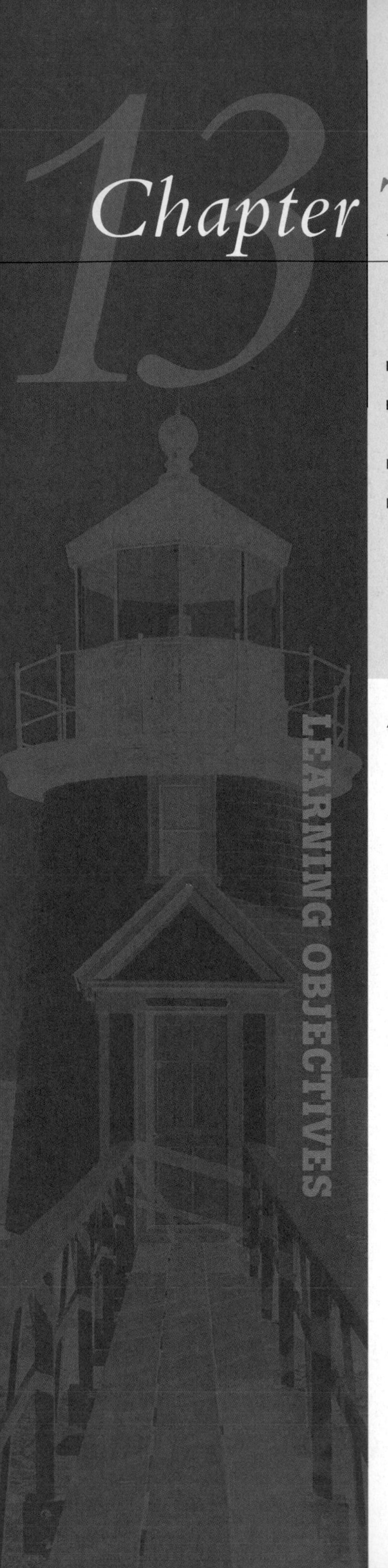

Chapter Thirteen

Relevant Costs for Decision Making

After studying Chapter 13, you should be able to:

1. Identify relevant and irrelevant costs and benefits in a decision situation.
2. Prepare an analysis showing whether a product line or other organizational segment should be dropped or retained.
3. Prepare a make or buy analysis.
4. Prepare an analysis showing whether a special order should be accepted.
5. Determine the most profitable use of a constrained resource and the value of obtaining more of the constrained resource.
6. Prepare an analysis showing whether joint products should be sold at the split-off point or processed further.

Traveling on a Sunk Cost

A failure to recognize the existence of sunk costs can lead to bad business decisions. As evidence, consider the following incident related by a business consultant after encountering a frustrated and angry fellow traveler ("Mr. Smith") whose flight home faced a lengthy delay:

Mr. Smith had recently flown into St. Louis on a commercial airline for a two-day business trip. While there, he learned that his company's private airplane had flown in the day before and would leave on the same day that he was scheduled to leave. Mr. Smith immediately cashed in his $200 commercial airline ticket and made arrangements to fly back on the company plane. He flew home feeling pretty good about saving his company the $200 fare and being able to depart on schedule.

About two weeks later, however, Mr. Smith's boss asked him why the department had been cross-charged $400 for his return trip when the commercial airfare was only $200. Mr. Smith explained that "the company plane was flying back regardless, and there were a number of empty seats."

How could Mr. Smith's attempt to save his company $200 end up "costing" his department $400? The problem is that Mr. Smith recognized something that his company's cost allocation system did not: namely, that the vast majority of the costs associated with flying the plane home were already sunk and, thus, unavoidable at the time he made the decision to fly home. By failing to distinguish between sunk (i.e., unavoidable) and avoidable costs, the cost allocation system was causing the firm and its managers to make uneconomic business decisions.

It is now clear why Mr. Smith was so frustrated the day I ran into him in St. Louis. His company's plane was sitting on the runway with a number of empty seats and ready to take off for the very same destination. Yet there was no way Mr. Smith was going to fly on that plane even though doing so was the "best business decision."

BUSINESS FOCUS

Source: Dennis L. Weisman, "How Cost Allocation Systems Can Lead Managers Astray," *Journal of Cost Management* 5, no. 1, p. 4. Used by permission.

Making decisions is one of the basic functions of a manager. Managers are constantly faced with problems of deciding what products to sell, what production methods to use, whether to make or buy component parts, what prices to charge, what channels of distribution to use, whether to accept special orders at special prices, and so forth. Decision making is often a difficult task that is complicated by the existence of numerous alternatives and massive amounts of data, only some of which may be relevant.

Every decision involves choosing from among at least two alternatives. In making a decision, the costs and benefits of one alternative must be compared to the costs and benefits of other alternatives. Costs that differ between alternatives are called **relevant costs.** Distinguishing between relevant and irrelevant costs and benefits is critical for two reasons. First, irrelevant data can be ignored and need not be analyzed. This can save decision makers tremendous amounts of time and effort. Second, bad decisions can easily result from erroneously including irrelevant cost and benefit data when analyzing alternatives. To be successful in decision making, managers must be able to tell the difference between relevant and irrelevant data and must be able to correctly use the relevant data in analyzing alternatives. The purpose of this chapter is to develop these skills by illustrating their use in a wide range of decision-making situations. We hasten to add that these decision-making skills are as important in your personal life as they are to managers. After completing your study of the material in this chapter, you should be able to think more clearly about decisions in many facets of your life.

Cost Concepts for Decision Making

Four cost terms discussed in Chapter 2 are particularly applicable to this chapter. These terms are *differential costs, incremental costs, opportunity costs,* and *sunk costs.* You may find it helpful to turn back to Chapter 2 and refresh your memory concerning these terms before reading on.

Identifying Relevant Costs and Benefits

LEARNING OBJECTIVE 1
Identify relevant and irrelevant costs and benefits in a decision situation.

Only those costs and benefits that differ in total between alternatives are relevant in a decision. If a cost will be the same regardless of the alternative selected, then the decision has no effect on the cost and it can be ignored. For example, if you are trying to decide whether to go to a movie or to rent a videotape for the evening, the rent on your apartment is irrelevant. Whether you go to a movie or rent a videotape, the rent on your apartment will be exactly the same and is therefore irrelevant in the decision. On the other hand, the cost of the movie ticket and the cost of renting the videotape would be relevant in the decision since they are *avoidable costs.*

An **avoidable cost** is a cost that can be eliminated in whole or in part by choosing one alternative over another. By choosing the alternative of going to the movie, the cost of renting the videotape can be avoided. By choosing the alternative of renting the videotape, the cost of the movie ticket can be avoided. Therefore, the cost of the movie ticket and the cost of renting the videotape are both avoidable costs. On the other hand, the rent on the apartment is not an avoidable cost of either alternative. You would continue to rent your apartment under either alternative. Avoidable costs are relevant costs. Unavoidable costs are irrelevant costs.

Two broad categories of costs are never relevant in decisions. These irrelevant costs are:

1. Sunk costs.
2. Future costs that do not differ between the alternatives.

As we learned in Chapter 2, a **sunk cost** is a cost that has already been incurred and that cannot be avoided regardless of what a manager decides to do. Sunk costs are always the same, no matter what alternatives are being considered, and they are therefore always irrelevant and should be ignored. On the other hand, future costs that do differ between alternatives *are* relevant. For example, when deciding whether to go to a movie or rent a videotape, the cost of buying a movie ticket and the cost of renting a videotape have not yet been incurred. These are future costs that differ between alternatives when the decision is being made and therefore are relevant.

Along with sunk cost, the term **differential cost** was introduced in Chapter 2. In managerial accounting, the terms *avoidable cost, differential cost, incremental cost,* and *relevant cost* are often used interchangeably. To identify the costs that are avoidable (differential) in a particular decision situation and are therefore relevant, these steps can be followed:

1. Eliminate costs and benefits that do not differ between alternatives. These irrelevant costs consist of (a) sunk costs and (b) future costs that do not differ between alternatives.
2. Use the remaining costs and benefits that do differ between alternatives in making the decision. The costs that remain are the differential, or avoidable, costs.

It Isn't Easy to Be Smart about Money

In Business

Most of us commonly suffer from psychological quirks that make it very difficult for us to actually ignore irrelevant costs when making decisions. As Dan Seligman puts it: "Higher primates do not like to admit, even to themselves, that they have screwed up." Humans have "the deep-seated, egoistic human need—evidenced in numerous psychological experiments—to justify the sunk costs in one's life. . . . Many people do not feel liberated by the news that sunk costs are irrelevant. Quite the contrary—they wish to resist the news."

What's the evidence? A lot of it comes from psychology labs, but much of it is recognizable in daily life. Homeowners commonly refuse to sell their homes for less than they paid for them even though the original price they paid is a sunk cost that is wholly irrelevant in the pricing decision. No matter what price they charge now, they will have paid exactly the same price when they originally bought the house and hence the original cost of the house is completely irrelevant. So why do people refuse to sell houses for less than they paid? Probably to avoid admitting to themselves that they made a mistake.

One of the authors of this text knows about this quirk from personal experience. He sold all of the mutual funds in his retirement accounts and transferred the funds into safe money market funds when the Dow-Jones Industrial stock market average was at 7200. The market subsequently climbed to over 10000, but he has refused to buy back into the stock market until it falls back below 7200. However, this is irrational. The fact that he bailed out of the market when it was at 7200 should be completely irrelevant in the decision of whether and when to buy back into the market. However, buying back at a price above 7200 would be an admission that it was a mistake to sell at that level, so he refuses to do it.

Sources: Dan Seligman, "Of Mice and Economics," *Forbes,* August 24, 1998, p. 62; Brian O'Reilley, "Why Johnny Can't Invest," *FORTUNE,* November 9, 1998, pp. 173–178; John S. Hammond, Ralph L. Keeney, and Howard Raiffa, "The Hidden Traps in Decision Making," *Harvard Business Review,* September–October 1998, pp. 47–58; and one of the authors' personal investment portfolio records.

Different Costs for Different Purposes

We need to recognize from the outset of our discussion that costs that are relevant in one decision situation are not necessarily relevant in another. Simply put, this means that *the manager needs different costs for different purposes.* For one purpose, a particular group of costs may be relevant; for another purpose, an entirely different group of costs may be relevant.

Thus, in *each* decision situation the manager must examine the data at hand and isolate the relevant costs. Otherwise, the manager runs the risk of being misled by irrelevant data.

The concept of "different costs for different purposes" is basic to managerial accounting; we shall see its application frequently in the pages that follow.

In Business

What Is Cost Anyway?

The wine newsletter *Liquid Assets* sent out a survey to its readers posing the following question:

> Suppose you bought a case of good 1982 Bordeaux [wine] for $20 a bottle and it now sells for $75. You give the bottle to a friend. Which of the following best captures your feeling of the cost to you as a gift?

The responses were:

		Gift	Drop
Nothing	I paid for the bottle already.	30%	8%
$20	The amount I paid for the bottle	16%	24%
$20+	The amount I paid for the bottle plus interest.	9%	11%
$75	The amount it would take to replace the bottle.	30%	54%
($55)	I am saving $55. I only paid $20 for a $75 gift.	15%	2%
		100%	100%

The last column in the above table reports the responses to a slightly different question in which readers were asked what they would feel about the cost of the bottle of wine if they had dropped it. From a economist's viewpoint—and the correct viewpoint for making decisions about the wine—the cost of the bottle is $75 whether given as a gift or dropped. Interestingly, only 30% of the respondents gave the correct response when the bottle was given as a gift, but 54% gave the correct response when the bottle was dropped.

Source: Samuel Brittan, "Glad Tidings of Dear Joy," *Financial Times (U.K.),* December 1995.

An Example of Identifying Relevant Costs and Benefits

Cynthia is currently a student in an MBA program in Boston and would like to visit a friend in New York City over the weekend. She is trying to decide whether to drive or take the train. Because she is on a tight budget, she wants to carefully consider the costs of the two alternatives. If one alternative is far less expensive than the other, that may be decisive in her choice. By car, the distance between her apartment in Boston and her friend's apartment in New York City is 230 miles. Cynthia has compiled the following list of items to consider:

Automobile Costs

	Item	Annual Cost of Fixed Items	Cost per Mile (based on 10,000 miles per year)
(a)	Annual straight-line depreciation on car [($18,000 original cost − $4,000 estimated resale value in 5 years)/5 years]	$2,800	$0.280
(b)	Cost of gasoline ($1.60 per gallon ÷ 32 miles per gallon)		0.050
(c)	Annual cost of auto insurance and license	1,380	0.138
(d)	Maintenance and repairs		0.065
(e)	Parking fees at school ($45 per month × 8 months)	360	0.036
(f)	Total average cost per mile		$0.569

Additional Data

	Item	
(g)	Reduction in the resale value of car due solely to wear and tear	$0.026 per mile
(h)	Cost of round-trip Amtrak ticket from Boston to New York City	$104
(i)	Benefit of relaxing and being able to study during the train ride rather than having to drive	?
(j)	Cost of putting the dog in a kennel while gone	$40
(k)	Benefit of having a car available in New York City	?
(l)	Hassle of parking the car in New York City	?
(m)	Cost of parking the car in New York City	$25 per day

Which costs and benefits are relevant in this decision? Remember, only those costs and benefits that differ between alternatives are relevant. Everything else is irrelevant and can be ignored.

Start at the top of the list with item (a): the original cost of the car is a sunk cost. This cost has already been incurred and therefore can never differ between alternatives. Consequently, it is irrelevant and can be ignored. The same is true of the accounting depreciation of $2,800 per year, which simply spreads the sunk cost across a number of years.

Move down the list to item (b): the cost of gasoline consumed by driving to New York City would clearly be a relevant cost in this decision. If Cynthia takes the train, this cost would not be incurred. Hence, the cost differs between alternatives and is therefore relevant.

Item (c), the annual cost of auto insurance and license, is not relevant. Whether Cynthia takes the train or drives on this particular trip, her annual auto insurance premium and her auto license fee will remain the same.[1]

Item (d), the cost of maintenance and repairs, is relevant. While maintenance and repair costs have a large random component, over the long run they should be more or less proportional to the amount the car is driven. Thus, the average cost of $0.065 per mile is a reasonable estimate to use.

Item (e), the monthly fee that Cynthia pays to park at her school during the academic year, would not be relevant in the decision of how to get to New York City. Regardless of which alternative she selects—driving or taking the train—she will still need to pay for parking at school.

Item (f) is the total average cost of $0.569 per mile. As discussed above, some elements of this total are relevant, but some are not relevant. Since it contains some irrelevant costs, it would be incorrect to estimate the cost of driving to New York City and back by simply multiplying the $0.569 by 460 miles (230 miles each way × 2). This erroneous approach would yield a cost of driving of $261.74. Unfortunately, such mistakes are often made in both personal life and in business. Since the total cost is stated on a per-mile basis, people are easily misled. Often people think that if the cost is stated as $0.569 per mile, the cost of driving 100 miles is $56.90. But it is not. Many of the costs included in the $0.569 cost per mile are sunk and/or fixed and will not increase if the car is driven another 100 miles. The $0.569 is an average cost, not an incremental cost. Beware of such unitized costs (i.e., costs stated in terms of a dollar amount per unit, per mile, per direct labor-hour, per machine-hour, and so on)—they are often misleading.

Item (g), the decline in the resale value of the car that occurs as a consequence of driving it more miles, is relevant in the decision. Because she uses the car, its resale value declines. Eventually, she will be able to get less for the car when she sells it or trades it in on another car. This reduction in resale value is a real cost of using the car that should be taken into account. Cynthia estimates this cost by accessing the *Kelly Blue Book* website at www.kbb.com. The reduction in resale value of an asset through use or over time is often

[1] If Cynthia has an accident while driving to New York City or back, this might affect her insurance premium when the policy is renewed. The increase in the insurance premium would be a relevant cost of this particular trip, but the normal amount of the insurance premium is not relevant in any case.

called *real* or *economic depreciation.* This is different from accounting depreciation, which attempts to match the sunk cost of the asset with the periods that benefit from that cost.

Item (h), the $104 cost of a round-trip ticket on Amtrak, is clearly relevant in this decision. If she drives, she would not have to buy the ticket.

Item (i) is relevant to the decision, even if it is difficult to put a dollar value on relaxing and being able to study while on the train. It is relevant because it is a benefit that is available under one alternative but not under the other.

Item (j), the cost of putting Cynthia's dog in the kennel while she is gone, is clearly irrelevant in this decision. Whether she takes the train or drives to New York City, she will still need to put her dog in a kennel.

Like item (i), items (k) and (l) are relevant to the decision even if it is difficult to measure their dollar impacts.

Item (m), the cost of parking in New York City, is relevant to the decision.

Bringing together all of the relevant data, Cynthia would estimate the relative costs of driving and taking the train as follows:

Relevant financial cost of driving to New York City:	
Gasoline (460 miles at $0.050 per mile)	$ 23.00
Maintenance and repairs (460 miles @ $0.065 per mile)	29.90
Reduction in the resale value of car due solely to wear and tear (460 miles @ $0.026 per mile)	11.96
Cost of parking the car in New York City (2 days @ $25 per day)	50.00
Total	$114.86
Relevant financial cost of taking the train to New York City:	
Cost of round-trip Amtrak ticket from Boston to New York City	$104.00

What should Cynthia do? From a purely financial standpoint, it would be cheaper by $10.86 ($114.86 − $104.00) to take the train than to drive. Cynthia has to decide if the convenience of having a car in New York City outweighs the additional cost and the disadvantages of being unable to relax and study on the train and the hassle of finding parking in the city.

In this example, we focused on identifying the relevant costs and benefits—everything else was ignored. In the next example, we will begin the analysis by including all of the costs and benefits—relevant or not. We will see that if we are very careful, we will still get the correct answer because the irrelevant costs and benefits will cancel out when we compare the alternatives.

In Business

Cruising on the Cheap

Princess Cruises, along with other cruise ship operators like Carnival Cruise Lines, sometimes offers deep discounts on popular cruises. Recently, a 10-day Mediterranean cruise on the Norwegian Dream was being offered at up to 75% off the list price. A seven-day cruise to Alaska could be booked for a $499–$700 discount. The cause? "An ambitious fleet expansion left the cruise industry grappling with a tidal wave of capacity. . . . Most cruise costs are fixed whether all the ship's berths are filled or not, so it is better to sell cheap than not at all. . . . In the current glut, discounting has made it possible for the cruise lines to keep berths nearly full."

Source: Martin Brannigan, *The Wall Street Journal,* July 17, 2000, pp. B1 & B4.

Reconciling the Total and Differential Approaches

Oak Harbor Woodworks is considering a new labor-saving machine that rents for $3,000 per year. The machine will be used on the company's butcher block production line. Data concerning the company's annual sales and costs of butcher blocks with and without the new machine are shown below:

	Current Situation	Situation with the New Machine
Units produced and sold	5,000	5,000
Selling price per unit	$ 40	$ 40
Direct materials cost per unit	14	14
Direct labor cost per unit	8	5
Variable overhead cost per unit	2	2
Fixed costs, other	62,000	62,000
Fixed costs, new machine	—	3,000

Given the annual sales and the price and cost data above, the net operating income for the product under the two alternatives can be computed as shown in Exhibit 13–1.

Note that the net operating income is higher by $12,000 with the new machine, so that is the better alternative. Note also that the $12,000 advantage for the new machine can be obtained in two different ways. It is the difference between the $30,000 net operating income with the new machine and the $18,000 net operating income for the current situation. It is also the sum of the differential costs and benefits as shown in the last column of Exhibit 13–1. A positive number in the Differential Costs and Benefits column indicates that the difference between the alternatives favors the new machine; a negative number indicates that the difference favors the current situation. A zero in that column simply means that the total amount for the item is exactly the same for both alternatives. Thus, since the difference in the net operating incomes equals the sum of the differences for the individual items, any cost or benefit that is the same for both alternatives will have no impact on which alternative is preferred. This is the reason that costs and benefits that do not differ between alternatives are irrelevant and can be ignored. If we properly account for them, they will cancel out when we compare the alternatives.

We could have arrived at the same solution much more quickly by ignoring altogether the irrelevant costs and benefits.

- The selling price per unit and the number of units sold do not differ between the alternatives. Therefore the total sales revenues are exactly the same for the two alternatives as shown in Exhibit 13–1. Since the sales revenues are exactly the same, they have no effect on the difference in net operating income between the two alternatives. That is shown in the last column in Exhibit 13–1, which shows a $0 differential benefit.

Exhibit 13–1
Total and Differential Costs

	Current Situation	Situation with New Machine	Differential Costs and Benefits
Sales (5,000 units @ $40 per unit)	$200,000	$200,000	$ 0
Less variable expenses:			
Direct materials (5,000 units @ $14 per unit)	70,000	70,000	0
Direct labor (5,000 units @ $8 and $5 per unit)	40,000	25,000	15,000
Variable overhead (5,000 units @ $2 per unit)	10,000	10,000	0
Total variable expenses	120,000	105,000	
Contribution margin	80,000	95,000	
Less fixed expenses:			
Other	62,000	62,000	0
Rent of new machine	0	3,000	(3,000)
Total fixed expenses	62,000	65,000	
Net operating income	$ 18,000	$ 30,000	$12,000

- The direct materials cost per unit, the variable overhead cost per unit, and the number of units produced and sold do not differ between the alternatives. Consequently, the direct materials cost and the variable overhead cost will be the same for the two alternatives and can be ignored.
- The "other" fixed expenses do not differ between the alternatives, so they can be ignored as well.

Indeed, the only costs that do differ between the alternatives are direct labor costs and the fixed rental cost of the new machine. Hence, these are the only relevant costs. The two alternatives can be compared based on just these relevant costs:

Net advantage to renting the new machine:	
Decrease in direct labor costs (5,000 units at a cost savings of $3 per unit)	$15,000
Increase in fixed expenses	(3,000)
Net annual cost savings from renting the new machine	$12,000

Thus, if we focus on just the relevant costs and benefits, we get exactly the same answer that we got when we listed all of the costs and benefits—including those that do not differ between the alternatives and hence are irrelevant. We get the same answer because the only costs and benefits that matter in the final comparison of the net operating incomes are those that differ between the two alternatives and hence are not zero in the last column of Exhibit 13–1. Those two relevant costs are both listed in the above analysis showing the net advantage to renting the new machine.

In Business

Future Costs that Do Not Differ

In the early 1990s, General Motors Corp. laid off tens of thousands of its hourly workers who would nevertheless continue to receive full pay under union contracts. GM entered into an agreement with one of its suppliers, Android Industries, Inc., to use laid-off GM workers. GM agreed to pay the wages of the workers who would be supervised by Android Industries. In return, Android subtracted the wages from the bills it submitted to GM under their current contract. This reduction in contract price is pure profit to GM, since GM would have had to pay the laid-off workers in any case.

Source: "GM Agrees to Allow a Parts Supplier to Use Some of Its Idled Employees," *The Wall Street Journal,* November 30, 1992, p. B3.

Why Isolate Relevant Costs?

In the preceding example, we used two different approaches to analyze the alternatives. First, we considered all costs, both those that were relevant and those that were not; and second, we considered only the relevant costs. We obtained the same answer under both approaches. It would be natural to ask, "Why bother to isolate relevant costs when total costs will do the job just as well?" Isolating relevant costs is desirable for at least two reasons.

First, only rarely will enough information be available to prepare a detailed income statement for both alternatives such as we have done in the preceding examples. Assume, for example, that you are called on to make a decision relating to just a portion of a single operation of a multidepartmental, multiproduct firm. Under these circumstances, it would be virtually impossible to prepare an income statement of any type. You would have to rely on your ability to recognize which costs are relevant and which are not in order to assemble that data necessary to make a decision.

Second, mingling irrelevant costs with relevant costs may cause confusion and distract attention from the matters that are really critical. Furthermore, the danger always exists that an irrelevant piece of data may be used improperly, resulting in an incorrect decision. The best approach is to ignore irrelevant data and base the decision entirely on the relevant data.

Relevant cost analysis, combined with the contribution approach to the income statement, provides a powerful tool for making decisions. We will investigate various uses of this tool in the remaining sections of this chapter.

Environmental Costs Add Up

In Business

A decision analysis can be flawed by incorrectly including irrelevant costs such as sunk costs and future costs that do not differ between alternatives. It can also be flawed by omitting future costs that *do* differ between alternatives. This is a problem particularly with environmental costs that have dramatically increased in recent years and about which many managers have little knowledge.

Consider the environmental complications posed by a decision of whether to install a solvent-based or powder-based system for spray-painting parts. In a solvent painting system, parts are sprayed as they move along a conveyor. The paint that misses the part is swept away by a wall of water, called a water curtain. The excess paint accumulates in a pit as sludge that must be removed each month. Environmental regulations classify this sludge as hazardous waste. As a result, the company must obtain a permit to produce the waste and must maintain meticulous records of how the waste is transported, stored, and disposed of. The annual costs of complying with these regulations can easily exceed $140,000 in total for a painting facility that initially costs only $400,000 to build. The costs of complying with environmental regulations include the following:

- The waste sludge must be hauled to a special disposal site. The typical disposal fee is about $300 per barrel, or $55,000 per year for a modest solvent-based painting system.
- Workers must be specially trained to handle the paint sludge.
- The company must carry special insurance.
- The company must pay substantial fees to the state for releasing pollutants (i.e., the solvent) into the air.
- The water in the water curtain must be specially treated to remove contaminants. This cost can run into tens of thousands of dollars per year.

In contrast, a powder-based painting system avoids almost all of those environmental costs. Excess powder used in the painting process can be recovered and reused without creating a hazardous waste. Additionally, the powder-based system does not release contaminants into the atmosphere. Therefore, even though the cost of building a powder-based system may be higher than the cost of building a solvent-based system, over the long run the costs of the powder-based system may be far lower due to the high environmental costs of a solvent-based system. Managers need to be aware of such environmental costs and take them fully into account when making decisions.

Source: Germain Böer, Margaret Curtin, and Louis Hoyt, "Environmental Cost Management," *Management Accounting,* September 1998, pp. 28–38. Used with permission from the IMA, Montvale, NJ, USA, www.imanet.org.

Adding and Dropping Product Lines and Other Segments

Decisions relating to whether old product lines or other segments of a company should be dropped and new ones added are among the most difficult that a manager has to make. In such decisions, many qualitative and quantitative factors must be considered. Ultimately, however, any final decision to drop an old segment or to add a new one is going to hinge primarily on the impact the decision will have on net operating income. To assess this impact, it is necessary to carefully analyze the costs.

LEARNING OBJECTIVE 2
Prepare an analysis showing whether a product line or other organizational segment should be dropped or retained.

An Illustration of Cost Analysis

Consider the three major product lines of the Discount Drug Company—drugs, cosmetics, and housewares. Sales and cost information for the preceding month for each separate product line and for the store in total are given in Exhibit 13–2.

What can be done to improve the company's overall performance? One product line—housewares—shows a net operating loss for the month. Perhaps dropping this line would cause profits in the company as a whole to improve. However, the report in Exhibit 13–2 may be misleading. Unlike the segmented income statements presented in Chapter 12, no attempt has been made in Exhibit 13–2 to distinguish between traceable fixed expenses, which may be avoidable if a product line is dropped, and common fixed expenses, which cannot be avoided by dropping any particular product line. The alternatives under consideration are keeping the housewares product line and dropping the housewares product line. Only those costs that differ between the two alternatives (i.e., that can be avoided by dropping the housewares product line) are relevant. In deciding whether to drop a product line, it is crucial for managers to clearly identify which costs can be avoided, and hence are relevant to the decision, and which costs cannot be avoided, and hence are irrelevant. The decision should be approached as follows:

Concept 13–1

If the housewares line is dropped, then the company will lose $20,000 per month in contribution margin, but by dropping the line it may be possible to avoid some fixed costs. It may be possible, for example, to discharge certain employees, or it may be possible to reduce advertising costs. If by dropping the housewares line the company is able to avoid more in fixed costs than it loses in contribution margin, then it will be better off if the product line is eliminated, since overall net operating income should improve. On the other hand, if the company is not able to avoid as much in fixed costs as it loses in contribution margin, then the housewares line should be retained. In short, the manager should ask, "What costs can I avoid if I drop this product line?"

As we have seen from our earlier discussion, not all costs are avoidable. For example, some of the costs associated with a product line may be sunk costs. Other costs may be allocated common costs, as discussed in Chapter 12, that will not differ in total regardless of whether the product line is dropped or retained. As discussed in Chapter 8, an activity-based costing analysis may be used to help identify the relevant costs.

Exhibit 13–2
Discount Drug Company Product Lines

		Product Line		
	Total	Drugs	Cosmetics	Housewares
Sales	$250,000	$125,000	$75,000	$50,000
Less variable expenses	105,000	50,000	25,000	30,000
Contribution margin	145,000	75,000	50,000	20,000
Less fixed expenses:				
Salaries	50,000	29,500	12,500	8,000
Advertising	15,000	1,000	7,500	6,500
Utilities	2,000	500	500	1,000
Depreciation—fixtures	5,000	1,000	2,000	2,000
Rent	20,000	10,000	6,000	4,000
Insurance	3,000	2,000	500	500
General administrative	30,000	15,000	9,000	6,000
Total fixed expenses	125,000	59,000	38,000	28,000
Net operating income (loss)	$ 20,000	$ 16,000	$12,000	$(8,000)

To show how one should proceed in a product-line analysis, suppose that the management of the Discount Drug Company has analyzed the fixed costs being charged to the three product lines and has determined the following:

1. The salaries expense represents salaries paid to employees working directly on a product. All of the employees working in housewares would be discharged if the product line is dropped.
2. The advertising expense represents product advertising specific to each product line and is avoidable if the line is dropped.
3. The utilities expense represents utilities costs for the entire company. The amount charged to each product line is an allocation based on space occupied and is not avoidable if the product line is dropped.
4. The depreciation expense represents depreciation on fixtures used for display of the various product lines. Although the fixtures are nearly new, they are custom-built and will have no resale value if the housewares line is dropped.
5. The rent expense represents rent on the entire building housing the company; it is allocated to the product lines on the basis of sales dollars. The monthly rent of $20,000 is fixed under a long-term lease agreement.
6. The insurance expense represents insurance carried on inventories within each of the three product lines.
7. The general administrative expense represents the costs of accounting, purchasing, and general management, which are allocated to the product lines on the basis of sales dollars. Total administrative costs will not change if the housewares line is dropped.

With this information, management can identify fixed costs that can and cannot be avoided if the product line is dropped:

Fixed Expenses	Total Cost Assigned to Housewares	Not Avoidable*	Avoidable
Salaries	$ 8,000		$ 8,000
Advertising	6,500		6,500
Utilities	1,000	$ 1,000	
Depreciation—fixtures	2,000	2,000	
Rent	4,000	4,000	
Insurance	500		500
General administrative	6,000	6,000	
Total	$28,000	$13,000	$15,000

*These fixed costs represent either (1) sunk costs or (2) future costs that will not change whether the housewares line is retained or discontinued.

To determine how dropping the line will affect the overall profits of the company, we can compare the contribution margin that will be lost to the costs that can be avoided if the line is dropped:

Contribution margin lost if the housewares line is discontinued (see Exhibit 13–2)	$(20,000)
Less fixed costs that can be avoided if the housewares line is discontinued (see above)	15,000
Decrease in overall company net operating income	$ (5,000)

In this case, the fixed costs that can be avoided by dropping the product line are less than the contribution margin that will be lost. Therefore, based on the data given, the housewares line should not be discontinued unless a more profitable use can be found for the floor and counter space that it is occupying.

Exhibit 13–3
A Comparative Format for Product-Line Analysis

	Keep Housewares	Drop Housewares	Difference: Net Operating Income Increase (or Decrease)
Sales	$50,000	$ 0	$(50,000)
Less variable expenses	30,000	0	30,000
Contribution margin	20,000	0	(20,000)
Less fixed expenses:			
Salaries	8,000	0	8,000
Advertising	6,500	0	6,500
Utilities	1,000	1,000	0
Depreciation—fixtures	2,000	2,000	0
Rent	4,000	4,000	0
Insurance	500	0	500
General administrative	6,000	6,000	0
Total fixed expenses	28,000	13,000	15,000
Net operating income (loss)	$ (8,000)	$(13,000)	$ (5,000)

A Comparative Format

Some managers prefer to approach decisions of this type by preparing comparative income statements showing the effects on the company as a whole of either keeping or dropping the product line in question as we did in Exhibit 13–1. A comparative analysis of this type for the Discount Drug Company is shown in Exhibit 13–3.

As shown in the last column in the exhibit, overall company net operating income will decrease by $5,000 each period if the housewares line is dropped. This is the same answer, of course, as we obtained when we focused just on the lost contribution margin and avoidable fixed costs.

Beware of Allocated Fixed Costs

Our conclusion that the housewares line should not be dropped seems to conflict with the data shown earlier in Exhibit 13–2. Recall from the exhibit that the housewares line is showing a loss rather than a profit. Why keep a line that is showing a loss? The explanation for this apparent inconsistency lies at least in part with the common fixed costs that are being allocated to the product lines. As we observed in Chapter 12, one of the great dangers in allocating common fixed costs is that such allocations can make a product line (or other segment of a business) *look* less profitable than it really is. By allocating the common fixed costs among all product lines, the housewares line has been made to *look* as if it were unprofitable, whereas, in fact, dropping the line would result in a decrease in overall company net operating income. This point can be seen clearly if we recast the data in Exhibit 13–2 and eliminate the allocation of the common fixed costs. This recasting of data—using the segmented approach from Chapter 12—is shown in Exhibit 13–4.

Exhibit 13–4 gives us a much different perspective of the housewares line than does Exhibit 13–2. As shown in Exhibit 13–4, the housewares line is covering all of its own traceable fixed costs and is generating a $3,000 segment margin toward covering the common fixed costs of the company. Unless another product line can be found that will generate a greater segment margin than this, the company would be better off keeping the housewares line. By keeping the line, the company's overall net operating income will be higher than if the product line were dropped.

Exhibit 13–4
Discount Drug Company Product Lines—Recast in Contribution Format (from Exhibit 13–2)

		Product Line		
	Total	Drugs	Cosmetics	House-wares
Sales	$250,000	$125,000	$75,000	$50,000
Less variable expenses	105,000	50,000	25,000	30,000
Contribution margin	145,000	75,000	50,000	20,000
Less traceable fixed expenses:				
Salaries	50,000	29,500	12,500	8,000
Advertising	15,000	1,000	7,500	6,500
Depreciation—fixtures	5,000	1,000	2,000	2,000
Insurance	3,000	2,000	500	500
Total traceable fixed expenses	73,000	33,500	22,500	17,000
Product-line segment margin	72,000	$ 41,500	$27,500	$ 3,000*
Less common fixed expenses:				
Utilities	2,000			
Rent	20,000			
General administrative	30,000			
Total common fixed expenses	52,000			
Net operating income	$ 20,000			

*If the housewares line is dropped, this $3,000 in segment margin will be lost to the company. In addition, we have seen that the $2,000 depreciation on the fixtures is a sunk cost that cannot be avoided. The sum of these two figures ($3,000 + $2,000 = $5,000) would be the decrease in the company's overall profits if the housewares line were discontinued.

Faking Out Taxpayers

In Business

Owners of sports teams almost always succeed in tapping the general taxpayer to help build fancy new stadiums that include luxurious skyboxes for wealthy fans. How do they do this? Partly by paying consultants to produce studies that purport to show the big favorable economic impact on the area of the new stadium. The trouble is that these studies are bogus. Voters in the state of Washington turned down public funding for the new Safeco baseball field in Seattle, but the state legislature went into special session to pass a tax bill to fund construction anyway. And shortly thereafter, taxpayers were asked to pay $325 million to tear down the old Kingdome football stadium to build a new stadium for Paul Allen, the cofounder of Microsoft who owns the Seattle Seahawks. When asked why public funds should finance private facilities for professional sports, the response was: "Even if you aren't a football fan, the high level of economic activity generated by the Seahawks does affect you. . . . The Seahawks' total annual economic impact in Washington State is $129 million." Sounds impressive, but the argument contains a fallacy. Most of this money would have been spent in Washington State anyway even if the Seahawks had left Seattle for another city. If a local fan did not have a Seahawks game to attend, what would he/she have done with the money? Burn it? Hardly. Almost all of this money would have been spent locally anyway. An independent estimate of the *additional* spending that would come to Washington State as a result of keeping the Seahawks in Seattle put the total economic impact at less than half that erroneously claimed by proponents of the stadium. To put this in perspective, Seattle's Fred Hutchinson Cancer Research Center alone has over twice the economic impact of professional sports teams in Seattle.

Source: Tom Griffin, "Only a Game," *Columns—The University of Washington Alumni Magazine,* June 1997, pp. 15–17.

Additionally, we should note that managers may choose to retain an unprofitable product line if the line is necessary to the sale of other products or if it serves as a "magnet" to attract customers. Bread, for example, may not be an especially profitable line in food stores, but customers expect it to be available, and many would undoubtedly shift their buying elsewhere if a particular store decided to stop carrying it.

The Make or Buy Decision

LEARNING OBJECTIVE 3
Prepare a make or buy analysis.

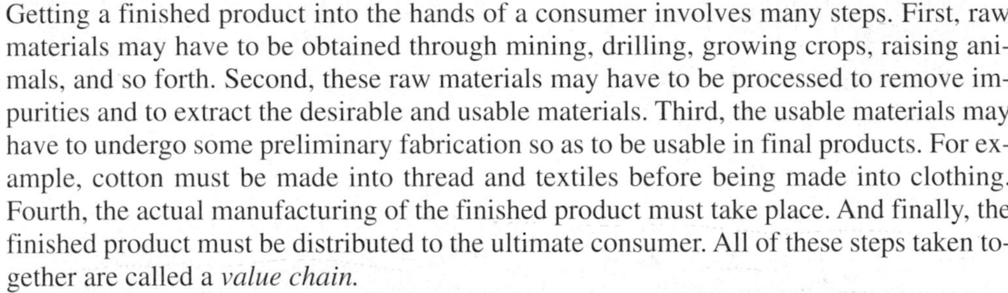

Getting a finished product into the hands of a consumer involves many steps. First, raw materials may have to be obtained through mining, drilling, growing crops, raising animals, and so forth. Second, these raw materials may have to be processed to remove impurities and to extract the desirable and usable materials. Third, the usable materials may have to undergo some preliminary fabrication so as to be usable in final products. For example, cotton must be made into thread and textiles before being made into clothing. Fourth, the actual manufacturing of the finished product must take place. And finally, the finished product must be distributed to the ultimate consumer. All of these steps taken together are called a *value chain.*

Separate companies may carry out each of the steps in the value chain or a single company may carry out several of the steps. When a company is involved in more than one of these steps in the entire value chain, it is **vertically integrated**. Vertical integration is very common. Some companies control *all* of the activities in the value chain from producing basic raw materials right up to the final distribution of finished goods. Other companies are content to integrate on a smaller scale by purchasing many of the parts and materials that go into their finished products.

Concept 13–2

A decision to produce a fabricated part internally, rather than to buy the part externally from a supplier, is called a **make or buy decision.** Actually, any decision relating to vertical integration is a make or buy decision, since the company is deciding whether to meet its own needs internally or to buy externally.

Strategic Aspects of the Make or Buy Decision

Integration provides certain advantages. An integrated company is less dependent on its suppliers and may be able to ensure a smoother flow of parts and materials for production than a nonintegrated company. For example, a strike against a major parts supplier can interrupt the operations of a nonintegrated company for many months, whereas an integrated company that is producing its own parts might be able to continue operations. Also, many companies feel that they can control quality better by producing their own parts and materials, rather than by relying on the quality control standards of outside suppliers. In addition, the integrated company realizes profits from the parts and materials that it is "making" rather than "buying," as well as profits from its regular operations.

The advantages of integration are counterbalanced by the advantages of using external suppliers. By pooling demand from a number of companies, a supplier may be able to enjoy economies of scale in research and development and in manufacturing. These economies of scale can result in higher quality and lower costs than would be possible if the company were to attempt to make the parts on its own. A company must be careful, however, to retain control over activities that are essential to maintaining its competitive position. For example, Hewlett-Packard controls the software for laser printers that it makes in cooperation with Canon Inc. of Japan to prevent Canon from coming out with a competing product. The present trend appears to be toward less vertical integration, with companies like Sun Microsystems and Hewlett-Packard concentrating on hardware and software design and relying on outside suppliers for almost everything else in the value chain. These factors suggest that the make or buy decision should be weighed very carefully.

An Example of Make or Buy

To provide an illustration of a make or buy decision, consider Mountain Goat Cycles. The company is now producing the heavy-duty gear shifters used in its most popular line of mountain bikes. The company's Accounting Department reports the following costs of producing 8,000 units of the shifter internally each year:

	Per Unit	8,000 Units
Direct materials	$ 6	$ 48,000
Direct labor	4	32,000
Variable overhead	1	8,000
Supervisor's salary	3	24,000
Depreciation of special equipment	2	16,000
Allocated general overhead	5	40,000
Total cost	$21	$168,000

An outside supplier has offered to sell Mountain Goat Cycles 8,000 shifters a year at a price of only $19 each. Should the company stop producing the shifters internally and start purchasing them from the outside supplier? To approach the decision from a financial point of view, the manager should again focus on the relevant costs. As we have seen, the relevant (i.e., differential or avoidable) costs can be obtained by eliminating those costs that are not avoidable—that is, by eliminating (1) the sunk costs and (2) the future costs that will continue regardless of whether the shifters are produced internally or purchased outside. The costs that remain after making these eliminations are the costs that are avoidable to the company by purchasing outside. If these avoidable costs are less than the outside purchase price, then the company should continue to manufacture its own shifters and reject the outside supplier's offer. That is, the company should purchase outside only if the outside purchase price is less than the costs that can be avoided by halting its own production of the shifters.

Looking at the cost data for producing the shifter internally, note first that depreciation of special equipment is listed as one of the costs of producing the shifters internally. Since the equipment has already been purchased, this depreciation is a sunk cost and is therefore irrelevant. If the equipment could be sold, its salvage value would be relevant. Or if the machine could be used to make other products, this could be relevant as well. However, we will assume that the equipment has no salvage value and that it has no other use except making the heavy-duty gear shifters.

Also note that the company is allocating a portion of its general overhead costs to the shifters. Any portion of this general overhead cost that would actually be eliminated if the gear shifters were purchased rather than made would be relevant in the analysis. However, it is likely that the general overhead costs allocated to the gear shifters are in fact common to all items produced in the factory and would continue unchanged even if the shifters were purchased from the outside. Such allocated common costs are not relevant costs (since they do not differ between the make or buy alternatives) and should be eliminated from the analysis along with the sunk costs.

The variable costs of producing the shifters (materials, labor, and variable overhead) are relevant costs, since they can be avoided by buying the shifters from the outside supplier. If the supervisor can be discharged and his or her salary avoided by buying the shifters, then it too will be relevant to the decision. Assuming that both the variable costs and the supervisor's salary can be avoided by buying from the outside supplier, then the analysis takes the form shown in Exhibit 13–5.

Since it costs $40,000 less to continue to make the shifters internally, Mountain Goat Cycles should reject the outside supplier's offer. However, the company may wish to consider one additional factor before coming to a final decision. This factor is the opportunity cost of the space now being used to produce the shifters.

Exhibit 13–5
Mountain Goat Cycles Make or Buy Analysis

	Total Relevant Costs— 8,000 units	
	Make	Buy
Direct materials (8,000 units @ $6 per unit)	$ 48,000	
Direct labor ($8,000 units @ $4 per unit)	32,000	
Variable overhead (8,000 units @ $1 per unit)	8,000	
Supervisor's salary	24,000	
Depreciation of special equipment (not relevant)		
Allocated general overhead (not relevant)		
Outside purchase price		$152,000
Total cost	$112,000	$152,000
Difference in favor of continuing to make	$ 40,000	

Opportunity Cost

If the space now being used to produce the shifters *would otherwise be idle,* then Mountain Goat Cycles should continue to produce its own shifters and the supplier's offer should be rejected, as stated above. Idle space that has no alternative use has an opportunity cost of zero.

But what if the space now being used to produce shifters could be used for some other purpose? In that case, the space would have an opportunity cost that should be considered in assessing the desirability of the supplier's offer. What would this opportunity cost be? It would be the segment margin that could be derived from the best alternative use of the space.

In Business

The Other Side of the Coin

This section of the chapter focuses on a company's decision of whether to make or buy a part. We can also look at this situation from the standpoint of the potential supplier for the part. It isn't always easy to be a supplier. Steven Keller, founder and CEO of Keller Design, a small maker of pet accessories, found this out the hard way after landing a contract with Target, the big retailing chain. Eventually, sales to Target grew to be 80% of Keller Design's business. "Then reality bit. Target suddenly decided to drop . . . four kinds of can lids and food scoops. . . . Later, an unexpected $100,000 charge for airfreighting devoured Keller's profits on a $300,000 shipment. Target also changed its mind about 6,000 specially made ceramic dog bowls, which will probably have to be dumped on a close-out firm for a fraction of Keller's investment. . . ." "The odds are pretty well stacked against you. Contracts with large customers tend to be boilerplate, shifting most of the risk to the supplier." Protect yourself by having your own lawyer go over all contracts, contest unreasonable charges, and don't rely too much on one big customer.

Source: Leigh Gallagher, "Holding the Bag," *Forbes*, June 14, 1999, pp. 164 and 168.

To illustrate, assume that the space now being used to produce shifters could be used to produce a new cross-country bike that would generate a segment margin of $60,000 per year. Under these conditions, Mountain Goat Cycles would be better off to accept the supplier's offer and to use the available space to produce the new product line:

	Make	Buy
Total annual cost (see Exhibit 13–5)	112,000	152,000
Opportunity cost—segment margin forgone on a potential new product line	60,000	

continued

Total cost	$172,000	$152,000
Difference in favor of purchasing from the outside supplier	$ 20,000	

Opportunity costs are not recorded in the organization's formal accounts since they do not represent actual dollar outlays. Rather, they represent economic benefits that are *forgone* as a result of pursuing some course of action. The opportunity costs of Mountain Goat Cycles are sufficiently large in this case to change the decision.

Special Orders

LEARNING OBJECTIVE 4
Prepare an analysis showing whether a special order should be accepted.

Managers must often evaluate whether a *special order* should be accepted, and if the order is accepted, the price that should be charged. A **special order** is a one-time order that is not considered part of the company's normal ongoing business. To illustrate, Mountain Goat Cycles has just received a request from the Seattle Police Department to produce 100 specially modified mountain bikes at a price of $179 each. The bikes would be used to patrol some of the more densely populated residential sections of the city. Mountain Goat Cycles can easily modify its City Cruiser model to fit the specifications of the Seattle Police. The normal selling price of the City Cruiser bike is $249, and its unit product cost is $182 as shown below:

Direct materials	$ 86
Direct labor	45
Manufacturing overhead	51
Unit product cost	$182

The variable portion of the above manufacturing overhead is $6 per unit. The order would have no effect on the company's total fixed manufacturing overhead costs.

The modifications requested by the Seattle Police Department consist of welded brackets to hold radios, nightsticks, and other gear. These modifications would require $17 in incremental variable costs. In addition, the company would have to pay a graphics design studio $1,200 to design and cut stencils that would be used for spray painting the Seattle Police Department's logo and other identifying marks on the bikes.

This order should have no effect on the company's other sales. The production manager says that she can handle the special order without disrupting any of the company's regular scheduled production.

What effect would accepting this order have on the company's net operating income?

Only the incremental costs and benefits are relevant. Since the existing fixed manufacturing overhead costs would not be affected by the order, they are not relevant. The incremental net operating income can be computed as follows:

	Per Unit	Total 100 Bikes
Incremental revenue	$179	$17,900
Less incremental costs:		
Variable costs:		
Direct materials	86	8,600
Direct labor	45	4,500
Variable manufacturing overhead	6	600
Special modifications	17	1,700
Total variable cost	$154	15,400

continued

Fixed cost:	
Purchase of stencils	1,200
Total incremental cost	16,600
Incremental net operating income	$ 1,300

Therefore, even though the $179 price on the special order is below the normal $182 unit product cost and the order would require incurring additional costs, the order would result in an increase in net operating income. In general, a special order is profitable as long as the incremental revenue from the special order exceeds the incremental costs of the order. We must note, however, that it is important to make sure that there is indeed idle capacity and that the special order does not cut into normal sales or undercut normal prices. For example, if the company was operating at capacity, opportunity costs would have to be taken into account as well as the incremental costs that have already been detailed above.

In Business **Fly the Friendly Aisles**

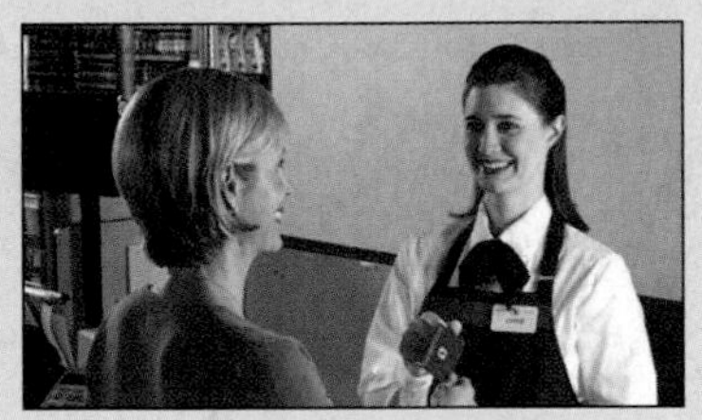

Shoppers at Safeway can now earn United Airlines frequent flier miles when they buy their groceries. Airlines charge marketing partners such as Safeway about 2¢ per mile. Since airlines typically charge 25,000 miles for a domestic round-trip ticket, United is earning about $500 per frequent-flier ticket issued to Safeway customers. This income to United is higher than many discounted fares. Moreover, United carefully manages its frequent flier program so that few frequent flier passengers displace regular fare-paying customers. The only costs of adding a frequent flier passenger to a flight under these circumstances are food, a little extra fuel, and some administrative costs. All of the other costs of the flight would be incurred anyway. Thus, the miles that United sells to Safeway are almost pure profit.

S

Source: Wendy Zellner, *Business Week,* March 6, 2000, pp. 152–154.

Utilization of a Constrained Resource

LEARNING OBJECTIVE 5
Determine the most profitable use of a constrained resource and the value of obtaining more of the constrained resource.

Managers are routinely faced with the problem of deciding how constrained resources are going to be utilized. A department store, for example, has a limited amount of floor space and therefore cannot stock every product that may be available. A manufacturer has a limited number of machine-hours and a limited number of direct labor-hours at its disposal. When a limited resource of some type restricts the company's ability to satisfy demand, the company is said to have a **constraint.** Since the company cannot fully satisfy demand, the manager must decide how the constrained resource should be used. Fixed costs are usually unaffected by such choices, so the course of action that will maximize the firm's *total* contribution margin should ordinarily be selected.

Contribution in Relation to a Constrained Resource

To maximize total contribution margin, a company should not necessarily promote those products that have the highest *unit* contribution margins. Rather, total contribution margin will be maximized by promoting those products or accepting those orders that provide the highest unit contribution margin *in relation to the constrained resource*. To illustrate, Mountain Goat Cycles makes a line of panniers—saddlebags for bicycles. There are two models of panniers—a touring model and a mountain model. Cost and revenue data for the two models of panniers follow:

	Model	
	Mountain Pannier	Touring Pannier
Selling price per unit	$25	$30
Variable cost per unit	10	18
Contribution margin per unit	$15	$12
Contribution margin (CM) ratio	60%	40%

The mountain pannier appears to be much more profitable than the touring pannier. It has a $15 per unit contribution margin as compared to only $12 per unit for the touring model, and it has a 60% CM ratio as compared to only 40% for the touring model.

But now let us add one more piece of information—the plant that makes the panniers is operating at capacity. This does not mean that every machine and every person in the plant is working at the maximum possible rate. Because machines have different capacities, some machines will be operating at less than 100% of capacity. However, if the plant as a whole cannot produce any more units, some machine or process must be operating at capacity. The machine or process that is limiting overall output is called the **bottleneck**—it is the constraint.

At Mountain Goat Cycles, the bottleneck is a particular stitching machine. The mountain pannier requires 2 minutes of stitching time, and the touring pannier requires 1 minute of stitching time. Since this stitching machine already has more work than it can handle, something will have to be cut back. In this situation, which product is more profitable? To answer this question, the manager should look at the *contribution margin per unit of the constrained resource.* This figure is computed by dividing the contribution margin by the amount of the constrained resource a unit of product requires. These calculations are carried out below for the mountain and touring panniers.

	Model	
	Mountain Pannier	Touring Pannier
Contribution margin per unit (above) (a)	$15.00	$12.00
Time on the stitching machine required to produce one unit (b)	2 minutes	1 minute
Contribution margin per unit of the constrained resource, (a) ÷ (b)	$ 7.50 per minute	$12.00 per minute

It is now easy to decide which product is less profitable and should be deemphasized. Each minute of processing time on the stitching machine that is devoted to the touring pannier results in an increase of $12 in contribution margin and profits. The comparable figure for the mountain pannier is only $7.50 per minute. Therefore, the touring model should be emphasized. Even though the mountain model has the larger per unit contribution margin and the larger CM ratio, the touring model provides the larger contribution margin in relation to the constrained resource.

To verify that the touring model is indeed the more profitable product, suppose an hour of additional stitching time is available and that unfilled orders exist for both products. The additional hour on the stitching machine could be used to make either 30 mountain panniers (60 minutes ÷ 2 minutes per mountain pannier) or 60 touring panniers (60 minutes ÷ 1 minute per touring pannier), with the following consequences:

	Model	
	Mountain Pannier	Touring Pannier
Contribution margin per unit (above)	$ 15	$ 12
Additional units that can be processed in one hour	× 30	× 60
Additional contribution margin	$450	$720

Since the additional contribution margin would be $720 for the touring panniers and only $450 for the mountain panniers, the touring panniers are the more profitable product given the current situation in which the stitching machine is the company's constraint.

This example clearly shows that looking at unit contribution margins alone is not enough; the contribution margin must be viewed in relation to the amount of the constrained resource each product requires.

In Business **Coping with Power Shortages**

Tata Iron and Steel Company Ltd. is one of the largest companies in India, employing about 75,000 people. The company has had to cope with electrical power shortages that have been severe enough to force it to shut down some of its mills. But which ones? In these situations, electrical power is the company's constraint and it became imperative to manage this constraint effectively. The first step was to estimate the electrical loads of running each of the company's mills using least-squares regression. These data were then used to compute the contribution margin per KWH (kilowatt-hour) for each mill. The model indicated which mills should be shut down, and in what order, and which products should be cut back. The model also indicated that it would be profitable for the company to install its own diesel generating units—the contribution margin from the additional output more than paid for the costs of buying and running the diesel generators.

Source: "How Tata Steel Optimized Its Results," *The Management Accountant (India),* July 1997, pp. 372–375.

Managing Constraints

Profits can be increased by effectively managing the organization's constraints. One aspect of managing constraints is to decide how to best utilize them. As discussed above, if the constraint is a bottleneck in the production process, the manager should select the product mix that maximizes the total contribution margin. In addition, the manager should take an active role in managing the constraint itself. Management should focus efforts on increasing the efficiency of the bottleneck operation and on increasing its capacity. Such efforts directly increase the output of finished goods and will often pay off in an almost immediate increase in profits.

It is often possible for a manager to effectively increase the capacity of the bottleneck, which is called **relaxing (or elevating) the constraint.** For example, the stitching machine operator could be asked to work overtime. This would result in more available stitching time and hence more finished goods that can be sold. The benefits from relaxing the constraint in such a manner are often enormous and can be easily quantified. The manager should first ask, "What would I do with additional capacity at the bottleneck if it were available?" In the example, if unfilled orders exist for both the touring and mountain panniers, the additional capacity would be used to process more touring panniers, since that would be a better use of the additional capacity. In that situation, the additional capacity would be worth $12 per minute or $720 per hour. This is because adding an hour of capacity would generate an additional $720 of contribution margin if it would be used solely to process more touring panniers. Since overtime pay for the operator is likely to be much less than $720 per hour, running the stitching machine on overtime would be an excellent way to increase the profits of the company while at the same time satisfying customers.

To reinforce this concept, suppose that making touring panniers has already been given top priority and consequently there are only unfilled orders for the mountain pannier. How much would it be worth to the company to run the stitching machine overtime in this situation? Since the additional capacity would be used to make the mountain pannier, the value of that additional capacity would drop to $7.50 per minute or $450 per hour. Nevertheless, the value of relaxing the constraint would still be quite high.

The Real Costs of Setups

In Business

The bottleneck at Southwestern Ohio Steel is the blanking line on which large rolls of steel up to 60 inches wide are cut into flat sheets. Setting up the blanking line between jobs takes an average of 2.5 hours, and during this time, the blanking line is shut down.

Management estimates the opportunity cost of lost sales at $225 per hour, which is the contribution margin per hour of the blanking line for a typical order. Under these circumstances, a new loading device with an annual fixed cost of $36,000 that would save 720 setup hours per year looked like an excellent investment. The new loading device would have an average cost of only $50 per hour ($36,000 ÷ 720 hours = $50) compared to the $225 per hour the company would generate in added contribution margin.

Source: Robert J. Campbell, "Steeling Time with ABC or TOC," *Management Accounting,* January 1995, pp. 31–36.

These calculations indicate that managers should pay great attention to bottleneck operations. If a bottleneck machine breaks down or is ineffectively utilized, the losses to the company can be quite large. In our example, for every minute the stitching machine is down due to breakdowns or setups, the company loses between $7.50 and $12.00. The losses on an hourly basis are between $450 and $720! In contrast, there is no such loss of contribution margin if time is lost on a machine that is not a bottleneck—such machines have excess capacity anyway.

The implications are clear. Managers should focus much of their attention on managing bottlenecks. As we have discussed, managers should emphasize products that most profitably utilize the constrained resource. They should also make sure that products are processed smoothly through the bottlenecks, with minimal lost time due to breakdowns and setups. And they should try to find ways to increase the capacity at the bottlenecks.

The capacity of a bottleneck can be effectively increased in a number of ways, including:

- Working overtime on the bottleneck.
- Subcontracting some of the processing that would be done at the bottleneck.
- Investing in additional machines at the bottleneck.
- Shifting workers from processes that are not bottlenecks to the process that is a bottleneck.
- Focusing business process improvement efforts such as TQM and Business Process Reengineering on the bottleneck.
- Reducing defective units. Each defective unit that is processed through the bottleneck and subsequently scrapped takes the place of a good unit that could be sold.

The last three methods of increasing the capacity of the bottleneck are particularly attractive, since they are essentially free and may even yield additional cost savings.

The methods and ideas discussed in this section are all part of the Theory of Constraints, which was introduced in Chapter 1. A number of organizations have successfully used the Theory of Constraints to improve their performance, including Avery Dennison, Bethlehem Steel, Boeing, Champion International, General Motors, ITT, National Semiconductor, Pratt and Whitney Canada, Procter and Gamble, Texas Instruments, United Airlines, United Electrical Controls, the United States Air Force Logistics Command, and the United States Navy Transportation Corps.

The Problem of Multiple Constraints

What does a firm do if it has more than one potential constraint? For example, a firm may have limited raw materials, limited direct labor-hours available, limited floor space, and limited advertising dollars to spend on product promotion. How would it proceed to find the right combination of products to produce? The proper combination or "mix" of products can be found by use of a quantitative method known as *linear programming,* which is covered in quantitative methods and operations management courses.

In Business

Look Before You Leap

It is often possible to elevate the constraint at very low cost. Western Textile Products makes pockets, waistbands, and other clothing components. The constraint at the company's plant in Greenville, South Carolina, was the slitting machines. These large machines slit huge rolls of textiles into appropriate widths for use on other machines. Management was contemplating adding a second shift to elevate the constraint. However, investigation revealed that the slitting machines were actually being run only one hour in a nine-hour shift. "The other eight hours were required to get materials, load and unload the machine, and do setups. Instead of adding a second shift, a second person was assigned to each machine to fetch materials and do as much of the setting up as possible off-line while the machine was running." This approach resulted in increasing the run time to four hours. If another shift had been added without any improvement in how the machines were being used, the cost would have been much higher and there would have been only a one-hour increase in run time.

Source: Eric Noreen, Debra Smith, and James T. Mackey, *The Theory of Constraints and Its Implications for Management Accounting* (Croton-on-Hudson, NY: The North River Press, 1995), pp. 84–85.

Joint Product Costs and the Contribution Approach

LEARNING OBJECTIVE 6
Prepare an analysis showing whether joint products should be sold at the split-off point or processed further.

In some industries, a number of end products are produced from a single raw material input. For example, in the petroleum refining industry a large number of products are extracted from crude oil, including gasoline, jet fuel, home heating oil, lubricants, asphalt, and various organic chemicals. Another example is provided by the Santa Maria Wool Cooperative of New Mexico. The company buys raw wool from local sheepherders, separates the wool into three grades—coarse, fine, and superfine—and then dyes the wool using traditional methods that rely on pigments from local materials. The production process, together with cost and revenue data, is diagrammed in Exhibit 13–6.

At Santa Maria Wool Cooperative, coarse wool, fine wool, and superfine wool are produced from one input—raw wool. Two or more products that are produced from a common input are known as **joint products.** The **split-off point** is the point in the manufacturing process at which the joint products can be recognized as separate products. This does not occur at Santa Maria Cooperative until the raw wool has been processed through the separating process. The term **joint cost** is used to describe the costs incurred up to the split-off point. At Santa Maria Wool Cooperative, the joint costs are the \$200,000 cost of the raw wool and the \$40,000 cost of separating the wool. The undyed wool is called an *intermediate product* because it is not finished at this point. Nevertheless, a market does exist for undyed wool—albeit at a significantly lower price than finished, dyed wool.

The Pitfalls of Allocation

Joint costs are common costs incurred to simultaneously produce a variety of end products. These joint costs are traditionally allocated among the different products at the split-off point. A typical approach is to allocate the joint costs according to the relative sales value of the end products.

Although allocation of joint product costs is needed for some purposes, such as balance sheet inventory valuation, allocations of this kind are extremely misleading for decision making. The In Business box on page 608 discusses an actual business situation illustrating an incorrect decision that resulted from using such an allocated joint cost.

Exhibit 13–6 Santa Maria Wool Cooperative

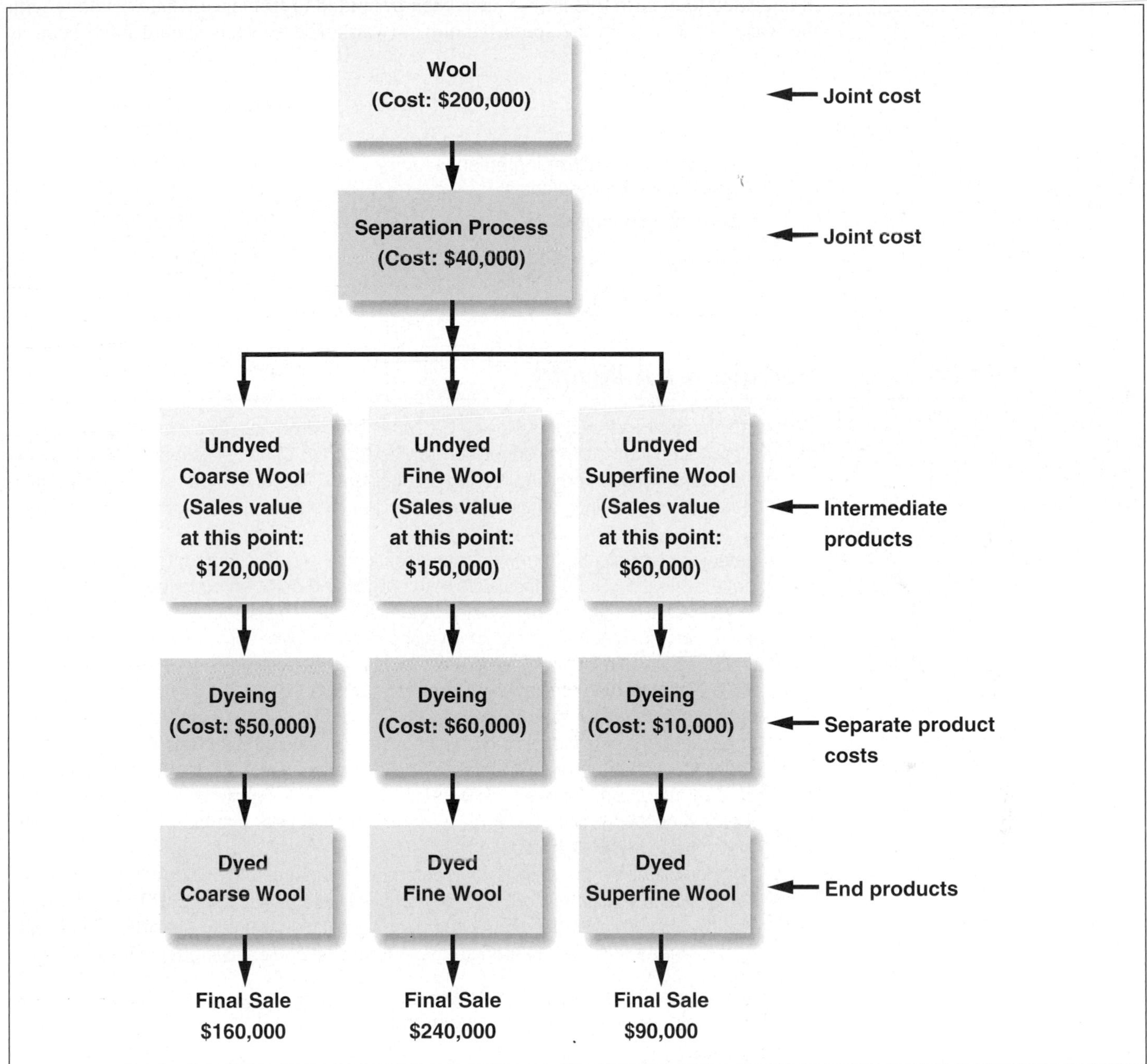

Sell or Process Further Decisions

Joint costs are irrelevant in decisions regarding what to do with a product from the split-off point forward. The reason is that regardless of what is done with the product after the split-off point, the joint costs must be incurred to get the product to the split-off point. Moreover, even if the product were disposed of in a landfill without any further processing, all of the joint costs must be incurred to obtain the other products that come out of the joint process. Therefore, none of the joint costs are economically attributable to any one of the intermediate or end products that emerge from the system. The joint costs are a common cost of all of the intermediate and end products and should not be allocated to them for purposes of making decisions about the products. In the case of the soap company (see the accompanying In Business box "Getting It All Wrong"), the $150,000 in allocated joint costs should not have been permitted to influence what was done with the waste product from the split-off point forward. The analysis should have been as follows:

	Dump in Gulf	Process Further
Sales value of fertilizer ingredient	0	$300,000
Additional processing costs	0	175,000
Contribution margin	0	$125,000
Advantage of processing further	$125,000	

In Business | Getting It All Wrong

A company located on the Gulf of Mexico produces soap products. Its six main soap product lines are produced from common inputs. Joint product costs up to the split-off point constitute the bulk of the production costs for all six product lines. These joint product costs are allocated to the six product lines on the basis of the relative sales value of each line at the split-off point.

A waste product results from the production of the six main product lines. Until a few years ago, the company loaded the waste onto barges and dumped it into the Gulf of Mexico, since the waste was thought to have no commercial value. The dumping was stopped, however, when the company's research division discovered that with some further processing the waste could be sold as a fertilizer ingredient. The further processing costs $175,000 per year. The waste was then sold to fertilizer manufacturers for $300,000.

The accountants responsible for allocating manufacturing costs included the sales value of the waste product along with the sales value of the six main product lines in their allocation of the joint product costs at the split-off point. This allocation resulted in the waste product being allocated $150,000 in joint product cost. This $150,000 allocation, when added to the further processing costs of $175,000 for the waste, made it appear that the waste product was unprofitable—as shown in the table below.

When presented with this analysis, the company's management decided that further processing of the waste should be stopped. The company went back to dumping the waste in the Gulf. In addition to foolishly reducing the company's profit, this dumping also raises questions regarding the company's social responsibility and the environmental impact of its actions.

Sales value of the waste product after further processing	$300,000
Less costs assignable to the waste product	325,000
Net loss	$ (25,000)

Decisions of this type are known as **sell or process further decisions.** It will always be profitable to continue processing a joint product after the split-off point *so long as the incremental revenue from such processing exceeds the incremental processing cost incurred after the split-off point.* Joint costs that have already been incurred up to the split-off point are always irrelevant in decisions concerning what to do from the split-off point forward.

To provide a detailed example of the sell or process further decision, return to the data for Santa Maria Wool Cooperative in Exhibit 13–6. We can answer several important questions using this data. First, is the company making money if it runs the entire process from beginning to end? Assuming there are no costs other than those displayed in Exhibit 13–6, the company is indeed making money as follows:

Analysis of the profitability of the overall operation:

Combined final sales value ($160,000 + $240,000 + $90,000)		$490,000
Less costs of producing the end products:		
Cost of wool	$200,000	
Cost of separating wool	40,000	
Combined costs of dyeing ($50,000 + $60,000 + $10,000)	120,000	360,000
Profit		$130,000

However, even though the company is making money overall, it may be losing money on one or more of the products. If the company buys wool and runs the separation process, it will get all three intermediate products. Nothing can be done about that. However, each of these products can be sold *as is* without further processing. It may be that the company would be better off selling one or more of the products prior to dyeing to avoid the costs of the dyeing. The appropriate way to make this choice is to compare the incremental revenues to the incremental costs from further processing as follows:

Analysis of sell or process further:

	Coarse Wool	Fine Wool	Superfine Wool
Final sales value after further processing	$160,000	$240,000	$90,000
Less sales value at the split-off point	120,000	150,000	60,000
Incremental revenue from further processing	40,000	90,000	30,000
Less cost of further processing (dyeing)	50,000	60,000	10,000
Profit (loss) from further processing	$ (10,000)	$ 30,000	$20,000

As this analysis shows, the company would be better off selling the undyed coarse wool as is rather than processing it further. The other two products should be processed further and dyed before selling them.

Note that the joint costs of the wool ($200,000) and of the wool separation process ($40,000) have played no role in the decision of whether to sell or further process the intermediate products. These joint costs are relevant in a decision of whether to buy wool and to run the wool separation process, but they are not relevant in decisions about what to do with the intermediate products once they have been separated.

Activity-Based Costing and Relevant Costs

As discussed in Chapter 8, activity-based costing can be used to help identify potentially relevant costs for decision-making purposes. Activity-based costing improves the traceability of costs by focusing on the activities caused by a product or other segment. However, managers should exercise caution against reading more into this "traceability" than really exists. People have a tendency to assume that if a cost is traceable to a segment, then the cost is automatically an avoidable cost. That is not true. As emphasized in Chapter 8, the costs provided by a well-designed activity-based costing system are only *potentially* relevant. Before making a decision, managers must still decide which of the potentially relevant costs are actually avoidable. Only those costs that are avoidable are relevant and the others should be ignored.

To illustrate, refer again to the data relating to the housewares line in Exhibit 13–4. The $2,000 fixtures depreciation is a traceable cost of the housewares lines because it relates to activities in that department. We found, however, that the $2,000 is not avoidable if the housewares line is dropped. The key lesson here is that the method used to assign a cost to a product or other segment does not change the basic nature of the cost. A sunk cost such as depreciation of old equipment is still a sunk cost regardless of whether it is traced directly to a particular segment on an activity basis, allocated to all segments on the basis of labor-hours, or treated in some other way in the costing process. Regardless of the method used to assign costs to products or other segments, the manager still must apply the principles discussed in this chapter to determine the costs that are avoidable in each situation.

Summary

All of the material in this chapter consists of applications of one simple but powerful idea. Only those costs and benefits that differ between alternatives are relevant in a decision. All other costs and benefits are irrelevant and can and should be ignored. In particular, sunk costs are irrelevant as are future costs that do not differ between alternatives.

This simple idea was applied in a variety of situations including decisions that involve making or buying a component, adding or dropping a product line, processing a joint product further, and using a constrained resource. This list includes only a small sample of the possible applications of the relevant cost concept. Indeed, any decision involving costs hinges on the proper identification and analysis of the costs that are relevant. We will continue to focus on the concept of relevant costs in the following chapter where long-run investment decisions are considered.

Review Problem: Relevant Costs

Charter Sports Equipment manufactures round, rectangular, and octagonal trampolines. Data on sales and expenses for the past month follow:

		Trampoline		
	Total	Round	Rectangular	Octagonal
Sales	$1,000,000	$140,000	$500,000	$360,000
Less variable expenses	410,000	60,000	200,000	150,000
Contribution margin	590,000	80,000	300,000	210,000
Less fixed expenses:				
Advertising—traceable	216,000	41,000	110,000	65,000
Depreciation of special equipment	95,000	20,000	40,000	35,000
Line supervisors' salaries	19,000	6,000	7,000	6,000
General factory overhead*	200,000	28,000	100,000	72,000
Total fixed expenses	530,000	95,000	257,000	178,000
Net operating income (loss)	$ 60,000	$ (15,000)	$ 43,000	$ 32,000

*A common fixed cost that is allocated on the basis of sales dollars.

Management is concerned about the continued losses shown by the round trampolines and wants a recommendation as to whether or not the line should be discontinued. The special equipment used to produce the trampolines has no resale value. If the round trampoline model is dropped, the two line supervisors assigned to the model would be discharged.

Required:

1. Should production and sale of the round trampolines be discontinued? You may assume that the company has no other use for the capacity now being used to produce the round trampolines. Show computations to support your answer.
2. Recast the above data in a format that would be more usable to management in assessing the long-run profitability of the various product lines.

Solution to Review Problem

1. No, production and sale of the round trampolines should not be discontinued. Computations to support this answer follow:

Contribution margin lost if the round trampolines are discontinued . . .		$(80,000)
Less fixed costs that can be avoided:		
Advertising—traceable	$41,000	
Line supervisors' salaries	6,000	47,000
Decrease in net operating income for the company as a whole		$(33,000)

The depreciation of the special equipment represents a sunk cost, and therefore it is not relevant to the decision. The general factory overhead is allocated and will presumably continue regardless of whether or not the round trampolines are discontinued; thus, it is not relevant.

2. If management wants a clear picture of the profitability of the segments, the general factory overhead should not be allocated. It is a common cost and therefore should be deducted from the total product-line segment margin, as shown in Chapter 12. A more useful income statement format would be as follows:

		Trampoline		
	Total	Round	Rectangular	Octagonal
Sales	$1,000,000	$140,000	$500,000	$360,000
Less variable expenses	410,000	60,000	200,000	150,000
Contribution margin	590,000	80,000	300,000	210,000
Less traceable fixed expenses:				
Advertising—traceable	216,000	41,000	110,000	65,000
Depreciation of special equipment	95,000	20,000	40,000	35,000
Line supervisors' salaries	19,000	6,000	7,000	6,000
Total traceable fixed expenses	330,000	67,000	157,000	106,000
Product-line segment margin	260,000	$ 13,000	$143,000	$104,000
Less common fixed expenses	200,000			
Net operating income (loss)	$ 60,000			

Glossary

Avoidable cost A cost that can be eliminated (in whole or in part) by choosing one alternative over another in a decision-making situation. This term is synonymous with *relevant cost* and *differential cost.* (p. 586)

Bottleneck A machine or some other part of a process that limits the total output of the entire system. (p. 603)

Constraint A limitation under which a company must operate, such as limited available machine time or raw materials, that restricts the company's ability to satisfy demand. (p. 602)

Differential cost Any cost that differs between alternatives in a decision-making situation. This term is synonymous with *avoidable cost* and *relevant cost.* (p. 587)

Joint costs Costs that are incurred up to the split-off point in a process that produces joint products. (p. 606)

Joint products Two or more items that are produced from a common input. (p. 606)

Make or buy decision A decision concerning whether an item should be produced internally or purchased from an outside supplier. (p. 598)

Relaxing (or elevating) the constraint An action that increases the amount of a constrained resource. (p. 604)

Relevant cost A cost that differs between alternatives in a particular decision. This term is synonymous with *avoidable cost* and *differential cost.* (p. 586)

Sell or process further decision A decision as to whether a joint product should be sold at the split-off point or sold after further processing. (p. 608)

Special order A one-time order that is not considered part of the company's normal ongoing business. (p. 601)

Split-off point That point in the manufacturing process where some or all of the joint products can be recognized as individual products. (p. 606)

Sunk cost Any cost that has already been incurred and that cannot be changed by any decision made now or in the future. (p. 587)

Cost per fishing trip:	
Depreciation on fishing boat* (annual depreciation of $1,500 ÷ 10 trips)	$150
Boat moorage fees (annual rental of $1,200 ÷ 10 trips)	120
Expenditures on fishing gear, except for snagged lures (annual expenditures of $200 ÷ 10 trips)	20
Snagged fishing lures	7
Fishing license (yearly license of $40 ÷ 10 trips)	4
Fuel and upkeep on boat per trip	25
Junk food consumed during trip	8
Total cost per fishing trip	$334
Cost per salmon ($334 ÷ 2 salmon)	$167

*The original cost of the boat was $15,000. It has an estimated useful life of 10 years, after which it will have no resale value. The boat does not wear out through use, but it does become less desirable for resale as it becomes older.

Required:

1. Assuming that the salmon fishing trip Steve has just completed is typical, what costs are relevant to a decision as to whether he should go on another trip this year?
2. Suppose that on Steve's next fishing trip he gets lucky and catches three salmon in the amount of time it took him to catch two salmon on his last trip. How much would the third salmon have cost him to catch? Explain.
3. Discuss the costs that are relevant in a decision of whether Steve should give up fishing.

EXERCISE 13–9 Dropping or Retaining a Segment [LO2]

Dexter Products, Inc., manufactures and sells a number of items, including an overnight case. The company has been experiencing losses on the overnight case for some time, as shown on the following income statement:

DEXTER PRODUCTS, INC.
Income Statement—Overnight Cases
For the Quarter Ended June 30

Sales		$450,000
Less variable expenses:		
Variable manufacturing expenses	$130,000	
Sales commissions	48,000	
Shipping	12,000	
Total variable expenses		190,000
Contribution margin		260,000
Less fixed expenses:		
Salary of product line manager	21,000	
General factory overhead	104,000*	
Depreciation of equipment (no resale value)	36,000	
Advertising—traceable	110,000	
Insurance on inventories	9,000	
Purchasing department expenses	50,000†	
Total fixed expenses		330,000
Net operating loss		$ (70,000)

*Allocated on the basis of machine-hours.
†Allocated on the basis of sales dollars.

Discontinuing the overnight cases would not affect sales of other product lines and would have no noticeable effect on the company's total general factory overhead or total purchasing department expenses.

Required:

Would you recommend that the company discontinue the manufacture and sale of overnight cases? Support your answer with appropriate computations.

EXERCISE 13–10 Make or Buy a Component [LO3]

Royal Company manufactures 20,000 units of part R-3 each year for use on its production line. The cost per unit for part R-3 follows:

Direct materials	$ 4.80
Direct labor	7.00
Variable manufacturing overhead	3.20
Fixed manufacturing overhead	10.00
Total cost per part	$25.00

An outside supplier has offered to sell 20,000 units of part R-3 each year to Royal Company for $23.50 per part. If Royal Company accepts this offer, the facilities now being used to manufacture part R-3 could be rented to another company at an annual rental of $150,000. However, Royal Company has determined that $6 of the fixed manufacturing overhead being applied to part R-3 would continue even if part R-3 were purchased from the outside supplier.

Required:

Prepare computations to show the net dollar advantage or disadvantage of accepting the outside supplier's offer.

Problems

PROBLEM 13–11 Dropping or Retaining a Tour [LO2]

Blueline Tours, Inc., operates tours throughout the United States. A study has indicated that some of the tours are not profitable, and consideration is being given to dropping these tours to improve the company's overall operating performance.

One such tour is a two-day Historic Mansions bus tour conducted in the southern states. An income statement from a typical Historic Mansions tour is given below:

Ticket revenue (100 seat capacity × 40% occupancy × $75 ticket price per person)	$3,000	100.0%
Less variable expenses ($22.50 per person)	900	30
Contribution margin	2,100	70%
Less tour expenses:		
Tour promotion	$ 600	
Salary of bus driver	350	
Fee, tour guide	700	
Fuel for bus	125	
Depreciation of bus	450	
Liability insurance, bus	200	
Overnight parking fee, bus	50	
Room and meals, bus driver and tour guide	175	
Bus maintenance and preparation	300	
Total tour expenses	2,950	
Net operating loss	$ (850)	

The following additional information is available about the tour:

a. Bus drivers are paid fixed annual salaries; tour guides are paid for each tour conducted.

b. The "Bus maintenance and preparation" cost above is an allocation of the salaries of mechanics and other service personnel who are responsible for keeping the company's fleet of buses in good operating condition.

c. Depreciation is due to obsolescence. Depreciation due to wear and tear is negligible.

d. Liability insurance premiums are based on the number of buses in the company's fleet.

e. Dropping the Historic Mansions bus tour would not allow Blueline Tours to reduce the number of buses in its fleet, the number of bus drivers on the payroll, or the size of the maintenance and preparation staff.

Required:

1. Prepare an analysis showing what the impact will be on the company's profits if this tour is discontinued.
2. The company's tour director has been criticized because only about 50% of the seats on Blueline's tours are being filled as compared to an average of 60% for the industry. The tour director has explained that Blueline's average seat occupancy could be improved considerably by eliminating about 10% of the tours, but that doing so would reduce profits. Explain how this could happen.

PROBLEM 13–12 Relevant Cost Potpourri [LO2, LO3, LO4, LO5, LO6]

Unless otherwise indicated, each of the following parts is independent. In all cases, show computations to support your answer.

1. Boyle's Home Center has two departments, Bath and Kitchen. The most recent income statement for the company follows:

		Department	
	Total	**Bath**	**Kitchen**
Sales	$5,000,000	$1,000,000	$4,000,000
Less variable expenses	1,900,000	300,000	1,600,000
Contribution margin	3,100,000	700,000	2,400,000
Less fixed expenses	2,700,000	900,000	1,800,000
Net operating income (loss)	$ 400,000	$ (200,000)	$ 600,000

A study indicates that $370,000 of the fixed expenses being charged to the Bath Department are sunk costs or allocated costs that will continue even if the Bath Department is dropped. In addition, the elimination of the Bath Department would result in a 10% decrease in the sales of the Kitchen Department. If the Bath Department is dropped, what will be the effect on the net operating income of the company as a whole?

2. Morrell Company produces several products from the processing of krypton, a rare mineral. Material and processing costs total $30,000 per ton, one-third of which is allocated to the product merifulon. The merifulon produced from a ton of krypton can either be sold at the split-off point or processed further at a cost of $13,000 and then sold for $60,000. The sales value of merifulon at the split-off point is $40,000. Should merifulon be processed further or sold at the split-off point?
3. Shelby Company produces three products, X, Y, and Z. Data concerning the three products follow (per unit):

		Product	
	X	**Y**	**Z**
Selling price	$80	$56	$70
Less variable expenses:			
Direct materials	24	15	9
Labor and overhead	24	27	40
Total variable expenses	48	42	49
Contribution margin	$32	$14	$21
Contribution margin ratio	40%	25%	30%

Demand for the company's products is very strong, with far more orders each month than the company can produce with the available raw materials. The same material is used in each product. The material costs $3 per pound, with a maximum of 5,000 pounds available each month. Which orders would you advise the company to accept first, those for X, for Y, or for Z? Which orders second? Third?

4. For many years, Diehl Company has produced a small electrical part that it uses in the production of its standard line of diesel tractors. The company's unit product cost, based on a production level of 60,000 parts per year, is as follows:

	Per Part	Total
Direct materials	$ 4.00	
Direct labor	2.75	
Variable manufacturing overhead	0.50	
Fixed manufacturing overhead, traceable	3.00	$180,000
Fixed manufacturing overhead, common (allocated on the basis of labor-hours)	2.25	135,000
Unit product cost	$12.50	

An outside supplier has offered to supply the electrical parts to the Diehl Company for only $10 per part. One-third of the traceable fixed manufacturing costs represent supervisory salaries and other costs that can be eliminated if the parts are purchased. The other two-thirds of the traceable fixed manufacturing costs represent depreciation of special equipment that has no resale value. Economic depreciation on this equipment is due to obsolescence rather than wear and tear. The decision would have no effect on the common fixed costs of the company, and the space being used to produce the parts would otherwise be idle. Show the dollar advantage or disadvantage of accepting the supplier's offer.

5. Glade Company produces a single product. The cost of producing and selling a single unit of this product at the company's current activity level of 8,000 units per month is as follows:

Direct materials	$2.50
Direct labor	3.00
Variable manufacturing overhead	0.50
Fixed manufacturing overhead	4.25
Variable selling and administrative expenses	1.50
Fixed selling and administrative expenses	2.00

The normal selling price is $15 per unit. The company's capacity is 10,000 units per month. An order has been received from an overseas source for 2,000 units at a price of $12 per unit. This order would not affect regular sales. If the order is accepted, by how much will monthly profits be increased or decreased? (The order would not change the company's total fixed costs.)

6. Refer to the data in (5) above. Assume the company has 500 units of this product left over from last year that are inferior to the current model. The units must be sold through regular channels at reduced prices. What unit cost is relevant for establishing a minimum selling price for these units? Explain.

PROBLEM 13–13 Sell or Process Further [LO6]

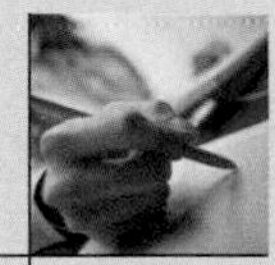

(Prepared from a situation suggested by Professor John W. Hardy.) Abilene Meat Processing Corporation is a major processor of beef and other meat products. The company has a large amount of T-bone steak on hand, and it is trying to decide whether to sell the T-bone steaks as is or to process them further into filet mignon and New York cut steaks.

Management believes that a 1-pound T-bone steak would yield the following profit:

Wholesale selling price ($2.25 per pound)	$2.25
Less joint costs incurred up to the split-off point where T-bone steak can be identified as a separate product	1.70
Profit per pound	$0.55

As mentioned above, instead of being sold as is, the T-bone steaks could be further processed into filet mignon and New York cut steaks. Cutting one side of a T-bone steak provides the filet mignon, and cutting the other side provides the New York cut. One 16-ounce T-bone steak cut in this way will yield one 6-ounce filet mignon and one 8-ounce New York cut; the remaining ounces are waste. The cost of processing the T-bone steaks into these cuts is $0.20 per pound. The filet mignon can be sold for $3.60 per pound, and the New York cut can be sold wholesale for $2.90 per pound.

Required:

1. Determine the profit per pound from processing the T-bone steaks further into filet mignon and New York cut steaks.
2. Would you recommend that the T-bone steaks be sold as is or processed further? Why?

PROBLEM 13–14 Shutting Down or Continuing to Operate a Plant [LO2]
(Note: This type of decision is similar to dropping a product line.)

Hallas Company manufactures a fast-bonding glue in its Northwest plant. The company normally produces and sells 40,000 gallons of the glue each month. This glue, which is known as MJ-7, is used in the wood industry to manufacture plywood. The selling price of MJ-7 is $35 per gallon, variable costs are $21 per gallon, fixed manufacturing overhead costs in the plant total $230,000 per month, and the fixed selling costs total $310,000 per month.

Strikes in the mills that purchase the bulk of the MJ-7 glue have caused Hallas Company's sales to temporarily drop to only 11,000 gallons per month. Hallas Company's management estimates that the strikes will last for about two months, after which sales of MJ-7 should return to normal. Due to the current low level of sales, however, Hallas Company's management is thinking about closing down the Northwest plant during the two months that the strikes are on.

If Hallas Company does close down the Northwest plant, fixed manufacturing overhead costs can be reduced to $170,000 per month and fixed selling costs can be reduced by 10%. Start-up costs at the end of the shutdown period would total $14,000. Since Hallas Company uses JIT production methods, no inventories are on hand.

Required:

1. Assuming that the strikes continue for two months, would you recommend that Hallas Company close the Northwest plant? Explain. Show computations in good form to support your answer.
2. At what level of sales (in gallons) for the two-month period should Hallas Company be indifferent between closing the plant or keeping it open? Show computations. (Hint: This is a type of break-even analysis, except that the fixed cost portion of your break-even computation should include only those fixed costs that are relevant [i.e., avoidable] over the two-month period.)

PROBLEM 13–15 Make or Buy Decision [LO3]

Bronson Company manufactures a variety of ballpoint pens. The company has just received an offer from an outside supplier to provide the ink cartridge for the company's Zippo pen line, at a price of $0.48 per dozen cartridges. The company is interested in this offer, since its own production of cartridges is at capacity.

Bronson Company estimates that if the supplier's offer were accepted, the direct labor and variable overhead costs of the Zippo pen line would be reduced by 10% and the direct materials cost would be reduced by 20%.

Under present operations, Bronson Company manufactures all of its own pens from start to finish. The Zippo pens are sold through wholesalers at $4 per box. Each box contains one dozen pens. Fixed overhead costs charged to the Zippo pen line total $50,000 each year. (The same equipment and facilities are used to produce several pen lines.) The present cost of producing one dozen Zippo pens (one box) is given below:

Direct materials	$1.50
Direct labor	1.00
Manufacturing overhead	0.80*
Total cost	$3.30

*Includes both variable and fixed manufacturing overhead, based on production of 100,000 boxes of pens each year.

Required:

1. Should Bronson Company accept the outside supplier's offer? Show computations.
2. What is the maximum price that Bronson Company should be willing to pay the outside supplier per dozen cartridges?
3. Due to the bankruptcy of a competitor, Bronson Company expects to sell 150,000 boxes of Zippo pens next year. As stated above, the company presently has enough capacity to produce the cartridges for only 100,000 boxes of Zippo pens annually. By incurring $30,000 in added fixed cost each year, the company could expand its production of cartridges to satisfy the anticipated demand for Zippo pens. The variable cost per unit to produce the additional cartridges would be the same as at present. Under these circumstances, should all 150,000 boxes be purchased from the outside supplier, or should some of the 150,000 boxes be made by Bronson? Show computations to support your answer.

4. What qualitative factors should Bronson Company consider in determining whether it should make or buy the ink cartridges?

(CMA, adapted)

PROBLEM 13–16 Accept or Reject a Special Order [LO4]

Pietarsaari Oy, a Finnish company, produces cross-country ski poles that it sells for 32 mk a pair. (The Finnish unit of currency, the markka, is abbreviated as "mk.") Operating at capacity, the company can produce 50,000 pairs of ski poles a year. Costs associated with this level of production and sales are given below:

	Per Pair	Total
Direct materials	12 mk	600,000 mk
Direct labor	3	150,000
Variable manufacturing overhead	1	50,000
Fixed manufacturing overhead	5	250,000
Variable selling expenses	2	100,000
Fixed selling expenses	4	200,000
Total cost	27 mk	1,350,000 mk

Required:

1. The Finnish army would like to make a one-time-only purchase of 10,000 pairs of ski poles for its mountain troops. The army would pay a fixed fee of 4 mk per pair, and in addition it would reimburse the Pietarsaari Oy company for its unit manufacturing costs (both fixed and variable). Due to a recession, the company would otherwise produce and sell only 40,000 pairs of ski poles this year. (Total fixed manufacturing overhead cost would be the same whether 40,000 pairs or 50,000 pairs of ski poles were produced.) The company would not incur its usual variable selling expenses with this special order.

   If the Pietarsaari Oy company accepts the army's offer, by how much would net operating income be increased or decreased from what it would be if only 40,000 pairs of ski poles were produced and sold during the year?
2. Assume the same situation as described in (1) above, except that the company is already operating at capacity and could sell 50,000 pairs of ski poles through regular channels. Thus, accepting the army's offer would require giving up sales of 10,000 pairs at the normal price of 32 mk a pair. If the army's offer is accepted, by how much will net operating income be increased or decreased from what it would be if the 10,000 pairs were sold through regular channels?

PROBLEM 13–17 Close or Retain a Store [LO2]

Thrifty Markets, Inc., operates three stores in a large metropolitan area. The company's segmented income statement for the last quarter is given below:

THRIFTY MARKETS, INC.
Income Statement
For the Quarter Ended March 31

	Total	Uptown Store	Downtown Store	Westpark Store
Sales	$2,500,000	$900,000	$600,000	$1,000,000
Cost of goods sold	1,450,000	513,000	372,000	565,000
Gross margin	1,050,000	387,000	228,000	435,000
Operating expenses:				
Selling expenses:				
Direct advertising	118,500	40,000	36,000	42,500
General advertising*	20,000	7,200	4,800	8,000
Sales salaries	157,000	52,000	45,000	60,000
Delivery salaries	30,000	10,000	10,000	10,000
Store rent	215,000	70,000	65,000	80,000
Depreciation of store fixtures	46,950	18,300	8,800	19,850
Depreciation of delivery equipment	27,000	9,000	9,000	9,000
Total selling expenses	614,450	206,500	178,600	229,350

continued

Store management salaries	63,000	20,000	18,000	25,000
General office salaries*	50,000	18,000	12,000	20,000
Utilities	89,800	31,000	27,200	31,600
Insurance on fixtures and inventory	25,500	8,000	9,000	8,500
Employment taxes	36,000	12,000	10,200	13,800
General office expenses—other*	25,000	9,000	6,000	10,000
Total administrative expenses	289,300	98,000	82,400	108,900
Total operating expenses	903,750	304,500	261,000	338,250
Net operating income (loss)	$ 146,250	$ 82,500	$ (33,000)	$ 96,750

*Allocated on the basis of sales dollars.

Management is very concerned about the Downtown Store's inability to show a profit, and consideration is being given to closing the store. The company has asked you to make a recommendation as to what course of action should be taken. The following additional information is available on the store:

a. The manager of the store has been with the company for many years; he would be retained and transferred to another position in the company if the store were closed. His salary is $6,000 per month, or $18,000 per quarter. If the store were not closed, a new employee would be hired to fill the other position at a salary of $5,000 per month.
b. The lease on the building housing the Downtown Store can be broken with no penalty.
c. The fixtures being used in the Downtown Store would be transferred to the other two stores if the Downtown Store were closed.
d. The company's employment taxes are 12% of salaries.
e. A single delivery crew serves all three stores. One delivery person could be discharged if the Downtown Store were closed; this person's salary amounts to $7,000 per quarter. The delivery equipment would be distributed to the other stores. The equipment does not wear out through use, but it does eventually become obsolete.
f. One-third of the Downtown Store's insurance relates to its fixtures.
g. The general office salaries and other expenses relate to the general management of Thrifty Markets, Inc. The employee in the general office who is responsible for the Downtown Store would be discharged if the store were closed. This employee's salary amounts to $8,000 per quarter.

Required:

1. Prepare a schedule showing the change in revenues and expenses and the impact on the overall company net income that would result if the Downtown Store were closed.
2. Based on your computations in (1) above, what recommendation would you make to the management of Thrifty Markets, Inc.?
3. Assume that if the Downtown Store were closed, sales in the Uptown Store would increase by $200,000 per quarter due to loyal customers shifting their buying to the Uptown Store. The Uptown Store has ample capacity to handle the increased sales, and its gross profit rate is 43%. What effect would these factors have on your recommendation concerning the Downtown Store? Show computations.

PROBLEM 13–18 Make or Buy Analysis [LO3]

"That old equipment for producing subassemblies is worn out," said Paul Taylor, president of Timkin Company. "We need to make a decision quickly." The company is trying to decide whether it should rent new equipment and continue to make its subassemblies internally or whether it should discontinue production of its subassemblies and purchase them from an outside supplier. The alternatives follow:

Alternative 1: New equipment for producing the subassemblies can be rented for $60,000 per year.

Alternative 2: The subassemblies can be purchased from an outside supplier who has offered to provide them for $8 each.

Timkin Company's present costs per unit of producing the subassemblies internally (with the old equipment) are given below. These costs are based on a current activity level of 40,000 subassemblies per year:

Direct materials	$ 2.75
Direct labor	4.00
Variable overhead	0.60
Fixed overhead ($0.75 supervision, $0.90 depreciation, and $2 general company overhead)	3.65
Total cost per unit	$11.00

The new equipment would be more efficient and, according to the manufacturer, would reduce direct labor costs and variable overhead costs by 25%. Supervision cost ($30,000 per year) and direct materials cost per unit would not be affected by the new equipment. The new equipment's capacity would be 60,000 subassemblies per year.

The total general company overhead would be unaffected by this decision.

Required:

1. The president is unsure what the company should do and would like an analysis showing what unit costs and what total costs would be under each of the two alternatives given above. Assume that 40,000 subassemblies are needed each year. Which course of action would you recommend to the president?
2. Would your recommendation in (1) above be the same if the company's needs were (*a*) 50,000 subassemblies per year, or (*b*) 60,000 subassemblies per year? Show computations in good form.
3. What other factors would you recommend that the company consider before making a decision?

PROBLEM 13–19 Relevant Cost Analysis in a Variety of Situations [LO2, LO3, LO4]

Barker Company has a single product called a Zet. The company normally produces and sells 80,000 Zets each year at a selling price of $40 per unit. The company's unit costs at this level of activity are given below:

Direct materials	$ 9.50
Direct labor	10.00
Variable manufacturing overhead	2.80
Fixed manufacturing overhead	5.00 ($400,000 total)
Variable selling expenses	1.70
Fixed selling expenses	4.50 ($360,000 total)
Total cost per unit	$33.50

A number of questions relating to the production and sale of Zets are given below. Each question is independent.

Required:

1. Assume that Barker Company has sufficient capacity to produce 100,000 Zets each year without any increase in fixed manufacturing overhead costs. The company could increase sales by 25% above the present 80,000 units each year if it were willing to increase the fixed selling expenses by $150,000. Would the increased fixed expenses be justified?
2. Assume again that Barker Company has sufficient capacity to produce 100,000 Zets each year. The company has an opportunity to sell 20,000 units in an overseas market. Import duties, foreign permits, and other special costs associated with the order would total $14,000. The only selling costs that would be associated with the order would be $1.50 per unit shipping cost. You have been asked by the president to compute the per unit break-even price on this order.
3. One of the materials used in the production of Zets is obtained from a foreign supplier. Civil unrest in the supplier's country has caused a cutoff in material shipments that is expected to last for three months. Barker Company has enough material on hand to continue to operate at 25% of normal levels for the three-month period. As an alternative, the company could close the plant down entirely for the three months. Closing the plant would reduce fixed overhead

costs by 40% during the three-month period; the fixed selling costs would continue at two-thirds of their normal level while the plant was closed. What would be the dollar advantage or disadvantage of closing the plant for the three-month period?

4. The company has 500 Zets on hand that were produced last month and have small blemishes. Due to the blemishes, it will be impossible to sell these units at the normal price. If the company wishes to sell them through regular distribution channels, what unit cost figure is relevant for setting a minimum selling price? Explain.
5. An outside manufacturer has offered to produce Zets for Barker Company and to ship them directly to Barker's customers. If Barker Company accepts this offer, the facilities that it uses to produce Zets would be idle; however, fixed overhead costs would continue at 30% of their present level. Since the outside manufacturer would pay for all the costs of shipping, the variable selling costs would be reduced by 60%. Compute the unit cost figure that is relevant for comparison to whatever quoted price is received from the outside manufacturer.

PROBLEM 13–20 Dropping or Retaining a Product [LO2]

Mrs. Agatha Spencer-Atwood is managing director of the British company, Imperial Reflections, Ltd. The company makes reproductions of antique dressing room mirrors. Mrs. Spencer-Atwood would like guidance on the advisability of eliminating the Kensington line of mirrors. These mirrors have never been among the company's best-selling products, although their sales have been stable for many years.

Below is a condensed statement of operating income for the company and for the Kensington product line for the quarter ended June 30:

	Total Company	Kensington Product Line
Sales	£5,000,000	£480,000
Cost of sales:		
Direct materials	420,000	32,000
Direct labor	1,600,000	200,000
Fringe benefits (30% of labor)	480,000	60,000
Variable manufacturing overhead	340,000	30,000
Building rent and maintenance	120,000	15,000
Depreciation	80,000	10,000
Royalties (5% of sales)	250,000	24,000
Total cost of sales	3,290,000	371,000
Gross margin	1,710,000	109,000
Selling and administrative expenses:		
Product-line managers' salaries	75,000	8,000
Sales commissions (10% of sales)	500,000	48,000
Fringe benefits (30% of salaries and commissions)	172,500	16,800
Shipping	120,000	10,000
Advertising	350,000	15,000
General administrative expenses	250,000	24,000
Total selling and administrative expenses	1,467,500	121,800
Net operating income (loss)	£ 242,500	£ (12,800)

The following additional data have been supplied by the company:

a. The company pays royalties to the owners of the original pieces of furniture from which the reproductions are copied.
b. All of the company's products are manufactured in the same facility and use the same equipment. The building rent and maintenance and the depreciation are allocated to products on the basis of direct labor dollars. The equipment does not wear out through use; rather it eventually becomes obsolete.
c. There is ample capacity to fill all orders.
d. Dropping the Kensington product line would have little (if any) effect on sales of other product lines.
e. All products are made to order, so there are no inventories.
f. Shipping costs are traced to the product lines.

g. Advertising costs are for ads to promote specific product lines. These costs have been traced directly to the product lines.
h. General administrative expenses are allocated to products on the basis of sales dollars. There would be no effect on the total general administrative expenses if the Kensington product line were dropped.

Required:

1. Would you recommend that the Kensington product line be dropped, given the current level of sales? Prepare appropriate computations to support your answer.
2. What would sales of the Kensington product line have to be, at a minimum, to justify retaining the product line? Explain your answer. (Hint: Set this up as a break-even problem, but include only the relevant costs.)

PROBLEM 13–21 Utilization of a Constrained Resource [LO5]

The Brandilyn Toy Company manufactures a line of dolls and a doll dress sewing kit. Demand for the dolls is increasing, and management requests assistance from you in determining the best sales and production mix for the coming year. The company has provided data for you to use in the form of an Excel worksheet:

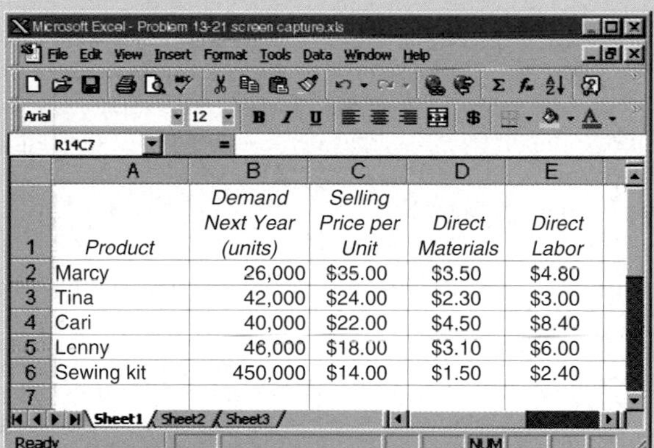

Product	Demand Next Year (units)	Selling Price per Unit	Direct Materials	Direct Labor
Marcy	26,000	$35.00	$3.50	$4.80
Tina	42,000	$24.00	$2.30	$3.00
Cari	40,000	$22.00	$4.50	$8.40
Lenny	46,000	$18.00	$3.10	$6.00
Sewing kit	450,000	$14.00	$1.50	$2.40

The following additional information is available:

a. The company's plant has a capacity of 150,000 direct labor-hours per year on a single-shift basis. The company's present employees and equipment can produce all five products.
b. The direct labor rate is $12.00 per hour; this rate is expected to remain unchanged during the coming year.
c. Fixed costs total $356,000 per year. Variable overhead costs are $4.00 per direct labor-hour.
d. All of the company's nonmanufacturing costs are fixed.
e. The company's present inventory of finished products is negligible and can be ignored.

Required:

1. Determine the contribution margin per direct labor-hour expended on each product.
2. Prepare a schedule showing the total direct labor-hours that will be required to produce the units estimated to be sold during the coming year.
3. Examine the data you have computed in (1) and (2) above. Indicate how much of each product should be made so that total production time is equal to the 150,000 direct labor-hours available.
4. What is the highest price, in terms of a rate per hour, that Brandilyn Toy Company should be willing to pay for additional capacity (that is, for added direct labor time)?
5. Identify ways in which the company might be able to obtain additional output so that it would not have to leave some demand for its products unsatisfied.

(CMA, adapted)

PROBLEM 13–22 Sell or Process Further [LO6]

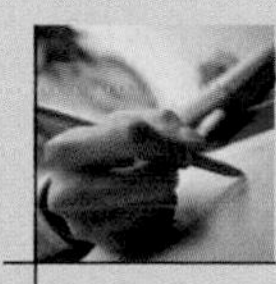

The Heather Honey Company purchases honeycombs from beekeepers for $2.00 a pound. The company produces two main products from the honeycombs—honey and beeswax. Honey is drained from the honeycombs, and then the honeycombs are melted down to form cubes of beeswax. The beeswax is sold for $1.50 a pound.

The honey can be sold in raw form for $3.00 a pound. However, some of the raw honey is used by the company to make honey drop candies. The candies are packed in a decorative container and are sold in gift and specialty shops. A container of honey drop candies sells for $4.40.

Each container of honey drop candies contains three quarters of a pound of honey. The other variable costs associated with making the candies are as follows:

Decorative container	$0.40
Other ingredients	0.25
Direct labor	0.20
Variable manufacturing overhead	0.10
Total variable manufacturing cost	$0.95

The monthly fixed manufacturing overhead costs associated with making the candies follow:

Master candy maker's salary	$3,880
Depreciation of candy making equipment	400
Total fixed manufacturing cost	$4,280

The master candy maker has no duties other than to oversee production of the honey drop candies. The candy making equipment is special-purpose equipment that was constructed specifically to make this particular candy. The equipment has no resale value and does not wear out through use.

A salesperson is paid $2,000 per month plus a commission of 5% of sales to market the honey drop candies.

The company had enjoyed robust sales of the candies for several years, but the recent entrance of a competing product into the marketplace has depressed sales of the candies. The management of the company is now wondering whether it would be more profitable to sell all of the honey rather than converting some of it into candies.

Required:

1. What is the incremental contribution margin per container from further processing the honey into candies?
2. What is the minimum number of containers of candy that must be sold each month to justify the continued processing of honey into candies? Explain. Show all computations in good form.

(CMA, adapted)

Cases

CASE 13–23 Ethics and the Manager; Shut Down or Continue Operations [LO2]

Marvin Braun had just been appointed vice president of the Great Basin Region of the Financial Services Corporation (FSC). The company provides check processing services for small banks. The banks send checks presented for deposit or payment to FSC, which then records the data on each check in a computerized database. FSC sends the data electronically to the nearest Federal Reserve Bank check-clearing center where the appropriate transfers of funds are made between banks. The Great Basin Region consists of three check processing centers in Eastern Idaho—Pocatello, Idaho Falls, and Ashton. Prior to his promotion to vice president, Mr. Braun had been manager of a check processing center in Indiana.

Immediately upon assuming his new position, Mr. Braun requested a complete financial report for the just-ended fiscal year from the region's controller, Lance Whiting. Mr. Braun specified that the financial report should follow the standardized format required by corporate headquarters for all regional performance reports. That report appears below:

Financial Performance
Great Basin Region

		Check Processing Centers		
	Total	**Pocatello**	**Idaho Falls**	**Ashton**
Revenues	$20,000,000	$7,000,000	$8,000,000	$5,000,000
Operating expenses:				
Direct labor	12,200,000	4,400,000	4,700,000	3,100,000
Variable overhead	400,000	150,000	160,000	90,000
Equipment depreciation	2,100,000	700,000	800,000	600,000
Facility expenses	2,000,000	600,000	500,000	900,000

continued

Local administrative expenses* . . .	450,000	150,000	180,000	120,000
Regional administrative expenses† . . .	400,000	140,000	160,000	100,000
Corporate administrative expenses‡ . . .	1,600,000	560,000	640,000	400,000
Total operating expense . . .	19,150,000	6,700,000	7,140,000	5,310,000
Net operating income . . .	$ 850,000	$ 300,000	$ 860,000	$ (310,000)

*Local administrative expenses are the administrative expenses incurred at the check processing centers.

†Regional administrative expenses are allocated to the check processing centers based on revenues.

‡Corporate administrative expenses represent a standard 8% charge against revenues.

Upon seeing this report, Mr. Braun summoned Lance Whiting for an explanation.

Braun: What's the story on Ashton? It didn't have a loss the previous year, did it?

Whiting: No, the Ashton facility has had a nice profit every year since it was opened six years ago, but Ashton lost a big contract this year.

Braun: Why?

Whiting: One of our national competitors entered the local market and bid very aggressively on the contract. We couldn't afford to meet the bid. Ashton's costs—particularly their facility expenses—are just too high. When Ashton lost the contract, we had to lay off a lot of employees, but we could not reduce the fixed costs of the Ashton facility.

Braun: Why is Ashton's facility expense so high? It's a smaller facility than either Pocatello or Idaho Falls and yet its facility expense is higher.

Whiting: The problem is that we are able to rent suitable facilities very cheaply at Pocatello and Idaho Falls. No such facilities were available at Ashton, so we had them built. Unfortunately, there were big cost overruns. The contractor we hired was inexperienced at this kind of work and in fact went bankrupt before the project was completed. After hiring another contractor to finish the work, we were way over budget. The large depreciation charges on the facility didn't matter at first because we didn't have much competition at the time and could charge premium prices.

Braun: Well, we can't do that anymore. The Ashton facility will obviously have to be shut down. Its business can be shifted to the other two check processing centers in the region.

Whiting: I would advise against that. The $900,000 in depreciation charges at the Ashton facility are misleading. That facility should last indefinitely with proper maintenance. And it has no resale value; there is no other commercial activity around Ashton.

Braun: What about the other costs at Ashton?

Whiting: If we shifted Ashton's business over to the other two processing centers in the region, we wouldn't save anything on direct labor or variable overhead costs. We might save $60,000 or so in local administrative expenses, but we would not save any regional administrative expense. And corporate headquarters would still charge us 8% of our revenues as corporate administrative expenses.

In addition, we would have to rent more space in Pocatello and Idaho Falls to handle the work transferred from Ashton; that would probably cost us at least $400,000 a year. And don't forget that it will cost us something to move the equipment from Ashton to Pocatello and Idaho Falls. And the move will disrupt service to customers.

Braun: I understand all of that, but a money-losing processing center on my performance report is completely unacceptable.

Whiting: And if you do shut down Ashton, you are going to throw some loyal employees out of work.

Braun: That's unfortunate, but we have to face hard business realities.

Whiting: And you would have to write off the investment in the facilities at Ashton.

Braun: I can explain a write-off to corporate headquarters; hiring an inexperienced contractor to build the Ashton facility was my predecessor's mistake. But they'll have my head at headquarters if I show operating losses every year at one of my processing centers. Ashton has to go. At the next corporate board meeting, I am going to recommend that the Ashton facility be closed.

Required:

1. From the standpoint of the company as a whole, should the Ashton processing center be shut down and its work redistributed to the other processing centers in the region? Explain.

2. Do you think Marvin Braun's decision to shut down the Ashton facility is ethical? Explain.
3. What influence should the depreciation on the facilities at Ashton have on prices charged by Ashton for its services?

CASE 13–24 Decentralization and Relevant Costs [LO4]

Whitmore Products consists of three decentralized divisions—Bayside Division, Cole Division, and Diamond Division. The president of Whitmore Products has given the managers of the three divisions the authority to decide whether they will sell to outside customers on the intermediate market or sell to other divisions within the company. The divisions are autonomous in that each divisional manager has power to set selling prices to outside customers and to set transfer prices to other divisions. (A transfer price is a price one division charges another division of the same company for a product or service it supplies to that division.) Each divisional manager is anxious to maximize his or her division's contribution margin.

To fill capacity for the remainder of the current year, the manager of the Cole Division is considering two alternative orders. Data on the orders are provided below:

a. The Diamond Division is in need of 3,000 motors that can be supplied by the Cole Division at a transfer price of $2,000 per motor. To manufacture these motors, Cole would purchase component parts from the Bayside Division at a transfer price of $800 per part. (Each motor would require one part.) Bayside would incur variable costs for these parts of $400 each. In addition, each part would require 3.5 hours of machine time at a general fixed overhead rate of $40 per hour. Cole Division would then further process these parts, incurring variable costs of $900 per motor. The motors would require seven hours of machine time each in Cole's plant at a general fixed overhead rate of $25 per hour.

   If the Diamond Division can't obtain the motors from the Cole Division, it will purchase the motors from London Company, which has offered to supply the same motors to Diamond Division at a price of $2,000 per motor. To manufacture these motors, London Company would also have to purchase a component part from Bayside Division. This would be a different component part than that needed by the Cole Division. It would cost Bayside $250 in variable cost to produce, and Bayside would sell it to London Company for $500 per part on an order of 3,000 parts. Because of its intricate design, this part would also require 3.5 hours of machine time to manufacture.

b. The Wales Company wants to place an order with the Cole Division for 3,500 units of a motor that is similar to the motor needed by the Diamond Division. The Wales Company has offered to pay $1,800 per motor. To manufacture these motors, Cole Division would again have to purchase a component part from the Bayside Division. This part would cost Bayside Division $200 per part in variable cost to produce, and Bayside would sell it to Cole Division at a transfer price of $400 per part. This part would require three hours of machine time to manufacture in Bayside's plant. Cole Division would further process these parts, incurring variable costs of $1,000 per motor. This work would require six hours of machine time per motor to complete.

The Cole Division's plant capacity is limited, and the division can accept only the order from the Diamond Division or the order from the Wales Company, but not both. The president of Whitmore Products and the manager of the Cole Division both agree that it would not be beneficial to increase capacity at this time. The company's total general fixed overhead would not be affected by this decision.

Required:

1. If the manager of the Cole Division is anxious to maximize the division's profits, which order should be accepted—the order from the Diamond Division or the order from the Wales Company? Support your answer with appropriate computations.
2. For the sake of discussion, assume that the Cole Division decides to accept the order from the Wales Company. Determine if this decision is in the best interests of Whitmore Products *as a whole.* Explain your answer. Support your answer with appropriate computations.

(CMA, adapted)

CASE 13–25 Integrative Case: Relevant Costs; Pricing [LO1, LO4]

Jenco, Inc., manufactures a combination fertilizer-weed killer under the name Fertikil. This is the only product that Jenco produces at present. Fertikil is sold nationwide through normal marketing channels to retail nurseries and garden stores.

Taylor Nursery plans to sell a similar fertilizer weed killer compound through its regional nursery chain under its own private label. Taylor does not have manufacturing facilities of its own, so it has asked Jenco (and several other companies) to submit a bid for manufacturing and delivering a 25,000-pound order of the private brand compound to Taylor. While the chemical composition of the Taylor compound differs from that of Fertikil, the manufacturing processes are very similar.

The Taylor compound would be produced in 1,000-pound lots. Each lot would require 30 direct labor-hours and the following chemicals:

Chemicals	Quantity in Pounds
CW–3	400
JX–6	300
MZ–8	200
BE–7	100

The first three chemicals (CW–3, JX–6, and MZ–8) are all used in the production of Fertikil. BE–7 was used in another compound that Jenco discontinued several months ago. The supply of BE–7 that Jenco had on hand when the other compound was discontinued was not discarded. Jenco could sell its supply of BE–7 at the prevailing market price less $0.10 per pound selling and handling expenses.

Jenco also has on hand a chemical called CN–5, which was manufactured for use in another product that is no longer produced. CN–5, which cannot be used in Fertikil, can be substituted for CW–3 on a one-for-one basis without affecting the quality of the Taylor compound. The CN–5 in inventory has a salvage value of $500.

Inventory and cost data for the chemicals that can be used to produce the Taylor compound are as shown below:

Raw Material	Pounds in Inventory	Actual Price per Pound When Purchased	Current Market Price per Pound
CW–3	22,000	$0.80	$0.90
JX–6	5,000	0.55	0.60
MZ–8	8,000	1.40	1.60
BE–7	4,000	0.60	0.65
CN–5	5,500	0.75	(Salvage)

The current direct labor rate is $14 per hour. The manufacturing overhead rate is established at the beginning of the year and is applied consistently throughout the year using direct labor-hours (DLH) as the base. The predetermined overhead rate for the current year, based on a two-shift capacity of 400,000 total DLH with no overtime, is as follows:

Variable manufacturing overhead	$ 4.50 per DLH
Fixed manufacturing overhead	7.50 per DLH
Combined rate	$12.00 per DLH

Jenco's production manager reports that the present equipment and facilities are adequate to manufacture the Taylor compound. Therefore, the order would have no effect on total fixed manufacturing overhead costs. However, Jenco is within 400 hours of its two-shift capacity this month before it must schedule overtime. If need be, the Taylor compound could be produced on regular time by shifting a portion of Fertikil production to overtime. Jenco's rate for overtime hours is 1½ times the regular pay rate, or $21 per hour. There is no allowance for any overtime premium in the manufacturing overhead rate.

Required:

1. Assume that Jenco, Inc., has decided to submit a bid for a 25,000-pound order of Taylor's new compound. The order must be delivered by the end of the current month. Taylor has indicated that this is a one-time order that will not be repeated. Calculate the lowest price that Jenco could bid for the order without reducing its net income.
2. Refer to the original data. Assume that Taylor Nursery plans to place regular orders for 25,000-pound lots of the new compound during the coming year. Jenco expects the demand for Fertikil to remain strong again in the coming year. Therefore, the recurring orders from Taylor would put Jenco over its two-shift capacity. However, production could be scheduled so that 60% of each Taylor order could be completed during regular hours. As another option, some

Fertikil production could be shifted temporarily to overtime so that the Taylor orders could be produced on regular time. Jenco's production manager has estimated that the prices of all chemicals will stabilize at the current market rates for the coming year; also, the variable and fixed overhead costs are expected to continue at the same rates per direct labor-hour.

Jenco's standard markup policy for new products is 40% of the full manufacturing cost, including fixed manufacturing overhead. Calculate the price that Jenco, Inc., would quote Taylor Nursery for each 25,000-pound lot of the new compound, assuming that it is to be treated as a new product and this pricing policy is followed.

(CMA, adapted)

CASE 13–26 Sell or Process Further Decision [LO6]

Midwest Mills has a plant that can mill wheat grain into a cracked wheat cereal and then further mill the cracked wheat into flour. The company can sell all the cracked wheat cereal that it can produce at a selling price of $490 per ton. In the past, the company has sold only part of its cracked wheat as cereal and has retained the rest for further milling into flour. The flour has been selling for $700 per ton, but recently the price has become unstable and has dropped to $625 per ton. The costs and revenues associated with a ton of flour follow:

		Per Ton of Flour
Selling price		$625
Cost to manufacture:		
Raw materials:		
Enrichment materials	$ 80	
Cracked wheat	470	
Total raw materials	550	
Direct labor	20	
Manufacturing overhead	60	630
Manufacturing profit (loss)		$ (5)

Because of the weak price for flour, the sales manager believes that the company should discontinue milling flour and use its entire milling capacity to produce cracked wheat to sell as cereal. (The same milling equipment is used for both products.) Current cost and revenue data on the cracked wheat cereal follow:

		Per Ton of Cracked Wheat
Selling price		$490
Cost to manufacture:		
Wheat grain	$390	
Direct labor	20	
Manufacturing overhead	60	470
Manufacturing profit		$ 20

The sales manager argues that since the present $625 per ton price for the flour results in a $5 per ton loss, the milling of flour should not be resumed until the price per ton rises above $630.

The company assigns manufacturing overhead cost to the two products on the basis of milling hours. The same amount of time is required to mill either a ton of cracked wheat or a ton of flour. Virtually all manufacturing overhead costs are fixed. Materials and labor costs are variable.

The company can sell all of the cracked wheat and flour it can produce at the current market prices.

Required:

1. Do you agree with the sales manager that the company should discontinue milling flour and use the entire milling capacity to mill cracked wheat if the price of flour remains at $625 per ton? Support your answer with appropriate computations and explanations.
2. What is the lowest price that the company should accept for a ton of flour? Again support your answer with appropriate computations and explanations.

CASE 13–27 Plant Closing Decision [LO1, LO2]

Mobile Seating Corporation manufactures seats for automobiles, vans, trucks, and boats. The company has a number of plants around North America, including the Greenville Cover Plant. Seat covers made of upholstery fabric are sewn at the Greenville Cover Plant..

Miriam Restin is the plant manager at the Greenville Cover Plant but also serves as the regional production manager for the company. Her budget as the regional manager is charged to the Greenville Cover Plant.

Restin has just heard that Mobile Seating has received a bid from an outside vendor to supply the equivalent of the entire annual output of the Greenville Cover Plant for $21 million. Restin was astonished at the low outside bid because the budget for the Greenville Cover Plant's operating costs for the coming year was set at $24.3 million. If this bid is accepted, the Greenville Cover Plant will be closed down

The budget for the Greenville Cover Plant's operating costs for the coming year is presented below. Additional facts regarding the plant's operations are as follows:

a. Due to the Greenville Cover Plant's commitment to use high-quality fabrics in all its products, the Purchasing Department was instructed to place blanket purchase orders with major suppliers to ensure the receipt of sufficient materials for the coming year. If these orders are canceled as a consequence of the plant closing, termination charges would amount to 25% of the cost of direct materials.
b. Approximately 350 employees will lose their jobs if the plant is closed. This includes all of the direct laborers and supervisors, management and staff, and the plumbers, electricians, and other skilled workers classified as indirect plant workers. Some of these workers would have difficulty finding new jobs. Nearly all the production workers would have difficulty matching the Greenville Cover Plant's base pay of $12.50 per hour, which is the highest in the area. A clause in Greenville Cover's contract with the union may help some employees; the company must provide employment assistance and job training to its former employees for 12 months after a plant closing. The estimated cost to administer this service would be $0.8 million.
c. Some employees would probably choose early retirement because Mobile Seating Corporation has an excellent pension plan. In fact, $0.7 million of the annual pension expense would continue whether the Greenville Cover Plant is open or not.
d. Restin and her regional staff would not be affected by the closing of the Greenville Cover Plant. They would still be responsible for running three other area plants.
e. If the Greenville Cover Plant were closed, the company would realize about $2 million salvage value for the equipment in the plant. If the plant remains open, there are no plans to make any significant investments in new equipment or buildings. The old equipment is adequate for the job and should last indefinitely.

GREENVILLE COVER PLANT
Annual Budget for Operating Costs

Materials		$ 8,000,000
Labor:		
Direct	$6,700,000	
Supervision	400,000	
Indirect plant	1,900,000	9,000,000
Overhead:		
Depreciation—equipment	1,300,000	
Depreciation—building	2,100,000	
Pension expense	1,600,000	
Plant manager and staff	600,000	
Corporate expenses*	1,700,000	7,300,000
Total budgeted costs		$24,300,000

*Fixed corporate expenses allocated to plants and other operating units based on total budgeted wage and salary costs.

Required:

1. Without regard to costs, identify the advantages to Mobile Seating Corporation of continuing to obtain covers from its own Greenville Cover Plant.
2. Mobile Seating Corporation plans to prepare a financial analysis that will be used in deciding whether or not to close the Greenville Cover Plant. Management has asked you to identify:

a. The annual budgeted costs that are relevant to the decision regarding closing the plant (show the dollar amounts).

b. The annual budgeted costs that are not relevant to the decision regarding closing the plant and explain why they are not relevant (again show the dollar amounts).

c. Any nonrecurring costs that would arise due to the closing of the plant and explain how they would affect the decision (again show any dollar amounts).

3. Looking at the data you have prepared in (2) above, should the plant be closed? Show computations and explain your answer.
4. Identify any revenues or costs not specifically mentioned in the problem that Mobile Seating Corporation should consider before making a decision.

(CMA, adapted)

CASE 13–28 Make or Buy; Utilization of a Constrained Resource [LO1, LO3, LO5]

Storage Systems, Inc., sells a wide range of drums, bins, boxes, and other containers that are used in the chemical industry. One of the company's products is a very heavy-duty corrosion-resistant metal drum, called the XSX drum, used to store toxic wastes. Production is constrained by the capacity of an automated welding machine that is used to make precision welds. A total of 2,000 hours of welding time are available annually on the machine. Since each drum requires 0.8 hours of welding time, annual production is limited to 2,500 drums. At present, the welding machine is used exclusively to make the XSX drums. The accounting department has provided the following financial data concerning the XSX drums:

	XSX Drums	
Selling price per drum		$154.00
Cost per drum:		
Materials	$44.50	
Direct labor ($18 per hour)	4.50	
Manufacturing overhead	3.15	
Selling and administrative cost	15.40	67.55
Margin per drum		$ 86.45

Management believes 3,000 XSX drums could be sold each year if the company had sufficient manufacturing capacity. As an alternative to adding another welding machine, management has looked into the possibility of buying additional drums from an outside supplier. Metal Products, Inc., a supplier of quality products, would be able to provide up to 1,800 XSX-type drums per year at a price of $120 per drum.

Jasmine Morita, Storage Systems' production manager, has suggested that the company could make better use of the welding machine by manufacturing premium mountain bike frames, which would require only 0.2 hours of welding time per frame. Jasmine believes that Storage Systems could sell up to 3,500 mountain bike frames per year to mountain bike manufacturers at a price of $65 per frame. The accounting department has provided the following data concerning the proposed new product:

Mountain Bike Frames		
Selling price per frame		$65.00
Cost per frame:		
Materials	$17.50	
Direct labor ($18 per hour)	22.50	
Manufacturing overhead	15.75	
Selling and administrative cost	6.50	62.25
Margin per frame		$ 2.75

The mountain bike frames could be produced with existing equipment and personnel. Manufacturing overhead is allocated to products on the basis of direct labor-hours. Most of the manufacturing overhead consists of fixed common costs such as rent on the factory building, but some of it is variable. The variable manufacturing overhead has been estimated at $1.05 per XSX drum and $0.60 per mountain bike frame. The variable manufacturing overhead cost would not be incurred on drums acquired from the outside supplier.

Selling and administrative costs are allocated to products on the basis of revenues. Almost all of the selling and administrative costs are fixed common costs, but it has been estimated that variable selling and administrative costs amount to $0.85 per XSX drum and would be $0.40 per mountain bike frame. The variable selling and administrative costs of $0.85 per drum would be incurred when drums acquired from the outside supplier are sold to the company's customers.

All of the company's employees—direct and indirect—are paid for full 40-hour workweeks and the company has a policy of laying off workers only in major recessions.

Required:

1. Given the margins of the two products as indicated in the reports submitted by the accounting department, does it make any sense to even consider producing the mountain bike frames? Explain.
2. Compute the contribution margin per unit for:
   a. Purchased XSX drums.
   b. Manufactured XSX drums.
   c. Manufactured mountain bike frames.
3. Determine the number of XSX drums (if any) that should be purchased and the number of XSX drums and/or mountain bike frames (if any) that should be manufactured. What is the improvement in net income that would result from this plan over current operations?

As soon as your analysis was shown to the top management team at Storage Systems, several managers got into an argument concerning how direct labor costs should be treated when making this decision. One manager argued that direct labor is always treated as a variable cost in textbooks and in practice and has always been considered a variable cost at Storage Systems. After all, "direct" means you can directly trace the cost to products. If direct labor is not a variable cost, what is? Another manager argued just as strenuously that direct labor should be considered a fixed cost at Storage Systems. No one had been laid off in over a decade, and for all practical purposes, everyone at the plant is on a monthly salary. Everyone classified as direct labor works a regular 40-hour workweek and overtime has not been necessary since the company adopted just-in-time techniques. Whether the welding machine is used to make drums or frames, the total payroll would be exactly the same. There is enough slack, in the form of idle time, to accommodate any increase in total direct labor time that the mountain bike frames would require.

4. Redo requirements (2) and (3) above, making the opposite assumption about direct labor from the one you originally made. In other words, if you treated direct labor as a variable cost, redo the analysis treating it as a fixed cost. If you treated direct labor as a fixed cost, redo the analysis treating it as a variable cost.
5. What do you think is the correct way to treat direct labor in this situation—as a variable cost or as a fixed cost?

Group and Internet Exercises

GROUP EXERCISE 13–29 Outsourcing May Be Hazardous to Your Health

Outsourcing, when a company contracts with third parties to produce some of its parts or products, has become commonplace among U.S. manufacturers. Thirty years ago, when factories were a lot less complex, predetermined manufacturing overhead rates of 50% or less of direct labor cost were deemed reasonable. But today, predetermined manufacturing overhead rates of 200% of direct labor are common and rates of 500% or more are not unusual. As a result, outsourcing has gained widespread acceptance over the past several decades. Products with high direct labor content are especially susceptible to being outsourced to parts of the world where labor rates are a lot less than they are in the United States.

Required:

1. What is the meaning of manufacturing overhead rates of 500% or more of direct labor?
2. What implications do such high manufacturing overhead rates hold for products high in direct labor content?
3. What happens to the costs of the remaining products when a product is outsourced?
4. Can you think of any drawbacks to outsourcing in a less-developed foreign land or any limitations to a strategy dependent on labor cost savings?
5. Continuing with the line of thinking developed in (1)–(3) above, what happens next?

INTERNET EXERCISE 13–30

As you know, the World Wide Web is a medium that is constantly evolving. Sites come and go, and change without notice. To enable periodic update of site addresses, this problem has been posted to the textbook website (www.mhhe.com/garrison10e). After accessing the site, enter the Student Center and select this chapter. Select and complete the Internet Exercise.

Chapter Fourteen

Capital Budgeting Decisions

After studying Chapter 14, you should be able to:

1. Evaluate the acceptability of an investment project using the net present value method.
2. Evaluate the acceptability of an investment project using the internal rate of return method.
3. Evaluate an investment project that has uncertain cash flows.
4. Rank investment projects in order of preference.
5. Determine the payback period for an investment.
6. Compute the simple rate of return for an investment.
7. (Appendix 14A) Understand present value concepts and the use of present value tables.
8. (Appendix 14D) Include income taxes in a capital budgeting analysis.

Invest Less, Make More

When Steven Burd became the CEO of Safeway, he slashed annual capital spending from $550 million to $290 million. Burd gave the following reason: "We had projects that were not returning the cost of money. So we cut spending back, which made the very best projects come to the surface."

Safeway set a minimum 22.5% pretax return on investment in all new store and remodeling projects. With that discipline in place, Safeway again increased capital spending. Recently it spent about $1 billion in a single year, adding 40 to 45 new stores and remodeling more than 200. Burd says he has emphasized expanding existing stores because the older stores generally have excellent real estate locations and the added size brings strong increases in sales.

Source: Robert Berner, "Safeway's Resurgence Is Built on Attention to Detail," *The Wall Street Journal,* October 2, 1998, p. B4.

BUSINESS FOCUS

The term **capital budgeting** is used to describe how managers plan significant outlays on projects that have long-term implications such as the purchase of new equipment and the introduction of new products. Most companies have many more potential projects than can actually be funded. Hence, managers must carefully select those projects that promise the greatest future return. How well managers make these capital budgeting decisions is a critical factor in the long-run profitability of the company.

Capital budgeting involves *investment*—a company must commit funds now in order to receive a return in the future. Investments are not limited to stocks and bonds. Purchase of inventory or equipment is also an investment. For example, Tri-Con Global Restaurants, Inc. makes an investment when it opens a new Pizza Hut restaurant. L. L. Bean makes an investment when it installs a new computer to handle customer billing. DaimlerChrysler makes an investment when it redesigns a product such as the Jeep Eagle and must retool its production lines. Merck & Co. invests in medical research. Amazon.com makes an investment when it redesigns its website. All of these investments are characterized by a commitment of funds today in the expectation of receiving a return in the future in the form of additional cash inflows or reduced cash outflows.

Capital Budgeting—Planning Investments

Typical Capital Budgeting Decisions

What types of business decisions require capital budgeting analysis? Virtually any decision that involves an outlay now in order to obtain some return (increase in revenue or reduction in costs) in the future. Typical capital budgeting decisions include:

1. Cost reduction decisions. Should new equipment be purchased to reduce costs?
2. Expansion decisions. Should a new plant, warehouse, or other facility be acquired to increase capacity and sales?
3. Equipment selection decisions. Which of several available machines would be the most cost effective to purchase?
4. Lease or buy decisions. Should new equipment be leased or purchased?
5. Equipment replacement decisions. Should old equipment be replaced now or later?

In Business

The Yukon Goes Online

Canada's Yukon Territory, which is two-thirds the size of Texas, has only 31,000 residents. Most of those live in Whitehorse, the territory's capital. All are about to get higher-speed Internet access as part of an ambitious Canadian government program to connect the Yukon with the rest of the world. To date, the Yukon's physical isolation has precluded economic growth in the area. The Internet may change all that. In some ways, it already has. A variety of organizations in the Yukon have made significant outlays on Internet projects that will have long-term implications.

After struggling to stay in business with annual sales of only $10,000, Herbie Croteau, the founder of Midnight Sun Plant Food, spent $1,600 to build a website for the company (www.midnightsunplantfood.com). Just two years later, sales are expected to exceed $65,000. Croteau is in the process of spending another $2,000 to redesign the company's website.

The town of Haines Junction is spending $10,000 to redesign its website. The town's chief administrative office estimates that printing costs for tourist brochures will drop by 75% since tourist information can now be obtained online at www.yukon.com/community/kluane/hj.html.

Source: David H. Freedman, "Cold Comfort," *Forbes ASAP*, May 29, 2000, pp. 174–182.

Capital budgeting decisions tend to fall into two broad categories—*screening decisions* and *preference decisions.* **Screening decisions** relate to whether a proposed project meets some preset standard of acceptance. For example, a firm may have a policy of accepting projects only if they promise a return of, say, 20% on the investment. The required rate of return is the minimum rate of return a project must yield to be acceptable.

Preference decisions, by contrast, relate to selecting from among several *competing* courses of action. To illustrate, a firm may be considering several different machines to replace an existing machine on the assembly line. The choice of which machine to purchase is a *preference* decision.

In this chapter, we initially discuss ways of making screening decisions. Preference decisions are discussed toward the end of the chapter.

The Time Value of Money

As stated earlier, investments commonly involve returns that extend over fairly long periods of time. Therefore, in approaching capital budgeting decisions, it is necessary to employ techniques that recognize *the time value of money.* A dollar today is worth more than a dollar a year from now. The same concept applies in choosing between investment projects. Those projects that promise earlier returns are preferable to those that promise later returns.

The capital budgeting techniques that recognize the above two characteristics of business investments most fully are those that involve *discounted cash flows.* We will spend most of this chapter illustrating the use of discounted cash flow methods in making capital budgeting decisions. If you are not already familiar with discounting and the use of present value tables, you should read Appendix 14A, The Concept of Present Value, at the end of this chapter before proceeding any further.

Discounted Cash Flows—The Net Present Value Method

LEARNING OBJECTIVE 1
Evaluate the acceptability of an investment project using the net present value method.

Two approaches to making capital budgeting decisions use discounted cash flows. One is the *net present value method,* and the other is the *internal rate of return method* (sometimes called the *time-adjusted rate of return method*). The net present value method is discussed in this section; the internal rate of return method is discussed in the following section.

The Net Present Value Method Illustrated

Under the net present value method, the present value of a project's cash inflows is compared to the present value of the project's cash outflows. The difference between the present value of these cash flows, called the **net present value,** determines whether or not the project is an acceptable investment. To illustrate, consider the following data:

Example A
Harper Company is contemplating the purchase of a machine capable of performing certain operations that are now performed manually. The machine will cost $5,000, and it will last for five years. At the end of the five-year period, the machine will have a zero scrap value. Use of the machine will reduce labor costs by $1,800 per year. Harper Company requires a minimum pretax return of 20% on all investment projects.[1]

Should the machine be purchased? Harper Company must determine whether a cash investment now of $5,000 can be justified if it will result in an $1,800 reduction in cost

[1] For simplicity, we ignore inflation and taxes. The impact of inflation on discounted cash flow analysis is discussed in Appendix 14B. The impact of income taxes on capital budgeting decisions is discussed in Appendix 14D.

Exhibit 14–1

Net Present Value Analysis of a Proposed Project

Concept 14–1

Initial cost.	$5,000
Life of the project (years)	5
Annual cost savings.	$1,800
Salvage value	0
Required rate of return.	20%

Item	Year(s)	Amount of Cash Flow	20% Factor	Present Value of Cash Flows
Annual cost savings	1–5	$1,800	2.991*	$ 5,384
Initial investment.	Now	(5,000)	1.000	(5,000)
Net present value				$ 384

*From Table 14C–4 in Appendix 14C at the end of this chapter.

each year over the next five years. It may appear that the answer is obvious since the total cost savings is $9,000 (5 × $1,800). However, the company can earn a 20% return by investing its money elsewhere. It is not enough that the cost reductions cover just the original cost of the machine; they must also yield at least a 20% return or the company would be better off investing the money elsewhere.

To determine whether the investment is desirable, the stream of annual $1,800 cost savings is discounted to its present value and then compared to the cost of the new machine. Since Harper Company requires a minimum return of 20% on all investment projects, this rate is used in the discounting process and is called the *discount rate.* Exhibit 14–1 shows how this analysis is done.

According to the analysis, Harper Company should purchase the new machine. The present value of the cost savings is $5,384, as compared to a present value of only $5,000 for the required investment (cost of the machine). Deducting the present value of the required investment from the present value of the cost savings gives a *net present value* of $384. Whenever the net present value is zero or greater, as in our example, an investment project is acceptable. Whenever the net present value is negative (the present value of the cash outflows exceeds the present value of the cash inflows), an investment project is not acceptable. In sum:

If the Net Present Value Is . . .	Then the Project Is . . .
Positive.	Acceptable, since it promises a return greater than the required rate of return.
Zero	Acceptable, since it promises a return equal to the required rate of return.
Negative	Not acceptable, since it promises a return less than the required rate of return.

A full interpretation of the solution would be as follows: The new machine promises more than the required 20% rate of return. This is evident from the positive net present value of $384. Harper Company could spend up to $5,384 for the new machine and still obtain the minimum required 20% rate of return. The net present value of $384, therefore, shows the amount of "cushion" or "margin of error." One way to look at this is that the company could underestimate the cost of the new machine by up to $384, or overestimate the net present value of the future cash savings by up to $384, and the project would still be financially attractive.

Emphasis on Cash Flows

In capital budgeting decisions, the focus is on cash flows and not on accounting net income. The reason is that accounting net income is based on accruals that ignore the timing of cash flows into and out of an organization. From a capital budgeting standpoint, the timing of cash flows is important, since a dollar received today is more valuable than a dollar received in the future. Therefore, even though accounting net income is useful for many things, it is not ordinarily used in discounted cash flow analysis.[2] Instead of determining accounting net income, the manager concentrates on identifying the specific cash flows of the investment project.

What kinds of cash flows should the manager look for? Although the specific cash flows will vary from project to project, certain types of cash flows tend to recur as explained in the following paragraphs.

Typical Cash Outflows Most projects will have an immediate cash outflow in the form of an initial investment in equipment or other assets. Any salvage value realized from the sale of old equipment can be recognized as a cash inflow or as a reduction in the required investment. In addition, some projects require that a company expand its working capital. **Working capital** is current assets (cash, accounts receivable, and inventory) less current liabilities. When a company takes on a new project, the balances in the current asset accounts will often increase. For example, opening a new Nordstrom's department store would require additional cash in sales registers, increased accounts receivable for new customers, and more inventory to stock the shelves. These additional working capital needs should be treated as part of the initial investment in a project. Also, many projects require periodic outlays for repairs and maintenance and for additional operating costs. These should all be treated as cash outflows for capital budgeting purposes.

Typical Cash Inflows On the cash inflow side, a project will normally either increase revenues or reduce costs. Either way, the amount involved should be treated as a cash inflow for capital budgeting purposes. Notice that so far as cash flows are concerned, a reduction in costs is equivalent to an increase in revenues. Cash inflows are also frequently realized from salvage of equipment when a project ends, although the company may actually have to pay to dispose of some low-value or hazardous items. In addition, any working capital that was tied up in the project can be released for use elsewhere at the end of the project and should be treated as a cash inflow at that time. Working capital is released, for example, when a company sells off its inventory or collects its receivables.

Hazardous PCs

In Business

Disposing of old equipment can be difficult—particularly when environmental regulations are involved. For example, computer equipment often contains lead and other substances that could contaminate the air, soil, or groundwater. Cindy Brethauer, the network administrator for 1st Choice Bank, in Greeley, Colorado, was faced with the mounting problem of storing old monitors, printers, and personal computers that could not be simply thrown away. These bulky items were constantly being shuttled back and forth from one storage space to another. For help, she turned to Technology Recycling LLC, which hauls away old computers and peripherals for $35 per component. Technology LLC employs disabled people to strip the machines. Many of the materials taken from the machines are recycled, while the environmentally sensitive materials are taken to disposal facilities approved by the Environmental Protection Agency. Technology LLC handles the complicated paperwork for its customers. One benefit for customers of finally disposing of the old equipment is a reduction in personal property taxes.

Source: Jill Hecht Maxwell, *Inc. Tech*, 2000, 1, p. 25.

---

[2] Under certain conditions, capital budgeting decisions can be correctly made by discounting appropriately defined accounting net income. However, this approach requires advanced techniques that are beyond the scope of this book.

In summary, the following types of cash flows are common in business investment projects:

Cash outflows:
- Initial investment (including installation costs).
- Increased working capital needs.
- Repairs and maintenance.
- Incremental operating costs.

Cash inflows:
- Incremental revenues.
- Reduction in costs.
- Salvage value.
- Release of working capital.

Recovery of the Original Investment

When computing the present value of a project, depreciation is not deducted for two reasons.

First, depreciation is not a current cash outflow.[3] As discussed above, discounted cash flow methods of making capital budgeting decisions focus on *cash flows.* Although depreciation is used to compute net income for financial statements, it is not relevant in an analytical framework that focuses on cash flows.

A second reason for not deducting depreciation is that discounted cash flow methods *automatically* provide for return of the original investment, thereby making a deduction for depreciation unnecessary. To demonstrate this point, consider the following data:

Example B
Carver Hospital is considering the purchase of an attachment for its X-ray machine that will cost $3,170. The attachment will be usable for four years, after which time it will have no salvage value. It will increase net cash inflows by $1,000 per year in the X-ray department. The hospital's board of directors has instructed that no investments are to be made unless they have an annual return of at least 10%.

A present value analysis of the desirability of purchasing the X-ray attachment is presented in Exhibit 14–2. Notice that the attachment promises exactly a 10% return on the original investment, since the net present value is zero at a 10% discount rate.

Each annual $1,000 cash inflow arising from use of the attachment is made up of two parts. One part represents a recovery of a portion *of* the original $3,170 paid for the attachment, and the other part represents a return *on* this investment. The breakdown of each year's $1,000 cash inflow between recovery *of* investment and return *on* investment is shown in Exhibit 14–3.

The first year's $1,000 cash inflow consists of a $317 interest return (10%) *on* the $3,170 original investment, plus a $683 return *of* that investment. Since the amount of the unrecovered investment decreases over the four years, the dollar amount of the interest return also decreases. By the end of the fourth year, all $3,170 of the original investment has been recovered.

Simplifying Assumptions

Two simplifying assumptions are usually made in net present value analysis.

The first assumption is that all cash flows other than the initial investment occur at the end of periods. This is somewhat unrealistic in that cash flows typically occur *throughout* a period rather than just at its end. The purpose of this assumption is just to simplify computations.

---

[3] Although depreciation itself is not a cash outflow, it does have an effect on cash outflows for income taxes. This is discussed in Appendix 14D.

Exhibit 14–2
Carver Hospital—Net Present Value Analysis of X-Ray Attachment

Initial cost	$3,170
Life of the project (years)	4
Annual net cash inflow	$1,000
Salvage value	0
Required rate of return	10%

Item	Year(s)	Amount of Cash Flow	10% Factor	Present Value of Cash Flows
Annual net cash inflow	1–4	$ 1,000	3.170*	$ 3,170
Initial investment	Now	(3,170)	1.000	(3,170)
Net present value				$ 0

*From Table 14C–4 in Appendix 14C.

Exhibit 14–3 Carver Hospital—Breakdown of Annual Cash Inflows

Year	(1) Investment Outstanding during the Year	(2) Cash Inflow	(3) Return on Investment (1) × 10%	(4) Recovery of Investment during the Year (2) − (3)	(5) Unrecovered Investment at the End of the Year (1) − (4)
1	$3,170	$1,000	$317	$ 683	$2,487
2	2,487	1,000	249	751	1,736
3	1,736	1,000	173	827	909
4	909	1,000	91	909	0
Total investment recovered				$3,170	

The second assumption is that all cash flows generated by an investment project are immediately reinvested at a rate of return equal to the discount rate. Unless these conditions are met, the net present value computed for the project will not be accurate. To illustrate, we used a discount rate of 10% for Carver Hospital in Exhibit 14–2. Unless the funds released each period are immediately reinvested at a 10% return, the net present value computed for the X-ray attachment will be misstated.

Choosing a Discount Rate

A positive net present value means that the project's return exceeds the discount rate. A negative net present value means that the project's return is less than the discount rate. Therefore, if the company's minimum required rate of return is used as the discount rate, a project with a positive net present value is acceptable and a project with a negative net present value is unacceptable.

What is a company's minimum required rate of return? The company's *cost of capital* is usually regarded as the minimum required rate of return. The **cost of capital** is the average rate of return the company must pay to its long-term creditors and to shareholders for the use of their funds. The cost of capital is the minimum required rate of return because if a project's rate of return is less than the cost of capital, the company does not earn enough to compensate its creditors and shareholders. Therefore, any project with a rate of return less than the cost of capital should not be accepted.

The cost of capital serves as a *screening device* in net present value analysis. When the cost of capital is used as the discount rate, any project with a negative net present value does not cover the company's cost of capital and should be discarded as unacceptable.

An Extended Example of the Net Present Value Method

To conclude our discussion of the net present value method, we present below an extended example of how it is used to analyze an investment proposal. This example will also help to tie together (and to reinforce) many of the ideas developed thus far.

Example C

Under a special licensing arrangement, Swinyard Company has an opportunity to market a new product in the western United States for a five-year period. The product would be purchased from the manufacturer, with Swinyard Company responsible for all costs of promotion and distribution. The licensing arrangement could be renewed at the end of the five-year period. After careful study, Swinyard Company has estimated the following costs and revenues for the new product:

Cost of equipment needed	$ 60,000
Working capital needed	100,000
Overhaul of the equipment in four years	5,000
Salvage value of the equipment in five years	10,000
Annual revenues and costs:	
Sales revenues	200,000
Cost of goods sold	125,000
Out-of-pocket operating costs (for salaries, advertising, and other direct costs)	35,000

At the end of the five-year period, the working capital would be released for investment elsewhere if Swinyard decides not to renew the licensing arrangement. Swinyard Company uses a 14% discount rate. Would you recommend that the new product be introduced?

This example involves a variety of cash inflows and cash outflows. The solution is given in Exhibit 14–4.

Notice particularly how the working capital is handled in this exhibit. It is counted as a cash outflow at the beginning of the project and as a cash inflow when it is released at the end of the project. Also notice how the sales revenues, cost of goods sold, and out-of-pocket costs are handled. **Out-of-pocket costs** are actual cash outlays for salaries, advertising, and other operating expenses. Depreciation would not be an out-of-pocket cost, since it involves no current cash outlay.

Exhibit 14–4 The Net Present Value Method—An Extended Example

Sales revenues	$200,000
Less cost of goods sold	125,000
Less out-of-pocket costs for salaries, advertising, etc.	35,000
Annual net cash inflows	$ 40,000

Item	Year(s)	Amount of Cash Flows	14% Factor	Present Value of Cash Flows
Purchase of equipment	Now	$ (60,000)	1.000	$ (60,000)
Working capital needed	Now	(100,000)	1.000	(100,000)
Overhaul of equipment	4	(5,000)	0.592*	(2,960)
Annual net cash inflows from sales of the product line	1–5	40,000	3.433†	137,320
Salvage value of the equipment	5	10,000	0.519*	5,190
Working capital released	5	100,000	0.519*	51,900
Net present value				$ 31,450

*From Table 14C–3 in Appendix 14C.

†From Table 14C–4 in Appendix 14C.

Since the overall net present value is positive, the new product should be added assuming the company has no better use for the investment funds.

Discounted Cash Flows—The Internal Rate of Return Method

LEARNING OBJECTIVE 2
Evaluate the acceptability of an investment project using the internal rate of return method.

The **internal rate of return** is the rate of return promised by an investment project over its useful life. It is sometimes referred to simply as the **yield** on a project. The internal rate of return is computed by finding the discount rate that equates the present value of a project's cash outflows with the present value of its cash inflows. In other words, the internal rate of return is that discount rate that will cause the net present value of a project to be equal to zero.

The Internal Rate of Return Method Illustrated

To illustrate the internal rate of return method, consider the following data:

Example D
Glendale School District is considering the purchase of a large tractor-pulled lawn mower. At present, the lawn is mowed using a small hand-pushed gas mower. The large, tractor-pulled mower will cost $16,950 and will have a useful life of 10 years. It will have only a negligible scrap value, which can be ignored. The tractor-pulled mower would do the job much more quickly than the old mower and would result in a labor savings of $3,000 per year.

To compute the internal rate of return promised by the new mower, we must find the discount rate that will cause the net present value of the project to be zero. How do we do this? The simplest and most direct approach *when the net cash inflow is the same every year* is to divide the investment in the project by the expected net annual cash inflow. This computation will yield a factor from which the internal rate of return can be determined. The formula is as follows:

$$\text{Factor of the internal rate of return} = \frac{\text{Investment required}}{\text{Net annual cash inflow}} \qquad (1)$$

The factor derived from formula (1) is then located in the present value tables to see what rate of return it represents. Using formula (1) and the data for Glendale School District's proposed project, we get:

$$\frac{\text{Investment required}}{\text{Net annual cash inflow}} = \frac{\$16{,}950}{\$3{,}000} = 5.650$$

Thus, the discount factor that will equate a series of $3,000 cash inflows with a present investment of $16,950 is 5.650. Now we need to find this factor in Table 14C–4 in Appendix 14C to see what rate of return it represents. We should use the 10-period line in Table 14C–4 since the cash flows for the project continue for 10 years. If we scan along the 10-period line, we find that a factor of 5.650 represents a 12% rate of return. Therefore, the internal rate of return promised by the mower project is 12%. We can verify this by computing the project's net present value using a 12% discount rate. This computation is made in Exhibit 14–5.

Notice from Exhibit 14–5 that using a 12% discount rate equates the present value of the annual cash inflows with the present value of the investment required in the project, leaving a zero net present value. The 12% rate therefore represents the internal rate of return promised by the project.

Salvage Value and Other Cash Flows

The technique just demonstrated works very well if a project's cash flows are identical every year. But what if they are not? For example, what if a project will have some salvage

Exhibit 14–5
Evaluation of the Mower Purchase Using a 12% Discount Rate

Initial cost	$16,950
Life of the project (years)	10
Annual cost savings	$3,000
Salvage value	0

Item	Year(s)	Amount of Cash Flow	12% Factor	Present Value of Cash Flows
Annual cost savings	1–10	$ 3,000	5.650*	$ 16,950
Initial investment	Now	(16,950)	1.000	(16,950)
Net present value				$ 0

*From Table 14C–4 in Appendix 14C.

value at the end of its life in addition to the annual cash inflows? Under these circumstances, a trial-and-error process may be used to find the rate of return that will equate the cash inflows with the cash outflows. The trial-and-error process can be carried out by hand; however, computer software programs such as spreadsheets can perform the necessary computations in seconds. In short, erratic or uneven cash flows should not prevent a manager from determining a project's internal rate of return.

Using the Internal Rate of Return

Once the internal rate of return has been computed, what does the manager do with the information? The internal rate of return is compared to the company's *required rate of return.* The **required rate of return** is the minimum rate of return that an investment project must yield to be acceptable. If the internal rate of return is *equal* to or *greater* than the required rate of return, then the project is acceptable. If it is less than the required rate of return, then the project is rejected. Quite often, the company's cost of capital is used as the required rate of return. The reasoning is that if a project can't provide a rate of return at least as great as the cost of the funds invested in it, then it is not profitable.

In the case of the Glendale School District example used earlier, let us assume that the district has set a minimum required rate of return of 15% on all projects. Since the large mower promises a rate of return of only 12%, it does not clear this hurdle and would therefore be rejected as a project.

The Cost of Capital as a Screening Tool

As we have seen in preceding examples, the cost of capital often operates as a *screening* device, helping the manager screen out undesirable investment projects. This screening is accomplished in different ways, depending on whether the company is using the internal rate of return method or the net present value method in its capital budgeting analysis.

When the internal rate of return method is used, the cost of capital is used as the *hurdle rate* that a project must clear for acceptance. If the internal rate of return of a project is not great enough to clear the cost of capital hurdle, then the project is ordinarily rejected. We saw the application of this idea in the Glendale School District example, where the hurdle rate was set at 15%.

When the net present value method is used, the cost of capital is the *discount rate* used to compute the net present value of a proposed project. Any project yielding a negative net present value is rejected unless other factors are significant enough to require its acceptance.

The use of the cost of capital as a screening tool is summarized in Exhibit 14–6.

Comparison of the Net Present Value and the Internal Rate of Return Methods

The net present value method has several important advantages over the internal rate of return method.

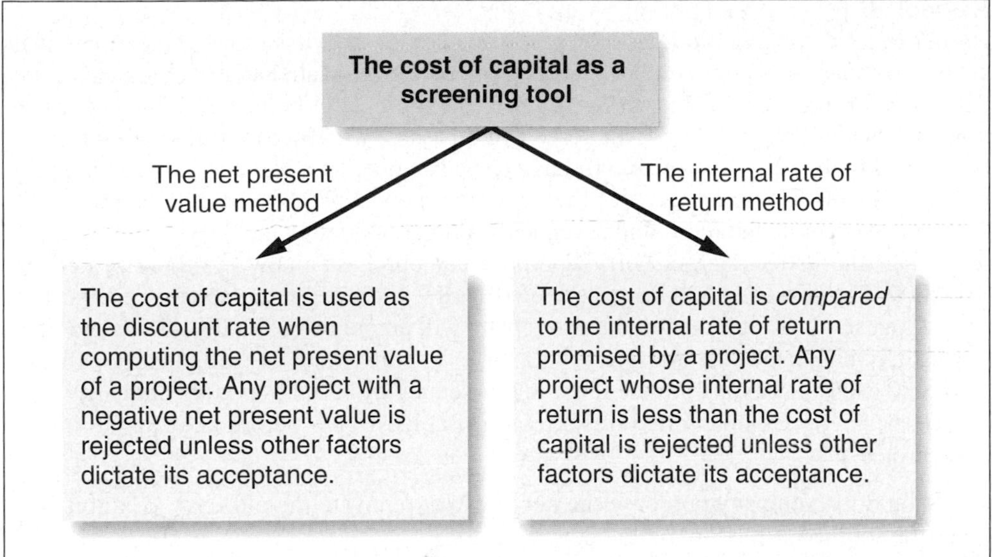

Exhibit 14–6
Capital Budgeting Screening Decisions

First, the net present value method is often simpler to use. As mentioned earlier, the internal rate of return method may require hunting for the discount rate that results in a net present value of zero. This can be a very laborious trial-and-error process, although it can be automated to some degree using a computer spreadsheet.

Second, a key assumption made by the internal rate of return method is questionable. Both methods assume that cash flows generated by a project during its useful life are immediately reinvested elsewhere. However, the two methods make different assumptions concerning the rate of return that is earned on those cash flows. The net present value method assumes the rate of return is the discount rate, whereas the internal rate of return method assumes the rate of return is the internal rate of return on the project. Specifically, if the internal rate of return of the project is high, this assumption may not be realistic. It is generally more realistic to assume that cash inflows can be reinvested at a rate of return equal to the discount rate—particularly if the discount rate is the company's cost of capital or an opportunity rate of return. For example, if the discount rate is the company's cost of capital, this rate of return can be actually realized by paying off the company's creditors and buying back the company's stock with cash flows from the project. In short, when the net present value method and the internal rate of return method do not agree concerning the attractiveness of a project, it is best to go with the net present value method. Of the two methods, it makes the more realistic assumption about the rate of return that can be earned on cash flows from the project.

Expanding the Net Present Value Method

So far all of our examples have involved only a single investment alternative. We will now expand the net present value method to include two alternatives. In addition, we will integrate the concept of relevant costs into the discounted cash flow analysis.

The net present value method can be used to compare competing investment projects in two ways. One is the *total-cost approach,* and the other is the *incremental-cost approach.* Each approach is illustrated below.

The Total-Cost Approach

The total-cost approach is the most flexible method for comparing competing projects. To illustrate the mechanics of the approach, consider the following data:

Example E

Harper Ferry Company provides a ferry service across the Mississippi River. One of its small ferryboats is in poor condition. This ferry can be renovated at an immediate cost of $200,000. Further repairs and an overhaul of the motor will be needed five years from now at a cost of $80,000. In all, the ferry will be usable for 10 years if this work is done. At the end of 10 years, the ferry will have to be scrapped at a salvage value of approximately $60,000. The scrap value of the ferry right now is $70,000. It will cost $300,000 each year to operate the ferry, and revenues will total $400,000 annually.

As an alternative, Harper Ferry Company can purchase a new ferryboat at a cost of $360,000. The new ferry will have a life of 10 years, but it will require some repairs at the end of 5 years. It is estimated that these repairs will amount to $30,000. At the end of 10 years, it is estimated that the ferry will have a scrap value of $60,000. It will cost $210,000 each year to operate the ferry, and revenues will total $400,000 annually.

Harper Ferry Company requires a return of at least 14% before taxes on all investment projects.

Should the company purchase the new ferry or renovate the old ferry? Exhibit 14–7 gives the solution using the total-cost approach.

Two points should be noted from the exhibit. First, observe that *all* cash inflows and *all* cash outflows are included in the solution under each alternative. No effort has been made to isolate those cash flows that are relevant to the decision and those that are not relevant. The inclusion of all cash flows associated with each alternative gives the approach its name—the *total-cost* approach.

Second, notice that a net present value is computed for each of the two alternatives. This is a distinct advantage of the total-cost approach in that an unlimited number of alternatives can be compared side by side to determine the best action. For example, another alternative for Harper Ferry Company would be to get out of the ferry business

Exhibit 14–7 The Total-Cost Approach to Project Selection

	New Ferry	Old Ferry
Annual revenues	$400,000	$400,000
Annual cash operating costs	210,000	300,000
Net annual cash inflows	$190,000	$100,000

Item	Year(s)	Amount of Cash Flows	14% Factor*	Present Value of Cash Flows
Buy the new ferry:				
Initial investment	Now	$(360,000)	1.000	$(360,000)
Repairs in five years	5	(30,000)	0.519	(15,570)
Net annual cash inflows	1–10	190,000	5.216	991,040
Salvage of the old ferry	Now	70,000	1.000	70,000
Salvage of the new ferry	10	60,000	0.270	16,200
Net present value				701,670
Keep the old ferry:				
Initial repairs	Now	$(200,000)	1.000	(200,000)
Repairs in five years	5	(80,000)	0.519	(41,520)
Net annual cash inflows	1–10	100,000	5.216	521,600
Salvage of the old ferry	10	60,000	0.270	16,200
Net present value				296,280
Net present value in favor of buying the new ferry				$ 405,390

*All present value factors are from Tables 14C–3 and 14C–4 in Appendix 14C.

entirely. If management desired, the net present value of this alternative could be computed to compare with the alternatives shown in Exhibit 14–7. Still other alternatives might be open to the company. Once management has determined the net present value of each alternative that it wishes to consider, it can select the course of action that promises to be the most profitable. In the case at hand, given only the two alternatives, the data indicate that the most profitable course is to purchase the new ferry.[4]

Does It Really Need to Be New?

In Business

Tom Copeland, the director of Corporate Finance Practice at the consulting firm Monitor Group, observes: "If they could afford it, most people would like to drive a new car. Managers are no different . . . [I]n my experience, . . . [managers] routinely spend millions of dollars on new machines years earlier than they need to. In most cases, the overall cost (including the cost of breakdowns) is 30% to 40% lower if a company continues servicing an existing machine for five more years instead of buying a new one. In order to fight impulsive acquisitions of new machinery, companies should require unit managers to run the numbers on all alternative investment options open to them—including maintaining the existing assets or buying used ones."

Source: Tom Copeland, "Cutting Costs Without Drawing Blood," *Harvard Business Review*, September-October 2000, pp. 3–7.

The Incremental-Cost Approach

When only two alternatives are being considered, the incremental-cost approach offers a simpler and more direct route to a decision. Unlike the total-cost approach, it focuses only on differential costs.[5] The procedure is to include in the discounted cash flow analysis only those costs and revenues that *differ* between the two alternatives being considered. To illustrate, refer again to the data in Example E relating to Harper Ferry Company. The solution using only differential costs is presented in Exhibit 14–8.

Two things should be noted from the data in this exhibit. First, notice that the net present value in favor of buying the new ferry of $405,390 shown in Exhibit 14–8 agrees with the net present value shown under the total-cost approach in Exhibit 14–7. This

Exhibit 14–8 The Incremental-Cost Approach to Project Selection

Item	Year(s)	Amount of Cash Flows	14% Factor*	Present Value of Cash Flows
Incremental investment to buy the new ferry	Now	$(160,000)	1.000	$(160,000)
Difference in repairs in five years.	5	50,000	0.519	25,950
Increase in net annual cash inflows	1–10	90,000	5.216	469,440
Salvage of the old ferry now.	Now	70,000	1.000	70,000
Difference in salvage value in 10 years	10	0	0.270	0
Net present value in favor of buying the new ferry.				$ 405,390

*All present value factors are from Tables 14C–3 and 14C–4 in Appendix 14C.

[4] The alternative with the highest net present value is not always the best choice, although it is the best choice in this case. For further discussion, see the section Preference Decisions—The Ranking of Investment Projects.

[5] Technically, the incremental-cost approach is misnamed, since it focuses on differential costs (that is, on both cost increases and decreases) rather than just on incremental costs. As used here, the term *incremental costs* should be interpreted broadly to include both cost increases and cost decreases.

agreement should be expected, since the two approaches are just different roads to the same destination.

Second, notice that the costs used in Exhibit 14–8 are just the differences between the costs shown for the two alternatives in the prior exhibit. For example, the $160,000 incremental investment required to purchase the new ferry in Exhibit 14–8 is the difference between the $360,000 cost of the new ferry and the $200,000 cost required to renovate the old ferry from Exhibit 14–7. The other figures in Exhibit 14–8 have been computed in the same way.

Least-Cost Decisions

Revenues are not directly involved in some decisions. For example, a company that does not charge for delivery service may need to replace an old delivery truck, or a company may be trying to decide whether to lease or to buy its fleet of executive cars. In situations such as these, where no revenues are involved, the most desirable alternative will be the one that promises the *least total cost* from the present value perspective. Hence, these are known as least-cost decisions. To illustrate a least-cost decision, consider the following data:

Example F

Val-Tek Company is considering the replacement of an old threading machine. A new threading machine is available that could substantially reduce annual operating costs. Selected data relating to the old and the new machines are presented below:

	Old Machine	New Machine
Purchase cost when new.	$200,000	$250,000
Salvage value now.	30,000	—
Annual cash operating costs	150,000	90,000
Overhaul needed immediately.	40,000	—
Salvage value in six years	0	50,000
Remaining life	6 years	6 years

Val-Tek Company uses a 10% discount rate.

Exhibit 14–9 provides an analysis of the alternatives using the total-cost approach.

Exhibit 14–9 The Total-Cost Approach (Least-Cost Decision)

Item	Year(s)	Amount of Cash Flows	10% Factor*	Present Value of Cash Flows
Buy the new machine:				
Initial investment.	Now	$(250,000)	1.000	$(250,000)†
Salvage of the old machine	Now	30,000	1.000	30,000†
Annual cash operating costs	1–6	(90,000)	4.355	(391,950)
Salvage of the new machine	6	50,000	0.564	28,200
Present value of net cash outflows.				(583,750)
Keep the old machine:				
Overhaul needed now	Now	$ (40,000)	1.000	$ (40,000)
Annual cash operating costs	1–6	(150,000)	4.355	(653,250)
Present value of net cash outflows.				(693,250)
Net present value in favor of buying the new machine				$ 109,500

*All factors are from Tables 14C–3 and 14C–4 in Appendix 14C.

†These two items could be netted into a single $220,000 incremental-cost figure ($250,000 − $30,000 = $220,000).

As shown in the exhibit, the new machine has the lowest total cost when the present value of the net cash outflows is considered. An analysis of the two alternatives using the incremental-cost approach is presented in Exhibit 14–10. As before, the data in this exhibit represent the differences between the alternatives as shown under the total-cost approach.

Trading in that Old Car?

In Business

Consumer Reports magazine provides the following data concerning the alternatives of keeping a four-year-old Ford Taurus for three years or buying a similar new car to replace it. The illustration assumes the car would be purchased and used in suburban Chicago.

	Keep the Old Taurus	Buy a New Taurus
Annual maintenance	$1,180	$ 650
Annual insurance	370	830
Annual license	15	100
Trade-in value in three years	605	7,763
Purchase price, including sales tax		17,150

Consumer Reports is ordinarily extremely careful in its analysis, but it has omitted in this case one financial item that would clearly differ substantially between the alternatives and hence would be relevant. What is it? To check your answer, go to the textbook website at www.mhhe.com/garrison10e. After accessing the site, click on the link to the Internet Exercises and then the link to this chapter.

Source: "When to Give Up on Your Clunker," *Consumer Reports*, August 2000, pp. 12–16.

Uncertain Cash Flows

LEARNING OBJECTIVE 3
Evaluate an investment project that has uncertain cash flows.

The analysis to this point in the chapter has assumed that all of the future cash flows are known with certainty. However, future cash flows are often uncertain or difficult to estimate. A number of techniques are available for handling this complication. Some of these techniques are quite technical—involving computer simulations or advanced mathematical skills—and are beyond the scope of this book. However, we can provide some very useful information to managers without getting too technical.

Exhibit 14–10 The Incremental-Cost Approach (Least-Cost Decision)

Item	Year(s)	Amount of Cash Flows	10% Factor*	Present Value of Cash Flows
Incremental investment required to purchase the new machine	Now	$(210,000)	1.000	$(210,000)†
Salvage of the old machine	Now	30,000	1.000	30,000†
Savings in annual cash operating costs	1–6	60,000	4.355	261,300
Difference in salvage value in six years	6	50,000	0.564	28,200
Net present value in favor of buying the new machine				$ 109,500

*All factors are from Tables 14C–3 and 14C–4 in Appendix 14C.

†These two items could be netted into a single $180,000 incremental-cost figure ($210,000 − $30,000 = $180,000).

In Business **Managing the Financial Risks of Drug Research**

Several different techniques can be used to take into account uncertainties about future cash flows in capital budgeting. The uncertainties are particularly apparent in the drug business where it costs an average of $359 million and 10 years to bring a new drug through the governmental approval process and to market. And once on the market, 7 out of 10 products fail to return the company's cost of capital.

Merck & Co. manages the financial risks and uncertainties of drug research using a Research Planning Model it has developed. The model, which produces net present value estimates and other key statistics, is based on a wide range of scientific and financial variables—most of which are uncertain. For example, the future selling price of any drug resulting from current research is usually highly uncertain, but managers at Merck & Co. can at least specify a range within which the selling price is likely to fall. The computer is used to draw a value at random, within the permissible range, for each of the variables in the model. The model then computes a net present value. This process is repeated many times, and each time a new value of each of the variables is drawn at random. In this way, Merck is able to produce a probability distribution for the net present value. This can be used, for example, to estimate the probability that the project's net present value will exceed a certain level. "What are the payoffs of all this sophistication? In short, better decisions."

Source: Nancy A. Nichols, "Scientific Management at Merck: An Interview with CFO Judy Lewent," *Harvard Business Review,* January–February 1994, pp. 89–99.

An Example

As an example of difficult-to-estimate future cash flows, consider the case of investments in automated equipment. The up-front costs of automated equipment and the tangible benefits, such as reductions in operating costs and lower wastage, tend to be relatively easy to estimate. However, the intangible benefits, such as greater reliability, greater speed, and higher quality, are more difficult to quantify in terms of future cash flows. These intangible benefits certainly impact future cash flows—particularly in terms of increased sales and perhaps higher selling prices—but the cash flow effects are difficult to estimate. What can be done?

A fairly simple procedure can be followed when the intangible benefits are likely to be significant. Suppose, for example, that a company with a 12% discount rate is considering purchasing automated equipment that would have a 10-year useful life. Also suppose that a discounted cash flow analysis of just the tangible costs and benefits shows a negative net present value of $226,000. Clearly, if the intangible benefits are large enough, they could turn this negative net present value into a positive net present value. In this case, the amount of additional cash flow per year from the intangible benefits that would be needed to make the project financially attractive can be computed as follows:

Net present value excluding the intangible benefits (negative)	$(226,000)
Present value factor for an annuity at 12% for 10 periods (from Table 14C–4 in Appendix 14C).	5.650

$$\frac{\text{Negative net present value to be offset, \$226,000}}{\text{Present value factor, 5.650}} = \$40{,}000$$

Thus, if the intangible benefits of the automated equipment are worth at least $40,000 a year to the company, then the automated equipment should be purchased. If, in the judgment of management, these intangible benefits are not worth $40,000 a year, then the automated equipment should not be purchased.

This technique can be used in other situations in which future cash flows are uncertain or difficult to estimate. For example, this technique can be used when the salvage value is difficult to estimate. To illustrate, suppose that all of the cash flows from an investment in a supertanker have been estimated—other than its salvage value in 20 years. Using a discount rate of 12%, management has determined that the net present value of all of these cash flows is a negative $1.04 million. This negative net present value would be offset by the salvage value of the supertanker. How large would the salvage value have to be to make this investment attractive?

Net present value excluding salvage value (negative)	$(1,040,000)
Present value factor at 12% for 20 periods (from Table 14C–4 in Appendix 14C)	0.104

$$\frac{\text{Negative net present value to be offset, \$1,040,000}}{\text{Present value factor, 0.104}} = \$10,000,000$$

Thus, if the salvage value of the tanker is at least $10 million, its net present value would be positive and the investment would be made. However, if management believes the salvage value is unlikely to be as large as $10 million, the investment should not be made.

Real Options

The analysis in this chapter has assumed that an investment cannot be postponed and that, once started, nothing can be done to alter the course of the project. In reality, investments can often be postponed. Postponement is a particularly attractive option when the net present value of a project is modest using current estimates of future cash flows, but the future cash flows involve a great deal of uncertainty that may be resolved over time. Similarly, once an investment is made, management can often exploit changes in the business environment and take actions that enhance future cash flows. For example, buying a supertanker provides management with a number of options, some of which may become more attractive as time unfolds. Instead of operating the supertanker itself, the company may decide to lease it to another operator if the rental rates become high enough. Or, if a supertanker shortage develops, management may decide to sell the supertanker and take a gain. In the case of an investment in automated equipment, management may initially buy only the basic model without costly add-ons, but keep the option open to add more capacity and capability later. The ability to delay the start of a project, to expand it if conditions are favorable, to cut losses if they are unfavorable, and to otherwise modify plans as business conditions change confers additional value on many investments. These advantages can be quantified using what is called *real option* analysis, but the techniques are beyond the scope of this book.

Thinking Ahead

In Business

With an eye on environmental concerns, the board of directors of Royal Dutch/Shell, the Anglo-Dutch energy company, has decided that all big projects must explicitly take into account the likely future costs of abating carbon emissions. Calculations must assume a cost of $5 per ton of carbon dioxide emission in 2005 through 2009, rising to $20 per ton from 2010 onward. A Shell manager explains: "We know that $5 and $20 are surely the wrong price, but everyone else who assumes a carbon price of zero in future will be more wrong. This is not altruism. We see it as giving us a competitive edge."

Source: "Big Business Bows to Global Warming," *The Economist*, December 2, 2000, p. 81.

Preference Decisions—The Ranking of Investment Projects

Recall that when considering investment opportunities, managers must make two types of decisions—screening decisions and preference decisions. Screening decisions, which

LEARNING OBJECTIVE 4
Rank investment projects in order of preference.

come first, pertain to whether or not some proposed investment is basically acceptable. Preference decisions come *after* screening decisions and attempt to answer the following question: "How do the remaining investment proposals, all of which have been screened and provide an acceptable rate of return, rank in terms of preference? That is, which one(s) would be *best* for the firm to accept?"

Preference decisions are more difficult to make than screening decisions because investment funds are usually limited. This often requires that some (perhaps many) otherwise very profitable investment opportunities must be passed up.

Sometimes preference decisions are called rationing decisions, or ranking decisions. Limited investment funds must be rationed among many competing alternatives, or the alternatives must be ranked. Either the internal rate of return method or the net present value method can be used in making preference decisions. However, as discussed earlier, if the two methods are in conflict, it is best to use the net present value method, which is more reliable.

Internal Rate of Return Method

When using the internal rate of return method to rank competing investment projects, the preference rule is: *The higher the internal rate of return, the more desirable the project.* An investment project with an internal rate of return of 18% is usually considered preferable to another project that promises a return of only 15%. Internal rate of return is widely used to rank projects.

Net Present Value Method

Unfortunately, the net present value of one project cannot be directly compared to the net present value of another project unless the investments are of equal size. For example, assume that a company is considering two competing investments, as shown below:

	Investment	
	A	B
Investment required	$(80,000)	$(5,000)
Present value of cash inflows	81,000	6,000
Net present value	$ 1,000	$ 1,000

Each project has a net present value of $1,000, but the projects are not equally desirable. When funds are limited, the project requiring an investment of only $5,000 is much more desirable than the project requiring an investment of $80,000. To compare the two projects on a valid basis, the present value of the cash inflows should be divided by the investment required. The result is called the **profitability index.** The formula for the profitability index follows:

$$\text{Profitability index} = \frac{\text{Present value of cash inflows}}{\text{Investment required}} \qquad (2)$$

The profitability indexes for the two investments above would be computed as follows:

	Investment	
	A	B
Present value of cash inflows(a)	$81,000	$6,000
Investment required (b)	$80,000	$5,000
Profitability index, (a) ÷ (b)	1.01	1.20

When using the profitability index to rank competing investments projects, the preference rule is: *The higher the profitability index, the more desirable the project.* Applying this rule to the two investments above, investment B should be chosen over investment A.

The profitability index is an application of the techniques for utilizing scarce resources discussed in Chapter 13. In this case, the scarce resource is the limited funds available for investment, and the profitability index is similar to the contribution margin per unit of the scarce resource.

A few details should be clarified with respect to the computation of the profitability index. The "Investment required" refers to any cash outflows that occur at the beginning of the project, reduced by any salvage value recovered from the sale of old equipment. The "Investment required" also includes any investment in working capital that the project may need. Finally, we should note that the "Present value of cash inflows" is net of all *outflows* that occur after the project starts.

Other Approaches to Capital Budgeting Decisions

The net present value and internal rate of return methods have gained widespread acceptance as decision-making tools. Other methods of making capital budgeting decisions are also used, however, and are preferred by some managers. In this section, we discuss two such methods known as *payback* and *simple rate of return.* Both methods have been in use for many years, but have been declining in popularity as primary tools for project evaluation.

The Payback Method

LEARNING OBJECTIVE 5
Determine the payback period for an investment.

The payback method focuses on the *payback period.* The **payback period** is the length of time that it takes for a project to recoup its initial cost out of the cash receipts that it generates. This period is sometimes referred to as "the time that it takes for an investment to pay for itself." The basic premise of the payback method is that the more quickly the cost of an investment can be recovered, the more desirable is the investment.

The payback period is expressed in years. *When the net annual cash inflow is the same every year,* the following formula can be used to compute the payback period:

$$\text{Payback period} = \frac{\text{Investment required}}{\text{Net annual cash inflow*}} \qquad (3)$$

*If new equipment is replacing old equipment, this becomes incremental net annual cash inflow.

To illustrate the payback method, consider the following data:

Concept 14–2

Example G
York Company needs a new milling machine. The company is considering two machines: machine A and machine B. Machine A costs $15,000 and will reduce operating costs by $5,000 per year. Machine B costs only $12,000 but will also reduce operating costs by $5,000 per year.

Required:
Which machine should be purchased according to the payback method?

$$\text{Machine A payback period} = \frac{\$15{,}000}{\$5{,}000} = 3.0 \text{ years}$$

$$\text{Machine B payback period} = \frac{\$12{,}000}{\$5{,}000} = 2.4 \text{ years}$$

According to the payback calculations, York Company should purchase machine B, since it has a shorter payback period than machine A.

In Business | Investing in an MBA

The financial benefit of earning an MBA degree is the enhanced earning power; the costs include both tuition and the opportunity cost of lost salary for two years. *Forbes* magazine computed both the net present value and the payback period for 80 full-time MBA programs. *Forbes* looked at the first five years of enhanced earnings after the degree is granted and the costs of getting the degree. The net present value of an MBA varies a great deal—ranging from over $100,000 at Harvard to $1,000 or less at some institutions. The payback periods show less variation. The quickest paybacks are at Harvard and Ohio State—3.3 years. The slowest payback is about five years. Why would a degree that has a five-year payback period have such a small net present value—$1,000 or less? If the payback period is five years for a particular school and the net present value analysis includes only the first five years of enhanced earnings, then the net present value must be zero or negative. Earnings that extend beyond the five-year horizon are ignored in the *Forbes* analysis. If these earnings had been included, the net present values of degrees at even the lowest-ranked schools would have increased substantially.

Source: Kurt Brandenhausen, "The Bottom Line on B-Schools," *Forbes*, February 7, 2000, pp. 100–104.

Evaluation of the Payback Method

The payback method is not a true measure of the profitability of an investment. Rather, it simply tells the manager how many years will be required to recover the original investment. Unfortunately, a shorter payback period does not always mean that one investment is more desirable than another.

To illustrate, consider again the two machines used in the example above. Since machine B has a shorter payback period than machine A, it *appears* that machine B is more desirable than machine A. But if we add one more piece of information, this illusion quickly disappears. Machine A has a projected 10-year life, and machine B has a projected 5-year life. It would take two purchases of machine B to provide the same length of service as would be provided by a single purchase of machine A. Under these circumstances, machine A would be a much better investment than machine B, even though machine B has a shorter payback period. Unfortunately, the payback method has no inherent mechanism for highlighting differences in useful life between investments. Such differences can be very important, and relying on payback alone may result in incorrect decisions.

A further criticism of the payback method is that it does not consider the time value of money. A cash inflow to be received several years in the future is weighed equally with a cash inflow to be received right now. To illustrate, assume that for an investment of $8,000 you can purchase either of the two following streams of cash inflows:

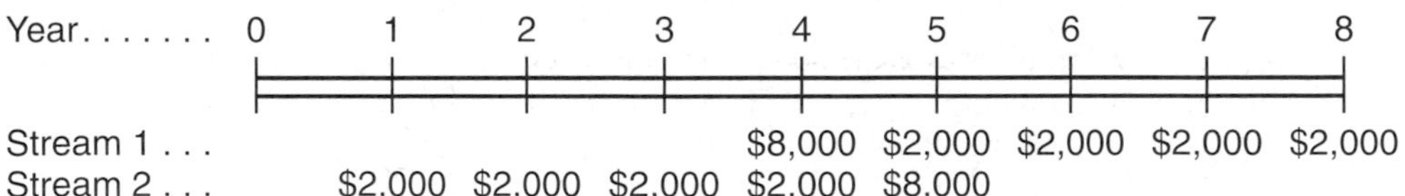

Which stream of cash inflows would you prefer to receive in return for your $8,000 investment? Each stream has a payback period of 4.0 years. Therefore, if payback alone were relied on in making the decision, you would be forced to say that the streams are equally desirable. However, from the point of view of the time value of money, stream 2 is much more desirable than stream 1.

On the other hand, under certain conditions the payback method can be very useful. For one thing, it can help identify which investment proposals are in the "ballpark." That is, it can be used as a screening tool to help answer the question, "Should I consider this proposal further?" If a proposal doesn't provide a payback within some specified period, then there may be no need to consider it further. In addition, the payback period is often of great importance to new firms that are "cash poor." When a firm is cash poor, a project with a short payback period but a low rate of return might be preferred over another project with a high rate of return but a long payback period. The reason is that the company may simply need a faster return of its cash investment. And finally, the payback method is sometimes used in industries where products become obsolete very rapidly—such as consumer electronics. Since products may last only a year or two, the payback period on investments must be very short.

Capital Budgeting in Academia

In Business

Capital budgeting techniques are widely used in large nonprofit organizations. A survey of universities in the United Kingdom revealed that 41% use the net present value method, 23% use the internal rate of return method, 29% use the payback method, and 11% use the accounting rate of return method. (Some universities use more than one method.) The central Funding Council of the United Kingdom requires that the net present value method be used for projects whose lifespans exceed 20 years.

Source: Paul Cooper, "Management Accounting Practices in Universities," *Management Accounting (U.K.),* February 1996, pp. 28–30.

An Extended Example of Payback

As shown by formula (3) given earlier, the payback period is computed by dividing the investment in a project by the net annual cash inflows that the project will generate. If new equipment is replacing old equipment, then any salvage to be received on disposal of the old equipment should be deducted from the cost of the new equipment, and only the *incremental* investment should be used in the payback computation. In addition, any depreciation deducted in arriving at the project's net operating income must be added back to obtain the project's expected net annual cash inflow. To illustrate, consider the following data:

Example H

Goodtime Fun Centers, Inc., operates many outlets in the eastern states. Some of the vending machines in one of its outlets provide very little revenue, so the company is considering removing the machines and installing equipment to dispense soft ice cream. The equipment would cost $80,000 and have an eight-year useful life. Incremental annual revenues and costs associated with the sale of ice cream would be as follows:

Sales	$150,000
Less cost of ingredients	90,000
Contribution margin	60,000
Less fixed expenses:	
Salaries	27,000
Maintenance	3,000
Depreciation	10,000
Total fixed expenses	40,000
Net operating income	$ 20,000

The vending machines can be sold for a $5,000 scrap value. The company will not purchase equipment unless it has a payback of three years or less. Should the equipment to dispense ice cream be purchased?

Exhibit 14–11
Computation of the Payback Period

Step 1: *Compute the net annual cash inflow.* Since the net annual cash inflow is not given, it must be computed before the payback period can be determined:

Net operating income (given above)	$20,000
Add: Noncash deduction for depreciation	10,000
Net annual cash inflow	$30,000

Step 2: *Compute the payback period.* Using the net annual cash inflow figure from above, the payback period can be determined as follows:

Cost of the new equipment	$80,000
Less salvage value of old equipment	5,000
Investment required	$75,000

$$\text{Payback period} = \frac{\text{Investment required}}{\text{Net annual cash inflow}}$$

$$= \frac{\$75,000}{\$30,000} = 2.5 \text{ years}$$

An analysis of the payback period for the proposed equipment is given in Exhibit 14–11. Several things should be noted. First, notice that depreciation is added back to net operating income to obtain the net annual cash inflow from the new equipment. Depreciation is not a cash outlay; thus, it must be added back to net operating income to adjust it to a cash basis. Second, notice in the payback computation that the salvage value from the old machines has been deducted from the cost of the new equipment, and that only the incremental investment has been used in computing the payback period.

Since the proposed equipment has a payback period of less than three years, the company's payback requirement has been met.

In Business

Counting the Environmental Costs

Companies often grossly underestimate how much they are spending on environmental costs. Many of these costs are buried in broad cost categories such as manufacturing overhead. Kestrel Management Services, LLC, a management consulting firm specializing in environmental matters, found that one chemical facility was spending five times as much on environmental expenses as its cost system reported. At another site, a small manufacturer with $840,000 in pretax profits thought that its annual safety and environmental compliance expenses were about $50,000 but, after digging into the accounts, found that the total was closer to $300,000. Alerted to this high cost, management of the company invested about $125,000 in environmental improvements, anticipating a three- to six-month payback period. By taking steps such as more efficient dust collection, the company improved its product quality, reduced scrap rates, decreased its consumption of city water for cooling, and reduced the expense of discharging wastewater into the city's sewer system. Further analysis revealed that spending $50,000 to improve energy efficiency would reduce annual energy costs by about $45,000. Few of these costs were visible in the company's traditional cost accounting system.

Source: Thomas P. Kunes, "A Green and *Lean* Workplace?" *Strategic Finance*, February 2001, pp. 71–73, 83.

Year	(1) Beginning Unrecovered Investment	(2) Investment	(3) Cash Inflow	(4) Ending Unrecovered Investment (1) + (2) − (3)
1.	$ 0	$4,000	$1,000	$3,000
2.	3,000		0	3,000
3.	3,000		2,000	1,000
4.	1,000	2,000	1,000	2,000
5.	2,000		500	1,500
6.	1,500		3,000	0
7.	0		2,000	0
8.	0		2,000	0

Exhibit 14–12
Payback and Uneven Cash Flows

Rapid Obsolescence

In Business

Intel Corporation invests a billion to a billion and a half dollars in plants to fabricate computer processor chips such as the Pentium IV. But the fab plants can only be used to make state-of-the-art chips for about two years. By the end of that time, the equipment is obsolete and the plant must be converted to making less complicated chips. Under such conditions of rapid obsolescence, the payback method may be the most appropriate way to evaluate investments. If the project does not pay back within a few years, it may never pay back its initial investment.

Source: "Pentium at a Glance," *Forbes ASAP*, February 26, 1996, p. 66.

Payback and Uneven Cash Flows

When the cash flows associated with an investment project change from year to year, the simple payback formula that we outlined earlier cannot be used. Consider the following data:

Year	Investment	Cash Inflow
1	$4,000	$1,000
2		0
3		2,000
4	2,000	1,000
5		500
6		3,000
7		2,000
8		2,000

What is the payback period on this investment? The answer is 5.5 years, but to obtain this figure it is necessary to track the unrecovered investment year by year. The steps involved in this process are shown in Exhibit 14–12. By the middle of the sixth year, sufficient cash inflows will have been realized to recover the entire investment of $6,000 ($4,000 + $2,000).

The Simple Rate of Return Method

LEARNING OBJECTIVE 6
Compute the simple rate of return for an investment.

The **simple rate of return** method is another capital budgeting technique that does not involve discounted cash flows. The method is also known as the accounting rate of return, the unadjusted rate of return, and the financial statement method.

Unlike the other capital budgeting methods that we have discussed, the simple rate of return method does not focus on cash flows. Rather, it focuses on accounting net operating income. The approach is to estimate the revenues that will be generated by a proposed investment and then to deduct from these revenues all of the projected operating expenses associated with the project. The net operating income is then related to the initial investment in the project, as shown in the following formula:

$$\text{Simple rate of return} = \frac{\text{Incremental revenues} - \text{Incremental expenses, including depreciation} = \text{Incremental net operating income}}{\text{Initial investment}^*} \qquad (4)$$

*The investment should be reduced by any salvage from the sale of old equipment.

Or, if a cost reduction project is involved, formula (4) becomes:

$$\text{Simple rate of return} = \frac{\text{Cost savings} - \text{Depreciation on new equipment}}{\text{Initial investment}^*} \qquad (5)$$

*The investment should be reduced by any salvage from the sale of old equipment.

Example I

Brigham Tea, Inc., is a processor of a low-acid tea. The company is contemplating purchasing equipment for an additional processing line. The additional processing line would increase revenues by $90,000 per year. Incremental cash operating expenses would be $40,000 per year. The equipment would cost $180,000 and have a nine-year life. No salvage value is projected.

$$\text{Simple rate of return} = \frac{\begin{bmatrix}\$90{,}000\\ \text{Incremental revenues}\end{bmatrix} - \begin{bmatrix}\$40{,}000 \text{ Cash operating expenses}\\ + \$20{,}000 \text{ Depreciation}\end{bmatrix}}{\$180{,}000 \text{ Initial investment}}$$

$$= \frac{\$30{,}000}{\$180{,}000}$$

$$= 16.7\%$$

Example J

Midwest Farms, Inc., hires people on a part-time basis to sort eggs. The cost of this hand-sorting process is $30,000 per year. The company is investigating the purchase of an egg-sorting machine that would cost $90,000 and have a 15-year useful life. The machine would have negligible salvage value, and it would cost $10,000 per year to operate and maintain. The egg-sorting equipment currently being used could be sold now for a scrap value of $2,500.

A cost reduction project is involved in this situation. By applying equation (5), we can compute the simple rate of return as follows:

$$\text{Simple rate of return} = \frac{\$20{,}000^* \text{ Cost savings} - \$6{,}000^\dagger \text{ Depreciation on new equipment}}{\$90{,}000 - \$2{,}500}$$

$$= 16.0\%$$

*$30,000 − $10,000 = $20,000 cost savings.

†$90,000 ÷ 15 years = $6,000 depreciation.

Criticisms of the Simple Rate of Return

The most damaging criticism of the simple rate of return method is that it does not consider the time value of money. The simple rate of return method considers a dollar received 10 years from now as just as valuable as a dollar received today. Thus, the simple rate of return method can be misleading if the alternatives being considered have different cash flow patterns. Additionally, many projects do not have constant incremental revenues and expenses over their useful lives. As a result, the simple rate of return will fluctuate from year to year, with the possibility that a project may appear to be desirable in some years and undesirable in other years. In contrast, the net present value method provides a single number that summarizes all of the cash flows over the entire useful life of the project.

Watching the Really Long Term

In Business

Forest product companies have some of the longest horizons in industry—trees they plant today may not reach their peak for decades. Of the 29 forest product companies that responded to a questionnaire, 9% use the simple rate of return as the primary criterion to evaluate timber investments, 15% use the payback period, 38% use the internal rate of return, and 38% use the net present value. None of the largest forest products firms use either the simple rate of return or the payback method to evaluate timber projects. For other investment decisions—that typically have shorter horizons—the method used shifted away from net present value and toward the payback period.

Source: Jack Bailes, James Nielsen, and Stephen Lawton, "How Forest Product Companies Analyze Capital Budgets," *Management Accounting*, October 1998, pp. 24–30.

Postaudit of Investment Projects

After an investment project has been approved and implemented, a *postaudit* should be conducted. A **postaudit** involves checking whether or not expected results are actually realized. This is a key part of the capital budgeting process. It helps to keep managers honest in their investment proposals. Any tendency to inflate the benefits or downplay the costs in a proposal should become evident after a few postaudits have been conducted. The postaudit also provides an opportunity to reinforce and possibly expand successful projects and to cut losses on floundering projects.

The same technique should be used in the postaudit as was used in the original approval process. That is, if a project was approved on the basis of a net present value analysis, then the same procedure should be used in performing the postaudit. However, the data used in the postaudit analysis should be *actual observed data* rather than estimated data. This affords management with an opportunity to make a side-by-side comparison to see how well the project has worked out. It also helps assure that estimated data received on future proposals will be carefully prepared, since the persons submitting the data will know that their estimates will be given careful scrutiny in the postaudit process. Actual results that are far out of line with original estimates should be carefully reviewed.

Summary

Investment decisions should take into account the time value of money since a dollar today is more valuable than a dollar received in the future. The net present value and internal rate of return methods both reflect this fact. In the net present value method, future cash flows are discounted to their present value so that they can be compared on a valid basis with current cash outlays. The difference between the present value of the cash inflows and the present value of the cash outflows is called the project's net present value. If the net present value of the project is negative, the project is rejected. The discount rate in the net present value method is usually a minimum required rate of return such as the company's cost of capital.

The internal rate of return is the rate of return that equates the present value of the cash inflows and the present value of the cash outflows, resulting in a zero net present value. If the internal rate of return is less than the company's minimum required rate of return, the project is rejected.

After rejecting projects whose net present values are negative or whose internal rates of return are less than the minimum required rate of return, the company may still have more projects than can be supported with available funds. The remaining projects can be ranked using either the profitability index or internal rate of return. The profitability index is computed by dividing the present value of the project's future net cash inflows by the required initial investment.

Some companies prefer to use either payback or the simple rate of return to evaluate investment proposals. The payback period is the number of periods that are required to fully recover the initial investment in the project. The simple rate of return is determined by dividing a project's accounting net operating income by the initial investment in the project.

Review Problem 1: Basic Present Value Computations

Each of the following situations is independent. Work out your own solution to each situation, and then check it against the solution provided.

1. John has just reached age 58. In 12 years, he plans to retire. Upon retiring, he would like to take an extended vacation, which he expects will cost at least $4,000. What lump-sum amount must he invest now to have the needed $4,000 at the end of 12 years if the rate of return is:
   a. Eight percent?
   b. Twelve percent?
2. The Morgans would like to send their daughter to an expensive music camp at the end of each of the next five years. The camp costs $1,000 a year. What lump-sum amount would have to be invested now to have the $1,000 at the end of each year if the rate of return is:
   a. Eight percent?
   b. Twelve percent?
3. You have just received an inheritance from a relative. You can invest the money and either receive a $20,000 lump-sum amount at the end of 10 years or receive $1,400 at the end of each year for the next 10 years. If your minimum desired rate of return is 12%, which alternative would you prefer?

Solution to Review Problem 1

1. *a.* The amount that must be invested now would be the present value of the $4,000, using a discount rate of 8%. From Table 14C–3 in Appendix 14C, the factor for a discount rate of 8% for 12 periods is 0.397. Multiplying this discount factor by the $4,000 needed in 12 years will give the amount of the present investment required: $4,000 × 0.397 = $1,588.
   b. We will proceed as we did in (*a*) above, but this time we will use a discount rate of 12%. From Table 14C–3 in Appendix 14C, the factor for a discount rate of 12% for 12 periods is 0.257. Multiplying this discount factor by the $4,000 needed in 12 years will give the amount of the present investment required: $4,000 × 0.257 = $1,028.
   Notice that as the discount rate (desired rate of return) increases, the present value decreases.
2. This part differs from (1) above in that we are now dealing with an annuity rather than with a single future sum. The amount that must be invested now will be the present value of the $1,000 needed at the end of each year for five years. Since we are dealing with an annuity, or a series of annual cash flows, we must refer to Table 14C–4 in Appendix 14C for the appropriate discount factor.
   a. From Table 14C–4 in Appendix 14C, the discount factor for 8% for five periods is 3.993. Therefore, the amount that must be invested now to have $1,000 available at the end of each year for five years is $1,000 × 3.993 = $3,993.
   b. From Table 14C–4 in Appendix 14C, the discount factor for 12% for five periods is 3.605. Therefore, the amount that must be invested now to have $1,000 available at the end of each year for five years is $1,000 × 3.605 = $3,605.
   Again, notice that as the discount rate (desired rate of return) increases, the present value decreases. At a higher rate of return we can invest less than would have been needed if a lower rate of return were being earned.
3. For this part we will need to refer to both Tables 14C–3 and 14C–4 in Appendix 14C. From Table 14C–3, we will need to find the discount factor for 12% for 10 periods, then apply it to the $20,000 lump sum to be received in 10 years. From Table 14C–4, we will need to find the discount factor for 12% for 10 periods, then apply it to the series of $1,400 payments to be received over the 10-year period. Whichever alternative has the higher present value is the one that should be selected.

$\$20{,}000 \times 0.322 = \$6{,}440$

$\$1{,}400 \times 5.650 = \$7{,}910$

Thus, you would prefer to receive the $1,400 per year for 10 years rather than the $20,000 lump sum.

Review Problem 2: Comparison of Capital Budgeting Methods

Lamar Company is studying a project that would have an eight-year life and require a $2,400,000 investment in equipment. At the end of eight years, the project would terminate and the equipment would have no salvage value. The project would provide net operating income each year as follows:

Sales		$3,000,000
Less variable expenses		1,800,000
Contribution margin		1,200,000
Less fixed expenses:		
Advertising, salaries, and other fixed out-of-pocket costs	$700,000	
Depreciation	300,000	
Total fixed expenses		1,000,000
Net operating income		$ 200,000

The company's discount rate is 12%.

Required:

1. Compute the net annual cash inflow from the project.
2. Compute the project's net present value. Is the project acceptable?
3. Find the project's internal rate of return to the nearest whole percent.
4. Compute the project's payback period.
5. Compute the project's simple rate of return.

Solution to Review Problem 2

1. The net annual cash inflow can be computed by deducting the cash expenses from sales:

Sales	$3,000,000
Less variable expenses	1,800,000
Contribution margin	1,200,000
Less advertising, salaries, and other fixed out-of-pocket costs	700,000
Net annual cash inflow	$ 500,000

Or it can be computed by adding depreciation back to net operating income:

Net operating income	$200,000
Add: Noncash deduction for depreciation	300,000
Net annual cash inflow	$500,000

2. The net present value can be computed as follows:

Item	Year(s)	Amount of Cash Flows	12% Factor	Present Value of Cash Flows
Cost of new equipment	Now	$(2,400,000)	1.000	$(2,400,000)
Net annual cash inflow	1–8	500,000	4.968	2,484,000
Net present value				$ 84,000

Yes, the project is acceptable since it has a positive net present value.

3. The formula for computing the factor of the internal rate of return is:

$$\text{Factor of the internal rate of return} = \frac{\text{Investment required}}{\text{Net annual cash inflow}}$$

$$= \frac{\$2{,}400{,}000}{\$500{,}000} = 4.800$$

Looking in Table 14C–4 in Appendix 14C at the end of the chapter and scanning along the 8-period line, we find that a factor of 4.800 represents a rate of return of about 13%.

4. The formula for the payback period is:

$$\text{Payback period} = \frac{\text{Investment required}}{\text{Net annual cash inflow}}$$

$$= \frac{\$2{,}400{,}000}{\$500{,}000}$$

$$= 4.8 \text{ years}$$

5. The formula for the simple rate of return is:

$$\text{Simple rate of return} = \frac{\text{Incremental revenues} - \text{Incremental expenses, including depreciation} = \text{Net operating income}}{\text{Initial investment}}$$

$$= \frac{\$200{,}000}{\$2{,}400{,}000}$$

$$= 8.3\%$$

Glossary

Capital budgeting The process of planning significant outlays on projects that have long-term implications such as the purchase of new equipment or the introduction of a new product. (p. 636)

Cost of capital The average rate of return a company must pay to its long-term creditors and shareholders for the use of their funds. (p. 641)

Internal rate of return The discount rate at which the net present value of an investment project is zero; thus, the internal rate of return is the rate of return promised by a project over its useful life. (p. 643)

Net present value The difference between the present value of the cash inflows and the present value of the cash outflows of an investment project. (p. 637)

Out-of-pocket costs Actual cash outlays for salaries, advertising, repairs, and similar costs. (p. 642)

Payback period The length of time that it takes for a project to fully recover its initial cost out of the cash receipts that it generates. (p. 653)

Postaudit The follow-up after a project has been approved and implemented to determine whether expected results are actually realized. (p. 659)

Preference decision A decision as to which of several competing acceptable investment proposals is best. (p. 637)

Profitability index The ratio of the present value of a project's cash inflows to the investment required. (p. 652)

Required rate of return The minimum rate of return that an investment project must yield to be acceptable. (p. 644)

Screening decision A decision as to whether a proposed investment meets some preset standard of acceptance. (p. 637)

Simple rate of return The rate of return computed by dividing a project's annual accounting net operating income by the initial investment required. (p. 657)

Working capital The excess of current assets over current liabilities. (p. 639)

Yield A term synonymous with *internal rate of return.* (p. 643)

Appendix 14A: The Concept of Present Value

LEARNING OBJECTIVE 7
Understand present value concepts and the use of present value tables.

A dollar received today is more valuable than a dollar received a year from now for the simple reason that if you have a dollar today, you can put it in the bank and have more than a dollar a year from now. Since dollars today are worth more than dollars in the future, we need some means of weighting cash flows that are received at different times so that they can be compared. Mathematics provides us with the means of making such comparisons. With a few simple calculations, we can adjust the value of a dollar received any number of years from now so that it can be compared with the value of a dollar in hand today.

The Mathematics of Interest

If a bank pays 5% interest, then a deposit of $100 today will be worth $105 one year from now. This can be expressed in mathematical terms by means of the following equation:

$$F_1 = P(1 + r) \tag{6}$$

where F_1 = the balance at the end of one period, P = the amount invested now, and r = the rate of interest per period.

If the investment made now is $100 deposited in a bank savings account that is to earn interest at 5%, then P = $100 and r = 0.05. Under these conditions, F_1 = $105, the amount to be received in one year.

The $100 present outlay is called the **present value** of the $105 amount to be received in one year. It is also known as the *discounted value* of the future $105 receipt. The $100 figure represents the value in present terms of $105 to be received a year from now when the interest rate is 5%.

Compound Interest What if the $105 is left in the bank for a second year? In that case, by the end of the second year the original $100 deposit will have grown to $110.25:

Original deposit.	$100.00
Interest for the first year:	
$100 × 0.05	5.00
Balance at the end of the first year.	105.00
Interest for the second year:	
$105 × 0.05	5.25
Balance at the end of the second year	$110.25

Notice that the interest for the second year is $5.25, as compared to only $5.00 for the first year. The reason for the greater interest earned during the second year is that during the second year, interest is being paid *on interest.* That is, the $5.00 interest earned during the first year has been left in the account and has been added to the original $100 deposit when computing interest for the second year. This is known as **compound interest.** In this case, the compounding is annual. Interest can be compounded on a semiannual, quarterly, monthly, or even more frequent basis. The more frequently compounding is done, the more rapidly the balance will grow.

We can determine the balance in an account after n periods of compounding using the following equation:

$$F_n = P(1 + r)^n \tag{7}$$

where n = the number of periods.

If n = 2 years and the interest rate is 5% per year, then the balance in two years will be as follows:

$$F_2 = \$100(1 + 0.05)^2$$

$$F_2 = \$110.25$$

Exhibit 14A–1
The Relationship between Present Value and Future Value

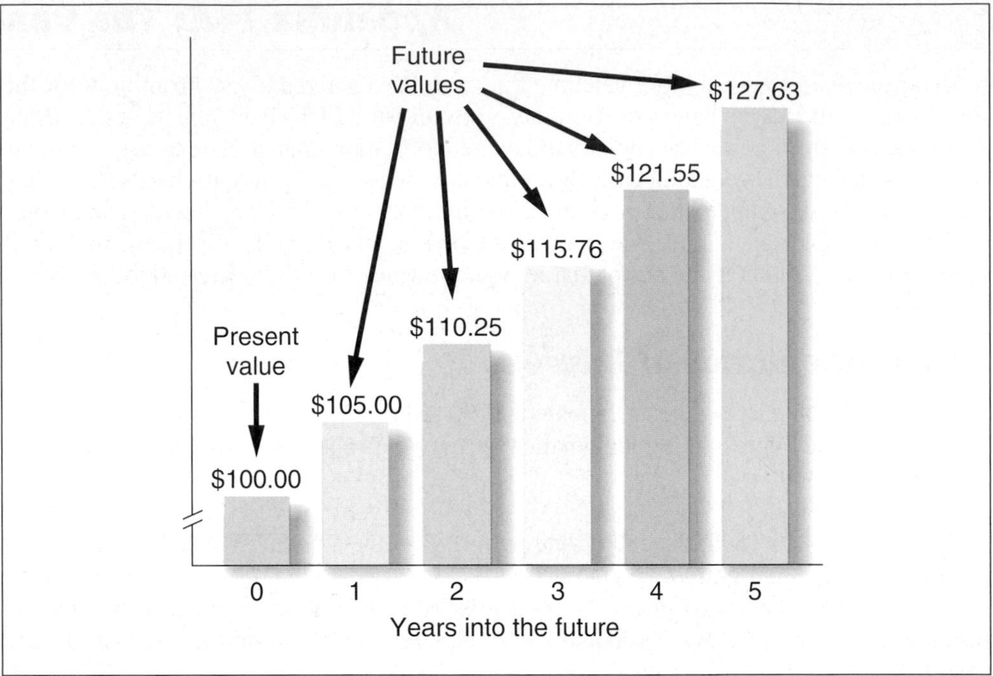

Present Value and Future Value Exhibit 14A–1 shows the relationship between present value and future value. As shown in the exhibit, if $100 is deposited in a bank at 5% interest, it will grow to $127.63 by the end of five years if interest is compounded annually.

Computation of Present Value

An investment can be viewed in two ways. It can be viewed either in terms of its future value or in terms of its present value. We have seen from our computations above that if we know the present value of a sum (such as our $100 deposit), it is a relatively simple task to compute the sum's future value in n years by using equation (7). But what if the tables are reversed and we know the *future* value of some amount but we do not know its present value?

For example, assume that you are to receive $200 two years from now. You know that the future value of this sum is $200, since this is the amount that you will be receiving in two years. But what is the sum's present value—what is it worth *right now?* The present value of any sum to be received in the future can be computed by turning equation (7) around and solving for P:

$$P = \frac{F_n}{(1 + r)^n} \qquad (8)$$

In our example, F = $200 (the amount to be received in the future), $r = 0.05$ (the annual rate of interest), and $n = 2$ (the number of years in the future that the amount is to be received).

$$P = \frac{\$200}{(1 + 0.05)^2}$$

$$P = \frac{\$200}{1.1025}$$

$$P = \$181.40$$

Exhibit 14A–2
Present Value of a Series of Cash Receipts

Year	Factor at 12% (Table 14C–3)	Interest Received	Present Value
1	0.893	$15,000	$13,395
2	0.797	15,000	11,955
3	0.712	15,000	10,680
4	0.636	15,000	9,540
5	0.567	15,000	8,505
			$54,075

As shown by the computation above, the present value of a $200 amount to be received two years from now is $181.40 if the interest rate is 5%. In effect, $181.40 received *right now* is equivalent to $200 received two years from now if the rate of return is 5%. The $181.40 and the $200 are just two ways of looking at the same thing.

The process of finding the present value of a future cash flow, which we have just completed, is called **discounting.** We have *discounted* the $200 to its present value of $181.40. The 5% interest figure that we have used to find this present value is called the **discount rate.** Discounting future sums to their present value is a common practice in business, particularly in capital budgeting decisions.

If you have a power key (y^x) on your calculator, the above calculations are fairly easy. However, some of the present value formulas we will be using are more complex and difficult to use. Fortunately, tables are available in which many of the calculations have already been done for you. For example, Table 14C–3 in Appendix 14C shows the discounted present value of $1 to be received at various periods in the future at various interest rates. The table indicates that the present value of $1 to be received two periods from now at 5% is 0.907. Since in our example we want to know the present value of $200 rather than just $1, we need to multiply the factor in the table by $200:

$$\$200 \times 0.907 = \$181.40$$

This answer is the same as we obtained earlier using the formula in equation (8).

Present Value of a Series of Cash Flows

Although some investments involve a single sum to be received (or paid) at a single point in the future, other investments involve a *series* of cash flows. A series (or stream) of identical cash flows is known as an **annuity.** To provide an example, assume that a firm has just purchased some government bonds in order to temporarily invest funds that are being held for future plant expansion. The bonds will yield interest of $15,000 each year and will be held for five years. What is the present value of the stream of interest receipts from the bonds? As shown in Exhibit 14A–2, the present value of this stream is $54,075 if we assume a discount rate of 12% compounded annually. The discount factors used in this exhibit were taken from Table 14C–3 in Appendix 14C.

Two points are important in connection with Exhibit 14A–2. First, notice that the present value of the $15,000 interest declines the further it is into the future. The present value of $15,000 received a year from now is $13,395, as compared to only $8,505 for the $15,000 interest payment to be received five years from now. This point simply underscores the fact that money has a time value.

The second point is that the computations involved in Exhibit 14A–2 involved unnecessary work. The same present value of $54,075 could have been obtained more easily by referring to Table 14C–4 in Appendix 14C. Table 14C–4 contains the present value of $1 to be received each year over a *series* of years at various interest rates. Table 14C–4 has been derived by simply adding together the factors from Table 14C–3, as follows:

Year	Table 14C–3 Factors at 12%
1	0.893
2	0.797
3	0.712
4	0.636
5	0.567
	3.605

The sum of the five factors above is 3.605. Notice from Table 14C–4 that the factor for $1 to be received each year for five years at 12% is also 3.605. If we use this factor and multiply it by the $15,000 annual cash inflow, then we get the same $54,075 present value that we obtained earlier in Exhibit 14A–2.

$$\$15{,}000 \times 3.605 = \$54{,}075$$

Therefore, when computing the present value of a series (or stream) of equal cash flows that begins at the end of period 1, Table 14C–4 should be used.

To summarize, the present value tables in Appendix 14C should be used as follows:

Table 14C–3: This table should be used to find the present value of a single cash flow (such as a single payment or receipt) occurring in the future.

Table 14C–4: This table should be used to find the present value of a series (or stream) of identical cash flows beginning at the end of the current period and continuing into the future.

The use of both of these tables is illustrated in various exhibits in the main body of the chapter. *When a present value factor appears in an exhibit, you should take the time to trace it back into either Table 14C–3 or Table 14C–4 to get acquainted with the tables and how they work.* (Review Problem 1 at the end of the chapter is designed for those who would like some practice in present value analysis before attempting the homework exercises and problems.)

Glossary (Appendix 14A)

Annuity A series, or stream, of identical cash flows. (p. 665)
Compound interest The process of paying interest on interest in an investment. (p. 663)
Discount rate The rate of return that is used to find the present value of a future cash flow. (p. 665)
Discounting The process of finding the present value of a future cash flow. (p. 665)
Present value The value now of an amount that will be received in some future period. (p. 663)

Appendix 14B: Inflation and Capital Budgeting

Doesn't inflation have an impact in a capital budgeting analysis? The answer is a qualified yes in that inflation does have an impact on the *numbers* that are used in a capital budgeting analysis, but it does not have an impact on the *results* of the analysis if certain conditions are satisfied. To show what we mean by this statement, we will use the following data:

Example K
Martin Company wants to purchase a new machine that costs $36,000. The machine would provide annual cost savings of $20,000, and it would have a three-year life with no salvage value. For each of the next three years, the company expects a 10% inflation rate in the cash flows associated with the new machine. If the company's cost of capital is 23.2%, should the new machine be purchased?

Exhibit 14B–1 Capital Budgeting and Inflation

Reconciliation of the Market-Based and Real Costs of Capital

The real cost of capital	12.0%
The inflation factor	10.0
The combined effect (12% × 10% = 1.2%)	1.2
The market-based cost of capital	23.2%

Solution A: Inflation Not Considered

Item	Year(s)	Amount of Cash Flows	12% Factor	Present Value of Cash Flows
Initial investment	Now	$(36,000)	1.000	$(36,000)
Annual cost savings	1–3	20,000	2.402	48,040
Net present value				$ 12,040‡

Solution B: Inflation Considered

Item	Year(s)	Amount of Cash Flows	Price Index Number*	Price-Adjusted Cash Flows	23.2% Factor†	Present Value of Cash Flows
Initial investment	Now	$(36,000)	1.000	$(36,000)	1.000	$(36,000)
Annual cost savings	1	20,000	1.100	22,000	0.812	17,864
	2	20,000	1.210	24,200	0.659	15,948
	3	20,000	1.331	26,620	0.535	14,242
Net present value						$ 12,054‡

*Computation of the price-index numbers, assuming a 10% inflation rate each year: Year 1, $(1.10)^1 = 1.10$; Year 2, $(1.10)^2 = 1.21$; and Year 3, $(1.10)^3 = 1.331$.

†Discount formulas are computed using the formula $1/(1 + r)^n$, where r is the discount factor and n is the number of years. The computations are $1/1.232 = 0.812$ for Year 1; $1/(1.232)^2 = 0.659$ for Year 2; and $1/(1.232)^3 = 0.535$ for Year 3.

‡These amounts are different only because of rounding error.

To answer this question, it is important to know how the cost of capital was derived. Ordinarily, it is based on the market rates of return on the company's various sources of financing—both debt and equity. This market rate of return includes expected inflation; the higher the expected rate of inflation, the higher the market rate of return on debt and equity. When the inflationary effect is removed from the market rate of return, the result is called a real rate of return. For example, if the inflation rate of 10% is removed from Martin's cost of capital of 23.2%, the "real cost of capital" is only 12%, as shown in Exhibit 14B–1. (You can't simply subtract the inflation rate from the market cost of capital to obtain the real cost of capital. The computations are a bit more complex than that.)

When performing a net present value analysis, one must be consistent. The market-based cost of capital reflects inflation. Therefore, if a market-based cost of capital is used to discount cash flows, then the cash flows should be adjusted upwards to reflect the effects of inflation in forthcoming periods. Computations for Martin Company under this approach are given in solution B in Exhibit 14B–1.

On the other hand, there is no need to adjust the cash flows upward if the "real cost of capital" is used in the analysis (since the inflationary effects have been taken out of the discount rate). Computations for Martin Company under this approach are given in solution A in Exhibit 14B–1. Note that under solutions A and B that the answer will be the same (within rounding error) regardless of which approach is used, so long as one is consistent and all of the cash flows associated with the project are affected in the same way by inflation.

Several points should be noted about solution B, where the effects of inflation are explicitly taken into account. First, note that the annual cost savings are adjusted for the effects of inflation by multiplying each year's cash savings by a price-index number that reflects a 10% inflation rate. (Observe from the footnotes to the exhibit how the index number is computed for each year.) Second, note that the net present value obtained in solution B, where inflation is explicitly taken into account, is the same, within rounding error, to that obtained in solution A, where the inflation effects are ignored. This result may seem surprising, but it is logical. The reason is that we have adjusted both the cash flows and the discount rate so that they are consistent, and these adjustments cancel each other out across the two solutions.

Throughout the chapter we assume for simplicity that there is no inflation. In that case, the market-based and real costs of capital are the same, and there is no reason to adjust the cash flows for inflation since there is none. When there is inflation, the unadjusted cash flows can be used in the analysis if all of the cash flows are affected identically by inflation and the real cost of capital is used to discount the cash flows. Otherwise, the cash flows should be adjusted for inflation and the market-based cost of capital should be used in the analysis.

Exhibit 14C–1 Future Value of $1; $(1 + r)^n$

Periods	4%	5%	6%	7%	8%	9%	10%	11%	12%	13%	14%	15%	16%	17%	18%	19%	20%
1	1.040	1.050	1.060	1.070	1.080	1.090	1.100	1.110	1.120	1.130	1.140	1.150	1.160	1.170	1.180	1.190	1.200
2	1.082	1.103	1.124	1.145	1.166	1.188	1.210	1.232	1.254	1.277	1.300	1.323	1.346	1.369	1.392	1.416	1.440
3	1.125	1.158	1.191	1.225	1.260	1.295	1.331	1.368	1.405	1.443	1.482	1.521	1.561	1.602	1.643	1.685	1.728
4	1.170	1.216	1.262	1.311	1.360	1.412	1.464	1.518	1.574	1.630	1.689	1.749	1.811	1.874	1.939	2.005	2.074
5	1.217	1.276	1.338	1.403	1.469	1.539	1.611	1.685	1.762	1.842	1.925	2.011	2.100	2.192	2.288	2.386	2.488
6	1.265	1.340	1.419	1.501	1.587	1.677	1.772	1.870	1.974	2.082	2.195	2.313	2.436	2.565	2.700	2.840	2.986
7	1.316	1.407	1.504	1.606	1.714	1.828	1.949	2.076	2.211	2.353	2.502	2.660	2.826	3.001	3.185	3.379	3.583
8	1.369	1.477	1.594	1.718	1.851	1.993	2.144	2.305	2.476	2.658	2.853	3.059	3.278	3.511	3.759	4.021	4.300
9	1.423	1.551	1.689	1.838	1.999	2.172	2.358	2.558	2.773	3.004	3.252	3.518	3.803	4.108	4.435	4.785	5.160
10	1.480	1.629	1.791	1.967	2.159	2.367	2.594	2.839	3.106	3.395	3.707	4.046	4.411	4.807	5.234	5.695	6.192
11	1.539	1.710	1.898	2.105	2.332	2.580	2.853	3.152	3.479	3.836	4.226	4.652	5.117	5.624	6.176	6.777	7.430
12	1.601	1.796	2.012	2.252	2.518	2.813	3.138	3.498	3.896	4.335	4.818	5.350	5.936	6.580	7.288	8.064	8.916
13	1.665	1.886	2.133	2.410	2.720	3.066	3.452	3.883	4.363	4.898	5.492	6.153	6.886	7.699	8.599	9.596	10.699
14	1.732	1.980	2.261	2.579	2.937	3.342	3.797	4.310	4.887	5.535	6.261	7.076	7.988	9.007	10.147	11.420	12.839
15	1.801	2.079	2.397	2.759	3.172	3.642	4.177	4.785	5.474	6.254	7.138	8.137	9.266	10.539	11.974	13.590	15.407
16	1.873	2.183	2.540	2.952	3.426	3.970	4.595	5.311	6.130	7.067	8.137	9.358	10.748	12.330	14.129	16.172	18.488
17	1.948	2.292	2.693	3.159	3.700	4.328	5.054	5.895	6.866	7.986	9.276	10.761	12.468	14.426	16.672	19.244	22.186
18	2.026	2.407	2.854	3.380	3.996	4.717	5.560	6.544	7.690	9.024	10.575	12.375	14.463	16.879	19.673	22.901	26.623
19	2.107	2.527	3.026	3.617	4.316	5.142	6.116	7.263	8.613	10.197	12.056	14.232	16.777	19.748	23.214	27.252	31.948
20	2.191	2.653	3.207	3.870	4.661	5.604	6.727	8.062	9.646	11.523	13.743	16.367	19.461	23.106	27.393	32.429	38.338
30	3.243	4.322	5.743	7.612	10.063	13.268	17.449	22.892	29.960	39.116	50.950	66.212	85.850	111.065	143.371	184.675	237.376

Exhibit 14C–2 Future Value of an Annuity of $1 in Arrears; $\frac{(1+r)^n - 1}{r}$

Periods	4%	5%	6%	7%	8%	9%	10%	11%	12%	13%	14%	15%	16%	17%	18%	19%	20%
1	1.000	1.000	1.000	1.000	1.000	1.000	1.000	1.000	1.000	1.000	1.000	1.000	1.000	1.000	1.000	1.000	1.000
2	2.040	2.050	2.060	2.070	2.080	2.090	2.100	2.110	2.120	2.130	2.140	2.150	2.160	2.170	2.180	2.190	2.200
3	3.122	3.153	3.184	3.215	3.246	3.278	3.310	3.342	3.374	3.407	3.440	3.473	3.506	3.539	3.572	3.606	3.640
4	4.246	4.310	4.375	4.440	4.506	4.573	4.641	4.710	4.779	4.850	4.921	4.993	5.066	5.141	5.215	5.291	5.368
5	5.416	5.526	5.637	5.751	5.867	5.985	6.105	6.228	6.353	6.480	6.610	6.742	6.877	7.014	7.154	7.297	7.442
6	6.633	6.802	6.975	7.153	7.336	7.523	7.716	7.913	8.115	8.323	8.536	8.754	8.977	9.207	9.442	9.683	9.930
7	7.898	8.142	8.394	8.654	8.923	9.200	9.487	9.783	10.089	10.405	10.730	11.067	11.414	11.772	12.142	12.523	12.916
8	9.214	9.549	9.897	10.260	10.637	11.028	11.436	11.859	12.300	12.757	13.233	13.727	14.240	14.773	15.327	15.902	16.499
9	10.583	11.027	11.491	11.978	12.488	13.021	13.579	14.164	14.776	15.416	16.085	16.786	17.519	18.285	19.086	19.923	20.799
10	12.006	12.578	13.181	13.816	14.487	15.193	15.937	16.722	17.549	18.420	19.337	20.304	21.321	22.393	23.521	24.709	25.959
11	13.486	14.207	14.972	15.784	16.645	17.560	18.531	19.561	20.655	21.814	23.045	24.349	25.733	27.200	28.755	30.404	32.150
12	15.026	15.917	16.870	17.888	18.977	20.141	21.384	22.713	24.133	25.650	27.271	29.002	30.850	32.824	34.931	37.180	39.581
13	16.627	17.713	18.882	20.141	21.495	22.953	24.523	26.212	28.029	29.985	32.089	34.352	36.786	39.404	42.219	45.244	48.497
14	18.292	19.599	21.015	22.550	24.215	26.019	27.975	30.095	32.393	34.883	37.581	40.505	43.672	47.103	50.818	54.841	59.196
15	20.024	21.579	23.276	25.129	27.152	29.361	31.772	34.405	37.280	40.417	43.842	47.580	51.660	56.110	60.965	66.261	72.035
16	21.825	23.657	25.673	27.888	30.324	33.003	35.950	39.190	42.753	46.672	50.980	55.717	60.925	66.649	72.939	79.850	87.442
17	23.698	25.840	28.213	30.840	33.750	36.974	40.545	44.501	48.884	53.739	59.118	65.075	71.673	78.979	87.068	96.022	105.931
18	25.645	28.132	30.906	33.999	37.450	41.301	45.599	50.396	55.750	61.725	68.394	75.836	84.141	93.406	103.740	115.266	128.117
19	27.671	30.539	33.760	37.379	41.446	46.018	51.159	56.939	63.440	70.749	78.969	88.212	98.603	110.285	123.414	138.166	154.740
20	29.778	33.066	36.786	40.995	45.762	51.160	57.275	64.203	72.052	80.947	91.025	102.444	115.380	130.033	146.628	165.418	186.688
30	56.085	66.439	79.058	94.461	113.283	136.308	164.494	199.021	241.333	293.199	356.787	434.745	530.312	647.439	790.948	966.712	1181.882

Exhibit 14C–3 Present Value of $1; $\frac{1}{(1 + r)^n}$

Periods	4%	5%	6%	7%	8%	9%	10%	11%	12%	13%	14%	15%	16%	17%	18%	19%	20%	21%	22%	23%	24%	25%
1	0.962	0.952	0.943	0.935	0.926	0.917	0.909	0.901	0.893	0.885	0.877	0.870	0.862	0.855	0.847	0.840	0.833	0.826	0.820	0.813	0.806	0.800
2	0.925	0.907	0.890	0.873	0.857	0.842	0.826	0.812	0.797	0.783	0.769	0.756	0.743	0.731	0.718	0.706	0.694	0.683	0.672	0.661	0.650	0.640
3	0.889	0.864	0.840	0.816	0.794	0.772	0.751	0.731	0.712	0.693	0.675	0.658	0.641	0.624	0.609	0.593	0.579	0.564	0.551	0.537	0.524	0.512
4	0.855	0.823	0.792	0.763	0.735	0.708	0.683	0.659	0.636	0.613	0.592	0.572	0.552	0.534	0.516	0.499	0.482	0.467	0.451	0.437	0.423	0.410
5	0.822	0.784	0.747	0.713	0.681	0.650	0.621	0.593	0.567	0.543	0.519	0.497	0.476	0.456	0.437	0.419	0.402	0.386	0.370	0.355	0.341	0.328
6	0.790	0.746	0.705	0.666	0.630	0.596	0.564	0.535	0.507	0.480	0.456	0.432	0.410	0.390	0.370	0.352	0.335	0.319	0.303	0.289	0.275	0.262
7	0.760	0.711	0.665	0.623	0.583	0.547	0.513	0.482	0.452	0.425	0.400	0.376	0.354	0.333	0.314	0.296	0.279	0.263	0.249	0.235	0.222	0.210
8	0.731	0.677	0.627	0.582	0.540	0.502	0.467	0.434	0.404	0.376	0.351	0.327	0.305	0.285	0.266	0.249	0.233	0.218	0.204	0.191	0.179	0.168
9	0.703	0.645	0.592	0.544	0.500	0.460	0.424	0.391	0.361	0.333	0.308	0.284	0.263	0.243	0.225	0.209	0.194	0.180	0.167	0.155	0.144	0.134
10	0.676	0.614	0.558	0.508	0.463	0.422	0.386	0.352	0.322	0.295	0.270	0.247	0.227	0.208	0.191	0.176	0.162	0.149	0.137	0.126	0.116	0.107
11	0.650	0.585	0.527	0.475	0.429	0.388	0.350	0.317	0.287	0.261	0.237	0.215	0.195	0.178	0.162	0.148	0.135	0.123	0.112	0.103	0.094	0.086
12	0.625	0.557	0.497	0.444	0.397	0.356	0.319	0.286	0.257	0.231	0.208	0.187	0.168	0.152	0.137	0.124	0.112	0.102	0.092	0.083	0.076	0.069
13	0.601	0.530	0.469	0.415	0.368	0.326	0.290	0.258	0.229	0.204	0.182	0.163	0.145	0.130	0.116	0.104	0.093	0.084	0.075	0.068	0.061	0.055
14	0.577	0.505	0.442	0.388	0.340	0.299	0.263	0.232	0.205	0.181	0.160	0.141	0.125	0.111	0.099	0.088	0.078	0.069	0.062	0.055	0.049	0.044
15	0.555	0.481	0.417	0.362	0.315	0.275	0.239	0.209	0.183	0.160	0.140	0.123	0.108	0.095	0.084	0.074	0.065	0.057	0.051	0.045	0.040	0.035
16	0.534	0.458	0.394	0.339	0.292	0.252	0.218	0.188	0.163	0.141	0.123	0.107	0.093	0.081	0.071	0.062	0.054	0.047	0.042	0.036	0.032	0.028
17	0.513	0.436	0.371	0.317	0.270	0.231	0.198	0.170	0.146	0.125	0.108	0.093	0.080	0.069	0.060	0.052	0.045	0.039	0.034	0.030	0.026	0.023
18	0.494	0.416	0.350	0.296	0.250	0.212	0.180	0.153	0.130	0.111	0.095	0.081	0.069	0.059	0.051	0.044	0.038	0.032	0.028	0.024	0.021	0.018
19	0.475	0.396	0.331	0.277	0.232	0.194	0.164	0.138	0.116	0.098	0.083	0.070	0.060	0.051	0.043	0.037	0.031	0.027	0.023	0.020	0.017	0.014
20	0.456	0.377	0.312	0.258	0.215	0.178	0.149	0.124	0.104	0.087	0.073	0.061	0.051	0.043	0.037	0.031	0.026	0.022	0.019	0.016	0.014	0.012
21	0.439	0.359	0.294	0.242	0.199	0.164	0.135	0.112	0.093	0.077	0.064	0.053	0.044	0.037	0.031	0.026	0.022	0.018	0.015	0.013	0.011	0.009
22	0.422	0.342	0.278	0.226	0.184	0.150	0.123	0.101	0.083	0.068	0.056	0.046	0.038	0.032	0.026	0.022	0.018	0.015	0.013	0.011	0.009	0.007
23	0.406	0.326	0.262	0.211	0.170	0.138	0.112	0.091	0.074	0.060	0.049	0.040	0.033	0.027	0.022	0.018	0.015	0.012	0.010	0.009	0.007	0.006
24	0.390	0.310	0.247	0.197	0.158	0.126	0.102	0.082	0.066	0.053	0.043	0.035	0.028	0.023	0.019	0.015	0.013	0.010	0.008	0.007	0.006	0.005
25	0.375	0.295	0.233	0.184	0.146	0.116	0.092	0.074	0.059	0.047	0.038	0.030	0.024	0.020	0.016	0.013	0.010	0.009	0.007	0.006	0.005	0.004
26	0.361	0.281	0.220	0.172	0.135	0.106	0.084	0.066	0.053	0.042	0.033	0.026	0.021	0.017	0.014	0.011	0.009	0.007	0.006	0.005	0.004	0.003
27	0.347	0.268	0.207	0.161	0.125	0.098	0.076	0.060	0.047	0.037	0.029	0.023	0.018	0.014	0.011	0.009	0.007	0.006	0.005	0.004	0.003	0.002
28	0.333	0.255	0.196	0.150	0.116	0.090	0.069	0.054	0.042	0.033	0.026	0.020	0.016	0.012	0.010	0.008	0.006	0.005	0.004	0.003	0.002	0.002
29	0.321	0.243	0.185	0.141	0.107	0.082	0.063	0.048	0.037	0.029	0.022	0.017	0.014	0.011	0.008	0.006	0.005	0.004	0.003	0.002	0.002	0.002
30	0.308	0.231	0.174	0.131	0.099	0.075	0.057	0.044	0.033	0.026	0.020	0.015	0.012	0.009	0.007	0.005	0.004	0.003	0.003	0.002	0.002	0.001
40	0.208	0.142	0.097	0.067	0.046	0.032	0.022	0.015	0.011	0.008	0.005	0.004	0.003	0.002	0.001	0.001	0.001	0.000	0.000	0.000	0.000	0.000

Exhibit 14C–4 Present Value of an Annuity of $1 in Arrears; $\frac{1}{r}\left[1 - \frac{1}{(1+r)^n}\right]$

Periods	4%	5%	6%	7%	8%	9%	10%	11%	12%	13%	14%	15%	16%	17%	18%	19%	20%	21%	22%	23%	24%	25%
1	0.962	0.952	0.943	0.935	0.926	0.917	0.909	0.901	0.893	0.885	0.877	0.870	0.862	0.855	0.847	0.840	0.833	0.826	0.820	0.813	0.806	0.800
2	1.886	1.859	1.833	1.808	1.783	1.759	1.736	1.713	1.690	1.668	1.647	1.626	1.605	1.585	1.566	1.547	1.528	1.509	1.492	1.474	1.457	1.440
3	2.775	2.723	2.673	2.624	2.577	2.531	2.487	2.444	2.402	2.361	2.322	2.283	2.246	2.210	2.174	2.140	2.106	2.074	2.042	2.011	1.981	1.952
4	3.630	3.546	3.465	3.387	3.312	3.240	3.170	3.102	3.037	2.974	2.914	2.855	2.798	2.743	2.690	2.639	2.589	2.540	2.494	2.448	2.404	2.362
5	4.452	4.329	4.212	4.100	3.993	3.890	3.791	3.696	3.605	3.517	3.433	3.352	3.274	3.199	3.127	3.058	2.991	2.926	2.864	2.803	2.745	2.689
6	5.242	5.076	4.917	4.767	4.623	4.486	4.355	4.231	4.111	3.998	3.889	3.784	3.685	3.589	3.498	3.410	3.326	3.245	3.167	3.092	3.020	2.951
7	6.002	5.786	5.582	5.389	5.206	5.033	4.868	4.712	4.564	4.423	4.288	4.160	4.039	3.922	3.812	3.706	3.605	3.508	3.416	3.327	3.242	3.161
8	6.733	6.463	6.210	5.971	5.747	5.535	5.335	5.146	4.968	4.799	4.639	4.487	4.344	4.207	4.078	3.954	3.837	3.726	3.619	3.518	3.421	3.329
9	7.435	7.108	6.802	6.515	6.247	5.995	5.759	5.537	5.328	5.132	4.946	4.772	4.607	4.451	4.303	4.163	4.031	3.905	3.786	3.673	3.566	3.463
10	8.111	7.722	7.360	7.024	6.710	6.418	6.145	5.889	5.650	5.426	5.216	5.019	4.833	4.659	4.494	4.339	4.192	4.054	3.923	3.799	3.682	3.571
11	8.760	8.306	7.887	7.499	7.139	6.805	6.495	6.207	5.938	5.687	5.453	5.234	5.029	4.836	4.656	4.486	4.327	4.177	4.035	3.902	3.776	3.656
12	9.385	8.863	8.384	7.943	7.536	7.161	6.814	6.492	6.194	5.918	5.660	5.421	5.197	4.988	4.793	4.611	4.439	4.278	4.127	3.985	3.851	3.725
13	9.986	9.394	8.853	8.358	7.904	7.487	7.103	6.750	6.424	6.122	5.842	5.583	5.342	5.118	4.910	4.715	4.533	4.362	4.203	4.053	3.912	3.780
14	10.563	9.899	9.295	8.745	8.244	7.786	7.367	6.982	6.628	6.302	6.002	5.724	5.468	5.229	5.008	4.802	4.611	4.432	4.265	4.108	3.962	3.824
15	11.118	10.380	9.712	9.108	8.559	8.061	7.606	7.191	6.811	6.462	6.142	5.847	5.575	5.324	5.092	4.876	4.675	4.489	4.315	4.153	4.001	3.859
16	11.652	10.838	10.106	9.447	8.851	8.313	7.824	7.379	6.974	6.604	6.265	5.954	5.668	5.405	5.162	4.938	4.730	4.536	4.357	4.189	4.033	3.887
17	12.166	11.274	10.477	9.763	9.122	8.544	8.022	7.549	7.120	6.729	6.373	6.047	5.749	5.475	5.222	4.990	4.775	4.576	4.391	4.219	4.059	3.910
18	12.659	11.690	10.828	10.059	9.372	8.756	8.201	7.702	7.250	6.840	6.467	6.128	5.818	5.534	5.273	5.033	4.812	4.608	4.419	4.243	4.080	3.928
19	13.134	12.085	11.158	10.336	9.604	8.950	8.365	7.839	7.366	6.938	6.550	6.198	5.877	5.584	5.316	5.070	4.843	4.635	4.442	4.263	4.097	3.942
20	13.590	12.462	11.470	10.594	9.818	9.129	8.514	7.963	7.469	7.025	6.623	6.259	5.929	5.628	5.353	5.101	4.870	4.657	4.460	4.279	4.110	3.954
21	14.029	12.821	11.764	10.836	10.017	9.292	8.649	8.075	7.562	7.102	6.687	6.312	5.973	5.665	5.384	5.127	4.891	4.675	4.476	4.292	4.121	3.963
22	14.451	13.163	12.042	11.061	10.201	9.442	8.772	8.176	7.645	7.170	6.743	6.359	6.011	5.696	5.410	5.149	4.909	4.690	4.488	4.302	4.130	3.970
23	14.857	13.489	12.303	11.272	10.371	9.580	8.883	8.266	7.718	7.230	6.792	6.399	6.044	5.723	5.432	5.167	4.925	4.703	4.499	4.311	4.137	3.976
24	15.247	13.799	12.550	11.469	10.529	9.707	8.985	8.348	7.784	7.283	6.835	6.434	6.073	5.746	5.451	5.182	4.937	4.713	4.507	4.318	4.143	3.981
25	15.622	14.094	12.783	11.654	10.675	9.823	9.077	8.422	7.843	7.330	6.873	6.464	6.097	5.766	5.467	5.195	4.948	4.721	4.514	4.323	4.147	3.985
26	15.983	14.375	13.003	11.826	10.810	9.929	9.161	8.488	7.896	7.372	6.906	6.491	6.118	5.783	5.480	5.206	4.956	4.728	4.520	4.328	4.151	3.988
27	16.330	14.643	13.211	11.987	10.935	10.027	9.237	8.548	7.943	7.409	6.935	6.514	6.136	5.798	5.492	5.215	4.964	4.734	4.524	4.332	4.154	3.990
28	16.663	14.898	13.406	12.137	11.051	10.116	9.307	8.602	7.984	7.441	6.961	6.534	6.152	5.810	5.502	5.223	4.970	4.739	4.528	4.335	4.157	3.992
29	16.984	15.141	13.591	12.278	11.158	10.198	9.370	8.650	8.022	7.470	6.983	6.551	6.166	5.820	5.510	5.229	4.975	4.743	4.531	4.337	4.159	3.994
30	17.292	15.372	13.765	12.409	11.258	10.274	9.427	8.694	8.055	7.496	7.003	6.566	6.177	5.829	5.517	5.235	4.979	4.746	4.534	4.339	4.160	3.995
40	19.793	17.159	15.046	13.332	11.925	10.757	9.779	8.951	8.244	7.634	7.105	6.642	6.233	5.871	5.548	5.258	4.997	4.760	4.544	4.347	4.166	3.999

Appendix 14D: Income Taxes in Capital Budgeting Decisions

LEARNING OBJECTIVE 8
Include income taxes in a capital budgeting analysis.

In our discussion of capital budgeting, we ignored income taxes for two reasons. First, many organizations do not pay income taxes. Not-for-profit organizations, such as hospitals and charitable foundations, and governmental agencies are exempt from income taxes. Second, capital budgeting is complex and is best absorbed in small doses. Now that we have a solid groundwork in the concepts of present value and discounting, we can explore the effects of income taxes on capital budgeting decisions.

The U.S. income tax code is enormously complex. We only scratch the surface in this text. To keep the subject within reasonable bounds, we have made many simplifying assumptions about the tax code throughout the chapter. Among the most important of these assumptions are: (1) taxable income equals net income as computed for financial reports; and (2) the tax rate is a flat percentage of taxable income. The actual tax code is far more complex than this; indeed, experts acknowledge that no one person knows or can know it all. However, the simplifications that we make throughout this appendix allow us to cover the most important implications of income taxes for capital budgeting without getting bogged down in details.

The Concept of After-Tax Cost

Businesses, like individuals, must pay income taxes. In the case of businesses, the amount of income tax that must be paid is determined by the company's net taxable income. Tax deductible expenses (tax deductions) decrease the company's net taxable income and hence reduce the taxes the company must pay. For this reason, expenses are often stated on an *after-tax* basis. For example, if a company pays rent of $10 million a year but this expense results in a reduction in income taxes of $3 million, the after-tax cost of the rent is $7 million. An expenditure net of its tax effect is known as **after-tax cost.**

To illustrate, assume that a company with a tax rate of 30% is contemplating a training program that costs $60,000. What impact will this have on the company's taxes? To keep matters simple, let's suppose the training program has no immediate effect on sales. How much does the company actually pay for the training program after taking into account the impact of this expense on taxes? The answer is $42,000 as shown in Exhibit 14D–1. While the training program costs $60,000 before taxes, it would reduce the company's taxes by $18,000, so its *after-tax* cost would be only $42,000.

Exhibit 14D–1
The Computation of After-Tax Cost

	Without Training Program		With Training Program
Sales	$850,000		$850,000
Less tax deductible expenses:			
Salaries, insurance, and other	700,000		700,000
New training program			60,000
Total expenses	700,000		760,000
Taxable income	$150,000		$ 90,000
Income taxes (30%)	$ 45,000		$ 27,000
Cost of new training program		$60,000	
Less: Reduction in income taxes ($45,000 − $27,000)		18,000	
After-tax cost of the new training program		$42,000	

The after-tax cost of any tax-deductible cash expense can be determined using the following formula:[1]

$$\begin{array}{c}\text{After-tax cost}\\ \text{(net cash outflow)}\end{array} = (1 - \text{Tax rate}) \times \text{Tax-deductible cash expense} \qquad (1)$$

We can verify the accuracy of this formula by applying it to the $60,000 training program expenditure:

$$(1 - 0.30) \times \$60{,}000 = \$42{,}000 \text{ after-tax cost of the training program}$$

This formula is very useful since it provides the actual amount of cash a company must pay after taking into consideration tax effects. It is this actual, after-tax, cash outflow that should be used in capital budgeting decisions.

Similar reasoning applies to revenues and other *taxable* cash inflows. Since these cash receipts are taxable, the company must pay out a portion of them in taxes. The **after-tax benefit,** or net cash inflow, realized from a particular cash receipt can be obtained by applying a simple variation of the cash expenditure formula used above:

$$\begin{array}{c}\text{After-tax benefit}\\ \text{(net cash inflow)}\end{array} = (1 - \text{Tax rate}) \times \text{Taxable cash receipt} \qquad (2)$$

We emphasize the term *taxable cash receipts* because not all cash inflows are taxable. For example, the release of working capital at the termination of an investment project would not be a taxable cash inflow. It is not counted as income for either financial accounting or income tax reporting purposes since it is simply a recovery of the initial investment.

Depreciation Tax Shield

Depreciation is not a cash flow. For this reason, depreciation was ignored in Chapter 14 in all discounted cash flow computations. However, depreciation does affect the taxes that must be paid and therefore has an indirect effect on the company's cash flows.

To illustrate the effect of depreciation deductions on tax payments, consider a company with annual cash sales of $500,000 and cash operating expenses of $310,000. In addition, the company has a depreciable asset on which the depreciation deduction is $90,000 per year. The tax rate is 30%. As shown in Exhibit 14D–2, the depreciation deduction reduces the company's taxes by $27,000. In effect, the depreciation deduction of $90,000 *shields* $90,000 in revenues from taxation and thereby *reduces* the amount of taxes that the company must pay. Because depreciation deductions shield revenues from taxation, they are generally referred to as a **depreciation tax shield.**[2] The reduction in tax payments made possible by the depreciation tax shield is equal to the amount of the depreciation deduction, multiplied by the tax rate as follows:

$$\begin{array}{c}\text{Tax savings from the}\\ \text{depreciation tax shield}\end{array} = \text{Tax rate} \times \text{Depreciation deduction} \qquad (3)$$

We can verify this formula by applying it to the $90,000 depreciation deduction in our example:

$$0.30 \times \$90{,}000 = \$27{,}000 \text{ reduction in tax payments}$$

[1] This formula assumes that a company is operating at a profit; if it is operating at a loss, the tax situation can be very complex. For simplicity, we assume in all examples, exercises, and problems that the company is operating at a profit.

[2] The term *depreciation tax shield* may convey the impression that there is something underhanded about depreciation deductions—that companies are getting some sort of a special tax break. However, to use the depreciation deduction, a company must have already acquired a depreciable asset—which typically requires a cash outflow. Essentially, the tax code requires companies to delay recognizing the cash outflow as an expense until depreciation charges are recorded.

Exhibit 14D–2
The Impact of Depreciation Deductions on Tax Payments

	Without Depreciation Deduction	With Depreciation Deduction
Sales	$500,000	$500,000
Cash operating expenses	310,000	310,000
Cash flow from operations	190,000	190,000
Depreciation expense	—	90,000
Taxable income	$190,000	$100,000
Income taxes (30%)	$ 57,000	$ 30,000
	$27,000 lower taxes with the depreciation deduction	
Cash flow comparison:		
Cash flow from operations (above)	$190,000	$190,000
Income taxes (above)	57,000	30,000
Net cash flow	$133,000	$160,000
	$27,000 greater cash flow with the depreciation deduction	

Exhibit 14D–3
Tax Adjustments Required in a Capital Budgeting Analysis

Item	Treatment
Tax-deductible cash expense*	Multiply by (1 − Tax rate) to get after-tax cost.
Taxable cash receipt*	Multiply by (1 − Tax rate) to get after-tax cash inflow.
Depreciation deduction	Multiply by the tax rate to get the tax savings from the depreciation tax shield.

*Cash expenses can be deducted from the cash receipts and the difference multiplied by (1 − Tax rate). See the example at the top of Exhibit 14D–4.

In this appendix, when we estimate after-tax cash flows for capital budgeting decisions, we will include the tax savings provided by the depreciation tax shield.

To keep matters simple, we will assume in all of our examples and problem materials that depreciation reported for tax purposes is straight-line depreciation, with no deduction for zero salvage. In other words, we will assume that the entire original cost of the asset is written off evenly over its useful life. Since the net book value of the asset at the end of its useful life will be zero under this depreciation method, we will assume that any proceeds received on disposal of the asset at the end of its useful life will be taxed as ordinary income.

In actuality, the rules for depreciation are more complex than this and most companies take advantage of accelerated depreciation methods allowed under the tax code. These accelerated methods usually result in a reduction in current taxes and an offsetting increase in future taxes. This shifting of part of the tax burden from the current year to future years is advantageous from a present value point of view, since a dollar today is worth more than a dollar in the future. A summary of the concepts we have introduced so far is given in Exhibit 14D–3.

Example of Income Taxes and Capital Budgeting

Armed with an understanding of after-tax cost, after-tax revenue, and the depreciation tax shield, we are now prepared to examine a comprehensive example of income taxes and capital budgeting.

Holland Company owns the mineral rights to land that has a deposit of ore. The company is uncertain as to whether it should purchase equipment and open a mine on the property. After careful study, the following data have been assembled by the company:

Cost of equipment needed	$300,000
Working capital needed	75,000
Estimated annual cash receipts from sales of ore	250,000
Estimated annual cash expenses for salaries, insurance, utilities, and other cash expenses of mining the ore	170,000
Cost of road repairs needed in 6 years	40,000
Salvage value of the equipment in 10 years	100,000

The ore in the mine would be exhausted after 10 years of mining activity, at which time the mine would be closed. The equipment would then be sold for its salvage value. Holland Company uses the straight-line method, assuming no salvage value, to compute depreciation deductions for tax purposes. The company's after-tax cost of capital is 12% and its tax rate is 30%.

Should Holland Company purchase the equipment and open a mine on the property? The solution to the problem is given in Exhibit 14D–4. We suggest that you go through this solution item by item and note the following points:

Cost of new equipment. The initial investment of $300,000 in the new equipment is included in full with no reductions for taxes. This represents an *investment,* not an expense, so no tax adjustment is made. (Only revenues and expenses are adjusted for the effects of taxes.) However, this investment does affect taxes through the depreciation deductions that are considered below.

Working capital. Observe that the working capital needed for the project is included in full with no reductions for taxes. Like the cost of new equipment, working

Exhibit 14D–4 Example of Income Taxes and Capital Budgeting

	Per Year
Cash receipts from sales of ore	$250,000
Less payments for salaries, insurance, utilities, and other cash expenses	170,000
Net cash receipts	$ 80,000

Items and Computations	Year(s)	(1) Amount	(2) Tax Effect*	After-Tax Cash Flows (1) × (2)	12% Factor	Present Value of Cash Flows
Cost of new equipment	Now	$(300,000)	—	$(300,000)	1.000	$(300,000)
Working capital needed	Now	(75,000)	—	(75,000)	1.000	(75,000)
Net annual cash receipts (above)	1–10	80,000	1 – 0.30	56,000	5.650	316,400
Road repairs	6	(40,000)	1 – 0.30	(28,000)	0.507	(14,196)
Annual depreciation deductions	1–10	30,000	0.30	9,000	5.650	50,850
Salvage value of equipment	10	100,000	1 – 0.30	70,000	0.322	22,540
Release of working capital	10	75,000	—	75,000	0.322	24,150
Net present value						$ 24,744

*Taxable cash receipts and tax-deductible cash expenses are multiplied by (1 − Tax rate) to determine the after-tax cash flow. Depreciation deductions are multiplied by the tax rate itself to determine the after-tax cash flow (i.e., tax savings from the depreciation tax shield).

capital is an investment and not an expense so no tax adjustment is made. Also observe that no tax adjustment is made when the working capital is released at the end of the project's life. The release of working capital is not a taxable cash flow, since it merely represents a return of investment funds back to the company.

Net annual cash receipts. The net annual cash receipts from sales of ore are adjusted for the effects of income taxes, as discussed earlier in the chapter. Note at the top of Exhibit 14D–4 that the annual cash expenses are deducted from the annual cash receipts to obtain the net cash receipts. This just simplifies computations.

Road repairs. Since the road repairs occur just once (in the sixth year), they are treated separately from other expenses. Road repairs would be a tax-deductible cash expense, and therefore they are adjusted for the effects of income taxes, as discussed earlier in the chapter.

Depreciation deductions. The equipment is in the MACRS seven-year property class. The tax savings provided by depreciation deductions is essentially an annuity that is included in the present value computations in the same way as other cash flows.

Salvage value of equipment. Since the company does not consider salvage value when computing depreciation deductions, book value will be zero at the end of the life of an asset. Thus, any salvage value received is taxable as income to the company. The after-tax benefit is determined by multiplying the salvage value by (1 − Tax rate).

Since the net present value of the proposed mining project is positive, the equipment should be purchased and the mine opened. Study Exhibit 14D–4 thoroughly. *Exhibit 14D–4 is the key exhibit!*

Summary (Appendix 14D)

Unless a company is a tax-exempt organization, such as a not-for-profit school or a governmental unit, income taxes should be considered in making capital budgeting decisions. Tax-deductible cash expenditures and taxable cash receipts are placed on an after-tax basis by multiplying them by (1 − Tax rate). Only the after-tax amount should be used in determining the desirability of an investment proposal.

Although depreciation is not a cash outflow, it is a valid deduction for tax purposes and as such affects income tax payments. The depreciation tax shield—computed by multiplying the depreciation deduction by the tax rate itself—also results in savings in income taxes.

Glossary (Appendix 14D)

After-tax benefit The amount of net cash inflow realized from a taxable cash receipt after income tax effects have been considered. The amount is determined by multiplying the taxable cash receipt by (1 − Tax rate). (p. 674)

After-tax cost The amount of net cash outflow resulting from a tax-deductible cash expense after income tax effects have been considered. The amount is determined by multiplying the tax-deductible cash expense by (1 − Tax rate). (p. 673)

Depreciation tax shield A reduction in tax that results from depreciation deductions. The reduction in tax is computed by multiplying the depreciation deduction by the tax rate. (p. 674)

Questions

14–1 What is the difference between capital budgeting screening decisions and capital budgeting preference decisions?

14–2 What is meant by the term *time value of money?*

14–3 What is meant by the term *discounting?*

14–4 Why isn't accounting net income used in the net present value and internal rate of return methods of making capital budgeting decisions?

14–5 Why are discounted cash flow methods of making capital budgeting decisions superior to other methods?

14–6 What is net present value? Can it ever be negative? Explain.

14–7 Identify two simplifying assumptions associated with discounted cash flow methods of making capital budgeting decisions.

14–8 If a firm has to pay interest of 14% on long-term debt, then its cost of capital is 14%. Do you agree? Explain.

14–9 What is meant by an investment project's internal rate of return? How is the internal rate of return computed?

14–10 Explain how the cost of capital serves as a screening tool when dealing with (*a*) the net present value method and (*b*) the internal rate of return method.

14–11 As the discount rate increases, the present value of a given future cash flow also increases. Do you agree? Explain.

14–12 Refer to Exhibit 14–4. Is the return on this investment proposal exactly 14%, more than 14%, or less than 14%? Explain.

14–13 How is the profitability index computed, and what does it measure?

14–14 Can an investment with a profitability index of less than 1.00 be an acceptable investment? Explain.

14–15 What is meant by the term *payback period?* How is the payback period determined? How can the payback method be useful?

14–16 What is the major criticism of the payback and simple rate of return methods of making capital budgeting decisions?

14–17 (Appendix 14D) What is meant by after-tax cost and how is the concept used in capital budgeting decisions?

14–18 (Appendix 14D) What is a depreciation tax shield and how does it affect capital budgeting decisions?

14–19 (Appendix 14D) Ludlow Company is considering the introduction of a new product line. Would an increase in the income tax rate tend to make the new investment more or less attractive? Explain.

14–20 (Appendix 14D) Assume that an old piece of equipment is sold at a loss. From a capital budgeting point of view, what two cash inflows will be associated with the sale?

14–21 (Appendix 14D) Assume that a new piece of equipment costs $40,000 and that the tax rate is 30%. Should the new piece of equipment be shown in the capital budgeting analysis as a cash outflow of $40,000, or should it be shown as a cash outflow of $28,000 [$40,000 × (1 − 0.30)]? Explain.

Exercises

EXERCISE 14–1 (Appendix 14A) Basic Present Value Concepts [LO7]

Consider each of the following situations independently. (Ignore income taxes.)

1. Annual cash inflows from two competing investment opportunities are given below. Each investment opportunity will require the same initial investment. Compute the present value of the cash inflows for each investment using a 20% discount rate.

	Investment	
Year	X	Y
1	$ 1,000	$ 4,000
2	2,000	3,000
3	3,000	2,000
4	4,000	1,000
	$10,000	$10,000

2. At the end of three years, when you graduate from college, your father has promised to give you a used car that will cost $12,000. What lump sum must he invest now to have the $12,000 at the end of three years if he can invest money at:

a. Six percent?
b. Ten percent?

3. Mark has just won the grand prize on the "Hoot 'n' Holler" quiz show. He has a choice between (*a*) receiving $500,000 immediately and (*b*) receiving $60,000 per year for eight years plus a lump sum of $200,000 at the end of the eight-year period. If Mark can get a return of 10% on his investments, which option would you recommend that he accept? (Use present value analysis, and show all computations.)
4. You have just learned that you are a beneficiary in the will of your late Aunt Susan. The executrix of her estate has given you three options as to how you may receive your inheritance:
   a. You may receive $50,000 immediately.
   b. You may receive $75,000 at the end of six years.
   c. You may receive $12,000 at the end of each year for six years (a total of $72,000).
   If you can invest money at a 12% return, which option would you prefer?

EXERCISE 14–2 Basic Net Present Value Analysis [LO1]

On January 2, Fred Critchfield paid $18,000 for 900 shares of the common stock of Acme Company. Mr. Critchfield received an $0.80 per share dividend on the stock at the end of each year for four years. At the end of four years, he sold the stock for $22,500. Mr. Critchfield has a goal of earning a minimum return of 12% on all of his investments.

Required:

Did Mr. Critchfield earn a 12% return on the stock? Use the net present value method and the general format shown in Exhibit 14–4. (Ignore income taxes. Round all computations to the nearest whole dollar.)

EXERCISE 14–3 Internal Rate of Return [LO2]

Pisa Pizza Parlor is investigating the purchase of a new delivery truck that would contain specially designed warming racks. The new truck would cost $45,000 and have a six-year useful life. It would save $5,400 per year over the present method of delivering pizzas. In addition, it would result in delivery of about 1,800 more pizzas each year. The company realizes a contribution margin of $2 per pizza.

Required:

(Ignore income taxes.)

1. What would be the total annual cash inflows associated with the new truck for capital budgeting purposes?
2. Find the internal rate of return promised by the new truck to the nearest whole percent.
3. In addition to the data above, assume that due to the unique warming racks, the truck will have a $13,000 salvage value at the end of six years. Under these conditions, compute the internal rate of return to the nearest whole percent. (Hint: You may find it helpful to use the net present value approach; find the discount rate that will cause the net present value to be closest to zero. Use the format shown in Exhibit 14–4.)

EXERCISE 14–4 Present Value Potpourri [LO1, LO3]

Solve the three following present value exercises.

1. Mountain View Hospital has purchased new lab equipment for $134,650. The equipment is expected to last for three years and to provide cash inflows as follows:

Year 1	$45,000
Year 2	60,000
Year 3	?

   Assuming that the equipment will yield exactly a 16% rate of return, what is the expected cash inflow for year 3?
2. Union Bay Plastics is investigating the purchase of a piece of automated equipment that will save $100,000 each year in direct labor and inventory carrying costs. This equipment costs $750,000 and is expected to have a 10-year useful life with no salvage value. The company requires a minimum 15% return on all equipment purchases. Management anticipates that this equipment will provide intangible benefits such as greater flexibility and higher quality output. What dollar value per year would these intangible benefits have to have in order to make the equipment an acceptable investment?
3. Worldwide Travel Service has made an investment in certain equipment that cost the company $307,100. The equipment is expected to generate cash inflows of $50,000 each year. How

many years will the equipment have to be used in order to provide the company with a 14% return on its investment?

EXERCISE 14–5 Preference Ranking [LO4]

Information on four investment proposals is given below:

	Investment Proposal			
	A	B	C	D
Investment required	$(85,000)	$(200,000)	$(90,000)	$(170,000)
Present value of cash inflows. . . .	119,000	184,000	135,000	221,000
Net present value.	$ 34,000	$ (16,000)	$ 45,000	$ 51,000
Life of the project	5 years	7 years	6 years	6 years

Required:

1. Compute the profitability index for each investment proposal.
2. Rank the proposals in terms of preference.

EXERCISE 14–6 Basic Payback Period and Simple Rate of Return Computations [LO5, LO6]

Martin Company is considering the purchase of a new piece of equipment. Relevant information concerning the equipment follows:

Purchase cost	$180,000
Annual cost savings that will be provided by the equipment.	37,500
Life of the equipment	12 years

Required:

(Ignore income taxes.)

1. Compute the payback period for the equipment. If the company rejects all proposals with a payback period of more than four years, would the equipment be purchased?
2. Compute the simple rate of return on the equipment. Use straight-line depreciation based on the equipment's useful life. Would the equipment be purchased if the company requires a rate of return of at least 14%?

EXERCISE 14–7 (Appendix 14A) Basic Present Value Concepts [LO7]

Each of the following parts is independent. (Ignore income taxes.)

1. Largo Freightlines plans to build a new garage in three years to have more space for repairing its trucks. The garage will cost $400,000. What lump-sum amount should the company invest now to have the $400,000 available at the end of the three-year period? Assume that the company can invest money at:
   a. Eight percent.
   b. Twelve percent.
2. Martell Products, Inc., can purchase a new copier that will save $5,000 per year in copying costs. The copier will last for six years and have no salvage value. What is the maximum purchase price that Martell Products would be willing to pay for the copier if the company's required rate of return is:
   a. Ten percent.
   b. Sixteen percent.
3. Sally has just won the million-dollar Big Slam jackpot at a gambling casino. The casino will pay her $50,000 per year for 20 years as the payoff. If Sally can invest money at a 10% rate of return, what is the present value of her winnings? Did she really win a million dollars? Explain.

EXERCISE 14–8 (Appendix 14D) After-Tax Costs [LO8]

a. Stoffer Company has hired a management consulting firm to review and make recommendations concerning Stoffer's organizational structure. The consulting firm's fee will be $100,000. What will be the after-tax cost of the consulting firm's fee if Stoffer's tax rate is 30%?

b. The Green Hills Riding Club has redirected its advertising toward a different sector of the market. As a result of this change in advertising, the club's annual revenues have increased by $40,000. If the club's tax rate is 30%, what is the after-tax benefit from the increased revenues?

c. The Golden Eagles Basketball Team has just installed an electronic scoreboard in its playing arena at a cost of $210,000. For tax purposes, the entire original cost of the electronic scoreboard will be depreciated over seven years, using the straight-line method. Determine the yearly tax savings from the depreciation tax shield. Assume that the income tax rate is 30%.

EXERCISE 14–9 Net Present Value Analysis of Two Alternatives [LO1]
Wriston Company has $300,000 to invest. The company is trying to decide between two alternative uses of the funds. The alternatives are as follows:

	A	B
Cost of equipment required	$300,000	$ 0
Working capital investment required	0	$300,000
Annual cash inflows	80,000	60,000
Salvage value of equipment in seven years	20,000	0
Life of the project	7 years	7 years

The working capital needed for project B will be released for investment elsewhere at the end of seven years. Wriston Company uses a 20% discount rate.

Required:
(Ignore income taxes.) Which investment alternative (if either) would you recommend that the company accept? Show all computations using the net present value format. Prepare a separate computation for each project.

EXERCISE 14–10 (Appendix 14D) After-Tax Cash Flows in Net Present Value Analysis [LO8]
Kramer Corporation is considering two investment projects, each of which would require $50,000. Cost and cash flow data concerning the two projects are given below:

	Project A	Project B
Investment in high-speed photocopier	$50,000	
Investment in working capital		$50,000
Net annual cash inflows	9,000	9,000
Life of the project	8 years	8 years

The high-speed photocopier will have a salvage value of $5,000 in eight years. For tax purposes, the company computes depreciation deductions assuming zero salvage value and uses straight-line depreciation. The photocopier would be depreciated over eight years. At the end of eight years, the investment in working capital would be released for use elsewhere. The company requires an after-tax return of 10% on all investments. The tax rate is 30%.

Required:
Compute the net present value of each investment project. (Round all dollar amounts to the nearest whole dollar.)

EXERCISE 14–11 Comparison of Projects Using Net Present Value [LO1]
Sharp Company has $15,000 to invest. The company is trying to decide between two alternative uses of the funds. The alternatives are as follows:

	Invest in Project A	Invest in Project B
Investment required	$15,000	$15,000
Annual cash inflows	4,000	0
Single cash inflow at the end of 10 years	—	60,000
Life of the project	10 years	10 years

Sharp Company uses a 16% discount rate.

Required:
(Ignore income taxes.) Which investment would you recommend that the company accept? Show all computations using net present value. Prepare a separate computation for each investment.

EXERCISE 14–12 Basic Net Present Value and Internal Rate of Return Analysis [LO1, LO2]
(Ignore income taxes.) Consider each case below independently.

PROBLEM 14–18 Simple Rate of Return; Payback [LO5, LO6]

Lugano's Pizza Parlor is considering the purchase of a large oven and related equipment for mixing and baking "crazy bread." The oven and equipment would cost $120,000 delivered and installed. It would be usable for about 15 years, after which it would have a 10% scrap value. The following additional information is available:

a. Mr. Lugano estimates that purchase of the oven and equipment would allow the pizza parlor to bake and sell 72,000 loaves of crazy bread each year. The bread sells for $1.25 per loaf.

b. The cost of the ingredients in a loaf of bread is 40% of the selling price. Mr. Lugano estimates that other costs each year associated with the bread would be the following: salaries, $18,000; utilities, $9,000; and insurance, $3,000.

c. The pizza parlor uses straight-line depreciation on all assets, deducting salvage value from original cost.

Required:

(Ignore income taxes.)

1. Prepare an income statement showing the net operating income each year from production and sale of the crazy bread. Use the contribution format.
2. Compute the simple rate of return for the new oven and equipment. If a simple rate of return above 12% is acceptable to Mr. Lugano, will he purchase the oven and equipment?
3. Compute the payback period on the oven and equipment. If Mr. Lugano purchases any equipment with less than a six-year payback, will he purchase this equipment?

PROBLEM 14–19 Basic Net Present Value Analysis [LO1]

Renfree Mines, Inc., owns the mining rights to a large tract of land in a mountainous area. The tract contains a mineral deposit that the company believes might be commercially attractive to mine and sell. An engineering and cost analysis has been made, and it is expected that the following cash flows would be associated with opening and operating a mine in the area:

Cost of equipment required	$850,000
Net annual cash receipts	230,000*
Working capital required	100,000
Cost of road repairs in three years	60,000
Salvage value of equipment in five years	200,000

*Receipts from sales of ore, less out-of-pocket costs for salaries, utilities, insurance, and so forth.

It is estimated that the mineral deposit would be exhausted after five years of mining. At that point, the working capital would be released for reinvestment elsewhere. The company's required rate of return is 14%.

Required:

(Ignore income taxes.) Determine the net present value of the proposed mining project. Should the project be accepted? Explain.

PROBLEM 14–20 Preference Ranking of Investment Projects [LO4]

Austin Company is investigating five different investment opportunities. Information on the five projects under study is given below:

	Project Number				
	1	2	3	4	5
Investment required	$(480,000)	$(360,000)	$(270,000)	$(450,000)	$(400,000)
Present value of cash inflows at a 10% discount rate	567,270	433,400	336,140	522,970	379,760
Net present value	$ 87,270	$ 73,400	$ 66,140	$ 72,970	$ (20,240)
Life of the project	6 years	12 years	6 years	3 years	5 years
Internal rate of return	16%	14%	18%	19%	8%

Since the company's required rate of return is 10%, a 10% discount rate has been used in the present value computations above. Limited funds are available for investment, so the company can't accept all of the available projects.

Required:

1. Compute the profitability index for each investment project.
2. Rank the five projects according to preference, in terms of:
   a. Net present value.
   b. Profitability index.
   c. Internal rate of return.
3. Which ranking do you prefer? Why?

PROBLEM 14–21 (Appendix 14D) Basic Net Present Value Analysis Including Income Taxes [LO8]

Rapid Parcel Service has been offered an eight-year contract to deliver mail and small parcels between army installations. To accept the contract, the company would have to purchase several new delivery trucks at a total cost of $450,000. Other data relating to the contract follow:

Net annual cash receipts (before taxes) from the contract	$108,000
Cost of overhauling the motors in the trucks in five years.	45,000
Salvage value of the trucks at termination of the contract.	20,000

If the contract were accepted, several old, fully depreciated trucks would be sold at a total price of $30,000. These funds would be used to help purchase the new trucks. For tax purposes, the company computes depreciation deductions assuming zero salvage value and uses straight-line depreciation. The trucks would be depreciated over eight years. The company requires a 12% after-tax return on all equipment purchases. The tax rate is 30%.

Required:

Compute the net present value of this investment opportunity. Round all dollar amounts to the nearest whole dollar. Would you recommend that the contract be accepted?

PROBLEM 14–22 Net Present Value Analysis [LO1]

Frank White will retire in six years. He wants to open some type of small business operation that can be managed in the free time he has available from his regular occupation, but that can be closed easily when he retires. He is considering several investment alternatives, one of which is to open a laundromat.

After careful study, Mr. White has determined the following:

a. Washers, dryers, and other equipment needed to open the laundromat would cost $194,000. In addition, $6,000 in working capital would be required to purchase an inventory of soap, bleaches, and related items and to provide change for change machines. (The soap, bleaches, and related items would be sold to customers basically at cost.) After six years, the working capital would be released for investment elsewhere.
b. The laundromat would charge $1.50 per use for the washers and $0.75 per use for the dryers. Mr. White expects the laundromat to gross $1,800 each week from the washers and $1,125 each week from the dryers.
c. The only variable costs in the laundromat would be 7½ cents per use for water and electricity for the washers and 9 cents per use for gas and electricity for the dryers.
d. Fixed costs would be $3,000 per month for rent, $1,500 per month for cleaning, and $1,875 per month for maintenance, insurance, and other items.
e. The equipment would have a 10% disposal value in six years.

Mr. White will not open the laundromat unless it provides at least a 12% return, since this is the amount that he could earn from an alternative investment opportunity.

Required:

(Ignore income taxes.)

1. Assuming that the laundromat would be open 52 weeks a year, compute the expected net annual cash receipts from its operation (gross cash receipts less cash disbursements). (Do not include the cost of the equipment, the working capital, or the salvage values in these computations.)
2. Would you advise Mr. White to open the laundromat? Show computations using the net present value method of investment analysis. Round all dollar amounts to the nearest whole dollar.

PROBLEM 14–23 Internal Rate of Return; Sensitivity Analysis [LO2]
Dr. Heidi Black is the managing partner of the Crestwood Dental Clinic. Dr. Black is trying to determine whether or not the clinic should move patient files and other items out of a spare room in the clinic and use the room for dental work. She has determined that it would require an investment of $142,950 for equipment and related costs of getting the room ready for use. Based on receipts being generated from other rooms in the clinic, Dr. Black estimates that the new room would generate a net cash inflow of $37,500 per year. The equipment purchased for the room would have a seven-year estimated useful life.

Required:
(Ignore income taxes.)

1. Compute the internal rate of return on the equipment for the new room to the nearest whole percent. Verify your answer by computing the net present value of the equipment using the internal rate of return you have computed as the discount rate.
2. Assume that Dr. Black will not purchase the new equipment unless it promises a return of at least 14%. Compute the amount of annual cash inflow that would provide this return on the $142,950 investment.
3. Although seven years is the average life for dental equipment, Dr. Black knows that due to changing technology this life can vary substantially. Compute the internal rate of return to the nearest whole percent if the life of the equipment were (*a*) five years and (*b*) nine years, rather than seven years. Is there any information provided by these computations that you would be particularly anxious to show Dr. Black?
4. Dr. Black is unsure about the estimated $37,500 annual cash inflow from the room. She thinks that the actual cash inflow could be as much as 20% greater or less than this figure.
   a. Assume that the actual cash inflow each year is 20% greater than estimated. Recompute the internal rate of return to the nearest whole percent.
   b. Assume that the actual cash inflow each year is 20% less than estimated. Recompute the internal rate of return to the nearest whole percent.
5. Refer to the original data. Assume that the equipment is purchased and that the room is opened for dental use. However, due to an increasing number of dentists in the area, the clinic is able to generate only $30,000 per year in net cash receipts from the new room. At the end of five years, the clinic closes the room and sells the equipment to a newly licensed dentist for a cash price of $61,375. Compute the internal rate of return (to the nearest whole percent) that the clinic earned on its investment over the five-year period. Round all dollar amounts to the nearest whole dollar. (Hint: A useful way to proceed is to find the discount rate that will cause the net present value of the investment to be equal to, or near, zero).

PROBLEM 14–24 Preference Ranking of Investment Projects [LO4]
Yancey Company has limited funds available for investment and must ration the funds among five competing projects. Selected information on the five projects follows:

Project	Investment Required	Net Present Value	Life of the Project (years)	Internal Rate of Return (percent)
A	$800,000	$221,615	7	18
B	675,000	210,000	12	16
C	500,000	175,175	7	20
D	700,000	152,544	3	22
E	900,000	(52,176)	6	8

The net present values above have been computed using a 10% discount rate. The company wants your assistance in determining which project to accept first, which to accept second, and so forth. The company's investment funds are limited.

Required:

1. Compute the profitability index for each project.
2. In order of preference, rank the five projects in terms of:
   a. Net present value.
   b. Profitability index.
   c. Internal rate of return.
3. Which ranking do you prefer? Why?

PROBLEM 14–25 Simple Rate of Return; Payback [LO5, LO6]
Nagoya Amusements Corporation places electronic games and other amusement devices in supermarkets and similar outlets throughout Japan. Nagoya Amusements is investigating the purchase of a new electronic game called Mystic Invaders. The manufacturer will sell 20 games to Nagoya Amusements for a total price of ¥180,000. (The Japanese currency is yen, which is denoted by the symbol ¥.) Nagoya Amusements has determined the following additional information about the game:

a. The game would have a five-year useful life and only a negligible salvage value. The company uses straight-line depreciation.
b. The game would replace other games that are unpopular and generating little revenue. These other games would be sold for a total of ¥30,000.
c. Nagoya Amusements estimates that Mystic Invaders would generate incremental revenues of ¥200,000 per year (total for all 20 games). Incremental out-of-pocket costs each year would be (in total): maintenance, ¥50,000; and insurance, ¥10,000. In addition, Nagoya Amusements would have to pay a commission of 40% of total revenues to the supermarkets and other outlets in which the games were placed.

Required:
(Ignore income taxes.)

1. Prepare an income statement showing the net operating income each year from Mystic Invaders. Use the contribution approach.
2. Compute the simple rate of return on Mystic Invaders. Will the game be purchased if Nagoya Amusements accepts any project with a simple rate of return greater than 14%?
3. Compute the payback period on Mystic Invaders. If the company accepts any investment with a payback period of less than three years, will the game be purchased?

PROBLEM 14–26 Net Present Value; Total and Incremental Approaches [LO1]
Eastbay Hospital has an auxiliary generator that is used when power failures occur. The generator is in bad repair and must be either overhauled or replaced with a new generator. The hospital has assembled the following information:

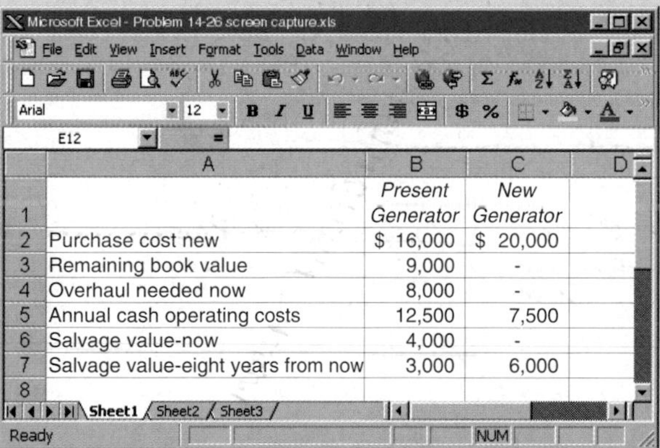

	A	B	C
1		*Present Generator*	*New Generator*
2	Purchase cost new	$ 16,000	$ 20,000
3	Remaining book value	9,000	-
4	Overhaul needed now	8,000	-
5	Annual cash operating costs	12,500	7,500
6	Salvage value-now	4,000	-
7	Salvage value-eight years from now	3,000	6,000

If the company keeps and overhauls its present generator, then the generator will be usable for eight more years. If a new generator is purchased, it will be used for eight years, after which it will be replaced. The new generator would be diesel-powered, resulting in a substantial reduction in annual operating costs, as shown above.

The hospital computes depreciation on a straight-line basis. All equipment purchases are evaluated using a 16% discount rate.

Required:
(Ignore income taxes.)

1. Should Eastbay Hospital keep the old generator or purchase the new one? Use the total-cost approach to net present value in making your decision.
2. Redo (1) above, this time using the incremental-cost approach.

PROBLEM 14–27 Simple Rate of Return; Payback; Internal Rate of Return [LO2, LO5, LO6]

Chateau Beaune is a family-owned winery located in the Burgundy region of France, which is headed by Gerard Despinoy. The harvesting season in early fall is the busiest part of the year for the winery, and many part-time workers are hired to help pick and process grapes. Mr. Despinoy is investigating the purchase of a harvesting machine that would significantly reduce the amount of labor required in the picking process. The harvesting machine is built to straddle grapevines, which are laid out in low-lying rows. Two workers are carried on the machine just above ground level, one on each side of the vine. As the machine slowly crawls through the vineyard, the workers cut bunches of grapes from the vines, which then fall into a hopper. The machine separates the grapes from the stems and other woody debris. The debris are then pulverized and spread behind the machine as a rich ground mulch. Mr. Despinoy has gathered the following information relating to the decision of whether to purchase the machine:

a. The winery would save €190,000 per year in labor costs with the new harvesting machine. In addition, the company would no longer have to purchase and spread ground mulch—at an annual savings of €10,000. (The French currency is the euro, which is denoted by the symbol €.)
b. The harvesting machine would cost €480,000. It would have an estimated 12-year useful life and zero salvage value. The winery uses straight-line depreciation.
c. Annual out-of-pocket costs associated with the harvesting machine would be insurance, €1,000; fuel, €9,000; and a maintenance contract, €12,000. In addition, two operators would be hired and trained for the machine, and they would be paid a total of €70,000 per year, including all benefits.
d. Mr. Despinoy feels that the investment in the harvesting machine should earn at least a 16% rate of return.

Required:

(Ignore income taxes.)

1. Determine the annual net savings in cash operating costs that would be realized if the harvesting machine were purchased.
2. Compute the simple rate of return expected from the harvesting machine. (Hint: This is a cost reduction project.)
3. Compute the payback period on the harvesting machine. Mr. Despinoy will not purchase equipment unless it has a payback period of five years or less. Under this criterion, should the harvesting machine be purchased?
4. Compute (to the nearest whole percent) the internal rate of return promised by the harvesting machine. Based on this computation, does it appear that the simple rate of return is an accurate guide in investment decisions?

PROBLEM 14–28 (Appendix 14D) Net Present Value Analysis Including Income Taxes [LO8]

The Crescent Drilling Company owns the drilling rights to several tracts of land on which natural gas has been found. The amount of gas on some of the tracts is somewhat marginal, and the company is unsure whether it would be profitable to extract and sell the gas that these tracts contain. One such tract is tract 410, on which the following information has been gathered:

Investment in equipment needed for extraction work	$600,000
Working capital investment needed	85,000
Annual cash receipts from sale of gas, net of related cash operating expenses (before taxes)	110,000
Cost of restoring land at completion of extraction work	70,000

The natural gas in tract 410 would be exhausted after 10 years of extraction work. The equipment would have a useful life of 15 years, but it could be sold for only 15% of its original cost when extraction was completed. For tax purposes, the company would depreciate the equipment over 10 years using straight-line depreciation and assuming zero salvage value. The tax rate is 30%, and the company's after-tax discount rate is 10%. The working capital would be released for use elsewhere at the completion of the project.

Required:

1. Compute the net present value of tract 410. Round all dollar amounts to the nearest whole dollar.
2. Would you recommend that the investment project be undertaken?

PROBLEM 14–29 Net Present Value Analysis of a Lease or Buy Decision [LO1]

Blinko Products wants an airplane available for use by its corporate staff. The airplane that the company wishes to acquire, a Zephyr II, can be either purchased or leased from the manufacturer. The company has made the following evaluation of the two alternatives:

Purchase alternative. If the Zephyr II is purchased, then the costs incurred by the company would be as follows:

Purchase cost of the plane	$850,000
Annual cost of servicing, licenses, and taxes	9,000
Repairs:	
First three years, per year	3,000
Fourth year	5,000
Fifth year	10,000

The plane would be sold after five years. Based on current resale values, the company would be able to sell it for about one-half of its original cost at the end of the five-year period.

Lease alternative. If the Zephyr II is leased, then the company would have to make an immediate deposit of $50,000 to cover any damage during use. The lease would run for five years, at the end of which time the deposit would be refunded. The lease would require an annual rental payment of $200,000 (the first payment is due at the end of year 1). As part of this lease cost, the manufacturer would provide all servicing and repairs, license the plane, and pay all taxes. At the end of the five-year period, the plane would revert to the manufacturer, as owner.

Blinko Products' cost of capital is 18%.

Required:

(Ignore income taxes.)

1. Use the total-cost approach to determine the present value of the cash flows associated with each alternative.
2. Which alternative would you recommend that the company accept? Why?

PROBLEM 14–30 Net Present Value; Uncertain Future Cash Flows; Postaudit [LO1, LO3]

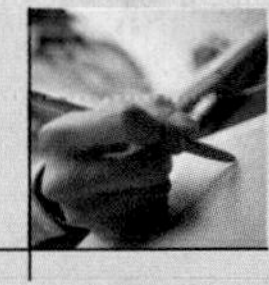

"If we can get that new robot to combine with our other automated equipment, we'll have a complete flexible manufacturing system in place in our Northridge plant," said Hal Swain, production manager for Diller Products.

"Let's just hope that reduced labor and inventory costs can justify its acquisition," replied Linda Wycoff, the controller. "Otherwise, we'll never get it. You know how the president feels about equipment paying for itself out of reduced costs."

Selected data relating to the robot are provided below:

Cost of the robot	$1,600,000
Software and installation	700,000
Annual savings in labor costs	?
Annual savings in inventory carrying costs	190,000
Monthly increase in power and maintenance costs	2,500
Salvage value in 12 years	90,000
Useful life	12 years

Engineering studies suggest that use of the robot will result in a savings of 20,000 direct labor-hours each year. The labor rate is $16 per hour. Also, the smoother work flow made possible by the FMS will allow the company to reduce the amount of inventory on hand by $300,000. The released funds will be available for use elsewhere in the company. This inventory reduction will take place in the first year of operation. The company requires a 20% return on all investments in automated equipment.

Required:

(Ignore income taxes.)

1. Determine the net *annual* cost savings if the robot is purchased. (Do not include the $300,000 inventory reduction or the salvage value in this computation.)
2. Compute the net present value of the proposed investment in the robot. Based on these data, would you recommend that the robot be purchased? Explain.
3. Assume that the robot is purchased. At the end of the first year, Linda Wycoff has found that some items didn't work out as planned. Due to unforeseen problems, software and installation costs were $125,000 more than estimated, and direct labor has been reduced by only 17,500 hours per year, rather than by 20,000 hours. Assuming that all other cost data were accurate, does it appear that the company made a wise investment? Show computations, using the net present value format as in (2) above. (Hint: It might be helpful to place yourself back at the beginning of the first year, with the new data.)
4. Upon seeing your analysis in (3) above, the president stated, "That robot is the worst investment we've ever made. And here we'll be stuck with it for years."
   a. Explain to the president what benefits other than cost savings might accrue from use of the new robot and FMS.
   b. Compute for the president the dollar amount of cash inflow that would be needed each year from the benefits in (*a*) above in order for the equipment to yield a 20% rate of return.

PROBLEM 14–31 (Appendix 14D) A Comparison of Investment Alternatives Including Income Taxes [LO8]

Ms. Keri Lee, an expert in retro-fitting buildings to meet seismic safety standards, has just received a $200,000 after-tax bonus for the successful completion of a project on time and under budget. Business has been so good that she is planning to retire in 12 years, spending her time relaxing in the sun, skiing, and doing charitable work. Ms. Lee is considering two alternatives for investing her bonus.

Alternative 1. Municipal bonds can be purchased that mature in 12 years and that bear interest at 8%. This interest would be tax-free and paid semiannually. (In discounting a cash flow that occurs semiannually, the procedure is to halve the discount rate and double the number of periods. Use the same procedure for discounting the principal returned when the bonds reach maturity.)

Alternative 2. A small discount perfume shop is available for sale at a nearby factory outlet center. The business can be purchased from its current owner for $200,000. The following information relates to this alternative:

a. Of the purchase price, $80,000 would be for fixtures and other depreciable items. The remainder would be for the company's working capital (inventory, accounts receivable, and cash). The fixtures and other depreciable items would have a remaining useful life of at least 12 years but would be depreciated for tax reporting purposes over eight years using the following allowances published by the Internal Revenue Service:

Year	Percentage of Original Cost Depreciated
1	14.3%
2	24.5
3	17.5
4	12.5
5	8.9
6	8.9
7	8.9
8	4.5
	100.0%

   Salvage value is not deducted when computing depreciation for tax purposes. At any rate, at the end of 12 years, these depreciable items would have a negligible salvage value; however, the working capital would be released for reinvestment elsewhere.

b. Store records indicate that sales have averaged $400,000 per year, and out-of-pocket costs have averaged $370,000 per year (*not* including income taxes). These out-of-pocket costs include rent on the building, cost of goods sold, utilities, and wages and salaries for the sales staff and the store manager. Ms. Lee plans to entrust the day-to-day operations of the store to the manager.
c. Ms. Lee's tax rate is 40%.
d. Ms. Lee wants an after-tax return on her investment of at least 8%.

Required:

Advise Ms. Lee as to which alternative should be selected. Use the total-cost approach to discounted cash flow in your analysis. (Round all dollar amounts to the nearest whole dollar.)

PROBLEM 14–32 Net Present Value Analysis of a New Product [LO1]

Atwood Company has an opportunity to produce and sell a revolutionary new smoke detector for homes. To determine whether this would be a profitable venture, the company has gathered the following data on probable costs and market potential:

a. New equipment would have to be acquired to produce the smoke detector. The equipment would cost $100,000 and be usable for 12 years. After 12 years, it would have a salvage value equal to 10% of the original cost.
b. Production and sales of the smoke detector would require a working capital investment of $40,000 to finance accounts receivable, inventories, and day-to-day cash needs. This working capital would be released for use elsewhere after 12 years.
c. An extensive marketing study projects sales in units over the next 12 years as follows:

Year	Sales in Units
1	4,000
2	7,000
3	10,000
4–12	12,000

d. The smoke detectors would sell for $45 each; variable costs for production, administration, and sales would be $25 per unit.
e. To gain entry into the market, the company would have to advertise heavily in the early years of sales. The advertising program follows:

Year	Amount of Advertising
1–2	$70,000
3	50,000
4–12	40,000

f. Other fixed costs for salaries, insurance, maintenance, and straight-line depreciation on equipment would total $127,500 per year. (Depreciation is based on cost less salvage value.)
g. Atwood Company views the smoke detector as a somewhat risky venture; therefore, the company would require a minimum 20% rate of return in order to accept it as a new product.

Required:

(Ignore income taxes.)

1. Compute the net cash inflow (cash receipts less yearly cash operating expenses) anticipated from sale of the smoke detectors for each year over the next 12 years.
2. Using the data computed in (1) above and other data provided in the problem, determine the net present value of the proposed investment. Would you recommend that Atwood Company accept the smoke detector as a new product?

Cases

CASE 14–33 Ethics and the Manager; Postaudit

After five years with a national CPA firm with mostly large manufacturing clients, Amy Kimbell joined Hi-Quality Productions Inc. (Hi-Q) as manager of Manufacturing Accounting. Amy has both CPA and CMA credentials.

Hi-Q is a publicly held company producing automotive components. One operation in the Alpha Division requires a highly automated process. Hi-Q's top management and board of directors had outsourced this particular high-tech operation to another company to avoid making a large investment in technology they viewed as constantly changing.

Each operating division of Hi-Q has a budget committee. Two years ago, the Alpha Division budget committee presented to the board its proposal to bring the high-tech operation in house. This would require a capital investment of approximately $4 million but would lead to more than enough cost savings to justify this expenditure. The board approved the proposal, and the investment was made. Later the same year, Amy Kimbell was promoted to assistant corporate controller. In this position, she sits on the budget committee of all divisions.

A little more than a year after the high-tech process was put into operation, the board requested a postaudit review of the actual cost savings. When the board requests such a review, the data are supplied by the management of the affected division and are reviewed by the division's budget committee. When the data were sent to the budget committee for review, Amy Kimbell noted that several of the projections in the original proposal were very aggressive. These included a very high salvage value for the equipment as well as a very long useful life over which cost savings were projected to occur. If more realistic projections had been used, Amy doubted that the board would have agreed to make the investment.

Also in the postaudit review, Amy noted that substantial amounts of incremental service department operating costs directly caused by the new investment were not being attributed to the high-tech operation. Instead, these costs were being allocated as general overhead to all departments. In addition, she noted that the estimated rate for spoiled and defective work contained in the proposal was being used in the review rather than the actual rate, which was considerably higher.

When Amy Kimbell brought these points to the attention of the division's budget committee, she was told that as a new member of the committee she would not be held responsible for decisions, such as the investment in the high-tech operation, that were made prior to her arrival. Accordingly, she should let the seasoned members of the committee handle this particular review. When Amy continued to express her concerns, she was firmly informed that it had been the unanimous decision of the committee to approve the original proposal because it was thought to be in the best long-run interest of the company. And given this consensus, it was felt that certain "adjustments and exceptions" to the postaudit review were justified to ensure the overall long-run well-being of the company.

Required:

1. What should Amy do? (Refer to the IMA Standards of Ethical Conduct for guidance.)
2. Do you have any suggestions for revising the way in which postaudits are conducted at Hi-Q?

(Adapted from Roland L. Madison and Curtis C. Verschoor, "New Position Brings Ethical Dilemma," *Strategic Finance*, December 2000, pp. 22, 24. Used with permission from the IMA, Montvale, NJ, USA, www.imanet.org.)

CASE 14–34 Net Present Value Analysis of a Lease or Buy Decision [LO1]

Wyndham Stores operates a regional chain of upscale department stores. The company is going to open another store soon in a prosperous and growing suburban area. In discussing how the company can acquire the desired building and other facilities needed to open the new store, Harry Wilson, the company's marketing vice president, stated, "I know most of our competitors are starting to lease facilities, rather than buy, but I just can't see the economics of it. Our development people tell me that we can buy the building site, put a building on it, and get all the store fixtures we need for $14 million. They also say that property taxes, insurance, maintenance, and repairs would run $200,000 a year. When you figure that we plan to keep a site for 20 years, that's a total cost of $18 million. But then when you realize that the building and property will be worth at least $5 million in 20 years, that's a net cost to us of only $13 million. Leasing costs a lot more than that."

"I'm not so sure," replied Erin Reilley, the company's executive vice president. "Guardian Insurance Company is willing to purchase the building site, construct a building and install fixtures to our specifications, and then lease the facility to us for 20 years for an annual lease payment of only $1 million."

"That's just my point," said Harry. "At $1 million a year, it would cost us $20 million over the 20 years instead of just $13 million. And what would we have left at the end? Nothing! The building would belong to the insurance company! I'll bet they would even want the first lease payment in advance."

"That's right," replied Erin. "We would have to make the first payment immediately and then one payment at the beginning of each of the following 19 years. However, you're overlooking a few things. For one thing, we would have to tie up a lot of our funds for 20 years under the purchase alternative. We would have to put $6 million down immediately if we buy the property, and then we would have to pay the other $8 million off over four years at $2 million a year."

"But that cost is nothing compared to $20 million for leasing," said Harry. "Also, if we lease, I understand we would have to put up a $400,000 security deposit that we wouldn't get back until the end. And besides that, we would still have to pay all the repair and maintenance costs just like we owned the property. No wonder those insurance companies are so rich if they can swing deals like this."

"Well, I'll admit that I don't have all the figures sorted out yet," replied Erin. "But I do have the operating cost breakdown for the building, which includes $90,000 annually for property taxes, $60,000 for insurance, and $50,000 for repairs and maintenance. If we lease, Guardian will handle its own insurance costs and will pay the property taxes, but we'll have to pay for the repairs and maintenance. I need to put all this together and see if leasing makes any sense with our 12% before-tax required rate of return. The president wants a presentation and recommendation in the executive committee meeting tomorrow."

Required:

(Ignore income taxes.)

1. Using the net present value approach, determine whether Wyndham Stores should lease or buy the new store. Assume that you will be making your presentation before the company's executive committee and remember that the president detests sloppy, disorganized reports.
2. What reply will you make in the meeting if Harry Wilson brings up the issue of the building's future sales value?

CASE 14–35 Comparison of Alternatives Using Net Present Value Analysis [LO1]

Woolrich Company's market research division has projected a substantial increase in demand over the next several years for one of the company's products. To meet this demand, the company will need to produce units as follows:

Year	Production in Units
1	20,000
2	30,000
3	40,000
4–10	45,000

At present, the company is using a single model 2600 machine to manufacture this product. To increase its productive capacity, the company is considering two alternatives:

Alternative 1. The company could purchase another model 2600 machine that would operate along with the one it now owns. The following information is available on this alternative:

a. The model 2600 machine now in use was purchased for $165,000 four years ago. Its present book value is $99,000, and its present market value is $90,000.
b. A new model 2600 machine costs $180,000 now. The old model 2600 machine will have to be replaced in six years at a cost of $200,000. The replacement machine will have a market value of about $100,000 when it is four years old.
c. The variable cost required to produce one unit of product using the model 2600 machine is given under the "general information" below.
d. Repairs and maintenance costs each year on a single model 2600 machine total $3,000.

Alternative 2. The company could purchase a model 5200 machine and use the old model 2600 machine as standby equipment. The model 5200 machine is a high-speed unit with double the capacity of the model 2600 machine. The following information is available on this alternative:

a. The cost of a new model 5200 machine is $250,000.
b. The variable cost required to produce one unit of product using the model 5200 machine is given under the "general information" below.
c. The model 5200 machine is more costly to maintain than the model 2600 machine. Repairs and maintenance on a model 5200 machine and on a model 2600 machine used as standby would total $4,600 per year.

The following general information is available on the two alternatives:

a. Both the model 2600 machine and the model 5200 machine have a 10-year life from the time they are first used in production. The scrap value of both machines is negligible and can be ignored. Straight-line depreciation is used by the company.
b. The two machine models are not equally efficient. Comparative variable costs per unit of product are as follows:

	Model 2600	Model 5200
Direct materials per unit	$0.36	$0.40
Direct labor per unit	0.50	0.22
Supplies and lubricants per unit	0.04	0.08
Total variable cost per unit	$0.90	$0.70

c. No other factory costs would change as a result of the decision between the two machines.
d. Woolrich Company uses an 18% discount rate.

Required:

(Ignore income taxes.)

1. Which alternative should the company choose? Use the net present value approach. (Round to the nearest whole dollar.)
2. Suppose that the cost of materials increases by 50%. Would this make the model 5200 machine more or less desirable? Explain. No computations are needed.
3. Suppose that the cost of labor increases by 25%. Would this make the model 5200 machine more or less desirable? Explain. No computations are needed.

CASE 14–36 (Appendix 14D) Break-Even and Net Present Value Analysis; Income Taxes [LO3, LO8]

VanDyk Enterprises has been operating a large gold mine for many years. The company wants to acquire equipment that will allow it to extract gold ore from a currently inaccessible area of the mine. Rich Salzman, VanDyk's controller, has gathered the following data:

a. The initial cost of the extraction equipment is $2,500,000. In addition to this cost, the equipment will require a large concrete foundation at a cost of $300,000. The vendor has quoted an additional cost of $200,000 to install and test the equipment. All of these costs are considered part of the cost of acquiring the equipment.
b. The useful life of the equipment is 10 years with no salvage value at the end of this period. However, the company will use the following depreciation allowances permitted under the tax code for computing its depreciation deductions for taxes:

Year	Percentage of Original Cost
1	14.3%
2	24.5
3	17.5
4	12.5
5	8.9
6	8.9
7	8.9
8	4.5
	100.0%

Salvage value is not deducted from original cost when determining the depreciation deductions.

c. Using the new equipment, 300 pounds of gold can be extracted annually for the next 10 years from the previously inaccessible area of the mine.
d. The cost to extract and separate gold from the ore is $1,000 per pound of gold. After separation, the gold must undergo further processing and testing that costs $400 per pound of gold. These are all out-of-pocket variable costs.
e. Two skilled technicians will be hired to operate the new equipment. The total salary and fringe benefit expense for these two employees will be $110,000 annually over the 10 years.
f. Periodic maintenance on the equipment is expected to cost $50,000 per year.
g. The project would require an investment in additional working capital of $200,000. This working capital would be released for use elsewhere at the conclusion of the project in 10 years.
h. Environmental and safety regulations require that the mine be extensively restored at the conclusion of the project and toxic chemicals be safely disposed of. The cost of this restoration work is expected to be $4,000,000.
i. The current market price of gold is $5,600 per pound.
j. VanDyk's tax rate is 30%.
k. VanDyk uses a 12% after-tax minimum required rate of return.

Required:

1. Determine the net present value of the extraction equipment assuming that the gold is sold for $5,600 per pound.
2. In reality, the future market value of gold is uncertain. What is the market price of gold at which VanDyk's acquisition of the extraction equipment will break even from a present value perspective?

(CMA, adapted)

Group and Internet Exercises

GROUP EXERCISE 14–37 Capital Budgets in Colleges

In recent years, your college or university has probably undertaken a capital budgeting project such as building or renovating a facility. Investigate one of these capital budgeting projects. You will probably need the help of your university's or college's accounting or finance office.

Required:

1. Determine the total cost of the project and the source of the funds for the project. Did the money come from state funds, gifts, grants, endowments, or the school's general fund?
2. Did the costs of the project stay within budget?
3. What financial criteria were used to evaluate the project?
4. If the net present value method or internal rate of return method was used, review the calculations. Do you agree with the calculations and methods used?
5. If the net present value method was not used to evaluate the project, estimate the project's net present value. If all of the required data are not available, make reasonable estimates for the missing data. What discount rate did you use? Why?
6. Evaluate the capital budgeting procedures that were actually used by your college or university.

INTERNET EXERCISE 14–38

As you know, the World Wide Web is a medium that is constantly evolving. Sites come and go, and change without notice. To enable periodic update of site addresses, this problem has been posted to the textbook website (www.mhhe.com/garrison10e). After accessing the site, enter the Student Center and select this chapter. Select and complete the Internet Exercise.

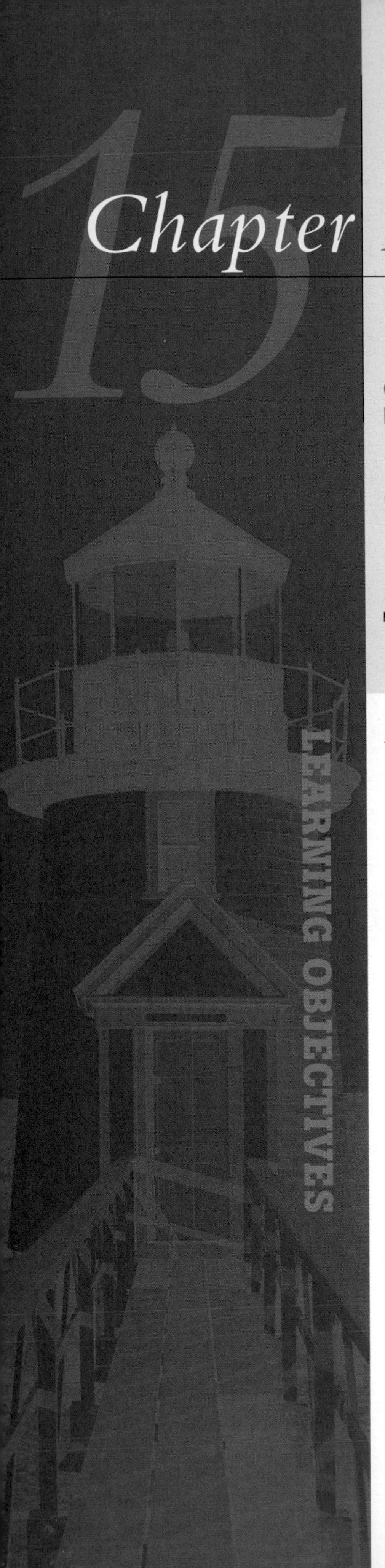

Chapter Fifteen

Service Department Costing: An Activity Approach

After studying Chapter 15, you should be able to:

1. Allocate service department costs to other departments, using the direct method.
2. Allocate service department costs to other departments, using the step method.
3. Allocate variable and fixed service department costs separately at the beginning of a period and at the end of the period.

Type It Yourself

Bellcore (Bell Communications Research) has 25 service centers that provide support to the company's operating units. Some service center rates had increased to intolerable levels because of an antiquated costing system.

For example, at one point the company's word processing service center was charging $50 per typed page. This very high charge forced engineers, researchers, and other highly paid people to type their own documents. The exorbitant rates forced other users to go outside the company for typing, graphics, and related services. After a major restructuring of the cost allocation system, including better tracing of costs to the service centers, rates in word processing, graphics, and other service centers were brought into line with competing rates elsewhere.

Source: Edward J. Kovac and Henry P. Troy, "Getting Transfer Prices Right: What Bellcore Did," *Harvard Business Review* 89, no. 5.

Most large organizations have both *operating departments* and *service departments*. The central purposes of the organization are carried out in the **operating departments**. In contrast, **service departments** do not directly engage in operating activities. Instead, they provide services or assistance to the operating departments. Examples of operating departments include the Surgery Department at Mt. Sinai Hospital, the Geography Department at the University of Washington, the Marketing Department at Allstate Insurance Company, and production departments at manufacturers such as Mitsubishi, Hewlett-Packard, and Michelin. Examples of service departments include Cafeteria, Internal Auditing, Human Resources, Cost Accounting, and Purchasing.

The costs incurred by service departments are usually allocated to the operating departments, and from the operating departments to products and services. Several different allocation methods will be considered in this chapter. The method that is selected can have a significant impact on the computed costs of goods and services and can affect an operating department's performance evaluation.

Allocations Using the Direct and Step Methods

Regardless of the allocation method that is ultimately selected, an allocation base must be selected for each service department.

Selecting Allocation Bases

Costs are ordinarily assigned to products and services by using a two-stage process. In the first stage, service department and other costs are allocated to operating departments. In the second stage, the costs that have been assigned to operating departments are allocated to products and services. We focused on the second stage of this costing process in Chapter 3. In this chapter, we focus on the first stage, in which service department costs are allocated to operating departments.

In the first stage, service department costs are allocated to operating departments by using a unique allocation base for each service department. The allocation base that is used to allocate a particular service department's costs should "drive" those costs. For example, the number of meals served would commonly be used as the allocation base for cafeteria costs because the costs incurred in the cafeteria are driven to a large extent by the number of meals served. Ideally, the total cost incurred in the service department should be directly proportional to the allocation base. If the allocation base increases or decreases by 10%, the service department cost should increase or decrease by 10% as well. Managers also often argue that an allocation base should reflect as accurately as possible the benefits that the various departments receive from the service department.

For example, most managers would argue that the square feet of building space occupied by each operating department should be used as the allocation base for janitorial services because both the benefits and costs of janitorial services tend to be proportional to the amount of space occupied by a department. Examples of allocation bases for some service departments are listed in Exhibit 15–1. A given service department's costs may be allocated using more than one base. For example, data processing costs may be allocated on the basis of CPU minutes for mainframe computers *and* on the basis of the number of personal computers used in each operating department.

Although the previous paragraph explains how to select an allocation base, another critical factor should not be overlooked. The allocations should be clear and straightforward and easily understood by the managers to whom the costs are being allocated.

Exhibit 15–1
Examples of Bases Commonly Used to Allocate Service Department Costs

Service Department	Bases (cost drivers) Involved
Laundry	Pounds of laundry
Airport Ground Services	Number of flights
Cafeteria	Number of meals
Medical Facilities	Cases handled; number of employees; hours worked
Materials Handling	Hours of service; volume handled
Data Processing	CPU minutes; lines printed; disk storage used; number of personal computers
Custodial Services (building and grounds)	Square footage occupied
Cost Accounting	Labor-hours; clients or patients serviced
Power	KWH used; capacity of machines
Human Resources	Number of employees; employee turnover; training hours
Receiving, Shipping, and Stores	Units handled; number of requisitions; space occupied
Factory Administration	Total labor-hours
Maintenance	Machine-hours

Increasing Accuracy at Hughes Aircraft

In Business

For many years, Hughes Aircraft allocated service department costs to operating departments using headcount as the allocation base. This method, while simple, was inaccurate because most service department costs are not driven by the number of employees (i.e., headcount) in the operating departments. To overcome this problem, the company adopted an activity-based approach in which each service department's costs are allocated based on the activities that are believed to drive the service department's costs. For example, the costs of the Human Resources Department are now allocated on the basis of headcount, new hires, union employees, and training hours in each operating department. Operating managers can control the amount of Human Resources cost allocated to their departments by controlling headcount, number of new hires, number of union employees, and number of training hours in their departments.

Source: Jack Haedicke and David Feil, "Hughes Aircraft Sets the Standard for ABC," *Management Accounting* 72, no. 8, pp. 31–32.

Interdepartmental Services

Many service departments provide services to each other, as well as to operating departments. The Cafeteria Department, for example, provides food for all employees, including those assigned to other service departments. In turn, the Cafeteria Department may receive services from other service departments, such as from Custodial Services or from Personnel. Services provided between service departments are known as **interdepartmental** or **reciprocal services.**

Three approaches are used to allocate the costs of service departments to other departments. These are known as the *direct method,* the *step method,* and the *reciprocal method.* All three methods are discussed in the following paragraphs.

LEARNING OBJECTIVE 1
Allocate service department costs to other departments, using the direct method.

Direct Method The **direct method** is the simplest of the three cost allocation methods. It ignores the services provided by a service department to other service departments and allocates all of its costs directly to operating departments. Even if a service department (such as Personnel) provides a large amount of service to another service department (such as the cafeteria), no allocations are made between the two departments. Rather, all costs are allocated *directly* to the operating departments, bypassing the other service departments. Hence the term *direct method.*

In Business

A Losing Football Program

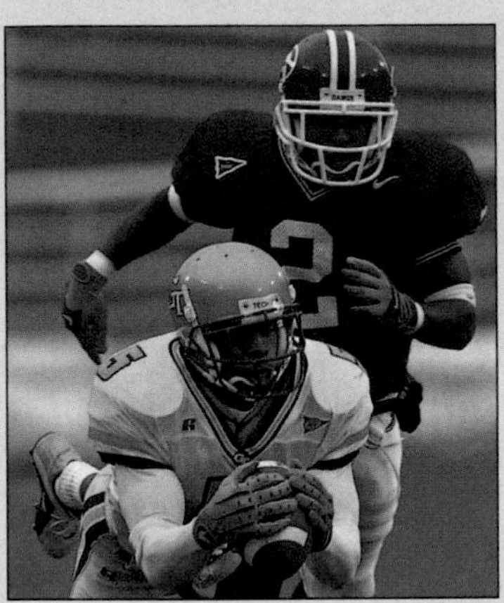

At Georgia Tech, service department costs are allocated to intercollegiate sports programs by using the direct method. For example, the costs of the Sports Medicine Department are allocated on the basis of the number of student athletes in each intercollegiate sport. Some costs, such as a sport's operating budget, recruiting costs, scholarships, and salaries, can be traced directly to the sport and are called direct costs. Service department costs, which are allocated, include Sports Medicine, Facilities, Sports Information, Academic Center, Student-Athlete Program, Office Supplies, Legal and Audit, Accounting Office, Marketing, and Administrative. Allocations of these service department costs to the sports programs can make a big difference in their apparent profitability. For example, the football program shows a margin of over $1 million based on just its direct costs, but a loss of over $800,000 when service department costs are allocated to the program.

Source: C. David Strupeck, Ken Milani, and James E. Murphy III, "Financial Management at Georgia Tech," *Management Accounting* 74, no. 8, pp. 58–63.

To provide an example of the direct method, consider Mountain View Hospital, which has two service departments and two operating departments as shown below:

	Service Department		Operating Department		
	Hospital Administration	Custodial Services	Laboratory	Daily Patient Care	Total
Departmental costs before allocation	$360,000	$90,000	$261,000	$689,000	$1,400,000
Employee hours	12,000	6,000	18,000	30,000	66,000
Space occupied—square feet	10,000	200	5,000	45,000	60,200

Hospital Administration costs will be allocated on the basis of employee-hours and Custodial Services costs will be allocated on the basis of square feet occupied.

The direct method of allocating the hospital's service department costs to the operating departments is shown in Exhibit 15–2. Several things should be carefully noted in this exhibit. First, even though both the Hospital Administration Department and the Custodial Services Department have recorded employee-hours, these employee-hours are ignored when allocating service department costs using the direct method. *Under the direct method, any of the allocation base attributable to the service departments themselves is ignored; only the amount of the allocation base attributable to the operating departments is used in the allocation.* Note that the same rule is used when allocating the costs of the Custodial Services Department. Even though the Hospital Administration and Custodial Services departments occupy some space, this is ignored when the Custodial Services costs are allocated. Finally, note that after all allocations have been completed, all of the departmental costs are contained in the two operating departments. These costs will be used to prepare overhead rates for purposes of costing products and services produced in the operating departments.

Concept 15–1

Exhibit 15–2 Direct Method of Allocation

	Service Department		Operating Department		
	Hospital Administration	Custodial Services	Laboratory	Daily Patient Care	Total
Departmental costs before allocation	$ 360,000	$ 90,000	$261,000	$689,000	$1,400,000
Allocation:					
Hospital Administration costs (18⁄48, 30⁄48)* .	(360,000)		135,000	225,000	
Custodial Services costs (5⁄50, 45⁄50)†		(90,000)	9,000	81,000	
Total costs after allocation	$ 0	$ 0	$405,000	$995,000	$1,400,000

*Based on the employee-hours in the two operating departments, which are 18,000 hours + 30,000 hours = 48,000 hours.
†Based on the space occupied by the two operating departments, which is 5,000 square feet + 45,000 square feet = 50,000 square feet.

Although the direct method is simple, it is less accurate than the other methods since it ignores interdepartmental services. This can lead to distorted product and service costs. Even so, many organizations use the direct method because of its simplicity.

LEARNING OBJECTIVE 2
Allocate service department costs to other departments, using the step method.

Concept 15–2

Step Method Unlike the direct method, the **step method** provides for allocation of a service department's costs to other service departments, as well as to operating departments. The step method is sequential. The sequence typically begins with the department that provides the greatest amount of service to other service departments. After its costs have been allocated, the process continues, step by step, ending with the department that provides the least amount of services to other service departments. This step procedure is illustrated in graphic form in Exhibit 15–3, assuming that Hospital Administration costs are allocated first at Mountain View Hospital.

Exhibit 15–4 shows the details of the step method. Note the following three key points about these allocations. First, under the Allocation heading in Exhibit 15–4, you see two allocations, or steps. In the first step, the costs of Hospital Administration are allocated to another service department (Custodial Services) as well as to the operating departments. In contrast to the direct method, the allocation base for Hospital Administration costs now includes the employee-hours for Custodial Services as well as for the operating departments. However, the allocation base still excludes the employee-hours for Hospital Administration itself. *In both the direct and step methods, any amount of the allocation base attributable to the service department whose cost is being allocated is always ignored.* Second, looking again at Exhibit 15–4, note that in the second step under the Allocation heading, the cost of Custodial Services is allocated to the two operating departments, and none of the cost is allocated to Hospital Administration even though Hospital Administration occupies space in the building. *In the step method, any amount of the allocation base that is attributable to a service department whose cost has already been allocated is ignored.* After a service department's costs have been allocated, costs of other service departments are not reallocated back to it. Third, note that the cost of Custodial Services allocated to other departments in the second step ($130,000) in Exhibit 15–4 includes the costs of Hospital Administration that were allocated to Custodial Services in the first step in Exhibit 15–4.

Exhibit 15–3
Graphic Illustration—Step Method

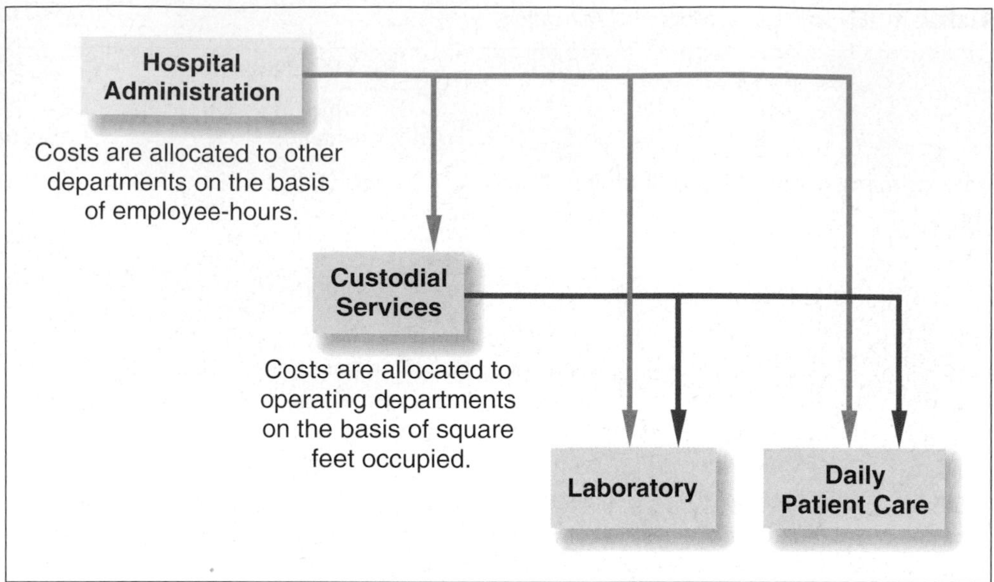

Exhibit 15–4 Step Method of Allocation

	Service Department		Operating Department		
	Hospital Administration	Custodial Services	Laboratory	Daily Patient Care	Total
Departmental costs before allocation	$360,000	$90,000	$261,000	$689,000	$1,400,000
Allocation:					
Hospital Administration costs (6/54, 18/54, 30/54)*	(360,000)	40,000	120,000	200,000	
Custodial Services costs (5/50, 45/50)†		(130,000)	13,000	117,000	
Total costs after allocation	$0	$0	$394,000	$1,006,000	$1,400,000

*Based on the employee-hours in Custodial Services and the two operating departments, which are 6,000 hours + 18,000 hours + 30,000 hours = 54,000 hours.
†As in Exhibit 15–2, this allocation is based on the space occupied by the two operating departments.

In Business

Stepping Down at Group Health

Group Health Cooperative of Puget Sound is a large health maintenance organization with 500 service departments that account for 30% of Group Health's total costs. The step method is used to allocate these costs to patient care departments and then to patients. These allocations are done so that costs can be summarized in a variety of ways including "by consumers, by diagnostic groupings, by employer groups, and by specific populations, such as Medicare, Medicaid, AIDS, Heart Care, and so on."

Source: John Y. Lee and Pauline Nefcy, "The Anatomy of an Effective HMO Cost Management System," *Management Accounting,* January 1997, p. 52.

Reciprocal Method The **reciprocal method** gives full recognition to interdepartmental services. Under the step method discussed above only partial recognition of interdepartmental services is possible. The step method always allocates costs forward—never backward. The reciprocal method, by contrast, allocates service department costs in *both* directions. Thus, since Custodial Services in the prior example provides services for Hospital Administration, part of Custodial Services' costs will be allocated *back* to Hospital Administration if the reciprocal method is used. At the same time, part of Hospital Administration's costs will be allocated *forward* to Custodial Services. This type of reciprocal allocation requires the use of simultaneous linear equations and is beyond the scope of this book. Examples of the reciprocal method can be found in more advanced cost accounting texts.

The reciprocal method is rarely used in practice for two reasons. First, the computations are relatively complex. Although the complexity issue could be overcome by use of computers, there is no evidence that computers have made the reciprocal method more popular. Second, the step method usually provides results that are a reasonable approximation of the results that the reciprocal method would provide. Thus, companies have little motivation to use the more complex reciprocal method.

Revenue Producing Departments To conclude our discussion of allocation methods, it is important to note that even though most service departments are cost centers and therefore generate no revenues, a few service departments such as the cafeteria may charge for the services they perform. If a service department generates revenues, those revenues should be offset against the department's costs, and only the net amount of cost remaining after this offset should be allocated to other departments within the organization. In this manner, the other departments will not be required to bear costs for which the service department has already been reimbursed.

Allocating Costs by Behavior

Whenever possible, service department costs should be separated into variable and fixed classifications and allocated separately to provide more useful data for planning and control of departmental operations.

Variable Costs

Variable costs vary in total in proportion to changes in the level of service provided. For example, the cost of food in a cafeteria is a variable cost that varies in proportion to the number of persons using the cafeteria or the number of meals served.

As a general rule, a variable cost should be charged to consuming departments according to whatever activity causes the incurrence of the cost. For example, variable costs of a maintenance department that are caused by the number of machine-hours worked in the producing departments should be allocated to the producing departments using machine-hours as the allocation basis. This will ensure that these costs are properly traced to departments, products, and customers.

Fixed Costs

The fixed costs of service departments represent the costs of making capacity available for use. These costs should be allocated to consuming departments in *predetermined lump-sum amounts.* By predetermined lump-sum amounts we mean that the total amount charged to each consuming department is determined in advance and, once determined, does not change. The lump-sum amount charged to a department can be based either on the department's peak-period or long-run average servicing needs. The logic behind lump-sum allocations of this type is as follows:

When a service department is first established, its capacity will be determined by the needs of the departments that it will service. This capacity may reflect the peak-period needs of the other departments, or it may reflect their long-run average or "normal" servicing needs. Depending on how much servicing capacity is provided for, it will be necessary to make a commitment of resources to the servicing unit, which will be reflected in its fixed costs. These fixed costs should be borne by the consuming departments in proportion to the amount of capacity each consuming department requires. That is, if available capacity in the service department has been provided to meet the peak-period needs of consuming departments, then the fixed costs of the service department should be allocated in predetermined lump-sum amounts to consuming departments on that basis. If available capacity has been provided only to meet "normal" or long-run average needs, then the fixed costs should be allocated on that basis.

Once set, allocations should not vary from period to period, since they represent the cost of having a certain level of service capacity available and on line for each consuming department. The fact that a consuming department does not need a peak level or even a "normal" level of servicing every period is immaterial; if it requires such servicing at certain times, then the capacity to deliver it must be available. It is the responsibility of the consuming departments to bear the cost of that availability.

To illustrate this idea, assume that Novak Company has just organized a Maintenance Department to service all machines in the Cutting, Assembly, and Finishing Departments. In determining the capacity of the newly organized Maintenance Department, the various producing departments estimated that they would have the following peak-period needs for maintenance:

Department	Peak-Period Maintenance Needs in Terms of Number of Hours of Maintenance Work Required	Percent of Total Hours
Cutting	900	30%
Assembly	1,800	60
Finishing	300	10
	3,000	100%

Therefore, in allocating the Maintenance Department fixed costs to the producing departments, 30% (i.e., 900/3,000 = 30%) should be allocated to the Cutting Department, 60% to the Assembly Department, and 10% to the Finishing Department. These lump-sum allocations *will not change* from period to period unless there is some shift in peak-period servicing needs.

Should Actual or Budgeted Costs Be Allocated?

Should the *actual* or *budgeted* costs of a service department be allocated to operating departments? The answer is that budgeted costs should be allocated. What's wrong with allocating actual costs? Allocating actual costs burdens the operating departments with any inefficiencies in the service department. If actual costs are allocated, then any lack of cost control on the part of the service department is simply buried in a routine allocation to other departments.

Any variance over budgeted costs should be retained in the service department and closed out at year-end against the company's revenues or against cost of goods sold, along with other variances. Operating department managers justifiably complain bitterly if they are forced to absorb service department inefficiencies.

Technically, preset charges based on budgeted costs are not allocations. Instead of dividing actual costs among the operating departments, they are charged a fixed amount per unit of service provided. In effect, management says, "You will be charged X dollars for every unit of service that you consume or capacity that you require. You can consume as much or as little as you desire; the total charge you bear will vary proportionately." The purpose of making such charges is to ensure that the managers of the operating departments are fully aware of all of the costs of their actions—including costs that are incurred in service departments. Only in this way can the managers of the operating departments make appropriate trade-offs when deciding, for example, whether to purchase a service from an external provider or to obtain it from a service department inside the company.

A Summary of Cost Allocation Guidelines

The following guidelines summarize the preceding discussion concerning allocations of service department costs.

1. If possible, the distinction between variable and fixed costs in service departments should be maintained.
2. Variable costs should be allocated at the budgeted rate, according to whatever activity (miles driven, direct labor-hours, number of employees) causes the incurrence of the cost.
   a. If the allocations are being made at the beginning of the year, they should be based on the budgeted activity level planned for the consuming departments. The allocation formula would be:

   $$\text{Variable cost allocated at the beginning of the period} = \text{Budgeted rate} \times \text{Budgeted activity}$$

   b. If the allocations are being made at the end of the year, they should be based on the actual activity level that has occurred during the year. The allocation formula would be:

   $$\text{Variable cost allocated at the end of the period} = \text{Budgeted rate} \times \text{Actual activity}$$

   Allocations made at the beginning of the year provide data for pricing and other decisions. Allocations made at the end of the year provide data for comparing actual performance to planned performance.
3. Fixed costs represent the costs of having service capacity available. Where feasible, these costs should be allocated in predetermined lump-sum amounts. The lump-sum amount going to each department should be in proportion to the servicing needs that gave rise to the investment in the service department in the first place. (This might be either peak-period needs for servicing or long-run average needs.) Budgeted fixed costs, rather than actual fixed costs, should always be allocated.

Implementing the Allocation Guidelines

LEARNING OBJECTIVE 3
Allocate variable and fixed service department costs separately at the beginning of a period and at the end of the period.

Specific examples will show how to implement the three guidelines given above. First, we focus on the allocation of costs for a single department, and then we will develop a more extended example involving multiple departments.

Basic Allocation Techniques Seaboard Airlines has two operating divisions: a Freight Division and a Passenger Division. The company has a single aircraft Maintenance Department that provides servicing to both divisions. Variable servicing costs are budgeted at $10 per flight-hour. The department's fixed costs are budgeted at $750,000 for the year. The fixed costs of the Maintenance Department are budgeted based on the peak-period demand, which occurs during the Thanksgiving to New Year's holiday period. The airline wants to make sure that none of its aircraft are grounded during this key period due to unavailability of maintenance facilities. Approximately 40% of the maintenance during this period is performed on the Freight Division's equipment, and 60% is performed on the Passenger Division's equipment. These figures and the budgeted flight-hours for the coming year are as follows:

	Percent of Peak Period Capacity Required	Budgeted Flight-Hours
Freight Division	40%	9,000
Passenger Division	60	15,000
Total	100%	24,000

Given these data, the amount of cost that would be allocated to each division from the Maintenance Department at the beginning of the coming year would be as follows:

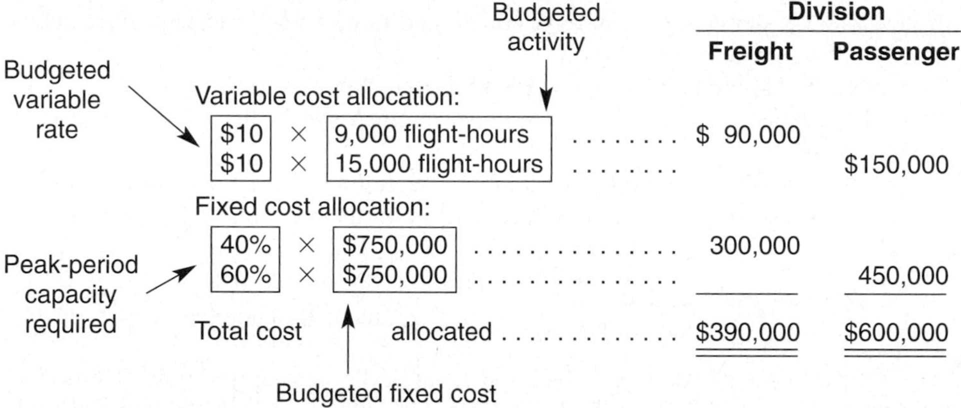

	Division: Freight	Division: Passenger
Variable cost allocation:		
$10 × 9,000 flight-hours	$ 90,000	
$10 × 15,000 flight-hours		$150,000
Fixed cost allocation:		
40% × $750,000	300,000	
60% × $750,000		450,000
Total cost allocated	$390,000	$600,000

These allocated Maintenance Department costs would be included in the flexible budgets of the respective divisions and included in the computation of divisional overhead rates.

At the end of the year, Seaboard Airlines' management may want to make a second allocation, this time based on actual activity, in order to compare actual performance for the year against planned performance. To illustrate, year-end records show that actual costs in the aircraft Maintenance Department for the year were variable costs, $260,000; and fixed costs, $780,000. One division logged more flight-hours during the year than planned, and the other division logged fewer flight-hours than planned, as shown below:

	Flight-Hours: Budgeted (see above)	Flight-Hours: Actual
Freight Division	9,000	8,000
Passenger Division	15,000	17,000
Total flight-hours	24,000	25,000

The amount of actual Maintenance Department cost charged to each division for the year would be as follows:

	Division: Freight	Division: Passenger
Variable cost allocation:		
$10 × 8,000 flight-hours	$ 80,000	
$10 × 17,000 flight-hours		$170,000
Fixed cost allocation:		
40% × $750,000	300,000	
60% × $750,000		450,000
Total cost allocated	$380,000	$620,000

Budgeted variable rate (arrow to the $10 boxes); Actual activity (arrow to the flight-hours boxes); Peak-period capacity required (arrow to the percentage boxes); Budgeted fixed cost (arrow to the $750,000 boxes)

Notice that variable servicing cost is charged to the operating divisions based on the budgeted rate ($10 per hour) and the *actual activity* for the year. In contrast, the charges for fixed costs are exactly the same as they were at the beginning of the year. Also note that the two operating divisions are *not* charged for the actual costs of the service department, which may be influenced by inefficiency in the service department and be beyond the control of the managers of the operating divisions. Instead, the service department is held responsible for the unallocated actual costs as shown below:

	Variable	Fixed
Total actual costs incurred	$260,000	$780,000
Costs allocated (above)	250,000*	750,000
Spending variance—not allocated	$ 10,000	$ 30,000

*$10 per flight-hour × 25,000 actual flight-hours = $250,000.

These variances will be closed out against the company's overall revenues for the year, along with any other variances that may occur.

Effect of Allocations on Operating Departments

Once allocations have been completed, what do the operating departments do with the allocated service department costs? The allocations are typically included in performance evaluations of the operating departments and also included in determining their profitability.

In addition, if the operating departments are responsible for developing overhead rates for costing products or services, then the allocated costs are combined with the other costs of the operating departments, and the total is used as a basis for rate computations. This rate development process is illustrated in Exhibit 15–5.

The budget serves as the means for combining allocated service department costs with operating department costs and for computing overhead rates. An example is presented in Exhibit 15–6. Note from the exhibit that both variable and fixed service department costs have been allocated to Superior Company's Milling Department and are

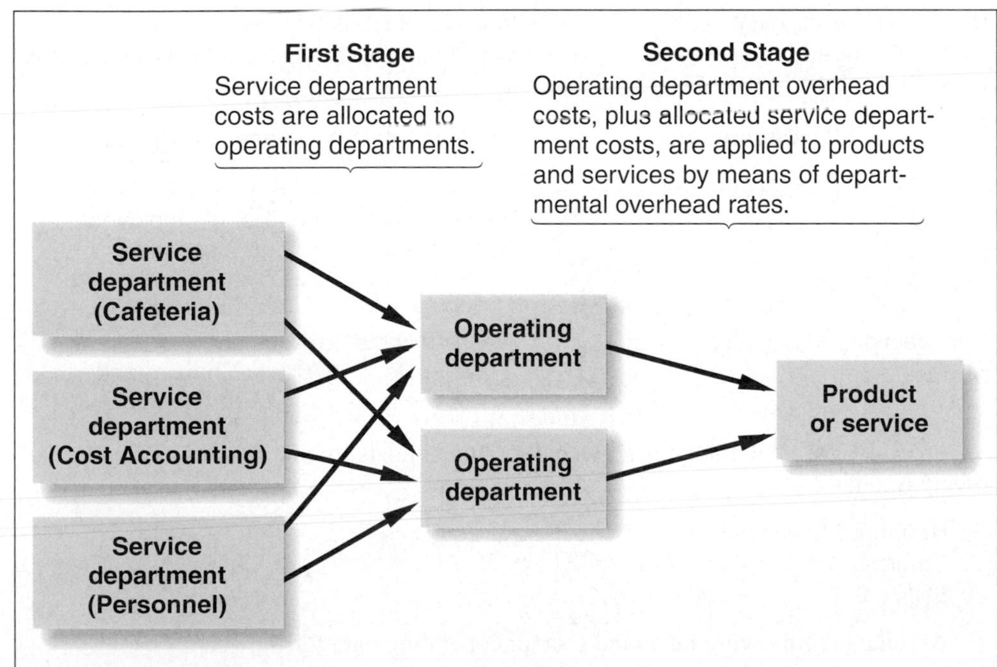

Exhibit 15–5
Effect of Allocations on Products and Services

Exhibit 15–6
Budget Containing Allocated Service Department Costs

SUPERIOR COMPANY Budget—Milling Department		
Budgeted direct labor-hours	50,000	
	Cost Formula (per direct labor-hour)	**Overhead**
Variable overhead costs:		
Indirect labor	$1.45	$ 72,500
Indirect material	0.90	45,000
Utilities	0.10	5,000
Allocation—Cafeteria	0.15	7,500
Total variable overhead cost	$2.60	130,000
Fixed overhead costs:		
Depreciation		85,000
Supervisory salaries		110,000
Property taxes		9,000
Allocation—Cafeteria		21,000
Allocation—Human Resources		45,000
Total fixed overhead cost		270,000
Total overhead cost		$400,000

$$\text{Predetermined overhead rate} = \frac{\$400{,}000}{50{,}000 \text{ DLHs}} = \$8 \text{ per direct labor-hour}$$

included on the latter's budget. Since allocated service department costs become an integral part of the budget, they are automatically included in overhead rate computations, as shown at the bottom of the exhibit.

An Extended Example

Proctor Company has three service departments—Building Maintenance, Cafeteria, and Inspection. The company also has two operating departments—Shaping and Assembly. The service departments provide services to each other, as well as to the operating departments. Types of costs in the service departments and bases for allocation are given below:

Department	Type of Cost	Base for Allocation
Building Maintenance	Fixed costs	Square footage occupied
Cafeteria	Variable costs	Number of employees
	Fixed costs	10% to Inspection, 40% to Shaping, and 50% to Assembly
Inspection	Variable costs	Direct labor-hours
	Fixed costs	70% to Shaping and 30% to Assembly

Proctor Company allocates service department costs by the step method in the following order:

1. Building Maintenance.
2. Cafeteria.
3. Inspection.

Assume the following budgeted cost and operating data for the year:

Department	Variable Cost	Fixed Cost
Building Maintenance	—	$130,000
Cafeteria	$200 per employee	$250,000
Inspection	$0.06 per direct labor-hour	$548,000

Department	Number of Employees	Direct Labor-Hours	Square Footage of Space Occupied (square feet)
Building Maintenance	6*	—	3,000
Cafeteria	9*	—	4,000
Inspection	30	—	1,000
Shaping	190	300,000	8,000
Assembly	250	500,000	13,000
Total	485	800,000	29,000

*Although there are employees in both of these service departments, under the step method, costs are only allocated *forward*—never backward. For this reason, the costs of the Cafeteria Department will be allocated *forward* on the basis of the number of employees in the Inspection, Shaping, and Assembly departments.

In addition to the service department costs listed above, the company's Shaping Department has budgeted $1,340,000 in overhead costs, and its Assembly Department has budgeted $1,846,000 in overhead costs.

Cost allocations from the service departments to the operating departments are shown in Exhibit 15–7. In the first panel of Exhibit 15–7, the variable costs of the service departments are allocated using the step method and budgeted rates and budgeted activity. For example, the variable cost of the Cafeteria Department is $200 per employee, so the Inspection Department, with 30 employees, is allocated $6,000 of this variable cost. In the second panel of Exhibit 15–7, the fixed costs of the service departments are allocated. Building Maintenance is allocated first using the square feet occupied by each of the other departments as the allocation base. Then the fixed costs of the Cafeteria and Inspection departments are allocated based on the given percentages. After both the variable and fixed service department costs have been allocated, the predetermined overhead rates for the two operating departments are computed toward the bottom of the exhibit.

Some Cautions in Allocating Service Department Costs

Pitfalls in Allocating Fixed Costs

Rather than charge fixed costs to using departments in predetermined lump-sum amounts, some firms allocate them using a *variable* allocation base that fluctuates from period to period. This practice can distort decisions and create serious inequities between departments. The inequities will arise from the fact that the fixed costs allocated to one department will be heavily influenced by what happens in *other* departments.

To illustrate, assume that Kolby Products has an auto service center that provides maintenance work on the fleet of autos used in the company's two sales territories. The auto service center costs are all fixed. Contrary to good practice, the company allocates these fixed costs to the sales territories on the basis of actual miles driven (a variable base). Selected cost data for the last two years follow:

Exhibit 15–7

THE PROCTOR COMPANY
Beginning-of-Year Cost Allocations for Purposes of Preparing Predetermined Overhead Rates

	Building Maintenance	Cafeteria	Inspection	Shaping	Assembly
Variable costs to be allocated	$ 0	$94,000	$ 42,000	$ —	$ —
Cafeteria allocation at $200 per employee:					
$200 × 30 employees	—	(6,000)	6,000	—	—
$200 × 190 employees	—	(38,000)	—	38,000	—
$200 × 250 employees	—	(50,000)	—	—	50,000
Inspection allocation at $0.06 per direct labor-hour:					
$0.06 × 300,000 DLH	—	—	(18,000)	18,000	—
$0.06 × 500,000 DLH	—	—	(30,000)	—	30,000
Total	0	0	0	56,000	80,000
Fixed costs to be allocated	130,000	250,000	548,000		
Building Maintenance allocation at $5 per square foot:*					
$5 × 4,000 square feet	(20,000)	20,000	—	—	—
$5 × 1,000 square feet	(5,000)	—	5,000	—	—
$5 × 8,000 square feet	(40,000)	—	—	40,000	—
$5 ×13,000 square feet	(65,000)	—	—	—	65,000
Cafeteria allocation:†					
10% × $270,000	—	(27,000)	27,000	—	—
40% × $270,000	—	(108,000)	—	108,000	—
50% × $270,000	—	(135,000)	—	—	135,000
Inspection allocation:‡					
70% × $580,000	—	—	(406,000)	406,000	—
30% × $580,000	—	—	(174,000)	—	174,000
Total	0	0	0	554,000	374,000
Total allocated costs	$ 0	$ 0	$ 0	610,000	454,000
Other budgeted costs				1,340,000	1,846,000
Total budgeted overhead costs (a)				$1,950,000	$2,300,000
Budgeted direct labor-hours (b)				300,000	500,000
Predetermined overhead rate, (a) ÷ (b)				$6.50	$4.60

*Square footage of space	29,000 square feet
Less Building Maintenance space	3,000 square feet
Net space for allocation	26,000 square feet

$$\frac{\text{Building Maintenance fixed costs, \$130,000}}{\text{Net space for allocation, 26,000 square feet}} = \text{\$5 per square foot}$$

†Cafeteria fixed costs	$250,000
Allocated from Building Maintenance	20,000
Total cost to be allocated	$270,000

Allocation percentages are given in the problem.

‡Inspection fixed costs	$548,000
Allocated from Building Maintenance	5,000
Allocated from Cafeteria	27,000
Total cost to be allocated	$580,000

Allocation percentages are given.

	Year 1	Year 2
Auto service center costs (all fixed) (a)	$120,000	$120,000
Western sales territory—miles driven	1,500,000	1,500,000
Eastern sales territory—miles driven	1,500,000	900,000
Total miles driven (b)	3,000,000	2,400,000
Allocation rate per mile, (a) ÷ (b)	$0.04	$0.05

Notice that the Western sales territory maintained an activity level of 1,500,000 miles driven in both years. On the other hand, activity in the Eastern sales territory dropped from 1,500,000 miles in Year 1 to only 900,000 miles in Year 2. The auto service center costs that would have been allocated to the two sales territories over the two-year span using actual miles driven as the allocation base are as follows:

Year 1:	
Western sales territory: 1,500,000 miles at $0.04 per mile	$ 60,000
Eastern sales territory: 1,500,000 miles at $0.04 per mile	60,000
Total cost allocated	$120,000
Year 2:	
Western sales territory: 1,500,000 miles at $0.05 per mile	$ 75,000
Eastern sales territory: 900,000 miles at $0.05 per mile	45,000
Total cost allocated	$120,000

In Year 1, the two sales territories share the service department costs equally. In Year 2, however, the bulk of the service department costs are allocated to the Western sales territory. This is not because of any increase in activity in the Western sales territory; rather, it is because of the *decrease* in activity in the Eastern sales territory. Even though the Western sales territory maintained the same level of activity in both years, the use of a variable allocation base has caused it to be penalized with a heavier cost allocation in Year 2 because of what has happened in *another* part of the company.

This kind of inequity is almost inevitable when a variable allocation base is used to allocate fixed costs. The manager of the Western sales territory undoubtedly will be upset about the inequity forced on his territory, but he will feel powerless to do anything about it. The result will be a loss of confidence in the system and considerable ill feeling.

Beware of Sales Dollars as an Allocation Base

Over the years, sales dollars have been a popular allocation base for service department costs. One reason is that a sales dollars base is simple, straightforward, and easy to work with. Another reason is that people tend to view sales dollars as a measure of well-being, or "ability to pay," and, hence, as a measure of how readily costs can be absorbed from other parts of the organization.

Unfortunately, sales dollars are often a very poor allocation base, for the reason that sales dollars vary from period to period, whereas the costs being allocated are often largely *fixed* in nature. As discussed earlier, if a variable base is used to allocate fixed costs, inequities can result between departments, since the costs being allocated to one department will depend in large part on what happens in *other* departments. For example, a letup in sales effort in one department will shift allocated costs from that department to other, more productive departments. In effect, the departments putting forth the best sales efforts are penalized in the form of higher allocations, simply because of inefficiencies elsewhere that are beyond their control. The result is often bitterness and resentment on the part of the managers of the better departments.

Consider the following situation encountered by one of the authors:

A large men's clothing store has one service department and three sales departments—Suits, Shoes, and Accessories. The Service Department's costs total $60,000 per period and are allocated to the three sales departments according to sales dollars. A recent period showed the following allocation:

	Department			
	Suits	**Shoes**	**Accessories**	**Total**
Sales by department	$260,000	$40,000	$100,000	$400,000
Percentage of total sales	65%	10%	25%	100%
Allocation of service department costs, based on percentage of total sales	$ 39,000	$ 6,000	$ 15,000	$ 60,000

In a following period, the manager of the Suits Department launched a very successful program to expand sales by $100,000 in his department. Sales in the other two departments remained unchanged. Total service department costs also remained unchanged, but the allocation of these costs changed substantially, as shown below:

	Department			
	Suits	**Shoes**	**Accessories**	**Total**
Sales by department	$360,000	$40,000	$100,000	$500,000
Percentage of total sales	72%	8%	20%	100%
Allocation of service department costs, based on percentage of total sales	$ 43,200	$ 4,800	$ 12,000	$ 60,000
Increase (or decrease) from prior allocation	4,200	(1,200)	(3,000)	0

The manager of the Suits Department complained that as a result of his successful effort to expand sales in his department, he was being forced to carry a larger share of the service department costs. On the other hand, the managers of the departments that showed no improvement in sales were relieved of a portion of the costs that they had been carrying. Yet there had been no change in the amount of services provided for any department.

The manager of the Suits Department viewed the increased service department cost allocation to his department as a penalty for his outstanding performance, and he wondered whether his efforts had really been worthwhile after all in the eyes of top management.

Sales dollars should be used as an allocation base only in those cases where service department costs are driven by sales. In those situations where service department costs are fixed, they should be allocated according to the three guidelines discussed earlier in the chapter.

Summary

Service departments are organized to provide some needed service in a single, centralized place, rather than have all units within the organization provide the service for themselves. Although service departments do not engage directly in production or other operating activities, the costs that they incur are vital to the overall success of an organization and therefore are properly included as part of the cost of its products and services.

Service department costs are charged to operating departments by an allocation process. In turn, the operating departments include the allocated costs in their budgets, from which overhead rates are computed for purposes of costing of products or services.

Variable and fixed service department costs should be allocated separately. The variable costs should be allocated according to whatever activity causes their incurrence. The fixed costs should be allocated in predetermined lump-sum amounts according to either the peak-period or the long-run average servicing needs of the consuming departments. Budgeted costs, rather than actual costs, should always be allocated. If actual costs are allocated, the operating departments would be implicitly held responsible for any inefficiency in the service departments. Any variances between budgeted and actual service department costs should be kept within the service departments and should be the responsibility of the service department managers.

Review Problem: Direct and Step Methods

Kovac Printing Company has three service departments and two operating departments. Selected data for the five departments relating to the most recent period follow:

	Service Department			Operating Department		
	Training	Janitorial	Maintenance	Offset Printing	Lithography	Total
Overhead costs	$360,000	$210,000	$96,000	$400,000	$534,000	$1,600,000
Number of employees	120	70	280	630	420	1,520
Square feet of space occupied	10,000	20,000	40,000	80,000	200,000	350,000
Hours of press time	—	—	—	30,000	60,000	90,000

The company allocates service department costs in the following order and using the bases indicated: Training (number of employees), Janitorial (space occupied), and Maintenance (hours of press time). The company makes no distinction between variable and fixed service department costs.

Required:

1. Use the direct method to allocate service department costs to the operating departments.
2. Use the step method to allocate service department costs to the operating departments.

Solution to Review Problem

1. Under the direct method, service department costs are allocated directly to the operating departments. Supporting computations for these allocations follow:

	Allocation Bases					
	Training		Janitorial		Maintenance	
Offset Printing data	630 employees	3/5	80,000 square feet	2/7	30,000 hours	1/3
Lithography data	420 employees	2/5	200,000 square feet	5/7	60,000 hours	2/3
Total	1,050 employees	5/5	280,000 square feet	7/7	90,000 hours	3/3

Given these allocation rates, the allocations to the operating departments would be as follows:

	Service Department			Operating Department		
	Training	Janitorial	Maintenance	Offset Printing	Lithography	Total
Overhead costs	$ 360,000	$ 210,000	$ 96,000	$400,000	$534,000	$1,600,000
Allocation:						
Training (3/5; 2/5)	(360,000)			216,000	144,000	
Janitorial (2/7; 5/7)		(210,000)		60,000	150,000	
Maintenance (1/3; 2/3)			(96,000)	32,000	64,000	
Total overhead cost after allocations	$ 0	$ 0	$ 0	$708,000	$892,000	$1,600,000

2. Under the step method, services rendered between service departments are recognized when costs are allocated to other departments. Starting with the Training service department, supporting computations for these allocations follow:

	Allocation Bases					
	Training		Janitorial		Maintenance	
Janitorial data	70 employees	5%	—		—	
Maintenance data .	280 employees	20%	40,000 square feet	1/8	—	
Offset Printing data	630 employees	45%	80,000 square feet	2/8	30,000 hours	1/3
Lithography data ..	420 employees	30%	200,000 square feet	5/8	60,000 hours	2/3
Total	1,400 employees	100%	320,000 square feet	8/8	90,000 hours	3/3

Given these ratios, the allocations to the various departments would be as follows:

	Service Department			Operating Department		
	Training	Janitorial	Maintenance	Offset Printing	Lithography	Total
Overhead costs	$ 360,000	$ 210,000	$ 96,000	$400,000	$534,000	$1,600,000
Allocation:						
Training (5%; 20%; 45%; 30%)*	(360,000)	18,000	72,000	162,000	108,000	
Janitorial (1/8; 2/8; 5/8)		(228,000)	28,500	57,000	142,500	
Maintenance (1/3; 2/3)			(196,500)	65,500	131,000	
Total overhead cost after allocations	$ 0	$ 0	$ 0	$684,500	$915,500	$1,600,000

*Allocation rates can be shown either in percentages, in fractions, or as a dollar rate per unit of activity. Both percentages and fractions are shown in this problem for sake of illustration. *It is better to use fractions if the use of percentages would result in rounding errors.*

Glossary

Direct method The allocation of all of a service department's costs directly to operating departments without recognizing services provided to other service departments. (p. 699)

Interdepartmental services Services provided between service departments. Also see *Reciprocal services.* (p. 699)

Operating department A department or similar unit in an organization within which the central purposes of the organization are carried out. (p. 698)

Reciprocal method A method of allocating service department costs that gives full recognition to interdepartmental services. (p. 702)

Reciprocal services Services provided between service departments. Also see *Interdepartmental services.* (p. 699)

Service department A department that provides support or assistance to operating departments and that does not engage directly in production or in other operating activities of an organization. (p. 698)

Step method The allocation of a service department's costs to other service departments, as well as to operating departments, in a sequential manner. The sequence typically starts with the service department that provides the greatest amount of service to other departments. (p. 701)

Questions

15–1 What is the difference between a service department and an operating department? Give several examples of service departments.

15–2 How are service department costs assigned to products and services?

15–3 What are interdepartmental service costs? How are such costs allocated to other departments under the step method?

15–4 How are service department costs allocated to other departments under the direct method?

15–5 If a service department generates revenues, how do these revenues enter into the allocation of the department's costs to other departments?

15–6 What guidelines should govern the allocation of fixed service department costs to other departments? The allocation of variable service department costs?

15–7 "A variable base should never be used in allocating fixed service department costs to operating departments." Explain.

Exercises

EXERCISE 15–1 Step Method [LO2]

Arbon Company has three service departments and two operating departments. Selected data on the five departments are presented below:

	Service Department			Operating Department		
	Administrative	Janitorial	Equipment Maintenance	Prep	Finishing	Total
Overhead costs	$84,000	$67,800	$36,000	$256,100	$498,600	$942,500
Number of employees	80	60	240	600	300	1,280
Square feet of space occupied	3,000	12,000	10,000	20,000	70,000	115,000
Machine-hours	—	—	—	10,000	30,000	40,000

The company allocates service department costs by the step method in the following order: Administrative (number of employees), Janitorial (space occupied), and Equipment Maintenance (machine-hours). The company makes no distinction between fixed and variable service department costs.

Required:

Using the step method, allocate the service department costs to the operating departments.

EXERCISE 15–2 Direct Method [LO1]

Refer to the data for Arbon Company in Exercise 15–1. Assume that the company allocates service department costs by the direct method, rather than by the step method.

Required:

Assuming that the company uses the direct method, how much overhead cost would be assigned to each operating department?

EXERCISE 15–3 Allocations by Cost Behavior at the Beginning of the Period [LO3]

Gutherie Oil Company has a Transport Services Department that provides trucks to transport crude oil from docks to the company's Arbon Refinery and Beck Refinery. Budgeted costs for the transport services consist of $0.30 per gallon variable cost and $200,000 fixed cost. The level of fixed cost is determined by peak-period requirements. During the peak period, Arbon Refinery requires 60% of the capacity and the Beck Refinery requires 40%.

During the coming year, 270,000 gallons of crude oil are budgeted to be hauled to the Arbon Refinery and 130,000 gallons of crude oil to the Beck Refinery.

Required:

Compute the amount of Transport Services Department cost that should be allocated to each refinery at the beginning of the year for purposes of computing predetermined overhead rates. (The company allocates variable and fixed costs separately.)

EXERCISE 15–4 Allocations by Cost Behavior at the End of the Period [LO3]

Refer to the data in Exercise 15–3. Assume that it is now the end of the year. During the year, the Transport Services Department actually hauled the following amounts of crude oil for the two refineries: Arbon Refinery, 260,000 gallons; and Beck Refinery, 140,000 gallons. The Transport Services Department incurred $365,000 in cost during the year, of which $148,000 was variable cost and $217,000 was fixed cost.

Management wants end-of-year service department cost allocations in order to compare actual performance to planned performance.

Required:

1. Determine how much of the $148,000 in variable cost should be allocated to each refinery.
2. Determine how much of the $217,000 in fixed cost should be allocated to each refinery.
3. Will any of the $365,000 in the Transport Services Department cost not be allocated to the refineries? Explain.

EXERCISE 15–5 Allocating Variable Costs at the End of the Year [LO3]
Reed Company operates a Medical Services Department for its employees. The variable costs of the department are allocated to operating departments on the basis of the number of employees in each department. Budgeted and actual data for last year are given below:

	Variable Costs	
	Budgeted	**Actual**
Medical Services Department	$60 per employee	$72 per employee

The budgeted and actual number of employees in each operating department during the year appear below.

	Department		
	Cutting	**Milling**	**Assembly**
Budgeted number of employees	600	300	900
Actual number of employees	500	400	800

Required:
Determine the amount of Medical Services Department variable cost that should have been allocated to each of the three operating departments at the end of the year, for purposes of comparing actual performance to planned performance.

EXERCISE 15–6 Allocations of Fixed Costs [LO3]
Refer to the data for Reed Company in Exercise 15–5. In addition to the Medical Services Department, the company also has a Janitorial Services Department that provides services to all other departments in the company. The fixed costs of the two service departments are allocated on the following bases:

Department	Basis for Allocation	
Janitorial Services	Square footage of space occupied:	
	Medical Services Department . . .	6,000 square feet
	Cutting Department	30,000 square feet
	Milling Department	24,000 square feet
	Assembly Department	90,000 square feet
Medical Services	Long-run average number of employees:	
	Janitorial Services Department . .	20 employees
	Cutting Department	600 employees
	Milling Department	400 employees
	Assembly Department	1,000 employees

Budgeted and actual fixed costs in the two service departments for the year follow:

	Janitorial Services	Medical Services
Budgeted fixed costs	$350,000	$596,000
Actual fixed costs	361,000	605,000

Required:
1. Show the allocation of the fixed costs of the two service departments at the beginning of the year. The company uses the step method of allocation, starting with the Janitorial Services Department.
2. Show the allocation of the fixed costs of the two service departments at the end of the year for purposes of comparing actual performance to planned performance.

EXERCISE 15–7 Sales Dollars as an Allocation Base for Fixed Costs [LO3]
Lacey's Department Store allocates its fixed administrative expenses to its four operating departments on the basis of sales dollars. During 2001, the fixed administrative expenses totaled $900,000. These expenses were allocated as follows:

	Department				
	Men's	Women's	Shoes	House-wares	Total
Total sales—2001	$600,000	$1,500,000	$2,100,000	$1,800,000	$6,000,000
Percentage of total sales	10%	25%	35%	30%	100%
Allocation (based on the above percentages)	$90,000	$225,000	$315,000	$270,000	$900,000

During 2002, the following year, the Women's Department doubled its sales. The sales levels in the other three departments remained unchanged. The company's 2002 sales data were as follows:

	Department				
	Men's	Women's	Shoes	House-wares	Total
Total sales—2002	$600,000	$3,000,000	$2,100,000	$1,800,000	$7,500,000
Percent of total sales ...	8%	40%	28%	24%	100%

Fixed administrative expenses remained unchanged at $900,000 during 2002.

Required:

1. Using sales dollars as an allocation base, show the allocation of the fixed administrative expenses among the four departments for 2002.
2. Compare your allocation from (1) above to the allocation for 2001. As the manager of the Women's Department, how would you feel about the administrative expenses that have been charged to you for 2002?
3. Comment on the usefulness of sales dollars as an allocation base.

Problems

PROBLEM 15–8 Step Method versus Direct Method; Predetermined Overhead Rates [LO1, LO2]

Petah, Ltd., of Tel Aviv, Israel, has budgeted costs in its various departments as follows for the coming year:

Factory Administration	₪ 540,000
Custodial Services	137,520
Personnel	57,680
Maintenance	90,400
Stamping—overhead	752,600
Assembly—overhead	351,800
Total overhead cost	₪1,930,000

(The Israeli currency is the shekel, denoted by ₪.)

The company allocates service department costs to other departments, *in the order listed below.*

	Number of Employees	Total Labor-Hours	Square Meters of Space Occupied	Direct Labor-Hours	Machine-Hours
Factory Administration ...	22	—	5,000	—	—
Custodial Services	8	6,000	2,000	—	—
Personnel	10	10,000	3,000	—	—
Maintenance	50	44,000	10,000	—	—
Stamping—overhead	80	60,000	70,000	40,000	140,000
Assembly—overhead ...	120	180,000	20,000	160,000	20,000
	290	300,000	110,000	200,000	160,000

Stamping and Assembly are operating departments; the other departments all act in a service capacity. The company does not make a distinction between fixed and variable service department costs. Factory Administration is allocated on the basis of labor-hours; Custodial Services on the basis of square meters occupied; Personnel on the basis of number of employees; and Maintenance on the basis of machine-hours.

Required:

1. Allocate service department costs to consuming departments by the step method. Then compute predetermined overhead rates in the operating departments, using a machine-hours basis in Stamping and a direct labor-hours basis in Assembly.
2. Repeat (1) above, this time using the direct method. Again compute predetermined overhead rates in Stamping and Assembly.
3. Assume that the company doesn't want to bother with allocating service department costs but simply wants to compute a single plantwide overhead rate based on total overhead costs (both service department and operating department) divided by total direct labor-hours. Compute the overhead rate.
4. Suppose a job requires machine and labor time as follows:

	Machine-Hours	Direct Labor-Hours
Stamping Department	190	25
Assembly Department	10	75
Total hours	200	100

Using the overhead rates computed in (1), (2), and (3) above, compute the amount of overhead cost that would be assigned to the job if the overhead rates were developed using the step method, the direct method, and the plantwide method. (Round allocations to the nearest whole shekel.)

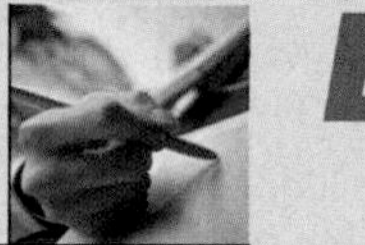

PROBLEM 15–9 Allocating by Cost Behavior [LO3]

Northstar Company has two operating divisions—Machine Tools and Special Products. The company has a maintenance department that services the equipment in both divisions. The costs of operating the maintenance department are budgeted at $80,000 per month plus $0.50 per machine-hour. The fixed costs of the maintenance department are determined by peak-period requirements. The Machine Tools Division requires 65% of the peak-period capacity, and the Special Products Division requires 35%.

For October, the Machine Tools Division has estimated that it will operate at a 90,000 machine-hours level of activity and the Special Products Division has estimated that it will operate at a 60,000 machine-hours level of activity.

Required:

1. At the beginning of October, how much maintenance department cost should be allocated to each division for planning purposes?
2. Assume that it is now the end of October. Cost records in the maintenance department show that actual fixed costs for the month totaled $85,000 and that actual variable costs totaled $78,000. Due to labor unrest and an unexpected strike, the Machine Tools Division worked only 60,000 machine-hours during the month. The Special Products Division also worked 60,000 machine-hours, as planned. How much of the actual maintenance department costs for the month should be allocated to each division? (Management uses these end-of-month allocations to compare actual performance against planned performance.)
3. Refer to the data in (2) above. Assume that the company follows the practice of allocating *all* maintenance department costs each month to the divisions in proportion to the actual machine-hours recorded in each division for the month. On this basis, how much cost would be allocated to each division for October?
4. What criticisms can you make of the allocation method used in (3) above?
5. If managers of producing departments know that fixed service costs are going to be allocated on the basis of peak-period requirements, what will be their probable strategy as they report their estimate of peak-period requirements to the company's budget committee? As a member of top management, what would you do to neutralize any such strategies?

PROBLEM 15–10 Beginning- and End-of-Year Allocations [LO3]

Björnson A/S of Norway has only one service department—a cafeteria, in which meals are provided for employees in the company's Milling and Finishing departments. The costs of the cafeteria are all paid by the company as a fringe benefit to its employees. These costs are allocated to the Milling and Finishing departments on the basis of meals served to employees in each department. Cost and other data relating to the Cafeteria and to the Milling and Finishing departments for the most recent year are provided below. (The Norwegian unit of currency is the krone, which is indicated below by K.)

Cafeteria:

	Budget	Actual
Variable costs for food	300,000K*	384,000K
Fixed costs	200,000	215,000

*Budgeted at 20K per meal served.

Milling and Finishing departments:

	Percent of Peak-Period Capacity Required	Number of Meals Served	
		Budget	Actual
Milling Department	70%	10,000	12,000
Finishing Department	30%	5,000	4,000
Total	100%	15,000	16,000

The company allocates variable and fixed costs separately. The level of fixed costs is determined by peak-period requirements.

Required:

1. Assume that it is the beginning of the year. How much of the budgeted Cafeteria cost above would be allocated to the Milling and Finishing departments?
2. Assume that it is now the end of the year. Management would like data to assist in comparing actual performance to planned performance in the Cafeteria and in the other departments.
   a. How much of the actual Cafeteria costs above would be allocated to the Milling Department and to the Finishing Department?
   b. Would any portion of the actual Cafeteria costs not be allocated to the other departments? If so, compute the amount that would not be allocated, and explain why it would not be allocated.

PROBLEM 15–11 Allocating Costs Equitably among Divisions [LO3]

First Bank maintains its own computer to service the needs of its three divisions. The company assigns the costs of the computer center to the three divisions on the basis of the number of lines of print prepared for each division during the month.

In July, Carol Benz, manager of the Lending Division, came to the company's controller seeking an explanation as to why her division had been charged a larger amount for computer services in June than in May, although her division had used the computer less in June. During the course of the discussion, the data in the worksheet on the next page were referred to by the controller:

"You see," said Eric Weller, the controller, "the computer center has large amounts of fixed costs that continue regardless of how much the computer is used. We have built into the computer enough capacity to handle the divisions' peak-period needs, and this cost must be absorbed by someone. I know it hurts, but the fact is that during June your division received a greater share of the computer's output than it did during May; therefore, it has been allocated a greater share of the cost."

Carol Benz was unhappy with this explanation. "I still don't understand why I would be charged more for the computer, when I used it less," she said. "There must be a better way to handle these cost allocations."

An analysis of the divisions' peak-period needs shows that the Lending Division requires 40% of the computer's peak-period capacity, the Retail Division requires 12%, and the Commercial Division requires 48%.

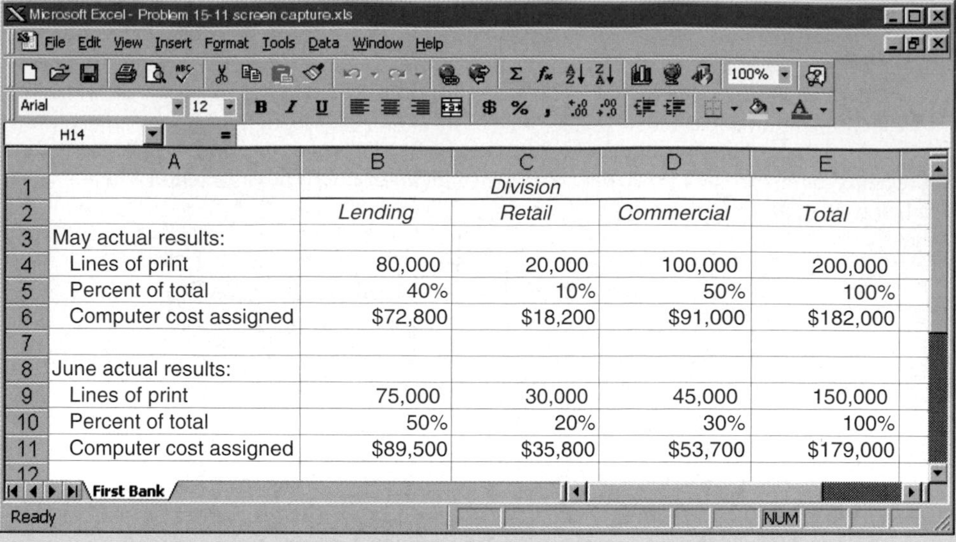

Microsoft Excel - Problem 15-11 screen capture.xls

	A	B	C	D	E
1			Division		
2		*Lending*	*Retail*	*Commercial*	*Total*
3	May actual results:				
4	Lines of print	80,000	20,000	100,000	200,000
5	Percent of total	40%	10%	50%	100%
6	Computer cost assigned	$72,800	$18,200	$91,000	$182,000
7					
8	June actual results:				
9	Lines of print	75,000	30,000	45,000	150,000
10	Percent of total	50%	20%	30%	100%
11	Computer cost assigned	$89,500	$35,800	$53,700	$179,000

Required:

1. Is there any merit to Carol Benz's complaint? Explain.
2. Using the high-low method, determine the monthly cost of the computer in terms of a variable rate per line of print and total fixed cost.
3. Reallocate the computer center costs for May and June in accordance with the cost allocation principles discussed in the chapter. Allocate the variable and fixed costs separately.

PROBLEM 15–12 Step Method [LO2, LO3]

Pleasant View Hospital has three service departments—Food Services, Administrative Services, and X-ray Services. The costs of these departments are allocated by the step method, using the bases and in the order shown below:

Service Department	Costs Incurred	Base for Allocation
Food Services	Variable	Meals served
	Fixed	Peak-period needs
Administrative Services	Variable	Files processed
	Fixed	10% X-ray Services, 20% Outpatient Clinic, 30% OB Care, and 40% General Hospital
X-ray Services	Variable	X-rays taken
	Fixed	Peak-period needs

Estimated cost and operating data for all departments in the hospital for the forthcoming month are presented in the following table:

	Food Services	Admin. Services	X-Ray Services	Outpatient Clinic	OB Care	General Hospital	Total
Variable costs	$ 73,150	$ 6,800	$38,100	$11,700	$ 14,850	$ 53,400	$198,000
Fixed costs	48,000	33,040	59,520	26,958	99,738	344,744	612,000
Total costs	$121,150	$39,840	$97,620	$38,658	$114,588	$398,144	$810,000
Files processed	—	—	1,500	3,000	900	12,000	17,400
X-rays taken	—	—	—	1,200	350	8,400	9,950
Percent of peak-period X-ray Services needs	—	—	—	13%	3%	84%	100%
Meals served	—	1,000	500	—	7,000	30,000	38,500
Percent of peak-period Food Services needs	—	2%	1%	—	17%	80%	100%

All billing in the hospital is done through the Outpatient Clinic, OB Care, or General Hospital. The hospital's administrator wants the costs of the three service departments allocated to these three billing centers.

Required:
Prepare the cost allocation desired by the hospital administrator. Include under each billing center the direct costs of the center as well as the costs allocated from the service departments.

PROBLEM 15–13 Step Method [LO2, LO3]
The Coral Lake Hotel has three service departments—Grounds and Maintenance, General Administration, and Laundry. The costs of these departments are allocated by the step method using the bases and in the order shown below:

Grounds and Maintenance:
 Fixed costs—allocated on the basis of square feet of space occupied.

General Administration:
 Variable costs—allocated on the basis of number of actual employees.
 Fixed costs—allocated 20% to Laundry, 14% to Convention Center, 36% to Food Services, and 30% to Lodging.

Laundry:
 Variable costs—allocated on the basis of number of items processed.
 Fixed costs—allocated on the basis of the percentage of peak-period requirements.

Cost and operating data for all departments in the hotel for a recent month are presented in the table below:

	Grounds and Maintenance	General Administration	Laundry	Convention Center	Food Services	Lodging	Total
Variable costs	$ 0	$ 915	$13,725	$ 0	$ 48,000	$ 36,450	$ 99,090
Fixed costs	17,500	12,150	18,975	28,500	64,000	81,000	222,125
Total overhead costs	$17,500	$13,065	$32,700	$28,500	$112,000	$117,450	$321,215
Square feet of space	2,000	2,500	3,750	15,000	6,250	97,500	127,000
Number of employees	9	5	10	5	25	21	75
Laundry items processed	—	—	—	1,000	5,250	40,000	46,250
Percent of peak-period laundry requirements	—	—	—	3%	13%	84%	100%

All billing in the hotel is done through the Convention Center, Food Services, and Lodging. The hotel's general manager wants the costs of the three service departments allocated to these three billing centers.

Required:
Prepare the cost allocation desired by the hotel's general manager. Include under each billing center the direct costs of the center, as well as the costs allocated from the service departments.

PROBLEM 15–14 Step Method; Predetermined Overhead Rates; Unit Costs [LO2, LO3]
Apsco Products has two service departments—Medical Services and Maintenance—and two producing departments—Metals and Plastics. Estimated monthly cost and operating data for the coming year are given below. These data have been prepared for purposes of computing predetermined overhead rates in the producing departments.

	Medical Services	Maintenance	Metals	Plastics
Direct labor cost	—	—	$ 30,000	$ 40,000
Maintenance labor cost	—	$ 5,000	—	—
Direct materials	—	—	50,000	80,000
Maintenance materials	—	7,536	—	—
Medical supplies	$ 3,630	—	—	—
Miscellaneous overhead costs	7,500	6,000	104,000	155,000
Total costs	$11,130	$18,536	$184,000	$275,000
Direct labor-hours	—	—	6,000	10,000
Number of employees:				
Currently employed	3	8	38	64
Long-run employee needs	3	10	60	80
Floor space occupied—square feet	800	1,500	8,000	12,000

Apsco Products allocates service department costs to producing departments for product costing purposes. The step method is used, starting with Medical Services. Allocation bases for the service departments are as follows:

Department	Costs Incurred	Base for Allocation
Medical Services	Variable	Currently employed workers
	Fixed	Long-run employee needs
Maintenance	Variable	Direct labor-hours
	Fixed	Square footage of floor space occupied

The behavior of various costs is shown below:

	Medical Services	Maintenance
Maintenance labor cost	—	V
Maintenance materials	—	V
Medical supplies	V	—
Miscellaneous overhead costs	F	F

V = Variable.
F = Fixed.

Required:

1. Show the allocation of the service department costs for the purpose of computing predetermined overhead rates. Round all allocations to the nearest whole dollar.
2. Compute the predetermined overhead rate in each of the producing departments (overhead rates are based on direct labor-hours).
3. Assume that production in the Plastics Department is planned at 20,000 units for the month. Compute the planned cost of one unit of product in the Plastics Department.

Cases

CASE 15–15 Step Method versus Direct Method [LO1, LO2]

"I can't understand what's happening here," said Mike Holt, president of Severson Products, Inc. "We always seem to bid too high on jobs that require a lot of labor time in the Finishing Department, and we always seem to get every job we bid on that requires a lot of machine time in the Milling Department. Yet we don't seem to be making much money on those Milling Department jobs. I wonder if the problem is in our overhead rates."

Severson Products manufactures high-quality wood products to customers' specifications. Some jobs take a large amount of machine work in the Milling Department, and other jobs take a large amount of hand finishing work in the Finishing Department. In addition to the Milling and Finishing departments, the company has three service departments. The costs of these service departments are allocated to other departments *in the order listed below.* (For each service department, use the most appropriate allocation base.)

	Total Labor-Hours	Square Feet of Space Occupied	Number of Employees	Machine-Hours	Direct Labor-Hours
Cafeteria	16,000	12,000	25	—	—
Custodial Services	9,000	3,000	40	—	—
Machinery Maintenance	15,000	10,000	60	—	—
Milling	30,000	40,000	100	160,000	20,000
Finishing	100,000	20,000	300	40,000	70,000
	170,000	85,000	525	200,000	90,000

Budgeted overhead costs in each department for the current year are as follows (no distinction is made between variable and fixed costs):

Cafeteria	$ 320,000*
Custodial Services	65,400
Machinery Maintenance	93,600
Milling	416,000
Finishing	166,000
Total budgeted costs	$1,061,000

*This represents the amount of cost subsidized by the company.

The company has always allocated service department costs to the producing departments (Milling and Finishing) using the direct method of allocation, because of its simplicity.

Required:

1. Allocate service department costs to using departments by the step method. Then compute predetermined overhead rates in the producing departments for the current year, using a machine-hours basis in the Milling Department and a direct labor-hours basis in the Finishing Department.
2. Repeat (1) above, this time using the direct method. Again compute predetermined overhead rates in the Milling and Finishing Departments.
3. Assume that during the current year the company bids on a job that requires machine and labor time as follows:

	Machine-Hours	Direct Labor-Hours
Milling Department	2,000	1,600
Finishing Department	800	13,000
Total hours	2,800	14,600

a. Determine the amount of overhead that would be assigned to the job if the company used the overhead rates developed in (1) above. Then determine the amount of overhead that would be assigned to the job if the company used the overhead rates developed in (2) above.

b. Explain to the president why the step method would provide a better basis for computing predetermined overhead rates than the direct method.

CASE 15–16 Direct Method; Plantwide versus Departmental Overhead Rates [LO1, LO3]

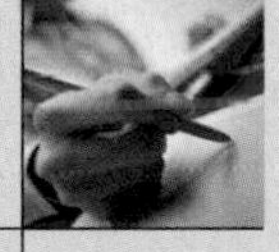

Sun Concepts, Inc., manufactures and markets a complete line of surfboards. Sun Concepts has three manufacturing departments—Molding, Assembly, and Finishing—and two service departments—Quality Control and Maintenance.

The basic fiberglass boards are fabricated in the Molding Department. Fittings are attached to the boards in the Assembly Department. The boards are painted, surfaces are sanded and polished, and the completed boards are packed in the Finishing Department. Varying amounts of materials, time, and effort are required for each of the various surfboards produced by the company. The Quality Control Department and Maintenance Department provide services to the manufacturing departments.

Sun Concepts has always used a plantwide overhead rate. Direct labor-hours are used to assign the overhead to products. The overhead rate is computed by dividing the company's total estimated overhead cost by the total estimated direct labor-hours to be worked in the three manufacturing departments.

Pui Lan Lee, manager of cost accounting, has recommended that the company use departmental overhead rates rather than a single, plantwide rate. Planned operating costs and expected levels of activity for the coming year have been developed by Lee and are presented below:

	Service Department Costs	
	Quality Control	Maintenance
Variable costs	$ 60,000	$ 8,000
Fixed costs	140,000	78,000
Total service department costs	$200,000	$86,000

	Manufacturing Department		
	Molding	**Assembly**	**Finishing**
Departmental activity measures:			
Direct labor-hours	10,000	40,000	30,000
Machine-hours	0	8,000	50,000
Department costs:			
Raw materials	$ 800,000	$2,000,000	$ 100,000
Direct labor	150,000	600,000	450,000
Variable overhead	100,000	200,000	50,000
Fixed overhead	1,200,300	702,300	597,400
Total department costs	$2,250,300	$3,502,300	$1,197,400

	Manufacturing Department		
	Molding	**Assembly**	**Finishing**
Use of service departments:			
Quality control:			
Estimated quality control hours	4,000	3,000	1,000
Percentage of peak-period requirements	50%	35%	15%
Maintenance:			
Estimated maintenance hours	200	600	800
Percentage of peak-period requirements	15%	40%	45%

Required:

1. Assume that the company will use a single, plantwide overhead rate for the coming year, the same as in the past. Compute the plantwide rate that would be used.
2. Assume that Pui Lan Lee has been asked to develop departmental overhead rates for the three manufacturing departments for comparison with the plantwide rate. To develop these rates, do the following:
   a. Using the direct method, allocate the service department costs to the manufacturing departments. In each case, allocate the variable and fixed costs separately. The fixed portion of the service department costs are incurred in order to support peak-period activity.
   b. Compute overhead rates for the three manufacturing departments for the coming year. In computing the rates, use a machine-hours basis in the Finishing Department and a direct labor-hours basis in the other two departments.
3. Assume that the Pipeline model surfboard has the following annual requirements for machine time and direct labor time in the various departments:

	Machine-Hours	**Direct Labor-Hours**
Molding Department	0	500
Assembly Department	200	1,000
Finishing Department	1,500	800
Total hours	1,700	2,300

   a. Compute the amount of overhead cost that would be allocated to the Pipeline model if a plantwide overhead rate is used. Repeat the computation, this time assuming that departmental overhead rates are used.
   b. Sun Concepts marks up its product costs by a preset percentage to determine its selling prices. Management is concerned because the Pipeline model is priced well below competing products of competitors. On the other hand, certain other of Sun Concepts' products are priced well above the prices of competitors with the result that profits in the company are deteriorating because of declining sales. Looking at the computations in (*a*) above, what effect is the use of a plantwide rate having on the costing of products and therefore on selling prices?
4. What additional steps could Sun Concepts, Inc., take to improve its overhead costing?

(CMA, adapted)

Group and Internet Exercises

GROUP EXERCISE 15–17 Understanding the Cost of Complexity

Service departments (or production support departments in the case of a manufacturer) make up a large and growing part of the cost structure of most businesses. This is as true in hospitals, financial institutions, universities, and other service industries as it is in manufacturing. The overall costs of service departments are high and rising. In many manufacturing firms, production support department costs can average 40% or more of total manufacturing costs. Yet, in reality, very little is known about the source or behavior of these discretionary fixed costs. If you don't know where these costs came from and you don't have a good understanding of how the costs behave, it is going to be very difficult to control and reduce these costs.

In an effort to reduce costs, many companies think all they have to do is reduce head count, a demoralizing and debilitating experience not only for those who lose their jobs, but also for those who remain employed. One sure sign of problems with this head-count-reduction approach is that more than half of firms refill these positions within a year after eliminating them.

Required:

1. Choose an industry with which you are somewhat familiar (or with which someone you know is familiar) and list seven or eight major production support or service departments in the factory or other facility in this industry. What is the output of each of these support or service departments?
2. Assume a relatively uncomplicated factory (facility) where just a single, standard product (or service) is mass produced. Describe the activity or work being done in each of the service areas of this focused firm.
3. Now assume a more complicated operation for another factory located close by where a wide range of products are made or services are offered—some are standard products/services while others are made to order, some are high-volume products/services while others are low volume, and some are fairly complex products/services while others are relatively simple. Describe the activity or work being done in the various service functions for this full-service firm.
4. Which factory or facility has higher production support costs? Why?
5. Explain the relationship between the range of products produced and the size of the support departments. When does the output of each of these support departments increase? When does the cost of each of these support departments increase?
6. Most firms are under increasing pressure to reduce costs. How would you go about bringing the overall level of service department costs down?

INTERNET EXERCISE 15–18

As you know, the World Wide Web is a medium that is constantly evolving. Sites come and go, and change without notice. To enable periodic update of site addresses, this problem has been posted to the textbook website (www.mhhe.com/garrison10e). After accessing the site, enter the Student Center and select this chapter. Select and complete the Internet Exercise.

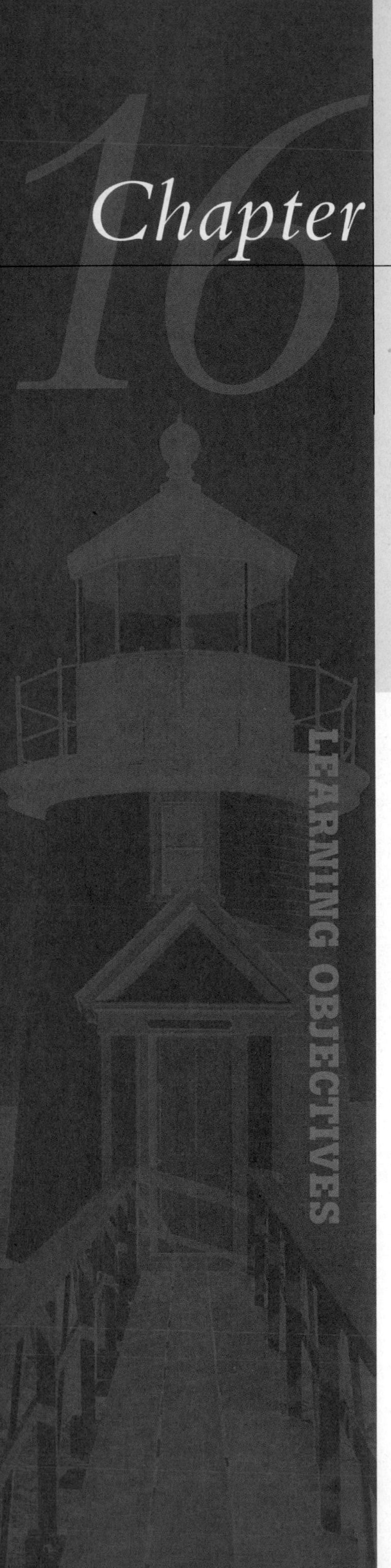

Chapter Sixteen

"How Well Am I Doing?" Statement of Cash Flows

After studying Chapter 16, you should be able to:

1. Know how to classify changes in noncash balance sheet accounts as sources or uses of cash.
2. State the general rules for determining whether transactions should be classified as operating activities, investing activities, or financing activities.
3. Prepare a statement of cash flows using the indirect method to determine the net cash provided by operating activities.
4. (Appendix 16A) Use the direct method to determine the net cash provided by operating activities.

Focus on Cash

One veteran entrepreneur describes the importance of cash flow in the following terms: "There's a hard lesson we all have to learn when we go into business. The lesson is that you live or die on cash flow. Sales are nice. Profits are even nicer. But it's cash flow that determines whether or not you survive. Where most first-time entrepreneurs trip up is in failing to understand that more sales almost always mean less cash flow—and less cash flow means trouble."

Source: Norm Brodsky, "Paying for Growth," *Inc.*, October 1996, p. 29.

Three major financial statements are ordinarily required for external reports—an income statement, a balance sheet, and a statement of cash flows. The purpose of the **statement of cash flows** is to highlight the major activities that directly and indirectly impact cash flows and hence affect the overall cash balance. Managers focus on cash for a very good reason—without sufficient cash at the right times, a company may miss golden opportunities or may even fall into bankruptcy.

The statement of cash flows answers questions that cannot be answered by the income statement and balance sheet. For example, the statement of cash flows can be used to answer questions like the following: Where did Delta Airlines get the cash to pay a dividend of nearly $140 million in a year in which, according to its income statement, it lost more than $1 billion? How was The Walt Disney Company able to invest nearly $800 million in expansion of its theme parks, including a major renovation of Epcot Center, despite a loss of more than $500 million on its investment in EuroDisney? Where did Wendy's International, Inc., get $125 million to expand its chain of fast-food restaurants in a year in which its net income was only $79 million and it did not raise any new debt? To answer such questions, familiarity with the statement of cash flows is required.

The statement of cash flows is a valuable analytical tool for managers as well as for investors and creditors, although managers tend to be more concerned with forecasted statements of cash flows that are prepared as part of the budgeting process. The statement of cash flows can be used to answer crucial questions such as the following:

1. Is the company generating sufficient positive cash flows from its ongoing operations to remain viable?
2. Will the company be able to repay its debts?
3. Will the company be able to pay its usual dividend?
4. Why is there a difference between net income and net cash flow for the year?
5. To what extent will the company have to borrow money in order to make needed investments?

In this chapter, our focus is on preparing the statement of cash flows and on its use as a tool for assessing the financial state of a company.

In Business

Watching the Cash Flow at a Dot.Com

George Pilla is a finance consultant who has been working with new businesses like AP Engines, a billing software firm for Internet Protocol phone and cable service. He has found that the burn rate (the rate at which cash is consumed by a company) is critical. "Running out of cash is the worst thing," says Pilla, "and we are usually working three to six months ahead, trying to figure out when we're going to run out of cash and how we're going to fund [the company]."

Source: George Donnelly, "Start Me Up," *CFO*, July 2000, pp. 77–84.

The Basic Approach to a Statement of Cash Flows

LEARNING OBJECTIVE 1
Know how to classify changes in noncash balance sheet accounts as sources or uses of cash.

For the statement of cash flows to be useful to managers and others, it is important that companies employ a common definition of cash. It is also important that the statement be constructed using consistent guidelines for identifying activities that are *sources* of cash and *uses* of cash. The proper definition of cash and the guidelines to use in identifying sources and uses of cash are discussed in this section.

Definition of Cash

In preparing a statement of cash flows, the term *cash* is broadly defined to include both cash and cash equivalents. **Cash equivalents** consist of short-term, highly liquid investments such as Treasury bills, commercial paper, and money market funds that are made solely for the purpose of generating a return on temporarily idle funds. Instead of simply holding cash, most companies invest their excess cash reserves in these types of interest-bearing assets that can be easily converted into cash. These short-term, liquid assets are usually included in *marketable securities* on the balance sheet. Since such assets are equivalent to cash, they are included with cash in preparing a statement of cash flows.

Constructing the Statement of Cash Flows Using Changes in Noncash Balance Sheet Accounts

While not the recommended procedure, a type of statement of cash flows could be constructed by simply summarizing all of the debits and credits to the Cash and Cash Equivalents accounts during a period. However, this approach would overlook all of the transactions that involved an implicit exchange of cash. For example, when a company purchases inventory on credit, cash is implicitly exchanged. In essence, the supplier loans the company cash, which the company then uses to acquire inventory from the supplier. Rather than just looking at the transactions that explicitly involve cash, financial statement users are interested in all of the transactions that implicitly or explicitly involve cash. When inventory is purchased on credit, the Inventory account increases, which is an implicit *use* of cash. At the same time, Accounts Payable increases, which is an implicit *source* of cash. In general, increases in the Inventory account are classified as uses of cash and increases in the Accounts Payable account are classified as sources of cash. This suggests that analyzing changes in balance sheet accounts, such as Inventory and Accounts Payable, will uncover both the explicit and implicit sources and uses of cash. And this is indeed the basic approach taken in the statement of cash flows. The logic underlying this approach is demonstrated in Exhibit 16–1.

Exhibit 16–1 requires some explanation. The exhibit shows how net cash flow can be explained in terms of net income, dividends, and changes in balance sheet accounts. The first line in the exhibit consists of the balance sheet equation: Assets = Liabilities + Stockholders' Equity. The first step is to recognize that assets consist of cash and non-

Exhibit 16–1 Explaining Net Cash Flow by Analysis of the Noncash Balance Sheet Accounts

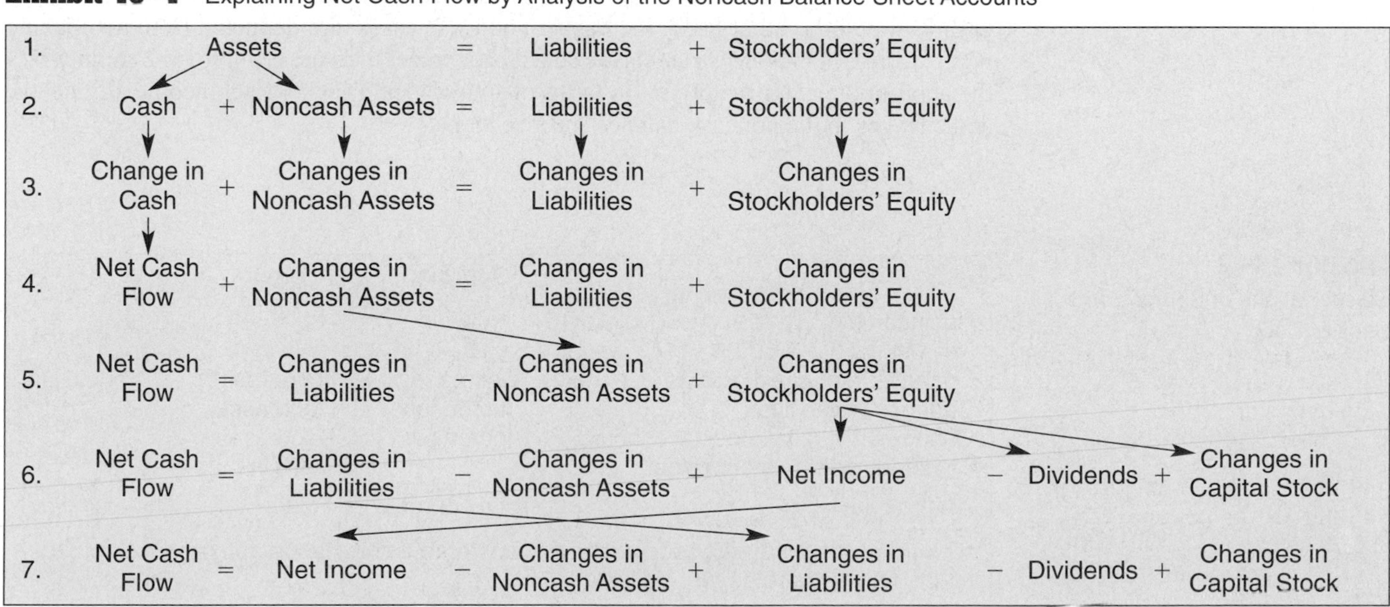

cash assets. This is shown in the second line of the exhibit. The third line in the exhibit recognizes that if the account balances are always equal, then the changes in the account balances must be equal too. The next step is simply to note that the change in cash for a period is by definition the company's net cash flow, which yields line 4 in the exhibit. The only difference between line 4 and line 5 is that the changes in noncash assets is moved from the left-hand side of the equation to the right-hand side. This is done because we are attempting to explain net cash flow, so it should be by itself on the left-hand side of the equation. To get from line 5 to line 6, we need to remember that stockholders' equity is affected by net income, dividends, and changes in capital stock. Net income increases stockholders' equity, while dividends reduce stockholders' equity. To get from line 6 of the exhibit to line 7, a few terms on the right-hand side of the equation are rearranged.

In Business

What's Up at Amazon?

Amazon.com, the online retailer of books and other merchandise, is often given the best chance of eventually succeeding of any Internet retailer. Even so, "[I]t's no news that Amazon has had troubles, but the numbers are worse than many on Wall Street have admitted." Robert Tracy, a CPA and an analyst on the staff of grantsinvestor.com, took a close look at Amazon's financial statements and found that the company is holding its bills longer than it used to, especially at year-end. The cash flow from this increase in accounts payable exceeded the cash flow from all other operating sources combined. "Bulls [i.e., those who are positive about Amazon.com stock] will commend the company on imaginative cash management. Bears [i.e., those who are skeptical about the stock] will accuse it of financial engineering. What is not debatable is that, by stretching out payments into the new year, Amazon has presented a more liquid face to the world than it could otherwise have done."

Source: James Grant, "Diving into Amazon," *Forbes*, January 22, 2001, p. 153.

According to equation 7 in Exhibit 16–1, the net cash flow for a period can be determined by starting with net income, then deducting changes in noncash assets, adding changes in liabilities, deducting dividends paid to stockholders, and finally adding changes in capital stock. It is important to realize that changes in accounts can be either increases (positive) or decreases (negative), and this affects how we should interpret equation 7 in Exhibit 16–1. For example, increases in liabilities are added back to net income, whereas decreases in liabilities are deducted from net income to arrive at the net cash flow. On the other hand, increases in noncash assets are deducted from net income while decreases in noncash assets are added back to net income. Exhibit 16–2 summarizes the appropriate classifications—in terms of sources and uses—of net income, dividends, and changes in the noncash balance sheet accounts.

Exhibit 16–2
Classifications of Sources and Uses of Cash

	Sources		Uses	
Net income	Always			
Net loss			Always	
Changes in noncash assets	Decreases		Increases	
Changes in liabilities*	Increases		Decreases	
Changes in capital stock accounts	Increases		Decreases	
Dividends paid to stockholders			Always	
	Total sources	−	Total uses	= Net cash flow

*Contra asset accounts, such as the Accumulated Depreciation and Amortization account, follow the rules for liabilities.

The classifications in Exhibit 16–2 seem to make sense. Positive net income generates cash, whereas a net loss consumes cash. Decreases in noncash assets, such as sale of inventories or property, are a source of cash. Increases in noncash assets, such as purchase of inventories or property, are a use of cash. Increases in liabilities, such as taking out a loan, are a source of cash. Decreases in liabilities, such as paying off a loan, are a use of cash. Increases in capital stock accounts, such as sale of common stock, are a source of cash. And payments of dividends to stockholders use cash.

Constructing a simple statement of cash flows is a straightforward process. Begin with net income (or net loss) and then add to it everything listed as sources in Exhibit 16–2 and subtract from it everything listed as uses. This will be illustrated with an example in the next section.

An Example of a Simplified Statement of Cash Flows

To illustrate the ideas introduced in the preceding section, we construct in this section a *simplified* statement of cash flows for Nordstrom, Inc., one of the leading fashion retailers in the United States. This simplified statement does not follow the format required by the FASB for external financial reports, but it shows where the numbers come from in a statement of cash flows and how they fit together. In later sections, we will show how the same basic data can be used to construct a full-fledged statement of cash flows that would be acceptable for external reports.

Constructing a Simplified Statement of Cash Flows

According to Exhibit 16–2, to construct a statement of cash flows we need the company's net income or loss, the changes in each of its balance sheet accounts, and the dividends paid to stockholders for the year. We can obtain this information from the Nordstrom financial statements that appear in Exhibits 16–3, 16–4, and 16–5. In a few instances, the actual statements have been simplified for ease of computation and discussion.

Exhibit 16–3

NORDSTROM, INC.*
Income Statement
(dollars in millions)

Net sales	$3,638
Less cost of sales	2,469
Gross margin	1,169
Less operating expenses	941
Net operating income	228
Nonoperating items:	
Gain on sale of store	3
Income before taxes	231
Less income taxes	91
Net income	$ 140

*This statement is loosely based on an actual income statement published by Nordstrom. Among other differences, there was no "Gain on sale of store" in the original statement. This "gain" has been included here to illustrate how to handle gains and losses on a statement of cash flows.

Exhibit 16–4

NORDSTROM, INC.*
Comparative Balance Sheet
(dollars in millions)

	Ending Balance	Beginning Balance	Change	Source or Use?
Assets				
Current assets:				
Cash and cash equivalents	$ 91	$ 29	$+62	
Accounts receivable	637	654	−17	Source
Merchandise inventory	586	537	+49	Use
Total current assets	1,314	1,220		
Property, buildings, and equipment	1,517	1,394	+123	Use
Less accumulated depreciation and amortization	654	561	+93	Source
Net property, buildings, and equipment	863	833		
Total assets	$2,177	$2,053		
Liabilities and Stockholders' Equity				
Current liabilities:				
Accounts payable	$ 264	$ 220	+44	Source
Accrued wages and salaries payable	193	190	+3	Source
Accrued income taxes payable	28	22	+6	Source
Notes payable	40	38	+2	Source
Total current liabilities	525	470		
Long-term debt	439	482	−43	Use
Deferred income taxes	47	49	−2	Use
Total liabilities	1,011	1,001		
Stockholders' equity:				
Common stock	157	155	+2	Source
Retained earnings	1,009	897	+112	†
Total stockholders' equity	1,166	1,052		
Total liabilities and stockholders' equity	$2,177	$2,053		

*This statement differs from the actual statement published by Nordstrom.

†The change in retained earnings of $112 million equals the net income of $140 million less the cash dividends paid to stockholders of $28 million. Net income is classified as a source and dividends as a use.

Exhibit 16–5

NORDSTROM, INC.*
Statement of Retained Earnings
(dollars in millions)

Retained earnings, beginning balance	$ 897
Add: Net income	140
	1,037
Deduct: Dividends paid	28
Retained earnings, ending balance	$1,009

*This statement differs in a few details from the actual statement published by Nordstrom.

Exhibit 16–6

NORDSTROM, INC.
Simplified Statement of Cash Flows
(dollars in millions)

Note: This simplified statement is for illustration purposes only. It should *not* be used to complete end-of-chapter homework assignments or for preparing an actual statement of cash flows. See Exhibit 16–12 for the proper format for a statement of cash flows.

Sources		
Net income	$140	
Decreases in noncash assets:		
Decrease in accounts receivable	17	
Increases in liabilities (and contra asset accounts):		
Increase in accumulated depreciation and amortization	93	
Increase in accounts payable	44	
Increase in accrued wages and salaries	3	
Increase in accrued income taxes	6	
Increase in notes payable	2	
Increases in capital stock accounts:		
Increase in common stock	2	
Total sources		$307
Uses		
Increases in noncash assets:		
Increase in merchandise inventory	49	
Increase in property, buildings, and equipment	123	
Decreases in liabilities:		
Decrease in long-term debt	43	
Decrease in deferred income taxes	2	
Dividends	28	
Total uses		245
Net cash flow		$ 62

Note that changes between the beginning and ending balances have been computed for each of the balance sheet accounts in Exhibit 16–4, and each change has been classified as a source or use of cash. For example, accounts receivable decreased by $17 million. And, according to Exhibit 16–2, a decrease in such an asset account is classified as a source of cash.

A *simplified* statement of cash flows appears in Exhibit 16–6. This statement was constructed by gathering together all of the entries listed as sources in Exhibit 16–4 and all of the entries listed as uses. The sources exceeded the uses by $62 million. This is the net cash flow for the year and is also, by definition, the change in cash and cash equivalents for the year. (Trace this $62 million figure back to Exhibit 16–4.)

The Need for a More Detailed Statement

While the simplified statement of cash flows in Exhibit 16–6 is not difficult to construct, it is not acceptable for external financial reports and is not as useful as it could be for internal reports. The FASB requires that the statement of cash flows follow a different format and that a few of the entries be modified. Nevertheless, almost all of the entries on a full-fledged statement of cash flows are the same as the entries on the simplified statement of cash flows—they are just in a different order.

In the following sections, we will discuss the modifications to the simplified statement that are necessary to conform to external reporting requirements.

In Business

Plugging the Cash Flow Leak

Ski clothes used to be made mainly of wool, but modern synthetic fabrics such as polyester fleece and Gore-Tex have almost completely replaced the traditional fabric. John Fernsell started Ibex Outdoor Clothing in Woodstock, Vermont, to buck this trend. Fernsell's five-person firm designs and sells jackets made of high-grade wool from Europe.

Fernsell quickly discovered an unfortunate fact of life about the wool clothing business—he faces a potentially ruinous cash crunch every year. Ibex orders wool from Europe in February but does not pay the mills until June when they ship fabric to the garment makers in California. The garment factories send finished goods to Ibex in July and August, and Ibex pays them on receipt. Ibex ships to retailers in September and October, but doesn't get paid until November, December, or even January. That means from June to December the company spends like crazy—and takes in virtually nothing. Fernsell tried to get by with a line of credit, but it was insufficient. To survive, he had to ask his suppliers to let him pay late, which is not a long-term solution. To reduce this cash flow problem, Fernsell is introducing a line of wool *summer* clothing so that some cash will be flowing in from May through July, when he must pay his suppliers for the winter clothing.

Source: Daniel Lyons, "Wool Gatherer," *Forbes*, April 16, 2001, p. 310.

Organization of the Full-Fledged Statement of Cash Flows

LEARNING OBJECTIVE 2
State the general rules for determining whether transactions should be classified as operating activities, investing activities, or financing activities.

To make it easier to compare statements of cash flows from different companies, the Financial Accounting Standards Board (FASB) requires that companies follow prescribed rules for preparing the statement of cash flows. Most companies follow these rules for internal reports as well as for external financial statements.

One of the FASB requirements is that the statement of cash flows be divided into three sections: *operating activities, investing activities,* and *financing activities.* The guidelines to be followed in classifying transactions under these three heads are summarized in Exhibit 16–7 and discussed below.

Operating Activities

Generally, **operating activities** are those activities that enter into the determination of net income. Technically, however, the FASB defines operating activities as all the transactions that are not classified as investing or financing activities. Generally speaking, this

Exhibit 16–7
Guidelines for Classifying Transactions as Operating, Investing, and Financing Activities

Operating activities:
- Net income
- Changes in current assets
- Changes in noncurrent assets that affect net income (e.g., depreciation)
- Changes in current liabilities (except for debts to lenders and dividends payable)
- Changes in noncurrent liabilities that affect net income

Investing activities:
- Changes in noncurrent assets that are not included in net income

Financing activities:
- Changes in the current liabilities that are debts to lenders rather than obligations to suppliers, employees, or the government
- Changes in noncurrent liabilities that are not included in net income
- Changes in capital stock accounts
- Dividends

includes all transactions affecting current assets. It also includes all transactions affecting current liabilities except for issuing and repaying a note payable. Operating activities also include changes in noncurrent balance sheet accounts that directly affect net income such as the Accumulated Depreciation and Amortization account.

Concept 16–1

Keep an Eye on the Cash Flow

In Business

Business Week advises taking a very close look at the statement of cash flows:

> If you really want to put the quality of a company's earnings to the test, you need to examine the cash flow statement . . . .
>
> To get a feeling for whether a company is playing games with its earnings, compare net income on the income statement with "cash flow from operating activities" . . . . "Generally, the closer a ratio of these two numbers is to one, the higher quality the earnings," says David Zion, a Bear Sterns accounting analyst.
>
> Next, compare the rates at which net income and operating cash are growing. If the two normally move in lockstep but cash flow lags, "it's a terrific early warning sign," says Howard Schllit, who heads the Center for Financial Research & Analysis . . . .
>
> [N]egative cash flow from operations isn't always bad. Because of the high costs of building a business, it is perfectly normal—even desirable—for fast-growing companies to consume more cash than they generate. Typically, such companies tide themselves over with bank loans or equity sales. In other words, they run a surplus in "financing" cash flows. Still, if operating cash doesn't pick up, bail out. Eventually, lenders lose patience with companies whose operations hemorrhage cash.

Source: Anne Tergeson, "The Ins and Outs of Cash Flow," *Business Week*, January 22, 2001, p. 102.

Investing Activities

Generally speaking, transactions that involve acquiring or disposing of noncurrent assets are classified as **investing activities.** These transactions include acquiring or selling property, plant, and equipment; acquiring or selling securities held for long-term investment, such as bonds and stocks of other companies; and lending money to another entity (such as a subsidiary) and the subsequent collection of the loan. However, as previously discussed, changes in noncurrent assets that directly affect net income, such as depreciation and amortization charges, are classified as operating activities.

Financing Activities

As a general rule, borrowing from creditors or repaying creditors as well as transactions with the company's owners are classified as **financing activities.** For example, when a company borrows money by issuing a bond, the transaction is classified as a financing activity. However, transactions with creditors that affect net income are classified as operating activities. For example, interest on the company's debt is included in operating activities rather than financing activities because interest is deducted as an expense in computing net income. In contrast, dividend payments to owners do not affect net income and therefore are classified as financing rather than operating activities.

Most changes in current liabilities are considered to be operating activities unless the transaction involves borrowing money directly from a lender, as with a note payable, or repaying such a debt. Transactions involving accounts payable, wages payable, and taxes payable are included in operating activities rather than financing activities, since these transactions occur on a routine basis and involve the company's suppliers, employees, and the government rather than lenders.

In Business | **Warning Signs on the Statement of Cash Flows**

Herb Greenberg, a columnist for *Fortune* magazine, emphasizes the importance of monitoring a company's cash flows:

> [S]tick with two basic indicators: cash flow from operations (how much money the company's core business generates day to day) and total cash flow (which includes the core business, financing, and any investments). Are these two numbers going up or down? Up, it almost goes without saying, is better than down. A slide in both suggested to Bill Fleckenstein of Fleckenstein Capital that Gateway was headed for earnings trouble back in June. Sure enough, in November the company warned of a profit shortfall. "If earnings are growing and the company is consuming cash, that's one of the largest red lights on the balance sheet decoder ring," Fleckenstein says.

Source: Herb Greenberg, "Minding Your K's and Q's," *Fortune*, January 8, 2001, p. 180.

Other Issues in Preparing the Statement of Cash Flows

We must consider several other issues before we can illustrate the preparation of a statement of cash flows that would be acceptable for external financial reports. These issues are (1) whether amounts on the statement should be presented gross or net, (2) whether operating activities should be presented using the direct or indirect method, and (3) whether direct exchanges should be reported on the statement.

Cash Flows: Gross or Net?

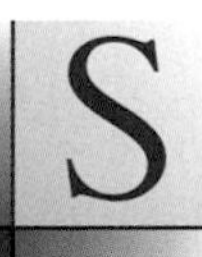

For both financing and investing activities, items on the statement of cash flows should be presented in gross amounts rather than in net amounts. To illustrate, suppose that Macy's Department Stores purchases $50 million in property during the year and sells other property for $30 million. Instead of showing the net change of $20 million, the company must show the gross amounts of both the purchases and the sales. The purchases would be recorded as a use of cash, and the sales would be recorded as a source of cash. In like manner, if Alcoa receives $80 million from the issue of long-term bonds and then pays out $30 million to retire other bonds, the two transactions must be reported separately on the statement of cash flows rather than being netted against each other.

The gross method of reporting does *not* extend to operating activities, where debits and credits to an account are ordinarily netted against each other on the statement of cash flows. For example, if Sears adds $600 million to its accounts receivable as a result of sales during the year and $520 million of receivables is collected, only the net increase of $80 million would be reported on the statement of cash flows.

Operating Activities: Direct or Indirect Method?

The net result of the cash inflows and outflows arising from operating activities is known formally as the **net cash provided by operating activities.** This figure can be computed by either the direct or the indirect method.

Under the **direct method,** the income statement is reconstructed on a cash basis from top to bottom. For example, in the direct method, cash collected from customers is used instead of revenue, and payments to suppliers is used instead of cost of sales. In essence, cash receipts are counted as revenues and cash disbursements are counted as expenses. The difference between the cash receipts and cash disbursements is the net cash provided by operating activities for the period.

Under the **indirect method,** the operating activities section of the statement of cash flows is constructed by starting with net income and adjusting it to a cash basis. That is, rather than directly computing cash sales, cash expenses, and so forth, these amounts are arrived at *indirectly* by removing from net income any items that do not affect cash flows. The indirect method has an advantage over the direct method in that it shows the reasons for any differences between net income and the net cash provided by operating activities. The indirect method is also known as the **reconciliation method.**

Concept 16–2

Which method should be used for constructing the operating activities section of the statement of cash flows—the direct method or the indirect method? Both methods will result in exactly the same figure for the net cash provided by operating activities. However, for external reporting purposes, the FASB *recommends* and *encourages* the use of the direct method. But there is a catch. If the direct method is used, there must be a supplementary reconciliation of net income with operating cash flows. In essence, if a company chooses to use the direct method, it must also go to the trouble of constructing a statement in which a form of the indirect method is used. However, if a company chooses to use the indirect method for determining the net cash flows from operating activities, there is no requirement that it also report the results of using the direct method.

Not surprisingly, a recent survey of 600 companies revealed that only 7, or about 1%, use the direct method to construct the statement of cash flows for external reports.[1] The remaining 99% probably use the indirect method because it is simply less work. While there are some good reasons for using the direct method, we use the indirect method in this chapter. The direct method is discussed and illustrated in Appendix 16A at the end of the chapter.

Direct Exchange Transactions

Companies sometimes enter into **direct exchange transactions** in which noncurrent balance sheet items are swapped. For example, a company might issue common stock that is directly exchanged for property. Or a company might induce its creditors to swap their long-term debt for common stock of the company. Or a company might acquire equipment under a long-term lease contract offered by the seller.

Direct exchange transactions are not reported on the statement of cash flows. However, such direct exchanges are disclosed in a separate schedule that accompanies the statement.

An Example of a Full-Fledged Statement of Cash Flows

LEARNING OBJECTIVE 3
Prepare a statement of cash flows using the indirect method to determine the net cash provided by operating activities.

In this section, we apply the FASB rules to construct a statement of cash flows for Nordstrom that would be acceptable for external reporting. The approach we take is based on an analysis of changes in balance sheet accounts, as in our earlier discussion of the simplified statement of cash flows. Indeed, as you will see, the full-fledged statement of cash flows is for the most part just a reorganized form of the simplified statement that appears in Exhibit 16–6.

The format for the operating activities part of the statement of cash flows is shown in Exhibit 16–8. For example, consider the effect of an increase in the Accounts Receivable account on the net cash provided by operating activities. Since the Accounts Receivable account is a noncash asset, we know from Exhibit 16–2 that increases in this account are treated as *uses* of cash. In other words, increases in Accounts Receivable are deducted when determining net cash flows. Intuitive explanations for this and other adjustments are sometimes slippery, but commonly given explanations are listed in Exhibit 16–9 for some of these adjustments. For example, Exhibit 16–9 suggests that an increase in Accounts Receivable is deducted from net income because sales have been recorded for which no

---

[1] American Institute of Certified Public Accountants, *Accounting Trends and Techniques: 2000* (Jersey City, NJ, 2000), p. 523.

Exhibit 16–8
General Model: Indirect Method of Determining the "Net Cash Provided by Operating Activities"

	Add (+) or Deduct (−) to Adjust Net Income
Net income	$XXX
Adjustments needed to convert net income to a cash basis:	
Depreciation, depletion, and amortization charges	+
Add (deduct) changes in current asset accounts affecting revenue or expense:*	
Increase in the account	−
Decrease in the account	+
Add (deduct) changes in current liability accounts affecting revenue or expense:†	
Increase in the account	+
Decrease in the account	−
Add (deduct) gains or losses on sales of assets:	
Gain on sales of assets	−
Loss on sales of assets	+
Add (deduct) changes in the Deferred Income Taxes account:	
Increase if a liability; decrease if an asset	+
Decrease if a liability; increase if an asset	−
Net cash provided by operating activities	$XXX

*Examples include accounts receivable, accrued receivables, inventory, and prepaid expenses.

†Examples include accounts payable, accrued liabilities, and taxes payable.

cash has been collected. Therefore, to adjust net income to a cash basis, the increase in the Accounts Receivable account must be deducted from net income to show that cash-basis sales are less than reported sales. However, we can more simply state that an increase in Accounts Receivable is deducted when computing net cash flows because, according to the logic of Exhibits 16–1 and 16–2, increases in all noncash assets must be deducted.

Eight Basic Steps to Preparing the Statement of Cash Flows

We recommend that you use a worksheet such as the one in Exhibit 16–10 to prepare the statement of cash flows. Preparing a statement of cash flows can be confusing, and important details can be easily overlooked without such an aid. The statement of cash flows worksheet in Exhibit 16–10 can be prepared using the eight steps that follow. This brief summary of the steps will be followed by more detailed explanations later.

1. Copy onto the worksheet the title of each account appearing on the comparative balance sheet except for cash and cash equivalents and retained earnings. To avoid confusion, contra asset accounts such as the Accumulated Depreciation and Amortization account should be listed with the liabilities. Contra asset accounts are treated the same way as liabilities on the statement of cash flows.
2. Compute the change from the beginning balance to the ending balance in each balance sheet account. Break the change in retained earnings down into net income and dividends paid to stockholders.
3. Using Exhibit 16–2 as a guide, code each entry on the worksheet as a source or a use.
4. Under the Cash Flow Effect column, write sources as positive numbers and uses as negative numbers.

Exhibit 16–9 Explanation of Adjustments for Changes in Current Asset and Current Liability Accounts (see Exhibit 16–8)

	Change in the Account	This Change Means That . . .	Therefore, to Adjust to a Cash Basis under the Indirect Method, We Must . . .
Accounts Receivable and Accrued Receivables	Increase	Sales (revenues) have been reported for which no cash has been collected.	Deduct the amount from net income to show that cash-basis sales are less than reported sales (revenues).
	Decrease	Cash has been collected for which no sales (revenues) have been reported for the current period.	Add the amount to net income to show that cash-basis sales are greater than reported sales (revenues).
Inventory	Increase	Goods have been purchased that are not included in cost of goods sold (COGS).	Deduct the amount from net income to show that cash-basis COGS is greater than reported COGS.
	Decrease	Goods have been included in COGS that were purchased in a prior period.	Add the amount to net income to show that cash-basis COGS is less than reported COGS.
Prepaid Expenses	Increase	More cash has been paid out for services than has been reported as expense.	Deduct the amount from net income to show that cash-basis expenses are greater than reported expenses.
	Decrease	More has been reported as expense for services than has been paid out in cash.	Add the amount to net income to show that cash-basis expenses are less than reported expenses.
Accounts Payable and Accrued Liabilities	Increase	More has been reported as expense for goods and services than has been paid out in cash.	Add the amount to net income to show that cash-basis expenses for goods and services are less than reported expenses.
	Decrease	More cash has been paid out for goods and services than has been reported as expense.	Deduct the amount from net income to show that cash-basis expenses for goods and services are greater than reported expenses.
Taxes Payable	Increase	More income tax expense has been reported than has been paid out in cash.	Add the amount to net income to show that cash-basis expenses are less than reported expenses.
	Decrease	More cash has been paid to the tax authorities than has been reported as income tax expense.	Deduct the amount from net income to show that cash-basis expenses are greater than reported expenses.

5. Make any necessary adjustments to reflect gross, rather than net, amounts involved in transactions—including adjustments for gains and losses. Some of these adjustments may require adding new entries to the bottom of the worksheet. The net effect of all such adjusting entries must be zero.
6. Classify each entry on the worksheet as an operating activity, investing activity, or financing activity according to the FASB's criteria, as given in Exhibit 16–7.
7. Copy the data from the worksheet to the statement of cash flows section by section, starting with the operating activities section.
8. At the bottom of the statement of cash flows prepare a reconciliation of the beginning and ending balances of cash and cash equivalents. The net change in cash and cash equivalents shown at the bottom of this statement should equal the change in the Cash and Cash Equivalents accounts during the year.

On the following pages we will apply these eight steps to the data contained in the comparative balance sheet for Nordstrom, Inc., found in Exhibit 16–4. *As we discuss each step, refer to Exhibit 16–4 and trace the data from this exhibit into the worksheet in Exhibit 16–10.*

Exhibit 16–10

NORDSTROM, INC. Statement of Cash Flows Worksheet (dollars in millions)	(1) Change	(2) Source or Use?	(3) Cash Flow Effect	(4) Adjustments	(5) Adjusted Effect (3) + (4)	(6) Classification*
Assets (except cash and cash equivalents)						
Current assets:						
Accounts receivable	$ −17	Source	$ +17		$ +17	Operating
Merchandise inventory	+49	Use	−49		−49	Operating
Noncurrent assets:						
Property, buildings, and equipment	+123	Use	−123	$−15	−138	Investing
Contra Assets, Liabilities, and Stockholders' Equity						
Contra assets:						
Accumulated depreciation and amortization	+93	Source	+93	+10	+103	Operating
Current liabilities:						
Accounts payable	+44	Source	+44		+44	Operating
Accrued wages and salaries payable	+3	Source	+3		+3	Operating
Accrued income taxes payable	+6	Source	+6		+6	Operating
Notes payable	+2	Source	+2		+2	Financing
Noncurrent liabilities:						
Long-term debt	−43	Use	−43		−43	Financing
Deferred income taxes	−2	Use	−2		−2	Operating
Stockholders' equity:						
Common stock	+2	Source	+2		+2	Financing
Retained earnings:						
Net income	+140	Source	+140		+140	Operating
Dividends	−28	Use	−28		−28	Financing
Additional Entries						
Proceeds from sale of store				+8	+8	Investing
Gain on sale of store				−3	−3	Operating
Total (net cash flow)			$ +62	$ 0	$ +62	

*See Exhibit 16–11 for the reasons for these classifications.

Setting Up the Worksheet (Steps 1–4)

As indicated above, step 1 in preparing the worksheet is to simply list all of the relevant account titles from the company's balance sheet. Note that we have done this for Nordstrom, Inc., on the worksheet in Exhibit 16–10. (The titles of Nordstrom's accounts have been taken from the company's comparative balance sheet, which is found in Exhibit 16–4.) The only significant differences between Nordstrom's balance sheet accounts and the worksheet listing are that (1) the Accumulated Depreciation and Amortization account has been moved down with the liabilities on the worksheet, (2) the Cash and Cash Equivalents accounts have been omitted, and (3) the change in retained earnings has been broken down into net income and dividends.

As stated in step 2, the change in each account's balance during the year is listed in the first column of the worksheet. We have entered these changes for Nordstrom's accounts onto the worksheet in Exhibit 16–10. (Refer to Nordstrom's comparative balance sheet in Exhibit 16–4 to see how these changes were computed.)

Then, as indicated in step 3, each change on the worksheet is classified as either a source or a use of cash. Whether a change is a source or a use can be determined by referring back to Exhibit 16–2, where we first discussed these classifications. For example, Nordstrom's Merchandise Inventory account increased by $49 million during the year. According to Exhibit 16–2, increases in noncash asset accounts are classified as uses of cash, so an entry has been made to that effect in the second column of the worksheet for the Merchandise Inventory account.

So far, nothing is new. All of this was done already in Exhibit 16–4 in preparation for constructing the simplified statement of cash flows. Step 4 is mechanical, but it helps prevent careless errors. Sources are coded as positive changes and uses as negative changes in the Cash Flow Effect column on the worksheet.

Adjustments to Reflect Gross, Rather than Net, Amounts (Step 5)

As discussed earlier, the FASB requires that gross, rather than net, amounts be disclosed in the investing and financing sections. This rule requires special treatment of gains and losses. To illustrate, suppose that Nordstrom decided to sell an old store and move its retail operations to a new location. Assume that the original cost of the old store was $15 million, its accumulated depreciation was $10 million, and that it was sold for $8 million in cash. The journal entry to record this transaction appears below:

Account	Debit	Credit
Cash	8,000,000	
Accumulated Depreciation and Amortization	10,000,000	
Property, Buildings, and Equipment		15,000,000
Gain on Sale		3,000,000

The $3 million gain is reflected in the income statement in Exhibit 16–3.

We can reconstruct the gross additions to the Property, Buildings, and Equipment account and the gross charges to the Accumulated Depreciation and Amortization account with the help of T-accounts:

Property, Buildings, and Equipment

	Debit	Credit	
Bal.	1,394		
Additions (plug*)	138	15	Disposal of store
Bal.	1,517		

Accumulated Depreciation and Amortization

	Debit	Credit	
		561	Bal.
Disposal of store	10	103	Depreciation charges (plug)
		654	Bal.

*By *plug* we mean the balancing figure in the account.

According to the FASB rules, the gross additions of $138 million to the Property, Buildings, and Equipment account should be disclosed on the statement of cash flows rather than the net change in the account of $123 million ($1,517 million − $1,394 million = $123 million). Likewise, the gross depreciation charges of $103 million should be disclosed rather than the net change in the Accumulated Depreciation and Amortization account of $93 million ($654 million − $561 million = $93 million). And the cash proceeds of $8 million from sale of the building should also be disclosed on the statement of cash flows. All of this is accomplished, while preserving the correct overall net cash flows on the statement, by using the above journal entry to make adjusting entries on the worksheet. As indicated in Exhibit 16–2, the debits are recorded as positive adjustments, and the credits are recorded as negative adjustments. These adjusting entries are recorded under the Adjustments column in Exhibit 16–10.

It may not be clear why the gain on the sale is *deducted* in the operating activities section of the statement of cash flows. The company's $140 million net income, which is part of the operating activities section, includes the $3 million gain on the sale of the store. But this $3 million gain must be reported in the *investing* activities section of the statement of cash flows as part of the $8 million proceeds from the sale transaction. Therefore, to avoid double counting, the $3 million gain is deducted from net income in the operating activities section of the statement. The adjustments we have made on the worksheet accomplish this. The $3 million gain will be deducted in the operating activities section, and all $8 million of the sale proceeds will be shown as an investing item. As a result, all of the gain will be included in the investing section of the statement of cash flows and none of it will be in the operating activities section. There will be no double-counting of the gain.

In the case of a loss on the sale of an asset, we do the opposite. The loss is added back to the net income figure in the operating activities section of the statement of cash flows. Whatever cash proceeds are received from the sale of the asset are reported in the investing activities section.

Before turning to step 6 in the process of building the statement of cash flows, one small step is required. Add the Adjustments in column (4) to the Cash Flow Effect in column (3) to arrive at the Adjusted Effect in column (5).

Classifying Entries as Operating, Investing, or Financing Activities (Step 6)

In step 6, each entry on the worksheet is classified as an operating, investing, or financing activity using the guidelines in Exhibit 16–7. These classifications are entered directly on the worksheet in Exhibit 16–10 and are explained in Exhibit 16–11. Most of these classifications are straightforward, but the classification of the change in the Deferred Income Taxes account may require some additional explanation. Because of the way income tax expense is determined for financial reporting purposes, the expense that appears on the income statement often differs from the taxes that are actually owed to the government. Usually, the income tax expense overstates the company's actual income tax liability for the year. When this happens, the journal entry to record income taxes includes a credit to Deferred Income Taxes:

Income Tax Expense	XXX	
Income Taxes Payable		XXX
Deferred Income Taxes (plug)		XXX

Since deferred income taxes arise directly from the computation of an expense, the change in the Deferred Income Taxes account is included in the operating activities section of the statement of cash flows.

In the case of Nordstrom, the Deferred Income Taxes account decreased during the year, so income tax expense was apparently less than the company's income tax liability for the year by $2 million. In other words, for some reason Nordstrom had to pay the government $2 million more than the income tax expense recorded on the income statement, and therefore this additional cash outflow must be deducted to convert net income to a cash basis. Or, looking back again to Exhibit 16–2, Deferred Income Taxes is a liability account for Nordstrom. Since this liability account decreased during the year, the change is counted as a use of cash and is deducted in determining net cash flow for the year.

The Completed Statement of Cash Flows (Steps 7 and 8)

Once the worksheet is completed, it is easy to complete step 7 by constructing an actual statement of cash flows. Nordstrom's statement of cash flows appears in Exhibit 16–12. Trace each item from the worksheet into this statement.

The operating activities section of the statement follows the format laid out in Exhibit 16–8, beginning with net income. The other entries in the operating activities section are

Exhibit 16–11 Classifications of Entries on Nordstrom's Statement of Cash Flows

Entry	Classification	Reason
• Changes in Accounts Receivable and Merchandise Inventory	Operating activity	Changes in current assets are included in operating activities.
• Change in Property, Buildings, and Equipment	Investing activity	Changes in noncurrent assets that do not directly affect net income are included in investing activities.
• Change in Accumulated Depreciation and Amortization	Operating activity	Depreciation and amortization directly affect net income and are therefore included in operating activities.
• Changes in Accounts Payable, Accrued Wages and Salaries Payable, and Accrued Income Taxes Payable	Operating activity	Changes in current liabilities (except for notes payable) are included in operating activities.
• Change in Notes Payable	Financing activity	Issuing or repaying notes payable is classified as a financing activity.
• Change in Long-Term Debt	Financing activity	Changes in noncurrent liabilities that do not directly affect net income are included in financing activities.
• Change in Deferred Income Taxes	Operating activity	Deferred income taxes result from income tax expense that directly affects net income. Therefore, this entry is included in operating activities.
• Change in Common Stock	Financing activity	Changes in capital stock accounts are always included in financing activities.
• Net income	Operating activity	Net income is always included in operating activities.
• Dividends	Financing activity	Dividends paid to stockholders are always included in financing activities.
• Proceeds from sale of store	Investing activity	The gross amounts received on disposal of noncurrent assets are included in investing activities.
• Gains from sale of store	Operating activity	Gains and losses directly affect net income and are therefore included in operating activities.

considered to be adjustments required to convert net income to a cash basis. The sum of all of the entries under the operating activities section is called the "Net cash provided by operating activities."

The investing activities section comes next on the statement of cash flows. The worksheet entries that have been classified as investing activities are recorded in this section in any order. The sum of all the entries in this section is called the "Net cash used in investing activities."

The financing activities section of the statement follows the investing activities section. The worksheet entries that have been classified as financing activities are recorded in this section in any order. The sum of all of the entries in this section is called the "Net cash used in financing activities."

Finally, for step 8, the bottom of the statement of cash flows contains a reconciliation of the beginning and ending balances of cash and cash equivalents.

Interpretation of the Statement of Cash Flows

The completed statement of cash flows in Exhibit 16–12 provides a very favorable picture of Nordstrom's cash flows. The net cash flow from operations is a healthy $259 million.

Exhibit 16–12
Summary of Cost Classifications

NORDSTROM, INC.* Statement of Cash Flows—Indirect Method (dollars in millions)	
Operating Activities	
Net income	$ 140
Adjustments to convert net income to a cash basis:	
Depreciation and amortization charges	103
Decrease in accounts receivable	17
Increase in merchandise inventory	(49)
Increase in accounts payable	44
Increase in accrued wages and salaries payable	3
Increase in accrued income taxes payable	6
Decrease in deferred income taxes	(2)
Gain on sale of store	(3)
Net cash provided by operating activities	259
Investing Activities	
Additions to property, buildings, and equipment	(138)
Proceeds from sale of store	8
Net cash used in investing activities	(130)
Financing Activities	
Increase in notes payable	2
Decrease in long-term debt	(43)
Increase in common stock	2
Cash dividends paid	(28)
Net cash used in financing activities	(67)
Net increase in cash and cash equivalents	62
Cash and cash equivalents at beginning of year	29
Cash and cash equivalents at end of year	$ 91

Reconciliation of the beginning and ending cash balances →

*This statement differs from the actual statement published by Nordstrom.

This positive cash flow permitted the company to make substantial additions to its property, buildings, and equipment and to pay off a substantial portion of its long-term debt. If similar conditions prevail in the future, the company can continue to finance substantial growth from its own cash flows without the necessity of raising debt or selling stock.

When interpreting a statement of cash flows, it is particularly important to scrutinize the net cash provided by operating activities. This figure provides a measure of how successful the company is in generating cash on a continuing basis. A negative cash flow from operations would usually be a sign of fundamental difficulties. A positive cash flow from operations is necessary to avoid liquidating assets or borrowing money just to sustain day-to-day operations.

Depreciation, Depletion, and Amortization

A few pitfalls can trap the unwary when reading a statement of cash flows. Perhaps the most common is to misinterpret the nature of the depreciation charges on the statement of cash flows. Since depreciation is added back to net income, there is a tendency to think that all you have to do to increase net cash flow is to increase depreciation charges. This is false. In a merchandising company like Nordstrom, increasing the depreciation charge by X dollars would decrease net income by X dollars because of the added expense taken. Adding back the depreciation charge to net income on the statement of cash flows simply cancels out the reduction in net income caused by the depreciation charge. Referring back to Exhibit 16–2, depreciation, depletion, and amortization charges are added back to net income on the statement of cash flows because they are a decrease in an asset (or an increase in a contra asset)—not because they generate cash.

What's Wrong with This Picture?

In Business

Getty Images is the world's biggest stock photo company—owning the rights to over 70 million images and 30,000 hours of film. The company gets its revenues from licensing the use of these images. The stock market is impressed with the potential in this market—despite losses of $63 million in the first six months of the year, the company's stock was worth $1.8 billion. "What is there for a growth company to talk about if earnings are so rotten? Anything but earnings. . . . Getty Images declared victory in its cash from operations, which it said had swelled to a robust $17.1 million in the second quarter, up from a deficit of $2.6 million in the first. Does that mean Getty collected its bills and whittled down its inventory? Nope. Both receivables and inventory are rising. The cash flow from operations, rather, comes from not paying bills."

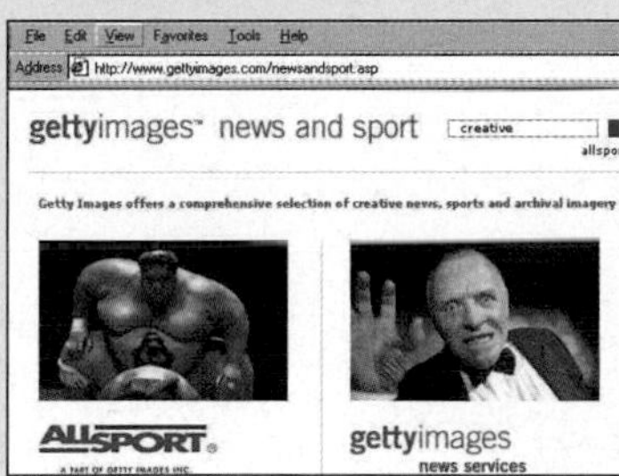

Source: Elizabeth MacDonald, "Image Problem," *Forbes*, October 16, 2000, pp. 104–106.

Summary

The statement of cash flows is one of the three major financial statements prepared by organizations. It explains how cash was generated and how it was used during a period. The statement of cash flows is widely used as a tool for assessing the financial health of organizations.

In general, sources of cash include net income, decreases in assets, increases in liabilities, and increases in stockholders' capital accounts. Uses of cash include increases in assets, decreases in liabilities, decreases in stockholders' capital accounts, and dividends. A simplified form of the statement of cash flows can be easily constructed using just these definitions and a comparative balance sheet.

For external reporting purposes, the statement of cash flows must be organized in terms of operating, investing, and financing activities. While there are some exceptions, changes in noncurrent assets are generally included in investing activities and changes in noncurrent liabilities are generally included in financing activities. And, with a few exceptions, operating activities include net income and changes in current assets and current liabilities.

An analyst should pay particularly close attention to the net cash provided by operating activities, since this provides a measure of how successful the company is in generating cash on a continuing basis.

Review Problem

Rockford Company's comparative balance sheet for 2002 and the company's income statement for the year follow:

ROCKFORD COMPANY
Comparative Balance Sheet
December 31, 2002, and 2001
(dollars in millions)

	2002	2001
Assets		
Cash	$ 26	$ 10
Accounts receivable	180	270
Inventory	205	160
Prepaid expenses	17	20
Plant and equipment	430	309
Less accumulated depreciation	(218)	(194)
Long-term investments	60	75
Total assets	$ 700	$ 650
Liabilities and Stockholders' Equity		
Accounts payable	$ 230	$ 310
Accrued liabilities	70	60
Bonds payable	135	40
Deferred income taxes	15	8
Common stock	140	140
Retained earnings	110	92
Total liabilities and stockholders' equity	$ 700	$ 650

ROCKFORD COMPANY
Income Statement
For the Year Ended December 31, 2002
(dollars in millions)

Sales	$1,000
Less cost of sales	530
Gross margin	470
Less operating expenses	352
Net operating income	118
Nonoperating items:	
Loss on sale of equipment	(4)
Income before taxes	114
Less income taxes	48
Net income	$ 66

Notes: Dividends of $48 million were paid in 2002. The loss on sale of equipment of $4 million reflects a transaction in which equipment with an original cost of $12 million and accumulated depreciation of $5 million was sold for $3 million in cash.

Required:
Using the indirect method, determine the net cash provided by operating activities for 2002 and construct a statement of cash flows for the year.

Solution to Review Problem

A worksheet for Rockford Company appears on the next page. Using the worksheet, it is a simple matter to construct the statement of cash flows, including the net cash provided by operating activities.

ROCKFORD COMPANY
Statement of Cash Flows Worksheet
For the Year Ended December 31, 2002
(dollars in millions)

	(1) Change	(2) Source or Use?	(3) Cash Flow Effect	(4) Adjust-ments	(5) Adjusted Effect (3) + (4)	(6) Classi-fication
Assets (except cash and cash equivalents)						
Current assets:						
Accounts receivable	$ −90	Source	$+90		$+90	Operating
Inventory	+45	Use	−45		−45	Operating
Prepaid expenses	−3	Source	+3		+3	Operating
Noncurrent assets:						
Property, buildings, and equipment	+121	Use	−121	$−12	−133	Investing
Long-term investments	−15	Source	+15		+15	Investing
Contra Assets, Liabilities, and Stockholders' Equity						
Contra assets:						
Accumulated depreciation	+24	Source	+24	+5	+29	Operating
Current liabilities:						
Accounts payable	−80	Use	−80		−80	Operating
Accrued liabilities	+10	Source	+10		+10	Operating
Noncurrent liabilities:						
Bonds payable	+95	Source	+95		+95	Financing
Deferred income taxes	+7	Source	+7		+7	Operating
Stockholders' equity:						
Common stock	+0	—	+0		+0	Financing
Retained earnings:						
Net income	+66	Source	+66		+66	Operating
Dividends	−48	Use	−48		−48	Financing
Additional Entries						
Proceeds from sale of equipment				+3	+3	Investing
Loss on sale of equipment				+4	+4	Operating
Total (net cash flow)			$+16	$ 0	$+16	

ROCKFORD COMPANY
Statement of Cash Flows—Indirect Method
For the Year Ended December 31, 2002
(dollars in millions)

Operating Activities:	
Net income	$ 66
Adjustments to convert net income to a cash basis:	
Depreciation and amortization charges	29
Decrease in accounts receivable	90
Increase in inventory	(45)
Decrease in prepaid expenses	3
Decrease in accounts payable	(80)
Increase in accrued liabilities	10
Increase in deferred income taxes	7
Loss on sale of equipment	4
Net cash provided by operating activities	84

continued

Investing Activities:	
Additions to property, buildings, and equipment	(133)
Decrease in long-term investments	15
Proceeds from sale of equipment	3
Net cash used in investing activities	(115)
Financing Activities:	
Increase in bonds payable	95
Cash dividends paid	(48)
Net cash provided by financing activities	47
Net increase in cash and cash equivalents	16
Cash and cash equivalents at beginning of year	10
Cash and cash equivalents at end of year	$ 26

Note that the $16 increase in cash and cash equivalents agrees with the $16 increase in the company's Cash account shown in the balance sheet on page 746, and it agrees with the total in column (5) of the worksheet shown on page 747.

Glossary

Cash equivalents Short-term, highly liquid investments such as Treasury bills, commercial paper, and money market funds that are made solely for the purpose of generating a return on funds that are temporarily idle. (p. 729)

Direct exchange transactions Transactions involving only noncurrent balance sheet accounts. For example, a company might issue common stock that is directly exchanged for property. (p. 737)

Direct method A method of computing the cash provided by operating activities in which the income statement is reconstructed on a cash basis from top to bottom. (p. 736)

Financing activities All transactions (other than payment of interest) involving borrowing from creditors or repaying creditors as well as transactions with the company's owners (except stock dividends and stock splits). (p. 735)

Indirect method A method of computing the cash provided by operating activities that starts with net income and adjusts it to a cash basis. It is also known as the *reconciliation method.* (p. 736)

Investing activities Transactions that involve acquiring or disposing of noncurrent assets. (p. 735)

Net cash provided by operating activities The net result of the cash inflows and outflows arising from day-to-day operations. (p. 736)

Operating activities Transactions that enter into the determination of net income. (p. 734)

Reconciliation method See *Indirect method.* (p. 737)

Statement of cash flows A financial statement that highlights the major activities that directly and indirectly impact cash flows and hence affect the overall cash balance. (p. 728)

Appendix 16A: The Direct Method of Determining the Net Cash Provided by Operating Activities

LEARNING OBJECTIVE 4
Use the direct method to determine the net cash provided by operating activities.

As stated in the main body of the chapter, to compute the net cash provided by operating activities under the direct method, we must reconstruct the income statement on a cash basis from top to bottom. A model is presented in Exhibit 16A–1 that shows the adjustments that must be made to adjust sales, expenses, and so forth, to a cash basis. To illustrate, we have included in the exhibit the Nordstrom data from the chapter.

Exhibit 16A–1
General Model: Direct Method of Determining the Net Cash Provided by Operating Activities

Revenue or Expense Item	Add (+) or Deduct (−) to Adjust to a Cash Basis	Illustration—Nordstrom (in millions)	
Sales revenue (as reported)		$3,638	
Adjustments to a cash basis:			
1. Increase in accounts receivable	−		
2. Decrease in accounts receivable	+	+17	
Total			$3,655
Cost of goods sold (as reported)		2,469	
Adjustments to a cash basis:			
3. Increase in merchandise inventory	+	+49	
4. Decrease in merchandise inventory	−		
5. Increase in accounts payable	−	−44	
6. Decrease in accounts payable	+		
Total			2,474
Operating expenses (as reported)		941	
Adjustments to a cash basis:			
7. Increase in prepaid expenses	+		
8. Decrease in prepaid expenses	−		
9. Increase in accrued liabilities	−	−3	
10. Decrease in accrued liabilities	+		
11. Period's depreciation, depletion, and amortization charges	−	−103	
Total			835
Income tax expense (as reported)		91	
Adjustments to a cash basis:			
12. Increase in accrued taxes payable	−	−6	
13. Decrease in accrued taxes payable	+		
14. Increase in deferred income taxes	−		
15. Decrease in deferred income taxes	+	+2	
Total			87
Net cash provided by operating activities			$ 259

Note that the net cash provided by operating activities figure ($259 million) agrees with the amount computed in the chapter by the indirect method. The two amounts agree, since the direct and indirect methods are just different roads to the same destination. The investing and financing activities sections of the statement will be exactly the same as shown for the indirect method in Exhibit 16–12. The only difference between the indirect and direct methods is in the operating activities section.

Similarities and Differences in the Handling of Data

Although we arrive at the same destination under either the direct or the indirect method, not all data are handled in the same way in the adjustment process. Stop for a moment, flip back to the general model for the indirect method in Exhibit 16–8 on page 738 and compare the adjustments made in that exhibit to the adjustments made for the direct method in Exhibit 16A–1. The adjustments for accounts that affect revenue are the same in the two methods. In either case, increases in the accounts are deducted and decreases in the accounts are added. The adjustments for accounts that affect expenses, however, are handled in *opposite* ways in the indirect and direct methods. This is because under the indirect method the adjustments are made to *net income,* whereas under the direct method the adjustments are made to the *expense accounts* themselves.

To illustrate this difference, note the handling of prepaid expenses and depreciation in the indirect and direct methods. Under the indirect method (Exhibit 16–8), an increase in the Prepaid Expenses account is *deducted* from net income in computing the amount of cash provided by operations. Under the direct method (Exhibit 16A–1), an increase in Prepaid Expenses is *added* to operating expenses. The reason for the difference can be explained as follows: An increase in Prepaid Expenses means that more cash has been paid out for items such as insurance than has been included as expense for the period. Therefore, to adjust net income to a cash basis, we must either deduct this increase from net income (indirect method) or we must add this increase to operating expenses (direct method). Either way, we will end up with the same figure for cash provided by operations. In like manner, depreciation is added to net income under the indirect method to cancel out its effect (Exhibit 16–8), whereas it is deducted from operating expenses under the direct method to cancel out its effect (Exhibit 16A–1). These differences in the handling of data are true for all other expense items in the two methods.

In the matter of gains and losses on sales of assets, no adjustments are needed at all under the direct method. These gains and losses are simply ignored, since they are not part of sales, cost of goods sold, operating expenses, or income taxes. Observe that in Exhibit 16A–1, Nordstrom's $3 million gain on the sale of the store is not listed as an adjustment in the operating activities section.

Special Rules—Direct and Indirect Methods

As stated earlier, when the direct method is used, the FASB requires a reconciliation between net income and the net cash provided by operating activities, as determined by the indirect method. Thus, *when a company elects to use the direct method, it must also present the indirect method* in a separate schedule accompanying the statement of cash flows.

On the other hand, if a company elects to use the indirect method to compute the net cash provided by operating activities, then it must also provide a special breakdown of data. The company must provide a separate disclosure of the amount of interest and the amount of income taxes paid during the year. The FASB requires this separate disclosure so that users can take the data provided by the indirect method and make estimates of what the amounts for sales, income taxes, and so forth, would have been if the direct method had been used instead.

Questions

16–1 What is the purpose of a statement of cash flows?

16–2 What are *cash equivalents,* and why are they included with cash on a statement of cash flows?

16–3 What are the three major sections on a statement of cash flows, and what are the general rules that determine the transactions that should be included in each section?

16–4 Why is interest paid on amounts borrowed from banks and other lenders considered to be an operating activity when the amounts borrowed are financing activities?

16–5 If an asset is sold at a gain, why is the gain deducted from net income when computing the cash provided by operating activities under the indirect method?

16–6 Why aren't transactions involving accounts payable considered to be financing activities?

16–7 Give an example of a direct exchange and explain how such exchanges are handled when preparing a statement of cash flows.

16–8 Assume that a company repays a $300,000 loan from its bank and then later in the same year borrows $500,000. What amount(s) would appear on the statement of cash flows?

16–9 How do the direct and the indirect methods differ in their approach to computing the cash provided by operating activities?

16–10 A business executive once stated, "Depreciation is one of our biggest sources of cash." Do you agree that depreciation is a source of cash? Explain.

16–11 If the balance in Accounts Receivable increases during a period, how will this increase be handled under the indirect method when computing the cash provided by operating activities?

16–12 (Appendix 16A) If the balance in Accounts Payable decreases during a period, how will this decrease be handled under the direct method in computing the cash provided by operating activities?

16–13 During the current year, a company declared and paid a $60,000 cash dividend and a 10% stock dividend. How will these two items be treated on the current year's statement of cash flows?

16–14 Would a sale of equipment for cash be considered a financing activity or an investing activity? Why?

16–15 (Appendix 16A) A merchandising company showed $250,000 in cost of goods sold on its income statement. The company's beginning inventory was $75,000, and its ending inventory was $60,000. The accounts payable balance was $50,000 at the beginning of the year and $40,000 at the end of the year. Using the direct method, adjust the company's cost of goods sold to a cash basis.

Exercises

EXERCISE 16–1 Classifying Transactions [LO1, LO2]

Below are certain events that took place at Hazzard, Inc., last year:

a. Short-term investment securities were purchased.
b. Equipment was purchased.
c. Accounts payable increased.
d. Deferred taxes decreased.
e. Long-term bonds were issued.
f. Common stock was sold.
g. A cash dividend was declared and paid.
h. Interest was paid to long-term creditors.
i. A long-term mortgage was entirely paid off.
j. Inventories decreased.
k. The company recorded net income of $1 million for the year.
l. Depreciation charges totaled $200,000 for the year.
m. Accounts receivable increased.

Required:
Prepare an answer sheet with the following headings:

	Activity				
Transaction	**Operating**	**Investing**	**Financing**	**Source**	**Use**
a.					
b.					
Etc.					

Enter the events above on your answer sheet and indicate how each of them would be classified on a statement of cash flows. Place an *X* in the Operating, Investing, or Financing column and an *X* in the Source or Use column as appropriate.

EXERCISE 16–2 Net Cash Provided by Operating Activities (Indirect Method) [LO3]

Changes in various accounts and gains and losses on sales of assets during the year for Weston Company are given below:

Item	Amount
Accounts Receivable	$ 70,000 decrease
Accrued Interest Receivable	6,000 increase
Inventory	110,000 increase
Prepaid Expenses	3,000 decrease
Accounts Payable	40,000 decrease
Accrued Liabilities	9,000 increase
Deferred Income Taxes	15,000 increase
Sale of equipment	8,000 gain
Sale of long-term investments	12,000 loss

Required:
For each item, place an *X* in the Add or Deduct column to indicate whether the dollar amount should be added to or deducted from net income under the indirect method when computing the cash provided by operating activities for the year. Use the following column headings in preparing your answers:

Item	Amount	Add	Deduct

EXERCISE 16–3 Net Cash Provided by Operating Activities (Indirect Method) [LO3]
For the year ended December 31, 2002, Strident Company reported a net income of $84,000. Balances in the company's current asset and current liability accounts at the beginning and end of the year were as follows:

	December 31	
	2002	2001
Current assets:		
Cash	$ 60,000	$ 80,000
Accounts receivable	250,000	190,000
Inventory	437,000	360,000
Prepaid expenses	12,000	14,000
Current liabilities:		
Accounts payable	420,000	390,000
Accrued liabilities	8,000	12,000

The Deferred Income Taxes account on the balance sheet increased by $6,000 during the year, and depreciation charges were $50,000 during the year.

Required:
Using the indirect method, determine the cash provided by operating activities for the year.

EXERCISE 16–4 (Appendix 16A) Net Cash Provided by Operating Activities (Direct Method) [LO4]
Refer to the data for Strident Company in Exercise 16–3. Assume that the company's income statement for the most recent year was as follows:

Sales	$1,000,000
Less cost of goods sold	580,000
Gross margin	420,000
Less operating expenses	300,000
Income before taxes	120,000
Less income taxes (30%)	36,000
Net income	$ 84,000

Required:
Using the direct method (and the data from Exercise 16–3), convert the company's income statement to a cash basis.

EXERCISE 16–5 Prepare a Statement of Cash Flows (Indirect Method) [LO2, LO3]
Comparative financial statement data for Holly Company are given below:

	December 31	
	2002	2001
Cash	$ 4	$ 7
Accounts receivable	36	29
Inventory	75	61
Plant and equipment	210	180
Accumulated depreciation	(40)	(30)
Total assets	$285	$247

continued

Accounts payable	$ 45	$ 39
Common stock	90	70
Retained earnings	150	138
Total liabilities and stockholders' equity	$285	$247

For 2002, the company reported net income as follows:

Sales	$500
Less cost of goods sold	300
Gross margin	200
Less operating expenses	180
Net income	$ 20

Dividends of $8 were declared and paid during 2002. There were no sales of plant and equipment during the year.

Required:

Using the indirect method, prepare a statement of cash flows for 2002.

EXERCISE 16–6 (Appendix 16A) Net Cash Provided by Operating Activities (Direct Method) [LO4]

Refer to the data for Holly Company in Exercise 16–5.

Required:

Using the direct method, convert the company's income statement to a cash basis.

EXERCISE 16–7 Prepare a Statement of Cash Flows (Indirect Method) [LO2, LO3]

The following changes took place last year in Herald Company's balance sheet accounts:

Debit Balance Accounts		Credit Balance Accounts	
Cash	$ 20 I	Accumulated Depreciation	$40 I
Accounts Receivable	10 D	Accounts Payable	20 I
Inventory	30 I	Accrued Liabilities	10 D
Prepaid Expenses	5 D	Taxes Payable	10 I
Long-Term Investments	30 D	Bonds Payable	20 D
Plant and Equipment	150 I	Deferred Income Taxes	5 I
Land	30 D	Common Stock	40 I
		Retained Earnings	40 I

D = Decrease; I = Increase.

Long-term investments that had cost the company $50 were sold during the year for $45, and land that had cost $30 was sold for $70. In addition, the company declared and paid $35 in cash dividends during the year. No sales or retirements of plant and equipment took place during the year.

The company's income statement for the year follows:

Sales		$600
Less cost of goods sold		250
Gross margin		350
Less operating expenses		280
Net operating income		70
Nonoperating items:		
Loss on sale of investments	$ (5)	
Gain on sale of land	40	35
Income before taxes		105
Less income taxes		30
Net income		$ 75

The company's cash balance at the beginning of the year was $100, and its balance at the end of the year was $120.

Required:

1. Use the indirect method to determine the cash provided by operating activities for the year.
2. Prepare a statement of cash flows for the year.

EXERCISE 16–8 (Appendix 16A) Adjust Net Income to a Cash Basis (Direct Method) [LO4]
Refer to the data for Herald Company in Exercise 16–7.

Required:
Use the direct method to convert the company's income statement to a cash basis.

Problems

PROBLEM 16–9 Classification of Transactions [LO1, LO2]
Below are several transactions that took place in Mohawk Company last year:

a. Bonds were retired by paying the principal amount due.
b. Equipment was purchased by giving a long-term note to the seller.
c. Interest was paid on a note, decreasing Interest Payable.
d. Accrued taxes were paid, reducing Taxes Payable.
e. A long-term loan was made to a supplier.
f. Interest was received on the long-term loan in (e) above, reducing Interest Receivable.
g. Cash dividends were declared and paid.
h. A building was acquired in exchange for shares of the company's common stock.
i. Common stock was sold for cash to investors.
j. Equipment was sold for cash.
k. Equipment was sold in exchange for a long-term note.
l. Convertible bonds were converted into common stock.

Required:
Prepare an answer sheet with the following headings:

	Activity			Source,	Reported
Transaction	Operating	Investing	Financing	Use, or Neither	in Separate Schedule?
a.					
b.					
Etc.					

Enter the transactions above on your answer sheet and indicate how each of them would be classified on a statement of cash flows. As appropriate, place an *X* in the Operating, Investing, or Financing column. Then indicate whether the transaction would be classified as a source, use, or neither. Finally, indicate if the transaction would be reported in a separate schedule rather than in the statement of cash flows itself.

PROBLEM 16–10 Prepare a Statement of Cash Flows (Indirect Method) [LO2, LO3]
A comparative balance sheet and income statement for Eaton Company follow:

EATON COMPANY
Comparative Balance Sheet
December 31, 2002, and 2001

	2002	2001
Assets		
Cash	$ 4	$ 11
Accounts receivable	310	230
Inventory	160	195
Prepaid expenses	8	6
Plant and equipment	500	420
Accumulated depreciation	(85)	(70)
Long-term investments	31	38
Total assets	$928	$830

continued

Liabilities and Stockholders' Equity		
Accounts payable	$300	$225
Accrued liabilities	70	80
Bonds payable	195	170
Deferred income taxes	71	63
Common stock	160	200
Retained earnings	132	92
Total liabilities and stockholders' equity	$928	$830

EATON COMPANY
Income Statement
For the Year Ended December 31, 2002

Sales		$750
Less cost of goods sold		450
Gross margin		300
Less operating expenses		223
Net operating income		77
Nonoperating items:		
Gain on sale of investments	$5	
Loss on sale of equipment	2	3
Income before taxes		80
Less income taxes		24
Net income		$ 56

During 2002, the company sold some equipment for $18 that had cost $30 and on which there was accumulated depreciation of $10. In addition, the company sold long-term investments for $12 that had cost $7 when purchased several years ago. Cash dividends totaling $16 were paid during 2002.

Required:

1. Using the indirect method, determine the cash provided by operating activities for 2002.
2. Use the information in (1) above, along with an analysis of the remaining balance sheet accounts, and prepare a statement of cash flows for 2002.

PROBLEM 16–11 (Appendix 16A) Prepare a Statement of Cash Flows (Direct Method) [LO2, LO4]

Refer to the financial statement data for Eaton Company in Problem 16–10.

Required:

1. Using the direct method, adjust the company's income statement for 2002 to a cash basis.
2. Use the information obtained in (1) above, along with an analysis of the remaining balance sheet accounts, and prepare a statement of cash flows for 2002.

PROBLEM 16–12 Prepare a Statement of Cash Flows (Indirect Method) [LO2, LO3]

Foxboro Company's income statement for Year 2 follows:

Sales	$700,000
Less cost of goods sold	400,000
Gross margin	300,000
Less operating expenses	216,000
Net operating income	84,000
Gain on sale of equipment	6,000
Income before taxes	90,000
Less income taxes	27,000
Net income	$ 63,000

Balance sheet accounts for Foxboro Company contained the following amounts at the end of Years 1 and 2:

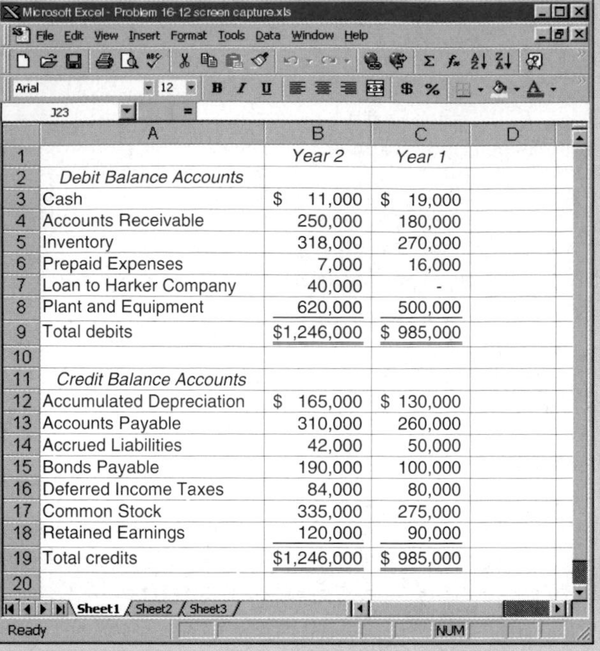

	A	B	C	D
1		*Year 2*	*Year 1*	
2	*Debit Balance Accounts*			
3	Cash	$ 11,000	$ 19,000	
4	Accounts Receivable	250,000	180,000	
5	Inventory	318,000	270,000	
6	Prepaid Expenses	7,000	16,000	
7	Loan to Harker Company	40,000	-	
8	Plant and Equipment	620,000	500,000	
9	Total debits	$1,246,000	$ 985,000	
10				
11	*Credit Balance Accounts*			
12	Accumulated Depreciation	$ 165,000	$ 130,000	
13	Accounts Payable	310,000	260,000	
14	Accrued Liabilities	42,000	50,000	
15	Bonds Payable	190,000	100,000	
16	Deferred Income Taxes	84,000	80,000	
17	Common Stock	335,000	275,000	
18	Retained Earnings	120,000	90,000	
19	Total credits	$1,246,000	$ 985,000	
20				

Equipment that had cost $30,000 and on which there was accumulated depreciation of $10,000 was sold during Year 2 for $26,000. Cash dividends totaling $33,000 were declared and paid during Year 2.

Required:

1. Using the indirect method, compute the cash provided by operating activities for Year 2.
2. Prepare a statement of cash flows for Year 2.
3. Prepare a brief explanation as to why cash declined so sharply during the year.

PROBLEM 16–13 (Appendix 16A) Prepare and Interpret a Statement of Cash Flows (Direct Method) [LO2, LO4]

Refer to the financial statement data for Foxboro Company in Problem 16–12. Mike Perry, president of the company, considers $15,000 to be a minimum cash balance for operating purposes. As can be seen from the balance sheet data, only $11,000 in cash was available at the end of the current year. The sharp decline is puzzling to Mr. Perry, particularly since sales and profits are at a record high.

Required:

1. Using the direct method, adjust the company's income statement to a cash basis for Year 2.
2. Using the data from (1) above and other data from the problem as needed, prepare a statement of cash flows for Year 2.
3. Explain to Mr. Perry why cash declined so sharply during the year.

PROBLEM 16–14 Prepare and Interpret a Statement of Cash Flows (Indirect Method) [LO2, LO3]

Sharon Feldman, president of Allied Products, considers $20,000 to be a minimum cash balance for operating purposes. As can be seen from the statements on the next page, only $15,000 in cash was available at the end of 2002. Since the company reported a large net income for the year, and also issued bonds and sold some long-term investments, the sharp decline in cash is puzzling to Ms. Feldman.

ALLIED PRODUCTS
Comparative Balance Sheet
December 31, 2002, and 2001

	2002	2001
Assets		
Current assets:		
Cash	$ 15,000	$ 33,000
Accounts receivable	300,000	210,000
Inventory	250,000	196,000
Prepaid expenses	7,000	15,000
Total current assets	572,000	454,000
Long-term investments	90,000	120,000
Plant and equipment	860,000	750,000
Less accumulated depreciation	210,000	190,000
Net plant and equipment	650,000	560,000
Total assets	$1,312,000	$1,134,000
Liabilities and Stockholders' Equity		
Current liabilities:		
Accounts payable	$ 275,000	$ 230,000
Accrued liabilities	8,000	15,000
Total current liabilities	283,000	245,000
Bonds payable	200,000	100,000
Deferred income taxes	42,000	39,000
Total liabilities	525,000	384,000
Stockholders' equity:		
Common stock	595,000	600,000
Retained earnings	192,000	150,000
Total stockholders' equity	787,000	750,000
Total liabilities and stockholders' equity	$1,312,000	$1,134,000

ALLIED PRODUCTS
Income Statement
For the Year Ended December 31, 2002

Sales		$ 800,000
Less cost of goods sold		500,000
Gross margin		300,000
Less operating expenses		214,000
Net operating income		86,000
Nonoperating items:		
Gain on sale of investments	$ 20,000	
Loss on sale of equipment	6,000	14,000
Income before taxes		100,000
Less income taxes		30,000
Net income		$ 70,000

The following additional information is available for the year 2002:

a. The company sold long-term investments with an original cost of $30,000 for $50,000 during the year.

b. Equipment that had cost $90,000 and on which there was $40,000 in accumulated depreciation was sold during the year for $44,000.

c. Cash dividends totaling $28,000 were declared and paid during the year.
d. The stock of a dissident stockholder was repurchased for cash and retired during the year. No issues of stock were made.

Required:

1. Using the indirect method, compute the cash provided by operating activities for 2002.
2. Using the data from (1) above and other data from the problem as needed, prepare a statement of cash flows for 2002.
3. Explain to the president the major reasons for the decline in the company's cash position.

PROBLEM 16–15 (Appendix 16A) Prepare and Interpret a Statement of Cash Flows (Direct Method) [LO2, LO4]
Refer to the financial statements for Allied Products in Problem 16–14. Since the Cash account decreased substantially during 2002, the company's executive committee is anxious to see how the income statement would appear on a cash basis.

Required:

1. Using the direct method, adjust the company's income statement for 2002 to a cash basis.
2. Using the data from (1) above and other data from the problem as needed, prepare a statement of cash flows for 2002.

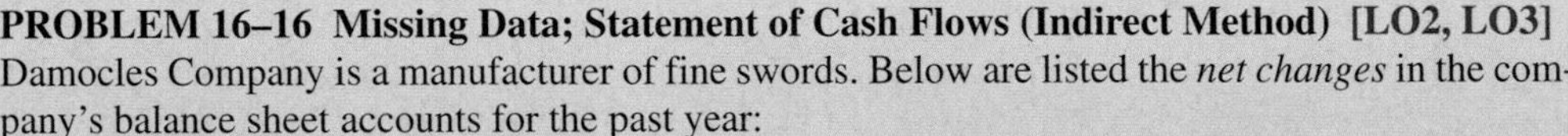

PROBLEM 16–16 Missing Data; Statement of Cash Flows (Indirect Method) [LO2, LO3]
Damocles Company is a manufacturer of fine swords. Below are listed the *net changes* in the company's balance sheet accounts for the past year:

	Debits	Credits
Cash	$ 51,000	
Accounts Receivable	170,000	
Inventory		$ 63,000
Prepaid Expenses	4,000	
Long-Term Loans to Subsidiaries		80,000
Long-Term Investments	90,000	
Plant and Equipment	340,000	
Accumulated Depreciation		65,000
Accounts Payable		48,000
Accrued Liabilities	5,000	
Bonds Payable		200,000
Deferred Income Taxes		9,000
Preferred Stock	180,000	
Common Stock		300,000
Retained Earnings		75,000
	$840,000	$840,000

The following additional information is available about last year's activities:

a. Net income for the year was $__?__.
b. The company sold equipment during the year for $35,000. The equipment had cost the company $160,000 when purchased, and it had $145,000 in accumulated depreciation at the time of sale.
c. The company declared and paid $10,000 in cash dividends during the year.
d. Depreciation charges for the year were $__?__.
e. The opening and closing balances in the Plant and Equipment and Accumulated Depreciation accounts are given below:

	Opening	Closing
Plant and Equipment	$2,850,000	$3,190,000
Accumulated Depreciation	$975,000	$1,040,000

f. There were no stock conversions (i.e., one class of stock converted to another class) during the year.
g. The balance in the Cash account at the beginning of the year was $109,000; the balance at the end of the year was $__?__.

h. If data are not given explaining the change in an account, make the most reasonable assumption as to the cause of the change.

Required:

Using the indirect method, prepare a statement of cash flows for the year.

PROBLEM 16–17 Worksheet; Prepare and Interpret a Statement of Cash Flows (Indirect Method) [LO2, LO3]

A comparative balance sheet for Alcorn Products containing data for the last two years is given below:

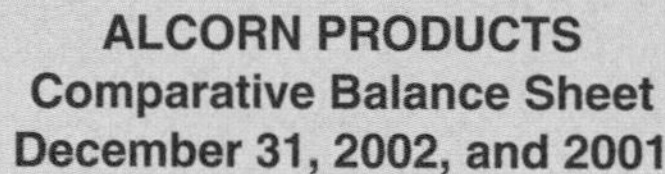

ALCORN PRODUCTS
Comparative Balance Sheet
December 31, 2002, and 2001

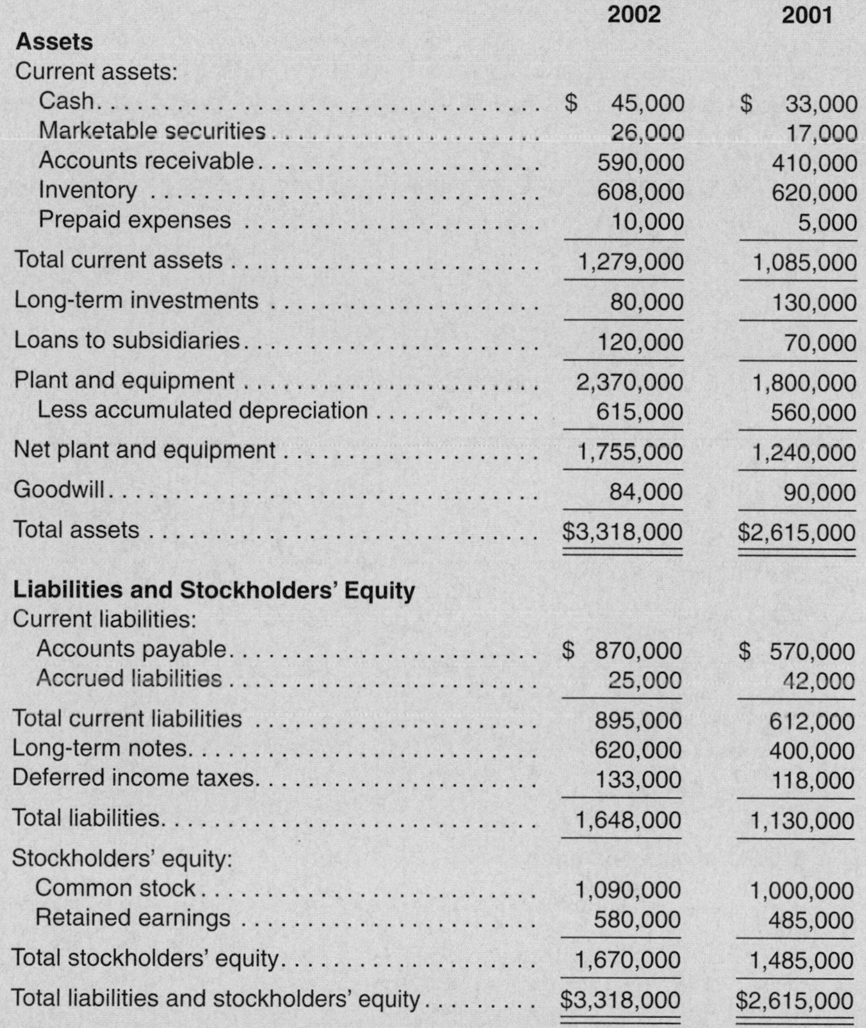

	2002	2001
Assets		
Current assets:		
Cash	$ 45,000	$ 33,000
Marketable securities	26,000	17,000
Accounts receivable	590,000	410,000
Inventory	608,000	620,000
Prepaid expenses	10,000	5,000
Total current assets	1,279,000	1,085,000
Long-term investments	80,000	130,000
Loans to subsidiaries	120,000	70,000
Plant and equipment	2,370,000	1,800,000
Less accumulated depreciation	615,000	560,000
Net plant and equipment	1,755,000	1,240,000
Goodwill	84,000	90,000
Total assets	$3,318,000	$2,615,000
Liabilities and Stockholders' Equity		
Current liabilities:		
Accounts payable	$ 870,000	$ 570,000
Accrued liabilities	25,000	42,000
Total current liabilities	895,000	612,000
Long-term notes	620,000	400,000
Deferred income taxes	133,000	118,000
Total liabilities	1,648,000	1,130,000
Stockholders' equity:		
Common stock	1,090,000	1,000,000
Retained earnings	580,000	485,000
Total stockholders' equity	1,670,000	1,485,000
Total liabilities and stockholders' equity	$3,318,000	$2,615,000

The following additional information is available about the company's activities during 2002, the current year:

a. Cash dividends declared and paid to the common stockholders totaled $75,000.
b. Long-term notes with a value of $380,000 were repaid during the year.
c. Equipment was sold during the year for $70,000. The equipment had cost $130,000 and had $40,000 in accumulated depreciation on the date of sale.
d. Long-term investments were sold during the year for $110,000. These investments had cost $50,000 when purchased several years ago.

The company reported net income during 2002 as follows:

Sales		$3,000,000
Less cost of goods sold		1,860,000
Gross margin		1,140,000
Less operating expenses		930,000
Net operating income		210,000
Nonoperating items:		
Gain on sale of investments	$60,000	
Loss on sale of equipment	20,000	40,000
Income before taxes		250,000
Less income taxes		80,000
Net income		$ 170,000

Required:

1. Prepare a worksheet like Exhibit 16–10 for Alcorn Products.
2. Using the indirect method, prepare a statement of cash flows for the year.
3. What problems relating to the company's activities are revealed by the statement of cash flows that you have prepared?

PROBLEM 16–18 (Appendix 16A) Adjusting Net Income to a Cash Basis (Direct Method) [LO4]

Refer to the data for Alcorn Products in Problem 16–17. All of the long-term notes issued during 2002 are being held by Alcorn's bank. The bank's management wants the income statement adjusted to a cash basis to see how the cash basis statement compares to the accrual basis statement.

Required:

Use the direct method to convert Alcorn Products' 2002 income statement to a cash basis.

PROBLEM 16–19 Missing Data; Statement of Cash Flows (Indirect Method) [LO2, LO3]

Listed below are the *changes* that have taken place in Luang Corporation's balance sheet accounts as a result of the past year's activities:

Debit Balance Accounts	Net Increase (Decrease)
Cash	$(30,000)
Accounts Receivable	20,000
Inventory	(60,000)
Prepaid Expenses	10,000
Long-Term Investments	50,000
Plant and Equipment	120,000
Net increase	$110,000
Credit Balance Accounts	
Accumulated Depreciation	$ 40,000
Accounts Payable	30,000
Accrued Liabilities	10,000
Taxes Payable	10,000
Bonds Payable	(40,000)
Deferred Income Taxes	(5,000)
Common Stock	20,000
Retained Earnings	45,000
Net increase	$110,000

The following additional information is available about last year's activities:

a. The company sold equipment during the year for $40,000. The equipment had cost the company $120,000 when purchased, and it had $70,000 in accumulated depreciation at the time of sale.
b. Net income for the year was $__?__.
c. The balance in the Cash account at the beginning of the year was $100,000; the balance at the end of the year was $__?__.

d. The company declared and paid $35,000 in cash dividends during the year.
e. Long-term investments that had cost $60,000 were sold during the year for $80,000.
f. The beginning and ending balances in the Plant and Equipment and Accumulated Depreciation accounts for the past year are given below:

	Ending	Beginning
Plant and Equipment	$620,000	$500,000
Accumulated Depreciation	$240,000	$200,000

g. If data are not given explaining the change in an account, make the most reasonable assumption as to the cause of the change.

Required:
Using the indirect method, prepare a statement of cash flows for the past year.

Group and Internet Exercises

GROUP EXERCISE 16–20 Reconciling the Statement of Cash Flows with the Balance Sheet
As shown in the chapter, it should be possible to reconcile the statement of cash flows with the changes in noncash balance sheet accounts. In practice, this is often difficult because the net change in a balance sheet account may have been decomposed into increases and decreases in the account or it may be netted against some other change in a balance sheet account when shown on the statement of cash flows. Find the most recent annual report of a company that interests you.

Required:
As far as you can, trace the changes in the company's noncash balance sheet accounts to the statement of cash flows.

INTERNET EXERCISE 16–21
As you know, the World Wide Web is a medium that is constantly evolving. Sites come and go, and change without notice. To enable periodic update of site addresses, this problem has been posted to the textbook website (www.mhhe.com/garrison10e). After accessing the site, enter the Student Center and select this chapter. Select and complete the Internet Exercise.

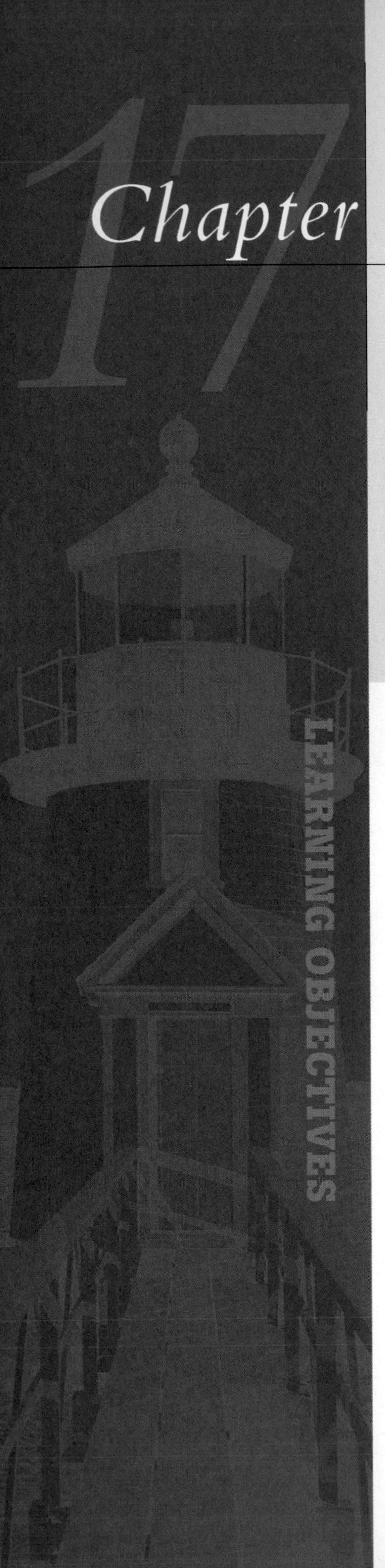

Chapter Seventeen

"How Well Am I Doing?" Financial Statement Analysis

After studying Chapter 17, you should be able to:

1. Prepare and interpret financial statements in comparative and common-size form.
2. Compute and interpret financial ratios that would be most useful to a common stockholder.
3. Compute and interpret financial ratios that would be most useful to a short-term creditor.
4. Compute and interpret financial ratios that would be most useful to a long-term creditor.

BUSINESS FOCUS

Getting Paid on Time

S

Rick Burrock, the managing director of an accounting firm based in Minneapolis, advises his small business clients to keep a tight rein on credit extended to customers. "You need to convey to your customers, right from the beginning, that you will work very hard to satisfy them and that in return, you expect to be paid on time. Start by investigating all new customers. A credit report helps, but with a business customer you can find out even more by requesting financial statements . . . Using the balance sheet, divide current assets by current liabilities to calculate the current ratio. If a company's current ratio is below 1.00, it will be paying out more than it expects to collect; you may want to reconsider doing business with that company or insist on stricter credit terms."

Source: Jill Andresky Fraser, "Hands on Collections: Get Paid Promptly," *Inc.,* November 1996, p. 87.

All financial statements are essentially historical documents. They tell what *has happened* during a particular period of time. However, most users of financial statements are concerned about what *will happen* in the future. Stockholders are concerned with future earnings and dividends. Creditors are concerned with the company's future ability to repay its debts. Managers are concerned with the company's ability to finance future expansion. Despite the fact that financial statements are historical documents, they can still provide valuable information bearing on all of these concerns.

Financial statement analysis involves careful selection of data from financial statements for the primary purpose of forecasting the financial health of the company. This is accomplished by examining trends in key financial data, comparing financial data across companies, and analyzing key financial ratios. In this chapter, we consider some of the more important ratios and other analytical tools that financial analysts use.

Managers are also vitally concerned with the financial ratios discussed in this chapter. First, the ratios provide indicators of how well the company and its business units are performing. Some of these ratios would ordinarily be used in a balanced scorecard approach as discussed in Chapter 10. The specific ratios selected depend on the company's strategy. For example, a company that wants to emphasize responsiveness to customers may closely monitor the inventory turnover ratio discussed later in this chapter. Second, since managers must report to shareholders and may wish to raise funds from external sources, managers must pay attention to the financial ratios used by external investors to evaluate the company's investment potential and creditworthiness.

Limitations of Financial Statement Analysis

Although financial statement analysis is a highly useful tool, it has two limitations that we must mention before proceeding any further. These two limitations involve the comparability of financial data between companies and the need to look beyond ratios.

Comparison of Financial Data

Comparisons of one company with another can provide valuable clues about the financial health of an organization. Unfortunately, differences in accounting methods between companies sometimes make it difficult to compare the companies' financial data. For example, if one firm values its inventories by the LIFO method and another firm by the average cost method, then direct comparisons of financial data such as inventory valuations and cost of goods sold between the two firms may be misleading. Sometimes enough data are presented in footnotes to the financial statements to restate data to a comparable basis. Otherwise, the analyst should keep in mind the lack of comparability of the data before drawing any definite conclusions. Nevertheless, even with this limitation in mind, comparisons of key ratios with other companies and with industry averages often suggest avenues for further investigation.

The Need to Look beyond Ratios

An inexperienced analyst may assume that ratios are sufficient in themselves as a basis for judgments about the future. Nothing could be further from the truth. Conclusions based on ratio analysis must be regarded as tentative. Ratios should not be viewed as an end, but rather they should be viewed as a *starting point,* as indicators of what to pursue in greater depth. They raise many questions, but they rarely answer any questions by themselves.

In addition to ratios, other sources of data should be analyzed in order to make judgments about the future of an organization. The analyst should look, for example, at industry trends, technological changes, changes in consumer tastes, changes in broad economic factors, and changes within the firm itself. A recent change in a key management position, for example, might provide a basis for optimism about the future, even though the past performance of the firm (as shown by its ratios) may have been mediocre.

Statements in Comparative and Common-Size Form

LEARNING OBJECTIVE 1
Prepare and interpret financial statements in comparative form and common-size form.

Few figures appearing on financial statements have much significance standing by themselves. It is the relationship of one figure to another and the amount and direction of change over time that are important in financial statement analysis. How does the analyst key in on significant relationships? How does the analyst dig out the important trends and changes in a company? Three analytical techniques are widely used:

1. Dollar and percentage changes on statements.
2. Common-size statements.
3. Ratios.

The first and second techniques are discussed in this section; the third technique is discussed in the remainder of the chapter. To illustrate these analytical techniques, we analyze the financial statements of Brickey Electronics, a producer of computer components.

Dollar and Percentage Changes on Statements

A good place to begin in financial statement analysis is to put statements in comparative form. This consists of little more than putting two or more years' data side by side. Statements cast in comparative form underscore movements and trends and may give the analyst valuable clues as to what to expect.

Examples of financial statements placed in comparative form are given in Exhibits 17–1 and 17–2. These statements of Brickey Electronics reveal the firm has been experiencing substantial growth. The data on these statements are used as a basis for discussion throughout the remainder of the chapter.

Concept 17–1

Horizontal Analysis Comparison of two or more years' financial data is known as **horizontal analysis,** or **trend analysis.** Horizontal analysis is facilitated by showing changes between years in both dollar *and* percentage form, as has been done in Exhibits 17–1 and 17–2. Showing changes in dollar form helps the analyst focus on key factors that have affected profitability or financial position. For example, observe in Exhibit 17–2 that sales for 2002 were up $4 million over 2001, but that this increase in sales was more than negated by a $4.5 million increase in cost of goods sold.

Showing changes between years in percentage form helps the analyst to gain *perspective* and to gain a feel for the *significance* of the changes that are taking place. A $1 million increase in sales is much more significant if the prior year's sales were $2 million than if the prior year's sales were $20 million. In the first situation, the increase would be 50%—undoubtedly a significant increase for any firm. In the second situation, the increase would be only 5%—perhaps just a reflection of normal growth.

Trend Percentages Horizontal analysis of financial statements can also be carried out by computing *trend percentages.* **Trend percentages** state several years' financial data in terms of a base year. The base year equals 100%, with all other years stated as some percentage of this base. To illustrate, consider McDonald's Corporation, the largest global food service retailer, with more than 26,000 restaurants worldwide. McDonald's enjoyed tremendous growth during the 1990s, as evidenced by the following data:

	2000	1999	1998	1997	1996	1995	1994	1993	1992	1991	1990
Sales (millions) . . .	$14,243	$13,259	$12,421	$11,409	$10,687	$9,795	$8,321	$7,408	$7,133	$6,695	$6,640
Net income (millions).	$ 1,977	$ 1,948	$ 1,550	$ 1,642	$ 1,573	$1,427	$1,224	$1,083	$ 959	$ 860	$ 802

Exhibit 17–1

BRICKEY ELECTRONICS
Comparative Balance Sheet
December 31, 2002, and 2001
(dollars in thousands)

	2002	2001	Increase (Decrease) Amount	Increase (Decrease) Percent
Assets				
Current assets:				
Cash	$ 1,200	$ 2,350	$(1,150)	(48.9)%*
Accounts receivable, net	6,000	4,000	2,000	50.0%
Inventory	8,000	10,000	(2,000)	(20.0)%
Prepaid expenses	300	120	180	150.0%
Total current assets	15,500	16,470	(970)	(5.9)%
Property and equipment:				
Land	4,000	4,000	0	0%
Buildings and equipment, net	12,000	8,500	3,500	41.2%
Total property and equipment	16,000	12,500	3,500	28.0%
Total assets	$31,500	$28,970	$ 2,530	8.7%
Liabilities and Stockholders' Equity				
Current liabilities:				
Accounts payable	$ 5,800	$ 4,000	$ 1,800	45.0%
Accrued payables	900	400	500	125.0%
Notes payable, short term	300	600	(300)	(50.0)%
Total current liabilities	7,000	5,000	2,000	40.0%
Long-term liabilities:				
Bonds payable, 8%	7,500	8,000	(500)	(6.3)%
Total liabilities	14,500	13,000	1,500	11.5%
Stockholders' equity:				
Preferred stock, $100 par, 6%, $100 liquidation value	2,000	2,000	0	0%
Common stock, $12 par	6,000	6,000	0	0%
Additional paid-in capital	1,000	1,000	0	0%
Total paid-in capital	9,000	9,000	0	0%
Retained earnings	8,000	6,970	1,030	14.8%
Total stockholders' equity	17,000	15,970	1,030	6.4%
Total liabilities and stockholders' equity	$31,500	$28,970	$ 2,530	8.7%

*Since we are measuring the amount of change between 2001 and 2002, the dollar amounts for 2001 become the base figures for expressing these changes in percentage form. For example, Cash decreased by $1,150 between 2001 and 2002. This decrease expressed in percentage form is computed as follows: $1,150 ÷ $2,350 = 48.9%. Other percentage figures in this exhibit and Exhibit 17–2 are computed in the same way.

By simply looking at these data, one can see that sales increased every year. But how rapidly have sales been increasing, and have the increases in net income kept pace with the increases in sales? It is difficult to answer these questions by looking at the raw data alone. The increases in sales and the increases in net income can be put into better perspective by stating them in terms of trend percentages, with 1990 as the base year. These percentages (all rounded) appear as follows:

Exhibit 17–2

BRICKEY ELECTRONICS
Comparative Income Statement and Reconciliation of Retained Earnings
For the Years Ended December 31, 2002, and 2001
(dollars in thousands)

	2002	2001	Increase (Decrease) Amount	Increase (Decrease) Percent
Sales	$52,000	$48,000	$4,000	8.3%
Cost of goods sold	36,000	31,500	4,500	14.3%
Gross margin	16,000	16,500	(500)	(3.0)%
Operating expenses:				
Selling expenses	7,000	6,500	500	7.7%
Administrative expenses	5,860	6,100	(240)	(3.9)%
Total operating expenses	12,860	12,600	260	2.1%
Net operating income	3,140	3,900	(760)	(19.5)%
Interest expense	640	700	(60)	(8.6)%
Net income before taxes	2,500	3,200	(700)	(21.9)%
Less income taxes (30%)	750	960	(210)	(21.9)%
Net income	1,750	2,240	$ (490)	(21.9)%
Dividends to preferred stockholders, $6 per share (see Exhibit 17–1)	120	120		
Net income remaining for common stockholders	1,630	2,120		
Dividends to common stockholders, $1.20 per share	600	600		
Net income added to retained earnings	1,030	1,520		
Retained earnings, beginning of year	6,970	5,450		
Retained earnings, end of year	$ 8,000	$ 6,970		

	2000	1999	1998	1997	1996	1995	1994	1993	1992	1991	1990
Sales*	215%	200%	187%	172%	161%	148%	125%	112%	107%	101%	100%
Net income	247%	243%	193%	205%	196%	178%	153%	135%	120%	107%	100%

*For 2000, $14,243 ÷ $6,640 = 215%; for 1999, $13,259 ÷ $6,640 = 200%, and so on.

The trend analysis is particularly striking when the data are plotted as in Exhibit 17–3. McDonald's sales growth was impressive throughout the entire 11-year period, but it was outpaced by even higher growth in the company's net income. A review of the company's income statement reveals that the dip in net income growth in 1998 was attributable, in part, to the $161.6 million that McDonald's spent to implement its "Made for You" program and a special charge of $160 million that related to a home office productivity initiative.

Common-Size Statements

Key changes and trends can also be highlighted by the use of *common-size statements.* A **common-size statement** is one that shows the items appearing on it in percentage form as well as in dollar form. Each item is stated as a percentage of some total of which that item is a part. The preparation of common-size statements is known as **vertical analysis.**

Exhibit 17–3 McDonald's Corporation: Trend Analysis of Sales and Net Income

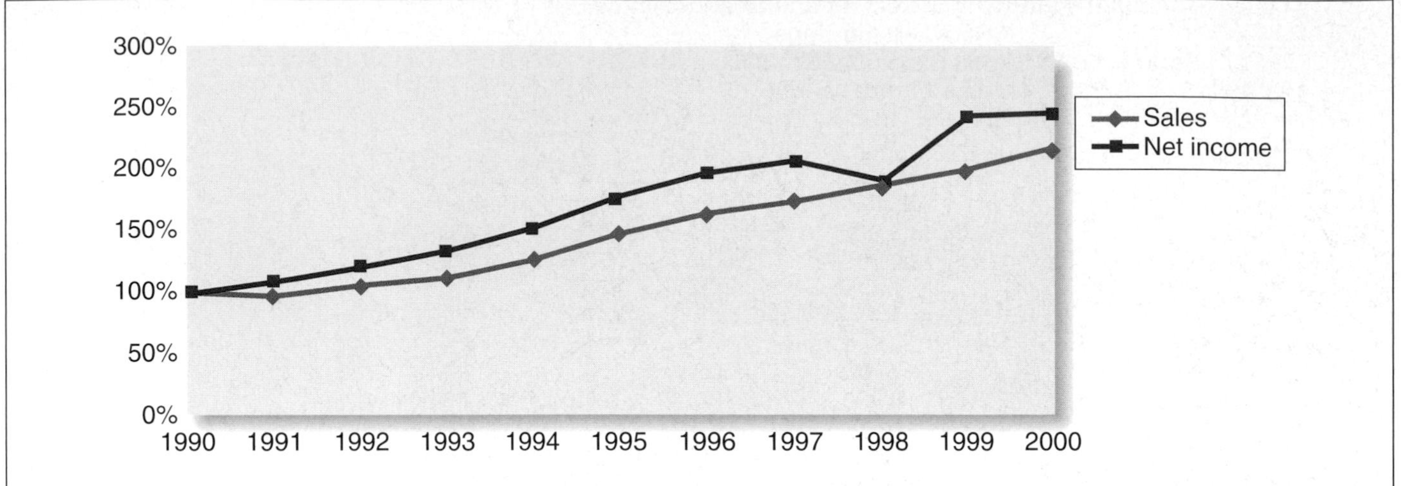

Common-size statements are particularly useful when comparing data from different companies. For example, in one year, Wendy's net income was about $110 million, whereas McDonald's was $1,427 million. This comparison is somewhat misleading because of the dramatically different sizes of the two companies. To put this in better perspective, the net income figures can be expressed as a percentage of the sales revenues of each company. Since Wendy's sales revenues were $1,746 million and McDonald's were $9,794 million, Wendy's net income as a percentage of sales was about 6.3% and McDonald's was about 14.6%. While the comparison still favors McDonald's, the contrast between the two companies has been placed on a more comparable basis.

The Balance Sheet One application of the vertical analysis idea is to state the separate assets of a company as percentages of total assets. A common-size statement of this type is shown in Exhibit 17–4 for Brickey Electronics.

Notice from Exhibit 17–4 that placing all assets in common-size form clearly shows the relative importance of the current assets as compared to the noncurrent assets. It also shows that significant changes have taken place in the *composition* of the current assets over the last year. Notice, for example, that the receivables have increased in relative importance and that both cash and inventory have declined in relative importance. Judging from the sharp increase in receivables, the deterioration in the cash position may be a result of inability to collect from customers.

The Income Statement Another application of the vertical analysis idea is to place all items on the income statement in percentage form in terms of sales. A common-size statement of this type is shown in Exhibit 17–5.

By placing all items on the income statement in common size in terms of sales, it is possible to see at a glance how each dollar of sales is distributed among the various costs, expenses, and profits. And by placing successive years' statements side by side, it is easy to spot interesting trends. For example, as shown in Exhibit 17–5, the cost of goods sold as a percentage of sales increased from 65.6% in 2001 to 69.2% in 2002. Or looking at this from a different viewpoint, the *gross margin percentage* declined from 34.4% in 2001 to 30.8% in 2002. Managers and investment analysts often pay close attention to the gross margin percentage since it is considered a broad gauge of profitability. The **gross margin percentage** is computed as follows:

$$\text{Gross margin percentage} = \frac{\text{Gross margin}}{\text{Sales}}$$

Exhibit 17–4

BRICKEY ELECTRONICS
Common-Size Comparative Balance Sheet
December 31, 2002, and 2001
(dollars in thousands)

	2002	2001	Common-Size Percentages 2002	Common-Size Percentages 2001
Assets				
Current assets:				
Cash	$ 1,200	$ 2,350	3.8%*	8.1%
Accounts receivable, net	6,000	4,000	19.0%	13.8%
Inventory	8,000	10,000	25.4%	34.5%
Prepaid expenses	300	120	1.0%	0.4%
Total current assets	15,500	16,470	49.2%	56.9%
Property and equipment:				
Land	4,000	4,000	12.7%	13.8%
Buildings and equipment, net	12,000	8,500	38.1%	29.3%
Total property and equipment	16,000	12,500	50.8%	43.1%
Total assets	$31,500	$28,970	100.0%	100.0%
Liabilities and Stockholders' Equity				
Current liabilities:				
Accounts payable	$ 5,800	$ 4,000	18.4%	13.8%
Accrued payables	900	400	2.9%	1.4%
Notes payable, short term	300	600	1.0%	2.1%
Total current liabilities	7,000	5,000	22.2%	17.3%
Long-term liabilities:				
Bonds payable, 8%	7,500	8,000	23.8%	27.6%
Total liabilities	14,500	13,000	46.0%	44.9%
Stockholders' equity:				
Preferred stock, $100, 6%, $100 liquidation value	2,000	2,000	6.3%	6.9%
Common stock, $12 par	6,000	6,000	19.0%	20.7%
Additional paid-in capital	1,000	1,000	3.2%	3.5%
Total paid-in capital	9,000	9,000	28.6%	31.1%
Retained earnings	8,000	6,970	25.4%	24.1%
Total stockholders' equity	17,000	15,970	54.0%	55.1%
Total liabilities and stockholders' equity	$31,500	$28,970	100.0%	100.0%

*Each asset account on a common-size statement is expressed in terms of total assets, and each liability and equity account is expressed in terms of total liabilities and stockholders' equity. For example, the percentage figure above for Cash in 2002 is computed as follows: $1,200 ÷ $31,500 = 3.8%.

The gross margin percentage tends to be more stable for retailing companies than for other service companies and for manufacturers since the cost of goods sold in retailing excludes fixed costs. When fixed costs are included in the cost of goods sold figure, the gross margin percentage tends to increase and decrease with sales volume. With increases in sales volume, the fixed costs are spread across more units and the gross margin percentage improves.

While a higher gross margin percentage is generally considered to be better than a lower gross margin percentage, there are exceptions. Some companies purposely choose a strategy emphasizing low prices (and hence low gross margins). An increasing gross

Exhibit 17–5

BRICKEY ELECTRONICS
Common-Size Comparative Income Statement
For the Years Ended December 31, 2002, and 2001
(dollars in thousands)

			Common-Size Percentages	
	2002	**2001**	**2002**	**2001**
Sales	$52,000	$48,000	100.0%	100.0%
Cost of goods sold	36,000	31,500	69.2%	65.6%
Gross margin	16,000	16,500	30.8%	34.4%
Operating expenses:				
Selling expenses	7,000	6,500	13.5%	13.5%
Administrative expenses	5,860	6,100	11.3%	12.7%
Total operating expenses	12,860	12,600	24.7%	26.2%
Net operating income	3,140	3,900	6.0%	8.1%
Interest expense	640	700	1.2%	1.5%
Net income before taxes	2,500	3,200	4.8%	6.7%
Income taxes (30%)	750	960	1.4%	2.0%
Net income	$ 1,750	$ 2,240	3.4%	4.7%

*Note that the percentage figures for each year are expressed in terms of total sales for the year. For example, the percentage figure for cost of goods sold in 2002 is computed as follows:
$36,000 ÷ $52,000 = 69.2%

margin in such a company might be a sign that the company's strategy is not being effectively implemented.

Common-size statements are also very helpful in pointing out efficiencies and inefficiencies that might otherwise go unnoticed. To illustrate, in 2002, Brickey Electronics' selling expenses increased by $500,000 over 2001. A glance at the common-size income statement shows, however, that on a relative basis, selling expenses were no higher in 2002 than in 2001. In each year they represented 13.5% of sales.

In Business

Gross Margins Can Make the Difference

After announcing a 42% increase in quarterly profits, Dell Computer Corp.'s shares fell over 6%. Why? According to *The Wall Street Journal,* investors focused on the company's eroding profit margins. "Analysts . . . said that a decline in gross margins was larger than they had expected and indicated a difficult pricing environment. Gross margins fell nearly a full percentage point to 21.5% of sales, from 22.4%." Dell had cut its prices to increase its market share, which worked, but at the cost of lowered profitability.

Source: Gary McWilliams, "Dell Net Rises, but Margins Spur Worries," *The Wall Street Journal*, May 19, 1999, p. A3.

Ratio Analysis—The Common Stockholder

A number of financial ratios are used to assess how well the company is doing from the standpoint of the stockholders. These ratios naturally focus on net income, dividends, and stockholders' equities.

Earnings per Share

LEARNING OBJECTIVE 2
Compute and interpret financial ratios that would be most useful to a common stockholder.

An investor buys a share of stock in the hope of realizing a return in the form of either dividends or future increases in the value of the stock. Since earnings form the basis for dividend payments, as well as the basis for future increases in the value of shares, investors are always interested in a company's reported *earnings per share.* Probably no single statistic is more widely quoted or relied on by investors than earnings per share, although it has some inherent limitations, as discussed below.

Earnings per share is computed by dividing net income available for common stockholders by the average number of common shares outstanding during the year. "Net income available for common stockholders" is net income less dividends paid to the owners of the company's preferred stock.[1]

$$\text{Earnings per share} = \frac{\text{Net income} - \text{Preferred dividends}}{\text{Average number of common shares outstanding}}$$

Using the data in Exhibits 17–1 and 17–2, we see that the earnings per share for Brickey Electronics for 2002 would be computed as follows:

$$\frac{\$1{,}750{,}000 - \$120{,}000}{(500{,}000 \text{ shares*} + 500{,}000 \text{ shares})/2} = \$3.26$$

*$6,000,000 ÷ 12 = 500,000 shares.

Price-Earnings Ratio

The relationship between the market price of a share of stock and the stock's current earnings per share is often quoted in terms of a **price-earnings ratio.** If we assume that the current market price for Brickey Electronics' stock is $40 per share, the company's price-earnings ratio would be computed as follows:

$$\text{Price-earnings ratio} = \frac{\text{Market price per share}}{\text{Earnings per share}}$$

$$= \frac{\$40}{\$3.26} = 12.3$$

The price-earnings ratio is 12.3; that is, the stock is selling for about 12.3 times its current earnings per share.

Concept 17–2

The price-earnings ratio is widely used by investors as a general guideline in gauging stock values. A high price-earnings ratio means that investors are willing to pay a premium for the company's stock—presumably because the company is expected to have higher than average future earnings growth. Conversely, if investors believe a company's future earnings growth prospects are limited, the company's price-earnings ratio would be relatively low. In the late 1990s, the stock prices of some dot.com companies—particularly those with little or no earnings—were selling at levels that resulted in unprecedented price-earnings ratios. Many commentators cautioned that these price-earnings ratios were unsustainable in the long run—and they were right. The stock prices of almost all dot.com companies subsequently crashed.

[1] Another complication can arise when a company has issued securities such as executive stock options or warrants that can be converted into shares of common stock. If these conversions were to take place, the same earnings would have to be distributed among a greater number of common shares. Therefore, a supplemental earnings per share figure, called diluted earnings per share, may have to be computed. Refer to a current intermediate financial accounting text for details.

In Business **Stickiness?**

The Internet stock market bubble of the late 1990s resulted in financial ratios for dot.com companies that were way out of line with traditional standards. Price-earnings ratios, in particular, reached dizzying heights. Investment analysts and dot.com enthusiasts developed new measures of performance in an attempt to justify the very high market valuations of these companies—most of whom had never earned a dime of profit. Thomas A. Weber of *The Wall Street Journal* has this to say about one measure that was widely used to evaluate the performance of dot.com companies: "Remember 'stickiness'? At the height of the dot.com hype, this cloyingly named concept set a new standard for buzzword-driven exuberance. Web sites sought it, and investors swooned over it. Everybody wanted to get sticky. Now the truth can be told: Sticky was stupid. Internet companies took a simple notion—namely, that products that engage customers for long stretches of time must be valuable—and elevated it into a cult . . . . If you want to gauge success, accountants have a much more useful number to obsess over. It's called net income."

Source: Thomas E. Weber, "A 'Sticky' Situation: How a Web Buzzword Spun Out of Control," *The Wall Street Journal*, March 5, 2001, p. B1.

Dividend Payout and Yield Ratios

Investors hold shares in a company because they anticipate an attractive return. The return sought isn't always dividends. Many investors prefer not to receive dividends. Instead, they prefer to have the company retain all earnings and reinvest them internally in order to support growth. The stocks of companies that adopt this approach, loosely termed *growth stocks,* may enjoy rapid upward movement in market price. Other investors prefer to have a dependable, current source of income through regular dividend payments. Such investors seek out stocks with consistent dividend records and payout ratios.

The Dividend Payout Ratio The **dividend payout ratio** gauges the portion of current earnings being paid out in dividends. Investors who seek growth in market price would like this ratio to be small, whereas investors who seek dividends prefer it to be large. This ratio is computed by relating dividends per share to earnings per share for common stock:

$$\text{Dividend payout ratio} = \frac{\text{Dividends per share}}{\text{Earnings per share}}$$

For Brickey Electronics, the dividend payout ratio for 2002 is computed as follows:

$$\frac{\$1.20 \text{ (see Exhibit 17–2)}}{\$3.26} = 36.8\%$$

There is no such thing as a "right" payout ratio, even though it should be noted that the ratio tends to be similar for companies within a particular industry. Industries with ample opportunities for growth at high rates of return on assets tend to have low payout ratios, whereas payout ratios tend to be high in industries with limited reinvestment opportunities.

The Dividend Yield Ratio The **dividend yield ratio** is obtained by dividing the current dividends per share by the current market price per share:

$$\text{Dividend yield ratio} = \frac{\text{Dividends per share}}{\text{Market price per share}}$$

The market price for Brickey Electronics' stock is $40 per share so the dividend yield is computed as follows:

$$\frac{\$1.20}{\$40} = 3.0\%$$

The dividend yield ratio measures the rate of return (in the form of cash dividends only) that would be earned by an investor who buys the common stock at the current market price. A low dividend yield ratio is neither bad nor good by itself. As discussed above, a company may pay out very little dividends because it has ample opportunities for reinvesting funds within the company at high rates of return.

Return on Total Assets

Managers have both *financing* and *operating* responsibilities. Financing responsibilities relate to how one *obtains* the funds needed to provide for the assets in an organization. Operating responsibilities relate to how one *uses* the assets once they have been obtained. Both are vital to a well-managed firm. However, care must be taken not to confuse or mix the two when assessing the performance of a manager. That is, whether funds have been obtained from creditors or from stockholders should not be allowed to influence one's assessment of *how well* the assets have been employed since being received by the firm.

The **return on total assets** is a measure of operating performance that shows how well assets have been employed. It is defined as follows:

$$\text{Return on total assets} = \frac{\text{Net income} + [\text{Interest expense} \times (1 - \text{Tax rate})]}{\text{Average total assets}}$$

Adding interest expense back to net income results in an adjusted earnings figure that shows what earnings would have been if the assets had been acquired solely by selling shares of stock. With this adjustment, the return on total assets can be compared for companies with differing amounts of debt or over time for a single company that has changed its mix of debt and equity. Thus, the measurement of how well the assets have been employed is not influenced by how the assets were financed. Notice that the interest expense is placed on an after-tax basis by multiplying it by the factor (1 − Tax rate).

The return on total assets for Brickey Electronics for 2002 would be computed as follows (from Exhibits 17–1 and 17–2):

Net income	$ 1,750,000
Add back interest expense: $640,000 × (1 − 0.30)	448,000
Total (a)	$ 2,198,000
Assets, beginning of year	$28,970,000
Assets, end of year	31,500,000
Total	$60,470,000
Average total assets: $60,470,000 ÷ 2 (b)	$30,235,000
Return on total assets, (a) ÷ (b)	7.3%

Brickey Electronics has earned a return of 7.3% on average assets employed over the last year.

Return on Common Stockholders' Equity

One of the primary reasons for operating a corporation is to generate income for the benefit of the common stockholders. One measure of a company's success in this regard is the **return on common stockholders' equity,** which divides the net income remaining for common stockholders by the average common stockholders' equity for the year. The formula is as follows:

$$\text{Return on common stockholders' equity} = \frac{\text{Net income} - \text{Preferred dividends}}{\text{Average common stockholders' equity}}$$

where $\frac{\text{Average common stockholders' equity}}{} = $ Average common stockholders' equity = Average total stockholders' equity − Average preferred stock

For Brickey Electronics, the return on common stockholders' equity is 11.3% for 2002 as shown below:

Net income	$ 1,750,000
Deduct preferred dividends	120,000
Net income remaining for common stockholders (a)	$ 1,630,000
Average stockholders' equity	$16,485,000*
Deduct average preferred stock	2,000,000†
Average common stockholders' equity (b)	$14,485,000
Return on common stockholders' equity, (a) ÷ (b)	11.3%

*$15,970,000 + $17,000,000 = $32,970,000; $32,970,000 ÷ 2 = $16,485,000.
†$2,000,000 + $2,000,000 = $4,000,000; $4,000,000 ÷ 2 = $2,000,000.

Compare the return on common stockholders' equity above (11.3%) with the return on total assets computed in the preceding section (7.3%). Why is the return on common stockholders' equity so much higher? The answer lies in the principle of *financial leverage*. Financial leverage is discussed in the following paragraphs.

In Business **Comparing Banks**

Deutsche Bank, the German banking giant, fares poorly in comparisons with its global rivals. Its net-income-to-assets ratio (i.e., return on assets) is only 0.26%, while its peers such as **Citigroup** and **Credit Suisse** have ratios of up to 0.92%. Its return on equity is only 10%, whereas the return on equity of almost all its peers is in the 14% to 16% range. One reason for Deutsche Bank's anemic performance is the bank's bloated and expensive payroll. Deutsche Bank's earnings average about $23,000 per employee. At **HSBC** (Hong Kong and Shanghai Banking Corporation) the figure is $32,000 per employee and at Credit Suisse it is $34,000.

Source: Justin Doebele, "Best Bank Bargain?" *Forbes,* August 9, 1999, pp. 89–90.

Financial Leverage

Financial leverage (often called *leverage* for short) involves acquiring assets with funds that have been obtained from creditors or from preferred stockholders at a fixed rate of return. If the assets in which the funds are invested are able to earn a rate of return *greater* than the fixed rate of return required by the funds' suppliers, then we have **positive financial leverage** and the common stockholders benefit.

For example, suppose that CBS is able to earn an after-tax return of 12% on its broadcasting assets. If the company can borrow from creditors at a 10% interest rate in order to expand its assets, then the common stockholders can benefit from positive leverage. The borrowed funds invested in the business will earn an after-tax return of 12%, but the after-tax interest cost of the borrowed funds will be only 7% [10% interest rate × (1 − 0.30) = 7%]. The difference will go to the common stockholders.

We can see this concept in operation in the case of Brickey Electronics. Notice from Exhibit 17–1 that the company's bonds payable bear a fixed interest rate of 8%. The after-tax interest cost of these bonds is only 5.6% [8% interest rate × (1 − 0.30) = 5.6%]. The company's assets are generating an after-tax return of 7.3%, as we computed earlier. Since this return on assets is greater than the after-tax interest cost of the bonds, leverage is positive, and the difference accrues to the benefit of the common stockholders. This explains in part why the return on common stockholders' equity (11.3%) is greater than the return on total assets (7.3%).

Unfortunately, leverage is a two-edged sword. If assets are unable to earn a high enough rate to cover the interest costs of debt, or to cover the preferred dividend due to the preferred stockholders, *then the common stockholder suffers.* Under these circumstances, we have **negative financial leverage.**

The Impact of Income Taxes Debt and preferred stock are not equally efficient in generating positive leverage. The reason is that interest on debt is tax deductible, whereas preferred dividends are not. This usually makes debt a much more effective source of positive leverage than preferred stock.

To illustrate this point, suppose that the Hospital Corporation of America is considering three ways of financing a $100 million expansion of its chain of hospitals:

1. $100 million from an issue of common stock.
2. $50 million from an issue of common stock, and $50 million from an issue of preferred stock bearing a dividend rate of 8%.
3. $50 million from an issue of common stock, and $50 million from an issue of bonds bearing an interest rate of 8%.

Assuming that the Hospital Corporation of America can earn an additional $15 million each year before interest and taxes as a result of the expansion, the operating results under each of the three alternatives are shown in Exhibit 17–6.

If the entire $100 million is raised from an issue of common stock, then the return to the common stockholders will be only 10.5%, as shown under alternative 1 in the exhibit. If half of the funds are raised from an issue of preferred stock, then the return to the common stockholders increases to 13%, due to the positive effects of leverage. However, if half of the funds are raised from an issue of bonds, then the return to the common stockholders jumps to 15.4%, as shown under alternative 3. Thus, long-term debt is much more efficient in generating positive leverage than is preferred stock. The reason is that the interest expense on long-term debt is tax deductible, whereas the dividends on preferred stock are not.

The Desirability of Leverage Because of leverage, having some debt in the capital structure can substantially benefit the common stockholder. For this reason, most companies today try to maintain a level of debt that is considered to be normal within the

Exhibit 17–6 Leverage from Preferred Stock and Long-Term Debt

	Alternatives: $100,000,000 Issue of Securities		
	Alternative 1: $100,000,000 Common Stock	Alternative 2: $50,000,000 Common Stock; $50,000,000 Preferred Stock	Alternative 3: $50,000,000 Common Stock; $50,000,000 Bonds
Earnings before interest and taxes	$ 15,000,000	$15,000,000	$15,000,000
Deduct interest expense (8% × $50,000,000)			4,000,000
Net income before taxes	15,000,000	15,000,000	11,000,000
Deduct income taxes (30%)	4,500,000	4,500,000	3,300,000
Net income	10,500,000	10,500,000	7,700,000
Deduct preferred dividends (8% × $50,000,000)		4,000,000	
Net income remaining for common (a)	$ 10,500,000	$ 6,500,000	$ 7,700,000
Common stockholders' equity (b)	$100,000,000	$50,000,000	$50,000,000
Return on common stockholders' equity (a) ÷ (b)	10.5%	13.0%	15.4%

industry. Many companies, such as commercial banks and other financial institutions, rely heavily on leverage to provide an attractive return on their common shares.

In Business

Looking at McDonald's Financials

McDonald's Corporation provides an interesting illustration of the use of financial ratios. The data below relate to the year ended December 31, 2000. (Averages were computed by adding together the beginning and end of year amounts reported on the balance sheet and dividing the total by two.)

Net income	$1,977 million
Interest expense	$430 million
Tax rate	31.4%
Average total assets	$21,334 million
Preferred stock dividends	$0 million
Average common stockholders' equity	$9,422 million
Common stock dividends per share	$0.22
Earnings per share	$1.49
Market price per share—end of year	$34.00
Book value per share—end of year	$7.05

Some key financial ratios from the standpoint of the common stockholder are computed below:

$$\text{Return on total assets} = \frac{\$1{,}977 + [\$430 \times (1 - 0.314)]}{\$21{,}334} = 10.6\%$$

$$\text{Return on common stockholders' equity} = \frac{\$1{,}977 - \$0}{\$9{,}422} = 21.0\%$$

$$\text{Dividend payout ratio} = \frac{\$0.22}{\$1.49} = 14.8\%$$

$$\text{Dividend yield ratio} = \frac{\$0.22}{\$34.00} = 0.65\%$$

The return on common stockholders' equity of 21.0% is higher than the return on total assets of 10.6%, and therefore the company has positive financial leverage. (Creditors provide about half of the company's financing; stockholders provide the remainder.) According to the management discussion in the annual report, "Given the Company's returns on equity and assets, management believes it is prudent to invest a significant portion of earnings back into the business and to use free cash flow for share repurchases. Accordingly, the common stock dividend is modest." Indeed, only 14.8% of earnings are paid out in dividends. In relation to the stock price, this is a dividend yield of less than 1%. Finally, note that the market value per share is over four times as large as the book value per share. This premium over book value reflects the market's perception that McDonald's earnings will continue to grow in the future.

Source: McDonald's Corporation annual report for the year 2000.

Book Value per Share

Another statistic frequently used in attempting to assess the well-being of the common stockholder is book value per share. The **book value per share** measures the amount that would be distributed to holders of each share of common stock if all assets were sold at their balance sheet carrying amounts (i.e., book values) and if all creditors were paid off. Thus, book value per share is based entirely on historical costs. The formula for computing it is as follows:

$$\text{Book value per share} = \frac{\text{Common stockholders' equity (Total stockholders' equity} - \text{Preferred stock)}}{\text{Number of common shares outstanding}}$$

Total stockholders' equity (see Exhibit 17–1)	$17,000,000
Deduct preferred stock (see Exhibit 17–1).	2,000,000
Common stockholders' equity	$15,000,000

The book value per share of Brickey Electronics' common stock is computed as follows:

$$\frac{\$15{,}000{,}000}{500{,}000 \text{ shares}} = \$30$$

If this book value is compared with the $40 market value of Brickey Electronics' stock, then the stock appears to be somewhat overpriced. However, as we discussed earlier, market prices reflect expectations about future earnings and dividends, whereas book value largely reflects the results of events that occurred in the past. Ordinarily, the market value of a stock exceeds its book value. For example, in a recent year, Microsoft's common stock often traded at over 4 times its book value, and Coca-Cola's market value was over 17 times its book value.

Ratio Analysis—The Short-Term Creditor

Short-term creditors, such as suppliers, want to be repaid on time. Therefore, they focus on the company's cash flows and on its working capital since these are the company's primary sources of cash in the short run.

LEARNING OBJECTIVE 3
Compute and interpret financial ratios that would be most useful to a short-term creditor.

Working Capital

The excess of current assets over current liabilities is known as **working capital.** The working capital for Brickey Electronics is computed below:

Concept 17–2

$$\text{Working capital} = \text{Current assets} - \text{Current liabilities}$$

	2002	2001
Current assets	$15,500,000	$16,470,000
Current liabilities.	7,000,000	5,000,000
Working capital.	$ 8,500,000	$11,470,000

The amount of working capital available to a firm is of considerable interest to short-term creditors, *since it represents assets financed from long-term capital sources that do not require near-term repayment.* Therefore, the greater the working capital, the greater is the cushion of protection available to short-term creditors and the greater is the assurance that short-term debts will be paid when due.

Although it is always comforting to short-term creditors to see a large working capital balance, a large balance by itself is no assurance that debts will be paid when due. Rather than being a sign of strength, a large working capital balance may simply mean that obsolete inventory is being accumulated. Therefore, to put the working capital figure into proper perspective, it must be supplemented with other analytical work. The following four ratios (the current ratio, the acid-test ratio, the accounts receivable turnover, and the inventory turnover) should all be used in connection with an analysis of working capital.

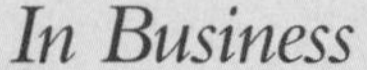

Bringing in the Cash

Burlington Northern Santa Fe, the second largest railroad system in the United States, goes to great lengths to minimize its investment in working capital. In fact, the company has negative working capital—its current assets are less than its current liabilities. To achieve this enviable record, the company has worked hard to improve many things—including its collections of receivables. A lot of the problems in collecting accounts receivable had to do with untimely billing and errors in bills, so the company automated and redesigned its billing process. As a result, the number of bills waiting to be processed and sent to customers dropped from about 50,000 to about 15,000. Once the bills had been sent out, the customer still might not pay—sometimes because of a dispute. The company's CFO Tom Hund explains: "Our average bill is a little over $1,000, so we have a lot of them. With some of our larger customers, we found that if they had a dispute with any of our bills, they wouldn't pay the whole batch. We said that was unreasonable, and started having the marketing arms of our business units work on why we had disputed bills and how we could correct them. We got great support from those folks. At the time, our days sales outstanding . . . was about 50. Now we've got it down to 29."

Source: Randy Myers, "Cash Crop," *CFO*, August 2000, pp. 58–81.

Current Ratio

The elements involved in the computation of working capital are frequently expressed in ratio form. A company's current assets divided by its current liabilities is known as the **current ratio:**

$$\text{Current ratio} = \frac{\text{Current assets}}{\text{Current liabilities}}$$

For Brickey Electronics, the current ratios for 2001 and 2002 would be computed as follows:

2002	**2001**
$\frac{\$15{,}500{,}000}{\$7{,}000{,}000} = 2.21 \text{ to } 1$	$\frac{\$16{,}470{,}000}{\$5{,}000{,}000} = 3.29 \text{ to } 1$

Although widely regarded as a measure of short-term debt-paying ability, the current ratio must be interpreted with great care. A *declining* ratio, as above, might be a sign of a deteriorating financial condition. On the other hand, it might be the result of eliminating obsolete inventories or other stagnant current assets. An *improving* ratio might be the result of an unwise stockpiling of inventory, or it might indicate an improving financial situation. In short, the current ratio is useful, but tricky to interpret. To avoid a blunder, the analyst must take a hard look at the individual assets and liabilities involved.

The general rule of thumb calls for a current ratio of 2 to 1. This rule is subject to many exceptions, depending on the industry and the firm involved. Some industries can operate quite successfully with a current ratio of slightly over 1 to 1. The adequacy of a current ratio depends heavily on the *composition* of the assets. For example, as we see in the table below, both Worthington Corporation and Greystone, Inc., have current ratios of 2 to 1. However, they are not in comparable financial condition. Greystone is likely to have difficulty meeting its current financial obligations, since almost all of its current assets consist of inventory rather than more liquid assets such as cash and accounts receivable.

	Worthington Corporation	**Greystone, Inc.**
Current assets:		
Cash	$ 25,000	$ 2,000
Accounts receivable, net	60,000	8,000

continued

Inventory	85,000	160,000
Prepaid expenses	5,000	5,000
Total current assets (a)	$175,000	$175,000
Current liabilities (b)	$ 87,500	$ 87,500
Current ratio, (a) ÷ (b)	2 to 1	2 to 1

Acid-Test (Quick) Ratio

The **acid-test (quick) ratio** is a much more rigorous test of a company's ability to meet its short-term debts. Inventories and prepaid expenses are excluded from total current assets, leaving only the more liquid (or "quick") assets to be divided by current liabilities.

$$\text{Acid-test ratio} = \frac{\text{Cash} + \text{Marketable securities} + \text{Current receivables}^*}{\text{Current liabilities}}$$

*Current receivables include both accounts receivable and any short-term notes receivable.

The acid-test ratio is designed to measure how well a company can meet its obligations without having to liquidate or depend too heavily on its inventory. Since inventory may be difficult to sell in times of economic stress, it is generally felt that to be properly protected, each dollar of liabilities should be backed by at least $1 of quick assets. Thus, an acid-test ratio of 1 to 1 is usually viewed as adequate.

The acid-test ratios for Brickey Electronics for 2001 and 2002 are computed below:

	2002	2001
Cash (see Exhibit 17–1)	$1,200,000	$2,350,000
Accounts receivable (see Exhibit 17–1)	6,000,000	4,000,000
Total quick assets (a)	$7,200,000	$6,350,000
Current liabilities (see Exhibit 17–1) (b)	$7,000,000	$5,000,000
Acid-test ratio, (a) ÷ (b)	1.03 to 1	1.27 to 1

Although Brickey Electronics has an acid-test ratio for 2002 that is within the acceptable range, an analyst might be concerned about several disquieting trends revealed in the company's balance sheet. Notice in Exhibit 17–1 that short-term debts are rising, while the cash position seems to be deteriorating. Perhaps the weakened cash position is a result of the greatly expanded volume of accounts receivable. One wonders why the accounts receivable have been allowed to increase so rapidly in so brief a time.

In short, as with the current ratio, the acid-test ratio should be interpreted with one eye on its basic components.

Accounts Receivable Turnover

The **accounts receivable turnover** is a rough measure of how many times a company's accounts receivable have been turned into cash during the year. It is frequently used in conjunction with an analysis of working capital, since a smooth flow from accounts receivable into cash is an important indicator of the "quality" of a company's working capital and is critical to the company's ability to operate. The accounts receivable turnover is computed by dividing sales on account (i.e., credit sales) by the average accounts receivable balance for the year.

$$\text{Accounts receivable turnover} = \frac{\text{Sales on account}}{\text{Average accounts receivable balance}}$$

Assuming that all sales for the year were on account, the accounts receivable turnover for Brickey Electronics for 2002 would be computed as follows:

$$\frac{\text{Sales on account}}{\text{Average accounts receivable balance}} = \frac{\$52{,}000{,}000}{\$5{,}000{,}000^*} = 10.4 \text{ times}$$

*$4,000,000 + $6,000,000 = $10,000,000; $10,000,000 ÷ 2 = $5,000,000 average.

The turnover figure can then be divided into 365 to determine the average number of days being taken to collect an account (known as the **average collection period**).

$$\text{Average collection period} = \frac{365 \text{ days}}{\text{Accounts receivable turnover}}$$

The average collection period for Brickey Electronics for 2002 is computed as follows:

$$\frac{365}{10.4 \text{ times}} = 35 \text{ days}$$

This simply means that on average it takes 35 days to collect on a credit sale. Whether the average of 35 days taken to collect an account is good or bad depends on the credit terms Brickey Electronics is offering its customers. If the credit terms are 30 days, then a 35-day average collection period would usually be viewed as very good. Most customers will tend to withhold payment for as long as the credit terms will allow and may even go over a few days. This factor, added to ever-present problems with a few slow-paying customers, can cause the average collection period to exceed normal credit terms by a week or so and should not cause great alarm.

On the other hand, if the company's credit terms are 10 days, then a 35-day average collection period is worrisome. The long collection period may result from many old unpaid accounts of doubtful collectability, or it may be a result of poor day-to-day credit management. The firm may be making sales with inadequate credit checks on customers, or perhaps no follow-ups are being made on slow accounts.

Inventory Turnover

The **inventory turnover ratio** measures how many times a company's inventory has been sold and replaced during the year. It is computed by dividing the cost of goods sold by the average level of inventory on hand:

$$\text{Inventory turnover} = \frac{\text{Cost of goods sold}}{\text{Average inventory balance}}$$

The average inventory figure is the average of the beginning and ending inventory figures. Since Brickey Electronics has a beginning inventory of $10,000,000 and an ending inventory of $8,000,000, its average inventory for the year would be $9,000,000. The company's inventory turnover for 2002 would be computed as follows:

$$\frac{\text{Cost of goods sold}}{\text{Average inventory balance}} = \frac{\$36{,}000{,}000}{\$9{,}000{,}000} = 4 \text{ times}$$

The number of days being taken to sell the entire inventory one time (called the **average sale period**) can be computed by dividing 365 by the inventory turnover figure:

$$\text{Average sale period} = \frac{365 \text{ days}}{\text{Inventory turnover}}$$

$$= \frac{365}{4 \text{ times}} = 91\tfrac{1}{4} \text{ days}$$

The average sale period varies from industry to industry. Grocery stores tend to turn their inventory over very quickly, perhaps as often as every 12 to 15 days. On the other hand, jewelry stores tend to turn their inventory over very slowly, perhaps only a couple of times each year.

If a firm has a turnover that is much slower than the average for its industry, then it may have obsolete goods on hand, or its inventory stocks may be needlessly high. Excessive inventories tie up funds that could be used elsewhere in operations. Managers sometimes argue that they must buy in very large quantities to take advantage of the best discounts being offered. But these discounts must be carefully weighed against the added costs of insurance, taxes, financing, and risks of obsolescence and deterioration that result from carrying added inventories.

Inventory turnover has been increasing in recent years as companies have adopted just-in-time (JIT) methods. Under JIT, inventories are purposely kept low, and thus a company utilizing JIT methods may have a very high inventory turnover as compared to other companies. Indeed, one of the goals of JIT is to increase inventory turnover by systematically reducing the amount of inventory on hand.

Watch Those Receivables and Inventories!

In Business

Herb Greenberg, an investment columnist for *Fortune* magazine, warns investors to look out for two "sure warning signs: receivables and inventory that rise faster than sales . . . . A fast rise in receivables could mean that the company is pulling out all the stops to get customers to take its products. That's good, *unless* it means stealing sales from future quarters. As for a rise in inventory: If finished goods are piling up in warehouses—absent some reasonable explanation, like a looming product launch—they must not be selling." To monitor these possibilities, watch the accounts receivable turnover or average collection period for the receivables and the inventory turnover or average sale period for the inventories.

Source: Herb Greenberg, "Minding Your K's and Q's," *Fortune*, January 8, 2001, p. 180.

Warning Signs at Amazon.com

In Business

Ravi Suria, a debt analyst at Lehman Brothers, sounded an early warning about Amazon.com's finances. Amazon's inventory turnover plummeted from 8.5 times to 2.9 times within two years. And in a year in which its sales grew 170%, its inventories skyrocketed by 650%. Suria points out that "When a company manages inventory properly, it should grow along with its sales growth rate." When inventory grows faster than sales, "it means simply that they're not selling as much as they are buying."

Source: Robert Hof, Debra Sparks, Ellen Neuborne, and Wendy Zellner, "Can Amazon Make It?" *Business Week*, July 10, 2000, pp. 38–43.

Ratio Analysis—The Long-Term Creditor

LEARNING OBJECTIVE 4
Compute and interpret financial ratios that would be most useful to a long-term creditor.

The position of long-term creditors differs from that of short-term creditors in that they are concerned with both the near-term *and* the long-term ability of a firm to meet its commitments. They are concerned with the near term since the interest they are entitled to is normally paid on a current basis. They are concerned with the long term since they want to be fully repaid on schedule.

Since the long-term creditor is usually faced with greater risks than the short-term creditor, firms are often required to agree to various restrictive covenants, or rules, for the long-term creditor's protection. Examples of such restrictive covenants include the maintenance of minimum working capital levels and restrictions on payment of dividends to common stockholders. Although these restrictive covenants are in widespread use, they are a poor second to adequate future *earnings* from the point of view of assessing protection

Concept 17–2

and safety. Creditors do not want to go to court to collect their claims; they would much prefer staking the safety of their claims for interest and eventual repayment of principal on an orderly and consistent flow of funds from operations.

Times Interest Earned Ratio

The most common measure of the ability of a firm's operations to provide protection to the long-term creditor is the **times interest earned ratio.** It is computed by dividing earnings *before* interest expense and income taxes (i.e., net operating income) by the yearly interest charges that must be met:

$$\text{Times interest earned} = \frac{\text{Earnings before interest expense and income taxes}}{\text{Interest expense}}$$

For Brickey Electronics, the times interest earned ratio for 2002 would be computed as follows:

$$\frac{\$3,140,000}{\$640,000} = 4.9 \text{ times}$$

Earnings before income taxes must be used in the computation, since interest expense deductions come *before* income taxes are computed. Creditors have first claim on earnings. Only those earnings remaining after all interest charges have been provided for are subject to income taxes.

Generally, earnings are viewed as adequate to protect long-term creditors if the times interest earned ratio is 2 or more. Before making a final judgment, however, it would be necessary to look at a firm's long-run *trend* of earnings and evaluate how vulnerable the firm is to cyclical changes in the economy.

Debt-to-Equity Ratio

Long-term creditors are also concerned with keeping a reasonable balance between the portion of assets provided by creditors and the portion of assets provided by the stockholders of a firm. This balance is measured by the **debt-to-equity ratio:**

$$\text{Debt-to-equity ratio} = \frac{\text{Total liabilities}}{\text{Stockholders' equity}}$$

	2002	2001
Total liabilities (a)	$14,500,000	$13,000,000
Stockholders' equity (b)	$17,000,000	$15,970,000
Debt-to-equity ratio, (a) ÷ (b).	0.85 to 1	0.81 to 1

The debt-to-equity ratio indicates the amount of assets being provided by creditors for each dollar of assets being provided by the owners of a company. In 2001, creditors of Brickey Electronics were providing 81 cents of assets for each $1 of assets being provided by stockholders; the figure increased only slightly to 85 cents by 2002.

Creditors would like the debt-to-equity ratio to be relatively low. The lower the ratio, the greater the amount of assets being provided by the owners of a company and the greater is the buffer of protection to creditors. By contrast, common stockholders would like the ratio to be relatively high, since through leverage, common stockholders can benefit from the assets being provided by creditors.

In most industries, norms have developed over the years that serve as guides to firms in their decisions as to the "right" amount of debt to include in the capital structure. Different industries face different risks. For this reason, the level of debt that is appropriate for firms in one industry is not necessarily a guide to the level of debt that is appropriate for firms in a different industry.

Revamping American Standard

In Business

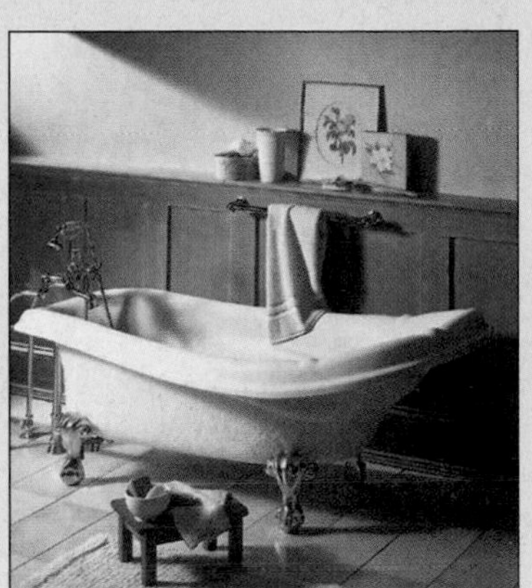

Emmanuel Kampouris, the Egyptian-born CEO of American Standard, has transformed the manufacturer of bathroom fixtures, coolers, and truck parts into a lean competitor. The key to this transformation has been "demand flow technology"—a sort of just-in-time (JIT) on steroids. In addition to cutting inventories, the aim is to slash manufacturing time. The end result is the capability to respond to the customer faster, at lower cost, and with greater variety than before. At Home Depot, Standard's plumbing, heating, and air-conditioning goods now arrive within days—not months—of being ordered. Overall, the company has reduced its inventories by more than 50%—realizing hundreds of millions of dollars of savings. Inventory turnover has improved from less than 5 times to over 11 times, and working capital has declined from 8.6% of sales to 4.9%. The interest savings alone on the reduced inventories are over $60 million per year. Kampouris has also slashed the company's debt by nearly $1 billion—dropping the company's debt-to-equity ratio from 87.5% down to about 39%.

Source: "American Standard Wises Up," *Business Week,* November 18, 1996, p. 50; Shawn Tully, "American Standard: Prophet of Zero Working Capital," *Fortune,* June 13, 1994, pp. 113–114.

Summary of Ratios and Sources of Comparative Ratio Data

Exhibit 17–7 contains a summary of the ratios discussed in this chapter. The formula for each ratio and a summary comment on each ratio's significance are included in the exhibit.

Exhibit 17–8 contains a listing of published sources that provide comparative ratio data organized by industry. These sources are used extensively by managers, investors, and analysts in doing comparative analyses and in attempting to assess the well-being of companies. The World Wide Web also contains a wealth of financial and other data. A search engine such as Alta Vista, Yahoo, or Excite can be used to track down information on individual companies. Many companies have their own websites on which they post their latest financial reports and news of interest to potential investors. The EDGAR database listed in Exhibit 17–8 is a particularly rich source of data. It contains copies of all reports filed by companies with the SEC since about 1995—including annual reports filed as Form 10-K.

Exhibit 17–7 Summary of Ratios

Ratio	Formula	Significance
Gross margin percentage	Gross margin ÷ Sales	A broad measure of profitability
Earnings per share (of common stock)	(Net income − Preferred dividends) ÷ Average number of common shares outstanding	Tends to have an effect on the market price per share, as reflected in the price-earnings ratio
Price-earnings ratio	Market price per share ÷ Earnings per share	An index of whether a stock is relatively cheap or relatively expensive in relation to current earnings
Dividend payout ratio	Dividends per share ÷ Earnings per share	An index showing whether a company pays out most of its earnings in dividends or reinvests the earnings internally
Dividend yield ratio	Dividends per share ÷ Market price per share	Shows the return in terms of cash dividends being provided by a stock
Return on total assets	{Net income + [Interest expense × (1 − Tax rate)]} ÷ Average total assets	Measure of how well assets have been employed by management
Return on common stockholders' equity	(Net income − Preferred dividends) ÷ Average common stockholders' equity (Average total stockholders' equity − Average preferred stock)	When compared to the return on total assets, measures the extent to which financial leverage is working for or against common stockholders
Book value per share	Common stockholders' equity (Total stockholders' equity − Preferred stock) ÷ Number of common shares outstanding	Measures the amount that would be distributed to holders of common stock if all assets were sold at their balance sheet carrying amounts and if all creditors were paid off
Working capital	Current assets − Current liabilities	Measures the company's ability to repay current liabilities using only current assets
Current ratio	Current assets ÷ Current liabilities	Test of short-term debt-paying ability
Acid-test (quick) ratio	(Cash + Marketable securities + Current receivables) ÷ Current liabilities	Test of short-term debt-paying ability without having to rely on inventory
Accounts receivable turnover	Sales on account ÷ Average accounts receivable balance	A rough measure of how many times a company's accounts receivable have been turned into cash during the year
Average collection period (age of receivables)	365 days ÷ Accounts receivable turnover	Measure of the average number of days taken to collect an account receivable
Inventory turnover	Cost of goods sold ÷ Average inventory balance	Measure of how many times a company's inventory has been sold during the year
Average sale period (turnover in days)	365 days ÷ Inventory turnover	Measure of the average number of days taken to sell the inventory one time
Times interest earned	Earnings before interest expense and income taxes ÷ Interest expense	Measure of the company's ability to make interest payments
Debt-to-equity ratio	Total liabilities ÷ Stockholders' equity	Measure of the amount of assets being provided by creditors for each dollar of assets being provided by the stockholders

Exhibit 17–8 Sources of Financial Ratios

Source	Content
Almanac of Business and Industrial Financial Ratios, Prentice-Hall; published annually	An exhaustive source that contains common-size income statements and financial ratios by industry and by size of companies within each industry.
Annual Statement Studies, Robert Morris Associates; published annually. See www.rmahq.org/Ann_Studies/asstudies.html for definitions and explanations of ratios and balance sheet and income statement data that are contained in the *Annual Statement Studies.*	A widely used publication that contains common-size statements and financial ratios on individual companies; companies arranged by industry.
Business & Company ASAP; database that is continually updated	Exhaustive database of business articles in periodicals for both industry and company information. Many of the articles are available in full text. Directory listings for over 150,000 companies are also included in the database.
EDGAR, Securities and Exchange Commission; website that is continually updated. www.sec.gov	An exhaustive database accessible on the World Wide Web that contains reports filed by companies with the SEC; these reports can be downloaded.
EBSCOhost (Business Source Elite index), EBSCO publishing; database that is continually updated	Exhaustive database of business articles in periodicals useful for both industry and company information. Full text is included from nearly 970 journals; indexing and abstracts are offered for over 1,650 journals.
FreeEdgar, EDGAR Online, Inc.; website that is continually updated; www.freeedgar.com	A site that allows you to search SEC filings; financial information can be downloaded directly into Excel worksheets.
Hoover's Online, Hoovers, Inc.; website that is continually updated; www.hoovers.com	A site that provides capsule profiles for 10,000 U.S. companies with links to company websites, annual reports, stock charts, news articles, and industry information.
Key Business Ratios, Dun & Bradstreet; published annually	Fourteen commonly used financial ratios are computed for over 800 major industry groupings.
Moody's Industrial Manual and Moody's Bank and Finance Manual, Dun & Bradstreet; published annually	An exhaustive source that contains financial ratios on all companies listed on the New York Stock Exchange, the American Stock Exchange, and regional American exchanges.
PricewaterhouseCoopers website that is continually updated; www.edgarscan.tc.pw.com	This source of financial statement data has an easier-to-use interface than other sources.
Standard & Poor's Industry Survey, Standard & Poor's; published annually	Various statistics, including some financial ratios, are given by industry and for leading companies within each industry grouping.

Summary

The data contained in financial statements represent a quantitative summary of a firm's operations and activities. Someone who is skillful at analyzing these statements can learn much about a company's strengths, weaknesses, emerging problems, operating efficiency, profitability, and so forth.

Many techniques are available to analyze financial statements and to assess the direction and importance of trends and changes. In this chapter, we have discussed three such analytical techniques—dollar and percentage changes in statements, common-size statements, and ratio analysis. Refer to Exhibit 17–7 for a detailed listing of the ratios. This listing also contains a brief statement as to the significance of each ratio.

Review Problem: Selected Ratios and Financial Leverage

Starbucks Coffee Company is the leading retailer and roaster of specialty coffee in North America with over 1,000 stores offering freshly brewed coffee, pastries, and coffee beans. Data from the company's financial statements are given below:

STARBUCKS COFFEE COMPANY
Comparative Balance Sheet
(dollars in thousands)

	End of Year	Beginning of Year
Assets		
Current assets:		
Cash	$126,215	$ 20,944
Marketable securities	103,221	41,507
Accounts receivable	17,621	9,852
Inventories	83,370	123,657
Other current assets	9,114	9,390
Total current assets	339,541	205,350
Property and equipment, net	369,477	244,728
Other assets	17,595	18,100
Total assets	$726,613	$468,178
Liabilities and Stockholders' Equity		
Current liabilities:		
Accounts payable	$ 38,034	$ 28,668
Short-term bank loans	16,241	13,138
Accrued payables	18,005	13,436
Other current liabilities	28,811	15,804
Total current liabilities	101,091	71,046
Long-term liabilities:		
Bonds payable	165,020	80,398
Other long-term liabilities	8,842	4,503
Total liabilities	274,953	155,947
Stockholders' equity:		
Preferred stock	0	0
Common stock and additional paid-in capital	361,309	265,679
Retained earnings	90,351	46,552
Total stockholders' equity	451,660	312,231
Total liabilities and stockholders' equity	$726,613	$468,178

Note: The effective interest rate on the bonds payable was about 5%.

STARBUCKS COFFEE COMPANY
Comparative Income Statement
(dollars in thousands)

	Current Year	Prior Year
Revenue	$696,481	$465,213
Cost of goods sold	335,800	211,279
Gross margin	360,681	253,934
Operating expenses:		
Store operating expenses	210,693	148,757
Other operating expenses	19,787	13,932
Depreciation and amortization	35,950	22,486
General and administrative expenses	37,258	28,643
Total operating expenses	303,688	213,818

continued

Net operating income	56,993	40,116
Gain on sale of investment	9,218	0
Plus interest income	11,029	6,792
Less interest expense	8,739	3,765
Net income before taxes	68,501	43,143
Less income taxes (about 38.5%)	26,373	17,041
Net income	$ 42,128	$ 26,102

Required:
For the current year:

1. Compute the return on total assets.
2. Compute the return on common stockholders' equity.
3. Is Starbucks' financial leverage positive or negative? Explain.
4. Compute the current ratio.
5. Compute the acid-test (quick) ratio.
6. Compute the inventory turnover.
7. Compute the average sale period.
8. Compute the debt-to-equity ratio.

Solution to Review Problem

1. Return on total assets:

$$\text{Return on total assets} = \frac{\text{Net income} + [\text{Interest expense} \times (1 - \text{Tax rate})]}{\text{Average total assets}}$$

$$= \frac{\$42{,}128 + [\$8{,}739 \times (1 - 0.385)]}{(\$726{,}613 + \$468{,}178)/2} = 8.0\%\ \text{(rounded)}$$

2. Return on common stockholders' equity:

$$\text{Return on common stockholders' equity} = \frac{\text{Net income} - \text{Preferred dividends}}{\text{Average common stockholders' equity}}$$

$$= \frac{\$42{,}128 - \$0}{(\$451{,}660 + \$312{,}231)/2} = 11.0\%\ \text{(rounded)}$$

3. The company has positive financial leverage, since the return on common stockholders' equity (11%) is greater than the return on total assets (8%). The positive financial leverage was obtained from current liabilities and the bonds payable. The interest rate on the bonds is substantially less than the return on total assets.
4. Current ratio:

$$\text{Current ratio} = \frac{\text{Current assets}}{\text{Current liabilities}}$$

$$= \frac{\$339{,}541}{\$101{,}091} = 3.36\ \text{(rounded)}$$

5. Acid-test (quick) ratio:

$$\text{Acid-test ratio} = \frac{\text{Cash} + \text{Marketable securities} + \text{Current receivables}}{\text{Current liabilities}}$$

$$= \frac{\$126{,}215 + \$103{,}221 + \$17{,}621}{\$101{,}091} = 2.44\ \text{(rounded)}$$

This acid-test ratio is quite high and provides Starbucks with the ability to fund rapid expansion.
6. Inventory turnover:

$$\text{Inventory turnover} = \frac{\text{Cost of goods sold}}{\text{Average inventory balance}}$$

$$= \frac{\$335{,}800}{(\$83{,}370 + \$123{,}657)/2} = 3.24 \text{ (rounded)}$$

7. Average sale period:

$$\text{Average sale period} = \frac{365 \text{ days}}{\text{Inventory turnover}}$$

$$= \frac{365 \text{ days}}{3.24} = 113 \text{ days (rounded)}$$

8. Debt-to-equity ratio:

$$\text{Debt-to-equity ratio} = \frac{\text{Total liabilities}}{\text{Stockholders' equity}}$$

$$= \frac{\$274{,}953}{\$451{,}660} = 0.61 \text{ (rounded)}$$

Glossary

(Note: Definitions and formulas for all financial ratios are shown in Exhibit 17–7. These definitions and formulas are not repeated here.)

Common-size statements A statement that shows the items appearing on it in percentage form as well as in dollar form. On the income statement, the percentages are based on total sales revenue; on the balance sheet, the percentages are based on total assets. (p. 767)

Financial leverage Acquiring assets with funds that have been obtained from creditors or from preferred stockholders at a fixed rate of return. (p. 774)

Horizontal analysis A side-by-side comparison of two or more years' financial statements. (p. 765)

Negative financial leverage A situation in which the fixed return to a company's creditors and preferred stockholders is greater than the return on total assets. In this situation, the return on common stockholders' equity will be *less* than the return on total assets. (p. 775)

Positive financial leverage A situation in which the fixed return to a company's creditors and preferred stockholders is less than the return on total assets. In this situation, the return on common stockholders' equity will be *greater* than the return on total assets. (p. 774)

Trend analysis See *Horizontal analysis.* (p. 765)

Trend percentages The expression of several years' financial data in percentage form in terms of a base year. (p. 765)

Vertical analysis The presentation of a company's financial statements in common-size form. (p. 767)

Questions

17–1 Distinguish between horizontal and vertical analysis of financial statement data.

17–2 What is the basic purpose for examining trends in a company's financial ratios and other data? What other kinds of comparisons might an analyst make?

17–3 Assume that two companies in the same industry have equal earnings. Why might these companies have different price-earnings ratios? If a company has a price-earnings ratio of 20 and reports earnings per share for the current year of $4, at what price would you expect to find the stock selling on the market?

17–4 Armcor, Inc., is in a rapidly growing technological industry. Would you expect the company to have a high or low dividend payout ratio?

17–5 What is meant by the dividend yield on a common stock investment?

17–6 What is meant by the term *financial leverage?*

17–7 The president of a medium-size plastics company was quoted in a business journal as stating, "We haven't had a dollar of interest-paying debt in over 10 years. Not many companies can say that." As a stockholder in this firm, how would you feel about its policy of not taking on interest-paying debt?

17–8 Why is it more difficult to obtain positive financial leverage from preferred stock than from long-term debt?

17–9 If a stock's market value exceeds its book value, then the stock is overpriced. Do you agree? Explain.

17–10 Weaver Company experiences a great deal of seasonal variation in its business activities. The company's high point in business activity is in June; its low point is in January. During which month would you expect the current ratio to be highest?

17–11 A company seeking a line of credit at a bank was turned down. Among other things, the bank stated that the company's 2 to 1 current ratio was not adequate. Give reasons why a 2 to 1 current ratio might not be adequate.

Exercises

EXERCISE 17–1 Common-Size Income Statement [LO1]
A comparative income statement is given below for Ryder Company:

RYDER COMPANY
Comparative Income Statement
For the Years Ended June 30, 2002, and 2001

	2002	2001
Sales	$5,000,000	$4,000,000
Less cost of goods sold	3,160,000	2,400,000
Gross margin	1,840,000	1,600,000
Selling expenses	900,000	700,000
Administrative expenses	680,000	584,000
Total expenses	1,580,000	1,284,000
Net operating income	260,000	316,000
Interest expense	70,000	40,000
Net income before taxes	$ 190,000	$ 276,000

The president is concerned that net income is down in 2002 even though sales have increased during the year. The president is also concerned that administrative expenses have increased, since the company made a concerted effort during 2002 to pare "fat" out of the organization.

Required:

1. Express each year's income statement in common-size percentages. Carry computations to one decimal place.
2. Comment briefly on the changes between the two years.

EXERCISE 17–2 Selected Financial Measures for Short-Term Creditors [LO3]
Rightway Products had a current ratio of 2.5 to 1 on June 30 of the current year. On that date, the company's assets were as follows:

Cash		$ 80,000
Accounts receivable	$530,000	
Less allowance for doubtful accounts	70,000	460,000
Inventory		750,000
Prepaid expenses		10,000
Plant and equipment, net		1,900,000
Total assets		$3,200,000

Required:

1. What was the company's working capital on June 30?
2. What was the company's acid-test ratio on June 30?
3. The company paid an account payable of $100,000 immediately after June 30.
   a. What effect did this transaction have on working capital? Show computations.
   b. What effect did this transaction have on the current ratio? Show computations.

EXERCISE 17–3 Selected Financial Ratios for Common Stockholders [LO2]
Selected financial data from the September 30 year-end statements of Kosanka Company are given below:

Total assets	$5,000,000
Long-term debt (12% interest rate)	750,000
Preferred stock, $100 par, 7%	800,000
Total stockholders' equity	3,100,000
Interest paid on long-term debt	90,000
Net income	470,000

Total assets at the beginning of the year were $4,800,000; total stockholders' equity was $2,900,000. There has been no change in the preferred stock during the year. The company's tax rate is 30%.

Required:
1. Compute the return on total assets.
2. Compute the return on common stockholders' equity.
3. Is the company's financial leverage positive or negative? Explain.

EXERCISE 17–4 Selected Financial Ratios [LO3, LO4]
Recent financial statements for Madison Company are given below:

MADISON COMPANY
Balance Sheet
June 30

Assets		
Current assets:		
Cash		$ 21,000
Accounts receivable, net		160,000
Merchandise inventory		300,000
Prepaid expenses		9,000
Total current assets		490,000
Property and equipment, net		810,000
Total assets		$1,300,000
Liabilities and Stockholders' Equity		
Liabilities:		
Current liabilities		$ 200,000
Bonds payable, 10%		300,000
Total liabilities		500,000
Stockholders' equity:		
Common stock, $5 par value	$100,000	
Retained earnings	700,000	
Total stockholders' equity		800,000
Total liabilities and stockholders' equity		$1,300,000

MADISON COMPANY
Income Statement
For the Year Ended June 30

Sales	$2,100,000
Less cost of goods sold	1,260,000
Gross margin	840,000
Less operating expenses	660,000
Net operating income	180,000
Less interest expense	30,000
Net income before taxes	150,000
Less income taxes	45,000
Net income	$ 105,000

Account balances at the beginning of the company's fiscal year were: accounts receivable, $140,000; and inventory, $260,000. All sales were on account.

Required:

Compute financial ratios as follows:

1. Gross margin percentage.
2. Current ratio.
3. Acid-test (quick) ratio.
4. Accounts receivable turnover in days.
5. Inventory turnover in days.
6. Debt-to-equity ratio.
7. Times interest earned.
8. Book value per share.

EXERCISE 17–5 Selected Financial Ratios for Common Stockholders [LO2]

Refer to the financial statements for Madison Company in Exercise 17–4. In addition to the data in these statements, assume that Madison Company paid dividends of $3.15 per share during the year. Also assume that the company's common stock had a market price of $63 per share on June 30 and there was no change in the number of outstanding shares of common stock during the fiscal year.

Required:

Compute the following:

1. Earnings per share.
2. Dividend payout ratio.
3. Dividend yield ratio.
4. Price-earnings ratio.

EXERCISE 17–6 Selected Financial Ratios for Common Stockholders [LO2]

Refer to the financial statements for Madison Company in Exercise 17–4. Assets at the beginning of the year totaled $1,100,000, and the stockholders' equity totaled $725,000.

Required:

Compute the following:

1. Return on total assets.
2. Return on common stockholders' equity.
3. Was financial leverage positive or negative for the year? Explain.

EXERCISE 17–7 Trend Percentages [LO1]

Starkey Company's sales, current assets, and current liabilities (all in thousands of dollars) have been reported as follows over the last five years (Year 5 is the most recent year):

	Year 5	Year 4	Year 3	Year 2	Year 1
Sales	$5,625	$5,400	$4,950	$4,725	$4,500
Current assets:					
Cash	$ 64	$ 72	$ 84	$ 88	$ 80
Accounts receivable	560	496	432	416	400
Inventory	896	880	816	864	800
Total current assets	$1,520	$1,448	$1,332	$1,368	$1,280
Current liabilities	$ 390	$ 318	$ 324	$ 330	$ 300

Required:

1. Express all of the asset, liability, and sales data in trend percentages. (Show percentages for each item.) Use Year 1 as the base year, and carry computations to one decimal place.
2. Comment on the results of your analysis.

Problems

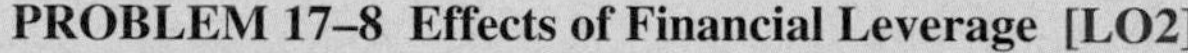

PROBLEM 17–8 Effects of Financial Leverage [LO2]

Vince Zolta and several other investors are in the process of organizing a new company to produce and distribute a household cleaning product. Mr. Zolta and his associates feel that $500,000 would be adequate to finance the new company's operations, and the group is studying three methods of raising this amount of money. The three methods are as follows:

Method A: All $500,000 obtained through issue of common stock.
Method B: $250,000 obtained through issue of common stock and the other $250,000 obtained through issue of $100 par value, 10% preferred stock.
Method C: $250,000 obtained through issue of common stock and the other $250,000 obtained through issue of bonds carrying an interest rate of 10%.

Mr. Zolta and his associates are confident that the company can earn $100,000 each year before interest and taxes. The tax rate is 30%.

Required:

1. Assuming that Mr. Zolta and his associates are correct in their earnings estimate, compute the net income that would go to the common stockholders under each of the three financing methods listed above.
2. Using the income data computed in (1) above, compute the return on common equity under each of the three methods.
3. Why do methods B and C provide a greater return on common equity than does method A? Why does method C provide a greater return on common equity than method B?

PROBLEM 17–9 Effects of Transactions on Various Ratios [LO3]

Selected amounts from Reingold Company's balance sheet from the beginning of the year follow:

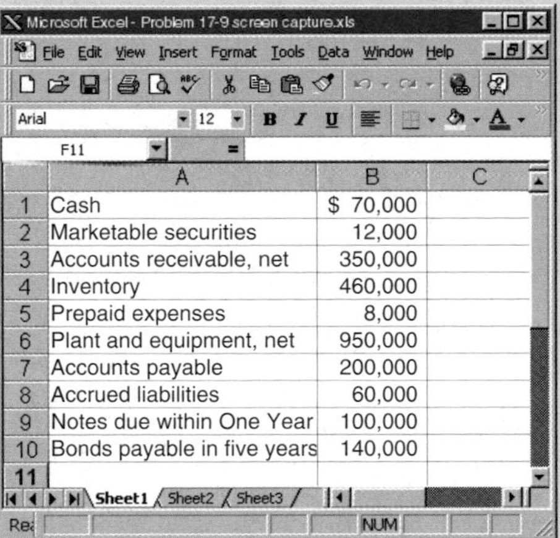

	A	B	C
1	Cash	$ 70,000	
2	Marketable securities	12,000	
3	Accounts receivable, net	350,000	
4	Inventory	460,000	
5	Prepaid expenses	8,000	
6	Plant and equipment, net	950,000	
7	Accounts payable	200,000	
8	Accrued liabilities	60,000	
9	Notes due within One Year	100,000	
10	Bonds payable in five years	140,000	
11			

During the year, the company completed the following transactions:

x. Purchased inventory on account, $50,000.
a. Declared a cash dividend, $30,000.
b. Paid accounts payable, $100,000.
c. Collected cash on accounts receivable, $80,000.
d. Purchased equipment for cash, $75,000.
e. Paid a cash dividend previously declared, $30,000.
f. Borrowed cash on a short-term note with the bank, $60,000.
g. Sold inventory costing $70,000 for $100,000, on account.
h. Wrote off uncollectible accounts in the amount of $10,000. The company uses the allowance method of accounting for bad debts.
i. Sold marketable securities costing $12,000 for cash, $9,000.
j. Issued additional shares of capital stock for cash, $200,000.
k. Paid off all short-term notes due, $160,000.

Required:

1. Compute the following amounts and ratios as of the beginning of the year:
   a. Working capital.
   b. Current ratio.
   c. Acid-test (quick) ratio.
2. Indicate the effect of each of the transactions given above on working capital, the current ratio, and the acid-test ratio. Give the effect in terms of increase, decrease, or none. Item (x) is given as an example of the format to use:

	The Effect on		
Transaction	Working Capital	Current Ratio	Acid-Test Ratio
(x) Purchased inventory on account.	None	Decrease	Decrease

PROBLEM 17–10 Common-Size Statements and Financial Ratios for Creditors [LO1, LO3, LO4]

Modern Building Supply sells various building materials to retail outlets. The company has just approached Linden State Bank requesting a $300,000 loan to strengthen the Cash account and to pay certain pressing short-term obligations. The company's financial statements for the most recent two years follow:

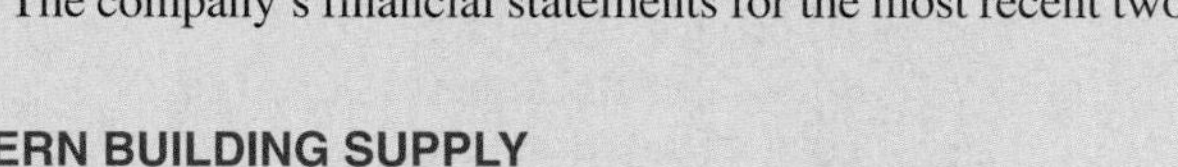

MODERN BUILDING SUPPLY
Comparative Balance Sheet

	This Year	Last Year
Assets		
Current assets:		
Cash	$ 90,000	$ 200,000
Marketable securities	0	50,000
Accounts receivable, net	650,000	400,000
Inventory	1,300,000	800,000
Prepaid expenses	20,000	20,000
Total current assets	2,060,000	1,470,000
Plant and equipment, net	1,940,000	1,830,000
Total assets	$4,000,000	$3,300,000
Liabilities and Stockholders' Equity		
Liabilities:		
Current liabilities	$1,100,000	$ 600,000
Bonds payable, 12%	750,000	750,000
Total liabilities	1,850,000	1,350,000
Stockholders' equity:		
Preferred stock, $50 par, 8%	200,000	200,000
Common stock, $10 par	500,000	500,000
Retained earnings	1,450,000	1,250,000
Total stockholders' equity	2,150,000	1,950,000
Total liabilities and stockholders' equity	$4,000,000	$3,300,000

MODERN BUILDING SUPPLY
Comparative Income Statement

	This Year	Last Year
Sales	$7,000,000	$6,000,000
Less cost of goods sold	5,400,000	4,800,000
Gross margin	1,600,000	1,200,000
Less operating expenses	970,000	710,000
Net operating income	630,000	490,000
Less interest expense	90,000	90,000
Net income before taxes	540,000	400,000
Less income taxes (40%)	216,000	160,000
Net income	324,000	240,000
Dividends paid:		
Preferred dividends	16,000	16,000
Common dividends	108,000	60,000
Total dividends paid	124,000	76,000
Net income retained	200,000	164,000
Retained earnings, beginning of year	1,250,000	1,086,000
Retained earnings, end of year	$1,450,000	$1,250,000

During the past year, the company has expanded the number of lines that it carries in order to stimulate sales and increase profits. It has also moved aggressively to acquire new customers. Sales terms are 2/10, n/30. All sales are on account.

Assume that the following ratios are typical of firms in the building supply industry:

Current ratio	2.5 to 1
Acid-test ratio	1.2 to 1
Average age of receivables	18 days
Inventory turnover in days	50 days
Debt-to-equity ratio	0.75 to 1
Times interest earned	6.0 times
Return on total assets	10%
Price-earnings ratio	9
Net income as a percentage of sales	4%

Required:

1. Linden State Bank is uncertain whether the loan should be made. To assist it in making a decision, you have been asked to compute the following ratios for both this year and last year:
   a. The amount of working capital.
   b. The current ratio.
   c. The acid-test ratio.
   d. The average age of receivables. (The accounts receivable at the beginning of last year totaled $350,000.)
   e. The inventory turnover in days. (The inventory at the beginning of last year totaled $720,000.)
   f. The debt-to-equity ratio.
   g. The number of times interest was earned.
2. For both this year and last year (carry computations to one decimal place):
   a. Present the balance sheet in common-size form.
   b. Present the income statement in common-size form down through net income.
3. From your analysis in (1) and (2) above, what problems or strengths do you see existing in Modern Building Supply? Make a recommendation as to whether the loan should be approved.

PROBLEM 17–11 Financial Ratios for Common Stockholders [LO2]

Refer to the financial statements and other data in Problem 17–10. Assume that you have just inherited several hundred shares of Modern Building Supply stock. Not being acquainted with the company, you decide to do some analytical work before making a decision about whether to retain or sell the stock you have inherited.

Required:

1. You decide first to assess the well-being of the common stockholders. For both this year and last year, compute the following:
   a. The earnings per share.
   b. The dividend yield ratio for common. The company's common stock is currently selling for $45 per share; last year it sold for $36 per share.
   c. The dividend payout ratio for common.
   d. The price-earnings ratio. How do investors regard Modern Building Supply as compared to other firms in the industry? Explain.
   e. The book value per share of common. Does the difference between market value and book value suggest that the stock at its current price is too high? Explain.
2. You decide next to assess the company's rate of return. Compute the following for both this year and last year:
   a. The return on total assets. (Total assets at the beginning of last year were $2,700,000.)
   b. The return on common equity. (Stockholders' equity at the beginning of last year was $1,786,000.)
   c. Is the company's financial leverage positive or negative? Explain.
3. Based on your analytical work (and assuming that you have no immediate need for cash), would you retain or sell the stock you have inherited? Explain.

PROBLEM 17–12 Comprehensive Ratio Analysis [LO2, LO3, LO4]

You have just been hired as a loan officer at Fairfield State Bank. Your supervisor has given you a file containing a request from Hedrick Company, a manufacturer of auto components, for a

$1,000,000 five-year loan. Financial statement data on the company for the last two years are given below:

HEDRICK COMPANY
Comparative Balance Sheet

	This Year	Last Year
Assets		
Current assets:		
Cash	$ 320,000	$ 420,000
Marketable securities	0	100,000
Accounts receivable, net	900,000	600,000
Inventory	1,300,000	800,000
Prepaid expenses	80,000	60,000
Total current assets	2,600,000	1,980,000
Plant and equipment, net	3,100,000	2,980,000
Total assets	$5,700,000	$4,960,000
Liabilities and Stockholders' Equity		
Liabilities:		
Current liabilities	$1,300,000	$ 920,000
Bonds payable, 10%	1,200,000	1,000,000
Total liabilities	2,500,000	1,920,000
Stockholders' equity:		
Preferred stock, 8%, $30 par value	600,000	600,000
Common stock, $40 par value	2,000,000	2,000,000
Retained earnings	600,000	440,000
Total stockholders' equity	3,200,000	3,040,000
Total liabilities and stockholders' equity	$5,700,000	$4,960,000

HEDRICK COMPANY
Comparative Income Statement

	This Year	Last Year
Sales (all on account)	$5,250,000	$4,160,000
Less cost of goods sold	4,200,000	3,300,000
Gross margin	1,050,000	860,000
Less operating expenses	530,000	520,000
Net operating income	520,000	340,000
Less interest expense	120,000	100,000
Net income before taxes	400,000	240,000
Less income taxes (30%)	120,000	72,000
Net income	280,000	168,000
Dividends paid:		
Preferred stock	48,000	48,000
Common stock	72,000	36,000
Total dividends paid	120,000	84,000
Net income retained	160,000	84,000
Retained earnings, beginning of year	440,000	356,000
Retained earnings, end of year	$ 600,000	$ 440,000

Marva Rossen, who just two years ago was appointed president of Hedrick Company, admits that the company has been "inconsistent" in its performance over the past several years. But Rossen argues that the company has its costs under control and is now experiencing strong sales growth, as evidenced by the more than 25% increase in sales over the last year. Rossen also argues that investors have recognized the improving situation at Hedrick Company, as shown by the jump in the price of its common stock from $20 per share last year to $36 per share this year. Rossen believes that with strong leadership and with the modernized equipment that the $1,000,000 loan will permit the company to buy, profits will be even stronger in the future.

Anxious to impress your supervisor, you decide to generate all the information you can about the company. You determine that the following ratios are typical of companies in Hedrick's industry:

Current ratio	2.3 to 1
Acid-test (quick) ratio	1.2 to 1
Average age of receivables	31 days
Inventory turnover	60 days
Return on assets	9.5%
Debt-to-equity ratio	0.65 to 1
Times interest earned	5.7
Price-earnings ratio	10

Required:

1. You decide first to assess the rate of return that the company is generating. Compute the following for both this year and last year:
   a. The return on total assets. (Total assets at the beginning of last year were $4,320,000.)
   b. The return on common equity. (Stockholders' equity at the beginning of last year totaled $3,016,000. There has been no change in preferred or common stock over the last two years.)
   c. Is the company's leverage positive or negative? Explain.
2. You decide next to assess the well-being of the common stockholders. For both this year and last year, compute:
   a. The earnings per share.
   b. The dividend yield ratio for common.
   c. The dividend payout ratio for common.
   d. The price-earnings ratio. How do investors regard Hedrick Company as compared to other firms in the industry? Explain.
   e. The book value per share of common. Does the difference between market value per share and book value per share suggest that the stock at its current price is a bargain? Explain.
   f. The gross margin percentage.
3. You decide, finally, to assess creditor ratios to determine both short-term and long-term debt paying ability. For both this year and last year, compute:
   a. Working capital.
   b. The current ratio.
   c. The acid-test ratio.
   d. The average age of receivables. (The accounts receivable at the beginning of last year totaled $520,000.)
   e. The inventory turnover. (The inventory at the beginning of last year totaled $640,000.)
   f. The debt-to-equity ratio.
   g. The number of times interest was earned.
4. Evaluate the data computed in (1) to (3) above, and using any additional data provided in the problem, make a recommendation to your supervisor as to whether the loan should be approved.

PROBLEM 17–13 Common-Size Financial Statements [LO1]

Refer to the financial statement data for Hedrick Company given in Problem 17–12.

Required:

For both this year and last year:

1. Present the balance sheet in common-size format.
2. Present the income statement in common-size format down through net income.
3. Comment on the results of your analysis.

PROBLEM 17–14 Interpretation of Financial Ratios [LO2, LO3]

Being a prudent investor, Sally Perkins always investigates a company thoroughly before purchasing shares of its stock for investment. At present, Ms. Perkins is interested in the common stock of Plunge Enterprises. All she has available on the company is a copy of its annual report for the current year (Year 3), which contains the Year 3 financial statements and the summary of ratios as follows:

	Year 3	Year 2	Year 1
Current ratio	2.8 to 1	2.5 to 1	2.0 to 1
Acid-test (quick) ratio	0.7 to 1	0.9 to 1	1.2 to 1
Accounts receivable turnover	8.6 times	9.5 times	10.4 times
Inventory turnover	5.0 times	5.7 times	6.8 times
Sales trend	130.0	118.0	100.0
Dividends paid per share*	$2.50	$2.50	$2.50
Dividend yield ratio	5%	4%	3%
Dividend payout ratio	40%	50%	60%
Return on total assets	13.0%	11.8%	10.4%
Return on common equity	16.2%	14.5%	9.0%

*There were no changes in common stock outstanding over the three-year period.

Ms. Perkins would like answers to a number of questions about the trend of events over the last three years in Plunge Enterprises. Her questions are as follows:

a. Is the market price of the company's stock going up or down?
b. Is the amount of the earnings per share increasing or decreasing?
c. Is the price-earnings ratio going up or down?
d. Is the company employing financial leverage to the advantage of the common stockholders?
e. Is it becoming easier for the company to pay its bills as they come due?
f. Are customers paying their bills at least as fast now as they did in Year 1?
g. Is the total of the accounts receivable increasing, decreasing, or remaining constant?
h. Is the level of inventory increasing, decreasing, or remaining constant?

Required:

Answer each of Ms. Perkins' questions using the data given above. In each case, explain how you arrived at your answer.

PROBLEM 17–15 Effects of Transactions on Various Financial Ratios [LO2, LO3, LO4]

In the right-hand column below, certain financial ratios are listed. To the left of each ratio is a business transaction or event relating to the operating activities of Graham Company.

1. Inventory was sold for cash at a profit.	Debt-to-equity ratio
2. Land was purchased for cash.	Earnings per share
3. The company sold inventory on account at cost.	Acid-test (quick) ratio
4. The company paid off some accounts payable.	Working capital
5. A customer paid an overdue bill.	Average collection period
6. The company declared, but did not yet pay, a cash dividend.	Current ratio
7. A previously declared cash dividend was paid.	Current ratio
8. The company's common stock price increased.	Book value per share
9. The company's common stock price increased. Earnings per share remained unchanged.	Dividend yield ratio
10. Property was sold for a profit.	Return on total assets
11. Obsolete inventory was written off as a loss.	Inventory turnover ratio
12. The company issued bonds with an interest rate less than the company's return on assets.	Return on common stockholders' equity
13. The company's common stock price decreased. The dividend paid per share remained the same.	Dividend payout ratio
14. The company's net income decreased, but long-term debt remained unchanged.	Times interest earned
15. An uncollectible account was written off against the Allowance for Bad Debts.	Current ratio
16. Inventory was purchased on credit.	Acid-test ratio
17. The company's common stock price increased. Earnings per share remained unchanged.	Price-earnings ratio
18. The company paid off some accounts payable.	Debt-to-equity ratio

Required:

Indicate the effect that each transaction or event would have on the ratio listed opposite to it. State the effect in terms of increase, decrease, or no effect on the ratio involved, and give the reason for your choice. In all cases, assume that the current assets exceed current liabilities both before and after the event or transaction. Use the following format for your answers:

	Effect on Ratio	Reason for Increase, Decrease, or No Effect
1.		
2.		
Etc.		

PROBLEM 17–16 Comprehensive Problem—Part 1: Financial Ratios for Common Stockholders [LO2]

(Problems 17–17 and 17–18 delve more deeply into the data presented below. Each problem is independent.) Microswift, Inc., was organized several years ago to develop and market computer software programs. The company is small but growing, and you are considering the purchase of some of its common stock as an investment. The following data on the company are available for the past two years:

MICROSWIFT, INC.
Comparative Income Statement
For the Years Ended December 31, This Year, and Last Year

	This Year	Last Year
Sales	$10,000,000	$7,500,000
Less cost of goods sold	6,500,000	4,500,000
Gross margin	3,500,000	3,000,000
Less operating expenses	2,630,000	2,280,000
Net operating income	870,000	720,000
Less interest expense	120,000	120,000
Net income before taxes	750,000	600,000
Less income taxes (30%)	225,000	180,000
Net income	$ 525,000	$ 420,000

MICROSWIFT, INC.
Comparative Retained Earnings Statement
For the Years Ended December 31, This Year, and Last Year

	This Year	Last Year
Retained earnings, January 1	$1,200,000	$ 980,000
Add net income (above)	525,000	420,000
Total	1,725,000	1,400,000
Deduct cash dividends paid:		
Preferred dividends	60,000	60,000
Common dividends	180,000	140,000
Total dividends paid	240,000	200,000
Retained earnings, December 31	$1,485,000	$1,200,000

MICROSWIFT, INC.
Comparative Balance Sheet
December 31, This Year, and Last Year

	This Year	Last Year
Assets		
Current assets:		
Cash	$ 100,000	$ 200,000
Accounts receivable, net	750,000	400,000
Inventory	1,500,000	600,000
Prepaid expenses	50,000	50,000
Total current assets	2,400,000	1,250,000
Plant and equipment, net	2,585,000	2,700,000
Total assets	$4,985,000	$3,950,000

continued

Liabilities and Stockholders' Equity		
Liabilities:		
Current liabilities	$1,250,000	$ 500,000
Bonds payable, 12%	1,000,000	1,000,000
Total liabilities	2,250,000	1,500,000
Stockholders' equity:		
Preferred stock, 8%, $10 par	750,000	750,000
Common stock, $5 par	500,000	500,000
Retained earnings	1,485,000	1,200,000
Total stockholders' equity	2,735,000	2,450,000
Total liabilities and stockholders' equity	$4,985,000	$3,950,000

After some research, you have determined that the following ratios are typical of companies in the computer software industry:

Dividend yield ratio	3%
Dividend payout ratio	40%
Price-earnings ratio	16
Return on total assets	13.5%
Return on common equity	20%

There has been no change in the preferred or common stock outstanding over the last three years. The company's common stock is currently selling for $60 per share. Last year, the stock sold for $45 per share.

Required:

1. In analyzing the company, you decide first to compute the earnings per share and related ratios. For both years, compute:
   a. The earnings per share.
   b. The dividend yield ratio.
   c. The dividend payout ratio.
   d. The price-earnings ratio.
   e. The book value per share of common stock.
   f. The gross margin percentage.
2. You decide next to determine the rate of return that the company is generating. For both years, compute:
   a. The return on total assets. (Total assets were $3,250,000 on January 1 of last year.)
   b. The return on common stockholders' equity. (Common stockholders' equity was $1,450,000 on January 1 of last year.)
   c. Is financial leverage positive or negative? Explain.
3. Based on your work in (1) and (2) above, does the company's common stock seem to be an attractive investment? Explain.

PROBLEM 17–17 Comprehensive Problem—Part 2: Creditor Ratios [LO3, LO4]

Refer to the data in Problem 17–16. Although Microswift, Inc., has been very profitable since it was organized several years ago, the company is beginning to experience some difficulty in paying its bills as they come due. Management has approached Guaranty National Bank requesting a two-year $250,000 loan to bolster the Cash account.

Guaranty National Bank has assigned you to evaluate the loan request. You have gathered the following data relating to companies in the computer software industry:

Current ratio	2.4 to 1
Acid-test (quick) ratio	1.2 to 1
Average age of receivables	16 days
Inventory turnover in days	40 days
Times interest earned	7 times
Debt-to-equity ratio	0.70 to 1

The following additional information is available on Microswift, Inc.:

a. All sales are on account.

b. At the beginning of last year, the accounts receivable balance was $300,000 and the inventory balance was $500,000.

Required:

1. Compute the following amounts and ratios for both years:
   a. The working capital.
   b. The current ratio.
   c. The acid-test ratio.
   d. The accounts receivable turnover (average collection period) in days.
   e. The inventory turnover (average sale period) in days.
   f. The times interest earned.
   g. The debt-to-equity ratio.
2. Comment on the results of your analysis in (1) above.
3. Would you recommend that the loan be approved? Explain.

PROBLEM 17–18 Comprehensive Problem—Part 3: Common-Size Statements [LO1]
Refer to the data in Problem 17–16. The president of Microswift, Inc., is very concerned. Sales increased by $2.5 million from last year to this year, yet the company's net income increased by only $105,000. Also, the company's operating expenses went up this year, even though a major effort was launched during the year to cut costs.

Required:

1. For both years, prepare the income statement and the balance sheet in common-size form. (Round computations to one decimal place.)
2. From your work in (1) above, explain to the president why the increase in profits was so small this year. Were any benefits realized from the company's cost-cutting efforts? Explain.

PROBLEM 17–19 Incomplete Statements; Analysis of Ratios [LO2, LO3, LO4]
Incomplete financial statements for Tanner Company are given below:

TANNER COMPANY
Income Statement
For the Year Ended December 31

Sales	$2,700,000
Less cost of goods sold	?
Gross margin	?
Less operating expenses	?
Net operating income	?
Less interest expense	45,000
Net income before taxes	?
Less income taxes (40%)	?
Net income	$?

TANNER COMPANY
Balance Sheet
December 31

Current assets:	
Cash	$?
Accounts receivable, net	?
Inventory	?
Total current assets	?
Plant and equipment, net	?
Total assets	$?

continued

Current liabilities	$250,000
Bonds payable, 10%	?
Total liabilities	?
Stockholders' equity:	
Common stock, $2.50 par value	?
Retained earnings	?
Total stockholders' equity	?
Total liabilities and stockholders' equity	$?

The following additional information is available about the company:

a. Selected financial ratios computed from the statements above are given below:

Current ratio	2.40 to 1
Acid-test (quick) ratio	1.12 to 1
Accounts receivable turnover	15.0 times
Inventory turnover	6.0 times
Debt-to-equity ratio	0.875 to 1
Times interest earned	7.0 times
Earnings per share	$4.05
Return on total assets	14%

b. All sales during the year were on account.

c. The interest expense on the income statement relates to the bonds payable; the amount of bonds outstanding did not change throughout the year.

d. There were no changes in the number of shares of common stock outstanding during the year.

e. Selected balances at the *beginning* of the current year (January 1) were as follows:

Accounts receivable	$ 160,000
Inventory	280,000
Total assets	1,200,000

Required:

Compute the missing amounts on the company's financial statements. (Hint: You may find it helpful to think about the difference between the current ratio and the acid-test ratio.)

PROBLEM 17–20 Ethics and the Manager [LO3]

Mountain Aerosport was founded by Jurgen Prinz to produce a ski he had designed for doing aerial tricks. Up to this point, Jurgen has financed the company from his own savings and from retained profits. However, Jurgen now faces a cash crisis. In the year just ended, an acute shortage of a vital tungsten steel alloy had developed just as the company was beginning production for the Christmas season. Jurgen had been assured by his suppliers that the steel would be delivered in time to make Christmas shipments, but the suppliers had been unable to fully deliver on this promise. As a consequence, Mountain Aerosport had large stocks of unfinished skis at the end of the year and had been unable to fill all of the orders that had come in from retailers for the Christmas season. Consequently, sales were below expectations for the year, and Jurgen does not have enough cash to pay his creditors.

Well before the accounts payable were to become due, Jurgen visited a local bank and inquired about obtaining a loan. The loan officer at the bank assured Jurgen that there should not be any problem getting a loan to pay off his accounts payable—providing that on his most recent financial statements the current ratio was above 2.0, the acid-test ratio was above 1.0, and net operating income was at least four times the interest on the proposed loan. Jurgen promised to return later with a copy of his financial statements.

Jurgen would like to apply for a $120 thousand six-month loan bearing an interest rate of 10% per year. The unaudited financial reports of the company appear below.

MOUNTAIN AEROSPORT
Comparative Balance Sheet
As of December 31, This Year and Last Year
(in thousands of dollars)

	This Year	Last Year
Assets		
Current assets:		
Cash	$105	$225
Accounts receivable, net	75	60
Inventory	240	150
Prepaid expenses	15	18
Total current assets	435	453
Property and equipment	405	270
Total assets	$840	$723
Liabilities and Stockholders' Equity		
Current liabilities:		
Accounts payable	$231	$135
Accrued payables	15	15
Total current liabilities	246	150
Long-term liabilities	0	0
Total liabilities	246	150
Stockholders' equity:		
Common stock and additional paid-in capital	150	150
Retained earnings	444	423
Total stockholders' equity	594	573
Total liabilities and stockholders' equity	$840	$723

MOUNTAIN AEROSPORT
Income Statement
For the Year Ended December 31, This Year
(in thousands of dollars)

Sales (all on account)	$630
Cost of goods sold	435
Gross margin	195
Operating expenses:	
Selling expenses	63
Administrative expenses	102
Total operating expenses	165
Net operating income	30
Interest expense	0
Net income before taxes	30
Less income taxes (30%)	9
Net income	$ 21

Required:

1. Based on the above unaudited financial statements and the statement made by the loan officer, would the company qualify for the loan?
2. Last year Jurgen purchased and installed new, more efficient equipment to replace an older heat-treating furnace. Jurgen had originally planned to sell the old equipment but found that it is still needed whenever the heat-treating process is a bottleneck. When Jurgen discussed his cash flow problems with his brother-in-law, he suggested to Jurgen that the old equipment be sold or at least reclassified as inventory on the balance sheet since it could be readily sold. At present, the equipment is carried in the Property and Equipment account and could be sold for

its net book value of $68 thousand. The bank does not require audited financial statements. What advice would you give to Jurgen concerning the machine?

Group and Internet Exercises

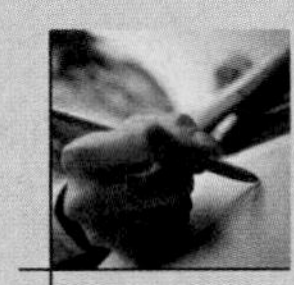

GROUP EXERCISE 17–21 Computing and Interpreting Financial Ratios
Obtain the most recent annual report or SEC filing 10-K of a publicly traded company that interests you. It may be a local company or it may be a company in an industry that you would like to know more about. Using the annual report, compute as many of the financial ratios covered in this chapter as you can for at least the past two years. This may pose some difficulties—particularly since companies often use different terms for many income statement and balance sheet items than were shown in the chapter. Nevertheless, do the best that you can. After you have computed the financial ratios, summarize the company's performance for the current year. Has it improved, gotten worse, or remained about the same? Do the ratios indicate any potential problems or any areas that have shown significant improvement? What recommendations, if any, would you make to a bank about extending short-term credit to this company? What recommendations, if any, would you make to an insurance company about extending long-term credit to this company? What recommendations, if any, would you make to an investor about buying or selling this company's stock?

INTERNET EXERCISE 17–22
As you know, the World Wide Web is a medium that is constantly evolving. Sites come and go, and change without notice. To enable periodic update of site addresses, this problem has been posted to the textbook website (www.mhhe.com/garrison10e). After accessing the site, enter the Student Center and select this chapter. Select and complete the Internet Exercise.

Appendix A

Pricing Products and Services

LEARNING OBJECTIVES

After studying this appendix, you should be able to:

1. Compute the profit-maximizing price of a product or service using the price elasticity of demand and variable cost.
2. Compute the selling price of a product using the absorption costing approach.
3. Compute the target cost for a new product or service.
4. Compute and use billing rates used in time and material pricing.

Introduction

Some businesses have no pricing problems. They make a product or provide a service that is in competition with other, identical products or services for which a market price already exists. Customers will not pay more than this price, and there is no reason to charge less. Under these circumstances, the company simply charges the prevailing market price. Markets for basic raw materials such as farm products and minerals follow this pattern.

In this appendix, we are concerned with the more common situation in which a company is faced with the problem of setting its own prices. Clearly, the pricing decision can be critical. If the price is set too high, customers will avoid purchasing the company's products. If the price is set too low, the company's costs may not be covered.

The usual approach in pricing is to *mark up* cost.[1] A product's **markup** is the difference between its selling price and its cost. The markup is usually expressed as a percentage of cost. This approach is called **cost-plus pricing** because the predetermined markup percentage is applied to the cost base to determine a target selling price.

Do Consumers Really Respond to Prices? You Bet They Do

In Business

Jess Stonestreet Jackson is the founder of Kendall-Jackson (K-J) winery, which specializes in making popular wines that are good enough to command a premium price. Jackson, who is now a billionaire, prices his wines a few dollars higher than other mainstream wines. For example, if a Clos du Bois chardonnay costs $9 at retail, Jackson will charge $11 for his chardonnay. When chardonnay became the rage in the late 1990s, Jackson tried pushing up his prices by another few dollars over the competition. But unit sales dropped by 18%. Jackson rolled back his prices and the volume recovered.

Source: Tim W. Ferguson, "Harvest Time," *Forbes*, October 16, 2000, pp. 112–118.

$$\text{Selling price} = \text{Cost} + (\text{Markup percentage} \times \text{Cost})$$

For example, if a company uses a markup of 50%, it adds 50% to the costs of its products to determine the selling price. If a product costs $10, then it would charge $15 for the product.

Two key issues must be addressed when the cost-plus approach to pricing is used. First, what cost should be used? Second, how should the markup be determined? Several alternative approaches are considered in this appendix, starting with the approach generally favored by economists.

The Economists' Approach to Pricing

LEARNING OBJECTIVE 1
Compute the profit-maximizing price of a product or service using the price elasticity of demand and variable cost.

If a company raises the price of a product, unit sales ordinarily fall. Because of this, pricing is a delicate balancing act in which the benefits of higher revenues per unit are traded off against the lower volume that results from charging higher prices. The sensitivity of unit sales to changes in price is called the *price elasticity of demand.*

[1] There are some legal restrictions on prices. Antitrust laws prohibit "predatory" prices, which are generally interpreted by the courts to mean a price below average variable cost. "Price discrimination"—charging different prices to customers in the same market for the same product or service—is also prohibited by the law.

In Business

Bringing in Skiers

Mike Shirley, the president and general manager of the Bogus Basin ski area in southern Idaho, started a price revolution in the ski resort industry by slashing the price of an adult season ticket from $500 to less than $200. Eight times as many passes were sold as the previous year, while generating four times as much revenue. Under the old price, a season pass holder skied on average 23 days. Under the new discounted price, the average dropped to only nine days. The reason? Lapsed skiers who don't ski all that much were buying the cheaper season passes. That year, the total skier visits jumped from 191,000 to over 303,000, but the average revenue per visit dropped by less than a dollar, from $24.84 to $23.89. Shirley notes, "When you have a huge increase in volume and you're collecting as much per skier as before, you're making out like a bandit." In ski resorts, almost all of the costs are fixed with respect to how many skiers are on the hill. Consequently, the increased revenue dropped almost directly to the bottom line as increased profits.

Source: Greg Trinker, "It's the Price, Stupid," *SKI*, October 1999, pp. 33–34.

Elasticity of Demand

A product's price elasticity should be a key element in setting its price. The **price elasticity of demand** measures the degree to which the unit sales of a product or service are affected by a change in price. Demand for a product is said to be *inelastic* if a change in price has little effect on the number of units sold. The demand for designer perfumes sold by trained personnel at cosmetic counters in department stores is relatively inelastic. Lowering prices on these luxury goods has little effect on sales volume; factors other than price are more important in generating sales. On the other hand, demand for a product is said to be *elastic* if a change in price has a substantial effect on the volume of units sold. An example of a product whose demand is elastic is gasoline. If a gas station raises its price for gasoline, there will usually be a substantial drop in volume as customers seek lower prices elsewhere.

In Business

Elasticity Depends on the Product

The demand for water is much more elastic than the demand for cigarettes. When cities raise the price of water by 10%, water usage goes down by as much as 12%. When the price of agricultural water goes up 10%, usage drops by about 20%. Agricultural users of water are much more sensitive to price than city dwellers, but both are much more sensitive to price than smokers. When the price of cigarettes increases by 10%, consumption drops by only 3% to 5%.

Sources: Terry L. Anderson and Clay J. Landry, "Trickle-Down Economics," *The Wall Street Journal*, August 23, 1999, p. A14; Gene Koretz, "Still Hooked on the Evil Weed," *Business Week*, July 5, 1999, p. 18.

Price elasticity is very important in determining prices. Managers should set higher markups over cost where customers are relatively insensitive to price (i.e., demand is inelastic) and lower markups where customers are relatively sensitive to price (i.e., demand is elastic). This principle is followed in department stores. Merchandise sold in the bargain basement has a much lower markup than merchandise sold elsewhere in the store because customers who shop in the bargain basement are much more sensitive to price (i.e., demand is elastic).

The price elasticity of demand for a product or service, ϵ_d, can be estimated using the following formula.[2,3]

$$\epsilon_d = \frac{\ln(1 + \%\text{ change in quantity sold})}{\ln(1 + \%\text{ change in price})}$$

For example, suppose that the managers of Nature's Garden believe that every 10% increase in the selling price of their apple-almond shampoo will result in a 15% decrease in the number of bottles of shampoo sold.[4] The price elasticity of demand for this product would be computed as follows:

$$\epsilon_d = \frac{\ln(1 + (-0.15))}{\ln(1 + (0.10))} = \frac{\ln(0.85)}{\ln(1.10)} = -1.71$$

For comparison purposes, the managers of Nature's Garden believe that another product, strawberry glycerin soap, will experience a 20% drop in unit sales if its price is increased by 10%. (Purchasers of this product are more sensitive to price than the purchasers of the apple-almond shampoo.) The price elasticity of demand for the strawberry glycerin soap is:

$$\epsilon_d = \frac{\ln(1 + (-0.20))}{\ln(1 + (0.10))} = \frac{\ln(0.80)}{\ln(1.10)} = -2.34$$

Both of these products, like other normal products, have a price elasticity that is less than −1. Note also that the price elasticity of demand for the strawberry glycerin soap is larger (in absolute value) than the price elasticity of demand for the apple-almond shampoo. The more sensitive customers are to price, the larger (in absolute value) is the price elasticity of demand. In other words, a larger (in absolute value) price elasticity of demand indicates a product whose demand is more elastic.

In the next subsection, the price elasticity of demand will be used to compute the selling price that maximizes the profits of the company.

The Profit-Maximizing Price

Under certain conditions, it can be shown that the profit-maximizing price can be determined by marking up *variable cost* using the following formula:[5]

$$\text{Profit-maximizing markup on variable cost} = \left(\frac{\epsilon_d}{1 + \epsilon_d}\right) - 1$$

Using the above markup is equivalent to setting the selling price using this formula:

$$\text{Profit-maximizing price} = \left(\frac{\epsilon_d}{1 + \epsilon_d}\right) \text{Variable cost per unit}$$

---

[2] The term "ln( )" is the natural log function. You can compute the natural log of any number using the LN or ln$x$ key on your calculator. For example, ln(0.85) = −0.1625.

[3] This formula assumes that the price elasticity of demand is constant. This occurs when the relation between the selling price, p, and the unit sales, q, can be expressed in the following form: $\ln(q) = a + \epsilon_d \ln(p)$. Even if this is not precisely true, the formula provides a useful way to estimate a product's real price elasticity.

[4] The estimated change in unit sales should take into account competitors' responses to a price change.

[5] The formula assumes that (a) the price elasticity of demand is constant; (b) Total cost = Total fixed cost + Variable cost per unit × q; and (c) the price of the product has no effect on the sales or costs of any other product. The formula can be derived using calculus.

In Business

What Did that Salmon Dish Cost?

Restaurants generally mark up food costs by an average of 300% to cover their overhead and generate a profit, but the markup is not the same for all items on the menu. Some ingredients—especially prime cuts of beef and exotic seafood such as fresh scallops—are so costly that diners would not tolerate a 300% markup. So restaurants make it up on the cheap stuff—vegetables, pasta, and salmon. Why salmon? The farmed variety is only $2.50 per pound wholesale, much cheaper than prime restaurant-quality beef. At the Docks restaurant in New York City, a 10-ounce salmon dinner garnished with potatoes and coleslaw is $19.50. The actual cost of the ingredients is only $1.90.

To take another example, the ingredients of the best-selling Angus beef tenderloin at the Sunset Grill in Nashville, Tennessee, costs the restaurant $8.42. Applying the average 300% markup, the price of the meal would be $33.68. But few diners would order the meal at that price. So instead the restaurant charges just $25. In contrast, the restaurant charges $9 for its Grill vegetable plate—whose ingredients cost only $1.55.

Source: Eileen Daspin, "Entrée Economics," *The Wall Street Journal*, March 10, 2000, pp. W1 and W4.

The profit-maximizing prices for the two Nature's Garden products are computed below using these formulas:

	Apple-Almond Shampoo	Strawberry Glycerin Soap
Price elasticity of demand (ϵ_d)	−1.71	−2.34
Profit-maximizing markup on variable cost (a)	$\left(\frac{-1.71}{-1.71 + 1}\right) - 1$	$\left(\frac{-2.34}{-2.34 + 1}\right) - 1$
	= 2.41 − 1 = 1.41 or 141%	= 1.75 − 1 = 0.75 or 75%
Variable cost per unit—given (b)	$2.00	$0.40
Markup, (a) × (b)	2.82	0.30
Profit-maximizing price	$4.82	$0.70

Note that the 75% markup for the strawberry glycerin soap is lower than the 141% markup for the apple-almond shampoo. The reason for this is that the purchasers of strawberry glycerin soap are more sensitive to price than the purchasers of apple-almond shampoo. This could be because strawberry glycerin soap is a relatively common product with close substitutes available in nearly every grocery store.

Exhibit A–1 shows how the profit-maximizing markup is affected by how sensitive unit sales are to price. For example, if a 10% increase in price leads to a 20% decrease in unit sales, then the optimal markup on variable cost according to the exhibit is 75%—the figure computed above for the strawberry glycerin soap. Note that the optimal markup drops as unit sales become more sensitive to price.

Caution is advised when using these formulas to establish a selling price. The assumptions underlying the formulas are probably not completely valid, and the estimate of the percentage change in unit sales that would result from a given percentage change in price is likely to be inexact. Nevertheless, the formulas can provide valuable clues regarding whether prices should be increased or decreased. Suppose, for example, that the strawberry glycerin soap is currently being sold for $0.60 per bar. The formula indicates that the profit-maximizing price is $0.70 per bar. Rather than increasing the price by $0.10, it would be prudent to increase the price by a more modest amount to observe what happens to unit sales and to profits.

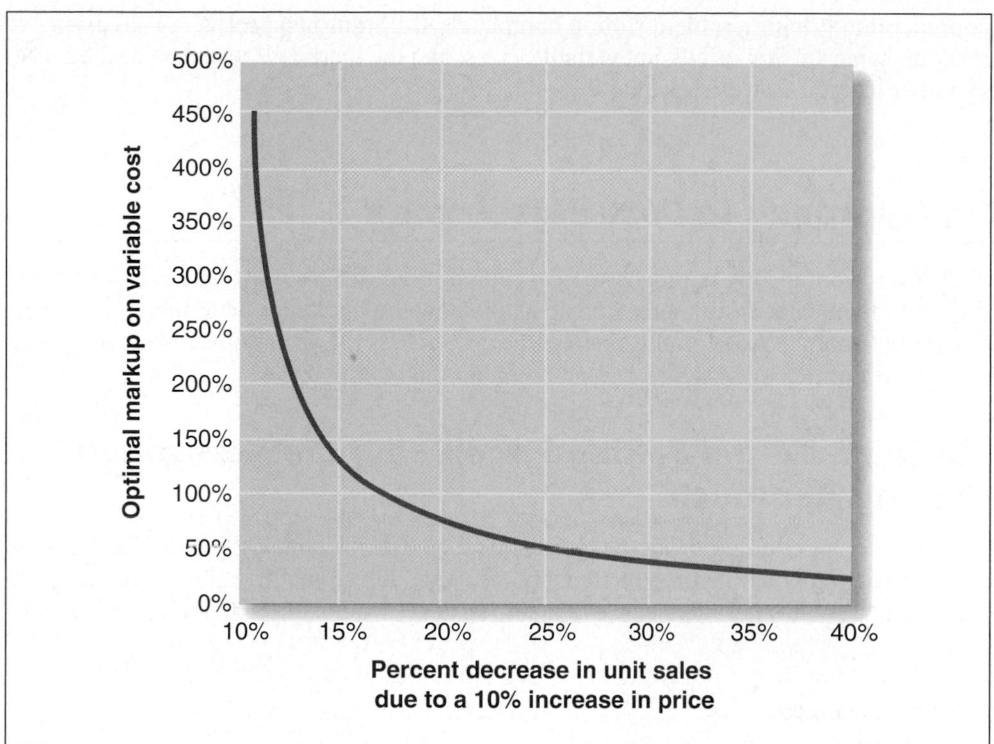

Exhibit A–1
The Optimal Markup on Variable Cost as a Function of the Sensitivity of Unit Sales to Price

The formula for the profit-maximizing price also conveys a very important lesson. The optimal selling price should depend on two factors—the variable cost per unit and how sensitive unit sales are to changes in price. In particular, fixed costs play no role in setting the optimal price. If the total fixed costs are the same whether the company charges $0.60 or $0.70, they cannot be relevant in the decision of which price to charge for the soap. Fixed costs are relevant when deciding whether to offer a product but are not relevant when deciding how much to charge for the product.

Incidentally, we can directly verify that an increase in selling price for the strawberry glycerin soap from the current price of $0.60 per bar is warranted, based just on the forecast that a 10% increase in selling price would lead to a 20% decrease in unit sales. Suppose, for example, that Nature's Garden is currently selling 200,000 bars of the soap per year at the price of $0.60 a bar. If the change in price has no effect on the company's fixed costs or on other products, the effect on profits of increasing the price by 10% can be computed as follows:

	Present Price	Higher Price
Selling price	$0.60	$0.60 + (0.10 × $0.60) = $0.66
Unit sales	200,000	200,000 − (0.20 × 200,000) = 160,000
Sales	$120,000	$105,600
Variable cost	80,000	64,000
Contribution margin	$ 40,000	$ 41,600

Despite the apparent optimality of prices based on marking up variable costs according to the price elasticity of demand, surveys consistently reveal that most managers approach the pricing problem from a completely different perspective.[6] They prefer to mark up some version of full, not variable, costs, and the markup is based on desired profits rather than on factors related to demand.

The Absorption Costing Approach to Cost-Plus Pricing

LEARNING OBJECTIVE 2
Compute the selling price of a product using the absorption costing approach.

The absorption costing approach to cost-plus pricing differs from the economists' approach both in what costs are marked up and in how the markup is determined. Under the absorption approach to cost-plus pricing, the cost base is the absorption costing unit product cost as defined in Chapters 2, 3, and 4 rather than variable cost.

Setting a Target Selling Price Using the Absorption Costing Approach

To illustrate, let us assume that the management of Ritter Company wants to set the selling price on a product that has just undergone some design modifications. The Accounting Department has provided cost estimates for the redesigned product as shown below:

	Per Unit	Total
Direct materials	$6	
Direct labor	4	
Variable manufacturing overhead	3	
Fixed manufacturing overhead		$70,000
Variable selling, general, and administrative expenses	2	
Fixed selling, general, and administrative expenses		60,000

The first step in the absorption costing approach to cost-plus pricing is to compute the unit product cost. For Ritter Company, this amounts to $20 per unit at a volume of 10,000 units, as computed below:

Direct materials	$ 6
Direct labor	4
Variable manufacturing overhead	3
Fixed manufacturing overhead ($70,000 ÷ 10,000 units)	7
Unit product cost	$20

Ritter Company has a general policy of marking up unit product costs by 50%. A price quotation sheet for the company prepared using the absorption approach is presented in Exhibit A-2. Note that selling, general, and administrative (SG&A) costs are not included in the cost base. Instead, the markup is supposed to cover these expenses. Let us see how some companies compute these markup percentages.

---

6 One study found that 83% of the 504 large manufacturing companies surveyed used some form of full cost (either absorption cost or absorption cost plus selling, general, and administrative expenses) as a basis for pricing. The remaining 17% used only variable costs as a basis for pricing decisions. See V. Govindarajan and Robert N. Anthony, "How Firms Use Cost Data in Pricing Decisions," *Management Accounting,* July 1983, pp. 30–36. A more recent, but less extensive, survey by Eunsup Shim and Ephraim F. Sudit, "How Manufacturers Price Products," *Management Accounting,* February 1995, pp. 37–39, found similar results.

On the other hand, a survey of small-company executives summarized in *Inc.*, November 1996, p. 84, revealed that only 41% set prices based on cost. The others charge what they think customers are willing to pay or what the market demands.

Direct materials	$ 6
Direct labor	4
Variable manufacturing overhead	3
Fixed manufacturing overhead (based on 10,000 units)	7
Unit product cost	20
Markup to cover selling, general, and administrative expenses and desired profit—50% of unit manufacturing cost	10
Target selling price	$30

Exhibit A–2
Price Quotation Sheet—Absorption Basis (10,000 Units)

The Politics of Pricing Medicines

In Business

The major international pharmaceutical companies often sell drugs for far more in developed countries than in poorer countries. For example, AIDS-fighting proteases cost about $14,000 a year in the U.S., but only $2,000 a year in Africa. This happens because most of the costs of a drug (i.e., research and development costs) are sunk by the time it actually is approved for patient use. Any price above the fairly small marginal (i.e., variable) costs of producing the drug will contribute to profits. Since patients in poorer countries simply cannot afford to pay the cost charged in the United States, the drug companies drop the price drastically in the poorer countries. At least initially, the discounted prices may be viewed by the public as a humanitarian gesture. However, pressures eventually mount to make the drug available to the uninsured (and to the elderly) at comparably low prices in the United States. But, as explained in *Forbes*, "Once you start making lifesaving drugs available at lower cost to the world's poorest people—or to 65-year-olds in the United States—you have to explain why you cannot deliver the product at a uniformly low price to everyone. Here come price controls. There goes the R&D budget."

Source: Robert Lenzner and Tomas Kellner, "Corporate Saboteurs," *Forbes*, November 27, 2000, pp. 156 168.

Determining the Markup Percentage

How did Ritter Company arrive at its markup percentage of 50%? This figure could be a widely used rule of thumb in the industry or just a company tradition that seems to work. The markup percentage may also be the result of an explicit computation. As we have discussed, the markup over cost ideally should be largely determined by market conditions. However, a popular approach is to at least start with a markup based on cost and desired profit. The reasoning goes like this. The markup must be large enough to cover SG&A expenses and provide an adequate return on investment (ROI). Given the forecasted unit sales, the markup can be computed as follows:

$$\text{Markup percentage on absorption cost} = \frac{(\text{Required ROI} \times \text{Investment}) + \text{SG\&A expenses}}{\text{Unit sales} \times \text{Unit product cost}}$$

To show how the formula above is applied, assume Ritter Company must invest $100,000 to produce and market 10,000 units of the product each year. The $100,000 investment covers purchase of equipment and funds needed to carry inventories and accounts receivable. If Ritter Company requires a 20% ROI, then the markup for the product would be determined as follows:

$$\text{Markup percentage on absorption cost} = \frac{(20\% \times 100{,}000) + (\$2 \times 10{,}000 + \$60{,}000)}{10{,}000 \times \$20}$$

$$= \frac{(\$20{,}000) + (\$80{,}000)}{\$200{,}000} = 50\%$$

Exhibit A–3
Income Statement and ROI Analysis—Ritter Company Actual Unit Sales = 10,000 Units; Selling Price = $30

Direct materials	$ 6
Direct labor	4
Variable manufacturing overhead	3
Fixed manufacturing overhead ($70,000 ÷ 10,000 units)	7
Unit product cost	$20

RITTER COMPANY
Absorption Costing Income Statement

Sales ($30 per unit × 10,000 units)	$300,000
Less cost of goods sold ($20 per unit × 10,000 units)	200,000
Gross margin	100,000
Less selling, general, and administration expenses ($2 per unit × 10,000 units + $60,000)	80,000
Net operating income	$ 20,000

ROI

$$\text{ROI} = \frac{\text{Net operating income}}{\text{Average operating assets}} = \frac{\$20{,}000}{\$100{,}000} = 20\%$$

As shown earlier, this markup of 50% leads to a target selling price of $30 for Ritter Company. As verified in Exhibit A–3, *if the company actually sells 10,000 units* of the product at this price, the company's ROI on this product will indeed be 20%. If it turns out that more than 10,000 units are sold at this price, the ROI will be greater than 20%. If less than 10,000 units are sold, the ROI will be less than 20%. *The required ROI will be attained only if the forecasted unit sales volume is attained.*

Problems with the Absorption Costing Approach

Using the absorption costing approach, the pricing problem looks deceptively simple. All you have to do is compute your unit product cost, decide how much profit you want, and then set your price. It appears that you can ignore demand and arrive at a price that will safely yield whatever profit you want. However, as noted above, the absorption costing approach relies on a forecast of unit sales. Neither the markup nor the unit product cost can be computed without such a forecast.

The absorption costing approach essentially assumes that customers *need* the forecasted unit sales and will pay whatever price the company decides to charge. However, customers have a choice. If the price is too high, they can buy from a competitor or they may choose not to buy at all. Suppose, for example, that when Ritter Company sets its price at $30, it sells only 7,000 units rather than the 10,000 units forecasted. As shown in Exhibit A–4, the company would then have a loss of $25,000 on the product instead of a profit of $20,000.[7] Some managers believe that the absorption costing approach to pricing is safe. This is an illusion. The absorption costing approach is safe only as long as customers choose to buy at least as many units as managers forecasted they would buy.

7 If there is only one product and it is inherently profitable, it is always possible to at least break even using the absorption costing approach. This is not true when the company has more than one product and common fixed costs. It may be *impossible* to break even using an absorption costing approach when there is more than one product—even when it would be possible to make substantial profits using the economists' approach to pricing. For details, see Eric Noreen and David Burgstahler, "Full Cost Pricing and the Illusion of Satisficing," *Journal of Management Accounting Research*, 9 (1997).

Direct materials	$ 6
Direct labor	4
Variable manufacturing overhead	3
Fixed manufacturing overhead ($70,000 ÷ 7,000 units)	10
Unit product cost	$23

RITTER COMPANY
Absorption Costing Income Statement

Sales ($30 per unit × 7,000 units)	$210,000
Less cost of goods sold ($23 per unit × 7,000 units)	161,000
Gross margin	49,000
Less selling, general, and administration expenses ($2 per unit × 7,000 units + $60,000)	74,000
Net operating income	$ (25,000)

ROI

$$\text{ROI} = \frac{\text{Net operating income}}{\text{Average operating assets}}$$

$$= \frac{-\$25{,}000}{\$100{,}000}$$

$$= -25\%$$

Exhibit A–4
Income Statement and ROI Analysis—Ritter Company Actual Unit Sales = 7,000 Units; Selling Price = $30

Sitting in the Customer's Seat

In Business

Rather than focusing on costs—which can be dangerous if forecasted unit volume does not materialize—many managers focus on customer value when making pricing decisions.

The ticket-services manager of the Washington Opera Company, Jimmy Legarreta, faced a difficult decision. After a financially unsuccessful season, he knew he had to do something about the opera company's pricing policy. Friday and Saturday performances were routinely sold out, and demand for the best seats far exceeded supply. Meanwhile, tickets for midweek performances were often left unsold. "Legarreta also knew that not all seats were equal, even in the sought-after orchestra section. So the ticket manager and his staff sat in every one of the opera house's 2,200 seats and gave each a value according to the view and the acoustics. . . . In the end, the opera raised prices for its most coveted seats by as much as 50% but also dropped the prices of some 600 seats. The gamble paid off in a 9% revenue increase during the next season."

Source: Susan Greco, "Are Your Prices Right?" *Inc.*, January 1997, p. 88.

Target Costing

LEARNING OBJECTIVE 3
Compute the target cost for a new product or service.

Our discussion thus far has presumed that a product has already been developed, has been costed, and is ready to be marketed as soon as a price is set. In many cases, the sequence of events is just the reverse. That is, the company already *knows* what price should be charged, and the problem is to *develop* a product that can be marketed profitably at the desired price. Even in this situation, where the normal sequence of events is reversed, cost is still a crucial factor. The company can use an approach called *target costing*. **Target costing** is the process of determining the maximum allowable cost for a new product and then developing a prototype that can be profitably made for that maximum target cost figure. A number of companies—primarily in Japan—use target costing, including Compaq, Culp, Cummins Engine, Daihatsu Motors, DaimlerChrysler, Ford, Isuzu Motors, ITT

Automotive, Komatsu, Matsushita Electric, Mitsubishi Kasei, NEC, Nippodenso, Nissan, Olympus, Sharp, Texas Instruments, and Toyota.

The target cost for a product is computed by starting with the product's anticipated selling price and then deducting the desired profit, as follows:

$$\text{Target cost} = \text{Anticipated selling price} - \text{Desired profit}$$

The product development team is then given the responsibility of designing the product so that it can be made for no more than the target cost.

In Business

Target Costing—An Iterative Process

Target costing is widely used in Japan. In the automobile industry, the target cost for a new model is decomposed into target costs for each of the elements of the car—down to a target cost for each of the individual parts. The designers draft a trial blueprint, and a check is made to see if the estimated cost of the car is within reasonable distance of the target cost. If not, design changes are made, and a new trial blueprint is drawn up. This process continues until there is sufficient confidence in the design to make a prototype car according to the trial blueprint. If there is still a gap between the target cost and estimated cost, the design of the car will be further modified.

After repeating this process a number of times, the final blueprint is drawn up and turned over to the production department. In the first several months of production, the target costs will ordinarily not be achieved due to problems in getting a new model into production. However, after that initial period, target costs are compared to actual costs and discrepancies between the two are investigated with the aim of eliminating the discrepancies and achieving target costs.

Source: Yasuhiro Monden and Kazuki Hamada, "Target Costing and Kaizen Costing in Japanese Automobile Companies," *Journal of Management Accounting Research* 3, pp. 16–34.

Reasons for Using Target Costing

The target costing approach was developed in recognition of two important characteristics of markets and costs. The first is that many companies have less control over price than they would like to think. The market (i.e., supply and demand) really determines prices, and a company that attempts to ignore this does so at its peril. Therefore, the anticipated market price is taken as a given in target costing. The second observation is that most of the cost of a product is determined in the design stage. Once a product has been designed and has gone into production, not much can be done to significantly reduce its cost. Most of the opportunities to reduce cost come from designing the product so that it is simple to make, uses inexpensive parts, and is robust and reliable. If the company has little control over market price and little control over cost once the product has gone into production, then it follows that the major opportunities for affecting profit come in the design stage where valuable features that customers are willing to pay for can be added and where most of the costs are really determined. So that is where the effort is concentrated—in designing and developing the product. The difference between target costing and other approaches to product development is profound. Instead of designing the product and then finding out how much it costs, the target cost is set first and then the product is designed so that the target cost is attained.

An Example of Target Costing

To provide a simple numerical example of target costing, assume the following situation: Handy Appliance Company feels that there is a market niche for a hand mixer with certain new features. Surveying the features and prices of hand mixers already on the market, the Marketing Department believes that a price of $30 would be about right for the new mixer. At that price, Marketing estimates that 40,000 of the new mixers could be sold annually. To design, develop, and produce these new mixers, an investment of $2,000,000 would be required. The company desires a 15% ROI. Given these data, the target cost to manufacture, sell, distribute, and service one mixer is $22.50 as shown below.

Projected sales (40,000 mixers × $30 per mixer)	$1,200,000
Less desired profit (15% × $2,000,000)	300,000
Target cost for 40,000 mixers	$ 900,000
Target cost per mixer ($900,000 ÷ 40,000 mixers)	$22.50

This $22.50 target cost would be broken down into target costs for the various functions: manufacturing, marketing, distribution, after-sales service, and so on. Each functional area would be responsible for keeping its actual costs within target.

Slow to Get on Target

In Business

Peter Zampino, director of research at the Consortium for Advanced Manufacturing—International (CAM-I), claims that only about 65 companies in the United States have embraced target costing despite widespread experience with target costing in Japan that has reduced product costs by 13 to 17%. "[M]ost American companies think they're already doing target costing. . . . The truth is, they're only doing part of it."

Many companies do market research to find out what customers want in new products and some even figure out how much customers are willing to pay, but very few deploy cross-functional teams that meet with customers and engineer the product to meet the target cost. "The hardest part is tearing down the silos, the individual power bases that describe most companies."

What gets companies interested in doing real target costing? In a word, crisis. "We haven't found one company [in the U.S.] that practices target costing that didn't initiate it in a crisis."

Source: Russ Banham, "Off Target? Why Target Costing Has Been Slow to Catch on Here, Despite Its Promises," *CFO*, May 2000, pp. 127–130.

Service Companies—Time and Material Pricing

LEARNING OBJECTIVE 4
Compute and use billing rates used in time and material pricing.

Some companies—particularly in service industries—use a variation on cost-plus pricing called **time and material pricing.** Under this method, two pricing rates are established—one based on direct labor time and the other based on the cost of direct material used. This pricing method is widely used in repair shops, in printing shops, and by many professionals such as physicians and dentists. The time and material rates are usually market-determined. In other words, the rates are determined by the interplay of supply and demand and by competitive conditions in the industry. However, some companies set the rates using a process similar to the process followed in the absorption costing approach to cost-plus pricing. In this case, the rates include allowances for selling, general, and administrative expenses; other direct and indirect costs; and a desired profit. This section will show how the rates might be set using the cost-plus approach.

Time Component

The time component is typically expressed as a rate per hour of labor. The rate is computed by adding together three elements: (1) the direct costs of the employee, including salary and fringe benefits; (2) a pro rata allowance for selling, general, and administrative expenses of the organization; and (3) an allowance for a desired profit per hour of employee time. In some organizations (such as a repair shop), the same hourly rate will be charged regardless of which employee actually works on the job; in other organizations, the rate may vary by employee. For example, in a public accounting firm, the rate charged for a new assistant accountant's time will generally be less than the rate charged for an experienced senior accountant or for a partner.

Material Component

The material component is determined by adding a **material loading charge** to the invoice price of any materials used on the job. The material loading charge is designed to cover the costs of ordering, handling, and carrying materials in stock, plus a profit margin on the materials themselves.

An Example of Time and Material Pricing

To provide a numerical example of time and material pricing, consider the following:

Quality Auto Shop uses time and material pricing for all of its repair work. The following costs have been budgeted for the coming year:

	Repairs	Parts
Mechanics' wages	$300,000	
Service manager—salary	40,000	
Parts manager—salary		$36,000
Clerical assistant—salary	18,000	15,000
Retirement and insurance—16% of salaries and wages	57,280	8,160
Supplies	720	540
Utilities	36,000	20,800
Property taxes	8,400	1,900
Depreciation	91,600	37,600
Invoice cost of parts used		400,000
Total budgeted cost	$552,000	$520,000

The company expects to bill customers for 24,000 hours of repair time. A profit of $7 per hour of repair time is considered to be feasible, given the competitive conditions in the market. For parts, the competitive markup on the invoice cost of parts used is 15%.

Exhibit A–5 shows the computation of the billing rate and the material loading charge to be used over the next year. Note that the billing rate, or time component, is $30 per hour of repair time and the material loading charge is 45% of the invoice cost of parts used. Using these rates, a repair job that requires 4.5 hours of mechanics' time and $200 in parts would be billed as follows:

Labor time: 4.5 hours × $30 per hour		$135
Parts used:		
Invoice cost	$200	
Material loading charge: 45% × $200	90	290
Total price of the job		$425

Rather than using labor-hours as the basis for computing the time rate, a machine shop, a printing shop, or a similar organization might use machine-hours.

This method of setting prices is a variation of the absorption costing approach. As such, it is not surprising that it suffers from the same problem. Customers may not be willing to pay the rates that have been computed. If actual business is less than the forecasted 24,000 hours and $400,000 worth of parts, the profit objectives will not be met and the company may not even break even.

Exhibit A–5 Time and Material Pricing

	Time Component: Repairs		Parts: Material Loading Charge	
	Total	**Per Hour***	**Total**	**Percent†**
Cost of mechanics' time:				
Mechanics' wages	$300,000			
Retirement and insurance (16% of wages)	48,000			
Total cost	348,000	$14.50		
For repairs—other cost of repair service. For parts—costs of ordering, handling, and storing parts:				
Repairs service manager—salary	40,000			
Parts manager—salary			$ 36,000	
Clerical assistant—salary	18,000		15,000	
Retirement and insurance (16% of salaries)	9,280		8,160	
Supplies	720		540	
Utilities	36,000		20,800	
Property taxes	8,400		1,900	
Depreciation	91,600		37,600	
Total cost	204,000	8.50	120,000	30%
Desired profit:				
24,000 hours × $7 per hour	168,000	7.00		
15% × $400,000			60,000	15%
Total amount to be billed	$720,000	$30.00	$180,000	45%

*Based on 24,000 hours.

†Based on $400,000 invoice cost of parts. The charge for ordering, handling, and storing parts, for example, is computed as follows: $120,000 cost ÷ $400,000 invoice cost = 30%.

Summary

Pricing involves a delicate balancing act. Higher prices result in more revenue per unit but drive down unit sales. Exactly where to set prices to maximize profit is a difficult problem, but, in general, the markup over cost should be highest for those products where customers are least sensitive to price. The demand for such products is said to be price inelastic.

Managers often rely on cost-plus formulas to set target prices. In the absorption costing approach, the cost base is the absorption costing unit product cost and the markup is computed to cover both nonmanufacturing costs and to provide an adequate return on investment. However, costs will not be covered and return on investment will not be adequate unless the unit sales forecast used in the cost-plus formula is accurate. If applying the cost-plus formula results in a price that is too high, the unit sales forecast will not be attained.

Some companies take a different approach to pricing. Instead of starting with costs and then determining prices, they start with prices and then determine allowable costs. Companies that use target costing estimate what a new product's market price is likely to be based on its anticipated features and prices of products already on the market. They subtract desired profit from the estimated market price to arrive at the product's target cost. The design and development team is then given the responsibility of ensuring that the actual cost of the new product does not exceed the target cost.

Glossary

Cost-plus pricing A pricing method in which a predetermined markup is applied to a cost base to determine the target selling price. (p. 805)

Markup The difference between the selling price of a product or service and its cost. The markup is usually expressed as a percentage of cost. (p. 805)

Material loading charge A markup applied to the cost of materials that is designed to cover the costs of ordering, handling, and carrying materials in stock and to provide for some profit. (p. 816)

Price elasticity of demand A measure of the degree to which the volume of unit sales for a product or service is affected by a change in price. (p. 806)

Target costing The process of determining the maximum allowable cost for a new product and then developing a prototype that can be profitably manufactured and distributed for that maximum target cost figure. (p. 813)

Time and material pricing A pricing method, often used in service firms, in which two pricing rates are established—one based on direct labor time and the other based on direct materials used. (p. 815)

Questions

A–1 What is meant by cost-plus pricing?

A–2 What does the price elasticity of demand measure? What is meant by inelastic demand? What is meant by elastic demand?

A–3 According to the economists' approach to setting prices, the profit-maximizing price should depend on what two factors?

A–4 Which product should have a larger markup over variable cost, a product whose demand is elastic or a product whose demand is inelastic?

A–5 When the absorption costing approach to cost-plus pricing is used, what is the markup supposed to cover?

A–6 What assumption does the absorption costing approach make about how consumers react to prices?

A–7 Discuss the following statement: "Full cost can be viewed as a floor of protection. If a firm always sets its prices above full cost, it will never have to worry about operating at a loss."

A–8 What is target costing? How do target costs enter into the pricing decision?

A–9 What is time and material pricing?

Exercises

EXERCISE A–1 The Economists' Approach to Pricing [LO1]

Kimio Nakimura owns an ice cream stand that she operates during the summer months in Jackson Hole, Wyoming. Her store caters primarily to tourists passing through town on their way to Yellowstone National Park.

Kimio is unsure of how she should price her ice cream cones and has experimented with two prices in successive weeks during the busy August season. The number of people who entered the store was roughly the same in the two weeks. During the first week, she priced the cones at $1.79 and 860 cones were sold. During the second week, she priced the cones at $1.39 and 1,340 cones were sold. The variable cost of a cone is $0.41 and consists solely of the costs of the ice cream and of the cone itself. The fixed expenses of the ice cream stand are $425 per week.

Required:

1. Did Kimio make more money selling the cones for $1.79 or for $1.39?
2. Estimate the price elasticity of demand for the ice cream cones.
3. Estimate the profit-maximizing price for ice cream cones.

EXERCISE A–2 Absorption Costing Approach to Setting a Selling Price [LO2]

Naylor Company is considering the introduction of a new product. Management has gathered the following information:

Number of units to be produced and sold each year	12,500
Unit product cost	$30
Projected annual selling and administrative expenses	$60,000
Estimated investment required by the company	$500,000
Desired return on investment (ROI)	18%

The company uses the absorption costing approach to cost-plus pricing.

Required:

1. Compute the markup the company will have to use to achieve the desired ROI.
2. Compute the target selling price per unit.

EXERCISE A–3 Target Costing [LO3]

Eastern Auto Supply, Inc., produces and distributes auto supplies. The company is anxious to enter the rapidly growing market for long-life batteries that is based on lithium technology. Management believes that to be fully competitive, the new battery that the company is planning can't be priced at more than $65. At this price, management is confident that the company can sell 50,000 batteries per year. The batteries would require an investment of $2,500,000, and the desired ROI is 20%.

Required:

Compute the target cost of one battery.

EXERCISE A–4 Time and Material Pricing [LO4]

Riteway Plumbing Company provides plumbing repair services and uses time and material pricing. The company has budgeted the following costs for next year:

Plumbers' wages and fringe benefits	$340,000
Other repair costs, except for parts-related costs	$160,000
Costs of ordering, handling, and storing parts	15% of invoice cost

In total, the company expects to log 20,000 hours of billable repair time next year. According to competitive conditions, the company believes it should aim for a profit of $5 per hour of plumber's time. The competitive markup on parts is 30% of invoice cost.

Required:

1. Compute the time rate and the material loading charge that would be used to bill jobs.
2. One of the company's plumbers has just completed a repair job that required three hours of time and $40 in parts (invoice cost). Compute the amount that would be billed for the job.

Problems

PROBLEM A–5 The Economists' Approach to Pricing [LO1]

The postal service of St. Lucia, an island in the West Indies, obtains a significant portion of its revenues from sales of special souvenir sheets to stamp collectors. The souvenir sheets usually contain several high-value St. Lucia stamps depicting a common theme, such as the anniversary of Princess Diana's funeral. The souvenir sheets are designed and printed for the postal service by Imperial Printing, a stamp agency service company in the United Kingdom. The souvenir sheets cost the postal service $0.60 each. (The currency in St. Lucia is the East Caribbean dollar.) St. Lucia has been selling these souvenir sheets for $5.00 each and ordinarily sells 50,000 units. To test the market, the postal service recently priced a new souvenir sheet at $6.00 and sales dropped to 40,000 units.

Required:

1. Does the postal service of St. Lucia make more money selling souvenir sheets for $5.00 each or $6.00 each?
2. Estimate the price elasticity of demand for the souvenir sheets.
3. Estimate the profit-maximizing price for souvenir sheets.
4. If Imperial Printing increases the price it charges to the St. Lucia postal service for souvenir sheets to $0.70 each, how much should the St. Lucia postal service charge its customers for the souvenir sheets?

PROBLEM A–6 Standard Costs; Absorption Costing Approach to Setting Prices [LO2]

Euclid Fashions, Inc., has designed a sports jacket that is about to be introduced on the market. A standard cost card has been prepared for the new jacket, as shown below:

	Standard Quantity or Hours	Standard Price or Rate	Standard Cost
Direct materials	2.0 yards	$ 4.60 per yard	$ 9.20
Direct labor	1.4 hours	10.00 per hour	14.00
Manufacturing overhead (1/6 variable)	1.4 hours	12.00 per hour	16.80
Total standard cost per jacket			$40.00

The following additional information relating to the new jacket is available:

a. The only variable selling, general, or administrative costs will be $4 per jacket for shipping. Fixed selling, general, and administrative costs will be (per year):

Salaries	$ 90,000
Advertising and other.	384,000
Total.	$474,000

b. Since the company manufactures many products, it is felt that no more than 21,000 hours of labor time per year can be devoted to production of the new jackets.

c. An investment of $900,000 will be necessary to carry inventories and accounts receivable and to purchase some new equipment. The company desires a 24% return on investment (ROI) in new product lines.

d. Manufacturing overhead costs are allocated to products on the basis of direct labor-hours.

Required:

1. Assume that the company uses the absorption approach to cost-plus pricing.
   a. Compute the markup that the company needs on the jackets to achieve a 24% ROI if it sells all of the jackets it can produce using 21,000 hours of labor time.
   b. Using the markup you have computed, prepare a price quote sheet for a single jacket.
   c. Assume that the company is able to sell all of the jackets that it can produce. Prepare an income statement for the first year of activity, and compute the company's ROI for the year on the jackets, using the ROI formula from Chapter 12.
2. After marketing the jackets for several years, the company is experiencing a falloff in demand due to an economic recession. A large retail outlet will make a bulk purchase of jackets if its label is sewn in and if an acceptable price can be worked out. What is the minimum acceptable price for this order?

PROBLEM A–7 Target Costing [LO3]

Choice Culinary Supply, Inc., sells restaurant equipment and supplies throughout most of the United States. Management is considering adding a gelato machine to its line of ice cream making machines. Management will negotiate the price of the gelato machine with its Italian manufacturer.

Management of Choice Culinary Supply believes the gelato machines can be sold to its customers in the United States for $3,795 each. At that price, annual sales of the gelato machine should be 80 units. If the gelato machine is added to Choice Culinary Supply's product lines, the company will have to invest $50,000 in inventories and special warehouse fixtures. The variable cost of selling the gelato machines would be $350 per machine.

Required:

1. If Choice Culinary Supply requires a 20% return on investment (ROI), what is the maximum amount the company would be willing to pay the Italian manufacturer for the gelato machines?
2. Management would like to know how the purchase price of the machines would affect Choice Culinary Supply's ROI. Construct a graph that shows Choice Culinary Supply's ROI as a function of the purchase price of the gelato machine. Put the purchase price on the *X*-axis and the resulting ROI on the *Y*-axis. Plot the ROI for purchase prices between $2,400 and $3,400 per machine.
3. After many hours of negotiations, management has concluded that the Italian manufacturer is unwilling to sell the gelato machine at a low enough price for Choice Culinary Supply to earn its 20% required ROI. Apart from simply giving up on the idea of adding the gelato machine to Choice Culinary Supply's product lines, what could management do?

PROBLEM A–8 Time and Material Pricing [LO4]

Superior TV Repair, Inc., uses time and material pricing, and each year it reviews its rates in light of the actual costs incurred in the prior year. Actual costs incurred last year in connection with repair work and in connection with the company's parts inventory are given below:

	Repairs	Parts
Repair technicians—wages	$280,000	
Repair service manager—salary.	30,000	
Parts manager—salary		$26,000

continued

Repairs and parts assistant—salary	16,000	4,000
Retirement benefits (20% of salaries and wages)	65,200	6,000
Health insurance (5% of salaries and wages)	16,300	1,500
Utilities	71,000	15,700
Truck operating costs	11,600	
Property taxes	5,200	3,200
Liability and fire insurance	3,800	1,800
Supplies	900	300
Rent—Building	24,000	16,500
Depreciation—trucks and equipment	36,000	
Invoice cost of parts used		300,000
Total costs for the year	$560,000	$375,000

Customers were billed for 20,000 hours of repair work last year.

The company has a target profit of $4 per hour of repair service time and a target profit of 15% of the invoice cost of parts used. During the past year, the company billed repair service time at $27.50 per hour and added a material loading charge of 35% to parts. There is some feeling in the company that these rates may now be inadequate, since costs have risen somewhat over the last year.

Required:

1. Using the above data, compute the following:
   a. The rate that would be charged per hour of repair service time using time and material pricing.
   b. The material loading charge that would be used in billing jobs. The material loading charge should be expressed as a percentage of the invoice cost.
2. Assume that the company adopts the rates that you have computed in (1) above. What should be the total price charged on a repair job that requires 1½ hours of service time and parts with an invoice cost of $69.50?
3. If the company adopts the rates that you have computed in (1) above, would you expect the company's profits to improve?

PROBLEM A–9 The Economists' Approach to Pricing; Absorption Costing Approach to Cost-Plus Pricing [LO1, LO2]

Softway, Inc., was started by two young software engineers to market AdBlocker, a software application they had written that blocks ads when surfing the Internet. Sales of the software have been good at 20,000 units a month, but the company has been losing money as shown below:

Sales (20,000 units × $18.95 per unit)	$379,000
Variable cost (20,000 units × $5.90 per unit)	118,000
Contribution margin	261,000
Fixed expenses	264,000
Net operating income (loss)	$ (3,000)

The company's only variable cost is the $5.90 fee it pays to another company to reproduce the software on CDs, print manuals, and package the result in an attractive box for sale to consumers. Monthly fixed selling, general, and administrative expenses total $264,000.

The company's marketing manager has been arguing for some time that the software is priced too high. She estimates that every 10% decrease in price will yield a 20% increase in unit sales. The marketing manager would like your help in preparing a presentation to the company's owners concerning the pricing issue.

Required:

1. To help the marketing manager prepare for her presentation, she has asked you to fill in the blanks in the following table. The selling prices in the table were computed by successively decreasing the selling price by 10%. The estimated unit sales were computed by successively increasing the unit sales by 20%. For example, $17.06 is 10% less than $18.95 and 24,000 units are 20% more than 20,000 units.

Selling Price	Unit Sales	Sales	Variable Cost	Fixed Cost	Net Operating Income
$18.95	20,000	$379,000	$118,000	$264,000	$(3,000)
$17.06	24,000	$409,440	$141,600	$264,000	$ 3,840
$15.35	28,800	?	?	?	?
$13.82	34,560	?	?	?	?
$12.44	41,472	?	?	?	?
$11.20	49,766	?	?	?	?
$10.08	59,719	?	?	?	?
$ 9.07	71,663	?	?	?	?
$ 8.16	85,996	?	?	?	?
$ 7.34	103,195	?	?	?	?

2. Using the data from the table, construct a graph that shows the net operating income as a function of the selling price. Put the selling price on the *X*-axis and the net operating income on the *Y*-axis. Using the graph, estimate the approximate selling price at which net operating income is maximized.
3. Compute the price elasticity of demand for the AdBlocker software. Based on this calculation, what is the profit-maximizing price?
4. The owners have invested $120,000 in the company and feel that they should be earning at least 2% per month on these funds. If the absorption costing approach to pricing were used, what would be the target selling price based on the current sales of 20,000 units? What do you think would happen to the net operating income of the company if this price were charged?
5. If the owners of the company are dissatisfied with the net operating income and return on investment at the selling price you computed in (3) above, should they increase the selling price? Explain.

PROBLEM A–10 Integrative Problem: Missing Data; Markup Computations; Return on Investment; Pricing [LO2]

Rest Easy, Inc., has designed a new puncture-proof, self-inflating sleeping pad that is unlike anything on the market. Because of the unique properties of the new sleeping pad, the company anticipates that it will be able to sell all the pads that it can produce. On this basis, the following budgeted income statement for the first year of activity is available:

Sales (__?__ pads at __?__ per pad)	$?
Less cost of goods sold (__?__ pads at __?__ per pad)	4,000,000
Gross margin	?
Less selling, general, and administrative expenses.	2,160,000
Net operating income.	$?

Additional information on the new sleeping pad is given below:

a. The company will hire enough workers to commit 100,000 direct labor-hours to the manufacture of the pads.
b. A partially completed standard cost card for the new sleeping pad follows:

	Standard Quantity or Hours	Standard Price or Rate	Standard Cost
Direct materials	5 yards	$6 per yard	$30
Direct labor.	2 hours	? per hour	?
Manufacturing overhead.	?	? per hour	?
Total standard cost per sleeping pad			$?

c. An investment of $3,500,000 will be necessary to carry inventories and accounts receivable and to purchase some new equipment. Management has decided that the design of the new pad is unique enough that the company should set a selling price that will yield a 24% return on investment (ROI).

d. Other information relating to production and costs follows:

Variable manufacturing overhead cost (per pad)	$7
Variable selling cost (per pad)	$5
Fixed manufacturing overhead cost (total)	$1,750,000
Fixed selling, general, and administrative cost (total)	?
Number of pads produced and sold (per year)	?

e. Manufacturing overhead costs are allocated to production on the basis of direct labor-hours.

Required:

1. Complete the standard cost card for a single pad.
2. Assume that the company uses the absorption approach to cost-plus pricing.
   a. Compute the markup that the company needs on the pads to achieve a 24% ROI.
   b. Using the markup you have computed, prepare a price quotation sheet for a single pad.
   c. Assume, as stated, that the company can sell all the pads that it can produce. Complete the income statement for the first year of activity, and then compute the company's ROI for the year.
3. Assume that direct labor is a variable cost. How many units would the company have to sell at the price you computed in (2) above to achieve the 24% ROI? How many units would have to be produced and sold to just break even without achieving the 24% ROI?

Photo Credits

page 3 AP/Wide World Photos
page 14 AP/Wide World Photos
page 15 AP/Wide World Photos
page 17 © Mark Richards/PhotoEdit, Inc.
page 39 © Mark Richards/PhotoEdit, Inc.
page 43 Courtesy of Benetton
page 51 © 1998 Jon Feingersh/The Stock Market
page 56 Courtesy of Corporate Angel Network
page 91 Everett Collection
page 97 Courtesy of Agricultural Data Systems
page 101 © J. Nordell/The Image Works
page 118 PhotoDisc
page 149 © Richard Hutchings
page 151 Bruce Ayers/Stone
page 152 Courtesy of HoneyTop Foods
page 190 © Scott Goodwin Photography
page 195 © Chris Sorensen
page 198 Luc Novovitch/Liaison Agency
page 233 © Mitchell Gerber/CORBIS
page 239 AP/Wide World Photos
page 247 Courtesy of The American
page 248 Martin A. Levick
page 284 © L. Mulvehill/The Image Works
page 291 AP/Wide World Photos
page 315 Christopher Bissell/Stone
page 321 Courtesy of Diamond Courier
page 323 © Christie's Images/CORBIS
page 340 Courtesy of Bertch Cabinet Manufacturing, Inc.
page 373 Walter Hodges/Stone
page 376 © Tony Freeman/PhotoEdit
page 383 © Jose L. Pelaez/The Stock Market
page 393 Courtesy of BNSF
page 423 © Photofest
page 430 © Christopher Morrow/Stock Boston/PictureQuest
page 445 Michelle D. Bridewell/PhotoEdit
page 481 Stephen W. Frisch/Stock Boston
page 487 Courtesy of Peter F. Drucker
page 492 © Michael Newman/PhotoEdit
page 525 © Bill Bachman/PhotoEdit
page 536 Courtesy of Great Harvest Franchising, Inc.
page 542 Photofest
page 549 Hugh Sitton/Stone
page 585 PhotoDisc
page 597 AP/Wide World Photos
page 602 Courtesy of Safeway, Inc.
page 635 © Eric Myer Photography
page 635 Bonnie Kamin/PhotoEdit
page 650 © Ted Horowitz/CORBIS Stock Market
page 659 Bruce Forster/Stone
page 697 Mark Richards/PhotoEdit
page 699 Chris Sorensen
page 700 AP/Wide World Photos
page 727 Eyewire
page 734 Michael Melford, Inc./The Image Bank
page 763 © Don Smetzer/Stone
page 776 © Mike Siluk/The Image Works
page 783 Courtesy of Impact Communications

Index